# Digital Media

Rimon Elias

# Digital Media

## A Problem-solving Approach for Computer Graphics

Springer

Rimon Elias
German University in Cairo
Cairo
Egypt

ISBN 978-3-319-05136-9 ISBN 978-3-319-05137-6 (eBook)
DOI 10.1007/978-3-319-05137-6
Springer Cham Heidelberg New York Dordrecht London

Library of Congress Control Number: 2014933528



Printed on acid-free paper

Springer is part of Springer Science+Business Media (www.springer.com)

*To my family;*
*my parents,*
*my wife,*
*and my daughters; Teodora and Eugenia*

# Preface

In the digital era, various media have received great attention in retrieving, displaying, manipulating, and communicating information. We may look at such digital media from two distinct perspectives, scientific and artistic. Due to the great importance of digital media, different university-level programs have been created to serve such areas of emerging science and arts. Some of these programs study the engineering and scientific aspects of digital media, e.g., video processing, audio processing, computer-generated imagery, etc. Other programs are concerned with the artistic creations built upon the advances in this area, e.g., digital photography, video production, audio production, etc.

Visual computing represents a section of the engineering and scientific aspects of digital media, where digital images become the core around which different fields of computer research are established. Such fields include computer vision, image processing, computer graphics, and visualization. Although digital imaging can be considered the greatest common divisor among those fields, essential differences are present among them. For instance, while computer graphics is the field concerned with representing descriptive data through artificial digital imaging form, computer vision is the field concerned with extracting descriptive data from real-world digital images. Another closely related and important research field is image processing that is concerned with manipulation of digital images. Algorithms developed in this field may be used as preprocessing steps to enhance the outcome of a vision system. All the fields are connected to some extent.

This book is concerned with the graphics part of visual computing. It handles the subject through explaining algorithms and concepts and providing plenty of solved problems. Our aim is that students understand and practice numeric problems. The target readers of this book are upper-division undergraduate students and other graduate students who did not take a computer graphics course before. The reader is expected to have a basic knowledge of mathematics and linear algebra (An appendix is provided at the end of the book). Since we talk about concepts and solving problems, no programming experience is needed to read the book.

Cairo, Egypt, December 2013 Rimon Elias
Ottawa, Canada

# Contents

# Abbreviations

| | |
|---|---|
| Ajax | Asynchronous JavaScript |
| API | Application Programming Interface |
| AR | Augmented Reality |
| ASP | Active Server Pages |
| AVC | Advanced Video Coding |
| B-rep | Boundary Representation |
| BSP | Binary Space Partitioning |
| CAD | Computer Aided Design |
| CAGD | Computer Aided Geometric Design |
| CG | Computer Graphics |
| CMY | Cyan Magenta Yellow (color space) |
| CODEC | COder-DECoder |
| COP | Center of Projection |
| CSG | Constructive Solid Geometry |
| CV | Computer Vision |
| DASP | Digital Audio Signal Processing |
| DDA | Digital Differential Analyzer |
| DOP | Direction of Projection |
| DSP | Digital Signal Processing |
| DVB | Digital Video Broadcasting |
| FOV | Field of View |
| GUI | Graphical User Interface |
| HCI | Human–Computer Interaction |
| HLS | Hue Luminance Saturation (color space) |
| HSB | Hue Saturation Brightness (color space) |
| HSL | Hue Saturation Luminance (color space) |
| HSV | Hue Saturation Value (color space) |
| HTML | HyperText Markup Language |
| IFS | Indexed Face Set |
| IP | Image Processing |
| JPEG | Joint Photographic Experts Group |
| MPEG | Moving Picture Experts Group |
| NDC | Normalized Device Coordinates |
| NURBS | Nonuniform Rational B-Splines |

| | |
|---|---|
| PHP | Hypertext Preprocessor |
| PRP | Projection Reference Point |
| QoS | Quality of Service |
| RGB | Red Green Blue (color space) |
| SQL | Sequential Query Language |
| VR | Virtual Reality |
| VRC | View Reference Coordinate System |
| VRP | View Reference Point |
| WCS | World Coordinate System |

# Examples

# Problems

# Chapter 1
# Introduction

**Abstract** Digital media have increasingly become an essential component of everyday life. In contrary to analog media, digital media are stored in digitized forms and transmitted over networks. Computer-generated movies, electronic newspapers, songs downloaded from the Web, live radio and TV streaming, etc. are examples of digital media. We can distinguish between two aspects of digital media. (1) The *engineering* aspect of digital media that represents the scientific foundation of creating and manipulating digital media. The persons dealing with this aspect of digital media are usually engineers (media engineers, software engineers, computer engineers, electrical engineers, etc.) and computer scientists. Our discussion in this book focuses on a part of this aspect. (2) The *artistic* aspect of digital media that applies the advances of digital media research to produce end-user products. The persons involved with this aspect include artists, photographers, architects, media designers, etc.

## 1.1 Digital Media Engineering

Digital media engineering programs focus on digital innovation and research in digital technologies. The core courses in such programs deal *at least* with the following areas:

- *Visual computing*: This term refers to a range of related computer research fields; all pertinent to images. This is discussed in Sect. 1.2.
- *Digital audio processing*: It can be regarded as an example of digital signal processing (DSP). It is also known as digital audio signal processing (DASP). Fundamentals of audio and acoustic environments are studied. Digital media engineering students are exposed to algorithms to analyze audio signals and evaluate the performance of different acoustic devices. In addition, students study audio compression techniques and other techniques to enhance audio signals (e.g., equalization, filtering, etc.). More can be found in Zölzer (2008).

R. Elias, *Digital Media*, DOI: 10.1007/978-3-319-05137-6_1,

- *Digital video processing*: Video processing includes operations dealing with video coding and compression, color space conversion, motion compensation and analysis, etc. Video codecs (i.e., coder-decoder) and standards (e.g., MPEG, H.264, AVC, JPEG2000, etc.) are studied. More on video processing can be found in Tekalp (1995), Bovik (2009), Wang et al. (2001).
- *Web programming*: Web-based multi-user applications can be built using various server-side (e.g., PHP, ASP, etc.) and client-side (e.g., HTML, JavaScript, Ajax, etc.) scripting languages. Different database systems (e.g., MySQL, Microsoft SQL Server) can be accessed through these applications. More can be found in Castro (2006), Flanagan (2011), Nixon (2012), Gilmore (2010).
- *Multimedia communications*: This area studies the use of networks to transmit images, video, audio, etc. Among the topics studied are multimedia synchronization, multimedia quality of service (QoS), multimedia conferencing, etc. Digital video broadcasting (DVB) can also be studied. More can be found in Halsall (2000), Fischer (2010).
- *Usability engineering*: Usability refers to a measure of how good (or bad) the experience of a user when dealing with a software or a hardware system or a product in general. Studying usability is important to help users save time when interacting with a system/product and increase their productivity utilizing such a system/product. Usability engineering is concerned with the study of *human-computer interaction* or HCI. Different aspects on both user and machine sides should be dealt with. Students should know how to prototype, design and evaluate interfaces (e.g., graphical user interface or GUI). More can be found in Nielsen (1993), Courage and Baxter (2005), Tullis and Albert (2008).

## 1.2 Visual Computing

Visual computing embraces a number of image-related fields. Among those fields are computer graphics, computer vision, image processing and visualization. Dealing with digital images may represent the main similarity among those fields; however, differences do exist. For example, computer graphics (CG) uses input description to produce artificial digital images representing the descriptive input data. On the other hand, computer vision (CV) (Szeliski 2011; Trucco and Verri 1998; Hartley and Zisserman 2004; Mitiche 1994; Faugeras 1993) focuses on extracting descriptive data from real-world digital images. Another closely related and important research field is image processing (IP) (Jain 1989; Gonzalez and Woods 2007; Gonzalez et al. 2009) that is concerned with treating input digital images to produce output digital images after processing. Moreover, visualization is the field with a focus on converting scientific information (e.g., scientific experimental results, software design, system hierarchy, etc.) into visual form; i.e., as easy-to-understand computer-generated images. Table 1.1 summarizes the role of each field. All the above fields in addition to others handling digital images (e.g., animation, virtual reality (VR), augmented reality (AR), etc.) are related to some extent.

**Table 1.1** Relationship between images and data/information as viewed by different visual computing fields

| Field | Input | | Output |
|---|---|---|---|
| Computer vision | **Image** | ⇒ | Description |
| Image processing | **Image** | ⇒ | **Image** |
| Computer graphics | Description | ⇒ | **Image** |
| Visualization | Information | ⇒ | **Image** |

## 1.3 Computer Graphics

Computer graphics is a field of visual computing where synthetic images are generated through a sequence of stages given some description.

Computer-generated images are used in entertainment applications like computer games, movies, commercials; training applications through virtual reality and simulated environments; and computer aided design (CAD) applications that help designers, engineers and architects design vehicles, parts, machines and buildings. Computer graphics can also help us create attractive user interfaces. In addition, computer graphics algorithms can help with different scientific visualization solutions.

### *1.3.1 Graphics Pipeline*

The term *graphics pipeline* (sometimes called *rendering pipeline*) refers to the sequence of steps a system follows to generate a 2D raster image (i.e., an array of picture elements or pixels) from a description of 3D models, lights, camera locations, etc. Traditionally, the graphics pipeline includes the following stages (Fig. 1.1):

1. *Modeling transformation*: This step refers to 3D geometry provided in world space. Different methods can be used to create models in 3D space. Those are discussed in Chaps. 4 and 7. The 3D models created in 3D space can be transformed to fit certain requirements. Various transformation operations are detailed in Chap. 5.
2. *Lighting*: Environments containing the 3D models created and transformed in Step 1 are lit by one or more light sources. Lighting calculations are performed per vertex. There are many types of light sources including directional, point and spotlights. Their influences differ according to factors pertaining to their locations and distances to the vertex being lit, their orientations, their intensities etc. (The shades between vertices are interpolated during rasterization of Step 6.) Lighting, illumination and shading are discussed in Chap. 11.
3. *Viewing transformation*: There are various coordinate systems that we should deal with along the graphics pipeline. In addition to the world coordinate system used in creating and transforming models and light, there is a camera coordinate system. In this coordinate system, the origin and the axes are determined according

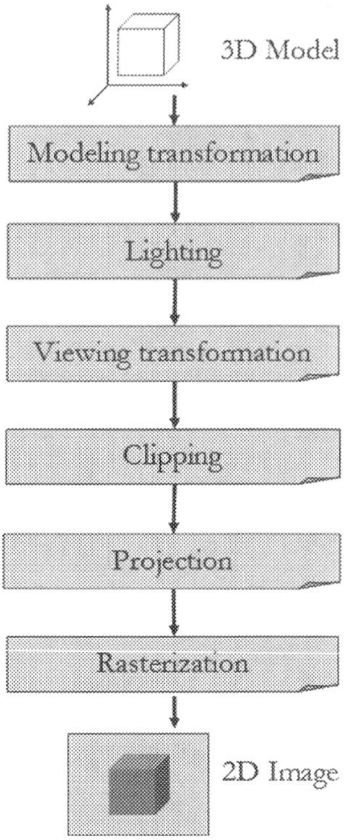


**Fig. 1.1** Graphics pipeline

to the camera location and orientation. Expressing the vertices in this 3D camera coordinate system is referred to as *viewing transformation*. We discuss this in Chap. 9.

4. *Clipping*: Step 3 may result in objects that reside outside the camera field of view (i.e., the viewing frustum). Those objects will not be visible in the final output image (unless reflected off or refracted through other visible objects). Hence, they are discarded. Keeping objects within a certain area/volume is referred to as *clipping*. This is discussed in Chap. 9.
5. *Projection transformation*: Projection transformation is applied to the 3D coordinates of the vertices obtained in Step 4 as discussed in Chap. 9. Details of various projection operations are studied in Chap. 8.
6. *Scan conversion and rasterization*: At this stage, the pixel intensity/color values are determined. *Shading* values are assigned to pixels between vertices as in Chap. 11. *Texturing* may be used to add realism to the outcome. This is done through various mapping techniques as in Chap. 12.

Note that scene objects may hide others with respect to the current camera location and orientation. A process that is referred to as *hidden-surface removal* or *hidden-surface elimination* is applied to remove object parts that are hidden. Methods to

solve the *visibility problem* (i.e., to determine what's visible and what's invisible) are discussed in Chap. 10.
7. *Displaying*: The last stage of the graphics pipeline is to display the output image on the screen.

Note that these stages of graphics pipeline are suitable for direct illumination; i.e., when light rays arrive directly to the surface being lit. Other situations when light rays are reflected off (or refracted through) other surfaces may alter the value of color assigned to a pixel.

## 1.4 Book Contents

This book covers many concepts and algorithms along the graphics pipeline. These concepts are supported by hundreds of solved numeric examples and unsolved problems for practice.

In this book, we concentrate on helping students who take the first course in computer graphics understand how concepts and algorithms work through practicing numeric examples. Pseudo codes are included when appropriate. We do not include any coding examples relying on specific language or library. Rather, we particularly emphasize on understanding the ideas.

### *1.4.1 Notations*

#### 1.4.1.1 Entities and Symbols

Different entities are used in computer graphics (e.g., 2D points, 3D points, vectors, matrices, etc.). Unless otherwise specified, in this book, we indicate a 2D point by a bold lowercase letter (e.g., $\mathbf{p}$ in case of homogeneous coordinates and $\dot{\mathbf{p}}$ in case of inhomogeneous coordinates) while a 3D point is indicated by a bold uppercase letter (e.g., $\mathbf{P}$ in case of homogeneous coordinates and $\dot{\mathbf{P}}$ in case of inhomogeneous coordinates). A matrix of any dimensions is represented by a fixed-size letter (e.g., $\mathtt{M}$). A vector of any length is represented by a bold face letter (e.g., $\mathbf{v}$).[1] A scalar variable is represented by an italic letter (e.g., $s$).

Some symbols may have multiple interpretations according to their context. For example, the symbol '$\times$' may be used to indicate scalar multiplication when the operands are scalar values or cross product operation when the operands are vectors. Table 1.2 lists the frequently used entities and symbols in this book.

[1] According to the context, distinguishing between vectors (e.g., those representing points and those representing directions) should be clear.

Table 1.2 Frequently used entities and symbols

| Symbol | Meaning |
|---|---|
| $\dot{\mathbf{p}}$ | 2D vector representing a 2D inhomogeneous point |
| $\mathbf{p}$ | 3D vector representing a 2D homogeneous point |
| $\mathbf{v}$ | A vector of any length; e.g., a direction vector (if context does not indicate a homogeneous 2D point) |
| $\dot{\mathbf{P}}$ | 3D vector representing a 3D inhomogeneous point |
| $\mathbf{P}$ | 4D vector representing a 3D homogeneous point |
| $\dot{\mathtt{M}}$ | A $2 \times 2$ transformation matrix used with inhomogeneous 2D points or a $3 \times 3$ transformation matrix used with inhomogeneous 3D points |
| $\mathtt{M}$ | A matrix of any dimensions |
| $s$ | A scalar variable |
| $u \times v$ | Scalar multiplication as both $u$ and $v$ are scalars |
| $\mathbf{u} \times \mathbf{v}$ | Cross product as both $\mathbf{u}$ and $\mathbf{v}$ are vectors |

#### 1.4.1.2 Working with Matrices and Vectors

In general and in this book as well, when not specified, a vector is considered to be a column vector. For example,

$$\mathbf{v} = \begin{bmatrix} v_1 \\ v_2 \\ v_3 \end{bmatrix} = [v_1, v_2, v_3]^T. \tag{1.1}$$

Notice that sometimes the column vector is written as a row vector with the transpose notation as in the above example.

In computer graphics literature, two different notations are used to multiply matrices and vectors. One notation uses *row* vectors, which are *right*-multiplied by matrices. For example,

$$\begin{aligned} \mathbf{v}_2 &= \mathbf{v}_1 \mathtt{A} \\ &= [\, v_1 \; v_2 \; v_3 \,] \begin{bmatrix} a_{11} & a_{12} & a_{13} \\ a_{21} & a_{22} & a_{23} \\ a_{31} & a_{32} & a_{33} \end{bmatrix} \\ &= [\, v_1 a_{11} + v_2 a_{21} + v_3 a_{31} \;\; v_1 a_{12} + v_2 a_{22} + v_3 a_{32} \;\; v_1 a_{13} + v_2 a_{23} + v_3 a_{33} \,]. \end{aligned} \tag{1.2}$$

The other notation uses *column* vectors, which are *left*-multiplied by matrices. For example,

$$\begin{aligned} \mathbf{v}_2^T &= \mathrm{A}^T \mathbf{v}_1^T \\ &= \begin{bmatrix} a_{11} & a_{21} & a_{31} \\ a_{12} & a_{22} & a_{32} \\ a_{13} & a_{23} & a_{33} \end{bmatrix} \begin{bmatrix} v_1 \\ v_2 \\ v_3 \end{bmatrix} \\ &= \begin{bmatrix} v_1 a_{11} + v_2 a_{21} + v_3 a_{31} \\ v_1 a_{12} + v_2 a_{22} + v_3 a_{32} \\ v_1 a_{13} + v_2 a_{23} + v_3 a_{33} \end{bmatrix}. \end{aligned} \tag{1.3}$$

In this book, we use the second notation. Refer to Appendix A that surveys the most important matrix and vector operations.

## References

Bovik, A.C. 2009. *The essential guide to video processing*, 1st ed. New York: Academic Press.
Castro, E. 2006. *HTML, XHTML, and CSS*, 6th ed. San Francisco: Peachpit Press.
Courage, C., and K. Baxter. 2005. *Understanding your users: A practical guide to user requirements methods, tools, and techniques*, 1st ed. Los Altos: Morgan Kaufmann.
Faugeras, O. 1993. *Three-dimensional computer vision: A geometric viewpoint*. Cambridge: MIT Press.
Fischer, W. 2010. *Digital video and audio broadcasting technology: A practical engineering guide*, 3rd ed. Berlin: Springer.
Flanagan, D. 2011. *JavaScript: The definitive guide: Activate your web pages*, 6th ed. Sebastopol: O'Reilly Media.
Gilmore, W.J. 2010. *Beginning PHP and MySQL: From novice to professional*, 4th ed. New York: Apress.
Gonzalez, R.C., and R.E. Woods. 2007. *Digital image processing*, 3rd ed. Englewood Cliffs: Prentice Hall.
Gonzalez, R.C., R.E. Woods., and S.L. Eddins. 2009. *Digital image processing using MATLAB*, 2nd ed. Gatesmark Publishing.
Halsall, F. 2000. *Multimedia communications: Applications, networks, protocols and standards*, 1st ed. Reading : Addison-Wesley.
Hartley, R.I., and A. Zisserman. 2004. *Multiple view geometry in computer vision*, 2nd ed. Cambridge: Cambridge University Press.
Jain, A.K. 1989. *Fundamentals of digital image processing*. Englewood Cliffs: Prentice Hall.
Mitiche, A. 1994. *Computational analysis of visual motion. Advances in computer vision and machine intelligence*. Berlin: Springer.
Nielsen, J. 1993. *Usability engineering. Interactive technologies*, 1st ed. Los Altos: Morgan Kaufmann.
Nixon, R. 2012. *Learning PHP, MySQL, JavaScript, and CSS: A step-by-step guide to creating dynamic websites*, 2nd ed. Sebastopol: O'Reilly Media.
Szeliski, R. 2011. *Computer vision: Algorithms and applications*. Texts in computer science. Berlin: Springer.
Tekalp, A.M. 1995. *Digital video processing*, 1st ed. Englewood Cliffs: Prentice Hall.
Trucco, E., and A. Verri. 1998. *Introductory techniques for 3-D computer vision*. Englewood Cliffs: Prentice Hall.

Tullis, T., and W. Albert. 2008. *Measuring the user experience: Collecting, analyzing, and presenting usability metrics*, 1st ed. Los Altos: Morgan Kaufmann.

Wang, Y., J. Ostermann, and Y.-Q. Zhang. 2001. *Video processing and communications*, 1st ed. Englewood Cliffs: Prentice Hall.

Zölzer, U. 2008. *Digital audio signal processing*, 2nd ed. London: Wiley.

# Chapter 2
# 2D Graphics

**Abstract** Objects can be drawn, edited and transformed in 2D and 3D spaces. One can create objects ranging from simple 2D primitives to complex 3D environments. Planar objects, sometimes called 2D shapes, are created on a single plane (usually the $xy$-plane) while 3D objects utilize all three dimensions of space. Focusing on planar objects, 2D primitives like lines, circles, etc. may be used to create more complex shapes. Thus, it is important to know how to create/draw such primitives as groups of pixels utilizing their equations; a process that is referred to as *scan conversion* (Working with graphics as mathematical equations is referred to as *vector graphics* while working with them as a series of pixels is called *raster graphics*.). A line can be scan-converted (i.e., expressed as a set of pixels that approximate its path) if we know its endpoints, which define its equation. Likewise, a circle is scan-converted if we know the location of its center as well as its radius; i.e., components that define its equation. The same concept applies to other primitives. Different operations may be applied to objects in 2D space. For example, an object can be clipped using a clip window or a clip polygon to preserve a part of that object. (Some systems refer to the clipping process as *trimming*.) Other operations that may be applied to such objects are called *transformations*. Such operations include translating (i.e., moving), rotating, scaling, stretching, reflecting (i.e., mirroring) and shearing the objects. In this chapter, we will look at how to create 2D primitives like lines and circles. Also, we will talk about polygons and polylines and how to clip line segments and polygons. We will dedicate Chap. 3 to talk about different transformations in 2D space. 3D object creation and operations will be discussed in subsequent chapters. Before starting the discussion, we should mention that there are two different Cartesian coordinate systems that could be used. These are left-handed and right-handed coordinate systems (see Sect. B.1.1). In the right-handed coordinate system, the origin is at the lower left corner of the screen and the $y$-axis is pointing upwards. On the contrary, in the left-handed coordinate system, the origin is at the upper left corner of the screen and the $y$-axis is pointing downwards. In this chapter, we will show a line drawn in both systems only once. Afterwards, we will stick to the right-handed coordinate system to avoid confusion. (The usual convention working with raster images is to use the

R. Elias, *Digital Media*, DOI: 10.1007/978-3-319-05137-6_2,

left-handed coordinate system where the origin is at the upper left corner and the $y$-axis is pointing downwards. However, switching between the left- and right-hand coordinate system is easy and can be done using Eq. (B.7).)

## 2.1 Lines

Drawing a line on a computer screen given its two endpoints is done by intensifying (or turning on) pixels along the path of this line. Figure 2.1a depicts an example of a line starting at pixel $[x_0, y_0]^T$ and ending at pixel $[x_1, y_1]^T$ where these pairs indicate the column and row numbers of the pixel respectively. The pixels to be intensified (i.e., those that are shaded in Fig. 2.1) could be *exactly on* or *close to* the linear path. Such a line can be expressed as

$$y - y_0 = \underbrace{\frac{y_1 - y_0}{x_1 - x_0}}_{slope}(x - x_0). \tag{2.1}$$

This can be written as

$$y = m(x - x_0) + y_0, \tag{2.2}$$

where $m = \frac{\Delta y}{\Delta x} = \frac{y_1 - y_0}{x_1 - x_0}$ is the slope of the line.

Note that the coordinate system used in Fig. 2.1a is a right-handed coordinate system where the origin is at the lower left corner of the screen and the $y$-axis is pointing upwards. (This is the coordinate system that will be used throughout this book unless otherwise specified.) Alternatively, the same line is drawn using a left-handed coordinate system in Fig. 2.1b where the origin is at the upper left corner and the $y$-axis is pointing downwards. Consequently, the slope of the line (i.e., $m$) in these cases is $<1$. Practically, the cases where the line is horizontal, vertical or having a slope of $\pm 1$ are handled as special cases.

### *2.1.1 Digital Differential Analyzer Algorithm*

A simple and direct way to draw the line is performed by looping or iterating through Eq. (2.2), incrementing the value of $x$ from $x_0$ to $x_1$ (i.e., moving from one column to the next) and obtaining the corresponding $y$ to plot the pixel $[x, y]^T$. There are some remarks to be mentioned here.

1. The $x$-value is an integer value as it is a column number; however, the resulting $y$-value could be a floating point number. In this case, the $y$-value must be rounded to the nearest integer in order to have the value $\lfloor y + 0.5 \rfloor$ where $\lfloor . \rfloor$ denotes the floor operation.

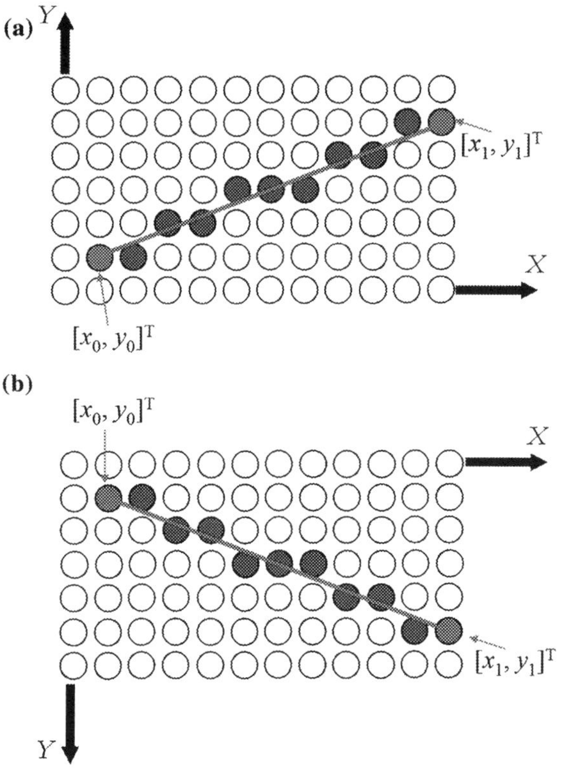


**Fig. 2.1** A 2D line as a path from $[x_0, y_0]^T$ to $[x_1, y_1]^T$. The slope of this line is <1. **a** The line is drawn using the *right-handed* coordinate system where the $y$-axis is pointing upwards. **b** The line is drawn using the *left-handed* coordinate system where the $y$-axis is pointing downwards

2. At each iteration, the slope $m$ is re-calculated although the slope is a constant number that does not change for the entire line. This could be time consuming. Thus, the value $m$ should be pre-calculated before looping.

Using Eq. (2.2) at iteration $i$, we can write

$$y_i = m(x_i - x_0) + y_0 = mx_i + \underbrace{y_0 - mx_0}_{B}, \tag{2.3}$$

where $B = y_0 - mx_0$ is the $y$-intercept, which is a constant value for the line. Since the $x$ increment is 1, the subsequent value of $y$ is obtained as

$$y_{i+1} = mx_{i+1} + B = m(x_i + 1) + B = \underbrace{mx_i + B}_{y_i} + m = y_i + m. \tag{2.4}$$

This means that subsequent $y$-values can be calculated by adding the value of the slope $m$ to the previous $y$-value at each iteration. Thus, for $|m| \leq 1$ as in Fig. 2.1, the algorithm can be written as follows:

**Algorithm 2.1** *DDA1 algorithm*

**Input:** $x_0, y_0, x_1, y_1$
1: $m = \frac{\Delta y}{\Delta x} = \frac{y_1 - y_0}{x_1 - x_0}$
2: $y = y_0$
3: **for** ($x = x_0$ to $x_1$) **do**
4: Plot $[x, \lfloor y + 0.5 \rfloor]^T$
5: $y = y + m$
6: **end for**

**end**

This algorithm is referred to as the *digital differential analyzer (DDA) algorithm*. Note that for $|m| \leq 1$, a fraction is added to the previous $y$-value each time. This means that, after rounding, $y$ may maintain the same value as in the previous iteration or be incremented by 1.

**Example 2.1:** [*DDA line drawing algorithm*]
Using the DDA line drawing algorithm, determine the pixels along a line segment that goes from $[3, 4]^T$ to $[8, 6]^T$.

**Solution 2.1:** According to Algorithm 2.1, the first step is to calculate the slope $m$ where

$$m = \frac{\Delta y}{\Delta x} = \frac{y_1 - y_0}{x_1 - x_0} = \frac{6 - 4}{8 - 3} = 0.4.$$

The second step is to loop along the $x$-direction from 3 to 8 using a step size of 1 and get the corresponding $y$-value by adding the value $m$ to the previous $y$ as listed in the following table:

| 3: $x$ | 4: $\lfloor y + 0.5 \rfloor$ | 4: Plot | 5: $y$ |
|---|---|---|---|
| 3 | 4 | $[3, 4]^T$ | $4.0 + 0.4 = 4.4$ |
| 4 | 4 | $[4, 4]^T$ | $4.4 + 0.4 = 4.8$ |
| 5 | 5 | $[5, 5]^T$ | $4.8 + 0.4 = 5.2$ |
| 6 | 5 | $[6, 5]^T$ | $5.2 + 0.4 = 5.6$ |
| 7 | 6 | $[7, 6]^T$ | $5.6 + 0.4 = 6.0$ |
| 8 | 6 | $[8, 6]^T$ | $6.0 + 0.4 = 6.4$ |

Each exact value of $y$ appearing in the last column is rounded and used in the next row to plot a pixel. Thus, the line segment is approximated by the pixels $[3, 4]^T$, $[4, 4]^T$, $[5, 5]^T$, $[6, 5]^T$, $[7, 6]^T$ and $[8, 6]^T$. □

Algorithm 2.1 assumes that $|m| \leq 1$. On the other hand, if $|m| > 1$, it can be written that

$$x_i = \frac{1}{m}(y_i - B). \tag{2.5}$$

Consequently, $x_{i+1}$ is calculated as by incrementing the value of $y$ by 1; so, we can write

$$x_{i+1} = \frac{1}{m}(y_{i+1} - B) = \frac{1}{m}(y_i + 1 - B) = \underbrace{\frac{1}{m}(y_i - B)}_{x_i} + \frac{1}{m} = x_i + \frac{1}{m}. \tag{2.6}$$

Thus, the roles of $x$ and $y$ are reversed by assigning an increment of 1 to $y$ and an increment of $\frac{1}{m}$ to $x$; consequently, the DDA algorithm can be modified as follows:

**Algorithm 2.2** *DDA2 algorithm*

**Input:** $x_0, y_0, x_1, y_1$
$m = \frac{\Delta y}{\Delta x} = \frac{y_1 - y_0}{x_1 - x_0}$
$x = x_0$
**for** ($y = y_0$ to $y_1$) **do**
    Plot $[\lfloor x + 0.5 \rfloor, y]^T$
    $x = x + \frac{1}{m}$
**end for**

**end**

### 2.1.2 Bresenham's Algorithm

In Example 2.1, notice that a difference could arise between the accurate value of $y$ and its integer value to be used for plotting or displaying the pixel. This difference represents an error value. Also, note that the $y$-value is incremented by 1 only if the fraction included in the accurate value of $y$ is $\geq 0.5$; otherwise, $y$ remains unchanged.

This suggests that each time $x$ is incremented, the slope $m$ can be added to an *error* value (indicating the vertical distance between the rounded $y$-value and the exact $y$-value) and if the new *error* is $\geq 0.5$ (i.e., the line gets closer to the next $y$-value), $y$ is incremented by 1 while the error is decremented by 1. This idea is listed in Algorithm 2.3.

**Algorithm 2.3** *Modified DDA algorithm*

**Input:** $x_0, y_0, x_1, y_1$
$m = \frac{\Delta y}{\Delta x} = \frac{y_1 - y_0}{x_1 - x_0}$
$y = y_0$
$error = 0$
**for** ($x = x_0$ to $x_1$) **do**
    Plot $[x, y]^T$

```
6:      error = error + m
7:      if (error ≥ 0.5) then
8:          y = y + 1
9:          error = error − 1
10:     end if
11: end for
```

**end**

**Example 2.2:** [*DDA and Bresenham's algorithm*] Re-solve Example 2.1 using Algorithm 2.3

**Solution 2.2:** The values are shown in the next table where the initial values for $x$, $y$ and *error* are $x_0$, $y_0$ and 0 respectively.

| 4: $x$ | 5: $y$ | 5: Plot | 6: *error* | 8: $y$ | 9: *error* |
|---|---|---|---|---|---|
| 3 | 4 | $[3, 4]^T$ | $0 + 0.4 = 0.4$ | | |
| 4 | 4 | $[4, 4]^T$ | $0.4 + 0.4 = 0.8$ | $4 + 1 = 5$ | $0.8 - 1 = -0.2$ |
| 5 | 5 | $[5, 5]^T$ | $-0.2 + 0.4 = 0.2$ | | |
| 6 | 5 | $[6, 5]^T$ | $0.2 + 0.4 = 0.6$ | $5 + 1 = 6$ | $0.6 - 1 = -0.4$ |
| 7 | 6 | $[7, 6]^T$ | $-0.4 + 0.4 = 0$ | | |
| 8 | 6 | $[8, 6]^T$ | $0 + 0.4 = 0.4$ | | |

□

Algorithm 2.3 does not handle the general case of a line and cannot be used to draw an arbitrary line. In particular, there are three cases that need to be considered to generalize it. In a right-handed coordinate system, these cases are:

1. if the line goes up but the slope $m > 1$ or $|\Delta y| > |\Delta x|$ (i.e., a steep line) as shown in Fig. 2.2a;
2. if the line slopes upwards but heads in the opposite direction where $x_0 > x_1$ as shown in Fig. 2.2b; and
3. if the line goes down where $y_0 > y_1$ as shown in Fig. 2.2c.

The solutions to the three cases mentioned above are the following:

1. If the line is steep, reflect it about the line $y = x$ in order to obtain a line with smaller slope (i.e., with $m < 1$). This is done by swapping $x_0$ with $y_0$ and $x_1$ with $y_1$. The $x$ and $y$ parameters are swapped again for plotting (i.e., to plot $[y, x]^T$).
2. If the line slopes upwards but heads in the opposite direction, swap the endpoints $[x_0, y_0]^T$ and $[x_1, y_1]^T$.
3. If the line goes down, decrement $y$ by 1 instead of incrementing it (i.e., step $y$ by $-1$ instead of 1).

Algorithm 2.4 accommodates these changes.

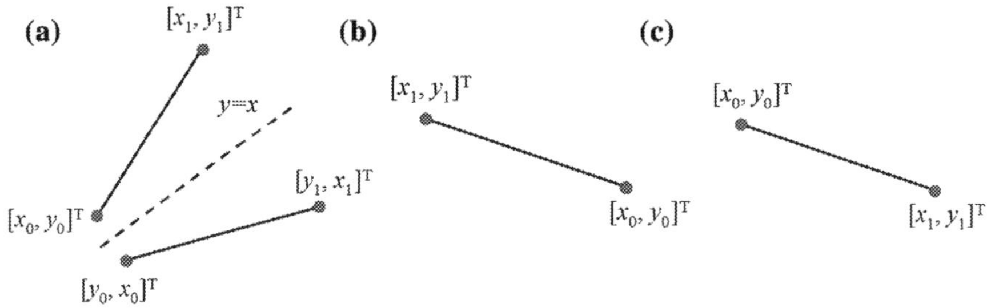

**Fig. 2.2** Cases considered to generalize the line algorithm. **a** If the slope is $>1$. **b** If the line slopes upwards but heads in the opposite direction. **c** If the line goes down

**Algorithm 2.4** *Modified Algorithm 2.3*

**Input:** $x_0, y_0, x_1, y_1$
1: $\Delta x = x_1 - x_0$
2: $\Delta y = y_1 - y_0$
3: $steep = \left| \frac{\Delta y}{\Delta x} \right| > 1$
4: **if** $(steep = TRUE)$ **then** . . . . . . $\Longleftarrow$ Fig. 2.2a
5:    swap $(x_0, y_0)$
6:    swap $(x_1, y_1)$
7: **end if**
8:
9: **if** $(x_0 > x_1)$ **then** . . . . . . $\Longleftarrow$ Fig. 2.2b
10:    swap $(x_0, x_1)$
11:    swap $(y_0, y_1)$
12: **end if**
13:
14: **if** $(y_0 > y_1)$ **then** . . . . . . $\Longleftarrow$ Fig. 2.2c
15:    $\delta y = -1$
16: **else**
17:    $\delta y = 1$
18: **end if**
19:
20: $m = \frac{|\Delta y|}{\Delta x} = \frac{|y_1 - y_0|}{x_1 - x_0}$
21: $y = y_0$
22: $error = 0$
23:
24: **for** $(x = x_0$ to $x_1)$ **do**
25:    **if** $(steep = TRUE)$ **then**
26:        Plot $[y, x]^T$
27:    **else**
28:        Plot $[x, y]^T$
29:    **end if**

30:     $error = error + m$
31:     **if** $(error \geq 0.5)$ **then**
32:         $y = y + \delta y$
33:         $error = error - 1$
34:     **end if**
35: **end for**

**end**

The main source of problem with Algorithm 2.4 is that it works with floating-point numbers (e.g., $m$ and $error$), which slows the process down and may result in error accumulation. Working with integer numbers will be much faster and more accurate. Switching to integers can be achieved easily by multiplying $m$ and $error$ by the denominator of the slope; i.e., $\Delta x$. Also, both sides of the condition $error \geq 0.5$ are doubled to get rid of the fraction. Such an algorithm is referred to as *Bresenham's algorithm* (Bresenham 1965). It is listed in Algorithm 2.5.

**Algorithm 2.5** *Bresenham's algorithm*

**Input:** $x_0, y_0, x_1, y_1$
1: $steep = |y_1 - y_0| > |x_1 - x_0|$
2: **if** $(steep = TRUE)$ **then**
3:     swap $(x_0, y_0)$
4:     swap $(x_1, y_1)$
5: **end if**
6:
7: **if** $(x_0 > x_1)$ **then**
8:     swap $(x_0, x_1)$
9:     swap $(y_0, y_1)$
10: **end if**
11:
12: **if** $(y_0 > y_1)$ **then**
13:     $\delta y = -1$
14: **else**
15:     $\delta y = 1$
16: **end if**
17:
18: $\Delta x = x_1 - x_0$
19: $\Delta y = |y_1 - y_0|$
20: $y = y_0$
21: $error = 0$
22:
23: **for** $(x = x_0$ to $x_1)$ **do**
24:     **if** $(steep = TRUE)$ **then**
25:         Plot $[y, x]^T$
26:     **else**

```
27:         Plot [x, y]^T
28:     end if
29:     error = error + Δy
30:     if (2 × error ≥ Δx) then
31:         y = y + δy
32:         error = error − Δx
33:     end if
34: end for
```

**end**

Note that Bresenham's algorithm can be tuned for integer computations of circumferential pixels in circles.

**Example 2.3:** [*Bresenham's line drawing algorithm*] You are asked to draw a line segment between the points $[1, 1]^T$ and $[4, 3]^T$. Use Bresenham's line drawing algorithm to specify the locations of pixels that should approximate the line.

**Solution 2.3:** We will follow the steps of Algorithm 2.5. The line is not steep as $|y_1 - y_0| < |x_1 - x_0|$. The $y$-step is 1 as $y_0 < y_1$. We have

$$\begin{aligned}
\delta y &= 1,\\
\Delta x = x_1 - x_0 &= 4 - 1 = 3,\\
\Delta y = y_1 - y_0 &= 3 - 1 = 2,\\
y &= 1,\\
error &= 0.
\end{aligned}$$

The following table shows the loop along the $x$-direction from 1 to 4 (i.e., the loop that starts at Line 23 in Algorithm 2.5):

| 23: $x$ | 27: Plot | 29: *error* | 31: $y$ | 32: *error* |
|---|---|---|---|---|
| 1 | $[1, 1]^T$ | $0 + 2 = 2$ | $1 + 1 = 2$ | $2 - 3 = -1$ |
| 2 | $[2, 2]^T$ | $-1 + 2 = 1$ | | |
| 3 | $[3, 2]^T$ | $1 + 2 = 3$ | $2 + 1 = 3$ | $3 - 3 = 0$ |
| 4 | $[4, 3]^T$ | $0 + 2 = 2$ | $3 + 1 = 4$ | $2 - 3 = -1$ |

Thus, the line is approximated by the pixels $[1, 1]^T$, $[2, 2]^T$, $[3, 2]^T$ and $[4, 3]^T$. □

### *2.1.3 The Midpoint Algorithm*

The *midpoint algorithm* (Pitteway 1967; Aken 1984; Van Aken and Novak 1985) can be used instead of Bresenham's algorithm to approximate straight lines. Actually, it produces the same line pixels; however, a difference does exist. In Bresenham's

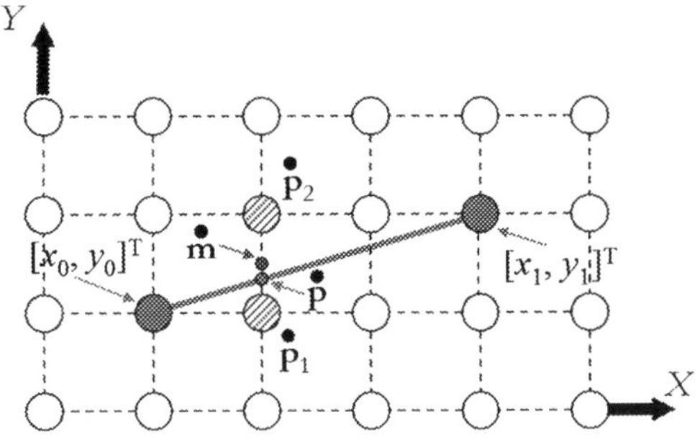


**Fig. 2.3** $\dot{\mathbf{m}} = [x_0 + 1, y_0 + \frac{1}{2}]^T$ is the midpoint between $[x_0 + 1, y_0]^T$ and $[x_0 + 1, y_0 + 1]^T$

algorithm, the smallest $y$-difference between the actual accurate $y$-value and the rounded integer $y$-value is used to pick up the nearest pixel to approximate the line. On the other hand, in the midpoint technique, we determine which side of the linear equation the midpoint between pixels lies.

Consider Fig. 2.3 where a line is to be drawn from $[x_0, y_0]^T$ to $[x_1, y_1]^T$. When $x$ is incremented at the second iteration as done before, the exact intersection happens at point $\dot{\mathbf{p}}$. Thus, there will be two choices for the pixels to be picked up at $x = x_0 + 1$; these choices are $\dot{\mathbf{p}}_1$ and $\dot{\mathbf{p}}_2$ (hatched in Fig. 2.3). The main idea of the previous formulation is to calculate the distances from $\dot{\mathbf{p}}$ to $\dot{\mathbf{p}}_1$ and from $\dot{\mathbf{p}}$ to $\dot{\mathbf{p}}_2$. According to the smaller distance, a pixel will be selected. Hence, $\dot{\mathbf{p}}_1$ is selected in our case.

In the midpoint algorithm, the equation of the line spanning from $[x_0, y_0]^T$ to $[x_1, y_1]^T$ is expressed [as in Eq. (2.3)] as

$$y = mx + B = \frac{\Delta y}{\Delta x} x + B, \tag{2.7}$$

where $m$ is the slope; $\Delta x = x_1 - x_0$; $\Delta y = y_1 - y_0$; and $B$ is the $y$-intercept. Equation (2.7) can be re-written in implicit form (i.e., $ax + by + c = 0$) as

$$\underbrace{\Delta y}_{a}\, x \underbrace{-\Delta x}_{b}\, y + \underbrace{\Delta x B}_{c} = 0, \tag{2.8}$$

where $a = \Delta y$; $b = -\Delta x$; and $c = \Delta x B$. Now, the midpoint $\dot{\mathbf{m}} = [x_0 + 1, y_0 + \frac{1}{2}]^T$ between $[x_0 + 1, y_0]^T$ and $[x_0 + 1, y_0 + 1]^T$ is applied to Eq. (2.8) to get

$$\begin{aligned} \mathscr{F}\left(x_0 + 1, y_0 + \frac{1}{2}\right) = d_{\dot{\mathbf{m}}} &= \Delta y(x_0 + 1) - \Delta x\left(y_0 + \frac{1}{2}\right) + \Delta x B \\ &= a(x_0 + 1) + b\left(y_0 + \frac{1}{2}\right) + c. \end{aligned} \tag{2.9}$$

There are three possibilities for $d_{\dot{\mathbf{m}}}$:

$$d_{\dot{\mathbf{m}}} = \begin{cases} +ve, & \text{the line is passing above } \dot{\mathbf{m}}\text{; thus, } \dot{\mathbf{p}}_2 \text{ is selected;} \\ -ve, & \text{the line is passing below } \dot{\mathbf{m}}\text{; thus, } \dot{\mathbf{p}}_1 \text{ is selected;} \\ 0, & \text{the midpoint } \dot{\mathbf{m}} \text{ is exactly on the line; thus, select either } \dot{\mathbf{p}}_1 \text{ or } \dot{\mathbf{p}}_2. \end{cases}$$

Choosing the pixel in the next column depends on whether $\dot{\mathbf{p}}_1$ or $\dot{\mathbf{p}}_2$ has been chosen. Assume that $\dot{\mathbf{p}}_1$ is selected. The midpoint $[x_0 + 2, y_0 + \frac{1}{2}]^T$ between $[x_0 + 2, y_0]^T$ and $[x_0 + 2, y_0 + 1]^T$ is applied to Eq. (2.8) to get

$$\begin{aligned} \mathscr{F}\left(x_0 + 2, y_0 + \frac{1}{2}\right) &= a(x_0 + 2) + b\left(y_0 + \frac{1}{2}\right) + c \\ &= \underbrace{a(x_0 + 1) + b\left(y_0 + \frac{1}{2}\right) + c}_{d_{\dot{\mathbf{m}}}} + a \\ &= d_{\dot{\mathbf{m}}} + a \\ &= d_{\dot{\mathbf{m}}} + \Delta y. \end{aligned} \tag{2.10}$$

On the other hand, if $\dot{\mathbf{p}}_2$ is selected, the midpoint $[x_0 + 2, y_0 + \frac{3}{2}]^T$ between $[x_0 + 2, y_0 + 1]^T$ and $[x_0 + 2, y_0 + 2]^T$ is applied to Eq. (2.8) to get

$$\begin{aligned} \mathscr{F}\left(x_0 + 2, y_0 + \frac{3}{2}\right) &= a(x_0 + 2) + b\left(y_0 + \frac{3}{2}\right) + c \\ &= \underbrace{a(x_0 + 1) + b\left(y_0 + \frac{1}{2}\right) + c}_{d_{\dot{\mathbf{m}}}} + a + b \\ &= d_{\dot{\mathbf{m}}} + a + b \\ &= d_{\dot{\mathbf{m}}} + \Delta y - \Delta x. \end{aligned} \tag{2.11}$$

This means that the subsequent sign of $d_{\dot{\mathbf{m}}}$ can be obtained by incrementing it by either $\Delta y$ if $\dot{\mathbf{p}}_1$ is selected or $\Delta y - \Delta x$ if $\dot{\mathbf{p}}_2$ is selected. An initial value for $d_{\dot{\mathbf{m}}}$ can be obtained using the start point $[x_0, y_0]^T$ and Eq. (2.9). So,

$$\begin{aligned} \mathscr{F}\left(x_0 + 1, y_0 + \frac{1}{2}\right) &= a(x_0 + 1) + b\left(y_0 + \frac{1}{2}\right) + c \\ &= \underbrace{ax_0 + by_0 + c}_{\mathscr{F}(x_0, y_0)} + a + \frac{b}{2}, \end{aligned} \tag{2.12}$$

where $a + \frac{b}{2} = \Delta y - \frac{\Delta x}{2}$ is the initial estimate of $d_{\dot{\mathbf{m}}}$. The midpoint algorithm is listed in Algorithm 2.6.

**Algorithm 2.6** *Midpoint algorithm—floating-point version*

**Input:** $x_0, y_0, x_1, y_1$
$\Delta x = x_1 - x_0$
$\Delta y = y_1 - y_0$
$d_{\dot{\mathbf{m}}} = \Delta y - \frac{\Delta x}{2}$
$d_{\dot{\mathbf{m}}}(\dot{\mathbf{p}}_1) = \Delta y$
$d_{\dot{\mathbf{m}}}(\dot{\mathbf{p}}_2) = \Delta y - \Delta x$
$y = y_0$

**for** $(x = x_0$ to $x_1)$ **do**
    Plot $[x, y]^T$
    **if** $(d_{\dot{\mathbf{m}}} \leq 0)$ **then**
        $d_{\dot{\mathbf{m}}} = d_{\dot{\mathbf{m}}} + d_{\dot{\mathbf{m}}}(\dot{\mathbf{p}}_1)$
    **else**
        $d_{\dot{\mathbf{m}}} = d_{\dot{\mathbf{m}}} + d_{\dot{\mathbf{m}}}(\dot{\mathbf{p}}_2)$
        $y = y + 1$
    **end if**
**end for**

**end**

Algorithm 2.6 uses floating-point numbers which slows the process down. This can be easily overcome as listed in Algorithm 2.7.

**Algorithm 2.7** *Midpoint algorithm – integer version*

**Input:** $x_0, y_0, x_1, y_1$
$\Delta x = x_1 - x_0$
$\Delta y = y_1 - y_0$
$d_{\dot{\mathbf{m}}} = 2\Delta y - \Delta x$
$d_{\dot{\mathbf{m}}}(\dot{\mathbf{p}}_1) = 2\Delta y$
$d_{\dot{\mathbf{m}}}(\dot{\mathbf{p}}_2) = 2\Delta y - 2\Delta x$
$y = y_0$

**for** $(x = x_0$ to $x_1)$ **do**
    Plot $[x, y]^T$
    **if** $(d_{\dot{\mathbf{m}}} \leq 0)$ **then**
        $d_{\dot{\mathbf{m}}} = d_{\dot{\mathbf{m}}} + d_{\dot{\mathbf{m}}}(\dot{\mathbf{p}}_1)$
    **else**
        $d_{\dot{\mathbf{m}}} = d_{\dot{\mathbf{m}}} + d_{\dot{\mathbf{m}}}(\dot{\mathbf{p}}_2)$
        $y = y + 1$
    **end if**
**end for**

**end**

**Example 2.4:** [*Midpoint line drawing algorithm*]

You are asked to draw a line segment between the points $[1, 1]^T$ and $[4, 3]^T$. Use the midpoint line drawing algorithm to specify the locations of pixels that should approximate the line.

**Solution 2.4:** We will follow the steps of Algorithm 2.7. So,

$$\begin{aligned}\Delta x &= x_1 - x_0 = 4 - 1 = 3,\\ \Delta y &= y_1 - y_0 = 3 - 1 = 2,\\ d_{\dot{\mathbf{m}}} &= 2\Delta y - \Delta x = 2 \times 2 - 3 = 1,\\ d_{\dot{\mathbf{m}}}(\dot{\mathbf{p}}_1) &= 2\Delta y = 2 \times 2 = 4,\\ d_{\dot{\mathbf{m}}}(\dot{\mathbf{p}}_2) &= 2\Delta y - 2\Delta x = 2 \times 2 - 2 \times 3 = -2,\\ y &= 1.\end{aligned}$$

The following table shows the loop along the $x$-direction from 1 to 4 (i.e., the loop that starts at Line 8 in Algorithm 2.7):

| 8: $x$ | 9: Plot | 11: $d_{\dot{\mathbf{m}}}$ | 13: $d_{\dot{\mathbf{m}}}$ | 14: $y$ |
|---|---|---|---|---|
| 1 | $[1, 1]^T$ | | $1 - 2 = -1$ | $1 + 1 = 2$ |
| 2 | $[2, 2]^T$ | $-1 + 4 = 3$ | | |
| 3 | $[3, 2]^T$ | | $3 - 2 = 1$ | $2 + 1 = 3$ |
| 4 | $[4, 3]^T$ | | $1 - 2 = -1$ | $3 + 1 = 4$ |

Thus, the line is approximated by the pixels $[1, 1]^T$, $[2, 2]^T$, $[3, 2]^T$ and $[4, 3]^T$. This is the same result obtained by Bresenham's algorithm in Example 2.3. □

## 2.2 Circles

As shown in Fig. 2.4, a pixel $[x, y]^T$ on the circumference of a circle can be estimated if the center $[x_0, y_0]^T$, the radius $r$ and the angle $\theta$ are known. The location of the pixel $[x, y]^T$ is obtained using trigonometric functions as

$$\begin{aligned}x &= x_0 + r\cos(\theta),\\ y &= y_0 + r\sin(\theta),\end{aligned} \tag{2.13}$$

which represent the parametric form of a circle where the parameter is the angle $\theta$.

In order to draw the whole circle, Eq. (2.13) can be used iteratively with different $\theta$-values going from 0° to 360° (i.e., $\theta \in [0°, 360°)$ or $0 \leq \theta < 2\pi$).[1] The problem with this approach is that working with trigonometric functions is time-consuming. The calculations could be very slow especially if the angle increment is small. On the other hand, if the angle increment is large, the algorithm will be fast; however,

[1] $[0°, 360°)$ represents a half-open interval where 0° is included while 360° is excluded.

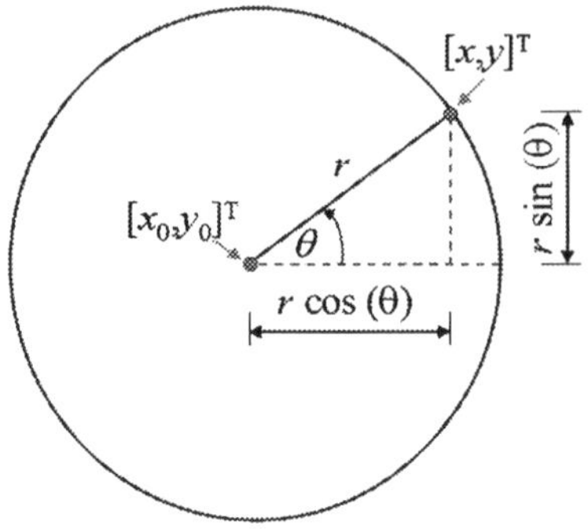


**Fig. 2.4** A pixel $[x, y]^T$ on the circumference of a circle can be estimated if the center $[x_0, y_0]^T$, the radius $r$ and the angle $\theta$ are known

some circumferential pixels may be missed. Also, if the radius value is too large, some pixels may be skipped as well. There must be a more efficient way to draw a circle.

### *2.2.1 Two-Way Symmetry Algorithm*

A circle equation may be expressed as

$$(x - x_0)^2 + (y - y_0)^2 = r^2, \tag{2.14}$$

where $[x_0, y_0]^T$ is the center point of the circle, $r$ is its radius in pixels and $[x, y]^T$ is a point on the circumference. Equation (2.14) can be re-written in an explicit form to solve for $y$ in terms of $x$ as

$$y = y_0 \pm \sqrt{r^2 - (x - x_0)^2}. \tag{2.15}$$

This explicit circle equation can be used to draw the circle by iterating along $x$-direction. Assuming that the center of the circle $[x_0, y_0]^T$ is at the origin $[0, 0]^T$, the $x$-values lie in the interval $[-r, r]$. Each iteration results in *two* values for $y$ which makes it faster than the previous method. Hence, comes the term *two-way symmetry* approach. However, discontinuities may appear with this approach when the slope is $<1$ (i.e., $\left|\frac{y-y_0}{x-x_0}\right| < 1$). An example showing a quarter of a circle is shown in Fig. 2.5 where discontinuities appear. Note that there is only one pixel marked for each $x$ in this upper quarter of the circle.

Algorithm 2.8 calculates the points comprising a circle centered at the origin and then moves the points estimated by the amount $[x_0, y_0]^T$ (i.e., the center of the circle) to get the correct positions.

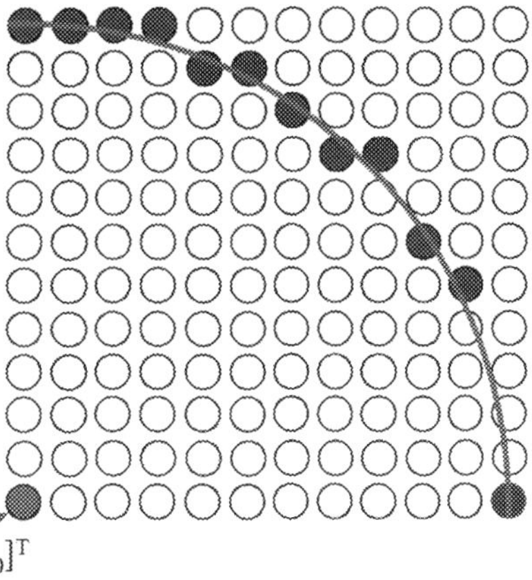


**Fig. 2.5** Two-way symmetry approach results in discontinuities where $\left|\frac{y-y_0}{x-x_0}\right| < 1$. Pixels selected to represent this quarter are shaded

**Algorithm 2.8** *Two-way symmetry algorithm*

**Input:** $x_0, y_0, r$
Plot $[x_0 + r, y_0]^T$
Plot $[x_0 - r, y_0]^T$
**for** $(x = -r + 1$ to $r - 1)$ **do**
  $y = \lfloor \sqrt{r^2 - x^2} + 0.5 \rfloor$
  Plot $[x_0 + x, y_0 + y]^T$
  Plot $[x_0 + x, y_0 - y]^T$
**end for**

**end**

Note that the start and endpoints of the horizontal diameter are treated as special cases before entering the loop. This is to avoid reflecting these points about themselves. Also, be careful that Algorithm 2.8 does not check if the points estimated lie inside the boundaries of the screen or viewport. In order to accommodate this constraint for a point $[x, y]^T$, check if $x \geq 0$, $y \geq 0$, $x < x_{max}$ and $y < y_{max}$ where $x_{max}$ and $y_{max}$ are the width and height of the screen or viewport in pixels.

**Example 2.5:** [*2-way symmetry algorithm*]
A circle having a radius of 5 pixels and centered at $[3, 4]^T$ is to be drawn on a computer screen. Use the 2-way symmetry algorithm to determine what pixels should constitute the circle.

**Solution 2.5:** The start and endpoints of the horizontal diameter are $[8, 4]^T$ and $[-2, 4]^T$. The rest of the points are listed in the following table:

| 3: $x$ | 4: $y$ | 5: Plot | 6: Plot |
|---|---|---|---|
| $-4$ | $\lfloor\sqrt{5^2-(-4)^2}+0.5\rfloor = 3$ | $[-1, 7]^T$ | $[-1, 1]^T$ |
| $-3$ | $\lfloor\sqrt{5^2-(-3)^2}+0.5\rfloor = 4$ | $[0, 8]^T$ | $[0, 0]^T$ |
| $-2$ | $\lfloor\sqrt{5^2-(-2)^2}+0.5\rfloor = 5$ | $[1, 9]^T$ | $[1, -1]^T$ |
| $-1$ | $\lfloor\sqrt{5^2-(-1)^2}+0.5\rfloor = 5$ | $[2, 9]^T$ | $[2, -1]^T$ |
| 0 | $\lfloor\sqrt{5^2-0^2}+0.5\rfloor = 5$ | $[3, 9]^T$ | $[3, -1]^T$ |
| 1 | $\lfloor\sqrt{5^2-1^2}+0.5\rfloor = 5$ | $[4, 9]^T$ | $[4, -1]^T$ |
| 2 | $\lfloor\sqrt{5^2-2^2}+0.5\rfloor = 5$ | $[5, 9]^T$ | $[5, -1]^T$ |
| 3 | $\lfloor\sqrt{5^2-3^2}+0.5\rfloor = 4$ | $[6, 8]^T$ | $[6, 0]^T$ |
| 4 | $\lfloor\sqrt{5^2-4^2}+0.5\rfloor = 3$ | $[7, 7]^T$ | $[7, 1]^T$ |

Of course, all points with negative coordinates are disregarded. Hence, the points considered are $[8, 4]^T$, $[0, 8]^T$, $[0, 0]^T$, $[1, 9]^T$, $[2, 9]^T$, $[3, 9]^T$, $[4, 9]^T$, $[5, 9]^T$, $[6, 8]^T$, $[6, 0]^T$, $[7, 7]^T$ and $[7, 1]^T$. □

### *2.2.2 Four-Way Symmetry Algorithm*

The symmetry of the circle can be utilized such that the circle may be split into four quadrants. In this four-way symmetry approach, the pixels of only one quadrant are estimated as done with the two-way symmetry approach while the pixels in the remaining three quadrants are mirrored/reflected. In this case, the number of iterations is reduced along the $x$-direction if compared with the two-way symmetry approach to almost half the number of iterations. This makes this approach faster than the previous one; however, it keeps the same problem of discontinuities as shown in Fig. 2.6 where the upper two quadrants of a circle are drawn using the four-way symmetry approach.

Assuming that the center of the circle $[x_0, y_0]^T$ is at the origin $[0, 0]^T$, Eq. (2.15) can be used to get a point $[x, y]^T$ on the circumference. This is followed by mirroring this point to obtain three other points $[x, -y]^T$, $[-x, y]^T$ and $[-x, -y]^T$ in the other three quadrants. In this case, the $x$-values lie within the interval $[0, r]$. In the general case where the circle is centered at an arbitrary point $[x_0, y_0]^T$, we calculate the points of the circle as if it is centered at the origin and then move the points estimated by the vector $[x_0, y_0]^T$ that represents the center point to get the correct positions. Algorithm 2.9 lists the four-way symmetry algorithm.

**Algorithm 2.9** *Four-way symmetry algorithm*

**Input:** $x_0, y_0, r$
Plot $[x_0, y_0 + r]^T$
Plot $[x_0, y_0 - r]^T$
Plot $[x_0 + r, y_0]^T$
Plot $[x_0 - r, y_0]^T$
**for** $(x = 1$ to $r - 1)$ **do**

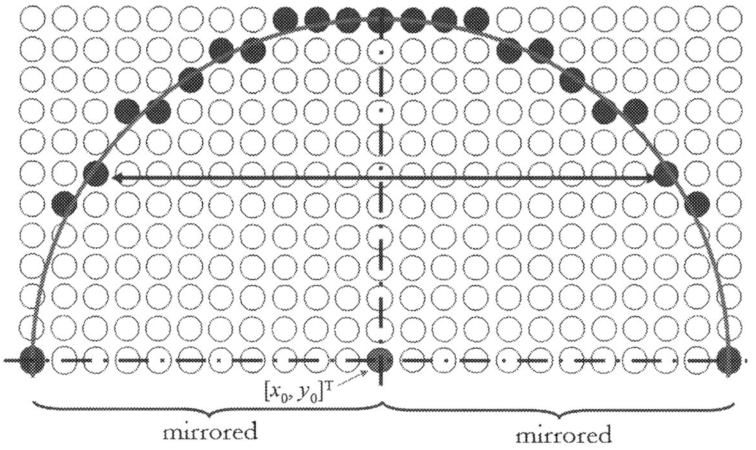


**Fig. 2.6** Four-way symmetry approach. Only two quadrants are shown

6: $\quad y = \lfloor\sqrt{r^2 - x^2} + 0.5\rfloor$
7: $\quad$ Plot $[x_0 + x, y_0 + y]^T$
8: $\quad$ Plot $[x_0 + x, y_0 - y]^T$
9: $\quad$ Plot $[x_0 - x, y_0 + y]^T$
10: $\quad$ Plot $[x_0 - x, y_0 - y]^T$
11: **end for**

**end**

Note that the start and endpoints of each quadrant are treated as special cases before entering the loop as done before with the two-way symmetry approach. This is to avoid reflecting these points about themselves. Also, you may tune Algorithm 2.9 to check if the points estimated lie inside the boundaries of the screen or viewport as mentioned before with the two-way symmetry approach.

**Example 2.6:** [*4-way symmetry algorithm*]
A circle having a radius of 5 pixels and centered at $[3, 4]^T$ is to be drawn on a computer screen. Use the 4-way symmetry algorithm to determine what pixels should constitute the circle.

**Solution 2.6:** The start and endpoints of each quadrant are $[3, 9]^T$, $[3, -1]^T$, $[8, 4]^T$ and $[-2, 4]^T$. The rest of the points are listed in the following table:

| 5: $x$ | 6: $y$ | 7: Plot | 8: Plot | 9: Plot | 10: Plot |
|---|---|---|---|---|---|
| 1 | $\lfloor\sqrt{5^2 - 1^2} + 0.5\rfloor = 5$ | $[4, 9]^T$ | $[4, -1]^T$ | $[2, 9]^T$ | $[2, -1]^T$ |
| 2 | $\lfloor\sqrt{5^2 - 2^2} + 0.5\rfloor = 5$ | $[5, 9]^T$ | $[5, -1]^T$ | $[1, 9]^T$ | $[1, -1]^T$ |
| 3 | $\lfloor\sqrt{5^2 - 3^2} + 0.5\rfloor = 4$ | $[6, 8]^T$ | $[6, 0]^T$ | $[0, 8]^T$ | $[0, 0]^T$ |
| 4 | $\lfloor\sqrt{5^2 - 4^2} + 0.5\rfloor = 3$ | $[7, 7]^T$ | $[7, 1]^T$ | $[-1, 7]^T$ | $[-1, 1]^T$ |

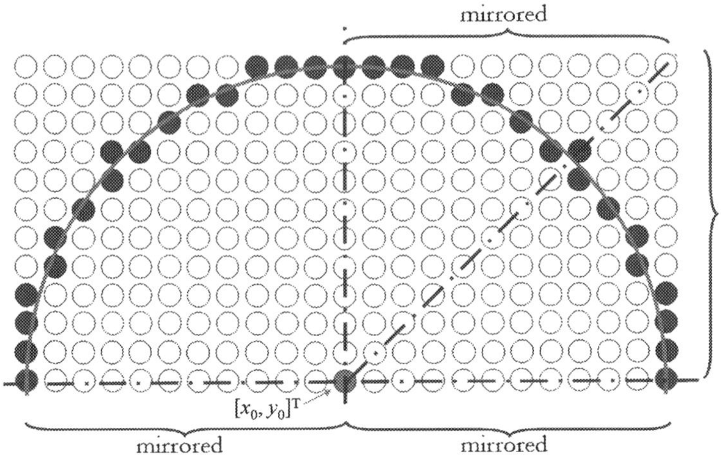


**Fig. 2.7** Eight-way symmetry approach. Only four octants are shown

We discard all points with negative coordinates. Hence, the points considered are $[3, 9]^T$, $[8, 4]^T$, $[4, 9]^T$, $[2, 9]^T$, $[5, 9]^T$, $[1, 9]^T$, $[6, 8]^T$, $[6, 0]^T$, $[0, 8]^T$, $[0, 0]^T$, $[7, 7]^T$ and $[7, 1]$. Note that those are the same points obtained in Example 2.5 using the 2-way symmetry algorithm but with less number of iterations. □

## 2.2.3 *Eight-Way Symmetry Algorithm*

The four-way symmetry approach can be further enhanced by splitting the circle into eight octants instead of only four quadrants. This is referred to as the *eight-way symmetry* approach in which the pixels of only one octant are estimated as done before while the pixels in the remaining seven octants are mirrored/reflected. In this case, the number of loop iterations is reduced more than before. This makes this approach much faster than the previous ones. In addition, it avoids the problem of discontinuities as shown in Fig. 2.7 where the upper four octants of a circle are drawn using the eight-way symmetry approach.

Assuming that the center of the circle $[x_0, y_0]^T$ is at the origin $[0, 0]^T$, Eq. (2.15) can be used to get a point $[x, y]^T$ on the circumference. This is followed by mirroring this point to obtain seven other points $[x, -y]^T$, $[-x, y]^T$, $[-x, -y]^T$, $[y, x]^T$, $[y, -x]^T$, $[-y, x]^T$ and $[-y, -x]^T$ in the other seven octants. Note that the $x$-values within the loop lie in the interval $\left[1, \left\lfloor \frac{r}{\sqrt{2}} \right\rfloor\right]$.

If the circle is centered at an arbitrary point $[x_0, y_0]^T$, we calculate the points comprising the circle as if it is centered at the origin and then move the points estimated by the amount $[x_0, y_0]^T$ to get the correct positions. Algorithm 2.10 lists the eight-way symmetry algorithm, which results in better and faster-to-generate circles.

**Algorithm 2.10** *Eight-way symmetry algorithm*

**Input:** $x_0, y_0, r$<br>
1: Plot $[x_0, y_0 + r]^T$<br>
2: Plot $[x_0, y_0 - r]^T$<br>
3: Plot $[x_0 + r, y_0]^T$<br>
4: Plot $[x_0 - r, y_0]^T$<br>
5: $x = 1$<br>
6: $y = \lfloor \sqrt{r^2 - x^2} + 0.5 \rfloor$<br>
7:<br>
8: **while** $(x < y)$ **do**<br>
9:     Plot $[x_0 + x, y_0 + y]^T$<br>
10:     Plot $[x_0 + x, y_0 - y]^T$<br>
11:     Plot $[x_0 - x, y_0 + y]^T$<br>
12:     Plot $[x_0 - x, y_0 - y]^T$<br>
13:     Plot $[x_0 + y, y_0 + x]^T$<br>
14:     Plot $[x_0 + y, y_0 - x]^T$<br>
15:     Plot $[x_0 - y, y_0 + x]^T$<br>
16:     Plot $[x_0 - y, y_0 - x]^T$<br>
17:     $x = x + 1$<br>
18:     $y = \lfloor \sqrt{r^2 - x^2} + 0.5 \rfloor$<br>
19: **end while**<br>
20:<br>
21: **if** $x = y$ **then**<br>
22:     Plot $[x_0 + x, y_0 + y]^T$<br>
23:     Plot $[x_0 + x, y_0 - y]^T$<br>
24:     Plot $[x_0 - x, y_0 + y]^T$<br>
25:     Plot $[x_0 - x, y_0 - y]^T$<br>
26: **end if**

**end**

Notice that the start and endpoints of each octant are treated as special cases as done with the two- and four-way symmetry approaches to avoid reflecting these points about themselves. (Check Lines 1–4 and 22–25.) You may also check if the points estimated lie inside the boundaries of the screen or viewport by testing if $x \geq 0$, $y \geq 0$, $x < x_{max}$ and $y < y_{max}$ where $x_{max}$ and $y_{max}$ are the width and height of the screen in pixels.

**Example 2.7:** [*8-way symmetry algorithm*]

A circle having a radius of 5 pixels and centered at $[3, 4]^T$ is to be drawn on a computer screen. Use the 8-way symmetry algorithm to determine what pixels should constitute the circle.

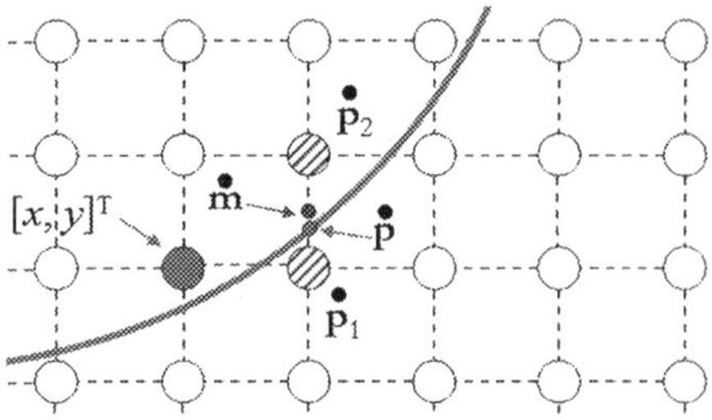


**Fig. 2.8** $\dot{\mathbf{m}} = [x+1, y+\frac{1}{2}]^T$ is the midpoint between $[x+1, y]^T$ and $[x+1, y+1]^T$

**Solution 2.7:** The start and endpoints of each quadrant are $[3, 9]^T$, $[3, -1]^T$, $[8, 4]^T$ and $[-2, 4]^T$. The rest of the points are listed in the following table:

| 5/17: $x$ | 6/18: $y$ | 9: Plot | 10: Plot | 11: Plot | 12: Plot | 13: Plot | 14: Plot | 15: Plot | 16: Plot |
|---|---|---|---|---|---|---|---|---|---|
| 1 | 5 | $[4, 9]^T$ | $[4, -1]^T$ | $[2, 9]^T$ | $[2, -1]^T$ | $[8, 5]^T$ | $[8, 3]^T$ | $[-2, 5]^T$ | $[-2, 3]^T$ |
| 2 | 5 | $[5, 9]^T$ | $[5, -1]^T$ | $[1, 9]^T$ | $[1, -1]^T$ | $[8, 6]^T$ | $[8, 2]^T$ | $[-2, 6]^T$ | $[-2, 2]^T$ |
| 3 | 4 | $[6, 8]^T$ | $[6, 0]^T$ | $[0, 8]^T$ | $[0, 0]^T$ | $[7, 7]^T$ | $[7, 1]^T$ | $[-1, 7]^T$ | $[-1, 1]^T$ |
| 4 | 3 | | | | no iteration as $x > y$ | | | | |

After neglecting all points with negative coordinates, the points considered are $[3, 9]^T$, $[8, 4]^T$, $[4, 9]^T$, $[2, 9]^T$, $[8, 5]^T$, $[8, 3]^T$, $[5, 9]^T$, $[1, 9]^T$, $[8, 6]^T$, $[8, 2]^T$, $[6, 8]^T$, $[6, 0]^T$, $[0, 8]^T$, $[0, 0]^T$, $[7, 7]^T$ and $[7, 1]^T$. Notice that the discontinuity problem has been overcome in this case. (Check out points $[8, 2]^T$, $[8, 3]^T$, $[8, 5]^T$ and $[8, 6]^T$.) In addition, calculations have been done with a faster algorithm.

Also, notice that the number of iterations along the $x$-direction may be calculated as

$$\left\lfloor \frac{r}{\sqrt{2}} \right\rfloor = \left\lfloor \frac{5}{\sqrt{2}} \right\rfloor = 3. \qquad \square$$

### *2.2.4 The Midpoint Algorithm*

The *midpoint algorithm* used to draw lines in Sect. 2.1.3 can be modified to draw circles (Foley et al. 1995). Similar to the 8-way symmetry algorithm (Sect. 2.2.3), only one octant is considered. The rest of the circle is obtained by symmetry as done before. Similar to the midpoint technique used to draw lines, we determine on which side of the circle equation the midpoint between pixels lies.

Consider Fig. 2.8 where a part of a circle is shown and where a pixel $[x, y]^T$ is determined to belong to the circle. When $x$ is incremented at the next iteration as done before, the exact intersection happens at point $\dot{\mathbf{p}}$. Thus, there will be two choices for the pixels to be picked up at $x+1$; these choices are $\dot{\mathbf{p}}_1$ and $\dot{\mathbf{p}}_2$.

The implicit form of a circle equation is given by

$$\mathscr{F}(x, y) = x^2 + y^2 - r^2 = 0, \tag{2.16}$$

where $r$ is the radius of the circle and $[x, y]^T$ is a point on the circle. Now, the midpoint $\dot{\mathbf{m}} = [x+1, y+\frac{1}{2}]^T$ between $[x+1, y]^T$ and $[x+1, y+1]^T$ is applied to Eq. (2.16) to get

$$\mathscr{F}\left(x+1, y+\frac{1}{2}\right) = d_{\dot{\mathbf{m}}} = (x+1)^2 + \left(y+\frac{1}{2}\right)^2 - r^2. \tag{2.17}$$

There are three possibilities for $d_{\dot{\mathbf{m}}}$:

$$d_{\dot{\mathbf{m}}} = \begin{cases} +ve, & \dot{\mathbf{m}} \text{ is outside the circle; thus, } \dot{\mathbf{p}}_2 \text{ is selected;} \\ -ve, & \dot{\mathbf{m}} \text{ is inside the circle; thus, } \dot{\mathbf{p}}_1 \text{ is selected;} \\ 0, & \text{the midpoint } \dot{\mathbf{m}} \text{ is exactly on the circle; thus, select either } \dot{\mathbf{p}}_1 \text{ or } \dot{\mathbf{p}}_2. \end{cases}$$

Choosing the pixel in the next column depends on whether $\dot{\mathbf{p}}_1$ or $\dot{\mathbf{p}}_2$ has been selected. Assume that $\dot{\mathbf{p}}_1$ is selected. The midpoint $[x+2, y+\frac{1}{2}]^T$ between $[x+2, y]^T$ and $[x+2, y+1]^T$ is applied to Eq. (2.16) to get

$$\begin{aligned} \mathscr{F}\left(x+2, y+\frac{1}{2}\right) &= (x+2)^2 + \left(y+\frac{1}{2}\right)^2 - r^2 \\ &= \underbrace{(x+1)^2 + \left(y+\frac{1}{2}\right)^2 - r^2}_{d_{\dot{\mathbf{m}}}} + 2x + 3 \\ &= d_{\dot{\mathbf{m}}} + 2x + 3. \end{aligned} \tag{2.18}$$

On the other hand, if $\dot{\mathbf{p}}_2$ is selected, the midpoint $[x+2, y+\frac{3}{2}]^T$ between $[x+2, y+1]^T$ and $[x+2, y+2]^T$ is applied to Eq. (2.16) to get

$$\begin{aligned} \mathscr{F}\left(x+2, y+\frac{3}{2}\right) &= (x+2)^2 + \left(y+\frac{3}{2}\right)^2 - r^2 \\ &= \underbrace{(x+1)^2 + \left(y+\frac{1}{2}\right)^2 - r^2}_{d_{\dot{\mathbf{m}}}} + 2x + 2y + 5 \\ &= d_{\dot{\mathbf{m}}} + 2x + 2y + 5. \end{aligned} \tag{2.19}$$

This means that the subsequent sign of $d_{\dot{\mathbf{m}}}$ can be obtained by incrementing it by either $2x+3$ if $\dot{\mathbf{p}}_1$ is selected or $2x+2y+5$ if $\dot{\mathbf{p}}_2$ is selected where $[x, y]^T$ is the previous point on the circle (i.e., the increments are functions rather than constants as in line midpoint algorithm). Assuming that the center point is at the origin, an initial value for $d_{\dot{\mathbf{m}}}$ can be obtained using the lowest point $[0, -r]^T$ and Eq. (2.17) where the next midpoint lies at $[1, -r + \frac{1}{2}]^T$. So,

$$\begin{aligned} \mathscr{F}\left(1, -r + \frac{1}{2}\right) &= 1^2 + \left(-r + \frac{1}{2}\right)^2 - r^2 \\ &= \underbrace{\frac{5}{4} - r}_{d_{\dot{\mathbf{m}}}}, \end{aligned} \tag{2.20}$$

where $\frac{5}{4} - r$ is the initial estimate of $d_{\dot{\mathbf{m}}}$. The midpoint algorithm for circles is listed in Algorithm 2.11. This algorithm assumes that the center of the circle is at $[x_0, y_0]^T$.

**Algorithm 2.11** *Midpoint algorithm for circles – floating-point version*

**Input:** $x_0, y_0, r$
1: $d_{\dot{\mathbf{m}}} = \frac{5}{4} - r$
2: $x = 0$
3: $y = -r$
4:
5: Plot $[x_0, y_0 + r]^T$
6: Plot $[x_0, y_0 - r]^T$
7: Plot $[x_0 + r, y_0]^T$
8: Plot $[x_0 - r, y_0]^T$
9:
10: **while** $(x < -(y + 1))$ **do**
11:     **if** $(d_{\dot{\mathbf{m}}} < 0)$ **then**
12:         $d_{\dot{\mathbf{m}}} = d_{\dot{\mathbf{m}}} + 2x + 3$
13:     **else**
14:         $d_{\dot{\mathbf{m}}} = d_{\dot{\mathbf{m}}} + 2x + 2y + 5$
15:         $y = y + 1$
16:     **end if**
17:     $x = x + 1$
18:     Plot $[x_0 + x, y_0 + y]^T$
19:     Plot $[x_0 + x, y_0 - y]^T$
20:     Plot $[x_0 - x, y_0 + y]^T$
21:     Plot $[x_0 - x, y_0 - y]^T$
22:     Plot $[x_0 + y, y_0 + x]^T$
23:     Plot $[x_0 + y, y_0 - x]^T$
24:     Plot $[x_0 - y, y_0 + x]^T$
25:     Plot $[x_0 - y, y_0 - x]^T$
26: **end while**

**end**

Notice that checking for the number of iterations $\left\lfloor \frac{r}{\sqrt{2}} \right\rfloor$ may be used to replace the condition of the "while" loop on Line 10. (See Problem 2.8.)

Algorithm 2.11 uses floating-point numbers which slows the process down. The initial value of $d_{\dot{\mathbf{m}}}$ contains a fraction; thus, a new variable $h_{\dot{\mathbf{m}}} = d_{\dot{\mathbf{m}}} - \frac{1}{4}$ is used (Foley et al. 1995) to replace the value of $d_{\dot{\mathbf{m}}}$ by $h_{\dot{\mathbf{m}}} + \frac{1}{4}$. Hence, Line 1 in Algorithm 2.11 can be $h_{\dot{\mathbf{m}}} = 1 - r$. In addition, the condition $d_{\dot{\mathbf{m}}} < 0$ of Line 11 is changed to $h_{\dot{\mathbf{m}}} < -\frac{1}{4}$. However, notice that $h_{\dot{\mathbf{m}}}$ is initialized to an integer (i.e., $1 - r$) and is incremented by integers (either by $2x+3$ or by $2x+2y+5$). So, the condition $h_{\dot{\mathbf{m}}} < -\frac{1}{4}$ can be modified to $h_{\dot{\mathbf{m}}} < 0$. Algorithm 2.12 applies all these changes.

**Algorithm 2.12** *Midpoint algorithm for circles – integer version*

**Input:** $x_0, y_0, r$

$h_{\dot{\mathbf{m}}} = 1 - r$
$x = 0$
$y = -r$

Plot $[x_0, y_0 + r]^T$
Plot $[x_0, y_0 - r]^T$
Plot $[x_0 + r, y_0]^T$
Plot $[x_0 - r, y_0]^T$

**while** $(x < -(y+1))$ **do**
  **if** $(h_{\dot{\mathbf{m}}} < 0)$ **then**
    $h_{\dot{\mathbf{m}}} = h_{\dot{\mathbf{m}}} + 2x + 3$
  **else**
    $h_{\dot{\mathbf{m}}} = h_{\dot{\mathbf{m}}} + 2x + 2y + 5$
    $y = y + 1$
  **end if**
  $x = x + 1$
  Plot $[x_0 + x, y_0 + y]^T$
  Plot $[x_0 + x, y_0 - y]^T$
  Plot $[x_0 - x, y_0 + y]^T$
  Plot $[x_0 - x, y_0 - y]^T$
  Plot $[x_0 + y, y_0 + x]^T$
  Plot $[x_0 + y, y_0 - x]^T$
  Plot $[x_0 - y, y_0 + x]^T$
  Plot $[x_0 - y, y_0 - x]^T$
**end while**

**end**

**Example 2.8:** [*Midpoint circle drawing algorithm*]

A circle having a radius of 5 pixels and centered at $[3, 4]^T$ is to be drawn on a computer screen. Use the midpoint algorithm to determine what pixels should approximate the circle.

**Solution 2.8:** The initial value of $h_{\dot{\mathbf{m}}}$ is given by

$$h_{\dot{\text{m}}} = 1 - r = 1 - 5 = -4.$$

The initial values for $x$ and $y$ are 0 and $-5$ respectively. The start and endpoints of each quadrant are $[3, 9]^T$, $[3, -1]^T$, $[8, 4]^T$ and $[-2, 4]^T$. The rest of the points are listed in the following table:

| 10: $x$ | 12/14: $h_{\dot{\text{m}}}$ | 15: $y$ | 17: $x$ | 18: Plot | 19: Plot | 20: Plot | 21: Plot | 22: Plot | 23: Plot | 24: Plot | 25: Plot |
|---|---|---|---|---|---|---|---|---|---|---|---|
| 0 | $-1$ | | 1 | $[4, -1]^T$ | $[4, 9]^T$ | $[2, -1]^T$ | $[2, 9]^T$ | $[-2, 5]^T$ | $[-2, 3]^T$ | $[8, 5]^T$ | $[8, 3]$ |
| 1 | 4 | | 2 | $[5, -1]^T$ | $[5, 9]^T$ | $[1, -1]^T$ | $[1, 9]^T$ | $[-2, 6]^T$ | $[-2, 2]^T$ | $[8, 6]^T$ | $[8, 2]$ |
| 2 | 3 | $-4$ | 3 | $[6, 0]^T$ | $[6, 8]^T$ | $[0, 0]^T$ | $[0, 8]^T$ | $[-1, 7]^T$ | $[-1, 1]^T$ | $[7, 7]^T$ | $[7, 1]$ |
| 3 | | | | | no iteration as $x = -(y + 1)$ | | | | | | |

Of course, all points with negative coordinates are disregarded. Hence, the points considered are $[3, 9]^T$, $[8, 4]^T$, $[4, 9]^T$, $[2, 9]^T$, $[8, 5]^T$, $[8, 3]^T$, $[5, 9]^T$, $[1, 9]^T$, $[8, 6]^T$, $[8, 2]^T$, $[6, 0]^T$, $[6, 8]^T$, $[0, 0]^T$, $[0, 8]^T$, $[7, 7]^T$ and $[7, 1]^T$. Note that those are the same points obtained in Example 2.7 using the 8-way symmetry algorithm but produced by a faster integer algorithm. □

## 2.3 Polygons

A 2D *polygon* is a closed planar path composed of a number of sequential straight line segments. Each line segment is called a *side* or an *edge*. The intersections between line segments are called *vertices*. The end vertex of the last edge is the start vertex of the first edge. A polygon encloses an area.

A *polyline* is similar to a polygon except that the end vertex of the last edge does not have to be the start vertex of the first edge. Hence, unlike polygons, no area is expected to emerge for a polyline.

### *2.3.1 Convexity Versus Concavity*

A polygon may be *convex* or *concave*. Examples of convex and concave polygons are shown in Fig. 2.9. A polygon is convex if the line connecting any two interior points is included completely in the interior of the polygon. Each interior angle in a convex polygon must be $\leq 180°$; otherwise, the polygon is considered concave.

A 2D polygon is stored as a set of vertex coordinates (i.e., $[x_i, y_i]^T$ where $i$ is the vertex number). These coordinates can be used to determine whether the polygon is convex or concave. Cross product or linear equations of the edges can be used to answer the question of convexity/concavity of a polygon.

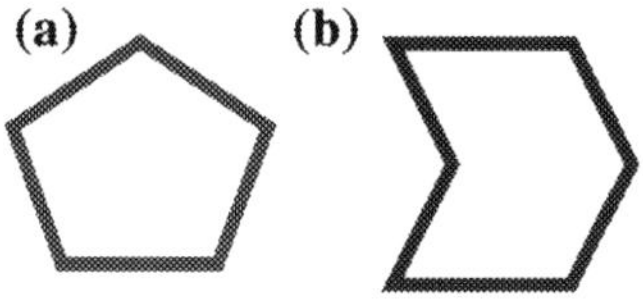


**Fig. 2.9** Examples of polygons. **a** Convex polygon where any interior angle is $\leq 180°$. **b** Concave polygon where at least one of the interior angles is $>180°$

**Cross product:** This method proceeds as follows:

1. For each edge:

   a. Define a vector for the edge $\mathbf{e}_i$ connecting the vertices $\dot{\mathbf{v}}_i$ and $\dot{\mathbf{v}}_{i+1}$. This is expressed as
$$\mathbf{e}_i = \dot{\mathbf{v}}_{i+1} - \dot{\mathbf{v}}_i. \tag{2.21}$$

   b. Compute the 2D cross product (Sect. A.4.3.4) along consecutive edges $\mathbf{e}_{i-1}$ and $\mathbf{e}_i$ as
$$\begin{aligned}\mathbf{e}_{i-1} \times \mathbf{e}_i &= [\dot{\mathbf{v}}_i - \dot{\mathbf{v}}_{i-1}] \times [\dot{\mathbf{v}}_{i+1} - \dot{\mathbf{v}}_i] \\ &= \begin{bmatrix} x_i - x_{i-1} \\ y_i - y_{i-1} \end{bmatrix} \times \begin{bmatrix} x_{i+1} - x_i \\ y_{i+1} - y_i \end{bmatrix} \\ &= (x_i - x_{i-1})(y_{i+1} - y_i) - (y_i - y_{i-1})(x_{i+1} - x_i).\end{aligned} \tag{2.22}$$

2. The polygon is convex if and only if all signs of cross products along all edges are the same; otherwise, the polygon is concave.

**Linear equations:** This method proceeds as follows:

1. For each edge:

   a. Estimate the linear equation of the edge connecting the vertices $\dot{\mathbf{v}}_i = [x_i, y_i]^T$ and $\dot{\mathbf{v}}_{i+1} = [x_{i+1}, y_{i+1}]^T$. This is expressed in explicit form as
$$y = \frac{y_{i+1} - y_i}{x_{i+1} - x_i}(x - x_i) + y_i \tag{2.23}$$

   or in $ax + by + c = 0$ implicit form as
$$\underbrace{(y_{i+1} - y_i)}_{a}\, x + \underbrace{(x_i - x_{i+1})}_{b}\, y + \underbrace{y_i x_{i+1} - x_i y_{i+1}}_{c} = 0. \tag{2.24}$$

   Another way to get the same equation is to calculate the cross product (Sect. A.4.3.4) of the homogeneous points (Sect. B.7) $\mathbf{v}_i = [x_i, y_i, 1]^T$ and $\mathbf{v}_{i+1} = [x_{i+1}, y_{i+1}, 1]^T$. Thus,

$$\begin{bmatrix} a \\ b \\ c \end{bmatrix} = \mathbf{v}_i \times \mathbf{v}_{i+1} = \begin{bmatrix} x_i \\ y_i \\ 1 \end{bmatrix} \times \begin{bmatrix} x_{i+1} \\ y_{i+1} \\ 1 \end{bmatrix}. \tag{2.25}$$

b. Apply each of the remaining vertices to the linear equation estimated above.

2. The polygon is convex if and only if all signs obtained are the same for each single edge; otherwise, the polygon is concave.

**Example 2.9:** [*Polygon concavity/convexity*]
At least two different methods may be used to decide whether or not a 2D polygon is concave or convex. Apply each of them to the 2D polygon specified by the vertices $[0, 0]^T$, $[5, 0]^T$, $[-1, 5]^T$ and $[-1, -5]^T$. Based on your calculations, determine whether this polygon is concave or convex.

**Solution 2.9:** This problem can be solved using 2D cross product or using linear equations.

1. Using 2D cross product:

   a. Substitute $\dot{\mathbf{v}}_{i-1} = [-1, -5]^T$, $\dot{\mathbf{v}}_i = [0, 0]^T$ and $\dot{\mathbf{v}}_{i+1} = [5, 0]^T$ in Eq. (2.22) and calculate $\mathbf{e}_{i-1} \times \mathbf{e}_i$ as

$$\begin{aligned} \mathbf{e}_{i-1} \times \mathbf{e}_i &= [\dot{\mathbf{v}}_i - \dot{\mathbf{v}}_{i-1}] \times [\dot{\mathbf{v}}_{i+1} - \dot{\mathbf{v}}_i] \\ &= (x_i - x_{i-1})(y_{i+1} - y_i) - (y_i - y_{i-1})(x_{i+1} - x_i) \\ &= (0 - (-1))(0 - 0) - (0 - (-5))(5 - 0) = -25 \Rightarrow -ve. \end{aligned}$$

   b. Substitute $\dot{\mathbf{v}}_{i-1} = [0, 0]^T$, $\dot{\mathbf{v}}_i = [5, 0]^T$ and $\dot{\mathbf{v}}_{i+1} = [-1, 5]^T$ in Eq. (2.22) and calculate $\mathbf{e}_{i-1} \times \mathbf{e}_i$ as

$$\begin{aligned} \mathbf{e}_{i-1} \times \mathbf{e}_i &= [\dot{\mathbf{v}}_i - \dot{\mathbf{v}}_{i-1}] \times [\dot{\mathbf{v}}_{i+1} - \dot{\mathbf{v}}_i] \\ &= (x_i - x_{i-1})(y_{i+1} - y_i) - (y_i - y_{i-1})(x_{i+1} - x_i) \\ &= (5 - 0)(5 - 0) - (0 - 0)(-1 - 5) = +25 \Rightarrow +ve. \end{aligned}$$

   The substitutions result in different signs. This implies that it is a concave polygon.

2. Using linear equations:

   a. Consider the linear equation given the points $[x_i, y_i]^T = [-1, -5]^T$ and $[x_{i+1}, y_{i+1}]^T = [0, 0]^T$. Using Eq. (2.23), we have

$$\begin{aligned} y &= \frac{y_{i+1} - y_i}{x_{i+1} - x_i}(x - x_i) + y_i \\ y &= 5x + 5 - 5 \\ y - 5x &= 0. \end{aligned}$$

b. Apply the other two points ($[5,0]^T$ and $[-1,5]^T$) to the previous equation to get

$$\begin{aligned} y - 5x &= 0 \\ 0 - 5(5) &= -25 \Rightarrow -ve, \\ 5 - 5(-1) &= +10 \Rightarrow +ve. \end{aligned}$$

The substitutions result in different signs. This implies that it is a concave polygon. □

## 2.4 Line Clipping

Given a 2D line or a group of 2D lines, a clip rectangle or window can be used to clip those lines so that only lines or portions of lines inside the clip window are preserved while the other lines or portions of lines are removed. Such an approach is referred to as a *2D line clipping* algorithm. It should be noted that even though there are many algorithms for rectangle and polygon clipping, a line clipping algorithm can be used repeatedly to clip polygons of any shape approximated by line segments.

An example of line clipping is shown in Fig. 2.10 where lines preserved after clipping appear thicker. There are three distinctive cases that may be observed:

1. Both endpoints of the line are *inside* the clip rectangle as line $\overline{\dot{\mathbf{a}}\mathbf{b}}$ shown in Fig. 2.10.
2. One endpoint is *inside* the clip rectangle while the other endpoint is *outside* the rectangle as line $\overline{\dot{\mathbf{c}}\mathbf{d}}$ shown in Fig. 2.10.
3. Both endpoints of the line are *outside* the clip rectangle as lines $\overline{\dot{\mathbf{e}}\mathbf{f}}$ and $\overline{\dot{\mathbf{g}}\mathbf{h}}$ shown in Fig. 2.10.

Dealing with each of the previous cases is different.

**Both endpoints are inside the clip rectangle**: A line is completely inside a clip rectangle or window if both endpoints are inside the window. Assume that the clip rectangle spans from $[x_{min}, y_{min}]^T$ to $[x_{max}, y_{max}]^T$ and a line goes from $[x_0, y_0]^T$ to $[x_1, y_1]^T$, the line is preserved and *trivially accepted* if all the following eight inequalities hold:

$$\begin{aligned} x_{min} &\leq x_0 \leq x_{max}, \\ y_{min} &\leq y_0 \leq y_{max}, \\ x_{min} &\leq x_1 \leq x_{max}, \\ y_{min} &\leq y_1 \leq y_{max}. \end{aligned} \tag{2.26}$$

**Only one endpoint is inside the clip rectangle:** A portion of the line is inside the clip rectangle in case only one endpoint is inside the clip rectangle. Assume that the clip rectangle spans from $[x_{min}, y_{min}]^T$ to $[x_{max}, y_{max}]^T$ and a line goes from $[x_0, y_0]^T$ to $[x_1, y_1]^T$. Perform the following steps:

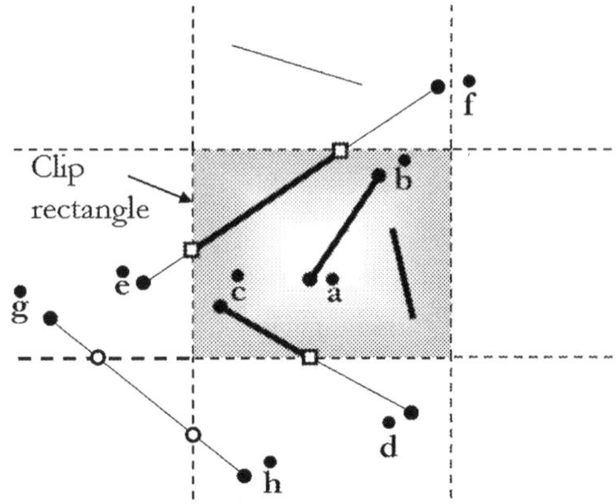


**Fig. 2.10** Example of 2D line clipping. Lines remained after clipping appear thicker

1. Check if only one endpoint falls inside the clip rectangle. The endpoint $[x_0, y_0]^T$ is inside the clip rectangle if the following tests are true:

$$\begin{aligned} x_{min} &\le x_0 \le x_{max}, \\ y_{min} &\le y_0 \le y_{max}. \end{aligned} \tag{2.27}$$

The endpoint $[x_1, y_1]^T$ is inside the clip rectangle if the following tests are true:

$$\begin{aligned} x_{min} &\le x_1 \le x_{max}, \\ y_{min} &\le y_1 \le y_{max}. \end{aligned} \tag{2.28}$$

Note that either Inequality (2.27) *or* Inequality (2.28) must be true but *not* both; otherwise, we will go back to the first case where both endpoints are inside the clip rectangle. (Note that either Inequality (2.27) or Inequality (2.28) can be used to keep or neglect isolated points; a process that is referred to as *point clipping*.)
2. Detect the intersection point between the line and the clip rectangle. Many methods exist to detect line intersections. The most suitable method in this situation is using the linear parametric form. There are four intersection points between the line and each of the clip rectangle edges to be detected. The intersection point $[x, y]^T$ along the line that goes from $[x_0, y_0]^T$ to $[x_1, y_1]^T$ can be expressed in parametric form as

$$\begin{bmatrix} x \\ y \end{bmatrix} = \begin{bmatrix} x_0 \\ y_0 \end{bmatrix} + t_{line} \begin{bmatrix} x_1 - x_0 \\ y_1 - y_0 \end{bmatrix}, \tag{2.29}$$

where $t_{line}$ is a parameter that determines the location of the point $[x, y]^T$ along the line such that $t_{line} \in [0, 1]$. The intersection point $[x, y]^T$ along the lower and upper horizontal clip rectangle edges can be expressed in parametric forms respectively as

$$\begin{bmatrix} x \\ y \end{bmatrix} = \begin{bmatrix} x_{min} \\ y_{min} \end{bmatrix} + t_{edge1} \begin{bmatrix} x_{max} - x_{min} \\ y_{min} - y_{min} \end{bmatrix} \tag{2.30}$$

and

$$\begin{bmatrix} x \\ y \end{bmatrix} = \begin{bmatrix} x_{min} \\ y_{max} \end{bmatrix} + t_{edge2} \begin{bmatrix} x_{max} - x_{min} \\ y_{max} - y_{max} \end{bmatrix}, \tag{2.31}$$

where $t_{edge1}$ and $t_{edge2}$ are parameters that determine the location of the intersection point $[x, y]^T$ along the clip rectangle lower and upper edges respectively such that $t_{edge1} \in [0, 1]$ and $t_{edge2} \in [0, 1]$. Note that a value of either 0 or 1 means that the line is going through a corner of the clip rectangle. Similarly, the intersection point $[x, y]^T$ along the left and right vertical clip rectangle edges can be expressed in parametric forms respectively as

$$\begin{bmatrix} x \\ y \end{bmatrix} = \begin{bmatrix} x_{min} \\ y_{min} \end{bmatrix} + t_{edge3} \begin{bmatrix} x_{min} - x_{min} \\ y_{max} - y_{min} \end{bmatrix} \tag{2.32}$$

and

$$\begin{bmatrix} x \\ y \end{bmatrix} = \begin{bmatrix} x_{max} \\ y_{min} \end{bmatrix} + t_{edge4} \begin{bmatrix} x_{max} - x_{max} \\ y_{max} - y_{min} \end{bmatrix}, \tag{2.33}$$

where $t_{edge3}$ and $t_{edge4}$ are parameters that determine the location of the point $[x, y]^T$ along the edges such that $t_{edge3} \in [0, 1]$ and $t_{edge4} \in [0, 1]$. To obtain the point $[x, y]^T$, solve Eq. (2.29) with each of Eqs. (2.30)–(2.33).

3. Check which intersection point $[x, y]^T$ falls inside the boundaries of the clip rectangle. Intersection points may occur at line and/or edge extensions. If this is the case, the following will be true: $t_{line} \notin [0, 1]$ and/or $t_{edgei} \notin [0, 1]$ where $i$ is the edge number. Thus, checking the value of $t_{line}$ and $t_{edgei}$ against the interval [0,1] determines whether the intersection point falls within the clip rectangle. Another way to determine if an intersection point $[x, y]^T$ falls within the clip rectangle is by checking

$$\begin{aligned} x_{min} &\le x \le x_{max}, \\ y_{min} &\le y \le y_{max}, \end{aligned} \tag{2.34}$$

which must be true so that the point $[x, y]^T$ is determined as falling within the clip rectangle.

Finally, the portion of the line from the intersection point to the inside endpoint is kept while the rest of the line is removed.

**Both endpoints are outside the clip rectangle:** If both endpoints are outside the clip rectangle, the line may be completely outside the clip rectangle as line $\overline{\dot{\mathbf{g}}\mathbf{h}}$ in Fig. 2.10 or part of the line is inside the clip rectangle as line $\overline{\dot{\mathbf{e}}\mathbf{f}}$ in the same figure. In this case, the intersection points between the line and the clip rectangle must be detected as in the previous case. However, in the current case we must differentiate between two type of intersection points.

1. The first type appears in white squares in Fig. 2.10. These intersection points fall within the boundaries of the clip rectangle (i.e., $t_{edgei} \in [0, 1]$ where $i$ is the edge

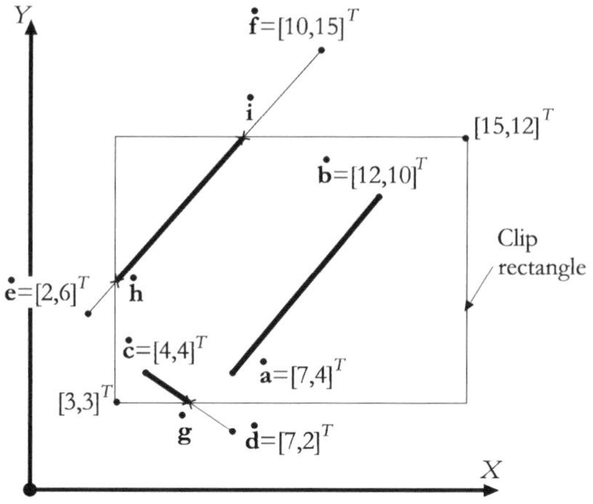


**Fig. 2.11** Three lines clipped by a rectangle

number). The portion of the line connecting these intersection points is inside the clip rectangle and must be kept.

2. The second type appears in white circles in Fig. 2.10. These intersection points are located outside the boundaries of the clip rectangle (i.e., $t_{edgei} \notin [0, 1]$ where $i$ is the edge number). The whole line must be removed.

The previous brute-force idea is inefficient and expensive as many calculations must be performed. The next example clarifies this claim.

**Example 2.10:** [*Line clipping*]

Figure 2.11 shows three line segments $\overline{\dot{\mathbf{a}}\dot{\mathbf{b}}}$, $\overline{\dot{\mathbf{c}}\dot{\mathbf{d}}}$ and $\overline{\dot{\mathbf{e}}\dot{\mathbf{f}}}$ where $\dot{\mathbf{a}} = [7, 4]^T$, $\dot{\mathbf{b}} = [12, 10]^T$, $\dot{\mathbf{c}} = [4, 4]^T$, $\dot{\mathbf{d}} = [7, 2]^T$, $\dot{\mathbf{e}} = [2, 6]^T$ and $\dot{\mathbf{f}} = [10, 15]^T$. If a clip rectangle spanning from $[3, 3]^T$ to $[15, 12]^T$ is used to clip these lines, what lines or portions of lines are preserved and kept?

**Solution 2.10: Working with line $\overline{\dot{\mathbf{a}}\dot{\mathbf{b}}}$**: Check if endpoints fall within the boundaries of the clip rectangle:

$$
\begin{aligned}
x_{min} \le x_{\dot{\mathbf{a}}} \le x_{max} &\Longrightarrow 3 \le 7 \le 15 \Longrightarrow \mathit{true},\\
y_{min} \le y_{\dot{\mathbf{a}}} \le y_{max} &\Longrightarrow 3 \le 4 \le 12 \Longrightarrow \mathit{true},\\
x_{min} \le x_{\dot{\mathbf{b}}} \le x_{max} &\Longrightarrow 3 \le 12 \le 15 \Longrightarrow \mathit{true},\\
y_{min} \le y_{\dot{\mathbf{b}}} \le y_{max} &\Longrightarrow 3 \le 10 \le 12 \Longrightarrow \mathit{true}.
\end{aligned}
$$

As all inequalities result in true condition, we conclude that the line $\overline{\dot{\mathbf{a}}\dot{\mathbf{b}}}$ falls completely within the boundaries of the clip rectangle and must be preserved.

**Working with line $\overline{\dot{\mathbf{c}}\dot{\mathbf{d}}}$**: Check if endpoints fall within the boundaries of the clip rectangle:

$$\begin{aligned}
x_{min} \le x_{\dot{\mathbf{c}}} \le x_{max} &\Longrightarrow 3 \le 4 \le 15 \Longrightarrow \mathit{true}, \\
y_{min} \le y_{\dot{\mathbf{c}}} \le y_{max} &\Longrightarrow 3 \le 4 \le 12 \Longrightarrow \mathit{true}, \\
x_{min} \le x_{\dot{\mathbf{d}}} \le x_{max} &\Longrightarrow 3 \le 7 \le 15 \Longrightarrow \mathit{true}, \\
y_{min} \le y_{\dot{\mathbf{d}}} \le y_{max} &\Longrightarrow 3 \le 2 \le 12 \Longrightarrow \mathit{false}.
\end{aligned}$$

Hence, the endpoint $\dot{\mathbf{c}}$ falls within the clip rectangle while the endpoint $\dot{\mathbf{d}}$ is outside it. Now, check the intersection point between the line and the lower horizontal edge:

$$\begin{bmatrix} x_{\dot{\mathbf{c}}} \\ y_{\dot{\mathbf{c}}} \end{bmatrix} + t_{line} \begin{bmatrix} x_{\dot{\mathbf{d}}} - x_{\dot{\mathbf{c}}} \\ y_{\dot{\mathbf{d}}} - y_{\dot{\mathbf{c}}} \end{bmatrix} = \begin{bmatrix} x_{min} \\ y_{min} \end{bmatrix} + t_{edge1} \begin{bmatrix} x_{max} - x_{min} \\ y_{min} - y_{min} \end{bmatrix}$$
$$\begin{bmatrix} 4 \\ 4 \end{bmatrix} + t_{line} \begin{bmatrix} 7-4 \\ 2-4 \end{bmatrix} = \begin{bmatrix} 3 \\ 3 \end{bmatrix} + t_{edge1} \begin{bmatrix} 15-3 \\ 3-3 \end{bmatrix}$$

or

$$\begin{aligned}
4 + 3\, t_{line} &= 3 + 12\, t_{edge1} \\
4 - 2\, t_{line} &= 3.
\end{aligned}$$

Solving these two equations results in values of $\frac{1}{2}$ and $\frac{2.5}{12}$ for $t_{line}$ and $t_{edge1}$ respectively. Since $t_{line} \in [0, 1]$ and $t_{edge1} \in [0, 1]$, the intersection point falls within the boundaries of the clip rectangle. Thus, using the line equation and $t_{line} = \frac{1}{2}$, the intersection point $[x, y]^T$ will be

$$\begin{aligned}
\begin{bmatrix} x \\ y \end{bmatrix} &= \begin{bmatrix} x_{\dot{\mathbf{c}}} \\ y_{\dot{\mathbf{c}}} \end{bmatrix} + t_{line} \begin{bmatrix} x_{\dot{\mathbf{d}}} - x_{\dot{\mathbf{c}}} \\ y_{\dot{\mathbf{d}}} - y_{\dot{\mathbf{c}}} \end{bmatrix} \\
&= \begin{bmatrix} 4 \\ 4 \end{bmatrix} + \frac{1}{2} \begin{bmatrix} 7-4 \\ 2-4 \end{bmatrix} = \begin{bmatrix} 5.5 \\ 3 \end{bmatrix}.
\end{aligned}$$

The same point is obtained when using $t_{edge1} = \frac{2.5}{12}$ with the parametric form of the edge. That is

$$\begin{aligned}
\begin{bmatrix} x \\ y \end{bmatrix} &= \begin{bmatrix} x_{min} \\ y_{min} \end{bmatrix} + t_{edge1} \begin{bmatrix} x_{max} - x_{min} \\ y_{min} - y_{min} \end{bmatrix} \\
&= \begin{bmatrix} 3 \\ 3 \end{bmatrix} + \frac{2.5}{12} \begin{bmatrix} 15-3 \\ 3-3 \end{bmatrix} = \begin{bmatrix} 5.5 \\ 3 \end{bmatrix}.
\end{aligned}$$

Because there is one endpoint inside the clip rectangle and one endpoint outside it, there is at most one intersection point that falls inside the borders of the clip rectangle. In other words, there is no need to check for intersection points with the rest of the edges. As $[4, 4]^T$ is the inside point, then the portion from $[4, 4]^T$ to $[5.5, 3]^T$ is kept while the rest of the line (i.e., from $[5.5, 3]^T$ to $[7, 2]^T$) is removed.

**Working with line $\overline{\dot{\mathbf{e}}\dot{\mathbf{f}}}$**: Check if endpoints fall within the boundaries of the clip rectangle:

$$\begin{aligned}
x_{min} \le x_{\dot{\mathbf{e}}} \le x_{max} &\Longrightarrow 3 \le 2 \le 15 \Longrightarrow \mathit{false}, \\
y_{min} \le y_{\dot{\mathbf{e}}} \le y_{max} &\Longrightarrow 3 \le 6 \le 12 \Longrightarrow \mathit{true}, \\
x_{min} \le x_{\dot{\mathbf{f}}} \le x_{max} &\Longrightarrow 3 \le 10 \le 15 \Longrightarrow \mathit{true}, \\
y_{min} \le y_{\dot{\mathbf{f}}} \le y_{max} &\Longrightarrow 3 \le 15 \le 12 \Longrightarrow \mathit{false}.
\end{aligned}$$

Thus, both endpoints are outside the clip rectangle. Hence, the line $\overline{\dot{\mathbf{e}}\dot{\mathbf{f}}}$ may be completely outside the clip rectangle or intersects its boundaries at two intersection points. We check the intersection point between the line and the lower horizontal edge:

$$\begin{bmatrix} x_{\dot{\mathbf{e}}} \\ y_{\dot{\mathbf{e}}} \end{bmatrix} + t_{line} \begin{bmatrix} x_{\dot{\mathbf{f}}} - x_{\dot{\mathbf{e}}} \\ y_{\dot{\mathbf{f}}} - y_{\dot{\mathbf{e}}} \end{bmatrix} = \begin{bmatrix} x_{min} \\ y_{min} \end{bmatrix} + t_{edge1} \begin{bmatrix} x_{max} - x_{min} \\ y_{min} - y_{min} \end{bmatrix}$$
$$\begin{bmatrix} 2 \\ 6 \end{bmatrix} + t_{line} \begin{bmatrix} 10 - 2 \\ 15 - 6 \end{bmatrix} = \begin{bmatrix} 3 \\ 3 \end{bmatrix} + t_{edge1} \begin{bmatrix} 15 - 3 \\ 3 - 3 \end{bmatrix}$$

or

$$\begin{aligned}
2 + 8\, t_{line} &= 3 + 12\, t_{edge1} \\
6 + 9\, t_{line} &= 3.
\end{aligned}$$

The value of $t_{line}$ is $-\frac{1}{3}$, which does not belong to the interval [0,1]; hence, this intersection point is outside the clip rectangle. Check the next possible intersection between the line and the upper horizontal edge:

$$\begin{bmatrix} x_{\dot{\mathbf{e}}} \\ y_{\dot{\mathbf{e}}} \end{bmatrix} + t_{line} \begin{bmatrix} x_{\dot{\mathbf{f}}} - x_{\dot{\mathbf{e}}} \\ y_{\dot{\mathbf{f}}} - y_{\dot{\mathbf{e}}} \end{bmatrix} = \begin{bmatrix} x_{min} \\ y_{max} \end{bmatrix} + t_{edge2} \begin{bmatrix} x_{max} - x_{min} \\ y_{max} - y_{max} \end{bmatrix}$$
$$\begin{bmatrix} 2 \\ 6 \end{bmatrix} + t_{line} \begin{bmatrix} 10 - 2 \\ 15 - 6 \end{bmatrix} = \begin{bmatrix} 3 \\ 12 \end{bmatrix} + t_{edge2} \begin{bmatrix} 15 - 3 \\ 12 - 12 \end{bmatrix}$$

or

$$\begin{aligned}
2 + 8\, t_{line} &= 3 + 12\, t_{edge2} \\
6 + 9\, t_{line} &= 12.
\end{aligned}$$

Solving these two equations results in values of $\frac{2}{3}$ and $\frac{13}{36}$ for $t_{line}$ and $t_{edge2}$ respectively. Since $t_{line} \in [0, 1]$ and $t_{edge2} \in [0, 1]$, the intersection point falls within the boundaries of the clip rectangle. Thus, using the line equation with $t_{line} = \frac{2}{3}$, the intersection point $[x, y]^T$ will be

$$\begin{aligned}
\begin{bmatrix} x \\ y \end{bmatrix} &= \begin{bmatrix} x_{\dot{\mathbf{e}}} \\ y_{\dot{\mathbf{e}}} \end{bmatrix} + t_{line} \begin{bmatrix} x_{\dot{\mathbf{f}}} - x_{\dot{\mathbf{e}}} \\ y_{\dot{\mathbf{f}}} - y_{\dot{\mathbf{e}}} \end{bmatrix} \\
&= \begin{bmatrix} 2 \\ 6 \end{bmatrix} + \frac{2}{3} \begin{bmatrix} 10 - 2 \\ 15 - 6 \end{bmatrix} = \begin{bmatrix} 7.3333 \\ 12 \end{bmatrix}.
\end{aligned}$$

The same point is obtained when using $t_{edge2} = \frac{13}{36}$ with the parametric form of the edge. That is

$$\begin{aligned}\begin{bmatrix} x \\ y \end{bmatrix} &= \begin{bmatrix} x_{min} \\ y_{max} \end{bmatrix} + t_{edge2} \begin{bmatrix} x_{max} - x_{min} \\ y_{max} - y_{max} \end{bmatrix} \\ &= \begin{bmatrix} 3 \\ 12 \end{bmatrix} + \frac{13}{36} \begin{bmatrix} 15 - 3 \\ 12 - 12 \end{bmatrix} = \begin{bmatrix} 7.3333 \\ 12 \end{bmatrix}.\end{aligned}$$

Because both endpoints are outside the clip rectangle and $t_{edge2}$ is neither 0 nor 1, we expect that there is only one more intersection point that falls inside the borders of the clip rectangle. So, we will go for the third edge (i.e., the left vertical edge):

$$\begin{gathered}\begin{bmatrix} x_{\dot{e}} \\ y_{\dot{e}} \end{bmatrix} + t_{line} \begin{bmatrix} x_{\dot{f}} - x_{\dot{e}} \\ y_{\dot{f}} - y_{\dot{e}} \end{bmatrix} = \begin{bmatrix} x_{min} \\ y_{min} \end{bmatrix} + t_{edge3} \begin{bmatrix} x_{min} - x_{min} \\ y_{max} - y_{min} \end{bmatrix} \\ \begin{bmatrix} 2 \\ 6 \end{bmatrix} + t_{line} \begin{bmatrix} 10 - 2 \\ 15 - 6 \end{bmatrix} = \begin{bmatrix} 3 \\ 3 \end{bmatrix} + t_{edge3} \begin{bmatrix} 3 - 3 \\ 12 - 3 \end{bmatrix}\end{gathered}$$

or

$$\begin{aligned} 2 + 8\, t_{line} &= 3 \\ 6 + 9\, t_{line} &= 3 + 9\, t_{edge3}. \end{aligned}$$

Solving these two equations results in values of $\frac{1}{8}$ and $\frac{11}{24}$ for $t_{line}$ and $t_{edge3}$ respectively. Since $t_{line} \in [0, 1]$ and $t_{edge2} \in [0, 1]$, the intersection point falls within the boundaries of the clip rectangle. So, using the line equation with $t_{line} = \frac{1}{8}$, the intersection point $[x, y]^T$ will be estimated as

$$\begin{aligned}\begin{bmatrix} x \\ y \end{bmatrix} &= \begin{bmatrix} x_{\dot{e}} \\ y_{\dot{e}} \end{bmatrix} + t_{line} \begin{bmatrix} x_{\dot{f}} - x_{\dot{e}} \\ y_{\dot{f}} - y_{\dot{e}} \end{bmatrix} \\ &= \begin{bmatrix} 2 \\ 6 \end{bmatrix} + \frac{1}{8} \begin{bmatrix} 10 - 2 \\ 15 - 6 \end{bmatrix} = \begin{bmatrix} 3 \\ 7.125 \end{bmatrix}.\end{aligned}$$

The same point is obtained when using $t_{edge3} = \frac{11}{24}$ with the parametric form of the edge. That is

$$\begin{aligned}\begin{bmatrix} x \\ y \end{bmatrix} &= \begin{bmatrix} x_{min} \\ y_{min} \end{bmatrix} + t_{edge3} \begin{bmatrix} x_{min} - x_{min} \\ y_{max} - y_{min} \end{bmatrix} \\ &= \begin{bmatrix} 3 \\ 3 \end{bmatrix} + \frac{11}{24} \begin{bmatrix} 3 - 3 \\ 12 - 3 \end{bmatrix} = \begin{bmatrix} 3 \\ 7.125 \end{bmatrix}.\end{aligned}$$

So, the portion from $[3, 7.125]^T$ to $[7.3333, 12]^T$ is kept while the portions from $[2, 6]^T$ to $[3, 7.125]^T$ and from $[7.3333, 12]^T$ to $[10, 15]^T$ are removed. □

In the literature, there are many 2D *line clipping* algorithms such as Liang-Barsky algorithm (Liang and Barsky 1984), Nicholl-Lee-Nicholl algorithm (Nicholl et al.

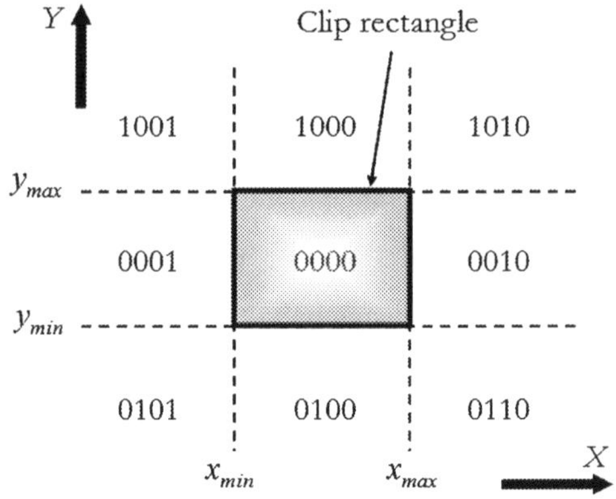


**Fig. 2.12** The space is divided into nine regions where the middle region represents the clip rectangle, window, polygon or the viewport. Each region is assigned a 4-bit outcode

**Table 2.1** Assigning outcodes for the nine regions

| Bit | Value | Meaning |
|---|---|---|
| 3 | = 1, if region is above the top edge | if $y > y_{max}$ |
| | = 0, otherwise | if $y \leq y_{max}$ |
| 2 | = 1, if region is below the bottom edge | if $y < y_{min}$ |
| | = 0, otherwise | if $y \geq y_{min}$ |
| 1 | = 1, if region is right to the right edge | if $x > x_{max}$ |
| | = 0, otherwise | if $x \leq x_{max}$ |
| 0 | = 1, if region is left to the left edge | if $x < x_{min}$ |
| | = 0, otherwise | if $x \geq x_{min}$ |

Bit 3 represents the most-significant bit while bit 0 represents the least-significant bit

1987), Cyrus-Beck algorithm (Cyrus and Beck 1978) and Cohen-Sutherland algorithm. We will discuss the Cohen-Sutherland algorithm in more details below.

### *2.4.1 Cohen-Sutherland Algorithm*

In Cohen-Sutherland clipping algorithm, the 2D space is divided into nine regions where the *middle region* represents the clip rectangle, window, polygon or the viewport as shown in Fig. 2.12.

Each region is assigned a 4-bit outcode. Each binary digit indicates where the region is with respect to the clip rectangle that is assigned the outcode 0000. The bits are arranged from left to right as top, bottom, right and left. Assuming that the clip rectangle spans from $[x_{min}, y_{min}]^T$ to $[x_{max}, y_{max}]^T$ as shown in Fig. 2.12, a point $[x, y]^T$ is assigned the bit values listed in Table 2.1 starting from the most-significant bit to the least-significant bit. For example, 1010 represents any point in the top right region while 0110 represents any point in the bottom right region. The outcodes are shown in Fig. 2.12. Note that in some implementations of this algorithm, the bits are arranged from left to right as left, right, bottom and top instead of top, bottom, right and left (which we are using). Also, some implementations deals with the

**Table 2.2** OR truth table and AND truth table

| $a$ | $b$ | $a$ OR $b$ | $a$ AND $b$ |
|---|---|---|---|
| 0 | 0 | 0 | 0 |
| 0 | 1 | 1 | 0 |
| 1 | 0 | 1 | 0 |
| 1 | 1 | 1 | 1 |

$y$-axis as pointing downwards. However, these discrepancies should not affect the final outcome of clipped lines.

The Cohen-Sutherland clipping algorithm clips a line as follows:

1. Determine the outcode for each endpoint. An outcode for a point $[x, y]^T$ is obtained by retrieving the *sign bit* of the following values:

$$\begin{aligned} \text{Bit 3} &\Longrightarrow y_{max} - y, \\ \text{Bit 2} &\Longrightarrow y - y_{min}, \\ \text{Bit 1} &\Longrightarrow x_{max} - x, \\ \text{Bit 0} &\Longrightarrow x - x_{min}, \end{aligned} \tag{2.35}$$

   where bit 3 represents the most-significant bit while bit 0 represents the least-significant bit. A sign bit is 1 for negative values and 0 otherwise. An alternative way to calculate the outcode is by ORing values. If *outcode* is initialized to 0000, it will take the following values:

$$\begin{aligned} outcode &= \begin{cases} outcode \text{ OR } 1000, & \text{if } y > y_{max}; \\ outcode \text{ OR } 0100, & \text{if } y < y_{min}, \end{cases} \\ \text{then} & \\ outcode &= \begin{cases} outcode \text{ OR } 0010, & \text{if } x > x_{max}; \\ outcode \text{ OR } 0001, & \text{if } x < x_{min}. \end{cases} \end{aligned} \tag{2.36}$$

   An algorithm to obtain the outcode for a point $[x, y]^T$ given the lower left and upper right corners (i.e., $[x_{min}, y_{min}]^T$ and $[x_{max}, y_{max}]^T$) of the clip rectangle is listed in Algorithm 2.13.
2. Consider the two outcodes determined above.
   a. If both endpoints are in the clip rectangle (i.e., having the same outcode of 0000), bitwise-OR the bits. This results in a value of 0000. In this case, *trivially accept* the line. The OR truth table is listed in Table 2.2.
   b. Otherwise, if both endpoints are outside the clip rectangle (i.e., having outcodes other than 0000), bitwise-AND the bits. If this results in a value other than 0000, *trivially reject* the line. The AND truth table is listed in Table 2.2.
   c. Otherwise, segment the line using the edges of the clip rectangle:
      i. Find an endpoint $[x_0, y_0]^T$ that is outside the clip rectangle (i.e., an outpoint) where its outcode $\neq$ 0000 (at least one endpoint is outside the clip rectangle).
      ii. Find the intersection point $[x, y]^T$ between the line and the clip rectangle. If the outpoint is $[x_0, y_0]^T$ and the other endpoint is $[x_1, y_1]^T$, the intersection point is given by:

$$
\begin{aligned}
\dot{\mathbf{p}}_{top} &= \begin{bmatrix} x \\ y \end{bmatrix} = \begin{bmatrix} x_0 + \frac{y_{max}-y_0}{m} \\ y_{max} \end{bmatrix}, \\
\dot{\mathbf{p}}_{bottom} &= \begin{bmatrix} x \\ y \end{bmatrix} = \begin{bmatrix} x_0 + \frac{y_{min}-y_0}{m} \\ y_{min} \end{bmatrix}, \\
\dot{\mathbf{p}}_{right} &= \begin{bmatrix} x \\ y \end{bmatrix} = \begin{bmatrix} x_{max} \\ y_0 + m(x_{max} - x_0) \end{bmatrix}, \\
\dot{\mathbf{p}}_{left} &= \begin{bmatrix} x \\ y \end{bmatrix} = \begin{bmatrix} x_{min} \\ y_0 + m(x_{min} - x_0) \end{bmatrix},
\end{aligned}
\tag{2.37}
$$

where $\dot{\mathbf{p}}_{top}$, $\dot{\mathbf{p}}_{bottom}$, $\dot{\mathbf{p}}_{right}$ and $\dot{\mathbf{p}}_{left}$ are the intersection points with the top, bottom, right and left edges of the clip rectangle respectively; $[x_{min}, y_{min}]^T$ and $[x_{max}, y_{max}]^T$ are the lower left and upper right points of the clip rectangle respectively; and $m$ is the line slope.

iii. The portion from the outpoint to the intersection point should be removed or rejected. The outpoint is replaced by the intersection point. Re-estimate the outcode for the outpoint.

iv. Go to Step 2.

3. If trivially accepted, draw the line.

Algorithm 2.14 lists the steps of the Cohen-Sutherland clipping algorithm (Foley et al. 1995).

**Algorithm 2.13** *Outcode calculation algorithm*

**Input:** $x, y, x_{min}, x_{max}, y_{min}, y_{max}$
**Output:** *outcode*

```
outcode = 0000
if (y > y_max) then
    outcode = outcode OR 1000
else if (y < y_min) then
    outcode = outcode OR 0100
end if
if (x > x_max) then
    outcode = outcode OR 0010
else if (x < x_min) then
    outcode = outcode OR 0001
end if
return outcode
```

**end**

**Algorithm 2.14** *Cohen-Sutherland clipping algorithm*

**Input:** $x_0$, $y_0$, $x_1$, $y_1$, $x_{min}$, $y_{min}$, $x_{max}$, $y_{max}$
1: $outcode0 = $ Call Algorithm 2.13 for $[x_0, y_0]^T$
2: $outcode1 = $ Call Algorithm 2.13 for $[x_1, y_1]^T$
3: $done = FALSE$
4: $in = FALSE$
5:
6: **while** $(done = FALSE)$ **do**
7:    **if** $(outcode0$ OR $outcode1 = 0000)$ **then**
8:       $done = TRUE$
9:       $in = TRUE$
10:    **else if** $(outcode0$ AND $outcode1 \neq 0000)$ **then**
11:       $done = TRUE$
12:    **else**
13:       $m = \frac{y_1 - y_0}{x_1 - x_0}$
14:       **if** $(outcode0 \neq 0000)$ **then**
15:          $outcode = outcode0$
16:       **else**
17:          $outcode = outcode1$
18:       **end if**
19:
20:       **if** $(outcode$ AND $1000 \neq 0000)$ **then**
21:          $x = x_0 + \frac{y_{max} - y_0}{m}$
22:          $y = y_{max}$
23:       **else if** $(outcode$ AND $0100 \neq 0000)$ **then**
24:          $x = x_0 + \frac{y_{min} - y_0}{m}$
25:          $y = y_{min}$
26:       **else if** $(outcode$ AND $0010 \neq 0000)$ **then**
27:          $x = x_{max}$
28:          $y = y_0 + m(x_{max} - x_0)$
29:       **else**
30:          $x = x_{min}$
31:          $y = y_0 + m(x_{min} - x_0)$
32:       **end if**
33:
34:       **if** $(outcode = outcode0)$ **then**
35:          $x_0 = x$
36:          $y_0 = y$
37:          $outcode0 = $ Call Algorithm 2.13 for $[x_0, y_0]^T$
38:       **else**
39:          $x_1 = x$
40:          $y_1 = y$
41:          $outcode1 = $ Call Algorithm 2.13 for $[x_1, y_1]^T$
42:       **end if**

43: **end if**
44: **end while**
45:
46: **if** $(in = TRUE)$ **then**
47: Call Algorithm 2.7 with parameters $x_0, y_0, x_1, y_1$
48: **end if**

**end**

One point to be mentioned here is that Algorithm 2.14 computes the slope $m$ on Line 13. This operation may be repeated for the same line if it intersects the clip rectangle more than once. In this case, it is better to compute the slope before the loop. However, if the slope is computed before the loop and the line is trivially accepted or trivially rejected, the slope will be computed but will never be used.

**Example 2.11:** [*Cohen-Sutherland clipping algorithm—outcodes*]

Figure 2.13 shows four line segments $\overline{\dot{\mathbf{a}}\dot{\mathbf{b}}}$, $\overline{\dot{\mathbf{c}}\dot{\mathbf{d}}}$, $\overline{\dot{\mathbf{e}}\dot{\mathbf{f}}}$ and $\overline{\dot{\mathbf{g}}\dot{\mathbf{h}}}$ where $\dot{\mathbf{a}} = [2, 6]^T$, $\dot{\mathbf{b}} = [4, 10]^T$, $\dot{\mathbf{c}} = [7, 18]^T$, $\dot{\mathbf{d}} = [10, 10]^T$, $\dot{\mathbf{e}} = [10, 1]^T$, $\dot{\mathbf{f}} = [18, 10]^T$, $\dot{\mathbf{g}} = [12, 12]^T$ and $\dot{\mathbf{h}} = [14, 10]^T$. If a clip rectangle spanning from $[5, 3]^T$ to $[15, 15]^T$ is used to clip these lines utilizing the Cohen-Sutherland clipping algorithm, get the outcodes for each of the endpoints.

**Solution 2.11:** Applying Algorithm 2.13 and since $[x_{min}, y_{min}]^T = [5, 3]^T$ and $[x_{max}, y_{max}]^T = [15, 15]^T$, the outcodes are listed in the following table:

| Point | $[x, y]^T$ | Condition | Outcode |
|---|---|---|---|
| $\dot{\mathbf{a}}$ | $[2, 6]^T$ | $x < x_{min}$ | 0001 |
| $\dot{\mathbf{b}}$ | $[4, 10]^T$ | $x < x_{min}$ | 0001 |
| $\dot{\mathbf{c}}$ | $[7, 18]^T$ | $y > y_{max}$ | 1000 |
| $\dot{\mathbf{d}}$ | $[10, 10]^T$ | within | 0000 |
| $\dot{\mathbf{e}}$ | $[10, 1]^T$ | $y < y_{min}$ | 0100 |
| $\dot{\mathbf{f}}$ | $[18, 10]^T$ | $x > x_{max}$ | 0010 |
| $\dot{\mathbf{g}}$ | $[12, 12]^T$ | within | 0000 |
| $\dot{\mathbf{h}}$ | $[14, 10]^T$ | within | 0000 |

□

**Example 2.12:** [*Cohen-Sutherland clipping algorithm—line category*] In Example 2.11, determine which lines are trivially accepted/rejected and which lines need intersection determination.

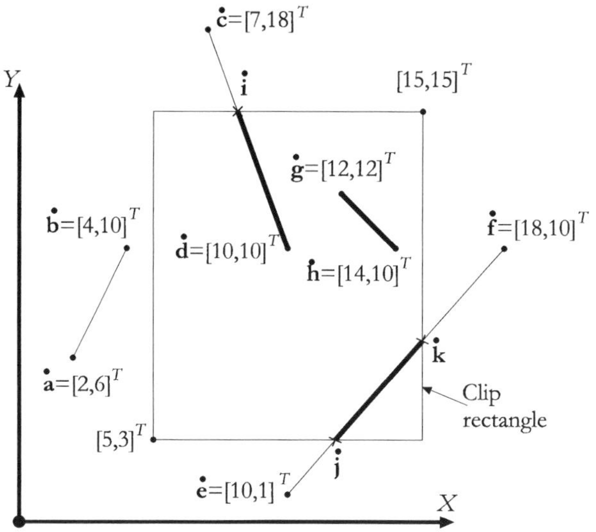


**Fig. 2.13** Four lines clipped by a rectangle

**Solution 2.12:** In order to determine line categories, we apply the first part of Algorithm 2.14 (i.e., performing ORing and ANDing operations).

| Line | ORing | ANDing | Decision |
|---|---|---|---|
| $\overline{\dot{\mathbf{a}}\dot{\mathbf{b}}}$ | 0001 | 0001 | Trivially reject |
| $\overline{\dot{\mathbf{c}}\dot{\mathbf{d}}}$ | 1000 | 0000 | Intersections |
| $\overline{\dot{\mathbf{e}}\dot{\mathbf{f}}}$ | 0110 | 0000 | Intersections |
| $\overline{\dot{\mathbf{g}}\dot{\mathbf{h}}}$ | 0000 | | Trivially accept |

Hence, only $\overline{\dot{\mathbf{c}}\dot{\mathbf{d}}}$ and $\overline{\dot{\mathbf{e}}\dot{\mathbf{f}}}$ need further intersection determination. □

**Example 2.13:** [*Cohen-Sutherland clipping algorithm—intersection points*] In Example 2.11, if the lines to be clipped intersect the clip rectangle, determine the intersection points between those lines and clip rectangle.

**Solution 2.13:** As we found in Example 2.12, intersections will be performed only for $\overline{\dot{\mathbf{c}}\dot{\mathbf{d}}}$ and $\overline{\dot{\mathbf{e}}\dot{\mathbf{f}}}$.

**Working with line $\overline{\dot{\mathbf{c}}\dot{\mathbf{d}}}$:** The slope is obtained as

$$m = \frac{y_{\dot{\mathbf{d}}} - y_{\dot{\mathbf{c}}}}{x_{\dot{\mathbf{d}}} - x_{\dot{\mathbf{c}}}} = \frac{10 - 18}{10 - 7} = -\frac{8}{3} = -2.6667.$$

We get the outpoint which has the outcode that is not equal to 0000 as

$$outcode = outcode_{\dot{\mathbf{c}}} = 1000.$$

Since

$$outcode \text{ AND } 1000 = 1000,$$

then the line extending from the outpoint (i.e., $\dot{\mathbf{c}}$) to $\dot{\mathbf{d}}$ intersects the top edge of the clip rectangle. The intersection point $\dot{\mathbf{i}}$ between the line and the clip rectangle is obtained as

$$\begin{aligned} x_{\dot{\mathbf{i}}} &= x_{\dot{\mathbf{c}}} + \frac{y_{max} - y_{\dot{\mathbf{c}}}}{m} = 7 + \frac{15 - 18}{-8/3} = 8\frac{1}{8} = 8.125, \\ y_{\dot{\mathbf{i}}} &= y_{max} = 15. \end{aligned}$$

Thus, the intersection point $\dot{\mathbf{i}}$ is $[8.125, 15]^T$. The intersection points between $\overline{\dot{\mathbf{e}}\dot{\mathbf{f}}}$ and the clip rectangle are obtained similarly. They are listed in the table below.

| Line | Outpoint | $m$ | Edge | Intersection |
|---|---|---|---|---|
| $\overline{\dot{\mathbf{c}}\dot{\mathbf{d}}}$ | $\dot{\mathbf{c}}$ | $-\frac{8}{3}$ | Top | $\dot{\mathbf{i}} = [8.125, 15]^T$ |
| $\overline{\dot{\mathbf{e}}\dot{\mathbf{f}}}$ | $\dot{\mathbf{e}}$ | $\frac{9}{8}$ | Bottom | $\dot{\mathbf{j}} = [11.7778, 3]^T$ |
| $\overline{\dot{\mathbf{j}}\dot{\mathbf{f}}}$ | $\dot{\mathbf{f}}$ | $\frac{9}{8}$ | Right | $\dot{\mathbf{k}} = [15, 6.625]^T$ |

□

**Example 2.14:** [*Cohen-Sutherland clipping algorithm*]

Figure 2.11 shows three line segments $\overline{\dot{\mathbf{a}}\dot{\mathbf{b}}}$, $\overline{\dot{\mathbf{c}}\dot{\mathbf{d}}}$ and $\overline{\dot{\mathbf{e}}\dot{\mathbf{f}}}$ where $\dot{\mathbf{a}} = [7, 4]^T$, $\dot{\mathbf{b}} = [12, 10]^T$, $\dot{\mathbf{c}} = [4, 4]^T$, $\dot{\mathbf{d}} = [7, 2]^T$, $\dot{\mathbf{e}} = [2, 6]^T$ and $\dot{\mathbf{f}} = [10, 15]^T$. If a clip rectangle spanning from $[3, 3]^T$ to $[15, 12]^T$ is used to clip these lines utilizing the Cohen-Sutherland clipping algorithm, what lines or portions of lines are preserved and kept?

**Solution 2.14: Working with line $\overline{\dot{\mathbf{a}}\dot{\mathbf{b}}}$:**

1. Get the outcodes for the endpoints $\dot{\mathbf{a}}$ and $\dot{\mathbf{b}}$:

$$\begin{aligned} outcode_{\dot{\mathbf{a}}} &= 0000, \\ outcode_{\dot{\mathbf{b}}} &= 0000. \end{aligned}$$

2. Perform a bitwise-ORing operation between $outcode_{\dot{\mathbf{a}}}$ and $outcode_{\dot{\mathbf{b}}}$:

$$outcode_{\dot{\mathbf{a}}} \text{ OR } outcode_{\dot{\mathbf{b}}} = 0000 \text{ OR } 0000 = 0000.$$

Since the result of the bitwise-ORing operation is 0000, both endpoints are in the clip rectangle.

3. Therefore, the line $\overline{\dot{\mathbf{a}}\dot{\mathbf{b}}}$ is trivially accepted.

**Working with line $\overline{\dot{\mathbf{c}}\dot{\mathbf{d}}}$:**

1. Get the outcodes for the endpoints $\dot{\mathbf{c}}$ and $\dot{\mathbf{d}}$:

$$\begin{aligned} outcode_{\dot{\mathbf{c}}} &= 0000, \\ outcode_{\dot{\mathbf{d}}} &= 0100. \end{aligned}$$

2.

   a. Perform a bitwise-ORing operation between $outcode_{\dot{\mathbf{c}}}$ and $outcode_{\dot{\mathbf{d}}}$:

$$outcode_{\dot{\mathbf{c}}} \text{ OR } outcode_{\dot{\mathbf{d}}} = 0000 \text{ OR } 0100 = 0100.$$

   b. Since the bitwise-ORing operation results in a value that is not 0000, perform a bitwise-ANDing operation between $outcode_{\dot{\mathbf{c}}}$ and $outcode_{\dot{\mathbf{d}}}$:

$$outcode_{\dot{\mathbf{c}}} \text{ AND } outcode_{\dot{\mathbf{d}}} = 0000 \text{ AND } 0100 = 0000.$$

   c.

      i. Since the bitwise-ANDing operation results in 0000, get the slope $m$ of the line, which is computed as

$$m = \frac{y_{\dot{\mathbf{d}}} - y_{\dot{\mathbf{c}}}}{x_{\dot{\mathbf{d}}} - x_{\dot{\mathbf{c}}}} = \frac{2-4}{7-4} = -\frac{2}{3} = -0.6667.$$

      ii. Get the outpoint which has the outcode that is not equal to 0000 as

$$outcode_{\dot{\mathbf{d}}} = 0100.$$

      iii. Since

$$outcode_{\dot{\mathbf{d}}} \text{ AND } 0100 = 0100,$$

then the line extending from the outpoint (i.e., $\dot{\mathbf{d}}$) to $\dot{\mathbf{c}}$ intersects the bottom edge of the clip rectangle. Split the line at the intersection point between the line and the clip rectangle. Utilizing the value of $m$, the intersection point $[x, y]^T$ is obtained as

$$\begin{aligned} x &= x_{\dot{\mathbf{d}}} + \frac{y_{min} - y_{\dot{\mathbf{d}}}}{m} = 7 + \frac{3-2}{-2/3} = 5.5, \\ y &= y_{min} = 3. \end{aligned}$$

In other words, the intersection point is $[5.5, 3]^T$. Let us call this point $\dot{\mathbf{g}}$.

iv. Remove the part between $\dot{\mathbf{d}} = [7, 2]^T$ and $\dot{\mathbf{g}} = [5.5, 3]^T$. The outcode for the intersection point now is

$$outcode_{\dot{\mathbf{g}}} = 0000.$$

v. The line to be tested now is extending from $\dot{\mathbf{c}} = [4, 4]^T$ to $\dot{\mathbf{g}} = [5.5, 3]^T$. The outcode for each of its endpoints is 0000.

3. The procedure is applied again to line $\overline{\dot{\mathbf{c}}\dot{\mathbf{g}}}$. Hence, line $\overline{\dot{\mathbf{c}}\dot{\mathbf{g}}}$ is trivially accepted.

**Working with line $\overline{\dot{\mathbf{e}}\dot{\mathbf{f}}}$**:

1. Get the outcodes for the endpoints $\dot{\mathbf{e}}$ and $\dot{\mathbf{f}}$:

$$\begin{aligned} outcode_{\dot{\mathbf{e}}} &= 0001, \\ outcode_{\dot{\mathbf{f}}} &= 1000. \end{aligned}$$

2.

a. Perform a bitwise-ORing operation between $outcode_{\dot{\mathbf{e}}}$ and $outcode_{\dot{\mathbf{f}}}$:

$$outcode_{\dot{\mathbf{e}}} \text{ OR } outcode_{\dot{\mathbf{f}}} = 0001 \text{ OR } 1000 = 1001.$$

b. Since the bitwise-ORing operation results in a value that is not 0000, perform a bitwise-ANDing operation between $outcode_{\dot{\mathbf{e}}}$ and $outcode_{\dot{\mathbf{f}}}$:

$$outcode_{\dot{\mathbf{e}}} \text{ AND } outcode_{\dot{\mathbf{f}}} = 0001 \text{ AND } 1000 = 0000.$$

c.

i. Since the bitwise-ANDing operation results in 0000, get the slope $m$ of the line that is obtained as

$$m = \frac{y_{\dot{\mathbf{f}}} - y_{\dot{\mathbf{e}}}}{x_{\dot{\mathbf{f}}} - x_{\dot{\mathbf{e}}}} = \frac{15 - 6}{10 - 2} = \frac{9}{8} = 1.125.$$

ii. check the first point (i.e., $\dot{\mathbf{e}} = [2, 6]^T$) if it has an outcode that is not equal to 0000 as

$$outcode_{\dot{\mathbf{e}}} = 0001.$$

iii. Since

$$outcode_{\dot{\mathbf{e}}} \text{ AND } 0001 = 0001,$$

then the line intersects the left edge of the clip rectangle. Split the line at the intersection point between the line and the clip rectangle. Utilizing the slope $m$, the intersection point $[x, y]^T$ is estimated as

$$x = x_{min} = 3,$$
$$y = y_{\dot{\mathbf{e}}} + m(x_{min} - x_{\dot{\mathbf{e}}}) = 6 + \tfrac{9}{8}(3-2) = 7\tfrac{1}{8} = 7.125.$$

In other words, the intersection point is $[3, 7.125]^T$. Let us call this point $\dot{\mathbf{h}}$.

iv. Remove the part between $\dot{\mathbf{e}} = [2, 6]^T$ and $\dot{\mathbf{h}} = [3, 7.125]^T$. The outcode for the intersection point now is

$$outcode_{\dot{\mathbf{h}}} = 0000.$$

v. The line to be tested now is extending from $\dot{\mathbf{h}} = [3, 7.125]^T$ to $\dot{\mathbf{f}} = [10, 15]^T$.

**Working with line $\overline{\dot{\mathbf{h}}\dot{\mathbf{f}}}$:**

a. Perform a bitwise-ORing operation between $outcode_{\dot{\mathbf{h}}}$ and $outcode_{\dot{\mathbf{f}}}$:

$$outcode_{\dot{\mathbf{h}}} \text{ OR } outcode_{\dot{\mathbf{f}}} = 0000 \text{ OR } 1000 = 1000.$$

b. Since the bitwise-ORing operation results in a value that is not 0000, perform a bitwise-ANDing operation between $outcode_{\dot{\mathbf{h}}}$ and $outcode_{\dot{\mathbf{f}}}$:

$$outcode_{\dot{\mathbf{h}}} \text{ AND } outcode_{\dot{\mathbf{f}}} = 0000 \text{ AND } 1000 = 0000.$$

c.

i. Since the bitwise-ANDing operation results in 0000, get the slope $m$ of the line that is obtained as

$$m = \frac{9}{8} = 1.125.$$

ii. Get the outpoint (i.e., $\dot{\mathbf{f}}$) as it has an outcode that is not equal to 0000 as

$$outcode_{\dot{\mathbf{f}}} = 1000.$$

iii. Since

$$outcode_{\dot{\mathbf{f}}} \text{ AND } 1000 = 1000,$$

then the line intersects the top edge of the clip rectangle. Split the line at the intersection point between the line and the clip rectangle. Using the slope $m$, the intersection point is estimated as

$$x = x_{\dot{\mathbf{f}}} + \frac{y_{max} - y_{\dot{\mathbf{f}}}}{m} = 10 + \frac{12 - 15}{9/8} = 7\frac{1}{3} = 7.3333,$$
$$y = y_{max} = 12.$$

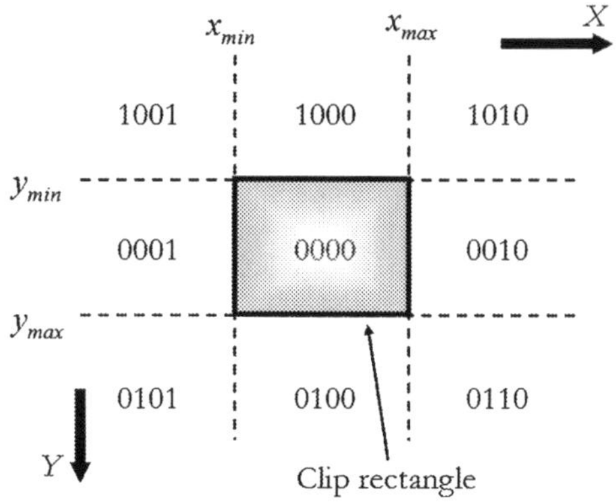


**Fig. 2.14** In a left-handed coordinate system, the $y$-axis is pointing downwards. The space is divided into nine regions where the middle region represents the clip rectangle, window, polygon or the viewport. Each region is assigned a 4-bit outcode

In other words, the intersection point is $[7.3333, 12]^T$. Let us call this point $\dot{\mathbf{i}}$.

iv. Remove the part between $\dot{\mathbf{f}} = [10, 15]^T$ and $\dot{\mathbf{i}} = [7.3333, 12]^T$. The outcode for the intersection point now is

$$outcode_{\dot{\mathbf{i}}} = 0000.$$

v. The line to be tested now is extending from $\dot{\mathbf{h}} = [3, 7.125]^T$ to $\dot{\mathbf{i}} = [7.3333, 12]^T$. The outcode for each of its endpoints is 0000.

3. The procedure is applied again to line $\overline{\dot{\mathbf{h}}\dot{\mathbf{i}}}$. Hence, line $\overline{\dot{\mathbf{h}}\dot{\mathbf{i}}}$ is trivially accepted.

Thus, the preserved lines are

1. $\overline{\dot{\mathbf{a}}\dot{\mathbf{b}}}$: extending from $\dot{\mathbf{a}} = [7, 4]^T$ to $\dot{\mathbf{b}} = [12, 10]^T$;
2. $\overline{\dot{\mathbf{c}}\dot{\mathbf{g}}}$: extending from $\dot{\mathbf{c}} = [4, 4]^T$ to $\dot{\mathbf{g}} = [5.5, 3]^T$; and
3. $\overline{\dot{\mathbf{h}}\dot{\mathbf{i}}}$: extending from $\dot{\mathbf{h}} = [3, 7.125]^T$ to $\dot{\mathbf{i}} = [7.3333, 12]^T$. □

**Example 2.15:** [*Cohen-Sutherland clipping algorithm—outcodes in a left-handed coordinate system*]
Assume that a left-handed coordinate system is used to assign outcode values to different regions of the Cohen-Sutherland clipping algorithm. Modify Table 2.1 so that each region keeps its outcode (e.g., the upper left region is assigned 1001, the lower right region is assigned 0110, etc.).

**Solution 2.15:** Since the $y$-axis is pointing downwards in a left-handed coordinate system as shown in Fig. 2.14, Table 2.1 is modified as follows:

□

## 2.5 Polygon Clipping

A 2D polygon represented by a set of three or more vertices ($\dot{\mathbf{v}}_i | i \in \{0, 1, 2, \ldots, n-1\}$ where $n$ is the number of vertices) can be clipped by another polygon. The output

| Bit | Value | Meaning |
|---|---|---|
| 3 | = 1, if region is above the top edge | if $y < y_{min}$ |
| | = 0, otherwise | if $y \geq y_{min}$ |
| 2 | = 1, if region is below the bottom edge | if $y > y_{max}$ |
| | = 0, otherwise | if $y \leq y_{max}$ |
| 1 | = 1, if region is right to the right edge | if $x > x_{max}$ |
| | = 0, otherwise | if $x \leq x_{max}$ |
| 0 | = 1, if region is left to the left edge | if $x < x_{min}$ |
| | = 0, otherwise | if $x \geq x_{min}$ |

of this clipping process is one or more polygons. The polygon after clipping may include vertices that are not part of the original vertices (i.e., new vertices may be created).

There are many 2D *polygon clippers* or *polygon clipping algorithms* such as Sutherland-Hodgman algorithm (Sutherland and Hodgman 1974), Patrick-Gilles Maillot algorithm (Maillot 1992), and Weiler-Atherton algorithm. We will discuss the Weiler-Atherton algorithm in more details.

### 2.5.1 Weiler-Atherton Algorithm

In Weiler-Atherton algorithm (Weiler and Atherton 1977), there are two types of polygons; a subject polygon that is to be clipped and a clip polygon or window as shown in Fig. 2.15a. The goal is to obtain the subject polygon after clipping as shown in Fig. 2.15b. In this algorithm, polygons are clockwise-oriented while holes are counter-clockwise-oriented. (Some researchers work with counter-clockwise-oriented polygons; however, this should not make a difference in the final outcome.) Also, in this algorithm, a polygon is represented as a circular list of vertices. The algorithm can be summarized by *walking* along the polygon boundaries as follows:

1. Compute the intersection points between the subject and clip polygons as depicted in Fig. 2.15c. Many methods to estimate the intersection points may be used. For example, given a subject edge $\overline{\dot{\mathbf{v}}_1\dot{\mathbf{v}}_2}$ bounded by $[x_{\dot{\mathbf{v}}_1}, y_{\dot{\mathbf{v}}_1}]^T$ and $[x_{\dot{\mathbf{v}}_2}, y_{\dot{\mathbf{v}}_2}]^T$ and a clipping horizontal (or vertical) edge $\overline{\dot{\mathbf{c}}_1\dot{\mathbf{c}}_2}$ bounded by $[x_{\dot{\mathbf{c}}_1}, y_{\dot{\mathbf{c}}_1}]^T$ and $[x_{\dot{\mathbf{c}}_2}, y_{\dot{\mathbf{c}}_2}]^T$, the intersection point $\dot{\mathbf{p}} = [x, y]^T$ may be estimated as done in Eq. (2.37). Alternatively, cross product (Sect. A.4.3.3) of homogeneous points (Sect. B.7) can also be used with lines with general slope values as

$$\mathbf{p} = [\mathbf{v}_1 \times \mathbf{v}_2] \times [\mathbf{c}_1 \times \mathbf{c}_2], \tag{2.38}$$

where $\times$ denotes the cross product; and $\mathbf{p}$, $\mathbf{v}_1$, $\mathbf{v}_2$, $\mathbf{c}_1$ and $\mathbf{c}_2$ are the homogeneous representation of the intersection point, subject polygon vertices and clip polygon vertices (i.e., $\mathbf{p} = [x, y, 1]^T$, $\mathbf{v}_1 = [x_{\mathbf{v}_1}, y_{\mathbf{v}_1}, 1]^T$, $\mathbf{v}_2 = [x_{\mathbf{v}_2}, y_{\mathbf{v}_2}, 1]^T$, $\mathbf{c}_1 = [x_{\mathbf{c}_1}, y_{\mathbf{c}_1}, 1]^T$ and $\mathbf{c}_2 = [x_{\mathbf{c}_2}, y_{\mathbf{c}_2}, 1]^T$).

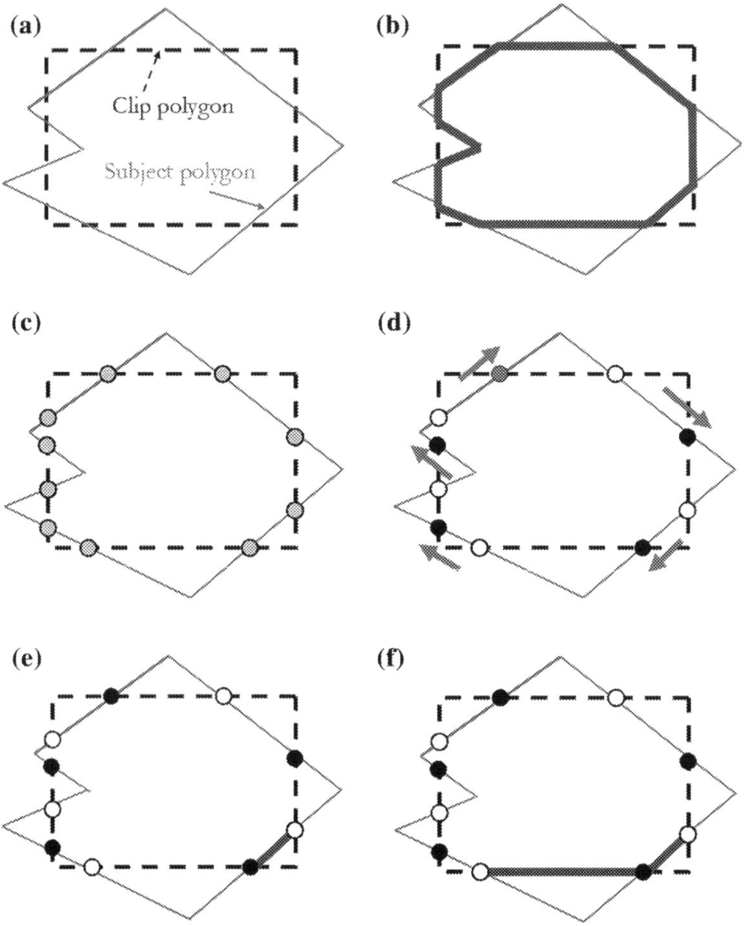


**Fig. 2.15** Weiler-Atherton algorithm. **a** The original subject and clip polygons. **b** The subject polygon after clipping. **c** The intersection points between the subject and clip polygons are computed. **d** Points where subject polygon enters clipping window are represented by *white* circles. **e** Out-to-in: Record clipped point and follow subject polygon boundary in a *clockwise* direction. **f** In-to-out: Record clipped point and follow clip polygon boundary in a *clockwise* direction

When a new intersection is detected, a new false vertex is added to the circular lists of the vertices representing the polygons. Links are established to permit travelling between polygons.

2. *Walking* along the boundaries of the subject polygon in a clockwise direction, mark points where the subject polygon enters the clip polygon. These points are represented in Fig. 2.15d as white circles where the previous subject vertex is outside the clip polygon and/or the following subject vertex is inside the clip polygon. The points where the subject polygon leaves the clip polygon are represented as black circles; i.e., when the previous subject vertex is inside the clip

polygon and/or the following subject vertex is outside the clip polygon. (One may prefer to *walking* along the boundaries of the clip polygon and detect intersections where clip polygon enters and leaves the subject polygon.) Note that intersections alternate from entering to leaving as the number of intersections is always even.

3. There are two types of point pairs; out-to-in and in-to-out:

    a. Out-to-in pair (i.e., from white to black circles): At a white circle (i.e., entering point), follow the subject polygon vertices in its circular list until the next leaving intersection. Figure 2.15e shows this case as following the subject polygon boundary in a clockwise direction.
    b. In-to-out pair (i.e., from black to white circles): At a black circle (i.e., leaving point), follow the clip polygon vertices in its circular list until the next entering intersection. Figure 2.15f shows this case as following the clip polygon boundary in a clockwise direction.

4. Repeat Step 3 until there are no more pairs to process.

The result of the above operation is the subject polygon after clipping as shown in Fig. 2.15b. The process is summarized in Algorithm 2.15.

**Algorithm 2.15** *Weiler-Atherton algorithm*

**Input:** Circular lists of vertices representing the subject and clip polygons
**Output:** Lists of vertices representing the clipped polygons

```
Get intersections between subject and clip polygons and add them to both lists.
Along the subject polygon, determine entering and leaving intersections.
while more vertices to process do
    If an entering or subject vertex is encountered, follow the subject circular list.
    If a leaving or clip vertex is encountered, follow the clip circular list.
    A loop of vertices is complete when arriving at the start vertex.
end while
```

**end**

**Example 2.16:** [*Weiler-Atherton clipping—circular lists and insertion of false vertices*]

Consider an irregular subject polygon to be clipped by a rectangular clip polygon as shown in Fig. 2.16. What are the steps that should be followed to populate circular lists for both the subject and clip polygons?

**Solution 2.16:** The steps are shown in Fig. 2.17.

1. To simplify the discussion, the vertices of both subject and clip polygons are numbered as shown in Fig. 2.17a and two circular lists are created; one for each polygon. The sequence of vertices of the subject polygon in a clockwise order is "0," "1," "2," "3" and "4." The sequence of vertices of the clip polygon in a clockwise order is "a," "b," "c" and "d." The circular lists are shown in Fig. 2.17b.

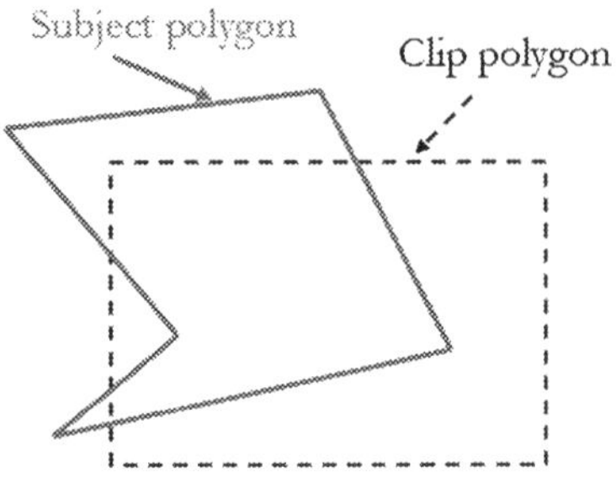


**Fig. 2.16** An irregular subject polygon is to be clipped by a rectangular clip polygon

2. The first intersection marked "e" is detected (Fig. 2.17c) and a new false vertex is linked to both lists as shown in Fig. 2.17d. The subject sequence now becomes "0," "e," "1," "2," "3" and "4" and the clip sequence becomes "a," "e," "b," "c" and "d."
3. Along the clockwise direction, the next intersection marked "f" is detected (Fig. 2.17e) and a new false vertex is linked to both lists as shown in Fig. 2.17f. Notice that "f" is between "1" and "2" in the subject polygon and between "d" and "a" in the clip polygon. Thus, the subject sequence now becomes "0," "e," "1," "f," "2," "3" and "4" and the clip sequence becomes "a," "e," "b," "c," "d" and "f."
4. The following intersection marked "g" is detected (Fig. 2.17g) and a new false vertex is linked to both lists as shown in Fig. 2.17h. The subject sequence now becomes "0," "e," "1," "f," "2," "g," "3" and "4" and the clip sequence becomes "a," "e," "b," "c," "d," "f" and "g."
5. The next intersection marked "h" is detected (Fig. 2.17i) and a new false vertex is linked to both lists as shown in Fig. 2.17j. The subject sequence now becomes "0," "e," "1," "f," "2," "g," "3," "h" and "4" and the clip sequence becomes "a," "e," "b," "c," "d," "f", "g" and "h."

In Fig. 2.17, the false vertices "e," "f," "g" and "h" are shown in gray. Also, in order to make the distinction clear, the edges and links of the subject polygon are illustrated as solid lines while the edges and links of the clip polygon are illustrated as dashed lines. Notice that this whole process is represented by Line 1 in Algorithm 2.15. □

**Example 2.17:** [*Weiler-Atherton clipping—clipped loops*]
Building on Example 2.16, determine the clipped polygon parts (i.e., loops of vertices).

**Solution 2.17:** The steps are shown in Fig. 2.18.

1. The entering and leaving vertices are determined. In Fig. 2.18a, b, the entering vertices "e" and "g" are marked in white and the leaving vertices "f" and "h" are marked in black.
2. Starting at the *entering* vertex "e," the *subject* polygon border is followed as shown in Fig. 2.18c. This process is performed on the *subject* polygon circular list by following the link out of that vertex. This is shown in Fig. 2.18d.

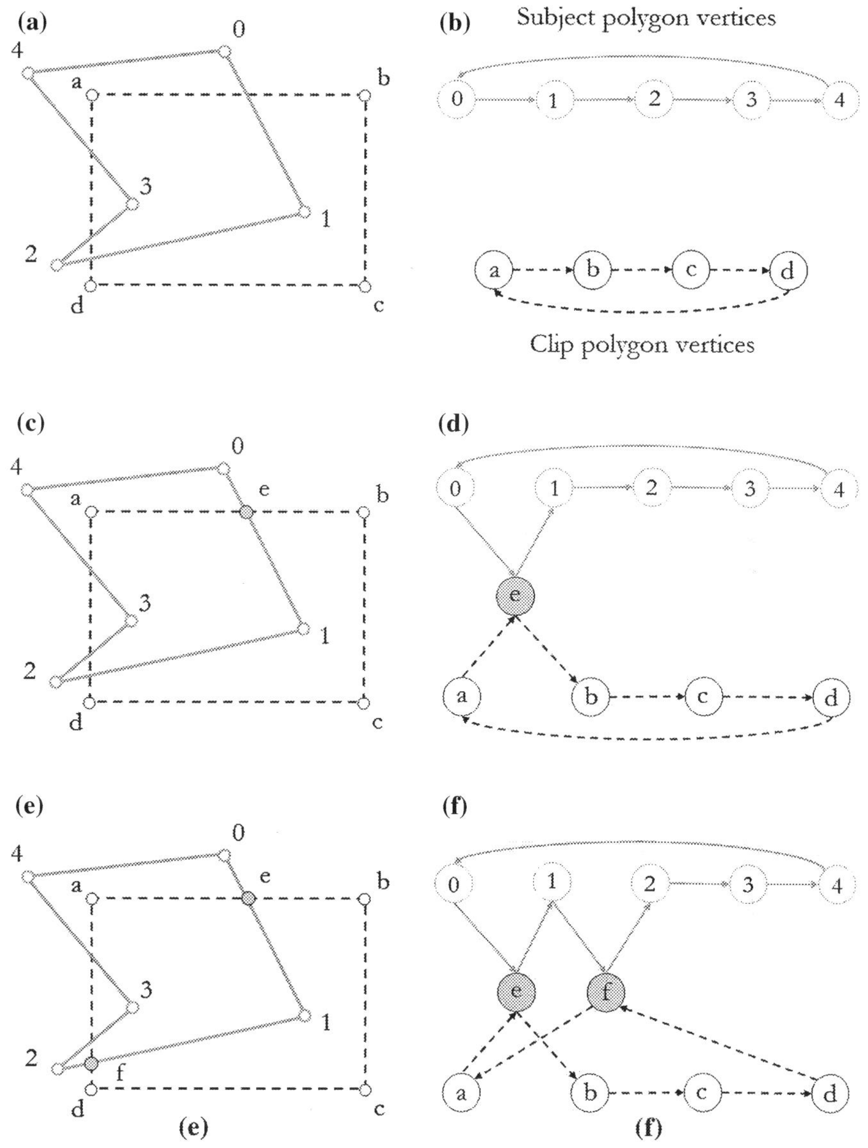


**Fig. 2.17** Getting intersection points and establishing *circular lists* for subject and clip polygons. This process is represented by Line 1 in Algorithm 2.15

3. Continuing from the subject vertex "1," the *subject* polygon is followed as in the previous step. This is shown in Fig. 2.18e, f.
4. At the *leaving* vertex "f," the *clip* polygon border is followed as shown in Fig. 2.18g. This process is performed on the *clip* polygon circular list by following the link out of that vertex. This is shown in Fig. 2.18h.

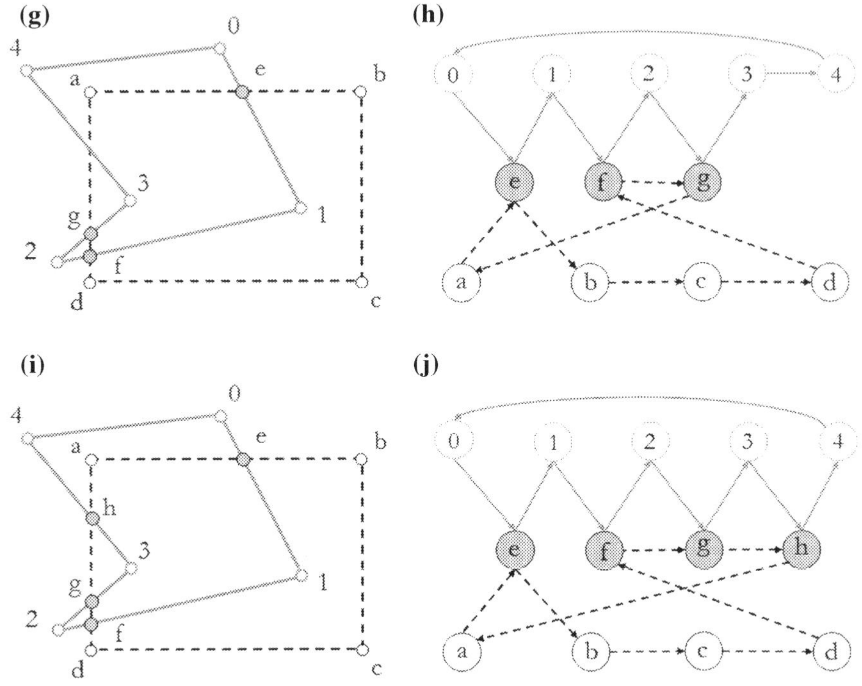

**Fig. 2.17** (continued)

5. As in Step 2 above, from the *entering* vertex "g," the *subject* polygon border is followed as shown in Fig. 2.18i. This process is performed on the *subject* polygon circular list by following the link out of that vertex. This is shown in Fig. 2.18j.
6. As in Step 3, continuing from the subject vertex "3," the *subject* polygon is followed as shown in Fig. 2.18k, l.
7. As in Step 4, at the *leaving* vertex "h," the *clip* polygon is followed as shown in Fig. 2.18m, n.
8. The loop is complete by following the *clip* path from the *clip* vertex "a" to the *entering* vertex "e," which is the start vertex in Step 1.
9. The final loop (i.e., the clipped part of the polygon) now is "e," "1," "f," "g," "3," "h," "a" and "e."

All the above steps appear as thick edges/arrows in Fig. 2.18. □

## 2.6 Problems

**Problem 2.1:** [*Bresenham's line drawing algorithm*]

Bresenham's algorithm is used to draw a line segment from $[28, 8]^T$ to $[26, 14]^T$. Determine whether the following pixels are part of the displayed line: $[28, 9]^T$, $[27, 9]^T$, $[27, 10]^T$, $[28, 10]^T$, $[26, 12]^T$, $[27, 13]^T$, $[26, 13]^T$, $[27, 14]^T$, $[27, 11]^T$ and $[27, 12]^T$.

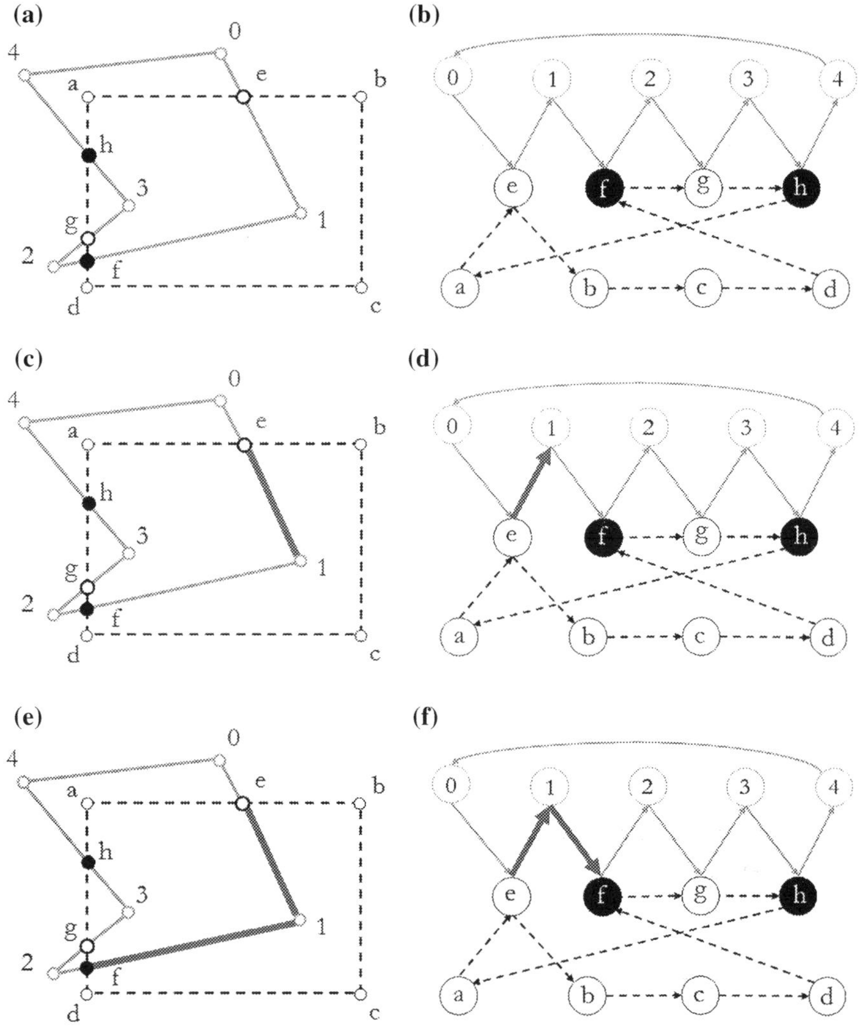


**Fig. 2.18** Determining the clipped polygon parts. This process is represented by Line 2 through Line 7 in Algorithm 2.15

**Problem 2.2:** [*8-way symmetry algorithm*]

Figure 2.19a shows the upper left corner of a computer screen. The horizontal and vertical axes are shown with values representing pixel locations. Suppose that a curve spanning from $[5, 15]^T$ to $[15, 5]^T$ is drawn as two circle quadrants. The centers of the circles are shown as black dots. Use the 8-way symmetry algorithm to determine what pixels should constitute the curve.

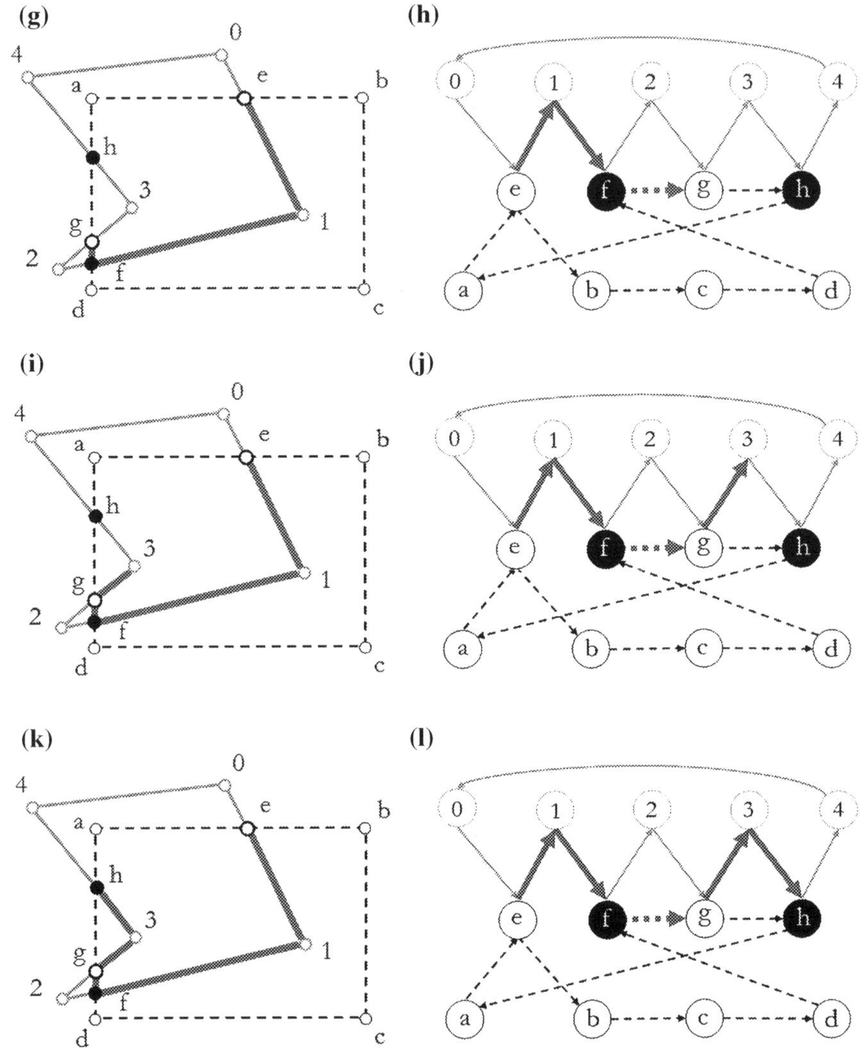


**Fig. 2.18** (continued)

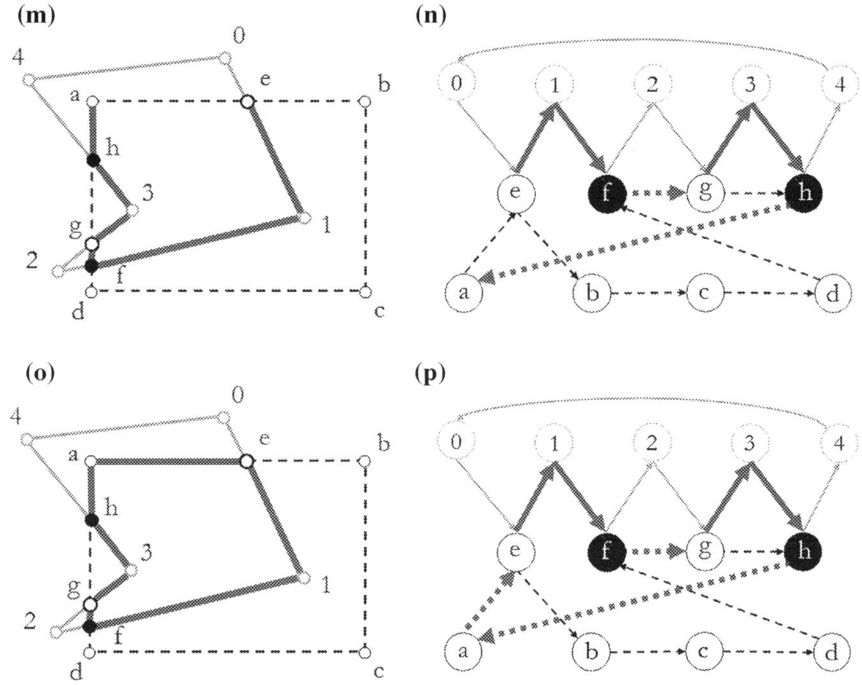


**Fig. 2.18** (continued)

**Problem 2.3:** [*4-way symmetry algorithm*]
Re-solve Problem 2.2 using the 4-way symmetry algorithm.

**Problem 2.4:** [*Line and circle drawing algorithms*]
Figure 2.19b shows the upper left corner of a computer screen. The horizontal and vertical axes are shown with values representing pixel locations. Suppose that the curve shown consists of three segments two of them are line segments and the third is one-eighth of a circle whose center is shown as a black dot. Use a line drawing algorithm (of your choice) and a circle drawing algorithm (of your choice) to determine what pixels should contribute to the curve.

**Problem 2.5:** [*8-way symmetry algorithm*]
A circle having a radius of 5 pixels and centered at $[4, 6]^T$ is to be drawn on a computer screen. Use the 8-way symmetry algorithm to determine whether the following pixels are part of the displayed circle: $[9, 6]^T$, $[9, 5]^T$, $[9, 4]^T$, $[9, 3]^T$, $[4, 11]^T$, $[4, 1]^T$, $[7, 10]^T$, $[1, 2]^T$, $[3, 1]^T$ and $[1, 3]^T$.

**Problem 2.6:** [*4-way symmetry algorithm*]
Re-solve Problem 2.5 using the 4-way symmetry algorithm.

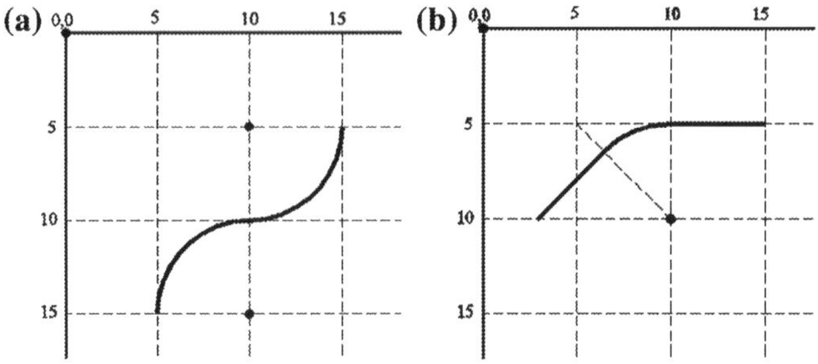


**Fig. 2.19** The *upper left corner* of a computer screen

**Problem 2.7:** [*8-way symmetry algorithm*]

Modify Algorithm 2.10 to use a "for" loop that goes from $x = 1$ to $x = \left\lfloor \frac{r}{\sqrt{2}} \right\rfloor$ where $\lfloor . \rfloor$ is the floor operation.

**Problem 2.8:** [*Midpoint algorithm for circles*]

Modify Algorithm 2.11 so that the condition of the "while" loop is

$$\left( x < \left\lfloor \frac{r}{\sqrt{2}} \right\rfloor \right),$$

where $x$ is the horizontal counter; and $r$ is the radius of the circle.

**Problem 2.9:** [*Midpoint and 8-way symmetry algorithms for circles*]

In order to draw a circle, Algorithm 2.12 starts from the point at the bottom of the circle while Algorithm 2.10 starts from the point at the top. Modify Algorithm 2.12 to start from the top.

**Problem 2.10:** [*Polygon concavity/convexity*]

Consider the polygon defined by the vertices $[3, 3]^T$, $[6, 3]^T$, $[8, 2]^T$ and $[6, 6]^T$. Determine if this polygon is convex or concave.

**Problem 2.11:** [*Polygon concavity/convexity*]

Given a 2D polygon specified by the vertices $[-3, 0]^T$, $[3, -1]^T$, $[1, 0]^T$ and $[4, 2]^T$, test whether it is convex or concave.

**Problem 2.12:** [*Cohen-Sutherland clipping algorithm—left-handed coordinate system*]

Suppose that a clip window is indicated by its upper left and lower right corners $[100, 50]^T$ and $[300, 200]^T$. Test whether each of the following line segments can be trivially accepted in the window, trivially rejected or needs further processing:

1. A line extending from $[171, 88]^T$ to $[233, 171]^T$.
2. A line extending from $[150, 101]^T$ to $[233, 39]^T$.
3. A line extending from $[52, 15]^T$ to $[98, 45]^T$.

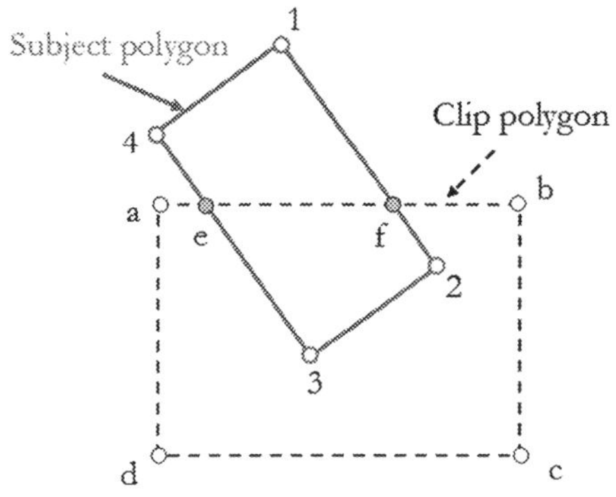


**Fig. 2.20** A subject polygon to be clipped by a clip polygon

**Problem 2.13:** [*Cohen-Sutherland clipping algorithm—left-handed coordinate system*]

Use the Cohen-Sutherland algorithm to determine what lines or portions of lines are preserved and kept in Problem 2.12.

**Problem 2.14:** [*Line clipping*]

Given a clip rectangle spanning from $[3, 3]^T$ to $[15, 12]^T$, use the brute-force algorithm discussed in this chapter to determine what lines or parts of lines are preserved and kept among the following:

1. A line extending from $[15, 12]^T$ to $[17, 10]^T$.
2. A line extending from $[16, 9]^T$ to $[10, 10]^T$.
3. A line extending from $[5, 5]^T$ to $[9, 8]^T$.
4. A line extending from $[12, 14]^T$ to $[7, 2]^T$.

**Problem 2.15:** [*Line intersection—parametric equation*]

Using the parametric equation of a line, determine the intersection point between the two line segments $\overline{\dot{\mathbf{p}}_1\dot{\mathbf{p}}_2}$ and $\overline{\dot{\mathbf{p}}_3\dot{\mathbf{p}}_4}$ where $\dot{\mathbf{p}}_1 = [1, 1]^T$, $\dot{\mathbf{p}}_2 = [9, 9]^T$, $\dot{\mathbf{p}}_3 = [9, 1]^T$ and $\dot{\mathbf{p}}_4 = [1, 9]^T$.

**Problem 2.16:** [*Line intersection—homogeneous coordinates*]

Re-solve Problem 2.15 using homogeneous coordinates (see Sect. B.7).

**Problem 2.17:** [*Line intersection*]

Use three different methods to determine the intersection point between the two line segments $\overline{\dot{\mathbf{p}}_1\dot{\mathbf{p}}_2}$ and $\overline{\dot{\mathbf{p}}_3\dot{\mathbf{p}}_4}$ where $\dot{\mathbf{p}}_1 = [1, 1]^T$, $\dot{\mathbf{p}}_2 = [3, 3]^T$, $\dot{\mathbf{p}}_3 = [1, 3]^T$ and $\dot{\mathbf{p}}_4 = [3, 1]^T$.

**Problem 2.18:** [*Weiler-Atherton clipping—circular lists and insertion of false vertices*]

Consider the subject and clip polygons shown in Fig. 2.20. What are the steps that should be followed to populate circular lists for both the subject and clip polygons?

**Problem 2.19:** [*Weiler-Atherton clipping—clipped loops*]

Determine the clipped polygon parts (i.e., loops of vertices) in Problem 2.18.

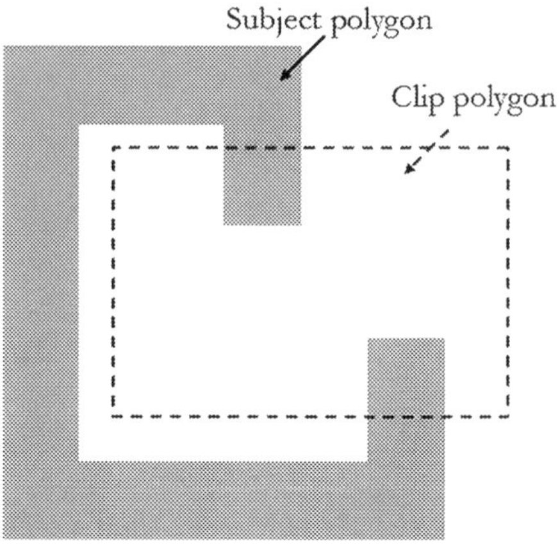


**Fig. 2.21** A subject polygon to be clipped by a clip polygon

**Problem 2.20:** [*Weiler-Atherton clipping—circular lists and insertion of false vertices*]

Consider the subject and clip polygons shown in Fig. 2.21. What are the steps that should be followed to populate circular lists for both the subject and clip polygons?

**Problem 2.21:** [*Weiler-Atherton clipping—clipped loops*]

Determine the clipped polygon parts (i.e., loops of vertices) in Problem 2.20.

## References


Aken, J.V. 1984. An efficient ellipse-drawing algorithm. *IEEE Computer Graphics and Applications* 4(9): 24–35.

Bresenham, J.E. 1965. Algorithm for computer control of a digital plotter. *IBM Systems Journal* 4(1): 25–30.

Cyrus, M., and J. Beck. 1978. Generalized two- and three-dimensional clipping. *Computers and Graphics* 3(1): 23–28.

Foley, J.D., A. van Dam, S.K. Feiner, and J. Hughes. 1995. *Computer Graphics: Principles and Practice in C*, 2nd ed. The systems programming series. Addison-Wesley, Reading, MA.

Liang, Y.-D., and B.A. Barsky. 1984. A new concept and method for line clipping. *ACM Transactions on Graphics (TOG)* 3(1): 1–22.

Maillot, P.-G. 1992. A new, fast method for 2d polygon clipping: analysis and software implementation. *ACM Transactions on Graphics (TOG)* 11(3): 276–290.

Nicholl, T.M., D.T. Lee, and R.A. Nicholl. 1987. An efficient new algorithm for 2-d line clipping: its development and analysis. *ACM SIGGRAPH Computer Graphics* 21(4): 253–262.

Pitteway, M. 1967. Algorithm for drawing ellipses or hyperbolae with a digital plotter. *Computer Journal* 10(3): 282–289.

Sutherland, I.E., and G.W. Hodgman. 1974. Reentrant polygon clipping. *Communications of the ACM* 17(1): 32–42.

Van Aken, J., and M. Novak. 1985. Curve-drawing algorithms for raster displays. *ACM Transactions on Graphics* 4(2): 147–169.

Weiler, K., and P. Atherton. 1977. Hidden surface removal using polygon area sorting. *ACM SIGGRAPH Computer Graphics* 11(2): 214–222.

# Chapter 3
# Transformations in 2D Space

**Abstract** Transformation operations in 2D space are a set of geometric operations that can be applied to 2D planar objects/shapes. The aim of any transformation operation is to alter the status of objects in space. In vector graphics, we are concerned mainly with specific points that shape the object to be transformed. For example, only four points surrounding a square (i.e., its vertices) can help us determine the shape after transformation; no matter how big or small the square is. This not the case with raster graphics where all the pixels inside the square should be transformed. However, raster graphics transformations are not the scope of this chapter. The basic 2D transformation operations include translation, rotation, scaling, reflection and shearing. We will discuss each of these operations in the rest of this chapter.

## 3.1 Translation in 2D Space

The translation operation in 2D space is performed when a 2D point is moved or *translated* from a position $\dot{\mathbf{p}}_1 = [x_1, y_1]^T$ to another position $\dot{\mathbf{p}}_2 = [x_2, y_2]^T$ as shown in Fig. 3.1a. In this case, the magnitude and direction of translation (or movement) are characterized by a 2D vector $\mathbf{t} = [t_x, t_y]^T = [x_2 - x_1, y_2 - y_1]^T$. This vector is referred to as the *translation vector*. In other words, the 2D translation operation can be expressed as

$$\underbrace{\begin{bmatrix} x_2 \\ y_2 \end{bmatrix}}_{\dot{\mathbf{p}}_2} = \underbrace{\begin{bmatrix} x_1 \\ y_1 \end{bmatrix}}_{\dot{\mathbf{p}}_1} + \underbrace{\begin{bmatrix} t_x \\ t_y \end{bmatrix}}_{\mathbf{t}}. \tag{3.1}$$

Hence, in order to translate an object in 2D space, each of its vertices is to be translated using Eq. (3.1). The same operation can be performed in homogeneous

R. Elias, *Digital Media*, DOI: 10.1007/978-3-319-05137-6_3,

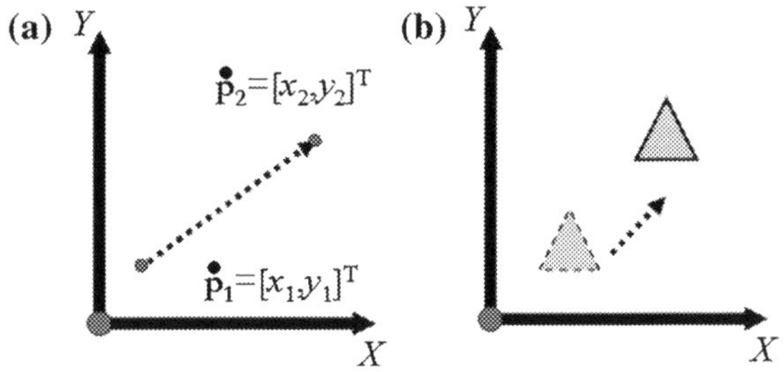


**Fig. 3.1** Translation (or movement) in 2D space. **a** An inhomogeneous point $\dot{\mathbf{p}}_1$ is translated to another 2D point $\dot{\mathbf{p}}_2$. **b** A triangle is translated in 2D space

coordinates (refer to Appendix B.7). To translate a homogeneous 2D point $\mathbf{p}_1 = [x_1, y_1, 1]^T$ to $\mathbf{p}_2 = [x_2, y_2, 1]^T$, we use

$$\underbrace{\begin{bmatrix} x_2 \\ y_2 \\ 1 \end{bmatrix}}_{\mathbf{p}_2} = \underbrace{\begin{bmatrix} 1 & 0 & t_x \\ 0 & 1 & t_y \\ 0 & 0 & 1 \end{bmatrix}}_{\mathtt{T}([t_x,t_y]^T)} \underbrace{\begin{bmatrix} x_1 \\ y_1 \\ 1 \end{bmatrix}}_{\mathbf{p}_1}, \tag{3.2}$$

where $\mathtt{T}$ is a $3 \times 3$ matrix representing the translation operation for homogeneous points in 2D space; and $[t_x, t_y]^T$ is the translation vector.

**Example 3.1:** [*2D translation*]

Consider a triangle with vertices located at $\dot{\mathbf{a}}_1 = [1, 0]^T$, $\dot{\mathbf{b}}_1 = [0, 1]^T$ and $\dot{\mathbf{c}}_1 = [-1, 0]^T$. This triangle is translated using a translation vector $\mathbf{t} = [2, 3]^T$. Determine the new locations of its vertices $\dot{\mathbf{a}}_2$, $\dot{\mathbf{b}}_2$ and $\dot{\mathbf{c}}_2$.

**Solution 3.1:** We may apply Eq. (3.1) to each of the vertices to get the new positions.

$$\dot{\mathbf{a}}_2 = \underbrace{\begin{bmatrix} 1 \\ 0 \end{bmatrix}}_{\dot{\mathbf{a}}_1} + \underbrace{\begin{bmatrix} 2 \\ 3 \end{bmatrix}}_{\mathbf{t}} = \underbrace{\begin{bmatrix} 3 \\ 3 \end{bmatrix}}_{\dot{\mathbf{a}}_2},$$

$$\dot{\mathbf{b}}_2 = \underbrace{\begin{bmatrix} 0 \\ 1 \end{bmatrix}}_{\dot{\mathbf{b}}_1} + \underbrace{\begin{bmatrix} 2 \\ 3 \end{bmatrix}}_{\mathbf{t}} = \underbrace{\begin{bmatrix} 2 \\ 4 \end{bmatrix}}_{\dot{\mathbf{b}}_2},$$

$$\dot{\mathbf{c}}_2 = \underbrace{\begin{bmatrix} -1 \\ 0 \end{bmatrix}}_{\dot{\mathbf{c}}_1} + \underbrace{\begin{bmatrix} 2 \\ 3 \end{bmatrix}}_{\mathbf{t}} = \underbrace{\begin{bmatrix} 1 \\ 3 \end{bmatrix}}_{\dot{\mathbf{c}}_2}.$$

Hence, after translation, the triangle is surrounded by the vertices $\dot{\mathbf{a}}_2 = [3, 3]^T$, $\dot{\mathbf{b}}_2 = [2, 4]^T$ and $\dot{\mathbf{c}}_2 = [1, 3]^T$. Alternatively, Eq. (3.2) may be used to achieve the same results in homogeneous coordinates as

$$\mathbf{a}_2 = \underbrace{\begin{bmatrix} 1 & 0 & 2 \\ 0 & 1 & 3 \\ 0 & 0 & 1 \end{bmatrix}}_{\mathtt{T}([2,3]^T)} \underbrace{\begin{bmatrix} 1 \\ 0 \\ 1 \end{bmatrix}}_{\mathbf{a}_1} = \underbrace{\begin{bmatrix} 3 \\ 3 \\ 1 \end{bmatrix}}_{\mathbf{a}_2},$$

$$\mathbf{b}_2 = \underbrace{\begin{bmatrix} 1 & 0 & 2 \\ 0 & 1 & 3 \\ 0 & 0 & 1 \end{bmatrix}}_{\mathtt{T}([2,3]^T)} \underbrace{\begin{bmatrix} 0 \\ 1 \\ 1 \end{bmatrix}}_{\mathbf{b}_1} = \underbrace{\begin{bmatrix} 2 \\ 4 \\ 1 \end{bmatrix}}_{\mathbf{b}_2},$$

$$\mathbf{c}_2 = \underbrace{\begin{bmatrix} 1 & 0 & 2 \\ 0 & 1 & 3 \\ 0 & 0 & 1 \end{bmatrix}}_{\mathtt{T}([2,3]^T)} \underbrace{\begin{bmatrix} -1 \\ 0 \\ 1 \end{bmatrix}}_{\mathbf{c}_1} = \underbrace{\begin{bmatrix} 1 \\ 3 \\ 1 \end{bmatrix}}_{\mathbf{c}_2},$$

which are the same points obtained before. □

## 3.2 Rotation in 2D Space

A point can be rotated in 2D space if the center of rotation (or the *pivot*), is specified as well as the angle of rotation. As depicted in Fig. 3.2, a point $\dot{\mathbf{p}}_1 = [x_1, y_1]^T$ is rotated about the origin through an angle $\theta$ to reach another point $\dot{\mathbf{p}}_2 = [x_2, y_2]^T$. If $\dot{\mathbf{p}}_1$ is at distance $r$ from the origin, its coordinates can be expressed as $[r\ \cos(\alpha), r\ \sin(\alpha)]^T$ where $\alpha$ is the inclination angle of the line $\overline{\dot{\mathbf{p}}_0\dot{\mathbf{p}}_1}$ with respect to the $x$-axis. (Note that the positive direction of rotation in 2D space is calculated anti-clockwise if the $y$-axis is pointing upwards and clockwise if the $y$-axis is pointing downwards. In the rest of this chapter, we will consider the $y$-axis as pointing upwards while the $x$-axis is pointing to the right.)

After the rotation, point $\dot{\mathbf{p}}_2$ can be expressed as $[r\ \cos(\alpha+\theta), r\ \sin(\alpha+\theta)]^T$. From basic trigonometry, we know that

$$\begin{aligned} \sin(\alpha+\theta) &= \sin(\alpha)\cos(\theta) + \cos(\alpha)\sin(\theta), \\ \cos(\alpha+\theta) &= \cos(\alpha)\cos(\theta) - \sin(\alpha)\sin(\theta). \end{aligned} \tag{3.3}$$

Applying Eq. (3.3) to the coordinates of the point after rotation, we get

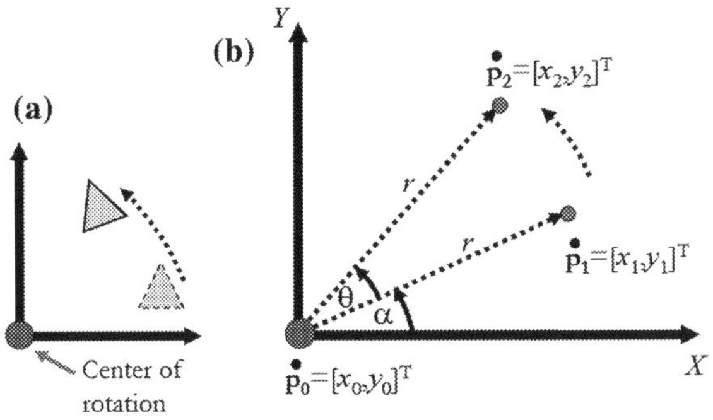


**Fig. 3.2** Rotation in 2D space. **a** A triangle is rotated in 2D space. **b** An inhomogeneous point $\dot{\mathbf{p}}_1$ is rotated about the origin through an angle $\theta$ to another 2D point $\dot{\mathbf{p}}_2$

$$\begin{aligned}
\underbrace{\begin{bmatrix} x_2 \\ y_2 \end{bmatrix}}_{\dot{\mathbf{p}}_2} &= \begin{bmatrix} r\cos(\alpha+\theta) \\ r\sin(\alpha+\theta) \end{bmatrix} \\
&= \begin{bmatrix} r\,(\cos(\alpha)\cos(\theta) - \sin(\alpha)\sin(\theta)) \\ r\,(\sin(\alpha)\cos(\theta) + \cos(\alpha)\sin(\theta)) \end{bmatrix} \\
&= \begin{bmatrix} \underbrace{r\cos(\alpha)}_{x_1}\cos(\theta) - \underbrace{r\sin(\alpha)}_{y_1}\sin(\theta) \\ \underbrace{r\sin(\alpha)}_{y_1}\cos(\theta) + \underbrace{r\cos(\alpha)}_{x_1}\sin(\theta) \end{bmatrix} \\
&= \underbrace{\begin{bmatrix} \cos(\theta) & -\sin(\theta) \\ \sin(\theta) & \cos(\theta) \end{bmatrix}}_{\dot{\mathrm{R}}(\theta)} \underbrace{\begin{bmatrix} x_1 \\ y_1 \end{bmatrix}}_{\dot{\mathbf{p}}_1},
\end{aligned} \tag{3.4}$$

where $\dot{\mathrm{R}}$ is a $2 \times 2$ matrix representing the rotation operation for inhomogeneous points in 2D space; and $\theta$ is the angle of rotation. Note that the center of rotation or the pivot in this case is the origin. Also, notice that Eq. (3.4) is used with inhomogeneous points (Appendix B.7).

In order to work with homogeneous coordinates, Eq. (3.4) is altered to rotate a 2D homogeneous point $\mathbf{p}_1 = [x_1, y_1, 1]^T$ to another 2D homogeneous point $\mathbf{p}_2 = [x_2, y_2, 1]^T$. We use

$$\underbrace{\begin{bmatrix} x_2 \\ y_2 \\ 1 \end{bmatrix}}_{\mathbf{p}_2} = \underbrace{\begin{bmatrix} \cos(\theta) & -\sin(\theta) & 0 \\ \sin(\theta) & \cos(\theta) & 0 \\ 0 & 0 & 1 \end{bmatrix}}_{\mathrm{R}(\theta)} \underbrace{\begin{bmatrix} x_1 \\ y_1 \\ 1 \end{bmatrix}}_{\mathbf{p}_1}, \tag{3.5}$$

where R is a $3 \times 3$ matrix representing the rotation operation for homogeneous points in 2D space; and $\theta$ is the angle of rotation.

**Example 3.2:** [*2D rotation about the origin—homogeneous coordinates*]

Consider a line segment spanning from $\dot{\mathbf{p}}_1 = [3, 4]^T$ to $\dot{\mathbf{p}}_2 = [10, 7]^T$. If this line is rotated through an angle of 45° about the origin, calculate the new positions of its endpoints. You may use homogeneous coordinates in your calculations. (Solving the same problem using inhomogeneous coordinates is left as an exercise.)

**Solution 3.2:** Let us assume that the homogeneous points $\mathbf{p}_1$ and $\mathbf{p}_2$ are rotated to $\mathbf{p}_3$ and $\mathbf{p}_4$ respectively. Using Eq. (3.5), the new positions can be obtained as

$$\underbrace{\begin{bmatrix} x_3 \\ y_3 \\ 1 \end{bmatrix}}_{\mathbf{p}_3} = \begin{bmatrix} \cos(\theta) & -\sin(\theta) & 0 \\ \sin(\theta) & \cos(\theta) & 0 \\ 0 & 0 & 1 \end{bmatrix} \begin{bmatrix} x_1 \\ y_1 \\ 1 \end{bmatrix}$$

$$= \underbrace{\begin{bmatrix} \cos(45) & -\sin(45) & 0 \\ \sin(45) & \cos(45) & 0 \\ 0 & 0 & 1 \end{bmatrix}}_{\mathtt{R}(45)} \underbrace{\begin{bmatrix} 3 \\ 4 \\ 1 \end{bmatrix}}_{\mathbf{p}_1} = \begin{bmatrix} -\frac{1}{\sqrt{2}} \\ \frac{7}{\sqrt{2}} \\ 1 \end{bmatrix} = \begin{bmatrix} -0.7071 \\ 4.9497 \\ 1 \end{bmatrix}$$

and

$$\underbrace{\begin{bmatrix} x_4 \\ y_4 \\ 1 \end{bmatrix}}_{\mathbf{p}_4} = \begin{bmatrix} \cos(\theta) & -\sin(\theta) & 0 \\ \sin(\theta) & \cos(\theta) & 0 \\ 0 & 0 & 1 \end{bmatrix} \begin{bmatrix} x_2 \\ y_2 \\ 1 \end{bmatrix}$$

$$= \underbrace{\begin{bmatrix} \cos(45) & -\sin(45) & 0 \\ \sin(45) & \cos(45) & 0 \\ 0 & 0 & 1 \end{bmatrix}}_{\mathtt{R}(45)} \underbrace{\begin{bmatrix} 10 \\ 7 \\ 1 \end{bmatrix}}_{\mathbf{p}_2} = \begin{bmatrix} \frac{3}{\sqrt{2}} \\ \frac{17}{\sqrt{2}} \\ 1 \end{bmatrix} = \begin{bmatrix} 2.1213 \\ 12.0208 \\ 1 \end{bmatrix}. \qquad \square$$

### 3.2.1 General Rotation in 2D Space

Most of the time, rotation operations are performed about a general point rather than the origin. In this case, the rotation matrix $\dot{\mathtt{R}}$ of Eq. (3.4) or $\mathtt{R}$ of Eq. (3.5) cannot be used directly. Instead, the center of rotation (with the point to be rotated) must be translated to the origin before applying the rotation. Afterwards, translation should be reversed. Hence, as depicted in Fig. 3.3, if a point $\dot{\mathbf{p}}_1$ is rotated about another point $\dot{\mathbf{p}}_0$ to get $\dot{\mathbf{p}}_2$, the following three steps should be performed:

1. Translate $\dot{\mathbf{p}}_0$ and $\dot{\mathbf{p}}_1$ by a translation vector $\mathbf{t}$ that moves $\dot{\mathbf{p}}_0$ to the origin (i.e., $\mathbf{t} = [-x_0, -y_0]^T$).
2. Rotate about the origin as done before.
3. Translate back using the vector $-\mathbf{t}$ or $[x_0, y_0]^T$.

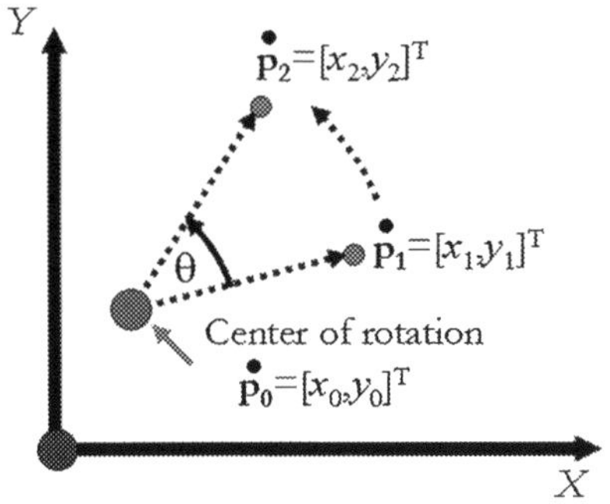


**Fig. 3.3** A point $\dot{\mathbf{p}}_1$ is rotated about an arbitrary point $\dot{\mathbf{p}}_0$

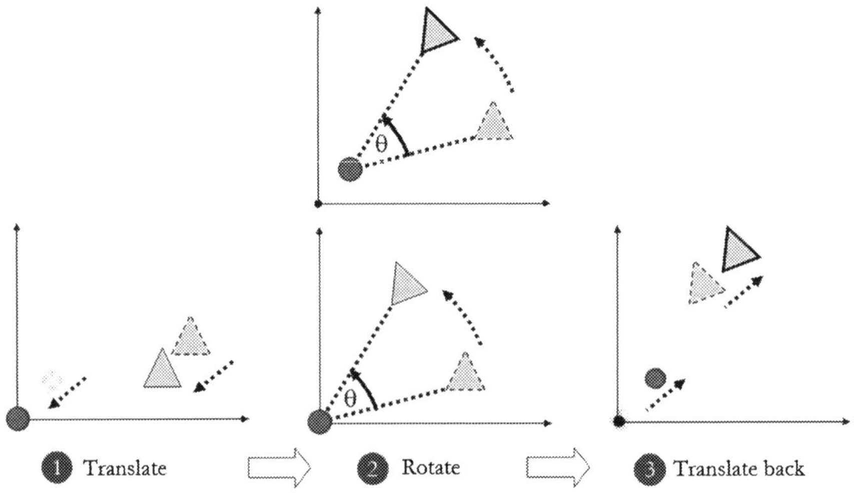


**Fig. 3.4** A triangle is rotated about an arbitrary point. The steps performed are: *1* Translate the center of rotation as well as the triangle so that the center of rotation coincides with the origin. *2* Perform the rotation operation about the origin. *3* Translate the triangle back using the same translation vector used before but in the opposite direction

An example is shown in Fig. 3.4. In this example, a triangle is rotated about an arbitrary point. In order to accomplish this action, three steps should be performed. The first step is to translate everything so that the center of rotation coincides with the origin. The second step applies the rotation operation as discussed above. The final step reverses the translation process by moving the triangle using the same translation vector used before but in the opposite direction (by switching the signs of the vector terms).

We can express the previous operations in mathematical form as

$$\begin{aligned} x_2 &= (x_1 - x_0)\cos(\theta) - (y_1 - y_0)\sin(\theta) + x_0, \\ y_2 &= (x_1 - x_0)\sin(\theta) + (y_1 - y_0)\cos(\theta) + y_0. \end{aligned} \tag{3.6}$$

In matrix form, the translation–rotation–translation process can be expressed as

$$\underbrace{\begin{bmatrix} x_2 \\ y_2 \end{bmatrix}}_{\dot{\mathbf{p}}_2} = \underbrace{\begin{bmatrix} \cos(\theta) & -\sin(\theta) \\ \sin(\theta) & \cos(\theta) \end{bmatrix}}_{\dot{\mathrm{R}}(\theta)} \underbrace{\begin{bmatrix} x_1 - x_0 \\ y_1 - y_0 \end{bmatrix}}_{\dot{\mathbf{p}}_1 - \dot{\mathbf{p}}_0} + \underbrace{\begin{bmatrix} x_0 \\ y_0 \end{bmatrix}}_{\dot{\mathbf{p}}_0}, \tag{3.7}$$

where $\dot{\mathrm{R}}$ is the rotation matrix; $\theta$ is the rotation angle; $[-x_0, -y_0]^T$ and $[x_0, y_0]^T$ are the translation vectors; $\dot{\mathbf{p}}_0$ is the center of rotation; $\dot{\mathbf{p}}_1$ is the point before rotation; and $\dot{\mathbf{p}}_2$ is the point after rotation.

The same general rotation operation about a homogeneous point $\mathbf{p}_0$ can be performed using the same steps mentioned above (i.e., translation, rotation and translation back). This can be expressed as

$$\begin{aligned} \underbrace{\begin{bmatrix} x_2 \\ y_2 \\ 1 \end{bmatrix}}_{\mathbf{p}_2} &= \underbrace{\begin{bmatrix} 1 & 0 & x_0 \\ 0 & 1 & y_0 \\ 0 & 0 & 1 \end{bmatrix}}_{\mathrm{T}([x_0,y_0]^T)} \underbrace{\begin{bmatrix} \cos(\theta) & -\sin(\theta) & 0 \\ \sin(\theta) & \cos(\theta) & 0 \\ 0 & 0 & 1 \end{bmatrix}}_{\mathrm{R}(\theta)} \underbrace{\begin{bmatrix} 1 & 0 & -x_0 \\ 0 & 1 & -y_0 \\ 0 & 0 & 1 \end{bmatrix}}_{\mathrm{T}([-x_0,-y_0]^T)} \underbrace{\begin{bmatrix} x_1 \\ y_1 \\ 1 \end{bmatrix}}_{\mathbf{p}_1} \\ &= \underbrace{\begin{bmatrix} \cos(\theta) & -\sin(\theta) & -x_0\cos(\theta) + y_0\sin(\theta) + x_0 \\ \sin(\theta) & \cos(\theta) & -x_0\sin(\theta) - y_0\cos(\theta) + y_0 \\ 0 & 0 & 1 \end{bmatrix}}_{\mathrm{T}([x_0,y_0]^T)\mathrm{R}(\theta)\mathrm{T}([-x_0,-y_0]^T)} \underbrace{\begin{bmatrix} x_1 \\ y_1 \\ 1 \end{bmatrix}}_{\mathbf{p}_1}, \end{aligned} \tag{3.8}$$

where R is the rotation matrix; $\theta$ is the rotation angle; T are the translation matrices; $[-x_0, -y_0]^T$ and $[x_0, y_0]^T$ are the translation vectors; $\mathbf{p}_0$ is the center of rotation; $\mathbf{p}_1$ is the point before rotation; and $\mathbf{p}_2$ is the point after rotation. (Notice the order of matrix multiplication.)

**Example 3.3:** [*2D general rotation—inhomogeneous coordinates*]

If the center of rotation in Example 3.2 is changed to $\dot{\mathbf{p}}_1 = [3, 4]^T$; one of the endpoints of the line segment, get the new positions of the endpoints. You may use inhomogeneous coordinates in your calculations.

**Solution 3.3:** Let us assume that point $\dot{\mathbf{p}}_1$ is rotated to $\dot{\mathbf{p}}_3$. Using Eq. (3.7), the new position can be obtained as

$$\begin{aligned} \underbrace{\begin{bmatrix} x_3 \\ y_3 \end{bmatrix}}_{\dot{\mathbf{p}}_3} &= \begin{bmatrix} \cos(\theta) & -\sin(\theta) \\ \sin(\theta) & \cos(\theta) \end{bmatrix} \begin{bmatrix} x_1 - x_0 \\ y_1 - y_0 \end{bmatrix} + \begin{bmatrix} x_0 \\ y_0 \end{bmatrix} \\ &= \underbrace{\begin{bmatrix} \cos(45) & -\sin(45) \\ \sin(45) & \cos(45) \end{bmatrix}}_{\dot{\mathrm{R}}(45)} \underbrace{\begin{bmatrix} 3 - 3 \\ 4 - 4 \end{bmatrix}}_{\dot{\mathbf{p}}_1 - \dot{\mathbf{p}}_0} + \underbrace{\begin{bmatrix} 3 \\ 4 \end{bmatrix}}_{\dot{\mathbf{p}}_0} = \begin{bmatrix} 3 \\ 4 \end{bmatrix}, \end{aligned}$$

which is expected as $\dot{\mathbf{p}}_1$ rotates about itself (i.e., $\dot{\mathbf{p}}_0$) to get $\dot{\mathbf{p}}_3 = \dot{\mathbf{p}}_1 = \dot{\mathbf{p}}_0$. Now, let us assume that point $\dot{\mathbf{p}}_2$ is rotated to $\dot{\mathbf{p}}_4$, which can be obtained using Eq. (3.7) as

$$\begin{aligned}
\underbrace{\begin{bmatrix} x_4 \\ y_4 \end{bmatrix}}_{\dot{\mathbf{p}}_4} &= \begin{bmatrix} \cos(\theta) & -\sin(\theta) \\ \sin(\theta) & \cos(\theta) \end{bmatrix} \begin{bmatrix} x_2 - x_0 \\ y_2 - y_0 \end{bmatrix} + \begin{bmatrix} x_0 \\ y_0 \end{bmatrix} \\
&= \underbrace{\begin{bmatrix} \cos(45) & -\sin(45) \\ \sin(45) & \cos(45) \end{bmatrix}}_{\dot{\mathtt{R}}(45)} \underbrace{\begin{bmatrix} 10-3 \\ 7-4 \end{bmatrix}}_{\dot{\mathbf{p}}_2 - \dot{\mathbf{p}}_0} + \underbrace{\begin{bmatrix} 3 \\ 4 \end{bmatrix}}_{\dot{\mathbf{p}}_0} \\
&= \begin{bmatrix} 2\sqrt{2}+3 \\ 5\sqrt{2}+4 \end{bmatrix} = \begin{bmatrix} 5.8284 \\ 11.0711 \end{bmatrix}.
\end{aligned}$$

□

**Example 3.4:** [*2D general rotation*]

Show that in order to rotate about $[t_x, t_y]^T$ through an angle $\theta$, a matrix $\mathtt{M}$ is required where

$$\mathtt{M} = \begin{bmatrix} \cos(\theta) & -\sin(\theta) & -t_x\cos(\theta) + t_y\sin(\theta) + t_x \\ \sin(\theta) & \cos(\theta) & -t_x\sin(\theta) - t_y\cos(\theta) + t_y \\ 0 & 0 & 1 \end{bmatrix}.$$

**Solution 3.4:** Three transformations should be performed in the following sequence:

1. Translate using the vector $[-t_x, -t_y]^T$. This is represented by $\mathtt{M}_1$ where

$$\mathtt{M}_1 = \mathtt{T}([-t_x, -t_y]^T) = \begin{bmatrix} 1 & 0 & -t_x \\ 0 & 1 & -t_y \\ 0 & 0 & 1 \end{bmatrix}.$$

2. Rotate through the angle $\theta$. This is represented by $\mathtt{M}_2$ where

$$\mathtt{M}_2 = \mathtt{R}(\theta) = \begin{bmatrix} \cos(\theta) & -\sin(\theta) & 0 \\ \sin(\theta) & \cos(\theta) & 0 \\ 0 & 0 & 1 \end{bmatrix}.$$

3. Translate back using the vector $[t_x, t_y]^T$. This is represented by $\mathtt{M}_3$ where

$$\mathtt{M}_3 = \mathtt{T}([t_x, t_y]^T) = \begin{bmatrix} 1 & 0 & t_x \\ 0 & 1 & t_y \\ 0 & 0 & 1 \end{bmatrix}.$$

Then, the overall transformation matrix is expressed as

$$\mathtt{M} = \mathtt{M}_3\mathtt{M}_2\mathtt{M}_1 = \begin{bmatrix} \cos(\theta) & -\sin(\theta) & -t_x\cos(\theta) + t_y\sin(\theta) + t_x \\ \sin(\theta) & \cos(\theta) & -t_x\sin(\theta) - t_y\cos(\theta) + t_y \\ 0 & 0 & 1 \end{bmatrix},$$

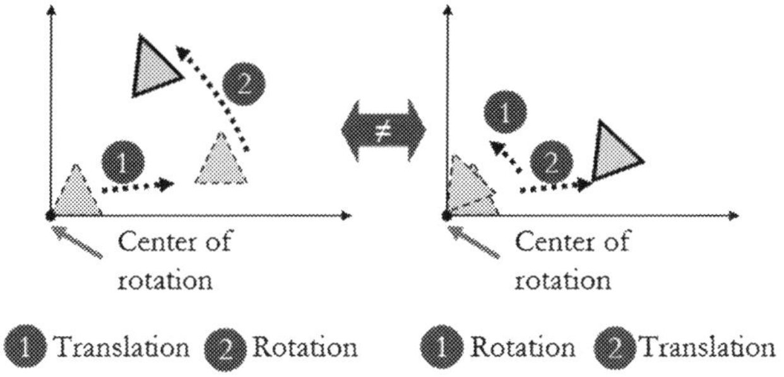


**Fig. 3.5** Transformations are *not* commutative. Translation followed by rotation is not the same as rotation followed by translation

which is the required matrix. □

One important point to be mentioned here is that transformations are *not* commutative. This means that the order of performing the transformation operations is important. For example, a translation operation followed by rotation would lead to a result that is totally different from that produced by a rotation operation followed by translation. An example is shown in Fig. 3.5.

**Example 3.5:** [*Order of transformations*]

Derive the overall transformation matrix if an object is translated by a vector $[t_x, t_y]^T$ and then rotated about the origin through an angle $\theta$. Re-estimate the matrix if the order of performing operations is reversed.

**Solution 3.5:** The following are the two cases:

- **Translation → Rotation**

$$\mathtt{RT} = \begin{bmatrix} \cos(\theta) & -\sin(\theta) & 0 \\ \sin(\theta) & \cos(\theta) & 0 \\ 0 & 0 & 1 \end{bmatrix} \begin{bmatrix} 1 & 0 & t_x \\ 0 & 1 & t_y \\ 0 & 0 & 1 \end{bmatrix}$$

$$= \begin{bmatrix} \cos(\theta) & -\sin(\theta) & t_x\cos(\theta) - t_y\sin(\theta) \\ \sin(\theta) & \cos(\theta) & t_x\sin(\theta) + t_y\cos(\theta) \\ 0 & 0 & 1 \end{bmatrix}.$$

- **Rotation → Translation**

$$\mathtt{TR} = \begin{bmatrix} 1 & 0 & t_x \\ 0 & 1 & t_y \\ 0 & 0 & 1 \end{bmatrix} \begin{bmatrix} \cos(\theta) & -\sin(\theta) & 0 \\ \sin(\theta) & \cos(\theta) & 0 \\ 0 & 0 & 1 \end{bmatrix}$$

$$= \begin{bmatrix} \cos(\theta) & -\sin(\theta) & t_x \\ \sin(\theta) & \cos(\theta) & t_y \\ 0 & 0 & 1 \end{bmatrix}.$$

It is clear that different orders of multiplications result in different outcomes. □

**Example 3.6:** [*2D general rotation*]

A circle with radius 4 is centered at $\dot{\mathbf{p}}_1 = [3, 5]^T$. If this circle is rotated through an angle of 10° about a point $\dot{\mathbf{p}}_0 = [1, 1]^T$, calculate its intersections with the $y$-axis.

**Solution 3.6:** Let us determine the location of the center point after rotation, $\dot{\mathbf{p}}_2$ through three steps:

1. Translate the circle using the translation vector $-\dot{\mathbf{p}}_0 = [-1, -1]^T$ in order to move the fixed point $\dot{\mathbf{p}}_0$ to the origin.
2. Rotate through an angle of 10°.
3. Translate back using the translation vector $\dot{\mathbf{p}}_0 = [1, 1]^T$ to reverse the translation of Step 1.

These steps are represented by Eq. (3.7), which can be applied directly as

$$\dot{\mathbf{p}}_2 = \begin{bmatrix} \cos(10) & -\sin(10) \\ \sin(10) & \cos(10) \end{bmatrix} \begin{bmatrix} 3-1 \\ 5-1 \end{bmatrix} + \begin{bmatrix} 1 \\ 1 \end{bmatrix} = \begin{bmatrix} 2.2750 \\ 5.2865 \end{bmatrix}.$$

The intersections with the $y$-axis can be calculated using the circle equation as

$$\begin{aligned} y &= y_2 \pm \sqrt{r^2 - (x - x_2)^2} \\ y &= 5.2865 \pm \sqrt{4^2 - (0 - 2.275)^2}. \end{aligned}$$

Hence, the intersection points between the circle and the $y$-axis are $[0, 8.5765]^T$ and $[0, 1.9965]^T$. □

## 3.3 Scaling in 2D Space

In order to scale (i.e., enlarge or shrink) an object in 2D space by a factor $s$ along both directions, the positions of its vertices $[x_i, y_i]^T$ are multiplied by this scaling factor to get $[s\ x_i, s\ y_i]^T$. Hence, to scale a point $[x_1, y_1]^T$ using scaling factors $s_x$ and $s_y$ to get $[x_2, y_2]^T$, we may use

$$\begin{aligned} x_2 &= s_x x_1 \\ y_2 &= s_y y_1 \end{aligned} \tag{3.9}$$

In a matrix form, for a vertex $\dot{\mathbf{p}}_1 = [x_1, y_1]^T$, this can be expressed as

$$\underbrace{\begin{bmatrix} x_2 \\ y_2 \end{bmatrix}}_{\dot{\mathbf{p}}_2} = \underbrace{\begin{bmatrix} s_x & 0 \\ 0 & s_y \end{bmatrix}}_{\dot{\mathsf{S}}(s_x, s_y)} \underbrace{\begin{bmatrix} x_1 \\ y_1 \end{bmatrix}}_{\dot{\mathbf{p}}_1}, \tag{3.10}$$

where $\dot{\mathsf{S}}$ is a $2 \times 2$ matrix representing the scaling operation for inhomogeneous points in 2D space; and $s_x$ and $s_y$ are the scaling factors along the $x$- and $y$-directions respectively. Note that if $s_x = s_y = s$, the object will be scaled by the same ratio in both directions. This is referred to as *2D uniform scaling*. If $s_x \neq s_y$, a different scaling ratio will be applied along each direction. This results in *2D non-uniform scaling*. In homogeneous coordinates, the scaling operation is applied as

$$\underbrace{\begin{bmatrix} x_2 \\ y_2 \\ 1 \end{bmatrix}}_{\mathbf{p}_2} = \underbrace{\begin{bmatrix} s_x & 0 & 0 \\ 0 & s_y & 0 \\ 0 & 0 & 1 \end{bmatrix}}_{\mathtt{S}(s_x, s_y)} \underbrace{\begin{bmatrix} x_1 \\ y_1 \\ 1 \end{bmatrix}}_{\mathbf{p}_1}, \tag{3.11}$$

where $\mathtt{S}$ is a $3 \times 3$ matrix representing the scaling operation for homogeneous points in 2D space; and $s_x$ and $s_y$ are the scaling factors along the $x$- and $y$-directions respectively.

### *3.3.1 General Scaling in 2D Space*

Any scaling operation must keep one fixed point at its original position while altering the rest of the points under consideration. This fixed point does not have to be one of the vertices considered. Moreover, this fixed point does not have to be inside the boundaries of the object. In Eq. (3.9) through Eq. (3.11), the fixed point assumed is the origin. Of course, in the general case, the fixed point can be any arbitrary point in 2D space. In this case, we should translate the object under scaling so that the fixed point coincides with the origin before applying Eqs. (3.9, 3.10) or Eq. (3.11). Afterwards, translation is performed again to reverse the effect of the first translation. This sequence of operations is similar to what was implemented in Sect. 3.2.1. Hence, given a vertex $\dot{\mathbf{p}}_1 = [x_1, y_1]^T$ and a fixed point $\dot{\mathbf{p}}_0 = [x_0, y_0]^T$, we can express the sequence of operations as

$$\underbrace{\begin{bmatrix} x_2 \\ y_2 \end{bmatrix}}_{\dot{\mathbf{p}}_2} = \underbrace{\begin{bmatrix} s_x & 0 \\ 0 & s_y \end{bmatrix}}_{\dot{\mathtt{S}}(s_x, s_y)} \underbrace{\begin{bmatrix} x_1 - x_0 \\ y_1 - y_0 \end{bmatrix}}_{\dot{\mathbf{p}}_1 - \dot{\mathbf{p}}_0} + \underbrace{\begin{bmatrix} x_0 \\ y_0 \end{bmatrix}}_{\dot{\mathbf{p}}_0}. \tag{3.12}$$

where $\dot{\mathtt{S}}$ is the scaling matrix; $s_x$ and $s_y$ are the scaling factors; $[-x_0, -y_0]^T$ and $[x_0, y_0]^T$ are the translation vectors; $\dot{\mathbf{p}}_0$ is the fixed point; $\dot{\mathbf{p}}_1$ is the point before

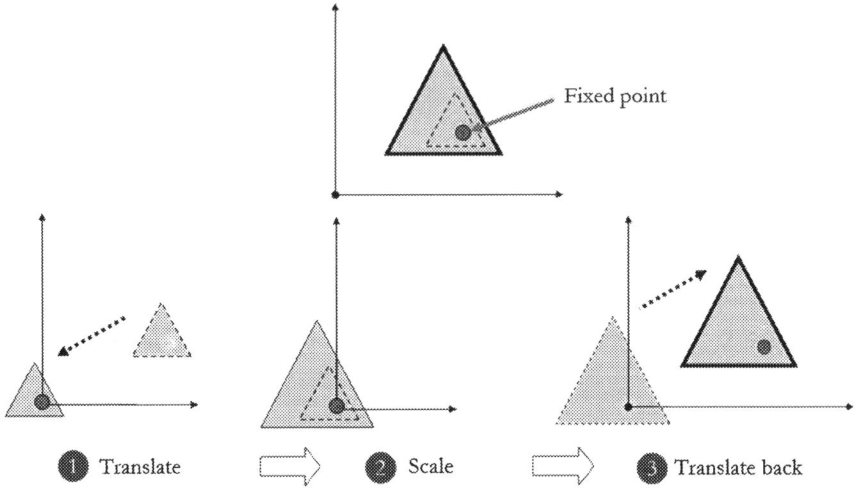


**Fig. 3.6** A triangle is scaled with respect to an arbitrary point. The steps performed are: *1* Translate the triangle so that the fixed point coincides with the origin. *2* Perform the scaling operation with respect to the origin. *3* Translate the triangle back using the same translation vector used before but in the opposite direction

scaling; and $\dot{\mathbf{p}}_2$ is the point after scaling.An illustrative example is depicted in Fig. 3.6. In homogeneous coordinates, the scaling operation is applied as

$$\begin{aligned}
\underbrace{\begin{bmatrix} x_2 \\ y_2 \\ 1 \end{bmatrix}}_{\mathbf{p}_2} &= \underbrace{\begin{bmatrix} 1 & 0 & x_0 \\ 0 & 1 & y_0 \\ 0 & 0 & 1 \end{bmatrix}}_{\mathtt{T}([x_0,y_0]^T)} \underbrace{\begin{bmatrix} s_x & 0 & 0 \\ 0 & s_y & 0 \\ 0 & 0 & 1 \end{bmatrix}}_{\mathtt{S}(s_x,s_y)} \underbrace{\begin{bmatrix} 1 & 0 & -x_0 \\ 0 & 1 & -y_0 \\ 0 & 0 & 1 \end{bmatrix}}_{\mathtt{T}([-x_0,-y_0]^T)} \underbrace{\begin{bmatrix} x_1 \\ y_1 \\ 1 \end{bmatrix}}_{\mathbf{p}_1} \\
&= \underbrace{\begin{bmatrix} s_x & 0 & -x_0 s_x + x_0 \\ 0 & s_y & -y_0 s_y + y_0 \\ 0 & 0 & 1 \end{bmatrix}}_{\mathtt{T}([x_0,y_0]^T)\mathtt{S}(s_x,s_y)\mathtt{T}([-x_0,-y_0]^T)} \underbrace{\begin{bmatrix} x_1 \\ y_1 \\ 1 \end{bmatrix}}_{\mathbf{p}_1},
\end{aligned} \tag{3.13}$$

where $\mathtt{S}$ is the scaling matrix; $s_x$ and $s_y$ are the scaling factors; $\mathtt{T}$ are the translation matrices; $[-x_0, -y_0]^T$ and $[x_0, y_0]^T$ are the translation vectors; $\mathbf{p}_0$ is the fixed point; $\mathbf{p}_1$ is the point before scaling; and $\mathbf{p}_2$ is the point after scaling.

**Example 3.7:** [*2D general transformation*]

Derive a single matrix that transforms a triangle bounded by $[1, 0]^T$, $[2, 0]^T$ and $[2, 2]^T$ to another triangle bounded by $[1, 0]^T$, $[3, 0]^T$ and $[3, 2]^T$.

**Solution 3.7:** Sketch it for better visualization. This is a three-step transformation operation that is performed as follows:

1. Translate the triangle using the vector $[-1, 0]^T$. Thus, the translation matrix is expressed as
$$\mathtt{M}_1 = \mathtt{T}([-1, 0]^T) = \begin{bmatrix} 1 & 0 & -1 \\ 0 & 1 & 0 \\ 0 & 0 & 1 \end{bmatrix}.$$

2. Scale the triangle using a factor of 2 in the $x$-direction. Thus, the scaling matrix is expressed as
$$\mathtt{M}_2 = \mathtt{S}(2, 1) = \begin{bmatrix} 2 & 0 & 0 \\ 0 & 1 & 0 \\ 0 & 0 & 1 \end{bmatrix}.$$

3. Translate the triangle back using the vector $[1, 0]^T$. Thus, the translation matrix is expressed as
$$\mathtt{M}_3 = \mathtt{T}([1, 0]^T) = \begin{bmatrix} 1 & 0 & 1 \\ 0 & 1 & 0 \\ 0 & 0 & 1 \end{bmatrix}.$$

Consequently, the overall transformation is estimated as

$$\begin{aligned} \mathtt{M} &= \mathtt{M}_3\mathtt{M}_2\mathtt{M}_1 \\ &= \begin{bmatrix} 1 & 0 & 1 \\ 0 & 1 & 0 \\ 0 & 0 & 1 \end{bmatrix} \begin{bmatrix} 2 & 0 & 0 \\ 0 & 1 & 0 \\ 0 & 0 & 1 \end{bmatrix} \begin{bmatrix} 1 & 0 & -1 \\ 0 & 1 & 0 \\ 0 & 0 & 1 \end{bmatrix} = \begin{bmatrix} 2 & 0 & -1 \\ 0 & 1 & 0 \\ 0 & 0 & 1 \end{bmatrix}. \end{aligned}$$ □

**Example 3.8:** [*2D general scaling—inhomogeneous coordinates*]

Consider the triangle $\triangle \dot{\mathbf{a}}_1\dot{\mathbf{b}}_1\dot{\mathbf{c}}_1$ where $\dot{\mathbf{a}}_1 = [0, 0]^T$, $\dot{\mathbf{b}}_1 = [1, 1]^T$ and $\dot{\mathbf{c}}_1 = [5, 2]^T$. If this triangle is magnified in both directions to twice its size while keeping point $\dot{\mathbf{c}}_1$ fixed, estimate the new positions $\dot{\mathbf{a}}_2$ and $\dot{\mathbf{b}}_2$. You must use inhomogeneous coordinates in all your calculations.

**Solution 3.8:** There are three steps to achieve the transformation:

1. Translate using the vector $-\dot{\mathbf{c}}_1$ so that point $\dot{\mathbf{c}}_1$ coincides with the origin.
2. Scale the triangle using scaling factors 2 and 2 in both $x$- and $y$-directions.
3. Translate back using the vector $\dot{\mathbf{c}}_1$ to reverse the effect of translation in Step 1.

Those steps are embedded in Eq. (3.12), which can be applied directly to get

$$\underbrace{\begin{bmatrix} x_2 \\ y_2 \end{bmatrix}}_{\dot{\mathbf{a}}_2} = \underbrace{\begin{bmatrix} 2 & 0 \\ 0 & 2 \end{bmatrix}}_{\dot{\mathtt{S}}(2,2)} \underbrace{\begin{bmatrix} 0-5 \\ 0-2 \end{bmatrix}}_{\dot{\mathbf{a}}_1-\dot{\mathbf{c}}_1} + \underbrace{\begin{bmatrix} 5 \\ 2 \end{bmatrix}}_{\dot{\mathbf{c}}_1} = \underbrace{\begin{bmatrix} -5 \\ -2 \end{bmatrix}}_{\dot{\mathbf{a}}_2}$$

and

$$\underbrace{\begin{bmatrix} x_2 \\ y_2 \end{bmatrix}}_{\dot{\mathbf{b}}_2} = \underbrace{\begin{bmatrix} 2 & 0 \\ 0 & 2 \end{bmatrix}}_{\dot{\mathtt{S}}(2,2)} \underbrace{\begin{bmatrix} 1-5 \\ 1-2 \end{bmatrix}}_{\dot{\mathbf{b}}_1 - \dot{\mathbf{c}}_1} + \underbrace{\begin{bmatrix} 5 \\ 2 \end{bmatrix}}_{\dot{\mathbf{c}}_1} = \underbrace{\begin{bmatrix} -3 \\ 0 \end{bmatrix}}_{\dot{\mathbf{b}}_2}. \qquad \square$$

## 3.4 Reflection in 2D Space

The reflection operation in 2D space mirrors an object about an axis. There are two basic reflection operations about the $x$-axis and the $y$-axis.

### *3.4.1 Reflection About the x-Axis*

A 2D reflection operation about the $x$-axis is equivalent to performing a non-uniform scaling using factors of 1 and $-1$ along the $x$-axis and $y$-axis respectively (i.e., the $x$-values remain unchanged while the $y$-values are flipped). Hence, to reflect a point $\dot{\mathbf{p}}_1 = [x_1, y_1]^T$ about the $x$-axis to get $\dot{\mathbf{p}}_2 = [x_2, y_2]^T$, we may use

$$\begin{aligned} x_2 &= x_1, \\ y_2 &= -y_1. \end{aligned} \tag{3.14}$$

In matrix form, we can write

$$\underbrace{\begin{bmatrix} x_2 \\ y_2 \end{bmatrix}}_{\dot{\mathbf{p}}_2} = \underbrace{\begin{bmatrix} 1 & 0 \\ 0 & -1 \end{bmatrix}}_{\dot{\mathtt{Ref}}_x} \underbrace{\begin{bmatrix} x_1 \\ y_1 \end{bmatrix}}_{\dot{\mathbf{p}}_1}, \tag{3.15}$$

where $\dot{\mathtt{Ref}}_x$ is a $2 \times 2$ matrix representing the reflection operation about the $x$-axis for inhomogeneous points in 2D space. In homogeneous coordinates, in order to reflect a 2D point $\mathbf{p}_1 = [x_1, y_1, 1]^T$ about the $x$-axis to get $\mathbf{p}_2 = [x_2, y_2, 1]^T$, we use

$$\underbrace{\begin{bmatrix} x_2 \\ y_2 \\ 1 \end{bmatrix}}_{\mathbf{p}_2} = \underbrace{\begin{bmatrix} 1 & 0 & 0 \\ 0 & -1 & 0 \\ 0 & 0 & 1 \end{bmatrix}}_{\mathtt{Ref}_x} \underbrace{\begin{bmatrix} x_1 \\ y_1 \\ 1 \end{bmatrix}}_{\mathbf{p}_1}, \tag{3.16}$$

where $\mathtt{Ref}_x$ is a $3 \times 3$ matrix representing the reflection operation about the $x$-axis for homogeneous points in 2D space.

### 3.4.2 Reflection About the y-Axis

A 2D reflection operation about the $y$-axis is equivalent to performing a non-uniform scaling using factors of $-1$ and 1 along the $x$-axis and $y$-axis respectively (i.e., the $y$-values remain unchanged while the $x$-values are flipped). Hence, to reflect a point $\dot{\mathbf{p}}_1 = [x_1, y_1]^T$ about the $y$-axis to get $\dot{\mathbf{p}}_2 = [x_2, y_2]^T$, we may use

$$\begin{aligned} x_2 &= -x_1, \\ y_2 &= y_1. \end{aligned} \tag{3.17}$$

Alternatively, we may write

$$\underbrace{\begin{bmatrix} x_2 \\ y_2 \end{bmatrix}}_{\dot{\mathbf{p}}_2} = \underbrace{\begin{bmatrix} -1 & 0 \\ 0 & 1 \end{bmatrix}}_{\dot{\mathtt{Ref}}_y} \underbrace{\begin{bmatrix} x_1 \\ y_1 \end{bmatrix}}_{\dot{\mathbf{p}}_1}, \tag{3.18}$$

where $\dot{\mathtt{Ref}}_y$ is a $2 \times 2$ matrix representing the reflection operation about the $y$-axis for inhomogeneous points in 2D space. In homogeneous coordinates, in order to reflect a 2D point $\mathbf{p}_1 = [x_1, y_1, 1]^T$ about the $y$-axis to get $\mathbf{p}_2 = [x_2, y_2, 1]^T$, we use

$$\underbrace{\begin{bmatrix} x_2 \\ y_2 \\ 1 \end{bmatrix}}_{\mathbf{p}_2} = \underbrace{\begin{bmatrix} -1 & 0 & 0 \\ 0 & 1 & 0 \\ 0 & 0 & 1 \end{bmatrix}}_{\mathtt{Ref}_y} \underbrace{\begin{bmatrix} x_1 \\ y_1 \\ 1 \end{bmatrix}}_{\mathbf{p}_1}, \tag{3.19}$$

where $\mathtt{Ref}_y$ is a $3 \times 3$ matrix representing the reflection operation about the $y$-axis for homogeneous points in 2D space.

### 3.4.3 General Reflection in 2D Space

You probably have noticed that Eq. (3.14) through Eq. (3.19) assume that the reflection axis is one of the coordinate axes. In the general case, the reflection operation can be performed about any arbitrary axis. In order to achieve this, the object to be reflected should be transformed (translated and/or rotated) so that the reflection axis coincides with one of the coordinate axes. According to which coordinate axis is referred to, an equation from Eq. (3.14) through Eq. (3.19) is used to perform reflection. Afterwards, the transformation done before (i.e., translation and/or rotation) is reversed. We can summarize the steps to be performed as:

1. Translate the object so that the reflection axis passes through the origin.
2. Rotate so that the reflection axis gets aligned with one of the coordinate axes.

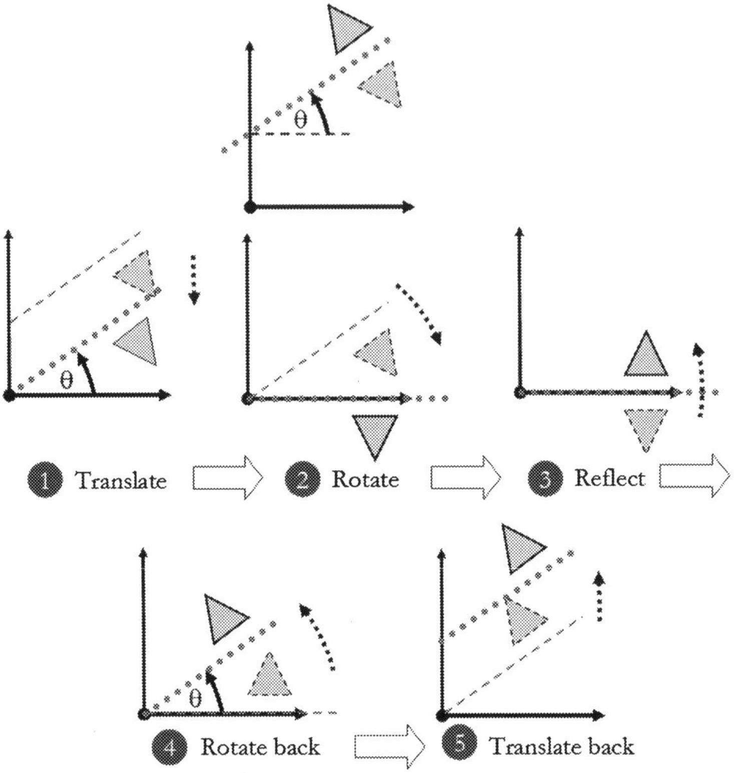


**Fig. 3.7** A triangle is reflected about an arbitrary axis which is inclined at an angle $\theta$ with respect to the $x$-axis. The steps performed are: *1* Translate the triangle using so that the axis of reflection passes through the origin. *2* Rotate the triangle through an angle $-\theta$ so that the axis of reflection coincides with the $x$-axis. *3* Reflect the triangle about the $x$-axis. *4* Rotate the triangle back through an angle $\theta$. *5* Translate the triangle back using the same translation vector used before but in the opposite direction

3. Reflect that coordinate axis using Eqs. (3.14, 3.15, 3.17) or Eq. (3.18) if inhomogeneous coordinates are used. Alternatively, utilize Eq. (3.16) or Eq. (3.19) if homogeneous coordinates are used.
4. Rotate back through the same angle of Step 2 in the opposite direction.
5. Translate back using the same vector of Step 1 in the opposite direction.

**Example 3.9:** [*2D general reflection—inhomogeneous coordinates*]
A triangle is to be reflected about an axis inclined at an angle $\theta$ with respect to the $x$-axis. Show the transformation steps.

**Solution 3.9:** There is a sequence of five operations depicted in Fig. 3.7. These steps are:

1. Translate the triangle such that the point of intersection between the axis of reflection and the $y$-axis is moved to the origin.

2. Rotate the triangle through an angle $-\theta$ such that the axis of reflection coincides with the $x$-axis.
3. Reflect the triangle about the $x$-axis.
4. Rotate back through an angle $\theta$.
5. Translate back using the same translation vector of Step 1 but along the opposite direction.

Assuming that the axis of reflection intersects the $y$-axis at point $\dot{\mathbf{p}}_0 = [0, y_0]^T$ and the reflection is to be performed about the $x$-axis, the previous five-step sequence of operations can be performed to a point $\dot{\mathbf{p}}_1$ to get $\dot{\mathbf{p}}_2$ using

$$\underbrace{\begin{bmatrix} x_2 \\ y_2 \end{bmatrix}}_{\dot{\mathbf{p}}_2} = \overbrace{\overbrace{\underbrace{\begin{bmatrix} \cos(\theta) & -\sin(\theta) \\ \sin(\theta) & \cos(\theta) \end{bmatrix}}_{\dot{\mathtt{R}}(\theta)} \overbrace{\underbrace{\begin{bmatrix} 1 & 0 \\ 0 & -1 \end{bmatrix}}_{\mathtt{R\dot{e}f}_x} \overbrace{\underbrace{\begin{bmatrix} \cos(-\theta) & -\sin(-\theta) \\ \sin(-\theta) & \cos(-\theta) \end{bmatrix}}_{\dot{\mathtt{R}}(-\theta)} \overbrace{\underbrace{\begin{bmatrix} x_1 \\ y_1 - y_0 \end{bmatrix}}_{\dot{\mathbf{p}}_1 - \dot{\mathbf{p}}_0}}^{Step\ 1}}^{Step\ 2}}^{Step\ 3}}^{Step\ 4} + \underbrace{\begin{bmatrix} 0 \\ y_0 \end{bmatrix}}_{\dot{\mathbf{p}}_0}}^{Step\ 5}, \tag{3.20}$$

where $\mathtt{R\dot{e}f}_x$ is the reflection matrix about the $x$-axis; $\dot{\mathtt{R}}$ are the rotation matrices through angles $\theta$ and $-\theta$; $[0, -y_0]^T$ and $[0, y_0]^T$ are the translation vectors; $\dot{\mathbf{p}}_1$ is the point before reflection; and $\dot{\mathbf{p}}_2$ is the point after reflection. Note that the same result can be obtained by rotating through an angle of $90° - \theta°$ (in Step 2) so that the axis of reflection coincides with the $y$-axis, reflecting about the $y$-axis (in Step 3) and rotating back through an angle of $\theta° - 90°$ (in Step 4). Noting that

$$\cos(\theta) = \sin(90 - \theta) = -\sin(\theta - 90) \tag{3.21}$$

and

$$\sin(\theta) = \cos(90 - \theta) = \cos(\theta - 90), \tag{3.22}$$

we may write

$$\underbrace{\begin{bmatrix} x_2 \\ y_2 \end{bmatrix}}_{\dot{\mathbf{p}}_2} = \underbrace{\begin{bmatrix} \sin(\theta) & \cos(\theta) \\ -\cos(\theta) & \sin(\theta) \end{bmatrix}}_{\dot{\mathtt{R}}(\theta-90)} \underbrace{\begin{bmatrix} -1 & 0 \\ 0 & 1 \end{bmatrix}}_{\mathtt{R\dot{e}f}_y} \underbrace{\begin{bmatrix} \sin(\theta) & -\cos(\theta) \\ \cos(\theta) & \sin(\theta) \end{bmatrix}}_{\dot{\mathtt{R}}(90-\theta)} \underbrace{\begin{bmatrix} x_1 \\ y_1 - y_0 \end{bmatrix}}_{\dot{\mathbf{p}}_1 - \dot{\mathbf{p}}_0} + \underbrace{\begin{bmatrix} 0 \\ y_0 \end{bmatrix}}_{\dot{\mathbf{p}}_0}, \tag{3.23}$$

where $\mathtt{R\dot{e}f}_y$ is the reflection matrix about the $y$-axis; $\dot{\mathtt{R}}$ are the rotation matrices through angles $\theta° - 90°$ and $90° - \theta°$; $[0, -y_0]^T$ and $[0, y_0]^T$ are the translation vectors; $\dot{\mathbf{p}}_1$ is the point before reflection; and $\dot{\mathbf{p}}_2$ is the point after reflection. □

**Example 3.10:** [*2D general reflection—homogeneous coordinates*]
Re-solve Example 3.9 using homogenous coordinates.

**Solution 3.10:** The five steps are represented by five matrices. Using the reflection matrix $\mathtt{Ref}_x$, we have

$$\mathtt{M}_1 = \mathtt{T}([0, -y_0]^T) = \begin{bmatrix} 1 & 0 & 0 \\ 0 & 1 & -y_0 \\ 0 & 0 & 1 \end{bmatrix},$$

$$\mathtt{M}_2 = \mathtt{R}(-\theta) = \begin{bmatrix} \cos(-\theta) & -\sin(-\theta) & 0 \\ \sin(-\theta) & \cos(-\theta) & 0 \\ 0 & 0 & 1 \end{bmatrix},$$

$$\mathtt{M}_3 = \mathtt{Ref}_x = \begin{bmatrix} 1 & 0 & 0 \\ 0 & -1 & 0 \\ 0 & 0 & 1 \end{bmatrix},$$

$$\mathtt{M}_4 = \mathtt{R}(\theta) = \begin{bmatrix} \cos(\theta) & -\sin(\theta) & 0 \\ \sin(\theta) & \cos(\theta) & 0 \\ 0 & 0 & 1 \end{bmatrix},$$

and

$$\mathtt{M}_5 = \mathtt{T}([0, y_0]^T) = \begin{bmatrix} 1 & 0 & 0 \\ 0 & 1 & y_0 \\ 0 & 0 & 1 \end{bmatrix}.$$

Since

$$\sin(2\theta) = 2\sin(\theta)\cos(\theta)$$

and

$$\cos(2\theta) = \cos^2(\theta) - \sin^2(\theta),$$

the overall transformation is expressed as

$$\begin{aligned} \mathtt{M} =& \ \mathtt{M}_5\mathtt{M}_4\mathtt{M}_3\mathtt{M}_2\mathtt{M}_1 \\ =& \begin{bmatrix} 1 & 0 & 0 \\ 0 & 1 & y_0 \\ 0 & 0 & 1 \end{bmatrix} \begin{bmatrix} \cos(\theta) & -\sin(\theta) & 0 \\ \sin(\theta) & \cos(\theta) & 0 \\ 0 & 0 & 1 \end{bmatrix} \begin{bmatrix} 1 & 0 & 0 \\ 0 & -1 & 0 \\ 0 & 0 & 1 \end{bmatrix} \dots \\ & \dots \begin{bmatrix} \cos(-\theta) & -\sin(-\theta) & 0 \\ \sin(-\theta) & \cos(-\theta) & 0 \\ 0 & 0 & 1 \end{bmatrix} \begin{bmatrix} 1 & 0 & 0 \\ 0 & 1 & -y_0 \\ 0 & 0 & 1 \end{bmatrix} \\ =& \begin{bmatrix} \cos(2\theta) & \sin(2\theta) & -y_0\sin(2\theta) \\ \sin(2\theta) & -\cos(2\theta) & y_0(\cos(2\theta)+1) \\ 0 & 0 & 1 \end{bmatrix}. \end{aligned}$$

Using the reflection matrix $\texttt{Ref}_y$, we have

$$\mathtt{M}_1 = \mathtt{T}([0, -y_0]^T) = \begin{bmatrix} 1 & 0 & 0 \\ 0 & 1 & -y_0 \\ 0 & 0 & 1 \end{bmatrix},$$

$$\mathtt{M}_2 = \mathtt{R}(90 - \theta) = \begin{bmatrix} \sin(\theta) & -\cos(\theta) & 0 \\ \cos(\theta) & \sin(\theta) & 0 \\ 0 & 0 & 1 \end{bmatrix},$$

$$\mathtt{M}_3 = \texttt{Ref}_y = \begin{bmatrix} -1 & 0 & 0 \\ 0 & 1 & 0 \\ 0 & 0 & 1 \end{bmatrix},$$

$$\mathtt{M}_4 = \mathtt{R}(\theta - 90) = \begin{bmatrix} \sin(\theta) & \cos(\theta) & 0 \\ -\cos(\theta) & \sin(\theta) & 0 \\ 0 & 0 & 1 \end{bmatrix},$$

and

$$\mathtt{M}_5 = \mathtt{T}([0, y_0]^T) = \begin{bmatrix} 1 & 0 & 0 \\ 0 & 1 & y_0 \\ 0 & 0 & 1 \end{bmatrix}.$$

Thus, the overall transformation is expressed as

$$\begin{aligned} \mathtt{M} &= \mathtt{M}_5\mathtt{M}_4\mathtt{M}_3\mathtt{M}_2\mathtt{M}_1 \\ &= \begin{bmatrix} 1 & 0 & 0 \\ 0 & 1 & y_0 \\ 0 & 0 & 1 \end{bmatrix} \begin{bmatrix} \sin(\theta) & \cos(\theta) & 0 \\ -\cos(\theta) & \sin(\theta) & 0 \\ 0 & 0 & 1 \end{bmatrix} \begin{bmatrix} -1 & 0 & 0 \\ 0 & 1 & 0 \\ 0 & 0 & 1 \end{bmatrix} \cdots \\ &\quad \cdots \begin{bmatrix} \sin(\theta) & -\cos(\theta) & 0 \\ \cos(\theta) & \sin(\theta) & 0 \\ 0 & 0 & 1 \end{bmatrix} \begin{bmatrix} 1 & 0 & 0 \\ 0 & 1 & -y_0 \\ 0 & 0 & 1 \end{bmatrix} \\ &= \begin{bmatrix} \cos(2\theta) & \sin(2\theta) & -y_0 \sin(2\theta) \\ \sin(2\theta) & -\cos(2\theta) & y_0(\cos(2\theta) + 1) \\ 0 & 0 & 1 \end{bmatrix}, \end{aligned}$$

which is the same transformation matrix obtained before as expected. □

**Example 3.11:** [*2D general reflection—homogeneous coordinates*]
In order to reflect about an axis having an inclination angle $\theta$ w ith respect to the $x$-axis and $y$-intercept as $[0, y_0]^T$, the following transformation matrix is used:

$$\mathtt{M} = \begin{bmatrix} \cos(2\theta) & \sin(2\theta) & -y_0 \sin(2\theta) \\ \sin(2\theta) & -\cos(2\theta) & y_0(\cos(2\theta)+1) \\ 0 & 0 & 1 \end{bmatrix}.$$

If the same axis is expressed using its slope $m$ rather than its inclination angle $\theta$, re-express the transformation matrix above in terms of $m$ instead of $\theta$.

**Solution 3.11:** We know that

$$\sin(2\theta) = 2\sin(\theta)\cos(\theta)$$

and

$$\cos(2\theta) = \cos^2(\theta) - \sin^2(\theta).$$

Hence, the transformation matrix can be expressed as

$$\mathtt{M} = \begin{bmatrix} \cos^2(\theta)-\sin^2(\theta) & 2\sin(\theta)\cos(\theta) & -2y_0\sin(\theta)\cos(\theta) \\ 2\sin(\theta)\cos(\theta) & -\cos^2(\theta)+\sin^2(\theta) & y_0(\cos^2(\theta)-\sin^2(\theta)+1) \\ 0 & 0 & 1 \end{bmatrix}.$$

Since the slope $m = \tan(\theta)$; hence, $\sin(\theta) = \frac{m}{\sqrt{m^2+1}}$ and $\cos(\theta) = \frac{1}{\sqrt{m^2+1}}$. Substituting the values of $\sin(\theta)$ and $\cos(\theta)$ in the previous matrix, we get

$$\mathtt{M} = \begin{bmatrix} \dfrac{1-m^2}{m^2+1} & \dfrac{2m}{m^2+1} & \dfrac{-2y_0m}{m^2+1} \\ \dfrac{2m}{m^2+1} & \dfrac{m^2-1}{m^2+1} & \dfrac{2y_0}{m^2+1} \\ 0 & 0 & 1 \end{bmatrix}, \tag{3.24}$$

which is the required transformation matrix. □

**Example 3.12:** [*2D general reflection—inhomogeneous coordinates*]

A point $\dot{\mathbf{p}}_1 = [5,5]^T$ is reflected about a line passing through the point $[2,0]^T$ with an inclination angle of 35° with respect to the $x$-axis. Determine the new location of the point (i.e., $\dot{\mathbf{p}}_2$). You must use inhomogeneous coordinates in all your calculations.

**Solution 3.12:** Consider the following five steps:

1. Translate using a translation vector $[-2,0]^T$ to ensure that the reflection line is passing through the origin.
2. Rotate through an angle of −35° so that the reflection line coincides with the $x$-axis.
3. Reflect about the $x$-axis.
4. Rotate through an angle of 35° to reverse the rotation operation performed in Step 2.
5. Translate back using the translation vector $[2,0]^T$ to reverse the translation operation performed in Step 1.

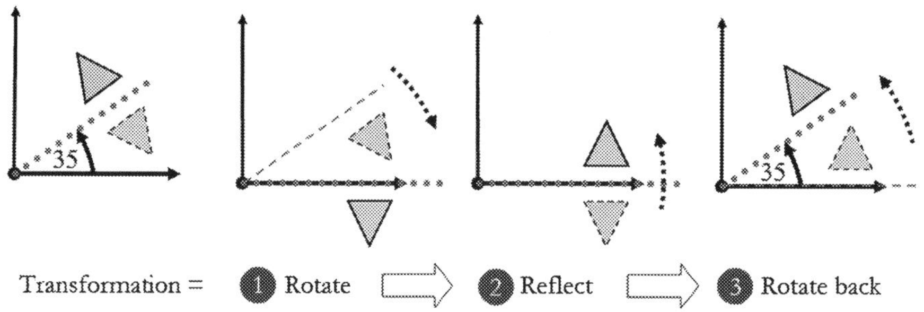


**Fig. 3.8** A triangle is reflected about a line passing through the origin with an inclination angle of 35°

Equation (3.20) represents these five steps and can be utilized as

$$\dot{\mathbf{p}}_2 = \begin{bmatrix} \cos(35) & -\sin(35) \\ \sin(35) & \cos(35) \end{bmatrix} \begin{bmatrix} 1 & 0 \\ 0 & -1 \end{bmatrix} \begin{bmatrix} \cos(-35) & -\sin(-35) \\ \sin(-35) & \cos(-35) \end{bmatrix} \begin{bmatrix} 5-2 \\ 5-0 \end{bmatrix} + \begin{bmatrix} 2 \\ 0 \end{bmatrix}$$
$$= \begin{bmatrix} 7.7245 \\ 1.1090 \end{bmatrix}. \qquad \square$$

**Example 3.13:** [*2D general reflection—homogeneous coordinates*]
Derive a transformation matrix to reflect an object about a line passing through the origin with an inclination angle of 35°.

**Solution 3.13:** Sketch it for better visualization as shown in Fig. 3.8. Notice that the axis of reflection is passing through the origin; hence, no translation is needed. A three-step transformation operation is performed:

1. Rotate the object through an angle of −35° about the origin. Let us call this rotation matrix $\mathtt{M}_1$ where

$$\mathtt{M}_1 = \mathtt{R}(-35) = \begin{bmatrix} \cos(-35) & -\sin(-35) & 0 \\ \sin(-35) & \cos(-35) & 0 \\ 0 & 0 & 1 \end{bmatrix}.$$

2. Reflect the object about the $x$-axis. Let us call this reflection matrix $\mathtt{M}_2$ where

$$\mathtt{M}_2 = \mathtt{Ref}_x = \begin{bmatrix} 1 & 0 & 0 \\ 0 & -1 & 0 \\ 0 & 0 & 1 \end{bmatrix}.$$

3. Rotate the object back through an angle of 35° about the origin. Let us call this rotation matrix $\mathtt{M}_3$ where

$$\mathtt{M}_3 = \mathtt{R}(35) = \begin{bmatrix} \cos(35) & -\sin(35) & 0 \\ \sin(35) & \cos(35) & 0 \\ 0 & 0 & 1 \end{bmatrix}.$$

Therefore, the overall transformation is expressed as

$$
\begin{aligned}
\mathtt{M} &= \mathtt{M}_3\mathtt{M}_2\mathtt{M}_1 \\
&= \begin{bmatrix} \cos(35) & -\sin(35) & 0 \\ \sin(35) & \cos(35) & 0 \\ 0 & 0 & 1 \end{bmatrix} \begin{bmatrix} 1 & 0 & 0 \\ 0 & -1 & 0 \\ 0 & 0 & 1 \end{bmatrix} \begin{bmatrix} \cos(-35) & -\sin(-35) & 0 \\ \sin(-35) & \cos(-35) & 0 \\ 0 & 0 & 1 \end{bmatrix} \\
&= \begin{bmatrix} 0.3420 & 0.9397 & 0 \\ 0.9397 & -0.3420 & 0 \\ 0 & 0 & 1 \end{bmatrix}.
\end{aligned}
$$

□

**Example 3.14:** [*2D general reflection—homogeneous coordinates*]

Derive the reflection matrix about a line parallel to the $x$-axis and passing through the point $[0, y_0]^T$.

**Solution 3.14:** A three-step solution can be applied:

1. Translate using a translation vector of $[0, -y_0]^T$. This forces the reflection axis to coincide with the $x$-axis. Let us call this translation matrix $\mathtt{M}_1$ where

$$
\mathtt{M}_1 = \mathtt{T}([0, -y_0]^T) = \begin{bmatrix} 1 & 0 & 0 \\ 0 & 1 & -y_0 \\ 0 & 0 & 1 \end{bmatrix}.
$$

2. Reflect about the $x$-axis. Let us call this reflection matrix $\mathtt{M}_2$ where

$$
\mathtt{M}_2 = \mathtt{Ref}_x = \begin{bmatrix} 1 & 0 & 0 \\ 0 & -1 & 0 \\ 0 & 0 & 1 \end{bmatrix}.
$$

3. Translate back using the translation vector $[0, y_0]^T$ to reverse the effect of Step 1. Let us call this translation matrix $\mathtt{M}_3$ where

$$
\mathtt{M}_3 = \mathtt{T}([0, y_0]^T) = \begin{bmatrix} 1 & 0 & 0 \\ 0 & 1 & y_0 \\ 0 & 0 & 1 \end{bmatrix}.
$$

Consequently, the overall transformation (i.e., reflection about a line parallel to the $x$-axis and passing through the point $[0, y_0]^T$) can be estimated as

$$
\begin{aligned}
\mathrm{M} &= \mathrm{M}_3\mathrm{M}_2\mathrm{M}_1 \\
&= \begin{bmatrix} 1 & 0 & 0 \\ 0 & 1 & y_0 \\ 0 & 0 & 1 \end{bmatrix} \begin{bmatrix} 1 & 0 & 0 \\ 0 & -1 & 0 \\ 0 & 0 & 1 \end{bmatrix} \begin{bmatrix} 1 & 0 & 0 \\ 0 & 1 & -y_0 \\ 0 & 0 & 1 \end{bmatrix} \\
&= \begin{bmatrix} 1 & 0 & 0 \\ 0 & -1 & 2y_0 \\ 0 & 0 & 1 \end{bmatrix}.
\end{aligned}
$$

In inhomogeneous coordinates, in order to reflect a point $\dot{\mathbf{p}}_1 = [x_1, y_1]^T$ about a line parallel to the $x$-axis and passing through $[0, y_0]^T$ to another point $\dot{\mathbf{p}}_2 = [x_2, y_2]^T$, we can apply the previous steps as

$$
\underbrace{\begin{bmatrix} x_2 \\ y_2 \end{bmatrix}}_{\dot{\mathbf{p}}_2} = \underbrace{\begin{bmatrix} 1 & 0 \\ 0 & -1 \end{bmatrix}}_{\dot{\mathtt{Ref}}_x} \underbrace{\begin{bmatrix} x_1 \\ y_1 - y_0 \end{bmatrix}}_{\dot{\mathbf{p}}_1 - \mathbf{t}} + \underbrace{\begin{bmatrix} 0 \\ y_0 \end{bmatrix}}_{\mathbf{t}}. \qquad \square
$$

## 3.5 Shearing in 2D Space

The 2D shearing operation results in shape distortion of the object by stretching the object with respect to an axis.

### *3.5.1 Shearing Along the x-Axis*

Shearing is performed along the $x$-axis by applying the following equations:

$$
\begin{aligned}
x_2 &= x_1 + sh_x y_1, \\
y_2 &= y_1,
\end{aligned} \tag{3.25}
$$

where $sh_x$ is a factor that controls shearing along the $x$-axis. This factor may be greater than or less than 0. The effect is shown in Fig. 3.9a, b. In matrix form, this operation is expressed as

$$
\underbrace{\begin{bmatrix} x_2 \\ y_2 \end{bmatrix}}_{\dot{\mathbf{p}}_2} = \underbrace{\begin{bmatrix} 1 & sh_x \\ 0 & 1 \end{bmatrix}}_{\dot{\mathtt{Sh}}_x(sh_x)} \underbrace{\begin{bmatrix} x_1 \\ y_1 \end{bmatrix}}_{\dot{\mathbf{p}}_1}, \tag{3.26}
$$

where $\dot{\mathtt{Sh}}_x$ is a $2 \times 2$ matrix representing the shearing operation along the $x$-axis for inhomogeneous points in 2D space; and $sh_x$ is the shearing factor. Note that all the

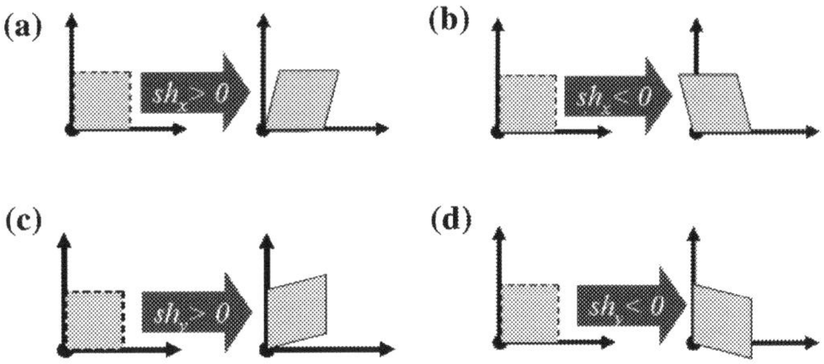


**Fig. 3.9** Shearing in 2D space. **a** $sh_x > 0$. **b** $sh_x < 0$. **c** $sh_y > 0$. **d** $sh_y < 0$

points on the $x$-axis (i.e., having $y$-coordinates of 0) are not affected by the matrix $\dot{\mathtt{Sh}}_x$. The shearing operation can be applied along the $x$-axis with homogeneous points as

$$\underbrace{\begin{bmatrix} x_2 \\ y_2 \\ 1 \end{bmatrix}}_{\mathbf{p}_2} = \underbrace{\begin{bmatrix} 1 & sh_x & 0 \\ 0 & 1 & 0 \\ 0 & 0 & 1 \end{bmatrix}}_{\mathtt{Sh}_x(sh_x)} \underbrace{\begin{bmatrix} x_1 \\ y_1 \\ 1 \end{bmatrix}}_{\mathbf{p}_1}, \tag{3.27}$$

where $\mathtt{Sh}_x$ is a $3 \times 3$ matrix representing the shearing operation along the $x$-axis for homogeneous points in 2D space; and $sh_x$ is the shearing factor.

### *3.5.2 Shearing Along the y-Axis*

Shearing is performed along the $y$-axis by applying the following equations:

$$\begin{aligned} x_2 &= x_1, \\ y_2 &= sh_y x_1 + y_1, \end{aligned} \tag{3.28}$$

where $sh_y$ is a factor that controls shearing along the $y$-axis. This factor may be greater than or less than 0. The effect is shown in Fig. 3.9c, d. In matrix form, this operation is expressed as

$$\underbrace{\begin{bmatrix} x_2 \\ y_2 \end{bmatrix}}_{\dot{\mathbf{p}}_2} = \underbrace{\begin{bmatrix} 1 & 0 \\ sh_y & 1 \end{bmatrix}}_{\dot{\mathtt{Sh}}_y(sh_y)} \underbrace{\begin{bmatrix} x_1 \\ y_1 \end{bmatrix}}_{\dot{\mathbf{p}}_1}, \tag{3.29}$$

where $\dot{\mathtt{Sh}}_y$ is a $2 \times 2$ matrix representing the shearing operation along the $y$-axis for inhomogeneous points in 2D space; and $sh_y$ is the shearing factor. Note that all the points on the $y$-axis (i.e., having $x$-coordinates of 0) are not affected by the matrix $\dot{\mathtt{Sh}}_y$. The shearing operation can be applied along the $y$-axis with homogeneous points as

$$\underbrace{\begin{bmatrix} x_2 \\ y_2 \\ 1 \end{bmatrix}}_{\mathbf{p}_2} = \underbrace{\begin{bmatrix} 1 & 0 & 0 \\ sh_y & 1 & 0 \\ 0 & 0 & 1 \end{bmatrix}}_{\mathtt{Sh}_y(sh_y)} \underbrace{\begin{bmatrix} x_1 \\ y_1 \\ 1 \end{bmatrix}}_{\mathbf{p}_1}, \tag{3.30}$$

where $\mathtt{Sh}_y$ is a $3 \times 3$ matrix representing the shearing operation along the $y$-axis for homogeneous points in 2D space; and $sh_y$ is the shearing factor.

### *3.5.3 General Shearing in 2D Space*

Note that 2D shearing with respect to an arbitrary axis is applicable as done in the previous operations provided that the axis under consideration is transformed to coincide with one of the coordinate axes before using any of Eq. (3.25) through Eq. (3.30). We can summarize the steps to be performed as:

1. Translate the object so that the arbitrary axis passes through the origin.
2. Rotate so that the axis gets aligned with one of the coordinate axes.
3. Shear along that coordinate axis using any of Eq. (3.25) through Eq. (3.30).
4. Rotate back through the same angle in the opposite direction.
5. Translate back using the same vector in the opposite direction.

**Example 3.15:** [*2D general shearing—inhomogeneous coordinates*]
A 2D object is to be sheared by an amount $\varepsilon$ along an axis inclined at an angle $\theta$ with respect to the $x$-axis. Show the steps of transformations.

**Solution 3.15:** There is a sequence of five operations. These steps are:

1. Translate the object such that the point of intersection between the axis of shearing and the $y$-axis $[0, y_0]^T$ is moved to the origin.
2. Rotate the object through an angle $-\theta$ such that the axis coincides with the $x$-axis.
3. Shear the object along the $x$-axis.
4. Rotate back through an angle $\theta$.
5. Translate back using the same translation vector but along the opposite direction (i.e., $[0, y_0]^T$).

This sequence of steps can be performed to a point $\dot{\mathbf{p}}_1$ to get $\dot{\mathbf{p}}_2$ using

$$\underbrace{\begin{bmatrix} x_2 \\ y_2 \end{bmatrix}}_{\dot{\mathbf{p}}_2} = \underbrace{\begin{bmatrix} \cos(\theta) & -\sin(\theta) \\ \sin(\theta) & \cos(\theta) \end{bmatrix}}_{\dot{\mathtt{R}}(\theta)} \underbrace{\begin{bmatrix} 1 & \varepsilon \\ 0 & 1 \end{bmatrix}}_{\dot{\mathtt{Sh}}_x(\varepsilon)} \underbrace{\begin{bmatrix} \cos(-\theta) & -\sin(-\theta) \\ \sin(-\theta) & \cos(-\theta) \end{bmatrix}}_{\dot{\mathtt{R}}(-\theta)} \underbrace{\begin{bmatrix} x_1 \\ y_1 - y_0 \end{bmatrix}}_{\dot{\mathbf{p}}_1 - \dot{\mathbf{p}}_0} + \underbrace{\begin{bmatrix} 0 \\ y_0 \end{bmatrix}}_{\dot{\mathbf{p}}_0}, \tag{3.31}$$

where $\dot{\mathtt{Sh}}_x$ is the shearing matrix along the $x$-axis using a factor of $\varepsilon$; and $\dot{\mathtt{R}}$ are the rotation matrices through angles $\theta$ and $-\theta$. Note that the same result can be obtained by rotating through an angle of $90° - \theta°$ (in Step 2) so that the axis of shearing coincides with the $y$-axis, shearing along the $y$-axis (in Step 3) and rotating back through an angle of $\theta° - 90°$ (in Step 4). Using Eqs. (3.21) and (3.22), we may write

$$\underbrace{\begin{bmatrix} x_2 \\ y_2 \end{bmatrix}}_{\dot{\mathbf{p}}_2} = \underbrace{\begin{bmatrix} \sin(\theta) & \cos(\theta) \\ -\cos(\theta) & \sin(\theta) \end{bmatrix}}_{\dot{\mathtt{R}}(\theta-90)} \underbrace{\begin{bmatrix} 1 & 0 \\ -\varepsilon & 1 \end{bmatrix}}_{\dot{\mathtt{Sh}}_y(-\varepsilon)} \underbrace{\begin{bmatrix} \sin(\theta) & -\cos(\theta) \\ \cos(\theta) & \sin(\theta) \end{bmatrix}}_{\dot{\mathtt{R}}(90-\theta)} \underbrace{\begin{bmatrix} x_1 \\ y_1 - y_0 \end{bmatrix}}_{\dot{\mathbf{p}}_1-\dot{\mathbf{p}}_0} + \underbrace{\begin{bmatrix} 0 \\ y_0 \end{bmatrix}}_{\dot{\mathbf{p}}_0}, \tag{3.32}$$

where $\dot{\mathtt{Sh}}_y$ is the shearing matrix along the $y$-axis using a factor of $-\varepsilon$; and $\dot{\mathtt{R}}$ are the rotation matrices through angles $\theta° - 90°$ and $90° - \theta°$. □

**Example 3.16:** [*2D general shearing—homogeneous coordinates*]
Re-solve Example 3.15 using homogeneous coordinates.

**Solution 3.16:** The five steps are represented by five matrices. Using the shearing matrix $\mathtt{Sh}_x$, we have

$$\mathtt{M}_1 = \mathtt{T}([0, -y_0]^T) = \begin{bmatrix} 1 & 0 & 0 \\ 0 & 1 & -y_0 \\ 0 & 0 & 1 \end{bmatrix},$$

$$\mathtt{M}_2 = \mathtt{R}(-\theta) = \begin{bmatrix} \cos(-\theta) & -\sin(-\theta) & 0 \\ \sin(-\theta) & \cos(-\theta) & 0 \\ 0 & 0 & 1 \end{bmatrix},$$

$$\mathtt{M}_3 = \mathtt{Sh}_x(\varepsilon) = \begin{bmatrix} 1 & \varepsilon & 0 \\ 0 & 1 & 0 \\ 0 & 0 & 1 \end{bmatrix},$$

$$\mathtt{M}_4 = \mathtt{R}(\theta) = \begin{bmatrix} \cos(\theta) & -\sin(\theta) & 0 \\ \sin(\theta) & \cos(\theta) & 0 \\ 0 & 0 & 1 \end{bmatrix}$$

and

$$\mathtt{M}_5 = \mathtt{T}([0, y_0]^T) = \begin{bmatrix} 1 & 0 & 0 \\ 0 & 1 & y_0 \\ 0 & 0 & 1 \end{bmatrix}.$$

Since

$$\sin^2(\theta) + \cos^2(\theta) = 1,$$

the overall transformation is expressed as

$$\begin{aligned}
\mathtt{M} &= \mathtt{M}_5\mathtt{M}_4\mathtt{M}_3\mathtt{M}_2\mathtt{M}_1\\
&= \begin{bmatrix} 1 & 0 & 0\\ 0 & 1 & y_0\\ 0 & 0 & 1 \end{bmatrix} \begin{bmatrix} \cos(\theta) & -\sin(\theta) & 0\\ \sin(\theta) & \cos(\theta) & 0\\ 0 & 0 & 1 \end{bmatrix} \begin{bmatrix} 1 & \varepsilon & 0\\ 0 & 1 & 0\\ 0 & 0 & 1 \end{bmatrix} \dots\\
&\quad \dots \begin{bmatrix} \cos(-\theta) & -\sin(-\theta) & 0\\ \sin(-\theta) & \cos(-\theta) & 0\\ 0 & 0 & 1 \end{bmatrix} \begin{bmatrix} 1 & 0 & 0\\ 0 & 1 & -y_0\\ 0 & 0 & 1 \end{bmatrix}\\
&= \begin{bmatrix} 1-\varepsilon\sin(\theta)\cos(\theta) & \varepsilon\cos^2(\theta) & -y_0\varepsilon\cos^2(\theta)\\ -\varepsilon\sin^2(\theta) & 1+\varepsilon\sin(\theta)\cos(\theta) & -y_0\varepsilon\sin(\theta)\cos(\theta)\\ 0 & 0 & 1 \end{bmatrix}.
\end{aligned}$$

Using the shearing matrix $\mathtt{Sh}_y$, we have

$$\begin{aligned}
\mathtt{M}_1 &= \mathtt{T}([0,-y_0]^T) = \begin{bmatrix} 1 & 0 & 0\\ 0 & 1 & -y_0\\ 0 & 0 & 1 \end{bmatrix},\\
\mathtt{M}_2 &= \mathtt{R}(90-\theta) = \begin{bmatrix} \sin(\theta) & -\cos(\theta) & 0\\ \cos(\theta) & \sin(\theta) & 0\\ 0 & 0 & 1 \end{bmatrix},\\
\mathtt{M}_3 &= \mathtt{Sh}_y(-\varepsilon) = \begin{bmatrix} 1 & 0 & 0\\ -\varepsilon & 1 & 0\\ 0 & 0 & 1 \end{bmatrix},\\
\mathtt{M}_4 &= \mathtt{R}(\theta-90) = \begin{bmatrix} \sin(\theta) & \cos(\theta) & 0\\ -\cos(\theta) & \sin(\theta) & 0\\ 0 & 0 & 1 \end{bmatrix}
\end{aligned}$$

and

$$\mathtt{M}_5 = \mathtt{T}([0,y_0]^T) = \begin{bmatrix} 1 & 0 & 0\\ 0 & 1 & y_0\\ 0 & 0 & 1 \end{bmatrix}.$$

Thus, the overall transformation is expressed as

$$
\begin{aligned}
\mathtt{M} &= \mathtt{M}_5\mathtt{M}_4\mathtt{M}_3\mathtt{M}_2\mathtt{M}_1 \\
&= \begin{bmatrix} 1 & 0 & 0 \\ 0 & 1 & y_0 \\ 0 & 0 & 1 \end{bmatrix} \begin{bmatrix} \sin(\theta) & \cos(\theta) & 0 \\ -\cos(\theta) & \sin(\theta) & 0 \\ 0 & 0 & 1 \end{bmatrix} \begin{bmatrix} 1 & 0 & 0 \\ -\varepsilon & 1 & 0 \\ 0 & 0 & 1 \end{bmatrix} \ldots \\
&\quad \ldots \begin{bmatrix} \sin(\theta) & -\cos(\theta) & 0 \\ \cos(\theta) & \sin(\theta) & 0 \\ 0 & 0 & 1 \end{bmatrix} \begin{bmatrix} 1 & 0 & 0 \\ 0 & 1 & -y_0 \\ 0 & 0 & 1 \end{bmatrix} \\
&= \begin{bmatrix} 1 - \varepsilon \sin(\theta)\cos(\theta) & \varepsilon \cos^2(\theta) & -y_0\varepsilon \cos^2(\theta) \\ -\varepsilon \sin^2(\theta) & 1 + \varepsilon \sin(\theta)\cos(\theta) & -y_0\varepsilon \sin(\theta)\cos(\theta) \\ 0 & 0 & 1 \end{bmatrix},
\end{aligned}
$$

which is the same transformation matrix obtained before as expected. □

## 3.6 Composite Transformations

A sequence of transformations of any type can be defined as a sequence of matrices; $\mathtt{M}_1, \mathtt{M}_2, \ldots, \mathtt{M}_n$. Thus, if a point $\mathbf{p}_1$ is transformed by $\mathtt{M}_1$, we get $\mathbf{p}_2 = \mathtt{M}_1\mathbf{p}_1$. If this operation is followed by another operation represented by $\mathtt{M}_2$, we get $\mathbf{p}_3 = \mathtt{M}_2\mathbf{p}_2$ and so on. Thus, it can be written

$$
\begin{aligned}
\mathbf{p}_2 &= \mathtt{M}_1\mathbf{p}_1, \\
\mathbf{p}_3 &= \mathtt{M}_2 \underbrace{\mathbf{p}_2}_{\mathtt{M}_1\mathbf{p}_1} = \mathtt{M}_2\mathtt{M}_1\mathbf{p}_1, \\
\mathbf{p}_4 &= \mathtt{M}_3 \underbrace{\mathbf{p}_3}_{\mathtt{M}_2\mathbf{p}_2} = \mathtt{M}_3\mathtt{M}_2\mathtt{M}_1\mathbf{p}_1, \\
\ldots &= \ldots\ldots
\end{aligned}
\tag{3.33}
$$

Thus, the general equation to transform a point $\mathbf{p}_1$ to another point $\mathbf{p}_2$ using a series of $n$ transformation operations can be expressed as

$$
\mathbf{p}_2 = \mathtt{M}_n \ldots \mathtt{M}_3\mathtt{M}_2\mathtt{M}_1\mathbf{p}_1. \tag{3.34}
$$

It is very important to notice that the order of multiplication is reversed (i.e., going from the last operation to the first). As mentioned before, transformations are not commutative.

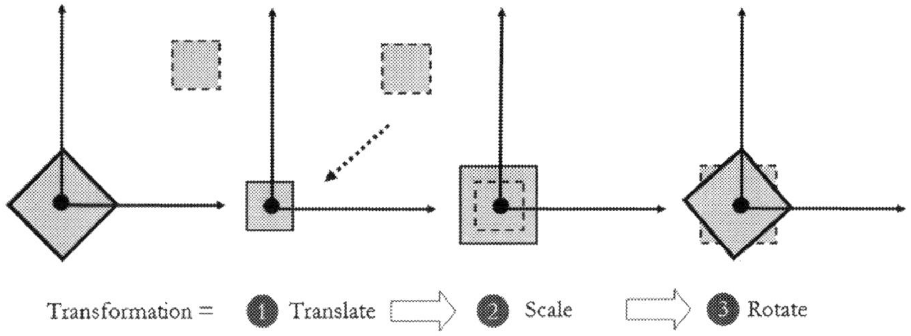


**Fig. 3.10** A square is translated, scaled and rotated

**Example 3.17:** [*2D composite transformations*]

Consider a unit square centered at the point $[5, 5]^T$ with sides parallel to the two coordinate axes. Find the 2D transformation matrix that transforms that square into another square whose vertices are at $[1, 0]^T$, $[0, 1]^T$, $[-1, 0]^T$ and $[0, -1]^T$.

**Solution 3.17:** Sketch it for better visualization as shown in Fig. 3.10. Three different transformations are required:

1. Translate the square using a translation vector of $[-5, -5]^T$ so that its center coincides with the origin. Let us call this translation matrix $\mathtt{M}_1$ where

$$\mathtt{M}_1 = \mathtt{T}([-5, -5]^T) = \begin{bmatrix} 1 & 0 & -5 \\ 1 & 0 & -5 \\ 0 & 0 & 1 \end{bmatrix}.$$

2. Scale the square by a scaling factor of $\sqrt{2}$. Let us call this scaling matrix $\mathtt{M}_2$ where

$$\mathtt{M}_2 = \mathtt{S}\left(\sqrt{2}, \sqrt{2}\right) = \begin{bmatrix} \sqrt{2} & 0 & 0 \\ 0 & \sqrt{2} & 0 \\ 0 & 0 & 1 \end{bmatrix}.$$

3. Rotate the square through an angle of 45° about the origin. Let us call this rotation matrix $\mathtt{M}_3$ where

$$\mathtt{M}_3 = \mathtt{R}(45) = \begin{bmatrix} \cos(45) & -\sin(45) & 0 \\ \sin(45) & \cos(45) & 0 \\ 0 & 0 & 1 \end{bmatrix}.$$

Then, the overall transformation matrix $\mathtt{M}$ is calculated as

$$\begin{aligned}
\mathtt{M} &= \mathtt{M}_3\mathtt{M}_2\mathtt{M}_1 \\
&= \begin{bmatrix} \cos(45) & -\sin(45) & 0 \\ \sin(45) & \cos(45) & 0 \\ 0 & 0 & 1 \end{bmatrix} \begin{bmatrix} \sqrt{2} & 0 & 0 \\ 0 & \sqrt{2} & 0 \\ 0 & 0 & 1 \end{bmatrix} \begin{bmatrix} 1 & 0 & -5 \\ 1 & 0 & -5 \\ 0 & 0 & 1 \end{bmatrix} \\
&= \begin{bmatrix} 1 & -1 & 0 \\ 1 & 1 & -10 \\ 0 & 0 & 1 \end{bmatrix}.
\end{aligned}$$

□

**Example 3.18:** [*2D composite transformations*]
Consider a triangle with vertices located at $\dot{\mathbf{a}}_1 = [1, 0]^T$, $\dot{\mathbf{b}}_1 = [0, 1]^T$ and $\dot{\mathbf{c}}_1 = [-1, 0]^T$. This triangle is sheared by a factor of 3 in the $x$-direction and then rotated through an angle of 35° about the origin. Determine the coordinates of the transformed triangle $\triangle\dot{\mathbf{a}}_2\dot{\mathbf{b}}_2\dot{\mathbf{c}}_2$.

**Solution 3.18:** A two-step transformation operation is performed:

1. Shear the triangle by a factor of 3 in the $x$-direction using a shearing matrix $\mathtt{M}_1$ where
$$\mathtt{M}_1 = \mathtt{Sh}_x(3) = \begin{bmatrix} 1 & 3 & 0 \\ 0 & 1 & 0 \\ 0 & 0 & 1 \end{bmatrix}.$$

2. Rotate the triangle through an angle of 35° about the origin using a rotation matrix $\mathtt{M}_2$ where
$$\mathtt{M}_2 = \mathtt{R}(35) = \begin{bmatrix} \cos(35) & -\sin(35) & 0 \\ \sin(35) & \cos(35) & 0 \\ 0 & 0 & 1 \end{bmatrix}.$$

Then, the overall transformation matrix $\mathtt{M}$ is calculated as

$$\begin{aligned}
\mathtt{M} &= \mathtt{M}_2\mathtt{M}_1 \\
&= \begin{bmatrix} \cos(35) & -\sin(35) & 0 \\ \sin(35) & \cos(35) & 0 \\ 0 & 0 & 1 \end{bmatrix} \begin{bmatrix} 1 & 3 & 0 \\ 0 & 1 & 0 \\ 0 & 0 & 1 \end{bmatrix} \\
&= \begin{bmatrix} 0.8192 & 1.8839 & 0 \\ 0.5736 & 2.5399 & 0 \\ 0 & 0 & 1 \end{bmatrix}.
\end{aligned}$$

Hence, the transformed coordinates are

$$\mathbf{a}_2 = \begin{bmatrix} 0.8192 & 1.8839 & 0 \\ 0.5736 & 2.5399 & 0 \\ 0 & 0 & 1 \end{bmatrix} \begin{bmatrix} 1 \\ 0 \\ 1 \end{bmatrix} = \begin{bmatrix} 0.8192 \\ 0.5736 \\ 1 \end{bmatrix},$$

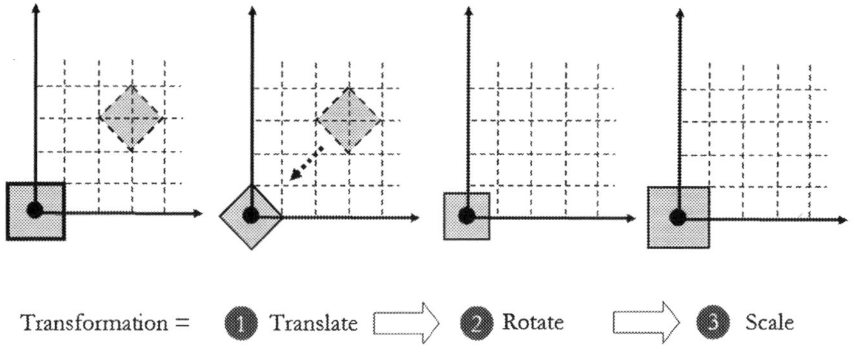


**Fig. 3.11** A square is translated, rotated and scaled

$$\mathbf{b}_2 = \begin{bmatrix} 0.8192 & 1.8839 & 0 \\ 0.5736 & 2.5399 & 0 \\ 0 & 0 & 1 \end{bmatrix} \begin{bmatrix} 0 \\ 1 \\ 1 \end{bmatrix} = \begin{bmatrix} 1.8839 \\ 2.5399 \\ 1 \end{bmatrix}$$

and

$$\mathbf{c}_2 = \begin{bmatrix} 0.8192 & 1.8839 & 0 \\ 0.5736 & 2.5399 & 0 \\ 0 & 0 & 1 \end{bmatrix} \begin{bmatrix} -1 \\ 0 \\ 1 \end{bmatrix} = \begin{bmatrix} -0.8192 \\ -0.5736 \\ 1 \end{bmatrix}.$$

As a result, the transformed vertices are $\dot{\mathbf{a}}_2 = [0.8192, 0.5736]^T$, $\dot{\mathbf{b}}_2 = [1.8839, 2.5399]^T$ and $\dot{\mathbf{c}}_2 = [-0.8192, -0.5736]^T$. □

**Example 3.19:** [*2D composite transformations*]
Consider a square with vertices located at $\dot{\mathbf{a}}_1 = [2, 3]^T$, $\dot{\mathbf{b}}_1 = [3, 2]^T$, $\dot{\mathbf{c}}_1 = [4, 3]^T$ and $\dot{\mathbf{d}}_1 = [3, 4]^T$. If this square is transformed so that its transformed vertices are $\dot{\mathbf{a}}_2 = [-1, -1]^T$, $\dot{\mathbf{b}}_2 = [1, -1]^T$, $\dot{\mathbf{c}}_2 = [1, 1]^T$ and $\dot{\mathbf{d}}_2 = [-1, 1]^T$, estimate one transformation matrix used to achieve the results.

**Solution 3.19:** Sketch it for better visualization as shown in Fig. 3.11. A three-step transformation operation is performed:

1. Translate using the translation vector $[-3, -3]^T$. This moves the center of the square to the origin. Let us call this translation matrix $\mathtt{M}_1$ where

$$\mathtt{M}_1 = \mathtt{T}([-3, -3]^T) = \begin{bmatrix} 1 & 0 & -3 \\ 0 & 1 & -3 \\ 0 & 0 & 1 \end{bmatrix}.$$

2. Rotate the square through an angle of 45° about the origin. Let us call this rotation matrix $\mathtt{M}_2$ where

$$\mathtt{M}_2 = \mathtt{R}(45) = \begin{bmatrix} \cos(45) & -\sin(45) & 0 \\ \sin(45) & \cos(45) & 0 \\ 0 & 0 & 1 \end{bmatrix}.$$

3. Scale the square along both directions using a scaling factor of $\sqrt{2}$. Let us call this scaling matrix $\mathtt{M}_3$ where

$$\mathtt{M}_3 = \mathtt{S}\left(\sqrt{2}, \sqrt{2}\right) = \begin{bmatrix} \sqrt{2} & 0 & 0 \\ 0 & \sqrt{2} & 0 \\ 0 & 0 & 1 \end{bmatrix}.$$

Hence, the overall transformation can be estimated as

$$\begin{aligned} \mathtt{M} &= \mathtt{M}_3\mathtt{M}_2\mathtt{M}_1 \\ &= \begin{bmatrix} \sqrt{2} & 0 & 0 \\ 0 & \sqrt{2} & 0 \\ 0 & 0 & 1 \end{bmatrix} \begin{bmatrix} \cos(45) & -\sin(45) & 0 \\ \sin(45) & \cos(45) & 0 \\ 0 & 0 & 1 \end{bmatrix} \begin{bmatrix} 1 & 0 & -3 \\ 0 & 1 & -3 \\ 0 & 0 & 1 \end{bmatrix} \\ &= \begin{bmatrix} 1 & -1 & 0 \\ 1 & 1 & -6 \\ 0 & 0 & 1 \end{bmatrix}. \end{aligned}$$

Note that switching Step 2 and Step 3 will not make a difference as both operations (i.e., rotation and scaling) are performed with respect to the origin. In other words, we can write $\mathtt{M}_3\mathtt{M}_2\mathtt{M}_1 = \mathtt{M}_2\mathtt{M}_3\mathtt{M}_1$. □

**Example 3.20:** [*2D composite transformations*]

If the polygon $\dot{\mathbf{a}}_1\dot{\mathbf{b}}_1\dot{\mathbf{c}}_1\dot{\mathbf{d}}_1$ specified by the vertices $\dot{\mathbf{a}}_1 = [0, 0]^T$, $\dot{\mathbf{b}}_1 = [5, 0]^T$, $\dot{\mathbf{c}}_1 = [-1, 5]^T$ and $\dot{\mathbf{d}}_1 = [-1, -5]^T$ is to be reflected about the $x$-axis and then rotated through an angle of 45° about the origin, determine the location of the transformed vertices $\dot{\mathbf{a}}_2$, $\dot{\mathbf{b}}_2$, $\dot{\mathbf{c}}_2$ and $\dot{\mathbf{d}}_2$.

**Solution 3.20:** There are two operations.

1. Reflect about the $x$-axis. Let us call this reflection matrix $\mathtt{M}_1$ where

$$\mathtt{M}_1 = \mathtt{Ref}_x = \begin{bmatrix} 1 & 0 & 0 \\ 0 & -1 & 0 \\ 0 & 0 & 1 \end{bmatrix}.$$

2. Rotate through an angle of 45° about the origin. Let us call this rotation matrix $\mathtt{M}_2$ where

$$\mathtt{M}_2 = \mathtt{R}(45) = \begin{bmatrix} \cos(45) & -\sin(45) & 0 \\ \sin(45) & \cos(45) & 0 \\ 0 & 0 & 1 \end{bmatrix}.$$

Thus, the overall transformation matrix can be expressed as

$$
\begin{aligned}
\mathtt{M} &= \mathtt{M}_2\mathtt{M}_1 \\
&= \begin{bmatrix} \cos(45) & -\sin(45) & 0 \\ \sin(45) & \cos(45) & 0 \\ 0 & 0 & 1 \end{bmatrix} \begin{bmatrix} 1 & 0 & 0 \\ 0 & -1 & 0 \\ 0 & 0 & 1 \end{bmatrix} \\
&= \begin{bmatrix} \frac{1}{\sqrt{2}} & \frac{1}{\sqrt{2}} & 0 \\ \frac{1}{\sqrt{2}} & -\frac{1}{\sqrt{2}} & 0 \\ 0 & 0 & 1 \end{bmatrix} = \begin{bmatrix} 0.7071 & 0.7071 & 0 \\ 0.7071 & -0.7071 & 0 \\ 0 & 0 & 1 \end{bmatrix}.
\end{aligned}
$$

Consequently, the transformed vertices will be as follows:

$$
\mathbf{a}_2 = \underbrace{\begin{bmatrix} \frac{1}{\sqrt{2}} & \frac{1}{\sqrt{2}} & 0 \\ \frac{1}{\sqrt{2}} & -\frac{1}{\sqrt{2}} & 0 \\ 0 & 0 & 1 \end{bmatrix}}_{\mathtt{M}} \underbrace{\begin{bmatrix} 0 \\ 0 \\ 1 \end{bmatrix}}_{\mathbf{a}_1} = \underbrace{\begin{bmatrix} 0 \\ 0 \\ 1 \end{bmatrix}}_{\mathbf{a}_2},
$$

$$
\mathbf{b}_2 = \underbrace{\begin{bmatrix} \frac{1}{\sqrt{2}} & \frac{1}{\sqrt{2}} & 0 \\ \frac{1}{\sqrt{2}} & -\frac{1}{\sqrt{2}} & 0 \\ 0 & 0 & 1 \end{bmatrix}}_{\mathtt{M}} \underbrace{\begin{bmatrix} 5 \\ 0 \\ 1 \end{bmatrix}}_{\mathbf{b}_1} = \underbrace{\begin{bmatrix} \frac{5}{\sqrt{2}} \\ \frac{5}{\sqrt{2}} \\ 1 \end{bmatrix}}_{\mathbf{b}_2} = \underbrace{\begin{bmatrix} 3.5355 \\ 3.5355 \\ 1 \end{bmatrix}}_{\mathbf{b}_2},
$$

$$
\mathbf{c}_2 = \underbrace{\begin{bmatrix} \frac{1}{\sqrt{2}} & \frac{1}{\sqrt{2}} & 0 \\ \frac{1}{\sqrt{2}} & -\frac{1}{\sqrt{2}} & 0 \\ 0 & 0 & 1 \end{bmatrix}}_{\mathtt{M}} \underbrace{\begin{bmatrix} -1 \\ 5 \\ 1 \end{bmatrix}}_{\mathbf{c}_1} = \underbrace{\begin{bmatrix} 2\sqrt{2} \\ -3\sqrt{2} \\ 1 \end{bmatrix}}_{\mathbf{c}_2} = \underbrace{\begin{bmatrix} 2.8284 \\ -4.2426 \\ 1 \end{bmatrix}}_{\mathbf{c}_2}
$$

and

$$
\mathbf{d}_2 = \underbrace{\begin{bmatrix} \frac{1}{\sqrt{2}} & \frac{1}{\sqrt{2}} & 0 \\ \frac{1}{\sqrt{2}} & -\frac{1}{\sqrt{2}} & 0 \\ 0 & 0 & 1 \end{bmatrix}}_{\mathtt{M}} \underbrace{\begin{bmatrix} -1 \\ -5 \\ 1 \end{bmatrix}}_{\mathbf{d}_1} = \underbrace{\begin{bmatrix} -3\sqrt{2} \\ 2\sqrt{2} \\ 1 \end{bmatrix}}_{\mathbf{d}_2} = \underbrace{\begin{bmatrix} -4.2426 \\ 2.8284 \\ 1 \end{bmatrix}}_{\mathbf{d}_2}.
$$

You can obtain the inhomogeneous representation of the transformed points. □

## 3.7 Same-Type Transformations

Generally, transformation operations are *not commutative* as changing the order of performing operations (i.e., changing the order of matrix multiplication) leads to different results as mentioned above. However, the following are considered special cases:

1. Two consecutive 2D translation operations are *commutative*:

$$\mathtt{T}([t_{x1}, t_{y1}]^T)\mathtt{T}([t_{x2}, t_{y2}]^T) = \mathtt{T}([t_{x2}, t_{y2}]^T)\mathtt{T}([t_{x1}, t_{y1}]^T). \tag{3.35}$$

2. Two consecutive 2D rotation operations are *commutative*:

$$\mathtt{R}(\theta_1)\mathtt{R}(\theta_2) = \mathtt{R}(\theta_2)\mathtt{R}(\theta_1). \tag{3.36}$$

3. Two consecutive 2D scaling operations are *commutative*:

$$\mathtt{S}(s_{x1}, s_{y1})\mathtt{S}(s_{x2}, s_{y2}) = \mathtt{S}(s_{x2}, s_{y2})\mathtt{S}(s_{x1}, s_{y1}). \tag{3.37}$$

4. Two consecutive 2D reflection operations about different axes are *commutative*:

$$\mathtt{Ref}_x\mathtt{Ref}_y = \mathtt{Ref}_y\mathtt{Ref}_x. \tag{3.38}$$

   Two consecutive 2D reflection operations about the same axis would result in the identity matrix:

$$\mathtt{Ref}_x\mathtt{Ref}_x = \mathtt{Ref}_y\mathtt{Ref}_y = \mathtt{I}. \tag{3.39}$$

5. Two consecutive 2D shearing operations with respect to the same axis are *commutative*:

$$\begin{aligned} \mathtt{Sh}_x(sh_1)\mathtt{Sh}_x(sh_2) &= \mathtt{Sh}_x(sh_2)\mathtt{Sh}_x(sh_1), \\ \mathtt{Sh}_y(sh_1)\mathtt{Sh}_y(sh_2) &= \mathtt{Sh}_y(sh_2)\mathtt{Sh}_y(sh_1). \end{aligned} \tag{3.40}$$

Also, in general, two matrices should be concatenated (i.e., multiplied) to express two consecutive transformations. Fortunately, it is much simpler in case the two operations are of the same type. In case of two successive translation operations, a single translation matrix, whose inputs are the two translation vectors added, can be used. Thus,

$$\begin{gathered} \mathtt{T}([t_{x1}, t_{y1}]^T)\mathtt{T}([t_{x2}, t_{y2}]^T) = \mathtt{T}([t_{x1} + t_{x2}, t_{y1} + t_{y1}]^T) \\ \begin{bmatrix} 1 & 0 & t_{x1} \\ 0 & 1 & t_{y1} \\ 0 & 0 & 1 \end{bmatrix} \begin{bmatrix} 1 & 0 & t_{x2} \\ 0 & 1 & t_{y2} \\ 0 & 0 & 1 \end{bmatrix} = \begin{bmatrix} 1 & 0 & t_{x1} + t_{x2} \\ 0 & 1 & t_{y1} + t_{y2} \\ 0 & 0 & 1 \end{bmatrix}. \end{gathered} \tag{3.41}$$

In case of two successive rotation operations, a single rotation matrix, whose inputs are the two rotation angles added, can be used. Thus,

$$\mathtt{R}(\theta_1)\mathtt{R}(\theta_2) = \mathtt{R}(\theta_1 + \theta_2)$$

$$\begin{bmatrix} \cos(\theta_1) & -\sin(\theta_1) & 0 \\ \sin(\theta_1) & \cos(\theta_1) & 0 \\ 0 & 0 & 1 \end{bmatrix} \begin{bmatrix} \cos(\theta_2) & -\sin(\theta_2) & 0 \\ \sin(\theta_2) & \cos(\theta_2) & 0 \\ 0 & 0 & 1 \end{bmatrix} = \begin{bmatrix} \cos(\theta_1 + \theta_2) & -\sin(\theta_1 + \theta_2) & 0 \\ \sin(\theta_1 + \theta_2) & \cos(\theta_1 + \theta_2) & 0 \\ 0 & 0 & 1 \end{bmatrix}. \tag{3.42}$$

In case of two successive scaling operations, a single scaling matrix, whose inputs are the two scaling factors (along each direction) multiplied, can be used. Thus,

$$\mathtt{S}(s_{x1}, s_{y1})\mathtt{S}(s_{x2}, s_{y2}) = \mathtt{S}(s_{x1}s_{x2}, s_{y1}s_{y1})$$

$$\begin{bmatrix} s_{x1} & 0 & 0 \\ 0 & s_{y1} & 0 \\ 0 & 0 & 1 \end{bmatrix} \begin{bmatrix} s_{x2} & 0 & 0 \\ 0 & s_{y2} & 0 \\ 0 & 0 & 1 \end{bmatrix} = \begin{bmatrix} s_{x1}s_{x2} & 0 & 0 \\ 0 & s_{y1}s_{y2} & 0 \\ 0 & 0 & 1 \end{bmatrix}. \tag{3.43}$$

The case of two successive reflection operations about different axes is the same as successive scaling mentioned above; hence, we have

$$\mathtt{Ref}_x\mathtt{Ref}_y = \mathtt{Ref}_y\mathtt{Ref}_x = \mathtt{S}(-1, -1). \tag{3.44}$$

In case of two successive shearing operations with respect to the same axis, a single shearing matrix, whose inputs are the two shearing factors added, can be used. Thus,

$$\mathtt{Sh}_x(sh_1)\mathtt{Sh}_x(sh_2) = \mathtt{Sh}_x(sh_1 + sh_2)$$

$$\begin{bmatrix} 1 & sh_1 & 0 \\ 0 & 1 & 0 \\ 0 & 0 & 1 \end{bmatrix} \begin{bmatrix} 1 & sh_2 & 0 \\ 0 & 1 & 0 \\ 0 & 0 & 1 \end{bmatrix} = \begin{bmatrix} 1 & sh_1 + sh_2 & 0 \\ 0 & 1 & 0 \\ 0 & 0 & 1 \end{bmatrix} \tag{3.45}$$

and

$$\mathtt{Sh}_y(sh_1)\mathtt{Sh}_y(sh_2) = \mathtt{Sh}_y(sh_1 + sh_2)$$

$$\begin{bmatrix} 1 & 0 & 0 \\ sh_1 & 1 & 0 \\ 0 & 0 & 1 \end{bmatrix} \begin{bmatrix} 1 & 0 & 0 \\ sh_2 & 1 & 0 \\ 0 & 0 & 1 \end{bmatrix} = \begin{bmatrix} 1 & 0 & 0 \\ sh_1 + sh_2 & 1 & 0 \\ 0 & 0 & 1 \end{bmatrix}. \tag{3.46}$$

## 3.8 Inverse Matrices

The inversion of a transformation operation can be represented as the inverse of a transformation matrix, which can be calculated easily as explained below.

**Translation matrix:** The inverse of a translation matrix is the same translation matrix but in the opposite direction. This is expressed as

$$\begin{aligned}\mathtt{T}^{-1}([t_x, t_y]^T) &= \mathtt{T}([-t_x, -t_y]^T)\\ \begin{bmatrix}1 & 0 & t_x\\ 0 & 1 & t_y\\ 0 & 0 & 1\end{bmatrix}^{-1} &= \begin{bmatrix}1 & 0 & -t_x\\ 0 & 1 & -t_y\\ 0 & 0 & 1\end{bmatrix}.\end{aligned} \tag{3.47}$$

**Rotation matrix:** The inverse of a rotation matrix is the same rotation matrix but in the opposite direction. It is also the transpose of the same rotation matrix. This is expressed as

$$\begin{aligned}\mathtt{R}^{-1}(\theta) &= \mathtt{R}(-\theta) = \mathtt{R}^T(\theta)\\ \begin{bmatrix}\cos(\theta) & -\sin(\theta) & 0\\ \sin(\theta) & \cos(\theta) & 0\\ 0 & 0 & 1\end{bmatrix}^{-1} &= \begin{bmatrix}\cos(-\theta) & -\sin(-\theta) & 0\\ \sin(-\theta) & \cos(-\theta) & 0\\ 0 & 0 & 1\end{bmatrix} = \begin{bmatrix}\cos(\theta) & \sin(\theta) & 0\\ -\sin(\theta) & \cos(\theta) & 0\\ 0 & 0 & 1\end{bmatrix}.\end{aligned} \tag{3.48}$$

**Scaling matrix:** The inverse of a scaling matrix is the same scaling matrix where the scaling factors are replaced by their reciprocals. This is expressed as

$$\begin{aligned}\mathtt{S}^{-1}(s_x, s_y) &= \mathtt{S}\left(\frac{1}{s_x}, \frac{1}{s_y}\right)\\ \begin{bmatrix}s_x & 0 & 0\\ 0 & s_y & 0\\ 0 & 0 & 1\end{bmatrix}^{-1} &= \begin{bmatrix}\frac{1}{s_x} & 0 & 0\\ 0 & \frac{1}{s_y} & 0\\ 0 & 0 & 1\end{bmatrix}.\end{aligned} \tag{3.49}$$

**Reflection matrix:** The inverse of a reflection matrix about any axis is the same reflection matrix. This is expressed as

$$\begin{aligned}\mathtt{Ref}_x^{-1} &= \mathtt{Ref}_x\\ \begin{bmatrix}1 & 0 & 0\\ 0 & -1 & 0\\ 0 & 0 & 1\end{bmatrix}^{-1} &= \begin{bmatrix}1 & 0 & 0\\ 0 & -1 & 0\\ 0 & 0 & 1\end{bmatrix}\end{aligned} \tag{3.50}$$

and

$$\begin{aligned}\mathtt{Ref}_y^{-1} &= \mathtt{Ref}_y\\ \begin{bmatrix}-1 & 0 & 0\\ 0 & 1 & 0\\ 0 & 0 & 1\end{bmatrix}^{-1} &= \begin{bmatrix}-1 & 0 & 0\\ 0 & 1 & 0\\ 0 & 0 & 1\end{bmatrix}.\end{aligned} \tag{3.51}$$

**Shearing matrix:** The inverse of a shearing matrix with respect to any axis is the same shearing matrix with the factor negated. This is expressed as

$$\begin{gathered}
\mathtt{Sh}_x^{-1}(sh_x) = \mathtt{Sh}_x(-sh_x) \\
\begin{bmatrix} 1 & sh_x & 0 \\ 0 & 1 & 0 \\ 0 & 0 & 1 \end{bmatrix}^{-1} = \begin{bmatrix} 1 & -sh_x & 0 \\ 0 & 1 & 0 \\ 0 & 0 & 1 \end{bmatrix}
\end{gathered} \tag{3.52}$$

and

$$\begin{gathered}
\mathtt{Sh}_y^{-1}(sh_y) = \mathtt{Sh}_y(-sh_y) \\
\begin{bmatrix} 1 & 0 & 0 \\ sh_y & 1 & 0 \\ 0 & 0 & 1 \end{bmatrix}^{-1} = \begin{bmatrix} 1 & 0 & 0 \\ -sh_y & 1 & 0 \\ 0 & 0 & 1 \end{bmatrix}.
\end{gathered} \tag{3.53}$$

## 3.9 Axes Transformations

All the previous transformation operations discussed above are applied to objects while fixing the coordinate axes. Similarly, the coordinate axes may be transformed while fixing the objects in 2D space. In this case, although the objects in space are not transformed; however, their vertex coordinates get affected by axes transformation (Xiang and Plastock 2000). We will talk about axes translation, rotation, scaling and reflection.

### *3.9.1 Axes Translation*

Consider Fig. 3.12 where the $x$- and $y$-axes are translated to the $x'$- and $y'$-axes respectively using a vector $[t_x, t_y]^T$. Thus, a point $\dot{\mathbf{p}} = [x, y]^T$ will have new coordinates $[x', y']^T$ expressed as

$$\begin{aligned} x' &= x - t_x, \\ y' &= y - t_y. \end{aligned} \tag{3.54}$$

In matrix notation, this can be written as

$$\begin{bmatrix} x' \\ y' \end{bmatrix} = \begin{bmatrix} x \\ y \end{bmatrix} + \begin{bmatrix} -t_x \\ -t_y \end{bmatrix}. \tag{3.55}$$

In homogeneous coordinates, this is expressed as

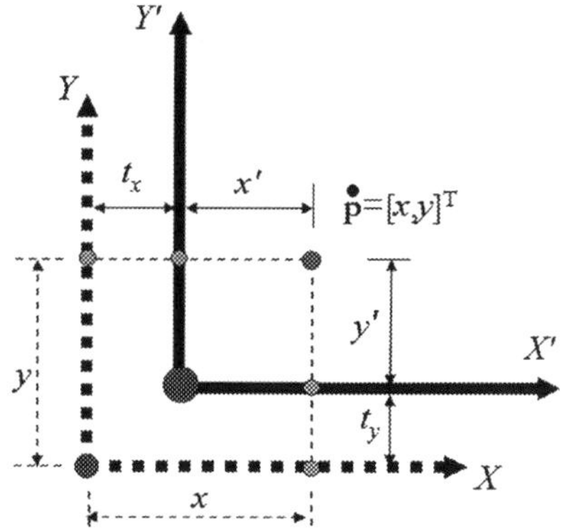


**Fig. 3.12** The $x$- and $y$-axes are translated using the vector $[t_x, t_y]^T$ to the $x'$- and $y'$-axes

$$\begin{bmatrix} x' \\ y' \\ 1 \end{bmatrix} = \begin{bmatrix} 1 & 0 & -t_x \\ 0 & 1 & -t_y \\ 0 & 0 & 1 \end{bmatrix} \begin{bmatrix} x \\ y \\ 1 \end{bmatrix}. \tag{3.56}$$

In other words, to translate the axes in 2D space using a vector $[t_x, t_y]^T$, Eq. (3.1) or Eq. (3.2) may be used with the translation vector $[t_x, t_y]^T$ but in the opposite direction (i.e., $[-t_x, -t_y]^T$).

**Example 3.21:** [*2D axes translation—inhomogeneous coordinates*]

The coordinates of the point $[3, 4]^T$ is considered with respect to the origin $[0, 0]^T$. What would the coordinates be with respect to the point $[-1, -1]^T$? Use inhomogeneous coordinates in your calculations.

**Solution 3.21:** This is an axes translation problem where the axes are translated so that the origin is placed at $[-1, -1]^T$. Therefore, the new coordinates are expressed using Eq. (3.55) as

$$\begin{aligned} \begin{bmatrix} x' \\ y' \end{bmatrix} &= \begin{bmatrix} x \\ y \end{bmatrix} + \begin{bmatrix} -t_x \\ -t_y \end{bmatrix} \\ &= \begin{bmatrix} 3 \\ 4 \end{bmatrix} + \begin{bmatrix} -(-1) \\ -(-1) \end{bmatrix} = \begin{bmatrix} 4 \\ 5 \end{bmatrix}. \end{aligned}$$

□

### 3.9.2 Axes Rotation

Consider Fig. 3.13 where the $x$- and $y$-axes are rotated through an angle $\theta$ to the $x'$- and $y'$-axes respectively. Thus, a point $\dot{\mathbf{p}} = [x, y]^T$ will have new coordinates $[x', y']^T$ expressed as

$$\begin{aligned} x' &= x\cos(\theta) + y\sin(\theta), \\ y' &= y\cos(\theta) - x\sin(\theta). \end{aligned} \tag{3.57}$$

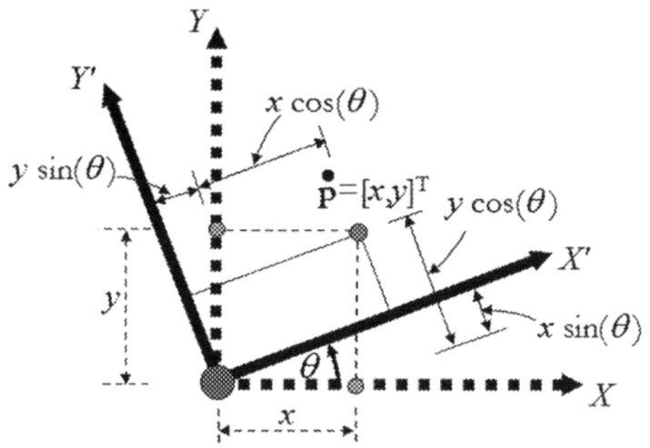


**Fig. 3.13** The $x$- and $y$-axes are rotated through an angle $\theta$ to the $x'$- and $y'$-axes

In matrix notation, this can be written as

$$\begin{bmatrix} x' \\ y' \end{bmatrix} = \begin{bmatrix} \cos(\theta) & \sin(\theta) \\ -\sin(\theta) & \cos(\theta) \end{bmatrix} \begin{bmatrix} x \\ y \end{bmatrix}. \tag{3.58}$$

In homogeneous coordinates, this is expressed as

$$\begin{bmatrix} x' \\ y' \\ 1 \end{bmatrix} = \begin{bmatrix} \cos(\theta) & \sin(\theta) & 0 \\ -\sin(\theta) & \cos(\theta) & 0 \\ 0 & 0 & 1 \end{bmatrix} \begin{bmatrix} x \\ y \\ 1 \end{bmatrix}. \tag{3.59}$$

In other words, to rotate the axes in 2D space through an angle $\theta$, Eq. (3.4) or Eq. (3.5) may be used with the same magnitude of the angle $\theta$ but in the opposite direction (i.e., $-\theta$).

**Example 3.22:** [*2D axes rotation—inhomogeneous coordinates*]
Consider a 2D line segment whose endpoints are $[x_1, y_1]^T = [3, 4]^T$ and $[x_2, y_2]^T = [9, 1]^T$. If the $x$- and $y$-axes are rotated through an angle of 45° about the origin to get the $x'$- and $y'$-axes, express the same line in the $x'y'$-coordinate system.

**Solution 3.22:** The endpoints after axes rotation are expressed using Eq. (3.57) as

$$\begin{aligned} x'_1 &= x_1 \cos(\theta) + y_1 \sin(\theta) \\ &= 3\cos(45) + 4\sin(45) = \tfrac{7}{\sqrt{2}}, \end{aligned}$$

$$\begin{aligned} y'_1 &= y_1 \cos(\theta) - x_1 \sin(\theta) \\ &= 4\cos(45) - 3\sin(45) = \tfrac{1}{\sqrt{2}} \end{aligned}$$

and

$$\begin{aligned} x'_2 &= x_2 \cos(\theta) + y_2 \sin(\theta) \\ &= 9\cos(45) + \sin(45) = \tfrac{10}{\sqrt{2}}, \end{aligned}$$

$$\begin{aligned} y'_2 &= y_2 \cos(\theta) - x_2 \sin(\theta) \\ &= \cos(45) - 9\sin(45) = -\tfrac{8}{\sqrt{2}}. \end{aligned}$$

The line equation is expressed in $x'y'$-coordinates as

$$y' = \frac{y'_2 - y'_1}{x'_2 - x'_1}(x' - x'_1) + y'_1.$$

Substituting the values of $x'_1$, $y'_1$, $x'_2$ and $y'_2$, the same line is expressed in $x'y'$-coordinates as

$$y' = \frac{-\frac{8}{\sqrt{2}} - \frac{1}{\sqrt{2}}}{\frac{10}{\sqrt{2}} - \frac{7}{\sqrt{2}}}\left(x' - \frac{7}{\sqrt{2}}\right) + \frac{1}{\sqrt{2}} = -3x' + 11\sqrt{2}.$$ □

**Example 3.23:** [*2D axes rotation—inhomogeneous coordinates*]
The equation of a 2D line segment is expressed in $x'y'$-coordinates as

$$y' = -3x' + 11\sqrt{2}.$$

If the $x'$- and $y'$-axes are obtained as the $x$- and $y$-axes are rotated through an angle of 45° about the origin, express the same linear equation in the old $xy$-coordinate system.

**Solution 3.23:** According to Eq. (3.57), we have

$$\begin{aligned} x' &= x\cos(\theta) + y\sin(\theta) \\ &= x\cos(45) + y\sin(45) = \frac{x+y}{\sqrt{2}}. \end{aligned}$$

$$\begin{aligned} y' &= y\cos(\theta) - x\sin(\theta) \\ &= y\cos(45) - x\sin(45) = \frac{y-x}{\sqrt{2}}. \end{aligned}$$

Substituting the values of $x'$ and $y'$ in the given linear equation, we get

$$\begin{aligned} y' &= -3x' + 11\sqrt{2} \\ \frac{y-x}{\sqrt{2}} &= \frac{-3(x+y)}{\sqrt{2}} + 11\sqrt{2}. \end{aligned}$$

Hence, we get the same equation in term of $x$ and $y$ as

$$y = 5.5 - 0.5x.$$ □

**Example 3.24:** [*2D axes transformations—inhomogeneous coordinates*]
If the $x$- and $y$-axes are rotated through an angle of 45° and then translated using the vector $[2, 1]^T$, determine the new coordinates $\dot{\mathbf{p}}_2$ of point $\dot{\mathbf{p}}_1 = [2, 1]^T$. Do your calculations using inhomogeneous coordinates.

**Solution 3.24:** A two-step transformation operation is performed:

1. Rotate the axes through an angle of 45° using the rotation matrix $\dot{\mathrm{R}}$.

2. Translate the axes using the translation vector $\mathbf{t} = [2, 1]^T$.

Note that both the rotation and translation directions are reversed as the axes are affected. Hence, we use $\dot{\mathrm{R}}(-45)$ and $\mathbf{t} = [-2, -1]^T$. Both operations can be expressed in inhomogeneous coordinates as

$$\underbrace{\begin{bmatrix} x_2 \\ y_2 \end{bmatrix}}_{\dot{\mathbf{p}}_2} = \underbrace{\begin{bmatrix} \cos(-45) & -\sin(-45) \\ \sin(-45) & \cos(-45) \end{bmatrix}}_{\dot{\mathrm{R}}(-45)} \underbrace{\begin{bmatrix} 2 \\ 1 \end{bmatrix}}_{\dot{\mathbf{p}}_1} + \underbrace{\begin{bmatrix} -2 \\ -1 \end{bmatrix}}_{\mathbf{t}}$$
$$= \begin{bmatrix} \frac{1}{\sqrt{2}} & \frac{1}{\sqrt{2}} \\ -\frac{1}{\sqrt{2}} & \frac{1}{\sqrt{2}} \end{bmatrix} \begin{bmatrix} 2 \\ 1 \end{bmatrix} + \begin{bmatrix} -2 \\ -1 \end{bmatrix} = \begin{bmatrix} 0.1213 \\ -1.7071 \end{bmatrix}. \qquad \square$$

**Example 3.25:** [*2D axes transformations—inhomogeneous coordinates*]
If the $x$- and $y$-axes are translated using the vector $[2, 1]^T$ and then rotated through an angle of 45°, determine the new coordinates of the point $[2, 1]^T$. Do your calculations in inhomogeneous coordinates.

**Solution 3.25:** A two-step transformation operation is performed:

1. Translate the axes using the translation vector $\mathbf{t} = [2, 1]^T$.
2. Rotate the axes through an angle of 45° using the rotation matrix $\dot{\mathrm{R}}$.

As done before, both the translation and rotation directions are reversed as the axes are affected. Hence, we use $\mathbf{t} = [-2, -1]^T$ and $\dot{\mathrm{R}}(-45)$. Both operations can be expressed in inhomogeneous coordinates as

$$\underbrace{\begin{bmatrix} x_2 \\ y_2 \end{bmatrix}}_{\dot{\mathbf{p}}_2} = \underbrace{\begin{bmatrix} \cos(-45) & -\sin(-45) \\ \sin(-45) & \cos(-45) \end{bmatrix}}_{\dot{\mathrm{R}}(-45)} \underbrace{\begin{bmatrix} 2-2 \\ 1-1 \end{bmatrix}}_{\dot{\mathbf{p}}_1 - \mathbf{t}} = \begin{bmatrix} 0 \\ 0 \end{bmatrix}. \qquad \square$$

### *3.9.3 Axes Scaling*

In addition to translation and rotation, coordinate axes may be scaled. However, in case of scaling and unlike axes translation, the origin keeps its location. Also, unlike axes rotation, the axes keep their orientations. The axes scaling process affects the units of the coordinate system, which are scaled along both directions using two scaling factors. As done before, let us refer to the scaled axes as the $x'$- and $y'$-axes. Thus, a point $\dot{\mathbf{p}} = [x, y]^T$ will have new coordinates $[x', y']^T$ expressed as

$$\begin{aligned} x' &= \frac{x}{s_x}, \\ y' &= \frac{y}{s_y}. \end{aligned} \tag{3.60}$$

In matrix notation, this can be written as

$$\begin{bmatrix} x' \\ y' \end{bmatrix} = \begin{bmatrix} \frac{1}{s_x} & 0 \\ 0 & \frac{1}{s_y} \end{bmatrix} \begin{bmatrix} x \\ y \end{bmatrix}. \tag{3.61}$$

In homogeneous coordinates, this is expressed as

$$\begin{bmatrix} x' \\ y' \\ 1 \end{bmatrix} = \begin{bmatrix} \frac{1}{s_x} & 0 & 0 \\ 0 & \frac{1}{s_y} & 0 \\ 0 & 0 & 1 \end{bmatrix} \begin{bmatrix} x \\ y \\ 1 \end{bmatrix}. \tag{3.62}$$

In other words, to scale the axes in 2D space, Eq. (3.10) or Eq. (3.11) may be used with the reciprocals of the scaling factors $s_x$ and $s_y$ along the $x$- and $y$-axes respectively.

**Example 3.26:** [*2D axes scaling—inhomogeneous coordinates*]
If the units of a 2D coordinate system are measured in inches, derive a transformation matrix that redefines those units in millimeters. Consider inhomogeneous coordinates in your calculations. (*Hint:* 1 inch = 25.4 mm.)

**Solution 3.26:** This problem can be treated as a 2D axes scaling problem. Since

$$1 \text{ mm} = \frac{1}{25.4} \text{ inches};$$

hence, the scaling factors are obtained as

$$s_x = s_y = \frac{1}{25.4}.$$

Therefore, a point $[x, y]^T$ expressed in inches may be re-expressed in millimeters using Eq. (3.61) as

$$\begin{aligned} \begin{bmatrix} x' \\ y' \end{bmatrix} &= \begin{bmatrix} \frac{1}{s_x} & 0 \\ 0 & \frac{1}{s_y} \end{bmatrix} \begin{bmatrix} x \\ y \end{bmatrix} \\ &= \begin{bmatrix} \frac{1}{1/25.4} & 0 \\ 0 & \frac{1}{1/25.4} \end{bmatrix} \begin{bmatrix} x \\ y \end{bmatrix} = \begin{bmatrix} 25.4x \\ 25.4y \end{bmatrix}. \end{aligned}$$ □

**Example 3.27:** [*2D axes scaling—inhomogeneous coordinates*]
The equation of a circle having a radius of $r$ and centered at the origin is expressed in $xy$-coordinates as

$$x^2 + y^2 = r^2.$$

If the $x$- and $y$-axes are scaled with respect to the origin to get the $x'$- and $y'$-axes such that every $r$ units along each direction become 1 unit in the new coordinate system, express the same circle equation in the new $x'y'$-coordinate system.

**Solution 3.27:** The scaling factors can be expressed as

$$s_x = s_y = r.$$

Therefore, a point $[x, y]^T$ expressed in the $xy$-coordinate system is re-expressed in the $x'y'$-coordinate system using Eq. (3.61) as

$$\begin{aligned}\begin{bmatrix} x' \\ y' \end{bmatrix} &= \begin{bmatrix} \frac{1}{s_x} & 0 \\ 0 & \frac{1}{s_y} \end{bmatrix} \begin{bmatrix} x \\ y \end{bmatrix} \\ &= \begin{bmatrix} \frac{1}{r} & 0 \\ 0 & \frac{1}{r} \end{bmatrix} \begin{bmatrix} x \\ y \end{bmatrix} = \begin{bmatrix} \frac{x}{r} \\ \frac{y}{r} \end{bmatrix}.\end{aligned}$$

Substituting the values of $x$ and $y$ in the circle equation, we get

$$\begin{aligned} x^2 + y^2 &= r^2 \\ r^2x'^2 + r^2y'^2 &= r^2 \\ x'^2 + y'^2 &= 1. \end{aligned}$$

□

### 3.9.4 Axes Reflection

The 2D axes may be reflected about the $x$-axis as shown in Fig. 3.14a to the $x'$- and $y'$-axes respectively. Thus, a point $\dot{\mathbf{p}} = [x, y]^T$ will have new coordinates $[x', y']^T$ expressed as

$$\begin{aligned} x' &= x, \\ y' &= -y. \end{aligned} \tag{3.63}$$

In matrix notation, this can be written as

$$\begin{bmatrix} x' \\ y' \end{bmatrix} = \begin{bmatrix} 1 & 0 \\ 0 & -1 \end{bmatrix} \begin{bmatrix} x \\ y \end{bmatrix}. \tag{3.64}$$

In homogeneous coordinates, this is expressed as

$$\begin{bmatrix} x' \\ y' \\ 1 \end{bmatrix} = \begin{bmatrix} 1 & 0 & 0 \\ 0 & -1 & 0 \\ 0 & 0 & 1 \end{bmatrix} \begin{bmatrix} x \\ y \\ 1 \end{bmatrix}. \tag{3.65}$$

In other words, to reflect the axes in 2D space about the $x$-axis, Eq. (3.15) or Eq. (3.16) may be used. Similarly, the 2D axes may be reflected about the $y$-axis as shown in Fig. 3.14b to the $x'$- and $y'$-axes respectively. Thus, a point $\dot{\mathbf{p}} = [x, y]^T$ will have new coordinates $[x', y']^T$ expressed as

$$\begin{aligned} x' &= -x, \\ y' &= y. \end{aligned} \tag{3.66}$$

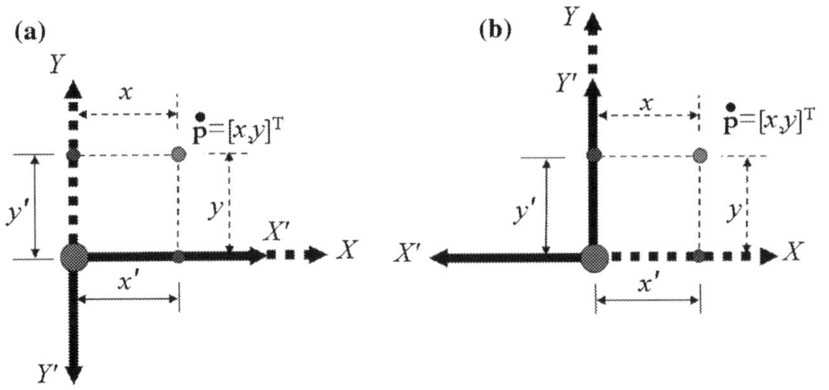


**Fig. 3.14** **a** The $x$- and $y$-axes are reflected about the $x$-axis to the $x'$- and $y'$-axes. **b** The $x$- and $y$-axes are reflected about the $y$-axis to the $x'$- and $y'$-axes

In matrix notation, this can be written as

$$\begin{bmatrix} x' \\ y' \end{bmatrix} = \begin{bmatrix} -1 & 0 \\ 0 & 1 \end{bmatrix} \begin{bmatrix} x \\ y \end{bmatrix}. \tag{3.67}$$

In homogeneous coordinates, this is expressed as

$$\begin{bmatrix} x' \\ y' \\ 1 \end{bmatrix} = \begin{bmatrix} -1 & 0 & 0 \\ 0 & 1 & 0 \\ 0 & 0 & 1 \end{bmatrix} \begin{bmatrix} x \\ y \\ 1 \end{bmatrix}. \tag{3.68}$$

In other words, to reflect the axes in 2D space about the $y$-axis, Eq. (3.18) or Eq. (3.19) may be used.

**Example 3.28:** [*2D reflection about the x-axis—inhomogeneous coordinates*]

A point $\dot{\mathbf{p}}$ is located at $[5, 8]^T$. If the positive $y$-axis is changed to point along its negative direction while fixing the location of point $\dot{\mathbf{p}}$, get the new coordinates of point $\dot{\mathbf{p}}$.

**Solution 3.28:** This is a 2D axes reflection problem. In this case, the reflection is performed about the $x$-axis. Using Eq. (3.64), the point is expressed as

$$\begin{aligned} \begin{bmatrix} x' \\ y' \end{bmatrix} &= \begin{bmatrix} 1 & 0 \\ 0 & -1 \end{bmatrix} \begin{bmatrix} x \\ y \end{bmatrix} \\ &= \begin{bmatrix} 1 & 0 \\ 0 & -1 \end{bmatrix} \begin{bmatrix} 5 \\ 8 \end{bmatrix} = \begin{bmatrix} 5 \\ -8 \end{bmatrix}. \end{aligned}$$

□

## 3.10 Problems

**Problem 3.1:** [*2D rotation about the origin—inhomogeneous coordinates*]
Consider a line segment spanning from $\dot{\mathbf{p}}_0 = [3, 4]^T$ to $\dot{\mathbf{p}}_1 = [10, 7]^T$. If this line is rotated through an angle of 45° about the origin, calculate the new positions of its endpoints. You may use inhomogeneous coordinates in your calculations.

**Problem 3.2:** [*2D general rotation—homogeneous coordinates*]
If the center of rotation in Problem 3.1 is changed to $\dot{\mathbf{p}}_0 = [3, 4]^T$; one of the endpoints of the line segment, get the new positions of the endpoints after rotation. You may use homogeneous coordinates in your calculations.

**Problem 3.3:** [*2D general reflection*]
Derive the reflection matrix about a line parallel to the $y$-axis and passing through the point $[x_0, y_0]^T$.

**Problem 3.4:** [*2D general reflection*]
Derive the reflection matrix about a line having a slope of 0.5 and $y$-intercept of 3.

**Problem 3.5:** [*2D general reflection*]
Use Eq. (3.24) to estimate the transformation matrix that reflects a point about the line $y = x$.

**Problem 3.6:** [*2D composite transformations—rotation/reflection*]
Consider a square whose vertices are $\dot{\mathbf{a}} = [2, 1]^T$, $\dot{\mathbf{b}} = [6, 1]^T$, $\dot{\mathbf{c}} = [6, 5]^T$ and $\dot{\mathbf{d}} = [2, 5]^T$. It is required to rotate that square about its center through an angle of 35°. This is followed by reflection about a line passing through the origin with an inclination angle of 35° (relative to the $x$-axis). Derive a single transformation matrix that can be used to perform all the transformations.

**Problem 3.7:** [*2D composite transformations—reflection/rotation*]
Given a 2D polygon specified by the vertices $[1, 1]^T$, $[3, 1]^T$, $[5, 3]^T$ and $[2, 4]^T$, develop a single transformation matrix that reflects it about the $x$-axis and rotates it about its center through an angle of 25°. Determine the coordinates of the transformed polygon. (*Hint:* The center of a 2D shape may be calculated as the average coordinates along the $x$- and $y$-directions.)

**Problem 3.8:** [*2D composite transformations—reflection/translation/rotation*]
Given the previous polygon, derive the transformation matrix that performs the following operations:

1. Reflecting the polygon about the line $y + x = 1$.
2. Translating it by $-1$ and 2 in the $x$- and $y$-directions respectively.
3. Rotating it about the point $[2, 2]^T$ through an angle of 180°.

Plot the original and transformed polygons.

**Problem 3.9:** [*2D composite transformations—scaling/rotation*]
Consider a square with vertices located at $[1, 0]^T$, $[0, -1]^T$, $[-1, 0]^T$ and $[0, 1]^T$. If this square is scaled up by a factor of 2 along the $x$-direction and then rotated through an angle of 35° about the origin, determine the coordinates of the transformed vertices.

**Problem 3.10:** [*2D composite transformations—translation/rotation*]
A triangle whose vertices are $\dot{\mathbf{a}} = [1, 0]^T$, $\dot{\mathbf{b}} = [0, 1]^T$ and $\dot{\mathbf{c}} = [-1, 0]^T$ is translated by the vector $[3, 2]^T$ and then rotated through an angle of 45° about the point $[1, -1]^T$, determine the coordinates and the area of the transformed triangle.

**Problem 3.11:** [*2D composite transformations—rotation/scaling*]
The points $\dot{\mathbf{a}} = [1, 1]^T$, $\dot{\mathbf{b}} = [-1, -1]^T$ and $\dot{\mathbf{c}} = [-4, 2]^T$ form a right triangle. Find a point $\dot{\mathbf{d}}$ such that $\dot{\mathbf{a}}\dot{\mathbf{b}}\dot{\mathbf{c}}\dot{\mathbf{d}}$ is a rectangle. The rectangle $\dot{\mathbf{a}}\dot{\mathbf{b}}\dot{\mathbf{c}}\dot{\mathbf{d}}$ is rotated through an angle of 45° about its center and then scaled to double its original size. Find the required transformation matrix and sketch the rectangle after the transformation.

**Problem 3.12:** [*2D composite transformations—shearing/rotation and homogeneous coordinates*]
A triangle whose vertices are $\dot{\mathbf{a}} = [1, 0]^T$, $\dot{\mathbf{b}} = [0, 1]^T$ and $\dot{\mathbf{c}} = [-1, 0]^T$ is sheared by a factor of 3 in the $x$-direction and then rotated through an angle of 45° about the point $[1, -1]^T$. Derive a single transformation matrix to perform these actions. Use homogeneous coordinates.

**Problem 3.13:** [*2D composite transformations—shearing/rotation and inhomogeneous coordinates*]
Re-solve Problem 3.12 using inhomogeneous coordinates. Determine the coordinates and area of the transformed triangle.

**Problem 3.14:** [*2D composite transformations—inhomogeneous equation*]
It is required that you transform the square $\dot{\mathbf{a}}\dot{\mathbf{b}}\dot{\mathbf{c}}\dot{\mathbf{d}}$ to have the coordinates $\dot{\mathbf{a}}'\dot{\mathbf{b}}'\dot{\mathbf{c}}'\dot{\mathbf{d}}'$. The coordinates of the vertices are $\dot{\mathbf{a}} = [0, 0]^T$, $\dot{\mathbf{b}} = [1, 1]^T$, $\dot{\mathbf{c}} = [0, 2]^T$, $\dot{\mathbf{d}} = [-1, 1]^T$, $\dot{\mathbf{a}}' = [4, 1]^T$, $\dot{\mathbf{b}}' = [7, 1]^T$, $\dot{\mathbf{c}}' = [7, 4]^T$ and $\dot{\mathbf{d}}' = [4, 4]^T$. Write down the inhomogeneous equation for that transformation in terms of $[x, y]^T$ and $[x', y']^T$.

**Problem 3.15:** [*2D composite transformations—inhomogeneous equation*]
Solve Problem 3.14 if the square $\dot{\mathbf{a}}'\dot{\mathbf{b}}'\dot{\mathbf{c}}'\dot{\mathbf{d}}'$ is transformed to $\dot{\mathbf{a}}\dot{\mathbf{b}}\dot{\mathbf{c}}\dot{\mathbf{d}}$.

**Problem 3.16:** [*2D transformations*]
Consider a triangle whose vertices are located at $\dot{\mathbf{a}}_1 = [-1, 0]^T$, $\dot{\mathbf{b}}_1 = [1, 0]^T$ and $\dot{\mathbf{c}}_1 = [0, 1]^T$. If this triangle is transformed to another triangle $\Delta\dot{\mathbf{a}}_2\dot{\mathbf{b}}_2\dot{\mathbf{c}}_2$ where $\dot{\mathbf{a}}_2 = [4, 4]^T$, $\dot{\mathbf{b}}_2 = [5, 4]^T$ and $\dot{\mathbf{c}}_2 = [4.5, 6]^T$, estimate the transformation matrix.

**Problem 3.17:** [*2D transformations*]
A unit square with sides parallel to the $x$- and $y$-axes and centered at $[5, 5]^T$ is to be transformed into a rectangle whose vertices are $[1, 1]^T$, $[-1, -1]^T$, $[-4, 2]^T$, $[-2, 4]^T$. Find the transformation matrix.

**Problem 3.18:** [*2D axes translation—homogeneous coordinates*]

The coordinates of the point $[7, 9]^T$ is considered with respect to the origin $[0, 0]^T$. What would the coordinates be with respect to the point $[1, -1]^T$? Use homogeneous coordinates in your calculations.

**Problem 3.19:** [*2D axes translation and point translation—inhomogeneous coordinates*]

A point $\dot{\mathbf{p}} = [7, 9]^T$ is translated to another location $\dot{\mathbf{p}}' = [6, 8]^T$. Then, the origin moves to $[-1, -1]^T$. What are the coordinates of $\dot{\mathbf{p}}$ and $\dot{\mathbf{p}}'$ after axes translation? Use inhomogeneous coordinates in your calculations.

**Problem 3.20:** [*2D axes rotation—inhomogeneous coordinates*]

The equation of a 2D line segment is expressed in $xy$-coordinates as

$$y = 5.5 - 0.5x.$$

If the $x$- and $y$-axes are rotated through an angle of 45° about the origin to get the $x'$- and $y'$-axes, express the same linear equation in the $x'y'$-coordinate system.

**Problem 3.21:** [*2D axes rotation—inhomogeneous coordinates*]

Consider a 2D line segment whose endpoints are $[x_1, y_1]^T$ and $[x_2, y_2]^T$. If the $x$- and $y$-axes are rotated through an angle of 45° about the origin to get the $x'$- and $y'$-axes, express the same line in the $x'y'$-coordinate system. Use inhomogeneous coordinates in your calculations.

**Problem 3.22:** [*2D axes scaling—homogeneous coordinates*]

If the units of a 2D coordinate system are measured in millimeters, derive a transformation matrix that redefines those units in inches. Use homogeneous coordinates in your calculations. (*Hint*: 1 inch = 25.4 mm.)

**Problem 3.23:** [*2D axes rotation*]

The equation of a circle having a radius of $r$ and centered at the origin is expressed in $xy$-coordinates as

$$x^2 + y^2 = r^2.$$

If the $x$- and $y$-axes are scaled with respect to the origin to get the $x'$- and $y'$-axes such that every $r$ units along the $x$-direction become 1 unit and every $r$ units along the $y$-direction become 2 units in the new coordinate system, express the same equation in the new $x'y'$-coordinate system. Will it remain a circle?

**Problem 3.24:** [*2D reflection about the $y$ -axis—inhomogeneous coordinates*]

A point $\dot{\mathbf{p}}$ is located at $[5, 8]^T$. If the positive $x$-axis is changed to point along its negative direction while fixing the location of point $\dot{\mathbf{p}}$, get the new coordinates of point $\dot{\mathbf{p}}$.

## Reference

Xiang, Z., and R.A. Plastock. 2000. *Computer graphics*. New York: McGraw-Hill. (Schaum's Outline Series).

# Chapter 4
# 3D Solid Modeling

**Abstract** Solids are 3D models that are used to represent objects in 3D space. Examples of simple solid primitives are cubes, cylinders, cones, spheres, etc. There are many techniques developed in the literature to construct solids in 3D space. These techniques can fall under certain categories (Requicha in ACM Computing Surveys 12(4):437–464, 1980; Foley et al in Computer graphics: principles and practice in C. Addison-Wesley, Boston 1995). Among these categories are constructive solid geometry, primitive instancing, cell decomposition, spatial enumeration, different tree representations, translational and rotational sweep representations in addition to boundary representation and polygonal modeling. In this chapter, we will discuss some of these solid modeling techniques.

## 4.1 Wireframes

A 3D model can be represented as a wireframe. An example is shown in Fig. 4.1. As a matter of fact, there are different methods to represent a wireframe model. One of these representations is referred to as *explicit edge listing*. In this representation, a 3D model is stored as two tables; a *vertex table* where an entry is composed of a vertex number and its $x$-, $y$- and $z$-coordinates and an *edge table* where an entry consists of an edge number and its starting and ending vertices.

Figure 4.2 shows an example of wireframe for a cube whose side length is 2 units and centered at the origin. As listed in Table 4.1, vertex table entries consist of vertex numbers and their coordinates while edge table entries contain edge numbers and starting and ending vertices.

**Example 4.1:** [*Wireframe modeling*]

Consider the tetrahedron shown in Fig. 4.3 where the vertices are indicated by lowercase letters (i.e., "a," "b," "c" and "d"), the faces by uppercase letters (i.e., "A," "B," "C" and "D") and the edges by digits (i.e., "1," "2," "3," "4," "5" and "6"). The coordinates of the vertices are $[x_a, y_a, z_a]^T$, $[x_b, y_b, z_b]^T$, etc. Write down the

R. Elias, *Digital Media*, DOI: 10.1007/978-3-319-05137-6_4,

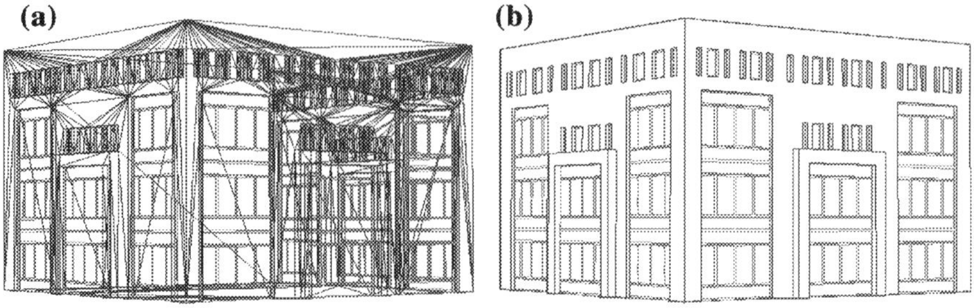


**Fig. 4.1** **a** A 3D model of a building as a wireframe. **b** The same model after removing hidden lines

**Fig. 4.2** A wireframe model is represented by vertices and edges only

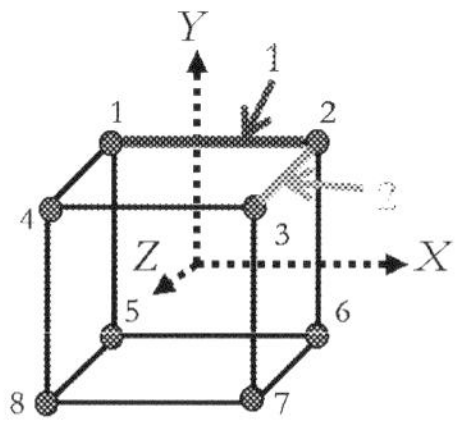


entries of the vertex and edge tables for this tetrahedron if it is to be represented as a wireframe model.

**Solution 4.1:** The vertex and edge tables of the tetrahedron shown in Fig. 4.3 are the following:

| Vertex # | $x$ | $y$ | $z$ |
|---|---|---|---|
| a | $x_a$ | $y_a$ | $z_a$ |
| b | $x_b$ | $y_b$ | $z_b$ |
| c | $x_c$ | $y_c$ | $z_c$ |
| d | $x_d$ | $y_d$ | $z_d$ |

| Edge # | Start vertex | End vertex |
|---|---|---|
| 1 | a | b |
| 2 | b | c |
| 3 | c | a |
| 4 | c | d |
| 5 | d | a |
| 6 | d | b |

□

**Table 4.1** Vertex and edge tables of a wireframe for a cube whose side length is 2 units and centered at the origin

| Vertex # | *x* | *y* | *z* |
|---|---|---|---|
| 1 | -1 | 1 | -1 |
| 2 | 1 | 1 | -1 |
| 3 | 1 | 1 | 1 |
| 4 | -1 | 1 | 1 |
| 5 | -1 | -1 | -1 |
| 6 | 1 | -1 | -1 |
| 7 | 1 | -1 | 1 |
| 8 | -1 | -1 | 1 |

| Edge # | Start vertex | End vertex |
|---|---|---|
| 1 | 1 | 2 |
| 2 | 2 | 3 |
| ⋮ | ⋮ | ⋮ |

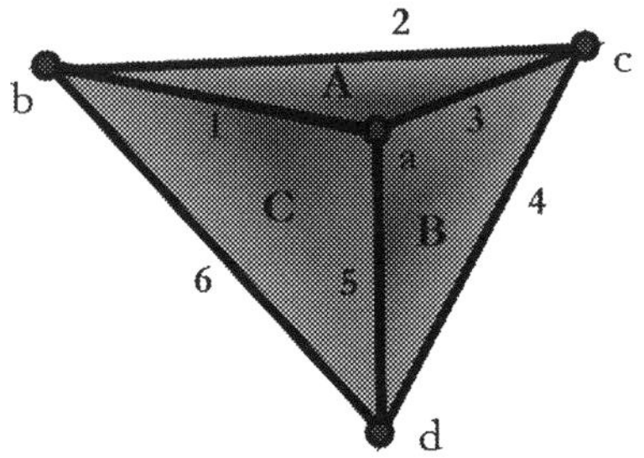


**Fig. 4.3** A tetrahedron represented by vertices and edges only

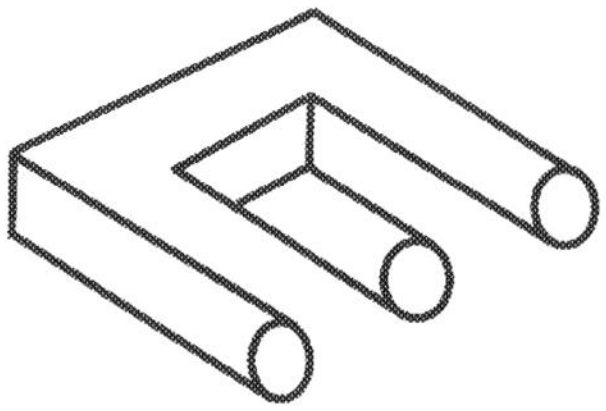

**Fig. 4.4** The devil's fork!

## *4.1.1 Wireframe Pros and Cons*

On the positive side, wireframe models are easy to construct, modify, clip and transform. They could be the best choice for previewing models since less information processes faster. On the negative side, however, representing a solid as a wireframe model could be ambiguous sometimes and could result in different interpretations for the same model due to the lack of face information. Sometimes, using wireframes might result in unrealistic models as the devil's fork shown in Fig. 4.4. In case edges are curves rather than straight line segments, more info will be required to store (e.g., curve equations).

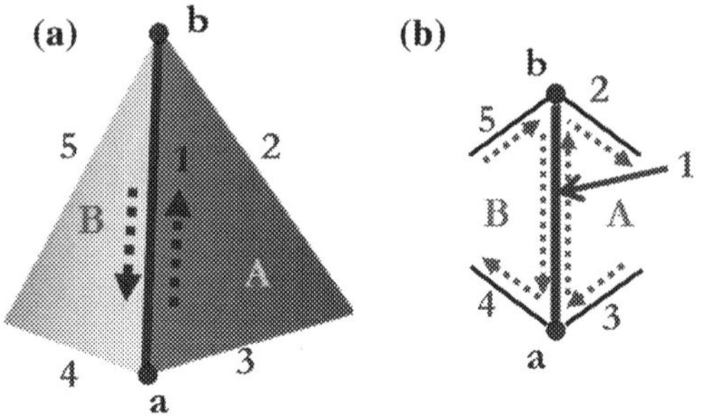


**Fig. 4.5** Baumgart's winged-edge data structure: **a** A pyramid. **b** Winged-edge "1"

## 4.2 Boundary Representations

*Boundary representations* or *B-reps* can be used to avoid the source of ambiguity arising in wireframe models. This is achieved by adding surface information to vertex and edge information that appears in wireframe modeling. Consequently, a solid is bounded by surface patches or faces forming exterior and interior for the solid. One of the renowned examples of B-reps is Baumgart's winged-edge data structure, which is discussed below.

### *4.2.1 Baumgart's Winged-Edge Data Structure*

Figure 4.5a shows a pyramid where edge "1" connects vertex "a" to vertex "b". This edge is the intersection between face "A" and face "B". Edges are clockwise-ordered while they are viewed from outside the model. For example, the edges of face "A" are ordered as "1," "2" and "3" while the edges of face "B" are ordered as "1," "4" and "5."

Faces, edges and vertices are traversed where the direction of traversal is important. For example, if you traverse edge "1" from vertex "a" to vertex "b," face "A" will be on the right while face "B" will be on the left. (They will switch position if traversal is done from vertex "b" to vertex "a".) Each edge is traversed once while traversing the face it surrounds. This means edge "1" is traversed twice; once while traversing face "A" and another time while traversing face "B"; however, this is done in different directions as shown in Fig. 4.5b.

In order to represent an edge, we need the vertices it connects, its left and right faces and the predecessor and successor of this edge when traversing its left as well as right faces; all combined in an *edge table*. This structure is referred to as *Baumgart's winged-edge data structure*. For edge "1" in Fig. 4.5, the information is listed in the edge table shown in Table 4.2a. Because the four edges "2," "3," "4" and "5" form wings for edge "1"; thus, edge "1" is said to be *winged* (Baumgart 1972, 1974, 1975).

Queries about which vertices, edges and faces are adjacent to an edge can be answered in constant time by using the edge table. In order to query about other

**Table 4.2** Baumgart's winged-edge tables: **a** Edge table. **b** Vertex table. **c** Face table

**(a)**

| Edge # | Vertices Start | End | Faces Left | Right | Left traverse Pred. | Succ. | Right traverse Pred. | Succ. |
|---|---|---|---|---|---|---|---|---|
| 1 | a | b | B | A | 5 | 4 | 3 | 2 |
| ⋮ | ⋮ | ⋮ | ⋮ | ⋮ | ⋮ | ⋮ | ⋮ | ⋮ |

**(b)**

| Vertex | Coordinates | Edge |
|---|---|---|
| a | $[x_a, y_a, z_a]^T$ | 1 |
| b | $[x_b, y_b, z_b]^T$ | 5 |
| ⋮ | ⋮ | ⋮ |

**(c)**

| Face | Edge |
|---|---|
| A | 2 |
| B | 5 |
| ⋮ | ⋮ |

adjacency relationships (i.e., which vertices, edges or faces are adjacent to which vertex or face), Baumgart's winged-edge data structure has, in addition to the edge table, two more tables; one for vertices and another one for faces. In the *vertex table*, each vertex is associated with an edge passing through it. In the *face table*, each face is associated with an edge surrounding it. Different choices of edges in both cases may result in different tables.

**Example 4.2:** [*Baumgart's winged-edge data structure*]
Consider the tetrahedron shown in Fig. 4.3 where the vertices are indicated by lowercase letters (i.e., "a," "b," "c" and "d"), the faces by uppercase letters (i.e., "A," "B," "C" and "D") and the edges by digits (i.e., "1," "2," "3," "4," "5" and "6"). Write down the entries of the edge table of Baumgart's winged-edge data structure for this model.

**Solution 4.2:** The entries are listed in the following table:

| Edge # | Vertices Start | End | Faces Left | Right | Left traverse Pred. | Succ. | Right traverse Pred. | Succ. |
|---|---|---|---|---|---|---|---|---|
| 1 | a | b | C | A | 6 | 5 | 3 | 2 |
| 2 | b | c | D | A | 4 | 6 | 1 | 3 |
| 3 | c | a | B | A | 5 | 4 | 2 | 1 |
| 4 | c | d | D | B | 6 | 2 | 3 | 5 |
| 5 | a | d | B | C | 4 | 3 | 1 | 6 |
| 6 | d | b | D | C | 2 | 4 | 5 | 1 |

The previous table represents the edge table for the tetrahedron shown in Fig. 4.3. □

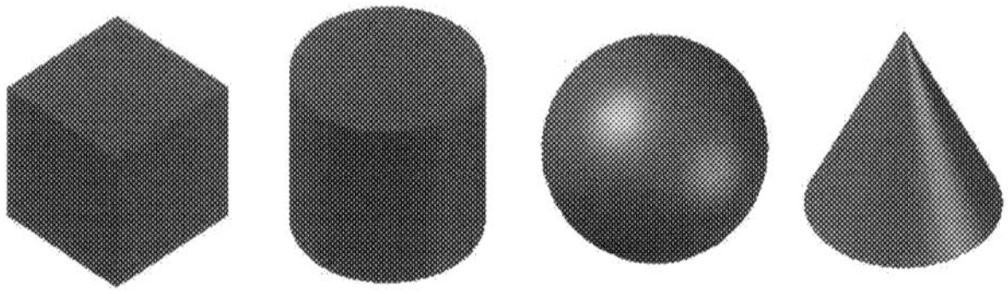

**Fig. 4.6** Examples of solid primitives

## 4.3 Constructive Solid Geometry

*Constructive solid geometry* (CSG) (Requicha 1980) is a technique used in solid modeling. The simplest solids used for the 3D modeling are called primitives. A *solid primitive* is an object of simple shape (e.g., cube, cylinder, sphere, etc.). Examples of solid primitives are shown in Fig. 4.6. A solid primitive is often created through a number of parameters. For example, a sphere is created by passing the location of its center point in addition to its radius. Once a primitive is instantiated, it can be transformed (e.g., translated, rotated or scaled) afterwards. (Transformations in 3D space is discussed in Chap. 5.)

Complex objects can also be created using CSG. This is done by combining two or more solid primitives through Boolean operations. The final complex 3D object or 3D model depends on the primitives used, their transformations (if any), the Boolean operations applied and their order of application.

### *4.3.1 Boolean Operations*

Boolean operations used with solids are similar to those used in set theory. These operations include union, subtraction and intersection. Processed solids for all operations may lie in any number of arbitrary planes. Examples of two solids $A$ and $B$ are shown in Fig. 4.7a.

#### 4.3.1.1 Solid Union

In set theory, the union of sets is a set that contains all the elements in all unionized sets. Thus, if $A$ and $B$ are two sets, the union of $A$ and $B$ (denoted as $A \cup B$) is a single set that contains all elements from $A$ or $B$. An element $x$ is an element in $A \cup B$ if and only if it is an element in $A$ *or* in $B$. For example, the union of the sets $A = \{1, 3, 5\}$ and $B = \{2, 4, 7\}$ is $A \cup B = \{1, 2, 3, 4, 5, 7\}$.

In solid modeling, the *union* operation combines two or more different solids into one composite solid. Figure 4.7b shows the union of two solids; $A$ and $B$. The resulting solid $A \cup B$ includes the total volume enclosed by both solids (i.e., $A$ and $B$). It should be mentioned that the resulting solid is not affected by the order of processing the solids as the overall volume remains unchanged by changing the order.

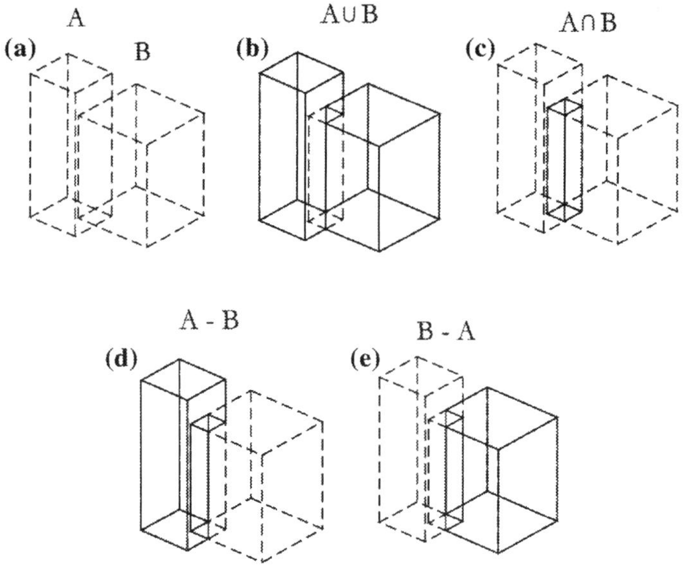


**Fig. 4.7** Boolean operations. **a** Two objects $A$ and $B$. **b** Union operation: $A \cup B$. **c** Intersection operation: $A \cap B$. **d** Subtraction operation: $A - B$. **e** Subtraction operation: $B - A$

#### 4.3.1.2 Solid Intersection

In set theory, the intersection of two sets is a set that contains all the elements that belong to both intersected sets. Thus, if $A$ and $B$ are two sets, the intersection of $A$ and $B$ (denoted as $A \cap B$) is a single set that contains all elements that appear both in $A$ and $B$. An element $x$ is an element in $A \cap B$ if and only if it is an element in $A$ *and* in $B$ as well. For example, the intersection of the sets $A = \{1, 3, 5\}$ and $B = \{3, 5, 7\}$ is $A \cap B = \{3, 5\}$.

In solid modeling, the *intersection* operation calculates the common (overlapping) volume of two or more solids. Figure 4.7c shows the intersection of two solids; $A$ and $B$. It is important to note that the resulting solid is not affected by the order of processing the solids as the overlapping volume remains unchanged by changing the order.

#### 4.3.1.3 Solid Subtraction

In set theory, the subtraction of two sets is a set that contains all the elements that belong to the first set but not the second set. Thus, if $A$ and $B$ are two sets, the subtraction of $A$ and $B$ (denoted as $A \backslash B$ or $A - B$) is a single set that contains all elements that appear in $A$ but not in $B$. An element $x$ is an element in $A \backslash B$ (or $A - B$) if and only if it is an element in $A$ but *not* in $B$. For example, the subtraction of the sets $A = \{1, 3, 5\}$ and $B = \{3, 5, 7\}$ is $A - B = \{1\}$. Unlike the previous two operations, the order in set subtraction is important as $A - B \neq B - A$ (or $A \backslash B \neq B \backslash A$). For the previous sets, $B - A = \{7\}$.

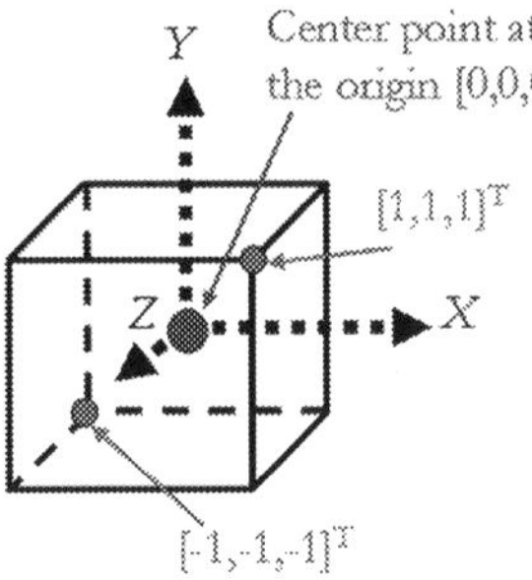


**Fig. 4.8** A cube whose side length is 2 units is centered at the origin $[0, 0, 0]^T$

In solid modeling, the *subtraction* or the *difference* operation calculates the difference volume resulting from subtracting two or more solids. The difference or subtraction operator is order-dependent. In other words, the order of processing the solids under consideration is very important as it results in quite different solids; e.g., consider Fig. 4.7d, e.

### 4.3.2 CSG Expressions and Trees

Consider the cube shown in Fig. 4.8. It extends from $[-1, -1, -1]^T$ to $[1, 1, 1]^T$ (i.e., each side is 2 units long). This cube is to be transformed into a rectangular block centered at $[1, 2, 3]^T$ and whose side lengths are 2, 3, 3 units along the $x$-, $y$- and $z$-directions respectively. In order to achieve this, the following operations are performed:

1. Scale the cube 1.5 times along the $y$- and $z$-directions. (The scale along the $x$-direction should remain unchanged.)
2. Translate it using a translation vector $[1, 2, 3]^T$.

These operations can be written as

$$translate(scale(Block, < 1, 1.5, 1.5 >), < 1, 2, 3 >).$$

The previous representation is called a *CSG expression*. This expression indicates that there is a solid called "Block" which is scaled using scaling factors of 1, 1.5 and 1.5 along the $x$-, $y$- and $z$-directions respectively. After scaling, this solid gets translated using a translation vector $[1, 2, 3]^T$. Notice that each of the "scale" and "translate" operations takes two arguments each (i.e., the solid to be operated on and the parameters of the operation). Generally, we can write any sequence of operations performed on a solid as a CSG expression.

CSG expressions extend to cover Boolean operations as well as transformation operations as clarified in the following examples.

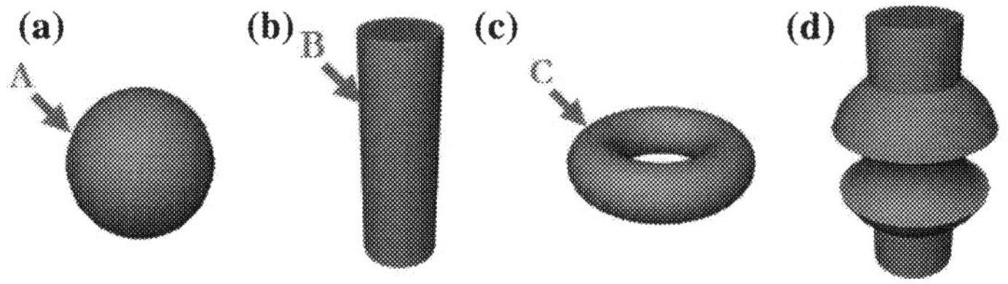


**Fig. 4.9** A CSG example. **a** A sphere $A$. **b** A cylinder $B$. **c** A torus $C$. **d** A solid made of solid primitives

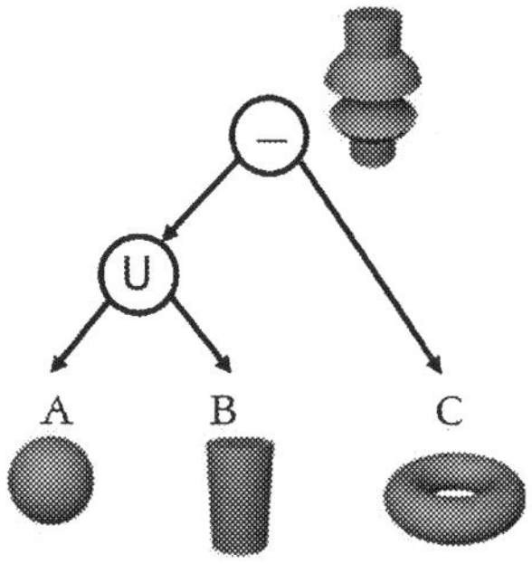


**Fig. 4.10** The CSG tree for the model shown in Fig. 4.9d

**Example 4.3:** [*CSG expressions*]

Suppose that you have three primitives as shown in Fig. 4.9; a sphere, $A$, a cylinder $B$ and a torus $C$. It is required to have the result shown in Fig. 4.9d. Determine the steps to follow and derive the CSG expression.

**Solution 4.3:** The result of Fig. 4.9d is achieved by unionizing $A$ and $B$ and subtracting $C$ from them. This can be written as a CSG expression:

$$diff(union(A, B), C)$$

or

$$A \cup B - C.$$

The CSG expression represents the final structure of the solid. □

Any solid can be expressed as a CSG expression. In turn, every CSG expression is associated with a *CSG tree*, which also represents the solid. The CSG tree representing the solid of Fig. 4.9d is shown in Fig. 4.10. A CSG tree may be implemented as a tree data structure with operators at the internal or branch nodes and simple primitives at the leaves. (Some internal nodes represent Boolean operators while others represent translation, rotation and scaling.)

**Example 4.4:** [*CSG expressions and trees*]

Suppose that you are asked to build a 3D modeling software. This software can create two types of solid primitives; cylinders and cubes. Every primitive instance is

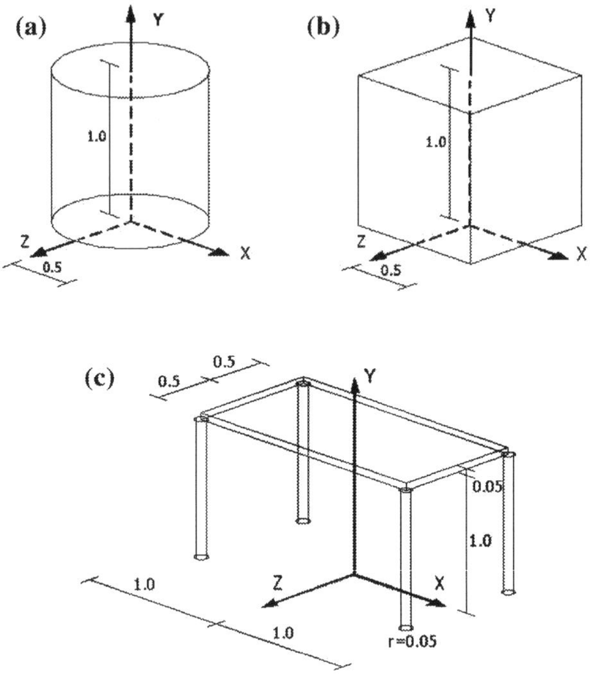


**Fig. 4.11** A CSG example. **a** A unit cylinder. **b** A unit cube. **c** A table made of solid primitives

initially created at the origin of the 3D coordinate space as shown in Fig. 4.11a and b with lengths equal to the unit. You will use these primitives to build a 3D model for a table as shown in Fig. 4.11c. Create the CSG expression required to represent this solid. Build the CSG tree representing the previous expression.

**Solution 4.4:** The top of the table is created as a cube and transformed as follows:

$$trans(Box) = translate(scale(Box, < 2, 0.05, 1 >), < 0, 1, 0 >).$$

Then the four legs are created as cylinders and transformed. This is expressed as

$$\begin{aligned}
trans(Cylinder1) &= translate(scale(Cylinder1, < 0.1, 1, 0.1 >), < 1, 0, 0.5 >),\\
trans(Cylinder2) &= translate(scale(Cylinder2, < 0.1, 1, 0.1 >), < 1, 0, -0.5 >),\\
trans(Cylinder3) &= translate(scale(Cylinder3, < 0.1, 1, 0.1 >), < -1, 0, 0.5 >),\\
trans(Cylinder4) &= translate(scale(Cylinder4, < 0.1, 1, 0.1 >), < -1, 0, -0.5 >).
\end{aligned}$$

All five solids are then unionized. Thus, the CSG expression can be written as

$$\begin{aligned}
&((((trans(Box) \cup trans(Cylinder1)) \cup trans(Cylinder2)) \cup trans(Cylinder3))\\
&\quad \cup trans(Cylinder4)).
\end{aligned}$$

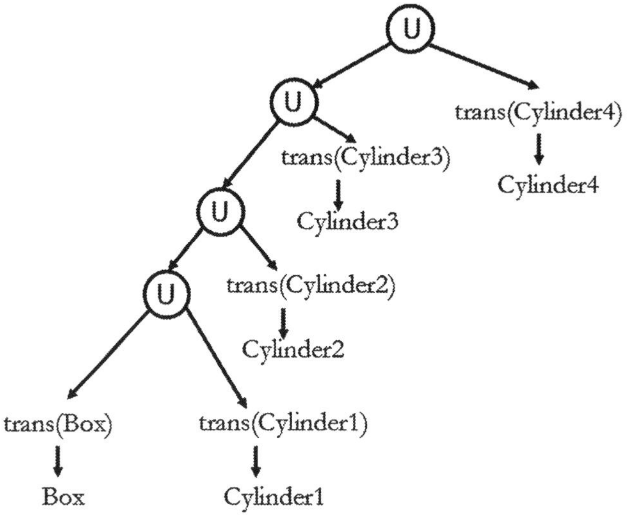


**Fig. 4.12** The CSG tree for the model shown in Fig. 4.11c

The corresponding CSG tree is shown in Fig. 4.12. Pay attention that the order of performing operations affects the nodes in the tree. In some implementations, intersection and union nodes may have any number of children. If this is the case in our example, the tree will contain one union node that has five children representing the transformed primitives. □

### *4.3.3 Regularized Boolean Operations*

The solid Boolean operations applied to solids should result in solids as well. An example is shown in Fig. 4.13a where two cubes are intersecting to produce a 3D solid. However, this is not always the case. In Fig. 4.13b–d, the intersections are a rectangular face, an edge and a point, which do *not* represent 3D solids. In Fig. 4.13e, there is no intersection at all (i.e., an empty set).

In order to avoid the above situation, we need to regularize the Boolean operations. This is done by using interior, closure and exterior of solids. The *interior* of a solid contains all points inside the solid. The *closure* of a solid contains the interior points in addition to the surface points. Boundary or surface points are those points at distance zero from the object and its complement. Finally, the *exterior* of a solid contains points that do not belong to the solid closure. Using these concepts, regularized Boolean operations are performed as follows:

1. The Boolean operation is performed as usual.
2. The interior of the result is computed, which may result in an empty set.
3. The closure of the last step is computed. This adds the boundaries back.

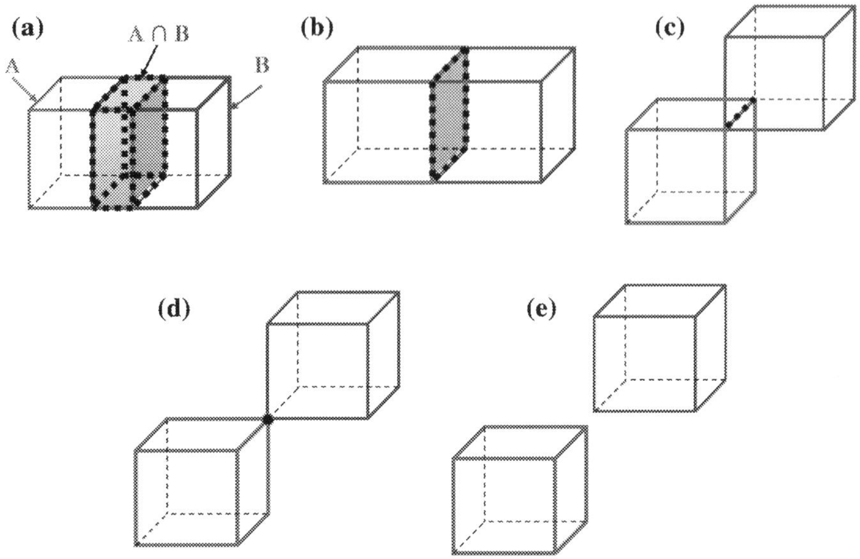


**Fig. 4.13** Boolean intersection operation. **a** The intersection between the cubes is a 3D object. **b** The intersection between the cubes is a rectangular face; i.e., *not* a 3D object. **c** The intersection between the cubes is an edge; i.e., *not* a 3D object. **d** The intersection between the cubes is a point; i.e., *not* a 3D object. **e** No intersection between the cubes

These operations can be expressed for two solids $A$ and $B$ as

$$A \cup^* B = closure(interior(A \cup B)), \tag{4.1}$$

where $\cup$ and $\cup^*$ represent the ordinary and regularized union operators respectively;

$$A \cap^* B = closure(interior(A \cap B)), \tag{4.2}$$

where $\cap$ and $\cap^*$ represent the ordinary and regularized intersection operators respectively; and

$$A -^* B = closure(interior(A - B)), \tag{4.3}$$

where $-$ and $-^*$ represent the ordinary and regularized difference or subtraction operators respectively. In the last example of Fig. 4.13b,

1. the Boolean intersection results in a rectangular face; hence,
2. the interior of a rectangular face is empty. Consequently,
3. the closure of the last step is empty as well.

Similar outcomes are obtained for cases c, d and e of Fig. 4.13.

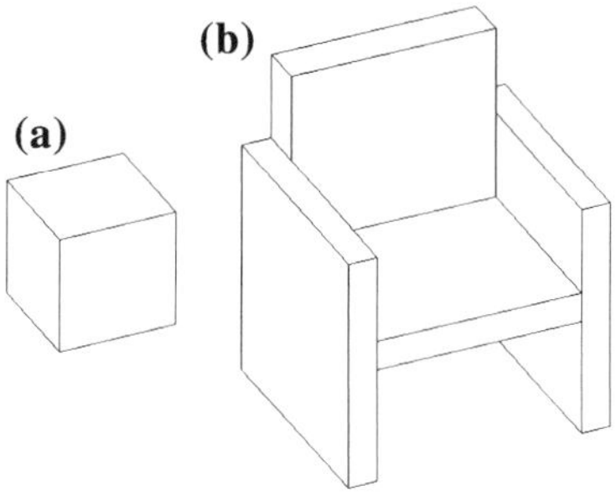


**Fig. 4.14** Cell decomposition. **a** A single cell defined. **b** The cell shown in (**a**) is repeatedly used and transformed to build the model of a chair

## 4.4 Spatial Representations

The *spatial representation* of a solid deals with the solid as a collection of adjacent non-overlapping more primitive solids. This decomposition differs from one representation to another as primitives' shapes vary in sizes, types, etc.

### 4.4.1 Cell Decomposition

*Cell decomposition* (Requicha 1980) is a spatial representation method used to build solids. A cell decomposition system defines a set of primitives that can be parameterized to produce parts of the model. Those parts should not intersect and each two adjacent parts should share at least a single point, edge or face. The parts are then glued together
(Foley et al. 1995) in a process that is similar to the union process that is used with CSG solids. Figure 4.14b shows an example of a chair built using the cell decomposition method where only one cell type (cuboid) is defined as shown in Fig. 4.14a. The parts (i.e., the cuboids) are transformed and glued together.

### 4.4.2 Spatial Enumeration

In *spatial enumeration*, (Requicha 1980) the space is split into equal-sized small *volume elements* or *voxels*. A voxel may be vacant or occupied. Voxels that belong to the solid are flagged as occupied. Although not necessary, a voxel is usually a cube. An example of square pyramid built using spatial enumeration is shown in Fig. 4.15 where each voxel is shown as a little cube.

Any 3D model can be represented as a list of occupied voxels. It can be decided if a voxel is occupied or vacant by testing its position and coordinates against the borders of the 3D object represented.

**Fig. 4.15** Spatial enumeration: a square pyramid built as a collection of voxels

**Example 4.5:** [*Spatial enumeration*]

A sphere whose radius is 5 units and centered at the origin is to be represented as voxels. The voxel size is $1 \times 1 \times 1$ units. The center point of each voxel has integer coordinates (e.g., $[0, 0, 0]^T$, $[1, 2, 0]^T$, $[2, 4, 3]^T$, ...). A voxel is declared occupied if its center point is inside the sphere. Determine whether the following voxels are declared vacant or occupied: $[2, 4, 2]^T$, $[2, 3, 3]^T$ and $[0, 5, 1]^T$ where these coordinates represent the center points of the voxels.

**Solution 4.5:** A voxel is occupied if the distance from its center to the origin (i.e., the center of the sphere) is less than or equal to the radius of the sphere. The Euclidean distance is given by Eq. (B.9) as

$$d(\dot{\mathbf{P}}_1, \dot{\mathbf{P}}_2) = \sqrt{(x_2 - x_1)^2 + (y_2 - y_1)^2 + (z_2 - z_1)^2};$$

thus,

$$\begin{aligned} d([0, 0, 0]^T, [2, 4, 2]^T) &= \sqrt{(2 - 0)^2 + (4 - 0)^2 + (2 - 0)^2} \\ &= 2\sqrt{6} = 4.899 \leq 5 \Longrightarrow \text{occupied}, \end{aligned}$$

$$\begin{aligned} d([0, 0, 0]^T, [2, 3, 3]^T) &= \sqrt{(2 - 0)^2 + (3 - 0)^2 + (3 - 0)^2} \\ &= \sqrt{22} = 4.6904 \leq 5 \Longrightarrow \text{occupied}, \end{aligned}$$

$$\begin{aligned} d([0, 0, 0]^T, [0, 5, 1]^T) &= \sqrt{(0 - 0)^2 + (5 - 0)^2 + (1 - 0)^2} \\ &= \sqrt{26} = 5.099 > 5 \Longrightarrow \text{vacant}. \end{aligned}$$

Alternatively, a voxel may be declared occupied or vacant when applying its coordinates in the surface equation of a sphere centered at the origin, which is given by

$$x^2 + y^2 + z^2 - r^2 = 0,$$

where $[x, y, z]^T$ and $r$ represent the surface point coordinates and the radius of the sphere respectively. Hence,

$$
\begin{aligned}
2^2+4^2+2^2-5^2 &= -1 \leq 0 \Longrightarrow \text{occupied},\\
2^2+3^2+3^2-5^2 &= -3 \leq 0 \Longrightarrow \text{occupied},\\
0^2+5^2+1^2-5^2 &= +1 > 0 \Longrightarrow \text{vacant}.
\end{aligned}
$$

Once the surface equation is known, determining voxel occupancy is easy. □

Because a voxel can be assigned one of two cases; either vacant or occupied, partially occupied voxels must be approximated. Figure 4.15 illustrates this problem. This approximation can only disappear if all faces of the 3D object being modelled are parallel to voxel sides and its vertices coincide with the voxel grid. Note that increasing the resolution of the voxel grid (by decreasing the voxel size) may increase the accuracy of the representation; however, this will increase the memory space required to represent the same 3D object in addition to consume more time for processing the whole space.

Spatial enumeration is particularly useful in medical imaging that deals with volumetric data. For example, stacks of 2D images detailing scanned slices of an organ can be converted into volumetric data represented by voxels.

### *4.4.3 Quadtrees*

The *quadtree* idea for partitioning or subdividing a 2D plane is based on a divide-and-conquer approach (Samet 1984). Such a tree is generated by dividing the 2D plane along two directions into quadrants. Each quadrant could be full, partially full or empty. In case of partially full quadrants, subdivision continues recursively until quadrants are either full or empty (or until a specific tree depth or a minimum area is reached). Following this idea, leaf nodes will represent full and empty quadrants while internal nodes represent partially full quadrants. Quadrants could be numbered from 0 to 3 or named with respect to the center of their parent as SW (south west), SE (south east), NW (north west) and NE (north east); however, no standard numbering or naming exists.

Figure 4.16a shows an example of a 2D pattern. It is required to construct a quadtree representing this pattern using the numbering scheme shown in Fig. 4.16b.

The whole pattern contains both filled and empty parts; thus, the root of the quadtree is represented as a partially full node. A new level is generated and the pattern is divided into four quadrants, which are numbered as shown. It is obvious that the quadrants "0," "1," and "3" are full while quadrant "2" is partially full. Hence, a new level is generated and quadrant "2" is divided into four sub-quadrants and so on. The whole tree is shown in Fig. 4.16c.

**Example 4.6:** [*Quadtree partitioning*] Construct a quadtree to partition the 2D pattern shown in Fig. 4.17a. The order of constructing nodes is given by

| | |
|---|---|
| 2 | 3 |
| 0 | 1 |

.

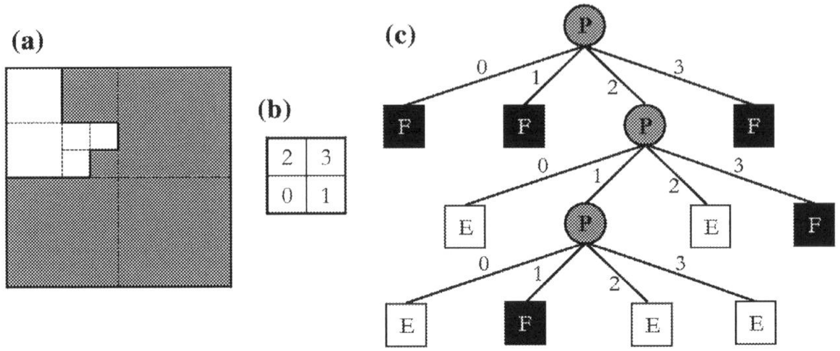


**Fig. 4.16** **a** A 2D pattern. **b** The numbering of quadrants. **c** A quadtree constructed for the pattern shown in (**a**). "F" represents full quadrants, "P" represents partially full quadrants and "E" represents empty quadrants

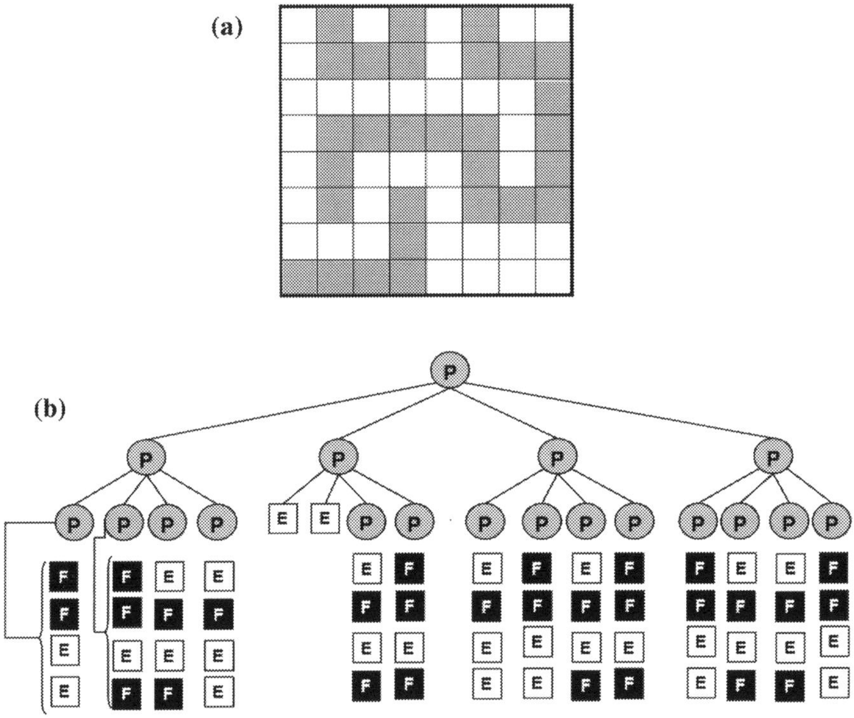


**Fig. 4.17** **a** A 2D pattern. **b** A quadtree constructed for the pattern shown in (**a**). "F" represents full quadrants, "P" represents partially full quadrants and "E" represents empty quadrants

**Solution 4.6:** The quadtree for the 2D pattern shown in Fig. 4.17a is constructed and shown in Fig. 4.17b. □

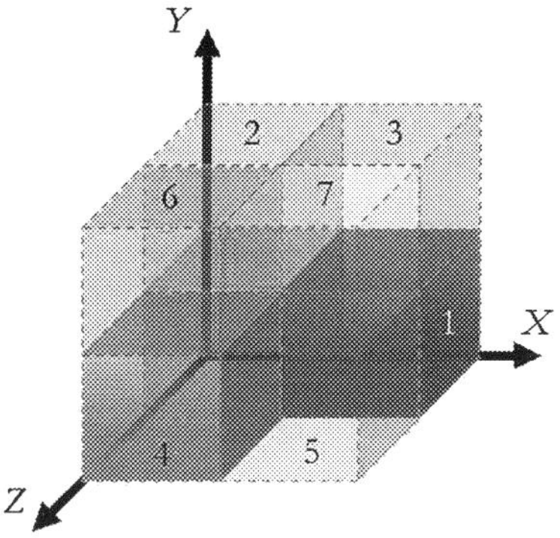


**Fig. 4.18** In octrees, a node is split into eight octants. An example of octant numbering is shown

### 4.4.4 Octrees

*Octrees* (Meagher 1982) can be regarded as the extension of quadtrees in 3D space. Similar to quadtrees, octrees are based on a divide-and-conquer approach; however, splitting or division is performed in 3D space along all three directions so that eight octants are generated for each partially full node at the next level instead of four quadrants in the quadtree case.

Each octant could be full, partially full or empty. In case of partially full octants, subdivision continues recursively until octants are either full or empty (or until a specific tree depth or a minimum volume is reached). Following this idea, leaf nodes will represent full and empty octants while internal nodes represent partially full octants. An example of numbering the octants is shown in Fig. 4.18.

**Example 4.7:** [*Solids as octrees*]

Figure 4.19a shows a 3D model. It is required to construct an octree representing this model using the numbering scheme shown in Fig. 4.18.

**Solution 4.7:** The octree for the model of Fig. 4.19a is shown in Fig. 4.19b. Note that there are filled and empty parts (indicated by solid and dashed lines); thus, the root of the octree is represented as a partially full node. A new level is generated and the partially filled root is divided into eight octants, which are numbered as shown. It is obvious that octants "0," "1," "2," "4" and "5" are full, octant "7" is empty while octants "3" and "6" are partially full. Hence, a new level is generated and each of octants "3" and "6" are divided into eight sub-octants where each of those sub-octants is either full or empty. □

### 4.4.5 Bintrees

Instead of dividing along all three axes in octrees, a bintree divides a partially full node about a single axis into two halves alternating among axes at each level

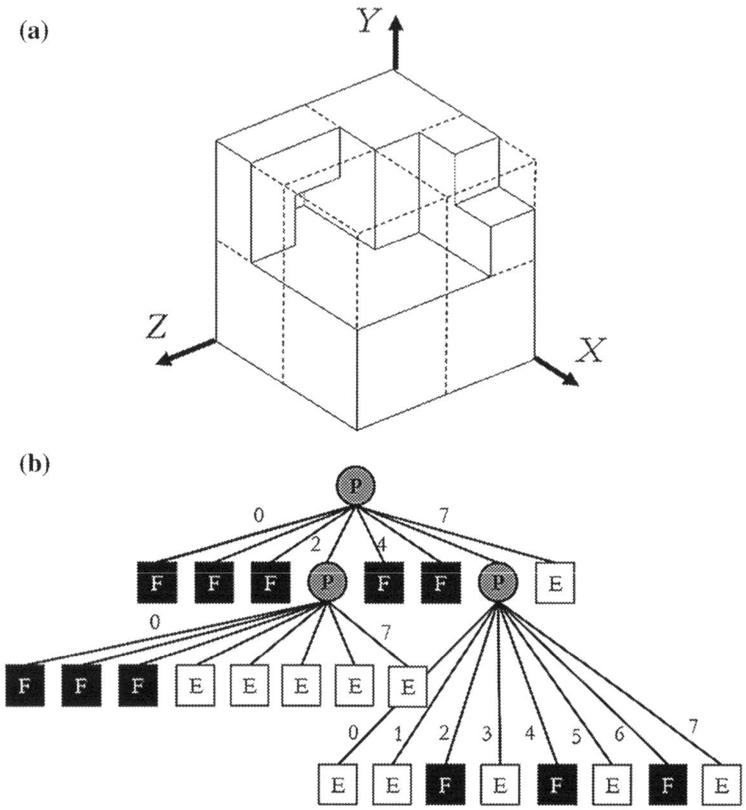


**Fig. 4.19** **a** A 3D model. **b** The octree constructed for the model shown in (**a**). "F" represents full octants, "P" represents partially full octants and "E" represents empty octants

**Fig. 4.20** A 2D pattern.

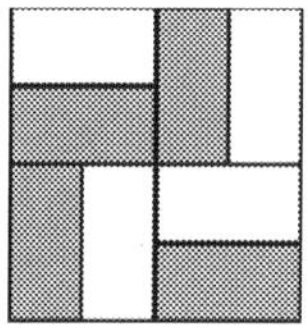

(Tamminen 1984; Samet and Tamminen 1985; Bao and Grabowski 1998). However, the number of nodes in a bintree is greater than those in quadtrees and octrees.

**Example 4.8:** [*Bintree partitioning*]

If a bintree is constructed to partition the 2D pattern shown in Fig. 4.17a, what would be the maximum depth of that bintree? (The depth of a node is the length of the path from the root to the node.)

**Solution 4.8:** The max depth of a bintree is 6. (If the whole pattern is $8 \times 8$, the nodes of the subsequent levels will be $4 \times 8$, $4 \times 4$, $2 \times 4$, $2 \times 2$, $1 \times 2$ and $1 \times 1$.) □

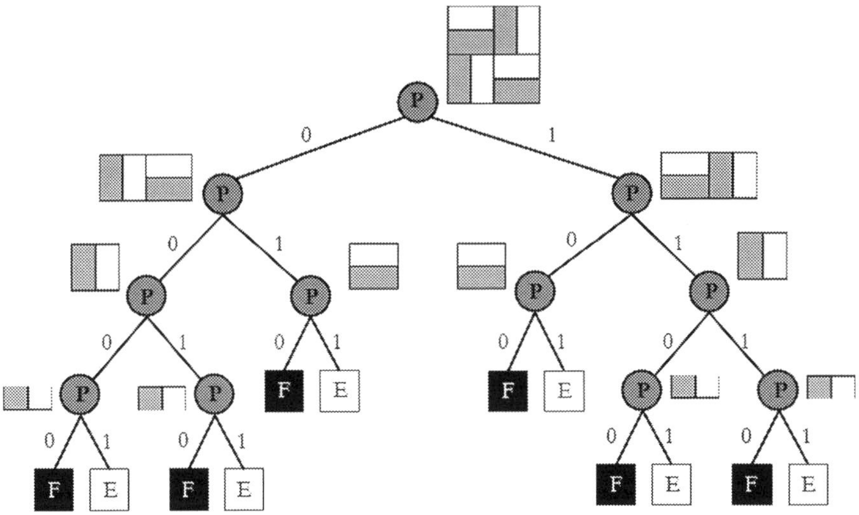


**Fig. 4.21** The bintree constructed for the pattern shown in Fig. 4.20. The letter “F” represents full nodes, “P” represents partially full nodes and “E” represents empty nodes

**Example 4.9:** [*Bintree partitioning*]

Construct the bintree for the pattern shown in Fig. 4.20. The splitting is to be done horizontally then vertically and continues until each leaf node is either empty or full. The order of constructing nodes is given by

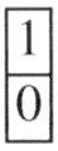


and

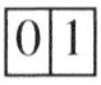


for horizontal and vertical splitting respectively.

**Solution 4.9:** The bintree is constructed and shown in Fig. 4.21. The order of the nodes is shown as numbers “0” and “1”. The letter “F” represents full nodes, “P” represents partially full nodes and “E” represents empty nodes. □

### 4.4.6 Binary Space-Partitioning Trees

A *binary space partitioning* (BSP) *tree* splits the space into two sub-spaces. The subdivision process continues recursively until a stopping condition is met. Unlike other partitioning processes, planes used for partitioning may be of any orientation and location. In fact, surfaces of the solid being represented are used as the dividing planes.

The process of building the BSP tree starts by choosing a dividing plane to represent the root of the tree. This plane splits the whole space into two sub-spaces representing two children for the root; in front and in back of this plane. The direction can be determined by the normal to the plane. (We assume that all normals are

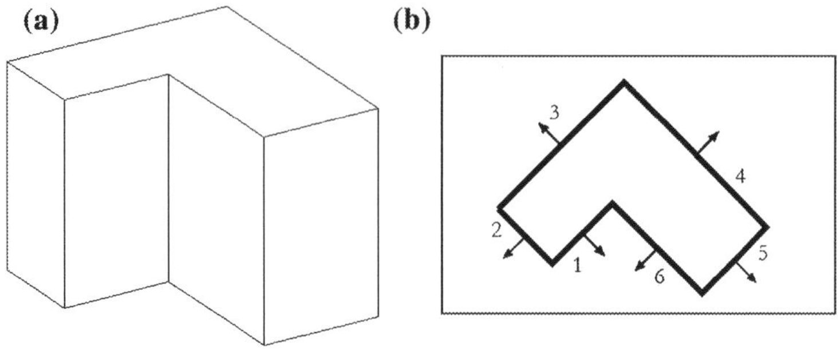


**Fig. 4.22** **a** A 3D model. **b** The top view of the 3D model

pointing out of the object.) Hence, one child represents the "in" sub-space while the other one represents the "out" sub-space. The process is repeated recursively for each sub-space. It stops when the sub-space is entirely "in" or "out" the solid. More details may be found in Thibault and Naylor (1987a,b).

Note that BSP trees can also be used to solve the visibility problem. This is discussed in Sect. 10.5.1.

**Example 4.10:** [*Models as BSP trees*]

A 3D model is shown in Fig. 4.22a. The top view of this model is shown in Fig. 4.22b. The arrows shown indicate the outside directions of the faces. Represent this model using a BSP tree. For simplicity, you may work with the top view (i.e., ignore top and bottom surfaces). Also, you may start with face "3."

**Solution 4.10:** The partitioning process starts with splitting the space along face "3" as shown in Fig. 4.23a. This step corresponds to creating the root of the BSP tree. Also, it creates two sub-spaces; one in front of face "3" (i.e., the "out" sub-space) and the other behind it (i.e., the "in" sub-space) as shown in Fig. 4.23b. The "out" sub-space is empty while the "in" sub-space contains the other faces; i.e., faces "4," "5," "6," "1" and "2".

Face "4" is considered to partition the "in" sub-space as shown in Fig. 4.23c. Hence, a node is created for face "4". Also, two sub-spaces are created; one in front of face "4" (i.e., the "out" sub-space) and the other behind it (i.e., the "in" sub-space) as shown in Fig. 4.23d. The "out" sub-space is empty while the "in" sub-space contains the other faces; i.e., faces "5," "6," "1" and "2". The steps of partitioning continue the same way as shown in the rest of Fig. 4.23. □

## 4.5 Sweep Representations

Sweeping an object (usually but not necessarily a 2D shape) along a path or about an axis defines another object that is called a *sweep*. Sweeping an object along a path creates a *translational sweep* while sweeping or revolving an object about an axis creates a *rotational sweep* (Requicha 1980). Note that sweeping a 2D shape in its own plane does not generate a 3D object.

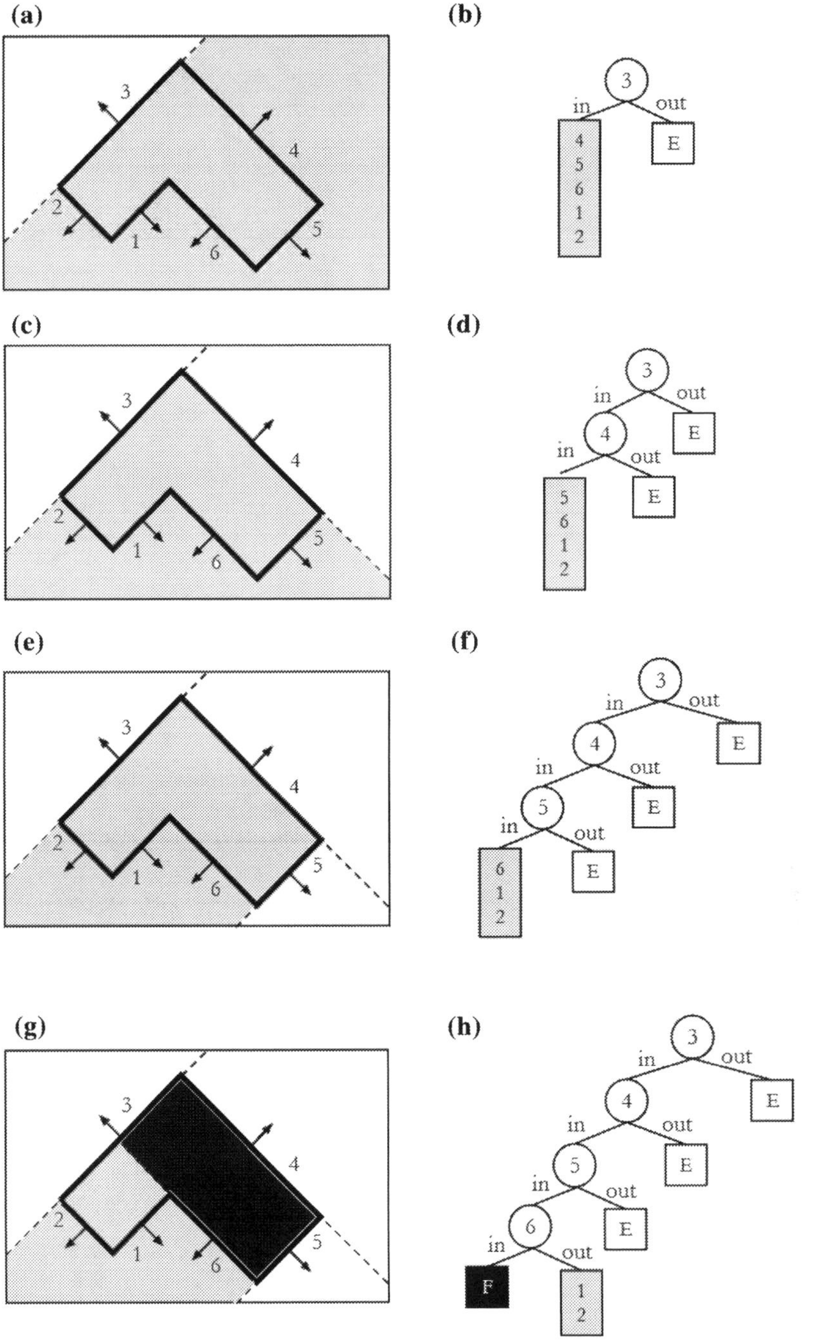


**Fig. 4.23** Binary space partitioning to represent the model shown in Fig. 4.22. *White* nodes represent empty space and *black* nodes represent occupied space while *gray* nodes are those that need further processing

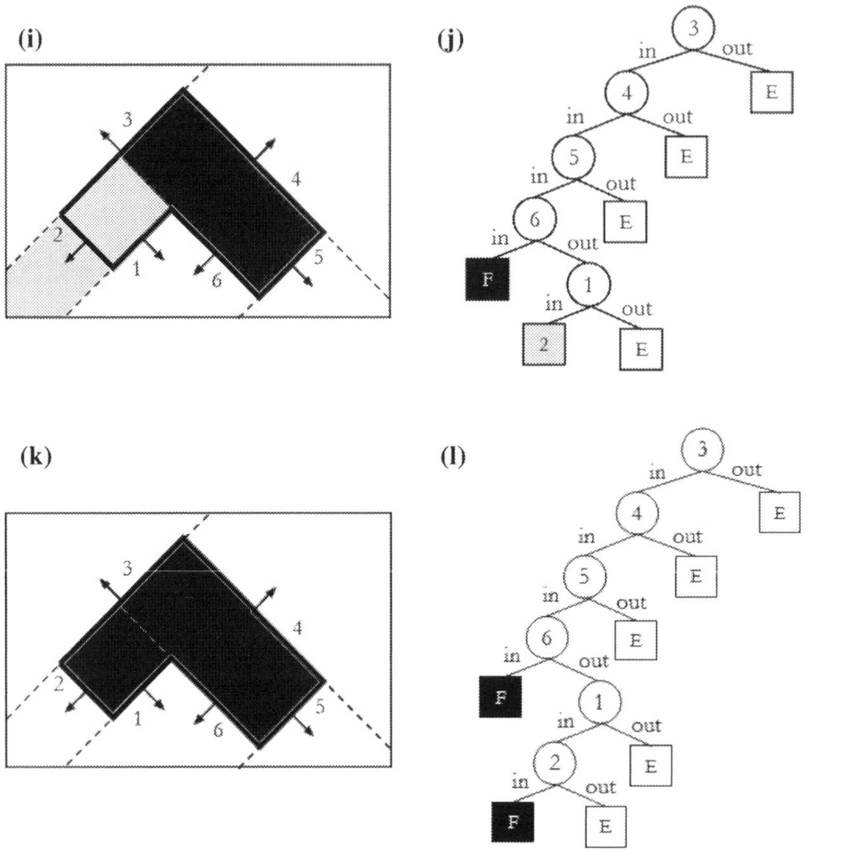


Fig. 4.23 continued

Fig. 4.24 Translational sweeps. **a** A 2D shape and a direction of extrusion. **b** A 3D object created by extruding the 2D shape shown in (**a**) along the direction of extrusion

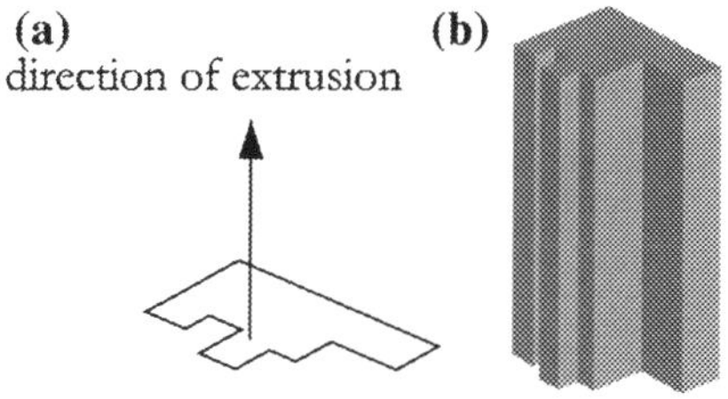


## 4.5.1 Translational Sweeps

The *extrusion*, a *translational sweep* (Rottensteiner 2001), is an important operation that converts a 2D shape located on a plane into a 3D solid model by adding thickness to it. In order to extrude the 2D shape shown in Fig. 4.24a, inputs are required to obtain the result of Fig. 4.24b. The inputs are

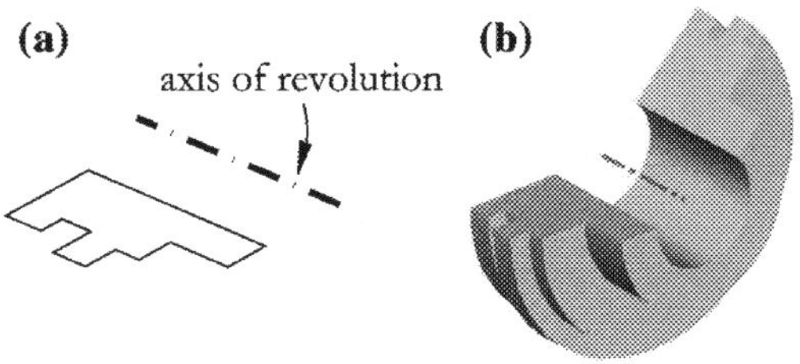


**Fig. 4.25** Rotational sweeps. **a** A 2D shape and an axis of revolution. **b** A 3D object created by revolving the 2D shape shown in (**a**) about the axis of revolution

1. a plan for this object, a cross-section or even an elevation (i.e., orthogonal projections of the object under consideration); and
2. the height and direction of extrusion, which is usually (but not necessarily) perpendicular to the plane of our profile. Note that the direction of extrusion may be linear or curved.

In case the direction of extrusion is perpendicular to the 2D shape being extruded, the volume generated equals to the original 2D area times the length of extrusion. In some cases, the cross section may be scaled along the direction of extrusion; a situation that results in a tapered object. Although a lot of details can be embedded in the profile prior to extrude the object, needs may arise to use Boolean operations afterwards to subtract cavities or add more 3D features.

### *4.5.2 Rotational Sweeps*

The *revolution*, a *rotational sweep*, is another important operation that converts a 2D shape located on a plane into a 3D solid model by revolving it about an axis. In order to revolve the 2D shape shown in Fig. 4.25a, inputs are required to obtain the result of Fig. 4.25b. The inputs are

1. a cross-section for the object;
2. the angle of revolution; and
3. the axis of revolution.

Note that *lathing* is a similar revolving operation where a curve can rotate about an axis.

## 4.6 Polygonal Modeling

In *polygonal modeling*, surfaces or faces are approximated by 3-sided polygons (i.e., triangular faces) where a polygon edge is a straight line connecting two vertices. In this case, each face is a planar surface for which a normal vector can be calculated easily as a cross product of two edges to help with shading and rendering. A group of adjacent faces comprises what is called a *polygonal mesh*. An example of a polygonal

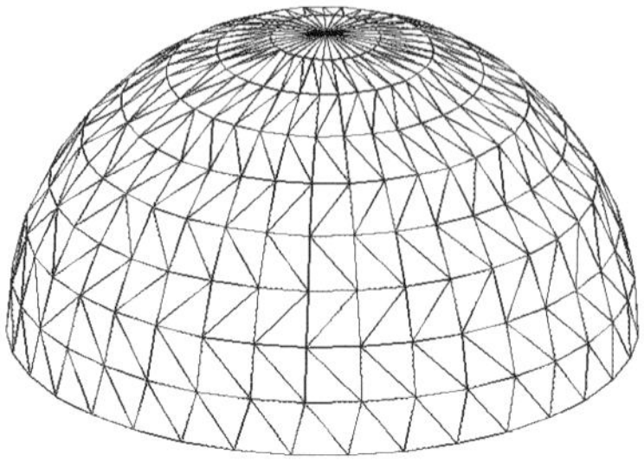

**Fig. 4.26** A semi-sphere represented as a polygonal mesh consisting of vertices, edges and polygons. In general, a mesh may not take the form of a regular pattern

**Table 4.3** Face table for independent faces representation

| Face | Vertices |
|---|---|
| A | $[x_1, y_1, z_1]^T, [x_2, y_2, z_2]^T, [x_3, y_3, z_3]^T$ |
| B | $[x_2, y_2, z_2]^T, [x_4, y_4, z_4]^T, [x_3, y_3, z_3]^T$ |
| ⋮ | ⋮ |

**Table 4.4** Vertex and face tables: **a** Vertex table. **b** Face table

**(a)**

| Vertex | Coordinates |
|---|---|
| 1 | $[x_1, y_1, z_1]^T$ |
| 2 | $[x_2, y_2, z_2]^T$ |
| ⋮ | ⋮ |

**(b)**

| Face | Vertices |
|---|---|
| A | 1, 2, 3 |
| B | 2, 4, 3 |
| ⋮ | ⋮ |

mesh consisting of vertices, edges and polygons is shown in Fig. 4.26. (Generating a polygonal approximation for a smooth surface is referred to as *tessellation.*) In other cases, a face may be approximated by a 4-sided polygon (i.e., quadrilateral face). In such cases, care must be given to ensure that the surrounding four vertices are coplanar. Extrusion and revolution (Sect. 4.5) are among the ways used to create polygonal meshes.

Polygonal meshes are represented through different ways. Among them are winged-edge data structure (discussed in Sect. 4.2.1) independent faces, vertex and face tables, adjacency list and triangle meshes.

**Independent faces:** In this representation, each face is indicated as a sequence of vertex coordinates. An example of face table for independent faces representation is shown in Table 4.3.

**Vertex and face tables**: This representation uses two tables; one for vertices showing vertex numbers and coordinates and another table showing faces and their surrounding vertex numbers. This is also referred to as *indexed face sets* or IFS. An example of this representation is shown in Table 4.4.

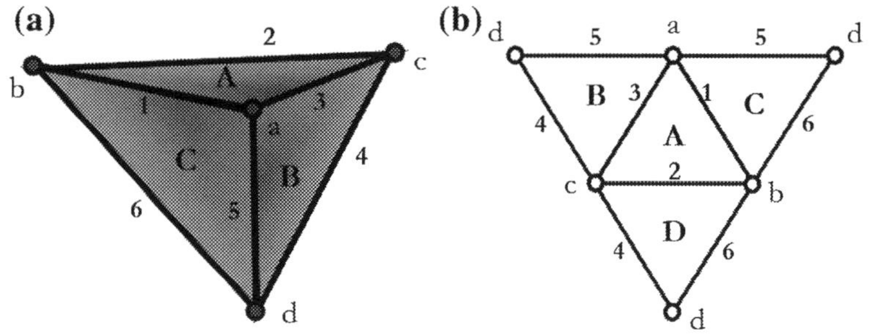


**Fig. 4.27** **a** A tetrahedron. **b** The tetrahedron unfolded

**Adjacency lists** : In this representation, a face is associated with three lists of adjacent vertices, edges and faces, an edge is associated with three lists of adjacent vertices, edges and faces and a vertex is associated with three lists of adjacent vertices, edges and faces. This type of representation provides an efficient way for traversal at the cost of more storage space.

**Triangle meshes**: Here, only triangular faces are considered; hence, three vertices exist per face. However, a vertex may be shared among many faces. For each face, surrounding vertices and adjacent faces are stored.

**Example 4.11:** [*Polygonal modeling*]

Consider the tetrahedron shown in Fig. 4.27a where the vertices are indicated by lowercase letters (i.e., "a," "b," "c" and "d"), the faces by uppercase letters (i.e., "A," "B," "C" and "D") and the edges by digits (i.e., "1," "2," "3," "4," "5" and "6"). The coordinates of the vertices are $[x_a, y_a, z_a]^T$, $[x_b, y_b, z_b]^T$, etc. Write down the entries of the various tables required for the following polygonal modeling representations: Independent faces and vertex and face tables.

**Solution 4.11:** It may be a good idea to unfold the tetrahedron as shown in Fig. 4.27b to simplify the answer. The independent faces are listed below.

| Face | Vertices |
|---|---|
| A | $[x_a, y_a, z_a]^T$, $[x_b, y_b, z_b]^T$, $[x_c, y_c, z_c]^T$ |
| B | $[x_a, y_a, z_a]^T$, $[x_c, y_c, z_c]^T$, $[x_d, y_d, z_d]^T$ |
| C | $[x_a, y_a, z_a]^T$, $[x_d, y_d, z_d]^T$, $[x_b, y_b, z_b]^T$ |
| D | $[x_b, y_b, z_b]^T$, $[x_d, y_d, z_d]^T$, $[x_c, y_c, z_c]^T$ |

The vertex and face tables are listed below.

Fig. 4.28 A roof of a house

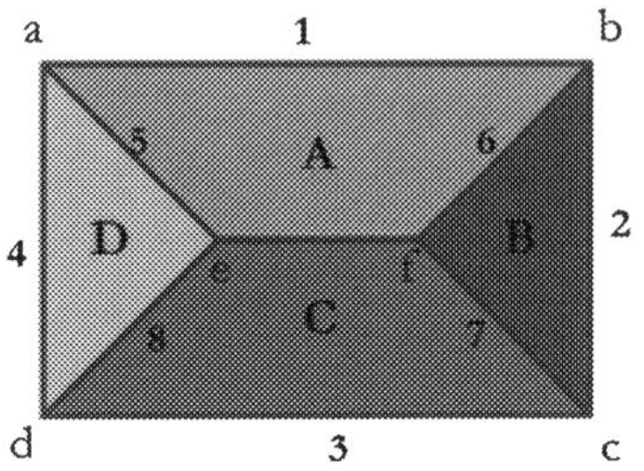


| Vertex | Coordinates | Face | Vertices |
|---|---|---|---|
| a | $[x_a, y_a, z_a]^T$ | A | a, b, c |
| b | $[x_b, y_b, z_b]^T$ | B | a, c, d |
| c | $[x_c, y_c, z_c]^T$ | C | a, d, b |
| d | $[x_d, y_d, z_d]^T$ | D | b, d, c |

□

**Example 4.12:** [*Polygonal modeling* ]

In Example 4.11, determine the adjacency lists for face "A," edge "1" and vertex "a."

**Solution 4.12:** Let us use the unfolded tetrahedron of Fig. 4.27b. The adjacency lists are listed below.

| Entity | Faces | Edges | Vertices |
|---|---|---|---|
| Face A | B, C, D | 3, 1, 2 | a, b, c |
| Edge 1 | A, C | 2, 3, 5, 6 | b, a |
| Vertex a | B, C, A | 3, 5, 1 | c, d, b |

□

## 4.7 Problems

**Problem 4.1:** [*Wireframe modeling*]

The roof of a house shown in Fig. 4.28 is represented as a wireframe where the vertices are indicated by lowercase letters (i.e., "a," "b," "c," ...), the faces by uppercase letters (i.e., "A," "B," "C," ...) and the edges by digits (i.e., "1," "2," "3," ...). The coordinates of the vertices are $[x_a, y_a, z_a]^T$, $[x_b, y_b, z_b]^T$, etc. Write down the entries of the vertex and edge tables.

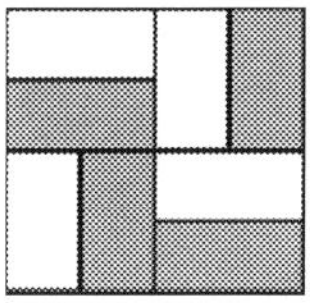

Fig. 4.29 A 2D pattern

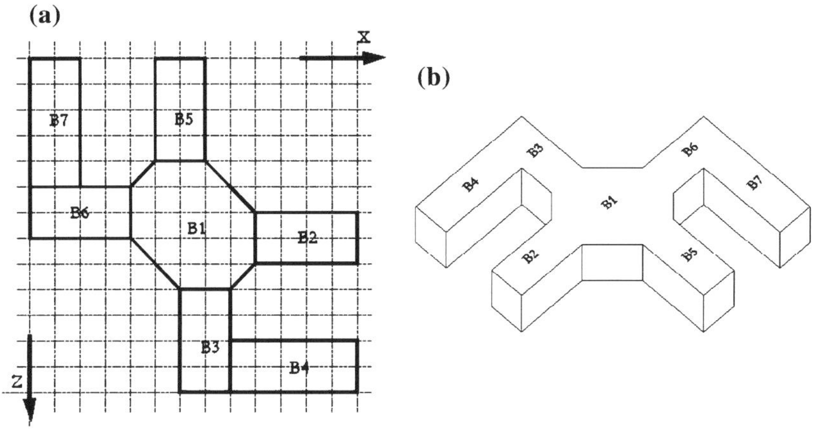


**Fig. 4.30** **a** A plan (i.e., a *top* view) of a series of connected buildings. **b** The buildings as a 3D object

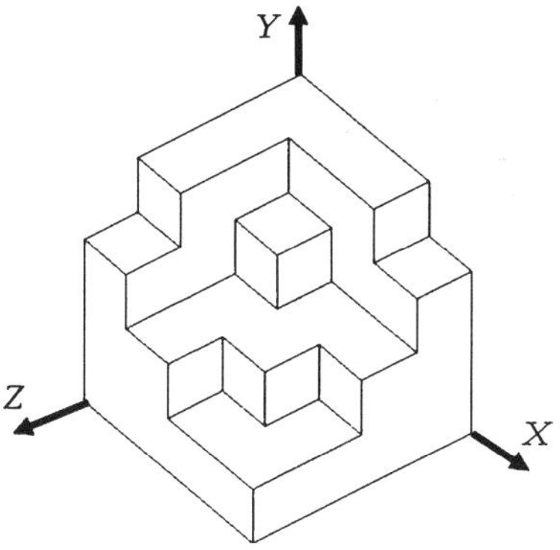


**Fig. 4.31** A 3D model

**Problem 4.2:** [*Quadtree partitioning*]

Construct a quadtree representing the pattern shown in Fig. 4.20. The order of constructing nodes is given by

| | |
|---|---|
| 2 | 3 |
| 0 | 1 |

.

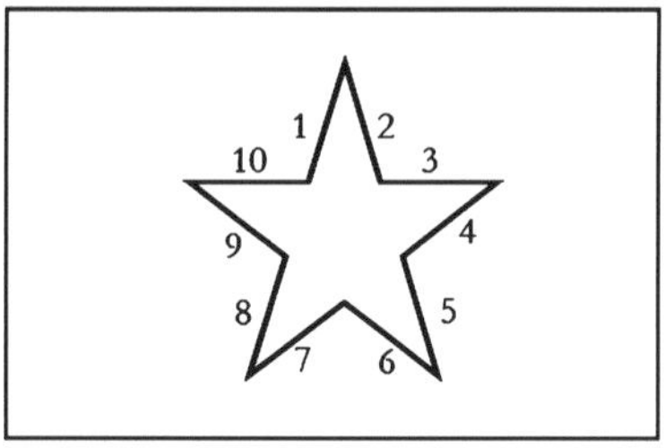


**Fig. 4.32** A top view of a 3D model

**Problem 4.3:** [*Bintree partitioning*]

Construct a bintree to represent the pattern shown in Fig. 4.29. The splitting is to be done horizontally then vertically and continues until each leaf node is either empty or full. The order of constructing nodes is given by

$$\begin{array}{|c|}\hline 1\\\hline 0\\\hline\end{array} \quad \text{and} \quad \begin{array}{|c|c|}\hline 0&1\\\hline\end{array}$$

for horizontal and vertical splitting respectively.

**Problem 4.4:** [*Bintree partitioning*]

Construct a bintree to represent the pattern shown in Fig. 4.16a. The splitting is to be done horizontally then vertically and continues until each leaf node is either empty or full. The order of constructing nodes is given by

$$\begin{array}{|c|}\hline 1\\\hline 0\\\hline\end{array} \quad \text{and} \quad \begin{array}{|c|c|}\hline 0&1\\\hline\end{array}$$

for horizontal and vertical splitting respectively.

**Problem 4.5:** [*CSG expressions and trees*]

Suppose that you are asked to build a 3D modeling software. This software can create only one type of solid primitives; cubes. Every primitive instance is initially created at the origin of the 3D coordinate space as shown in Fig. 4.11b with lengths equal to 1 m.

Figure 4.30a shows a plan (or a top view) for a series of connected buildings B1, B2, ..., B7. These buildings are placed on a grid of $10 \times 10$ m (i.e., every side of each grid square has a length of 10 m). The $x$- and $z$-axes are shown and the $y$-axis is perpendicular to both of them and pointing outwards. This means that the origin is at the upper left corner of B7. A 3D model representing the buildings is shown in Fig. 4.30b.

If the height of each of the buildings is 16 m, construct each of these buildings as a solid, transform and unionize them showing the CSG expression including the transformation. Also show the CSG tree as well as the transformation matrices for B1 and B2. (For the part of transformation matrices, refer to Chap. 5.)

**Problem 4.6:** [*Solids as octrees*]

Construct an octree to represent the 3D solid shown in Fig. 4.31. The numbering of octants is given in Fig. 4.18.

**Problem 4.7:** [*BSP trees*]

Construct a BSP tree to represent a 3D solid whose top view is shown in Fig. 4.32. Assume that all normals are pointing outwards. Ignore the top and bottom surfaces of the model.

**Problem 4.8:** [*Polygonal modeling*]

The roof of a house is shown in Fig. 4.28 where the vertices are indicated by lowercase letters (i.e., "a," "b," "c," ...), the faces by uppercase letters (i.e., "A," "B," "C," ...) and the edges by digits (i.e., "1," "2," "3," ...). The coordinates of the vertices are $[x_a, y_a, z_a]^T$, $[x_b, y_b, z_b]^T$, etc. Write down the entries of the various tables required for the following polygonal modeling representations: Independent faces and vertex and face tables.

**Problem 4.9:** [*Polygonal modeling*]

Determine the rest of adjacency lists in Example 4.12. Also, determine the lists required for triangle mesh representation.

## References


Bao, Z., and H. Grabowski. 1998. Converting boundary representations to exact bintrees. *Computers in Industry* 37(1): 55–66.

Baumgart, B.G. 1972. Winged edge polyhedron representation. Technical report, Stanford: Stanford University.

Baumgart, B.G. 1974. Geometric modeling for computer vision. PhD thesis, Stanford: Stanford University. AAI7506806.

Baumgart, B.G. 1975. A polyhedron representation for computer vision. *Proceedings of the May 19–22, 1975, national computer conference and exposition, AFIPS '75*, pages 589–596, New York, ACM.

Foley, J.D., van Dam, A., Feiner, S.K. and Hughes, J. 1995. *Computer graphics: Principles and practice in C.* The systems programming series, Boston: Addison-Wesley, 2nd ed.

Meagher, D. 1982. Geometric modeling using octree encoding. *Computer Graphics and Image Processing* 19: 129–147.

Requicha, A.G. 1980. Representations for rigid solids: Theory, methods, and systems. *ACM Computing Surveys* 12(4): 437–464.

Rottensteiner, F. 2001. *Semi-automatic extraction of buildings based on hybrid adjustment using 3D surface models and management of building data in a TIS.* Wien: Geowissenschaftliche Mitteilungen. Inst. für Photogrammetrie u. Fernerkundung d. Techn. Univ.

Samet, H. 1984. The quadtree and related hierarchical data structures. *Computing Surveys* 16(2): 187–260.

Samet, H. and Tamminen, M. 1985. Bintrees, csg trees, and time. *Proceedings of the 12th annual conference on computer graphics and interactive techniques, SIGGRAPH '85*, pages 121–130, New York, NY, USA. ACM.

Tamminen, M. 1984. Comment on quad—and octrees. *Communications of the ACM* 27(3): 248–249.

Thibault, W.C., and B.F. Naylor. 1987a. Set operations on polyhedra using binary space partitioning trees. *SIGGRAPH Computer Graphics* 21(4): 153–162.

Thibault, W.C. and Naylor, B.F. 1987b. Set operations on polyhedra using binary space partitioning trees. *Proceedings of the 14th annual conference on computer graphics and interactive techniques, SIGGRAPH '87*, pages 153–162, New York, NY, USA. ACM.

# Chapter 5
# Transformations in 3D Space

**Abstract** Similar to transformations in 2D space discussed in Chap. 3, transformation operations can be applied to objects in 3D space. Those operations change the status of objects. Points of interest like vertices are those that undergo the transformation operations. For example, in order to rotate a tetrahedron that is composed of four triangular faces, only its four vertices need to be rotated. The basic 3D transformation operations include translation, rotation, scaling, reflection and shearing. Many publications handled such operations (e.g., Foley et al. 1995, Vince11, Ammeraal07). We will discuss each of these operations in the rest of this chapter.

## 5.1 Translation in 3D Space

The translation operation in 3D space is performed when a 3D point is moved or *translated* from a position $\dot{\mathbf{P}}_1 = [x_1, y_1, z_1]^T$ to another position $\dot{\mathbf{P}}_2 = [x_2, y_2, z_2]^T$ (Fig. 5.1). In this case, the magnitude and direction of translation (or movement) are characterized by the 3D vector $\mathbf{t} = [t_x, t_y, t_z]^T = [x_2 - x_1, y_2 - y_1, z_2 - z_1]^T$. This vector is referred to as the *translation vector*. In other words, the 3D translation operation can be expressed as

$$\underbrace{\begin{bmatrix} x_2 \\ y_2 \\ z_2 \end{bmatrix}}_{\dot{\mathbf{P}}_2} = \underbrace{\begin{bmatrix} x_1 \\ y_1 \\ z_1 \end{bmatrix}}_{\dot{\mathbf{P}}_1} + \underbrace{\begin{bmatrix} t_x \\ t_y \\ t_z \end{bmatrix}}_{\mathbf{t}}. \tag{5.1}$$

As done previously in 2D space, translation in 3D space can be expressed in homogeneous coordinates (Sect. B.7). In order to translate a homogeneous 3D point $\mathbf{P} = [x_1, y_1, z_1, 1]^T$ to another homogeneous 3D point $\mathbf{P}_2 = [x_2, y_2, z_2, 1]^T$, we use

R. Elias, *Digital Media*, DOI: 10.1007/978-3-319-05137-6_5,

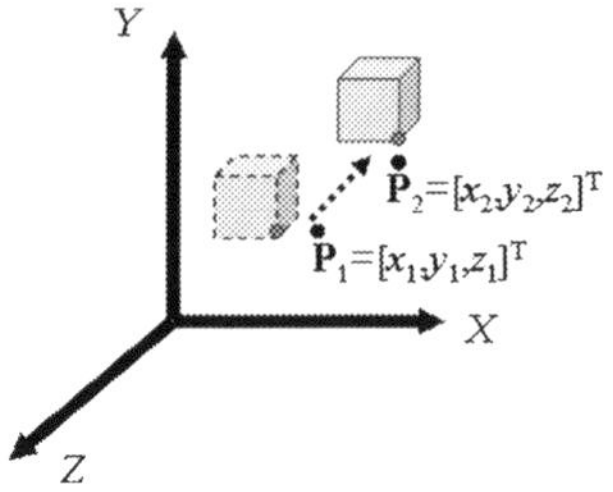


**Fig. 5.1** Translation (or movement) in 3D space. An inhomogeneous 3D point $\dot{\mathbf{P}}_1$ is translated to another 3D point $\dot{\mathbf{P}}_2$

$$\underbrace{\begin{bmatrix} x_2 \\ y_2 \\ z_2 \\ 1 \end{bmatrix}}_{\mathbf{P}_2} = \underbrace{\begin{bmatrix} 1 & 0 & 0 & t_x \\ 0 & 1 & 0 & t_y \\ 0 & 0 & 1 & t_z \\ 0 & 0 & 0 & 1 \end{bmatrix}}_{\mathtt{T}([t_x,t_y,t_z]^T)} \underbrace{\begin{bmatrix} x_1 \\ y_1 \\ z_1 \\ 1 \end{bmatrix}}_{\mathbf{P}_1}, \tag{5.2}$$

where $\mathtt{T}$ is a $4 \times 4$ matrix representing the translation operation for homogeneous points in 3D space; and $[t_x, t_y, t_z]^T$ is the translation vector.

**Example 5.1:** [*3D translation*]
Translate a point $\dot{\mathbf{P}}_1 = [-2, 6, 3]^T$ using a translation vector $\mathbf{t} = [4, -3, 8]^T$.

**Solution 5.1:** In inhomogeneous coordinates, point $\dot{\mathbf{P}}_2$ (i.e., after translation) is expressed as

$$\dot{\mathbf{P}}_2 = \underbrace{\begin{bmatrix} -2 \\ 6 \\ 3 \end{bmatrix}}_{\dot{\mathbf{P}}_1} + \underbrace{\begin{bmatrix} 4 \\ -3 \\ 8 \end{bmatrix}}_{\mathbf{t}} = \underbrace{\begin{bmatrix} 2 \\ 3 \\ 11 \end{bmatrix}}_{\dot{\mathbf{P}}_2}$$

and in homogeneous coordinates, point $\mathbf{P}_2$ (i.e., after translation) is expressed as

$$\mathbf{P}_2 = \underbrace{\begin{bmatrix} 1 & 0 & 0 & 4 \\ 0 & 1 & 0 & -3 \\ 0 & 0 & 1 & 8 \\ 0 & 0 & 0 & 1 \end{bmatrix}}_{\mathtt{T}([4,-3,8]^T)} \underbrace{\begin{bmatrix} -2 \\ 6 \\ 3 \\ 1 \end{bmatrix}}_{\mathbf{P}_1} = \underbrace{\begin{bmatrix} 2 \\ 3 \\ 11 \\ 1 \end{bmatrix}}_{\mathbf{P}_2}. \qquad \square$$

## 5.2 Rotation in 3D Space

A point can be rotated in 3D space if the axis of rotation as well as the angle of rotation are specified. Rotation in 3D can be performed about any of the principal axes or even about an arbitrary axis.

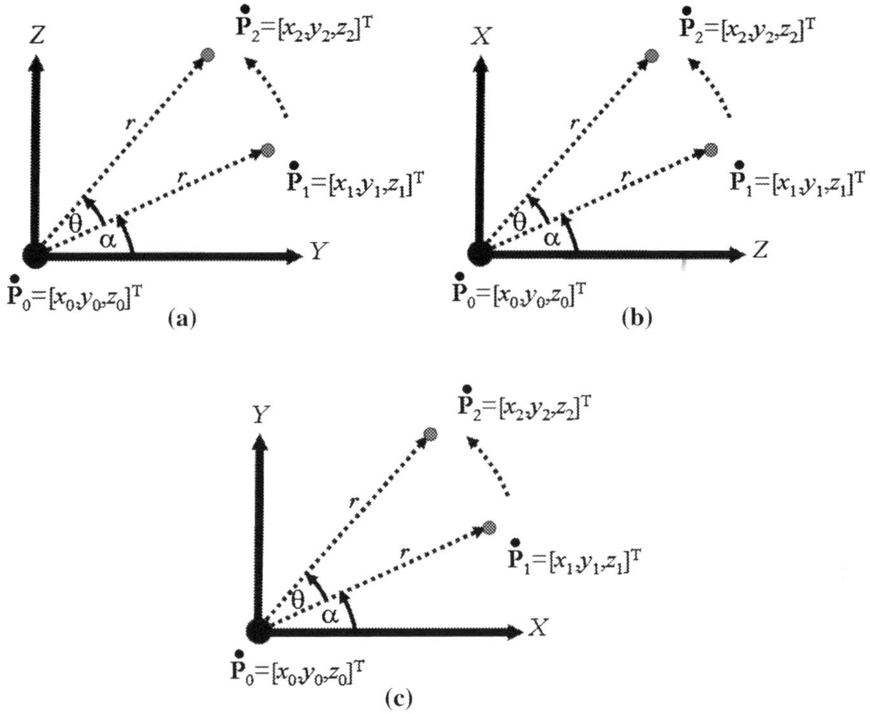


**Fig. 5.2** Rotation in 3D space. **a** An inhomogeneous point $\dot{\mathbf{P}}_1 = [x_1, y_1, z_1]^T$ is rotated about the $x$-axis to another point $\dot{\mathbf{P}}_2 = [x_2, y_2, z_2]^T$. The $x$-axis is perpendicular to both $y$- and $z$-axes and pointing outwards. **b** An inhomogeneous point $\dot{\mathbf{P}}_1 = [x_1, y_1, z_1]^T$ is rotated about the $y$-axis to another point $\dot{\mathbf{P}}_2 = [x_2, y_2, z_2]^T$. The $y$-axis is perpendicular to both $z$- and $x$-axes and pointing outwards. **c** An inhomogeneous point $\dot{\mathbf{P}}_1 = [x_1, y_1, z_1]^T$ is rotated about the $z$-axis to another point $\dot{\mathbf{P}}_2 = [x_2, y_2, z_2]^T$. The $z$-axis is perpendicular to both $x$- and $y$-axes and pointing outwards

### *5.2.1 Rotation About the x-Axis*

As depicted in Fig. 5.2a, a point $\dot{\mathbf{P}}_1 = [x_1, y_1, z_1]^T$ is rotated about the $x$-axis through an angle $\theta$ to another point $\dot{\mathbf{P}}_2 = [x_2, y_2, z_2]^T$. If $\dot{\mathbf{P}}_1$ is at a distance $r$ from the origin, its coordinates can be expressed as $[x_1, r\ \cos(\alpha), r\ \sin(\alpha)]^T$ where $\alpha$ is the inclination angle[1] of the projection of the line $\overline{\dot{\mathbf{P}}_0\dot{\mathbf{P}}_1}$ onto the $yz$-plane with respect to the $y$-axis.

After the rotation, point $\dot{\mathbf{P}}_2$ can be expressed as $[x_1, r\ \cos(\alpha+\theta), r\ \sin(\alpha+\theta)]^T$. From basic trigonometry, we know that

$$\sin(\alpha+\theta) = \sin(\alpha)\cos(\theta) + \cos(\alpha)\sin(\theta) \tag{5.3}$$

[1] Note that the positive direction of the rotation about the $x$-axis in 3D space is the direction of rotation from the $y$-axis to the $z$-axis.

and

$$\cos(\alpha + \theta) = \cos(\alpha)\cos(\theta) - \sin(\alpha)\sin(\theta). \tag{5.4}$$

Applying Eqs. (5.3) and (5.4) to the coordinates of the point after rotation, we get

$$\begin{aligned}
\underbrace{\begin{bmatrix} x_2 \\ y_2 \\ z_2 \end{bmatrix}}_{\dot{\mathbf{P}}_2} &= \begin{bmatrix} x_1 \\ r\cos(\alpha+\theta) \\ r\sin(\alpha+\theta) \end{bmatrix} \\
&= \begin{bmatrix} x_1 \\ r\,(\cos(\alpha)\cos(\theta) - \sin(\alpha)\sin(\theta)) \\ r\,(\sin(\alpha)\cos(\theta) + \cos(\alpha)\sin(\theta)) \end{bmatrix} \\
&= \begin{bmatrix} x_1 \\ \underbrace{r\cos(\alpha)}_{y_1}\cos(\theta) - \underbrace{r\sin(\alpha)}_{z_1}\sin(\theta) \\ \underbrace{r\sin(\alpha)}_{z_1}\cos(\theta) + \underbrace{r\cos(\alpha)}_{y_1}\sin(\theta) \end{bmatrix} \\
&= \begin{bmatrix} x_1 \\ y_1\cos(\theta) - z_1\sin(\theta) \\ y_1\sin(\theta) + z_1\cos(\theta) \end{bmatrix}.
\end{aligned}$$

Hence,

$$\underbrace{\begin{bmatrix} x_2 \\ y_2 \\ z_2 \end{bmatrix}}_{\dot{\mathbf{P}}_2} = \underbrace{\begin{bmatrix} 1 & 0 & 0 \\ 0 & \cos(\theta) & -\sin(\theta) \\ 0 & \sin(\theta) & \cos(\theta) \end{bmatrix}}_{\dot{\mathrm{R}}_x(\theta)} \underbrace{\begin{bmatrix} x_1 \\ y_1 \\ z_1 \end{bmatrix}}_{\dot{\mathbf{P}}_1}, \tag{5.5}$$

where $\dot{\mathrm{R}}_x$ is a $3 \times 3$ matrix representing the rotation operation about the $x$-axis for inhomogeneous points in 3D space; and $\theta$ is the angle of rotation. The same operation can be expressed in homogeneous coordinates as

$$\underbrace{\begin{bmatrix} x_2 \\ y_2 \\ z_2 \\ 1 \end{bmatrix}}_{\mathbf{P}_2} = \underbrace{\begin{bmatrix} 1 & 0 & 0 & 0 \\ 0 & \cos(\theta) & -\sin(\theta) & 0 \\ 0 & \sin(\theta) & \cos(\theta) & 0 \\ 0 & 0 & 0 & 1 \end{bmatrix}}_{\mathrm{R}_x(\theta)} \underbrace{\begin{bmatrix} x_1 \\ y_1 \\ z_1 \\ 1 \end{bmatrix}}_{\mathbf{P}_1}, \tag{5.6}$$

where $\mathrm{R}_x$ is a $4 \times 4$ matrix representing the rotation operation about the $x$-axis for homogeneous points in 3D space; and $\theta$ is the angle of rotation.

### 5.2.2 Rotation About the y-Axis

Also, as depicted in Fig. 5.2b, a point $\dot{\mathbf{P}}_1 = [x_1, y_1, z_1]^T$ is rotated about the $y$-axis through an angle $\theta$ to another point $\dot{\mathbf{P}}_2 = [x_2, y_2, z_2]^T$. If $\dot{\mathbf{P}}_1$ is at a distance $r$ from the origin, its coordinates can be expressed as $[r\ \sin(\alpha), y_1, r\ \cos(\alpha)]^T$ where $\alpha$ is the inclination angle[2] of the projection of the line $\overline{\dot{\mathbf{P}}_0\dot{\mathbf{P}}_1}$ onto the $zx$-plane with respect to the $z$-axis.

After the rotation, point $\dot{\mathbf{P}}_2$ can be expressed as $[r\ \sin(\alpha+\theta), y_1, r\ \cos(\alpha+\theta)]^T$. Applying Eqs. (5.3) and (5.4) to the coordinates of the point after rotation, we get

$$\begin{aligned}
\underbrace{\begin{bmatrix} x_2 \\ y_2 \\ z_2 \end{bmatrix}}_{\dot{\mathbf{P}}_2} &= \begin{bmatrix} r\sin(\alpha+\theta) \\ y_1 \\ r\cos(\alpha+\theta) \end{bmatrix} \\
&= \begin{bmatrix} r\,(\sin(\alpha)\cos(\theta)+\cos(\alpha)\sin(\theta)) \\ y_1 \\ r\,(\cos(\alpha)\cos(\theta)-\sin(\alpha)\sin(\theta)) \end{bmatrix} \\
&= \begin{bmatrix} \underbrace{r\sin(\alpha)}_{x_1}\cos(\theta)+\underbrace{r\cos(\alpha)}_{z_1}\sin(\theta) \\ y_1 \\ \underbrace{r\cos(\alpha)}_{z_1}\cos(\theta)-\underbrace{r\sin(\alpha)}_{x_1}\sin(\theta) \end{bmatrix} \\
&= \begin{bmatrix} x_1\cos(\theta)+z_1\sin(\theta) \\ y_1 \\ -x_1\sin(\theta)+z_1\cos(\theta) \end{bmatrix}.
\end{aligned}$$

Hence,

$$\underbrace{\begin{bmatrix} x_2 \\ y_2 \\ z_2 \end{bmatrix}}_{\dot{\mathbf{P}}_2} = \underbrace{\begin{bmatrix} \cos(\theta) & 0 & \sin(\theta) \\ 0 & 1 & 0 \\ -\sin(\theta) & 0 & \cos(\theta) \end{bmatrix}}_{\dot{\mathrm{R}}_y(\theta)} \underbrace{\begin{bmatrix} x_1 \\ y_1 \\ z_1 \end{bmatrix}}_{\dot{\mathbf{P}}_1}, \tag{5.7}$$

where $\dot{\mathrm{R}}_y$ is a $3 \times 3$ matrix representing the rotation operation about the $y$-axis for inhomogeneous points in 3D space; and $\theta$ is the angle of rotation. The same operation can be expressed in homogeneous coordinates as

[2] Note that the positive direction of the rotation about the $y$-axis in 3D space is the direction of rotation from the $z$-axis to the $x$-axis.

$$\underbrace{\begin{bmatrix} x_2 \\ y_2 \\ z_2 \\ 1 \end{bmatrix}}_{\mathbf{P}_2} = \underbrace{\begin{bmatrix} \cos(\theta) & 0 & \sin(\theta) & 0 \\ 0 & 1 & 0 & 0 \\ -\sin(\theta) & 0 & \cos(\theta) & 0 \\ 0 & 0 & 0 & 1 \end{bmatrix}}_{\mathtt{R}_y(\theta)} \underbrace{\begin{bmatrix} x_1 \\ y_1 \\ z_1 \\ 1 \end{bmatrix}}_{\mathbf{P}_1}, \tag{5.8}$$

where $\mathtt{R}_y$ is a $4 \times 4$ matrix representing the rotation operation about the $y$-axis for homogeneous points in 3D space; and $\theta$ is the angle of rotation.

### 5.2.3 Rotation About the z-Axis

Applying the same procedure as done before, the rotation about the $z$-axis can be expressed as

$$\begin{aligned} \underbrace{\begin{bmatrix} x_2 \\ y_2 \\ z_2 \end{bmatrix}}_{\dot{\mathbf{P}}_2} &= \begin{bmatrix} r\cos(\alpha+\theta) \\ r\sin(\alpha+\theta) \\ z_1 \end{bmatrix} \\ &= \begin{bmatrix} x_1\cos(\theta) - y_1\sin(\theta) \\ x_1\sin(\theta) + y_1\cos(\theta) \\ z_1 \end{bmatrix} \\ &= \underbrace{\begin{bmatrix} \cos(\theta) & -\sin(\theta) & 0 \\ \sin(\theta) & \cos(\theta) & 0 \\ 0 & 0 & 1 \end{bmatrix}}_{\dot{\mathtt{R}}_z(\theta)} \underbrace{\begin{bmatrix} x_1 \\ y_1 \\ z_1 \end{bmatrix}}_{\dot{\mathbf{P}}_1}, \end{aligned} \tag{5.9}$$

where $\dot{\mathtt{R}}_z$ is a $3 \times 3$ matrix representing the rotation operation about the $z$-axis for inhomogeneous points in 3D space; and $\theta$ is the angle of rotation. Again, the same operation can be expressed in homogeneous coordinates as

$$\underbrace{\begin{bmatrix} x_2 \\ y_2 \\ z_2 \\ 1 \end{bmatrix}}_{\mathbf{P}_2} = \underbrace{\begin{bmatrix} \cos(\theta) & -\sin(\theta) & 0 & 0 \\ \sin(\theta) & \cos(\theta) & 0 & 0 \\ 0 & 0 & 1 & 0 \\ 0 & 0 & 0 & 1 \end{bmatrix}}_{\mathtt{R}_z(\theta)} \underbrace{\begin{bmatrix} x_1 \\ y_1 \\ z_1 \\ 1 \end{bmatrix}}_{\mathbf{P}_1}, \tag{5.10}$$

where $\mathtt{R}_z$ is a $4 \times 4$ matrix representing the rotation operation about the $z$-axis for homogeneous points in 3D space; and $\theta$ is the angle of rotation.

### 5.2.4 Properties of the Rotation Matrix

The rotation matrix is a special orthogonal matrix that has the following properties:

1. The inverse of the rotation matrix is its transpose. Thus, we can write

$$\mathtt{R}\mathtt{R}^{-1} = \mathtt{R}\mathtt{R}^{T} = \mathtt{I} \text{ or } \mathtt{R}^{-1} = \mathtt{R}^{T}. \tag{5.11}$$

2. The determinant of the rotation matrix has a unit value. Thus,

$$\det(\mathtt{R}) = +1. \tag{5.12}$$

3. The rotation matrix is normalized. This means that the squares of the elements in any row or column sum to 1.
4. The rotation matrix is orthogonal. This means that the dot product of any pair of rows or any pair of columns is 0.

You may utilize these properties to make sure that you are on the right track when calculating a rotation matrix.

**Example 5.2:** [*3D rotation matrices*]

Check if each of the following inhomogeneous matrices can be a rotation matrix. Mention at least one reason if a matrix cannot be a rotation matrix and at least two reasons if it may. The matrices are:

$$\mathtt{M}_1 = \begin{bmatrix} 1 & 0 & 0 \\ 0 & 0.9 & -0.2 \\ 0 & 0.2 & 0.9 \end{bmatrix},$$

$$\mathtt{M}_2 = \begin{bmatrix} 1 & 0 & 0 \\ 0 & \frac{3}{\sqrt{10}} & -\frac{1}{\sqrt{10}} \\ 0 & \frac{1}{\sqrt{10}} & \frac{3}{\sqrt{10}} \end{bmatrix},$$

$$\mathtt{M}_3 = \begin{bmatrix} 1 & 0 & 0 \\ 0 & 0 & -\frac{1}{\sqrt{10}} \\ 0 & \frac{1}{\sqrt{10}} & 0 \end{bmatrix},$$

$$\mathtt{M}_4 = \begin{bmatrix} \frac{\sqrt{3}}{2} & 0 & \frac{1}{2} \\ 0 & 1 & 0 \\ -\frac{1}{2} & 0 & \frac{\sqrt{3}}{2} \end{bmatrix}$$

and

$$\mathtt{M}_5 = \begin{bmatrix} 1 & 0 & 0 \\ 0 & 1 & 0 \\ 0 & 0 & 1 \end{bmatrix}.$$

**Solution 5.2:**

1. $\mathtt{M}_1$ cannot be a rotation matrix as it is not normalized. In addition, $\det(\mathtt{M}_1) \neq +1$ and $\mathtt{M}_1^{-1} \neq \mathtt{M}_1^T$.
2. $\mathtt{M}_2$ can be a rotation matrix as it is normalized and orthogonal. In addition, $\det(\mathtt{M}_2) = +1$ and $\mathtt{M}_2^{-1} = \mathtt{M}_2^T$.
3. $\mathtt{M}_3$ cannot be a rotation matrix as it is not normalized. In addition, $\det(\mathtt{M}_3) \neq +1$ and $\mathtt{M}_3^{-1} \neq \mathtt{M}_3^T$.
4. $\mathtt{M}_4$ can be a rotation matrix as it is normalized and orthogonal. In addition, $\det(\mathtt{M}_4) = +1$ and $\mathtt{M}_4^{-1} = \mathtt{M}_4^T$.
5. $\mathtt{M}_5$ can be a rotation matrix as it is normalized and orthogonal. In addition, $\det(\mathtt{M}_5) = +1$ and $\mathtt{M}_5^{-1} = \mathtt{M}_5^T$. □

## *5.2.5 General Rotation in 3D Space*

We talked about how to rotate a point (or an object) about one of the principal axes; however, in general, rotation may be performed about an arbitrary axis. In this case, the rotation matrices of Eq. (5.5) through Eq. (5.10) cannot be used directly. Instead, the axis of rotation (along with the point/object to be rotated) must be translated and/or rotated in order to coincide with one of the principal axes before applying the rotation. Afterwards, initial translation and/or rotation should be reversed.

Thus, in order to rotate a point about an arbitrary axis that does not coincide with any of the main coordinate axes, do the following:

1. If the arbitrary rotation axis does not pass through the origin $[0, 0, 0]^T$, translate the point/object and the arbitrary axis by a translation vector that causes this axis to pass through the origin.
2. If the arbitrary rotation axis does not coincide with a principal axis (i.e., $x$-, $y$- or $z$-axis), rotate the point/object as well as the arbitrary axis so that the arbitrary axis coincide with one of the principal axes.
3. Perform the specified point rotation about the selected principal axis.
4. Apply inverse rotation (if Step 2 has been performed).
5. Apply inverse translation (if Step 1 has been performed).

**Example 5.3:** [*3D general rotation*]

Rotate a point $\dot{\mathbf{P}}_1 = [3, 8, 7]^T$ about a 2D line having the equation $x = y$ through an angle of 45°. Derive the required 3D transformation matrix.

**Solution 5.3:** The steps can be performed as follows:

1. Rotate through an angle of 45° about the $z$-axis using the matrix $\mathtt{M}_1$ where

$$\mathtt{M}_1 = \mathrm{R}_z(45) = \begin{bmatrix} \cos(45) & -\sin(45) & 0 & 0 \\ \sin(45) & \cos(45) & 0 & 0 \\ 0 & 0 & 1 & 0 \\ 0 & 0 & 0 & 1 \end{bmatrix} = \begin{bmatrix} \frac{1}{\sqrt{2}} & -\frac{1}{\sqrt{2}} & 0 & 0 \\ \frac{1}{\sqrt{2}} & \frac{1}{\sqrt{2}} & 0 & 0 \\ 0 & 0 & 1 & 0 \\ 0 & 0 & 0 & 1 \end{bmatrix}.$$

   This enforces the rotation axis to coincide with the $y$-axis.
2. Rotate through an angle of 45° about the $y$-axis using the matrix $\mathtt{M}_2$ where

$$\mathtt{M}_2 = \mathrm{R}_y(45) = \begin{bmatrix} \cos(45) & 0 & \sin(45) & 0 \\ 0 & 1 & 0 & 0 \\ -\sin(45) & 0 & \cos(45) & 0 \\ 0 & 0 & 0 & 1 \end{bmatrix} = \begin{bmatrix} \frac{1}{\sqrt{2}} & 0 & \frac{1}{\sqrt{2}} & 0 \\ 0 & 1 & 0 & 0 \\ -\frac{1}{\sqrt{2}} & 0 & \frac{1}{\sqrt{2}} & 0 \\ 0 & 0 & 0 & 1 \end{bmatrix}.$$

3. Rotate through an angle of −45° about the $z$-axis to reverse the rotation done in Step 1 using the matrix $\mathtt{M}_3$ where

$$\mathtt{M}_3 = \mathrm{R}_z(-45) = \begin{bmatrix} \cos(-45) & -\sin(-45) & 0 & 0 \\ \sin(-45) & \cos(-45) & 0 & 0 \\ 0 & 0 & 1 & 0 \\ 0 & 0 & 0 & 1 \end{bmatrix} = \begin{bmatrix} \frac{1}{\sqrt{2}} & \frac{1}{\sqrt{2}} & 0 & 0 \\ -\frac{1}{\sqrt{2}} & \frac{1}{\sqrt{2}} & 0 & 0 \\ 0 & 0 & 1 & 0 \\ 0 & 0 & 0 & 1 \end{bmatrix}.$$

The overall transformation can be expressed as

$$
\begin{aligned}
\mathtt{M} &= \mathtt{M}_3\mathtt{M}_2\mathtt{M}_1 \\
&= \mathtt{R}_z(-45)\mathtt{R}_y(45)\mathtt{R}_z(45) \\
&= \begin{bmatrix} \frac{1}{\sqrt{2}} & \frac{1}{\sqrt{2}} & 0 & 0 \\ -\frac{1}{\sqrt{2}} & \frac{1}{\sqrt{2}} & 0 & 0 \\ 0 & 0 & 1 & 0 \\ 0 & 0 & 0 & 1 \end{bmatrix}
\begin{bmatrix} \frac{1}{\sqrt{2}} & 0 & \frac{1}{\sqrt{2}} & 0 \\ 0 & 1 & 0 & 0 \\ -\frac{1}{\sqrt{2}} & 0 & \frac{1}{\sqrt{2}} & 0 \\ 0 & 0 & 0 & 1 \end{bmatrix}
\begin{bmatrix} \frac{1}{\sqrt{2}} & -\frac{1}{\sqrt{2}} & 0 & 0 \\ \frac{1}{\sqrt{2}} & \frac{1}{\sqrt{2}} & 0 & 0 \\ 0 & 0 & 1 & 0 \\ 0 & 0 & 0 & 1 \end{bmatrix} \\
&= \begin{bmatrix} \frac{\sqrt{2}+1}{2\sqrt{2}} & \frac{\sqrt{2}-1}{2\sqrt{2}} & \frac{1}{2} & 0 \\ \frac{\sqrt{2}-1}{2\sqrt{2}} & \frac{\sqrt{2}+1}{2\sqrt{2}} & -\frac{1}{2} & 0 \\ -\frac{1}{2} & \frac{1}{2} & \frac{1}{\sqrt{2}} & 0 \\ 0 & 0 & 0 & 1 \end{bmatrix}
= \begin{bmatrix} 0.8536 & 0.1464 & 0.5 & 0 \\ 0.1464 & 0.8536 & -0.5 & 0 \\ -0.5 & 0.5 & 0.7071 & 0 \\ 0 & 0 & 0 & 1 \end{bmatrix}.
\end{aligned}
$$

Hence, the transformed point can be obtained as

$$
\begin{aligned}
\mathbf{P}_2 &= \mathtt{M}\mathbf{P}_1 \\
&= \begin{bmatrix} \frac{\sqrt{2}+1}{2\sqrt{2}} & \frac{\sqrt{2}-1}{2\sqrt{2}} & \frac{1}{2} & 0 \\ \frac{\sqrt{2}-1}{2\sqrt{2}} & \frac{\sqrt{2}+1}{2\sqrt{2}} & -\frac{1}{2} & 0 \\ -\frac{1}{2} & \frac{1}{2} & \frac{1}{\sqrt{2}} & 0 \\ 0 & 0 & 0 & 1 \end{bmatrix}
\begin{bmatrix} 3 \\ 8 \\ 7 \\ 1 \end{bmatrix}
= \begin{bmatrix} 9 - \frac{5}{2\sqrt{2}} \\ 2 + \frac{5}{2\sqrt{2}} \\ \frac{5+7\sqrt{2}}{2} \\ 1 \end{bmatrix}
= \begin{bmatrix} 7.2322 \\ 3.7678 \\ 7.4497 \\ 1 \end{bmatrix}.
\end{aligned}
$$

The same action can be performed by applying the following steps:

1. Rotate through an angle of $-45°$ about the $z$-axis using the matrix $\mathtt{M}_1$ where

$$
\begin{aligned}
\mathtt{M}_1 &= \mathtt{R}_z(-45) \\
&= \begin{bmatrix} \cos(-45) & -\sin(-45) & 0 & 0 \\ \sin(-45) & \cos(-45) & 0 & 0 \\ 0 & 0 & 1 & 0 \\ 0 & 0 & 0 & 1 \end{bmatrix} \\
&= \begin{bmatrix} \frac{1}{\sqrt{2}} & \frac{1}{\sqrt{2}} & 0 & 0 \\ -\frac{1}{\sqrt{2}} & \frac{1}{\sqrt{2}} & 0 & 0 \\ 0 & 0 & 1 & 0 \\ 0 & 0 & 0 & 1 \end{bmatrix}.
\end{aligned}
$$

This enforces the rotation axis to coincide with the $x$-axis.

2. Rotate through an angle of 45° about the $x$-axis using the matrix $\mathtt{M}_2$ where

$$\mathtt{M}_2 = \mathtt{R}_x(45) = \begin{bmatrix} 1 & 0 & 0 & 0 \\ 0 & \cos(45) & -\sin(45) & 0 \\ 0 & \sin(45) & \cos(45) & 0 \\ 0 & 0 & 0 & 1 \end{bmatrix} = \begin{bmatrix} 1 & 0 & 0 & 0 \\ 0 & \frac{1}{\sqrt{2}} & -\frac{1}{\sqrt{2}} & 0 \\ 0 & \frac{1}{\sqrt{2}} & \frac{1}{\sqrt{2}} & 0 \\ 0 & 0 & 0 & 1 \end{bmatrix}.$$

3. Rotate through an angle of 45° about the $z$-axis to reverse the rotation done in Step 1 using the matrix $\mathtt{M}_3$ where

$$\mathtt{M}_3 = \mathtt{R}_z(45) = \begin{bmatrix} \cos(45) & -\sin(45) & 0 & 0 \\ \sin(45) & \cos(45) & 0 & 0 \\ 0 & 0 & 1 & 0 \\ 0 & 0 & 0 & 1 \end{bmatrix} = \begin{bmatrix} \frac{1}{\sqrt{2}} & -\frac{1}{\sqrt{2}} & 0 & 0 \\ \frac{1}{\sqrt{2}} & \frac{1}{\sqrt{2}} & 0 & 0 \\ 0 & 0 & 1 & 0 \\ 0 & 0 & 0 & 1 \end{bmatrix}.$$

In this case, the overall transformation can be expressed as

$$\begin{aligned} \mathtt{M} &= \mathtt{M}_3\mathtt{M}_2\mathtt{M}_1 \\ &= \mathtt{R}_z(45)\mathtt{R}_x(45)\mathtt{R}_z(-45) \\ &= \begin{bmatrix} \frac{1}{\sqrt{2}} & -\frac{1}{\sqrt{2}} & 0 & 0 \\ \frac{1}{\sqrt{2}} & \frac{1}{\sqrt{2}} & 0 & 0 \\ 0 & 0 & 1 & 0 \\ 0 & 0 & 0 & 1 \end{bmatrix} \begin{bmatrix} 1 & 0 & 0 & 0 \\ 0 & \frac{1}{\sqrt{2}} & -\frac{1}{\sqrt{2}} & 0 \\ 0 & \frac{1}{\sqrt{2}} & \frac{1}{\sqrt{2}} & 0 \\ 0 & 0 & 0 & 1 \end{bmatrix} \begin{bmatrix} \frac{1}{\sqrt{2}} & \frac{1}{\sqrt{2}} & 0 & 0 \\ -\frac{1}{\sqrt{2}} & \frac{1}{\sqrt{2}} & 0 & 0 \\ 0 & 0 & 1 & 0 \\ 0 & 0 & 0 & 1 \end{bmatrix} \\ &= \begin{bmatrix} \frac{\sqrt{2}+1}{2\sqrt{2}} & \frac{\sqrt{2}-1}{2\sqrt{2}} & \frac{1}{2} & 0 \\ \frac{\sqrt{2}-1}{2\sqrt{2}} & \frac{\sqrt{2}+1}{2\sqrt{2}} & -\frac{1}{2} & 0 \\ -\frac{1}{2} & \frac{1}{2} & \frac{1}{\sqrt{2}} & 0 \\ 0 & 0 & 0 & 1 \end{bmatrix} = \begin{bmatrix} 0.8536 & 0.1464 & 0.5 & 0 \\ 0.1464 & 0.8536 & -0.5 & 0 \\ -0.5 & 0.5 & 0.7071 & 0 \\ 0 & 0 & 0 & 1 \end{bmatrix}, \end{aligned}$$

which is the same matrix obtained before. □

**Example 5.4:** [*3D general rotation*]

Consider the pyramid $\dot{\mathbf{A}}_1\dot{\mathbf{B}}_1\dot{\mathbf{C}}_1\dot{\mathbf{D}}_1$ where $\dot{\mathbf{A}}_1 = [0, 0, 0]^T$, $\dot{\mathbf{B}}_1 = [1, 0, 0]^T$, $\dot{\mathbf{C}}_1 = [0, 1, 0]^T$ and $\dot{\mathbf{D}}_1 = [0, 0, 1]^T$. The pyramid is to be rotated through an angle of 45° about a line passing through $\dot{\mathbf{C}}_1$ and having the direction $[0, 1, 1]^T$. Find the coordinates of the rotated vertices.

**Solution 5.4:** The steps are as follows:

1. Translate the pyramid using the vector $[0, -1, 0]^T$ so that point $\dot{\mathbf{C}}_1$ coincides with the origin. This is using the matrix $\mathtt{M}_1$ where

$$\begin{aligned}\mathtt{M}_1 &= \mathtt{T}([0, -1, 0]^T)\\ &= \begin{bmatrix} 1 & 0 & 0 & 0 \\ 0 & 1 & 0 & -1 \\ 0 & 0 & 1 & 0 \\ 0 & 0 & 0 & 1 \end{bmatrix}.\end{aligned}$$

2. Rotate through an angle of 45° about the $x$-axis using the matrix $\mathtt{M}_2$ where

$$\begin{aligned}\mathtt{M}_2 &= \mathtt{R}_x(45)\\ &= \begin{bmatrix} 1 & 0 & 0 & 0 \\ 0 & \cos(45) & -\sin(45) & 0 \\ 0 & \sin(45) & \cos(45) & 0 \\ 0 & 0 & 0 & 1 \end{bmatrix}\\ &= \begin{bmatrix} 1 & 0 & 0 & 0 \\ 0 & \frac{1}{\sqrt{2}} & -\frac{1}{\sqrt{2}} & 0 \\ 0 & \frac{1}{\sqrt{2}} & \frac{1}{\sqrt{2}} & 0 \\ 0 & 0 & 0 & 1 \end{bmatrix}.\end{aligned}$$

This enforces the rotation axis to coincide with the $z$-axis.

3. Rotate through an angle of 45° about the $z$-axis using the matrix $\mathtt{M}_3$ where

$$\begin{aligned}\mathtt{M}_3 &= \mathtt{R}_z(45)\\ &= \begin{bmatrix} \cos(45) & -\sin(45) & 0 & 0 \\ \sin(45) & \cos(45) & 0 & 0 \\ 0 & 0 & 1 & 0 \\ 0 & 0 & 0 & 1 \end{bmatrix}\\ &= \begin{bmatrix} \frac{1}{\sqrt{2}} & -\frac{1}{\sqrt{2}} & 0 & 0 \\ \frac{1}{\sqrt{2}} & \frac{1}{\sqrt{2}} & 0 & 0 \\ 0 & 0 & 1 & 0 \\ 0 & 0 & 0 & 1 \end{bmatrix}.\end{aligned}$$

4. Rotate through an angle of $-45°$ about the $x$-axis to reverse the rotation done in Step 2 using the matrix $\mathtt{M}_4$ where

$$\mathtt{M}_4 = \mathtt{R}_x(-45) = \begin{bmatrix} 1 & 0 & 0 & 0 \\ 0 & \cos(-45) & -\sin(-45) & 0 \\ 0 & \sin(-45) & \cos(-45) & 0 \\ 0 & 0 & 0 & 1 \end{bmatrix} = \begin{bmatrix} 1 & 0 & 0 & 0 \\ 0 & \frac{1}{\sqrt{2}} & \frac{1}{\sqrt{2}} & 0 \\ 0 & -\frac{1}{\sqrt{2}} & \frac{1}{\sqrt{2}} & 0 \\ 0 & 0 & 0 & 1 \end{bmatrix}.$$

5. Translate the pyramid using the vector $[0, 1, 0]^T$ to reverse the translation done in Step 1. This is using the matrix $\mathtt{M}_5$ where

$$\mathtt{M}_5 = \mathtt{T}([0, 1, 0]^T) = \begin{bmatrix} 1 & 0 & 0 & 0 \\ 0 & 1 & 0 & 1 \\ 0 & 0 & 1 & 0 \\ 0 & 0 & 0 & 1 \end{bmatrix}.$$

The overall transformation can be expressed as

$$\begin{aligned} \mathtt{M} &= \mathtt{M}_5\mathtt{M}_4\mathtt{M}_3\mathtt{M}_2\mathtt{M}_1 \\ &= \mathtt{T}([0, 1, 0]^T)\mathtt{R}_x(-45)\mathtt{R}_z(45)\mathtt{R}_x(45)\mathtt{T}([0, -1, 0]^T) \\ &= \begin{bmatrix} 1 & 0 & 0 & 0 \\ 0 & 1 & 0 & 1 \\ 0 & 0 & 1 & 0 \\ 0 & 0 & 0 & 1 \end{bmatrix} \begin{bmatrix} 1 & 0 & 0 & 0 \\ 0 & \frac{1}{\sqrt{2}} & \frac{1}{\sqrt{2}} & 0 \\ 0 & -\frac{1}{\sqrt{2}} & \frac{1}{\sqrt{2}} & 0 \\ 0 & 0 & 0 & 1 \end{bmatrix} \begin{bmatrix} \frac{1}{\sqrt{2}} & -\frac{1}{\sqrt{2}} & 0 & 0 \\ \frac{1}{\sqrt{2}} & \frac{1}{\sqrt{2}} & 0 & 0 \\ 0 & 0 & 1 & 0 \\ 0 & 0 & 0 & 1 \end{bmatrix} \cdots \\ &\cdots \begin{bmatrix} 1 & 0 & 0 & 0 \\ 0 & \frac{1}{\sqrt{2}} & -\frac{1}{\sqrt{2}} & 0 \\ 0 & \frac{1}{\sqrt{2}} & \frac{1}{\sqrt{2}} & 0 \\ 0 & 0 & 0 & 1 \end{bmatrix} \begin{bmatrix} 1 & 0 & 0 & 0 \\ 0 & 1 & 0 & -1 \\ 0 & 0 & 1 & 0 \\ 0 & 0 & 0 & 1 \end{bmatrix} \\ &= \begin{bmatrix} \frac{\sqrt{2}}{2} & -\frac{1}{2} & \frac{1}{2} & \frac{1}{2} \\ \frac{1}{2} & \frac{2+\sqrt{2}}{4} & \frac{2-\sqrt{2}}{4} & \frac{2-\sqrt{2}}{4} \\ -\frac{1}{2} & \frac{2-\sqrt{2}}{4} & \frac{2+\sqrt{2}}{4} & \frac{-2+\sqrt{2}}{4} \\ 0 & 0 & 0 & 1 \end{bmatrix} = \begin{bmatrix} 0.7071 & -0.5 & 0.5 & 0.5 \\ 0.5 & 0.8536 & 0.1464 & 0.1464 \\ -0.5 & 0.1464 & 0.8536 & -0.1464 \\ 0 & 0 & 0 & 1 \end{bmatrix}. \end{aligned}$$

Hence, the transformed points can be obtained as

$$\mathbf{A}_2 = \mathtt{M}\mathbf{A}_1 = \begin{bmatrix} \frac{\sqrt{2}}{2} & -\frac{1}{2} & \frac{1}{2} & \frac{1}{2} \\ \frac{1}{2} & \frac{2+\sqrt{2}}{4} & \frac{2-\sqrt{2}}{4} & \frac{2-\sqrt{2}}{4} \\ -\frac{1}{2} & \frac{2-\sqrt{2}}{4} & \frac{2+\sqrt{2}}{4} & \frac{-2+\sqrt{2}}{4} \\ 0 & 0 & 0 & 1 \end{bmatrix} \begin{bmatrix} 0 \\ 0 \\ 0 \\ 1 \end{bmatrix} = \begin{bmatrix} \frac{1}{2} \\ \frac{2-\sqrt{2}}{4} \\ \frac{-2+\sqrt{2}}{4} \\ 1 \end{bmatrix} = \begin{bmatrix} 0.5 \\ 0.1464 \\ -0.1464 \\ 1 \end{bmatrix},$$

$$\mathbf{B}_2 = \mathtt{M}\mathbf{B}_1 = \begin{bmatrix} \frac{\sqrt{2}}{2} & -\frac{1}{2} & \frac{1}{2} & \frac{1}{2} \\ \frac{1}{2} & \frac{2+\sqrt{2}}{4} & \frac{2-\sqrt{2}}{4} & \frac{2-\sqrt{2}}{4} \\ -\frac{1}{2} & \frac{2-\sqrt{2}}{4} & \frac{2+\sqrt{2}}{4} & \frac{-2+\sqrt{2}}{4} \\ 0 & 0 & 0 & 1 \end{bmatrix} \begin{bmatrix} 1 \\ 0 \\ 0 \\ 1 \end{bmatrix} = \begin{bmatrix} \frac{1+\sqrt{2}}{2} \\ \frac{4-\sqrt{2}}{4} \\ \frac{-4+\sqrt{2}}{4} \\ 1 \end{bmatrix} = \begin{bmatrix} 1.2071 \\ 0.6464 \\ -0.6464 \\ 1 \end{bmatrix},$$

$$\mathbf{C}_2 = \mathtt{M}\mathbf{C}_1 = \begin{bmatrix} \frac{\sqrt{2}}{2} & -\frac{1}{2} & \frac{1}{2} & \frac{1}{2} \\ \frac{1}{2} & \frac{2+\sqrt{2}}{4} & \frac{2-\sqrt{2}}{4} & \frac{2-\sqrt{2}}{4} \\ -\frac{1}{2} & \frac{2-\sqrt{2}}{4} & \frac{2+\sqrt{2}}{4} & \frac{-2+\sqrt{2}}{4} \\ 0 & 0 & 0 & 1 \end{bmatrix} \begin{bmatrix} 0 \\ 1 \\ 0 \\ 1 \end{bmatrix} = \begin{bmatrix} 0 \\ 1 \\ 0 \\ 1 \end{bmatrix}$$

and

$$\mathbf{D}_2 = \mathtt{M}\mathbf{D}_1 = \begin{bmatrix} \frac{\sqrt{2}}{2} & -\frac{1}{2} & \frac{1}{2} & \frac{1}{2} \\ \frac{1}{2} & \frac{2+\sqrt{2}}{4} & \frac{2-\sqrt{2}}{4} & \frac{2-\sqrt{2}}{4} \\ -\frac{1}{2} & \frac{2-\sqrt{2}}{4} & \frac{2+\sqrt{2}}{4} & \frac{-2+\sqrt{2}}{4} \\ 0 & 0 & 0 & 1 \end{bmatrix} \begin{bmatrix} 0 \\ 0 \\ 1 \\ 1 \end{bmatrix} = \begin{bmatrix} 1 \\ \frac{2-\sqrt{2}}{2} \\ \frac{\sqrt{2}}{2} \\ 1 \end{bmatrix} = \begin{bmatrix} 1 \\ 0.2929 \\ 0.7071 \\ 1 \end{bmatrix}.$$

The same results can obtained through the following steps:

1. Translate the pyramid using the vector $[0, -1, 0]^T$ so that point $\dot{\mathbf{C}}_1$ coincides with the origin.
2. Rotate through an angle of $-45°$ about the $x$-axis. This enforces the rotation axis to coincide with the $y$-axis.
3. Rotate through an angle of $45°$ about the $y$-axis.
4. Rotate through an angle of $45°$ about the $x$-axis to reverse the rotation done in Step 2.
5. Translate the pyramid using the vector $[0, 1, 0]^T$ to reverse the translation done in Step 1.

The calculations are left for you as an exercise. □

**Example 5.5:** [*3D general rotation—angles*]

A point is rotated through an angle of $30°$ about a line passing through the origin $\dot{\mathbf{A}} = [0, 0, 0]^T$ and a point $\dot{\mathbf{B}} = [7, 7, 7]^T$. Get the required rotation angles and rotation sequence.

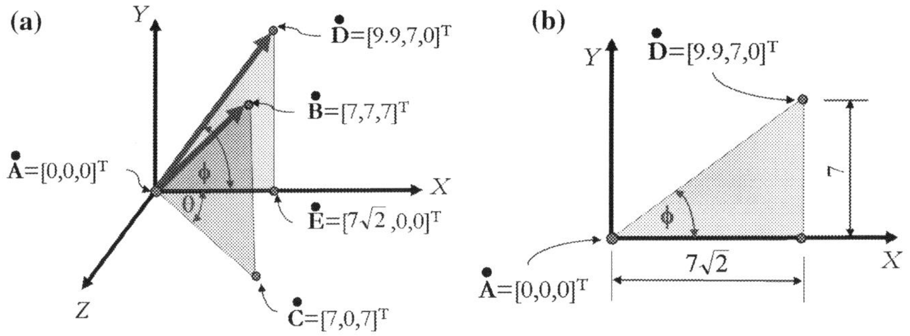


**Fig. 5.3** Rotation in 3D space. **a** 3D representation of the relationships. **b** Projection onto the $xy$-plane

**Solution 5.5:** Consider Fig. 5.3a. The rotation axis is indicated by the line $\overline{\dot{\mathbf{A}}\dot{\mathbf{B}}}$. We need that line to coincide with one of the principal axes; e.g., the $x$-axis. We will do this in two steps:

1. Rotate the line $\overline{\dot{\mathbf{A}}\dot{\mathbf{B}}}$ about the $y$-axis through an angle $\theta$ so that we get the line $\overline{\dot{\mathbf{A}}\dot{\mathbf{D}}}$ on the $xy$-plane.
2. Rotate the line $\overline{\dot{\mathbf{A}}\dot{\mathbf{D}}}$ about the $z$-axis through an angle $-\phi$ to coincide with the $x$-axis.

*But, how can we get the angles $\theta$ and $\phi$?* The angle $\theta$ is the inclination angle of the line $\overline{\dot{\mathbf{A}}\dot{\mathbf{C}}}$ with respect to the $x$-axis where the line $\overline{\dot{\mathbf{A}}\dot{\mathbf{C}}}$ is the projection of $\overline{\dot{\mathbf{A}}\dot{\mathbf{B}}}$ onto the $zx$-plane. (Consider the triangle $\triangle\dot{\mathbf{A}}\dot{\mathbf{B}}\dot{\mathbf{C}}$ as intersecting the $zx$-plane.) In our case, $\theta$ should be 45°.

Note that when you rotate the line $\overline{\dot{\mathbf{A}}\dot{\mathbf{B}}}$, the origin $\dot{\mathbf{A}}$ will not change. However, point $\dot{\mathbf{B}}$ will be rotated to $\dot{\mathbf{D}}$. Apply the rotation matrix about the $y$-axis. Thus, the homogeneous point $\mathbf{D}$ is expressed as

$$\begin{aligned}
\mathbf{D} &= \mathrm{R}_y(45)\mathbf{B} \\
&= \begin{bmatrix} \cos(45) & 0 & \sin(45) & 0 \\ 0 & 1 & 0 & 0 \\ -\sin(45) & 0 & \cos(45) & 0 \\ 0 & 0 & 0 & 1 \end{bmatrix} \begin{bmatrix} 7 \\ 7 \\ 7 \\ 1 \end{bmatrix} \\
&= \begin{bmatrix} 7\sqrt{2} \\ 7 \\ 0 \\ 1 \end{bmatrix} = \begin{bmatrix} 9.8995 \\ 7 \\ 0 \\ 1 \end{bmatrix}.
\end{aligned}$$

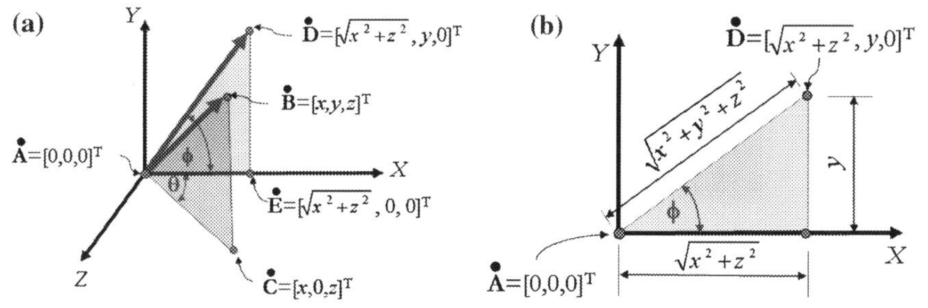


**Fig. 5.4** Rotation in 3D space of a vector $\dot{\mathbf{B}} = [x, y, z]^T$. **a** 3D representation of the relationships. **b** Projection onto the $xy$-plane

Figure 5.3b shows the location of point $\dot{\mathbf{D}}$ on the $xy$-plane where $\phi$ is the inclination angle of the line $\dot{\mathbf{A}}\dot{\mathbf{D}}$ with respect to the $x$-axis. Thus,

$$\phi = \tan^{-1}\left(\frac{7}{7\sqrt{2}}\right) = 35.26°.$$

Hence, the rotation sequence will be as follows: $\mathrm{R}_y(45°) \rightarrow \mathrm{R}_z(-35.26°) \rightarrow \mathrm{R}_x(30°) \rightarrow \mathrm{R}_z(35.26°) \rightarrow \mathrm{R}_y(-45°)$. Note that the following sequences of transformations are also valid:

- $\mathrm{R}_y(45°) \rightarrow \mathrm{R}_z(54.74°) \rightarrow \mathrm{R}_y(30°) \rightarrow \mathrm{R}_z(-54.74°) \rightarrow \mathrm{R}_y(-45°)$;
- $\mathrm{R}_y(-45°) \rightarrow \mathrm{R}_x(35.26°) \rightarrow \mathrm{R}_z(30°) \rightarrow \mathrm{R}_x(-35.26°) \rightarrow \mathrm{R}_y(45°)$; and
- $\mathrm{R}_y(-45°) \rightarrow \mathrm{R}_x(-54.74°) \rightarrow \mathrm{R}_y(30°) \rightarrow \mathrm{R}_x(54.74°) \rightarrow \mathrm{R}_y(45°)$.

You may also start by rotating about the $x$- or the $z$-axis instead of the $y$-axis. This will add 8 more alternatives to solve the same problem. However, note that all the solutions should lead to the same transformation matrix. Try them out. □

**Example 5.6:** [*3D general rotation—rotating vectors*]

Derive a rotation matrix that rotates a vector $\dot{\mathbf{B}} = [x, y, z]^T$ so that it coincides with the $x$-axis.

**Solution 5.6:** Consider Fig. 5.4a where the vector under consideration goes from the origin to point $\dot{\mathbf{B}}$. We denote this vector as $\overrightarrow{\dot{\mathbf{A}}\dot{\mathbf{B}}}$. In order to enforce the vector to coincide with the $x$-axis, we will perform two steps:

1. Rotate the vector $\overrightarrow{\dot{\mathbf{A}}\dot{\mathbf{B}}}$ through an angle $\theta$ about the $y$-axis so that we get the vector $\overrightarrow{\dot{\mathbf{A}}\dot{\mathbf{D}}}$ on the $xy$-plane. Since $\dot{\mathbf{A}}$ is the origin, its position will not change. We only need to get the position of point $\dot{\mathbf{D}}$ where

$$
\begin{aligned}
\mathbf{D} &= \mathtt{M}_1\mathbf{B} = \mathtt{R}_y(\theta)\mathbf{B} \\
&= \begin{bmatrix} \cos(\theta) & 0 & \sin(\theta) & 0 \\ 0 & 1 & 0 & 0 \\ -\sin(\theta) & 0 & \cos(\theta) & 0 \\ 0 & 0 & 0 & 1 \end{bmatrix} \begin{bmatrix} x \\ y \\ z \\ 1 \end{bmatrix} \\
&= \begin{bmatrix} x\ \cos(\theta) + z\ \sin(\theta) \\ y \\ -x\ \sin(\theta) + z\ \cos(\theta) \\ 1 \end{bmatrix}.
\end{aligned}
$$

The angle $\theta$ is the inclination angle of the vector $\overrightarrow{\dot{\mathbf{A}}\dot{\mathbf{C}}}$ with respect to the $x$-axis where the vector $\overrightarrow{\dot{\mathbf{A}}\dot{\mathbf{C}}}$ is the projection of $\overrightarrow{\dot{\mathbf{A}}\dot{\mathbf{B}}}$ onto the $zx$-plane. (Consider the triangle $\triangle\dot{\mathbf{A}}\dot{\mathbf{B}}\dot{\mathbf{C}}$ in Fig. 5.4a as intersecting the $zx$-plane.) Thus,

$$
\theta = \tan^{-1}\left(\frac{z}{x}\right),
$$

$$
\sin(\theta) = \frac{z}{\sqrt{x^2 + z^2}} = \frac{z}{\|\dot{\mathbf{C}}\|}
$$

and

$$
\cos(\theta) = \frac{x}{\sqrt{x^2 + z^2}} = \frac{x}{\|\dot{\mathbf{C}}\|}.
$$

Therefore, point $\mathbf{D}$ is expressed as

$$
\begin{aligned}
\mathbf{D} &= \mathtt{M}_1\mathbf{B} = \mathtt{R}_y(\theta)\mathbf{B} \\
&= \begin{bmatrix} \frac{x}{\sqrt{x^2+z^2}} & 0 & \frac{z}{\sqrt{x^2+z^2}} & 0 \\ 0 & 1 & 0 & 0 \\ -\frac{z}{\sqrt{x^2+z^2}} & 0 & \frac{x}{\sqrt{x^2+z^2}} & 0 \\ 0 & 0 & 0 & 1 \end{bmatrix} \begin{bmatrix} x \\ y \\ z \\ 1 \end{bmatrix} \\
&= \begin{bmatrix} x\left(\frac{x}{\sqrt{x^2+z^2}}\right) + z\left(\frac{z}{\sqrt{x^2+z^2}}\right) \\ y \\ -x\left(\frac{z}{\sqrt{x^2+z^2}}\right) + z\left(\frac{x}{\sqrt{x^2+z^2}}\right) \\ 1 \end{bmatrix} \\
&= \begin{bmatrix} \sqrt{x^2 + z^2} \\ y \\ 0 \\ 1 \end{bmatrix} = \begin{bmatrix} \|\dot{\mathbf{C}}\| \\ y \\ 0 \\ 1 \end{bmatrix}.
\end{aligned}
$$

2. Rotate the vector $\overrightarrow{\dot{\mathbf{A}}\dot{\mathbf{D}}}$ about the $z$-axis through an angle $-\phi$ to coincide with the $x$-axis. Figure 5.4b shows the location of point $\dot{\mathbf{D}}$ on the $xy$-plane where $\phi$ is the inclination angle of the vector $\overrightarrow{\dot{\mathbf{A}}\dot{\mathbf{D}}}$ with respect to the $x$-axis. Thus,

$$\phi = \tan^{-1}\left(\frac{y}{\sqrt{x^2+z^2}}\right) = \tan^{-1}\left(\frac{y}{\|\dot{\mathbf{C}}\|}\right),$$

$$\sin(\phi) = \frac{y}{\sqrt{x^2+y^2+z^2}} = \frac{y}{\|\dot{\mathbf{B}}\|} = \frac{y}{\|\dot{\mathbf{D}}\|}$$

and

$$\cos(\phi) = \frac{\sqrt{x^2+z^2}}{\sqrt{x^2+y^2+z^2}} = \frac{\|\dot{\mathbf{C}}\|}{\|\dot{\mathbf{B}}\|} = \frac{\|\dot{\mathbf{C}}\|}{\|\dot{\mathbf{D}}\|}.$$

The second rotation matrix $\mathtt{M}_2$ is expressed as

$$\begin{aligned}
\mathtt{M}_2 &= \mathtt{R}_z(-\phi) \\
&= \begin{bmatrix} \cos(-\phi) & -\sin(-\phi) & 0 & 0 \\ \sin(-\phi) & \cos(-\phi) & 0 & 0 \\ 0 & 0 & 1 & 0 \\ 0 & 0 & 0 & 1 \end{bmatrix} \\
&= \begin{bmatrix} \cos(\phi) & \sin(\phi) & 0 & 0 \\ -\sin(\phi) & \cos(\phi) & 0 & 0 \\ 0 & 0 & 1 & 0 \\ 0 & 0 & 0 & 1 \end{bmatrix} \\
&= \begin{bmatrix} \frac{\sqrt{x^2+z^2}}{\sqrt{x^2+y^2+z^2}} & \frac{y}{\sqrt{x^2+y^2+z^2}} & 0 & 0 \\ -\frac{y}{\sqrt{x^2+y^2+z^2}} & \frac{\sqrt{x^2+z^2}}{\sqrt{x^2+y^2+z^2}} & 0 & 0 \\ 0 & 0 & 1 & 0 \\ 0 & 0 & 0 & 1 \end{bmatrix}.
\end{aligned}$$

Finally, the overall rotation matrix $\mathtt{M}$ (i.e., $\mathtt{R}_{zy}([x, y, z]^T)$) is estimated as the concatenation of $\mathtt{M}_2\mathtt{M}_1$ where

$$\begin{aligned}
\mathtt{M} &= \mathtt{M}_2\mathtt{M}_1 \\
&= \mathtt{R}_{zy}([x, y, z]^T) \\
&= \mathtt{R}_z(-\phi)\mathtt{R}_y(\theta) \\
&= \begin{bmatrix} \frac{\sqrt{x^2+z^2}}{\sqrt{x^2+y^2+z^2}} & \frac{y}{\sqrt{x^2+y^2+z^2}} & 0 & 0 \\ -\frac{y}{\sqrt{x^2+y^2+z^2}} & \frac{\sqrt{x^2+z^2}}{\sqrt{x^2+y^2+z^2}} & 0 & 0 \\ 0 & 0 & 1 & 0 \\ 0 & 0 & 0 & 1 \end{bmatrix} \begin{bmatrix} \frac{x}{\sqrt{x^2+z^2}} & 0 & \frac{z}{\sqrt{x^2+z^2}} & 0 \\ 0 & 1 & 0 & 0 \\ -\frac{z}{\sqrt{x^2+z^2}} & 0 & \frac{x}{\sqrt{x^2+z^2}} & 0 \\ 0 & 0 & 0 & 1 \end{bmatrix}
\end{aligned}$$

$$
= \begin{bmatrix}
\frac{x}{\sqrt{x^2+y^2+z^2}} & \frac{y}{\sqrt{x^2+y^2+z^2}} & \frac{z}{\sqrt{x^2+y^2+z^2}} & 0 \\
-\frac{xy}{\sqrt{x^2+z^2}\sqrt{x^2+y^2+z^2}} & \frac{\sqrt{x^2+z^2}}{\sqrt{x^2+y^2+z^2}} & -\frac{yz}{\sqrt{x^2+z^2}\sqrt{x^2+y^2+z^2}} & 0 \\
-\frac{z}{\sqrt{x^2+z^2}} & 0 & \frac{x}{\sqrt{x^2+z^2}} & 0 \\
0 & 0 & 0 & 1
\end{bmatrix} \tag{5.13}
$$

$$
= \begin{bmatrix}
\frac{x}{\|\dot{\mathbf{B}}\|} & \frac{y}{\|\dot{\mathbf{B}}\|} & \frac{z}{\|\dot{\mathbf{B}}\|} & 0 \\
-\frac{xy}{\|\dot{\mathbf{C}}\|\|\dot{\mathbf{B}}\|} & \frac{\|\dot{\mathbf{C}}\|}{\|\dot{\mathbf{B}}\|} & -\frac{yz}{\|\dot{\mathbf{C}}\|\|\dot{\mathbf{B}}\|} & 0 \\
-\frac{z}{\|\dot{\mathbf{C}}\|} & 0 & \frac{x}{\|\dot{\mathbf{C}}\|} & 0 \\
0 & 0 & 0 & 1
\end{bmatrix}.
$$

The previous matrix rotates a general vector to align with the $x$-axis except for vectors along the $y$-axis (e.g., $[0, y, 0]^T$) because the location of $\dot{\mathbf{C}}$ in this case coincides with the origin (i.e., $\|\dot{\mathbf{C}}\| = 0$). In such a case, only $\mathtt{R}_z(-\phi)$ is needed where $\phi = 90°$. Thus, we have

$$
\begin{aligned}
\mathtt{M} &= \mathtt{M}_2 \\
&= \mathtt{R}_z(-\phi) \\
&= \begin{bmatrix}
\cos(90) & \sin(90) & 0 & 0 \\
-\sin(90) & \cos(90) & 0 & 0 \\
0 & 0 & 1 & 0 \\
0 & 0 & 0 & 1
\end{bmatrix} \\
&= \begin{bmatrix}
\frac{\sqrt{x^2+z^2}}{\sqrt{x^2+y^2+z^2}} & \frac{y}{\sqrt{x^2+y^2+z^2}} & 0 & 0 \\
-\frac{y}{\sqrt{x^2+y^2+z^2}} & \frac{\sqrt{x^2+z^2}}{\sqrt{x^2+y^2+z^2}} & 0 & 0 \\
0 & 0 & 1 & 0 \\
0 & 0 & 0 & 1
\end{bmatrix} \\
&= \begin{bmatrix}
0 & 1 & 0 & 0 \\
-1 & 0 & 0 & 0 \\
0 & 0 & 1 & 0 \\
0 & 0 & 0 & 1
\end{bmatrix}.
\end{aligned}
$$

□

**Example 5.7:** [*3D general rotation—rotating vectors*]

Derive a rotation matrix to undo the previous rotation of Example 5.6.

**Solution 5.7:** The inverse of the final rotation matrix defined in Example 5.6 is the answer to this problem. This inverse can also be obtained in two steps (opposite to the steps used in Example 5.6).

1. Rotate through an angle $\phi$ about the $z$-axis using the matrix $\mathtt{M}_1$ where

$$\begin{aligned}
\mathtt{M}_1 &= \mathrm{R}_z(\phi)\\
&= \begin{bmatrix} \cos(\phi) & -\sin(\phi) & 0 & 0\\ \sin(\phi) & \cos(\phi) & 0 & 0\\ 0 & 0 & 1 & 0\\ 0 & 0 & 0 & 1 \end{bmatrix}\\
&= \begin{bmatrix} \frac{\sqrt{x^2+z^2}}{\sqrt{x^2+y^2+z^2}} & -\frac{y}{\sqrt{x^2+y^2+z^2}} & 0 & 0\\ \frac{y}{\sqrt{x^2+y^2+z^2}} & \frac{\sqrt{x^2+z^2}}{\sqrt{x^2+y^2+z^2}} & 0 & 0\\ 0 & 0 & 1 & 0\\ 0 & 0 & 0 & 1 \end{bmatrix}.
\end{aligned}$$

2. Rotate through an angle $-\theta$ about the $y$-axis using the matrix $\mathtt{M}_2$ where

$$\begin{aligned}
\mathtt{M}_2 &= \mathrm{R}_y(-\theta)\\
&= \begin{bmatrix} \cos(-\theta) & 0 & \sin(-\theta) & 0\\ 0 & 1 & 0 & 0\\ -\sin(-\theta) & 0 & \cos(-\theta) & 0\\ 0 & 0 & 0 & 1 \end{bmatrix}\\
&= \begin{bmatrix} \cos(\theta) & 0 & -\sin(\theta) & 0\\ 0 & 1 & 0 & 0\\ \sin(\theta) & 0 & \cos(\theta) & 0\\ 0 & 0 & 0 & 1 \end{bmatrix}\\
&= \begin{bmatrix} \frac{x}{\sqrt{x^2+z^2}} & 0 & -\frac{z}{\sqrt{x^2+z^2}} & 0\\ 0 & 1 & 0 & 0\\ \frac{z}{\sqrt{x^2+z^2}} & 0 & \frac{x}{\sqrt{x^2+z^2}} & 0\\ 0 & 0 & 0 & 1 \end{bmatrix}.
\end{aligned}$$

The overall rotation matrix $\mathtt{M}$ is estimated as the concatenation $\mathtt{M}_2\mathtt{M}_1$ where

$$\begin{aligned}
\mathtt{M} &= \mathtt{M}_2\mathtt{M}_1\\
&= \mathrm{R}_{zy}^{-1}([x,y,z]^T)\\
&= \mathrm{R}_y(-\theta)\mathrm{R}_z(\phi)\\
&= \begin{bmatrix} \frac{x}{\sqrt{x^2+z^2}} & 0 & -\frac{z}{\sqrt{x^2+z^2}} & 0\\ 0 & 1 & 0 & 0\\ \frac{z}{\sqrt{x^2+z^2}} & 0 & \frac{x}{\sqrt{x^2+z^2}} & 0\\ 0 & 0 & 0 & 1 \end{bmatrix} \begin{bmatrix} \frac{\sqrt{x^2+z^2}}{\sqrt{x^2+y^2+z^2}} & -\frac{y}{\sqrt{x^2+y^2+z^2}} & 0 & 0\\ \frac{y}{\sqrt{x^2+y^2+z^2}} & \frac{\sqrt{x^2+z^2}}{\sqrt{x^2+y^2+z^2}} & 0 & 0\\ 0 & 0 & 1 & 0\\ 0 & 0 & 0 & 1 \end{bmatrix}
\end{aligned}$$

$$= \begin{bmatrix} \frac{x}{\sqrt{x^2+y^2+z^2}} & -\frac{xy}{\sqrt{x^2+z^2}\sqrt{x^2+y^2+z^2}} & -\frac{z}{\sqrt{x^2+z^2}} & 0 \\ \frac{y}{\sqrt{x^2+y^2+z^2}} & \frac{\sqrt{x^2+z^2}}{\sqrt{x^2+y^2+z^2}} & 0 & 0 \\ \frac{z}{\sqrt{x^2+y^2+z^2}} & -\frac{yz}{\sqrt{x^2+z^2}\sqrt{x^2+y^2+z^2}} & \frac{x}{\sqrt{x^2+z^2}} & 0 \\ 0 & 0 & 0 & 1 \end{bmatrix}$$

$$= \begin{bmatrix} \frac{x}{\|\dot{\mathbf{B}}\|} & -\frac{xy}{\|\dot{\mathbf{C}}\|\|\dot{\mathbf{B}}\|} & -\frac{z}{\|\dot{\mathbf{C}}\|} & 0 \\ \frac{y}{\|\dot{\mathbf{B}}\|} & \frac{\|\dot{\mathbf{C}}\|}{\|\dot{\mathbf{B}}\|} & 0 & 0 \\ \frac{z}{\|\dot{\mathbf{B}}\|} & -\frac{yz}{\|\dot{\mathbf{C}}\|\|\dot{\mathbf{B}}\|} & \frac{x}{\|\dot{\mathbf{C}}\|} & 0 \\ 0 & 0 & 0 & 1 \end{bmatrix}. \tag{5.14}$$

Notice that $\mathtt{R}_{zy}^T([x, y, z]^T) = \mathtt{R}_{zy}^{-1}([x, y, z]^T)$. □

**Example 5.8:** [*3D general rotation—rotating vectors*]

Derive a transformation matrix that rotates a point through an angle $\theta$ about an axis passing through the origin and having the direction $[x, y, z]^T$.

**Solution 5.8:** The matrix is obtained by applying the following steps:

1. Align the rotation axis with the $x$-axis using Eq. (5.13). Thus,

$$\mathtt{M}_1 = \begin{bmatrix} \frac{x}{\|\dot{\mathbf{B}}\|} & \frac{y}{\|\dot{\mathbf{B}}\|} & \frac{z}{\|\dot{\mathbf{B}}\|} & 0 \\ -\frac{xy}{\|\dot{\mathbf{C}}\|\|\dot{\mathbf{B}}\|} & \frac{\|\dot{\mathbf{C}}\|}{\|\dot{\mathbf{B}}\|} & -\frac{yz}{\|\dot{\mathbf{C}}\|\|\dot{\mathbf{B}}\|} & 0 \\ -\frac{z}{\|\dot{\mathbf{C}}\|} & 0 & \frac{x}{\|\dot{\mathbf{C}}\|} & 0 \\ 0 & 0 & 0 & 1 \end{bmatrix},$$

where $\|\dot{\mathbf{B}}\| = \sqrt{x^2 + y^2 + z^2}$ and $\|\dot{\mathbf{C}}\| = \sqrt{x^2 + z^2}$.

2. Rotate about the $x$-axis through an angle $\theta$. This is using the matrix $\mathtt{M}_2$ where

$$\mathtt{M}_2 = \begin{bmatrix} 1 & 0 & 0 & 0 \\ 0 & \cos(\theta) & -\sin(\theta) & 0 \\ 0 & \sin(\theta) & \cos(\theta) & 0 \\ 0 & 0 & 0 & 1 \end{bmatrix}.$$

3. Reverse the rotation of Step 1 using Eq. (5.14). Hence,

$$\mathtt{M}_3 = \begin{bmatrix} \frac{x}{\|\dot{\mathbf{B}}\|} & -\frac{xy}{\|\dot{\mathbf{C}}\|\|\dot{\mathbf{B}}\|} & -\frac{z}{\|\dot{\mathbf{C}}\|} & 0 \\ \frac{y}{\|\dot{\mathbf{B}}\|} & \frac{\|\dot{\mathbf{C}}\|}{\|\dot{\mathbf{B}}\|} & 0 & 0 \\ \frac{z}{\|\dot{\mathbf{B}}\|} & -\frac{yz}{\|\dot{\mathbf{C}}\|\|\dot{\mathbf{B}}\|} & \frac{x}{\|\dot{\mathbf{C}}\|} & 0 \\ 0 & 0 & 0 & 1 \end{bmatrix}.$$

Therefore, the overall transformation is expressed as

$$
\begin{aligned}
\mathtt{M} &= \mathtt{M}_3\mathtt{M}_2\mathtt{M}_1 \\
&= \begin{bmatrix} \frac{x}{\|\dot{\mathbf{B}}\|} & -\frac{xy}{\|\dot{\mathbf{C}}\|\,\|\dot{\mathbf{B}}\|} & -\frac{z}{\|\dot{\mathbf{C}}\|} & 0 \\ \frac{y}{\|\dot{\mathbf{B}}\|} & \frac{\|\dot{\mathbf{C}}\|}{\|\dot{\mathbf{B}}\|} & 0 & 0 \\ \frac{z}{\|\dot{\mathbf{B}}\|} & -\frac{yz}{\|\dot{\mathbf{C}}\|\,\|\dot{\mathbf{B}}\|} & \frac{x}{\|\dot{\mathbf{C}}\|} & 0 \\ 0 & 0 & 0 & 1 \end{bmatrix} \begin{bmatrix} 1 & 0 & 0 & 0 \\ 0 & \cos(\theta) & -\sin(\theta) & 0 \\ 0 & \sin(\theta) & \cos(\theta) & 0 \\ 0 & 0 & 0 & 1 \end{bmatrix} \cdots \\
&\cdots \begin{bmatrix} \frac{x}{\|\dot{\mathbf{B}}\|} & \frac{y}{\|\dot{\mathbf{B}}\|} & \frac{z}{\|\dot{\mathbf{B}}\|} & 0 \\ -\frac{xy}{\|\dot{\mathbf{C}}\|\,\|\dot{\mathbf{B}}\|} & \frac{\|\dot{\mathbf{C}}\|}{\|\dot{\mathbf{B}}\|} & -\frac{yz}{\|\dot{\mathbf{C}}\|\,\|\dot{\mathbf{B}}\|} & 0 \\ -\frac{z}{\|\dot{\mathbf{C}}\|} & 0 & \frac{x}{\|\dot{\mathbf{C}}\|} & 0 \\ 0 & 0 & 0 & 1 \end{bmatrix}.
\end{aligned}
$$

Get the final matrix yourself! □

**Example 5.9:** [*3D general rotation—vector alignment*]
Get the transformation matrix that makes the vector $\mathbf{u} = [3, 5, 4]$ align with the vector $\mathbf{v} = [7, 8, 7]$. Use inhomogeneous coordinates.

**Solution 5.9:** The matrix is obtained by applying the following steps:

1. Align the vector $\mathbf{u}$ with the $x$-axis using Eq. (5.13) after removing the last row and column. Thus,

$$
\mathtt{M}_1 = \begin{bmatrix} \frac{x_\mathbf{u}}{\|\dot{\mathbf{B}}_\mathbf{u}\|} & \frac{y_\mathbf{u}}{\|\dot{\mathbf{B}}_\mathbf{u}\|} & \frac{z_\mathbf{u}}{\|\dot{\mathbf{B}}_\mathbf{u}\|} \\ -\frac{x_\mathbf{u} y_\mathbf{u}}{\|\dot{\mathbf{C}}_\mathbf{u}\|\,\|\dot{\mathbf{B}}_\mathbf{u}\|} & \frac{\|\dot{\mathbf{C}}_\mathbf{u}\|}{\|\dot{\mathbf{B}}_\mathbf{u}\|} & -\frac{y_\mathbf{u} z_\mathbf{u}}{\|\dot{\mathbf{C}}_\mathbf{u}\|\,\|\dot{\mathbf{B}}_\mathbf{u}\|} \\ -\frac{z_\mathbf{u}}{\|\dot{\mathbf{C}}_\mathbf{u}\|} & 0 & \frac{x_\mathbf{u}}{\|\dot{\mathbf{C}}_\mathbf{u}\|} \end{bmatrix},
$$

where $\|\dot{\mathbf{B}}_\mathbf{u}\| = \sqrt{x_\mathbf{u}^2 + y_\mathbf{u}^2 + z_\mathbf{u}^2} = \sqrt{3^2 + 4^2 + 5^2} = 5\sqrt{2}$ and $\|\dot{\mathbf{C}}_\mathbf{u}\| = \sqrt{x_\mathbf{u}^2 + z_\mathbf{u}^2} = \sqrt{3^2 + 4^2} = 5$. Thus,

$$
\begin{aligned}
\mathtt{M}_1 &= \begin{bmatrix} \frac{3}{5\sqrt{2}} & \frac{5}{5\sqrt{2}} & \frac{4}{5\sqrt{2}} \\ -\frac{3 \times 5}{5 \times 5\sqrt{2}} & \frac{5}{5\sqrt{2}} & -\frac{5 \times 4}{5 \times 5\sqrt{2}} \\ -\frac{4}{5} & 0 & \frac{3}{5} \end{bmatrix} = \begin{bmatrix} \frac{3}{5\sqrt{2}} & \frac{1}{\sqrt{2}} & \frac{4}{5\sqrt{2}} \\ -\frac{3}{5\sqrt{2}} & \frac{1}{\sqrt{2}} & -\frac{4}{5\sqrt{2}} \\ -\frac{4}{5} & 0 & \frac{3}{5} \end{bmatrix} \\
&= \begin{bmatrix} 0.4243 & 0.7071 & 0.5657 \\ -0.4243 & 0.7071 & -0.5657 \\ -0.8000 & 0 & 0.6000 \end{bmatrix}.
\end{aligned}
$$

2. Align the rotated vector in the previous step with the vector **v** using Eq. (5.14) after removing the last row and column. Thus,

$$\mathrm{M}_2 = \begin{bmatrix} \frac{x_\mathbf{v}}{\|\dot{\mathbf{B}}_\mathbf{v}\|} & -\frac{x_\mathbf{v} y_\mathbf{v}}{\|\dot{\mathbf{C}}_\mathbf{v}\|\|\dot{\mathbf{B}}_\mathbf{v}\|} & -\frac{z_\mathbf{v}}{\|\dot{\mathbf{C}}_\mathbf{v}\|} \\ \frac{y_\mathbf{v}}{\|\dot{\mathbf{B}}_\mathbf{v}\|} & \frac{\|\dot{\mathbf{C}}_\mathbf{v}\|}{\|\dot{\mathbf{B}}_\mathbf{v}\|} & 0 \\ \frac{z_\mathbf{v}}{\|\dot{\mathbf{B}}_\mathbf{v}\|} & -\frac{y_\mathbf{v} z_\mathbf{v}}{\|\dot{\mathbf{C}}_\mathbf{v}\|\|\dot{\mathbf{B}}_\mathbf{v}\|} & \frac{x_\mathbf{v}}{\|\dot{\mathbf{C}}_\mathbf{v}\|} \end{bmatrix},$$

where $\|\dot{\mathbf{B}}_\mathbf{v}\| = \sqrt{x_\mathbf{v}^2 + y_\mathbf{v}^2 + z_\mathbf{v}^2} = \sqrt{7^2 + 8^2 + 7^2} = 9\sqrt{2}$ and $\|\dot{\mathbf{C}}_\mathbf{v}\| = \sqrt{x_\mathbf{v}^2 + z_\mathbf{v}^2} = \sqrt{7^2 + 7^2} = 7\sqrt{2}$. Thus,

$$\mathrm{M}_2 = \begin{bmatrix} \frac{7}{9\sqrt{2}} & -\frac{7 \times 8}{7\sqrt{2} \times 9\sqrt{2}} & -\frac{7}{7\sqrt{2}} \\ \frac{8}{9\sqrt{2}} & \frac{7\sqrt{2}}{9\sqrt{2}} & 0 \\ \frac{7}{9\sqrt{2}} & -\frac{8 \times 7}{7\sqrt{2} \times 9\sqrt{2}} & \frac{7}{7\sqrt{2}} \end{bmatrix} = \begin{bmatrix} \frac{7}{9\sqrt{2}} & -\frac{4}{9} & -\frac{1}{\sqrt{2}} \\ \frac{8}{9\sqrt{2}} & \frac{7}{9} & 0 \\ \frac{7}{9\sqrt{2}} & -\frac{4}{9} & \frac{1}{\sqrt{2}} \end{bmatrix}$$
$$= \begin{bmatrix} 0.5500 & -0.4444 & -0.7071 \\ 0.6285 & 0.7778 & 0 \\ 0.5500 & -0.4444 & 0.7071 \end{bmatrix}.$$

Therefore, the overall transformation is expressed as

$$\begin{aligned} \mathrm{M} &= \mathrm{M}_2\mathrm{M}_1 \\ &= \begin{bmatrix} \frac{7}{9\sqrt{2}} & -\frac{4}{9} & -\frac{1}{\sqrt{2}} \\ \frac{8}{9\sqrt{2}} & \frac{7}{9} & 0 \\ \frac{7}{9\sqrt{2}} & -\frac{4}{9} & \frac{1}{\sqrt{2}} \end{bmatrix} \begin{bmatrix} \frac{3}{5\sqrt{2}} & \frac{1}{\sqrt{2}} & \frac{4}{5\sqrt{2}} \\ -\frac{3}{5\sqrt{2}} & \frac{1}{\sqrt{2}} & -\frac{4}{5\sqrt{2}} \\ -\frac{4}{5} & 0 & \frac{3}{5} \end{bmatrix} \\ &= \begin{bmatrix} \frac{7}{30} + \frac{16}{15\sqrt{2}} & \frac{7}{18} - \frac{4}{9\sqrt{2}} & \frac{14}{45} - \frac{11}{45\sqrt{2}} \\ \frac{4}{15} - \frac{7}{15\sqrt{2}} & \frac{4}{9} + \frac{7}{9\sqrt{2}} & \frac{16}{45} - \frac{28}{45\sqrt{2}} \\ \frac{7}{30} - \frac{8}{15\sqrt{2}} & \frac{7}{18} - \frac{4}{9\sqrt{2}} & \frac{14}{45} + \frac{43}{45\sqrt{2}} \end{bmatrix} \\ &= \begin{bmatrix} 0.9876 & 0.0746 & 0.1383 \\ -0.0633 & 0.9944 & -0.0844 \\ -0.1438 & 0.0746 & 0.9868 \end{bmatrix}. \end{aligned}$$

□

**Example 5.10:** [*3D general rotation—vector alignment*]
In Example 5.9, what would the length of the aligned vector be?

**Solution 5.10:** The above-estimated matrix aligns the vector **u** with the vector **v** to be along the same direction (i.e., $[7, 8, 7]^T$); however, the vector **u** keeps its length (i.e., $\|\mathbf{u}\|$) after alignment. Multiplying the above-estimated matrix by the vector **u**, we get

$$\mathbf{u}' = \begin{bmatrix} 0.9876 & 0.0746 & 0.1383 \\ -0.0633 & 0.9944 & -0.0844 \\ -0.1438 & 0.0746 & 0.9868 \end{bmatrix} \begin{bmatrix} 3 \\ 5 \\ 4 \end{bmatrix} = \begin{bmatrix} 3.8889 \\ 4.4444 \\ 3.8889 \end{bmatrix},$$

which means

$$\|\mathbf{u}\| = \|\mathbf{u}'\| \neq \|\mathbf{v}\|.$$

□

**Example 5.11:** [*3D general rotation/transformation*]
Consider the triangle $\triangle\dot{\mathbf{A}}\dot{\mathbf{B}}\dot{\mathbf{C}}$ where $\dot{\mathbf{A}} = [0, 0, 0]^T$, $\dot{\mathbf{B}} = [1, 1, 1]^T$ and $\dot{\mathbf{C}} = [-2, -3, 3]^T$. The triangle is to be rotated so that the vertex $\dot{\mathbf{A}}$ remains at the origin, the edge $\overline{\dot{\mathbf{A}}\dot{\mathbf{B}}}$ coincides with the $x$-axis and the triangle $\triangle\dot{\mathbf{A}}\dot{\mathbf{B}}\dot{\mathbf{C}}$ coincides with the $xy$-plane. Estimate the transformation matrix used.

**Solution 5.11:** In order to solve this problem, apply the following steps:

1. Adjust the edge $\overline{\dot{\mathbf{A}}\dot{\mathbf{B}}}$ to coincide with the $x$-axis.

   (a) Project the edge $\overline{\dot{\mathbf{A}}\dot{\mathbf{B}}}$ onto the $zx$-plane and get the inclination angle $\alpha$ with respect to the $x$-axis. It is easy to show that $\alpha = 45°$.
   
   (b) Rotate through angle $\alpha$ about the $y$-axis using the matrix $\mathtt{R}_y(\alpha)$. Get the position of $\dot{\mathbf{B}}$ after rotation as $\dot{\mathbf{B}}_2$. Hence,

$$\begin{aligned} \mathbf{B}_2 &= \mathtt{R}_y(45)\mathbf{B} \\ &= \begin{bmatrix} \cos(45) & 0 & \sin(45) & 0 \\ 0 & 1 & 0 & 0 \\ -\sin(45) & 0 & \cos(45) & 0 \\ 0 & 0 & 0 & 1 \end{bmatrix} \begin{bmatrix} 1 \\ 1 \\ 1 \\ 1 \end{bmatrix} \\ &= \begin{bmatrix} \sqrt{2} \\ 1 \\ 0 \\ 1 \end{bmatrix} = \begin{bmatrix} 1.4142 \\ 1 \\ 0 \\ 1 \end{bmatrix}. \end{aligned}$$

   (c) The edge $\overline{\dot{\mathbf{A}}\dot{\mathbf{B}}_2}$ now is on the $xy$-plane. Get its inclination angle $\beta$ with respect to the $x$-axis as shown in Fig. 5.5a. The angle $\beta$ can be estimated as

$$\beta = \tan^{-1}\left(\frac{1}{\sqrt{2}}\right) = 35.26°.$$

   (d) Rotate through angle $-\beta$ about the $z$-axis; i.e., using $\mathtt{R}_z(-\beta)$.

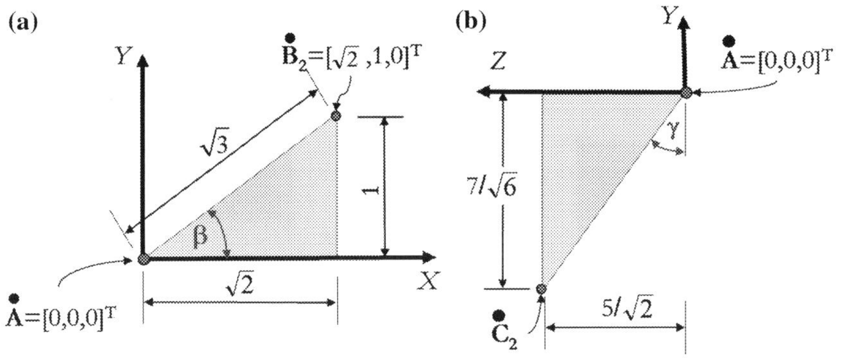


**Fig. 5.5** Rotation in 3D space. **a** Get the inclination angle $\beta$ of $\overline{\dot{\mathbf{A}}\dot{\mathbf{B}}_2}$ with respect to the $x$-axis in order to rotate about the $z$-axis. **b** Get the inclination angle $\gamma$ of $\overline{\dot{\mathbf{A}}\dot{\mathbf{C}}_2}$ with respect to the $y$-axis in order to rotate about the $x$-axis

2. Get the position of point $\dot{\mathbf{C}}_2$ after rotating $\dot{\mathbf{C}}$ using $\mathrm{R}_z(-\beta)\mathrm{R}_y(\alpha)$. Thus,

$$\begin{aligned}
\mathbf{C}_2 &= \mathrm{R}_z(-\beta)\mathrm{R}_y(\alpha)\mathbf{C} \\
&= \mathrm{R}_z(-35.26)\mathrm{R}_y(45)\mathbf{C} \\
&= \begin{bmatrix} \cos(-35.26) & -\sin(-35.26) & 0 & 0 \\ \sin(-35.26) & \cos(-35.26) & 0 & 0 \\ 0 & 0 & 1 & 0 \\ 0 & 0 & 0 & 1 \end{bmatrix} \begin{bmatrix} \cos(45) & 0 & \sin(45) & 0 \\ 0 & 1 & 0 & 0 \\ -\sin(45) & 0 & \cos(45) & 0 \\ 0 & 0 & 0 & 1 \end{bmatrix} \begin{bmatrix} -2 \\ -3 \\ 3 \\ 1 \end{bmatrix} \\
&= \begin{bmatrix} \frac{1}{\sqrt{3}} & \frac{1}{\sqrt{3}} & \frac{1}{\sqrt{3}} & 0 \\ -\frac{1}{\sqrt{6}} & \frac{\sqrt{2}}{\sqrt{3}} & -\frac{1}{\sqrt{6}} & 0 \\ -\frac{1}{\sqrt{2}} & 0 & \frac{1}{\sqrt{2}} & 0 \\ 0 & 0 & 0 & 1 \end{bmatrix} \begin{bmatrix} -2 \\ -3 \\ 3 \\ 1 \end{bmatrix} \\
&= \begin{bmatrix} -\frac{2}{\sqrt{3}} \\ -\frac{7}{\sqrt{6}} \\ \frac{5}{\sqrt{2}} \\ 1 \end{bmatrix} = \begin{bmatrix} -1.1547 \\ -2.8577 \\ 3.5355 \\ 1 \end{bmatrix}.
\end{aligned}$$

3. Get the inclination angle $\gamma$ of $\overline{\dot{\mathbf{A}}\dot{\mathbf{C}}_2}$ with respect to the $y$-axis (Fig. 5.5b) where

$$\gamma = \tan^{-1}\left(\frac{5\sqrt{6}}{7\sqrt{2}}\right) = 51.05^\circ.$$

4. Rotate through angle $\gamma$ about the $x$-axis using the matrix $\mathtt{R}_x(\gamma)$, which is estimated as

$$\mathtt{R}_x(\gamma) = \mathtt{R}_x(51.05) = \begin{bmatrix} 1 & 0 & 0 & 0 \\ 0 & \cos(51.05) & -\sin(51.05) & 0 \\ 0 & \sin(51.05) & \cos(51.05) & 0 \\ 0 & 0 & 0 & 1 \end{bmatrix}.$$

5. Hence, the overall rotation $\mathtt{R}$ can be estimated as $\mathtt{R}_x(\gamma)\mathtt{R}_z(\beta)\mathtt{R}_y(\alpha)$ where

$$\begin{aligned}
\mathtt{R} &= \mathtt{R}_x(\gamma)\mathtt{R}_z(-\beta)\mathtt{R}_y(\alpha) \\
&= \mathtt{R}_x(51.05)\mathtt{R}_z(-35.26)\mathtt{R}_y(45) \\
&= \begin{bmatrix} 1 & 0 & 0 & 0 \\ 0 & \cos(51.05) & -\sin(51.05) & 0 \\ 0 & \sin(51.05) & \cos(51.05) & 0 \\ 0 & 0 & 0 & 1 \end{bmatrix} \begin{bmatrix} \cos(-35.26) & -\sin(-35.26) & 0 & 0 \\ \sin(-35.26) & \cos(-35.26) & 0 & 0 \\ 0 & 0 & 1 & 0 \\ 0 & 0 & 0 & 1 \end{bmatrix} \cdots \\
&\cdots \begin{bmatrix} \cos(45) & 0 & \sin(45) & 0 \\ 0 & 1 & 0 & 0 \\ -\sin(45) & 0 & \cos(45) & 0 \\ 0 & 0 & 0 & 1 \end{bmatrix} \\
&= \begin{bmatrix} 0.5774 & 0.5774 & 0.5774 & 0 \\ 0.2933 & 0.5133 & -0.8066 & 0 \\ -0.762 & 0.635 & 0.127 & 0 \\ 0 & 0 & 0 & 1 \end{bmatrix}.
\end{aligned}$$

Also, the following matrix:

$$\begin{aligned}
\mathtt{R} &= \mathtt{R}_x(\gamma + 180)\mathtt{R}_z(-\beta)\mathtt{R}_y(\alpha) \\
&= \mathtt{R}_x(51.05 + 180.0)\mathtt{R}_z(-35.26)\mathtt{R}_y(45) \\
&= \begin{bmatrix} 0.5774 & 0.5774 & 0.5774 & 0 \\ -0.2933 & -0.5133 & 0.8066 & 0 \\ 0.762 & -0.635 & -0.127 & 0 \\ 0 & 0 & 0 & 1 \end{bmatrix}
\end{aligned}$$

is considered true as well.

Notice that the matrix $\mathtt{R}_z(-\beta)\mathtt{R}_y(\alpha)$, used to align $\overline{\dot{\mathbf{A}}\dot{\mathbf{B}}}$ with the $x$-axis, can be obtained using Eq. (5.13) where $x = y = z = 1$, $\|\dot{\mathbf{B}}\| = \sqrt{3}$ and $\|\dot{\mathbf{C}}\| = \sqrt{2}$. So,

$$
\begin{aligned}
\mathrm{R} &= \mathrm{R}_x(\gamma)\mathrm{R}_{zy}([x, y, z]^T) \\
&= \mathrm{R}_x(51.05)\mathrm{R}_{zy}([1, 1, 1]^T) \\
&= \begin{bmatrix} 1 & 0 & 0 & 0 \\ 0 & \cos(\gamma) & -\sin(\gamma) & 0 \\ 0 & \sin(\gamma) & \cos(\gamma) & 0 \\ 0 & 0 & 0 & 1 \end{bmatrix}
\begin{bmatrix} \frac{x}{\|\dot{\mathbf{B}}\|} & \frac{y}{\|\dot{\mathbf{B}}\|} & \frac{z}{\|\dot{\mathbf{B}}\|} & 0 \\ -\frac{xy}{\|\dot{\mathbf{C}}\|\|\dot{\mathbf{B}}\|} & \frac{\|\dot{\mathbf{C}}\|}{\|\dot{\mathbf{B}}\|} & -\frac{yz}{\|\dot{\mathbf{C}}\|\|\dot{\mathbf{B}}\|} & 0 \\ -\frac{z}{\|\dot{\mathbf{C}}\|} & 0 & \frac{x}{\|\dot{\mathbf{C}}\|} & 0 \\ 0 & 0 & 0 & 1 \end{bmatrix} \\
&= \begin{bmatrix} 1 & 0 & 0 & 0 \\ 0 & \cos(51.05) & -\sin(51.05) & 0 \\ 0 & \sin(51.05) & \cos(51.05) & 0 \\ 0 & 0 & 0 & 1 \end{bmatrix}
\begin{bmatrix} \frac{1}{\sqrt{3}} & \frac{1}{\sqrt{3}} & \frac{1}{\sqrt{3}} & 0 \\ -\frac{1}{\sqrt{2}\sqrt{3}} & \frac{\sqrt{2}}{\sqrt{3}} & -\frac{1}{\sqrt{2}\sqrt{3}} & 0 \\ -\frac{1}{\sqrt{2}} & 0 & \frac{1}{\sqrt{2}} & 0 \\ 0 & 0 & 0 & 1 \end{bmatrix} \\
&= \begin{bmatrix} 0.5774 & 0.5774 & 0.5774 & 0 \\ 0.2933 & 0.5133 & -0.8066 & 0 \\ -0.762 & 0.635 & 0.127 & 0 \\ 0 & 0 & 0 & 1 \end{bmatrix}.
\end{aligned}
$$

□

## 5.3 Scaling in 3D Space

In order to scale an object in 3D space by a factor $s$ along all directions, the positions of its vertices $[x_i, y_i, z_i]^T$ are multiplied by this scaling factor to get $[s\,x_i, s\,y_i, s\,z_i]^T$. Note that scaling is performed with respect to the origin of the coordinate system. Different scaling factors $s_x$, $s_y$ and $s_z$ can be used along the $x$-, $y$- and $z$-directions respectively as

$$
\begin{aligned}
x_2 &= s_x x_1, \\
y_2 &= s_y y_1, \\
z_2 &= s_z z_1.
\end{aligned}
\tag{5.15}
$$

In a matrix form, this can be expressed as

$$
\underbrace{\begin{bmatrix} x_2 \\ y_2 \\ z_2 \end{bmatrix}}_{\dot{\mathbf{P}}_2} = \underbrace{\begin{bmatrix} s_x & 0 & 0 \\ 0 & s_y & 0 \\ 0 & 0 & s_z \end{bmatrix}}_{\dot{\mathrm{S}}(s_x, s_y, s_z)} \underbrace{\begin{bmatrix} x_1 \\ y_1 \\ z_1 \end{bmatrix}}_{\dot{\mathbf{P}}_1},
\tag{5.16}
$$

where $\dot{\mathrm{S}}$ is a $3 \times 3$ matrix representing the scaling operation for inhomogeneous points in 3D space; and $s_x$, $s_y$ and $s_z$ are the scaling factors along the $x$-, $y$- and $z$-directions respectively. Note that if $s_x = s_y = s_z$, the object will be scaled by the same ratio along all directions. This is referred to as *3D uniform scaling*; otherwise, this is referred to as *3D non-uniform scaling*. As done previously with rotation, the scaling operation can be expressed in homogeneous coordinates as

$$\underbrace{\begin{bmatrix} x_2 \\ y_2 \\ z_2 \\ 1 \end{bmatrix}}_{\mathbf{P}_2} = \underbrace{\begin{bmatrix} s_x & 0 & 0 & 0 \\ 0 & s_y & 0 & 0 \\ 0 & 0 & s_z & 0 \\ 0 & 0 & 0 & 1 \end{bmatrix}}_{\mathsf{S}(s_x,s_y,s_z)} \underbrace{\begin{bmatrix} x_1 \\ y_1 \\ z_1 \\ 1 \end{bmatrix}}_{\mathbf{P}_1}, \tag{5.17}$$

where $\mathsf{S}$ is a $4 \times 4$ matrix representing the scaling operation for homogeneous points in 3D space; and $s_x$, $s_y$ and $s_z$ are the scaling factors along the $x$-, $y$- and $z$-directions respectively.

### 5.3.1 General Scaling in 3D Space

In general, scaling in 3D space may be performed with respect to an arbitrary point. In this case, translation must be applied prior to using the above scaling operation. Thus, if the arbitrary point $\dot{\mathbf{P}}_0$ is located at $[x_0, y_0, z_0]^T$ then the following steps should be performed to apply general scaling:

1. Translate the object to be scaled using a translation vector $[-x_0, -y_0, -z_0]^T$. This step shifts the arbitrary point $\dot{\mathbf{P}}_0$ (with the object to be scaled) to the origin.
2. Apply scaling in inhomogeneous coordinates using either Eq. (5.15) or Eq. (5.16) or in homogeneous coordinates using Eq. (5.17).
3. Translate the object back using a translation vector $[x_0, y_0, z_0]^T$. This reverses the translation operation done in Step 1.

This series of steps can be expressed in inhomogeneous coordinates as

$$\underbrace{\begin{bmatrix} x_2 \\ y_2 \\ z_2 \end{bmatrix}}_{\dot{\mathbf{P}}_2} = \underbrace{\begin{bmatrix} s_x & 0 & 0 \\ 0 & s_y & 0 \\ 0 & 0 & s_z \end{bmatrix}}_{\dot{\mathsf{S}}(s_x,s_y,s_z)} \underbrace{\begin{bmatrix} x_1 - x_0 \\ y_1 - y_0 \\ z_1 - z_0 \end{bmatrix}}_{\dot{\mathbf{P}}_1 - \dot{\mathbf{P}}_0} + \underbrace{\begin{bmatrix} x_0 \\ y_0 \\ z_0 \end{bmatrix}}_{\dot{\mathbf{P}}_0}, \tag{5.18}$$

where $\dot{\mathsf{S}}$ is the scaling matrix; $s_x$, $s_y$ and $s_z$ are the scaling factors; $[-x_0, -y_0, -z_0]^T$ and $[x_0, y_0, z_0]^T$ are the translation vectors; $\dot{\mathbf{P}}_0$ is the fixed point; $\dot{\mathbf{P}}_1$ is the point before scaling; and $\dot{\mathbf{P}}_2$ is the point after scaling. The same operation can be performed in homogeneous coordinates as

$$\underbrace{\begin{bmatrix} x_2 \\ y_2 \\ z_2 \\ 1 \end{bmatrix}}_{\mathbf{P}_2} = \underbrace{\begin{bmatrix} 1 & 0 & 0 & x_0 \\ 0 & 1 & 0 & y_0 \\ 0 & 0 & 1 & z_0 \\ 0 & 0 & 0 & 1 \end{bmatrix}}_{\mathtt{T}([x_0,y_0,z_0]^T)} \underbrace{\begin{bmatrix} s_x & 0 & 0 & 0 \\ 0 & s_y & 0 & 0 \\ 0 & 0 & s_z & 0 \\ 0 & 0 & 0 & 1 \end{bmatrix}}_{\mathtt{S}(s_x,s_y,s_z)} \underbrace{\begin{bmatrix} 1 & 0 & 0 & -x_0 \\ 0 & 1 & 0 & -y_0 \\ 0 & 0 & 1 & -z_0 \\ 0 & 0 & 0 & 1 \end{bmatrix}}_{\mathtt{T}([-x_0,-y_0,-z_0]^T)} \underbrace{\begin{bmatrix} x_1 \\ y_1 \\ z_1 \\ 1 \end{bmatrix}}_{\mathbf{P}_1}$$
$$= \underbrace{\begin{bmatrix} s_x & 0 & 0 & x_0 - s_x x_0 \\ 0 & s_y & 0 & y_0 - s_y y_0 \\ 0 & 0 & s_z & z_0 - s_z z_0 \\ 0 & 0 & 0 & 1 \end{bmatrix}}_{\mathtt{T}([x_0,y_0,z_0]^T)\mathtt{S}\mathtt{T}([-x_0,-y_0,-z_0]^T)} \underbrace{\begin{bmatrix} x_1 \\ y_1 \\ z_1 \\ 1 \end{bmatrix}}_{\mathbf{P}_1}, \tag{5.19}$$

where $\mathtt{S}$ is the scaling matrix; $s_x$, $s_y$ and $s_z$ are the scaling factors; $[-x_0, -y_0, -z_0]^T$ and $[x_0, y_0, z_0]^T$ are the translation vectors; $\mathbf{P}_0$ is the fixed point; $\mathbf{P}_1$ is the point before scaling; and $\mathbf{P}_2$ is the point after scaling.

**Example 5.12:** [*3D scaling*]

A vertex of a pyramid is located at $\dot{\mathbf{P}}_1 = [2, 2, 1]^T$. If the pyramid is to be scaled using scaling factors of 0.5, 1.5, 1 along the $x$-, $y$- and $z$-directions respectively with respect to the point $[2, -2, -2]^T$, find the location of $\dot{\mathbf{P}}_1$ after scaling.

**Solution 5.12:** As mentioned above, we will apply the following steps:

1. Translate the pyramid using the translation vector $[-2, 2, 2]^T$ to move the fixed point to the origin. We may use a translation matrix in homogeneous coordinates that can be expressed as

$$\mathtt{T}([-2, 2, 2]^T) = \begin{bmatrix} 1 & 0 & 0 & -2 \\ 0 & 1 & 0 & 2 \\ 0 & 0 & 1 & 2 \\ 0 & 0 & 0 & 1 \end{bmatrix}.$$

2. Perform scaling operation using factors of 0.5, 1.5 and 1 along the $x$-, $y$- and $z$-directions respectively. This is done using the scaling matrix $\mathtt{S}$, which is expressed as

$$\mathtt{S}(0.5, 1.5, 1) = \begin{bmatrix} 0.5 & 0 & 0 & 0 \\ 0 & 1.5 & 0 & 0 \\ 0 & 0 & 1 & 0 \\ 0 & 0 & 0 & 1 \end{bmatrix}.$$

3. Translate the pyramid back using the translation vector $[2, -2, -2]^T$. This is to reverse the translation operation performed in Step 1. The translation matrix is expressed as

$$\mathtt{T}([2, -2, -2]^T) = \begin{bmatrix} 1 & 0 & 0 & 2 \\ 0 & 1 & 0 & -2 \\ 0 & 0 & 1 & -2 \\ 0 & 0 & 0 & 1 \end{bmatrix}.$$

Thus, the point after scaling is expressed as

$$
\begin{bmatrix} x_2 \\ y_2 \\ z_2 \\ 1 \end{bmatrix} = \mathtt{T}([2,-2,-2]^T)\mathtt{S}(0.5,1.5,1)\mathtt{T}([-2,2,2]^T)
$$
$$
= \begin{bmatrix} 1 & 0 & 0 & 2 \\ 0 & 1 & 0 & -2 \\ 0 & 0 & 1 & -2 \\ 0 & 0 & 0 & 1 \end{bmatrix} \begin{bmatrix} 0.5 & 0 & 0 & 0 \\ 0 & 1.5 & 0 & 0 \\ 0 & 0 & 1 & 0 \\ 0 & 0 & 0 & 1 \end{bmatrix} \begin{bmatrix} 1 & 0 & 0 & -2 \\ 0 & 1 & 0 & 2 \\ 0 & 0 & 1 & 2 \\ 0 & 0 & 0 & 1 \end{bmatrix} \begin{bmatrix} 2 \\ 2 \\ 1 \\ 1 \end{bmatrix}
$$
$$
= \begin{bmatrix} 2 \\ 4 \\ 1 \\ 1 \end{bmatrix}.
$$

□

## 5.4 Reflection in 3D Space

In 3D space, an object may be reflected about an axis or a plane. The process of 3D reflection about an axis is similar to the 2D case discussed in Chap. 3. Basically, reflection with respect to an axis is equivalent to a 180°-rotation about that axis. A reflection with respect to one of the coordinate planes (i.e. $xy$-, $yz$- or $zx$-plane) is equivalent to a conversion between a right-handed frame and a left-handed frame (Sect. B.1.1).

### *5.4.1 Reflection About the $xy$-Plane*

As depicted in Fig. 5.6a, an object may be reflected about the $xy$-plane. 3D reflection about the $xy$-plane reverses the sign of the $z$-coordinates, leaving the $x$- and $y$-coordinates unchanged. Thus, if a point $\dot{\mathbf{P}}_1 = [x_1, y_1, z_1]^T$ is reflected about the $xy$-plane to another point $\dot{\mathbf{P}}_2 = [x_2, y_2, z_2]^T$, we can write

$$
\begin{aligned}
x_2 &= x_1, \\
y_2 &= y_1, \\
z_2 &= -z_1.
\end{aligned} \tag{5.20}
$$

Alternatively, this can be written as

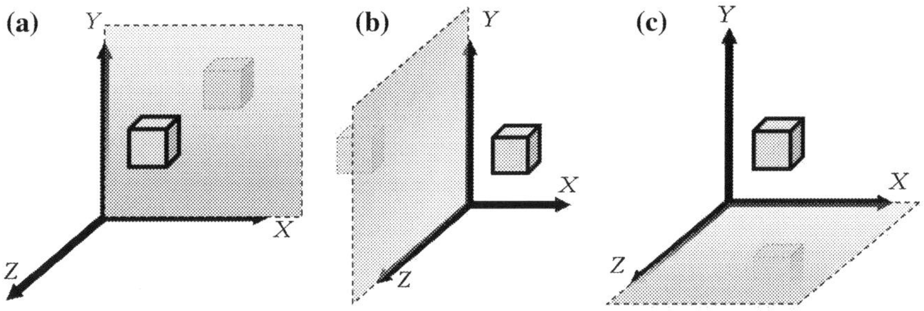


**Fig. 5.6** Reflection in 3D space. **a** Reflection about the $xy$-plane. **b** Reflection about the $yz$-plane. **c** Reflection about the $zx$-plane

$$\underbrace{\begin{bmatrix} x_2 \\ y_2 \\ z_2 \end{bmatrix}}_{\dot{\mathbf{P}}_2} = \underbrace{\begin{bmatrix} 1 & 0 & 0 \\ 0 & 1 & 0 \\ 0 & 0 & -1 \end{bmatrix}}_{\dot{\texttt{Ref}}_{xy}} \underbrace{\begin{bmatrix} x_1 \\ y_1 \\ z_1 \end{bmatrix}}_{\dot{\mathbf{P}}_1}, \tag{5.21}$$

where $\dot{\texttt{Ref}}_{xy}$ is a $3 \times 3$ matrix representing the reflection operation about the $xy$-plane for inhomogeneous points in 3D space. In homogenous coordinates, reflection about the $xy$-plane can be expressed as

$$\underbrace{\begin{bmatrix} x_2 \\ y_2 \\ z_2 \\ 1 \end{bmatrix}}_{\mathbf{P}_2} = \underbrace{\begin{bmatrix} 1 & 0 & 0 & 0 \\ 0 & 1 & 0 & 0 \\ 0 & 0 & -1 & 0 \\ 0 & 0 & 0 & 1 \end{bmatrix}}_{\texttt{Ref}_{xy}} \underbrace{\begin{bmatrix} x_1 \\ y_1 \\ z_1 \\ 1 \end{bmatrix}}_{\mathbf{P}_1}, \tag{5.22}$$

where $\texttt{Ref}_{xy}$ is a $4 \times 4$ matrix representing the reflection operation about the $xy$-plane for homogeneous points in 3D space.

### 5.4.2 *Reflection About the yz-Plane*

As depicted in Fig. 5.6b, an object may be reflected about the $yz$-plane. 3D reflection about the $yz$-plane reverses the sign of the $x$-coordinates, leaving the $y$- and $z$-coordinates unchanged. Thus, if a point $\dot{\mathbf{P}}_1 = [x_1, y_1, z_1]^T$ is reflected about the $yz$-plane to another point $\dot{\mathbf{P}}_2 = [x_2, y_2, z_2]^T$, we can write

$$\begin{aligned} x_2 &= -x_1, \\ y_2 &= y_1, \\ z_2 &= z_1. \end{aligned} \tag{5.23}$$

Alternatively, this can be written as

$$\underbrace{\begin{bmatrix} x_2 \\ y_2 \\ z_2 \end{bmatrix}}_{\dot{\mathbf{P}}_2} = \underbrace{\begin{bmatrix} -1 & 0 & 0 \\ 0 & 1 & 0 \\ 0 & 0 & 1 \end{bmatrix}}_{\dot{\mathtt{Ref}}_{yz}} \underbrace{\begin{bmatrix} x_1 \\ y_1 \\ z_1 \end{bmatrix}}_{\dot{\mathbf{P}}_1}, \tag{5.24}$$

where $\dot{\mathtt{Ref}}_{yz}$ is a $3 \times 3$ matrix representing the reflection operation about the $yz$-plane for inhomogeneous points in 3D space. In homogenous coordinates, reflection about the $yz$-plane can be expressed as

$$\underbrace{\begin{bmatrix} x_2 \\ y_2 \\ z_2 \\ 1 \end{bmatrix}}_{\mathbf{P}_2} = \underbrace{\begin{bmatrix} -1 & 0 & 0 & 0 \\ 0 & 1 & 0 & 0 \\ 0 & 0 & 1 & 0 \\ 0 & 0 & 0 & 1 \end{bmatrix}}_{\mathtt{Ref}_{yz}} \underbrace{\begin{bmatrix} x_1 \\ y_1 \\ z_1 \\ 1 \end{bmatrix}}_{\mathbf{P}_1}, \tag{5.25}$$

where $\mathtt{Ref}_{yz}$ is a $4 \times 4$ matrix representing the reflection operation about the $yz$-plane for homogeneous points in 3D space.

### *5.4.3 Reflection About the zx-Plane*

Also, as depicted in Fig. 5.6c, an object may be reflected about the $zx$-plane. 3D reflection about the $zx$-plane reverses the sign of the $y$-coordinates, leaving the $z$- and $x$-coordinates unchanged. Thus, if a point $\dot{\mathbf{P}}_1 = [x_1, y_1, z_1]^T$ is reflected about the $zx$-plane to another point $\dot{\mathbf{P}}_2 = [x_2, y_2, z_2]^T$, we can write

$$\begin{aligned} x_2 &= x_1, \\ y_2 &= -y_1, \\ z_2 &= z_1. \end{aligned} \tag{5.26}$$

Alternatively, this can be written as

$$\underbrace{\begin{bmatrix} x_2 \\ y_2 \\ z_2 \end{bmatrix}}_{\dot{\mathbf{P}}_2} = \underbrace{\begin{bmatrix} 1 & 0 & 0 \\ 0 & -1 & 0 \\ 0 & 0 & 1 \end{bmatrix}}_{\dot{\mathtt{Ref}}_{zx}} \underbrace{\begin{bmatrix} x_1 \\ y_1 \\ z_1 \end{bmatrix}}_{\dot{\mathbf{P}}_1}, \tag{5.27}$$

where $\dot{\mathtt{Ref}}_{zx}$ is a $3 \times 3$ matrix representing the reflection operation about the $zx$-plane for inhomogeneous points in 3D space. In homogenous coordinates, reflection about the $zx$-plane can be expressed as

$$\underbrace{\begin{bmatrix} x_2 \\ y_2 \\ z_2 \\ 1 \end{bmatrix}}_{\mathbf{P}_2} = \underbrace{\begin{bmatrix} 1 & 0 & 0 & 0 \\ 0 & -1 & 0 & 0 \\ 0 & 0 & 1 & 0 \\ 0 & 0 & 0 & 1 \end{bmatrix}}_{\texttt{Ref}_{zx}} \underbrace{\begin{bmatrix} x_1 \\ y_1 \\ z_1 \\ 1 \end{bmatrix}}_{\mathbf{P}_1}, \tag{5.28}$$

where $\texttt{Ref}_{zx}$ is a $4 \times 4$ matrix representing the reflection operation about the $zx$-plane for homogeneous points in 3D space.

### *5.4.4 General Reflection in 3D Space*

We talked about how to reflect a point (or an object) about one of the $xy$-, $yz$- and $zx$-planes; however, in general, reflection may be performed about an arbitrary plane. In this case, the reflection operations of Eq. (5.20) through Eq. (5.28) cannot be used directly. Instead, the plane of reflection (along with the point/object to be reflected) must be translated and/or rotated in order to coincide with one of the principal planes before applying the reflection. Afterwards, initial translation and/or rotation should be reversed.

Thus, in order to reflect a point about an arbitrary plane that does not coincide with any of the principal planes, do the following:

1. If the reflection plane does not pass through the origin $[0, 0, 0]^T$, translate the point and the arbitrary plane by a translation vector that causes this plane to pass through the origin.
2. If the reflection plane does not coincide with a principal plane, rotate the point as well as the arbitrary plane so that the arbitrary plane coincide with one of the principal planes; i.e., $xy$-, $yz$- or $zx$-plane. Note that more that a single rotation may be needed to satisfy this step.
3. Perform the specified point reflection about the selected principal plane.
4. Apply inverse rotation (if Step 2 has been performed).
5. Apply inverse translation (if Step 1 has been performed).

**Example 5.13:** [*3D general reflection—plane parallel to $zx$-plane*]
Derive a matrix that reflects a point $[x, y, z]^T$ about the plane $y = \delta$ where $\delta$ is a real number.

**Solution 5.13:** Notice that the plane $y = \delta$ is parallel to the $zx$-plane. In order to get the overall transformation, perform the following steps:

1. Translate the plane $y = \delta$ so that it coincides with the $zx$-plane using the matrix $\texttt{M}_1$ where

$$\mathtt{M}_1 = \mathtt{T}([0, -\delta, 0]^T) = \begin{bmatrix} 1 & 0 & 0 & 0 \\ 0 & 1 & 0 & -\delta \\ 0 & 0 & 1 & 0 \\ 0 & 0 & 0 & 1 \end{bmatrix}.$$

2. Reflect about the $zx$-plane using the matrix $\mathtt{M}_2$ where

$$\mathtt{M}_2 = \mathtt{Ref}_{zx} = \begin{bmatrix} 1 & 0 & 0 & 0 \\ 0 & -1 & 0 & 0 \\ 0 & 0 & 1 & 0 \\ 0 & 0 & 0 & 1 \end{bmatrix}.$$

3. Translate back using the vector $[0, \delta, 0]^T$ and the matrix $\mathtt{M}_3$ where

$$\mathtt{M}_3 = \mathtt{T}([0, \delta, 0]^T) = \begin{bmatrix} 1 & 0 & 0 & 0 \\ 0 & 1 & 0 & \delta \\ 0 & 0 & 1 & 0 \\ 0 & 0 & 0 & 1 \end{bmatrix}.$$

The overall transformation matrix can be calculated as

$$\begin{aligned} \mathtt{M} &= \mathtt{M}_3\mathtt{M}_2\mathtt{M}_1 \\ &= \begin{bmatrix} 1 & 0 & 0 & 0 \\ 0 & 1 & 0 & \delta \\ 0 & 0 & 1 & 0 \\ 0 & 0 & 0 & 1 \end{bmatrix} \begin{bmatrix} 1 & 0 & 0 & 0 \\ 0 & -1 & 0 & 0 \\ 0 & 0 & 1 & 0 \\ 0 & 0 & 0 & 1 \end{bmatrix} \begin{bmatrix} 1 & 0 & 0 & 0 \\ 0 & 1 & 0 & -\delta \\ 0 & 0 & 1 & 0 \\ 0 & 0 & 0 & 1 \end{bmatrix} \\ &= \begin{bmatrix} 1 & 0 & 0 & 0 \\ 0 & -1 & 0 & 2\delta \\ 0 & 0 & 1 & 0 \\ 0 & 0 & 0 & 1 \end{bmatrix}. \end{aligned}$$

□

**Example 5.14:** [*3D general reflection—plane passing through the origin*]
Derive a matrix that reflects a point $[x, y, z]^T$ about the plane $z = \sqrt{3}y$.

**Solution 5.14:** The plane $z = \sqrt{3}y$ is drawn in Fig. 5.7a. In order to get the overall transformation, perform the following steps:

1. Calculate the angle between the plane $z = \sqrt{3}y$ and the $zx$-plane. It is easy to show that this angle is 30°. This is illustrated in Fig. 5.7b.
2. Rotate through an angle of 30° about the $x$-axis using the matrix $\mathtt{M}_1$ where

$$\mathtt{M}_1 = \mathrm{R}_x(30) = \begin{bmatrix} 1 & 0 & 0 & 0 \\ 0 & \cos(30) & 0 & -\sin(30) \\ 0 & \sin(30) & 0 & \cos(30) \\ 0 & 0 & 0 & 1 \end{bmatrix}.$$

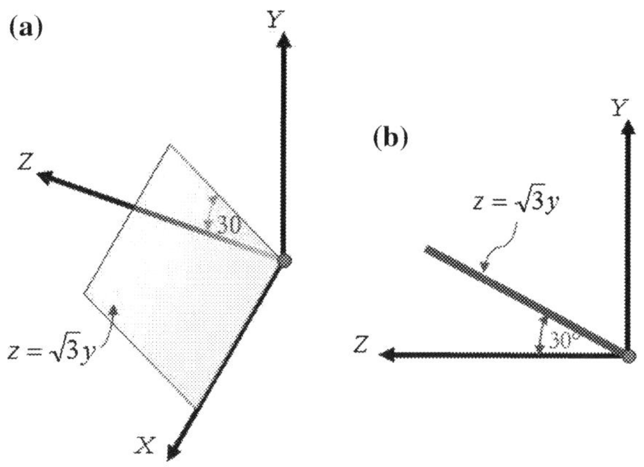


**Fig. 5.7** **a** The plane $z = \sqrt{3}y$. **b** The angle between the plane $z = \sqrt{3}y$ and the $zx$-plane is 30°

This step enforces the reflection plane to coincide with the $zx$-plane.

3. Reflect about the $zx$-plane using the matrix $\mathtt{M}_2$ where

$$\mathtt{M}_2 = \mathtt{Ref}_{zx} = \begin{bmatrix} 1 & 0 & 0 & 0 \\ 0 & -1 & 0 & 0 \\ 0 & 0 & 1 & 0 \\ 0 & 0 & 0 & 1 \end{bmatrix}.$$

4. Rotate through an angle of −30° about the $x$-axis using the matrix $\mathtt{M}_3$ where

$$\mathtt{M}_3 = \mathtt{R}_x(-30) = \begin{bmatrix} 1 & 0 & 0 & 0 \\ 0 & \cos(-30) & 0 & -\sin(-30) \\ 0 & \sin(-30) & 0 & \cos(-30) \\ 0 & 0 & 0 & 1 \end{bmatrix}.$$

The overall transformation matrix can be calculated as

$$\begin{aligned}
\mathtt{M} &= \mathtt{M}_3\mathtt{M}_2\mathtt{M}_1 \\
&= \begin{bmatrix} 1 & 0 & 0 & 0 \\ 0 & \cos(-30) & -\sin(-30) & 0 \\ 0 & \sin(-30) & \cos(-30) & 0 \\ 0 & 0 & 0 & 1 \end{bmatrix} \begin{bmatrix} 1 & 0 & 0 & 0 \\ 0 & -1 & 0 & 0 \\ 0 & 0 & 1 & 0 \\ 0 & 0 & 0 & 1 \end{bmatrix} \begin{bmatrix} 1 & 0 & 0 & 0 \\ 0 & \cos(30) & -\sin(30) & 0 \\ 0 & \sin(30) & \cos(30) & 0 \\ 0 & 0 & 0 & 1 \end{bmatrix} \\
&= \begin{bmatrix} 1 & 0 & 0 & 0 \\ 0 & \frac{\sqrt{3}}{2} & \frac{1}{2} & 0 \\ 0 & -\frac{1}{2} & \frac{\sqrt{3}}{2} & 0 \\ 0 & 0 & 0 & 1 \end{bmatrix} \begin{bmatrix} 1 & 0 & 0 & 0 \\ 0 & -1 & 0 & 0 \\ 0 & 0 & 1 & 0 \\ 0 & 0 & 0 & 1 \end{bmatrix} \begin{bmatrix} 1 & 0 & 0 & 0 \\ 0 & \frac{\sqrt{3}}{2} & -\frac{1}{2} & 0 \\ 0 & \frac{1}{2} & \frac{\sqrt{3}}{2} & 0 \\ 0 & 0 & 0 & 1 \end{bmatrix} \\
&= \begin{bmatrix} 1 & 0 & 0 & 0 \\ 0 & -\frac{1}{2} & \frac{\sqrt{3}}{2} & 0 \\ 0 & \frac{\sqrt{3}}{2} & \frac{1}{2} & 0 \\ 0 & 0 & 0 & 1 \end{bmatrix} = \begin{bmatrix} 1 & 0 & 0 & 0 \\ 0 & -0.5 & 0.866 & 0 \\ 0 & 0.866 & 0.5 & 0 \\ 0 & 0 & 0 & 1 \end{bmatrix}.
\end{aligned}$$

Alternatively, the same overall transformation can be obtained by performing the following steps:

1. Calculate the angle between the plane $z = \sqrt{3}y$ and the $xy$-plane. It is easy to show that this angle is 60°.
2. Rotate through an angle of −60° about the $x$-axis using the matrix $\mathtt{M}_1$ where

$$\mathtt{M}_1 = \mathtt{R}_x(-60) = \begin{bmatrix} 1 & 0 & 0 & 0 \\ 0 & \cos(-60) & -\sin(-60) & 0 \\ 0 & \sin(-60) & \cos(-60) & 0 \\ 0 & 0 & 0 & 1 \end{bmatrix}.$$

   This step enforces the reflection plane to coincide with the $xy$-plane.
3. Reflect about the $xy$-plane using the matrix $\mathtt{M}_2$ where

$$\mathtt{M}_2 = \mathtt{Ref}_{xy} = \begin{bmatrix} 1 & 0 & 0 & 0 \\ 0 & 1 & 0 & 0 \\ 0 & 0 & -1 & 0 \\ 0 & 0 & 0 & 1 \end{bmatrix}.$$

4. Rotate through an angle of 60° about the $x$-axis using the matrix $\mathtt{M}_3$ where

$$\mathtt{M}_3 = \mathtt{R}_x(60) = \begin{bmatrix} 1 & 0 & 0 & 0 \\ 0 & \cos(60) & -\sin(60) & 0 \\ 0 & \sin(60) & \cos(60) & 0 \\ 0 & 0 & 0 & 1 \end{bmatrix}.$$

The overall transformation matrix can be calculated as

$$\begin{aligned}
\mathtt{M} &= \mathtt{M}_3\mathtt{M}_2\mathtt{M}_1 \\
&= \begin{bmatrix} 1 & 0 & 0 & 0 \\ 0 & \cos(60) & -\sin(60) & 0 \\ 0 & \sin(60) & \cos(60) & 0 \\ 0 & 0 & 0 & 1 \end{bmatrix} \begin{bmatrix} 1 & 0 & 0 & 0 \\ 0 & 1 & 0 & 0 \\ 0 & 0 & -1 & 0 \\ 0 & 0 & 0 & 1 \end{bmatrix} \begin{bmatrix} 1 & 0 & 0 & 0 \\ 0 & \cos(-60) & -\sin(-60) & 0 \\ 0 & \sin(-60) & \cos(-60) & 0 \\ 0 & 0 & 0 & 1 \end{bmatrix} \\
&= \begin{bmatrix} 1 & 0 & 0 & 0 \\ 0 & \frac{1}{2} & -\frac{\sqrt{3}}{2} & 0 \\ 0 & -\frac{\sqrt{3}}{2} & \frac{1}{2} & 0 \\ 0 & 0 & 0 & 1 \end{bmatrix} \begin{bmatrix} 1 & 0 & 0 & 0 \\ 0 & 1 & 0 & 0 \\ 0 & 0 & -1 & 0 \\ 0 & 0 & 0 & 1 \end{bmatrix} \begin{bmatrix} 1 & 0 & 0 & 0 \\ 0 & \frac{1}{2} & \frac{\sqrt{3}}{2} & 0 \\ 0 & -\frac{\sqrt{3}}{2} & \frac{1}{2} & 0 \\ 0 & 0 & 0 & 1 \end{bmatrix} \\
&= \begin{bmatrix} 1 & 0 & 0 & 0 \\ 0 & -\frac{1}{2} & \frac{\sqrt{3}}{2} & 0 \\ 0 & \frac{\sqrt{3}}{2} & \frac{1}{2} & 0 \\ 0 & 0 & 0 & 1 \end{bmatrix} = \begin{bmatrix} 1 & 0 & 0 & 0 \\ 0 & -0.5 & 0.866 & 0 \\ 0 & 0.866 & 0.5 & 0 \\ 0 & 0 & 0 & 1 \end{bmatrix},
\end{aligned}$$

which is the same matrix obtained above as expected. □

**Example 5.15:** [*3D general reflection—a plane and rotating vectors*]
Derive a transformation matrix that reflects a point about the plane $ax + by + cz = 0$.

**Solution 5.15:** The general plane equation is expressed as

$$ax + by + cz = d, \tag{5.29}$$

where $[a, b, c]^T$ is the normal vector to the plane. In case that this vector is normalized to a unit magnitude, $d$ becomes the perpendicular distance from the origin to the plane. In our case, since $d = 0$, the plane is passing through the origin. The required transformation matrix is obtained by applying the following steps:

1. Align the normal to the plane with the $x$-axis using Eq. (5.13). Thus,

$$\begin{aligned}\mathtt{M}_1 &= \mathtt{R}_{zy}([a, b, c]^T) \\ &= \begin{bmatrix} \frac{a}{\|\dot{\mathbf{B}}\|} & \frac{b}{\|\dot{\mathbf{B}}\|} & \frac{c}{\|\dot{\mathbf{B}}\|} & 0 \\ -\frac{ab}{\|\dot{\mathbf{C}}\|\|\dot{\mathbf{B}}\|} & \frac{\|\dot{\mathbf{C}}\|}{\|\dot{\mathbf{B}}\|} & -\frac{bc}{\|\dot{\mathbf{C}}\|\|\dot{\mathbf{B}}\|} & 0 \\ -\frac{c}{\|\dot{\mathbf{C}}\|} & 0 & \frac{a}{\|\dot{\mathbf{C}}\|} & 0 \\ 0 & 0 & 0 & 1 \end{bmatrix},\end{aligned}$$

where $\|\dot{\mathbf{B}}\| = \sqrt{a^2 + b^2 + c^2}$ and $\|\dot{\mathbf{C}}\| = \sqrt{a^2 + c^2}$.

2. Reflect about the $yz$-plane using Eq. (5.25). Thus,

$$\begin{aligned}\mathtt{M}_2 &= \mathtt{Ref}_{yz} \\ &= \begin{bmatrix} -1 & 0 & 0 & 0 \\ 0 & 1 & 0 & 0 \\ 0 & 0 & 1 & 0 \\ 0 & 0 & 0 & 1 \end{bmatrix}.\end{aligned}$$

3. Reverse the rotation of Step 1 using Eq. (5.14). Thus,

$$\begin{aligned}\mathtt{M}_3 &= \mathtt{R}_{zy}^{-1}([a, b, c]^T) \\ &= \begin{bmatrix} \frac{a}{\|\dot{\mathbf{B}}\|} & -\frac{ab}{\|\dot{\mathbf{C}}\|\|\dot{\mathbf{B}}\|} & -\frac{c}{\|\dot{\mathbf{C}}\|} & 0 \\ \frac{b}{\|\dot{\mathbf{B}}\|} & \frac{\|\dot{\mathbf{C}}\|}{\|\dot{\mathbf{B}}\|} & 0 & 0 \\ \frac{c}{\|\dot{\mathbf{B}}\|} & -\frac{bc}{\|\dot{\mathbf{C}}\|\|\dot{\mathbf{B}}\|} & \frac{a}{\|\dot{\mathbf{C}}\|} & 0 \\ 0 & 0 & 0 & 1 \end{bmatrix}.\end{aligned}$$

Therefore, the overall transformation is expressed as

$$\mathtt{M} = \mathtt{M}_3\mathtt{M}_2\mathtt{M}_1$$
$$= \begin{bmatrix} \frac{a}{\|\dot{\mathbf{B}}\|} & -\frac{ab}{\|\dot{\mathbf{C}}\|\|\dot{\mathbf{B}}\|} & -\frac{c}{\|\dot{\mathbf{C}}\|} & 0 \\ \frac{b}{\|\dot{\mathbf{B}}\|} & \frac{\|\dot{\mathbf{C}}\|}{\|\dot{\mathbf{B}}\|} & 0 & 0 \\ \frac{c}{\|\dot{\mathbf{B}}\|} & -\frac{bc}{\|\dot{\mathbf{C}}\|\|\dot{\mathbf{B}}\|} & \frac{a}{\|\dot{\mathbf{C}}\|} & 0 \\ 0 & 0 & 0 & 1 \end{bmatrix} \begin{bmatrix} -1 & 0 & 0 & 0 \\ 0 & 1 & 0 & 0 \\ 0 & 0 & 1 & 0 \\ 0 & 0 & 0 & 1 \end{bmatrix} \begin{bmatrix} \frac{a}{\|\dot{\mathbf{B}}\|} & \frac{b}{\|\dot{\mathbf{B}}\|} & \frac{c}{\|\dot{\mathbf{B}}\|} & 0 \\ -\frac{ab}{\|\dot{\mathbf{C}}\|\|\dot{\mathbf{B}}\|} & \frac{\|\dot{\mathbf{C}}\|}{\|\dot{\mathbf{B}}\|} & -\frac{bc}{\|\dot{\mathbf{C}}\|\|\dot{\mathbf{B}}\|} & 0 \\ -\frac{c}{\|\dot{\mathbf{C}}\|} & 0 & \frac{a}{\|\dot{\mathbf{C}}\|} & 0 \\ 0 & 0 & 0 & 1 \end{bmatrix}.$$

Get the final matrix yourself! □

## 5.5 Shearing in 3D Space

In 3D space, one can push in two coordinate axis directions and keep the third one fixed. Thus, with respect to the principal axes, there are three different shearing situations relative to these axes.

### 5.5.1 *Shearing Relative to the x-Axis*

The 3D shearing transformation can be performed relative to the $x$-axis in both $y$- and $z$-directions with shearing factors $sh_{xy}$ and $sh_{xz}$ respectively, keeping the $x$-coordinate the same. Hence, if a point $\dot{\mathbf{P}}_1 = [x_1, y_1, z_1]^T$ is sheared relative to the $x$-axis to another point $\dot{\mathbf{P}}_2 = [x_2, y_2, z_2]^T$, we can write

$$\begin{aligned} x_2 &= x_1, \\ y_2 &= y_1 + x_1 sh_{xy}, \\ z_2 &= z_1 + x_1 sh_{xz}. \end{aligned} \tag{5.30}$$

Alternatively, this can be written as

$$\underbrace{\begin{bmatrix} x_2 \\ y_2 \\ z_2 \end{bmatrix}}_{\dot{\mathbf{P}}_2} = \underbrace{\begin{bmatrix} 1 & 0 & 0 \\ sh_{xy} & 1 & 0 \\ sh_{xz} & 0 & 1 \end{bmatrix}}_{\dot{\mathtt{Sh}}_x(sh_{xy}, sh_{xz})} \underbrace{\begin{bmatrix} x_1 \\ y_1 \\ z_1 \end{bmatrix}}_{\dot{\mathbf{P}}_1}, \tag{5.31}$$

where $\dot{\mathtt{Sh}}_x$ is a $3 \times 3$ matrix representing the shearing operation relative the $x$-axis for inhomogeneous points in 3D space; and $sh_{xy}$ and $sh_{xz}$ are the shearing factors. In homogenous coordinates, the same operation can be expressed as

$$\underbrace{\begin{bmatrix} x_2 \\ y_2 \\ z_2 \\ 1 \end{bmatrix}}_{\mathbf{P}_2} = \underbrace{\begin{bmatrix} 1 & 0 & 0 & 0 \\ sh_{xy} & 1 & 0 & 0 \\ sh_{xz} & 0 & 1 & 0 \\ 0 & 0 & 0 & 1 \end{bmatrix}}_{\mathtt{Sh}_x(sh_{xy},sh_{xz})} \underbrace{\begin{bmatrix} x_1 \\ y_1 \\ z_1 \\ 1 \end{bmatrix}}_{\mathbf{P}_1}, \tag{5.32}$$

where $\mathtt{Sh}_x$ is a $4 \times 4$ matrix representing the shearing operation relative the $x$-axis for homogeneous points in 3D space; and $sh_{xy}$ and $sh_{xz}$ are the shearing factors.

### 5.5.2 Shearing Relative to the y-Axis

The 3D shearing transformation can be performed relative to the $y$-axis in both $x$- and $z$-directions with shearing factors $sh_{yx}$ and $sh_{yz}$ respectively, keeping the $y$-coordinate the same. Hence, if a point $\dot{\mathbf{P}}_1 = [x_1, y_1, z_1]^T$ is sheared relative to the $y$-axis to another point $\dot{\mathbf{P}}_2 = [x_2, y_2, z_2]^T$, we can write

$$\begin{aligned} x_2 &= x_1 + y_1 sh_{yx}, \\ y_2 &= y_1, \\ z_2 &= z_1 + y_1 sh_{yz}. \end{aligned} \tag{5.33}$$

Alternatively, this can be written as

$$\underbrace{\begin{bmatrix} x_2 \\ y_2 \\ z_2 \end{bmatrix}}_{\dot{\mathbf{P}}_2} = \underbrace{\begin{bmatrix} 1 & sh_{yx} & 0 \\ 0 & 1 & 0 \\ 0 & sh_{yz} & 1 \end{bmatrix}}_{\dot{\mathtt{Sh}}_y(sh_{yx},sh_{yz})} \underbrace{\begin{bmatrix} x_1 \\ y_1 \\ z_1 \end{bmatrix}}_{\dot{\mathbf{P}}_1}, \tag{5.34}$$

where $\dot{\mathtt{Sh}}_y$ is a $3 \times 3$ matrix representing the shearing operation relative the $y$-axis for inhomogeneous points in 3D space; and $sh_{yx}$ and $sh_{yz}$ are the shearing factors. In homogenous coordinates, the same operation can be expressed as

$$\underbrace{\begin{bmatrix} x_2 \\ y_2 \\ z_2 \\ 1 \end{bmatrix}}_{\mathbf{P}_2} = \underbrace{\begin{bmatrix} 1 & sh_{yx} & 0 & 0 \\ 0 & 1 & 0 & 0 \\ 0 & sh_{yz} & 1 & 0 \\ 0 & 0 & 0 & 1 \end{bmatrix}}_{\mathtt{Sh}_y(sh_{yx},sh_{yz})} \underbrace{\begin{bmatrix} x_1 \\ y_1 \\ z_1 \\ 1 \end{bmatrix}}_{\mathbf{P}_1}, \tag{5.35}$$

where $\mathtt{Sh}_y$ is a $4 \times 4$ matrix representing the shearing operation relative the $y$-axis for homogeneous points in 3D space; and $sh_{yx}$ and $sh_{yz}$ are the shearing factors.

### 5.5.3 Shearing Relative to the z-Axis

The 3D shearing transformation can be performed relative to the $z$-axis in both $x$- and $y$-directions with shearing factors $sh_{zx}$ and $sh_{zy}$ respectively, keeping the $z$-coordinate the same. Hence, if a point $\dot{\mathbf{P}}_1 = [x_1, y_1, z_1]^T$ is sheared relative to the $z$-axis to another point $\dot{\mathbf{P}}_2 = [x_2, y_2, z_2]^T$, we can write

$$\begin{aligned} x_2 &= x_1 + z_1 sh_{zx}, \\ y_2 &= y_1 + z_1 sh_{zy}, \\ z_2 &= z_1. \end{aligned} \tag{5.36}$$

Alternatively, this can be written as

$$\underbrace{\begin{bmatrix} x_2 \\ y_2 \\ z_2 \end{bmatrix}}_{\dot{\mathbf{P}}_2} = \underbrace{\begin{bmatrix} 1 & 0 & sh_{zx} \\ 0 & 1 & sh_{zy} \\ 0 & 0 & 1 \end{bmatrix}}_{\dot{\mathtt{Sh}}_z(sh_{zx}, sh_{zy})} \underbrace{\begin{bmatrix} x_1 \\ y_1 \\ z_1 \end{bmatrix}}_{\dot{\mathbf{P}}_1}, \tag{5.37}$$

where $\dot{\mathtt{Sh}}_z$ is a $3 \times 3$ matrix representing the shearing operation relative the $z$-axis for inhomogeneous points in 3D space; and $sh_{zx}$ and $sh_{zy}$ are the shearing factors. In homogenous coordinates, the same operation can be expressed as

$$\underbrace{\begin{bmatrix} x_2 \\ y_2 \\ z_2 \\ 1 \end{bmatrix}}_{\mathbf{P}_2} = \underbrace{\begin{bmatrix} 1 & 0 & sh_{zx} & 0 \\ 0 & 1 & sh_{zy} & 0 \\ 0 & 0 & 1 & 0 \\ 0 & 0 & 0 & 1 \end{bmatrix}}_{\mathtt{Sh}_z(sh_{zx}, sh_{zy})} \underbrace{\begin{bmatrix} x_1 \\ y_1 \\ z_1 \\ 1 \end{bmatrix}}_{\mathbf{P}_1}, \tag{5.38}$$

where $\mathtt{Sh}_z$ is a $4 \times 4$ matrix representing the shearing operation relative the $z$-axis for homogeneous points in 3D space; and $sh_{zx}$ and $sh_{zy}$ are the shearing factors.

### 5.5.4 General Shearing in 3D Space

As with general transformation (e.g., general reflection discussed in Sect. 5.4.4), shearing may be performed relative to an arbitrary axis. In this case, the shearing operations of Eq. (5.30) through Eq. (5.38) cannot be used directly. Instead, the axis (along with the point/object to be sheared) must be translated and/or rotated in order to coincide with one of the principal axes before applying the shearing. Afterwards, initial translation and/or rotation should be reversed. The steps are as follows:

1. If the axis does not pass through the origin $[0, 0, 0]^T$, translate the axis and the object under consideration by a translation vector that causes this axis to pass through the origin.
2. If the axis does not coincide with one of the principal axes (i.e., $x$-, $y$- or $z$-axis), rotate the axis and the object under consideration so that the axis coincides with one of the principal axes. Note that more that a single rotation may be needed to satisfy this step.
3. Perform the shearing operation relative to the selected principal axis.
4. Apply inverse rotation (if Step 2 has been performed).
5. Apply inverse translation (if Step 1 has been performed).

**Example 5.16:** [*3D general shearing*]
Derive a transformation matrix that shears an object using amounts 0.2 and 0.5 relative to an axis passing through the points $[0, 0, 0]^T$ and $[7, 7, 7]^T$.

**Solution 5.16:** The axis passing through the points $[0, 0, 0]^T$ and $[7, 7, 7]^T$ must be rotated to coincide with one of the principal axes then the appropriate shearing matrix is used and the transformation is reversed back. According to the values we calculated before in Sect. 5.2.5, we apply the following steps:

1. Rotate through an angle of 45° about the $y$-axis. This is using $\mathtt{M}_1$ where

$$\begin{aligned}\mathtt{M}_1 &= \mathrm{R}_y(45)\\ &= \begin{bmatrix} \cos(45) & 0 & \sin(45) & 0\\ 0 & 1 & 0 & 0\\ -\sin(45) & 0 & \cos(45) & 0\\ 0 & 0 & 0 & 1 \end{bmatrix}\\ &= \begin{bmatrix} \frac{1}{\sqrt{2}} & 0 & \frac{1}{\sqrt{2}} & 0\\ 0 & 1 & 0 & 0\\ -\frac{1}{\sqrt{2}} & 0 & \frac{1}{\sqrt{2}} & 0\\ 0 & 0 & 0 & 1 \end{bmatrix}.\end{aligned}$$

2. Rotate through an angle of $-35.26°$ about the $z$-axis. This is using $\mathtt{M}_2$ where

$$\begin{aligned}\mathtt{M}_2 &= \mathrm{R}_z(-35.26)\\ &= \begin{bmatrix} \cos(-35.26) & -\sin(-35.26) & 0 & 0\\ \sin(-35.26) & \cos(-35.26) & 0 & 0\\ 0 & 0 & 1 & 0\\ 0 & 0 & 0 & 1 \end{bmatrix}\\ &= \begin{bmatrix} \frac{\sqrt{2}}{\sqrt{3}} & \frac{1}{\sqrt{3}} & 0 & 0\\ -\frac{1}{\sqrt{3}} & \frac{\sqrt{2}}{\sqrt{3}} & 0 & 0\\ 0 & 0 & 1 & 0\\ 0 & 0 & 0 & 1 \end{bmatrix}.\end{aligned}$$

3. Shear relative to the $x$-axis using amounts 0.2 and 0.5. This is using $\mathtt{M}_3$ where

$$\begin{aligned}\mathtt{M}_3 &= \mathtt{Sh}_x(0.2, 0.5)\\ &= \begin{bmatrix} 1 & 0 & 0 & 0 \\ 0.2 & 1 & 0 & 0 \\ 0.5 & 0 & 1 & 0 \\ 0 & 0 & 0 & 1 \end{bmatrix}.\end{aligned}$$

4. Rotate through an angle of 35.26° about the $z$-axis. This is using $\mathtt{M}_4$ where

$$\begin{aligned}\mathtt{M}_4 &= \mathtt{R}_z(35.26)\\ &= \begin{bmatrix} \cos(35.26) & -\sin(35.26) & 0 & 0 \\ \sin(35.26) & \cos(35.26) & 0 & 0 \\ 0 & 0 & 1 & 0 \\ 0 & 0 & 0 & 1 \end{bmatrix}\\ &= \begin{bmatrix} \frac{\sqrt{2}}{\sqrt{3}} & -\frac{1}{\sqrt{3}} & 0 & 0 \\ \frac{1}{\sqrt{3}} & \frac{\sqrt{2}}{\sqrt{3}} & 0 & 0 \\ 0 & 0 & 1 & 0 \\ 0 & 0 & 0 & 1 \end{bmatrix}.\end{aligned}$$

5. Rotate through an angle of −45° about the $y$-axis. This is using $\mathtt{M}_5$ where

$$\begin{aligned}\mathtt{M}_5 &= \mathtt{R}_y(-45)\\ &= \begin{bmatrix} \cos(-45) & 0 & \sin(-45) & 0 \\ 0 & 1 & 0 & 0 \\ -\sin(-45) & 0 & \cos(-45) & 0 \\ 0 & 0 & 0 & 1 \end{bmatrix}\\ &= \begin{bmatrix} \frac{1}{\sqrt{2}} & 0 & -\frac{1}{\sqrt{2}} & 0 \\ 0 & 1 & 0 & 0 \\ \frac{1}{\sqrt{2}} & 0 & \frac{1}{\sqrt{2}} & 0 \\ 0 & 0 & 0 & 1 \end{bmatrix}.\end{aligned}$$

Thus, the overall transformation is expressed as

$$\begin{aligned}\mathtt{M} &= \mathtt{M}_5\mathtt{M}_4\mathtt{M}_3\mathtt{M}_2\mathtt{M}_1\\ &= \begin{bmatrix} \frac{1}{\sqrt{2}} & 0 & -\frac{1}{\sqrt{2}} & 0 \\ 0 & 1 & 0 & 0 \\ \frac{1}{\sqrt{2}} & 0 & \frac{1}{\sqrt{2}} & 0 \\ 0 & 0 & 0 & 1 \end{bmatrix} \begin{bmatrix} \frac{\sqrt{2}}{\sqrt{3}} & -\frac{1}{\sqrt{3}} & 0 & 0 \\ \frac{1}{\sqrt{3}} & \frac{\sqrt{2}}{\sqrt{3}} & 0 & 0 \\ 0 & 0 & 1 & 0 \\ 0 & 0 & 0 & 1 \end{bmatrix} \begin{bmatrix} 1 & 0 & 0 & 0 \\ 0.2 & 1 & 0 & 0 \\ 0.5 & 0 & 1 & 0 \\ 0 & 0 & 0 & 1 \end{bmatrix} \cdots\end{aligned}$$

$$
\cdots \begin{bmatrix} \frac{\sqrt{2}}{\sqrt{3}} & \frac{1}{\sqrt{3}} & 0 & 0 \\ -\frac{1}{\sqrt{3}} & \frac{\sqrt{2}}{\sqrt{3}} & 0 & 0 \\ 0 & 0 & 1 & 0 \\ 0 & 0 & 0 & 1 \end{bmatrix} \begin{bmatrix} \frac{1}{\sqrt{2}} & 0 & \frac{1}{\sqrt{2}} & 0 \\ 0 & 1 & 0 & 0 \\ -\frac{1}{\sqrt{2}} & 0 & \frac{1}{\sqrt{2}} & 0 \\ 0 & 0 & 0 & 1 \end{bmatrix}
$$

$$
= \begin{bmatrix} 1 - \frac{1}{15\sqrt{2}} - \frac{1}{2\sqrt{6}} & -\frac{1}{15\sqrt{2}} - \frac{1}{2\sqrt{6}} & -\frac{1}{15\sqrt{2}} - \frac{1}{2\sqrt{6}} & 0 \\ \frac{\sqrt{2}}{15} & 1 + \frac{\sqrt{2}}{15} & \frac{\sqrt{2}}{15} & 0 \\ -\frac{1}{15\sqrt{2}} + \frac{1}{2\sqrt{6}} & -\frac{1}{15\sqrt{2}} + \frac{1}{2\sqrt{6}} & 1 - \frac{1}{15\sqrt{2}} + \frac{1}{2\sqrt{6}} & 0 \\ 0 & 0 & 0 & 1 \end{bmatrix}
$$

$$
= \begin{bmatrix} 0.7487 & -0.2513 & -0.2513 & 0 \\ 0.0943 & 1.0943 & 0.0943 & 0 \\ 0.1570 & 0.1570 & 1.1570 & 0 \\ 0 & 0 & 0 & 1 \end{bmatrix}.
$$

Think about using Eq. (5.13) to align the axis passing through the points $[0, 0, 0]^T$ and $[7, 7, 7]^T$ with the $x$-axis. Using another principal axis (i.e., $y$- or $z$-axis) is left as an exercise. □

## 5.6 Composite 3D Transformations

In general, transformations of one type (e.g., rotation) will *not* be commutative with transformations of another type (e.g., translation). Furthermore, *in general*, a rotation about one axis will *not* be commutative with another rotation about a different axis. For example, a rotation of 90° about the $x$-axis followed by another rotation of 90° about the $y$-axis is not equal to a rotation of 90° about the $y$-axis followed by another rotation of 90° about the $x$-axis.

**Example 5.17:** [*3D composite transformations*]

Derive the transformation matrix that performs this series of 3D transformations applied to a 3D object.

1. Scale the object using a factor 5 in the $x$-direction.
2. Rotate it through an angle of 30° about the $z$-axis.
3. Shear it in the $x$- and $y$-directions using shearing factors 2 and 3, respectively.
4. Translate it using a translation vector $[2, 1, 2]^T$.

**Solution 5.17:** Using homogeneous coordinates, the transformations are performed in the following sequence:

1. Scaling:

$$\mathtt{M}_1 = \mathtt{S}(5, 1, 1) = \begin{bmatrix} 5 & 0 & 0 & 0 \\ 0 & 1 & 0 & 0 \\ 0 & 0 & 1 & 0 \\ 0 & 0 & 0 & 1 \end{bmatrix}.$$

2. Rotating:

$$\mathtt{M}_2 = \mathtt{R}_z(30) = \begin{bmatrix} \cos(30) & -\sin(30) & 0 & 0 \\ \sin(30) & \cos(30) & 0 & 0 \\ 0 & 0 & 1 & 0 \\ 0 & 0 & 0 & 1 \end{bmatrix}.$$

3. Shearing:

$$\mathtt{M}_3 = \mathtt{Sh}_z(2, 3) = \begin{bmatrix} 1 & 0 & 2 & 0 \\ 0 & 1 & 3 & 0 \\ 0 & 0 & 1 & 0 \\ 0 & 0 & 0 & 1 \end{bmatrix}.$$

4. Translating:

$$\mathtt{M}_4 = \mathtt{T}([2, 1, 2]^T) = \begin{bmatrix} 1 & 0 & 0 & 2 \\ 0 & 1 & 0 & 1 \\ 0 & 0 & 1 & 2 \\ 0 & 0 & 0 & 1 \end{bmatrix}.$$

The overall transformation can be obtained as

$$\begin{aligned} \mathtt{M} &= \mathtt{M}_4\mathtt{M}_3\mathtt{M}_2\mathtt{M}_1 \\ &= \begin{bmatrix} 1 & 0 & 0 & 2 \\ 0 & 1 & 0 & 1 \\ 0 & 0 & 1 & 2 \\ 0 & 0 & 0 & 1 \end{bmatrix} \begin{bmatrix} 1 & 0 & 2 & 0 \\ 0 & 1 & 3 & 0 \\ 0 & 0 & 1 & 0 \\ 0 & 0 & 0 & 1 \end{bmatrix} \begin{bmatrix} \cos(30) & -\sin(30) & 0 & 0 \\ \sin(30) & \cos(30) & 0 & 0 \\ 0 & 0 & 1 & 0 \\ 0 & 0 & 0 & 1 \end{bmatrix} \begin{bmatrix} 5 & 0 & 0 & 0 \\ 0 & 1 & 0 & 0 \\ 0 & 0 & 1 & 0 \\ 0 & 0 & 0 & 1 \end{bmatrix} \\ &= \begin{bmatrix} 5\cos(30) & -\sin(30) & 2 & 2 \\ 5\sin(30) & \cos(30) & 3 & 1 \\ 0 & 0 & 1 & 2 \\ 0 & 0 & 0 & 1 \end{bmatrix} \\ &= \begin{bmatrix} \frac{5\sqrt{3}}{2} & -\frac{1}{2} & 2 & 2 \\ 2\frac{1}{2} & \frac{\sqrt{3}}{2} & 3 & 1 \\ 0 & 0 & 1 & 2 \\ 0 & 0 & 0 & 1 \end{bmatrix} = \begin{bmatrix} 4.3301 & -0.5 & 2 & 2 \\ 2.5 & 0.866 & 3 & 1 \\ 0 & 0 & 1 & 2 \\ 0 & 0 & 0 & 1 \end{bmatrix}. \end{aligned}$$

□

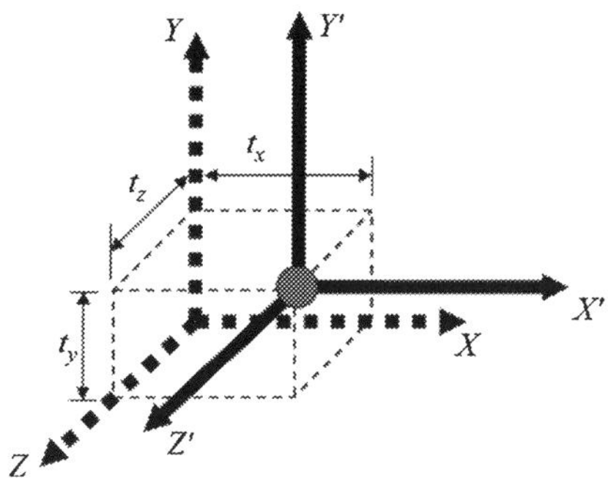


**Fig. 5.8** The $x$-, $y$- and $z$-axes are translated using the vector $[t_x, t_y, t_z]^T$ to the $x'$-, $y'$- and $z'$-axes

## 5.7 Axes Transformations

Similar to 2D space, axes may be transformed in 3D space. Although objects in space do not transform; however, their vertex coordinates get affected by axes transformation.

### *5.7.1 Axes Translation*

Consider Fig. 5.8 where the $x$-, $y$- and $z$-axes are translated to the $x'$-, $y'$- and $z'$-axes using a translation vector $[t_x, t_y, t_z]^T$. Thus, a point $\dot{\mathbf{P}} = [x, y, z]^T$ will have new coordinates $[x', y', z']^T$ expressed as

$$\begin{aligned} x' &= x - t_x, \\ y' &= y - t_y, \\ z' &= z - t_z. \end{aligned} \tag{5.39}$$

In matrix notation, this can be written as

$$\begin{bmatrix} x' \\ y' \\ z' \end{bmatrix} = \begin{bmatrix} x \\ y \\ z \end{bmatrix} + \begin{bmatrix} -t_x \\ -t_y \\ -t_z \end{bmatrix}. \tag{5.40}$$

In homogeneous coordinates, this is expressed as

$$\begin{bmatrix} x' \\ y' \\ z' \\ 1 \end{bmatrix} = \begin{bmatrix} 1 & 0 & 0 & -t_x \\ 0 & 1 & 0 & -t_y \\ 0 & 0 & 1 & -t_z \\ 0 & 0 & 0 & 1 \end{bmatrix} \begin{bmatrix} x \\ y \\ z \\ 1 \end{bmatrix}. \tag{5.41}$$

In other words, to translate the axes in 3D space using a vector $[t_x, t_y, t_z]^T$, Eq. (5.1) or Eq. (5.2) may be used with the translation vector $[t_x, t_y, t_z]^T$ but in the opposite direction (i.e., $[-t_x, -t_y, -t_z]^T$).

**Example 5.18:** [*Axes translation—point locations*]
Consider a point $\dot{\mathbf{P}} = [-2, 6, 3]^T$. If the axes are translated so that the origin is at $[3, 4, 5]^T$, find the coordinates of $\dot{\mathbf{P}}$ after axes translation.

**Solution 5.18:** Eqs. (5.39, 5.40) or Eq. (5.41) can be applied. Let us use Eq. (5.40).

$$\begin{aligned}\begin{bmatrix} x' \\ y' \\ z' \end{bmatrix} &= \begin{bmatrix} x \\ y \\ z \end{bmatrix} + \begin{bmatrix} -t_x \\ -t_y \\ -t_z \end{bmatrix} \\ &= \begin{bmatrix} -2 \\ 6 \\ 3 \end{bmatrix} + \begin{bmatrix} -3 \\ -4 \\ -5 \end{bmatrix} = \begin{bmatrix} -5 \\ 2 \\ -2 \end{bmatrix}.\end{aligned}$$

□

## 5.7.2 Axes Rotation

Axes may be rotated about any of the principal axes; i.e., the $x$-, $y$- or $z$-axis.

### 5.7.2.1 Axes Rotation About the $x$-Axis

Consider Fig. 5.9 where the $y$- and $z$-axes are rotated through an angle $\theta$ about the $x$-axis to the $y'$- and $z'$-axes respectively. Thus, a point $\dot{\mathbf{P}} = [x, y, z]^T$ will have new coordinates $[x', y', z']^T$ expressed as

$$\begin{aligned} x' &= x, \\ y' &= y\cos(\theta) + z\sin(\theta), \\ z' &= z\cos(\theta) - y\sin(\theta). \end{aligned} \tag{5.42}$$

In matrix notation, this can be written as

$$\begin{bmatrix} x' \\ y' \\ z' \end{bmatrix} = \begin{bmatrix} 1 & 0 & 0 \\ 0 & \cos(\theta) & \sin(\theta) \\ 0 & -\sin(\theta) & \cos(\theta) \end{bmatrix} \begin{bmatrix} x \\ y \\ z \end{bmatrix}. \tag{5.43}$$

In homogeneous coordinates, this is expressed as

$$\begin{bmatrix} x' \\ y' \\ z' \\ 1 \end{bmatrix} = \begin{bmatrix} 1 & 0 & 0 & 0 \\ 0 & \cos(\theta) & \sin(\theta) & 0 \\ 0 & -\sin(\theta) & \cos(\theta) & 0 \\ 0 & 0 & 0 & 1 \end{bmatrix} \begin{bmatrix} x \\ y \\ z \\ 1 \end{bmatrix}. \tag{5.44}$$

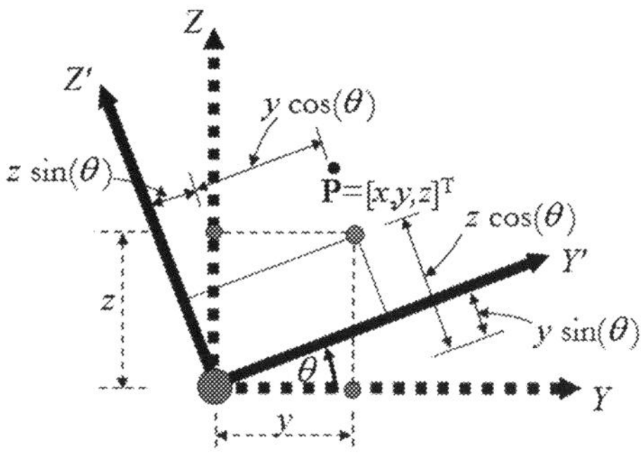


**Fig. 5.9** The $y$- and $z$-axes are rotated about the $x$-axis to the $y'$- and $z'$-axes

In other words, to rotate the axes in 3D space about the $x$-axis, Eq. (5.5) or Eq. (5.6) may be used with the same magnitude of angle $\theta$ but in the opposite direction (i.e., $-\theta$).

**Example 5.19:** [*Axes rotation—point locations*]
Consider a point $\dot{\mathbf{P}} = [-2, 6, 3]^T$. If the $y$- and $z$-axes are rotated through an angle of 45° about the $x$-axis, find the coordinates of $\dot{\mathbf{P}}$ after axes rotation.

**Solution 5.19:** Eqs. (5.42, 5.43) or Eq. (5.44) can be applied. Let us use Eq. (5.43).

$$\begin{bmatrix} x' \\ y' \\ z' \end{bmatrix} = \begin{bmatrix} 1 & 0 & 0 \\ 0 & \cos(\theta) & \sin(\theta) \\ 0 & -\sin(\theta) & \cos(\theta) \end{bmatrix} \begin{bmatrix} x \\ y \\ z \end{bmatrix}$$
$$= \begin{bmatrix} 1 & 0 & 0 \\ 0 & \cos(45) & \sin(45) \\ 0 & -\sin(45) & \cos(45) \end{bmatrix} \begin{bmatrix} -2 \\ 6 \\ 3 \end{bmatrix} = \begin{bmatrix} -2 \\ 6.3640 \\ -2.1213 \end{bmatrix}.$$

Notice that the $x$-coordinate did not change as the rotation is about the $x$-axis. □

#### 5.7.2.2 Axes Rotation About the $y$-Axis

Consider Fig. 5.10 where the $z$- and $x$-axes are rotated through an angle $\theta$ about the $y$-axis to the $z'$- and $x'$-axes respectively. Thus, a point $\dot{\mathbf{P}} = [x, y, z]^T$ will have new coordinates $[x', y', z']^T$ expressed as

$$\begin{aligned} x' &= x\cos(\theta) - z\sin(\theta), \\ y' &= y, \\ z' &= z\cos(\theta) + x\sin(\theta). \end{aligned} \qquad (5.45)$$

In matrix notation, this can be written as

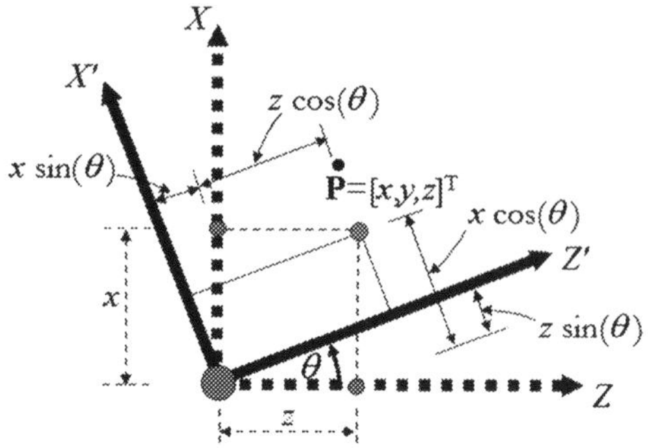


**Fig. 5.10** The $z$- and $x$-axes are rotated about the $y$-axis to the $z'$- and $x'$-axes

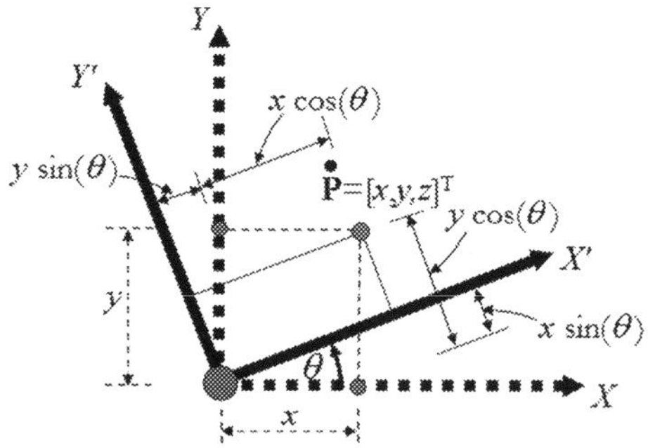


**Fig. 5.11** The $x$- and $y$-axes are rotated about the $z$-axis to the $x'$- and $y'$-axes

$$\begin{bmatrix} x' \\ y' \\ z' \end{bmatrix} = \begin{bmatrix} \cos(\theta) & 0 & -\sin(\theta) \\ 0 & 1 & 0 \\ \sin(\theta) & 0 & \cos(\theta) \end{bmatrix} \begin{bmatrix} x \\ y \\ z \end{bmatrix}. \tag{5.46}$$

In homogeneous coordinates, this is expressed as

$$\begin{bmatrix} x' \\ y' \\ z' \\ 1 \end{bmatrix} = \begin{bmatrix} \cos(\theta) & 0 & -\sin(\theta) & 0 \\ 0 & 1 & 0 & 0 \\ \sin(\theta) & 0 & \cos(\theta) & 0 \\ 0 & 0 & 0 & 1 \end{bmatrix} \begin{bmatrix} x \\ y \\ z \\ 1 \end{bmatrix}. \tag{5.47}$$

In other words, to rotate the axes in 3D space about the $y$-axis, Eq. (5.7) or Eq. (5.8) may be used with the same magnitude of angle $\theta$ but in the opposite direction (i.e., $-\theta$).

#### 5.7.2.3 Axes Rotation About the $z$-Axis

Consider Fig. 5.11 where the $x$- and $y$-axes are rotated through an angle $\theta$ about the $z$-axis to the $x'$- and $y'$-axes respectively. Thus, a point $\dot{\mathbf{P}} = [x, y, z]^T$ will have new coordinates $[x', y', z']^T$ expressed as

$$\begin{aligned} x' &= x\cos(\theta) + y\sin(\theta), \\ y' &= y\cos(\theta) - x\sin(\theta), \\ z' &= z. \end{aligned} \tag{5.48}$$

In matrix notation, this can be written as

$$\begin{bmatrix} x' \\ y' \\ z' \end{bmatrix} = \begin{bmatrix} \cos(\theta) & \sin(\theta) & 0 \\ -\sin(\theta) & \cos(\theta) & 0 \\ 0 & 0 & 1 \end{bmatrix} \begin{bmatrix} x \\ y \\ z \end{bmatrix}. \tag{5.49}$$

In homogeneous coordinates, this is expressed as

$$\begin{bmatrix} x' \\ y' \\ z' \\ 1 \end{bmatrix} = \begin{bmatrix} \cos(\theta) & \sin(\theta) & 0 & 0 \\ -\sin(\theta) & \cos(\theta) & 0 & 0 \\ 0 & 0 & 1 & 0 \\ 0 & 0 & 0 & 1 \end{bmatrix} \begin{bmatrix} x \\ y \\ z \\ 1 \end{bmatrix}. \tag{5.50}$$

In other words, to rotate the axes in 3D space about the $z$-axis, Eq. (5.9) or Eq. (5.10) may be used with the same magnitude of angle $\theta$ but in the opposite direction (i.e., $-\theta$).

### 5.7.3 Axes Scaling

Coordinate axes may be scaled in 3D space fixing the location of the origin and the orientations of the axes while changing the scaling of units. In this case, a point $\dot{\mathbf{P}} = [x, y, z]^T$ will have new coordinates $[x', y', z']^T$ expressed as

$$\begin{aligned} x' &= \frac{x}{s_x}, \\ y' &= \frac{y}{s_y}, \\ z' &= \frac{z}{s_z}. \end{aligned} \tag{5.51}$$

In matrix notation, this can be written as

$$\begin{bmatrix} x' \\ y' \\ z' \end{bmatrix} = \begin{bmatrix} \frac{1}{s_x} & 0 & 0 \\ 0 & \frac{1}{s_y} & 0 \\ 0 & 0 & \frac{1}{s_z} \end{bmatrix} \begin{bmatrix} x \\ y \\ z \end{bmatrix}. \tag{5.52}$$

In homogeneous coordinates, this is expressed as

$$\begin{bmatrix} x' \\ y' \\ z' \\ 1 \end{bmatrix} = \begin{bmatrix} \frac{1}{s_x} & 0 & 0 & 0 \\ 0 & \frac{1}{s_y} & 0 & 0 \\ 0 & 0 & \frac{1}{s_z} & 0 \\ 0 & 0 & 0 & 1 \end{bmatrix} \begin{bmatrix} x \\ y \\ z \\ 1 \end{bmatrix}. \tag{5.53}$$

In other words, to scale the axes in 3D space, Eq. (5.16) or Eq. (5.17) may be used with the reciprocals of the scaling factors $s_x$, $s_y$ and $s_z$ along the $x$-, $y$- and $z$-axes respectively.

**Example 5.20:** [*Axes scaling—point coordinates*]
Assume that the units of the 3D world coordinates are measured in meters where 1 unit = 1 m. If we decided to change the units to centimeters instead, estimate the coordinates of a point $[x, y, z]^T$ after this operation.

**Solution 5.20:** This is an axes scaling problem where the scaling factors to switch from meters to centimeters are $\frac{1}{100}$, $\frac{1}{100}$ and $\frac{1}{100}$ along the $x$-, $y$- and $z$-axes. Equations (5.51, 5.52) or Eq. (5.53) can be applied. Let us use Eq. (5.51):

$$\begin{aligned} x' &= \frac{x}{s_x} = 100x, \\ y' &= \frac{y}{s_y} = 100y, \\ z' &= \frac{z}{s_z} = 100z. \end{aligned}$$

□

## 5.7.4 Axes Reflection

Axes reflection in 3D space is equivalent to switching between left-handed and right-handed coordinate systems (Sect. B.1.1). Reflection can be performed about any of the principal planes.

### 5.7.4.1 Axes Reflection About the *xy*-Plane

Only the $z$-coordinates are affected by axes reflection about the $xy$-plane as depicted in Fig. 5.12. Thus, a point $\dot{\mathbf{P}} = [x, y, z]^T$ will have new coordinates $[x', y', z']^T$ expressed as

$$\begin{aligned} x' &= x, \\ y' &= y, \\ z' &= -z. \end{aligned} \tag{5.54}$$

In matrix notation, this can be written as

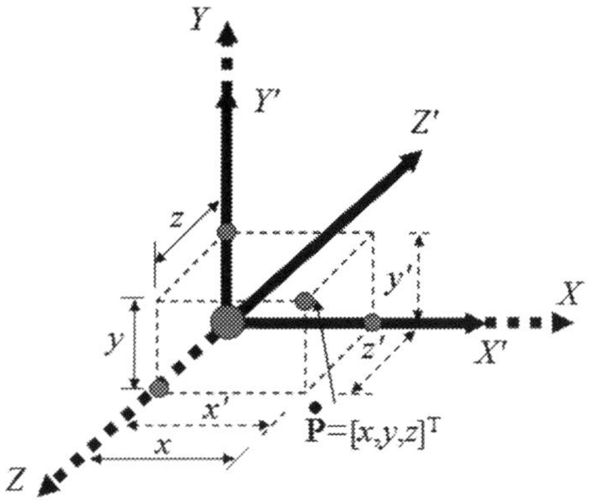


**Fig. 5.12** Reflection of axes about the $xy$-plane affects the $z$-coordinates only

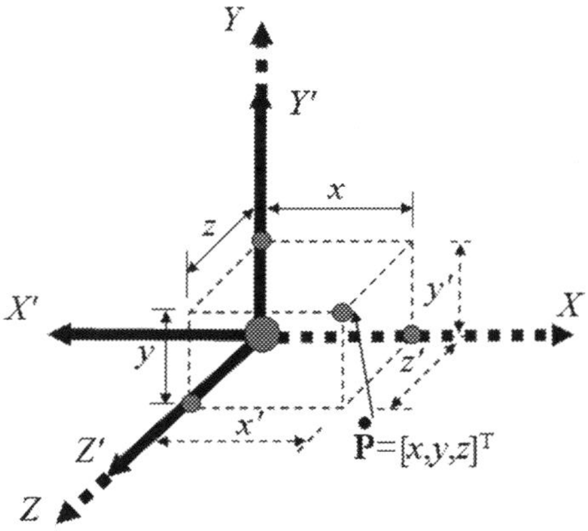


**Fig. 5.13** Reflection of axes about the $yz$-plane affects the $x$-coordinates only

$$\begin{bmatrix} x' \\ y' \\ z' \end{bmatrix} = \begin{bmatrix} 1 & 0 & 0 \\ 0 & 1 & 0 \\ 0 & 0 & -1 \end{bmatrix} \begin{bmatrix} x \\ y \\ z \end{bmatrix}. \tag{5.55}$$

In homogeneous coordinates, this is expressed as

$$\begin{bmatrix} x' \\ y' \\ z' \\ 1 \end{bmatrix} = \begin{bmatrix} 1 & 0 & 0 & 0 \\ 0 & 1 & 0 & 0 \\ 0 & 0 & -1 & 0 \\ 0 & 0 & 0 & 1 \end{bmatrix} \begin{bmatrix} x \\ y \\ z \\ 1 \end{bmatrix}. \tag{5.56}$$

In other words, to reflect the axes in 3D space about the $xy$-plane, Eq. (5.21) or Eq. (5.22) may be used.

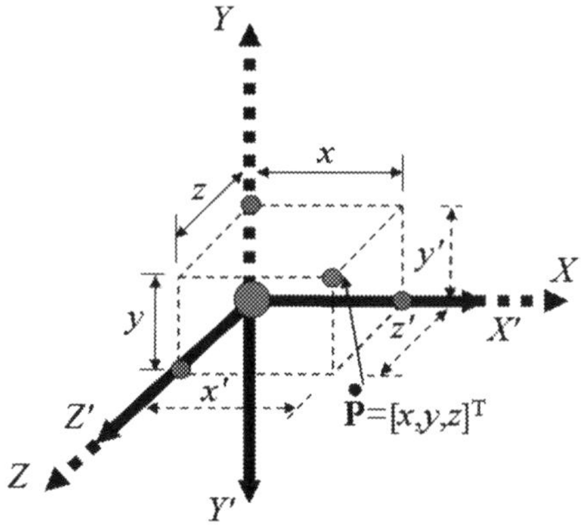


**Fig. 5.14** Reflection of axes about the $zx$-plane affects the $y$-coordinates only

#### 5.7.4.2 Axes Reflection About the $yz$-Plane

Only the $x$-coordinates are affected by axes reflection about the $yz$-plane as depicted in Fig. 5.13. Thus, a point $\dot{\mathbf{P}} = [x, y, z]^T$ will have new coordinates $[x', y', z']^T$ expressed as

$$\begin{aligned} x' &= -x, \\ y' &= y, \\ z' &= z. \end{aligned} \tag{5.57}$$

In matrix notation, this can be written as

$$\begin{bmatrix} x' \\ y' \\ z' \end{bmatrix} = \begin{bmatrix} -1 & 0 & 0 \\ 0 & 1 & 0 \\ 0 & 0 & 1 \end{bmatrix} \begin{bmatrix} x \\ y \\ z \end{bmatrix}. \tag{5.58}$$

In homogeneous coordinates, this is expressed as

$$\begin{bmatrix} x' \\ y' \\ z' \\ 1 \end{bmatrix} = \begin{bmatrix} -1 & 0 & 0 & 0 \\ 0 & 1 & 0 & 0 \\ 0 & 0 & 1 & 0 \\ 0 & 0 & 0 & 1 \end{bmatrix} \begin{bmatrix} x \\ y \\ z \\ 1 \end{bmatrix}. \tag{5.59}$$

In other words, to reflect the axes in 3D space about the $yz$-plane, Eq. (5.24) or Eq. (5.25) may be used.

#### 5.7.4.3 Axes Reflection About the $zx$-Plane

Only the $y$-coordinates are affected by axes reflection about the $zx$-plane as depicted in Fig. 5.14. Thus, a point $\dot{\mathbf{P}} = [x, y, z]^T$ will have new coordinates $[x', y', z']^T$

expressed as

$$\begin{aligned} x' &= x, \\ y' &= -y, \\ z' &= z. \end{aligned} \tag{5.60}$$

In matrix notation, this can be written as

$$\begin{bmatrix} x' \\ y' \\ z' \end{bmatrix} = \begin{bmatrix} 1 & 0 & 0 \\ 0 & -1 & 0 \\ 0 & 0 & 1 \end{bmatrix} \begin{bmatrix} x \\ y \\ z \end{bmatrix}. \tag{5.61}$$

In homogeneous coordinates, this is expressed as

$$\begin{bmatrix} x' \\ y' \\ z' \\ 1 \end{bmatrix} = \begin{bmatrix} 1 & 0 & 0 & 0 \\ 0 & -1 & 0 & 0 \\ 0 & 0 & 1 & 0 \\ 0 & 0 & 0 & 1 \end{bmatrix} \begin{bmatrix} x \\ y \\ z \\ 1 \end{bmatrix}. \tag{5.62}$$

In other words, to reflect the axes in 3D space about the $zx$-plane, Eq. (5.27) or Eq. (5.28) may be used.

## 5.8 Problems

**Problem 5.1:** [*3D general rotation*]
A tetrahedron is to be rotated through an angle of 45° about a line passing through the points $[2, 1, 0]^T$ and $[6, 5, 0]^T$. Derive the required 3D transformation matrix.

**Problem 5.2:** [*3D general rotation*]
A unit cube is centered at $[2, 5, 3]^T$. Rotate it through an angle of 45° about a line passing through its center and parallel to the $y$-axis. Derive the required 3D transformation matrix.

**Problem 5.3:** [*3D general rotation*]
A unit cube is centered at $[2, 5, 3]^T$. Rotate it through an angle of 45° about a line passing through the origin and having a direction vector $[7, 7, 7]^T$. Derive the required 3D transformation matrix.

**Problem 5.4:** [*3D general rotation*]
We want to rotate a point through an angle of 34.87° about a line passing through the origin and the point $[1, 1, \sqrt{3}]^T$. Determine the series of transformations (with their parameters) required. You must start with rotation about the $z$-axis. Also, you must avoid rotating about the $y$-axis. *Hint*: Note that there are four different routes that start with rotation about the $z$-axis but only one of them does not involve rotation about the $y$-axis.

**Problem 5.5:** [*3D general rotation*]

We want to rotate a point through an angle of 34.87° about a line passing through the origin and the point $[1, 1, \sqrt{3}]^T$. Determine the series of transformations (with their parameters) required. You must start with rotation about the $x$-axis. Also, you must avoid rotating about the $z$-axis.

**Problem 5.6:** [*3D general rotation*]

Consider the pyramid $\dot{\mathbf{A}}\dot{\mathbf{B}}\dot{\mathbf{C}}\dot{\mathbf{D}}$ where $\dot{\mathbf{A}} = [0, 0, 0]^T$, $\dot{\mathbf{B}} = [1, 0, 0]^T$, $\dot{\mathbf{C}} = [0, 1, 0]^T$ and $\dot{\mathbf{D}} = [0, 0, 1]^T$. The pyramid is to be rotated 45° about a line passing through $\dot{\mathbf{B}}$ and having the direction $[0, 1, 1]^T$. Find the coordinates of the rotated vertices.

**Problem 5.7:** [*3D general rotation*]

A cube with faces parallel to the planes $x = 0$, $y = 0$ and $z = 0$ and two corners located at $[2, 4, 6]^T$ and $[4, 6, 8]^T$ is to be rotated through an angle of 30° about a line passing through the points $[2, 1, 4]^T$ and $[4, 1, 6]^T$. Determine the locations of the above two corners after transformation.

**Problem 5.8:** [*3D general rotation*]

If a tetrahedron is to be rotated through an angle of 45° about a line passing through the points $[2, 1, 0]^T$ and $[6, 5, 0]^T$. Derive the required 3D transformation matrix.

**Problem 5.9:** [*3D general rotation*]

A unit cube with edges parallel to the principal axes and a center point located at $[2, 4, 6]^T$ is to be rotated through an angle of 45° about a line passing through the origin and determined by the direction vector $[0, 1, 1]^T$. Derive the transformation matrix that performs this 3D transformation. Determine the location of the center point after rotation.

**Problem 5.10:** [*3D general rotation—rotating vectors*]

Derive a rotation matrix that rotates a vector $[x, y, z]^T$ so that it coincides with the $y$-axis.

**Problem 5.11:** [*3D general rotation—rotating vectors*]

Derive a rotation matrix that rotates a vector $[x, y, z]^T$ so that it coincides with the $z$-axis.

**Problem 5.12:** [*3D general rotation—rotating vectors*]

Given two direction vectors $\mathbf{u}$ and $\mathbf{v}$ intersecting at the origin, verify that the vector $\mathbf{u}$ is aligned with the vector $\mathbf{v}$ when $\mathbf{u}$ is rotated through a rotation angle $\theta$ about the vector $\mathbf{n}$ that passes through the origin such that

$$\theta = \cos^{-1}\left(\frac{\mathbf{u} \bullet \mathbf{v}}{\|\mathbf{u}\|\,\|\mathbf{v}\|}\right)$$

and

$$\mathbf{n} = \mathbf{u} \times \mathbf{v},$$

where $\bullet$ and $\times$ denote the dot and cross products respectively.

**Problem 5.13:** [*3D general reflection*]
Derive a matrix that reflects a point $[x, y, z]^T$ about the plane $x = \delta$ where $\delta$ is a real number.

**Problem 5.14:** [*3D general reflection*]
Derive a matrix that reflects a point $[x, y, z]^T$ about the plane $z = \delta$ where $\delta$ is a real number.

**Problem 5.15:** [*3D general reflection—plane passing through the origin*]
Derive a transformation matrix that reflects a point about a plane having the equation $3x + 5y + 6z = 0$.

**Problem 5.16:** [*3D general reflection—general plane and rotating vectors*]
Derive a transformation matrix that reflects a point about the plane $ax + by + cz = d$.

**Problem 5.17:** [*3D composite transformations—translation/shearing/scaling/rotation*]
Derive the transformation matrix that performs this series of 3D transformations applied to a 3D object.

1. Translate it using a translation vector $[2, 4, 6]^T$.
2. Shear it in the $x$- and $y$-directions using shearing factors of 5 and 3 respectively.
3. Scale it using factors of 5 and 3 in the $x$- and $y$-directions respectively.
4. Rotate it through an angle of 70° about the $z$-axis.

## References

Ammeraal, L., and K. Zhang. 2007. *Computer graphics for Java programmers*, 2nd ed. New York: Wiley

Foley, J.D., A. van Dam, S.K. Feiner, and J. Hughes. 1995. *Computer graphics: principles and practice in C*, 2nd ed. The systems programming series. Reading: Addison-Wesley

Vince, J. 2011. *Rotation transforms for computer graphics*. Berlin: Springer.

# Chapter 6
# Curves

**Abstract** Representing curves is a main and important topic in different fields such as computer aided geometric design (CAGD) (Farin in Curves and surfaces for CAGD: a practical guide. Morgan Kaufmann Publishers Inc., San Francisco, 2002; Goldman in An integrated introduction to computer graphics and geometric modeling, Chapman&Hall/CRC Computer Graphics, London, 2009) and computer graphics (Mukundan in Advanced methods in computer graphics: with examples in OpenGL. Springer, Berlin, 2012; McConnell in Computer graphics: theory into practice. Jones & Bartlett, Boston, 2005; Lengyel in Mathematics for 3D game programming and computer graphics, Course Technology PTR, 2011; Salomon in Curves and surfaces for computer graphics. Springer, Berlin, 2006; Buss in 3D computer graphics: a mathematical introduction with OpenGL. Cambridge University Press, New York, 2003). Given a set of points, a curve may be constructed to pass through (i.e., *interpolate*) those points. Alternatively, points can be used to *approximate* the shape of the curve. The number of points used to construct the curve affects its degree; and consequently, its shape. Curves may be created using functions of degree 2 (i.e. of order 3) and higher. Lines created through linear equations of degree 1 may be considered as a special case of curves although other methods are usually used to create lines (see Chap. 2). Points in 2D space create planar curve while 3D points are used to create 3D curves passing through different planes in 3D space. Different equations used to generate 2D curves can easily be extended to 3D space. In this chapter, we explore different curves representations. We discuss various methods and equations to construct curves.

## 6.1 Curve Representations

There are different ways to write an equation for a curve (Salomon 2006; Goldman 2009; Mukundan 2012; Lengyel 2011).

R. Elias, *Digital Media*, DOI: 10.1007/978-3-319-05137-6_6,

1. Explicit representation.
2. Implicit representation.
3. Parametric representation.

### 6.1.1 Explicit Representation

A polynomial is used to represent lines and curves mathematically. A polynomial may take the form

$$y = f(x), \tag{6.1}$$

where $f(x)$ consists of powers of $x$ only. A linear (i.e., first degree) polynomial is used to represent a line as

$$y = mx + b, \tag{6.2}$$

where $m$ is the slope and $b$ is the $y$-intercept. A quadratic (i.e., second degree) polynomial is used to represent a curve as

$$y = ax^2 + bx + c, \tag{6.3}$$

where $a$, $b$ and $c$ are coefficients. Also, a cubic (i.e., third degree) polynomial is used to represent a curve as

$$y = ax^3 + bx^2 + cx + d, \tag{6.4}$$

where $a$, $b$, $c$ and $d$ are coefficients. In fact, polynomials higher than first degree are used to represent curves. In other words, an equation of a curve may be of degree 2 or higher where the *degree* of a polynomial equation is the largest exponent in the equation. The curve's freedom to bend is affected by the number of points available for modeling.

Equations (6.3) and (6.4) are the explicit quadratic and cubic curve representations. Having these polynomials and a range or an interval for $x$-values, a curve can be drawn.

**Example 6.1:** [*Curve drawing*]
Given the quadratic polynomial

$$y = x^2 + x + 1,$$

where $x$-values range from 0 to 2, draw the curve that is represented by this polynomial equation.

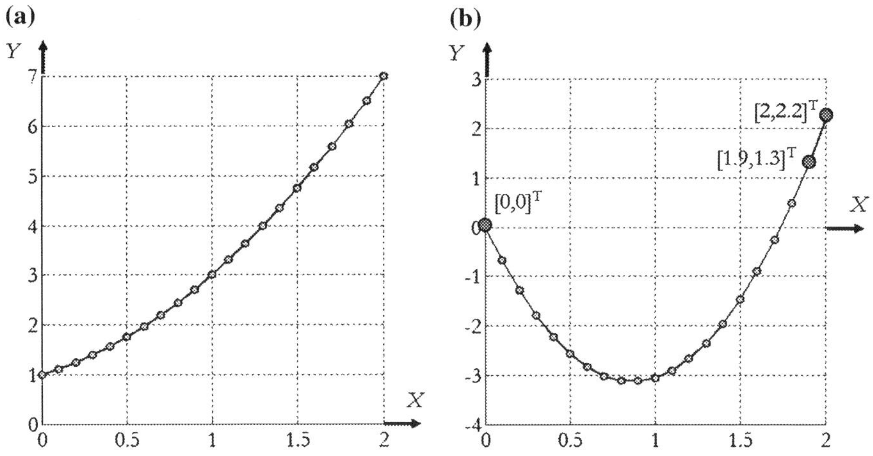


**Fig. 6.1** Quadratic curves. **a** Marks appear at each 0.1 units along the $x$-direction. **b** Marks appear at each 0.1 units along the $x$-direction. The big circles represent the input points

**Solution 6.1:** The curve is shown in Fig. 6.1a. □

**Curve Points and Equation Coefficients:** If the coefficients (i.e., $a$, $b$, etc.) are not known, the curve polynomial equation can still be obtained if points on the curve are of known positions. The number of points required depends on the degree of the curve. If the degree of the curve is $p$ then the number of required points is $p+1$. (The value $p+1$ is referred to as the *order* of the curve as well.) For example, a *second* degree polynomial can be obtained and a *quadratic* curve can be drawn if *three* points are known of which two are endpoints. Similarly, a *third* degree polynomial can be obtained and a *cubic* curve can be drawn if *four* points are known of which two are endpoints.

Let us consider a quadratic curve that is to be drawn using three points $[x_0, y_0]^T$, $[x_1, y_1]^T$ and $[x_2, y_2]^T$. In this case, three simultaneous equations should be solved to get one solution. These equations are:

$$
\begin{aligned}
y_0 &= ax_0^2 + bx_0 + c,\\
y_1 &= ax_1^2 + bx_1 + c,\\
y_2 &= ax_2^2 + bx_2 + c.
\end{aligned}
$$

Hence, the quadratic polynomial equation of the curve is expressed as

$$y = ax^2 + bx + c, \tag{6.5}$$

where

$$a = \frac{x_0(y_1 - y_2) + y_0(x_2 - x_1) + x_1 y_2 - x_2 y_1}{(x_1 - x_0)(x_2 - x_0)(x_2 - x_1)},$$

$$b = \frac{y_2 - y_0}{x_2 - x_0} - (x_2 + x_0)a$$

and

$$c = y_0 - ax_0^2 - bx_0.$$

The previous idea can be extended to higher degree curves.

**Example 6.2:** [*Explicit representation—coefficients for quadratic curves*]
Consider a quadratic curve whose endpoints are $[0, 0]^T$ and $[2, 2.2]^T$. If the point $[1.9, 1.3]^T$ is on the curve, get its polynomial equation and draw the curve.

**Solution 6.2:** Using Eq. (6.5), the coefficients can be obtained as

$$\begin{aligned} a &= \frac{x_0(y_1 - y_2) + y_0(x_2 - x_1) + x_1y_2 - x_2y_1}{(x_1 - x_0)(x_2 - x_0)(x_2 - x_1)} \\ &= \frac{0 \times (1.3 - 2.2) + 0 \times (2 - 1.9) + 1.9 \times 2.2 - 2 \times 1.3}{(1.9 - 0)(2 - 0)(2 - 1.9)} = 4.1579, \\ b &= \frac{y_2 - y_0}{x_2 - x_0} - (x_2 + x_0)a \\ &= \frac{2.2 - 0}{2 - 0} - (2 + 0) \times 4.1579 = -7.2158 \end{aligned}$$

and

$$\begin{aligned} c &= y_0 - ax_0^2 - bx_0 \\ &= 0 - 4.1579 \times 0^2 - (-7.2158) \times 0 = 0. \end{aligned}$$

Hence, the polynomial equation of the quadratic curve is expressed as

$$y = 4.1579x^2 - 7.2158x,$$

where $x \in [0, 2]$. The curve is drawn and shown in Fig. 6.1b. □

**Example 6.3:** [*Explicit representation—points on curves*]
A quadratic curve is represented explicitly as

$$y = ax^2 + bx + c.$$

Assume that a quadratic curve is passing through the points $[2, 2]^T$, $[4, 5]^T$ and $[9, 8]^T$. Estimate the values of $y$ at $x = 5$ and $x = 8$.

**Solution 6.3:** In order to estimate the values of $y$, the coefficients $a$, $b$ and $c$ are obtained using Eq. (6.5) as

$$
\begin{aligned}
a &= \frac{x_0(y_1 - y_2) + y_0(x_2 - x_1) + x_1 y_2 - x_2 y_1}{(x_1 - x_0)(x_2 - x_0)(x_2 - x_1)} \\
&= \frac{2 \times (5 - 8) + 2 \times (9 - 4) + 4 \times 8 - 9 \times 5}{(4 - 2)(9 - 2)(9 - 4)} = -0.1286, \\
b &= \frac{y_2 - y_0}{x_2 - x_0} - (x_2 + x_0)a \\
&= \frac{8 - 2}{9 - 2} - (9 + 2) \times (-0.1286) = 2.2714
\end{aligned}
$$

and

$$
\begin{aligned}
c &= y_0 - a x_0^2 - b x_0 \\
&= 2 - (-0.1286) \times 2^2 - 2.2714 \times 2 = -2.0286.
\end{aligned}
$$

Hence, the quadratic equation is written as

$$y = -0.1286x^2 + 2.2714x - 2.0286.$$

When $x = 5$,

$$y = -0.1286 \times 5^2 + 2.2714 \times 5 - 2.0286 = 6.1143.$$

When $x = 8$,

$$y = -0.1286 \times 8^2 + 2.2714 \times 8 - 2.0286 = 7.9143. \qquad \square$$

Notice that multiple $y$-values cannot be obtained for a single $x$-value; hence, conic sections like circles and ellipses cannot be explicitly represented unless they are split into curve segments. Also, describing curves with vertical tangents (i.e., slope of $\infty$) is difficult. Moreover, explicit representation of curves is not rotationally invariant (Foley et al. 1995).

**Example 6.4:** [*Explicit representation—transformations of quadratic curves*]
If the curve of Example 6.3 is rotated through an angle of 30° about the origin, determine the locations of the previously calculated points. Re-solve the same problem by rotating the given curve points before calculating the required $y$-values. Are the same points obtained in both cases?

**Solution 6.4:** Rotation can be performed using homogeneous or inhomogeneous coordinates as discussed in Chap. 3. Let us consider the inhomogeneous solution here using Eq. (3.4); however, the same result should be obtained using homogeneous coordinates. Consider the curve point $[5, 6.1143]^T$. After rotation, this point becomes

$$\dot{\mathbf{p}}' = \begin{bmatrix} \cos(\theta) & -\sin(\theta) \\ \sin(\theta) & \cos(\theta) \end{bmatrix} \begin{bmatrix} x_{\dot{\mathbf{p}}} \\ y_{\dot{\mathbf{p}}} \end{bmatrix}$$
$$= \begin{bmatrix} \cos(30) & -\sin(30) \\ \sin(30) & \cos(30) \end{bmatrix} \begin{bmatrix} 5 \\ 6.1143 \end{bmatrix} = \begin{bmatrix} 1.2730 \\ 7.7951 \end{bmatrix},$$

where $\dot{\mathbf{p}} = [x_{\dot{\mathbf{p}}}, y_{\dot{\mathbf{p}}}]^T = [5, 6.1143]^T$ is the point to be rotated. Similarly, the point $[8, 7.9143]^T$ is rotated to be

$$\dot{\mathbf{p}}' = \begin{bmatrix} \cos(30) & -\sin(30) \\ \sin(30) & \cos(30) \end{bmatrix} \begin{bmatrix} 8 \\ 7.9143 \end{bmatrix} = \begin{bmatrix} 2.9711 \\ 10.8540 \end{bmatrix}.$$

Now, we will rotate the points $[2, 2]^T$, $[4, 5]^T$ and $[9, 8]^T$ to get

$$\dot{\mathbf{p}}'_0 = \begin{bmatrix} \cos(30) & -\sin(30) \\ \sin(30) & \cos(30) \end{bmatrix} \begin{bmatrix} 2 \\ 2 \end{bmatrix} = \begin{bmatrix} 0.7321 \\ 2.7321 \end{bmatrix},$$

$$\dot{\mathbf{p}}'_1 = \begin{bmatrix} \cos(30) & -\sin(30) \\ \sin(30) & \cos(30) \end{bmatrix} \begin{bmatrix} 4 \\ 5 \end{bmatrix} = \begin{bmatrix} 0.9641 \\ 6.3301 \end{bmatrix}$$

and

$$\dot{\mathbf{p}}'_2 = \begin{bmatrix} \cos(30) & -\sin(30) \\ \sin(30) & \cos(30) \end{bmatrix} \begin{bmatrix} 9 \\ 8 \end{bmatrix} = \begin{bmatrix} 3.7942 \\ 11.4282 \end{bmatrix}.$$

Then, we use points $\dot{\mathbf{p}}'_0 = [0.7321, 2.7321]^T$, $\dot{\mathbf{p}}'_1 = [0.9641, 6.3301]^T$ and $\dot{\mathbf{p}}'_2 = [3.7942, 11.4282]^T$ to get the coefficients $a'$, $b'$ and $c'$. Thus,

$$\begin{aligned}
a' &= \frac{x'_0(y'_1 - y'_2) + y'_0(x'_2 - x'_1) + x'_1 y'_2 - x'_2 y'_1}{(x'_1 - x'_0)(x'_2 - x'_0)(x'_2 - x'_1)} \\
&= \frac{0.7321(6.3301 - 11.4282) + 2.7321(3.7942 - 0.9641) + 0.9641 \times 11.4282 - 3.7942 \times 6.3301}{(0.9641 - 0.7321)(3.7942 - 0.7321)(3.7942 - 0.9641)} \\
&= -4.4753, \\
b' &= \frac{y'_2 - y'_0}{x'_2 - x'_0} - (x'_2 + x'_0)a' \\
&= \frac{11.4282 - 2.7321}{3.7942 - 0.7321} - (3.7942 + 0.7321) \times -4.4753 = 23.0964
\end{aligned}$$

and

$$\begin{aligned}
c' &= y'_0 - a' x_0'^2 - b' x'_0 \\
&= 2.7321 - (-4.4753) \times 0.7321^2 - 23.0964 \times 0.7321 = -11.7773.
\end{aligned}$$

Hence, the quadratic equation is written as

$$y' = -4.4753 x'^2 + 23.0964 x' - 11.7773.$$

When $x' = 1.2730$,

$$y' = -4.4753 \times 1.2730^2 + 23.0964 \times 1.2730 - 11.7773 = 10.3720.$$

When $x' = 2.9711$,

$$y' = -4.4753 \times 2.9711^2 + 23.0964 \times 2.9711 - 11.7773 = 17.3387.$$

These are not the same points obtained before. □

### 6.1.2 Implicit Representation

The *implicit representation* of curves combines the variables (i.e., $x$ and $y$ in 2D space or $x$, $y$ and $z$ in 3D space) in an equation. Generally, the implicit representation functions take the forms

$$f(x, y) = 0 \tag{6.6}$$

and

$$f(x, y, z) = 0 \tag{6.7}$$

in 2D and 3D spaces respectively. A linear equation may be represented implicitly as

$$ax + by + c = 0, \tag{6.8}$$

where $a$, $b$ and $c$ are coefficients. Higher-degree equations represent curves. For example,

$$ax^3 + by^2 + 3cxy + 3dx + 3ey + f = 0,$$

where $a$, $b$, $c$, $d$, $e$ and $f$ are coefficients, is an implicit representation of a curve. Here, the entire equation must be solved in order to calculate $x$ and $y$ (or $x$, $y$ and $z$ in 3D space).

In some cases, implicit representation might not be the perfect type of representation one may use. For example,

$$x^2 + y^2 = r^2$$

is an implicit representation of a circle that can be used to draw a whole circle of radius $r$ at the origin. In this example, note that there are two $y$-values for each $x$ and two $x$-values for each $y$. This implies that such an equation cannot be used by itself to draw a part of a circle or an arc as more solutions than needed are found. More constraints (such as $x$- and $y$-domains) are required, which cannot be imbedded in this equation.

## 6.1.3 Parametric Representation

The parametric representation of curves writes short and easily-solved curve equations that translate one variable into values for the others. The parametric representation uses a parameter $t$ that usually goes from 0 at the start of the curve to 1 at the end. All intermediate points can be obtained as functions of $t$.

### 6.1.3.1 Linear Parametric Representation

For linear 2D curves, the following linear polynomials are used to get a curve point $\dot{\mathbf{p}}(t) = [x(t), y(t)]^T$:

$$\begin{aligned} x(t) &= a_x t + b_x, \\ y(t) &= a_y t + b_y, \end{aligned} \tag{6.9}$$

where $a_x$, $b_x$, $a_y$ and $b_y$ are coefficients for the $x$- and $y$-directions respectively; and $t \in [0, 1]$ is a parameter that determines the location of the curve point $\dot{\mathbf{p}}(t) = [x(t), y(t)]^T$ along the curve. In vector form, Eq. (6.9) can be re-written as

$$\begin{aligned} x(t) &= \underbrace{\begin{bmatrix} t & 1 \end{bmatrix}}_{\mathbf{t}} \underbrace{\begin{bmatrix} a_x \\ b_x \end{bmatrix}}_{\mathbf{x}} = \mathbf{t} \cdot \mathbf{x}^T, \\ y(t) &= \underbrace{\begin{bmatrix} t & 1 \end{bmatrix}}_{\mathbf{t}} \underbrace{\begin{bmatrix} a_y \\ b_y \end{bmatrix}}_{\mathbf{y}} = \mathbf{t} \cdot \mathbf{y}^T, \end{aligned} \tag{6.10}$$

where $\mathbf{x}$ and $\mathbf{y}$ are vectors representing coefficients for the $x$- and $y$-directions respectively; and $\cdot$ denotes the dot product. Equation (6.10) can be re-written in a compact matrix form as

$$\dot{\mathbf{p}}^T(t) = \mathbf{t} \begin{bmatrix} \mathbf{x} & \mathbf{y} \end{bmatrix}. \tag{6.11}$$

Note that Eq. (6.9) can be extended to cover linear parametric curves in 3D space by adding an entry for the third dimension (i.e., the $z$-direction). Hence, the location of a curve point $\dot{\mathbf{P}}(t) = [x(t), y(t), z(t)]^T$ along the curve can be obtained as

$$\begin{aligned} x(t) &= a_x t + b_x, \\ y(t) &= a_y t + b_y, \\ z(t) &= a_z t + b_z, \end{aligned} \tag{6.12}$$

where $a_z$ and $b_z$ are coefficients for the $z$-direction. Furthermore, Eq. (6.12) can be written in vector form as

$$
\begin{aligned}
x(t) &= \underbrace{\begin{bmatrix} t & 1 \end{bmatrix}}_{\mathbf{t}} \underbrace{\begin{bmatrix} a_x \\ b_x \end{bmatrix}}_{\mathbf{x}} = \mathbf{t} \cdot \mathbf{x}^T, \\
y(t) &= \underbrace{\begin{bmatrix} t & 1 \end{bmatrix}}_{\mathbf{t}} \underbrace{\begin{bmatrix} a_y \\ b_y \end{bmatrix}}_{\mathbf{y}} = \mathbf{t} \cdot \mathbf{y}^T, \\
z(t) &= \underbrace{\begin{bmatrix} t & 1 \end{bmatrix}}_{\mathbf{t}} \underbrace{\begin{bmatrix} a_z \\ b_z \end{bmatrix}}_{\mathbf{z}} = \mathbf{t} \cdot \mathbf{z}^T,
\end{aligned}
\tag{6.13}
$$

where $\mathbf{z}$ is a vector representing the coefficients for the $z$-direction; and $\cdot$ denotes the dot product. Finally, Eq. (6.13) is written in a compact matrix form as

$$
\dot{\mathbf{P}}^T(t) = \mathbf{t}\begin{bmatrix} \mathbf{x} \; \mathbf{y} \; \mathbf{z} \end{bmatrix}. \tag{6.14}
$$

#### 6.1.3.2 Quadratic Parametric Representation

For quadratic 2D curves, the following quadratic polynomials are used to get a curve point $\dot{\mathbf{p}}(t) = [x(t), y(t)]^T$:

$$
\begin{aligned}
x(t) &= a_x t^2 + b_x t + c_x, \\
y(t) &= a_y t^2 + b_y t + c_y,
\end{aligned}
\tag{6.15}
$$

where $a_x, b_x, c_x, a_y, b_y$ and $c_y$ are coefficients for the $x$- and $y$-directions respectively; and $t \in [0, 1]$ is a parameter that determines the location of the curve point $\dot{\mathbf{p}}(t) = [x(t), y(t)]^T$ along the curve. In vector form, Eq. (6.15) can be re-written as

$$
\begin{aligned}
x(t) &= \underbrace{\begin{bmatrix} t^2 & t & 1 \end{bmatrix}}_{\mathbf{t}} \underbrace{\begin{bmatrix} a_x \\ b_x \\ c_x \end{bmatrix}}_{\mathbf{x}} = \mathbf{t} \cdot \mathbf{x}^T, \\
y(t) &= \underbrace{\begin{bmatrix} t^2 & t & 1 \end{bmatrix}}_{\mathbf{t}} \underbrace{\begin{bmatrix} a_y \\ b_y \\ c_y \end{bmatrix}}_{\mathbf{y}} = \mathbf{t} \cdot \mathbf{y}^T,
\end{aligned}
\tag{6.16}
$$

where $\mathbf{x}$ and $\mathbf{y}$ are vectors representing coefficients for the $x$- and $y$-directions respectively; and $\cdot$ denotes the dot product. Equation (6.16) can be re-written in a compact matrix form as

$$
\dot{\mathbf{p}}^T(t) = \mathbf{t}\begin{bmatrix} \mathbf{x} \; \mathbf{y} \end{bmatrix}. \tag{6.17}
$$

Note that Eq. (6.15) can be extended to cover quadratic parametric curves in 3D space by adding an entry for the third dimension (i.e., the $z$-direction). Hence, the location of a curve point $\dot{\mathbf{P}}(t) = [x(t), y(t), z(t)]^T$ along the curve can be obtained by extending Eq. (6.15) as

$$\begin{aligned} x(t) &= a_x t^2 + b_x t + c_x, \\ y(t) &= a_y t^2 + b_y t + c_y, \\ z(t) &= a_z t^2 + b_z t + c_z, \end{aligned} \tag{6.18}$$

where $a_z$, $b_z$ and $c_z$ are coefficients for the $z$-direction. Furthermore, Eq. (6.18) can be written in vector form as

$$\begin{aligned} x(t) &= \underbrace{\begin{bmatrix} t^2 & t & 1 \end{bmatrix}}_{\mathbf{t}} \underbrace{\begin{bmatrix} a_x \\ b_x \\ c_x \end{bmatrix}}_{\mathbf{x}} = \mathbf{t} \cdot \mathbf{x}^T, \\ y(t) &= \underbrace{\begin{bmatrix} t^2 & t & 1 \end{bmatrix}}_{\mathbf{t}} \underbrace{\begin{bmatrix} a_y \\ b_y \\ c_y \end{bmatrix}}_{\mathbf{y}} = \mathbf{t} \cdot \mathbf{y}^T, \\ z(t) &= \underbrace{\begin{bmatrix} t^2 & t & 1 \end{bmatrix}}_{\mathbf{t}} \underbrace{\begin{bmatrix} a_z \\ b_z \\ c_z \end{bmatrix}}_{\mathbf{z}} = \mathbf{t} \cdot \mathbf{z}^T, \end{aligned} \tag{6.19}$$

where $\mathbf{z}$ is a vector representing coefficients for the $z$-direction; and $\cdot$ denotes the dot product. Equation (6.19) is written in a compact matrix form as

$$\dot{\mathbf{P}}^T(t) = \mathbf{t} \begin{bmatrix} \mathbf{x} & \mathbf{y} & \mathbf{z} \end{bmatrix}. \tag{6.20}$$

It is important to mention that although the previous equation defines a quadratic curve in 3D space, such a curve must reside on a single plane. (The coefficients can be obtained by three 3D points, which define a plane.)

**How to solve the quadratic parametric equations**? Given two 2D endpoints $\dot{\mathbf{p}}_0$ and $\dot{\mathbf{p}}_2$ of a quadratic curve in addition to a 2D curve point $\dot{\mathbf{p}}_1$ whose parameter is $t$, the coefficients of the quadratic parametric equation can be estimated. Equation (6.15) can be written as

$$\dot{\mathbf{p}}(t) = \mathbf{a}t^2 + \mathbf{b}t + \mathbf{c}, \tag{6.21}$$

where $\dot{\mathbf{p}}(t) = [x(t), y(t)]^T$ is a curve point; $\mathbf{a} = [a_x, a_y]^T$, $\mathbf{b} = [b_x, b_y]^T$ and $\mathbf{c} = [c_x, c_y]^T$ are coefficients for the $x$- and $y$-directions; and $t \in [0, 1]$ is a parameter that determines the location of the curve point $\dot{\mathbf{p}}(t)$. At the start point $\dot{\mathbf{p}}_0$ where $t = 0$, we have

$$\dot{\mathbf{p}}_0(0) = \mathbf{c}. \tag{6.22}$$

At the endpoint $\dot{\mathbf{p}}_2$ where $t = 1$, we have

$$\dot{\mathbf{p}}_2(1) = \mathbf{a} + \mathbf{b} + \mathbf{c}. \tag{6.23}$$

At an intermediate point $\dot{\mathbf{p}}_1$ whose parameter is $t$, we have

$$\dot{\mathbf{p}}_1(t) = \mathbf{a}t^2 + \mathbf{b}t + \mathbf{c}. \tag{6.24}$$

Solving Eqs. (6.22–6.24), the coefficients can be written as

$$\begin{aligned}
\mathbf{c} &= \dot{\mathbf{p}}_0, \\
\mathbf{a} &= \frac{t(\dot{\mathbf{p}}_2 - \dot{\mathbf{p}}_0) + (\dot{\mathbf{p}}_0 - \dot{\mathbf{p}}_1)}{t(1-t)}, \\
\mathbf{b} &= \dot{\mathbf{p}}_2 - \dot{\mathbf{p}}_0 - \mathbf{a}.
\end{aligned} \tag{6.25}$$

The previous operation can be expressed in matrix form. Using Eqs. (6.22–6.24), we can write

$$\begin{bmatrix} \dot{\mathbf{p}}_0 \\ \dot{\mathbf{p}}_1 \\ \dot{\mathbf{p}}_2 \end{bmatrix} = \begin{bmatrix} 0 & 0 & 1 \\ t^2 & t & 1 \\ 1 & 1 & 1 \end{bmatrix} \begin{bmatrix} \mathbf{a} \\ \mathbf{b} \\ \mathbf{c} \end{bmatrix}. \tag{6.26}$$

Hence, the coefficients are written as

$$\begin{bmatrix} \mathbf{a} \\ \mathbf{b} \\ \mathbf{c} \end{bmatrix} = \underbrace{\begin{bmatrix} 0 & 0 & 1 \\ t^2 & t & 1 \\ 1 & 1 & 1 \end{bmatrix}^{-1}}_{\mathtt{M}} \begin{bmatrix} \dot{\mathbf{p}}_0 \\ \dot{\mathbf{p}}_1 \\ \dot{\mathbf{p}}_2 \end{bmatrix}, \tag{6.27}$$

where $\mathtt{M}$ is the interpolation matrix used with quadratic parametric curves.

Note that Eqs. (6.25) and (6.27) can also be used for parametric quadratic curves in 3D space. In that case, 3D points $\dot{\mathbf{P}}_0$, $\dot{\mathbf{P}}_1$ and $\dot{\mathbf{P}}_2$ are used instead of 2D points $\dot{\mathbf{p}}_0$, $\dot{\mathbf{p}}_1$ and $\dot{\mathbf{p}}_2$. In addition, the coefficient vectors will be $\mathbf{a} = [a_x, a_y, a_z]^T$, $\mathbf{b} = [b_x, b_y, b_z]^T$ and $\mathbf{c} = [c_x, c_y, c_z]^T$.

**Example 6.5:** [*Parametric representation—interpolation matrix for quadratic curves*]

What are the entries of the interpolation matrix used to generate a quadratic parametric curve given three points $\dot{\mathbf{p}}_0$, $\dot{\mathbf{p}}_1$ and $\dot{\mathbf{p}}_2$ at $t = 0$, $t = \frac{1}{2}$ and $t = 1$ respectively?

**Solution 6.5:** Using Eq. (6.27), the interpolation matrix is written as

$$\mathtt{M} = \begin{bmatrix} 0 & 0 & 1 \\ t^2 & t & 1 \\ 1 & 1 & 1 \end{bmatrix}^{-1}$$

$$
= \begin{bmatrix} 0 & 0 & 1 \\ \left(\frac{1}{2}\right)^2 & \frac{1}{2} & 1 \\ 1 & 1 & 1 \end{bmatrix}^{-1}
= \begin{bmatrix} 2 & -4 & 2 \\ -3 & 4 & -1 \\ 1 & 0 & 0 \end{bmatrix}.
$$

Notice that the entries of this matrix are constant regardless of the locations of the points as long as $\dot{\mathbf{p}}_0$, $\dot{\mathbf{p}}_1$ and $\dot{\mathbf{p}}_2$ are at $t = 0$, $t = \frac{1}{2}$ and $t = 1$ respectively. Notice also that applying this matrix results in the following coefficients:

$$
\begin{bmatrix} \mathbf{a} \\ \mathbf{b} \\ \mathbf{c} \end{bmatrix} = \begin{bmatrix} 2 & -4 & 2 \\ -3 & 4 & -1 \\ 1 & 0 & 0 \end{bmatrix} \begin{bmatrix} \dot{\mathbf{p}}_0 \\ \dot{\mathbf{p}}_1 \\ \dot{\mathbf{p}}_2 \end{bmatrix}.
$$

Thus,

$$
\begin{aligned}
\mathbf{a} &= 2\dot{\mathbf{p}}_0 - 4\dot{\mathbf{p}}_1 + 2\dot{\mathbf{p}}_2, \\
\mathbf{b} &= -3\dot{\mathbf{p}}_0 + 4\dot{\mathbf{p}}_1 - \dot{\mathbf{p}}_2, \\
\mathbf{c} &= \dot{\mathbf{p}}_0,
\end{aligned}
$$

which are the same values obtained using Eq. (6.25) when $t = \frac{1}{2}$. □

**Example 6.6:** [*Parametric representation—general equation for quadratic curves*]
Write down a general equation to estimate the location of a point $\dot{\mathbf{p}}$ at parameter $t$ on a quadratic curve passing through three points $\dot{\mathbf{p}}_0$, $\dot{\mathbf{p}}_1$ and $\dot{\mathbf{p}}_2$. These three points are at 0, $t_1$ and 1 respectively.

**Solution 6.6:** Utilizing the coefficients of Eq. (6.27), the general equation to estimate a point $\dot{\mathbf{p}}$ at parameter $t$ on a quadratic curve given three points can be written as

$$
\dot{\mathbf{p}}(t) = \begin{bmatrix} t^2 & t & 1 \end{bmatrix} \underbrace{\begin{bmatrix} 0 & 0 & 1 \\ t_1^2 & t_1 & 1 \\ 1 & 1 & 1 \end{bmatrix}^{-1} \begin{bmatrix} \dot{\mathbf{p}}_0 \\ \dot{\mathbf{p}}_1 \\ \dot{\mathbf{p}}_2 \end{bmatrix}}_{\begin{bmatrix} \mathbf{a} & \mathbf{b} & \mathbf{c} \end{bmatrix}^T} \quad \text{such that} \quad t \in [0, 1],
$$

where $t_1$ is the value of $t$ at point $\dot{\mathbf{p}}_1$. □

**Example 6.7:** [*Parametric representation—coefficients for quadratic curves*]
A quadratic curve whose endpoints are $[0, 0]^T$ and $[3, 3]^T$ is represented parametrically. If the point $[3, 8]^T$ is on the curve at $t = 0.5$, get the coefficients of the curve equation.

**Solution 6.7:** The coefficients can be estimated using Eq. (6.25) as

$$\begin{aligned}\mathbf{c} &= \dot{\mathbf{p}}_0\\ &= \begin{bmatrix}0\\0\end{bmatrix},\end{aligned}$$

$$\begin{aligned}\mathbf{a} &= \frac{t(\dot{\mathbf{p}}_2 - \dot{\mathbf{p}}_0) + (\dot{\mathbf{p}}_0 - \dot{\mathbf{p}}_1)}{t(1-t)}\\ &= \frac{0.5 \times \left(\begin{bmatrix}3\\3\end{bmatrix} - \begin{bmatrix}0\\0\end{bmatrix}\right) + \left(\begin{bmatrix}0\\0\end{bmatrix} - \begin{bmatrix}3\\8\end{bmatrix}\right)}{0.5 \times (1-0.5)} = \begin{bmatrix}-6\\-26\end{bmatrix}\end{aligned}$$

and

$$\begin{aligned}\mathbf{b} &= \dot{\mathbf{p}}_2 - \dot{\mathbf{p}}_0 - \mathbf{a}\\ &= \begin{bmatrix}3\\3\end{bmatrix} - \begin{bmatrix}0\\0\end{bmatrix} - \begin{bmatrix}-6\\-26\end{bmatrix} = \begin{bmatrix}9\\29\end{bmatrix}.\end{aligned}$$

Alternatively, we may use the interpolation matrix of Example 6.5 in order to get the coefficients **a**, **b** and **c**:

$$\begin{bmatrix}\mathbf{a}\\ \mathbf{b}\\ \mathbf{c}\end{bmatrix} = \begin{bmatrix}2 & -4 & 2\\ -3 & 4 & -1\\ 1 & 0 & 0\end{bmatrix}\begin{bmatrix}\dot{\mathbf{p}}_0\\ \dot{\mathbf{p}}_1\\ \dot{\mathbf{p}}_2\end{bmatrix}.$$

Thus,

$$\begin{aligned}\mathbf{a} &= 2\dot{\mathbf{p}}_0 - 4\dot{\mathbf{p}}_1 + 2\dot{\mathbf{p}}_2\\ &= 2\begin{bmatrix}0\\0\end{bmatrix} - 4\begin{bmatrix}3\\8\end{bmatrix} + 2\begin{bmatrix}3\\3\end{bmatrix}\\ &= -\begin{bmatrix}6\\26\end{bmatrix},\end{aligned}$$

$$\begin{aligned}\mathbf{b} &= -3\dot{\mathbf{p}}_0 + 4\dot{\mathbf{p}}_1 - \dot{\mathbf{p}}_2\\ &= -3\begin{bmatrix}0\\0\end{bmatrix} + 4\begin{bmatrix}3\\8\end{bmatrix} - \begin{bmatrix}3\\3\end{bmatrix}\\ &= \begin{bmatrix}9\\29\end{bmatrix}\end{aligned}$$

and

$$\begin{aligned}\mathbf{c} &= \dot{\mathbf{p}}_0\\ &= \begin{bmatrix}0\\0\end{bmatrix}.\end{aligned}$$

Hence, a point $\dot{\mathbf{p}}(t)$ on the curve is obtained as

$$\begin{aligned}\dot{\mathbf{p}}(t) &= \mathbf{a}t^2 + \mathbf{b}t + \mathbf{c}\\ &= -\begin{bmatrix}6\\26\end{bmatrix}t^2 + \begin{bmatrix}9\\29\end{bmatrix}t + \begin{bmatrix}0\\0\end{bmatrix}.\end{aligned}$$

The $x$- and $y$-values drawn against $t$, when the point $[3, 8]^T$ is at $t = 0.5$, are shown in Fig. 6.2a, c respectively. The final curve is shown in Fig. 6.2e. □

**Example 6.8:** [*Parametric representation—coefficients for quadratic curves*]
Re-solve Example 6.7 if the point $[3, 8]^T$ is on the curve where $t = 0.2$.

**Solution 6.8:** The coefficients can be estimated using Eq. (6.25) as

$$\begin{aligned}\mathbf{c} &= \dot{\mathbf{p}}_0\\ &= \begin{bmatrix}0\\0\end{bmatrix},\end{aligned}$$

$$\begin{aligned}\mathbf{a} &= \frac{t(\dot{\mathbf{p}}_2 - \dot{\mathbf{p}}_0) + (\dot{\mathbf{p}}_0 - \dot{\mathbf{p}}_1)}{t(1-t)}\\ &= \frac{0.2 \times \left(\begin{bmatrix}3\\3\end{bmatrix} - \begin{bmatrix}0\\0\end{bmatrix}\right) + \left(\begin{bmatrix}0\\0\end{bmatrix} - \begin{bmatrix}3\\8\end{bmatrix}\right)}{0.2 \times (1 - 0.2)} = \begin{bmatrix}-15\\-46.25\end{bmatrix}\end{aligned}$$

and

$$\begin{aligned}\mathbf{b} &= \dot{\mathbf{p}}_2 - \dot{\mathbf{p}}_0 - \mathbf{a}\\ &= \begin{bmatrix}3\\3\end{bmatrix} - \begin{bmatrix}0\\0\end{bmatrix} - \begin{bmatrix}-15\\-46.25\end{bmatrix} = \begin{bmatrix}18\\49.25\end{bmatrix}.\end{aligned}$$

Hence, a point $\dot{\mathbf{p}}(t)$ on the curve is obtained as

$$\begin{aligned}\dot{\mathbf{p}}(t) &= \mathbf{a}t^2 + \mathbf{b}t + \mathbf{c}\\ &= -\begin{bmatrix}15\\46.25\end{bmatrix}t^2 + \begin{bmatrix}18\\49.25\end{bmatrix}t + \begin{bmatrix}0\\0\end{bmatrix}.\end{aligned}$$

The $x$- and $y$-values drawn against $t$, when the point $[3, 8]^T$ is at $t = 0.2$, are shown in Fig. 6.2b, d respectively. The final curve is shown in Fig. 6.2f.

Notice the difference between this curve and that of Fig. 6.2e where $[3, 8]^T$ is at $t = 0.5$. □

**Example 6.9:** [*Parametric representation—transformations of quadratic curves*]
Consider a quadratic curve that is represented parametrically. This curve is passing through the points $[0, 0]^T$, $[2, 3]^T$, $[8, 6]^T$ that are at $t = 0$, $t = 0.3$ and $t = 1$

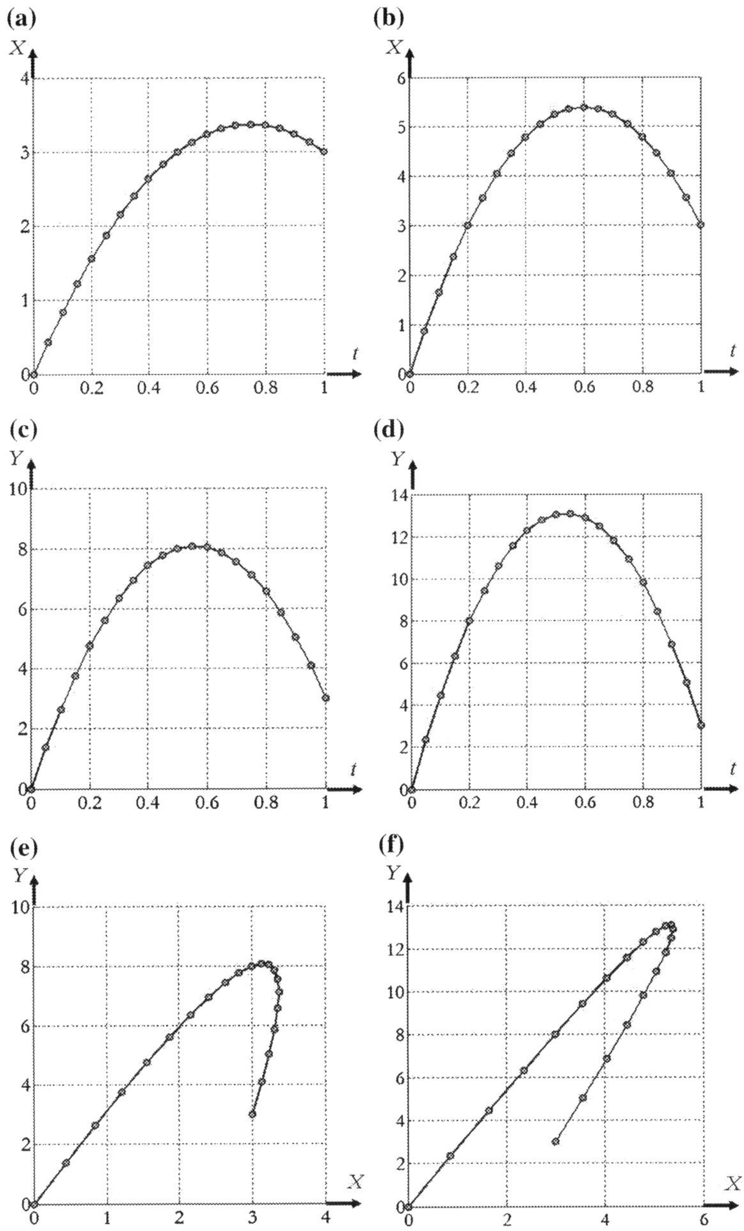


**Fig. 6.2** Parametric quadratic curves passing through $[0, 0]^T$, $[3, 8]^T$ and $[3, 3]^T$. Points are marked at each $0.05t$. **a** The $x$-values against the $t$-values when $[3, 8]^T$ is at $t = 0.5$. **b** The $x$-values against the $t$-values when $[3, 8]^T$ is at $t = 0.2$. **c** The $y$-values against the $t$-values when $[3, 8]^T$ is at $t = 0.5$. **d** The $y$-values against the $t$-values when $[3, 8]^T$ is at $t = 0.2$. **e** The $x$-values against the $y$-values when $[3, 8]^T$ is at $t = 0.5$. **f** The $x$-values against the $y$-values when $[3, 8]^T$ is at $t = 0.2$

respectively. If this curve is rotated through an angle of 45° about a point $\dot{\mathbf{r}} = [3, 3]^T$, estimate the location of the curve at $t = 0.5$ after rotation.

**Solution 6.9:** The coefficients can be estimated using Eq. (6.25) as

$$\mathbf{c} = \dot{\mathbf{p}}_0 = \begin{bmatrix} 0 \\ 0 \end{bmatrix},$$

$$\mathbf{a} = \frac{t(\dot{\mathbf{p}}_2 - \dot{\mathbf{p}}_0) + (\dot{\mathbf{p}}_0 - \dot{\mathbf{p}}_1)}{t(1-t)} = \frac{0.3 \times \left(\begin{bmatrix} 8 \\ 6 \end{bmatrix} - \begin{bmatrix} 0 \\ 0 \end{bmatrix}\right) + \left(\begin{bmatrix} 0 \\ 0 \end{bmatrix} - \begin{bmatrix} 2 \\ 3 \end{bmatrix}\right)}{0.3 \times (1 - 0.3)} = \begin{bmatrix} 1.9048 \\ -5.7143 \end{bmatrix}$$

and

$$\mathbf{b} = \dot{\mathbf{p}}_2 - \dot{\mathbf{p}}_0 - \mathbf{a} = \begin{bmatrix} 8 \\ 6 \end{bmatrix} - \begin{bmatrix} 0 \\ 0 \end{bmatrix} - \begin{bmatrix} 1.9048 \\ -5.7143 \end{bmatrix} = \begin{bmatrix} 6.0952 \\ 11.7143 \end{bmatrix}.$$

Hence, point $\dot{\mathbf{p}}(0.5)$ on the curve is obtained as

$$\dot{\mathbf{p}}(0.5) = \mathbf{a}t^2 + \mathbf{b}t + \mathbf{c} = \begin{bmatrix} 1.9048 \\ -5.7143 \end{bmatrix} \times 0.5^2 + \begin{bmatrix} 6.0952 \\ 11.7143 \end{bmatrix} \times 0.5 + \begin{bmatrix} 0 \\ 0 \end{bmatrix} = \begin{bmatrix} 3.5238 \\ 4.4286 \end{bmatrix}.$$

In order to rotate the curve about $\dot{\mathbf{r}} = [3, 3]^T$, the following steps are performed (refer to Chap. 3):

1. Translate using the vector $[-3, -3]^T$ so that the center of rotation coincides with the origin. The translation process is expressed by a translation matrix $\mathtt{T}([-3, -3]^T)$ that is used with homogeneous points where

$$\mathtt{M}_1 = \mathtt{T}([-3, -3]^T) = \begin{bmatrix} 1 & 0 & -3 \\ 0 & 1 & -3 \\ 0 & 0 & 1 \end{bmatrix}.$$

2. Rotate about the origin through an angle of 45° using the rotation matrix $\mathtt{R}(45°)$ where

$$\mathtt{M}_2 = \mathtt{R}(45) = \begin{bmatrix} \cos(45) & -\sin(45) & 0 \\ \sin(45) & \cos(45) & 0 \\ 0 & 0 & 1 \end{bmatrix}.$$

3. Translate back using the vector $[3, 3]^T$. This translation process is expressed by the translation matrix $\mathtt{T}([3, 3]^T)$ where

$$\mathtt{M}_3 = \mathtt{T}([3,3]^T) = \begin{bmatrix} 1 & 0 & 3 \\ 0 & 1 & 3 \\ 0 & 0 & 1 \end{bmatrix}.$$

Therefore, the transformation process is expressed as

$$\begin{aligned}
\mathtt{M} &= \mathtt{M}_3\mathtt{M}_2\mathtt{M}_1 \\
&= \begin{bmatrix} 1 & 0 & 3 \\ 0 & 1 & 3 \\ 0 & 0 & 1 \end{bmatrix} \begin{bmatrix} \cos(45) & -\sin(45) & 0 \\ \sin(45) & \cos(45) & 0 \\ 0 & 0 & 1 \end{bmatrix} \begin{bmatrix} 1 & 0 & -3 \\ 0 & 1 & -3 \\ 0 & 0 & 1 \end{bmatrix} \\
&= \begin{bmatrix} \frac{1}{\sqrt{2}} & -\frac{1}{\sqrt{2}} & 3 \\ \frac{1}{\sqrt{2}} & \frac{1}{\sqrt{2}} & -\frac{6}{\sqrt{2}} + 3 \\ 0 & 0 & 1 \end{bmatrix} = \begin{bmatrix} 0.7071 & -0.7071 & 3 \\ 0.7071 & 0.7071 & -1.2426 \\ 0 & 0 & 1 \end{bmatrix}.
\end{aligned}$$

Hence, the point after rotation is obtained as

$$\begin{aligned}
\mathbf{p}' &= \mathtt{M}\mathbf{p} \\
&= \begin{bmatrix} \frac{1}{\sqrt{2}} & -\frac{1}{\sqrt{2}} & 3 \\ \frac{1}{\sqrt{2}} & \frac{1}{\sqrt{2}} & -\frac{6}{\sqrt{2}} + 3 \\ 0 & 0 & 1 \end{bmatrix} \begin{bmatrix} 3.5238 \\ 4.4286 \\ 1 \end{bmatrix} = \begin{bmatrix} 2.3602 \\ 4.3805 \\ 1 \end{bmatrix} \Longrightarrow \dot{\mathbf{p}}' = \begin{bmatrix} 2.3602 \\ 4.3805 \end{bmatrix},
\end{aligned}$$

where $\dot{\mathbf{p}} = [3.5238, 4.4286]^T$ is the point to be rotated. The same result can be obtained using Eq. (3.7) as

$$\begin{aligned}
\dot{\mathbf{p}}' &= \begin{bmatrix} \cos(\theta) & -\sin(\theta) \\ \sin(\theta) & \cos(\theta) \end{bmatrix} \begin{bmatrix} x_{\dot{\mathbf{p}}} - x_{\dot{\mathbf{r}}} \\ y_{\dot{\mathbf{p}}} - y_{\dot{\mathbf{r}}} \end{bmatrix} + \begin{bmatrix} x_{\dot{\mathbf{r}}} \\ y_{\dot{\mathbf{r}}} \end{bmatrix} \\
&= \begin{bmatrix} \cos(45) & -\sin(45) \\ \sin(45) & \cos(45) \end{bmatrix} \begin{bmatrix} 3.5238 - 3 \\ 4.4286 - 3 \end{bmatrix} + \begin{bmatrix} 3 \\ 3 \end{bmatrix} = \begin{bmatrix} 2.3602 \\ 4.3805 \end{bmatrix},
\end{aligned}$$

where $[x_{\dot{\mathbf{p}}}, y_{\dot{\mathbf{p}}}]^T$ is the point to be rotated; and $[x_{\dot{\mathbf{r}}}, y_{\dot{\mathbf{r}}}]^T$ is the center of rotation.

Note that this form of curve representation is invariant under affine transformation (e.g., translation, rotation, etc.). In other words, the same result would be achieved if the transformation is applied first to the given points (i.e., $[0, 0]^T$, $[2, 3]^T$ and $[8, 6]^T$) and the curve point is estimated afterwards using the transformed points. This is illustrated in Example 6.10. □

**Example 6.10:** [*Parametric representation—transformations of quadratic curves*]
Re-solve Example 6.9 where the curve point at $t = 0.5$ is obtained after transforming the given curve points $[0, 0]^T$, $[2, 3]^T$ and $[8, 6]^T$.

**Solution 6.10:** We will work with inhomogeneous coordinates to rotate the points. However, the same results must be obtained when using homogeneous points. Thus,

$$\dot{\mathbf{p}}'_0 = \begin{bmatrix} \cos(\theta) & -\sin(\theta) \\ \sin(\theta) & \cos(\theta) \end{bmatrix} \begin{bmatrix} x_{\dot{\mathbf{p}}} - x_{\dot{\mathbf{r}}} \\ y_{\dot{\mathbf{p}}} - y_{\dot{\mathbf{r}}} \end{bmatrix} + \begin{bmatrix} x_{\dot{\mathbf{r}}} \\ y_{\dot{\mathbf{r}}} \end{bmatrix}$$

$$= \begin{bmatrix} \cos(45) & -\sin(45) \\ \sin(45) & \cos(45) \end{bmatrix} \begin{bmatrix} 0-3 \\ 0-3 \end{bmatrix} + \begin{bmatrix} 3 \\ 3 \end{bmatrix} = \begin{bmatrix} 3 \\ -1.2426 \end{bmatrix},$$

where $[x_{\dot{\mathbf{p}}}, y_{\dot{\mathbf{p}}}]^T$ is the point to be rotated; and $[x_{\dot{\mathbf{r}}}, y_{\dot{\mathbf{r}}}]^T$ is the center of rotation. Similarly, the other two rotated points are estimated as

$$\dot{\mathbf{p}}'_1 = \begin{bmatrix} \cos(45) & -\sin(45) \\ \sin(45) & \cos(45) \end{bmatrix} \begin{bmatrix} 2-3 \\ 3-3 \end{bmatrix} + \begin{bmatrix} 3 \\ 3 \end{bmatrix} = \begin{bmatrix} 2.2929 \\ 2.2929 \end{bmatrix}$$

and

$$\dot{\mathbf{p}}'_2 = \begin{bmatrix} \cos(45) & -\sin(45) \\ \sin(45) & \cos(45) \end{bmatrix} \begin{bmatrix} 8-3 \\ 6-3 \end{bmatrix} + \begin{bmatrix} 3 \\ 3 \end{bmatrix} = \begin{bmatrix} 4.4142 \\ 8.6569 \end{bmatrix}.$$

Now the coefficients are obtained as

$$\mathbf{c}' = \dot{\mathbf{p}}'_0 = \begin{bmatrix} 3 \\ -1.2426 \end{bmatrix},$$

$$\mathbf{a}' = \frac{t(\dot{\mathbf{p}}'_2 - \dot{\mathbf{p}}'_0) + (\dot{\mathbf{p}}'_0 - \dot{\mathbf{p}}'_1)}{t(1-t)}$$

$$= \frac{0.3 \times \left( \begin{bmatrix} 4.4142 \\ 8.6569 \end{bmatrix} - \begin{bmatrix} 3.0 \\ -1.2426 \end{bmatrix} \right) + \left( \begin{bmatrix} 3 \\ -1.2426 \end{bmatrix} - \begin{bmatrix} 2.2929 \\ 2.2929 \end{bmatrix} \right)}{0.3 \times (1-0.3)}$$

$$= \begin{bmatrix} 5.3875 \\ -2.6937 \end{bmatrix}$$

and

$$\mathbf{b}' = \dot{\mathbf{p}}'_2 - \dot{\mathbf{p}}'_0 - \mathbf{a}'$$

$$= \begin{bmatrix} 4.4142 \\ 8.6569 \end{bmatrix} - \begin{bmatrix} 3 \\ -1.2426 \end{bmatrix} - \begin{bmatrix} 5.3875 \\ -2.6937 \end{bmatrix} = \begin{bmatrix} -3.9733 \\ 12.5932 \end{bmatrix}.$$

Hence, point $\dot{\mathbf{p}}'(0.5)$ on the curve is obtained as

$$\dot{\mathbf{p}}'(0.5) = \mathbf{a}'t^2 + \mathbf{b}'t + \mathbf{c}'$$

$$= \begin{bmatrix} 5.3875 \\ -2.6937 \end{bmatrix} \times 0.5^2 + \begin{bmatrix} -3.9733 \\ 12.5932 \end{bmatrix} \times 0.5 + \begin{bmatrix} 3 \\ -1.2426 \end{bmatrix} = \begin{bmatrix} 2.3602 \\ 4.3805 \end{bmatrix},$$

which is the same point obtained in Example 6.9. □

#### 6.1.3.3 Cubic Parametric Representation

For cubic 2D curves, the following cubic polynomials are used to get a curve point $\dot{\mathbf{p}}(t) = [x(t), y(t)]^T$:

$$\begin{aligned} x(t) &= a_x t^3 + b_x t^2 + c_x t + d_x, \\ y(t) &= a_y t^3 + b_y t^2 + c_y t + d_y, \end{aligned} \tag{6.28}$$

where $a_x$, $b_x$, $c_x$, $d_x$, $a_y$, $b_y$, $c_y$ and $d_y$ are coefficients for the $x$- and $y$-directions respectively; and $t \in [0, 1]$ is a parameter that determines the location of the curve point $\dot{\mathbf{p}}(t) = [x(t), y(t)]^T$ along the curve. In vector form, Eq. (6.28) can be re-written as

$$\begin{aligned} x(t) &= \underbrace{\begin{bmatrix} t^3 & t^2 & t & 1 \end{bmatrix}}_{\mathbf{t}} \underbrace{\begin{bmatrix} a_x \\ b_x \\ c_x \\ d_x \end{bmatrix}}_{\mathbf{x}} = \mathbf{t} \cdot \mathbf{x}^T, \\ y(t) &= \underbrace{\begin{bmatrix} t^3 & t^2 & t & 1 \end{bmatrix}}_{\mathbf{t}} \underbrace{\begin{bmatrix} a_y \\ b_y \\ c_y \\ d_y \end{bmatrix}}_{\mathbf{y}} = \mathbf{t} \cdot \mathbf{y}^T, \end{aligned} \tag{6.29}$$

where $\mathbf{x}$ and $\mathbf{y}$ are vectors representing coefficients for the $x$- and $y$-directions respectively; and $\cdot$ denotes the dot product. Equation (6.29) can be re-written in a compact matrix form as

$$\dot{\mathbf{p}}^T(t) = \mathbf{t}\begin{bmatrix} \mathbf{x} & \mathbf{y} \end{bmatrix}. \tag{6.30}$$

Note that Eq. (6.28) can be extended to cover cubic parametric curves in 3D space by adding an entry for the third dimension (i.e., the $z$-direction). Hence, the location of a curve point $\dot{\mathbf{P}}(t) = [x(t), y(t), z(t)]^T$ along the curve can be obtained as

$$\begin{aligned} x(t) &= a_x t^3 + b_x t^2 + c_x t + d_x, \\ y(t) &= a_y t^3 + b_y t^2 + c_y t + d_y, \\ z(t) &= a_z t^3 + b_z t^2 + c_z t + d_z, \end{aligned} \tag{6.31}$$

where $a_z$, $b_z$, $c_z$ and $d_z$ are coefficients for the $z$-direction. Furthermore, Eq. (6.31) can be written in vector form as

$$
\begin{aligned}
x(t) &= \underbrace{\left[t^3\ t^2\ t\ 1\right]}_{\mathbf{t}} \underbrace{\begin{bmatrix} a_x \\ b_x \\ c_x \\ d_x \end{bmatrix}}_{\mathbf{x}} = \mathbf{t} \cdot \mathbf{x}^T, \\
y(t) &= \underbrace{\left[t^3\ t^2\ t\ 1\right]}_{\mathbf{t}} \underbrace{\begin{bmatrix} a_y \\ b_y \\ c_y \\ d_y \end{bmatrix}}_{\mathbf{y}} = \mathbf{t} \cdot \mathbf{y}^T, \\
z(t) &= \underbrace{\left[t^3\ t^2\ t\ 1\right]}_{\mathbf{t}} \underbrace{\begin{bmatrix} a_z \\ b_z \\ c_z \\ d_z \end{bmatrix}}_{\mathbf{z}} = \mathbf{t} \cdot \mathbf{z}^T,
\end{aligned}
\tag{6.32}
$$

where $\mathbf{z}$ is a vector representing coefficients for the $z$-direction; and $\cdot$ denotes the dot product. Finally, Eq. (6.32) is written in a compact matrix form as

$$\dot{\mathbf{P}}^T(t) = \mathbf{t}\left[\mathbf{x}\ \mathbf{y}\ \mathbf{z}\right]. \tag{6.33}$$

**How to solve the cubic parametric equations**? Given two 2D endpoints $\dot{\mathbf{p}}_0$ and $\dot{\mathbf{p}}_3$ of a cubic curve in addition to two 2D points $\dot{\mathbf{p}}_1$ and $\dot{\mathbf{p}}_2$ whose parameters are $t_1$ and $t_2$, the coefficients of the cubic parametric equation can be estimated. Equation (6.28) can be written as

$$\dot{\mathbf{p}}(t) = \mathbf{a}t^3 + \mathbf{b}t^2 + \mathbf{c}t + \mathbf{d}, \tag{6.34}$$

where $\dot{\mathbf{p}}(t) = [x(t), y(t)]^T$ is a curve point; $\mathbf{a} = [a_x, a_y]^T$, $\mathbf{b} = [b_x, b_y]^T$, $\mathbf{c} = [c_x, c_y]^T$ and $\mathbf{d} = [d_x, d_y]^T$ are coefficients for the $x$- and $y$-directions; and $t \in [0, 1]$ is a parameter that determines the location of the curve point. At the start point $\dot{\mathbf{p}}_0$ where $t = 0$, we have

$$\dot{\mathbf{p}}_0(0) = \mathbf{d}. \tag{6.35}$$

At the endpoint $\dot{\mathbf{p}}_3$ where $t = 1$, we have

$$\dot{\mathbf{p}}_3(1) = \mathbf{a} + \mathbf{b} + \mathbf{c} + \mathbf{d}. \tag{6.36}$$

At the intermediate points $\dot{\mathbf{p}}_1$ and $\dot{\mathbf{p}}_2$ whose parameters are $t_1$ and $t_2$, we have

$$\dot{\mathbf{p}}_1(t_1) = \mathbf{a}t_1^3 + \mathbf{b}t_1^2 + \mathbf{c}t_1 + \mathbf{d} \tag{6.37}$$

and

$$\dot{\mathbf{p}}_2(t_2) = \mathbf{a}t_2^3 + \mathbf{b}t_2^2 + \mathbf{c}t_2 + \mathbf{d}. \tag{6.38}$$

As done with quadratic curves, Eq. (6.35) through Eq. (6.38) can be solved simultaneously to get the coefficients **a**, **b**, **c** and **d**. In matrix form, those equations can be written as

$$\begin{bmatrix} \dot{\mathbf{p}}_0 \\ \dot{\mathbf{p}}_1 \\ \dot{\mathbf{p}}_2 \\ \dot{\mathbf{p}}_3 \end{bmatrix} = \begin{bmatrix} 0 & 0 & 0 & 1 \\ t_1^3 & t_1^2 & t_1 & 1 \\ t_2^3 & t_1^2 & t_2 & 1 \\ 1 & 1 & 1 & 1 \end{bmatrix} \begin{bmatrix} \mathbf{a} \\ \mathbf{b} \\ \mathbf{c} \\ \mathbf{d} \end{bmatrix}. \tag{6.39}$$

Hence, the coefficients are written as

$$\begin{bmatrix} \mathbf{a} \\ \mathbf{b} \\ \mathbf{c} \\ \mathbf{d} \end{bmatrix} = \underbrace{\begin{bmatrix} 0 & 0 & 0 & 1 \\ t_1^3 & t_1^2 & t_1 & 1 \\ t_2^3 & t_2^2 & t_2 & 1 \\ 1 & 1 & 1 & 1 \end{bmatrix}^{-1}}_{\mathtt{M}} \begin{bmatrix} \dot{\mathbf{p}}_0 \\ \dot{\mathbf{p}}_1 \\ \dot{\mathbf{p}}_2 \\ \dot{\mathbf{p}}_3 \end{bmatrix}, \tag{6.40}$$

where $\mathtt{M}$ is the interpolation matrix used with cubic parametric curves.

Note that Eq. (6.40) may also be used for parametric cubic curves in 3D space. In that case, 3D points $\dot{\mathbf{P}}_0$, $\dot{\mathbf{P}}_1$, $\dot{\mathbf{P}}_2$ and $\dot{\mathbf{P}}_3$ are used instead of 2D points $\dot{\mathbf{p}}_0$, $\dot{\mathbf{p}}_1$, $\dot{\mathbf{p}}_2$ and $\dot{\mathbf{p}}_3$. In addition, the coefficient vectors will be $\mathbf{a} = [a_x, a_y, a_z]^T$, $\mathbf{b} = [b_x, b_y, b_z]^T$, $\mathbf{c} = [c_x, c_y, c_z]^T$ and $\mathbf{d} = [d_x, d_y, d_z]^T$.

**Example 6.11:** [*Parametric representation—general equation of cubic curves*]

Write down a general equation to estimate a point $\dot{\mathbf{p}}$ at parameter $t$ on a cubic curve passing through four points $\dot{\mathbf{p}}_0$, $\dot{\mathbf{p}}_1$, $\dot{\mathbf{p}}_2$ and $\dot{\mathbf{p}}_3$. These four points are at 0, $t_1$, $t_2$ and 1 respectively.

**Solution 6.11:** Utilizing the coefficients of Eq. (6.40), the general equation to estimate a point $\dot{\mathbf{p}}$ at parameter $t$ on a cubic curve given four points can be written as

$$\dot{\mathbf{p}}(t) = \begin{bmatrix} t^3 & t^2 & t & 1 \end{bmatrix} \underbrace{\begin{bmatrix} 0 & 0 & 0 & 1 \\ t_1^3 & t_1^2 & t_1 & 1 \\ t_2^3 & t_2^2 & t_2 & 1 \\ 1 & 1 & 1 & 1 \end{bmatrix}^{-1} \begin{bmatrix} \dot{\mathbf{p}}_0 \\ \dot{\mathbf{p}}_1 \\ \dot{\mathbf{p}}_2 \\ \dot{\mathbf{p}}_3 \end{bmatrix}}_{\begin{bmatrix} \mathbf{a} & \mathbf{b} & \mathbf{c} & \mathbf{d} \end{bmatrix}^T}. \qquad \square$$

**Example 6.12:** [*Parametric representation—interpolation matrix for cubic curves*]

What are the entries of the interpolation matrix used for cubic parametric curves when $t_0 = 0$, $t_1 = \frac{1}{3}$, $t_2 = \frac{2}{3}$ and $t_3 = 1$ for $\dot{\mathbf{p}}_0$, $\dot{\mathbf{p}}_1$, $\dot{\mathbf{p}}_2$ and $\dot{\mathbf{p}}_3$ respectively?

**Solution 6.12:** Using Eq. (6.40), the interpolation matrix is written as

$$\mathtt{M} = \begin{bmatrix} 0 & 0 & 0 & 1 \\ t_1^3 & t_1^2 & t_1 & 1 \\ t_2^3 & t_2^2 & t_2 & 1 \\ 1 & 1 & 1 & 1 \end{bmatrix}^{-1}$$

$$= \begin{bmatrix} 0 & 0 & 0 & 1 \\ \left(\frac{1}{3}\right)^3 & \left(\frac{1}{3}\right)^2 & \frac{1}{3} & 1 \\ \left(\frac{2}{3}\right)^3 & \left(\frac{2}{3}\right)^2 & \frac{2}{3} & 1 \\ 1 & 1 & 1 & 1 \end{bmatrix}^{-1} = \begin{bmatrix} -4.5 & 13.5 & -13.5 & 4.5 \\ 9 & -22.5 & 18 & -4.5 \\ -5.5 & 9 & -4.5 & 1 \\ 1 & 0 & 0 & 0 \end{bmatrix}.$$

Notice that the entries of this matrix are constant regardless of the locations of the points as long as $\dot{\mathbf{p}}_0$, $\dot{\mathbf{p}}_1$, $\dot{\mathbf{p}}_2$ and $\dot{\mathbf{p}}_3$ are at $t = 0$, $t = \frac{1}{3}$, $t = \frac{2}{3}$ and $t = 1$ respectively. □

**Example 6.13:** [*Parametric representation—equation of cubic curves*]
A cubic curve is passing through points $\dot{\mathbf{p}}_0$, $\dot{\mathbf{p}}_1$, $\dot{\mathbf{p}}_2$ and $\dot{\mathbf{p}}_3$ where the values of the parameter $t$ at these points are 0, $\frac{1}{3}$, $\frac{2}{3}$ and 1 respectively. Write down the equation for a general point $\dot{\mathbf{p}}$ on this curve.

**Solution 6.13:** Using the interpolation matrix from Example 6.12, the coefficients **a**, **b**, **c** and **d** are written as

$$\begin{bmatrix} \mathbf{a} \\ \mathbf{b} \\ \mathbf{c} \\ \mathbf{d} \end{bmatrix} = \begin{bmatrix} -4.5 & 13.5 & -13.5 & 4.5 \\ 9 & -22.5 & 18 & -4.5 \\ -5.5 & 9 & -4.5 & 1 \\ 1 & 0 & 0 & 0 \end{bmatrix} \begin{bmatrix} \dot{\mathbf{p}}_0 \\ \dot{\mathbf{p}}_1 \\ \dot{\mathbf{p}}_2 \\ \dot{\mathbf{p}}_3 \end{bmatrix}$$

or

$$\begin{aligned} \mathbf{a} &= -4.5\dot{\mathbf{p}}_0 + 13.5\dot{\mathbf{p}}_1 - 13.5\dot{\mathbf{p}}_2 + 4.5\dot{\mathbf{p}}_3, \\ \mathbf{b} &= 9\dot{\mathbf{p}}_0 - 22.5\dot{\mathbf{p}}_1 + 18\dot{\mathbf{p}}_2 - 4.5\dot{\mathbf{p}}_3, \\ \mathbf{c} &= -5.5\dot{\mathbf{p}}_0 + 9\dot{\mathbf{p}}_1 - 4.5\dot{\mathbf{p}}_2 + \dot{\mathbf{p}}_3, \\ \mathbf{d} &= \dot{\mathbf{p}}_0. \end{aligned}$$

Hence, a point $\dot{\mathbf{p}}(t)$ on this curve is calculated as

$$\begin{aligned} \dot{\mathbf{p}}(t) &= \mathbf{a}t^3 + \mathbf{b}t^2 + \mathbf{c}t + \mathbf{d} \\ &= [\, t^3 \; t^2 \; t \; 1 \,] \begin{bmatrix} -4.5 & 13.5 & -13.5 & 4.5 \\ 9 & -22.5 & 18 & -4.5 \\ -5.5 & 9 & -4.5 & 1 \\ 1 & 0 & 0 & 0 \end{bmatrix} \begin{bmatrix} \dot{\mathbf{p}}_0 \\ \dot{\mathbf{p}}_1 \\ \dot{\mathbf{p}}_2 \\ \dot{\mathbf{p}}_3 \end{bmatrix}. \end{aligned}$$ □

**Example 6.14:** [*Parametric representation—points on curves*]
In the previous cubic curve of Example 6.13 where $t_1$ and $t_2$ are $\frac{1}{3}$ and $\frac{2}{3}$ respectively, determine the location of the curve where $t = \frac{1}{2}$ if $\dot{\mathbf{p}}_0 = [1, 1]^T$, $\dot{\mathbf{p}}_1 = [3, 3]^T$, $\dot{\mathbf{p}}_2 = [6, 3]^T$ and $\dot{\mathbf{p}}_3 = [9, 2]^T$.

**Solution 6.14:** The coefficients **a**, **b**, **c** and **d** are calculated as

$$\begin{aligned}\mathbf{a} &= -4.5\dot{\mathbf{p}}_0 + 13.5\dot{\mathbf{p}}_1 - 13.5\dot{\mathbf{p}}_2 + 4.5\dot{\mathbf{p}}_3\\ &= -4.5\begin{bmatrix}1\\1\end{bmatrix} + 13.5\begin{bmatrix}3\\3\end{bmatrix} - 13.5\begin{bmatrix}6\\3\end{bmatrix} + 4.5\begin{bmatrix}9\\2\end{bmatrix}\\ &= \begin{bmatrix}-4.5\\4.5\end{bmatrix},\end{aligned}$$

$$\begin{aligned}\mathbf{b} &= 9\dot{\mathbf{p}}_0 - 22.5\dot{\mathbf{p}}_1 + 18\dot{\mathbf{p}}_2 - 4.5\dot{\mathbf{p}}_3\\ &= 9\begin{bmatrix}1\\1\end{bmatrix} - 22.5\begin{bmatrix}3\\3\end{bmatrix} + 18\begin{bmatrix}6\\3\end{bmatrix} - 4.5\begin{bmatrix}9\\2\end{bmatrix}\\ &= \begin{bmatrix}9\\-13.5\end{bmatrix},\end{aligned}$$

$$\begin{aligned}\mathbf{c} &= -5.5\dot{\mathbf{p}}_0 + 9\dot{\mathbf{p}}_1 - 4.5\dot{\mathbf{p}}_2 + \dot{\mathbf{p}}_3\\ &= -5.5\begin{bmatrix}1\\1\end{bmatrix} + 9\begin{bmatrix}3\\3\end{bmatrix} - 4.5\begin{bmatrix}6\\3\end{bmatrix} + \begin{bmatrix}9\\2\end{bmatrix}\\ &= \begin{bmatrix}3.5\\10\end{bmatrix}\end{aligned}$$

and

$$\mathbf{d} = \begin{bmatrix}1\\1\end{bmatrix}.$$

Hence, the curve point at $t = \frac{1}{2}$ is obtained as

$$\begin{aligned}\dot{\mathbf{p}}(t) &= \mathbf{a}t^3 + \mathbf{b}t^2 + \mathbf{c}t + \mathbf{d}\\ \dot{\mathbf{p}}\left(\tfrac{1}{2}\right) &= \begin{bmatrix}-4.5\\4.5\end{bmatrix}\left(\tfrac{1}{2}\right)^3 + \begin{bmatrix}9\\-13.5\end{bmatrix}\left(\tfrac{1}{2}\right)^2 + \begin{bmatrix}3.5\\10\end{bmatrix}\left(\tfrac{1}{2}\right) + \begin{bmatrix}1\\1\end{bmatrix}\\ &= \begin{bmatrix}4.4375\\3.1875\end{bmatrix}.\end{aligned}$$

The curve is drawn in Fig. 6.3 where the locations of curve points at 0, $\frac{1}{3}$, $\frac{1}{2}$, $\frac{2}{3}$ and 1 are marked. The small marks on the curve represent the values of $t$ at 0.05, 0.1, 0.15, 0.2, etc. □

#### 6.1.3.4 Higher Order Parametric Representation

Note that in all the previous equations, each dimension is dealt with independently. Thus, parametric representation can be extended to any number of dimensions even higher than 3D space.

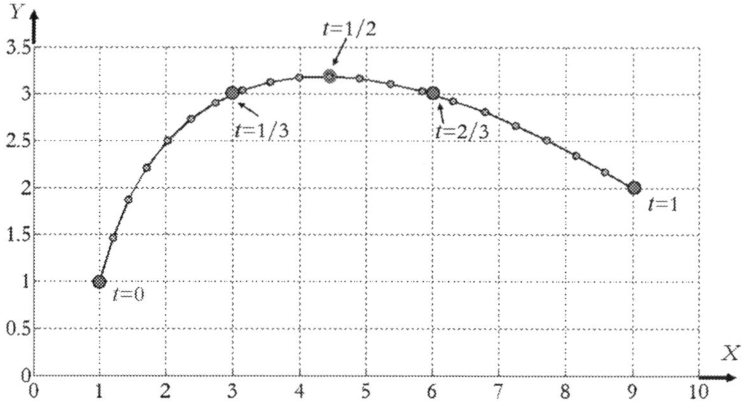


**Fig. 6.3** A parametric cubic curve passing through $[1, 1]^T$, $[3, 3]^T$, $[6, 3]^T$ and $[9, 2]^T$. The values of parameter $t$ at these points are 0, $\frac{1}{3}$, $\frac{2}{3}$ and 1 respectively. The indicated curve point at $t = \frac{1}{2}$ is $[4.4375, 3.1875]^T$. The small dots on the curve represent the values of $t$ at 0.05, 0.1, 0.15, 0.2, etc.

#### 6.1.3.5 Curve Continuity

Equation (6.17) defines a quadratic curve equation in 2D space. The derivative of $\dot{\mathbf{p}}^T(t)$ is obtained as

$$\begin{aligned}\frac{d}{dt}\dot{\mathbf{p}}^T(t) &= \frac{d}{dt}[x(t)\ \ y(t)] \\ &= \frac{d}{dt}\mathbf{t}\begin{bmatrix}\mathbf{x} & \mathbf{y}\end{bmatrix} \\ &= \begin{bmatrix}2t & 1 & 0\end{bmatrix}\begin{bmatrix}\mathbf{x} & \mathbf{y}\end{bmatrix} \\ &= [\,2a_xt + b_x\ \ 2a_yt + b_y\,].\end{aligned} \tag{6.41}$$

The resulting vector $[2a_xt + b_x, 2a_yt + b_y]$ is called the parametric *tangent vector*. Similarly, for quadratic curve in 3D space, the derivative of $\dot{\mathbf{P}}^T(t)$ is obtained as

$$\begin{aligned}\frac{d}{dt}\dot{\mathbf{P}}^T(t) &= \frac{d}{dt}[x(t)\ \ y(t)\ \ z(t)] \\ &= \frac{d}{dt}\mathbf{t}\begin{bmatrix}\mathbf{x} & \mathbf{y} & \mathbf{z}\end{bmatrix} \\ &= \begin{bmatrix}2t & 1 & 0\end{bmatrix}\begin{bmatrix}\mathbf{x} & \mathbf{y} & \mathbf{z}\end{bmatrix} \\ &= [\,2a_xt + b_x\ \ 2a_yt + b_y\ \ 2a_zt + b_z\,].\end{aligned} \tag{6.42}$$

For 2D cubic curve, the tangent vector or the derivative of $\dot{\mathbf{p}}^T(t)$ is obtained as

$$\begin{aligned}
\frac{d}{dt}\dot{\mathbf{p}}^T(t) &= \frac{d}{dt}[x(t) \;\; y(t)] \\
&= \frac{d}{dt}\mathbf{t}\left[\mathbf{x} \; \mathbf{y}\right] \\
&= \left[3t^2 \; 2t \; 1 \; 0\right]\left[\mathbf{x} \; \mathbf{y}\right] \\
&= [\, 3a_x t^2 + 2b_x t + c_x \;\; 3a_y t^2 + 2b_y t + c_y \,].
\end{aligned} \tag{6.43}$$

Similarly, the tangent vector or the derivative for a 3D cubic curve is obtained as

$$\begin{aligned}
\frac{d}{dt}\dot{\mathbf{P}}^T(t) &= \frac{d}{dt}[x(t) \;\; y(t) \;\; z(t)] \\
&= \frac{d}{dt}\mathbf{t}\left[\mathbf{x} \; \mathbf{y} \; \mathbf{z}\right] \\
&= \left[3t^2 \; 2t \; 1 \; 0\right]\left[\mathbf{x} \; \mathbf{y} \; \mathbf{z}\right] \\
&= [\, 3a_x t^2 + 2b_x t + c_x \;\; 3a_y t^2 + 2b_y t + c_y \;\; 3a_z t^2 + 2b_z t + c_z \,].
\end{aligned} \tag{6.44}$$

**$G^n$ geometric continuity:** If two curve segments join at a point, the curve is said to be $G^0$ *continuous*. If the directions of the tangent vectors of the segments at the join point are equal, the curve is said to be $G^1$ *continuous*. Note that the directions of the vectors may be equal while their magnitudes are different. The $G^1$ geometric continuity is concerned with the direction only. Two tangent vectors $\mathbf{t}_1$ and $\mathbf{t}_2$ are having the same direction when one of them is a scalar multiple of the other (Foley et al. 1995) (i.e., $\mathbf{t}_1 = s\mathbf{t}_2$ where $s$ is a scalar value). $G^1$ geometric continuity is a good condition to ensure curve smoothness at join points. As with $G^1$ continuity, if the directions of the 2nd derivative of the segments at the join point are equal, the curve is said to be $G^2$ *continuous*.

**$C^n$parametric continuity:** As with $G^0$ *continuous* curves, $C^0$ parametric continuity happens when two curve segments join at a point. In case the magnitudes as well as the directions of the tangent vectors are equal at the join points, the curve is said to be $C^1$ *continuous*. Note that a $C^1$ continuous curve is $G^1$ continuous at the same time as $C^1$ continuity requires equal directions (unless tangent vectors are zero or null vectors). A curve is $C^2$ continuous if the magnitudes as well as the directions of the 2nd derivative are equal. In general, a curve is $C^n$ continuous if the magnitudes as well as the directions of the $n$th derivative are equal.

## 6.2 Approximating Curves

All the curves that we have seen so far are referred to as interpolating curves. Given a number of points, an *interpolating curve* passes through those points (Parent 2012). Increasing the number of these points increases the degree of the curve so as the computational time required to determine all the pixels comprising the curve. Sometimes, it may be a good idea to split the higher-degree curve into a sequence of lower-degree curve segments. (A curve segment is sometimes called a *span* or a *patch*.)

Notice that in order to maintain smoothness of the curves, we have to match not only the locations of join points but the slopes (i.e., the gradients) of curve segments at those points as well (refer to Sect. 6.1.3.5). An idea to keep the smoothness of curves is by using approximating curves. An *approximating curve* does not pass through all specified points (i.e., *control points*). Rather, the control points are used to control the shape of the curve. (Sometimes, a curve interpolates the ending control points only and uses the rest of the points to determine its shape.) Examples include Bézier curves, B-splines and NURBS (Buss 2003; McConnell 2005; Farin 2002). Those curves are discussed in the rest of this chapter.

## 6.2.1 Bézier Curves

A Bézier curve (Bezier 1972, 1974) is an approximating curve that is generated as a blend of a number of control points. The number of control points varies according to the degree of the curve. The minimum acceptable number of control points is two, which defines a linear Bézier curve (i.e., a line). In case more control points are available, two of them will mark the start and end of the curve while the rest of points contribute to shape the curve as a blend of these points. We will talk about linear, quadratic and cubic Bézier curves.

### 6.2.1.1 Linear Bézier Curves

In order to generate a *linear* Bézier curve, *two* points are required. These points represent the start and endpoints of the curve, which is a simple straight line in this case. Assuming that two 2D points $\dot{\mathbf{p}}_0$ and $\dot{\mathbf{p}}_1$ are available. The linear Bézier curve is given by

$$\dot{\mathbf{p}}(t) = (1-t)\dot{\mathbf{p}}_0 + t\dot{\mathbf{p}}_1, \tag{6.45}$$

where $t \in [0, 1]$ is a parameter that increases from 0 at the start point $\dot{\mathbf{p}}_0$ to 1 at the endpoint $\dot{\mathbf{p}}_1$; and $\dot{\mathbf{p}}(t)$ is a point on the line at parameter $t$. Note that Eq. (6.45) represents the parametric equation of a line. In matrix form, Eq. (6.45) is re-written as

$$\dot{\mathbf{p}}(t) = \begin{bmatrix} t & 1 \end{bmatrix} \underbrace{\begin{bmatrix} -1 & 1 \\ 1 & 0 \end{bmatrix}}_{\dot{\mathrm{B}}_1} \begin{bmatrix} \dot{\mathbf{p}}_0 \\ \dot{\mathbf{p}}_1 \end{bmatrix}, \tag{6.46}$$

where $\dot{\mathrm{B}}_1$ is the geometry matrix for linear Bézier curves.

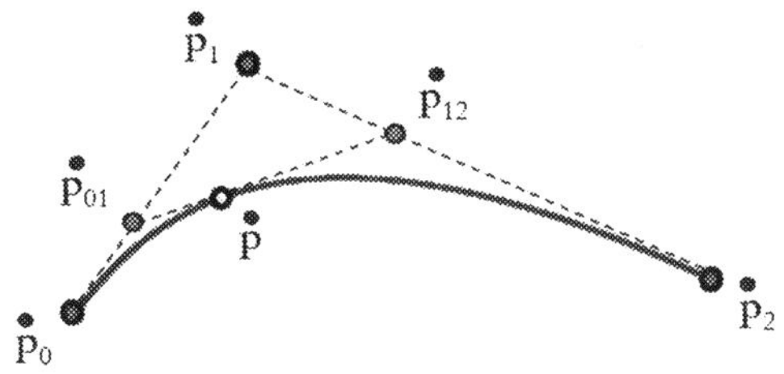


**Fig. 6.4** A quadratic Bézier curve

#### 6.2.1.2 Quadratic Bézier Curves

In order to generate a *quadratic* Bézier curve, *three* points are required. Two of those points represent the start and endpoints of the curve while the third point gives directional information for the curve. The polyline that passes through all these three control points is referred to as the *Bézier polygon* or the *control polygon* (although, in general, it is not a closed polygon as mentioned in Sect. 2.3). Also, it can be said that the convex hull of all control points contains the curve completely.

Given three 2D control points $\dot{\mathbf{p}}_0$, $\dot{\mathbf{p}}_1$ and $\dot{\mathbf{p}}_2$, the quadratic curve starts at $\dot{\mathbf{p}}_0$ and ends at $\dot{\mathbf{p}}_2$; however, it does not pass through $\dot{\mathbf{p}}_1$. The directions of the tangent vectors at the curve endpoints $\dot{\mathbf{p}}_0$ and $\dot{\mathbf{p}}_2$ are the same as the directions of the first and last segments of the control polygon; i.e., $\overline{\dot{\mathbf{p}}_0\dot{\mathbf{p}}_1}$ and $\overline{\dot{\mathbf{p}}_1\dot{\mathbf{p}}_2}$. As shown in Fig. 6.4, a point $\dot{\mathbf{p}}$ at $t$ on a quadratic Bézier curve is estimated through the following steps:

1. A point $\dot{\mathbf{p}}_{01}$ is obtained at $t$ along the linear Bézier curve connecting $\dot{\mathbf{p}}_0$ and $\dot{\mathbf{p}}_1$ using Eq. (6.45) as
$$\dot{\mathbf{p}}_{01}(t) = (1-t)\dot{\mathbf{p}}_0 + t\dot{\mathbf{p}}_1. \tag{6.47}$$
2. A point $\dot{\mathbf{p}}_{12}$ is obtained at $t$ along the linear Bézier curve connecting $\dot{\mathbf{p}}_1$ and $\dot{\mathbf{p}}_2$ using Eq. (6.45) as
$$\dot{\mathbf{p}}_{12}(t) = (1-t)\dot{\mathbf{p}}_1 + t\dot{\mathbf{p}}_2. \tag{6.48}$$
3. The point $\dot{\mathbf{p}}$ is obtained at $t$ along the linear Bézier curve connecting $\dot{\mathbf{p}}_{01}$ and $\dot{\mathbf{p}}_{12}$ using Eq. (6.45) as
$$\dot{\mathbf{p}}(t) = (1-t)\dot{\mathbf{p}}_{01} + t\dot{\mathbf{p}}_{12}. \tag{6.49}$$

   Substituting the values of $\dot{\mathbf{p}}_{01}$ and $\dot{\mathbf{p}}_{12}$ from Eqs. (6.47) and (6.48) respectively, we get

$$\begin{aligned}\dot{\mathbf{p}}(t) &= (1-t)\dot{\mathbf{p}}_{01} + t\dot{\mathbf{p}}_{12} \\ &= (1-t)\big[(1-t)\dot{\mathbf{p}}_0 + t\dot{\mathbf{p}}_1\big] + t\big[(1-t)\dot{\mathbf{p}}_1 + t\dot{\mathbf{p}}_2\big].\end{aligned} \tag{6.50}$$

   Thus, a point $\dot{\mathbf{p}}$ on a quadratic Bézier curve is given by

$$\dot{\mathbf{p}}(t) = (1-t)^2\dot{\mathbf{p}}_0 + 2t(1-t)\dot{\mathbf{p}}_1 + t^2\dot{\mathbf{p}}_2, \tag{6.51}$$

where $t \in [0, 1]$ is a parameter that increases from 0 at the start point $\dot{\mathbf{p}}_0$ to 1 at the endpoint $\dot{\mathbf{p}}_2$; and $\dot{\mathbf{p}}(t)$ is a point on the curve at parameter $t$. In matrix form, Eq. (6.51) is re-written as (Vince 2005; Salomon 2011)

$$\dot{\mathbf{p}}(t) = \begin{bmatrix} t^2 & t & 1 \end{bmatrix} \underbrace{\begin{bmatrix} 1 & -2 & 1 \\ -2 & 2 & 0 \\ 1 & 0 & 0 \end{bmatrix}}_{\dot{\mathrm{B}}_2} \begin{bmatrix} \dot{\mathbf{p}}_0 \\ \dot{\mathbf{p}}_1 \\ \dot{\mathbf{p}}_2 \end{bmatrix}, \tag{6.52}$$

where $\dot{\mathrm{B}}_2$ is the geometry matrix for quadratic Bézier curves. It is important to mention that

$$\begin{bmatrix} t^2 & t & 1 \end{bmatrix} \begin{bmatrix} 1 & -2 & 1 \\ -2 & 2 & 0 \\ 1 & 0 & 0 \end{bmatrix} = \begin{bmatrix} (1-t)^2 & 2t(1-t) & t^2 \end{bmatrix} \tag{6.53}$$

represent functions that shape the quadratic Bézier curve. These functions are referred to as *Bernstein polynomials* Such polynomials are defined as

$$\begin{aligned} B_{i,p}(t) &= \binom{p}{i} t^i (1-t)^{p-i} \\ &= \frac{p!}{i!(p-i)!} t^i (1-t)^{p-i}, \end{aligned} \tag{6.54}$$

where $\binom{p}{i}$ is a binomial coefficient (i.e., $p$–choose–$i$); $p$ is the curve degree; and $i$ is the control point number. In case of quadratic Bézier curves, $p = 2$ and $i \in \{0, 1, 2\}$. So, $B_{0,2}(t) = (1-t)^2$, $B_{1,2}(t) = 2t(1-t)$ and $B_{2,2}(t) = t^2$ as in Eq. (6.53). Notice that

$$\begin{aligned} \sum_{i=0}^{2} B_{i,2}(t) &= B_{0,2}(t) + B_{1,2}(t) + B_{2,2}(t) \\ &= (1-t)^2 + 2t(1-t) + t^2 = 1 \end{aligned}$$

These polynomials are shown in Fig. 6.5.

Equation (6.54) is used to generate the polynomials of linear Bézier curves where $p = 1$ and $i \in \{0, 1\}$. These polynomials are $B_{0,1}(t) = (1-t)$ and $B_{1,1}(t) = t$, which are the same those listed in Eq. (6.46). Moreover, notice that

$$\begin{aligned} \sum_{i=0}^{1} B_{i,1}(t) &= B_{0,1}(t) + B_{1,1}(t) \\ &= (1-t) + t = 1. \end{aligned}$$

**Fig. 6.5** The Bernstein polynomials of degree 2

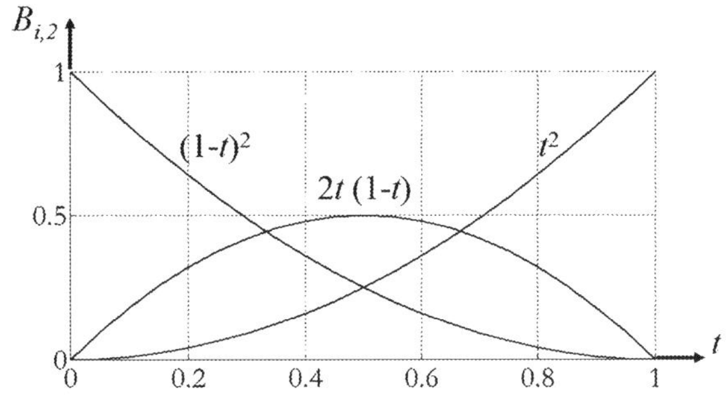


**Example 6.15:** [*Bézier curves—points on quadratic curves*]

A quadratic Bézier curve is created using three control points; $[30, 127]^T$, $[104, 24]^T$ and $[299, 115]^T$. Get the curve location at $t = 0.3$.

**Solution 6.15:** The quadratic Bézier curve Eq. (6.51) or Eq. (6.52) can be used directly with the control points provided and the value of $t = 0.3$ to obtain the curve location as

$$
\begin{aligned}
\dot{\mathbf{p}}(t) &= (1-t)^2\dot{\mathbf{p}}_0 + 2t(1-t)\dot{\mathbf{p}}_1 + t^2\dot{\mathbf{p}}_2 \\
\dot{\mathbf{p}}(0.3) &= (1-0.3)^2\begin{bmatrix} 30 \\ 127 \end{bmatrix} + 2\times 0.3(1-0.3)\begin{bmatrix} 104 \\ 24 \end{bmatrix} + 0.3^2\begin{bmatrix} 299 \\ 115 \end{bmatrix} \\
&= \begin{bmatrix} 85.29 \\ 82.66 \end{bmatrix}.
\end{aligned}
$$

The curve is shown in Fig. 6.6 where the control points as well as point $\dot{\mathbf{p}}(0.3)$ are identified. Alternatively, one may want to use linear Bézier equations:

$$
\begin{aligned}
\dot{\mathbf{p}}_{01}(t) &= (1-t)\dot{\mathbf{p}}_0 + t\dot{\mathbf{p}}_1 \\
\dot{\mathbf{p}}_{01}(0.3) &= (1-0.3)\begin{bmatrix} 30 \\ 127 \end{bmatrix} + 0.3\begin{bmatrix} 104 \\ 24 \end{bmatrix} \\
&= \begin{bmatrix} 52.2 \\ 96.1 \end{bmatrix}
\end{aligned}
$$

and

$$
\begin{aligned}
\dot{\mathbf{p}}_{12}(t) &= (1-t)\dot{\mathbf{p}}_1 + t\dot{\mathbf{p}}_2 \\
\dot{\mathbf{p}}_{12}(0.3) &= (1-0.3)\begin{bmatrix} 104 \\ 24 \end{bmatrix} + 0.3\begin{bmatrix} 299 \\ 115 \end{bmatrix} \\
&= \begin{bmatrix} 162.5 \\ 51.3 \end{bmatrix}.
\end{aligned}
$$

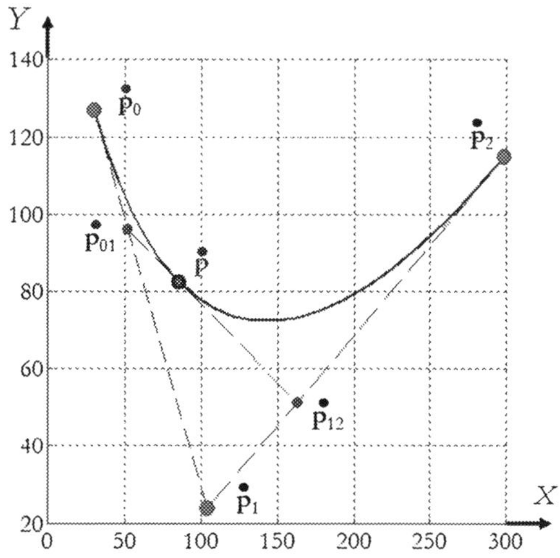


**Fig. 6.6** A quadratic Bézier curve whose control points are $[30, 127]^T$, $[104, 24]^T$ and $[299, 115]^T$. The point $\dot{\mathbf{p}}$ is the curve location at $t = 0.3$

Those points [i.e., $\dot{\mathbf{p}}_{01}(0.3)$ and $\dot{\mathbf{p}}_{12}(0.3)$] are identified in Fig. 6.6. Hence,

$$\begin{aligned}
\dot{\mathbf{p}}(t) &= (1-t)\dot{\mathbf{p}}_{01} + t\dot{\mathbf{p}}_{12} \\
\dot{\mathbf{p}}(0.3) &= (1-0.3)\begin{bmatrix} 52.2 \\ 96.1 \end{bmatrix} + 0.3\begin{bmatrix} 162.5 \\ 51.3 \end{bmatrix} \\
&= \begin{bmatrix} 85.29 \\ 82.66 \end{bmatrix},
\end{aligned}$$

which is the result obtained above. In fact, higher order Bézier curves can be obtained the same way. □

#### 6.2.1.3 Cubic Bézier Curves

In order to generate a *cubic* Bézier curve, *four* points are required. Two of those points represent the start and endpoints of the curve while the other two points give directional information for the curve. As with the quadratic case, the polyline that passes through all these four control points is called the Bézier polygon or the control polygon.

Given four 2D points $\dot{\mathbf{p}}_0$, $\dot{\mathbf{p}}_1$, $\dot{\mathbf{p}}_2$ and $\dot{\mathbf{p}}_3$, the cubic curve starts at $\dot{\mathbf{p}}_0$ and ends at $\dot{\mathbf{p}}_3$; however, it does not pass through $\dot{\mathbf{p}}_1$ or $\dot{\mathbf{p}}_2$. The directions of the tangent vectors at the curve endpoints $\dot{\mathbf{p}}_0$ and $\dot{\mathbf{p}}_3$ are the same as the directions of the first and last segments of the control polygon; i.e., $\overline{\dot{\mathbf{p}}_0\dot{\mathbf{p}}_1}$ and $\overline{\dot{\mathbf{p}}_2\dot{\mathbf{p}}_3}$. As shown in Fig. 6.7, a point $\dot{\mathbf{p}}$ at $t$ on a cubic Bézier curve is estimated through the following steps:

1. A point $\dot{\mathbf{p}}_{01}$ is obtained at $t$ along the linear Bézier curve connecting $\dot{\mathbf{p}}_0$ and $\dot{\mathbf{p}}_1$ using Eq. (6.45) as

$$\dot{\mathbf{p}}_{01}(t) = (1-t)\dot{\mathbf{p}}_0 + t\dot{\mathbf{p}}_1. \tag{6.55}$$

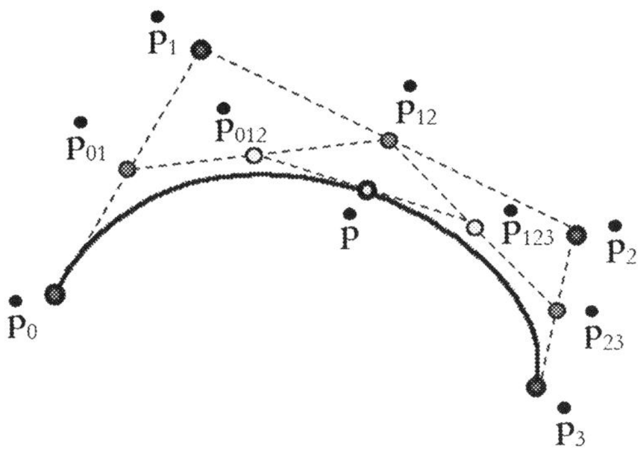


**Fig. 6.7** A cubic Bézier curve

2. A point $\dot{\mathbf{p}}_{12}$ is obtained at $t$ along the linear Bézier curve connecting $\dot{\mathbf{p}}_1$ and $\dot{\mathbf{p}}_2$ using Eq. (6.45) as

$$\dot{\mathbf{p}}_{12}(t) = (1-t)\dot{\mathbf{p}}_1 + t\dot{\mathbf{p}}_2. \tag{6.56}$$

3. A point $\dot{\mathbf{p}}_{23}$ is obtained at $t$ along the linear Bézier curve connecting $\dot{\mathbf{p}}_2$ and $\dot{\mathbf{p}}_3$ using Eq. (6.45) as

$$\dot{\mathbf{p}}_{23}(t) = (1-t)\dot{\mathbf{p}}_2 + t\dot{\mathbf{p}}_3. \tag{6.57}$$

4. A point $\dot{\mathbf{p}}_{012}$ is obtained at $t$ along the linear Bézier curve connecting $\dot{\mathbf{p}}_{01}$ and $\dot{\mathbf{p}}_{12}$ using Eq. (6.45) as

$$\dot{\mathbf{p}}_{012}(t) = (1-t)\dot{\mathbf{p}}_{01} + t\dot{\mathbf{p}}_{12}. \tag{6.58}$$

Substituting the values of $\dot{\mathbf{p}}_{01}$ and $\dot{\mathbf{p}}_{12}$ from Eqs. (6.55) and (6.56), Eq. (6.58) can be re-written as

$$\begin{aligned}\dot{\mathbf{p}}_{012}(t) &= (1-t)\dot{\mathbf{p}}_{01} + t\dot{\mathbf{p}}_{12}\\ &= (1-t)^2\dot{\mathbf{p}}_0 + 2t(1-t)\dot{\mathbf{p}}_1 + t^2\dot{\mathbf{p}}_2.\end{aligned} \tag{6.59}$$

The point $\dot{\mathbf{p}}_{012}(t)$ represents a point on a quadratic curve connecting $\dot{\mathbf{p}}_0$, $\dot{\mathbf{p}}_1$ and $\dot{\mathbf{p}}_2$ as in Eq. (6.51).

5. A point $\dot{\mathbf{p}}_{123}$ is obtained at $t$ along the linear Bézier curve connecting $\dot{\mathbf{p}}_{12}$ and $\dot{\mathbf{p}}_{23}$ using Eq. (6.45) as

$$\dot{\mathbf{p}}_{123}(t) = (1-t)\dot{\mathbf{p}}_{12} + t\dot{\mathbf{p}}_{23}. \tag{6.60}$$

Similar to $\dot{\mathbf{p}}_{012}(t)$, $\dot{\mathbf{p}}_{123}(t)$ is expressed as

$$\begin{aligned}\dot{\mathbf{p}}_{123}(t) &= (1-t)\dot{\mathbf{p}}_{12} + t\dot{\mathbf{p}}_{23}\\ &= (1-t)^2\dot{\mathbf{p}}_1 + 2t(1-t)\dot{\mathbf{p}}_2 + t^2\dot{\mathbf{p}}_3.\end{aligned} \tag{6.61}$$

The point $\dot{\mathbf{p}}_{123}(t)$ represents a point on a quadratic curve connecting $\dot{\mathbf{p}}_1$, $\dot{\mathbf{p}}_2$ and $\dot{\mathbf{p}}_3$ as in Eq. (6.51).

6. The point $\dot{\mathbf{p}}$ is obtained at $t$ along the linear Bézier curve connecting $\dot{\mathbf{p}}_{012}$ and $\dot{\mathbf{p}}_{123}$ using Eq. (6.45) as

$$\dot{\mathbf{p}}(t) = (1-t)\dot{\mathbf{p}}_{012} + t\dot{\mathbf{p}}_{123}. \tag{6.62}$$

Substituting the values of $\dot{\mathbf{p}}_{012}$ and $\dot{\mathbf{p}}_{123}$ from Eqs. (6.59) and (6.61) respectively, we get

$$\begin{aligned}\dot{\mathbf{p}}(t) &= (1-t)\dot{\mathbf{p}}_{012} + t\dot{\mathbf{p}}_{123}\\ &= (1-t)\left[(1-t)^2\dot{\mathbf{p}}_0 + 2t(1-t)\dot{\mathbf{p}}_1 + t^2\dot{\mathbf{p}}_2\right]\\ &\quad + t\left[(1-t)^2\dot{\mathbf{p}}_1 + 2t(1-t)\dot{\mathbf{p}}_2 + t^2\dot{\mathbf{p}}_3\right].\end{aligned} \tag{6.63}$$

Thus, a point $\dot{\mathbf{p}}$ on a cubic Bézier curve is given by

$$\dot{\mathbf{p}}(t) = (1-t)^3\dot{\mathbf{p}}_0 + 3t(1-t)^2\dot{\mathbf{p}}_1 + 3t^2(1-t)\dot{\mathbf{p}}_2 + t^3\dot{\mathbf{p}}_3, \tag{6.64}$$

where $t \in [0, 1]$ is a parameter that increases from 0 at the start point $\dot{\mathbf{p}}_0$ to 1 at the endpoint $\dot{\mathbf{p}}_3$; and $\dot{\mathbf{p}}(t)$ is a point on the curve at parameter $t$. In matrix form, Eq. (6.64) is re-written as (Vince 2005)

$$\dot{\mathbf{p}}(t) = \begin{bmatrix} t^3 & t^2 & t & 1\end{bmatrix} \underbrace{\begin{bmatrix} -1 & 3 & -3 & 1\\ 3 & -6 & 3 & 0\\ -3 & 3 & 0 & 0\\ 1 & 0 & 0 & 0\end{bmatrix}}_{\dot{\mathrm{B}}_3} \begin{bmatrix}\dot{\mathbf{p}}_0\\ \dot{\mathbf{p}}_1\\ \dot{\mathbf{p}}_2\\ \dot{\mathbf{p}}_3\end{bmatrix}, \tag{6.65}$$

where $\dot{\mathrm{B}}_3$ is the geometry matrix for cubic Bézier curves. It is important to mention that

$$\begin{bmatrix} t^3 & t^2 & t & 1\end{bmatrix} \begin{bmatrix} -1 & 3 & -3 & 1\\ 3 & -6 & 3 & 0\\ -3 & 3 & 0 & 0\\ 1 & 0 & 0 & 0\end{bmatrix} = \begin{bmatrix}(1-t)^3 & 3t(1-t)^2 & 3t^2(1-t) & t^3\end{bmatrix} \tag{6.66}$$

represent functions that shape the cubic Bézier curve. These are Bernstein polynomials of Eq. (6.54) where $p = 3$ and $i \in \{0, 1, 2, 3\}$. So, $B_{0,3}(t) = (1-t)^3$, $B_{1,3}(t) = 3t(1-t)^2$, $B_{2,3}(t) = 3t^2(1-t)$ and $B_{3,3}(t) = t^3$ as in Eq. (6.66). Notice that

$$\begin{aligned}\sum_{i=0}^{3} B_{i,3}(t) &= B_{0,3}(t) + B_{1,3}(t) + B_{2,3}(t) + B_{3,3}(t)\\ &= (1-t)^3 + 3t(1-t)^2 + 3t^2(1-t) + t^3 = 1\end{aligned}$$

The polynomials are shown in Fig. 6.8.

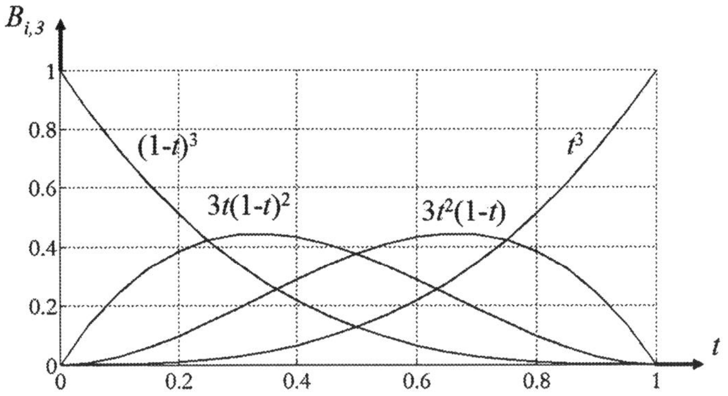


**Fig. 6.8** The Bernstein polynomials of degree 3

In general, a point on a Bézier curve is defined as

$$\dot{\mathbf{p}}(t) = \sum_{i=0}^{p} \dot{\mathbf{p}}_i B_{i,p}(t), \tag{6.67}$$

where $\dot{\mathbf{p}}(t)$ is a curve point at $t$; $p$ is the degree of the curve; $\dot{\mathbf{p}}_i$ is the control point $i$ such that $i \in \{0, 1, 2, \ldots, p\}$; and $B_{i,p}(t)$ is the Bernstein polynomial.

**Example 6.16:** [*Bézier curves—transformations of cubic curves*]
Consider a cubic Bézier curve whose control points are $[0, 0]^T$, $[3, 4]^T$, $[7, 8]^T$ and $[10, 11]^T$. If this curve is rotated through an angle of 45° about the point $[3, 3]^T$, estimate the curve location at $t = 0.3$ after rotation.

**Solution 6.16:** We will get the location of the curve point at $t = 0.3$ before rotation using Eq. (6.64) as

$$\begin{aligned}
\dot{\mathbf{p}}(t) &= (1-t)^3\dot{\mathbf{p}}_0 + 3t(1-t)^2\dot{\mathbf{p}}_1 + 3t^2(1-t)\dot{\mathbf{p}}_2 + t^3\dot{\mathbf{p}}_3 \\
\dot{\mathbf{p}}(0.3) &= (1-0.3)^3\begin{bmatrix}0\\0\end{bmatrix} + 3\times 0.3(1-0.3)^2\begin{bmatrix}3\\4\end{bmatrix} + 3\times 0.3^2(1-0.3)\begin{bmatrix}7\\8\end{bmatrix} \\
&\quad + 0.3^3\begin{bmatrix}10\\11\end{bmatrix} \\
&= \begin{bmatrix}2.916\\3.573\end{bmatrix}.
\end{aligned}$$

In order to rotate the curve about $[3, 3]^T$, the following steps are performed (refer to Chap. 3):

1. Translate using the vector $[-3, -3]^T$ so that the center of rotation coincides with the origin. The translation process is expressed by the translation matrix

$\mathtt{T}([-3,-3]^T)$ that is used with homogeneous points as

$$\mathtt{M}_1 = \mathtt{T}([-3,-3]^T) = \begin{bmatrix} 1 & 0 & -3 \\ 0 & 1 & -3 \\ 0 & 0 & 1 \end{bmatrix}.$$

2. Rotate through an angle of 45° about the origin using the rotation matrix $\mathtt{R}(45°)$ as

$$\mathtt{M}_2 = \mathtt{R}(45) = \begin{bmatrix} \cos(45) & -\sin(45) & 0 \\ \sin(45) & \cos(45) & 0 \\ 0 & 0 & 1 \end{bmatrix}.$$

3. Translate back using the vector $[3,3]^T$. This translation process is expressed by the translation matrix $\mathtt{T}([3,3]^T)$ as

$$\mathtt{M}_3 = \mathtt{T}([3,3]^T) = \begin{bmatrix} 1 & 0 & 3 \\ 0 & 1 & 3 \\ 0 & 0 & 1 \end{bmatrix}.$$

The transformation process is expressed as

$$\begin{aligned} \mathtt{M} &= \mathtt{M}_3\mathtt{M}_2\mathtt{M}_1 \\ &= \begin{bmatrix} 1 & 0 & 3 \\ 0 & 1 & 3 \\ 0 & 0 & 1 \end{bmatrix} \begin{bmatrix} \cos(45) & -\sin(45) & 0 \\ \sin(45) & \cos(45) & 0 \\ 0 & 0 & 1 \end{bmatrix} \begin{bmatrix} 1 & 0 & -3 \\ 0 & 1 & -3 \\ 0 & 0 & 1 \end{bmatrix} \\ &= \begin{bmatrix} \frac{1}{\sqrt{2}} & -\frac{1}{\sqrt{2}} & 3 \\ \frac{1}{\sqrt{2}} & \frac{1}{\sqrt{2}} & -\frac{6}{\sqrt{2}}+3 \\ 0 & 0 & 1 \end{bmatrix} = \begin{bmatrix} 0.7071 & -0.7071 & 3 \\ 0.7071 & 0.7071 & -1.2426 \\ 0 & 0 & 1 \end{bmatrix}. \end{aligned}$$

Hence, the point after rotation is obtained as

$$\begin{aligned} \mathbf{p}' &= \mathtt{M}\mathbf{p} \\ &= \begin{bmatrix} \frac{1}{\sqrt{2}} & -\frac{1}{\sqrt{2}} & 3 \\ \frac{1}{\sqrt{2}} & \frac{1}{\sqrt{2}} & -\frac{6}{\sqrt{2}}+3 \\ 0 & 0 & 1 \end{bmatrix} \begin{bmatrix} 2.916 \\ 3.573 \\ 1 \end{bmatrix} = \begin{bmatrix} 2.5354 \\ 3.3458 \\ 1 \end{bmatrix} \Longrightarrow \dot{\mathbf{p}}' = \begin{bmatrix} 2.5354 \\ 3.3458 \end{bmatrix}, \end{aligned}$$

where $\dot{\mathbf{p}} = [2.916, 3.573]^T$ is the curve point to be rotated; and $\dot{\mathbf{p}}' = [2.5354, 3.3458]^T$ is the point after rotation. The same result can be obtained using Eq. (3.7) as

$$\dot{\mathbf{p}}' = \begin{bmatrix} \cos(\theta) & -\sin(\theta) \\ \sin(\theta) & \cos(\theta) \end{bmatrix} \begin{bmatrix} x_{\dot{\mathbf{p}}} - x_{\dot{\mathbf{r}}} \\ y_{\dot{\mathbf{p}}} - y_{\dot{\mathbf{r}}} \end{bmatrix} + \begin{bmatrix} x_{\dot{\mathbf{r}}} \\ y_{\dot{\mathbf{r}}} \end{bmatrix}$$

$$= \begin{bmatrix} \cos(45) & -\sin(45) \\ \sin(45) & \cos(45) \end{bmatrix} \begin{bmatrix} 2.916 - 3 \\ 3.573 - 3 \end{bmatrix} + \begin{bmatrix} 3 \\ 3 \end{bmatrix} = \begin{bmatrix} 2.5354 \\ 3.3458 \end{bmatrix},$$

where $\dot{\mathbf{p}} = [x_{\dot{\mathbf{p}}}, y_{\dot{\mathbf{p}}}]^T$ is the point to be rotated; and $\dot{\mathbf{r}} = [x_{\dot{\mathbf{r}}}, y_{\dot{\mathbf{r}}}]^T$ is the center of rotation.

Note that Bézier curves are invariant under affine transformation (e.g., translation, rotation, etc.). In other words, the same result would be achieved if the transformation is applied first to the given control points and the curve point is estimated afterwards using the transformed points. □

**Example 6.17:** [*Bézier curves—transformations of cubic curves*]
Re-solve Example 6.16 where the curve point at $t = 0.3$ is obtained after transforming the given control points.

**Solution 6.17:** We will work with inhomogeneous coordinates to rotate the control points. However, the same results must be obtained when using homogeneous points. Thus,

$$\dot{\mathbf{p}}'_0 = \begin{bmatrix} \cos(\theta) & -\sin(\theta) \\ \sin(\theta) & \cos(\theta) \end{bmatrix} \begin{bmatrix} x_{\dot{\mathbf{p}}} - x_{\dot{\mathbf{r}}} \\ y_{\dot{\mathbf{p}}} - y_{\dot{\mathbf{r}}} \end{bmatrix} + \begin{bmatrix} x_{\dot{\mathbf{r}}} \\ y_{\dot{\mathbf{r}}} \end{bmatrix}$$

$$= \begin{bmatrix} \cos(45) & -\sin(45) \\ \sin(45) & \cos(45) \end{bmatrix} \begin{bmatrix} 0 - 3 \\ 0 - 3 \end{bmatrix} + \begin{bmatrix} 3 \\ 3 \end{bmatrix} = \begin{bmatrix} 3.0 \\ -1.2426 \end{bmatrix},$$

where $\dot{\mathbf{p}} = [x_{\dot{\mathbf{p}}}, y_{\dot{\mathbf{p}}}]$ is the point to be rotated; and $\dot{\mathbf{r}} = [x_{\dot{\mathbf{r}}}, y_{\dot{\mathbf{r}}}]$ is the center of rotation. Similarly, the other three rotated points are estimated as

$$\dot{\mathbf{p}}'_1 = \begin{bmatrix} \cos(45) & -\sin(45) \\ \sin(45) & \cos(45) \end{bmatrix} \begin{bmatrix} 3 - 3 \\ 4 - 3 \end{bmatrix} + \begin{bmatrix} 3 \\ 3 \end{bmatrix} = \begin{bmatrix} 2.2929 \\ 3.7071 \end{bmatrix},$$

$$\dot{\mathbf{p}}'_2 = \begin{bmatrix} \cos(45) & -\sin(45) \\ \sin(45) & \cos(45) \end{bmatrix} \begin{bmatrix} 7 - 3 \\ 8 - 3 \end{bmatrix} + \begin{bmatrix} 3 \\ 3 \end{bmatrix} = \begin{bmatrix} 2.2929 \\ 9.3640 \end{bmatrix}$$

and

$$\dot{\mathbf{p}}'_3 = \begin{bmatrix} \cos(45) & -\sin(45) \\ \sin(45) & \cos(45) \end{bmatrix} \begin{bmatrix} 10 - 3 \\ 11 - 3 \end{bmatrix} + \begin{bmatrix} 3 \\ 3 \end{bmatrix} = \begin{bmatrix} 2.2929 \\ 13.6066 \end{bmatrix}.$$

The location of the rotated curve point at $t = 0.3$ is obtained using Eq. (6.64) as

$$\begin{aligned}
\dot{\mathbf{p}}'(t) &= (1-t)^3\dot{\mathbf{p}}'_0 + 3t(1-t)^2\dot{\mathbf{p}}'_1 + 3t^2(1-t)\dot{\mathbf{p}}'_2 + t^3\dot{\mathbf{p}}'_3 \\
\dot{\mathbf{p}}'(0.3) &= (1-0.3)^3 \begin{bmatrix} 3.0 \\ -1.2426 \end{bmatrix} + 3 \times 0.3(1-0.3)^2 \begin{bmatrix} 2.2929 \\ 3.7071 \end{bmatrix} \\
&\quad + 3 \times 0.3^2(1-0.3) \begin{bmatrix} 2.2929 \\ 9.3640 \end{bmatrix} + 0.3^3 \begin{bmatrix} 2.2929 \\ 13.6066 \end{bmatrix} \\
&= \begin{bmatrix} 2.5354 \\ 3.3458 \end{bmatrix},
\end{aligned}$$

which is the same point obtained in Example 6.16. □

**Example 6.18:** [*Bézier curves—cubic curves in 3D space*]

Equations (6.64) and (6.65) are used to construct a cubic Bézier curve in 2D space. Modify these equations to accommodate a cubic Bézier curve in 3D space.

**Solution 6.18:** 3D points are used with the same equations. Thus, given four 3D control points $\dot{\mathbf{P}}_0$, $\dot{\mathbf{P}}_1$, $\dot{\mathbf{P}}_2$ and $\dot{\mathbf{P}}_3$, a point $\dot{\mathbf{P}}(t)$ on a cubic Bézier curve is given by

$$\dot{\mathbf{P}}(t) = (1-t)^3\dot{\mathbf{P}}_0 + 3t(1-t)^2\dot{\mathbf{P}}_1 + 3t^2(1-t)\dot{\mathbf{P}}_2 + t^3\dot{\mathbf{P}}_3, \tag{6.68}$$

where $t \in [0, 1]$ is a parameter that increases from 0 at the start point $\dot{\mathbf{P}}_0$ to 1 at the endpoint $\dot{\mathbf{P}}_3$. In matrix form, Eq. (6.68) is re-written as

$$\dot{\mathbf{P}}(t) = \begin{bmatrix} t^3 & t^2 & t & 1 \end{bmatrix} \begin{bmatrix} -1 & 3 & -3 & 1 \\ 3 & -6 & 3 & 0 \\ -3 & 3 & 0 & 0 \\ 1 & 0 & 0 & 0 \end{bmatrix} \begin{bmatrix} \dot{\mathbf{P}}_0 \\ \dot{\mathbf{P}}_1 \\ \dot{\mathbf{P}}_2 \\ \dot{\mathbf{P}}_3 \end{bmatrix}. \qquad \square \tag{6.69}$$

**Example 6.19:** [*Bézier curves—points on cubic curves*]

A cubic Bézier curve is controlled by points $\dot{\mathbf{P}}_0 = [5, 5, 0]^T$, $\dot{\mathbf{P}}_1 = [10, 15, 0]^T$, $\dot{\mathbf{P}}_2 = [15, 5, 0]^T$ and $\dot{\mathbf{P}}_3 = [15, 15, 3]^T$. Determine the locations of curve points at each $0.05t$.

**Solution 6.19:** Using Eq. (6.69), the locations of curve points are as listed in the following table:

| $t$ | $x$ | $y$ | $z$ |
|---|---|---|---|
| 0.00 | 5.0000 | 5.0000 | 0.0000 |
| 0.05 | 5.7494 | 6.3550 | 0.0004 |
| 0.10 | 6.4950 | 7.4400 | 0.0030 |
| 0.15 | 7.2331 | 8.2850 | 0.0101 |
| 0.20 | 7.9600 | 8.9200 | 0.0240 |
| 0.25 | 8.6719 | 9.3750 | 0.0469 |
| 0.30 | 9.3650 | 9.6800 | 0.0810 |
| 0.35 | 10.0356 | 9.8650 | 0.1286 |
| 0.40 | 10.6800 | 9.9600 | 0.1920 |
| 0.45 | 11.2944 | 9.9950 | 0.2734 |
| 0.50 | 11.8750 | 10.0000 | 0.3750 |
| 0.55 | 12.4181 | 10.0050 | 0.4991 |
| 0.60 | 12.9200 | 10.0400 | 0.6480 |
| 0.65 | 13.3769 | 10.1350 | 0.8239 |
| 0.70 | 13.7850 | 10.3200 | 1.0290 |
| 0.75 | 14.1406 | 10.6250 | 1.2656 |
| 0.80 | 14.4400 | 11.0800 | 1.5360 |
| 0.85 | 14.6794 | 11.7150 | 1.8424 |
| 0.90 | 14.8550 | 12.5600 | 2.1870 |
| 0.95 | 14.9631 | 13.6450 | 2.5721 |
| 1.00 | 15.0000 | 15.0000 | 3.0000 |

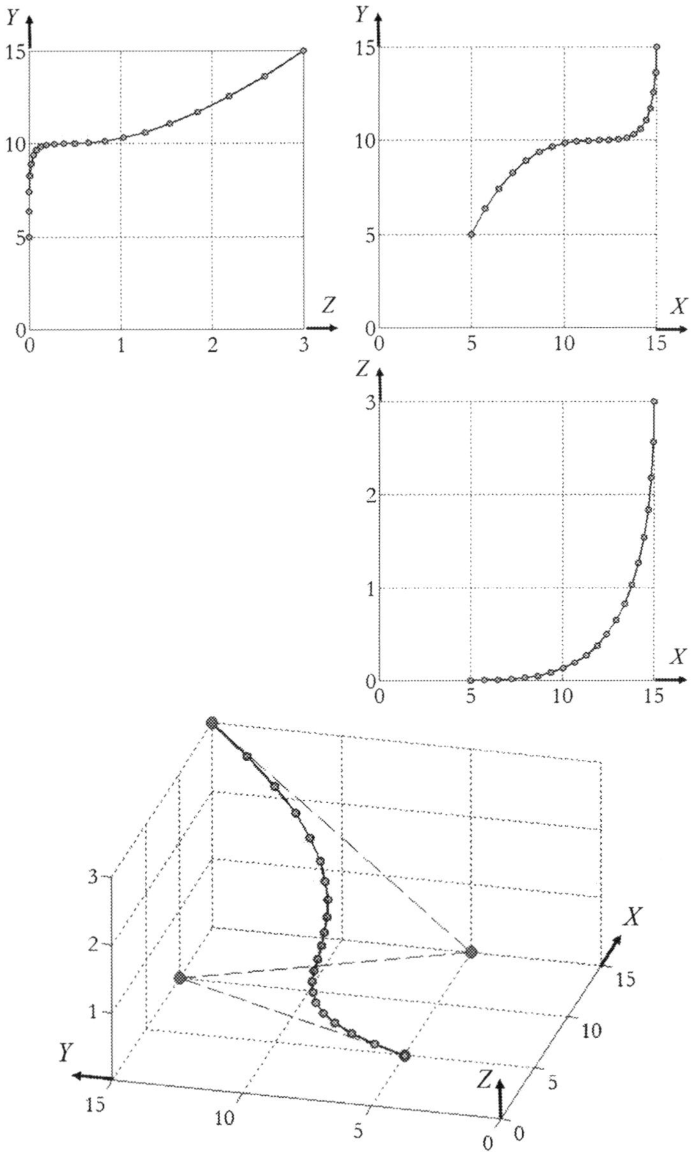


**Fig. 6.9** A cubic Bézier curve passing through $\dot{\mathbf{P}}_0 = [5, 5, 0]^T$, $\dot{\mathbf{P}}_1 = [10, 15, 0]^T$, $\dot{\mathbf{P}}_2 = [15, 5, 0]^T$ and $\dot{\mathbf{P}}_3 = [15, 15, 3]^T$. The locations of curve points are marked at each $0.05t$

Figure 6.9 shows the orthogonal projections (i.e., multi-view projections) of the curve on each of the principal planes and the curve in 3D space as well. The locations of curve points are marked at each $0.05t$. □

#### 6.2.1.4 Higher Order Bézier Curves

More complex Bézier curves that are higher than third degree curves can be constructed as a sequence of lower-degree Bézier curve segments. In this case, the joints should always look smooth. Splitting the curve into many lower-degree curve segments brings us to the concept of B-splines, which is discussed in the following section.

### *6.2.2 B-Spline Curves*

In B-spline curves, the curve whole $t$ interval or domain (previously denoted as [0,1]) is split into subintervals resulting in curve segments. The join points between curve segments are called *knots*. The values of $t$ at the knots or the *knot values* are those of span bounds (i.e., $t_0, t_1, \ldots$) where the $i$th knot span is $[t_{i-1}, t_i)$; e.g., the 5th knot span covers the half-open interval $[t_4, t_5)$. In order to generate a curve of degree $p$ given a set of $n+1$ control points (i.e., $\dot{\mathbf{p}}_0, \dot{\mathbf{p}}_1, \ldots, \dot{\mathbf{p}}_n$), the vector $[t_0, t_1, \ldots, t_{n+p+1}]$, where $t_0 \leq t_1 \leq \cdots \leq t_{n+p+1}$, is used. This vector is referred to as the *knot vector*. Different types of knot vectors are discussed in Sect. 6.2.2.1.

Unlike the previous curves discussed where each control point contributes to all points of the curve, a B-spline control point affects only a portion of the curve around it (i.e., the curve segment or segments containing it). This is referred to as the *local control* property where control points away from a given curve point contributes nothing to its location. According to the type of knot vector used, a B-spline curve may (or may not) pass through the start and end control points. (Remember that Bézier curves pass through the start and end control points.)

The local control property is achieved using polynomial *basis* or blending functions; hence, comes the letter "B" in B-spline. In this case, a curve point is estimated as a weighted sum of basis functions, which distinguishes B-splines from the parametric curves discussed in Sect. 6.1.3. A B-spline curve point $\dot{\mathbf{p}}(t)$ at parameter $t$ is then defined as

$$\dot{\mathbf{p}}(t) = \sum_{i=0}^{n} \dot{\mathbf{p}}_i N_{i,p}(t), \tag{6.70}$$

where $\dot{\mathbf{p}}_i$ is the control point $i$ such that $i \in \{0, 1, 2, \ldots, n\}$; $n+1$ is the number of control points; $p$ is the curve degree[1]; and $N_{i,p}(t)$ is the basis function estimated as explained in Sect. 6.2.2.3. The basis functions applied to a curve segment should sum to 1. The meaning of Eq. (6.70) is that it adds up all control point positions; however, the contribution of each control point varies according to the basis function $N_{i,p}(t)$. As a control point gets farther away from the current curve point, the contribution gets smaller until it diminishes.

[1] Recall that a curve degree is the largest exponent in its equations. A curve of degree $p$ is of order $p+1$ where the order cannot be greater than the number of control points $n+1$; i.e., $p \not> n$.

#### 6.2.2.1 The Knot Vector

The knot vector (e.g., $[t_0, t_1, t_2, \ldots, t_m]$) comprises the $t$ values at the knots. If the number of control points is $n+1$ and the degree of the curve is $p$, then the number of knots will be $m+1$ where

$$m = \underbrace{(n+1)}_{\#\text{ control points}} + \underbrace{p}_{\text{degree}}. \tag{6.71}$$

For example, if the number of control points for a quadratic curve is 3 (i.e., $p = 2$ and $n = 2$), then $m = n + 1 + p = 2 + 1 + 2 = 5$; hence, the knot vector is considered as $[t_0, t_1, t_2, t_3, t_4, t_5]$. There are three types of knot vectors:

1. **Uniform knot vector:** If the spaces among consecutive knots are equal, the knot vector is called *uniform*. This is expressed as

$$t_{i+1} - t_i = C, \tag{6.72}$$

where $C$ is a constant for all $i$ such that $0 \le i \le m-1$. In this case, the parameter range or domain is defined as $t_p \le t \le t_{n+1}$ (shown in bold below). Examples of uniform knot vectors are listed in the following table:

| $p$ | $n$ | $m$ | Knot vector | $C$ | Domain | # Segments |
|---|---|---|---|---|---|---|
| 2 | 2 | 5 | [0, 1, **2**, **3**, 4, 5] | 1 | $t_2 \le t \le t_3$ | 1 |
| 2 | 4 | 7 | [0, 0.2, **0.4**, **0.6**, **0.8**, **1**, 1.2, 1.4] | 0.2 | $t_2 \le t \le t_5$ | 3 |
| 2 | 2 | 5 | [−1.7, −0.8, **0.1**, **1**, 1.9, 2.8] | 0.9 | $t_2 \le t \le t_3$ | 1 |
| 3 | 3 | 7 | [1, 2, 3, **4**, **5**, 6, 7, 8] | 1 | $t_3 \le t \le t_4$ | 1 |

The curve using this types of knot vectors does not interpolate the start and end control points. Some authors refer to this type as a *periodic knot vector*.

2. **Open uniform knot vector:** If $p$ is the curve degree, an *open uniform knot vector* places $p+1$ repeated knot values at each end (i.e., $t_0 = t_1 = \cdots = t_p$ and $t_{m-p} = t_{m-p+1} = \cdots = t_m$). In the parameter range or domain $t_p \le t \le t_{n+1}$, the knots are uniformly spaced as with the previous knot vector type. This is expressed as

$$\begin{aligned} t_0 &= t_1 = \cdots = t_p, \\ t_i &= (i-p)C + t_0 \quad \text{if } p \le i \le n+1, \\ t_{n+1}\ (\text{i.e., } t_{m-p}) &= t_{n+2}\ (\text{i.e., } t_{m-p+1}) = \cdots = t_m. \end{aligned} \tag{6.73}$$

Examples of open uniform knot vectors are listed in the following table:

| $p$ | $n$ | $m$ | Knot vector | $C$ | Domain | # Segments |
|---|---|---|---|---|---|---|
| 2 | 2 | 5 | $[0, 0, \mathbf{0}, \mathbf{1}, 1, 1]$ | 1 | $t_2 \le t \le t_3$ | 1 |
| 3 | 3 | 7 | $[0, 0, 0, \mathbf{0}, \mathbf{1}, 1, 1, 1]$ | 1 | $t_3 \le t \le t_4$ | 1 |
| 3 | 6 | 10 | $[0, 0, 0, \mathbf{0}, \mathbf{1}, \mathbf{2}, \mathbf{3}, \mathbf{4}, 4, 4, 4]$ | 1 | $t_3 \le t \le t_7$ | 4 |
| 2 | 3 | 6 | $[1, 1, \mathbf{1}, \mathbf{2.5}, \mathbf{4}, 4, 4]$ | 1.5 | $t_2 \le t \le t_4$ | 2 |

In this case, the curve interpolates the start and end control points. Some authors refer to this type as a *non-periodic knot vector*.
Getting uniformly-spaced internal knots while keeping the whole range or domain within the interval [0,1] means that we should have $t_0 = t_1 = \cdots = t_p = 0, t_{p+1}, t_{p+2}, \ldots, t_{m-p} = t_{m-p+1} = \cdots = t_m = 1$. In this case, internal knots are uniformly-spaced if we divide the interval [0,1] into $n - p + 1$ subintervals. Hence, Eq. (6.73) is modified to

$$\begin{aligned} t_0 &= t_1 = \cdots = t_p = 0, \\ t_i &= \tfrac{i-p}{n-p+1} \quad \text{if } p+1 \le i \le n, \\ t_{n+1} \text{ (i.e., } t_{m-p}) &= t_{n+2} \text{ (i.e., } t_{m-p+1}) = \cdots = t_m = 1. \end{aligned} \tag{6.74}$$

Examples are listed in the following table:

| $p$ | $n$ | $m$ | Knot vector | $C$ | Domain | # Segments |
|---|---|---|---|---|---|---|
| 2 | 3 | 6 | $[0, 0, \mathbf{0}, \mathbf{0.5}, \mathbf{1}, 1, 1]$ | 0.5 | $t_2 \le t \le t_4$ | 2 |
| 2 | 5 | 8 | $[0, 0, \mathbf{0}, \mathbf{0.25}, \mathbf{0.5}, \mathbf{0.75}, \mathbf{1}, 1, 1]$ | 0.25 | $t_2 \le t \le t_6$ | 4 |

3. **Non-uniform knot vector:** Unlike the uniform knot vectors, if the spaces among knots are not equal, the knot vector is called *non-uniform*. The only constraint in this case is

$$t_i \le t_{i+1}. \tag{6.75}$$

Examples of non-uniform knot vectors are listed in the following table:

| $p$ | $n$ | $m$ | Knot vector | Domain | # Segments |
|---|---|---|---|---|---|
| 2 | 2 | 5 | $[0, 2, \mathbf{5}, \mathbf{6}, 7, 9]$ | $t_2 \le t \le t_3$ | 1 |
| 2 | 8 | 11 | $[0, 0, \mathbf{0}, \frac{\pi}{\mathbf{2}}, \frac{\pi}{\mathbf{2}}, \pi, \pi, \frac{\mathbf{3}\pi}{\mathbf{2}}, \frac{\mathbf{3}\pi}{\mathbf{2}}, \mathbf{2}\pi, 2\pi, 2\pi]$ | $t_2 \le t \le t_9$ | 7 |

#### 6.2.2.2 Multiplicity and Continuity

A knot value may be repeated within the knot vector. This increases that value's *multiplicity*. For example, the open uniform vector [0, 0, 0, 1, 2, 2, 2] has repeated 0's and 2's. These repeated knots are said to be of *multiplicity* 3 because they are repeated 3 times each. This can be written as 0(3) and 2(3). The maximum number of repetitions (i.e., maximum multiplicity) for a knot is the order of the curve or $p+1$ where $p$ is the degree of the curve. (Recall that $order = degree + 1$.)

It should be mentioned that increasing the multiplicity of a knot decreases the continuity of the curve at that knot. The relationship between multiplicity and continuity is expressed as

$$Continuity = order - (multiplicity + 1). \tag{6.76}$$

In other words, the maximum continuity of a B-spline curve is its $order - 2$. This happens when the multiplicity of each knot does not exceed 1. In this case, the curve is said to be $C^{p-1}$ continuous, where $p$ is its degree. Thus, the maximum continuity for quadratic curves is $C^1$ and the maximum continuity for cubic curves is $C^2$. Finally, the case of maximum multiplicity (i.e., the *order* of the curve) implies $C^{-1}$ continuity; i.e., a discontinuous curve.

#### 6.2.2.3 The Basis Function

A *basis function* specifies how strong or weak a control point contributes to a curve point at parameter $t$. The $i$th basis function $N_{i,p}(t)$ of degree $p$ is expressed by the Cox–de Boor recursion formula as

$$\begin{aligned} N_{i,0}(t) &= \begin{cases} 1, & \text{if } t_i \le t < t_{i+1}; \\ 0, & \text{otherwise}, \end{cases} \\ N_{i,p}(t) &= \frac{t - t_i}{t_{i+p} - t_i} N_{i,p-1}(t) + \frac{t_{i+p+1} - t}{t_{i+p+1} - t_{i+1}} N_{i+1,p-1}(t), \end{aligned} \tag{6.77}$$

where $p$ is the curve degree. This formula has two cases; a base case that is used when $p = 0$ and a recursive case that is used when $p > 0$. In this section, we assume that $t_0 = 0$, $t_1 = 1$, $t_2 = 2$ and so on unless otherwise specified.

When the degree is zero (i.e., $p = 0$), the base case is invoked to get $N_{i,0}(t)$, which is 1 when $t \in [t_i, t_{i+1})$ and 0 otherwise. For example, $N_{0,0}(t) = 1$ when $t \in [0, 1)$ and $N_{0,0}(t) = 0$ when $t \notin [0, 1)$. This is shown in Fig. 6.10a. Also, $N_{1,0}(t) = 1$ when $t \in [1, 2)$ and $N_{1,0}(t) = 0$ when $t \notin [1, 2)$ as shown in Fig. 6.10b. Similarly, $N_{2,0}(t) = 1$ when $t \in [2, 3)$ and $N_{2,0}(t) = 0$ when $t \notin [2, 3)$ as shown in Fig. 6.10c and so on.

Figure 6.11 depicts a diagram showing various $i$ and $p$ values contributing to $N_{i,p}(t)$. It shows that $N_{0,0}(t) = 1$ throughout the knot span $[0, 1)$, $N_{1,0}(t) = 1$ throughout the knot span $[1, 2)$, $N_{2,0}(t) = 1$ throughout the knot span $[2, 3)$, etc.

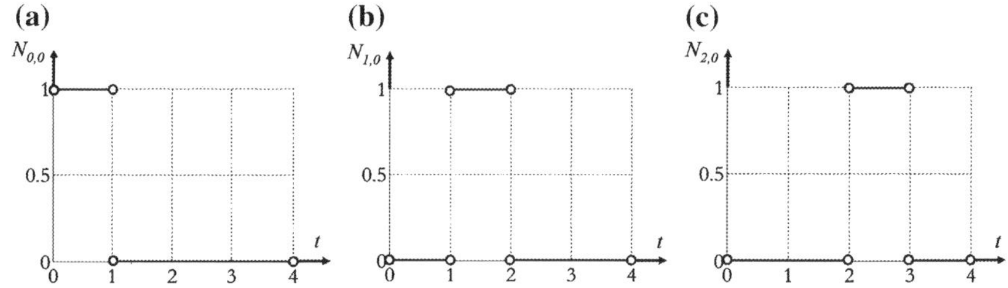


**Fig. 6.10** Basis functions using the knot vector [0, 1, 2, 3, 4]. **a** $N_{0,0}$. **b** $N_{1,0}$. **c** $N_{2,0}$

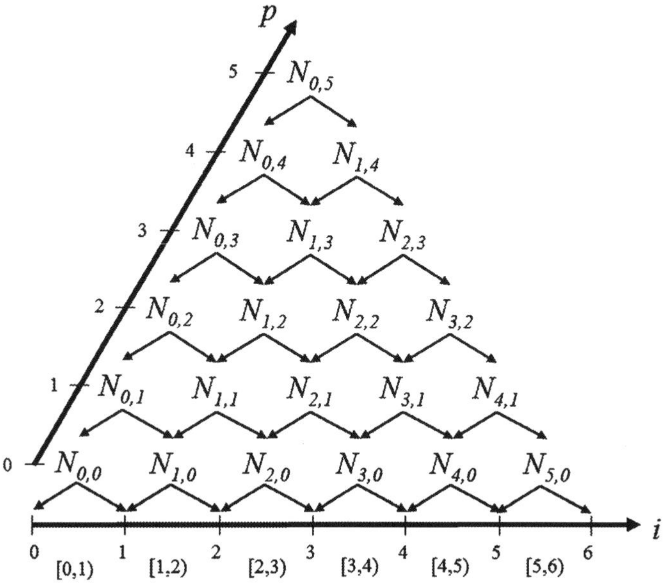


**Fig. 6.11** Basis function $N_{i,p}$. Intervals shown are for the uniform knot vector [0, 1, 2, 3, 4, 5, 6]

This way the lower row of basis functions (i.e., $N_{i,0}$) shown in Fig. 6.11 can be estimated.

We move to the recursive part starting from the second row in Fig. 6.11. In order to calculate $N_{i,1}(t)$, we need to have $N_{i,0}(t)$ and $N_{i+1,0}(t)$. Hence, we use $N_{0,0}(t)$ and $N_{1,0}(t)$ to calculate $N_{0,1}(t)$ and we use $N_{1,0}(t)$ and $N_{2,0}(t)$ to calculate $N_{1,1}(t)$ and so on. For example, $N_{0,1}(t)$ is calculated by applying Eq. (6.77) as

$$N_{0,1}(t) = \frac{t - t_0}{t_1 - t_0} N_{0,0}(t) + \frac{t_2 - t}{t_2 - t_1} N_{1,0}(t). \tag{6.78}$$

When $t_0 = 0$, $t_1 = 1$ and $t_2 = 2$, $N_{0,1}(t)$ is estimated as

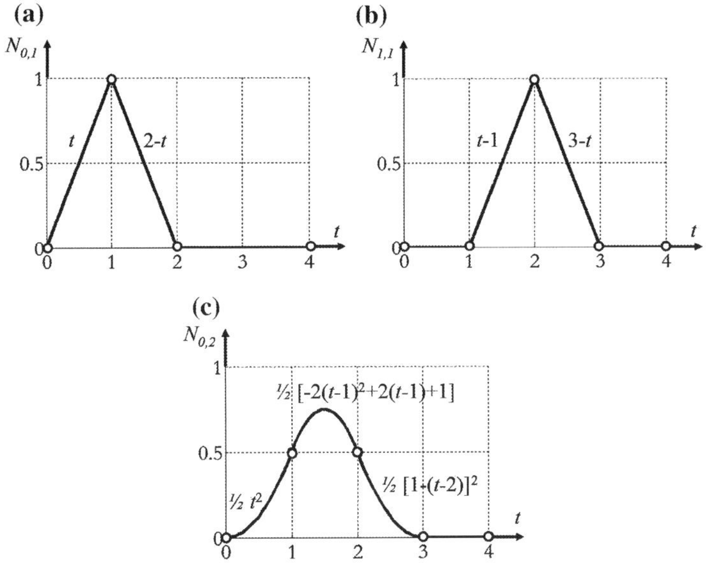


**Fig. 6.12** Basis functions using the knot vector [0, 1, 2, 3, 4]. **a** $N_{0,1}$. **b** $N_{1,1}$. **c** $N_{0,2}$

$$N_{0,1}(t) = tN_{0,0}(t) + (2-t)N_{1,0}(t). \tag{6.79}$$

As discussed above, $N_{0,0}(t) = 1$ when $t \in [0, 1)$ and $N_{0,0}(t) = 0$ when $t \notin [0, 1)$. The same goes for $N_{1,0}(t)$ and the knot span $[1, 2)$. Hence, by substituting in Eq. (6.79), $N_{0,1}(t)$ has the following values:

$$N_{0,1}(t) = \begin{cases} t, & \text{if } 0 \le t < 1 \text{ or } t \in [0, 1); \\ 2-t, & \text{if } 1 \le t < 2 \text{ or } t \in [1, 2); \\ 0, & \text{otherwise.} \end{cases} \tag{6.80}$$

$N_{0,1}(t)$ represented by Eq. (6.80) is shown in Fig. 6.12a. In this figure, notice that the value of $N_{0,1}(t)$ varies from $t$ to $2-t$ to 0 throughout [0,1), [1,2) and [2,4) respectively. Similarly, $N_{1,1}(t)$ has the following values:

$$N_{1,1}(t) = \begin{cases} t-1, & \text{if } 1 \le t < 2 \text{ or } t \in [1, 2); \\ 3-t, & \text{if } 2 \le t < 3 \text{ or } t \in [2, 3); \\ 0, & \text{otherwise.} \end{cases} \tag{6.81}$$

$N_{1,1}(t)$ represented by Eq. (6.81) is shown in Fig. 6.12b. Notice that the value of $N_{1,1}(t)$ varies from 0 to $t-1$ to $3-t$ to 0 throughout [0,1), [1,2), [2,3) and [3,4) respectively.

The above concept is applied to the third row. In order to calculate $N_{i,2}(t)$, we need to have $N_{i,1}(t)$ and $N_{i+1,1}(t)$. Hence, we use $N_{0,1}(t)$ and $N_{1,1}(t)$ to calculate $N_{0,2}(t)$ and so on. $N_{0,2}(t)$ is estimated as

$$N_{0,2}(t) = \frac{t - t_0}{t_2 - t_0} N_{0,1}(t) + \frac{t_3 - t}{t_3 - t_1} N_{1,1}(t). \tag{6.82}$$

When $t_0 = 0$, $t_1 = 1$, $t_2 = 2$ and $t_3 = 3$, $N_{0,2}(t)$ is estimated as

$$N_{0,2}(t) = \frac{t}{2} N_{0,1}(t) + \frac{3 - t}{2} N_{1,1}(t). \tag{6.83}$$

As discussed above, $N_{0,1}(t) = t$ when $t \in [0, 1)$ and $N_{0,1}(t) = 2 - t$ when $t \in [1, 2)$ [i.e., $N_{0,1}(t)$ has a value other than 0 when $t \in [0, 2)$] and $N_{0,1}(t) = 0$ when $t \notin [0, 2)$. The same goes for $N_{1,1}(t)$ and the knot span $[1, 3)$. Hence, by substituting in Eq. (6.83) when $t \in [0, 1)$, $N_{0,2}(t)$ has the value of

$$\begin{aligned} N_{0,2}(t) &= \frac{1}{2} t N_{0,1}(t) \\ &= \frac{1}{2} t^2. \end{aligned}$$

When $t \in [1, 2)$, $N_{0,2}(t)$ has the value of

$$\begin{aligned} N_{0,2}(t) &= \frac{1}{2} t N_{0,1}(t) + \frac{1}{2}(3 - t) N_{1,1}(t) \\ &= \frac{1}{2} t(2 - t) + \frac{1}{2}(3 - t)(t - 1) \\ &= \frac{1}{2}[-2(t - 1)^2 + 2(t - 1) + 1]. \end{aligned}$$

When $t \in [2, 3)$, $N_{0,2}(t)$ has the value of

$$\begin{aligned} N_{0,2}(t) &= \frac{1}{2}(3 - t) N_{1,1}(t) \\ &= \frac{1}{2}[1 - (t - 2)]^2. \end{aligned}$$

These values can be expressed as

$$N_{0,2}(t) = \begin{cases} \frac{1}{2} t^2, & \text{if } 0 \le t < 1 \text{ or } t \in [0, 1); \\ \frac{1}{2}[-2(t - 1)^2 + 2(t - 1) + 1], & \text{if } 1 \le t < 2 \text{ or } t \in [1, 2); \\ \frac{1}{2}[1 - (t - 2)]^2, & \text{if } 2 \le t < 3 \text{ or } t \in [2, 3); \\ 0, & \text{otherwise.} \end{cases} \tag{6.84}$$

$N_{0,2}(t)$ represented by Eq. (6.84) is shown in Fig. 6.12c. Notice that the value of $N_{0,2}(t)$ varies from $\frac{1}{2}t^2$ to $\frac{1}{2}[-2(t-1)^2 + 2(t-1) + 1]$ to $\frac{1}{2}[1-(t-2)]^2$ to 0 throughout [0,1), [1,2), [2,3) and [3,4) respectively.

**Example 6.20:** [*Basis function— $N_{0,2}(t)$ using uniform knot vector*]
Utilizing the uniform knot vector $\left[0, \frac{1}{3}, \frac{2}{3}, 1\right]$, estimate the values of $N_{0,2}(t)$ for different subintervals.

**Solution 6.20:** It is easy to get the values of the basis functions for degree 0. These are

$$N_{0,0}(t) = \begin{cases} 1, & \text{if } t \in \left[0, \dfrac{1}{3}\right); \\ 0, & \text{otherwise,} \end{cases}$$

$$N_{1,0}(t) = \begin{cases} 1, & \text{if } t \in \left[\dfrac{1}{3}, \dfrac{2}{3}\right); \\ 0, & \text{otherwise;} \end{cases}$$

and

$$N_{2,0}(t) = \begin{cases} 1, & \text{if } t \in \left[\dfrac{2}{3}, 1\right); \\ 0, & \text{otherwise.} \end{cases}$$

$N_{0,1}(t)$ is calculated by applying Eq. (6.77) as

$$N_{0,1}(t) = \frac{t - t_0}{t_1 - t_0} N_{0,0}(t) + \frac{t_2 - t}{t_2 - t_1} N_{1,0}(t).$$

When $t_0 = 0$, $t_1 = \frac{1}{3}$ and $t_2 = \frac{2}{3}$, $N_{0,1}(t)$ is estimated as

$$N_{0,1}(t) = 3t N_{0,0}(t) + (2 - 3t) N_{1,0}(t).$$

Hence,

$$N_{0,1}(t) = \begin{cases} 3t, & \text{if } t \in \left[0, \dfrac{1}{3}\right); \\ 2 - 3t, & \text{if } t \in \left[\dfrac{1}{3}, \dfrac{2}{3}\right); \\ 0, & \text{otherwise.} \end{cases}$$

The previous equations representing $N_{0,1}(t)$ are shown in Fig. 6.13a. Notice that the value of $N_{0,1}(t)$ varies from $3t$ to $2 - 3t$ to 0 throughout $[0, \frac{1}{3})$, $[\frac{1}{3}, \frac{2}{3})$ and $[\frac{2}{3}, 1)$ respectively. Similarly, $N_{1,1}(t)$ has the following values:

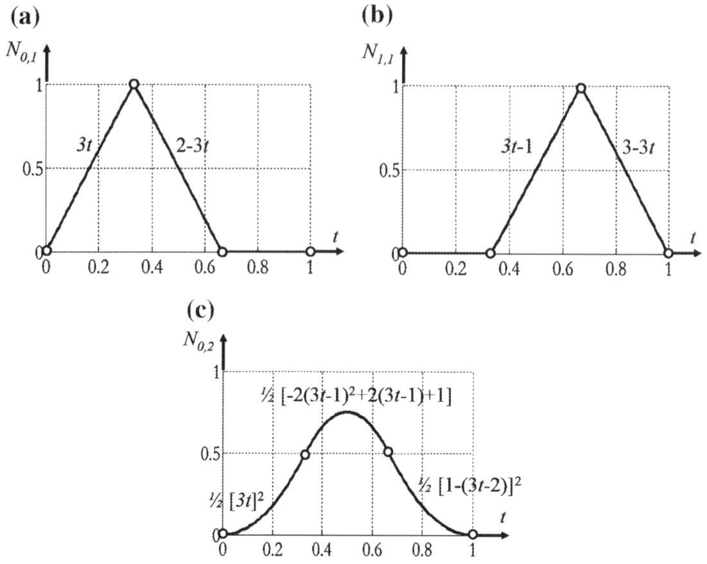


**Fig. 6.13** Basis functions using the knot vector $\left[0, \frac{1}{3}, \frac{2}{3}, 1\right]$. **a** $N_{0,1}$. **b** $N_{1,1}$. **c** $N_{0,2}$

$$N_{1,1}(t) = \begin{cases} 3t - 1, & \text{if } t \in \left[\frac{1}{3}, \frac{2}{3}\right); \\ 3 - 3t, & \text{if } t \in \left[\frac{2}{3}, 1\right); \\ 0, & \text{otherwise.} \end{cases}$$

The previous equations representing $N_{1,1}(t)$ are shown in Fig. 6.13b. Notice that the value of $N_{1,1}(t)$ varies from 0 to $3t - 1$ to $3 - 3t$ along $[0, \frac{1}{3})$, $[\frac{1}{3}, \frac{2}{3})$ and $[\frac{2}{3}, 1)$ respectively. At degree 2, $N_{0,2}(t)$ is calculated as

$$N_{0,2}(t) = \frac{t - t_0}{t_2 - t_0} N_{0,1}(t) + \frac{t_3 - t}{t_3 - t_1} N_{1,1}(t).$$

When $t_0 = 0$, $t_1 = \frac{1}{3}$, $t_2 = \frac{2}{3}$ and $t_3 = 1$, $N_{0,2}(t)$ is estimated as

$$N_{0,2}(t) = \frac{3t}{2} N_{0,1}(t) + \frac{3 - 3t}{2} N_{1,1}(t).$$

Thus, when $t \in [0, \frac{1}{3})$, $N_{0,2}(t)$ has the value of

$$\begin{aligned} N_{0,2}(t) &= \frac{1}{2} 3t N_{0,1}(t) \\ &= \tfrac{1}{2}(3t)^2. \end{aligned}$$

When $t \in [\frac{1}{3}, \frac{2}{3})$, $N_{0,2}(t)$ has the value of

$$\begin{aligned} N_{0,2}(t) &= \frac{1}{2}3tN_{0,1}(t) + \frac{1}{2}(3-3t)N_{1,1}(t) \\ &= \frac{1}{2}3t(2-3t) + \frac{1}{2}(3-3t)(3t-1) \\ &= \frac{1}{2}[-2(3t-1)^2 + 2(3t-1) + 1]. \end{aligned}$$

When $t \in [\frac{2}{3}, 1)$, $N_{0,2}(t)$ has the value of

$$\begin{aligned} N_{0,2}(t) &= \frac{1}{2}(3-3t)N_{1,1}(t) \\ &= \frac{1}{2}[1-(3t-2)]^2. \end{aligned}$$

These values can be expressed as

$$N_{0,2}(t) = \begin{cases} \frac{1}{2}(3t)^2, & \text{if } t \in \left[0, \frac{1}{3}\right); \\ \frac{1}{2}[-2(3t-1)^2 + 2(3t-1) + 1], & \text{if } t \in \left[\frac{1}{3}, \frac{2}{3}\right); \\ \frac{1}{2}[1-(3t-2)]^2, & \text{if } t \in \left[\frac{2}{3}, 1\right); \\ 0, & \text{otherwise.} \end{cases}$$

The equation representing $N_{0,2}(t)$ is shown in Fig. 6.13c. Notice that the value of $N_{0,2}(t)$ varies from $\frac{1}{2}(3t)^2$ to $\frac{1}{2}[-2(3t-1)^2 + 2(3t-1) + 1]$ to $\frac{1}{2}[1-(3t-2)]^2$ throughout $[0, \frac{1}{3})$, $[\frac{1}{3}, \frac{2}{3})$ and $[\frac{2}{3}, 1)$ respectively. □

**Example 6.21:** [*Basis function— $N_{0,3}(t)$ using uniform knot vector*]
Utilizing the uniform knot vector [0, 1, 2, 3, 4], estimate the value of $N_{0,3}(t)$ for different subintervals.

**Solution 6.21:** According the recursive steps shown in Fig. 6.11 and in order to estimate the value of $N_{0,3}(t)$, we need to estimate the values of $N_{0,2}(t)$ and $N_{1,2}(t)$. $N_{0,2}(t)$ values are listed in Eq. (6.84); hence, we will proceed by estimating the values of $N_{1,2}(t)$.

Again, to estimate the values of $N_{1,2}(t)$, we need to obtain the values of $N_{1,1}(t)$ and $N_{2,1}(t)$ according to Fig. 6.11. $N_{1,1}(t)$ values are listed in Eq. (6.81); hence, we will estimate the values of $N_{2,1}(t)$.

The values of $N_{2,0}(t)$ and $N_{3,0}(t)$ contribute to the estimation of $N_{2,1}(t)$. As discussed above, the values of $N_{2,0}(t)$ are 1 for the knot span [2, 3) and 0 otherwise. Similarly, the values of $N_{3,0}(t)$ are 1 for the knot span [3, 4) and 0 otherwise.

Now the values of $N_{2,1}(t)$ are calculated by applying Eq. (6.77) as

$$N_{2,1}(t) = \frac{t - t_2}{t_3 - t_2} N_{2,0}(t) + \frac{t_4 - t}{t_4 - t_3} N_{3,0}(t). \tag{6.85}$$

When $t_2 = 2$, $t_3 = 3$ and $t_4 = 4$, $N_{2,1}(t)$ is estimated as

$$N_{2,1}(t) = (t - 2)N_{2,0}(t) + (4 - t)N_{3,0}(t). \tag{6.86}$$

$N_{2,1}(t)$ covers the subinterval $[2, 4)$. $N_{2,0}(t) = 1$ and $N_{3,0}(t) = 1$ in the subintervals $[2, 3)$ and $[3, 4)$ respectively. Hence, $N_{2,1}(t)$ has the following values:

$$N_{2,1}(t) = \begin{cases} t - 2, & \text{if } 2 \le t < 3 \text{ or } t \in [2, 3); \\ 4 - t, & \text{if } 3 \le t < 4 \text{ or } t \in [3, 4); \\ 0, & \text{otherwise.} \end{cases} \tag{6.87}$$

The basis functions of degree 1; i.e., $N_{0,1}(t)$, $N_{1,1}(t)$ and $N_{2,1}(t)$, are shown in Fig. 6.14a, b and c respectively.

Similar to the above, the values of $N_{1,2}(t)$ are estimated by applying Eq. (6.77) as

$$N_{1,2}(t) = \frac{t - t_1}{t_3 - t_1} N_{1,1}(t) + \frac{t_4 - t}{t_4 - t_2} N_{2,1}(t). \tag{6.88}$$

When $t_1 = 1$, $t_2 = 2$, $t_3 = 3$ and $t_4 = 4$, $N_{1,2}(t)$ is estimated as

$$N_{1,2}(t) = \frac{t - 1}{2} N_{1,1}(t) + \frac{4 - t}{2} N_{2,1}(t). \tag{6.89}$$

Using the values of $N_{1,1}(t)$ and $N_{2,1}(t)$ listed in Eqs. (6.81) and (6.87), $N_{1,2}(t)$ value when $t \in [1, 2)$ is estimated as

$$\begin{aligned} N_{1,2}(t) &= \frac{t - 1}{2} N_{1,1}(t) \\ &= \tfrac{1}{2}(t - 1)^2. \end{aligned}$$

When $t \in [2, 3)$, $N_{1,2}(t)$ has the value of

$$\begin{aligned} N_{1,2}(t) &= \frac{t - 1}{2} N_{1,1}(t) + \frac{4 - t}{2} N_{2,1}(t) \\ &= \frac{t - 1}{2}(3 - t) + \frac{4 - t}{2}(t - 2) \\ &= \frac{1}{2}[(t - 1)(3 - t) + (4 - t)(t - 2)]. \end{aligned}$$

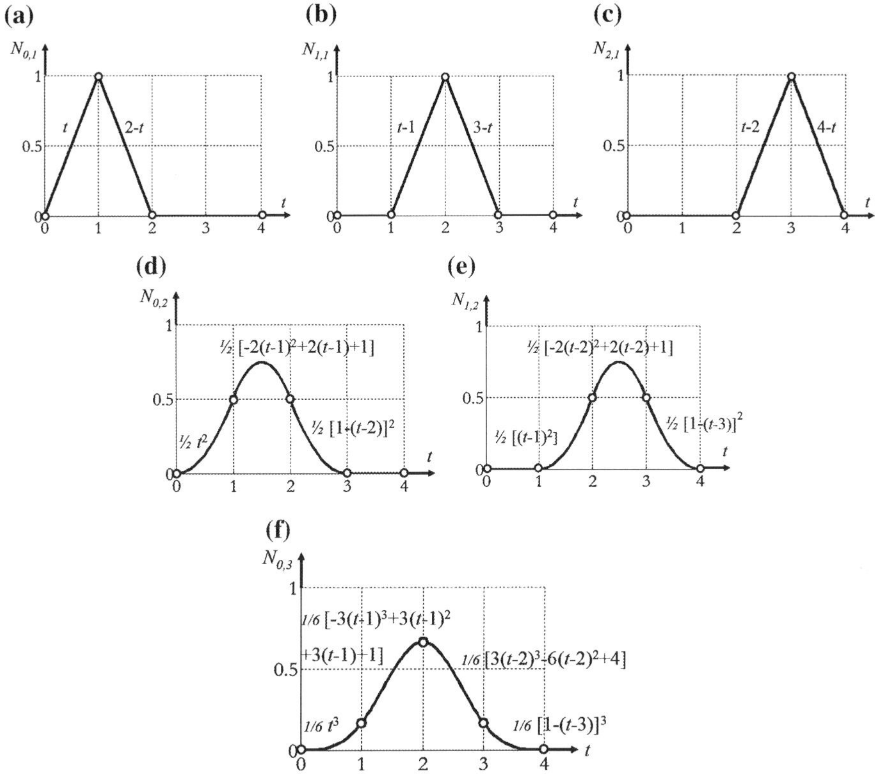


**Fig. 6.14** Basis functions using the knot vector [0, 1, 2, 3, 4]. **a** $N_{0,1}$. **b** $N_{1,1}$. **c** $N_{2,1}$. **d** $N_{0,2}$. **e** $N_{1,2}$. **f** $N_{0,3}$

When $t \in [3, 4)$, $N_{1,2}(t)$ has the value of

$$\begin{aligned} N_{1,2}(t) &= \frac{4-t}{2} N_{2,1}(t) \\ &= \frac{1}{2}(4-t)^2. \end{aligned}$$

These values can be expressed as

$$N_{1,2}(t) = \begin{cases} \frac{1}{2}[(t-1)^2], & \text{if } 1 \le t < 2 \text{ or } t \in [1,2); \\ \frac{1}{2}[-2(t-2)^2 + 2(t-2) + 1], & \text{if } 2 \le t < 3 \text{ or } t \in [2,3); \\ \frac{1}{2}[1-(t-3)]^2, & \text{if } 3 \le t < 4 \text{ or } t \in [3,4); \\ 0, & \text{otherwise.} \end{cases} \tag{6.90}$$

The basis functions of degree 2; i.e., $N_{0,2}(t)$ and $N_{1,2}(t)$, are shown in Fig. 6.14d, e respectively. Now, the values of $N_{0,3}(t)$ are estimated by applying Eq. (6.77) as

$$N_{0,3}(t) = \frac{t - t_0}{t_3 - t_0} N_{0,2}(t) + \frac{t_4 - t}{t_4 - t_1} N_{1,2}(t). \tag{6.91}$$

Substituting the values of $t_0$, $t_1$, $t_3$ and $t_4$ as 0, 1, 3 and 4 respectively, $N_{0,3}(t)$ is estimated as

$$N_{0,3}(t) = \frac{t}{3} N_{0,2}(t) + \frac{4 - t}{3} N_{1,2}(t). \tag{6.92}$$

Using the values of $N_{0,2}(t)$ and $N_{1,2}(t)$ listed in Eqs. (6.84) and (6.90), $N_{0,3}(t)$ value when $t \in [0, 1)$ is estimated as

$$\begin{aligned} N_{0,3}(t) &= \frac{t}{3} N_{0,2}(t) \\ &= \frac{1}{6} t^3. \end{aligned}$$

When $t \in [1, 2)$, $N_{0,3}(t)$ has the value of

$$\begin{aligned} N_{0,3}(t) &= \frac{t}{3} N_{0,2}(t) + \frac{4 - t}{3} N_{1,2}(t) \\ &= \frac{t}{3}\frac{1}{2}(6t - 2t^2 - 3) + \frac{4 - t}{3}\frac{1}{2}(t - 1)^2 \\ &= \frac{1}{6}[-3(t - 1)^3 + 3(t - 1)^2 + 3(t - 1) + 1]. \end{aligned}$$

When $t \in [2, 3)$, $N_{0,3}(t)$ has the value of

$$\begin{aligned} N_{0,3}(t) &= \frac{t}{3} N_{0,2}(t) + \frac{4 - t}{3} N_{1,2}(t) \\ &= \frac{t}{3}\frac{1}{2}(3 - t)^2 + \frac{4 - t}{3}\frac{1}{2}(10t - 2t^2 - 11) \\ &= \frac{1}{6}[3(t - 2)^3 - 6(t - 2)^2 + 4]. \end{aligned}$$

When $t \in [3, 4)$, $N_{0,3}(t)$ has the value of

$$\begin{aligned} N_{0,3}(t) &= \frac{4 - t}{3} N_{1,2}(t) \\ &= \frac{1}{6}(4 - t)^3. \end{aligned}$$

These values can be expressed as

$$N_{0,3}(t) = \begin{cases} \frac{1}{6}t^3, & \text{if } 0 \le t < 1 \text{ or } t \in [0, 1); \\ \frac{1}{6}[-3(t-1)^3 + 3(t-1)^2 + 3(t-1)+1], & \text{if } 1 \le t < 2 \text{ or } t \in [1, 2); \\ \frac{1}{6}[3(t-2)^3 - 6(t-2)^2 + 4], & \text{if } 2 \le t < 3 \text{ or } t \in [2, 3); \\ \frac{1}{6}[1-(t-3)]^3, & \text{if } 3 \le t < 4 \text{ or } t \in [3, 4); \\ 0, & \text{otherwise.} \end{cases} \tag{6.93}$$

The basis functions of degree 3; i.e., $N_{0,3}(t)$, are shown in Fig. 6.14f. □

**Example 6.22:** [*Basis function— $N_{i,p}(t)$ using uniform knot vector*]
Utilizing the uniform knot vector [0, 1, 2, 3, 4, 5, 6], estimate the values of basis functions for different subintervals in case of a quadratic curve.

**Solution 6.22:** From the given uniform knot vector [0, 1, 2, 3, 4, 5, 6], we understand the following:

1. This B-spline curve consists of two curve segments; the first segment is within the subinterval [2,3) while the second segment is within the subinterval [3,4). More on this point is explained in Sect. 6.2.2.4 and Table 6.3.
2. The number of elements in the knot vector is 7 ($m = 6$). Hence, the number of basis functions for degree 0 is $n+1$ where $n = m - p - 1 = 6 - 0 - 1 = 5$. These functions are $N_{0,0}(t)$, $N_{1,0}(t)$, $N_{2,0}(t)$, $N_{3,0}(t)$, $N_{4,0}(t)$ and $N_{5,0}(t)$. See Fig. 6.15.
3. The number of control points is $n + 1$ where $n = m - p - 1 = 6 - 2 - 1 = 3$.

Having $t_0 = 0$, $t_1 = 1$, $t_2 = 2$, $t_3 = 3$, $t_4 = 4$, $t_5 = 5$ and $t_6 = 6$, the basis functions are calculated as follows:

**Degree 0:** The values for $N_{0,0}(t)$ are calculated as

$$N_{0,0}(t) = \begin{cases} 1, & \text{if } t \in [0, 1); \\ 0, & \text{otherwise;} \end{cases}$$

and the values for $N_{1,0}(t)$ are calculated as

$$N_{1,0}(t) = \begin{cases} 1, & \text{if } t \in [1, 2); \\ 0, & \text{otherwise.} \end{cases}$$

The rest of the $N_{i,0}$ functions are obtained the same way. They have the following values:

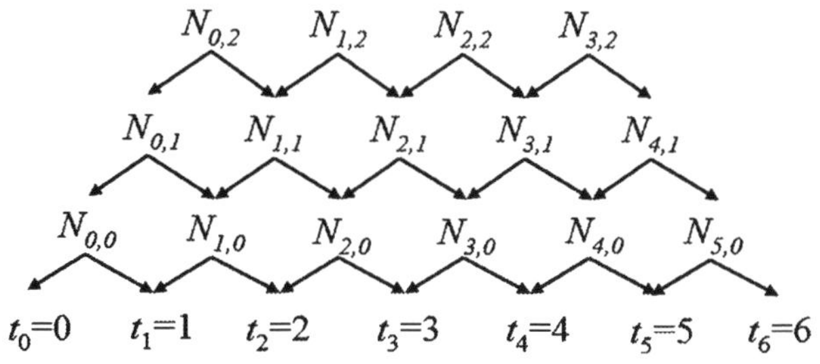


**Fig. 6.15** Basis functions using the knot vector [0, 1, 2, 3, 4, 5, 6]

| Basis function | Range | Equation |
|---|---|---|
| $N_{0,0}(t)$ | [0,1) | 1 |
| $N_{1,0}(t)$ | [1,2) | 1 |
| $N_{2,0}(t)$ | [2,3) | 1 |
| $N_{3,0}(t)$ | [3,4) | 1 |
| $N_{4,0}(t)$ | [4,5) | 1 |
| $N_{5,0}(t)$ | [5,6) | 1 |

**Degree 1:** $N_{0,1}(t)$ is calculated as

$$\begin{aligned} N_{0,1}(t) &= \frac{t-t_0}{t_1-t_0}N_{0,0}(t) + \frac{t_2-t}{t_2-t_1}N_{1,0}(t) \\ &= tN_{0,0}(t) + (2-t)N_{1,0}(t). \end{aligned}$$

Thus,

$$N_{0,1}(t) = \begin{cases} t, & \text{if } t \in [0,1); \\ 2-t, & \text{if } t \in [1,2); \\ 0, & \text{otherwise.} \end{cases}$$

Also, $N_{1,1}(t)$ is calculated as

$$\begin{aligned} N_{1,1}(t) &= \frac{t-t_1}{t_2-t_1}N_{1,0}(t) + \frac{t_3-t}{t_3-t_2}N_{2,0}(t) \\ &= (t-1)N_{1,0}(t) + (3-t)N_{2,0}(t). \end{aligned}$$

Thus,

$$N_{1,1}(t) = \begin{cases} t-1, & \text{if } t \in [1,2); \\ 3-t, & \text{if } t \in [2,3); \\ 0, & \text{otherwise.} \end{cases}$$

Similarly,

$$N_{2,1}(t) = \begin{cases} t-2, & \text{if } t \in [2,3); \\ 4-t, & \text{if } t \in [3,4); \\ 0, & \text{otherwise;} \end{cases}$$

$$N_{3,1}(t) = \begin{cases} t-3, & \text{if } t \in [3,4); \\ 5-t, & \text{if } t \in [4,5); \\ 0, & \text{otherwise;} \end{cases}$$

and

$$N_{4,1}(t) = \begin{cases} t-4, & \text{if } t \in [4,5); \\ 6-t, & \text{if } t \in [5,6); \\ 0, & \text{otherwise.} \end{cases}$$

Hence, the values for $N_{i,1}$ basis functions are as follows:

| Basis function | Range | Equation |
|---|---|---|
| $N_{0,1}(t)$ | [0,1) | $t$ |
| | [1,2) | $2-t$ |
| $N_{1,1}(t)$ | [1,2) | $t-1$ |
| | [2,3) | $3-t$ |
| $N_{2,1}(t)$ | [2,3) | $t-2$ |
| | [3,4) | $4-t$ |
| $N_{3,1}(t)$ | [3,4) | $t-3$ |
| | [4,5) | $5-t$ |
| $N_{4,1}(t)$ | [4,5) | $t-4$ |
| | [5,6) | $6-t$ |

The basis functions $N_{i,1}(t)$ are shown in Fig. 6.16a.

**Degree 2:** At degree 2, $N_{0,2}(t)$ is calculated as

$$\begin{aligned} N_{0,2}(t) &= \frac{t-t_0}{t_2-t_0} N_{0,1}(t) + \frac{t_3-t}{t_3-t_1} N_{1,1}(t) \\ &= \frac{t}{2} N_{0,1}(t) + \frac{3-t}{2} N_{1,1}(t). \end{aligned}$$

Hence,

$$N_{0,2}(t) = \begin{cases} \frac{1}{2}t^2, & \text{if } t \in [0,1); \\ \frac{1}{2}[-2(t-1)^2 + 2(t-1) + 1], & \text{if } t \in [1,2); \\ \frac{1}{2}[1-(t-2)]^2, & \text{if } t \in [2,3); \\ 0, & \text{otherwise.} \end{cases}$$

Also, $N_{1,2}(t)$ is calculated as

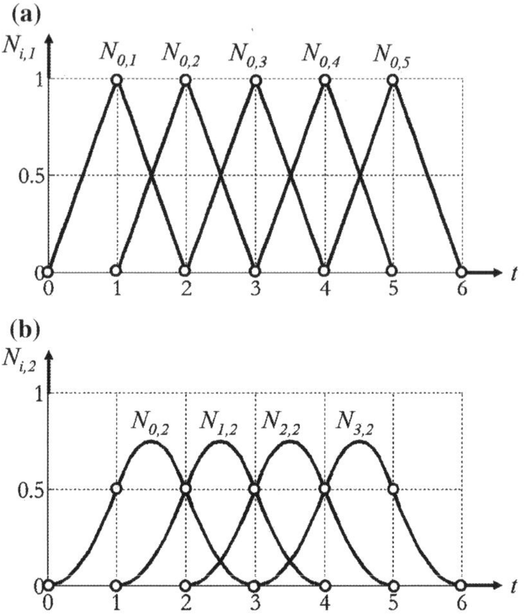


**Fig. 6.16** Basis functions using the knot vector [0, 1, 2, 3, 4, 5, 6]. **a** Degree 1. **b** Degree 2

$$\begin{aligned} N_{1,2}(t) &= \frac{t - t_1}{t_3 - t_1} N_{1,1}(t) + \frac{t_4 - t}{t_4 - t_2} N_{2,1}(t) \\ &= \frac{t-1}{2} N_{1,1}(t) + \frac{4-t}{2} N_{2,1}(t). \end{aligned}$$

Hence,

$$N_{1,2}(t) = \begin{cases} \frac{1}{2}[(t-1)]^2, & \text{if } t \in [1,2); \\ \frac{1}{2}[-2(t-2)^2 + 2(t-2) + 1], & \text{if } t \in [2,3); \\ \frac{1}{2}[1-(t-3)]^2, & \text{if } t \in [3,4); \\ 0, & \text{otherwise.} \end{cases}$$

Similarly,

$$N_{2,2}(t) = \begin{cases} \frac{1}{2}[(t-2)]^2, & \text{if } t \in [2,3); \\ \frac{1}{2}[-2(t-3)^2 + 2(t-3) + 1], & \text{if } t \in [3,4); \\ \frac{1}{2}[1-(t-4)]^2, & \text{if } t \in [4,5); \\ 0, & \text{otherwise;} \end{cases}$$

**Table 6.1** Basis functions for degree 2 generated by the knot vector [0, 1, 2, 3, 4, 5, 6]

| Basis function | Range | Equation |
|---|---|---|
| $N_{0,2}(t)$ | [0,1) | $\frac{1}{2}t^2$ |
| | [1,2) | $\frac{1}{2}[-2(t-1)^2+2(t-1)+1]$ |
| | [2,3) | $\frac{1}{2}[1-(t-2)]^2$ |
| $N_{1,2}(t)$ | [1,2) | $\frac{1}{2}[(t-1)^2]$ |
| | [2,3) | $\frac{1}{2}[-2(t-2)^2+2(t-2)+1]$ |
| | [3,4) | $\frac{1}{2}[1-(t-3)^2]$ |
| $N_{2,2}(t)$ | [2,3) | $\frac{1}{2}[(t-2)^2]$ |
| | [3,4) | $\frac{1}{2}[-2(t-3)^2+2(t-3)+1]$ |
| | [4,5) | $\frac{1}{2}[1-(t-4)^2]$ |
| $N_{3,2}(t)$ | [3,4) | $\frac{1}{2}[(t-3)^2]$ |
| | [4,5) | $\frac{1}{2}[-2(t-4)^2+2(t-4)+1]$ |
| | [5,6) | $\frac{1}{2}[1-(t-5)^2]$ |

and

$$N_{3,2}(t) = \begin{cases} \frac{1}{2}[(t-3)]^2, & \text{if } t \in [3,4); \\ \frac{1}{2}[-2(t-4)^2+2(t-4)+1], & \text{if } t \in [4,5); \\ \frac{1}{2}[1-(t-5)]^2, & \text{if } t \in [5,6); \\ 0, & \text{otherwise.} \end{cases}$$

The values for the basis functions $N_{i,2}(t)$ are listed in Table 6.1 and shown in Fig. 6.16b. Thus, given the four control points $\dot{\mathbf{p}}_0$, $\dot{\mathbf{p}}_1$, $\dot{\mathbf{p}}_2$ and $\dot{\mathbf{p}}_3$, a point $\dot{\mathbf{p}}(t)$ on the B-spline is estimated using Eq. (6.70) as

$$\begin{aligned} \dot{\mathbf{p}}(t) &= \sum_{i=0}^{n} \dot{\mathbf{p}}_i N_{i,p}(t) \\ &= \dot{\mathbf{p}}_0 N_{0,2} + \dot{\mathbf{p}}_1 N_{1,2} + \dot{\mathbf{p}}_2 N_{2,2} + \dot{\mathbf{p}}_3 N_{3,2}. \end{aligned}$$

Notice that the sum of the basis functions within any active subinterval is 1. For example, within [2,3), the sum of $N_{i,2}$ functions is

$$\sum_{i=0}^{n} N_{i,2} = \frac{1}{2}[1-(t-2)]^2 + \frac{1}{2}[-2(t-2)^2+2(t-2)+1] + \frac{1}{2}[(t-2)^2] = 1.$$

Try out the sum within [3,4) yourself! □

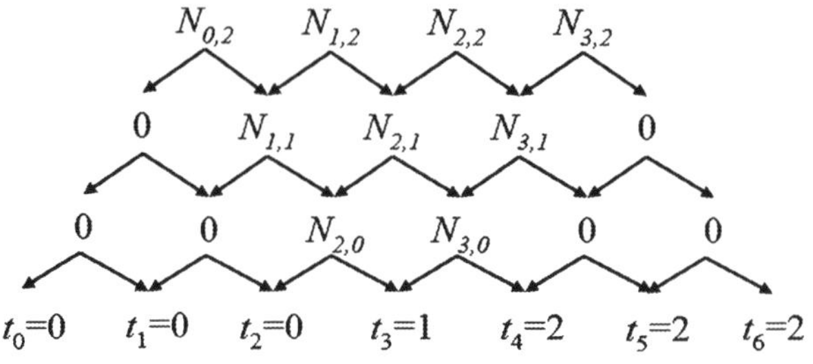


**Fig. 6.17** Basis functions using the knot vector [0, 0, 0, 1, 2, 2, 2]

**Example 6.23:** [*Basis function—* $N_{i,p}(t)$ *using open uniform knot vector*]
Utilizing the open uniform knot vector [0, 0, 0, 1, 2, 2, 2], estimate the values of basis functions for different subintervals.

**Solution 6.23:** From the given open uniform knot vector [0, 0, 0, 1, 2, 2, 2], we understand the following:

1. Since three values are repeated at both ends, this open uniform knot vector represents a quadratic B-spline curve.
2. This B-spline curve consists of two curve segments; the first segment is within the subinterval [0,1) while the second segment is within the subinterval [1,2). More on this point is explained in Sect. 6.2.2.4.
3. The number of elements in the knot vector is 7 ($m = 6$). Hence, the number of basis functions for degree 0 is $n + 1$ where $n = m - p - 1 = 6 - 0 - 1 = 5$. These functions are $N_{0,0}(t)$, $N_{1,0}(t)$, $N_{2,0}(t)$, $N_{3,0}(t)$, $N_{4,0}(t)$ and $N_{5,0}(t)$. See Fig. 6.17.
4. As mentioned in Sect. 6.2.2.2, repeated knots (0 and 2 in this example) are said to be of *multiplicity* 3. In this case, the subintervals $[t_0, t_1)$, $[t_1, t_2)$, $[t_4, t_5)$ and $[t_5, t_6)$ do not exist. Consequently, $N_{0,0}$, $N_{1,0}$, $N_{4,0}$ and $N_{5,0}$ are zeros for all $t$ values.
5. The number of control points is $n + 1$ where $n = m - p - 1 = 6 - 2 - 1 = 3$.

Having $t_0 = 0$, $t_1 = 0$, $t_2 = 0$, $t_3 = 1$, $t_4 = 2$, $t_5 = 2$ and $t_6 = 2$, the basis functions are calculated as follows:

**Degree 0:** As mentioned above, $N_{0,0} = N_{1,0} = N_{4,0} = N_{5,0} = 0$. In addition,

$$N_{2,0}(t) = \begin{cases} 1, & \text{if } t \in [0, 1); \\ 0, & \text{otherwise;} \end{cases}$$

and

$$N_{3,0}(t) = \begin{cases} 1, & \text{if } t \in [1, 2); \\ 0, & \text{otherwise.} \end{cases}$$

**Degree 1:** Since $N_{0,0}$, $N_{1,0}$, $N_{4,0}$ and $N_{5,0}$ are all zeros, $N_{0,1}$ and $N_{4,1}$ are zeros as well. $N_{1,1}(t)$ is calculated as

$$\begin{aligned}N_{1,1}(t) &= \frac{t - t_1}{t_2 - t_1} N_{1,0}(t) + \frac{t_3 - t}{t_3 - t_2} N_{2,0}(t)\\ &= (1 - t) N_{2,0}(t).\end{aligned}$$

Notice that $N_{1,0}(t)$ is always 0. Hence, the first term is 0 as well. Only the second term contributes to the result. Therefore, we have

$$N_{1,1}(t) = \begin{cases} 1 - t, & \text{if } t \in [0, 1);\\ 0, & \text{otherwise.}\end{cases}$$

Also,

$$\begin{aligned}N_{2,1}(t) &= \frac{t - t_2}{t_3 - t_2} N_{2,0}(t) + \frac{t_4 - t}{t_4 - t_3} N_{3,0}(t)\\ &= t N_{2,0}(t) + (2 - t) N_{3,0}(t).\end{aligned}$$

Hence,

$$N_{2,1}(t) = \begin{cases} t, & \text{if } t \in [0, 1);\\ 2 - t, & \text{if } t \in [1, 2);\\ 0, & \text{otherwise.}\end{cases}$$

Similarly,

$$\begin{aligned}N_{3,1}(t) &= \frac{t - t_3}{t_4 - t_3} N_{3,0}(t) + \frac{t_5 - t}{t_5 - t_4} N_{4,0}(t)\\ &= (t - 1) N_{3,0}(t).\end{aligned}$$

Hence,

$$N_{3,1}(t) = \begin{cases} t - 1, & \text{if } t \in [1, 2);\\ 0, & \text{otherwise.}\end{cases}$$

**Degree 2:** At degree 2, $N_{0,2}(t)$ is calculated as

$$\begin{aligned}N_{0,2}(t) &= \frac{t - t_0}{t_2 - t_0} N_{0,1}(t) + \frac{t_3 - t}{t_3 - t_1} N_{1,1}(t)\\ &= (1 - t) N_{1,1}(t).\end{aligned}$$

Hence,

$$N_{0,2}(t) = \begin{cases} (1 - t)^2, & \text{if } t \in [0, 1);\\ 0, & \text{otherwise.}\end{cases}$$

Also,

$$\begin{aligned}N_{1,2}(t) &= \frac{t - t_1}{t_3 - t_1} N_{1,1}(t) + \frac{t_4 - t}{t_4 - t_2} N_{2,1}(t)\\ &= t N_{1,1}(t) + \frac{2 - t}{2} N_{2,1}(t).\end{aligned}$$

Hence,

$$N_{1,2}(t) = \begin{cases} t(1-t) + \frac{1}{2}t(2-t), & \text{if } t \in [0, 1); \\ \frac{1}{2}(2-t)^2, & \text{if } t \in [1, 2); \\ 0, & \text{otherwise.} \end{cases}$$

Similarly,

$$\begin{aligned} N_{2,2}(t) &= \frac{t - t_2}{t_4 - t_2} N_{2,1}(t) + \frac{t_5 - t}{t_5 - t_3} N_{3,1}(t) \\ &= \frac{t}{2} N_{2,1}(t) + (2-t) N_{3,1}(t), \end{aligned}$$

$$N_{2,2}(t) = \begin{cases} \frac{1}{2}t^2, & \text{if } t \in [0, 1); \\ \frac{1}{2}t(2-t) + (2-t)(t-1), & \text{if } t \in [1, 2); \\ 0, & \text{otherwise,} \end{cases}$$

$$\begin{aligned} N_{3,2}(t) &= \frac{t - t_3}{t_5 - t_3} N_{3,1}(t) + \frac{t_6 - t}{t_6 - t_4} N_{4,1}(t) \\ &= (t-1) N_{3,1}(t), \end{aligned}$$

$$N_{3,2}(t) = \begin{cases} (t-1)^2, & \text{if } t \in [1, 2); \\ 0, & \text{otherwise.} \end{cases}$$

To summarize, the equations for degree 0 are as follows:

| Basis function | Range | Equation |
|---|---|---|
| $N_{0,0}(t)$ | [0,0) | 0 |
| $N_{1,0}(t)$ | [0,0) | 0 |
| $N_{2,0}(t)$ | [0,1) | 1 |
| $N_{3,0}(t)$ | [1,2) | 1 |
| $N_{4,0}(t)$ | [2,2) | 0 |
| $N_{5,0}(t)$ | [2,2) | 0 |

The equations for degree 1 are as follows:

| Basis function | Range | Equation |
|---|---|---|
| $N_{0,1}(t)$ | [0,0) | 0 |
| $N_{1,1}(t)$ | [0,1) | $1-t$ |
| $N_{2,1}(t)$ | [0,1) | $t$ |
| | [1,2) | $2-t$ |
| $N_{3,1}(t)$ | [1,2) | $t-1$ |
| $N_{4,1}(t)$ | [2,2) | 0 |

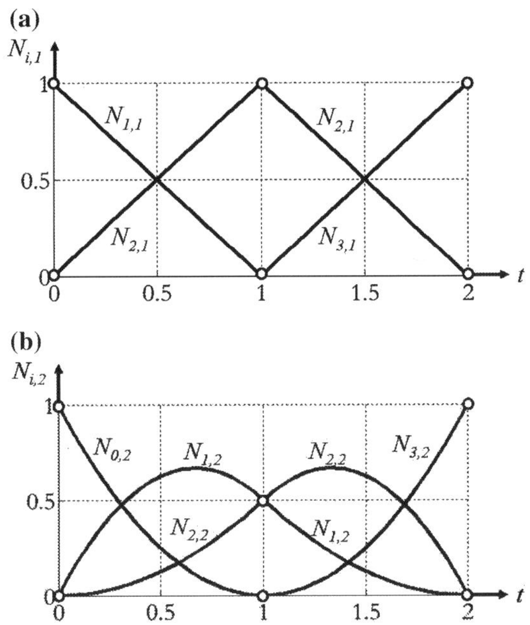


**Fig. 6.18** Basis functions using the knot vector [0, 0, 0, 1, 2, 2, 2]. **a** Degree 1. **b** Degree 2

**Table 6.2** Basis functions for degree 2 generated by the knot vector [0, 0, 0, 1, 2, 2, 2]

| Basis function | Range | Equation |
|---|---|---|
| $N_{0,2}(t)$ | [0,1) | $(1-t)^2$ |
| $N_{1,2}(t)$ | [0,1) | $t(1-t)+\frac{1}{2}t(2-t)$ |
| | [1,2) | $\frac{1}{2}(2-t)^2$ |
| $N_{2,2}(t)$ | [0,1) | $\frac{1}{2}t^2$ |
| | [1,2) | $\frac{1}{2}t(2-t)+(2-t)(t-1)$ |
| $N_{3,2}(t)$ | [1,2) | $(t-1)^2$ |

These basis functions are shown in Fig. 6.18a. The equations for degree 2 are listed in Table 6.2. These basis functions are shown in Fig. 6.18b. Thus, given the four control points $\dot{\mathbf{p}}_0$, $\dot{\mathbf{p}}_1$, $\dot{\mathbf{p}}_2$ and $\dot{\mathbf{p}}_3$, a point $\dot{\mathbf{p}}(t)$ on the B-spline is estimated using Eq. (6.70) as

$$\begin{aligned}\dot{\mathbf{p}}(t) &= \sum_{i=0}^{n} \dot{\mathbf{p}}_i N_{i,p}(t)\\ &= \dot{\mathbf{p}}_0 N_{0,2} + \dot{\mathbf{p}}_1 N_{1,2} + \dot{\mathbf{p}}_2 N_{2,2} + \dot{\mathbf{p}}_3 N_{3,2}.\end{aligned}$$

Notice that the sum of the basis functions within any active subinterval is 1. For example, within [0,1), the sum of $N_{i,2}$ functions is

$$\sum_{i=0}^{n} N_{i,2} = (1-t)^2 + t(1-t) + \frac{1}{2}t(2-t) + \frac{1}{2}t^2 = 1.$$

Try out the sum within [1,2) yourself! □

#### 6.2.2.4 Quadratic B-Splines

We may apply the basis functions with control points through Eq. (6.70) to get points on quadratic B-spline curves.

**Example 6.24:** [*B-spline curves—points on quadratic curves using uniform knot vector*]

A quadratic B-spline curve is to be generated using the control points $\dot{\mathbf{p}}_0 = [10, 30]^T$, $\dot{\mathbf{p}}_1 = [30, 50]^T$, $\dot{\mathbf{p}}_2 = [80, 30]^T$ and $\dot{\mathbf{p}}_3 = [120, 40]^T$ and the knot vector [0, 1, 2, 3, 4, 5, 6]. Determine the location of the curve point at $t = 2.5$.

**Solution 6.24:** According to Table 6.1, the basis functions for $t = 2.5$ are as follows:

| Basis function | Range | Equation |
|---|---|---|
| $N_{0,2}(t)$ | [2,3) | $\frac{1}{2}[1-(t-2)]^2$ |
| $N_{1,2}(t)$ | [2,3) | $\frac{1}{2}[-2(t-2)^2+2(t-2)+1]$ |
| $N_{2,2}(t)$ | [2,3) | $\frac{1}{2}[(t-2)^2]$ |
| $N_{3,2}(t)$ | [2,3) | 0 |

Using Eq. (6.70), the location of the curve point at $t = 2.5$ is estimated as

$$\begin{aligned}
\dot{\mathbf{p}}(t) &= \sum_{i=0}^{n} N_{i,p}(t)\dot{\mathbf{p}}_i \\
&= N_{0,2}(2.5)\dot{\mathbf{p}}_0 + N_{1,2}(2.5)\dot{\mathbf{p}}_1 + N_{2,2}(2.5)\dot{\mathbf{p}}_2 + N_{3,2}(2.5)\dot{\mathbf{p}}_3 \\
&= \tfrac{1}{2}[1-(t-2)]^2\dot{\mathbf{p}}_0 + \tfrac{1}{2}[-2(t-2)^2+2(t-2)+1]\dot{\mathbf{p}}_1 + \tfrac{1}{2}[(t-2)^2] \\
&\quad \dot{\mathbf{p}}_2 + 0\dot{\mathbf{p}}_3 \\
\dot{\mathbf{p}}(2.5) &= \frac{1}{2}[1-(2.5-2)]^2\begin{bmatrix}10\\30\end{bmatrix} + \frac{1}{2}[-2(2.5-2)^2+2(2.5-2)+1]\begin{bmatrix}30\\50\end{bmatrix} \\
&\quad + \frac{1}{2}[(2.5-2)^2]\begin{bmatrix}80\\30\end{bmatrix} + 0\begin{bmatrix}120\\40\end{bmatrix} \\
&= \begin{bmatrix}33.75\\45\end{bmatrix}.
\end{aligned}$$

The curve is drawn in Fig. 6.19a where $\dot{\mathbf{p}}(2.5)$ is marked. Notice that the uniform knot vector used *does not* interpolate the start and end control points. □

**Example 6.25:** [*B-spline curves—points on quadratic curves using open uniform knot vector*]

A quadratic B-spline curve is to be generated using the control points $\dot{\mathbf{p}}_0 = [10, 30]^T$, $\dot{\mathbf{p}}_1 = [30, 50]^T$, $\dot{\mathbf{p}}_2 = [80, 30]^T$ and $\dot{\mathbf{p}}_3 = [120, 40]^T$ and the knot vector [0, 0, 0, 1, 2, 2, 2]. Determine the location of the curve point at $t = 0.5$.

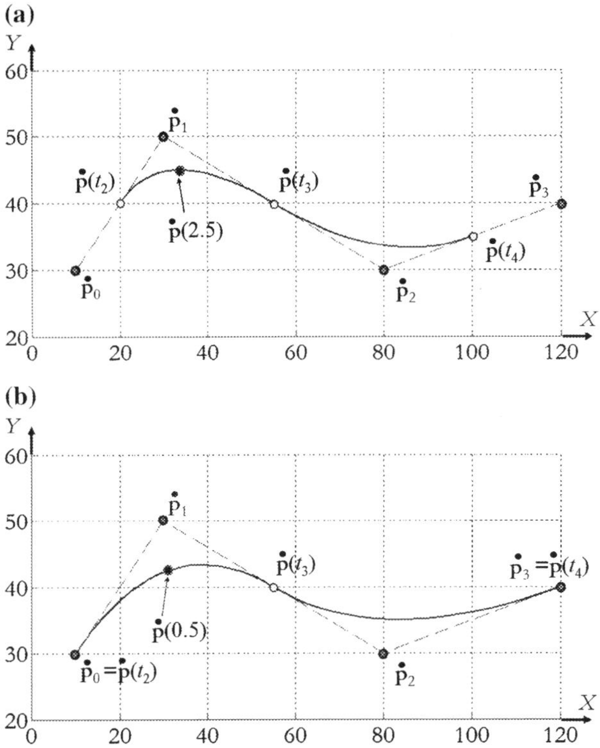


**Fig. 6.19** A quadratic B-spline curve generated using the control points $\dot{\mathbf{p}}_0 = [10, 30]^T$, $\dot{\mathbf{p}}_1 = [30, 50]^T$, $\dot{\mathbf{p}}_2 = [80, 30]^T$ and $\dot{\mathbf{p}}_3 = [120, 40]^T$. **a** The uniform knot vector [0, 1, 2, 3, 4, 5, 6] is used. The curve point at $t = 2.5$ is marked. **b** The open uniform knot vector [0, 0, 0, 1, 2, 2, 2] is used. The curve point at $t = 0.5$ is marked

**Solution 6.25:** According to Table 6.2, the basis functions for $t = 0.5$ are as follows:

| Basis function | Range | Equation |
|---|---|---|
| $N_{0,2}(t)$ | [0,1) | $(1-t)^2$ |
| $N_{1,2}(t)$ | [0,1) | $t(1-t) + \frac{1}{2}t(2-t)$ |
| $N_{2,2}(t)$ | [0,1) | $\frac{1}{2}t^2$ |
| $N_{3,2}(t)$ | [0,1) | 0 |

Using Eq. (6.70), the location of the curve point at $t = 0.5$ is estimated as

$$\dot{\mathbf{p}}(t) = \sum_{i=0}^{n} N_{i,p}(t)\dot{\mathbf{p}}_i$$

**Table 6.3** Quadratic curve segments and their associated control points

| Segment | Control points | Domain |
|---|---|---|
| $\mathscr{S}_2$ | $\dot{\mathbf{p}}_0, \dot{\mathbf{p}}_1, \dot{\mathbf{p}}_2$ | $t_2 \le t < t_3$ |
| $\mathscr{S}_3$ | $\dot{\mathbf{p}}_1, \dot{\mathbf{p}}_2, \dot{\mathbf{p}}_3$ | $t_3 \le t < t_4$ |
| $\vdots$ | $\vdots$ | $\vdots$ |
| $\mathscr{S}_n$ | $\dot{\mathbf{p}}_{n-2}, \dot{\mathbf{p}}_{n-1}, \dot{\mathbf{p}}_n$ | $t_n \le t < t_{n+1}$ |

Note that in quadratic B-splines, $n$ must be greater than or equal to 2. Also, note that $t$ has a value of $t_3$ at the knot between $\mathscr{S}_2$ and $\mathscr{S}_3$ and has a value of $t_4$ at the knot between $\mathscr{S}_3$ and $\mathscr{S}_4$, etc.

$$
\begin{aligned}
&= N_{0,2}(0.5)\dot{\mathbf{p}}_0 + N_{1,2}(0.5)\dot{\mathbf{p}}_1 + N_{2,2}(0.5)\dot{\mathbf{p}}_2 + N_{3,2}(0.5)\dot{\mathbf{p}}_3 \\
&= (1-t)^2\dot{\mathbf{p}}_0 + [t(1-t) + \frac{1}{2}t(2-t)]\dot{\mathbf{p}}_1 + \frac{1}{2}t^2\dot{\mathbf{p}}_2 + 0\dot{\mathbf{p}}_3 \\
\dot{\mathbf{p}}(0.5) &= (1-0.5)^2\begin{bmatrix}10\\30\end{bmatrix} + [0.5(1-0.5) + \frac{1}{2}0.5(2-0.5)]\begin{bmatrix}30\\50\end{bmatrix} \\
&\quad + \frac{1}{2}0.5^2\begin{bmatrix}80\\30\end{bmatrix} + 0\begin{bmatrix}120\\40\end{bmatrix} \\
&= \begin{bmatrix}31.25\\42.5\end{bmatrix}.
\end{aligned}
$$

The curve is drawn is Fig. 6.19b where $\dot{\mathbf{p}}(0.5)$ is marked. Notice that the open uniform knot vector used *does* interpolate the start and end control points. □

**Quadratic B-Spline Curve Segments:** Consider the control points $\dot{\mathbf{p}}_0, \dot{\mathbf{p}}_1, \ldots, \dot{\mathbf{p}}_n$. Those points can approximate a quadratic B-spline curve that consists of a sequence of $n-1$ (where $n \ge 2$) quadratic curve segments defined as listed in Table 6.3. The parameter $t$ along each curve segment may be defined as $0 \le t < 1$ or as a part of a sequence of domains bounded by $t_i, t_{i+1}, \ldots$, etc. as listed in the third column of Table 6.3.

Notice that the points at the start and end of each curve segment represent the knots including those at the start and end of the whole curve. Also, it should be mentioned that a quadratic curve segment is contained in the convex hull (i.e., the triangle) formed by its three control points.

As each quadratic curve segment is controlled by three control points, a control point (except for the first two points and the last two points) affects and contributes to three curve segments. For example, point $\dot{\mathbf{p}}_3$ affects segments $\mathscr{S}_3$, $\mathscr{S}_4$ and $\mathscr{S}_5$; however, it has no effect on $\mathscr{S}_2, \mathscr{S}_6, \mathscr{S}_7$, etc. Hence, if $\dot{\mathbf{p}}_3$ moves in a certain direction, only $\mathscr{S}_3$, $\mathscr{S}_4$ and $\mathscr{S}_5$ move in the same direction while the rest of the segments do not get affected to comply with the local control property. Notice in each of Example 6.24 and Example 6.25 that the points estimated lie on the first quadratic curve segment, which is affected by the first three control points; $\dot{\mathbf{p}}_0$, $\dot{\mathbf{p}}_1$ and $\dot{\mathbf{p}}_2$. Hence, point $\dot{\mathbf{p}}_3$ contributes nothing to the calculations ($N_{3,2} = 0$).

**Example 6.26:** [*B-spline curves—knots on quadratic curves using uniform knot vector*]

A quadratic B-spline curve is to be generated using the control points $\dot{\mathbf{p}}_0 = [10, 30]^T$, $\dot{\mathbf{p}}_1 = [30, 50]^T$, $\dot{\mathbf{p}}_2 = [80, 30]^T$ and $\dot{\mathbf{p}}_3 = [120, 40]^T$ and the uniform knot vector [0, 1, 2, 3, 4, 5, 6]. Determine the locations of the knots.

**Solution 6.26:** The parameter range is $t_p \leq t \leq t_{n+1}$ as discussed in Sect. 6.2.2.1. Since $p = 2$ and $n = 3$, the knots are located at $t_2$, $t_3$ and $t_4$ (i.e., at $t = 2$, $t = 3$ and $t = 4$ respectively).

Using Eq. (6.70), the location of the curve point at $t = 2$ is estimated as

$$\begin{aligned}
\dot{\mathbf{p}}(t) &= \sum_{i=0}^{n} N_{i,p}(t)\dot{\mathbf{p}}_i \\
&= N_{0,2}(2)\dot{\mathbf{p}}_0 + N_{1,2}(2)\dot{\mathbf{p}}_1 + N_{2,2}(2)\dot{\mathbf{p}}_2 + N_{3,2}(2)\dot{\mathbf{p}}_3 \\
&= \frac{1}{2}[1-(t-2)]^2\dot{\mathbf{p}}_0 + \frac{1}{2}[-2(t-2)^2 + 2(t-2) + 1]\dot{\mathbf{p}}_1 \\
&\quad + \frac{1}{2}[(t-2)^2]\dot{\mathbf{p}}_2 + 0\dot{\mathbf{p}}_3 \\
\dot{\mathbf{p}}(2) &= \frac{1}{2}[1-(2-2)]^2\begin{bmatrix}10\\30\end{bmatrix} + \frac{1}{2}[-2(2-2)^2 + 2(2-2) + 1]\begin{bmatrix}30\\50\end{bmatrix} \\
&\quad + \frac{1}{2}[(2-2)^2]\begin{bmatrix}80\\30\end{bmatrix} + 0\begin{bmatrix}120\\40\end{bmatrix} \\
&= \begin{bmatrix}20\\40\end{bmatrix}.
\end{aligned}$$

Notice that the basis functions used are for the interval [2,3) according to Table 6.1. Similarly, the location of the curve point at $t = 3$ is estimated as

$$\begin{aligned}
\dot{\mathbf{p}}(t) &= \sum_{i=0}^{n} N_{i,p}(t)\dot{\mathbf{p}}_i \\
&= N_{0,2}(3)\dot{\mathbf{p}}_0 + N_{1,2}(3)\dot{\mathbf{p}}_1 + N_{2,2}(3)\dot{\mathbf{p}}_2 + N_{3,2}(3)\dot{\mathbf{p}}_3 \\
&= \frac{1}{2}[1-(t-2)]^2\dot{\mathbf{p}}_0 + \frac{1}{2}[-2(t-2)^2 + 2(t-2) + 1]\dot{\mathbf{p}}_1 \\
&\quad + \frac{1}{2}[(t-2)^2]\dot{\mathbf{p}}_2 + 0\dot{\mathbf{p}}_3 \\
\dot{\mathbf{p}}(3) &= \frac{1}{2}[1-(3-2)]^2\begin{bmatrix}10\\30\end{bmatrix} + \frac{1}{2}[-2(3-2)^2 + 2(3-2) + 1]\begin{bmatrix}30\\50\end{bmatrix} \\
&\quad + \frac{1}{2}[(3-2)^2]\begin{bmatrix}80\\30\end{bmatrix} + 0\begin{bmatrix}120\\40\end{bmatrix} \\
&= \begin{bmatrix}55\\40\end{bmatrix}.
\end{aligned}$$

Again, notice that the basis functions used are for the interval [2,3) according to Table 6.1. Alternatively, the basis functions for the range [3,4) can be used when $t = 3$. Thus, according to Table 6.1, we may write

$$
\begin{aligned}
\dot{\mathbf{p}}(t) &= \sum_{i=0}^{n} N_{i,p}(t)\dot{\mathbf{p}}_i \\
&= N_{0,2}(3)\dot{\mathbf{p}}_0 + N_{1,2}(3)\dot{\mathbf{p}}_1 + N_{2,2}(3)\dot{\mathbf{p}}_2 + N_{3,2}(3)\dot{\mathbf{p}}_3 \\
&= 0\dot{\mathbf{p}}_0 + \frac{1}{2}[1-(t-3)]^2\dot{\mathbf{p}}_1 + \frac{1}{2}[-2(t-3)^2 + 2(t-3) + 1]\dot{\mathbf{p}}_2 \\
&\quad + \frac{1}{2}[(t-3)^2]\dot{\mathbf{p}}_3 \\
\dot{\mathbf{p}}(3) &= 0\begin{bmatrix} 10 \\ 30 \end{bmatrix} + \frac{1}{2}[1-(3-3)]^2\begin{bmatrix} 30 \\ 50 \end{bmatrix} + \frac{1}{2}[-2(3-3)^2 + 2(3-3) + 1]\begin{bmatrix} 80 \\ 30 \end{bmatrix} \\
&\quad + \frac{1}{2}[(3-3)^2]\begin{bmatrix} 120 \\ 40 \end{bmatrix} \\
&= \begin{bmatrix} 55 \\ 40 \end{bmatrix}.
\end{aligned}
$$

Similarly, $\dot{\mathbf{p}}(4) = [100, 35]^T$. The curve is drawn in Fig. 6.19a where the locations of the knots $\dot{\mathbf{p}}(2)$, $\dot{\mathbf{p}}(3)$ and $\dot{\mathbf{p}}(4)$ are marked and identified as $\dot{\mathbf{p}}(t_2)$, $\dot{\mathbf{p}}(t_3)$ and $\dot{\mathbf{p}}(t_4)$ respectively. □

**Example 6.27:** [*B-spline curves—knots on quadratic curves using open uniform knot vector*]

A quadratic B-spline curve is to be generated using the control points $\dot{\mathbf{p}}_0 = [10, 30]^T$, $\dot{\mathbf{p}}_1 = [30, 50]^T$, $\dot{\mathbf{p}}_2 = [80, 30]^T$ and $\dot{\mathbf{p}}_3 = [120, 40]^T$ and the open uniform knot vector [0, 0, 0, 1, 2, 2, 2]. Determine the locations of the knots.

**Solution 6.27:** The parameter range is $t_p \le t \le t_{n+1}$ as discussed in Sect. 6.2.2.1. Since $p = 2$ and $n = 3$, the knots are located at $t_2$, $t_3$ and $t_4$ (i.e., at $t = 0$, $t = 1$ and $t = 2$ respectively).

Similar to Example 6.26, the locations of the knots are obtained; however, the basis functions are retrieved from Table 6.2. The values are listed as follows:

| $t$ | Knot | Location | Remarks |
|---|---|---|---|
| $t_2 = 0$ | $\dot{\mathbf{p}}(0)$ | $[10, 30]^T$ | $= \dot{\mathbf{p}}_0$ |
| $t_3 = 1$ | $\dot{\mathbf{p}}(1)$ | $[55, 40]^T$ | Same as previous example |
| $t_4 = 2$ | $\dot{\mathbf{p}}(2)$ | $[120, 40]^T$ | $= \dot{\mathbf{p}}_3$ |

The curve is drawn in Fig. 6.19b where the locations of the knots $\dot{\mathbf{p}}(0)$, $\dot{\mathbf{p}}(1)$ and $\dot{\mathbf{p}}(2)$ are marked and identified as $\dot{\mathbf{p}}(t_2)$, $\dot{\mathbf{p}}(t_3)$ and $\dot{\mathbf{p}}(t_4)$ respectively. □

**Basis Matrix:** In matrix form, a quadratic B-spline segment spanning within [0,1] and generated by $\dot{\mathbf{p}}_0$, $\dot{\mathbf{p}}_1$ and $\dot{\mathbf{p}}_2$ is defined as

$$\dot{\mathbf{p}}(t) = \underbrace{\frac{1}{2}\begin{bmatrix} t^2 & t & 1 \end{bmatrix}\begin{bmatrix} 1 & -2 & 1 \\ -2 & 2 & 0 \\ 1 & 1 & 0 \end{bmatrix}}_{sum=1}\begin{bmatrix} \dot{\mathbf{p}}_0 \\ \dot{\mathbf{p}}_1 \\ \dot{\mathbf{p}}_2 \end{bmatrix}, \tag{6.94}$$

where $\frac{1}{2}\begin{bmatrix} 1 & -2 & 1 \\ -2 & 2 & 0 \\ 1 & 1 & 0 \end{bmatrix}$ is called the quadratic B-spline basis matrix. Notice that the elements of the vector $\frac{1}{2}\begin{bmatrix} t^2 & t & 1 \end{bmatrix}\begin{bmatrix} 1 & -2 & 1 \\ -2 & 2 & 0 \\ 1 & 1 & 0 \end{bmatrix}$ sum to 1. Alternatively, Eq. (6.94) can be re-written as

$$\dot{\mathbf{p}}(t) = \frac{1}{2}\left[(1-t)^2\dot{\mathbf{p}}_0 + (-2t^2+2t+1)\dot{\mathbf{p}}_1 + t^2\dot{\mathbf{p}}_2\right]. \tag{6.95}$$

Notice that

$$\frac{1}{2}\begin{bmatrix} t^2 & t & 1 \end{bmatrix}\begin{bmatrix} 1 & -2 & 1 \\ -2 & 2 & 0 \\ 1 & 1 & 0 \end{bmatrix} = \frac{1}{2}\begin{bmatrix} (1-t)^2 & -2t^2+2t+1 & t^2 \end{bmatrix} \tag{6.96}$$

represent functions that shape the quadratic B-spline curve. The polynomials are shown in Fig. 6.20. Equation (6.94) assumes that the lower bound of the $t$ interval is 0. Since the basis functions for each curve segment are the same and assuming a uniform knot vector, if the $t$ interval starts at $t_i$, Eq. (6.94) should be modified to

$$\dot{\mathbf{p}}(t) = \frac{1}{2}\begin{bmatrix} (t-t_i)^2 & (t-t_i) & 1 \end{bmatrix}\begin{bmatrix} 1 & -2 & 1 \\ -2 & 2 & 0 \\ 1 & 1 & 0 \end{bmatrix}\begin{bmatrix} \dot{\mathbf{p}}_{i-2} \\ \dot{\mathbf{p}}_{i-1} \\ \dot{\mathbf{p}}_i \end{bmatrix} \tag{6.97}$$

or

$$\dot{\mathbf{p}}(t) = \frac{1}{2}\left[(1-(t-t_i))^2\dot{\mathbf{p}}_{i-2} + (-2(t-t_i)^2+2(t-t_i)+1)\dot{\mathbf{p}}_{i-1} + (t-t_i)^2\dot{\mathbf{p}}_i\right]. \tag{6.98}$$

**Example 6.28:** [*B-spline curves—knots on quadratic curves using uniform knot vector*]

A quadratic B-spline curve is to be generated using the control points $\dot{\mathbf{p}}_0 = [10, 30]^T$, $\dot{\mathbf{p}}_1 = [30, 50]^T$, $\dot{\mathbf{p}}_2 = [80, 30]^T$ and $\dot{\mathbf{p}}_3 = [120, 40]^T$ and the uniform knot vector [0, 1, 2, 3, 4, 5, 6]. How many curve segments are generated? What are the locations of the knot points?

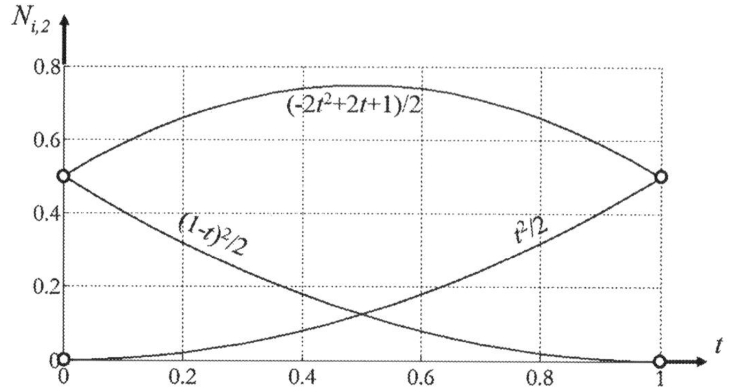


**Fig. 6.20** The basis functions for B-splines of degree 2

**Solution 6.28:** In the previous solutions, we used the values of $N_{0,2}$, $N_{1,2}$, $N_{2,2}$ and $N_{3,2}$ with all four points to get curve points and locations of knots. In this example, we will work with individual curve segments with their associated control points. A quadratic B-spline segment is generated using three control points. Hence, the given four points generate two segments; $\mathscr{S}_2$ that goes from $t_2$ to $t_3$ using $\dot{\mathbf{p}}_0$, $\dot{\mathbf{p}}_1$ and $\dot{\mathbf{p}}_2$ and $\mathscr{S}_3$ that goes from $t_3$ to $t_4$ using $\dot{\mathbf{p}}_1$, $\dot{\mathbf{p}}_2$ and $\dot{\mathbf{p}}_3$.

The knot at $t_2$ is obtained when substituting $t = t_i = 2$ in Eq. (6.98) with points $\dot{\mathbf{p}}_0$, $\dot{\mathbf{p}}_1$ and $\dot{\mathbf{p}}_2$. Thus,

$$\begin{aligned}
\dot{\mathbf{p}}(t) &= \tfrac{1}{2}\left[(1-(t-t_i))^2\dot{\mathbf{p}}_{i-2} + (-2(t-t_i)^2 + 2(t-t_i) + 1)\dot{\mathbf{p}}_{i-1} + (t-t_i)^2\dot{\mathbf{p}}_i\right] \\
\dot{\mathbf{p}}(2) &= \tfrac{1}{2}\left[(1-0)^2\begin{bmatrix}10\\30\end{bmatrix} + (-2\times 0^2 + 2\times 0 + 1)\begin{bmatrix}30\\50\end{bmatrix} + 0^2\begin{bmatrix}80\\30\end{bmatrix}\right] \\
&= \begin{bmatrix}20\\40\end{bmatrix}.
\end{aligned}$$

The knot at $t_3$ is obtained when substituting $t = 3$ and $t_i = 2$ in Eq. (6.98) with points $\dot{\mathbf{p}}_0$, $\dot{\mathbf{p}}_1$ and $\dot{\mathbf{p}}_2$. So,

$$\begin{aligned}
\dot{\mathbf{p}}(3) &= \tfrac{1}{2}\left[(1-1)^2\begin{bmatrix}10\\30\end{bmatrix} + (-2\times 1^2 + 2\times 1 + 1)\begin{bmatrix}30\\50\end{bmatrix} + 1^2\begin{bmatrix}80\\30\end{bmatrix}\right] \\
&= \begin{bmatrix}55\\40\end{bmatrix}.
\end{aligned}$$

Alternatively, the knot at $t_3$ may be obtained when substituting $t = 3$ and $t_i = 3$ in the same equation with points $\dot{\mathbf{p}}_1$, $\dot{\mathbf{p}}_2$ and $\dot{\mathbf{p}}_3$. Thus,

$$\begin{aligned}
\dot{\mathbf{p}}(3) &= \frac{1}{2}\left[(1-0)^2\begin{bmatrix}30\\50\end{bmatrix} + (-2\times 0^2 + 2\times 0 + 1)\begin{bmatrix}80\\30\end{bmatrix} + 0^2\begin{bmatrix}120\\40\end{bmatrix}\right] \\
&= \begin{bmatrix}55\\40\end{bmatrix}.
\end{aligned}$$

The knot at $t_4$ is obtained when substituting $t = 4$ and $t_i = 3$ in the same equation with points $\dot{\mathbf{p}}_1$, $\dot{\mathbf{p}}_2$ and $\dot{\mathbf{p}}_3$. So,

$$\begin{aligned}\dot{\mathbf{p}}(4) &= \frac{1}{2}\left[(1-1)^2\begin{bmatrix}30\\50\end{bmatrix} + (-2\times 1^2 + 2\times 1 + 1)\begin{bmatrix}80\\30\end{bmatrix} + 1^2\begin{bmatrix}120\\40\end{bmatrix}\right]\\ &= \begin{bmatrix}100\\35\end{bmatrix}.\end{aligned}$$

The curve as well as the control points and the knots were previously shown in Fig. 6.19a. □

**Example 6.29:** [*B-spline curves—effect of moving control points on quadratic curves*]

In Example 6.28, if the control point $\dot{\mathbf{p}}_3$ is moved to $[100, 55]^T$, what effect should we expect on the knots in this case?

**Solution 6.29:** The control point $\dot{\mathbf{p}}_3$ contributes to the second segment $\mathscr{S}_3$ only, which is bounded by the knots $t_3$ and $t_4$. Since the knot at $t_3$ is shared between both curve segments, we should expect that only the last knot (i.e., at $t = t_4 = 4$) will move. The new location is obtained when substituting $t = 4$ and $t_i = 3$ in Eq. (6.98) with points $\dot{\mathbf{p}}_1$, $\dot{\mathbf{p}}_2$ and $\dot{\mathbf{p}}_3$ as

$$\begin{aligned}\dot{\mathbf{p}}(t) &= \frac{1}{2}\left[(1-(t-t_i))^2\dot{\mathbf{p}}_1 + (-2(t-t_i)^2 + 2(t-t_i) + 1)\dot{\mathbf{p}}_2 + (t-t_i)^2\dot{\mathbf{p}}_3\right]\\ \dot{\mathbf{p}}(4) &= \frac{1}{2}\left[(1-1)^2\begin{bmatrix}30\\50\end{bmatrix} + (-2\times 1^2 + 2\times 1 + 1)\begin{bmatrix}80\\30\end{bmatrix} + 1^2\begin{bmatrix}100\\55\end{bmatrix}\right]\\ &= \begin{bmatrix}90\\42.5\end{bmatrix}.\end{aligned}$$

The curve as well as the control points and the knots are shown in Fig. 6.21. □

**Example 6.30:** [*B-spline curves—curve continuity*]

A quadratic B-spline curve is to be generated using the control points $\dot{\mathbf{p}}_0 = [10, 10]^T$, $\dot{\mathbf{p}}_1 = [30, 50]^T$, $\dot{\mathbf{p}}_2 = [90, 70]^T$, $\dot{\mathbf{p}}_3 = [130, 20]^T$, $\dot{\mathbf{p}}_4 = [170, 80]^T$ and $\dot{\mathbf{p}}_5 = [220, 60]^T$. Consider the following cases:

1. If the knot vector [0, 1, 2, 3, 4, 5, 6, 7, 8] is used, determine the location of the curve point at $t = 4$. What is the continuity of the curve in this case?
2. If the knot vector [0, 1, 2, 4, 4, 5, 6, 7, 8] is used, determine the location of the curve point at $t = 4$. What is the continuity of the curve in this case?

**Solution 6.30:** The continuity gets changed using these knot vectors.

**The knot vector [0, 1, 2, 3, 4, 5, 6, 7, 8]:** The curve is shown in Fig. 6.22a. The curve point at $t = 4$ is obtained when substituting $t_i = 3$ in Eq. (6.98) with points $\dot{\mathbf{p}}_1$, $\dot{\mathbf{p}}_2$ and $\dot{\mathbf{p}}_3$. So,

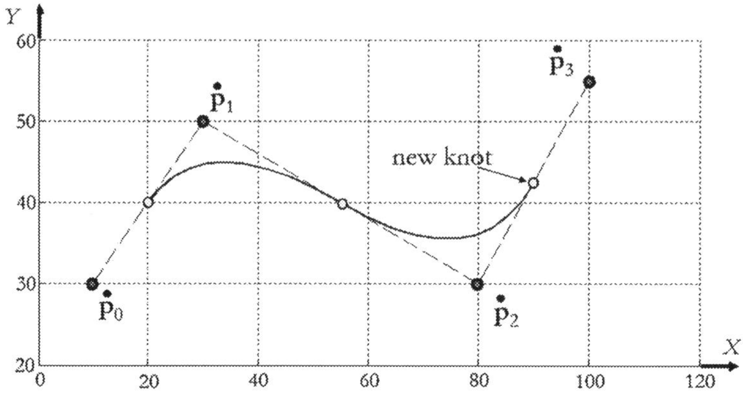


**Fig. 6.21** A quadratic B-spline curve is generated using the control points $\dot{\mathbf{p}}_0 = [10, 30]^T$, $\dot{\mathbf{p}}_1 = [30, 50]^T$, $\dot{\mathbf{p}}_2 = [80, 30]^T$ and $\dot{\mathbf{p}}_3 = [100, 55]^T$

$$\begin{aligned}
\dot{\mathbf{p}}(t) &= \frac{1}{2}\left[(1-(t-t_i))^2\dot{\mathbf{p}}_1 + (-2(t-t_i)^2 + 2(t-t_i)+1)\dot{\mathbf{p}}_2 + (t-t_i)^2\dot{\mathbf{p}}_3\right] \\
\dot{\mathbf{p}}(4) &= \frac{1}{2}\left[(1-1)^2\begin{bmatrix}30\\50\end{bmatrix} + (-2\times 1^2 + 2\times 1 + 1)\begin{bmatrix}90\\70\end{bmatrix} + 1^2\begin{bmatrix}130\\20\end{bmatrix}\right] \\
&= \begin{bmatrix}110\\45\end{bmatrix}.
\end{aligned}$$

The same result is obtained when substituting $t_i = 4$ in Eq. (6.98) with points $\dot{\mathbf{p}}_2$, $\dot{\mathbf{p}}_3$ and $\dot{\mathbf{p}}_4$. The curve point at $t = 4$; $\dot{\mathbf{p}}(t_4)$, is marked in Fig. 6.22a.

Note that at $t = 4$, the multiplicity is 1; hence, the continuity is expressed using Eq. (6.76) as

$$\begin{aligned}
Continuity &= order - (multiplicity + 1) \\
&= 3 - (1 + 1) = 1.
\end{aligned}$$

Thus, the curve is $C^1$ continuous.

**The knot vector [0, 1, 2, 4, 4, 5, 6, 7, 8]:** The curve is shown in Fig. 6.22b. The basis functions should be estimated for this knot vector. (This is left as an exercise.) For the interval, [4,5), we have the following basis functions:

| Basis function | Equation |
|---|---|
| $N_{2,2}(t)$ | $(5-t)^2$ |
| $N_{3,2}(t)$ | $(t-4)(5-t) + \frac{1}{2}(t-4)(6-t)$ |
| $N_{4,2}(t)$ | $\frac{1}{2}(t-4)^2$ |

Thus, the curve point at $t = 4$ is obtained as $[90, 70]^T$, which is the control point $\dot{\mathbf{p}}_2$. This is marked in Fig. 6.22b. In fact, the control polygon should coincide with the

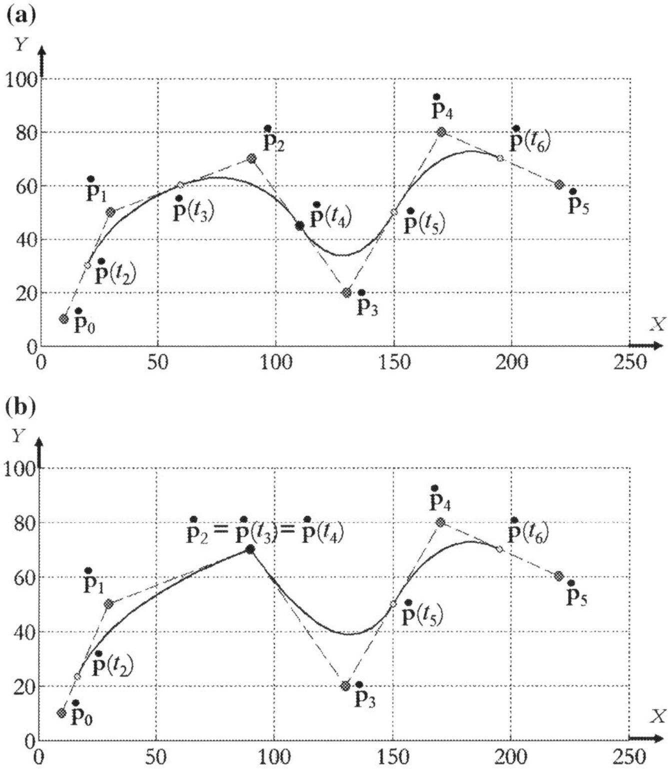


**Fig. 6.22** A quadratic B-spline curve generated using the control points $\dot{\mathbf{p}}_0 = [10, 10]^T$, $\dot{\mathbf{p}}_1 = [30, 50]^T$, $\dot{\mathbf{p}}_2 = [90, 70]^T$, $\dot{\mathbf{p}}_3 = [130, 20]^T$, $\dot{\mathbf{p}}_4 = [170, 80]^T$ and $\dot{\mathbf{p}}_5 = [220, 60]^T$. **a** The knot vector [0, 1, 2, 3, 4, 5, 6, 7, 8]. The curve point at $t = 4$ is marked. **b** The knot vector [0, 1, 2, 4, 4, 5, 6, 7, 8]. The curve point at $t = 4$ is marked

curve at points with multiplicity that is equal to the degree of the curve, which is 2 in our case. (Multiplicity of $p + 1$ at the ends of the knot vector forces the curve to coincide with start and end control points, which is the case with open uniform knot vectors.) Moreover, the continuity in the current case is expressed using Eq. (6.76) as

$$\begin{aligned} Continuity &= order - (multiplicity + 1) \\ &= 3 - (2 + 1) = 0. \end{aligned}$$

Thus, the curve is $C^0$ continuous. Compare it with the previous case when multiplicity was 1. (Recall that increasing the multiplicity of a knot decreases the continuity of the curve at that knot.)

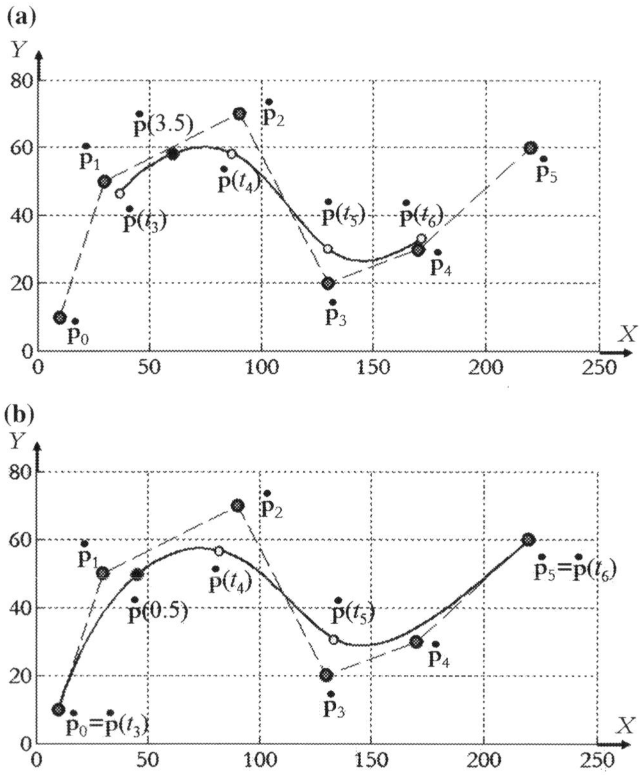


**Fig. 6.23** A cubic B-spline curve generated using the control points $\dot{\mathbf{p}}_0 = [10, 10]^T$, $\dot{\mathbf{p}}_1 = [30, 50]^T$, $\dot{\mathbf{p}}_2 = [90, 70]^T$, $\dot{\mathbf{p}}_3 = [130, 20]^T$, $\dot{\mathbf{p}}_4 = [170, 30]^T$ and $\dot{\mathbf{p}}_5 = [220, 60]^T$. **a** The uniform knot vector [0, 1, 2, 3, 4, 5, 6, 7, 8, 9] is used. The curve point at $t = 3.5$ is marked. **b** The open uniform knot vector [0, 0, 0, 0, 1, 2, 3, 3, 3, 3] is used. The curve point at $t = 0.5$ is marked

#### 6.2.2.5 Cubic B-Splines

As done with quadratic B-splines, we may apply the basis functions with control points through Eq. (6.70) to get points on cubic B-spline curves.

**Example 6.31:** [*B-spline curves—points on cubic curves using uniform knot vector*]
A cubic B-spline curve is to be generated using the control points $\dot{\mathbf{p}}_0 = [10, 10]^T$, $\dot{\mathbf{p}}_1 = [30, 50]^T$, $\dot{\mathbf{p}}_2 = [90, 70]^T$, $\dot{\mathbf{p}}_3 = [130, 20]^T$, $\dot{\mathbf{p}}_4 = [170, 30]^T$ and $\dot{\mathbf{p}}_5 = [220, 60]^T$ and the uniform knot vector [0, 1, 2, 3, 4, 5, 6, 7, 8, 9]. Determine the location of the curve point at $t = 3.5$.

**Solution 6.31:** The curve is shown in Fig. 6.23a where $\dot{\mathbf{p}}(3.5) = [60.4167, 58.1250]^T$ is marked. Notice that the uniform knot vector used *does not* interpolate the start and end control points. The steps of the solution are left as an exercise. □

**Table 6.4** Cubic curve segments and their associated control points

| Segment | Control points | Domain |
|---|---|---|
| $\mathscr{S}_3$ | $\dot{\mathbf{p}}_0, \dot{\mathbf{p}}_1, \dot{\mathbf{p}}_2, \dot{\mathbf{p}}_3$ | $t_3 \leq t < t_4$ |
| $\mathscr{S}_4$ | $\dot{\mathbf{p}}_1, \dot{\mathbf{p}}_2, \dot{\mathbf{p}}_3, \dot{\mathbf{p}}_4$ | $t_4 \leq t < t_5$ |
| $\vdots$ | $\vdots$ | $\vdots$ |
| $\mathscr{S}_n$ | $\dot{\mathbf{p}}_{n-3}, \dot{\mathbf{p}}_{n-2}, \dot{\mathbf{p}}_{n-1}, \dot{\mathbf{p}}_n$ | $t_n \leq t < t_{n+1}$ |

Note that in cubic B-splines, $n$ must be greater than or equal to 3. Also, note that $t$ has a value of $t_4$ at the knot between $\mathscr{S}_3$ and $\mathscr{S}_4$ and has a value of $t_5$ at the knot between $\mathscr{S}_4$ and $\mathscr{S}_5$, etc.

**Example 6.32:** [*B-spline curves—points on cubic curves using open uniform knot vector*]

A cubic B-spline curve is to be generated using the control points $\dot{\mathbf{p}}_0 = [10, 10]^T$, $\dot{\mathbf{p}}_1 = [30, 50]^T$, $\dot{\mathbf{p}}_2 = [90, 70]^T$, $\dot{\mathbf{p}}_3 = [130, 20]^T$, $\dot{\mathbf{p}}_4 = [170, 30]^T$ and $\dot{\mathbf{p}}_5 = [220, 60]^T$ and the open uniform knot vector $[0, 0, 0, 0, 1, 2, 3, 3, 3, 3]$. Determine the location of the curve point at $t = 0.5$.

**Solution 6.32:** The curve is shown in Fig. 6.23b where $\dot{\mathbf{p}}(3.5)=[45.2083, 49.5833]^T$ is marked. Notice that the open uniform knot vector used *does* interpolate the start and end control points. The steps of the solution are left as an exercise. □

**Cubic B-Spline Curve Segments:** Consider the control points $\dot{\mathbf{p}}_0, \dot{\mathbf{p}}_1, \ldots, \dot{\mathbf{p}}_n$. Those points can approximate a cubic B-spline curve that consists of a sequence of $n - 2$ (where $n \geq 3$) cubic curve segments defined as listed in Table 6.4. The parameter $t$ along each curve segment may be defined as $0 \leq t < 1$ or as a part of a sequence of domains bounded by $t_i, t_{i+1}, \ldots$, etc. as listed in the third column of Table 6.4.

Notice that the points at the start and end of each curve segment represent the knots including those at the start and end of the whole curve. As with quadratic B-spline curve segments, a cubic segment is contained in the convex hull (i.e., the quadrilateral) formed by its four control points.

Figure 6.24c shows a cubic B-spline curve that consists of two curve segments shown in Fig. 6.24a, b. The control points $\dot{\mathbf{p}}_0$, $\dot{\mathbf{p}}_1$, $\dot{\mathbf{p}}_2$ and $\dot{\mathbf{p}}_3$ form the first curve segment while the control points $\dot{\mathbf{p}}_1$, $\dot{\mathbf{p}}_2$, $\dot{\mathbf{p}}_3$ and $\dot{\mathbf{p}}_4$ form the second curve segment. The dashed lines represent the control polygon in Fig. 6.24a, c while they represent the convex hull that contains the second segment in Fig. 6.24b. Notice that the second knot of the first segment is the first knot of the second segment as identified.

As each cubic curve segment is controlled by four control points, a control point (except for the first three points and the last three points) affects and contributes to four curve segments. For example, point $\dot{\mathbf{p}}_3$ affects segments $\mathscr{S}_3$, $\mathscr{S}_4$, $\mathscr{S}_5$ and $\mathscr{S}_6$; however, it has no effect on $S_7$, $\mathscr{S}_8$, etc. Hence, the local control property is preserved as with the case of quadratic B-spline curves.

**Basis Matrix:** In matrix form, a cubic B-spline segment spanning within [0,1] and generated by $\dot{\mathbf{p}}_0$, $\dot{\mathbf{p}}_1$, $\dot{\mathbf{p}}_2$ and $\dot{\mathbf{p}}_3$ is defined as

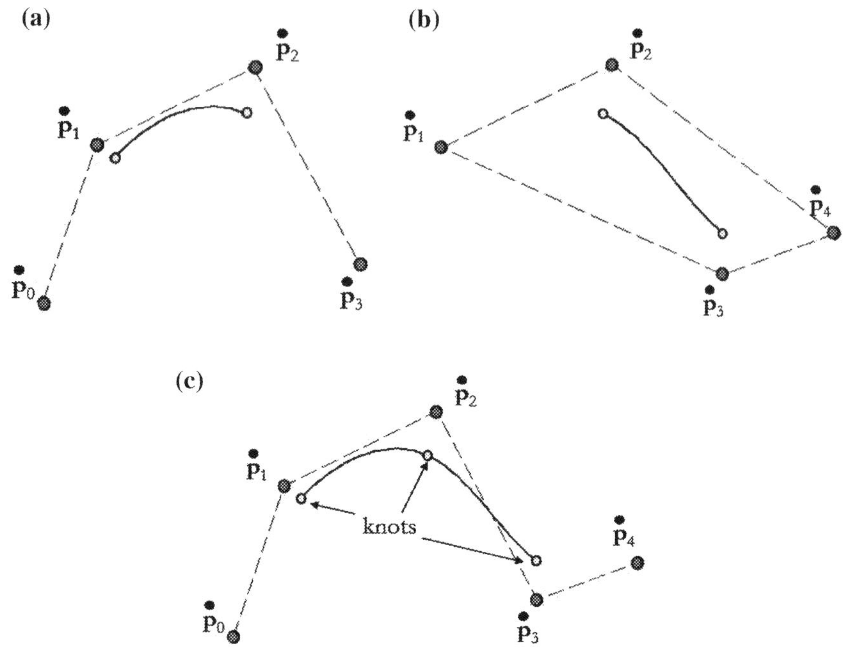


**Fig. 6.24** Cubic B-spline curve segments. **a** The control points $\dot{\mathbf{p}}_0$, $\dot{\mathbf{p}}_1$, $\dot{\mathbf{p}}_2$ and $\dot{\mathbf{p}}_3$ form the first cubic curve segment. The dashed lines represent the control polygon. The knots are indicated. **b** The control points $\dot{\mathbf{p}}_1$, $\dot{\mathbf{p}}_2$, $\dot{\mathbf{p}}_3$ and $\dot{\mathbf{p}}_4$ form the second cubic curve segment. The dashed lines represent the convex hull inside which the curve segment resides. The knots are indicated. **c** The control points $\dot{\mathbf{p}}_0$, $\dot{\mathbf{p}}_1$, $\dot{\mathbf{p}}_2$, $\dot{\mathbf{p}}_3$ and $\dot{\mathbf{p}}_4$ form a cubic B-spline curve consisting of two segments. All knots are indicated

$$\dot{\mathbf{p}}(t) = \underbrace{\frac{1}{6}\begin{bmatrix} t^3 & t^2 & t & 1 \end{bmatrix}\begin{bmatrix} -1 & 3 & -3 & 1 \\ 3 & -6 & 3 & 0 \\ -3 & 0 & 3 & 0 \\ 1 & 4 & 1 & 0 \end{bmatrix}}_{sum=1}\begin{bmatrix} \dot{\mathbf{p}}_0 \\ \dot{\mathbf{p}}_1 \\ \dot{\mathbf{p}}_2 \\ \dot{\mathbf{p}}_3 \end{bmatrix}, \tag{6.99}$$

where $\frac{1}{6}\begin{bmatrix} -1 & 3 & -3 & 1 \\ 3 & -6 & 3 & 0 \\ -3 & 0 & 3 & 0 \\ 1 & 4 & 1 & 0 \end{bmatrix}$ is called the cubic B-spline basis matrix. Notice that the elements of the vector $\frac{1}{6}\begin{bmatrix} t^3 & t^2 & t & 1 \end{bmatrix}\begin{bmatrix} -1 & 3 & -3 & 1 \\ 3 & -6 & 3 & 0 \\ -3 & 0 & 3 & 0 \\ 1 & 4 & 1 & 0 \end{bmatrix}$ sum to 1. Alternatively, Eq. (6.99) can be re-written as

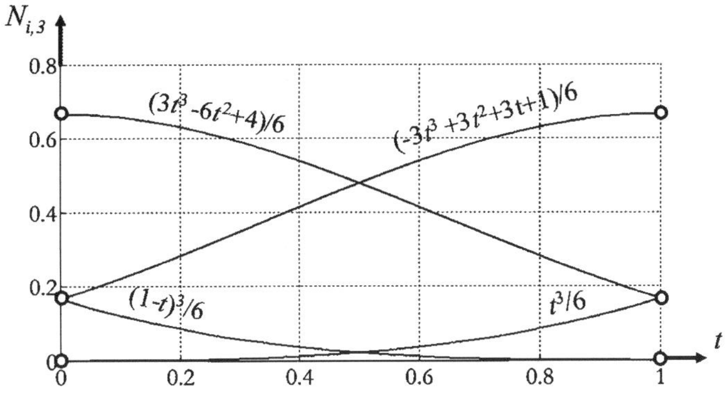


**Fig. 6.25** The basis functions for B-splines of degree 3

$$\dot{\mathbf{p}}(t) = \frac{1}{6}\left[(1-t)^3\dot{\mathbf{p}}_0 + (3t^3 - 6t^2 + 4)\dot{\mathbf{p}}_1 + (-3t^3 + 3t^2 + 3t + 1)\dot{\mathbf{p}}_2 + t^3\dot{\mathbf{p}}_3\right]. \tag{6.100}$$

Notice that

$$\frac{1}{6}\left[t^3\ t^2\ t\ 1\right]\begin{bmatrix} -1 & 3 & -3 & 1 \\ 3 & -6 & 3 & 0 \\ -3 & 0 & 3 & 0 \\ 1 & 4 & 1 & 0 \end{bmatrix} = \frac{1}{6}\begin{bmatrix} (1-t)^3 \\ 3t^3 - 6t^2 + 4 \\ -3t^3 + 3t^2 + 3t + 1 \\ t^3 \end{bmatrix}^T \tag{6.101}$$

represent functions that shape the cubic B-spline curve (Bartels et al. 1987). The polynomials are shown in Fig. 6.25. Equation (6.99) assumes that the lower bound of the $t$ interval is 0. Since the basis functions for each curve segment are the same and assuming a uniform knot vector, if the $t$ interval starts at $t_i$, Eq. (6.99) may be adjusted to

$$\dot{\mathbf{p}}(t) = \frac{1}{6}\left[(t-t_i)^3\ (t-t_i)^2\ (t-t_i)\ 1\right]\begin{bmatrix} -1 & 3 & -3 & 1 \\ 3 & -6 & 3 & 0 \\ -3 & 0 & 3 & 0 \\ 1 & 4 & 1 & 0 \end{bmatrix}\begin{bmatrix} \dot{\mathbf{p}}_{i-3} \\ \dot{\mathbf{p}}_{i-2} \\ \dot{\mathbf{p}}_{i-1} \\ \dot{\mathbf{p}}_i \end{bmatrix} \tag{6.102}$$

or

$$\begin{aligned} \dot{\mathbf{p}}(t) = \frac{1}{6}\big[&(1-(t-t_i))^3\dot{\mathbf{p}}_{i-3} + (3(t-t_i)^3 - 6(t-t_i)^2 + 4)\dot{\mathbf{p}}_{i-2} \\ &+ (-3(t-t_i)^3 + 3(t-t_i)^2 + 3(t-t_i) + 1)\dot{\mathbf{p}}_{i-1} + (t-t_i)^3\dot{\mathbf{p}}_i\big]. \end{aligned} \tag{6.103}$$

**Example 6.33:** [*B-spline curves—knots on cubic curves using uniform knot vector*]
A cubic B-spline curve is to be generated using the control points $\dot{\mathbf{p}}_0 = [10, 10]^T$, $\dot{\mathbf{p}}_1 = [30, 50]^T$, $\dot{\mathbf{p}}_2 = [90, 70]^T$, $\dot{\mathbf{p}}_3 = [130, 20]^T$, $\dot{\mathbf{p}}_4 = [170, 30]^T$ and

$\dot{\mathbf{p}}_5 = [220, 60]^T$ and the uniform knot vector [0, 1, 2, 3, 4, 5, 6, 7, 8, 9]. How many curve segments are generated? What are the locations of the knot points?

**Solution 6.33:** We will work with individual curve segments and their associated control points. A cubic B-spline segment is generated using four control points. Hence, three segments are generated; $\mathscr{S}_3$ using $\dot{\mathbf{p}}_0$, $\dot{\mathbf{p}}_1$, $\dot{\mathbf{p}}_2$ and $\dot{\mathbf{p}}_3$, $\mathscr{S}_4$ using $\dot{\mathbf{p}}_1$, $\dot{\mathbf{p}}_2$, $\dot{\mathbf{p}}_3$ and $\dot{\mathbf{p}}_4$ and $\mathscr{S}_5$ using $\dot{\mathbf{p}}_2$, $\dot{\mathbf{p}}_3$, $\dot{\mathbf{p}}_4$ and $\dot{\mathbf{p}}_5$.

The knot at $t_3$ is obtained when substituting $t = t_i = 3$ in Eq. (6.103) with points $\dot{\mathbf{p}}_0$, $\dot{\mathbf{p}}_1$, $\dot{\mathbf{p}}_2$ and $\dot{\mathbf{p}}_3$. Thus,

$$\begin{aligned}
\dot{\mathbf{p}}(t) &= \frac{1}{6}\Big[(1-(t-t_i))^3\dot{\mathbf{p}}_0 + (3(t-t_i)^3 - 6(t-t_i)^2 + 4)\dot{\mathbf{p}}_1 \\
&\quad + (-3(t-t_i)^3 + 3(t-t_i)^2 + 3(t-t_i) + 1)\dot{\mathbf{p}}_2 + (t-t_i)^3\dot{\mathbf{p}}_3\Big] \\
\dot{\mathbf{p}}(3) &= \frac{1}{6}\left[(1-0)^3\begin{bmatrix}10\\10\end{bmatrix} + (3\times 0^3 - 6\times 0^2 + 4)\begin{bmatrix}30\\50\end{bmatrix}\right. \\
&\quad \left. + (-3\times 0^3 + 3\times 0^2 + 3\times 0 + 1)\begin{bmatrix}90\\70\end{bmatrix} + 0^3\begin{bmatrix}130\\20\end{bmatrix}\right] \\
&= \begin{bmatrix}36.6667\\46.6667\end{bmatrix}.
\end{aligned}$$

The knot at $t_4$ is obtained when substituting $t = 4$ and $t_i = 3$ in the same equation with the same points. So,

$$\begin{aligned}
\dot{\mathbf{p}}(4) &= \frac{1}{6}\left[(1-1)^3\begin{bmatrix}10\\10\end{bmatrix} + (3\times 1^3 - 6\times 1^2 + 4)\begin{bmatrix}30\\50\end{bmatrix}\right. \\
&\quad \left. + (-3\times 1^3 + 3\times 1^2 + 3\times 1 + 1)\begin{bmatrix}90\\70\end{bmatrix} + 1^3\begin{bmatrix}130\\20\end{bmatrix}\right] \\
&= \begin{bmatrix}86.6667\\58.3333\end{bmatrix}.
\end{aligned}$$

Alternatively, the previous knot may be obtained when substituting $t = 4$ and $t_i = 4$ in the same equation with points $\dot{\mathbf{p}}_1$, $\dot{\mathbf{p}}_2$, $\dot{\mathbf{p}}_3$ and $\dot{\mathbf{p}}_4$. Thus,

$$\begin{aligned}
\dot{\mathbf{p}}(4) &= \frac{1}{6}\left[(1-0)^3\begin{bmatrix}30\\50\end{bmatrix} + (3\times 0^3 - 6\times 0^2 + 4)\begin{bmatrix}90\\70\end{bmatrix}\right. \\
&\quad \left. + (-3\times 0^3 + 3\times 0^2 + 3\times 0 + 1)\begin{bmatrix}130\\20\end{bmatrix} + 0^3\begin{bmatrix}170\\30\end{bmatrix}\right] \\
&= \begin{bmatrix}86.6667\\58.3333\end{bmatrix}.
\end{aligned}$$

The knot at $t_5$ is obtained when substituting $t = 5$ and $t_i = 4$ in the same equation with points $\dot{\mathbf{p}}_1$, $\dot{\mathbf{p}}_2$, $\dot{\mathbf{p}}_3$ and $\dot{\mathbf{p}}_4$. So,

$$\begin{aligned}\dot{\mathbf{p}}(5) &= \frac{1}{6}\left[(1-1)^3\begin{bmatrix}30\\50\end{bmatrix} + (3\times 1^3 - 6\times 1^2 + 4)\begin{bmatrix}90\\70\end{bmatrix}\right.\\ &\quad \left. + (-3\times 1^3 + 3\times 1^2 + 3\times 1 + 1)\begin{bmatrix}130\\20\end{bmatrix} + 1^3\begin{bmatrix}170\\30\end{bmatrix}\right]\\ &= \begin{bmatrix}130\\30\end{bmatrix}.\end{aligned}$$

The same location should be obtained when substituting $t = 5$ and $t_i = 5$ in the same equation with points $\dot{\mathbf{p}}_2$, $\dot{\mathbf{p}}_3$, $\dot{\mathbf{p}}_4$ and $\dot{\mathbf{p}}_5$. The knot at $t_6$ is estimated when substituting $t = 6$ and $t_i = 5$ in the same equation with points $\dot{\mathbf{p}}_2$, $\dot{\mathbf{p}}_3$, $\dot{\mathbf{p}}_4$ and $\dot{\mathbf{p}}_5$. Hence,

$$\begin{aligned}\dot{\mathbf{p}}(6) &= \frac{1}{6}\left[(1-1)^3\begin{bmatrix}90\\70\end{bmatrix} + (3\times 1^3 - 6\times 1^2 + 4)\begin{bmatrix}130\\20\end{bmatrix}\right.\\ &\quad \left. + (-3\times 1^3 + 3\times 1^2 + 3\times 1 + 1)\begin{bmatrix}170\\30\end{bmatrix} + 1^3\begin{bmatrix}220\\60\end{bmatrix}\right]\\ &= \begin{bmatrix}171.6667\\33.3333\end{bmatrix}.\end{aligned}$$

The curve as well as the control points and the knots were previously shown in Fig. 6.23a. □

**Example 6.34:** [*B-spline curves—effect of moving control points on cubic curves*]
In Example 6.33, if the control point $\dot{\mathbf{p}}_4$ is moved vertically to $[170, 80]^T$, what effect should we expect on the knots in this case?

**Solution 6.34:** The control point $\dot{\mathbf{p}}_4$ contributes to the second and third segments; $\mathscr{S}_4$ and $\mathscr{S}_5$. Hence, complying with the local control property, we should expect that only the knots at $t_5$ and $t_6$ be changed. Continuing as previously done, the knots will get the values listed in the following table:

| Knot | Before | After |
|---|---|---|
| $t_3$ | $[36.6667, 46.6667]^T$ | $[36.6667, 46.6667]^T$ |
| $t_4$ | $[86.6667, 58.3333]^T$ | $[86.6667, 58.3333]^T$ |
| $t_5$ | $[130, 30]^T$ | $[130, 38.3333]^T$ |
| $t_6$ | $[171.6667, 33.3333]^T$ | $[171.6667, 66.6667]^T$ |

The curve as well as the control points and the knots are shown in Fig. 6.26. □

### 6.2.3 NURBS Curves

Both Bézier and B-spline curves are polynomial parametric curves, which cannot represent some simple curves such as circles. The more powerful rational curves

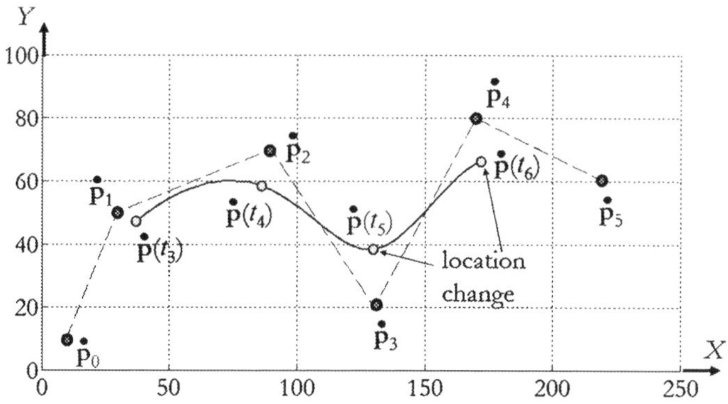


**Fig. 6.26** A cubic B-spline curve is generated using the control points $\dot{\mathbf{p}}_0 = [10, 10]^T$, $\dot{\mathbf{p}}_1 = [30, 50]^T$, $\dot{\mathbf{p}}_2 = [90, 70]^T$, $\dot{\mathbf{p}}_3 = [130, 20]^T$, $\dot{\mathbf{p}}_4 = [170, 80]^T$ and $\dot{\mathbf{p}}_5 = [220, 60]^T$. Compare the positions of the knots bounding the last segment (i.e. $t_5$ and $t_6$) with those of Example 6.33

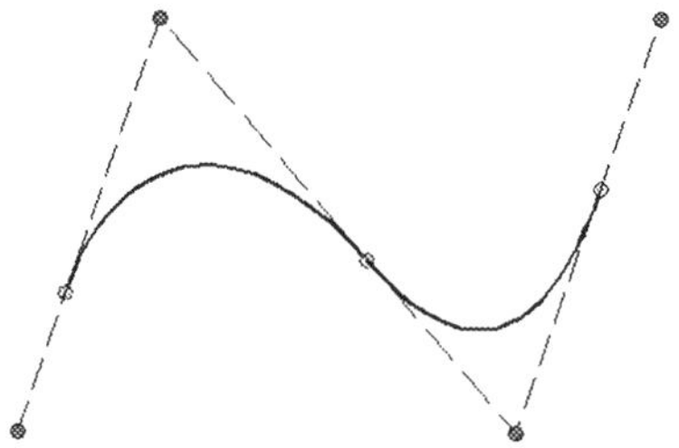

**Fig. 6.27** A quadratic NURBS curve. Lines between consecutive control points form the control hull or control polygon

use homogeneous coordinates (see Appendix B.7) by adding one dimension. *Rational Bézier* curves and *NURBS* (Forrest 1980) are the generalization of Bézier and B-spline curves respectively.

NURBS is an abbreviation for *non-uniform rational B-splines*. NU or *non-uniform* implies that the knots may be placed at non-equal intervals. R or *rational* refers to the underlying mathematical representation. BS or B-splines refer to piecewise polynomial curves. An example of NURBS curve is shown in Fig. 6.27. Lines between consecutive control points form the control hull or control polygon.

Unlike non-rational B-spline curves discussed previously, NURBS curves have the power of producing the correct result even under projective transformation. (Non-rational B-spline curves give the correct result under affine transformation only.)

A 2D control point may be represented in homogeneous coordinates as $\mathbf{p}_i = [xw_i, yw_i, w_i]^T$; hence, a 2D NURBS curve point is defined as

$$\mathbf{p}(t) = \begin{bmatrix} x(t) \\ y(t) \\ w(t) \end{bmatrix} = \sum_{i=0}^{n} \mathbf{p}_i N_{i,p}(t), \tag{6.104}$$

where $\mathbf{p}(t)$ is the curve point; $\mathbf{p}_i$ is the control point $i$ such that $i \in \{0, 1, \ldots, n\}$; and $N_{i,p}(t)$ is the $i$th basis function of degree $p$ as estimated in Eq. (6.77). The only difference between Eqs. (6.104) and (6.70) is that the curve point $\mathbf{p}(t)$ as well as the control point $\mathbf{p}_i$ are homogeneous points. Equation (6.104) may be re-written as

$$\begin{aligned} x(t) &= \sum_{i=0}^{n} x_i N_{i,p}(t) w_i, \\ y(t) &= \sum_{i=0}^{n} y_i N_{i,p}(t) w_i, \\ w(t) &= \sum_{i=0}^{n} N_{i,p}(t) w_i. \end{aligned} \tag{6.105}$$

To obtain the curve point in inhomogeneous coordinates, we divide by $w(t)$. Hence, point $\dot{\mathbf{p}}(t)$ is expressed as

$$\dot{\mathbf{p}}(t) = \begin{bmatrix} \frac{x(t)}{w(t)} \\ \frac{y(t)}{w(t)} \end{bmatrix}. \tag{6.106}$$

These steps can written in a single equation to estimate a NURBS curve point $\dot{\mathbf{p}}$ at parameter $t$ as (Rogers 2000; Piegl and Tiller 1997)

$$\dot{\mathbf{p}}(t) = \frac{\sum_{i=0}^{n} \dot{\mathbf{p}}_i N_{i,p}(t) w_i}{\sum_{i=0}^{n} N_{i,p}(t) w_i}, \tag{6.107}$$

where $n+1$ is the number of control points; $\dot{\mathbf{p}}_i$ is the control point number $i$; $p$ is the curve degree; $N_{i,p}(t)$ is the $i$th basis function of degree $p$ as estimated in Eq. (6.77); and $w_i$ is the weight of control point $\dot{\mathbf{p}}_i$ (i.e., $w_i$ is the last entry in the homogeneous representation of control point $\mathbf{p}_i$). If we set $w_i = 1$, the denominator becomes 1 and Eq. (6.107) turns to Eq. (6.70), which defines a non-rational B-spline. If $w_i > 1$, the curve is pulled closer to control point $\dot{\mathbf{p}}_i$. On the other hand, if $w_i < 1$, the curve is pushed away from control point $\dot{\mathbf{p}}_i$ while $w_i = 0$ means that control point $\dot{\mathbf{p}}_i$ has no effect on the curve. NURBS curves can also be extended to 3D space by adding the $z$-component to each of the previous equations.

#### 6.2.3.1 The Knot Vector

As in Eq. (6.71), the number of knots is $m+1$ such that

$$m = n + 1 + p,$$

where $n+1$ is the number of control points and $p$ is the curve degree. In other words, we can say that the number of knots (i.e., $m+1$) equals the number of control points (i.e., $n+1$) plus the order (i.e., $p+1$). Different types of knot vectors discussed before may be used. As with B-splines, knot values must be non-decreasing.

#### 6.2.3.2 Quadratic NURBS Curves

In order to estimate a point on a quadratic NURBS curve, Eq. (6.107) can be written as

$$\dot{\mathbf{p}}(t) = \frac{\sum\limits_{i=0}^{n} \dot{\mathbf{p}}_i N_{i,2}(t) w_i}{\sum\limits_{i=0}^{n} N_{i,2}(t) w_i}, \tag{6.108}$$

where $n+1$ is the number of control points such that $n \geq 2$; $\dot{\mathbf{p}}_i$ is the control point number $i$; $N_{i,2}$ is the $i$th basis function of degree 2; and $w_i$ is the weight of control point $\dot{\mathbf{p}}_i$.

**Example 6.35:** [*NURBS curves—points on quadratic curves using different knot vectors*]

A quadratic NURBS curve has its control points defined at $\dot{\mathbf{p}}_0 = [10, 30]^T$, $\dot{\mathbf{p}}_1 = [30, 50]^T$ and $\dot{\mathbf{p}}_2 = [80, 30]^T$.

1. If the uniform knot vector used is [0, 1, 2, 3, 4, 5] and $w_0 = w_1 = w_2 = 1$, determine the location of $\dot{\mathbf{p}}(2.5)$ as well as the locations of the knots. Repeat the calculations if $w_1$ is changed to 0.2, 1.8 and 0.
2. If the open uniform knot vector used is [0, 0, 0, 2, 2, 2] and $w_0 = w_1 = w_2 = 1$, determine the location of $\dot{\mathbf{p}}(1)$ as well as the locations of the knots. Repeat the calculations if $w_1$ is changed to 0.2, 1.8 and 0.
3. If the non-uniform knot vector used is [0, 1, 2, 4, 5, 7] and $w_0 = w_1 = w_2 = 1$, determine the location of $\dot{\mathbf{p}}(3)$ as well as the locations of the knots. Repeat the calculations if $w_1$ is changed to 0.2, 1.8 and 0.

Show the curve in each of these cases.

**Solution 6.35: Using the uniform knot vector [0, 1, 2, 3, 4, 5]:** To obtain a point on a quadratic NURBS curve, we may use Eq. (6.108) where

$$\dot{\mathbf{p}}(t) = \frac{\sum\limits_{i=0}^{n} \dot{\mathbf{p}}_i N_{i,2}(t) w_i}{\sum\limits_{i=0}^{n} N_{i,2}(t) w_i}.$$

Alternatively and similar to Eq. (6.98) when $t_i \leq t < t_{i+1}$ and $t_i = 2$ (or Table 6.1 when $t \in [2, 3)$), $\dot{\mathbf{p}}(t)$ is expressed as

$$\dot{\mathbf{p}}(t) = \begin{bmatrix} \dfrac{0.5[(1-(t-t_i))^2 x_{i-2}w_{i-2}+(-2(t-t_i)^2+2(t-t_i)+1)x_{i-1}w_{i-1}+(t-t_i)^2 x_i w_i]}{0.5[(1-(t-t_i))^2 w_{i-2}+(-2(t-t_i)^2+2(t-t_i)+1)w_{i-1}+(t-t_i)^2 w_i]} \\ \dfrac{0.5[(1-(t-t_i))^2 y_{i-2}w_{i-2}+(-2(t-t_i)^2+2(t-t_i)+1)y_{i-1}w_{i-1}+(t-t_i)^2 y_i w_i]}{0.5[(1-(t-t_i))^2 w_{i-2}+(-2(t-t_i)^2+2(t-t_i)+1)w_{i-1}+(t-t_i)^2 w_i]} \end{bmatrix}. \tag{6.109}$$

In our case, $t = 2.5$ and $t_i = 2$. Thus, a NURBS point $\dot{\mathbf{p}}(2.5)$ is computed as

$$\dot{\mathbf{p}}(2.5) = \begin{bmatrix} \dfrac{0.5[(1-0.5)^2 \times 10 + (-2 \times 0.5^2 + 2 \times 0.5 + 1) \times 30 + 0.5^2 \times 80]}{0.5[(1-0.5)^2 + (-2 \times 0.5^2 + 2 \times 0.5 + 1) + 0.5^2]} \\ \dfrac{0.5[(1-0.5)^2 \times 30 + (-2 \times 0.5^2 + 2 \times 0.5 + 1) \times 50 + 0.5^2 \times 30]}{0.5[(1-0.5)^2 + (-2 \times 0.5^2 + 2 \times 0.5 + 1) + 0.5^2]} \end{bmatrix}$$

$$= \begin{bmatrix} 33.75 \\ 45 \end{bmatrix}.$$

Similarly, the curve points can be computed at knots (i.e., when $t = t_2 = 2$ and $t = t_3 = 3$). Also, the curve points can be computed when $w_1$ is changed to 0.2, 1.8 and 0. The values are listed in the following table:

| $w_0$ | $w_1$ | $w_2$ | $\dot{\mathbf{p}}(2.5)$ | $\dot{\mathbf{p}}(2)$ | $\dot{\mathbf{p}}(3)$ |
|---|---|---|---|---|---|
| 1 | 1 | 1 | $[33.75, 45]^T$ | $[20, 40]^T$ | $[55, 40]^T$ |
| 1 | 0.2 | 1 | $[39.375, 37.5]^T$ | $[13.3333, 33.3333]^T$ | $[71.6667, 33.3333]^T$ |
| 1 | 1.8 | 1 | $[32.3438, 46.8750]^T$ | $[22.8571, 42.8571]^T$ | $[47.8571, 42.8571]^T$ |
| 1 | 0 | 1 | $[45, 30]^T$ | $[10, 30]^T$ | $[80, 30]^T$ |

The curves are shown in Fig. 6.28. Notice that in case of $w_1 = 0$, $\dot{\mathbf{p}}_1$ contributes nothing to the calculation. In other words, it is excluded from calculation, which results in a straight line connecting the remaining two points.

**Using the open uniform knot vector [0, 0, 0, 2, 2, 2]:** We may utilize Eq. (6.108) with different $w_i$ values. The next table lists the values obtained.

| $w_0$ | $w_1$ | $w_2$ | $\dot{\mathbf{p}}(1)$ | $\dot{\mathbf{p}}(0)$ | $\dot{\mathbf{p}}(2)$ |
|---|---|---|---|---|---|
| 1 | 1 | 1 | $[37.5, 40]^T$ | $[10, 30]^T$ | $[80, 30]^T$ |
| 1 | 0.2 | 1 | $[42.5, 33.3333]^T$ | $[10, 30]^T$ | $[80, 30]^T$ |
| 1 | 1.8 | 1 | $[35.3571, 42.8571]^T$ | $[10, 30]^T$ | $[80, 30]^T$ |
| 1 | 0 | 1 | $[45, 30]^T$ | $[10, 30]^T$ | $[80, 30]^T$ |

The steps of the solution are left as an exercise. The curves are shown in Fig. 6.29. Notice that in all these cases $\dot{\mathbf{p}}(0) = [10, 30]^T$ and $\dot{\mathbf{p}}(2) = [80, 30]^T$ (i.e., the curve interpolates the start and end control points). The reason is using the open uniform knot vector regardless of the values of $w_i$. Try other $w_i$ values yourself.

**Using the non-uniform knot vector [0, 1, 2, 4, 5, 7]:** As done before, we may utilize Eq. (6.108) with different $w_i$ values. The next table lists the values obtained.

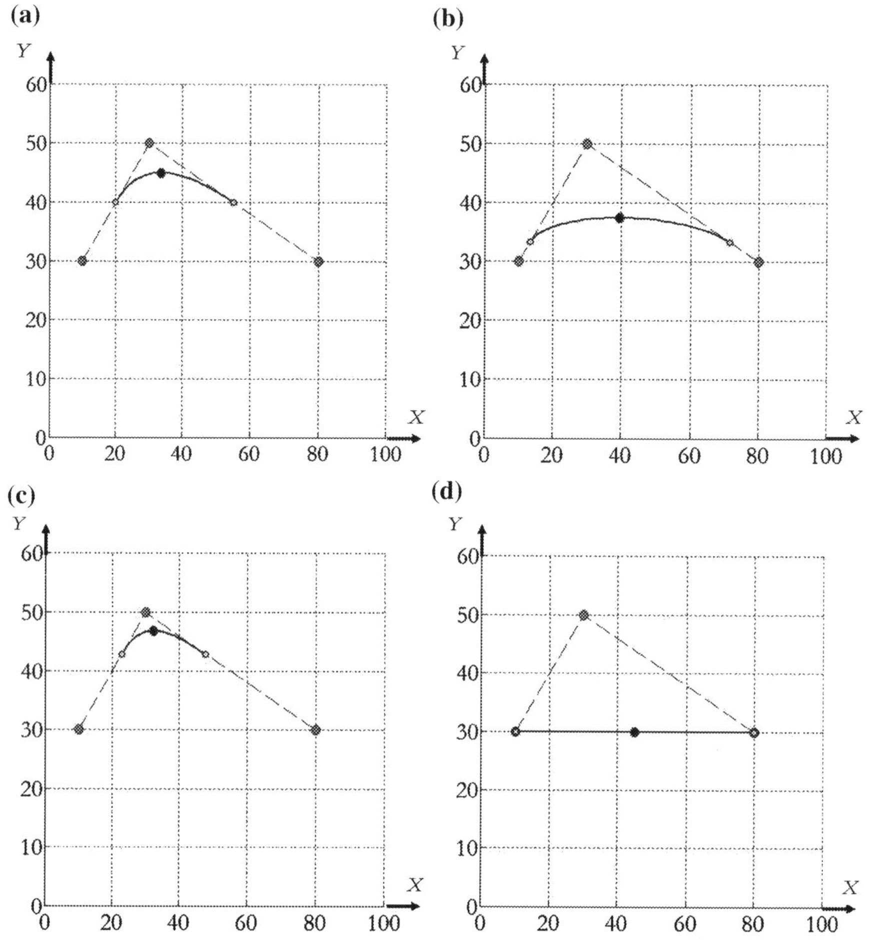


**Fig. 6.28** A quadratic NURBS curve where $w_0 = w_2 = 1$. **a** $w_1 = 1$. **b** $w_1 = 0.2$. **c** $w_1 = 1.8$. **d** $w_1 = 0$. All the cases use the uniform knot vector [0, 1, 2, 3, 4, 5]

| $w_0$ | $w_1$ | $w_2$ | $\dot{\mathbf{p}}(3)$ | $\dot{\mathbf{p}}(2)$ | $\dot{\mathbf{p}}(4)$ |
|---|---|---|---|---|---|
| 1 | 1 | 1 | $[35, 43.3333]^T$ | $[16.6667, 36.6667]^T$ | $[63.3333, 36.6667]^T$ |
| 1 | 0.2 | 1 | $[40.7143, 35.7143]^T$ | $[11.8182, 31.8182]^T$ | $[75.4545, 31.8182]^T$ |
| 1 | 1.8 | 1 | $[33.2609, 45.6522]^T$ | $[19.4737, 39.4737]^T$ | $[56.3158, 39.4737]^T$ |
| 1 | 0 | 1 | $[45, 30]^T$ | $[10, 30]^T$ | $[80, 30]^T$ |

The steps of the solution are left as an exercise. The curves are shown in Fig. 6.30.
□

**Example 6.36:** [*NURBS curves—changing homogeneous weights for quadratic curves using different knot vectors*]

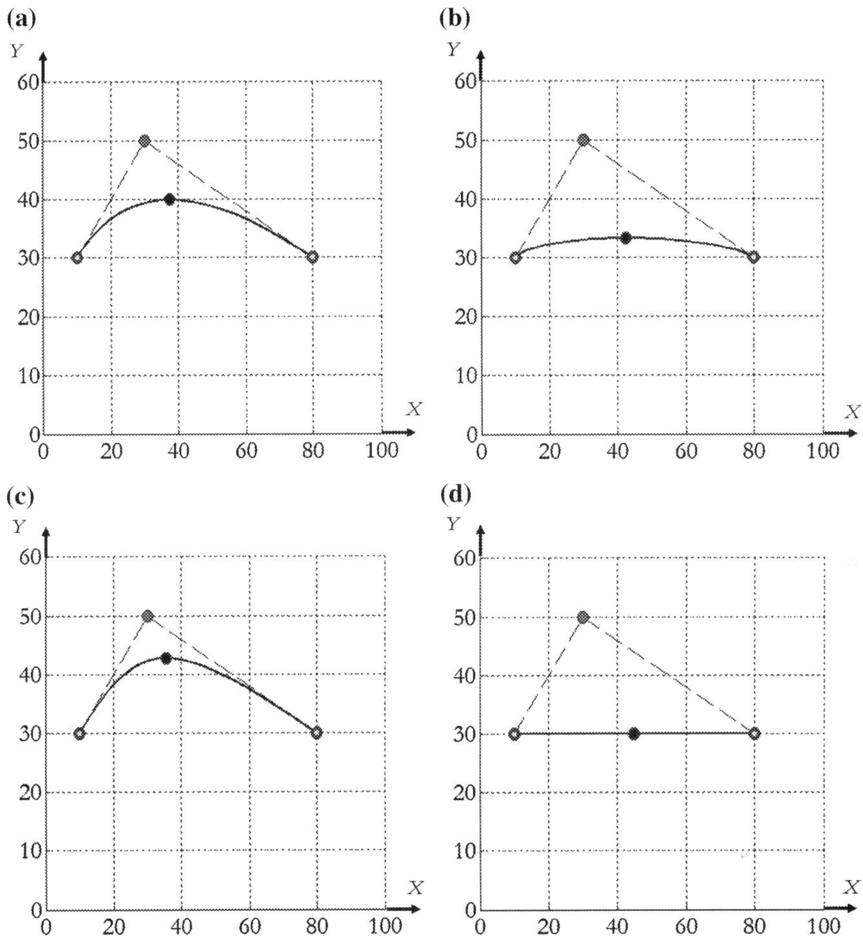


**Fig. 6.29** A quadratic NURBS curve where $w_0 = w_2 = 1$. **a** $w_1 = 1$. **b** $w_1 = 0.2$. **c** $w_1 = 1.8$. **d** $w_1 = 0$. All the cases use the open uniform knot vector [0, 0, 0, 2, 2, 2]

For the curve of Example 6.35, solve the following:

1. If the uniform knot vector used is [0, 1, 2, 3, 4, 5] and $w_0 = w_1 = w_2 = 0.2$, determine the location of $\dot{\mathbf{p}}(2.5)$ as well as the locations of the knots. Repeat the solution when $w_0 = w_1 = w_2 = 1.8$ and $w_0 = w_1 = w_2 = 0$.
2. If the open uniform knot vector used is [0, 0, 0, 2, 2, 2] and $w_0 = w_1 = w_2 = 1.8$, determine the location of $\dot{\mathbf{p}}(1)$ as well as the locations of the knots. Repeat the solution when $w_0 = w_1 = w_2 = 1.8$ and $w_0 = w_1 = w_2 = 0$.
3. If the non-uniform knot vector used is [0, 1, 2, 4, 5, 7] and $w_0 = w_1 = w_2 = 0$, determine the location of $\dot{\mathbf{p}}(3)$ as well as the locations of the knots. Repeat the solution when $w_0 = w_1 = w_2 = 1.8$ and $w_0 = w_1 = w_2 = 0$.

What are the differences if any?

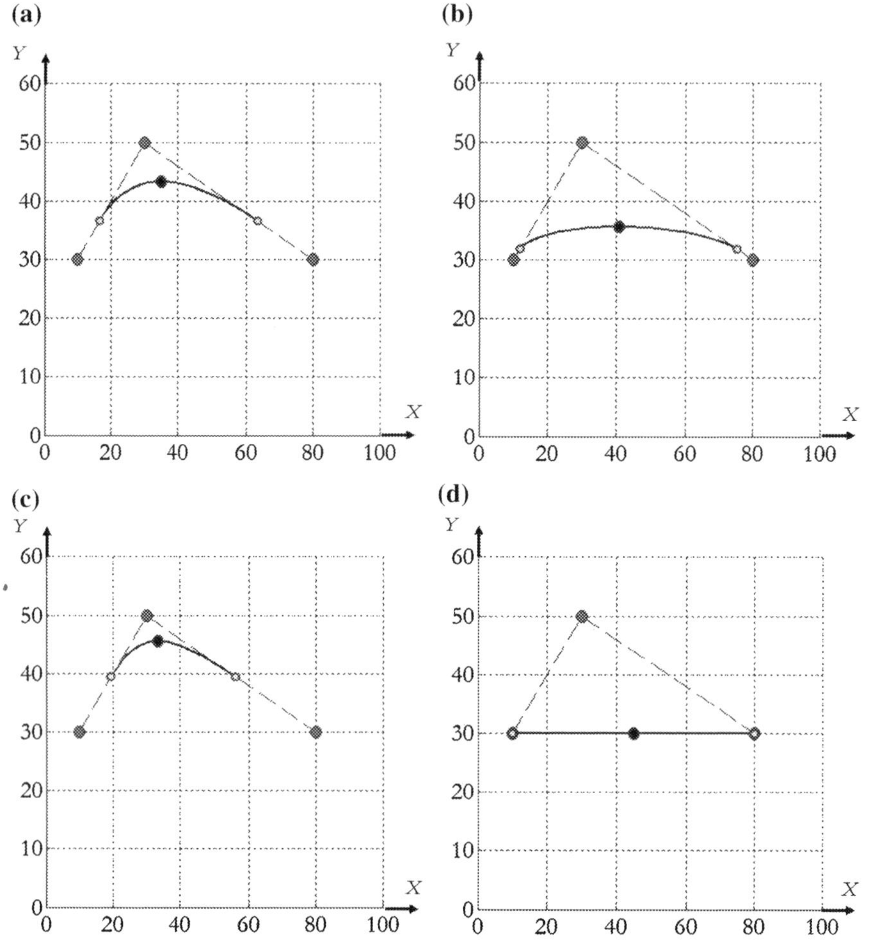


**Fig. 6.30** A quadratic NURBS curve where $w_0 = w_2 = 1$. **a** $w_1 = 1$. **b** $w_1 = 0.2$. **c** $w_1 = 1.8$. **d** $w_1 = 0$. All the cases use the non-uniform knot vector [0, 1, 2, 4, 5, 7]

**Solution 6.36:** We will use Eq. (6.109) when $w_i \in \{1, 0.2, 1.8, 0\}$ such that $i \in \{0, 1, 2\}$.

**Using the uniform knot vector [0, 1, 2, 3, 4, 5]:** The results are listed in the following table:

| $w_0$ | $w_1$ | $w_2$ | $\dot{\mathbf{p}}(2.5)$ | $\dot{\mathbf{p}}(2)$ | $\dot{\mathbf{p}}(3)$ |
|---|---|---|---|---|---|
| 1 | 1 | 1 | $[33.75, 45]^T$ | $[20, 40]^T$ | $[55, 40]^T$ |
| 0.2 | 0.2 | 0.2 | $[33.75, 45]^T$ | $[20, 40]^T$ | $[55, 40]^T$ |
| 1.8 | 1.8 | 1.8 | $[33.75, 45]^T$ | $[20, 40]^T$ | $[55, 40]^T$ |
| 0 | 0 | 0 | Not defined | | |

The first three cases (i.e., when $w_0 = w_1 = w_2 = 1$, $w_0 = w_1 = w_2 = 0.2$ and $w_0 = w_1 = w_2 = 1.8$) are identical to the case shown in Fig. 6.28a. When $w_0 = w_1 = w_2 = 0$, the curve is not defined.

**Using the open uniform knot vector [0, 0, 0, 2, 2, 2]:** The results are listed in the following table:

| $w_0$ | $w_1$ | $w_2$ | $\dot{\mathbf{p}}(1)$ | $\dot{\mathbf{p}}(0)$ | $\dot{\mathbf{p}}(2)$ |
|---|---|---|---|---|---|
| 1 | 1 | 1 | $[37.5, 40]^T$ | $[10, 30]^T$ | $[80, 30]^T$ |
| 0.2 | 0.2 | 0.2 | $[37.5, 40]^T$ | $[10, 30]^T$ | $[80, 30]^T$ |
| 1.8 | 1.8 | 1.8 | $[37.5, 40]^T$ | $[10, 30]^T$ | $[80, 30]^T$ |
| 0 | 0 | 0 | Not defined | | |

The first three cases (i.e., when $w_0 = w_1 = w_2 = 1$, $w_0 = w_1 = w_2 = 0.2$ and $w_0 = w_1 = w_2 = 1.8$) are identical to the case shown in Fig. 6.29a. When $w_0 = w_1 = w_2 = 0$, the curve is not defined.

**Using the non-uniform knot vector [0, 1, 2, 4, 5, 7]:** The results are listed in the following table:

| $w_0$ | $w_1$ | $w_2$ | $\dot{\mathbf{p}}(3)$ | $\dot{\mathbf{p}}(2)$ | $\dot{\mathbf{p}}(4)$ |
|---|---|---|---|---|---|
| 1 | 1 | 1 | $[35, 43.3333]^T$ | $[16.6667, 36.6667]^T$ | $[63.3333, 36.6667]^T$ |
| 0.2 | 0.2 | 0.2 | $[35, 43.3333]^T$ | $[16.6667, 36.6667]^T$ | $[63.3333, 36.6667]^T$ |
| 1.8 | 1.8 | 1.8 | $[35, 43.3333]^T$ | $[16.6667, 36.6667]^T$ | $[63.3333, 36.6667]^T$ |
| 0 | 0 | 0 | Not defined | | |

The first three cases (i.e., when $w_0 = w_1 = w_2 = 1$, $w_0 = w_1 = w_2 = 0.2$ and $w_0 = w_1 = w_2 = 1.8$) are identical to the case shown in Fig. 6.30a. When $w_0 = w_1 = w_2 = 0$, the curve is not defined.

Notice that in all these cases where $w_0 = w_1 = w_2 \neq 0$, Eq. (6.108), or in general Eq. (6.107), can be re-written as

$$\dot{\mathbf{p}}(t) = \frac{\sum\limits_{i=0}^{n} \dot{\mathbf{p}}_i N_{i,p}(t)}{\sum\limits_{i=0}^{n} N_{i,p}(t)}$$

and Eq. (6.109) can be re-written as

$$\dot{\mathbf{p}}(t) = \begin{bmatrix} \dfrac{(1-(t-t_i))^2 x_{i-2} + (-2(t-t_i)^2 + 2(t-t_i) + 1)x_{i-1} + (t-t_i)^2 x_i}{(1-(t-t_i))^2 + (-2(t-t_i)^2 + 2(t-t_i) + 1) + (t-t_i)^2} \\ \dfrac{(1-(t-t_i))^2 y_{i-2} + (-2(t-t_i)^2 + 2(t-t_i) + 1)y_{i-1} + (t-t_i)^2 y_i}{(1-(t-t_i))^2 + (-2(t-t_i)^2 + 2(t-t_i) + 1) + (t-t_i)^2} \end{bmatrix}. \quad \square$$

**Example 6.37:** [*NURBS curves—a circular arc as a quadratic curve segment*]
Given the control points $\dot{\mathbf{p}}_0 = [1, 1]^T$, $\dot{\mathbf{p}}_1 = [3, 4]^T$ and $\dot{\mathbf{p}}_2 = [5, 1]^T$, construct a circular arc passing through $\dot{\mathbf{p}}_0$ and $\dot{\mathbf{p}}_2$ as a quadratic NURBS curve.

**Solution 6.37:** Notice that the control points form an isosceles triangle. To solve this problem, we have to determine:

1. **The knot vector:** In order for a quadratic NURBS curve to pass through the start and end control points, we should use an open uniform knot vector. Since $n = p = 2$, then $m = n + p + 1 = 5$. Hence, the knot vector can be [0, 0, 0, 1, 1, 1].
2. **The values of** $w_0$, $w_1$, $w_2$: $w_1$ of the middle control point should be equal to $\cos(\phi)$ where $\phi$ is the angle $\angle\, \dot{\mathbf{p}}_2\dot{\mathbf{p}}_0\dot{\mathbf{p}}_1$ (which is equal to the angle $\angle\, \dot{\mathbf{p}}_1\dot{\mathbf{p}}_2\dot{\mathbf{p}}_0$). In this example,

$$\cos(\phi) = \frac{[\dot{\mathbf{p}}_2 - \dot{\mathbf{p}}_0] \cdot [\dot{\mathbf{p}}_1 - \dot{\mathbf{p}}_0]}{\|\dot{\mathbf{p}}_2 - \dot{\mathbf{p}}_0\| \, \|\dot{\mathbf{p}}_1 - \dot{\mathbf{p}}_0\|},$$

where $\cdot$ indicates the dot product (see Appendix A.4.3.2). Thus,

$$\dot{\mathbf{p}}_2 - \dot{\mathbf{p}}_0 = \begin{bmatrix} 5-1 \\ 1-1 \end{bmatrix} = \begin{bmatrix} 4 \\ 0 \end{bmatrix}$$

and

$$\dot{\mathbf{p}}_1 - \dot{\mathbf{p}}_0 = \begin{bmatrix} 3-1 \\ 4-1 \end{bmatrix} = \begin{bmatrix} 2 \\ 3 \end{bmatrix}.$$

Consequently,

$$\begin{aligned} w_1 &= \cos(\phi) \\ &= \frac{4 \times 2 + 0 \times 3}{\sqrt{4^2 + 0^2}\sqrt{2^2 + 3^2}} \\ &= 0.5547. \end{aligned}$$

Thus, the circular arc is drawn using $\mathbf{p}_0 = [1, 1, 1]^T$, $\mathbf{p}_1 = [3, 4, 0.5547]^T$ and $\mathbf{p}_2 = [5, 1, 1]^T$. The arc is shown in Fig. 6.31.

One last point to be mentioned is that some authors estimate $w_1$ of the middle control point $\dot{\mathbf{p}}_1$ to be equal to $\sin(\alpha)$ where $\alpha$ is half the angle $\angle\, \dot{\mathbf{p}}_0\dot{\mathbf{p}}_1\dot{\mathbf{p}}_2$. In other words, given the isosceles triangle $\Delta\dot{\mathbf{p}}_0\dot{\mathbf{p}}_1\dot{\mathbf{p}}_2$, it can be written that

$$w_1 = \sin(\alpha) = \sin\left(\frac{180^\circ - 2\phi}{2}\right) = \sin(90^\circ - \phi). \qquad \square$$

**Example 6.38:** [*NURBS curves—a full circle as quadratic curve segments*]
Construct a full circle as a sequence of quadratic NURBS curve segments. The circle is centered at $[2, 2]^T$ and has a radius of 1.

**Solution 6.38:** Building on the idea of Example 6.37, we may use isosceles triangles to construct circular arcs, which may comprise a full circle. All equal sides of these

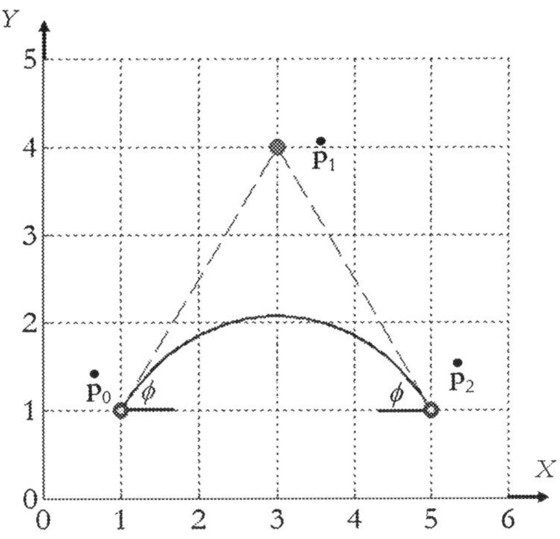


**Fig. 6.31** A circular arc drawn as a quadratic NURBS curve

triangles form a regular (i.e., equilateral) polygon inside which the circle resides. This equilateral polygon may be a triangle, a square, a pentagon, a hexagon, etc. To construct the full circle, we need to determine

1. the control points including vertices of the equilateral polygon;
2. the weights of the homogeneous representations at each of the control points; and
3. the knot vector used.

Let us look at two cases; a square and an equilateral triangle.

**A circle enclosed inside a square:** We need to determine:

1. *The control points:* Each circular arc or curve segment is generated by three control points; the first and third points represent the start and endpoints of the curve segment residing at the middle points of square sides and the second point represents a vertex of the square. Hence, a full circle in this case is made up of four curve segments or circular arcs.
   As shown in Fig. 6.32a, if the circle is having a radius $r$ and centered at $[x, y]^T$, its control points will be $\dot{\mathbf{p}}_0 = [x+r, y]^T$, $\dot{\mathbf{p}}_1 = [x+r, y+r]^T$, $\dot{\mathbf{p}}_2 = [x, y+r]^T$, $\dot{\mathbf{p}}_3 = [x-r, y+r]^T$, $\dot{\mathbf{p}}_4 = [x-r, y]^T$, $\dot{\mathbf{p}}_5 = [x-r, y-r]^T$, $\dot{\mathbf{p}}_6 = [x, y-r]^T$, $\dot{\mathbf{p}}_7 = [x+r, y-r]^T$ and $\dot{\mathbf{p}}_8 = [x+r, y]^T$. Notice that $\dot{\mathbf{p}}_0 = \dot{\mathbf{p}}_8$ to join up the curve. Hence, if $r = 1$ and $[x, y]^T = [2, 2]^T$, the control points will be $\dot{\mathbf{p}}_0 = [3, 2]^T$, $\dot{\mathbf{p}}_1 = [3, 3]^T$, $\dot{\mathbf{p}}_2 = [2, 3]^T$, $\dot{\mathbf{p}}_3 = [1, 3]^T$, $\dot{\mathbf{p}}_4 = [1, 2]^T$, $\dot{\mathbf{p}}_5 = [1, 1]^T$, $\dot{\mathbf{p}}_6 = [2, 1]^T$, $\dot{\mathbf{p}}_7 = [3, 1]^T$ and $\dot{\mathbf{p}}_8 = [3, 2]^T$.
2. *The weights:* Since each control point at the vertices has a weight of $\cos(\phi)$ as discussed in Example 6.37, it is easy to see that the weights at $\dot{\mathbf{p}}_1$, $\dot{\mathbf{p}}_3$, $\dot{\mathbf{p}}_5$ and $\dot{\mathbf{p}}_7$ are $\cos(45°) = \frac{1}{\sqrt{2}}$ each. As done with Example 6.37, a weight of 1 is assigned to each of the rest of control points; i.e., $\dot{\mathbf{p}}_0$, $\dot{\mathbf{p}}_2$, $\dot{\mathbf{p}}_4$, $\dot{\mathbf{p}}_6$ and $\dot{\mathbf{p}}_8$. Thus, the homogeneous control points will be $\mathbf{p}_0 = [3, 2, 1]^T$, $\mathbf{p}_1 = [3, 3, \frac{1}{\sqrt{2}}]^T$,

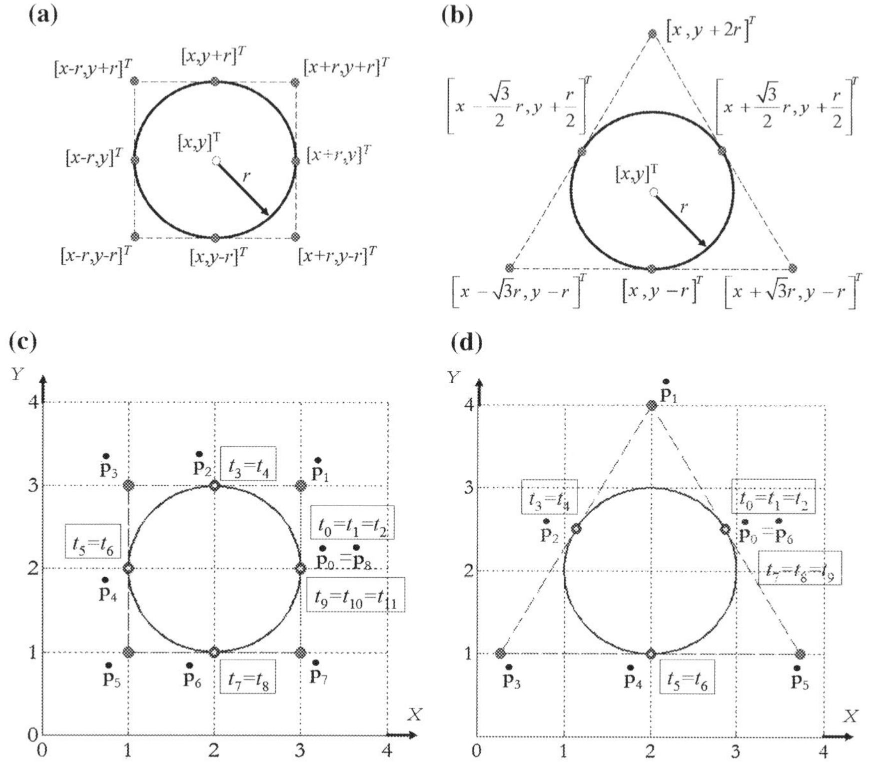


**Fig. 6.32** A circle can be constructed as a sequence of quadratic NURBS curve segments. **a** Locations of control points with respect to the center $[x, y]^T$ and the radius $r$ when a square is used. **b** Locations of control points with respect to the center $[x, y]^T$ and the radius $r$ when an equilateral triangle is used. **c** The circle is composed of four curve segments and enclosed inside a square. **d** The circle is composed of three curve segments and enclosed inside a triangle

$\mathbf{p}_2 = [2, 3, 1]^T$, $\mathbf{p}_3 = [1, 3, \frac{1}{\sqrt{2}}]^T$, $\mathbf{p}_4 = [1, 2, 1]^T$, $\mathbf{p}_5 = [1, 1, \frac{1}{\sqrt{2}}]^T$, $\mathbf{p}_6 = [2, 1, 1]^T$, $\mathbf{p}_7 = [3, 1, \frac{1}{\sqrt{2}}]^T$ and $\mathbf{p}_8 = [3, 2, 1]^T$.

3. *The knot vector:* In case of a full circle enclosed inside a square, $n = 8$, $p = 2$; hence, $m = n + p + 1 = 8 + 2 + 1 = 11$ (i.e., the knot vector is composed of 12 elements). In this case, $t_0 = t_1 = t_2$, $t_3 = t_4$, $t_5 = t_6$, $t_7 = t_8$ and $t_9 = t_{10} = t_{11}$. This means that the curve segments will pass through $\dot{\mathbf{p}}_0$, $\dot{\mathbf{p}}_2$, $\dot{\mathbf{p}}_4$, $\dot{\mathbf{p}}_6$ and $\dot{\mathbf{p}}_8$. The following knot vectors will have the same effect:

   (a) $[0, 0, 0, \frac{\pi}{2}, \frac{\pi}{2}, \pi, \pi, \frac{3\pi}{2}, \frac{3\pi}{2}, 2\pi, 2\pi, 2\pi]$.
   (b) $[0, 0, 0, 0.25, 0.25, 0.5, 0.5, 0.75, 0.75, 1, 1, 1]$.
   (c) $[0, 0, 0, 1, 1, 2, 2, 3, 3, 4, 4, 4]$.

The circle having the previous values is shown in Fig. 6.32c.

**A circle enclosed inside a triangle:** We need to determine:

1. *The control points:* As discussed above, each curve segment is generated by three control points; the first and third points reside at the middle points of the enclosing triangle sides and the second point represents a vertex of the triangle. In this case, a full circle is composed of three curve segments instead of four in the previous case.
   As shown in Fig. 6.32b, if the circle is having a radius $r$ and centered at $[x, y]^T$, its control points will be $\dot{\mathbf{p}}_0 = [x + \frac{\sqrt{3}}{2}r, y + \frac{r}{2}]^T$, $\dot{\mathbf{p}}_1 = [x, y + 2r]^T$, $\dot{\mathbf{p}}_2 = [x - \frac{\sqrt{3}}{2}r, y + \frac{r}{2}]^T$, $\dot{\mathbf{p}}_3 = [x - \sqrt{3}r, y - r]^T$, $\dot{\mathbf{p}}_4 = [x, y - r]^T$, $\dot{\mathbf{p}}_5 = [x + \sqrt{3}r, y - r]^T$ and $\dot{\mathbf{p}}_6 = [x + \frac{\sqrt{3}}{2}r, y + \frac{r}{2}]^T$. Notice that $\dot{\mathbf{p}}_0 = \dot{\mathbf{p}}_6$ to join up the curve. (Again, note that infinite choices of the locations of control points can be assumed; however, they will be rotated versions of the previous points about the center of the circle. Also, note that the start control point $\dot{\mathbf{p}}_0$ must be selected as the middle of the triangle's side; otherwise, the three control points generating a curve segment will be collinear. The same concepts apply to all equilateral polygons used to generate a circle.) Hence, if $r = 1$ and $[x, y]^T = [2, 2]^T$, the control points will be $\dot{\mathbf{p}}_0 = [2 + \frac{\sqrt{3}}{2}, 2\frac{1}{2}]^T$, $\dot{\mathbf{p}}_1 = [2, 4]^T$, $\dot{\mathbf{p}}_2 = [2 - \frac{\sqrt{3}}{2}, 2\frac{1}{2}]^T$, $\dot{\mathbf{p}}_3 = [2 - \sqrt{3}, 1]^T$, $\dot{\mathbf{p}}_4 = [2, 1]^T$, $\dot{\mathbf{p}}_5 = [2 + \sqrt{3}, 1]^T$ and $\dot{\mathbf{p}}_6 = [2 + \frac{\sqrt{3}}{2}, 2\frac{1}{2}]^T$.
2. *The weights:* Since each control point at the vertices has a weight of $\cos(\phi)$; thus, the weights at $\dot{\mathbf{p}}_1$, $\dot{\mathbf{p}}_3$ and $\dot{\mathbf{p}}_5$ are $\cos(60°) = \frac{1}{2}$ each. As done in Example 6.37, a weight of 1 is assigned to each of the rest of control points; i.e., $\dot{\mathbf{p}}_0$, $\dot{\mathbf{p}}_2$, $\dot{\mathbf{p}}_4$ and $\dot{\mathbf{p}}_6$. Thus, the homogeneous control points will be $\dot{\mathbf{p}}_0 = [2 + \frac{\sqrt{3}}{2}, 2\frac{1}{2}, 1]^T$, $\dot{\mathbf{p}}_1 = [2, 4, \frac{1}{2}]^T$, $\dot{\mathbf{p}}_2 = [2 - \frac{\sqrt{3}}{2}, 2\frac{1}{2}, 1]^T$, $\dot{\mathbf{p}}_3 = [2 - \sqrt{3}, 1, \frac{1}{2}]^T$, $\dot{\mathbf{p}}_4 = [2, 1, 1]^T$, $\dot{\mathbf{p}}_5 = [2 + \sqrt{3}, 1, \frac{1}{2}]^T$ and $\dot{\mathbf{p}}_6 = [2 + \frac{\sqrt{3}}{2}, 2\frac{1}{2}, 1]^T$.
3. *The knot vector:* In case of a full circle enclosed inside a triangle, $n = 6$, $p = 2$; hence, $m = n + p + 1 = 6 + 2 + 1 = 9$ (i.e., the knot vector is composed of 10 elements). In this case, $t_0 = t_1 = t_2$, $t_3 = t_4$, $t_5 = t_6$ and $t_7 = t_8 = t_9$. This means that the curve segments will pass through $\dot{\mathbf{p}}_0$, $\dot{\mathbf{p}}_2$, $\dot{\mathbf{p}}_4$ and $\dot{\mathbf{p}}_6$. The following knot vectors will have the same effect:
   (a) $[0, 0, 0, \frac{2\pi}{3}, \frac{2\pi}{3}, \frac{4\pi}{3}, \frac{4\pi}{3}, 2\pi, 2\pi, 2\pi]$.
   (b) $[0, 0, 0, \frac{1}{3}, \frac{1}{3}, \frac{2}{3}, \frac{2}{3}, 1, 1, 1]$.
   (c) $[0, 0, 0, 1, 1, 2, 2, 3, 3, 3]$.

The circle having the previous values is shown in Fig. 6.32d. □

#### 6.2.3.3 Cubic NURBS Curves

In order to estimate a point on a cubic NURBS curve, Eq. (6.107) can be written as

$$\dot{\mathbf{p}}(t) = \frac{\sum\limits_{i=0}^{n} \dot{\mathbf{p}}_i N_{i,3}(t) w_i}{\sum\limits_{i=0}^{n} N_{i,3}(t) w_i}, \tag{6.110}$$

where $n+1$ is the number of control points such that $n \geq 3$; $\dot{\mathbf{p}}_i$ is the control point number $i$; $N_{i,3}$ is $i$th basis function of degree 3; and $w_i$ is the weight of control point $\dot{\mathbf{p}}_i$.

**Example 6.39:** [*NURBS curves—changing homogeneous weights for cubic curves using different knot vectors*]

A 2D cubic NURBS curve has its control points defined at $\dot{\mathbf{p}}_0 = [10, 10]^T$, $\dot{\mathbf{p}}_1 = [30, 50]^T$, $\dot{\mathbf{p}}_2 = [90, 70]^T$, $\dot{\mathbf{p}}_3 = [130, 20]^T$, $\dot{\mathbf{p}}_4 = [170, 80]^T$ and $\dot{\mathbf{p}}_5 = [220, 60]^T$.

1. If the uniform knot vector used is [0, 1, 2, 3, 4, 5, 6, 7, 8, 9] and $w_0 = w_1 = w_2 = 1$, determine the locations of the knots. Repeat the calculations if $w_1$ is changed to 0.2, 1.8 and 0.
2. If the open uniform knot vector used is [0, 0, 0, 0, 1, 2, 3, 3, 3, 3] and $w_0 = w_1 = w_2 = 1$, determine the locations of the knots. Repeat the calculations if $w_1$ is changed to 0.2, 1.8 and 0.
3. If the non-uniform knot vector used is [0, 1, 2, 4, 5, 7, 10, 12, 14, 15] and $w_0 = w_1 = w_2 = 1$, determine the locations of the knots. Repeat the calculations if $w_1$ is changed to 0.2, 1.8 and 0.

Show the curve in each of these cases.

**Solution 6.39:** Each segment of a cubic NURBS curve is generated by four control points. Since there are six control points, three curve segments should be generated.

**Using the uniform knot vector [0, 1, 2, 3, 4, 5, 6, 7, 8, 9]:** To obtain a point on a cubic NURBS curve, we may use Eq. (6.110):

$$\dot{\mathbf{p}}(t) = \frac{\sum_{i=0}^{n} \dot{\mathbf{p}}_i N_{i,3}(t) w_i}{\sum_{i=0}^{n} N_{i,3}(t) w_i}.$$

Alternatively and similar to Eq. (6.109), a point $\dot{\mathbf{p}}(t)$ on a cubic NURBS curve is estimated as

$$\dot{\mathbf{p}}(t) = \begin{bmatrix} \dfrac{\frac{1}{6}[(1-(t-t_i))^3 x_{i-3} w_{i-3} + (3(t-t_i)^3 - 6(t-t_i)^2 + 4) x_{i-2} w_{i-2} + (-3(t-t_i)^3 + 3(t-t_i)^2 + 3(t-t_i) + 1) x_{i-1} w_{i-1} + (t-t_i)^3 x_i w_i]}{\frac{1}{6}[(1-(t-t_i))^3 w_{i-3} + (3(t-t_i)^3 - 6(t-t_i)^2 + 4) w_{i-2} + (-3(t-t_i)^3 + 3(t-t_i)^2 + 3(t-t_i) + 1) w_{i-1} + (t-t_i)^3 w_i]} \\ \dfrac{\frac{1}{6}[(1-(t-t_i))^3 y_{i-3} w_{i-3} + (3(t-t_i)^3 - 6(t-t_i)^2 + 4) y_{i-2} w_{i-2} + (-3(t-t_i)^3 + 3(t-t_i)^2 + 3(t-t_i) + 1) y_{i-1} w_{i-1} + (t-t_i)^3 y_i w_i]}{\frac{1}{6}[(1-(t-t_i))^3 w_{i-3} + (3(t-t_i)^3 - 6(t-t_i)^2 + 4) w_{i-2} + (-3(t-t_i)^3 + 3(t-t_i)^2 + 3(t-t_i) + 1) w_{i-1} + (t-t_i)^3 w_i]} \end{bmatrix}. \tag{6.111}$$

The locations of the knots are at $t_3$, $t_4$, $t_5$ and $t_6$. In order to obtain the location of the first knot, we use $\dot{\mathbf{p}}_0$, $\dot{\mathbf{p}}_1$, $\dot{\mathbf{p}}_2$ and $\dot{\mathbf{p}}_3$ with $t = t_3 = 3$. So,

$$\dot{\mathbf{p}}(3) = \begin{bmatrix} \frac{\frac{1}{6}[(1-0)^3 10\times 1+(3\times 0^3-6\times 0^2+4)30\times 1+(-3\times 0^3+3\times 0^2+3\times 0+1)90\times 1+(0^3)130\times 1]}{\frac{1}{6}[(1-0)^3 1+(3\times 0^3-6\times 0^2+4)1+(-3\times 0^3+3\times 0^2+3\times 0+1)1+(0^3)1]} \\ \frac{\frac{1}{6}[(1-0)^3 10\times 1+(3\times 0^3-6\times 0^2+4)50\times 1+(-3\times 0^3+3\times 0^2+3\times 0+1)70\times 1+(0^3)20\times 1]}{\frac{1}{6}[(1-0)^3 1+(3\times 0^3-6\times 0^2+4)1+(-3\times 0^3+3\times 0^2+3\times 0+1)1+(0^3)1]} \end{bmatrix}$$

$$= \begin{bmatrix} 36.6667 \\ 46.6667 \end{bmatrix}.$$

The other knots are computed the same way. Also, the knot points can be obtained when $w_1$ is changed to 0.2, 1.8 and 0. The values are listed in the following table:

| Segment | $t_i$ | Points | $w_1$ | $\dot{\mathbf{p}}(t_i)$ | $\dot{\mathbf{p}}(t_{i+1})$ |
|---|---|---|---|---|---|
| $\mathscr{S}_3$ | $t_3$ | $\dot{\mathbf{p}}_0, \dot{\mathbf{p}}_1, \dot{\mathbf{p}}_2, \dot{\mathbf{p}}_3$ | 1 | $[36.6667, 46.6667]^T$ | $[86.6667, 58.3333]^T$ |
| | | | 0.2 | $[44.2857, 42.8571]^T$ | $[95.3846, 59.6154]^T$ |
| | | | 1.8 | $[34.3478, 47.8261]^T$ | $[80, 57.3529]^T$ |
| | | | 0 | $[50, 40]^T$ | $[98, 60]^T$ |
| $\mathscr{S}_4$ | $t_4$ | $\dot{\mathbf{p}}_1, \dot{\mathbf{p}}_2, \dot{\mathbf{p}}_3, \dot{\mathbf{p}}_4$ | 1 | $[86.6667, 58.3333]^T$ | $[130, 38.3333]^T$ |
| | | | 0.2 | $[95.3846, 59.6154]^T$ | $[130, 38.3333]^T$ |
| | | | 1.8 | $[80, 57.3529]^T$ | $[130, 38.3333]^T$ |
| | | | 0 | $[98, 60]^T$ | $[130, 38.3333]^T$ |
| $\mathscr{S}_5$ | $t_5$ | $\dot{\mathbf{p}}_2, \dot{\mathbf{p}}_3, \dot{\mathbf{p}}_4, \dot{\mathbf{p}}_5$ | 1 | $[130, 38.3333]^T$ | $[171.6667, 66.6667]^T$ |
| | | | 0.2 | $[130, 38.3333]^T$ | $[171.6667, 66.6667]^T$ |
| | | | 1.8 | $[130, 38.3333]^T$ | $[171.6667, 66.6667]^T$ |
| | | | 0 | $[130, 38.3333]^T$ | $[171.6667, 66.6667]^T$ |

The curves are shown in Fig. 6.33. From the results, we can see that changing $w_1$ affects only the first two knots (i.e., points at $t_3$ and $t_4$) as control point $\dot{\mathbf{p}}_1$ contributes to $\mathscr{S}_3$ and $\mathscr{S}_4$ only. Notice that in case of $w_1 = 0$, $\dot{\mathbf{p}}_1$ contributes nothing to the calculation. In other words, it is excluded from calculation.

**Using the open uniform knot vector [0, 0, 0, 0, 1, 2, 3, 3, 3, 3]:** We may utilize Eq. (6.111) with different $w_1$ values. The next table lists the values obtained.

| $w_1$ | $\dot{\mathbf{p}}(t_3)$ | $\dot{\mathbf{p}}(t_4)$ | $\dot{\mathbf{p}}(t_5)$ | $\dot{\mathbf{p}}(t_6)$ |
|---|---|---|---|---|
| 1 | $[10, 10]^T$ | $[81.6667, 56.6667]^T$ | $[133.3333, 43.3333]^T$ | $[220, 60]^T$ |
| 0.2 | $[10, 10]^T$ | $[94.5833, 58.3333]^T$ | $[133.3333, 43.3333]^T$ | $[220, 60]^T$ |
| 1.8 | $[10, 10]^T$ | $[73.0556, 55.5556]^T$ | $[133.3333, 43.3333]^T$ | $[220, 60]^T$ |
| 0 | $[10, 10]^T$ | $[98.8889, 58.8889]^T$ | $[133.3333, 43.3333]^T$ | $[220, 60]^T$ |

The steps of the solution are left as an exercise. The curves are shown in Fig. 6.34. Notice that the curve interpolates the start and end control points as happened with quadratic NURBS and open uniform knot vector.

**Using the non-uniform knot vector [0, 1, 2, 4, 5, 7, 10, 12, 14, 15]:** As done before, we may utilize Eq. (6.111) with different $w_1$ values. The next table lists the values obtained.

The steps of the solution are left as an exercise. The curves are shown in Fig. 6.35. □

**Example 6.40:** [*NURBS curves—points on 3D curve*]

Write down an equation to estimate a 3D NURBS curve point.

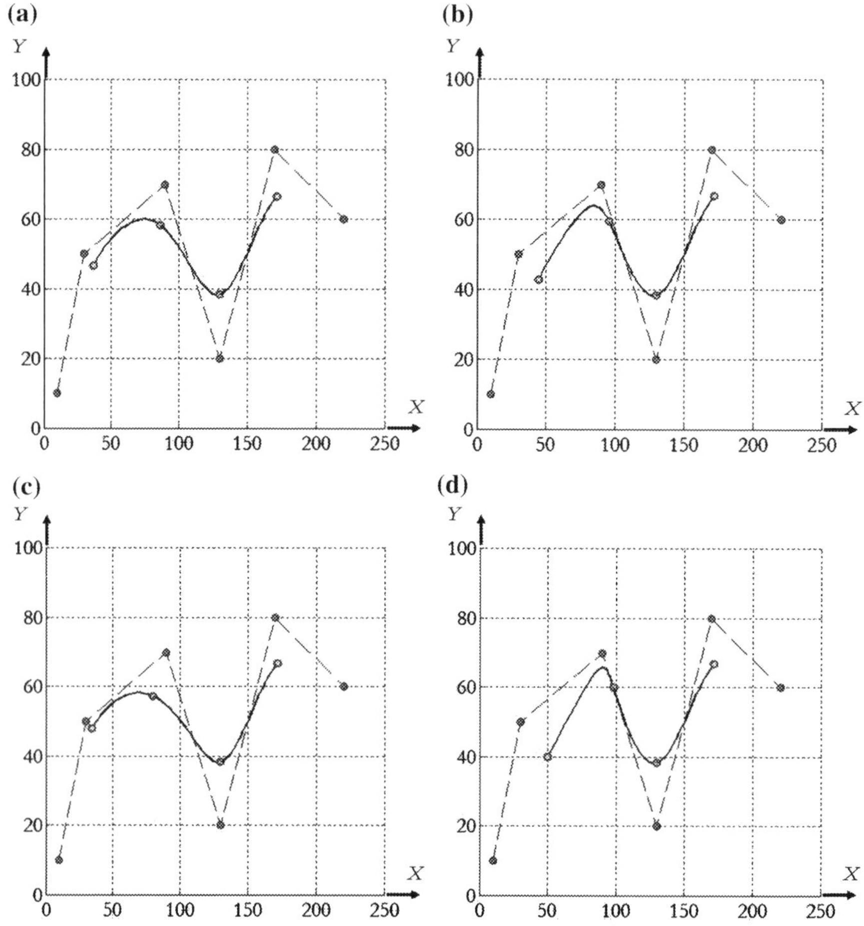


**Fig. 6.33** A cubic NURBS curve where $w_0 = w_2 = w_3 = w_4 = w_5 = 1$. **a** $w_1 = 1$. **b** $w_1 = 0.2$. **c** $w_1 = 1.8$. **d** $w_1 = 0$. All the cases use the uniform knot vector [0, 1, 2, 3, 4, 5, 6, 7, 8, 9]

| $w_1$ | $\dot{\mathbf{p}}(t_3)$ | $\dot{\mathbf{p}}(t_4)$ | $\dot{\mathbf{p}}(t_5)$ | $\dot{\mathbf{p}}(t_6)$ |
|---|---|---|---|---|
| 1 | $[44.3333, 52]^T$ | $[76.2222, 61.8889]^T$ | $[122.5714, 41.8571]^T$ | $[178.2857, 68]^T$ |
| 0.2 | $[59.8611, 54.1667]^T$ | $[88.7571, 65.1130]^T$ | $[122.5714, 41.8571]^T$ | $[178.2857, 68]^T$ |
| 1.8 | $[39.4298, 51.3158]^T$ | $[68.0952, 59.7985]^T$ | $[122.5714, 41.8571]^T$ | $[178.2857, 68]^T$ |
| 0 | $[70.9524, 55.7143]^T$ | $[93.0303, 66.2121]^T$ | $[122.5714, 41.8571]^T$ | $[178.2857, 68]^T$ |

**Solution 6.40:** A 3D control point may be represented in homogeneous coordinates as $\mathbf{P}_i = [xw_i, yw_i, zw_i, w_i]^T$; hence, a 3D NURBS curve point is defined as

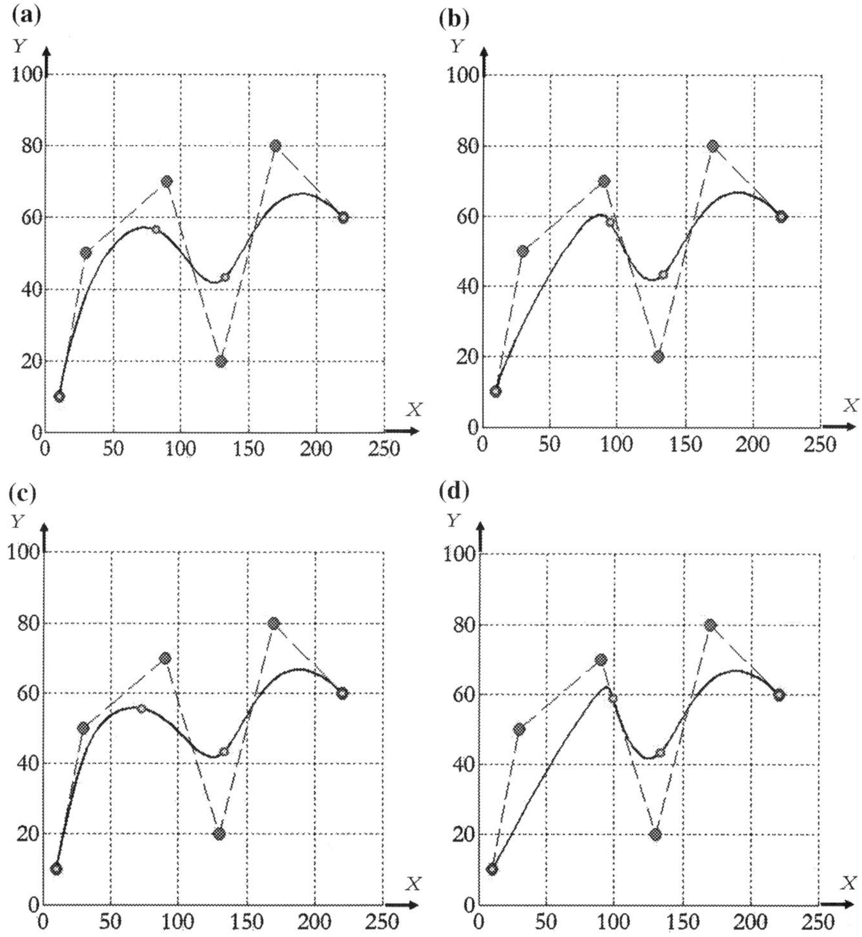


**Fig. 6.34** A cubic NURBS curve where $w_0 = w_2 = w_3 = w_4 = w_5 = 1$. **a** $w_1 = 1$. **b** $w_1 = 0.2$. **c** $w_1 = 1.8$. **d** $w_1 = 0$. All the cases use the open uniform knot vector [0, 0, 0, 0, 1, 2, 3, 3, 3, 3]

$$\mathbf{P}(t) = \begin{bmatrix} x(t) \\ y(t) \\ z(t) \\ w(t) \end{bmatrix} = \sum_{i=0}^{n} \mathbf{P}_i N_{i,p}(t), \tag{6.112}$$

where $\mathbf{P}(t)$ is the homogeneous curve point; $\mathbf{P}_i$ is the homogeneous control point $i$ such that $i \in \{0, 1, \ldots n\}$; and $N_{i,p}(t)$ is the $i$th basis function of degree $p$ as estimated in Eq. (6.77). Equation (6.112) may be re-written as

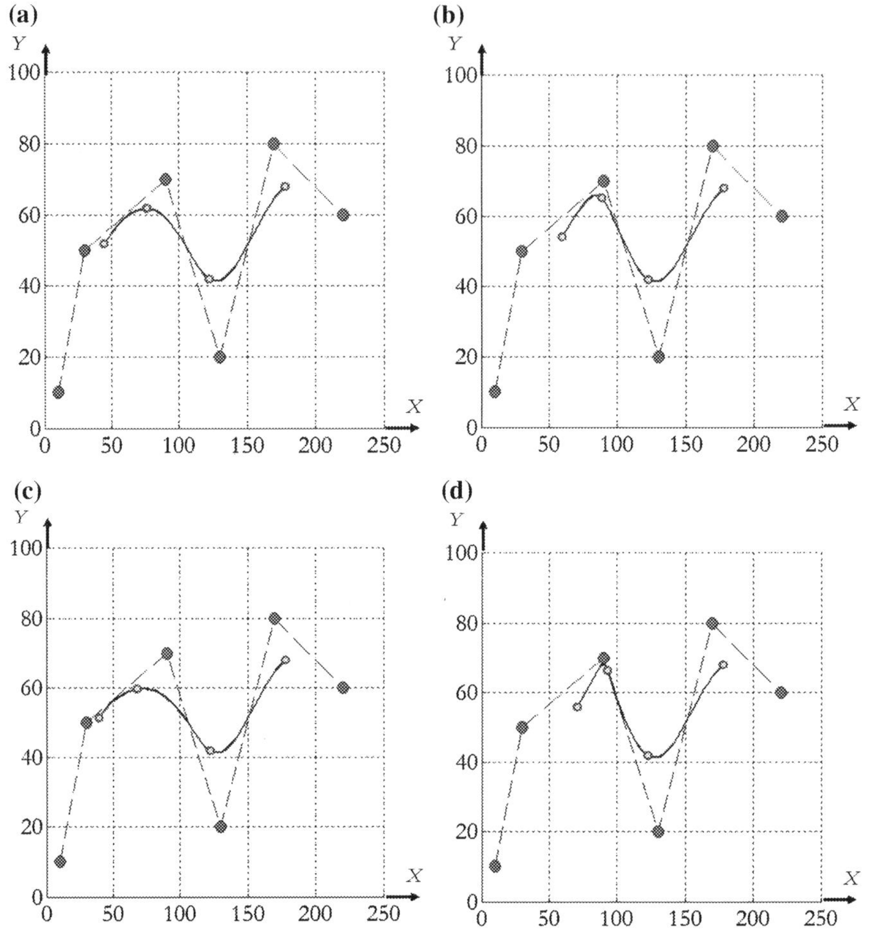


**Fig. 6.35** A cubic NURBS curve where $w_0 = w_2 = w_3 = w_4 = w_5 = 1$. **a** $w_1 = 1$. **b** $w_1 = 0.2$. **c** $w_1 = 1.8$. **d** $w_1 = 0$. All the cases use the non-uniform knot vector [0, 1, 2, 4, 5, 7, 10, 12, 14, 15]

$$
\begin{aligned}
x(t) &= \sum_{i=0}^{n} x_i N_{i,p}(t) w_i, \\
y(t) &= \sum_{i=0}^{n} y_i N_{i,p}(t) w_i, \\
z(t) &= \sum_{i=0}^{n} z_i N_{i,p}(t) w_i, \\
w(t) &= \sum_{i=0}^{n} N_{i,p}(t) w_i.
\end{aligned}
\tag{6.113}
$$

To obtain the curve point in inhomogeneous coordinates, we divide by $w(t)$. Hence, point $\dot{\mathbf{P}}(t)$ is expressed as

$$\dot{\mathbf{P}}(t) = \begin{bmatrix} \frac{x(t)}{w(t)} \\ \frac{y(t)}{w(t)} \\ \frac{z(t)}{w(t)} \end{bmatrix}. \tag{6.114}$$

Combining in a single equation, we estimate a 3D NURBS curve point $\dot{\mathbf{P}}$ at parameter $t$ as

$$\dot{\mathbf{P}}(t) = \frac{\sum_{i=0}^{n} \dot{\mathbf{P}}_i N_{i,p}(t) w_i}{\sum_{i=0}^{n} N_{i,p}(t) w_i}, \tag{6.115}$$

where $n+1$ is the number of control points; $\dot{\mathbf{P}}_i$ is the control point number $i$; $p$ is the curve degree; $N_{i,p}(t)$ is the $i$th basis function of degree $p$ as estimated in Eq. (6.77); and $w_i$ is the weight of control point $\dot{\mathbf{P}}_i$ (i.e., $w_i$ is the last entry in the homogeneous representation of control point $\mathbf{P}_i$). □

## 6.3 Problems

**Problem 6.1:** [*Explicit representation—points on curves*]
Assume that a quadratic curve is passing through the points $[4, 3]^T$, $[7, 8]^T$ and $[12, 10]^T$. Define the curve explicitly and estimate the values of $y$ at $x = 7$ and $x = 9$.

**Problem 6.2:** [*Parametric representation—coefficients for quadratic curves*]
A quadratic curve whose endpoints are $[0, 0]^T$ and $[3, 3]^T$ is represented parametrically. If the point $[3, 8]^T$ is on the curve where $t = 0.7$, get the coefficients of its equation.

**Problem 6.3:** [*Parametric representation—transformations of quadratic curves*]
If the curve in Problem 6.2 is rotated through an angle of 30° about the point $[5, 6]^T$ and then translated using a translation vector $[3, 4]^T$, estimate the location of $t = 0.4$ after transformation. Is this type of representation invariant under affine transformation?

**Problem 6.4:** [*Parametric representation—interpolation matrix for cubic curves*]
Write down the entries of the interpolation matrix for a cubic curve that is represented parametrically when the points $\dot{\mathbf{p}}_0$, $\dot{\mathbf{p}}_1$, $\dot{\mathbf{p}}_2$ and $\dot{\mathbf{p}}_3$ are at $t_0 = 0$, $t_1 = 0.2$, $t_2 = 0.8$ and $t_3 = 1$ respectively.

**Problem 6.5:** [*Parametric representation—coefficients for cubic curves*]
A point $\dot{\mathbf{p}}(t)$ on a cubic curve that is represented parametrically is estimated as

$$\dot{\mathbf{p}}(t) = \mathbf{a}t^3 + \mathbf{b}t^2 + \mathbf{c}t + \mathbf{d},$$

where **a**, **b**, **c** and **d** are vectors representing the coefficients of the cubic curve equation. Determine the values of these coefficients in terms of the curve points $\dot{\mathbf{p}}_0$, $\dot{\mathbf{p}}_1$, $\dot{\mathbf{p}}_2$ and $\dot{\mathbf{p}}_3$, which are at $t_0 = 0$, $t_1 = 0.2$, $t_2 = 0.8$ and $t_3 = 1$ respectively.

**Problem 6.6:** [*Parametric representation—coefficients for cubic curves*]
Draw a cubic curve that is specified by the points $\dot{\mathbf{p}}_0 = [5, 5]^T$, $\dot{\mathbf{p}}_1 = [10, 15]^T$, $\dot{\mathbf{p}}_2 = [15, 5]^T$ and $\dot{\mathbf{p}}_3 = [15, 15]^T$ such that $\dot{\mathbf{p}}_0, \dot{\mathbf{p}}_1, \dot{\mathbf{p}}_2$ and $\dot{\mathbf{p}}_3$ are at $t_0 = 0$, $t_1 = 0.2$, $t_2 = 0.8$ and $t_3 = 1$ respectively. (You may use the answers to Problem 6.4 and Problem 6.5.)

**Problem 6.7:** [*Parametric representation—coefficients for cubic curves*]
A cubic curve is passing through $\dot{\mathbf{p}}_0 = [x_0, y_0]^T$, $\dot{\mathbf{p}}_1 = [x_1, y_1]^T$, $\dot{\mathbf{p}}_2 = [x_2, y_2]^T$ and $\dot{\mathbf{p}}_3 = [x_3, y_3]^T$. This curve is represented parametrically where the $t$ values are $0$, $t_1$, $t_2$ and $1$ at points $\dot{\mathbf{p}}_0$, $\dot{\mathbf{p}}_1$, $\dot{\mathbf{p}}_2$ and $\dot{\mathbf{p}}_3$ respectively. If the parametric equation is expressed as

$$\dot{\mathbf{p}}(t) = \mathbf{a}_0 + \mathbf{a}_1 t + \mathbf{a}_2 t^2 + \mathbf{a}_3 t^3,$$

determine the coefficient vectors $\mathbf{a}_0$, $\mathbf{a}_1$, $\mathbf{a}_2$ and $\mathbf{a}_3$.

**Problem 6.8:** [*Parametric representation—coefficients for cubic curves*]
A cubic curve whose endpoints are $[0, 0]^T$ and $[13, 12]^T$ is represented parametrically. If the points $[2, 4]^T$ and $[5, 6]^T$ are on the curve at $t = 0.4$ and $t = 0.7$ respectively, get the coefficients of the curve equation.

**Problem 6.9:** [*Bézier curves—points on quadratic curves*]
Consider a quadratic Bézier curve whose control points are $[0, 0]^T$, $[2, 4]^T$ and $[13, 12]^T$. Get the curve point at $t = 0.4$.

**Problem 6.10:** [*Bézier curves—points on cubic curves*]
Consider a cubic Bézier curve whose control points are $[0, 0]^T$, $[2, 4]^T$, $[5, 7]^T$ and $[13, 12]^T$. Get the curve point at $t = 0.4$.

**Problem 6.11:** [*Bézier curves—transformations of cubic curves*]
If the curve in Problem 6.10 is rotated through 60° about the point $[5, 7]^T$, estimate the location at $t = 0.55$ after rotation. Is this type of representation invariant under affine transformation?

**Problem 6.12:** [*Bézier curves—cubic curves in 3D space*]
Equations (6.51) and (6.52) are used to construct a quadratic Bézier curve in 2D space. Modify these equations to accommodate a quadratic Bézier curve in 3D space.

**Problem 6.13:** [*Bézier curves—points on quadratic 3D curves*]
Consider a quadratic Bézier curve whose control points are $[0, 0, 0]^T$, $[2, 4, 5]^T$ and $[13, 12, 3]^T$. Get the curve point at $t = 0.4$.

**Problem 6.14:** [*Basis function—$N_{1,3}(t)$ using uniform knot vector*]
Estimate the values of the basis function $N_{1,3}(t)$ for different subintervals if the uniform knot vector [1, 2, 3, 4, 5] is used.

**Problem 6.15:** [*Basis function—$N_{i,p}(t)$ using uniform knot vector*]
Utilizing the uniform knot vector [0, 1, 2, 3, 4, 5, 6, 7, 8] for a quadratic curve, estimate the values of basis functions for different subintervals.

**Problem 6.16:** [*Basis function—$N_{i,p}(t)$ using open uniform knot vector*]
Utilizing the open uniform knot vector [0, 0, 0, 0, 1, 2, 2, 2, 2] for a cubic curve, estimate the values of basis functions for different subintervals.

**Problem 6.17:** [*Basis function—multiple knots*]
Utilizing the knot vector [0, 1, 2, 4, 4, 5, 6, 7, 8] for a quadratic curve, estimate the values of basis functions for different subintervals.

**Problem 6.18:** [*B-spline curves—points on cubic curves using uniform knot vector*]
A cubic B-spline curve is to be generated using the control points $\dot{\mathbf{p}}_0 = [10, 10]^T$, $\dot{\mathbf{p}}_1 = [30, 50]^T$, $\dot{\mathbf{p}}_2 = [90, 70]^T$, $\dot{\mathbf{p}}_3 = [130, 20]^T$, $\dot{\mathbf{p}}_4 = [170, 30]^T$ and $\dot{\mathbf{p}}_5 = [220, 60]^T$ and the uniform knot vector [0, 1, 2, 3, 4, 5, 6, 7, 8, 9]. Determine the location of the curve point at $t = 3.5$. Show the steps.

**Problem 6.19:** [*B-spline curves—points on cubic curves using open uniform knot vector*]
A cubic B-spline curve is to be generated using the control points $\dot{\mathbf{p}}_0 = [10, 10]^T$, $\dot{\mathbf{p}}_1 = [30, 50]^T$, $\dot{\mathbf{p}}_2 = [90, 70]^T$, $\dot{\mathbf{p}}_3 = [130, 20]^T$, $\dot{\mathbf{p}}_4 = [170, 30]^T$ and $\dot{\mathbf{p}}_5 = [220, 60]^T$ and the open uniform knot vector [0, 0, 0, 0, 1, 2, 3, 3, 3, 3]. Determine the location of the curve point at $t = 0.5$. Show the steps.

**Problem 6.20:** [*B-spline curves—points on quadratic curves using open uniform knot vector*]
Consider a quadratic B-spline curve segment whose control points are $[0, 0]^T$, $[2, 4]^T$ and $[13, 12]^T$. If the open uniform knot vector [0, 0, 0, 1, 1, 1] is used, get the curve point at $t = 0.4$.

**Problem 6.21:** [*B-spline curves—points on cubic curves using open uniform knot vector*]
Consider a cubic B-spline curve segment whose control points are $[2, 3]^T$, $[4, 7]^T$, $[10, 8]^T$ and $[13, 5]^T$. If the open uniform knot vector [0, 0, 0, 0, 1, 1, 1, 1] is used, get the curve point at $t = 0.7$.

**Problem 6.22:** [*B-spline curves—curves in 3D space*]
The general B-spline curve in 2D space is defined using Eq. (6.70) while a curve segment spanning from $t = 0$ to $t = 1$ is defined using Eq. (6.94) in quadratic case and Eq. (6.99) in cubic case. Extend these equations to cover points and curves in 3D space.

**Problem 6.23:** [*NURBS curves—a full circle as quadratic curve segments using a regular pentagon*]

A full circle is to be constructed inside a regular pentagon as a sequence of quadratic NURBS curve segments. The circle is centered at $[4, 3]^T$ and has a radius of 2.5. Determine the locations of control points, their homogeneous weights and the knot vector used.

**Problem 6.24:** [*NURBS curves—a full circle as quadratic curve segments using a regular hexagon*]

Re-solve Problem 6.23 if the circle is to be constructed inside a regular hexagon.

## References

Bartels, R.H., J.C. Beatty, B.A. Barsky, et al. 1987. *An introduction to splines for use in computer graphics and geometric modeling*. San Mateo: Morgan Kaufmann Publishers Inc.
Bézier, P. 1972. *Numerical control; mathematics and applications*. Wiley series in computing. London: Wiley.
Bézier, P. 1974. *Computer aided geometric design*. Mathematical and practical possibilities of UNISURF. New York: Academic Press.
Buss, S.R. 2003. *3D computer graphics: a mathematical introduction with OpenGL*. New York: Cambridge University Press.
Farin, G. 2002. *Curves and surfaces for CAGD: a practical guide*, 5th ed. San Francisco: Morgan Kaufmann Publishers Inc.
Foley, J.D., A. van Dam, S.K. Feiner, and J. Hughes. 1995. *Computer graphics: principles and practice in C*, 2nd ed., The systems programming series. Reading: Addison-Wesley.
Forrest, R.A. 1980. The twisted cubic curve: a computer-aided geometric design approach. *Computer Aided Design* 12(4): 165–172.
Goldman, R. 2009. *An integrated introduction to computer graphics and geometric modeling.*, Geometric modeling, and animation series. London: Chapman & Hall/CRC Computer Graphics, CRC Press.
Lengyel, E. (2011). *Mathematics for 3D game programming and computer graphics*, 3rd ed., Course Technology PTR.
McConnell, J. 2005. *Computer graphics: theory into practice*, 1st ed. Boston: Jones & Bartlett.
Mukundan, R. 2012. *Advanced methods in computer graphics: with examples in OpenGL*. Berlin: Springer.
Parent, R. 2012. *Computer animation: algorithms and techniques*, 3rd ed. Waltham: Morgan Kaufmann.
Piegl, L., and W. Tiller. 1997. *The NURBS book*, 2nd ed. New York: Springer.
Rogers, D.F. 2000. *An introduction to NURBS: with historical perspective*. San Francisco: Morgan Kaufmann.
Salomon, D. 2006. *Curves and surfaces for computer graphics*. Berlin: Springer.
Salomon, D. 2011. *The computer graphics manual*. Texts in computer science. New York: Springer.
Vince, J. 2005. *Geometry for computer graphics: formulae, examples and proofs*. New York: Springer.

# Chapter 7
# Surfaces

**Abstract** Surfaces are a way of representing 3D models in space; however, in general, a surface may not enclose a volume. In many aspects, surfaces can be seen as an extension to curves (Chap. 6) where a surface point is determined using two parameters. A surface may interpolate data points or be controlled by space points that may reside on different planes. In this chapter, we will discuss some surface representations.

## 7.1 Surface Representations

The concepts and mathematics of constructing 2D curves may be extended to surfaces to 3D space. Similar to curves, a surface may be represented *explicitly* by a polynomial of the form

$$z = f(x, y). \tag{7.1}$$

Thus, a point $\dot{\mathbf{P}}$ on the surface is expressed as $[x, y, f(x, y)]^T$. A surface may also be represented *implicitly* as

$$f(x, y, z) = 0. \tag{7.2}$$

For example, a plane equation is represented implicitly as

$$ax + by + cz - d = 0. \tag{7.3}$$

Higher-degree equations may represent curved surfaces implicitly as

R. Elias, *Digital Media*, DOI: 10.1007/978-3-319-05137-6_7,

$$x^2 + y^2 + z^2 - r^2 = 0, \tag{7.4}$$

which represents a spherical surface.

Also, similar to curves, a surface may be represented *parametrically*. In this case, two parameters are required instead of a single parameter used in case of curves. Generally, a point $\dot{\mathbf{P}}$ on a surface is represented parametrically as

$$\dot{\mathbf{P}}(u, v) = \begin{bmatrix} x(u, v) \\ y(u, v) \\ z(u, v) \end{bmatrix}, \tag{7.5}$$

where $u$ and $v$ are parameters covering two directions.

Moreover, surfaces may pass through data points while other surfaces use points to control the shape of the surface. Examples of the later type include Bézier surfaces and NURBS. Those surfaces are discussed below.

## 7.2 Bézier Surfaces

Bézier curves (Bézier 1972, 1974) can be generalized to Bézier surfaces. Instead of having one parameter $t$ along the curve, Bézier surfaces use two parameters $u$ and $v$. Given a set of $(p + 1)(q + 1)$ control points, a Bézier surface of degree $(p, q)$ is defined using these points as

$$\dot{\mathbf{P}}(u, v) = \sum_{i=0}^{p} \sum_{j=0}^{q} \dot{\mathbf{P}}_{ij} B_{i,p}(u) B_{j,q}(v), \tag{7.6}$$

where $\dot{\mathbf{P}}(u, v)$ is a point on the Bézier surface at parameters $u$ and $v$ such that $u \in [0, 1]$ and $v \in [0, 1]$; $i \in \{0, 1, 2, \ldots, p\}$; $j \in \{0, 1, 2, \ldots, q\}$; $\dot{\mathbf{P}}_{ij}$ is the control point number $(i, j)$; $B_{i,p}(u)$ and $B_{j,q}(v)$ are *Bernstein polynomials*. As defined in Eq. (6.54), such polynomials are expressed as

$$\begin{aligned} B_{i,p}(u) &= \binom{p}{i} u^i (1 - u)^{p-i} \\ &= \frac{p!}{i!(p - i)!} u^i (1 - u)^{p-i}, \end{aligned} \tag{7.7}$$

where $\binom{p}{i}$ is a binomial coefficient; $p$ is the surface degree along the $u$-direction; and $i$ is the control point number along that direction. Similarly,

$$B_{j,q}(v) = \binom{q}{j} v^j (1-v)^{q-j} \\ = \frac{q!}{j!(q-j)!} v^j (1-v)^{q-j}, \qquad (7.8)$$

where $\binom{q}{j}$ is a binomial coefficient; $q$ is the surface degree along the $v$-direction; and $j$ is the control point number along that direction. Thus, Eq. (7.6) can be re-written as

$$\dot{\mathbf{P}}(u,v) = \sum_{i=0}^{p}\sum_{j=0}^{q} \dot{\mathbf{P}}_{ij} \binom{p}{i} u^i (1-u)^{p-i} \binom{q}{j} v^j (1-v)^{q-j} \\ = \sum_{i=0}^{p}\sum_{j=0}^{q} \dot{\mathbf{P}}_{ij} \frac{p!}{i!(p-i)!} u^i (1-u)^{p-i} \frac{q!}{j!(q-j)!} v^j (1-v)^{q-j}. \qquad (7.9)$$

In general and similar to Bézier curves, a Bézier surface does not pass through its control points except for the corners of the grid of control points. Also, similar to Bézier curves, a Bézier surface must be within the convex hull of the control points. Each edge of the grid of control points defines a Bézier curve. The most usable Bézier surfaces (or patches) are of degrees (2, 2) and (3, 3).

### *7.2.1 Linear Bézier Surfaces*

A planar surface or a planar patch may be estimated as a linear Bézier surface of degree (1, 1) using four points (i.e., $2 \times 2$); $\dot{\mathbf{P}}_{00}$, $\dot{\mathbf{P}}_{10}$, $\dot{\mathbf{P}}_{01}$ and $\dot{\mathbf{P}}_{11}$, by substituting $p = q = 1$ in Eq. (7.9) to get

$$\dot{\mathbf{P}}(u,v) = \sum_{i=0}^{1}\sum_{j=0}^{1} \dot{\mathbf{P}}_{ij} \binom{1}{i} u^i (1-u)^{1-i} \binom{1}{j} v^j (1-v)^{1-j} \qquad (7.10)$$

or

$$\dot{\mathbf{P}}(u,v) = (1-v)\big[(1-u)\dot{\mathbf{P}}_{00} + u\dot{\mathbf{P}}_{10}\big] + v\big[(1-u)\dot{\mathbf{P}}_{01} + u\dot{\mathbf{P}}_{11}\big], \qquad (7.11)$$

where $\dot{\mathbf{P}}(u,v)$ is a point on the planar Bézier patch; $u$ and $v$ are parameters such that $u \in [0,1]$ and $v \in [0,1]$. Equation (7.11) can be written in matrix form as

$$\dot{\mathbf{P}}(u,v) = \begin{bmatrix} u & 1 \end{bmatrix} \underbrace{\begin{bmatrix} -1 & 1 \\ 1 & 0 \end{bmatrix}}_{\dot{\mathrm{B}}_1} \begin{bmatrix} \dot{\mathbf{P}}_{00} & \dot{\mathbf{P}}_{01} \\ \dot{\mathbf{P}}_{10} & \dot{\mathbf{P}}_{11} \end{bmatrix} \underbrace{\begin{bmatrix} -1 & 1 \\ 1 & 0 \end{bmatrix}}_{\dot{\mathrm{B}}_1^T} \begin{bmatrix} v \\ 1 \end{bmatrix}, \qquad (7.12)$$

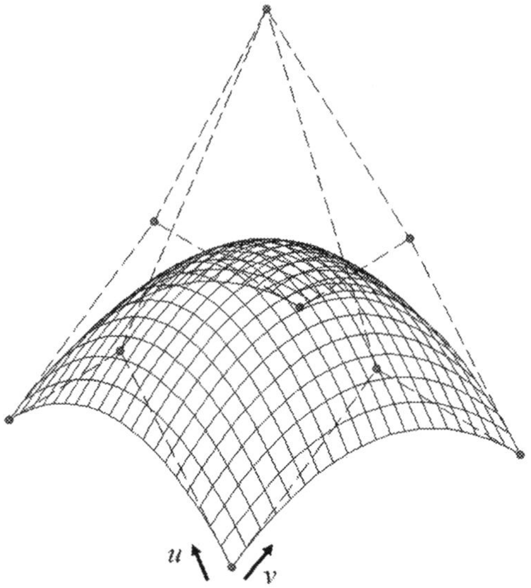


**Fig. 7.1** An example of a biquadratic Bézier surface

where $\dot{\mathrm{B}}_1$ is the geometry matrix for the surface. It is the same matrix used with linear Bézier curves in Eq. (6.46). Note that $\dot{\mathbf{P}}_{00}$, $\dot{\mathbf{P}}_{10}$, $\dot{\mathbf{P}}_{01}$ and $\dot{\mathbf{P}}_{11}$ are 3D points in general; however, 2D points could be used as well.

### 7.2.2 *Biquadratic Bézier Surfaces*

The number of control points defining a Bézier patch of degree (2, 2) is nine (i.e., 3 × 3). An example of a biquadratic Bézier surface is shown in Fig. 7.1 where two parameters $u$ and $v$ are considered along two directions.[1] Equation (7.9) can be tailored for this patch by substituting $p = q = 2$ to get

$$\dot{\mathbf{P}}(u, v) = \sum_{i=0}^{2}\sum_{j=0}^{2} \dot{\mathbf{P}}_{ij} \binom{2}{i} u^i (1-u)^{2-i} \binom{2}{j} v^j (1-v)^{2-j}, \tag{7.13}$$

where $\dot{\mathbf{P}}(u, v)$ is a point on the biquadratic Bézier patch; $u$ and $v$ are parameters such that $u \in [0, 1]$ and $v \in [0, 1]$; $i \in \{0, 1, 2\}$; $j \in \{0, 1, 2\}$; and $\dot{\mathbf{P}}_{ij}$ is the control point number $(i, j)$. Equation (7.13) can be written in matrix form as

[1] Curves shaping along the surface are called *isoparametric curves*. An isoparametric curve has a fixed $u$ value and a varying $v$ value or a fixed $v$ value and a varying $u$ value.

$$\dot{\mathbf{P}}(u,v)=\begin{bmatrix}u^2 & u & 1\end{bmatrix}\underbrace{\begin{bmatrix}1 & -2 & 1\\ -2 & 2 & 0\\ 1 & 0 & 0\end{bmatrix}}_{\dot{\text{B}}_2}\begin{bmatrix}\dot{\mathbf{P}}_{00} & \dot{\mathbf{P}}_{01} & \dot{\mathbf{P}}_{02}\\ \dot{\mathbf{P}}_{10} & \dot{\mathbf{P}}_{11} & \dot{\mathbf{P}}_{12}\\ \dot{\mathbf{P}}_{20} & \dot{\mathbf{P}}_{21} & \dot{\mathbf{P}}_{22}\end{bmatrix}\underbrace{\begin{bmatrix}1 & -2 & 1\\ -2 & 2 & 0\\ 1 & 0 & 0\end{bmatrix}}_{\dot{\text{B}}_2^T}\begin{bmatrix}v^2\\ v\\ 1\end{bmatrix}, \quad (7.14)$$

where $\dot{\text{B}}_2$ is the geometry matrix for the surface. It is the same matrix used with quadratic Bézier curves in Eq. (6.52).

**Example 7.1:** [*Bézier surfaces—points on biquadratic surfaces*]

A biquadratic Bézier surface is controlled by the following points: $\dot{\mathbf{P}}_{00}=[30, 30, 0]^T$, $\dot{\mathbf{P}}_{01}=[60, 30, 10]^T$, $\dot{\mathbf{P}}_{02}=[90, 30, 0]^T$, $\dot{\mathbf{P}}_{10}=[30, 60, 10]^T$, $\dot{\mathbf{P}}_{11}=[60, 60, 15]^T$, $\dot{\mathbf{P}}_{12}=[90, 60, 10]^T$, $\dot{\mathbf{P}}_{20}=[30, 90, 0]^T$, $\dot{\mathbf{P}}_{21}=[60, 90, 10]^T$ and $\dot{\mathbf{P}}_{22}=[90, 90, 0]^T$. Determine the surface point at $u=0.2$ and $v=0.5$.

**Solution 7.1:** We may use Eq. (7.14) to determine the required location $[x, y, z]^T$:

$$\begin{aligned}
x(0.2,0.5) &= \begin{bmatrix}0.2^2 & 0.2 & 1\end{bmatrix}\begin{bmatrix}1 & -2 & 1\\ -2 & 2 & 0\\ 1 & 0 & 0\end{bmatrix}\begin{bmatrix}30 & 60 & 90\\ 30 & 60 & 90\\ 30 & 60 & 90\end{bmatrix}\begin{bmatrix}1 & -2 & 1\\ -2 & 2 & 0\\ 1 & 0 & 0\end{bmatrix}\begin{bmatrix}0.5^2\\ 0.5\\ 1\end{bmatrix}\\
&= 60,\\
y(0.2,0.5) &= \begin{bmatrix}0.2^2 & 0.2 & 1\end{bmatrix}\begin{bmatrix}1 & -2 & 1\\ -2 & 2 & 0\\ 1 & 0 & 0\end{bmatrix}\begin{bmatrix}30 & 30 & 30\\ 60 & 60 & 60\\ 90 & 90 & 90\end{bmatrix}\begin{bmatrix}1 & -2 & 1\\ -2 & 2 & 0\\ 1 & 0 & 0\end{bmatrix}\begin{bmatrix}0.5^2\\ 0.5\\ 1\end{bmatrix}\\
&= 42,\\
z(0.2,0.5) &= \begin{bmatrix}0.2^2 & 0.2 & 1\end{bmatrix}\begin{bmatrix}1 & -2 & 1\\ -2 & 2 & 0\\ 1 & 0 & 0\end{bmatrix}\begin{bmatrix}0 & 10 & 0\\ 10 & 15 & 10\\ 0 & 10 & 0\end{bmatrix}\begin{bmatrix}1 & -2 & 1\\ -2 & 2 & 0\\ 1 & 0 & 0\end{bmatrix}\begin{bmatrix}0.5^2\\ 0.5\\ 1\end{bmatrix}\\
&= 7.4.
\end{aligned}$$

Hence, the surface point $\dot{\mathbf{P}}(0.2, 0.5)$ is $[60, 42, 7.4]^T$. The biquadratic Bézier surface is shown Fig. 7.2. The contours are drawn every 0.1 along both $u$- and $v$-directions. The surface point at $u=0.2$ and $v=0.5$ is marked. □

**Example 7.2:** [*Bézier surfaces—points on isoparametric curve*]

In Example 7.1, get surface locations for the isoparametric curve where $u=0$. Use steps of 0.1 $v$.

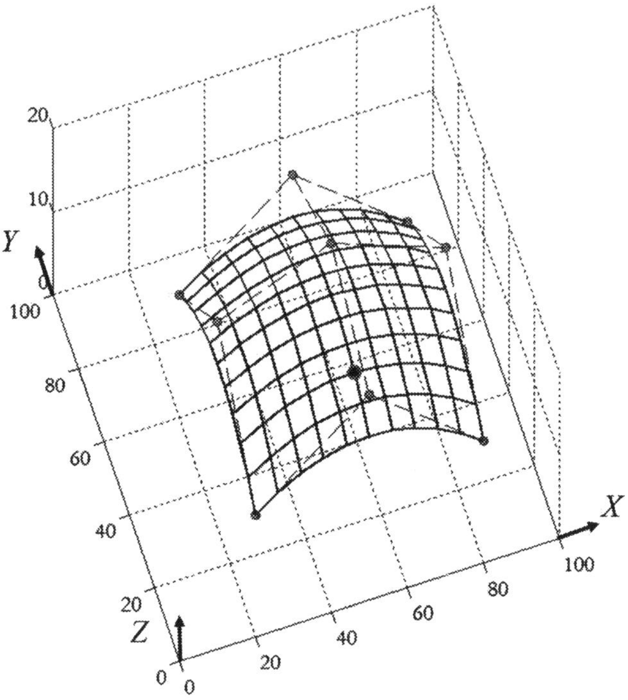


**Fig. 7.2** A biquadratic Bézier surface is controlled by $\dot{\mathbf{P}}_{00} = [30, 30, 0]^T$, $\dot{\mathbf{P}}_{01} = [60, 30, 10]^T$, $\dot{\mathbf{P}}_{02} = [90, 30, 0]^T$, $\dot{\mathbf{P}}_{10} = [30, 60, 10]^T$, $\dot{\mathbf{P}}_{11} = [60, 60, 15]^T$, $\dot{\mathbf{P}}_{12} = [90, 60, 10]^T$, $\dot{\mathbf{P}}_{20} = [30, 90, 0]^T$, $\dot{\mathbf{P}}_{21} = [60, 90, 10]^T$ and $\dot{\mathbf{P}}_{22} = [90, 90, 0]^T$. The surface point at $u = 0.2$ and $v = 0.5$ is marked. The dashed lines are connecting the control points

**Solution 7.2:** The required points have the parameters (0, 0), (0, 0.1), (0, 0.2), ..., (0, 1). We may use Eq. (7.14) to determine the required location at each of the required parameters. The isoparametric curve points are listed in the following table:

| $u$ | $v$ | $\dot{\mathbf{P}}(u, v)$ |
|---|---|---|
| 0 | 0 | $[30, 30, 0]^T$ |
| 0 | 0.1 | $[36, 30, 1.8]^T$ |
| 0 | 0.2 | $[42, 30, 3.2]^T$ |
| 0 | 0.3 | $[48, 30, 4.2]^T$ |
| 0 | 0.4 | $[54, 30, 4.8]^T$ |
| 0 | 0.5 | $[60, 30, 5]^T$ |
| 0 | 0.6 | $[66, 30, 4.8]^T$ |
| 0 | 0.7 | $[72, 30, 4.2]^T$ |
| 0 | 0.8 | $[78, 30, 3.2]^T$ |
| 0 | 0.9 | $[84, 30, 1.8]^T$ |
| 0 | 1 | $[90, 30, 0]^T$ |

Notice that a path of biquadratic Bézier surface points having a constant $u$ or a constant $v$; i.e., an isoparametric curve, is a quadratic Bézier curve. In our case, the path where $u = 0$ is a quadratic Bézier curve obtained using the control points $\dot{\mathbf{P}}_{00} = [30, 30, 0]^T$, $\dot{\mathbf{P}}_{01} = [60, 30, 10]^T$ and $\dot{\mathbf{P}}_{02} = [90, 30, 0]^T$. Check this out by using Eq. (6.52) with those control points where $t = \{0, 0.1, 0.2, \ldots, 1\}$. □

**Example 7.3:** [*Bézier surfaces—points on biquadratic surfaces*]
Consider the control points: $\dot{\mathbf{P}}_{00}, \dot{\mathbf{P}}_{01}, \dot{\mathbf{P}}_{02}, \dot{\mathbf{P}}_{10}, \dot{\mathbf{P}}_{11}, \dot{\mathbf{P}}_{12}, \dot{\mathbf{P}}_{20}, \dot{\mathbf{P}}_{21}$ and $\dot{\mathbf{P}}_{22}$. Utilize Eq. (6.52) to get the position of the surface point $\dot{\mathbf{P}}(u, v)$.

**Solution 7.3:** The idea is to use Eq. (6.52) along both directions to get the required surface point.

1. Obtain the intermediate control points along the $v$-direction.

   a. Using points $\dot{\mathbf{P}}_{00}$, $\dot{\mathbf{P}}_{01}$ and $\dot{\mathbf{P}}_{02}$, get $\dot{\mathbf{P}}_{0v}$ where

$$\dot{\mathbf{P}}_{0v} = \begin{bmatrix} v^2 & v & 1 \end{bmatrix} \begin{bmatrix} 1 & -2 & 1 \\ -2 & 2 & 0 \\ 1 & 0 & 0 \end{bmatrix} \begin{bmatrix} \dot{\mathbf{P}}_{00} \\ \dot{\mathbf{P}}_{01} \\ \dot{\mathbf{P}}_{02} \end{bmatrix}.$$

   b. Using points $\dot{\mathbf{P}}_{10}$, $\dot{\mathbf{P}}_{11}$ and $\dot{\mathbf{P}}_{12}$, get $\dot{\mathbf{P}}_{1v}$ where

$$\dot{\mathbf{P}}_{1v} = \begin{bmatrix} v^2 & v & 1 \end{bmatrix} \begin{bmatrix} 1 & -2 & 1 \\ -2 & 2 & 0 \\ 1 & 0 & 0 \end{bmatrix} \begin{bmatrix} \dot{\mathbf{P}}_{10} \\ \dot{\mathbf{P}}_{11} \\ \dot{\mathbf{P}}_{12} \end{bmatrix}.$$

   c. Using points $\dot{\mathbf{P}}_{20}$, $\dot{\mathbf{P}}_{21}$ and $\dot{\mathbf{P}}_{22}$, get $\dot{\mathbf{P}}_{2v}$ where

$$\dot{\mathbf{P}}_{2v} = \begin{bmatrix} v^2 & v & 1 \end{bmatrix} \begin{bmatrix} 1 & -2 & 1 \\ -2 & 2 & 0 \\ 1 & 0 & 0 \end{bmatrix} \begin{bmatrix} \dot{\mathbf{P}}_{20} \\ \dot{\mathbf{P}}_{21} \\ \dot{\mathbf{P}}_{22} \end{bmatrix}.$$

2. Obtain the surface point along the $u$-direction.

   a. Using points $\dot{\mathbf{P}}_{0v}$, $\dot{\mathbf{P}}_{1v}$ and $\dot{\mathbf{P}}_{2v}$, we have

$$\dot{\mathbf{P}}(u, v) = \begin{bmatrix} u^2 & u & 1 \end{bmatrix} \begin{bmatrix} 1 & -2 & 1 \\ -2 & 2 & 0 \\ 1 & 0 & 0 \end{bmatrix} \begin{bmatrix} \dot{\mathbf{P}}_{0v} \\ \dot{\mathbf{P}}_{1v} \\ \dot{\mathbf{P}}_{2v} \end{bmatrix}.$$

   Since

$$\begin{bmatrix} \dot{\mathbf{P}}_{0v} \\ \dot{\mathbf{P}}_{1v} \\ \dot{\mathbf{P}}_{2v} \end{bmatrix} = \left[ \begin{bmatrix} v^2 & v & 1 \end{bmatrix} \begin{bmatrix} 1 & -2 & 1 \\ -2 & 2 & 0 \\ 1 & 0 & 0 \end{bmatrix} \begin{bmatrix} \dot{\mathbf{P}}_{00} & \dot{\mathbf{P}}_{10} & \dot{\mathbf{P}}_{20} \\ \dot{\mathbf{P}}_{01} & \dot{\mathbf{P}}_{11} & \dot{\mathbf{P}}_{21} \\ \dot{\mathbf{P}}_{02} & \dot{\mathbf{P}}_{12} & \dot{\mathbf{P}}_{22} \end{bmatrix} \right]^T$$
$$= \begin{bmatrix} \dot{\mathbf{P}}_{00} & \dot{\mathbf{P}}_{01} & \dot{\mathbf{P}}_{02} \\ \dot{\mathbf{P}}_{10} & \dot{\mathbf{P}}_{11} & \dot{\mathbf{P}}_{12} \\ \dot{\mathbf{P}}_{20} & \dot{\mathbf{P}}_{21} & \dot{\mathbf{P}}_{22} \end{bmatrix} \begin{bmatrix} 1 & -2 & 1 \\ -2 & 2 & 0 \\ 1 & 0 & 0 \end{bmatrix} \begin{bmatrix} v^2 \\ v \\ 1 \end{bmatrix};$$

thus,

$$\dot{\mathbf{P}}(u,v) = \begin{bmatrix} u^2 & u & 1 \end{bmatrix} \begin{bmatrix} 1 & -2 & 1 \\ -2 & 2 & 0 \\ 1 & 0 & 0 \end{bmatrix} \begin{bmatrix} \dot{\mathbf{P}}_{00} & \dot{\mathbf{P}}_{01} & \dot{\mathbf{P}}_{02} \\ \dot{\mathbf{P}}_{10} & \dot{\mathbf{P}}_{11} & \dot{\mathbf{P}}_{12} \\ \dot{\mathbf{P}}_{20} & \dot{\mathbf{P}}_{21} & \dot{\mathbf{P}}_{22} \end{bmatrix} \begin{bmatrix} 1 & -2 & 1 \\ -2 & 2 & 0 \\ 1 & 0 & 0 \end{bmatrix} \begin{bmatrix} v^2 \\ v \\ 1 \end{bmatrix},$$

which is the same as Eq. (7.14). □

### *7.2.3 Bicubic Bézier Surfaces*

The number of control points defining a Bézier patch of degree (3, 3) is 16 (i.e., 4×4). An example of a bicubic Bézier surface is shown in Fig. 7.3 where two parameters $u$ and $v$ are considered along two directions. Equation (7.9) can be tailored for this patch by substituting $p = q = 3$ to get

$$\dot{\mathbf{P}}(u,v) = \sum_{i=0}^{3}\sum_{j=0}^{3} \dot{\mathbf{P}}_{ij} \binom{3}{i} u^i (1-u)^{3-i} \binom{3}{j} v^j (1-v)^{3-j}, \tag{7.15}$$

where $\dot{\mathbf{P}}(u,v)$ is a point on the bicubic Bézier surface; $u$ and $v$ are parameters such that $u \in [0,1]$ and $v \in [0,1]$; $i \in \{0,1,2,3\}$; $j \in \{0,1,2,3\}$; and $\dot{\mathbf{P}}_{ij}$ is the control point number $(i, j)$. Equation (7.15) can be written in matrix form as

$$\dot{\mathbf{P}}(u,v) = \begin{bmatrix} u^3 & u^2 & u & 1 \end{bmatrix} \underbrace{\begin{bmatrix} -1 & 3 & -3 & 1 \\ 3 & -6 & 3 & 0 \\ -3 & 3 & 0 & 0 \\ 1 & 0 & 0 & 0 \end{bmatrix}}_{\dot{\mathrm{B}}_3} \begin{bmatrix} \dot{\mathbf{P}}_{00} & \dot{\mathbf{P}}_{01} & \dot{\mathbf{P}}_{02} & \dot{\mathbf{P}}_{03} \\ \dot{\mathbf{P}}_{10} & \dot{\mathbf{P}}_{11} & \dot{\mathbf{P}}_{12} & \dot{\mathbf{P}}_{13} \\ \dot{\mathbf{P}}_{20} & \dot{\mathbf{P}}_{21} & \dot{\mathbf{P}}_{22} & \dot{\mathbf{P}}_{23} \\ \dot{\mathbf{P}}_{30} & \dot{\mathbf{P}}_{31} & \dot{\mathbf{P}}_{32} & \dot{\mathbf{P}}_{33} \end{bmatrix} \cdots$$
$$\cdots \underbrace{\begin{bmatrix} -1 & 3 & -3 & 1 \\ 3 & -6 & 3 & 0 \\ -3 & 3 & 0 & 0 \\ 1 & 0 & 0 & 0 \end{bmatrix}}_{\dot{\mathrm{B}}_3^T} \begin{bmatrix} v^3 \\ v^2 \\ v \\ 1 \end{bmatrix}, \tag{7.16}$$

where $\dot{\mathrm{B}}_3$ is the geometry matrix for the surface. It is the same matrix used with cubic Bézier curves in Eq. (6.65).

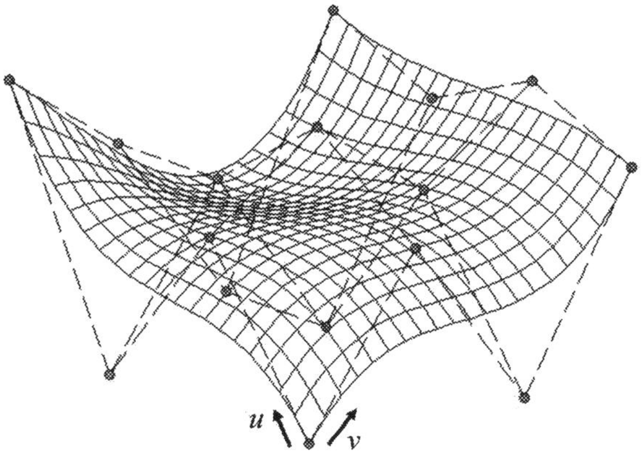


**Fig. 7.3** An example of a bicubic Bézier surface

**Example 7.4:** [*Bézier surfaces—points on bicubic surfaces*]

A bicubic Bézier surface is controlled by the following points: $\dot{\mathbf{P}}_{00} = [30, 30, 0]^T$, $\dot{\mathbf{P}}_{01} = [60, 30, 10]^T$, $\dot{\mathbf{P}}_{02} = [90, 30, 8]^T$, $\dot{\mathbf{P}}_{03} = [120, 30, 20]^T$, $\dot{\mathbf{P}}_{10} = [30, 60, 10]^T$, $\dot{\mathbf{P}}_{11} = [60, 60, 15]^T$, $\dot{\mathbf{P}}_{12} = [90, 60, 16]^T$, $\dot{\mathbf{P}}_{13} = [120, 60, 7]^T$, $\dot{\mathbf{P}}_{20} = [30, 90, 8]^T$, $\dot{\mathbf{P}}_{21} = [60, 90, 18]^T$, $\dot{\mathbf{P}}_{22} = [90, 90, 15]^T$, $\dot{\mathbf{P}}_{23} = [120, 90, 5]^T$, $\dot{\mathbf{P}}_{30} = [30, 120, 0]^T$, $\dot{\mathbf{P}}_{31} = [60, 120, 5]^T$, $\dot{\mathbf{P}}_{32} = [90, 120, 3]^T$ and $\dot{\mathbf{P}}_{33} = [120, 120, 1]^T$. Determine the surface point at $u = 0.8$ and $v = 0.5$.

**Solution 7.4:** We may use Eq. (7.16) to determine the required location $[x, y, z]^T$ as

$$
x(0.8, 0.5) = \begin{bmatrix} 0.8^3 & 0.8^2 & 0.8 & 1 \end{bmatrix} \begin{bmatrix} -1 & 3 & -3 & 1 \\ 3 & -6 & 3 & 0 \\ -3 & 3 & 0 & 0 \\ 1 & 0 & 0 & 0 \end{bmatrix} \begin{bmatrix} 30 & 30 & 30 & 30 \\ 60 & 60 & 60 & 60 \\ 90 & 90 & 90 & 90 \\ 120 & 120 & 120 & 120 \end{bmatrix} \cdots
$$

$$
\cdots \begin{bmatrix} -1 & 3 & -3 & 1 \\ 3 & -6 & 3 & 0 \\ -3 & 3 & 0 & 0 \\ 1 & 0 & 0 & 0 \end{bmatrix} \begin{bmatrix} 0.5^2 \\ 0.5 \\ 1 \end{bmatrix}
$$

$$
= 75,
$$

$$
y(0.8, 0.5) = \begin{bmatrix} 0.8^3 & 0.8^2 & 0.8 & 1 \end{bmatrix} \begin{bmatrix} -1 & 3 & -3 & 1 \\ 3 & -6 & 3 & 0 \\ -3 & 3 & 0 & 0 \\ 1 & 0 & 0 & 0 \end{bmatrix} \begin{bmatrix} 30 & 60 & 90 & 120 \\ 30 & 60 & 90 & 120 \\ 30 & 60 & 90 & 120 \\ 30 & 60 & 90 & 120 \end{bmatrix} \cdots
$$

$$
\cdots \begin{bmatrix} -1 & 3 & -3 & 1 \\ 3 & -6 & 3 & 0 \\ -3 & 3 & 0 & 0 \\ 1 & 0 & 0 & 0 \end{bmatrix} \begin{bmatrix} 0.5^2 \\ 0.5 \\ 1 \end{bmatrix}
$$

$$
= 102,
$$

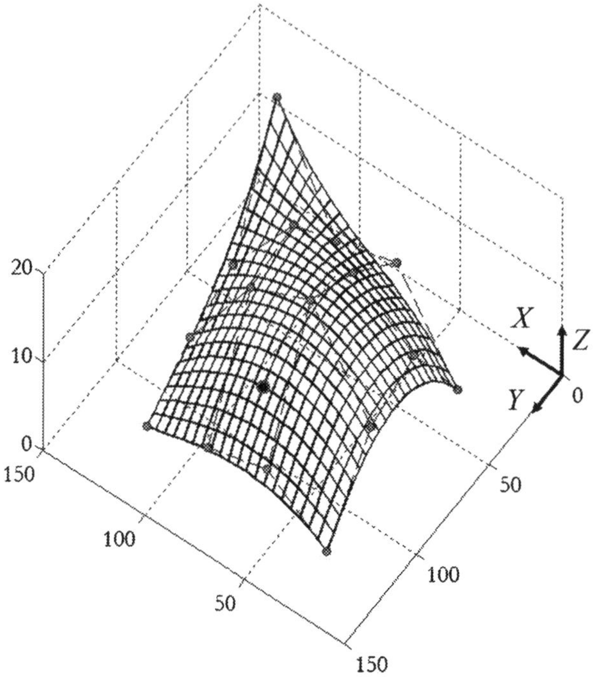


**Fig. 7.4** A bicubic Bézier surface is controlled by $\dot{\mathbf{P}}_{00} = [30, 30, 0]^T$, $\dot{\mathbf{P}}_{01} = [60, 30, 10]^T$, $\dot{\mathbf{P}}_{02} = [90, 30, 8]^T$, $\dot{\mathbf{P}}_{03} = [120, 30, 20]^T$, $\dot{\mathbf{P}}_{10} = [30, 60, 10]^T$, $\dot{\mathbf{P}}_{11} = [60, 60, 15]^T$, $\dot{\mathbf{P}}_{12} = [90, 60, 16]^T$, $\dot{\mathbf{P}}_{13} = [120, 60, 7]^T$, $\dot{\mathbf{P}}_{20} = [30, 90, 8]^T$, $\dot{\mathbf{P}}_{21} = [60, 90, 18]^T$, $\dot{\mathbf{P}}_{22} = [90, 90, 15]^T$, $\dot{\mathbf{P}}_{23} = [120, 90, 5]^T$, $\dot{\mathbf{P}}_{30} = [30, 120, 0]^T$, $\dot{\mathbf{P}}_{31} = [60, 120, 5]^T$, $\dot{\mathbf{P}}_{32} = [90, 120, 3]^T$ and $\dot{\mathbf{P}}_{33} = [120, 120, 1]^T$. The surface point at $u = 0.8$ and $v = 0.5$ is marked. The dashed lines are connecting the control points

and

$$
\begin{aligned}
z(0.8, 0.5) = \begin{bmatrix} 0.8^3 & 0.8^2 & 0.8 & 1 \end{bmatrix} & \begin{bmatrix} -1 & 3 & -3 & 1 \\ 3 & -6 & 3 & 0 \\ -3 & 3 & 0 & 0 \\ 1 & 0 & 0 & 0 \end{bmatrix} \begin{bmatrix} 0 & 10 & 8 & 0 \\ 10 & 15 & 18 & 5 \\ 8 & 16 & 15 & 3 \\ 20 & 7 & 5 & 1 \end{bmatrix} \cdots \\
& \cdots \begin{bmatrix} -1 & 3 & -3 & 1 \\ 3 & -6 & 3 & 0 \\ -3 & 3 & 0 & 0 \\ 1 & 0 & 0 & 0 \end{bmatrix} \begin{bmatrix} 0.5^2 \\ 0.5 \\ 1 \end{bmatrix} \\
& = 8.37.
\end{aligned}
$$

Hence, the surface point $\dot{\mathbf{P}}(0.8, 0.5)$ is $[75, 102, 8.37]^T$. The bicubic Bézier surface is shown Fig. 7.4. The contours are drawn every 0.05 along both $u$- and $v$-directions. The surface point at $u = 0.8$ and $v = 0.5$ is marked. □

## 7.3 NURBS Surfaces

As a Bézier curve having one parameter $t$ along one direction evolves to a Bézier surface having two parameters $u$ and $v$ along two directions, NURBS curves (Sect. 6.2.3) (Forrest 1980) can be extended to NURBS surfaces along both directions as well.

As in NURBS curves, NURBS surfaces are influenced by the locations of control points, the knot vectors and the weights of homogeneous points. However, in case of NURBS surfaces, two knot vectors are used to cover two directions; i.e., $u$ and $v$, instead of one direction $t$ in case of NURBS curves. Any knot vector type may be used; uniform, open uniform and non-uniform. Examples of NURBS surfaces built on the same control points but using different knots vectors are shown in Fig. 7.5.

A point $\dot{\mathbf{P}}$ having parameters $u$ and $v$ (i.e., $\dot{\mathbf{P}}(u, v)$) on a non-uniform rational B-spline surface of degree[2] $(p, q)$ is expressed as

$$\dot{\mathbf{P}}(u, v) = \frac{\sum\limits_{i=0}^{n}\sum\limits_{j=0}^{m} \dot{\mathbf{P}}_{ij} N_{i,p}(u) N_{j,q}(v) w_{ij}}{\sum\limits_{i=0}^{n}\sum\limits_{j=0}^{m} N_{i,p}(u) N_{j,q}(v) w_{ij}}, \tag{7.17}$$

where $(n+1)(m+1)$ is the number of control points; $i \in \{0, 1, 2, \ldots, n\}$; $j \in \{0, 1, 2, \ldots, m\}$; $\dot{\mathbf{P}}_{ij}$ is the control point number $(i, j)$; $p$ and $q$ represent the surface degree along the $u$- and $v$-directions respectively; $N_{i,p}(u)$ and $N_{j,q}(v)$ are the B-spline basis functions defined by Eq. (6.77) for the $u$- and $v$-directions respectively; and $w_{ij}$ is the weight of control point $\dot{\mathbf{P}}_{ij}$ (i.e., $w_{ij}$ is the last entry in the homogeneous representation of the control point $\mathbf{P}_{ij}$). In general, the surface degrees along both directions may not be equal (i.e., $p \neq q$). For all cases shown in Fig. 7.5, $p = 2$ and $q = 3$. This means that the whole surface is generated as two curved patches using a $4 \times 4$ grid of control points.

### *7.3.1 Biquadratic NURBS Surfaces*

A biquadratic NURBS surface is a surface of degree (2, 2); i.e., a surface of order 3 along each direction. The number of control points defining a NURBS surface of degree (2, 2) is nine (i.e., $3 \times 3$). Examples of biquadratic NURBS surfaces are shown in Fig. 7.6 where two parameters $u$ and $v$ are considered along two directions. Notice that using open uniform knot vectors interpolates the control endpoints while using uniform knot vectors does not. In both examples, all points are having homogeneous weights of 1. Equation (7.17) can be tailored for this surface by substituting $p = q = 2$ to get

[2] Recall that degree $(p, q)$ is equivalent to order $(p + 1, q + 1)$.

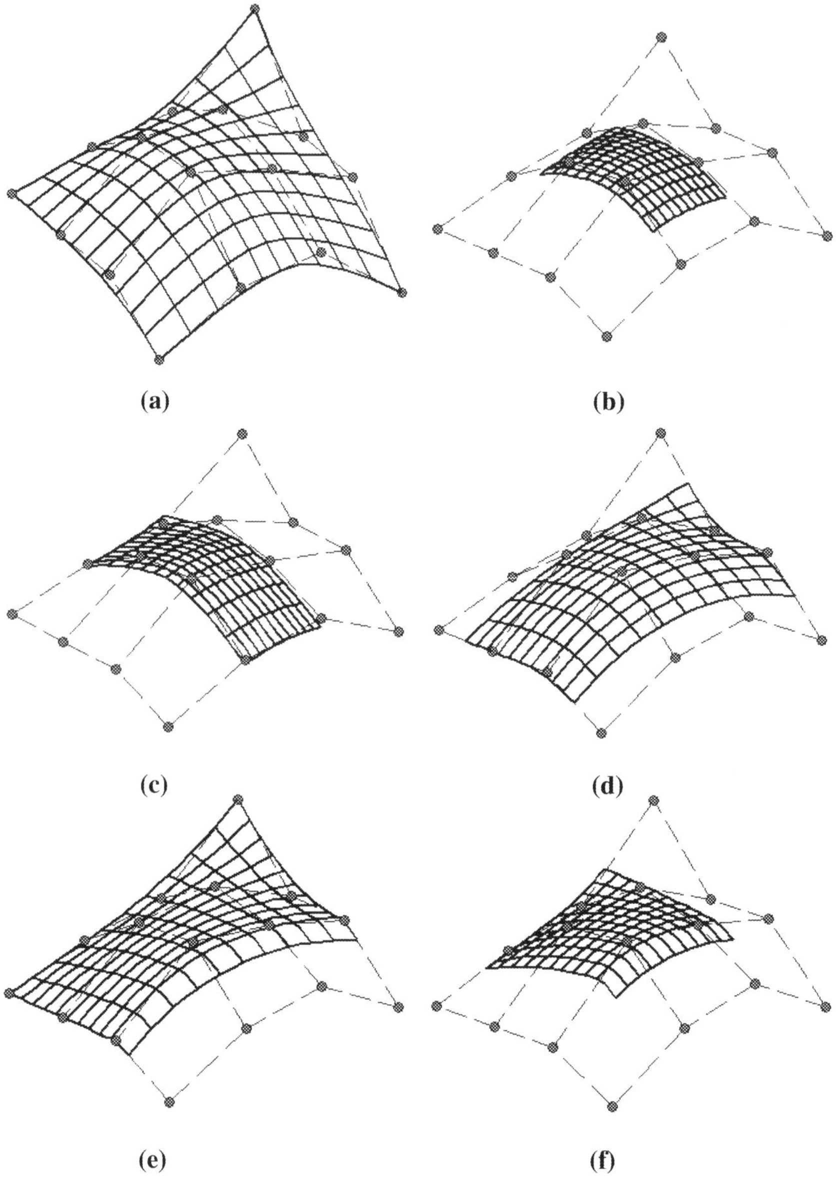

Fig. 7.5 Different NURBS surfaces can be generated using the same control points including their weights but with different knot vectors. **a** Using open uniform knot vectors along both directions. **b** Using uniform knot vectors along both directions. **c**, **d** Using uniform knot vector along one direction and open uniform knot vector along the other direction. **e** Using open uniform and non-uniform knot vectors. **f** Using uniform and non-uniform knot vectors

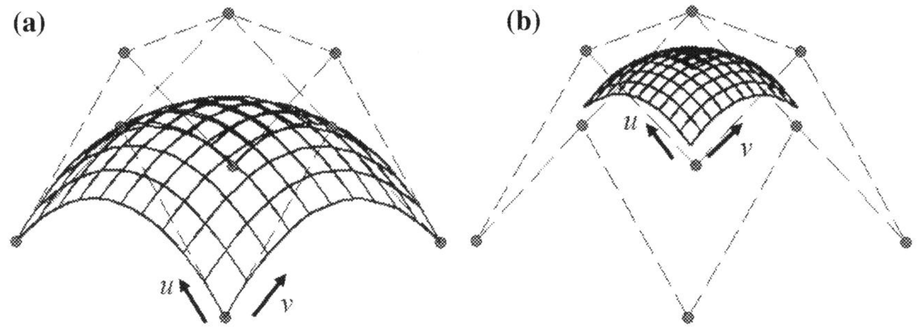


**Fig. 7.6** Examples of biquadratic NURBS surfaces using the same control points. **a** Using the open uniform knot vectors [0, 0, 0, 1, 1, 1]. **b** Using the uniform knot vectors [0, 1, 2, 3, 4, 5]

$$\dot{\mathbf{P}}(u, v) = \frac{\sum_{i=0}^{n} \sum_{j=0}^{m} \dot{\mathbf{P}}_{ij} N_{i,2}(u) N_{j,2}(v) w_{ij}}{\sum_{i=0}^{n} \sum_{j=0}^{m} N_{i,2}(u) N_{j,2}(v) w_{ij}}, \tag{7.18}$$

where $\dot{\mathbf{P}}(u, v)$ is a point on the biquadratic NURBS surface; $u$ and $v$ are parameters along two directions; $(n+1)(m+1)$ is the number of control points; $\dot{\mathbf{P}}_{ij}$ is the control point number $(i, j)$; $N_{i,2}(u)$ and $N_{j,2}(v)$ are the B-spline basis functions defined by Eq. (6.77) for the $u$- and $v$-directions respectively; and $w_{ij}$ is the weight of control point $\dot{\mathbf{P}}_{ij}$.

**Example 7.5:** [*NURBS surfaces—points on biquadratic surfaces using different knot vectors*]

A biquadratic NURBS surface is controlled by the following homogeneous points: $\mathbf{P}_{00} = [30, 30, 0, 1]^T$, $\mathbf{P}_{01} = [60, 30, 10, 1]^T$, $\mathbf{P}_{02} = [90, 30, 0, 1]^T$, $\mathbf{P}_{10} = [30, 60, 10, 1]^T$, $\mathbf{P}_{11} = [60, 60, 15, 1]^T$, $\mathbf{P}_{12} = [90, 60, 10, 1]^T$, $\mathbf{P}_{20} = [30, 90, 0, 1]^T$, $\mathbf{P}_{21} = [60, 90, 10, 1]^T$ and $\mathbf{P}_{22} = [90, 90, 0, 1]^T$ where the fourth term in each point representation denotes the homogeneous weight of that point.

1. If the same open uniform knot vector [0, 0, 0, 1, 1, 1] is used along both directions, determine the values of the basis functions $N_{i,2}(0.2)$ and $N_{j,2}(0.5)$ as well as the location of the surface point $\dot{\mathbf{P}}$ at $u = 0.2$ and $v = 0.5$.
2. If the same uniform knot vector [0, 1, 2, 3, 4, 5] is used along both directions, determine the values of the basis functions $N_{i,2}(2.2)$ and $N_{j,2}(2.5)$ as well as the location of the surface point $\dot{\mathbf{P}}$ at $u = 2.2$ and $v = 2.5$.

Show the curve generated in each case.

**Solution 7.5:** Different results are obtained using different knot vectors.

**Using the open uniform knot vectors [0, 0, 0, 1, 1, 1]:** The basis functions are calculated as

$$\begin{aligned}N_{0,2}(0.2) &= 0.64,\\ N_{1,2}(0.2) &= 0.32,\\ N_{2,2}(0.2) &= 0.04\end{aligned}$$

and

$$\begin{aligned}N_{0,2}(0.5) &= 0.25,\\ N_{1,2}(0.5) &= 0.50,\\ N_{2,2}(0.5) &= 0.25.\end{aligned}$$

Refer to Sect. 6.2.2.3 for information on how to get these values. We substitute these values in Eq. (7.18) that can be written as

$$\dot{\mathbf{P}}(u,v) = \frac{\begin{array}{l}\dot{\mathbf{P}}_{00}N_{0,2}(u)N_{0,2}(v)w_{00} + \dot{\mathbf{P}}_{01}N_{0,2}(u)N_{1,2}(v)w_{01} + \dot{\mathbf{P}}_{02}N_{0,2}(u)N_{2,2}(v)w_{02} + \cdots\\ +\dot{\mathbf{P}}_{10}N_{1,2}(u)N_{0,2}(v)w_{10} + \dot{\mathbf{P}}_{11}N_{1,2}(u)N_{1,2}(v)w_{11} + \dot{\mathbf{P}}_{12}N_{1,2}(u)N_{2,2}(v)w_{12} + \cdots\\ +\dot{\mathbf{P}}_{20}N_{2,2}(u)N_{0,2}(v)w_{20} + \dot{\mathbf{P}}_{21}N_{2,2}(u)N_{1,2}(v)w_{21} + \dot{\mathbf{P}}_{22}N_{2,2}(u)N_{2,2}(v)w_{22}\end{array}}{\begin{array}{l}N_{0,2}(u)N_{0,2}(v)w_{00} + N_{0,2}(u)N_{1,2}(v)w_{01} + N_{0,2}(u)N_{2,2}(v)w_{02} + \cdots\\ +N_{1,2}(u)N_{0,2}(v)w_{10} + N_{1,2}(u)N_{1,2}(v)w_{11} + N_{1,2}(u)N_{2,2}(v)w_{12} + \cdots\\ +N_{2,2}(u)N_{0,2}(v)w_{20} + N_{2,2}(u)N_{1,2}(v)w_{21} + N_{2,2}(u)N_{2,2}(v)w_{22}\end{array}}.$$

Hence,

$$x(0.2,0.5) = \frac{\begin{array}{l}30 \times 0.64 \times 0.25 \times 1 + 60 \times 0.64 \times 0.5 \times 1 + 90 \times 0.64 \times 0.25 \times 1 + \cdots\\ +30 \times 0.32 \times 0.25 \times 1 + 60 \times 0.32 \times 0.5 \times 1 + 90 \times 0.32 \times 0.25 \times 1 + \cdots\\ +30 \times 0.04 \times 0.25 \times 1 + 60 \times 0.04 \times 0.5 \times 1 + 90 \times 0.04 \times 0.25 \times 1\end{array}}{\begin{array}{l}0.64 \times 0.25 \times 1 + 0.64 \times 0.5 \times 1 + 0.64 \times 0.25 \times 1 + \cdots\\ +0.32 \times 0.25 \times 1 + 0.32 \times 0.5 \times 1 + 0.32 \times 0.25 \times 1 + \cdots\\ +0.04 \times 0.25 \times 1 + 0.04 \times 0.5 \times 1 + 0.04 \times 0.25 \times 1\end{array}} = 60,$$

$$y(0.2,0.5) = \frac{\begin{array}{l}30 \times 0.64 \times 0.25 \times 1 + 30 \times 0.64 \times 0.5 \times 1 + 30 \times 0.64 \times 0.25 \times 1 + \cdots\\ +60 \times 0.32 \times 0.25 \times 1 + 60 \times 0.32 \times 0.5 \times 1 + 60 \times 0.32 \times 0.25 \times 1 + \cdots\\ +90 \times 0.04 \times 0.25 \times 1 + 90 \times 0.04 \times 0.5 \times 1 + 90 \times 0.04 \times 0.25 \times 1\end{array}}{\begin{array}{l}0.64 \times 0.25 \times 1 + 0.64 \times 0.5 \times 1 + 0.64 \times 0.25 \times 1 + \cdots\\ +0.32 \times 0.25 \times 1 + 0.32 \times 0.5 \times 1 + 0.32 \times 0.25 \times 1 + \cdots\\ +0.04 \times 0.25 \times 1 + 0.04 \times 0.5 \times 1 + 0.04 \times 0.25 \times 1\end{array}} = 42$$

and

$$z(0.2, 0.5) = \frac{\begin{array}{l} 0 \times 0.64 \times 0.25 \times 1 + 10 \times 0.64 \times 0.5 \times 1 + 0 \times 0.64 \times 0.25 \times 1 + \cdots \\ +10 \times 0.32 \times 0.25 \times 1 + 15 \times 0.32 \times 0.5 \times 1 + 10 \times 0.32 \times 0.25 \times 1 + \cdots \\ +0 \times 0.04 \times 0.25 \times 1 + 10 \times 0.04 \times 0.5 \times 1 + 0 \times 0.04 \times 0.25 \times 1 \end{array}}{\begin{array}{l} 0.64 \times 0.25 \times 1 + 0.64 \times 0.5 \times 1 + 0.64 \times 0.25 \times 1 + \cdots \\ +0.32 \times 0.25 \times 1 + 0.32 \times 0.5 \times 1 + 0.32 \times 0.25 \times 1 + \cdots \\ +0.04 \times 0.25 \times 1 + 0.04 \times 0.5 \times 1 + 0.04 \times 0.25 \times 1 \end{array}} = 7.4.$$

Thus, the surface point $\dot{\mathbf{P}}$ at $u = 0.2$ and $v = 0.5$ is estimated as $[60, 42, 7.4]^T$ (i.e., same as Bézier surface in Example 7.1). (Notice that we did not have to calculate the denominator in the previous equations as it becomes 1 when $w_{ij} = 1$.) Using these open uniform vectors results in the biquadratic NURBS surface shown in Fig. 7.7a. The contours are drawn every $0.1u$ and $0.1v$. The surface point at $u = 0.2$ and $v = 0.5$ is marked.

**Using the uniform knot vectors [0, 1, 2, 3, 4, 5]:** According to Table 6.1, the basis functions are calculated as

$$N_{0,2}(2.2) = 0.32,$$
$$N_{1,2}(2.2) = 0.66,$$
$$N_{2,2}(2.2) = 0.02$$

and

$$N_{0,2}(2.5) = 0.125,$$
$$N_{1,2}(2.5) = 0.75,$$
$$N_{2,2}(2.5) = 0.125.$$

Substituting these values in Eq. (7.18) where $w_{ij} = 1$ for all points, the surface point $\dot{\mathbf{P}}$ at $u = 2.2$ and $v = 2.5$ is estimated as $[60, 51, 11.625]^T$. Using these uniform vectors results in the biquadratic NURBS surface shown in Fig. 7.7b. The contours are drawn every $0.1u$ and $0.1v$. The surface point at $u = 2.2$ and $v = 2.5$ is marked. □

**Example 7.6:** [*NURBS surfaces—changing homogeneous weights for biquadratic surfaces using open uniform knot vector*]

In Example 7.5, if the homogeneous weights $w_{i1}$ of points $\mathbf{P}_{i1}$ are changed to 0.2 and then to 1.8, determine the points of the isoparametric curve having $u = 0.2$ if the open uniform knot vector [0, 0, 0, 1, 1, 1] is used.

**Solution 7.6:** The isoparametric curve has a fixed $u$ value at 0.2 while $v$ values vary from 0 to 1. Equation (7.18) is utilized to get the points along that curve. The locations of these points are listed in the following table:

| $u$ | $v$ | $w_{i1} = 1$ | $w_{i1} = 0.2$ | $w_{i1} = 1.8$ |
|---|---|---|---|---|
| 0.2 | 0.0 | $[30, 42, 3.2]^T$ | $[30, 42, 3.2]^T$ | $[30, 42, 3.2]^T$ |
| 0.2 | 0.1 | $[36, 42, 4.712]^T$ | $[31.9626, 42, 3.5533]^T$ | $[39.021, 42, 5.579]^T$ |
| 0.2 | 0.2 | $[42, 42, 5.888]^T$ | $[35.8065, 42, 3.9226]^T$ | $[45.6688, 42, 7.0522]^T$ |
| 0.2 | 0.3 | $[48, 42, 6.728]^T$ | $[41.9277, 42, 4.2627]^T$ | $[51.018, 42, 7.9533]^T$ |
| 0.2 | 0.4 | $[54, 42, 7.232]^T$ | $[50.2597, 42, 4.5091]^T$ | $[55.6647, 42, 8.4439]^T$ |
| 0.2 | 0.5 | $[60, 42, 7.4]^T$ | $[60, 42, 4.6]^T$ | $[60, 42, 8.6]^T$ |
| 0.2 | 0.6 | $[66, 42, 7.232]^T$ | $[69.7403, 42, 4.5091]^T$ | $[64.3353, 42, 8.4439]^T$ |
| 0.2 | 0.7 | $[72, 42, 6.728]^T$ | $[78.0723, 42, 4.2627]^T$ | $[68.982, 42, 7.9533]^T$ |
| 0.2 | 0.8 | $[78, 42, 5.888]^T$ | $[84.1935, 42, 3.9226]^T$ | $[74.3312, 42, 7.0522]^T$ |
| 0.2 | 0.9 | $[84, 42, 4.712]^T$ | $[88.0374, 42, 3.5533]^T$ | $[80.979, 42, 5.579]^T$ |
| 0.2 | 1.0 | $[90, 42, 3.2]^T$ | $[90, 42, 3.2]^T$ | $[90, 42, 3.2]^T$ |

The surfaces where $w_{i1} = 0.2$ and $w_{i1} = 1.8$ are shown in Fig. 7.8a, b respectively while the surface where $w_{i1} = 1$ is shown in Fig. 7.7a. Notice that when $w_{i1} = 0.2$, the surface is pushed away from control points $\dot{\mathbf{P}}_{i1}$. On the other hand, when $w_{i1} = 1.8$, the surface is pulled closer to control points $\dot{\mathbf{P}}_{i1}$. □

### 7.3.2 Bicubic NURBS Surfaces

A bicubic NURBS surface is a surface of degree (3, 3); i.e., a surface of order 4 along both directions. The number of control points defining a NURBS surface of degree (3, 3) is 16 (i.e., $4 \times 4$). Examples of bicubic NURBS surfaces are shown in Fig. 7.9 where two parameters $u$ and $v$ are considered along two directions. Notice that using open uniform knot vectors interpolate the control endpoints while using uniform knot vectors do not. In both examples, all points are having homogeneous weights of 1. Equation (7.17) can be tailored for this surface by substituting $p = q = 3$ to get

$$\dot{\mathbf{P}}(u, v) = \frac{\sum\limits_{i=0}^{n} \sum\limits_{j=0}^{m} \dot{\mathbf{P}}_{ij} N_{i,3}(u) N_{j,3}(v) w_{ij}}{\sum\limits_{i=0}^{n} \sum\limits_{j=0}^{m} N_{i,3}(u) N_{j,3}(v) w_{ij}}. \tag{7.19}$$

where $\dot{\mathbf{P}}(u, v)$ is a point on the bicubic NURBS surface; $u$ and $v$ are parameters along two directions; $(n + 1)(m + 1)$ is the number of control points; $\dot{\mathbf{P}}_{ij}$ is the control point number $(i, j)$; $N_{i,3}(u)$ and $N_{j,3}(v)$ are the B-spline basis functions defined by Eq. (6.77) for the $u$- and $v$-directions respectively; and $w_{ij}$ is the weight of control point $\dot{\mathbf{P}}_{ij}$.

**Example 7.7:** [*NURBS surfaces—points on bicubic surfaces using different knot vectors*]

A bicubic NURBS surface is controlled by the following points: $\dot{\mathbf{P}}_{00} = [30, 30, 0]^T$, $\dot{\mathbf{P}}_{01} = [60, 30, 10]^T$, $\dot{\mathbf{P}}_{02} = [90, 30, 8]^T$, $\dot{\mathbf{P}}_{03} = [120, 30, 20]^T$, $\dot{\mathbf{P}}_{10} =$

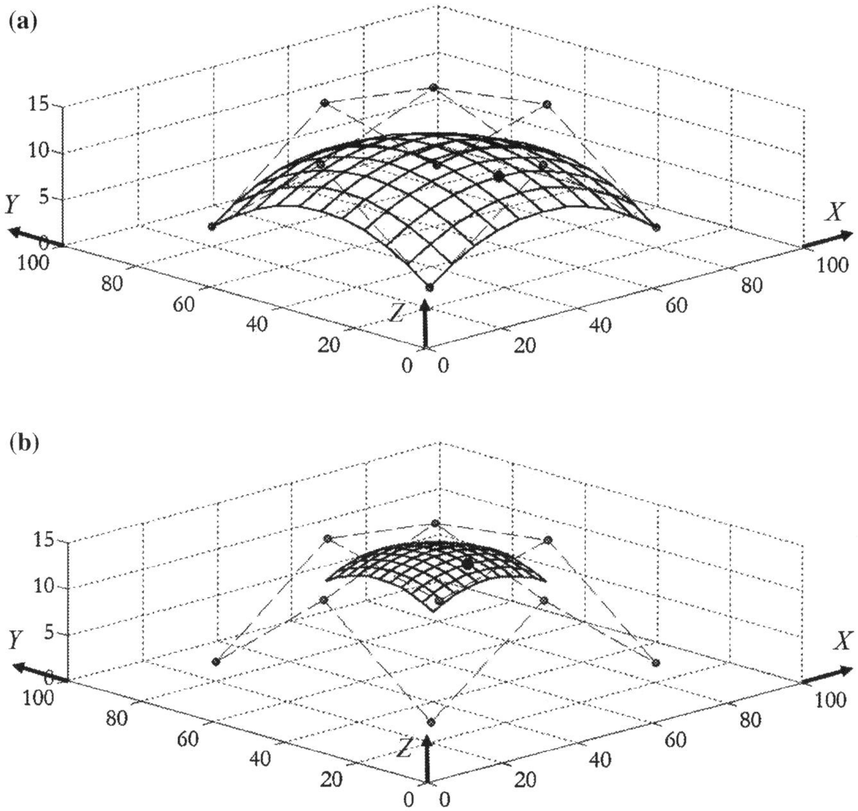


**Fig. 7.7** A biquadratic NURBS surface is controlled by $\mathbf{P}_{00} = [30, 30, 0, 1]^T$, $\mathbf{P}_{01} = [60, 30, 10, 1]^T$, $\mathbf{P}_{02} = [90, 30, 0, 1]^T$, $\mathbf{P}_{10} = [30, 60, 10, 1]^T$, $\mathbf{P}_{11} = [60, 60, 15, 1]^T$, $\mathbf{P}_{12} = [90, 60, 10, 1]^T$, $\mathbf{P}_{20} = [30, 90, 0, 1]^T$, $\mathbf{P}_{21} = [60, 90, 10, 1]^T$ and $\mathbf{P}_{22} = [90, 90, 0, 1]^T$. **a** The surface point at $u = 0.2$ and $v = 0.5$ is marked when the same open uniform knot vector [0, 0, 0, 1, 1, 1] is used along both directions. **b** The surface point at $u = 2.2$ and $v = 2.5$ is marked when the same uniform knot vector [0, 1, 2, 3, 4, 5] is used along both directions

$[30, 60, 10]^T$, $\dot{\mathbf{P}}_{11} = [60, 60, 15]^T$, $\dot{\mathbf{P}}_{12} = [90, 60, 16]^T$, $\dot{\mathbf{P}}_{13} = [120, 60, 7]^T$, $\dot{\mathbf{P}}_{20} = [30, 90, 8]^T$, $\dot{\mathbf{P}}_{21} = [60, 90, 18]^T$, $\dot{\mathbf{P}}_{22} = [90, 90, 15]^T$, $\dot{\mathbf{P}}_{23} = [120, 90, 5]^T$, $\dot{\mathbf{P}}_{30} = [30, 120, 0]^T$, $\dot{\mathbf{P}}_{31} = [60, 120, 5]^T$, $\dot{\mathbf{P}}_{32} = [90, 120, 3]^T$ and $\dot{\mathbf{P}}_{33} = [120, 120, 1]^T$. The homogeneous weight for each of these points is 1.

1. If the same open uniform knot vector [0, 0, 0, 0, 1, 1, 1, 1] is used along both directions, determine the values of the basis functions $N_{i,3}(0.8)$ and $N_{j,3}(0.5)$ as well as the location of the surface point $\dot{\mathbf{P}}$ at $u = 0.8$ and $v = 0.5$.
2. If the same uniform knot vector [0, 1, 2, 3, 4, 5, 6, 7] is used along both directions, determine the values of the basis functions $N_{i,3}(3.8)$ and $N_{j,3}(3.5)$ as well as the location of the surface point $\dot{\mathbf{P}}$ at $u = 3.8$ and $v = 3.5$.

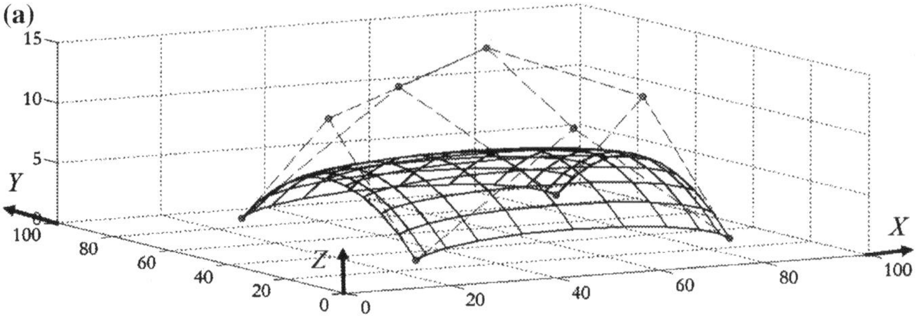


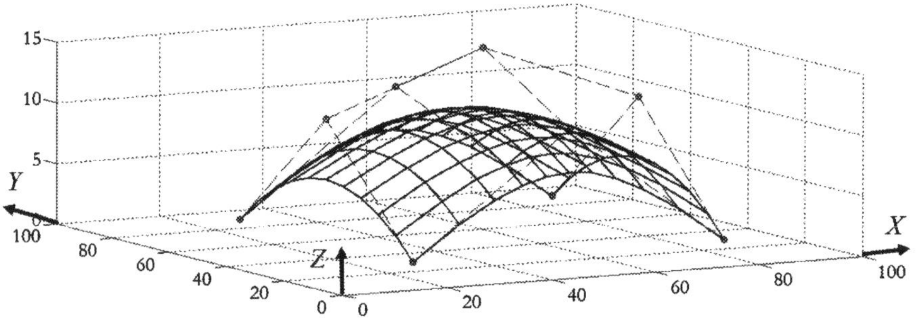


**Fig. 7.8** **a** A biquadratic NURBS surface is controlled by $\mathbf{P}_{00} = [30, 30, 0, 1]^T$, $\mathbf{P}_{01} = [60, 30, 10, 0.2]^T$, $\mathbf{P}_{02} = [90, 30, 0, 1]^T$, $\mathbf{P}_{10} = [30, 60, 10, 1]^T$, $\mathbf{P}_{11} = [60, 60, 15, 0.2]^T$, $\mathbf{P}_{12} = [90, 60, 10, 1]^T$, $\mathbf{P}_{20} = [30, 90, 0, 1]^T$, $\mathbf{P}_{21} = [60, 90, 10, 0.2]^T$ and $\mathbf{P}_{22} = [90, 90, 0, 1]^T$. **b** A biquadratic NURBS surface is controlled by $\mathbf{P}_{00} = [30, 30, 0, 1]^T$, $\mathbf{P}_{01} = [60, 30, 10, 1.8]^T$, $\mathbf{P}_{02} = [90, 30, 0, 1]^T$, $\mathbf{P}_{10} = [30, 60, 10, 1]^T$, $\mathbf{P}_{11} = [60, 60, 15, 1.8]^T$, $\mathbf{P}_{12} = [90, 60, 10, 1]^T$, $\mathbf{P}_{20} = [30, 90, 0, 1]^T$, $\mathbf{P}_{21} = [60, 90, 10, 1.8]^T$ and $\mathbf{P}_{22} = [90, 90, 0, 1]^T$. The open uniform knot vector [0, 0, 0, 1, 1, 1] is used in both cases

3. If the same non-uniform knot vector [0, 2, 3, 5, 6, 8, 10, 12] is used along both directions, determine the values of the basis functions $N_{i,3}(5.5)$ as well as the location of the surface point $\dot{\mathbf{P}}$ at $u = 5.5$ and $v = 5.5$.

Show the curve generated in each case.

**Solution 7.7:** Different results are obtained using different knot vectors.

**Using the open uniform knot vectors [0, 0, 0, 0, 1, 1, 1, 1]:** The basis functions are calculated as

$$\begin{aligned} N_{0,3}(0.8) &= 0.008, \\ N_{1,3}(0.8) &= 0.096, \\ N_{2,3}(0.8) &= 0.384, \\ N_{3,3}(0.8) &= 0.512 \end{aligned}$$

and

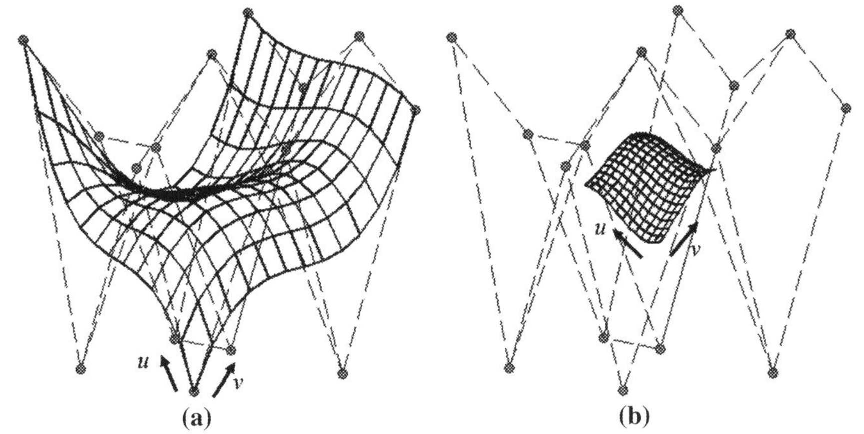


**Fig. 7.9** Examples of bicubic NURBS surfaces using the same control points. **a** Using the open knot vectors [0, 0, 0, 0, 1, 1, 1, 1]. **b** Using the uniform knot vectors [0, 1, 2, 3, 4, 5, 6, 7]

$$\begin{aligned}N_{0,3}(0.5) &= 0.125,\\ N_{1,3}(0.5) &= 0.375,\\ N_{2,3}(0.5) &= 0.375,\\ N_{3,3}(0.5) &= 0.125.\end{aligned}$$

Refer to Sect. 6.2.2.3 for information on how to get these values. Substituting these values in Eq. (7.19) where $w_{ij} = 1$ for all points, the surface point $\dot{\mathbf{P}}$ at $u = 0.8$ and $v = 0.5$ is estimated as $[75, 102, 8.37]^T$ (i.e., same as Bézier surface in Example 7.4). Using these open uniform vectors results in the bicubic NURBS surface shown in Fig. 7.10a. The contours are drawn every $0.1\,u$ and $0.1\,v$. The surface point at $u = 0.8$ and $v = 0.5$ is marked.

**Using the uniform knot vectors [0, 1, 2, 3, 4, 5, 6, 7]:** The basis functions are calculated as

$$\begin{aligned}N_{0,3}(3.8) &= 0.0013,\\ N_{1,3}(3.8) &= 0.2827,\\ N_{2,3}(3.8) &= 0.6307,\\ N_{3,3}(3.8) &= 0.0853\end{aligned}$$

and

$$\begin{aligned}N_{0,3}(3.5) &= 0.0208,\\ N_{1,3}(3.5) &= 0.4792,\\ N_{2,3}(3.5) &= 0.4792,\\ N_{3,3}(3.5) &= 0.0208.\end{aligned}$$

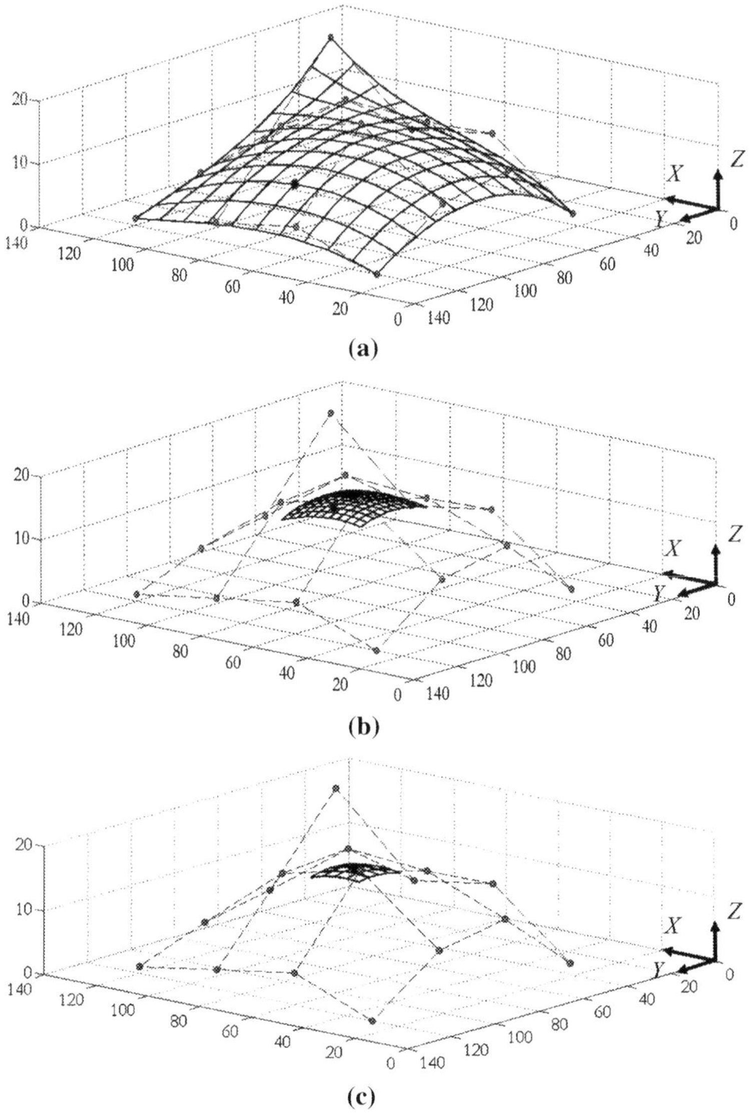


**Fig. 7.10** A bicubic NURBS surface is controlled by $\mathbf{P}_{00} = [30, 30, 0, 1]^T$, $\mathbf{P}_{01} = [60, 30, 10, 1]^T$, $\mathbf{P}_{02} = [90, 30, 8, 1]^T$, $\mathbf{P}_{03} = [120, 30, 20, 1]^T$, $\mathbf{P}_{10} = [30, 60, 10, 1]^T$, $\mathbf{P}_{11} = [60, 60, 15, 1]^T$, $\mathbf{P}_{12} = [90, 60, 16, 1]^T$, $\mathbf{P}_{13} = [120, 60, 7, 1]^T$, $\mathbf{P}_{20} = [30, 90, 8, 1]^T$, $\mathbf{P}_{21} = [60, 90, 18, 1]^T$, $\mathbf{P}_{22} = [90, 90, 15, 1]^T$, $\mathbf{P}_{23} = [120, 90, 5, 1]^T$, $\mathbf{P}_{30} = [30, 120, 0, 1]^T$, $\mathbf{P}_{31} = [60, 120, 5, 1]^T$, $\mathbf{P}_{32} = [90, 120, 3, 1]^T$ and $\mathbf{P}_{33} = [120, 120, 1, 1]^T$. **a** The knot vectors [0, 0, 0, 0, 1, 1, 1, 1] are used. **b** The knot vectors [0, 1, 2, 3, 4, 5, 6, 7] are used. **c** The knot vectors [0, 2, 3, 5, 6, 8, 10, 12] are used

Refer to Sect. 6.2.2.3 for information on how to get these values. Substituting these values in Eq. (7.19) where $w_{ij} = 1$ for all points, the surface point $\dot{\mathbf{P}}$ at $u = 3.8$ and $v = 3.5$ is estimated as $[75, 84, 14.7831]^T$. Using these uniform vectors results in the bicubic NURBS surface shown in Fig. 7.10b. The contours are drawn every $0.1u$ and $0.1v$. The surface point at $u = 3.8$ and $v = 3.5$ is marked.

**Using the non-uniform knot vectors [0, 2, 3, 5, 6, 8, 10, 12]:** The basis functions are calculated as

$$N_{0,3}(5.5) = 0.0104,$$
$$N_{1,3}(5.5) = 0.4896,$$
$$N_{2,3}(5.5) = 0.4917,$$
$$N_{3,3}(5.5) = 0.0083.$$

Refer to Sect. 6.2.2.3 for information on how to get these values. Substituting these values in Eq. (7.19) where $w_{ij} = 1$ for all points, the surface point $\dot{\mathbf{P}}$ at $u = 5.5$ and $v = 5.5$ is estimated as $[74.9375, 74.9375, 15.6731]^T$. Using these non-uniform vectors results in the bicubic NURBS surface shown in Fig. 7.10c. The contours are drawn every $0.25u$ and $0.25v$. The surface point at $u = 5.5$ and $v = 5.5$ is marked. □

**Example 7.8:** [*NURBS surfaces—changing homogeneous weights for bicubic surfaces using open uniform knot vector*]

In Example 7.7, if the homogeneous weights $w_{i1}$ of points $\mathbf{P}_{i1}$ are changed to 0.2 and then to 1.8, determine the points of the isoparametric curve having $u = 0.8$ if the open uniform knot vector [0, 0, 0, 0, 1, 1, 1, 1] is used.

**Solution 7.8:** As mentioned previously, the isoparametric curve has a fixed $u$ value at 0.8 while $v$ values vary from 0 to 1. Equation (7.19) is utilized to get the points along that curve. The locations of these points are listed in the following table:

| $u$ | $v$ | $w_{i1} = 1$ | $w_{i1} = 0.2$ | $w_{i1} = 1.8$ |
|---|---|---|---|---|
| 0.8 | 0.0 | $[30, 102, 4.032]^T$ | $[30, 102, 4.032]^T$ | $[30, 102, 4.032]^T$ |
| 0.8 | 0.1 | $[39, 102, 5.8538]^T$ | $[33.9325, 102, 4.6139]^T$ | $[42.418, 102, 6.6901]^T$ |
| 0.8 | 0.2 | $[48, 102, 7.1654]^T$ | $[42.679, 102, 5.4687]^T$ | $[50.8201, 102, 8.0647]^T$ |
| 0.8 | 0.3 | $[57, 102, 7.9999]^T$ | $[55.3646, 102, 6.3689]^T$ | $[57.7824, 102, 8.7802]^T$ |
| 0.8 | 0.4 | $[66, 102, 8.3904]^T$ | $[69.1687, 102, 7.0164]^T$ | $[64.459, 102, 9.0586]^T$ |
| 0.8 | 0.5 | $[75, 102, 8.37]^T$ | $[81.4286, 102, 7.2463]^T$ | $[71.5385, 102, 8.9751]^T$ |
| 0.8 | 0.6 | $[84, 102, 7.9718]^T$ | $[91.185, 102, 7.0677]^T$ | $[79.5059, 102, 8.5374]^T$ |
| 0.8 | 0.7 | $[93, 102, 7.229]^T$ | $[98.8784, 102, 6.5587]^T$ | $[88.6657, 102, 7.7233]^T$ |
| 0.8 | 0.8 | $[102, 102, 6.1747]^T$ | $[105.4939, 102, 5.774]^T$ | $[99.0045, 102, 6.5183]^T$ |
| 0.8 | 0.9 | $[111, 102, 4.842]^T$ | $[112.1259, 102, 4.7062]^T$ | $[109.9217, 102, 4.972]^T$ |
| 0.8 | 1.0 | $[120, 102, 3.264]^T$ | $[120, 102, 3.264]^T$ | $[120, 102, 3.264]^T$ |

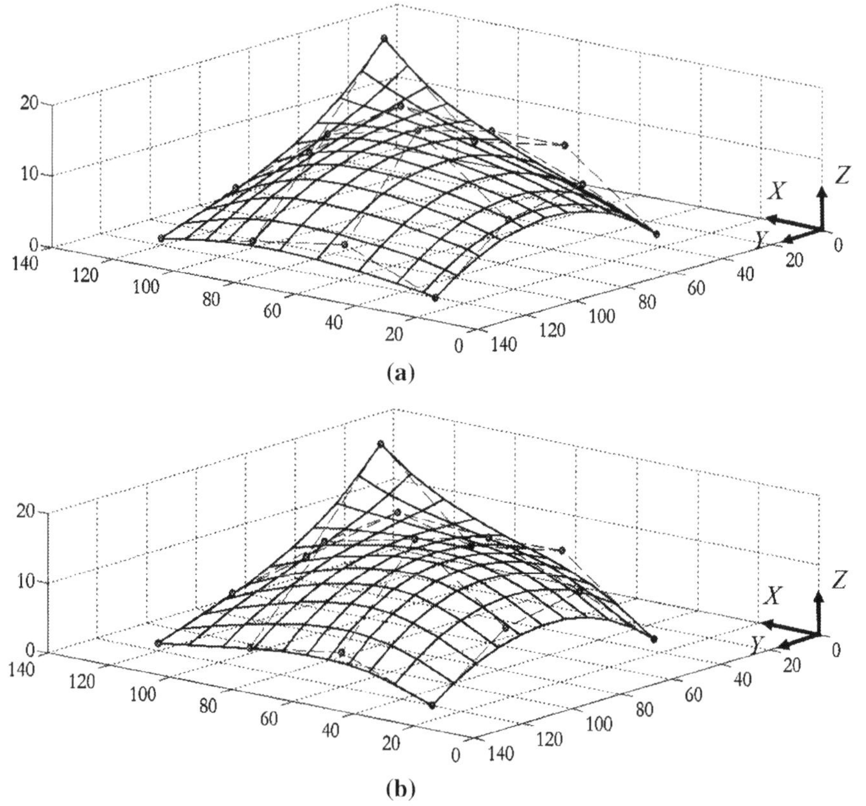


**Fig. 7.11** **a** A bicubic NURBS surface is controlled by $\mathbf{P}_{00} = [30, 30, 0, 1]^T$, $\mathbf{P}_{01} = [60, 30, 10, 0.2]^T$, $\mathbf{P}_{02} = [90, 30, 8, 1]^T$, $\mathbf{P}_{03} = [120, 30, 20, 1]^T$, $\mathbf{P}_{10} = [30, 60, 10, 1]^T$, $\mathbf{P}_{11} = [60, 60, 15, 0.2]^T$, $\mathbf{P}_{12} = [90, 60, 16, 1]^T$, $\mathbf{P}_{13} = [120, 60, 7, 1]^T$, $\mathbf{P}_{20} = [30, 90, 8, 1]^T$, $\mathbf{P}_{21} = [60, 90, 18, 0.2]^T$, $\mathbf{P}_{22} = [90, 90, 15, 1]^T$, $\mathbf{P}_{23} = [120, 90, 5, 1]^T$, $\mathbf{P}_{30} = [30, 120, 0, 1]^T$, $\mathbf{P}_{31} = [60, 120, 5, 0.2]^T$, $\mathbf{P}_{32} = [90, 120, 3, 1]^T$ and $\mathbf{P}_{33} = [120, 120, 1, 1]^T$. **b** A bicubic NURBS surface is controlled by $\mathbf{P}_{00} = [30, 30, 0, 1]^T$, $\mathbf{P}_{01} = [60, 30, 10, 1.8]^T$, $\mathbf{P}_{02} = [90, 30, 8, 1]^T$, $\mathbf{P}_{03} = [120, 30, 20, 1]^T$, $\mathbf{P}_{10} = [30, 60, 10, 1]^T$, $\mathbf{P}_{11} = [60, 60, 15, 1.8]^T$, $\mathbf{P}_{12} = [90, 60, 16, 1]^T$, $\mathbf{P}_{13} = [120, 60, 7, 1]^T$, $\mathbf{P}_{20} = [30, 90, 8, 1]^T$, $\mathbf{P}_{21} = [60, 90, 18, 1.8]^T$, $\mathbf{P}_{22} = [90, 90, 15, 1]^T$, $\mathbf{P}_{23} = [120, 90, 5, 1]^T$, $\mathbf{P}_{30} = [30, 120, 0, 1]^T$, $\mathbf{P}_{31} = [60, 120, 5, 1.8]^T$, $\mathbf{P}_{32} = [90, 120, 3, 1]^T$ and $\mathbf{P}_{33} = [120, 120, 1, 1]^T$. The open uniform knot vector [0, 0, 0, 0, 1, 1, 1, 1] is used in both cases

The surfaces where $w_{i1} = 0.2$ and $w_{i1} = 1.8$ are shown in Fig. 7.11a, b respectively while the surface where $w_{i1} = 1$ is shown in Fig. 7.10a. Notice that when $w_{i1} = 0.2$, the surface is pushed away from control points $\dot{\mathbf{P}}_{i1}$. On the other hand, when $w_{i1} = 1.8$, the surface is pulled closer to control points $\dot{\mathbf{P}}_{i1}$. □

## 7.4 Problems

**Problem 7.1:** [*Biquadratic surfaces—basis function*]
Utilizing the open uniform knot vector [0, 0, 0, 1, 1, 1], estimate the values of basis functions for different subintervals.

**Problem 7.2:** [*Bicubic surfaces—basis function*]
Utilizing the open uniform knot vector [0, 0, 0, 0, 1, 1, 1, 1], estimate the values of basis functions for different subintervals.

**Problem 7.3:** [*Bicubic surfaces—points*]
Consider the control points: $\dot{\mathbf{P}}_{00}$, $\dot{\mathbf{P}}_{01}$, $\dot{\mathbf{P}}_{02}$, $\dot{\mathbf{P}}_{03}$, $\dot{\mathbf{P}}_{10}$, $\dot{\mathbf{P}}_{11}$, $\dot{\mathbf{P}}_{12}$, $\dot{\mathbf{P}}_{13}$, $\dot{\mathbf{P}}_{20}$, $\dot{\mathbf{P}}_{21}$, $\dot{\mathbf{P}}_{22}$, $\dot{\mathbf{P}}_{23}$, $\dot{\mathbf{P}}_{30}$, $\dot{\mathbf{P}}_{31}$, $\dot{\mathbf{P}}_{32}$ and $\dot{\mathbf{P}}_{33}$. Utilize Eq. (6.65) to get the position of the bicubic surface point $\dot{\mathbf{P}}(u, v)$.

## References

Bézier, P. 1972. *Numerical control: Mathematics and applications*. Wiley series in computing London: Wiley.
Bézier, P. 1974. *Computer aided geometric design, chapter mathematical and practical possibilities of UNISURF*. New York: Academic Press.
Forrest, R.A. 1980. The twisted cubic curve: A computer-aided geometric design approach. *Computer Aided Design* 12(4): 165–172.

# Chapter 8
# Projections

**Abstract** When a virtual camera navigates a 3D scene taking shots at different positions along different orientations, different outcomes may be produced onto its view plane or projection plane depending on the viewpoint or the center of projection (COP) and the view volume that defines the projectors. In addition, a viewport (i.e., a window that displays the outcome of projection) on the screen should be specified. Viewing in 3D space handles different operations. Among them is projection transformation that is determined by different projection types. In this chapter, we will talk about various projection types including parallel and perspective projections. We will discuss the main differences among those types. We will investigate the result when the viewpoint is at an infinite distance from the view plane and the projectors are parallel to each other. We will also discuss the output when the COP is at a finite distance from the view plane and the projectors are intersecting at that COP.

## 8.1 Projection Types

Projection types can be split into two main categories; planar projections and non-planar projections. The main differences between these two categories reside in the viewing surfaces and the projectors. In planar projection, the viewing surface is planar (i.e., view plane) and the projectors are straight lines while in non-planar projections the viewing surface as well as the projectors may be curved as listed in Table 8.1. We will discuss the planar projections in more details in the rest of this chapter.

## 8.2 Planar Projections

Planar geometric projections embrace sub-types that share the planarity of the viewing surface and the straightness of the projectors. However, other essential differences exist. These differences include

R. Elias, *Digital Media*, DOI: 10.1007/978-3-319-05137-6_8,

**Table 8.1** Projection types

| Projection type | Viewing surface | Projectors |
|---|---|---|
| Planar | Planar | Lines |
| Non-planar | Curved | Curves |

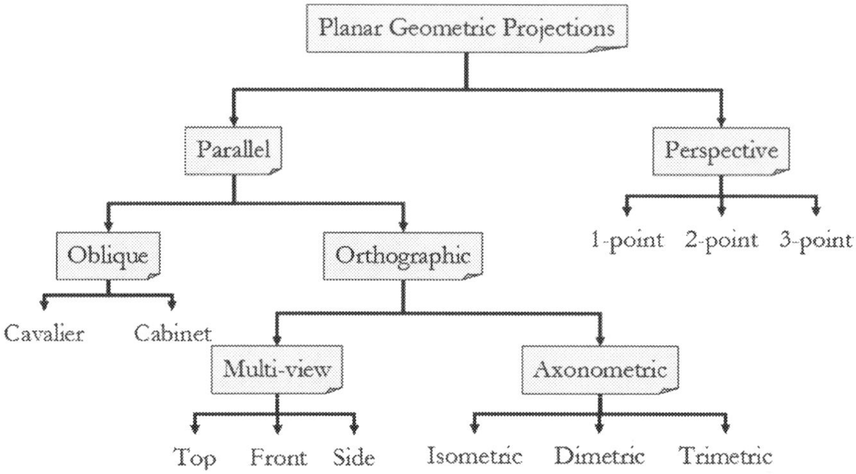


**Fig. 8.1** Different planar geometric projections

1. whether the straight projectors are parallel to each other or converging to a point. This signifies the difference between parallel and perspective projections.
2. whether the straight projectors are perpendicular to or oblique with respect to the viewing surface. This signifies the difference between orthographic and oblique projections.
3. whether two or three axes are visible in the projection. This signifies the difference between multi-view and axonometric projections.

Figure 8.1 shows the relationships among different planar projection sub-types. In the sections to follow, we will talk about each of these sub-types.

## 8.3 Parallel Projections

The main property characterizing all parallel projections is that the viewpoint or the center of projection is placed at infinity. Consequently, straight projectors are parallel to each other; hence comes the term *parallel projection*. This property forces the view volume to be parallelepiped. Also, in parallel projections, we find that the

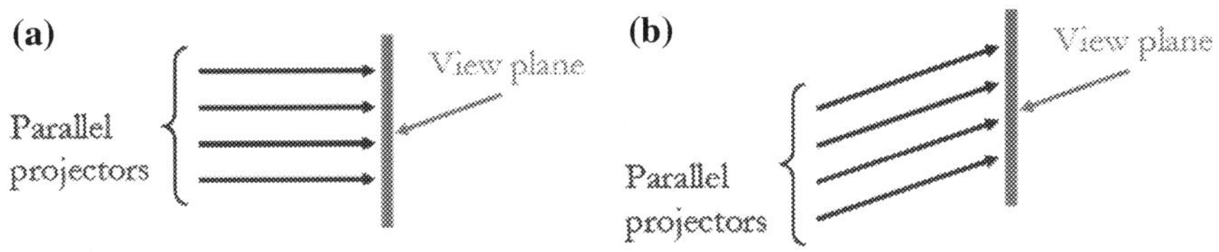


**Fig. 8.2** Parallel projections. **a** Orthographic projection. **b** Oblique projection

*proportions* of an object are maintained. In other words, the actual measurements are *not necessarily* maintained.

Parallel projectors may be either perpendicular to the view plane as shown in Fig. 8.2a to form orthographic projection or oblique with respect to the view plane as shown in Fig. 8.2b to form oblique projection.

## *8.3.1 Orthographic Projections*

As depicted in Fig. 8.2a, in orthographic projection, the straight projectors are parallel to each other and perpendicular to the view plane. Depending on the normal to the view plane, orthographic projections can be classified as either multi-view or axonometric projections.

### 8.3.1.1 Multi-view Projections

In multi-view projections, one dimension is suppressed leaving only two axes shown on the projection. Consequently, an object is not shown as a 3D model; rather, only a single face may be displayed. The projection depends on where the view plane is or in other words where the normal vector to the view plane is. As depicted in Fig. 8.3, a view plane normal must be parallel to one of the principal axes. This results in three main multi-view projections; i.e., front, side and top views. (Some systems handle front, back, left side, right side, top and bottom views.) In these projections, dimensions and angles are preserved; hence, they are used regularly in engineering and architectural drawings.

**Front view projection:** Figure 8.3a shows a right-handed coordinate system where the $y$-axis points upwards and the view plane normal is parallel to the positive $z$-axis. Equivalently, it can be said that the view plane is parallel to the $xy$-plane. In this projection type, all $z$-coordinates are neglected. Only the $x$- and $y$-coordinates are mapped to the view plane. If the view plane normal is parallel to the negative $z$-axis, the back view is created.

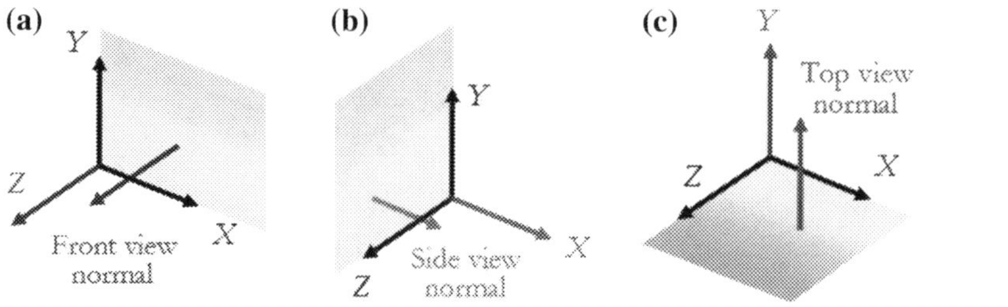


**Fig. 8.3** Multi-view projections. **a** Front view normal. **b** Side view normal. **c** Top view normal

We can estimate the location of a 3D point $\dot{\mathbf{P}} = [x, y, z]^T$ after front projection onto the $xy$-plane as

$$\begin{aligned} x' &= x, \\ y' &= y, \\ z' &= 0, \end{aligned} \tag{8.1}$$

where $[x', y', 0]^T$ is the point after front projection. In matrix form, this can be written as

$$\underbrace{\begin{bmatrix} x' \\ y' \\ 0 \end{bmatrix}}_{\dot{\mathbf{P}}'} = \begin{bmatrix} 1 & 0 & 0 \\ 0 & 1 & 0 \\ 0 & 0 & 0 \end{bmatrix} \underbrace{\begin{bmatrix} x \\ y \\ z \end{bmatrix}}_{\dot{\mathbf{P}}}, \tag{8.2}$$

where $\dot{\mathbf{P}} = [x, y, z]^T$ and $\dot{\mathbf{P}}' = [x', y', 0]^T$ are the inhomogeneous 3D points before and after front projection onto the $xy$-plane. In homogeneous coordinates (Sect. B.7), Eq. (8.2) can be re-written as

$$\underbrace{\begin{bmatrix} x' \\ y' \\ 0 \\ 1 \end{bmatrix}}_{\mathbf{P}'} = \begin{bmatrix} 1 & 0 & 0 & 0 \\ 0 & 1 & 0 & 0 \\ 0 & 0 & 0 & 0 \\ 0 & 0 & 0 & 1 \end{bmatrix} \underbrace{\begin{bmatrix} x \\ y \\ z \\ 1 \end{bmatrix}}_{\mathbf{P}}, \tag{8.3}$$

where $\mathbf{P} = [x, y, z, 1]^T$ and $\mathbf{P}' = [x', y', 0, 1]^T$ are the homogeneous 3D points before and after front projection onto the $xy$-plane. In order to project the same 3D point $\dot{\mathbf{P}} = [x, y, z]^T$ to a 2D point $\dot{\mathbf{p}}' = [x', y']^T$, a $2 \times 3$ matrix can be used as

$$\underbrace{\begin{bmatrix} x' \\ y' \end{bmatrix}}_{\dot{\mathbf{p}}'} = \begin{bmatrix} 1 & 0 & 0 \\ 0 & 1 & 0 \end{bmatrix} \underbrace{\begin{bmatrix} x \\ y \\ z \end{bmatrix}}_{\dot{\mathbf{P}}}, \tag{8.4}$$

where $\dot{\mathbf{P}} = [x, y, z]^T$ and $\dot{\mathbf{p}}' = [x', y']^T$ are the inhomogeneous points before and after front projection onto the $xy$-plane. The same result can be obtained using a $3 \times 4$ matrix with homogeneous points as

$$\underbrace{\begin{bmatrix} x' \\ y' \\ 1 \end{bmatrix}}_{\mathbf{p}'} = \begin{bmatrix} 1 & 0 & 0 & 0 \\ 0 & 1 & 0 & 0 \\ 0 & 0 & 0 & 1 \end{bmatrix} \underbrace{\begin{bmatrix} x \\ y \\ z \\ 1 \end{bmatrix}}_{\mathbf{P}'}, \tag{8.5}$$

where $\mathbf{P} = [x, y, z, 1]^T$ and $\mathbf{p}' = [x', y', 1]^T$ are the homogeneous points before and after front projection onto the $xy$-plane.

In general, an inhomogeneous 3D point $\dot{\mathbf{P}} = [x, y, z]^T$ can be projected to another inhomogeneous 2D point $\dot{\mathbf{p}} = [x', y']^T$ in front view after scaling and translating using scaling factors $s_x$ and $s_y$ and a translation vector $[t_x, t_x]^T$; hence, the projection can be expressed for front view as

$$\underbrace{\begin{bmatrix} x' \\ y' \end{bmatrix}}_{\dot{\mathbf{p}}'} = \begin{bmatrix} s_x & 0 & 0 \\ 0 & s_y & 0 \end{bmatrix} \underbrace{\begin{bmatrix} x \\ y \\ z \end{bmatrix}}_{\dot{\mathbf{P}}} + \begin{bmatrix} t_x \\ t_y \end{bmatrix}, \tag{8.6}$$

where $\dot{\mathbf{P}} = [x, y, z]^T$ and $\dot{\mathbf{p}}' = [x', y']^T$ are the inhomogeneous points before and after front projection onto the $xy$-plane. The same operation can be performed in homogeneous coordinates as

$$\underbrace{\begin{bmatrix} x' \\ y' \\ 1 \end{bmatrix}}_{\mathbf{p}'} = \begin{bmatrix} s_x & 0 & 0 & t_x \\ 0 & s_x & 0 & t_y \\ 0 & 0 & 0 & 1 \end{bmatrix} \underbrace{\begin{bmatrix} x \\ y \\ z \\ 1 \end{bmatrix}}_{\mathbf{P}}, \tag{8.7}$$

where $\mathbf{P} = [x, y, z, 1]^T$ and $\mathbf{p}' = [x', y', 1]^T$ are the homogeneous points before and after front projection onto the $xy$-plane.

**Side view projection:** Figure 8.3b shows a right-handed coordinate system where the $y$-axis points upwards and the view plane normal is parallel to the positive $x$-axis. Equivalently, it can be said that the view plane is parallel to the $yz$-plane. In this projection type, all $x$-coordinates are neglected. Only the $y$- and $z$-coordinates are mapped to the view plane. If the view plane normal is parallel to the negative $x$-axis, the other side view is created.

Similar to front projection, the location of a 3D point $\dot{\mathbf{P}} = [x, y, z]^T$ can be estimated after side projection onto the $yz$-plane as

$$\begin{aligned} x' &= 0, \\ y' &= y, \\ z' &= z, \end{aligned} \tag{8.8}$$

where $[0, y', z']^T$ is the point after side projection. In matrix form, this can be written as

$$\underbrace{\begin{bmatrix} 0 \\ y' \\ z' \end{bmatrix}}_{\dot{\mathbf{P}}'} = \begin{bmatrix} 0 & 0 & 0 \\ 0 & 1 & 0 \\ 0 & 0 & 1 \end{bmatrix} \underbrace{\begin{bmatrix} x \\ y \\ z \end{bmatrix}}_{\dot{\mathbf{P}}}, \tag{8.9}$$

where $\dot{\mathbf{P}} = [x, y, z]^T$ and $\dot{\mathbf{P}}' = [0, y', z']^T$ are the inhomogeneous 3D points before and after side projection onto the $yz$-plane. In homogeneous coordinates, Eq. (8.9) can be re-written as

$$\underbrace{\begin{bmatrix} 0 \\ y' \\ z' \\ 1 \end{bmatrix}}_{\mathbf{P}'} = \begin{bmatrix} 0 & 0 & 0 & 0 \\ 0 & 1 & 0 & 0 \\ 0 & 0 & 1 & 0 \\ 0 & 0 & 0 & 1 \end{bmatrix} \underbrace{\begin{bmatrix} x \\ y \\ z \\ 1 \end{bmatrix}}_{\mathbf{P}}, \tag{8.10}$$

where $\mathbf{P} = [x, y, z, 1]^T$ and $\mathbf{P}' = [0, y', z', 1]^T$ are the homogeneous 3D points before and after side projection onto the $yz$-plane. In order to project the same 3D point $\dot{\mathbf{P}} = [x, y, z]^T$ to a 2D point $\dot{\mathbf{p}}' = [y', z']^T$, a $2 \times 3$ matrix can be used as

$$\underbrace{\begin{bmatrix} y' \\ z' \end{bmatrix}}_{\dot{\mathbf{p}}'} = \begin{bmatrix} 0 & 1 & 0 \\ 0 & 0 & 1 \end{bmatrix} \underbrace{\begin{bmatrix} x \\ y \\ z \end{bmatrix}}_{\dot{\mathbf{P}}}, \tag{8.11}$$

where $\dot{\mathbf{P}} = [x, y, z]^T$ and $\dot{\mathbf{p}}' = [y', z']^T$ are the inhomogeneous points before and after side projection onto the $yz$-plane. The same result can be obtained using a $3 \times 4$ matrix with homogeneous points as

$$\underbrace{\begin{bmatrix} y' \\ z' \\ 1 \end{bmatrix}}_{\mathbf{p}'} = \begin{bmatrix} 0 & 1 & 0 & 0 \\ 0 & 0 & 1 & 0 \\ 0 & 0 & 0 & 1 \end{bmatrix} \underbrace{\begin{bmatrix} x \\ y \\ z \\ 1 \end{bmatrix}}_{\mathbf{P}'}, \tag{8.12}$$

where $\mathbf{P} = [x, y, z, 1]^T$ and $\mathbf{p}' = [y', z', 1]^T$ are the homogeneous points before and after side projection onto the $yz$-plane.

In general, an inhomogeneous 3D point $\dot{\mathbf{P}} = [x, y, z]^T$ can be projected to another inhomogeneous 2D point $\dot{\mathbf{p}} = [y', z']^T$ in side view after scaling and translating using scaling factors $s_y$ and $s_z$ and a translation vector $[t_y, t_z]^T$; hence, the projection can be expressed for side view as

$$\underbrace{\begin{bmatrix} y' \\ z' \end{bmatrix}}_{\dot{\mathbf{p}}'} = \begin{bmatrix} 0 & s_y & 0 \\ 0 & 0 & s_z \end{bmatrix} \underbrace{\begin{bmatrix} x \\ y \\ z \end{bmatrix}}_{\dot{\mathbf{P}}} + \begin{bmatrix} t_y \\ t_z \end{bmatrix}, \tag{8.13}$$

where $\dot{\mathbf{P}} = [x, y, z]^T$ and $\dot{\mathbf{p}}' = [y', z']^T$ are the inhomogeneous points before and after side projection onto the $yz$-plane. The same operation can be performed in homogeneous coordinates as

$$\underbrace{\begin{bmatrix} y' \\ z' \\ 1 \end{bmatrix}}_{\mathbf{p}'} = \begin{bmatrix} 0 & s_y & 0 & t_y \\ 0 & 0 & s_z & t_z \\ 0 & 0 & 0 & 1 \end{bmatrix} \underbrace{\begin{bmatrix} x \\ y \\ z \\ 1 \end{bmatrix}}_{\mathbf{P}}, \tag{8.14}$$

where $\mathbf{P} = [x, y, z, 1]^T$ and $\mathbf{p}' = [y', z', 1]^T$ are the homogeneous points before and after side projection onto the $yz$-plane.

**Top view projection:** Figure 8.3c shows a right-handed coordinate system where the $y$-axis points upwards and the view plane normal is parallel to the positive $y$-axis. Equivalently, it can be said that the view plane is parallel to the $zx$-plane. In this projection type, all $y$-coordinates are neglected. Only the $z$- and $x$-coordinates are mapped to the view plane. If the view plane normal is parallel to the negative $y$-axis, the bottom view is created.

Similar to other multi-view projections, the location of a 3D point $\dot{\mathbf{P}} = [x, y, z]^T$ can be estimated after top projection onto the $zx$-plane as

$$\begin{aligned} x' &= x, \\ y' &= 0, \\ z' &= z, \end{aligned} \tag{8.15}$$

where $[x', 0, z']^T$ is the point after top projection. In matrix form, this can be written as

$$\underbrace{\begin{bmatrix} x' \\ 0 \\ z' \end{bmatrix}}_{\dot{\mathbf{P}}'} = \begin{bmatrix} 1 & 0 & 0 \\ 0 & 0 & 0 \\ 0 & 0 & 1 \end{bmatrix} \underbrace{\begin{bmatrix} x \\ y \\ z \end{bmatrix}}_{\dot{\mathbf{P}}}, \tag{8.16}$$

where $\dot{\mathbf{P}} = [x, y, z]^T$ and $\dot{\mathbf{P}}' = [x', 0, z']^T$ are the inhomogeneous 3D points before and after top projection onto the $zx$-plane. In homogeneous coordinates, Eq. (8.16) can be re-written as

$$\underbrace{\begin{bmatrix} x' \\ 0 \\ z' \\ 1 \end{bmatrix}}_{\mathbf{P}'} = \begin{bmatrix} 1 & 0 & 0 & 0 \\ 0 & 0 & 0 & 0 \\ 0 & 0 & 1 & 0 \\ 0 & 0 & 0 & 1 \end{bmatrix} \underbrace{\begin{bmatrix} x \\ y \\ z \\ 1 \end{bmatrix}}_{\mathbf{P}}, \tag{8.17}$$

where $\mathbf{P} = [x, y, z, 1]^T$ and $\mathbf{P}' = [x', 0, z', 1]^T$ are the homogeneous 3D points before and after top projection onto the $zx$-plane. In order to project the same 3D point $\dot{\mathbf{P}} = [x, y, z]^T$ to a 2D point $\dot{\mathbf{p}}' = [x', z']^T$, a $2 \times 3$ matrix can be used as

$$\underbrace{\begin{bmatrix} x' \\ z' \end{bmatrix}}_{\dot{\mathbf{p}}'} = \begin{bmatrix} 1 & 0 & 0 \\ 0 & 0 & 1 \end{bmatrix} \underbrace{\begin{bmatrix} x \\ y \\ z \end{bmatrix}}_{\dot{\mathbf{P}}}, \tag{8.18}$$

where $\dot{\mathbf{P}} = [x, y, z]^T$ and $\dot{\mathbf{p}}' = [x', z']^T$ are the inhomogeneous points before and after top projection onto the $zx$-plane. (Switching the rows of the previous matrix would result in $\dot{\mathbf{p}}' = [z', x']^T$.) The same result can be obtained using a $3 \times 4$ matrix with homogeneous points as

$$\underbrace{\begin{bmatrix} x' \\ z' \\ 1 \end{bmatrix}}_{\mathbf{p}'} = \begin{bmatrix} 1 & 0 & 0 & 0 \\ 0 & 0 & 1 & 0 \\ 0 & 0 & 0 & 1 \end{bmatrix} \underbrace{\begin{bmatrix} x \\ y \\ z \\ 1 \end{bmatrix}}_{\mathbf{P}'}, \tag{8.19}$$

where $\mathbf{P} = [x, y, z, 1]^T$ and $\mathbf{p}' = [x', z', 1]^T$ are the homogeneous points before and after top projection onto the $zx$-plane.

In general, an inhomogeneous 3D point $\dot{\mathbf{P}} = [x, y, z]^T$ can be projected to another inhomogeneous 2D point $\dot{\mathbf{p}}' = [x', z']^T$ in top view after scaling and translating using scaling factors $s_x$ and $s_z$ and a translation vector $[t_x, t_z]^T$; hence, the projection can be expressed for top view as

$$\underbrace{\begin{bmatrix} x' \\ z' \end{bmatrix}}_{\dot{\mathbf{p}}'} = \begin{bmatrix} s_x & 0 & 0 \\ 0 & 0 & s_z \end{bmatrix} \underbrace{\begin{bmatrix} x \\ y \\ z \end{bmatrix}}_{\dot{\mathbf{P}}} + \begin{bmatrix} t_x \\ t_z \end{bmatrix}, \tag{8.20}$$

where $\dot{\mathbf{P}} = [x, y, z]^T$ and $\dot{\mathbf{p}}' = [x', z']^T$ are the inhomogeneous points before and after top projection onto the $zx$-plane. The same operation can be performed in

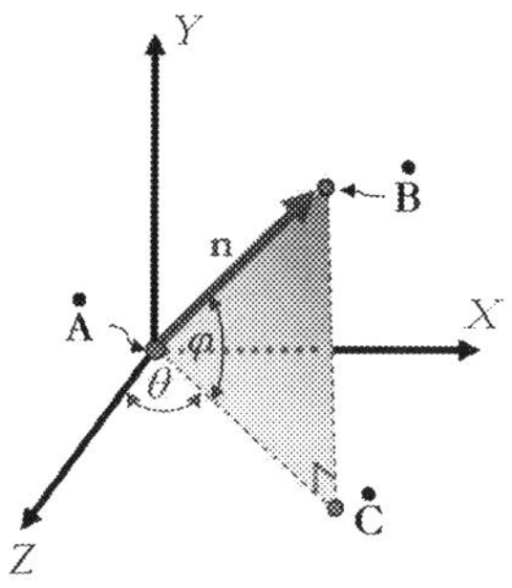


**Fig. 8.4** Axonometric projection

homogeneous coordinates as

$$\underbrace{\begin{bmatrix} x' \\ z' \\ 1 \end{bmatrix}}_{\mathbf{p}'} = \begin{bmatrix} s_x & 0 & 0 & t_x \\ 0 & 0 & s_z & t_z \\ 0 & 0 & 0 & 1 \end{bmatrix} \underbrace{\begin{bmatrix} x \\ y \\ z \\ 1 \end{bmatrix}}_{\mathbf{P}}, \tag{8.21}$$

where $\mathbf{P} = [x, y, z, 1]^T$ and $\mathbf{p}' = [x', z', 1]^T$ are the homogeneous points before and after top projection onto the $zx$-plane.

#### 8.3.1.2 Axonometric Projections

Unlike multi-view projections, in axonometric projections, the view plane normal is placed in any direction such that the three axes may be visible. In this case, the view plane should intersect *at least two* of the principal axes. If the view plane normal is placed parallel to *one* principal axis or if the view plane intersects only *one* principal axis, the projection turns to a multi-view projection as discussed in Sect. 8.3.1.1.

In an axonometric projection, parallel lines in reality remain parallel after projection. Also, if a line is parallel to the view plane, its length will be preserved; otherwise, line proportions (but not lengths) are maintained and equal lengths of parallel lines will be foreshortened equally.

Assume that the normal to the view plane is $\mathbf{n} = \dot{\mathbf{B}} - \dot{\mathbf{A}}$ as shown in Fig. 8.4. The top view projection of $\mathbf{n}$ is indicated by the vector $\dot{\mathbf{C}} - \dot{\mathbf{A}}$, which makes an *azimuth* angle $\theta$ with the $z$-axis. The *elevation* angle $\varphi$ is enclosed between the vectors $\dot{\mathbf{B}} - \dot{\mathbf{A}}$ and $\dot{\mathbf{C}} - \dot{\mathbf{A}}$. (In Sect. B.6, we refer to the *zenith* angle $\phi$ as the angle that is measured from the positive $y$-axis. In other words, $\varphi + \phi = 90°$.)

The axonometric projection matrix can be obtained by rotating the normal vector $\mathbf{n}$ to coincide with the $z$-axis; hence, the front projection matrix can be used. The steps are as follows:

1. Rotate through an angle $-\theta$ about the $y$-axis using the matrix $\dot{\mathrm{R}}_y$ of Eq. (5.7) where

$$\dot{\mathrm{R}}_y(-\theta) = \begin{bmatrix} \cos(-\theta) & 0 & \sin(-\theta) \\ 0 & 1 & 0 \\ -\sin(-\theta) & 0 & \cos(-\theta) \end{bmatrix} = \begin{bmatrix} \cos(\theta) & 0 & -\sin(\theta) \\ 0 & 1 & 0 \\ \sin(\theta) & 0 & \cos(\theta) \end{bmatrix}. \tag{8.22}$$

2. Rotate through an angle $\varphi$ about the $x$-axis using the matrix $\dot{\mathrm{R}}_x$ of Eq. (5.5) where

$$\dot{\mathrm{R}}_x(\varphi) = \begin{bmatrix} 1 & 0 & 0 \\ 0 & \cos(\varphi) & -\sin(\varphi) \\ 0 & \sin(\varphi) & \cos(\varphi) \end{bmatrix}. \tag{8.23}$$

3. Use the front view projection matrix of Eq. (8.2). Let us call it $\dot{\mathrm{P}}_f$ where

$$\dot{\mathrm{P}}_f = \begin{bmatrix} 1 & 0 & 0 \\ 0 & 1 & 0 \\ 0 & 0 & 0 \end{bmatrix}. \tag{8.24}$$

Hence, the overall axonometric projection onto the $xy$-plane for a point $[x, y, z]^T$ is estimated as

$$\begin{aligned} \underbrace{\begin{bmatrix} x' \\ y' \\ 0 \end{bmatrix}}_{\dot{\mathbf{P}}'} &= \begin{bmatrix} 1 & 0 & 0 \\ 0 & 1 & 0 \\ 0 & 0 & 0 \end{bmatrix} \begin{bmatrix} 1 & 0 & 0 \\ 0 & \cos(\varphi) & -\sin(\varphi) \\ 0 & \sin(\varphi) & \cos(\varphi) \end{bmatrix} \begin{bmatrix} \cos(\theta) & 0 & -\sin(\theta) \\ 0 & 1 & 0 \\ \sin(\theta) & 0 & \cos(\theta) \end{bmatrix} \begin{bmatrix} x \\ y \\ z \end{bmatrix} \\ &= \begin{bmatrix} \cos(\theta) & 0 & -\sin(\theta) \\ -\sin(\varphi)\sin(\theta) & \cos(\varphi) & -\sin(\varphi)\cos(\theta) \\ 0 & 0 & 0 \end{bmatrix} \underbrace{\begin{bmatrix} x \\ y \\ z \end{bmatrix}}_{\dot{\mathbf{P}}}, \end{aligned} \tag{8.25}$$

where $\dot{\mathbf{P}} = [x, y, z]^T$ and $\dot{\mathbf{P}}' = [x', y', 0]$ are the inhomogeneous points before and after axonometric projection. This can be written as

$$\begin{aligned} x' &= x\cos(\theta) - z\sin(\theta), \\ y' &= -x\sin(\varphi)\sin(\theta) + y\cos(\varphi) - z\cos(\theta)\sin(\varphi), \\ z' &= 0. \end{aligned} \tag{8.26}$$

In homogeneous coordinates, Eqs. (8.25) and (8.26) can be re-written as

$$\underbrace{\begin{bmatrix} x' \\ y' \\ 0 \\ 1 \end{bmatrix}}_{\mathbf{P}'} = \begin{bmatrix} \cos(\theta) & 0 & -\sin(\theta) & 0 \\ -\sin(\varphi)\sin(\theta) & \cos(\varphi) & -\sin(\varphi)\cos(\theta) & 0 \\ 0 & 0 & 0 & 0 \\ 0 & 0 & 0 & 1 \end{bmatrix} \underbrace{\begin{bmatrix} x \\ y \\ z \\ 1 \end{bmatrix}}_{\mathbf{P}}, \tag{8.27}$$

where $\mathbf{P} = [x, y, z, 1]^T$ and $\mathbf{P}' = [x', y', 0, 1]^T$ are the homogeneous 3D points before and after axonometric projection. In order to project the same 3D point $\dot{\mathbf{P}} = [x, y, z]^T$ to a 2D point $\dot{\mathbf{p}}' = [x', y']^T$, a $2 \times 3$ matrix can be used as

$$\underbrace{\begin{bmatrix} x' \\ y' \end{bmatrix}}_{\dot{\mathbf{p}}'} = \begin{bmatrix} \cos(\theta) & 0 & -\sin(\theta) \\ -\sin(\varphi)\sin(\theta) & \cos(\varphi) & -\sin(\varphi)\cos(\theta) \end{bmatrix} \underbrace{\begin{bmatrix} x \\ y \\ z \end{bmatrix}}_{\dot{\mathbf{P}}}, \tag{8.28}$$

where $\dot{\mathbf{P}} = [x, y, z]^T$ and $\dot{\mathbf{p}}' = [x', y']^T$ are the inhomogeneous points before and after axonometric projection. The same result can be obtained using a $3 \times 4$ matrix with homogeneous points as

$$\underbrace{\begin{bmatrix} x' \\ y' \\ 1 \end{bmatrix}}_{\mathbf{p}'} = \begin{bmatrix} \cos(\theta) & 0 & -\sin(\theta) & 0 \\ -\sin(\varphi)\sin(\theta) & \cos(\varphi) & -\sin(\varphi)\cos(\theta) & 0 \\ 0 & 0 & 0 & 1 \end{bmatrix} \underbrace{\begin{bmatrix} x \\ y \\ z \\ 1 \end{bmatrix}}_{\mathbf{P}'}, \tag{8.29}$$

where $\mathbf{P} = [x, y, z, 1]^T$ and $\mathbf{p}' = [x', y', 1]^T$ are the homogeneous points before and after axonometric projection. The variations of axonometric projections include isometric, dimetric and trimetric projections.

**Example 8.1:** [*Axonometric projection*]

Equation (8.25) estimates the axonometric projection onto the $xy$-plane by applying front view projection following the rotations about the $y$- and $x$-axes respectively. The same axonometric transformation may result in 3D outcome when omitting the front view projection. Estimate the projection matrix in this case.

**Solution 8.1:** In our case, the projection is estimated as

$$\begin{aligned} \underbrace{\begin{bmatrix} x' \\ y' \\ z' \end{bmatrix}}_{\dot{\mathbf{P}}'} &= \begin{bmatrix} 1 & 0 & 0 \\ 0 & \cos(\varphi) & -\sin(\varphi) \\ 0 & \sin(\varphi) & \cos(\varphi) \end{bmatrix} \begin{bmatrix} \cos(\theta) & 0 & -\sin(\theta) \\ 0 & 1 & 0 \\ \sin(\theta) & 0 & \cos(\theta) \end{bmatrix} \begin{bmatrix} x \\ y \\ z \end{bmatrix} \\ &= \begin{bmatrix} \cos(\theta) & 0 & -\sin(\theta) \\ -\sin(\varphi)\sin(\theta) & \cos(\varphi) & -\sin(\varphi)\cos(\theta) \\ \cos(\varphi)\sin(\theta) & \sin(\varphi) & \cos(\varphi)\cos(\theta) \end{bmatrix} \underbrace{\begin{bmatrix} x \\ y \\ z \end{bmatrix}}_{\dot{\mathbf{P}}}, \end{aligned} \tag{8.30}$$

where $\dot{\mathbf{P}} = [x, y, z]^T$ and $\dot{\mathbf{P}}' = [x', y', z']$ are the inhomogeneous 3D points before and after axonometric projection. This can be written as

Fig. 8.5 Isometric projection

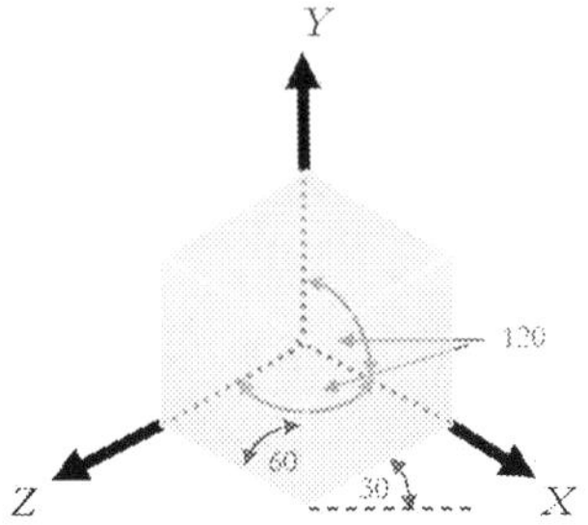


$$\begin{aligned} x' &= x\cos(\theta) - z\sin(\theta), \\ y' &= -x\sin(\varphi)\sin(\theta) + y\cos(\varphi) - z\sin(\varphi)\cos(\theta), \\ z' &= x\cos(\varphi)\sin(\theta) + y\sin(\varphi) + z\cos(\varphi)\cos(\theta). \end{aligned} \tag{8.31}$$

In homogeneous coordinates, Eqs. (8.30) and (8.31) can be re-written as

$$\underbrace{\begin{bmatrix} x' \\ y' \\ z' \\ 1 \end{bmatrix}}_{\mathbf{P}'} = \begin{bmatrix} \cos(\theta) & 0 & -\sin(\theta) & 0 \\ -\sin(\varphi)\sin(\theta) & \cos(\varphi) & -\sin(\varphi)\cos(\theta) & 0 \\ \cos(\varphi)\sin(\theta) & \sin(\varphi) & \cos(\varphi)\cos(\theta) & 0 \\ 0 & 0 & 0 & 1 \end{bmatrix} \underbrace{\begin{bmatrix} x \\ y \\ z \\ 1 \end{bmatrix}}_{\mathbf{P}}, \tag{8.32}$$

where $\mathbf{P} = [x, y, z, 1]^T$ and $\mathbf{P}' = [x', y', z', 1]^T$ are the homogeneous 3D points before and after axonometric projection. □

**Isometric projection:** In isometric projection, the view plane normal makes equal angles with the three principal axes and the angles between the projections of the $x$-, $y$- and $z$-axes are all the same, or 120° each as shown in Fig. 8.5. Consequently, the normal vector $\mathbf{n}$ is expressed as

$$\mathbf{n} = \begin{bmatrix} n_x \\ n_y \\ n_z \end{bmatrix} \text{ such that } |n_x| = |n_y| = |n_z|. \tag{8.33}$$

This leaves only one possible normal vector for each octant. In this type of projection, all parallel lines remain parallel and their lengths are preserved or scaled equally. Vertical lines remain vertical while horizontal lines are projected at 30° to the horizontal.

Assuming that the normal vector to the view plane is $[n, n, n]^T$, the azimuth angle $\theta$ must be 45°. As shown in Fig. 8.6, the elevation angle $\varphi$ is estimated as

$$\varphi = \tan^{-1}\left(\frac{n}{\sqrt{2}n}\right) = 35.2644°.$$

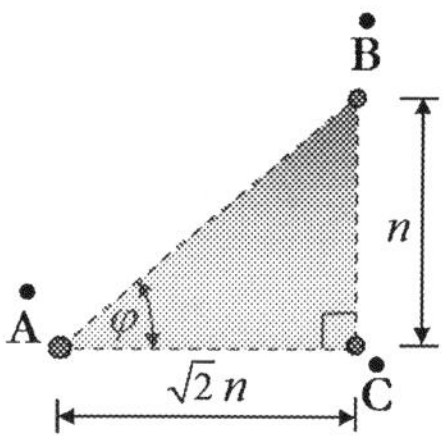


**Fig. 8.6** The elevation angle $\varphi$ of the isometric projection

Equation (8.28) can be re-written for isometric projection as

$$\underbrace{\begin{bmatrix} x' \\ y' \end{bmatrix}}_{\dot{\mathbf{p}}'} = \begin{bmatrix} \cos(45) & 0 & -\sin(45) \\ -\sin(35.2644)\sin(45) & \cos(35.2644) & -\sin(35.2644)\cos(45) \end{bmatrix} \begin{bmatrix} x \\ y \\ z \end{bmatrix}$$
$$= \begin{bmatrix} \frac{1}{\sqrt{2}} & 0 & -\frac{1}{\sqrt{2}} \\ -\frac{1}{\sqrt{6}} & \frac{\sqrt{2}}{\sqrt{3}} & -\frac{1}{\sqrt{6}} \end{bmatrix} \underbrace{\begin{bmatrix} x \\ y \\ z \end{bmatrix}}_{\dot{\mathbf{P}}}, \tag{8.34}$$

where $\dot{\mathbf{P}} = [x, y, z]^T$ and $\dot{\mathbf{p}}' = [x', y']^T$ are the inhomogeneous points before and after isometric projection. Similarly, Eq. (8.30) can be re-written for isometric projection as

$$\underbrace{\begin{bmatrix} x' \\ y' \\ z' \end{bmatrix}}_{\dot{\mathbf{P}}'} = \begin{bmatrix} \cos(45) & 0 & -\sin(45) \\ -\sin(35.2644)\sin(45) & \cos(35.2644) & -\sin(35.2644)\cos(45) \\ \cos(35.2644)\sin(45) & \sin(35.2644) & \cos(35.2644)\cos(45) \end{bmatrix} \begin{bmatrix} x \\ y \\ z \end{bmatrix}$$
$$= \begin{bmatrix} \frac{1}{\sqrt{2}} & 0 & -\frac{1}{\sqrt{2}} \\ -\frac{1}{\sqrt{6}} & \frac{\sqrt{2}}{\sqrt{3}} & -\frac{1}{\sqrt{6}} \\ \frac{1}{\sqrt{3}} & \frac{1}{\sqrt{3}} & \frac{1}{\sqrt{3}} \end{bmatrix} \underbrace{\begin{bmatrix} x \\ y \\ z \end{bmatrix}}_{\dot{\mathbf{P}}}, \tag{8.35}$$

where $\dot{\mathbf{P}} = [x, y, z]^T$ and $\dot{\mathbf{P}}' = [x', y', z']^T$ are the inhomogeneous points before and after isometric projection. Note that Eqs. (8.34) and (8.35) represent the isometric projection for the first octant (where all coordinates are positive).

**Example 8.2:** [*Isometric projection—points given a view plane normal vector*]
Consider a unit cube with two of its corners placed at $[0, 0, 0]^T$ and $[1, 1, 1]^T$. Given a view plane with a normal vector $[1, 1, 1]^T$, determine the isometric projection of its corners.

**Solution 8.2:** Equation (8.35) is used to get the locations of points after isometric transformation. Let us take the point $\dot{\mathbf{P}} = [1, 0, 0]^T$ as an example:

$$\underbrace{\begin{bmatrix} x' \\ y' \\ z' \end{bmatrix}}_{\dot{\mathbf{P}}'} = \begin{bmatrix} \cos(45) & 0 & -\sin(45) \\ -\sin(35.2644)\sin(45) & \cos(35.2644) & -\sin(35.2644)\cos(45) \\ \cos(35.2644)\sin(45) & \sin(35.2644) & \cos(35.2644)\cos(45) \end{bmatrix} \underbrace{\begin{bmatrix} x \\ y \\ z \end{bmatrix}}_{\dot{\mathbf{P}}}$$

$$= \begin{bmatrix} \frac{1}{\sqrt{2}} & 0 & -\frac{1}{\sqrt{2}} \\ -\frac{1}{\sqrt{6}} & \frac{\sqrt{2}}{\sqrt{3}} & -\frac{1}{\sqrt{6}} \\ \frac{1}{\sqrt{3}} & \frac{1}{\sqrt{3}} & \frac{1}{\sqrt{3}} \end{bmatrix} \begin{bmatrix} 1 \\ 0 \\ 0 \end{bmatrix} = \begin{bmatrix} \frac{1}{\sqrt{2}} \\ -\frac{1}{\sqrt{6}} \\ \frac{1}{\sqrt{3}} \end{bmatrix} = \begin{bmatrix} 0.7071 \\ -0.4082 \\ 0.5774 \end{bmatrix}.$$

Similarly, using Eq. (8.35), the 3D locations of the projected points are given in the following table:

| $\dot{\mathbf{P}} = [x, y, z]^T$ | $\dot{\mathbf{P}}' = [x', y', z']^T$ |
|---|---|
| $[0, 0, 0]^T$ | $[0, 0, 0]^T$ |
| $[1, 0, 0]^T$ | $[0.7071, -0.4082, 0.5774]^T$ |
| $[0, 1, 0]^T$ | $[0.0000, 0.8165, 0.5774]^T$ |
| $[1, 1, 0]^T$ | $[0.7071, 0.4082, 1.1547]^T$ |
| $[0, 0, 1]^T$ | $[-0.7071, -0.4082, 0.5774]^T$ |
| $[1, 0, 1]^T$ | $[0, -0.8165, 1.1547]^T$ |
| $[0, 1, 1]^T$ | $[-0.7071, 0.4082, 1.1547]^T$ |
| $[1, 1, 1]^T$ | $[0, 0, 1.7321]^T$ |

Projecting the same corners onto the $xy$-plane is discussed in Example 8.3. □

**Example 8.3:** [*Isometric projection—points given a view plane normal vector*]
Consider a unit cube with two of its corners placed at $[0, 0, 0]^T$ and $[1, 1, 1]^T$. Given a view plane with a normal vector $[1, 1, 1]^T$, determine the isometric projection of its corners onto the $xy$-plane.

**Solution 8.3:** Equation (8.34) is used to get the locations of points on the $xy$-plane after isometric transformation. Let us take the point $\dot{\mathbf{P}} = [1, 0, 0]^T$ as an example:

$$\underbrace{\begin{bmatrix} x' \\ y' \end{bmatrix}}_{\dot{\mathbf{p}}'} = \begin{bmatrix} \cos(45) & 0 & -\sin(45) \\ -\sin(35.2644)\sin(45) & \cos(35.2644) & -\sin(35.2644)\cos(45) \end{bmatrix} \underbrace{\begin{bmatrix} x \\ y \\ z \end{bmatrix}}_{\dot{\mathbf{P}}}$$

$$= \begin{bmatrix} \frac{1}{\sqrt{2}} & 0 & -\frac{1}{\sqrt{2}} \\ -\frac{1}{\sqrt{6}} & \frac{\sqrt{2}}{\sqrt{3}} & -\frac{1}{\sqrt{6}} \end{bmatrix} \begin{bmatrix} 1 \\ 0 \\ 0 \end{bmatrix} = \begin{bmatrix} \frac{1}{\sqrt{2}} \\ -\frac{1}{\sqrt{6}} \end{bmatrix} = \begin{bmatrix} 0.7071 \\ -0.4082 \end{bmatrix}.$$

Similarly, using Eq. (8.34), the locations of the projected points are given in the following table:

| $\dot{\mathbf{P}} = [x, y, z]^T$ | $\dot{\mathbf{p}}' = [x', y']^T$ |
|---|---|
| $[0, 0, 0]^T$ | $[0, 0]^T$ |
| $[1, 0, 0]^T$ | $[0.7071, -0.4082]^T$ |
| $[0, 1, 0]^T$ | $[0, 0.8165]^T$ |
| $[1, 1, 0]^T$ | $[0.7071, 0.4082]^T$ |
| $[0, 0, 1]^T$ | $[-0.7071, -0.4082]^T$ |
| $[1, 0, 1]^T$ | $[0, -0.8165]^T$ |
| $[0, 1, 1]^T$ | $[-0.7071, 0.4082]^T$ |
| $[1, 1, 1]^T$ | $[0, 0]^T$ |

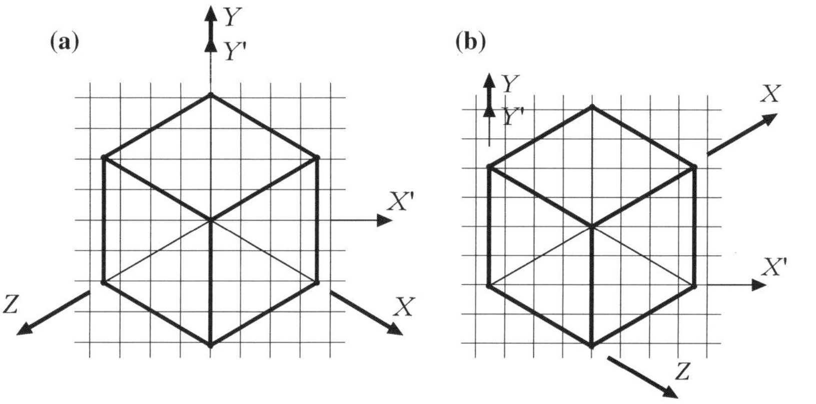


**Fig. 8.7** An isometric projection for a unit cube drawn on a 0.2 × 0.2 grid. Notice that there are two coordinate systems shown; the 3D coordinate system including $x$-, $y$- and $z$-axes as well as the 2D coordinate system including $x'$- and $y'$-axes. **a** When normal vector is $[1, 1, 1]^T$. **b** When normal vector is $[-1, 1, 1]^T$

These values are the same as those in Example 8.2 after removing the $z$-coordinates.

The isometric projection for the unit cube drawn on a 0.2 × 0.2 grid is shown in Fig. 8.7a. Notice that there are two coordinate systems shown; the 3D coordinate system including $x$-, $y$- and $z$-axes as well as the 2D coordinate system including $x'$- and $y'$-axes. Also, notice that the Euclidean distances between projected vertices sharing the same edge are equal. These distances can be calculated using Eq. (B.8). □

The matrix appearing in Eq. (8.34) does not represent a general isometric projection matrix. It is good for one octant only. Having a normal vector of $[-1, 1, 1]^T$ would change the rotation angle $\theta$ about the $y$-axis (i.e., azimuth angle) from $-45°$ to $45°$. Thus, Eq. (8.34) can be expressed as

$$\underbrace{\begin{bmatrix} x' \\ y' \end{bmatrix}}_{\dot{\mathbf{p}}'} = \begin{bmatrix} \cos(45) & 0 & \sin(45) \\ \sin(35.26)\sin(45) & \cos(35.26) & -\sin(35.26)\cos(45) \end{bmatrix} \begin{bmatrix} x \\ y \\ z \end{bmatrix}$$

$$= \begin{bmatrix} \frac{1}{\sqrt{2}} & 0 & \frac{1}{\sqrt{2}} \\ \frac{1}{\sqrt{6}} & \frac{\sqrt{2}}{\sqrt{3}} & -\frac{1}{\sqrt{6}} \end{bmatrix} \underbrace{\begin{bmatrix} x \\ y \\ z \end{bmatrix}}_{\dot{\mathbf{P}}}, \tag{8.36}$$

where $\dot{\mathbf{P}} = [x, y, z]^T$ and $\dot{\mathbf{p}}' = [x', y']^T$ are the inhomogeneous points before and after isometric projection.

**Example 8.4:** [*Isometric projection—points given a view plane normal vector*]
Consider a unit cube with two of its corners placed at $[0, 0, 0]^T$ and $[1, 1, 1]^T$. Given a view plane with a normal vector $[-1, 1, 1]^T$, determine the isometric projection of its corners onto the $xy$-plane.

**Solution 8.4:** Equation (8.36) is used to get the locations of points on the $xy$-plane after isometric transformation. Let us take the point $\dot{\mathbf{P}} = [1, 0, 0]^T$ as an example:

$$\underbrace{\begin{bmatrix} x' \\ y' \end{bmatrix}}_{\dot{\mathbf{p}}'} = \begin{bmatrix} \cos(-45) & 0 & -\sin(-45) \\ -\sin(35.2644)\sin(-45) & \cos(35.2644) & -\sin(35.2644)\cos(-45) \end{bmatrix} \underbrace{\begin{bmatrix} x \\ y \\ z \end{bmatrix}}_{\dot{\mathbf{P}}}$$

$$= \begin{bmatrix} \frac{1}{\sqrt{2}} & 0 & \frac{1}{\sqrt{2}} \\ \frac{1}{\sqrt{6}} & \frac{\sqrt{2}}{\sqrt{3}} & -\frac{1}{\sqrt{6}} \end{bmatrix} \begin{bmatrix} 1 \\ 0 \\ 0 \end{bmatrix} = \begin{bmatrix} \frac{1}{\sqrt{2}} \\ \frac{1}{\sqrt{6}} \end{bmatrix} = \begin{bmatrix} 0.7071 \\ 0.4082 \end{bmatrix}.$$

Similarly, using Eq. (8.36), the locations of the projected points onto the $xy$-plane are given in the following table:

| $\dot{\mathbf{P}} = [x, y, z]^T$ | $\dot{\mathbf{p}}' = [x', y']^T$ |
|---|---|
| $[0, 0, 0]^T$ | $[0, 0]^T$ |
| $[1, 0, 0]^T$ | $[0.7071, 0.4082]^T$ |
| $[0, 1, 0]^T$ | $[0.0000, 0.8165]^T$ |
| $[1, 1, 0]^T$ | $[0.7071, 1.2247]^T$ |
| $[0, 0, 1]^T$ | $[0.7071, -0.4082]^T$ |
| $[1, 0, 1]^T$ | $[1.4142, 0]^T$ |
| $[0, 1, 1]^T$ | $[0.7071, 0.4082]^T$ |
| $[1, 1, 1]^T$ | $[1.4142, 0.8165]^T$ |

As done in the previous example, the isometric projection for the unit cube drawn on a $0.2 \times 0.2$ grid is shown in Fig. 8.7b. Compare the difference between Fig. 8.7a,

**Fig. 8.8** Dimetric projection

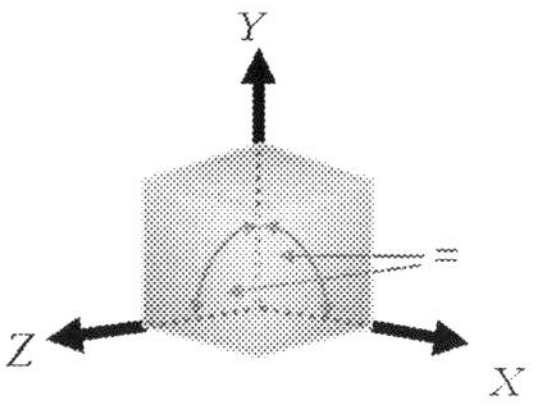


b. Again, the Euclidean distances between projected vertices sharing the same edge are equal. □

Isometric matrices change throughout octants according to the azimuth angle $\theta$ and elevation angle $\varphi$. Finding those matrices is left as an exercise.

**Dimetric projection:** In dimetric projection, the view plane normal makes equal angles with two of the principal axes. Equivalently, the view plane makes equal angles with two of the principal planes. Consequently, two of the angles enclosed between the projections of the principal axes are equal. Moreover, the normal vector $\mathbf{n}$ is expressed as

$$\mathbf{n} = \begin{bmatrix} n_x \\ n_y \\ n_z \end{bmatrix} \text{ such that } |n_x| = |n_y| \text{ or } |n_x| = |n_z| \text{ or } |n_y| = |n_z|. \tag{8.37}$$

Figure 8.8 shows an example of dimetric projection. In this type of projection, all parallel lines remain parallel and their lengths are preserved or scaled equally along the two equally foreshortened axes.

Assuming that the normal vector to the view plane is $[n, m, n]^T$, the azimuth angle $\theta$ must be 45°. In this case, the elevation angle $\varphi$ is estimated as

$$\varphi = \tan^{-1}\left(\frac{m}{\sqrt{2}n}\right).$$

Equation (8.28) can be re-written for dimetric projection as

$$\begin{aligned} \underbrace{\begin{bmatrix} x' \\ y' \end{bmatrix}}_{\dot{\mathbf{p}}'} &= \begin{bmatrix} \cos(45) & 0 & -\sin(45) \\ -\sin(\varphi)\sin(45) & \cos(\varphi) & -\sin(\varphi)\cos(45) \end{bmatrix} \begin{bmatrix} x \\ y \\ z \end{bmatrix} \\ &= \begin{bmatrix} \frac{1}{\sqrt{2}} & 0 & -\frac{1}{\sqrt{2}} \\ -\frac{\sin(\varphi)}{\sqrt{2}} & \cos(\varphi) & -\frac{\sin(\varphi)}{\sqrt{2}} \end{bmatrix} \underbrace{\begin{bmatrix} x \\ y \\ z \end{bmatrix}}_{\dot{\mathbf{P}}}, \end{aligned} \tag{8.38}$$

where $\dot{\mathbf{P}} = [x, y, z]^T$ and $\dot{\mathbf{p}}' = [x', y']^T$ are the inhomogeneous points before and after dimetric projection onto the $xy$-plane. Note that Eq. (8.38) represents the dimetric projection onto the $xy$-plane when the first and third terms of the normal vector are equal. Similarly, Eq. (8.30) can be re-written for dimetric projection as

$$\underbrace{\begin{bmatrix} x' \\ y' \\ z' \end{bmatrix}}_{\dot{\mathbf{P}}'} = \begin{bmatrix} \cos(45) & 0 & -\sin(45) \\ -\sin(\varphi)\sin(45) & \cos(\varphi) & -\sin(\varphi)\cos(45) \\ \cos(\varphi)\sin(45) & \sin(\varphi) & \cos(\varphi)\cos(45) \end{bmatrix} \begin{bmatrix} x \\ y \\ z \end{bmatrix}$$
$$= \begin{bmatrix} \frac{1}{\sqrt{2}} & 0 & -\frac{1}{\sqrt{2}} \\ -\frac{\sin(\varphi)}{\sqrt{2}} & \cos(\varphi) & -\frac{\sin(\varphi)}{\sqrt{2}} \\ \frac{\cos(\varphi)}{\sqrt{2}} & \sin(\varphi) & \frac{\cos(\varphi)}{\sqrt{2}} \end{bmatrix} \underbrace{\begin{bmatrix} x \\ y \\ z \end{bmatrix}}_{\dot{\mathbf{P}}}, \tag{8.39}$$

where $\dot{\mathbf{P}} = [x, y, z]^T$ and $\dot{\mathbf{P}}' = [x', y', z']^T$ are the inhomogeneous points before and after dimetric projection.

**Example 8.5:** [*Dimetric projection—points given a view plane normal vector*]
Consider a unit cube with two of its corners placed at $[0, 0, 0]^T$ and $[1, 1, 1]^T$. Given a view plane with a normal vector $[3\sqrt{2}, 6, 3\sqrt{2}]^T$, determine the dimetric projection of its corners onto the $xy$-plane.

**Solution 8.5:** The elevation angle $\varphi$ is estimated as

$$\varphi = \tan^{-1}\left(\frac{6}{6}\right) = 45^\circ.$$

Equation (8.38) is used to get the locations of points on the $xy$-plane after dimetric transformation. Let us take the point $\dot{\mathbf{P}} = [1, 0, 0]^T$ as an example:

$$\underbrace{\begin{bmatrix} x' \\ y' \end{bmatrix}}_{\dot{\mathbf{p}}'} = \begin{bmatrix} \cos(45) & 0 & -\sin(45) \\ -\sin(45)\sin(45) & \cos(45) & -\sin(45)\cos(45) \end{bmatrix} \underbrace{\begin{bmatrix} x \\ y \\ z \end{bmatrix}}_{\dot{\mathbf{P}}}$$
$$= \begin{bmatrix} \frac{1}{\sqrt{2}} & 0 & -\frac{1}{\sqrt{2}} \\ -\frac{1}{2} & \frac{1}{\sqrt{2}} & -\frac{1}{2} \end{bmatrix} \begin{bmatrix} 1 \\ 0 \\ 0 \end{bmatrix} = \begin{bmatrix} \frac{1}{\sqrt{2}} \\ -\frac{1}{2} \end{bmatrix} = \begin{bmatrix} 0.7071 \\ -0.5 \end{bmatrix}$$

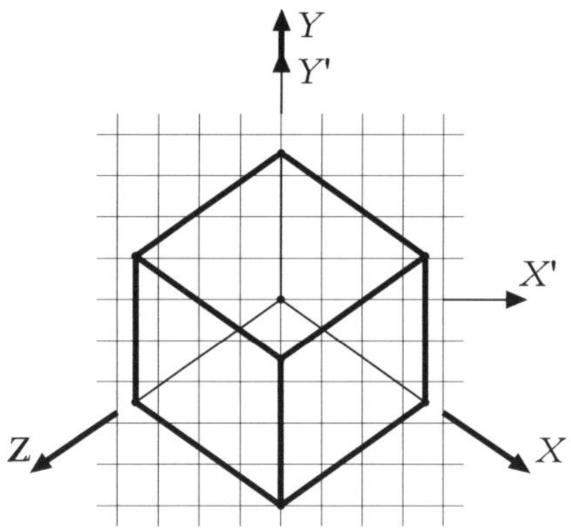


**Fig. 8.9** A dimetric projection for a unit cube drawn on a 0.2 × 0.2 grid. Notice that there are two coordinate systems shown; the 3D coordinate system including $x$-, $y$- and $z$-axes as well as the 2D coordinate system including $x'$- and $y'$-axes. The normal vector to the view plane is $[3\sqrt{2}, 6, 3\sqrt{2}]^T$

Similarly, using Eq. (8.38), the locations of the projected points onto the $xy$-plane are given in the following table:

| $\dot{\mathbf{P}} = [x, y, z]^T$ | $\dot{\mathbf{p}}' = [x', y']^T$ |
|---|---|
| $[0, 0, 0]^T$ | $[0, 0]^T$ |
| $[1, 0, 0]^T$ | $[0.7071, -0.5]^T$ |
| $[0, 1, 0]^T$ | $[0, 0.7071]^T$ |
| $[1, 1, 0]^T$ | $[0.7071, 0.2071]^T$ |
| $[0, 0, 1]^T$ | $[-0.7071, -0.5]^T$ |
| $[1, 0, 1]^T$ | $[0, -1]^T$ |
| $[0, 1, 1]^T$ | $[-0.7071, 0.2071]^T$ |
| $[1, 1, 1]^T$ | $[0, -0.2929]^T$ |

The dimetric projection for the unit cube drawn on a 0.2 × 0.2 grid is shown in Fig. 8.9. Compare it to Fig. 8.7a. Notice that the Euclidean distances of the projected edges parallel to the $x$- and $z$-axes are equal. □

**Example 8.6:** [*Dimetric projection—projection matrix given a view plane normal vector*]

Given a view plane with a normal vector $[3, 3, 4]^T$, determine the homogeneous dimetric projection matrix (onto the $xy$-plane) that can be used with it.

**Solution 8.6:** As shown in Fig. 8.10, the azimuth angle $\theta$ is estimated as

$$\theta = \tan^{-1}\left(\frac{3}{4}\right) = 36.8699°$$

and the elevation angle $\varphi$ is estimated as

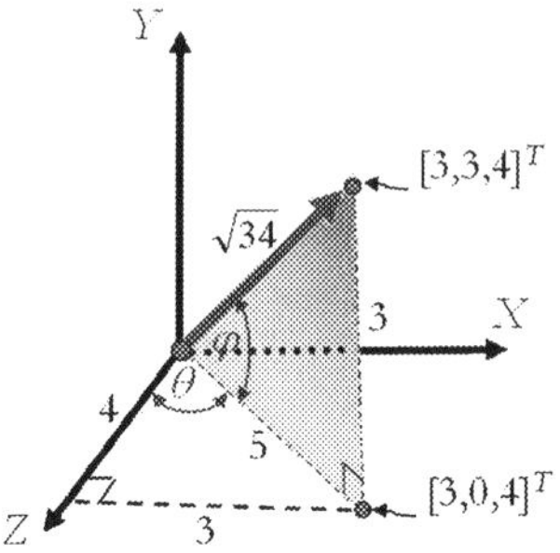


**Fig. 8.10** The azimuth angle $\theta$ and the elevation angle $\varphi$ for the normal vector $[3, 3, 4]^T$

$$\varphi = \tan^{-1}\left(\frac{3}{5}\right) = 30.9638^\circ.$$

Equation (8.29) can be used with the previous angles. Thus,

$$\underbrace{\begin{bmatrix} x' \\ y' \\ 1 \end{bmatrix}}_{\mathbf{p}'} = \begin{bmatrix} \cos(\theta) & 0 & -\sin(\theta) & 0 \\ -\sin(\varphi)\sin(\theta) & \cos(\varphi) & -\sin(\varphi)\cos(\theta) & 0 \\ 0 & 0 & 0 & 1 \end{bmatrix} \begin{bmatrix} x \\ y \\ z \\ 1 \end{bmatrix}$$
$$= \begin{bmatrix} \frac{4}{5} & 0 & -\frac{3}{5} & 0 \\ -\frac{9}{5\sqrt{34}} & \frac{5}{\sqrt{34}} & -\frac{12}{5\sqrt{34}} & 0 \\ 0 & 0 & 0 & 1 \end{bmatrix} \underbrace{\begin{bmatrix} x \\ y \\ z \\ 1 \end{bmatrix}}_{\mathbf{P}'}, \tag{8.40}$$

where $\mathbf{P} = [x, y, z, 1]^T$ and $\mathbf{p}' = [x', y', 1]^T$ are the homogeneous points before and after axonometric projection onto the $xy$-plane. □

**Trimetric projection:** In trimetric projection, the view plane normal makes different angles with the principal axes. Consequently, none of the angles enclosed between the projections of the principal axes are equal. Moreover, the normal vector $\mathbf{n}$ is expressed as

$$\mathbf{n} = \begin{bmatrix} n_x \\ n_y \\ n_z \end{bmatrix} \text{ such that } |n_x| \neq |n_y|, |n_x| \neq |n_z| \text{ and } |n_y| \neq |n_z|. \tag{8.41}$$

Figure 8.11 shows an example of trimetric projection. In this type of projection, lines are scaled differently along the principal axes. Equation (8.25) through Eq. (8.32) can be used with trimetric projection.

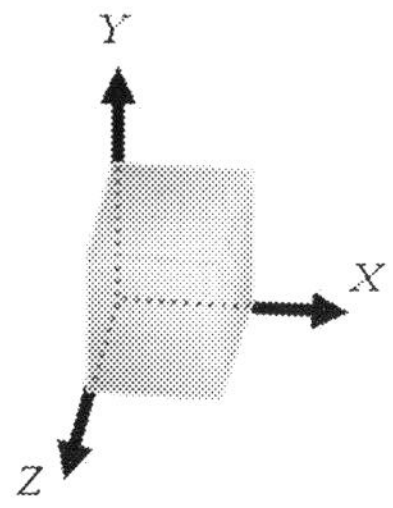


**Fig. 8.11** Trimetric projection

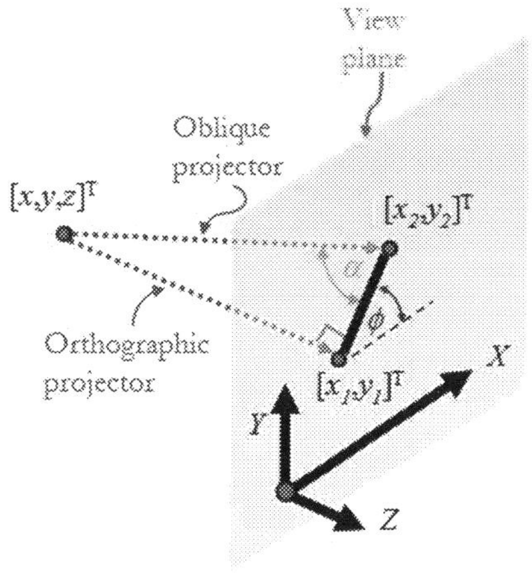


**Fig. 8.12** Oblique projection and angles $\alpha$ and $\phi$

## *8.3.2 Oblique Projections*

As shown in Fig. 8.2b, in oblique projections, the projectors are parallel to each other but *not* perpendicular to view plane as with orthographic (i.e., multi-view and axonometric) projections. Like orthographic multi-view projections, an oblique projection displays the exact shapes of faces parallel to the view plane preserving both angles and lengths (or length proportions). Like orthographic axonometric projections, an oblique projection displays 3D models (including the exact shapes of faces parallel to the view plane).

Consider Fig. 8.12 where a 3D point $[x, y, z]^T$ is projected onto a view plane. If the point is orthographically projected onto the plane (i.e., if the direction of projection (DOP) or the projectors make an angle of 90° with the view plane), the location of the projected point will appear at the point $[x_1, y_1]^T$. Alternatively, if the projectors make an angle other than 90° with the view plane, the location of the projected point will appear at another point $[x_2, y_2]^T$. Considering the triangle whose vertices are the 3D point $[x, y, z]^T$ and the projected points $[x_1, y_1]^T$ and $[x_2, y_2]^T$, the angle $\alpha$ that is enclosed between the oblique projector and the line connecting $[x_1, y_1]^T$ and $[x_2, y_2]^T$ determines the category of the oblique projection. Note that according to

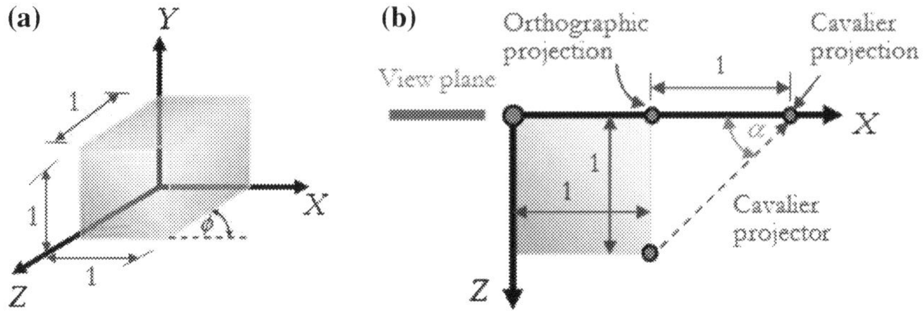


**Fig. 8.13** Oblique projections. **a** Cavalier projection. **b** When $\alpha = 45°$, lines parallel to the $z$-axis maintain their actual lengths

the direction of projection, the angle $\phi$[1] in Fig. 8.12 (i.e., the angle enclosed between the line connecting the projected points $[x_1, y_1]^T$ and $[x_2, y_2]^T$ and the horizontal axis) may not be 0° in general. Cavalier and cabinet projections are classified under oblique projections.

#### 8.3.2.1 Cavalier Projection

The oblique projection is referred to as *cavalier* projection if $\alpha = 45°$. Consider Fig. 8.13a, which shows a cavalier projection for a unit cube with faces parallel to the principal planes in the world coordinate system. In this figure, the view plane normal is parallel to the positive $z$-axis. One face that is parallel to the view plane will be orthographically projected as a front view. The lines perpendicular to that face (or parallel to the $z$-axis) will maintain their actual lengths since $\tan(\alpha) = 1$ as shown in Fig. 8.13b. The angle $\phi$ is typically 30° or 45°. However, the model does not seem to be a real 3D model!

Utilizing the angle $\phi$ and trigonometry, one can estimate the location of a 3D point $\dot{\mathbf{P}} = [x, y, z]^T$ after cavalier projection onto the $xy$-plane as

$$\begin{aligned} x' &= x + z\cos(\phi), \\ y' &= y + z\sin(\phi), \\ z' &= 0, \end{aligned} \tag{8.42}$$

where $[x', y', 0]^T$ is the point after cavalier projection. In matrix form, this can be written as

$$\underbrace{\begin{bmatrix} x' \\ y' \\ 0 \end{bmatrix}}_{\dot{\mathbf{P}}'} = \begin{bmatrix} 1 & 0 & \cos(\phi) \\ 0 & 1 & \sin(\phi) \\ 0 & 0 & 0 \end{bmatrix} \underbrace{\begin{bmatrix} x \\ y \\ z \end{bmatrix}}_{\dot{\mathbf{P}}}, \tag{8.43}$$

[1] The symbol $\phi$ refers to different entities throughout this book. For example, in Sect. 8.3.1.2, $\phi$ referred to the zenith angle (as in Sect. B.6).

where $\dot{\mathbf{P}} = [x, y, z]^T$ and $\dot{\mathbf{P}}' = [x', y', 0]^T$ are the inhomogeneous 3D points before and after cavalier projection onto the $xy$-plane. In homogeneous coordinates (Sect. B.7), Eq. (8.43) can be re-written as

$$\underbrace{\begin{bmatrix} x' \\ y' \\ 0 \\ 1 \end{bmatrix}}_{\mathbf{P}'} = \begin{bmatrix} 1 & 0 & \cos(\phi) & 0 \\ 0 & 1 & \sin(\phi) & 0 \\ 0 & 0 & 0 & 0 \\ 0 & 0 & 0 & 1 \end{bmatrix} \underbrace{\begin{bmatrix} x \\ y \\ z \\ 1 \end{bmatrix}}_{\mathbf{P}}, \tag{8.44}$$

where $\mathbf{P} = [x, y, z, 1]^T$ and $\mathbf{P}' = [x', y', 0, 1]^T$ are the homogeneous 3D points before and after cavalier projection onto the $xy$-plane. In order to project the same 3D point $\dot{\mathbf{P}} = [x, y, z]^T$ to a 2D point $\dot{\mathbf{p}}' = [x', y']^T$, a $2 \times 3$ matrix can be used as

$$\underbrace{\begin{bmatrix} x' \\ y' \end{bmatrix}}_{\dot{\mathbf{p}}'} = \begin{bmatrix} 1 & 0 & \cos(\phi) \\ 0 & 1 & \sin(\phi) \end{bmatrix} \underbrace{\begin{bmatrix} x \\ y \\ z \end{bmatrix}}_{\dot{\mathbf{P}}}, \tag{8.45}$$

where $\dot{\mathbf{P}} = [x, y, z]^T$ and $\dot{\mathbf{p}}' = [x', y']^T$ are the inhomogeneous points before and after cavalier projection onto the $xy$-plane. The same result can be obtained using a $3 \times 4$ matrix with homogeneous points as

$$\underbrace{\begin{bmatrix} x' \\ y' \\ 1 \end{bmatrix}}_{\mathbf{p}'} = \begin{bmatrix} 1 & 0 & \cos(\phi) & 0 \\ 0 & 1 & \sin(\phi) & 0 \\ 0 & 0 & 0 & 1 \end{bmatrix} \underbrace{\begin{bmatrix} x \\ y \\ z \\ 1 \end{bmatrix}}_{\mathbf{P}}, \tag{8.46}$$

where $\mathbf{P} = [x, y, z, 1]^T$ and $\mathbf{p}' = [x', y', 1]^T$ are the homogeneous points before and after cavalier projection onto the $xy$-plane.

#### 8.3.2.2 Cabinet Projection

The oblique projection is referred to as *cabinet* projection if $\alpha = 63.43°$. Consider Fig. 8.14a, which shows a cabinet projection for a unit cube with faces parallel to the principal planes in the world coordinate system. In this figure, the view plane normal is parallel to the positive $z$-axis. One face that is parallel to the view plane will be orthographically projected as a front view. The lines perpendicular to that face (or parallel to the $z$-axis) will be displayed at one-half of their actual lengths since $\tan(\alpha) = 2$ as shown in Fig. 8.14b. Also, in cabinet projection, the angle $\phi$ could be 30° or 45°.

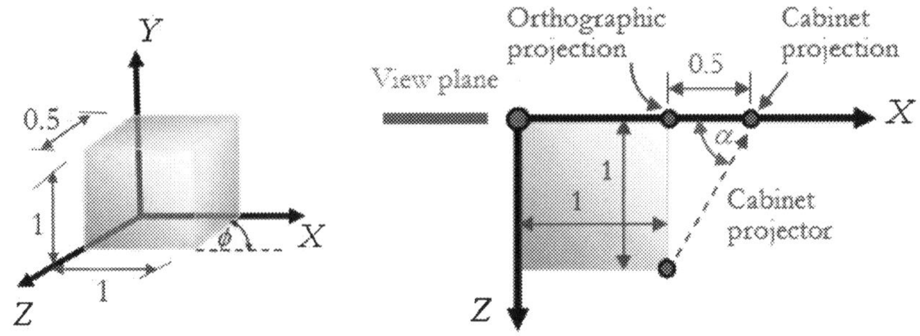


**Fig. 8.14** Oblique projections. **a** Cabinet projection. **b** When $\alpha = 63.43°$, lines parallel to the $z$-axis are displayed at one-half of their actual lengths

As done previously with cavalier projection, we can utilize the angle $\phi$ and trigonometry to estimate the location of a 3D point $\dot{\mathbf{P}} = [x, y, z]^T$ after cabinet projection onto the $xy$-plane as

$$\begin{aligned} x' &= x + \tfrac{1}{2}z\cos(\phi), \\ y' &= y + \tfrac{1}{2}z\sin(\phi), \\ z' &= 0, \end{aligned} \tag{8.47}$$

where $[x', y', 0]^T$ is the point after cabinet projection. In matrix form, this can be written as

$$\underbrace{\begin{bmatrix} x' \\ y' \\ 0 \end{bmatrix}}_{\dot{\mathbf{P}}'} = \begin{bmatrix} 1 & 0 & \frac{1}{2}\cos(\phi) \\ 0 & 1 & \frac{1}{2}\sin(\phi) \\ 0 & 0 & 0 \end{bmatrix} \underbrace{\begin{bmatrix} x \\ y \\ z \end{bmatrix}}_{\dot{\mathbf{P}}}, \tag{8.48}$$

where $\dot{\mathbf{P}} = [x, y, z]^T$ and $\dot{\mathbf{P}}' = [x', y', 0]^T$ are the inhomogeneous 3D points before and after cabinet projection onto the $xy$-plane. In homogeneous coordinates, Eq. (8.48) can be re-written as

$$\underbrace{\begin{bmatrix} x' \\ y' \\ 0 \\ 1 \end{bmatrix}}_{\mathbf{P}'} = \begin{bmatrix} 1 & 0 & \frac{1}{2}\cos(\phi) & 0 \\ 0 & 1 & \frac{1}{2}\sin(\phi) & 0 \\ 0 & 0 & 0 & 0 \\ 0 & 0 & 0 & 1 \end{bmatrix} \underbrace{\begin{bmatrix} x \\ y \\ z \\ 1 \end{bmatrix}}_{\mathbf{P}}, \tag{8.49}$$

where $\mathbf{P} = [x, y, z, 1]^T$ and $\mathbf{P}' = [x', y', 0, 1]^T$ are the homogeneous 3D points before and after cabinet projection onto the $xy$-plane. In order to project the same 3D point $\dot{\mathbf{P}} = [x, y, z]^T$ to a 2D point $\dot{\mathbf{p}}' = [x', y']^T$, a $2 \times 3$ matrix can be used as

$$\underbrace{\begin{bmatrix} x' \\ y' \end{bmatrix}}_{\dot{\mathbf{p}}'} = \begin{bmatrix} 1 & 0 & \frac{1}{2}\cos(\phi) \\ 0 & 1 & \frac{1}{2}\sin(\phi) \end{bmatrix} \underbrace{\begin{bmatrix} x \\ y \\ z \end{bmatrix}}_{\dot{\mathbf{P}}}, \tag{8.50}$$

where $\dot{\mathbf{P}} = [x, y, z]^T$ and $\dot{\mathbf{p}}' = [x', y']^T$ are the inhomogeneous points before and after cabinet projection onto the $xy$-plane. The same result can be obtained using a $3 \times 4$ matrix with homogeneous points as

$$\underbrace{\begin{bmatrix} x' \\ y' \\ 1 \end{bmatrix}}_{\mathbf{p}'} = \begin{bmatrix} 1 & 0 & \frac{1}{2}\cos(\phi) & 0 \\ 0 & 1 & \frac{1}{2}\sin(\phi) & 0 \\ 0 & 0 & 0 & 1 \end{bmatrix} \underbrace{\begin{bmatrix} x \\ y \\ z \\ 1 \end{bmatrix}}_{\mathbf{P}'}, \tag{8.51}$$

where $\mathbf{P} = [x, y, z, 1]^T$ and $\mathbf{p}' = [x', y', 1]^T$ are the homogeneous points before and after cabinet projection onto the $xy$-plane.

**General oblique projection:** If you compare between Eqs. (8.43) and (8.48) or between Eqs. (8.44) and (8.49), you will notice that the difference between both projections lie on the coefficients multiplying $\sin(\phi)$ and $\cos(\phi)$, which are 1 and 0.5 for cavalier and cabinet projections respectively. These values are equal to $\cot(\alpha)$. Thus, a general oblique projection is estimated in matrix form as

$$\underbrace{\begin{bmatrix} x' \\ y' \\ 0 \end{bmatrix}}_{\dot{\mathbf{P}}'} = \underbrace{\begin{bmatrix} 1 & 0 & \cot(\alpha)\cos(\phi) \\ 0 & 1 & \cot(\alpha)\sin(\phi) \\ 0 & 0 & 0 \end{bmatrix}}_{\dot{\mathrm{P}}_{oblique}} \underbrace{\begin{bmatrix} x \\ y \\ z \end{bmatrix}}_{\dot{\mathbf{P}}}, \tag{8.52}$$

where $\dot{\mathrm{P}}_{oblique}$ is a $3 \times 3$ matrix used to obliquely project a 3D point $\dot{\mathbf{P}} = [x, y, z]^T$ onto the $xy$-plane as $\dot{\mathbf{P}}' = [x', y', 0]^T$. In homogeneous coordinates, Eq. (8.52) can be re-written as

$$\underbrace{\begin{bmatrix} x' \\ y' \\ 0 \\ 1 \end{bmatrix}}_{\mathbf{P}'} = \underbrace{\begin{bmatrix} 1 & 0 & \cot(\alpha)\cos(\phi) & 0 \\ 0 & 1 & \cot(\alpha)\sin(\phi) & 0 \\ 0 & 0 & 0 & 0 \\ 0 & 0 & 0 & 1 \end{bmatrix}}_{\mathrm{P}_{oblique}} \underbrace{\begin{bmatrix} x \\ y \\ z \\ 1 \end{bmatrix}}_{\mathbf{P}}, \tag{8.53}$$

where $\mathrm{P}_{oblique}$ is a $4 \times 4$ homogeneous matrix used to obliquely project a homogeneous 3D point $\mathbf{P} = [x, y, z, 1]^T$ onto the $xy$-plane as $\mathbf{P}' = [x', y', 0, 1]^T$. As a matter of fact, both Eqs. (8.52) and (8.53) can be used for front view projection when $\alpha = 90°$.

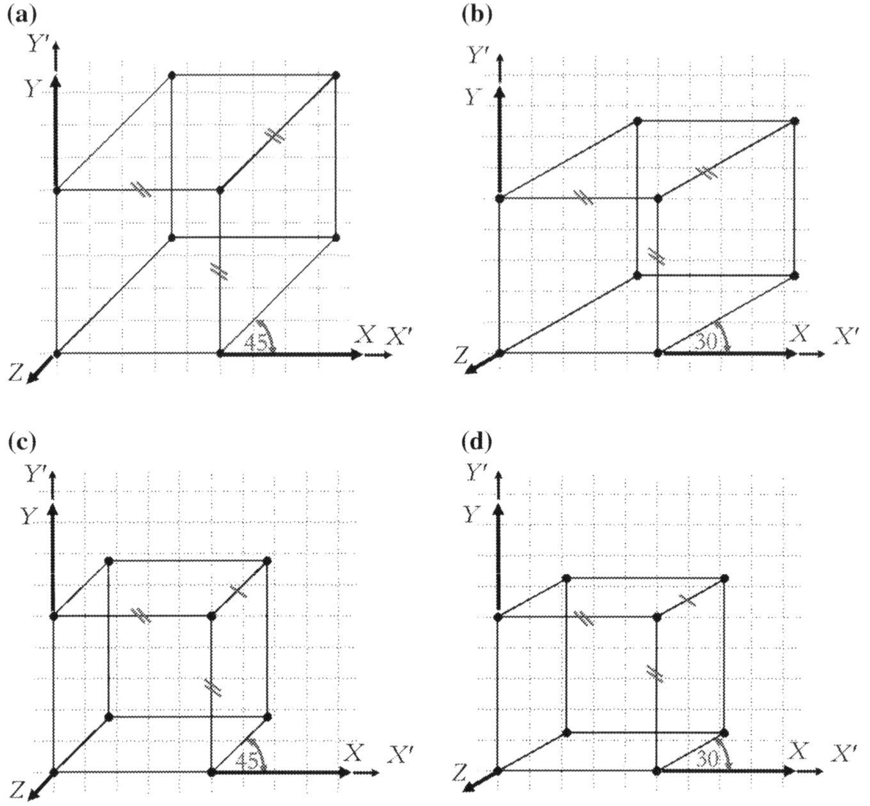


**Fig. 8.15** Oblique projections using Eq. (8.53). **a** Cavalier projection: $\alpha = 45°, \phi = 45°$. **b** Cavalier projection: $\alpha = 45°, \phi = 30°$. **c** Cabinet projection: $\alpha = 63.43°, \phi = 45°$. **d** Cabinet projection: $\alpha = 63.43°, \phi = 30°$

The projection matrix $\mathtt{P}_{oblique}$ of Eq. (8.53) is used to generate the unit cubes shown in Fig. 8.15. The angles and projection types are listed in the following table:

| Figure | $\alpha$ | $\phi$ | Type |
|---|---|---|---|
| 8.15(a) | 45° | 45° | Cavalier |
| 8.15(b) | 45° | 30° | Cavalier |
| 8.15(c) | 63.43° | 45° | Cabinet |
| 8.15(d) | 63.43° | 30° | Cabinet |

Closer faces look closer when the projection matrix $\mathtt{P}_{oblique}$ of Eq. (8.53) is tuned as

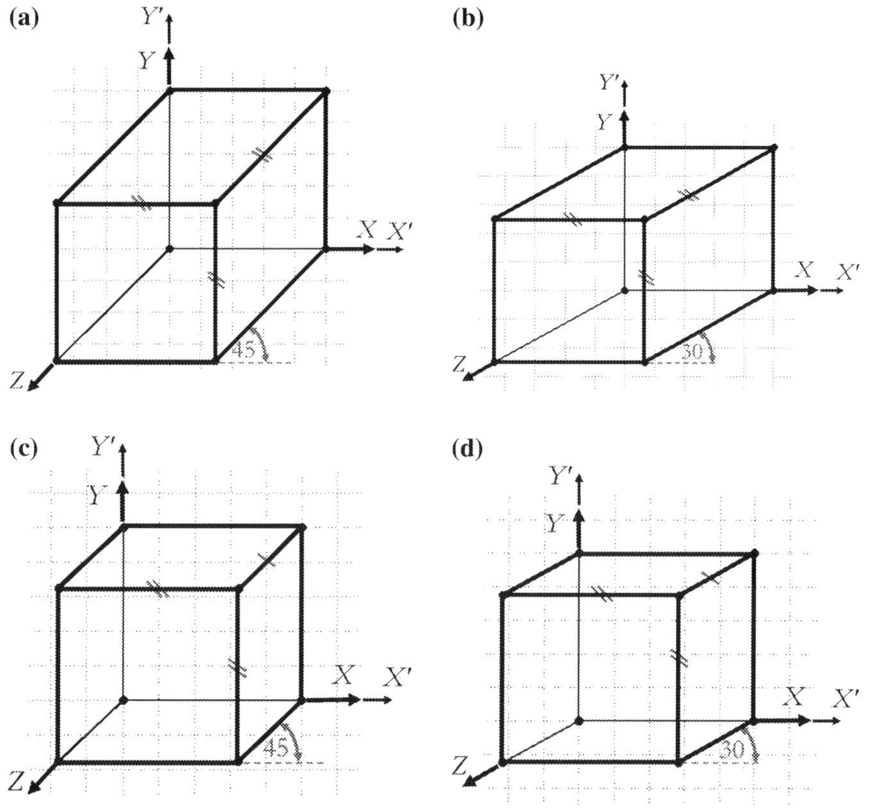


**Fig. 8.16** Oblique projections using Eq. (8.54). **a** Cavalier projection: $\alpha = 45°, \phi = 45°$. **b** Cavalier projection: $\alpha = 45°, \phi = 30°$. **c** Cabinet projection: $\alpha = 63.43°, \phi = 45°$. **d** Cabinet projection: $\alpha = 63.43°, \phi = 30°$

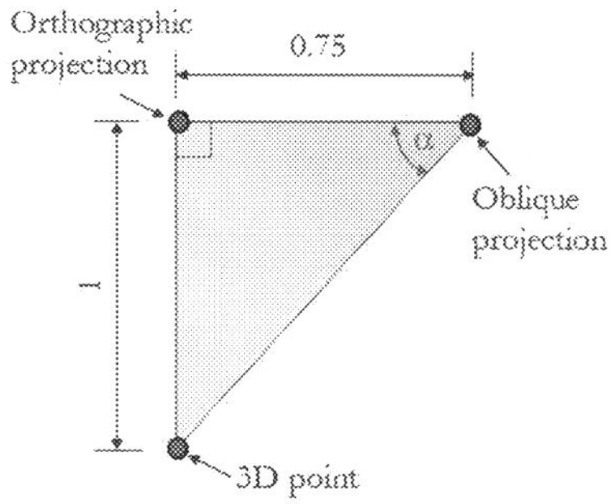


**Fig. 8.17** If the lines are to be projected at 0.75 of their actual lengths, what would the value of angle $\alpha$ be?

$$\underbrace{\begin{bmatrix} x' \\ y' \\ 0 \\ 1 \end{bmatrix}}_{\mathbf{P}'} = \underbrace{\begin{bmatrix} 1 & 0 & -\cot(\alpha)\cos(\phi) & 0 \\ 0 & 1 & -\cot(\alpha)\sin(\phi) & 0 \\ 0 & 0 & 0 & 0 \\ 0 & 0 & 0 & 1 \end{bmatrix}}_{\mathrm{P}_{oblique}} \underbrace{\begin{bmatrix} x \\ y \\ z \\ 1 \end{bmatrix}}_{\mathbf{P}}. \tag{8.54}$$

The unit cubes of Fig. 8.15 are re-drawn to get the results shown in Fig. 8.16.

**Example 8.7:** [*Oblique projection—length ratio given angle* $\alpha$]
Considering the $xy$-plane as the view plane, if the projectors are not parallel to the $z$-axis, oblique projection can be created. In cavalier projection with $\alpha = 45°$, the lines parallel to the $z$-axis maintain their actual lengths. In case of cabinet projection with $\alpha = 63.4°$, those lines are displayed at a ratio of 0.5 of their lengths. What would the ratio be if $\alpha = 30°$?

**Solution 8.7:** The ratio is estimated as

$$\cot(\alpha) = \cot(30) = \sqrt{3}. \qquad \square$$

**Example 8.8:** [*Oblique projection—angle* $\alpha$ *given length ratio*]
Consider a cube whose faces are parallel to the three principal planes. If an oblique projection is applied to this cube such that the view plane is parallel to the $xy$-plane, one face of the cube that is parallel to the view plane is orthographically projected. The lines perpendicular to that face maintain their actual lengths if $\alpha = 45°$ in case of cavalier projection. The same lines may be displayed at one-half of their actual lengths if $\alpha = 63.4°$ in case of cabinet projection. What would the value of angle $\alpha$ be if those lines are to be projected at 0.75 of their actual lengths?

**Solution 8.8:** Consider the triangle shown in Fig. 8.17 whose vertices are the 3D point and its orthographic and oblique projections. The angle $\alpha$ is obtained as

$$\alpha = \cot^{-1}(0.75) = \tan^{-1}\left(\frac{4}{3}\right) = 53.1301°. \qquad \square$$

**Example 8.9:** [*Oblique projection—orthographic projection*]
Orthographic projection can be considered as a special case of oblique projection. What would the value of angle $\alpha$ be in this case?

**Solution 8.9:** In this case, $\alpha = 90°$. Applying this value to Eq. (8.53) results in a front projection. □

## 8.4 Perspective Projections

Perspective projections represent the second sub-type of planar geometric projections. The main property characterizing all perspective projections is that the viewpoint or the center of projection (i.e., COP) is placed at a finite distance from the viewing surface (or the view plane). In other words, projectors are not parallel to each other as in parallel projections; instead, they meet at the COP as shown in Fig. 8.18. This figure also shows that the view volume in this case is pyramidal as opposite to parallelepiped viewing volume that appear in parallel projections.

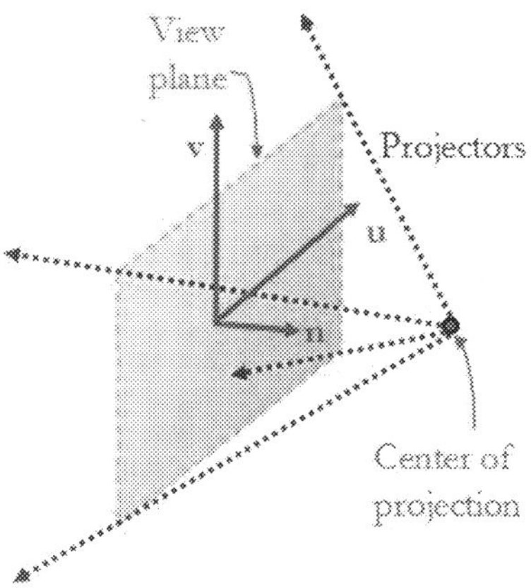


**Fig. 8.18** Perspective projection: The center of projection is placed at a finite distance from the view plane

In perspective projections, parallel lines that are not parallel to the view plane converge to a specific point that is referred to as a *vanishing point*. Objects away from the viewpoint or center of projection appear smaller comparing to identical objects closer to the center of projection, which provides a more realistic look of a 3D model!

According to the orientation of the view plane and the number of vanishing points, perspective projections can be further categorized into one-point projection, two-point projection and three-point projection. However, we should emphasize that the terms one-, two- and three-point perspective projections do *not* mean that the exact numbers of vanishing points in these projections are one, two and three points respectively. Instead, the number here is with respect to the principal axes. Practically, we may have many more vanishing points as every set of parallel lines will converge to a separate vanishing point. In order to avoid confusion, vanishing points for lines that are *not* parallel to the principal axes are sometimes referred to as *trace points*.

## *8.4.1 One-Point Perspective Projection*

The one-point perspective projection exists when the view plane is parallel to two of the principal axes or one principal plane; i.e., when the view plane intersects one of the principal axes. In Fig. 8.19, this situation happens as the view plane is parallel to the $x$- and $y$-axes. In other words, it is parallel to the $xy$-plane and intersecting the $z$-axis. In this case, the normal to the view plane is parallel to the $z$-axis.

Moreover, entities parallel to the view plane will be orthographically projected as a multi-view projection and lines parallel to the two principal axes (i.e., $x$- and $y$-axes in Fig. 8.19) remain parallel to these axes. On the other hand, lines parallel to the third axis intersecting the view plane (i.e., the axis that is parallel to the view plane normal) converge to a single vanishing point. In case of one-point perspective projection, two components of the normal vector to the view plane are zeros.

Consider Fig. 8.20a, which shows the view plane as placed at $z = d$ while the COP as placed at the origin. (The distance $d$ is referred to as the focal length.)

Fig. 8.19 One-point perspective projection: The view plane is parallel to two principal axes

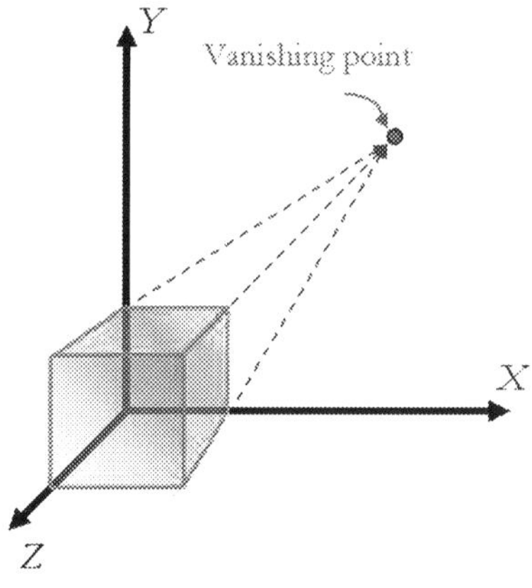


A 3D point $\dot{\mathbf{P}} = [x, y, z]^T$ is projected onto the view plane as another point $\dot{\mathbf{P}}' = [x', y', d]^T$. Figure 8.20b shows the relationships among the view plane, the 3D point $\dot{\mathbf{P}} = [x, y, z]^T$ and the projected point $\dot{\mathbf{P}}' = [x', y', d]^T$ where the $y$-axis is pointing outwards. Figure 8.20c shows another multi-view projection illustrating these relationships where the $x$-axis is pointing outwards. Considering similar triangles in these figures, we can write

$$\begin{aligned}\frac{x'}{d} &= \frac{x}{z},\\ \frac{y'}{d} &= \frac{y}{z}.\end{aligned} \tag{8.55}$$

Equivalently, we can write

$$\begin{aligned}x' &= \frac{x}{z/d},\\ y' &= \frac{y}{z/d}.\end{aligned} \tag{8.56}$$

Note that the existence of the division by $z$ gives the effect of making distant objects smaller than closer ones. Also, note that $z$ must not be zero. Eq. (8.56) can be written in homogeneous matrix form as (Foley et al. 1995)

$$\begin{aligned}\mathbf{P}' &= \underbrace{\begin{bmatrix} 1 & 0 & 0 & 0 \\ 0 & 1 & 0 & 0 \\ 0 & 0 & 1 & 0 \\ 0 & 0 & \frac{1}{d} & 0 \end{bmatrix}}_{\mathrm{P}_{per}} \underbrace{\begin{bmatrix} x \\ y \\ z \\ 1 \end{bmatrix}}_{\mathbf{P}} \\ &= \begin{bmatrix} x \\ y \\ z \\ \frac{z}{d} \end{bmatrix},\end{aligned} \tag{8.57}$$

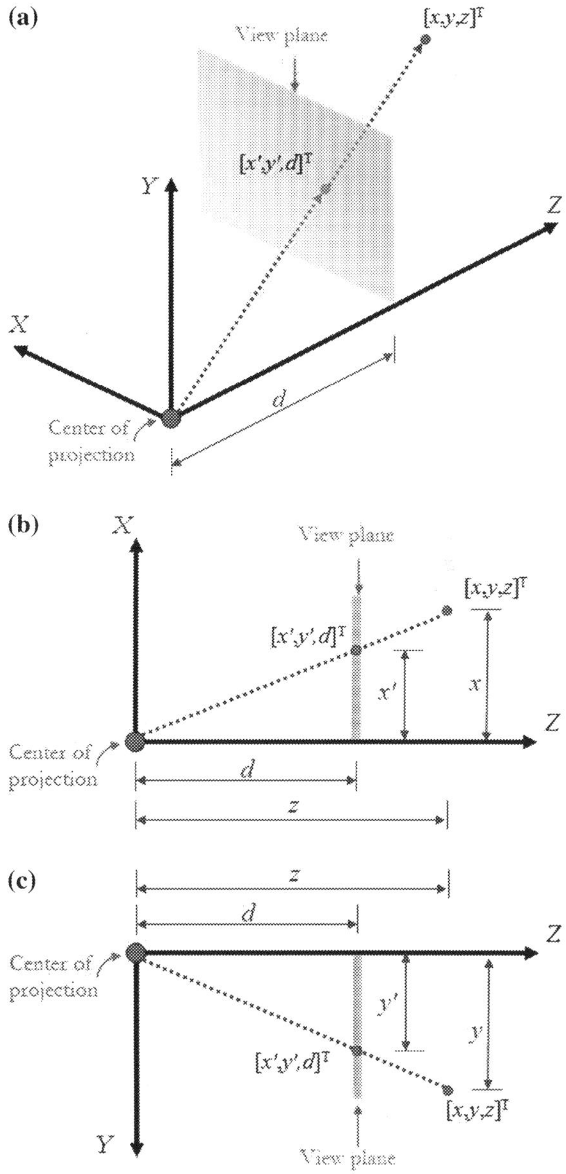


**Fig. 8.20** One-point perspective projection when the center of projection is at the origin and the view plane is at $z = d$. **a** The relationships are depicted in 3D space. **b** A multi-view projection illustrating the relationships as the $y$-axis is pointing outwards. **c** A multi-view projection illustrating the relationships as the $x$-axis is pointing outwards

where $\mathtt{P}_{per}$ is the one-point perspective projection matrix when the center of projection is at the origin and the view plane is at $z = d$; $\mathbf{P} = [x, y, z, 1]^T$ is the homogeneous representation of the point to be projected; and $\mathbf{P}' = [x, y, z, \frac{z}{d}]^T$ is the homogeneous representation of the point after projection. The inhomogeneous representation of $\mathbf{P}'$ is obtained by dividing by the fourth term of $\mathbf{P}'$. Thus,

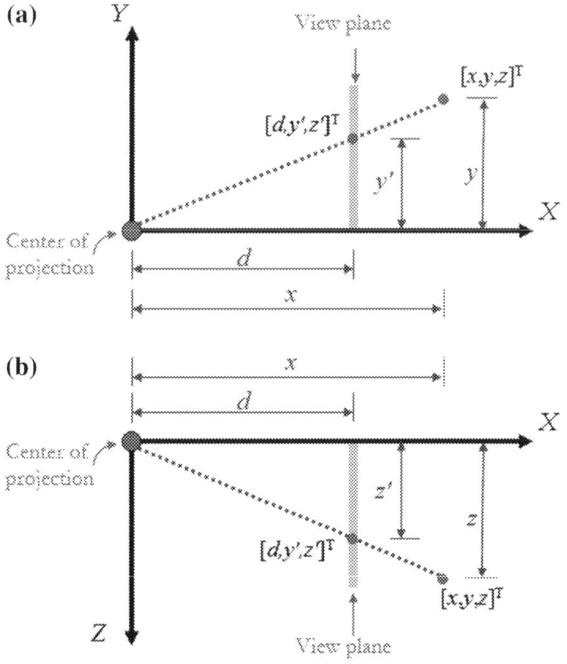


**Fig. 8.21** One-point perspective projection when the center of projection is at the origin and the view plane is at $x = d$. **a** The $z$-axis is pointing outwards. **b** The $y$-axis is pointing outwards

$$\underbrace{\begin{bmatrix} x' \\ y' \\ z' \end{bmatrix}}_{\dot{\mathbf{P}}'} = \begin{bmatrix} \frac{x}{z/d} \\ \frac{y}{z/d} \\ d \end{bmatrix}. \tag{8.58}$$

**Example 8.10:** [*One-point perspective projection—deriving the projection matrix when COP is at the origin and view plane is at $x = d$*]

If the center of projection is placed at $[0, 0, 0]^T$ and the view plane is placed at $x = d$, derive the projection matrix.

**Solution 8.10:** This situation is depicted as a multi-view projection in Fig. 8.21a where the $z$-axis is pointing outwards. Another multi-view projection is shown in Fig. 8.21b where the $y$-axis is pointing outwards. Considering similar triangles in these figures, we can write

$$\begin{aligned} \frac{y'}{d} &= \frac{y}{x}, \\ \frac{z'}{d} &= \frac{z}{x}. \end{aligned} \tag{8.59}$$

Equivalently, we can write

$$\begin{aligned} y' &= \frac{y}{x/d}, \\ z' &= \frac{z}{x/d}. \end{aligned} \tag{8.60}$$

Thus, the projection is performed in homogeneous coordinates as

$$\mathbf{P}' = \begin{bmatrix} 1 & 0 & 0 & 0 \\ 0 & 1 & 0 & 0 \\ 0 & 0 & 1 & 0 \\ \frac{1}{d} & 0 & 0 & 0 \end{bmatrix} \begin{bmatrix} x \\ y \\ z \\ 1 \end{bmatrix} = \begin{bmatrix} x \\ y \\ z \\ \frac{x}{d} \end{bmatrix}, \tag{8.61}$$

where the $\mathbf{P}' = [x, y, z, \frac{x}{d}]^T$ is the homogeneous representation of the point after projection onto the plane $x = d$. In this case, the inhomogeneous representation of $\mathbf{P}'$ is obtained as

$$\dot{\mathbf{P}}' = \begin{bmatrix} x' \\ y' \\ z' \end{bmatrix} = \begin{bmatrix} d \\ \frac{y}{x/d} \\ \frac{z}{x/d} \end{bmatrix}. \tag{8.62}$$

□

**Example 8.11:** [*One-point perspective projection—deriving the projection matrix when COP is at the origin and view plane is at $y = d$*]

Re-formulate the one-point perspective projection process when the center of projection remains at the origin while the view plane is placed at $y = d$.

**Solution 8.11:** In this case, the projection is modified to

$$\mathbf{P}' = \begin{bmatrix} 1 & 0 & 0 & 0 \\ 0 & 1 & 0 & 0 \\ 0 & 0 & 1 & 0 \\ 0 & \frac{1}{d} & 0 & 0 \end{bmatrix} \begin{bmatrix} x \\ y \\ z \\ 1 \end{bmatrix} = \begin{bmatrix} x \\ y \\ z \\ \frac{y}{d} \end{bmatrix}, \tag{8.63}$$

where the $\mathbf{P}' = [x, y, z, \frac{y}{d}]^T$ is the homogeneous representation of the point after projection onto the plane $y = d$. Thus, the inhomogeneous representation of $\mathbf{P}'$ is expressed as

$$\dot{\mathbf{P}}' = \begin{bmatrix} x' \\ y' \\ z' \end{bmatrix} = \begin{bmatrix} \frac{x}{y/d} \\ d \\ \frac{z}{y/d} \end{bmatrix}. \tag{8.64}$$

□

Consider Fig. 8.22a, which shows the view plane as placed at $z = 0$ while the center of projection as placed at $[0, 0, -d]^T$. A 3D point $\dot{\mathbf{P}} = [x, y, z]^T$ is projected onto the view plane as another point $\dot{\mathbf{P}}' = [x', y', 0]^T$. Figure 8.22b and 8.22c show the relationships among the view plane, the 3D point $\dot{\mathbf{P}} = [x, y, z]^T$ and the projected point $\dot{\mathbf{P}}' = [x', y', 0]^T$. Considering similar triangles in these figures, we can write

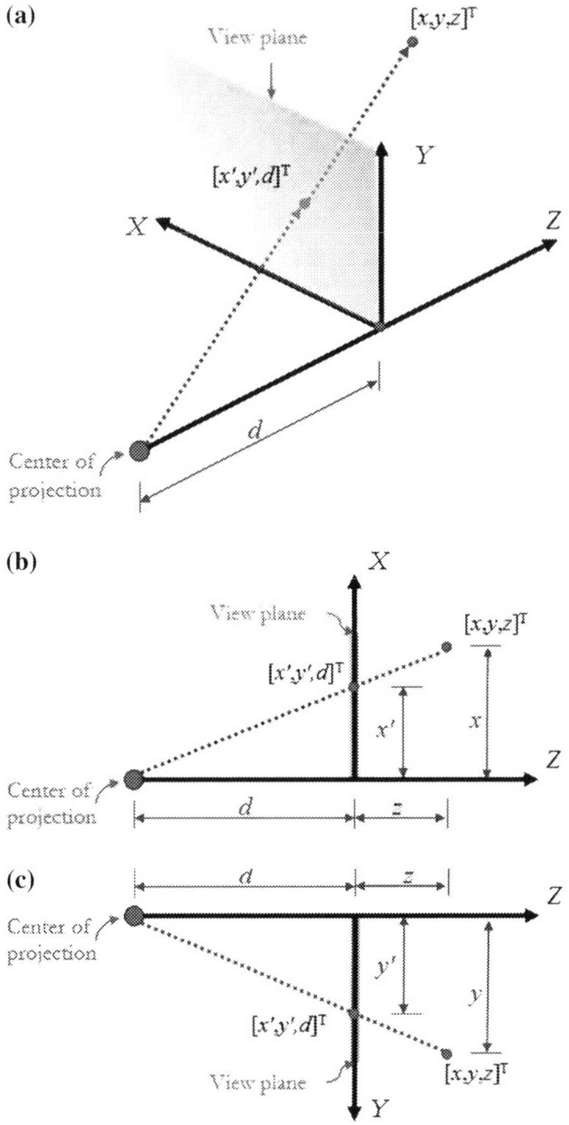


**Fig. 8.22** One-point perspective projection when the center of projection is at $[0, 0, -d]^T$ and the view plane is at $z = 0$. **a** The relationships are depicted in 3D space. **b** The $y$-axis is pointing outwards. **c** The $x$-axis is pointing outwards

$$\begin{aligned} \frac{x'}{d} &= \frac{x}{z+d}, \\ \frac{y'}{d} &= \frac{y}{z+d}. \end{aligned} \tag{8.65}$$

Equivalently, we can write

$$\begin{aligned} x' &= \frac{x}{(z/d)+1}, \\ y' &= \frac{y}{(z/d)+1}. \end{aligned} \tag{8.66}$$

Equation (8.66) can be written in homogeneous matrix form as

$$\begin{aligned} \mathbf{P}' &= \underbrace{\begin{bmatrix} 1 & 0 & 0 & 0 \\ 0 & 1 & 0 & 0 \\ 0 & 0 & 0 & 0 \\ 0 & 0 & \frac{1}{d} & 1 \end{bmatrix}}_{\mathtt{P}'_{per}} \underbrace{\begin{bmatrix} x \\ y \\ z \\ 1 \end{bmatrix}}_{\mathbf{P}} \\ &= \begin{bmatrix} x \\ y \\ 0 \\ \frac{z+d}{d} \end{bmatrix}, \end{aligned} \tag{8.67}$$

where $\mathtt{P}'_{per}$ is the one-point perspective projection matrix when the center of projection is at $[0, 0, -d]^T$ and the view plane is at $z = 0$; $\mathbf{P} = [x, y, z, 1]^T$ is the homogeneous representation of the point to be projected; and $\mathbf{P}' = [x, y, 0, \frac{z+d}{d}]^T$ is the homogeneous representation of the point after projection. The inhomogeneous representation of $\mathbf{P}'$ is obtained by dividing by the fourth term of $\mathbf{P}'$. Thus,

$$\underbrace{\begin{bmatrix} x' \\ y' \\ z' \end{bmatrix}}_{\dot{\mathbf{P}}'} = \begin{bmatrix} \frac{x}{(z/d)+1} \\ \frac{y}{(z/d)+1} \\ 0 \end{bmatrix}. \tag{8.68}$$

Notice that as $d$ tends to infinity, $\mathtt{P}'_{per}$ turns to be a front projection matrix as in Eq. (8.3).

**Example 8.12:** [*One-point perspective projection—projection matrix when COP is at* $[0, 0, -d]^T$ *and view plane is at* $z = 0$]

The projection matrix $\mathtt{P}_{per}$ of Eq. (8.57) is used when the center of projection is at the origin and the view plane has the equation $z = d$. Modify this matrix so that the center of projection moves to $[0, 0, -d]^T$ and view plane moves to $z = 0$.

**Solution 8.12:** 3D translation is applied in three steps.

1. Translate using the translation vector $[0, 0, d]^T$. This is using the matrix $\mathtt{M}_1$ where

$$\mathtt{M}_1 = \mathtt{T}([0, 0, d]^T) = \begin{bmatrix} 1 & 0 & 0 & 0 \\ 0 & 1 & 0 & 0 \\ 0 & 0 & 1 & d \\ 0 & 0 & 0 & 1 \end{bmatrix}.$$

2. Apply the projection of Eq. (8.57). This is using the matrix $\mathtt{M}_2$ where

$$\mathtt{M}_2 = \mathtt{P}_{per} = \begin{bmatrix} 1 & 0 & 0 & 0 \\ 0 & 1 & 0 & 0 \\ 0 & 0 & 1 & 0 \\ 0 & 0 & \frac{1}{d} & 0 \end{bmatrix}.$$

3. Translate back using the translation vector $[0, 0, -d]^T$. This is using the matrix $\mathtt{M}_3$ where

$$\mathtt{M}_3 = \mathtt{T}([0, 0, -d]^T) = \begin{bmatrix} 1 & 0 & 0 & 0 \\ 0 & 1 & 0 & 0 \\ 0 & 0 & 1 & -d \\ 0 & 0 & 0 & 1 \end{bmatrix}.$$

Then, the overall matrix $\mathtt{P}'_{per}$ is calculated as

$$\begin{aligned} \mathtt{P}'_{per} &= \mathtt{M}_3\mathtt{M}_2\mathtt{M}_1 \\ &= \begin{bmatrix} 1 & 0 & 0 & 0 \\ 0 & 1 & 0 & 0 \\ 0 & 0 & 1 & -d \\ 0 & 0 & 0 & 1 \end{bmatrix} \begin{bmatrix} 1 & 0 & 0 & 0 \\ 0 & 1 & 0 & 0 \\ 0 & 0 & 1 & 0 \\ 0 & 0 & \frac{1}{d} & 0 \end{bmatrix} \begin{bmatrix} 1 & 0 & 0 & 0 \\ 0 & 1 & 0 & 0 \\ 0 & 0 & 1 & d \\ 0 & 0 & 0 & 1 \end{bmatrix} \\ &= \begin{bmatrix} 1 & 0 & 0 & 0 \\ 0 & 1 & 0 & 0 \\ 0 & 0 & 0 & 0 \\ 0 & 0 & \frac{1}{d} & 1 \end{bmatrix}, \end{aligned}$$

which is the same matrix obtained in Eq. (8.67). □

**Example 8.13:** [*One-point perspective projection—points after projection when COP is at* $[0, 0, -d]^T$ *and view plane is at* $z = 0$]

Consider a unit cube with two of its corners placed at $[0, 0, 0]^T$ and $[1, 1, 1]^T$. If a one-point perspective projection is to be performed onto the $xy$-plane where the center of projection is at $[0, 0, -d]^T$ as shown in Fig. 8.23, determine the locations of the corners after projection.

**Solution 8.13:** Equation (8.67) is used to get the locations of points after the one-point perspective transformation. Let us take the point $\dot{\mathbf{P}} = [0, 0, 1]^T$ as an example:

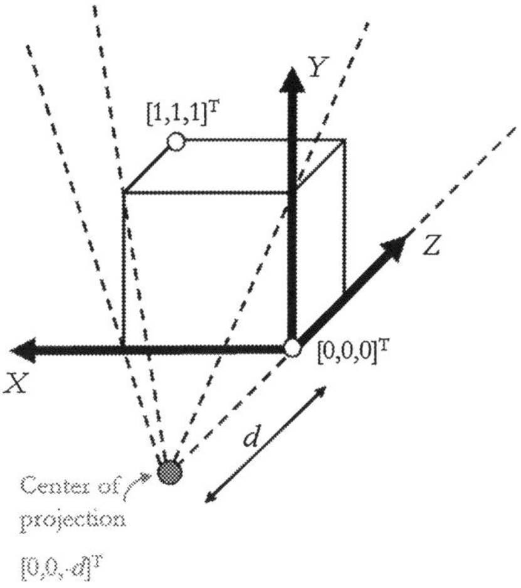


**Fig. 8.23** The center of projection is placed at $[0, 0, -d]^T$

$$
\mathbf{P}' = \underbrace{\begin{bmatrix} 1 & 0 & 0 & 0 \\ 0 & 1 & 0 & 0 \\ 0 & 0 & 0 & 0 \\ 0 & 0 & \frac{1}{d} & 1 \end{bmatrix}}_{\mathrm{P}'_{per}} \underbrace{\begin{bmatrix} x \\ y \\ z \\ 1 \end{bmatrix}}_{\mathbf{P}}
= \begin{bmatrix} 1 & 0 & 0 & 0 \\ 0 & 1 & 0 & 0 \\ 0 & 0 & 0 & 0 \\ 0 & 0 & \frac{1}{d} & 1 \end{bmatrix} \begin{bmatrix} 0 \\ 0 \\ 1 \\ 1 \end{bmatrix} = \begin{bmatrix} 0 \\ 0 \\ 0 \\ \frac{1}{d} + 1 \end{bmatrix}.
$$

Similarly, using Eq. (8.67), the locations of the projected points are given in the following table:

| $\dot{\mathbf{P}} = [x, y, z]^T$ | $\mathbf{P}' = \mathrm{P}'_{per}\mathbf{P}$ | $\dot{\mathbf{P}}' = [x', y', z']^T$ | $\dot{\mathbf{p}}' = [x', y']^T$ | $d = 1$ |
|---|---|---|---|---|
| $[0, 0, 0]^T$ | $[0, 0, 0, 1]^T$ | $[0, 0, 0]^T$ | $[0, 0]^T$ | $[0, 0]^T$ |
| $[1, 0, 0]^T$ | $[1, 0, 0, 1]^T$ | $[1, 0, 0]^T$ | $[1, 0]^T$ | $[1, 0]^T$ |
| $[0, 1, 0]^T$ | $[0, 1, 0, 1]^T$ | $[0, 1, 0]^T$ | $[0, 1]^T$ | $[0, 1]^T$ |
| $[1, 1, 0]^T$ | $[1, 1, 0, 1]^T$ | $[1, 1, 0]^T$ | $[1, 1]^T$ | $[1, 1]^T$ |
| $[0, 0, 1]^T$ | $\left[0, 0, 0, \frac{1}{d} + 1\right]^T$ | $[0, 0, 0]^T$ | $[0, 0]^T$ | $[0, 0]^T$ |
| $[1, 0, 1]^T$ | $\left[1, 0, 0, \frac{1}{d} + 1\right]^T$ | $\left[\frac{d}{d+1}, 0, 0\right]^T$ | $\left[\frac{d}{d+1}, 0\right]^T$ | $\left[\frac{1}{2}, 0\right]^T$ |
| $[0, 1, 1]^T$ | $\left[0, 1, 0, \frac{1}{d} + 1\right]^T$ | $\left[0, \frac{d}{d+1}, 0\right]^T$ | $\left[0, \frac{d}{d+1}\right]^T$ | $\left[0, \frac{1}{2}\right]^T$ |
| $[1, 1, 1]^T$ | $\left[1, 1, 0, \frac{1}{d} + 1\right]^T$ | $\left[\frac{d}{d+1}, \frac{d}{d+1}, 0\right]^T$ | $\left[\frac{d}{d+1}, \frac{d}{d+1}\right]^T$ | $\left[\frac{1}{2}, \frac{1}{2}\right]^T$ |

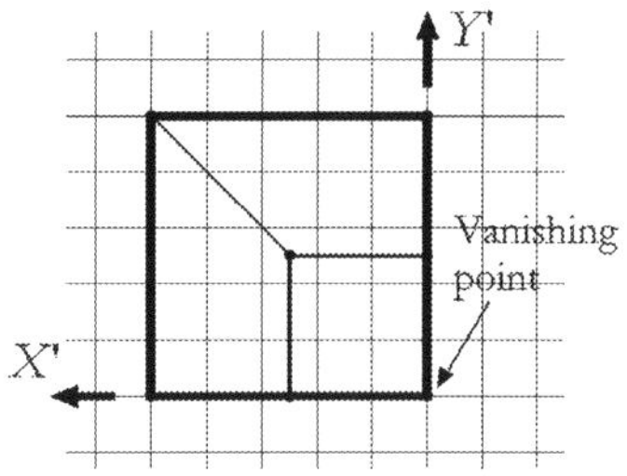


**Fig. 8.24** A one-point perspective projection for the unit cube of Fig. 8.23 drawn on a $0.2 \times 0.2$ grid where the center of projection is at $[0, 0, -1]^T$ and the normal vector to the view plane is $[0, 0, -1]^T$. The vanishing point is identified

The one-point perspective projection for the unit cube drawn on a $0.2 \times 0.2$ grid is shown in Fig. 8.24 where $d = 1$. □

**Example 8.14:** [*One-point perspective projection—vanishing point when COP is at* $[0, 0, -d]^T$ *and view plane is at* $z = 0$]

Determine the location of the vanishing point in Example 8.13 where $d = 1$.

**Solution 8.14:** A vanishing point is obtained by applying the perspective transformation to a point at infinity along the $z$-axis. A point at infinity can be expressed as $[0, 0, z, 0]^T$. (As discussed in Sect. B.7, the last term must be zero.) We use the same projection matrix obtained before:

$$\mathbf{P}' = \begin{bmatrix} 1 & 0 & 0 & 0 \\ 0 & 1 & 0 & 0 \\ 0 & 0 & 0 & 0 \\ 0 & 0 & \frac{1}{d} & 1 \end{bmatrix} \begin{bmatrix} 0 \\ 0 \\ z \\ 0 \end{bmatrix} = \begin{bmatrix} 0 \\ 0 \\ 0 \\ \frac{z}{d} \end{bmatrix}.$$

Dividing by the last term of the homogeneous point $\mathbf{P}'$, we get $\dot{\mathbf{P}}'$ as $[0, 0, 0]^T$. Hence, the vanishing point on the $xy$-plane is $\dot{\mathbf{p}}' = [0, 0]^T$. This point is identified in Fig. 8.24.

Another way to get the location of the vanishing point for the $z$-axis is by intersecting projected lines. This is discussed in Example 8.16. □

**Example 8.15:** [*One-point perspective projection—points after projection when COP is at* $\left[\frac{1}{2}, \frac{1}{2}, -d\right]^T$ *and view plane is at* $z = 0$]

Re-solve Example 8.13 if the center of projection is at $\left[\frac{1}{2}, \frac{1}{2}, -d\right]^T$ (as shown in Fig. 8.25) instead of $[0, 0, -d]^T$.

**Solution 8.15:** Transformation should be applied to the projection matrix of Eq. (8.67) before applying point transformation. The steps are as follows:

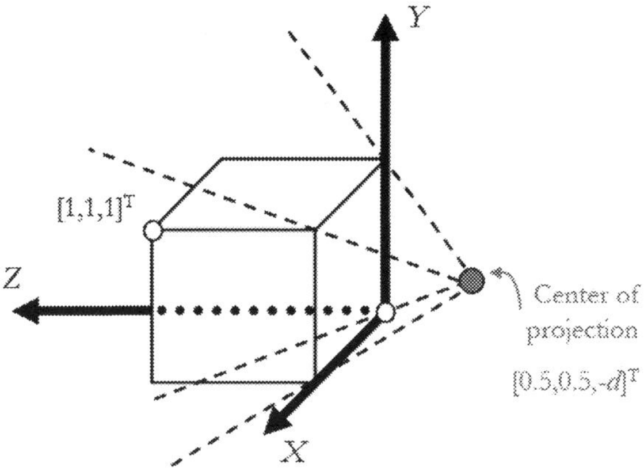


**Fig. 8.25** The center of projection is placed at $\left[\frac{1}{2}, \frac{1}{2}, -d\right]^T$

1. Translate using a translation vector $\left[-\frac{1}{2}, -\frac{1}{2}, 0\right]^T$. This is using the matrix $\mathtt{M}_1$ where
$$\mathtt{M}_1 = \mathtt{T}\left(\left[-\frac{1}{2}, -\frac{1}{2}, 0\right]^T\right) = \begin{bmatrix} 1 & 0 & 0 & -\frac{1}{2} \\ 0 & 1 & 0 & -\frac{1}{2} \\ 0 & 0 & 1 & 0 \\ 0 & 0 & 0 & 1 \end{bmatrix}.$$
Notice that this step does not affect the view plane.
2. Use the projection matrix of Eq. (8.67) to project onto the $xy$-plane from $[0, 0, -d]^T$. This is using the matrix $\mathtt{M}_2$ where
$$\mathtt{M}_2 = \mathtt{P}'_{per} = \begin{bmatrix} 1 & 0 & 0 & 0 \\ 0 & 1 & 0 & 0 \\ 0 & 0 & 0 & 0 \\ 0 & 0 & \frac{1}{d} & 1 \end{bmatrix}.$$
3. Translate using a translation vector $\left[\frac{1}{2}, \frac{1}{2}, 0\right]^T$. This is using the matrix $\mathtt{M}_3$ where
$$\mathtt{M}_3 = \mathtt{T}\left(\left[\frac{1}{2}, \frac{1}{2}, 0\right]^T\right) = \begin{bmatrix} 1 & 0 & 0 & \frac{1}{2} \\ 0 & 1 & 0 & \frac{1}{2} \\ 0 & 0 & 1 & 0 \\ 0 & 0 & 0 & 1 \end{bmatrix}.$$

Hence, the projection matrix is expressed as

$$
\begin{aligned}
M &= M_3 M_2 M_1 \\
&= \begin{bmatrix} 1 & 0 & 0 & \frac{1}{2} \\ 0 & 1 & 0 & \frac{1}{2} \\ 0 & 0 & 1 & 0 \\ 0 & 0 & 0 & 1 \end{bmatrix}
\begin{bmatrix} 1 & 0 & 0 & 0 \\ 0 & 1 & 0 & 0 \\ 0 & 0 & 0 & 0 \\ 0 & 0 & \frac{1}{d} & 1 \end{bmatrix}
\begin{bmatrix} 1 & 0 & 0 & -\frac{1}{2} \\ 0 & 1 & 0 & -\frac{1}{2} \\ 0 & 0 & 1 & 0 \\ 0 & 0 & 0 & 1 \end{bmatrix} \\
&= \begin{bmatrix} 1 & 0 & \frac{1}{2d} & 0 \\ 0 & 1 & \frac{1}{2d} & 0 \\ 0 & 0 & 0 & 0 \\ 0 & 0 & \frac{1}{d} & 1 \end{bmatrix}.
\end{aligned}
$$

Utilizing this matrix, the locations of the projected points are given in the following table:

| $\dot{\mathbf{P}} = [x, y, z]^T$ | $\mathbf{P}' = \mathtt{M}\mathbf{P}$ | $\dot{\mathbf{P}}' = [x', y', z']^T$ | $\dot{\mathbf{p}}' = [x', y']^T$ | $d = 1$ |
|---|---|---|---|---|
| $[0, 0, 0]^T$ | $[0, 0, 0, 1]^T$ | $[0, 0, 0]^T$ | $[0, 0]^T$ | $[0, 0]^T$ |
| $[1, 0, 0]^T$ | $[1, 0, 0, 1]^T$ | $[1, 0, 0]^T$ | $[1, 0]^T$ | $[1, 0]^T$ |
| $[0, 1, 0]^T$ | $[0, 1, 0, 1]^T$ | $[0, 1, 0]^T$ | $[0, 1]^T$ | $[0, 1]^T$ |
| $[1, 1, 0]^T$ | $[1, 1, 0, 1]^T$ | $[1, 1, 0]^T$ | $[1, 1]^T$ | $[1, 1]^T$ |
| $[0, 0, 1]^T$ | $\left[\frac{1}{2d}, \frac{1}{2d}, 0, \frac{1}{d} + 1\right]^T$ | $\left[\frac{1}{2(d+1)}, \frac{1}{2(d+1)}, 0\right]^T$ | $\left[\frac{1}{2(d+1)}, \frac{1}{2(d+1)}\right]^T$ | $\left[\frac{1}{4}, \frac{1}{4}\right]^T$ |
| $[1, 0, 1]^T$ | $\left[\frac{1}{2d} + 1, \frac{1}{2d}, 0, \frac{1}{d} + 1\right]^T$ | $\left[\frac{2d+1}{2(d+1)}, \frac{1}{2(d+1)}, 0\right]^T$ | $\left[\frac{2d+1}{2(d+1)}, \frac{1}{2(d+1)}\right]^T$ | $\left[\frac{3}{4}, \frac{1}{4}\right]^T$ |
| $[0, 1, 1]^T$ | $\left[\frac{1}{2d}, \frac{1}{2d} + 1, 0, \frac{1}{d} + 1\right]^T$ | $\left[\frac{1}{2(d+1)}, \frac{2d+1}{2(d+1)}, 0\right]^T$ | $\left[\frac{1}{2(d+1)}, \frac{2d+1}{2(d+1)}\right]^T$ | $\left[\frac{1}{4}, \frac{3}{4}\right]^T$ |
| $[1, 1, 1]^T$ | $\left[\frac{1}{2d} + 1, \frac{1}{2d} + 1, 0, \frac{1}{d} + 1\right]^T$ | $\left[\frac{2d+1}{2(d+1)}, \frac{2d+1}{2(d+1)}, 0\right]^T$ | $\left[\frac{2d+1}{2(d+1)}, \frac{2d+1}{2(d+1)}\right]^T$ | $\left[\frac{3}{4}, \frac{3}{4}\right]^T$ |

The one-point perspective projection for the unit cube drawn on a $0.2 \times 0.2$ grid is shown in Fig. 8.26 where $d = 1$. Compare it to the result shown in Fig. 8.24. □

**Example 8.16:** [*One-point perspective projection—vanishing point when COP is at* $\left[\frac{1}{2}, \frac{1}{2}, -d\right]^T$ *and view plane is at* $z = 0$]

Determine the location of the vanishing point in Example 8.15 where $d = 1$.

**Solution 8.16:** As done with Example 8.14, a vanishing point is obtained by applying the perspective transformation to a point at infinity along the $z$-axis (e.g., $[0, 0, z, 0]^T$). We use the same projection matrix obtained in Example 8.15:

$$
\mathbf{P}' = \begin{bmatrix} 1 & 0 & \frac{1}{2d} & 0 \\ 0 & 1 & \frac{1}{2d} & 0 \\ 0 & 0 & 0 & 0 \\ 0 & 0 & \frac{1}{d} & 1 \end{bmatrix}
\begin{bmatrix} 0 \\ 0 \\ z \\ 0 \end{bmatrix}
= \begin{bmatrix} \frac{z}{2d} \\ \frac{z}{2d} \\ 0 \\ \frac{z}{d} \end{bmatrix}.
$$

Dividing by the last term of the homogeneous point $\mathbf{P}'$, we get $\dot{\mathbf{P}}'$ as $\left[\frac{1}{2}, \frac{1}{2}, 0\right]^T$. Hence, the vanishing point on the $xy$-plane is $\dot{\mathbf{p}}' = \left[\frac{1}{2}, \frac{1}{2}\right]^T$. This point is identified in Fig. 8.26.

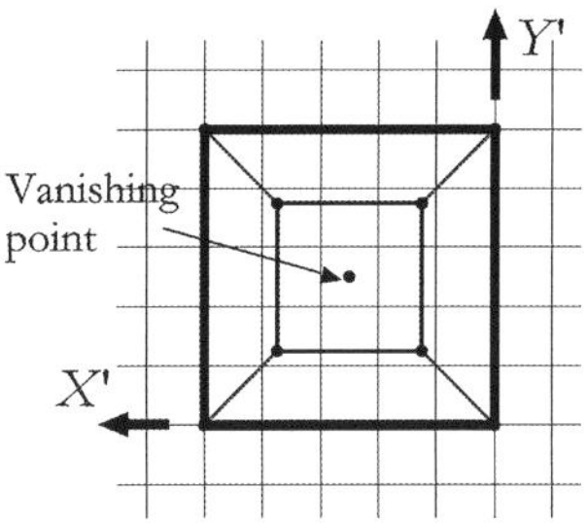


**Fig. 8.26** A one-point perspective projection for the unit cube of Fig. 8.25 drawn on a $0.2 \times 0.2$ grid where the center of projection is at $\left[\frac{1}{2}, \frac{1}{2}, -1\right]^T$ and the normal vector to the view plane is $[0, 0, -1]^T$. The vanishing point is identified

Another way to get the location of the vanishing point for the $z$-axis is by getting the intersection point between two projected lines that are parallel to the $z$-axis in reality. Let us consider the line passing through $[0, 0]^T$ and $[\frac{1}{4}, \frac{1}{4}]^T$ and the line passing through $[1, 0]^T$ and $[\frac{3}{4}, \frac{1}{4}]^T$; however, other lines may be as good as these two lines. The first linear equation is obtained as

$$\begin{aligned} y - y_1 &= \tfrac{y_2 - y_1}{x_2 - x_1}(x - x_1) \\ y - 0 &= \tfrac{\frac{1}{4} - 0}{\frac{1}{4} - 0}(x - 0) \\ y &= x. \end{aligned}$$

The same linear equation can be obtained using the cross product (see Sect. A.4.3.3) of the homogeneous 2D endpoints. This cross product represents the coefficients of the linear equation; that is,

$$\begin{bmatrix} 0 \\ 0 \\ 1 \end{bmatrix} \times \begin{bmatrix} \frac{1}{4} \\ \frac{1}{4} \\ 1 \end{bmatrix} = \begin{bmatrix} -\frac{1}{4} \\ \frac{1}{4} \\ 0 \end{bmatrix}.$$

Hence, the coefficients of the linear equation $ax + by + c = 0$ are $a = -\frac{1}{4}$, $b = \frac{1}{4}$ and $c = 0$. This is the same linear equation obtained before; i.e., $y = x$. Similarly, the other linear equation is obtained as $x + y = 1$.

Again, many methods may be used to get the intersection point between two 2D lines. For example, two linear equations may be solved simultaneously to get the intersection point. Substituting the value of $x$ from the first equation in the second, we get $y + y = 1$. Hence, $y = \frac{1}{2}$; consequently, $x = \frac{1}{2}$ (i.e., the intersection point $\dot{\mathbf{p}}'$ is obtained as $\left[\frac{1}{2}, \frac{1}{2}\right]^T$).

Alternatively, the cross product of the linear equation coefficients may be used to get the intersection point between lines. The two vectors representing the linear equations are $[1, -1, 0]^T$ and $[1, 1, -1]^T$. Hence, the homogeneous point $\mathbf{p}'$ representing the intersection is obtained as

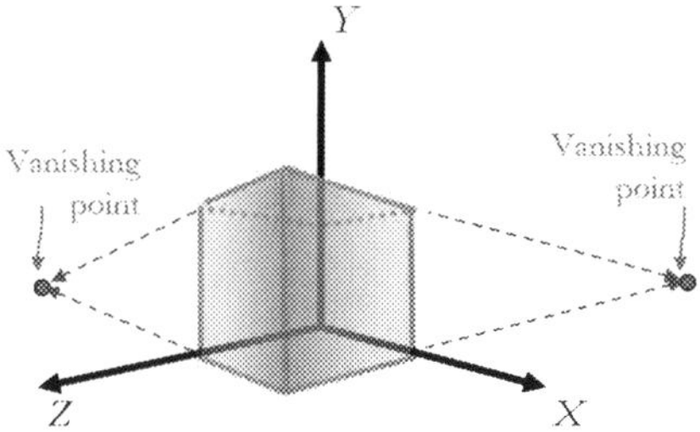


**Fig. 8.27** Two-point perspective projection: The view plane is parallel to one of the principal axes

$$\mathbf{p}' = \begin{bmatrix} 1 \\ -1 \\ 0 \end{bmatrix} \times \begin{bmatrix} 1 \\ 1 \\ -1 \end{bmatrix} = \begin{bmatrix} 1 \\ 1 \\ 2 \end{bmatrix}.$$

Thus, the inhomogeneous representation of the intersection point $\dot{\mathbf{p}}'$ is obtained as $\left[\frac{1}{2}, \frac{1}{2}\right]^T$, which is the same point obtained before. □

## 8.4.2 Two-point Perspective Projection

The two-point perspective projection exists when the view plane is parallel to one of the principal axes; i.e., when the view plane intersects two of the principal axes. In Fig. 8.27, this situation happens as the view plane is parallel to the $y$-axis and intersecting the $x$- and $z$-axes. In this case, the normal to the view plane is perpendicular to the $y$-axis.

Moreover, lines parallel to the $y$-axis (in Fig. 8.27) remain parallel to this axis. On the other hand, lines parallel to the other two axes intersecting the view plane converge to two different vanishing points. In case of two-point perspective projection, one component of the normal vector to the view plane is zero.

Assuming that the center of projection is at the origin and the normal to the view plane makes an angle $\theta$ with the $yz$-plane, the overall two-point perspective projection process can be achieved in three steps.

1. Rotate through an angle $-\theta$ about the $y$-axis so that the normal to the view plane coincides with the $z$-axis. This is using the matrix $\mathtt{M}_1$ where

$$\mathtt{M}_1 = \mathtt{R}_y(-\theta) = \begin{bmatrix} \cos(-\theta) & 0 & \sin(-\theta) & 0 \\ 0 & 1 & 0 & 0 \\ -\sin(-\theta) & 0 & \cos(-\theta) & 0 \\ 0 & 0 & 0 & 1 \end{bmatrix} = \begin{bmatrix} \cos(\theta) & 0 & -\sin(\theta) & 0 \\ 0 & 1 & 0 & 0 \\ \sin(\theta) & 0 & \cos(\theta) & 0 \\ 0 & 0 & 0 & 1 \end{bmatrix}.$$

2. Perform a one-point perspective projection using Eq. (8.57). This is using the matrix $\mathtt{M}_2$ where

$$\mathtt{M}_2 = \mathtt{P}_{per} = \begin{bmatrix} 1 & 0 & 0 & 0 \\ 0 & 1 & 0 & 0 \\ 0 & 0 & 1 & 0 \\ 0 & 0 & \frac{1}{d} & 0 \end{bmatrix}.$$

3. Rotate back through an angle $\theta$ about the $y$-axis. This is using the matrix $\mathtt{M}_3$ where

$$\mathtt{M}_3 = \mathtt{R}_y(\theta) = \begin{bmatrix} \cos(\theta) & 0 & \sin(\theta) & 0 \\ 0 & 1 & 0 & 0 \\ -\sin(\theta) & 0 & \cos(\theta) & 0 \\ 0 & 0 & 0 & 1 \end{bmatrix}.$$

Thus, the overall projection is estimated as

$$\begin{aligned} \mathtt{P}_{per2} &= \mathtt{M}_3\mathtt{M}_2\mathtt{M}_1 \\ &= \begin{bmatrix} \cos(\theta) & 0 & \sin(\theta) & 0 \\ 0 & 1 & 0 & 0 \\ -\sin(\theta) & 0 & \cos(\theta) & 0 \\ 0 & 0 & 0 & 1 \end{bmatrix} \begin{bmatrix} 1 & 0 & 0 & 0 \\ 0 & 1 & 0 & 0 \\ 0 & 0 & 1 & 0 \\ 0 & 0 & \frac{1}{d} & 0 \end{bmatrix} \begin{bmatrix} \cos(\theta) & 0 & -\sin(\theta) & 0 \\ 0 & 1 & 0 & 0 \\ \sin(\theta) & 0 & \cos(\theta) & 0 \\ 0 & 0 & 0 & 1 \end{bmatrix} \\ &= \begin{bmatrix} 1 & 0 & 0 & 0 \\ 0 & 1 & 0 & 0 \\ 0 & 0 & 1 & 0 \\ \frac{\sin(\theta)}{d} & 0 & \frac{\cos(\theta)}{d} & 0 \end{bmatrix}, \end{aligned} \tag{8.69}$$

where $\mathtt{P}_{per2}$ is the two-point perspective projection matrix when the center of projection is at the origin; $d$ is the perpendicular distance from the origin to the view plane that is parallel to the $y$-axis and whose normal vector makes an angle $\theta$ with the $yz$-plane.

**Example 8.17:** [*Two-point perspective projection—points after projection when COP is at the origin and view plane is parallel to the y-axis*]

A unit cube is placed in the world coordinate system such that two corners reside at $\left[2, -\frac{1}{2}, 2\right]^T$ and $\left[3, \frac{1}{2}, 3\right]^T$. A two-point perspective projection is to be generated for that cube where the center of projection is placed at the origin. As shown in Fig. 8.28a, the view plane is 1 unit away from the origin and its normal vector, which is perpendicular to the $y$-axis, makes an angle of 30° with the $z$-axis. Get the locations of the corners after performing a two-point perspective transformation and show the results on the $xy$-plane.

**Solution 8.17:** As the view plane is 1 unit away from the origin, $d = 1$. The projection matrix is estimated using Eq. (8.69) as

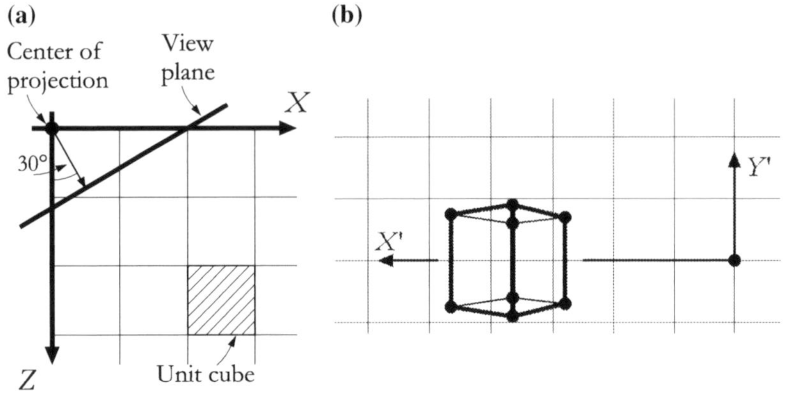


**Fig. 8.28** A two-point perspective projection for a unit cube placed such that two corners reside at $[2, -0.5, 2]^T$ and $[3, 0.5, 3]^T$ where the center of projection is at $[0, 0, 0]^T$ and the normal vector to the view plane is $[\sin(30), 0, \cos(30)]^T$. **a** The top view for the cube drawn on a $1 \times 1$ grid. **b** A two-point perspective projection drawn on a $0.2 \times 0.2$ grid

$$\mathrm{P}_{per2} = \begin{bmatrix} 1 & 0 & 0 & 0 \\ 0 & 1 & 0 & 0 \\ 0 & 0 & 1 & 0 \\ \frac{\sin(\theta)}{d} & 0 & \frac{\cos(\theta)}{d} & 0 \end{bmatrix} = \begin{bmatrix} 1 & 0 & 0 & 0 \\ 0 & 1 & 0 & 0 \\ 0 & 0 & 1 & 0 \\ \sin(30) & 0 & \cos(30) & 0 \end{bmatrix} = \begin{bmatrix} 1 & 0 & 0 & 0 \\ 0 & 1 & 0 & 0 \\ 0 & 0 & 1 & 0 \\ \frac{1}{2} & 0 & \frac{\sqrt{3}}{2} & 0 \end{bmatrix}.$$

Let us take the point $\dot{\mathbf{P}} = \left[2, \frac{1}{2}, 3\right]^T$ as an example:

$$\mathbf{P}' = \underbrace{\begin{bmatrix} 1 & 0 & 0 & 0 \\ 0 & 1 & 0 & 0 \\ 0 & 0 & 1 & 0 \\ \frac{1}{2} & 0 & \frac{\sqrt{3}}{2} & 0 \end{bmatrix}}_{\mathrm{P}_{per2}} \underbrace{\begin{bmatrix} x \\ y \\ z \\ 1 \end{bmatrix}}_{\mathbf{P}} = \begin{bmatrix} 1 & 0 & 0 & 0 \\ 0 & 1 & 0 & 0 \\ 0 & 0 & 1 & 0 \\ \frac{1}{2} & 0 & \frac{\sqrt{3}}{2} & 0 \end{bmatrix} \begin{bmatrix} 2 \\ \frac{1}{2} \\ 3 \\ 1 \end{bmatrix} = \begin{bmatrix} 2 \\ \frac{1}{2} \\ 3 \\ 1 + \frac{3\sqrt{3}}{2} \end{bmatrix} = \begin{bmatrix} 2 \\ 0.5 \\ 3 \\ 3.5981 \end{bmatrix}.$$

Similarly, the locations of the rest of projected points are given in the following table:

| $\dot{\mathbf{P}} = [x, y, z]^T$ | $\mathbf{P}' = \mathtt{P}_{per2}\mathbf{P}$ | $\dot{\mathbf{P}}' = [x', y', z']^T$ |
|---|---|---|
| $[2, -0.5, 2]^T$ | $[2.0, -0.5, 2.0, 2.7321]^T$ | $[0.7321, -0.1830, 0.7321]^T$ |
| $[2, 0.5, 2]^T$ | $[2.0, 0.5, 2.0, 2.7321]^T$ | $[0.7321, 0.1830, 0.7321]^T$ |
| $[2, -0.5, 3]^T$ | $[2.0, -0.5, 3.0, 3.5981]^T$ | $[0.5559, -0.1390, 0.8338]^T$ |
| $[2, 0.5, 3]^T$ | $[2.0, 0.5, 3.0, 3.5981]^T$ | $[0.5559, 0.1390, 0.8338]^T$ |
| $[3, -0.5, 2]^T$ | $[3.0, -0.5, 2.0, 3.2321]^T$ | $[0.9282, -0.1547, 0.6188]^T$ |
| $[3, 0.5, 2]^T$ | $[3.0, 0.5, 2.0, 3.2321]^T$ | $[0.9282, 0.1547, 0.6188]^T$ |
| $[3, -0.5, 3]^T$ | $[3.0, -0.5, 3.0, 4.0981]^T$ | $[0.7321, -0.1220, 0.7321]^T$ |
| $[3, 0.5, 3]^T$ | $[3.0, 0.5, 3.0, 4.0981]^T$ | $[0.7321, 0.1220, 0.7321]^T$ |

The two-point perspective projection for the unit cube drawn on a $0.2 \times 0.2$ grid is shown in Fig. 8.28b. □

**Example 8.18:** [*Two-point perspective projection—deriving projection matrix when COP is at an arbitrary point and view plane is parallel to the y-axis*]

If the center of projection is placed at an arbitrary point $[x, y, z]^T$, the normal to the view plane, which is perpendicular to the $y$-axis, makes an angle $\theta$ with the $z$-axis and the distance from the origin to the view plane is $d$, derive the two-point projection matrix in this case.

**Solution 8.18:** The matrix is obtained in three steps.

1. Translate the center of projection using the translation vector $[-x, -y, -z]^T$ so it coincides with the origin. Let us apply the matrix $\mathtt{M}_1$ where

$$\mathtt{M}_1 = \mathtt{T}([-x, -y, -z]^T) = \begin{bmatrix} 1 & 0 & 0 & -x \\ 0 & 1 & 0 & -y \\ 0 & 0 & 1 & -z \\ 0 & 0 & 0 & 1 \end{bmatrix}.$$

At this point, make sure that the view plane does not flip to another octant and the perpendicular distance $d$ remains unchanged. See Example 8.20.

2. Perform a two-point perspective projection using Eq. (8.69). Let us apply the matrix $\mathtt{M}_2$ where

$$\mathtt{M}_2 = \mathtt{P}_{per2} = \begin{bmatrix} 1 & 0 & 0 & 0 \\ 0 & 1 & 0 & 0 \\ 0 & 0 & 1 & 0 \\ \frac{\sin(\theta)}{d} & 0 & \frac{\cos(\theta)}{d} & 0 \end{bmatrix}.$$

3. Translate back using the translation vector $[x, y, z]^T$. Let us apply the matrix $\mathtt{M}_3$ where

$$\mathtt{M}_3 = \mathtt{T}([x, y, z]^T) = \begin{bmatrix} 1 & 0 & 0 & x \\ 0 & 1 & 0 & y \\ 0 & 0 & 1 & z \\ 0 & 0 & 0 & 1 \end{bmatrix}.$$

Thus, the overall projection is estimated as

$$\begin{aligned}
\mathtt{P}_{per2} &= \mathtt{M}_3\mathtt{M}_2\mathtt{M}_1 \\
&= \begin{bmatrix} 1 & 0 & 0 & x \\ 0 & 1 & 0 & y \\ 0 & 0 & 1 & z \\ 0 & 0 & 0 & 1 \end{bmatrix} \begin{bmatrix} 1 & 0 & 0 & 0 \\ 0 & 1 & 0 & 0 \\ 0 & 0 & 1 & 0 \\ \frac{\sin(\theta)}{d} & 0 & \frac{\cos(\theta)}{d} & 0 \end{bmatrix} \begin{bmatrix} 1 & 0 & 0 & -x \\ 0 & 1 & 0 & -y \\ 0 & 0 & 1 & -z \\ 0 & 0 & 0 & 1 \end{bmatrix} \\
&= \begin{bmatrix} 1+\frac{x\sin(\theta)}{d} & 0 & \frac{x\cos(\theta)}{d} & \frac{-x^2\sin(\theta)-zx\cos(\theta)}{d} - x \\ \frac{y\sin(\theta)}{d} & 1 & \frac{y\cos(\theta)}{d} & \frac{-xy\sin(\theta)-zy\cos(\theta)}{d} - y \\ \frac{z\sin(\theta)}{d} & 0 & 1+\frac{z\cos(\theta)}{d} & \frac{-xz\sin(\theta)-z^2\cos(\theta)}{d} - z \\ \frac{\sin(\theta)}{d} & 0 & \frac{\cos(\theta)}{d} & \frac{-x\sin(\theta)-z\cos(\theta)}{d} \end{bmatrix}.
\end{aligned} \tag{8.70}$$

□

**Example 8.19:** [*Two-point perspective projection—deriving projection matrix onto the $xy$-plane when COP is at an arbitrary point and view plane is parallel to the $y$-axis*]

Modify the general two-point perspective projection matrix of Eq. (8.70) so that all points are projected onto the $xy$-plane.

**Solution 8.19:** We apply the front projection matrix to the matrix of Eq. (8.70) to get

$$\begin{aligned}
\mathtt{P}'_{per2} &= \begin{bmatrix} 1 & 0 & 0 & 0 \\ 0 & 1 & 0 & 0 \\ 0 & 0 & 0 & 0 \\ 0 & 0 & 0 & 1 \end{bmatrix} \begin{bmatrix} 1+\frac{x\sin(\theta)}{d} & 0 & \frac{x\cos(\theta)}{d} & \frac{-x^2\sin(\theta)-zx\cos(\theta)}{d} - x \\ \frac{y\sin(\theta)}{d} & 1 & \frac{y\cos(\theta)}{d} & \frac{-xy\sin(\theta)-zy\cos(\theta)}{d} - y \\ \frac{z\sin(\theta)}{d} & 0 & 1+\frac{z\cos(\theta)}{d} & \frac{-xz\sin(\theta)-z^2\cos(\theta)}{d} - z \\ \frac{\sin(\theta)}{d} & 0 & \frac{\cos(\theta)}{d} & \frac{-x\sin(\theta)-z\cos(\theta)}{d} \end{bmatrix} \\
&= \begin{bmatrix} 1+\frac{x\sin(\theta)}{d} & 0 & \frac{x\cos(\theta)}{d} & \frac{-x^2\sin(\theta)-zx\cos(\theta)}{d} - x \\ \frac{y\sin(\theta)}{d} & 1 & \frac{y\cos(\theta)}{d} & \frac{-xy\sin(\theta)-zy\cos(\theta)}{d} - y \\ 0 & 0 & 0 & 0 \\ \frac{\sin(\theta)}{d} & 0 & \frac{\cos(\theta)}{d} & \frac{-x\sin(\theta)-z\cos(\theta)}{d} \end{bmatrix}.
\end{aligned} \tag{8.71}$$

□

**Example 8.20:** [*Two-point perspective projection—points after projection onto the $xy$-plane when COP is at an arbitrary point and view plane is parallel to the $y$-axis*]

Consider a unit cube with two of its corners placed at $[0, 0, 0]^T$ and $[1, 1, 1]^T$. If a camera is used to view the cube such that the view plane is parallel to the $y$-axis

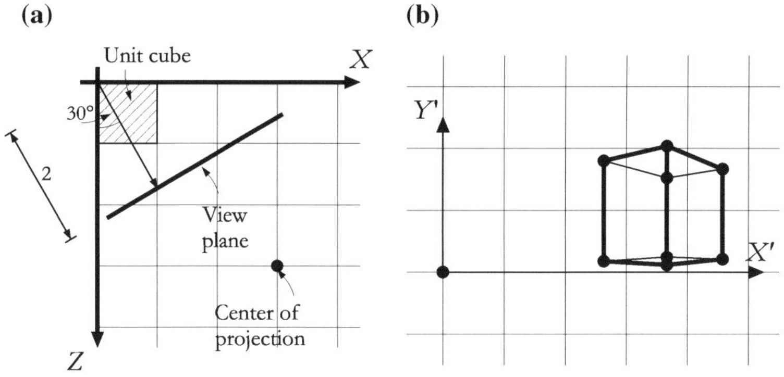


**Fig. 8.29** A two-point perspective projection for a unit cube placed such that two corners reside at $[0, 0, 0]^T$ and $[1, 1, 1]^T$ where the center of projection is at $[3, 0.2, 3]^T$ and the normal vector to the view plane is $[\sin(30), 0, \cos(30)]^T$. **a** The top view for the cube drawn on a $1 \times 1$ grid. **b** A two-point perspective projection drawn on a $0.4 \times 0.4$ grid

with a normal vector inclined at an angle of 30° with respect to the $yz$-plane and the center of projection is placed at $[3, 0.2, 3]^T$ as shown in Fig. 8.29a, determine the locations of the corners after performing a two-point perspective projection onto the $xy$-plane when $d = 2$.

**Solution 8.20:** The main idea in such a situation is use the projection matrix of Eq. (8.71); however, this matrix is obtained through a translation-projection-translation-projection sequence of operations. After the first translation that gets the COP at the origin, the view plane moves to another octant and the perpendicular distance from the origin to the view plane changes. Thus, assuming that the COP is initially at $[x, y, z]^T$, the operations done are as follows:

1. Translate the COP using the translation vector $[-x, -y, -z]^T$ so it coincides with the origin. Let us apply the matrix $\mathtt{M}_1$ where

$$\mathtt{M}_1 = \mathtt{T}([-x, -y, -z]^T) = \begin{bmatrix} 1 & 0 & 0 & -x \\ 0 & 1 & 0 & -y \\ 0 & 0 & 1 & -z \\ 0 & 0 & 0 & 1 \end{bmatrix}.$$

At this point, the perpendicular distance $d$ changes to $d'$.

2. Perform a two-point perspective projection using Eq. (8.69). Let us apply the matrix $\mathtt{M}_2$ where

$$\mathtt{M}_2 = \mathtt{P}_{per2} = \begin{bmatrix} 1 & 0 & 0 & 0 \\ 0 & 1 & 0 & 0 \\ 0 & 0 & 1 & 0 \\ \frac{\sin(\theta)}{d'} & 0 & \frac{\cos(\theta)}{d'} & 0 \end{bmatrix}.$$

3. Translate back using the translation vector $[x, y, z]^T$. Let us apply the matrix $\mathtt{M}_3$ where

$$\mathtt{M}_3 = \mathtt{T}([x, y, z]^T) = \begin{bmatrix} 1 & 0 & 0 & x \\ 0 & 1 & 0 & y \\ 0 & 0 & 1 & z \\ 0 & 0 & 0 & 1 \end{bmatrix}.$$

4. Apply the front projection matrix of Eq. (8.3). Let us call it $\mathtt{M}_4$ where

$$\mathtt{M}_4 = \begin{bmatrix} 1 & 0 & 0 & 0 \\ 0 & 1 & 0 & 0 \\ 0 & 0 & 0 & 0 \\ 0 & 0 & 0 & 1 \end{bmatrix}.$$

Thus, the overall projection is estimated as

$$\begin{aligned} \mathtt{P}'_{per2} &= \mathtt{M}_4\mathtt{M}_3\mathtt{M}_2\mathtt{M}_1 \\ &= \begin{bmatrix} 1 & 0 & 0 & 0 \\ 0 & 1 & 0 & 0 \\ 0 & 0 & 0 & 0 \\ 0 & 0 & 0 & 1 \end{bmatrix} \begin{bmatrix} 1 & 0 & 0 & x \\ 0 & 1 & 0 & y \\ 0 & 0 & 1 & z \\ 0 & 0 & 0 & 1 \end{bmatrix} \begin{bmatrix} 1 & 0 & 0 & 0 \\ 0 & 1 & 0 & 0 \\ 0 & 0 & 1 & 0 \\ \frac{\sin(\theta)}{d'} & 0 & \frac{\cos(\theta)}{d'} & 0 \end{bmatrix} \begin{bmatrix} 1 & 0 & 0 & -x \\ 0 & 1 & 0 & -y \\ 0 & 0 & 1 & -z \\ 0 & 0 & 0 & 1 \end{bmatrix} \\ &= \begin{bmatrix} 1 + \frac{x\sin(\theta)}{d'} & 0 & \frac{x\cos(\theta)}{d'} & \frac{-x^2\sin(\theta) - zx\cos(\theta)}{d'} - x \\ \frac{y\sin(\theta)}{d'} & 1 & \frac{y\cos(\theta)}{d'} & \frac{-xy\sin(\theta) - zy\cos(\theta)}{d'} - y \\ 0 & 0 & 0 & 0 \\ \frac{\sin(\theta)}{d'} & 0 & \frac{\cos(\theta)}{d'} & \frac{-x\sin(\theta) - z\cos(\theta)}{d'} \end{bmatrix}. \end{aligned} \tag{8.72}$$

**Perpendicular distance from COP to view plane:** The distance $d'$ can be estimated as

$$d' = d - |\mathrm{proj}_{\dot{\mathbf{R}}}\mathbf{n}|,$$

where $\dot{\mathbf{R}} = [3, 0.2, 3]^T$ is the location of the COP; $\mathbf{n} = [\sin(30), 0, \cos(30)]^T$ is the normal to the view plane; and $d$ is the perpendicular distance from the origin to the view plane when $\mathbf{n}$ is normalized. Utilizing Eq. (A.23), $d'$ can be re-written as

$$d' = d - \frac{\dot{\mathbf{R}} \cdot \mathbf{n}}{\|\mathbf{n}\|}.$$

Thus,

$$d' = 2 - \frac{\begin{bmatrix} 3 \\ 0.2 \\ 3 \end{bmatrix} \cdot \begin{bmatrix} \sin(30) \\ 0 \\ \cos(30) \end{bmatrix}}{\left\| \begin{bmatrix} \sin(30) \\ 0 \\ \cos(30) \end{bmatrix} \right\|} = -2.0981.$$

Now, using Eq. (8.72), $\mathtt{P}'_{per2}$ is estimated as

$$\mathtt{P}'_{per2} = \begin{bmatrix} 1 + \frac{3\sin(30)}{-2.0981} & 0 & \frac{3\cos(30)}{-2.0981} & \frac{-3^2\sin(30) - 3\times 3\cos(30)}{-2.0981} - 3 \\ \frac{0.2\sin(30)}{-2.0981} & 1 & \frac{y\cos(30)}{-2.0981} & \frac{-3\times 0.2\sin(30) - 3\times 0.2\cos(30)}{-2.0981} - 3 \\ 0 & 0 & 0 & 0 \\ \frac{\sin(30)}{-2.0981} & 0 & \frac{\cos(30)}{-2.0981} & \frac{-3\sin(30) - 3\cos(30)}{-2.0981} \end{bmatrix}$$

$$= \begin{bmatrix} 0.2851 & 0 & -1.2383 & 2.8598 \\ -0.0477 & 1 & -0.0826 & 0.1907 \\ 0 & 0 & 0 & 0 \\ -0.2383 & 0 & -0.4128 & 1.9533 \end{bmatrix}.$$

Let us take the point $\dot{\mathbf{P}} = [1, 1, 1]^T$ as an example:

$$\mathbf{P}' = \underbrace{\begin{bmatrix} 0.2851 & 0 & -1.2383 & 2.8598 \\ -0.0477 & 1 & -0.0826 & 0.1907 \\ 0 & 0 & 0 & 0 \\ -0.2383 & 0 & -0.4128 & 1.9533 \end{bmatrix}}_{\mathtt{P}'_{per2}} \underbrace{\begin{bmatrix} x \\ y \\ z \\ 1 \end{bmatrix}}_{\mathbf{P}}$$

$$= \begin{bmatrix} 0.2851 & 0 & -1.2383 & 2.8598 \\ -0.0477 & 1 & -0.0826 & 0.1907 \\ 0 & 0 & 0 & 0 \\ -0.2383 & 0 & -0.4128 & 1.9533 \end{bmatrix} \begin{bmatrix} 1 \\ 1 \\ 1 \\ 1 \end{bmatrix} = \begin{bmatrix} 1.9065 \\ 1.0604 \\ 0 \\ 1.3022 \end{bmatrix}.$$

Similarly, the locations of the rest of projected points onto the $xy$-plane are obtained using the previous matrix. They are listed in the following table:

| $\dot{\mathbf{P}} = [x, y, z]^T$ | $\mathbf{P}' = \mathtt{P}'_{per2}\mathbf{P}$ | $\dot{\mathbf{P}}' = [x', y', z']^T$ | $\dot{\mathbf{p}}' = [x', y']^T$ |
|---|---|---|---|
| $[0, 0, 0]^T$ | $[2.8598, 0.1907, 0, 1.9533]^T$ | $[1.4641, 0.0976, 0]^T$ | $[1.4641, 0.0976]^T$ |
| $[1, 0, 0]^T$ | $[3.1448, 0.1430, 0, 1.7149]^T$ | $[1.8338, 0.0834, 0]^T$ | $[1.8338, 0.0834]^T$ |
| $[0, 1, 0]^T$ | $[2.8598, 1.1907, 0, 1.9533]^T$ | $[1.4641, 0.6096, 0]^T$ | $[1.4641, 0.6096]^T$ |
| $[1, 1, 0]^T$ | $[3.1448, 1.1430, 0, 1.7149]^T$ | $[1.8338, 0.6665, 0]^T$ | $[1.8338, 0.6665]^T$ |
| $[0, 0, 1]^T$ | $[1.6214, 0.1081, 0, 1.5405]^T$ | $[1.0526, 0.0702, 0]^T$ | $[1.0526, 0.0702]^T$ |
| $[1, 0, 1]^T$ | $[1.9065, 0.0604, 0, 1.3022]^T$ | $[1.4641, 0.0464, 0]^T$ | $[1.4641, 0.0464]^T$ |
| $[0, 1, 1]^T$ | $[1.6214, 1.1081, 0, 1.5405]^T$ | $[1.0526, 0.7193, 0]^T$ | $[1.0526, 0.7193]^T$ |
| $[1, 1, 1]^T$ | $[1.9065, 1.0604, 0, 1.3022]^T$ | $[1.4641, 0.8144, 0]^T$ | $[1.4641, 0.8144]^T$ |

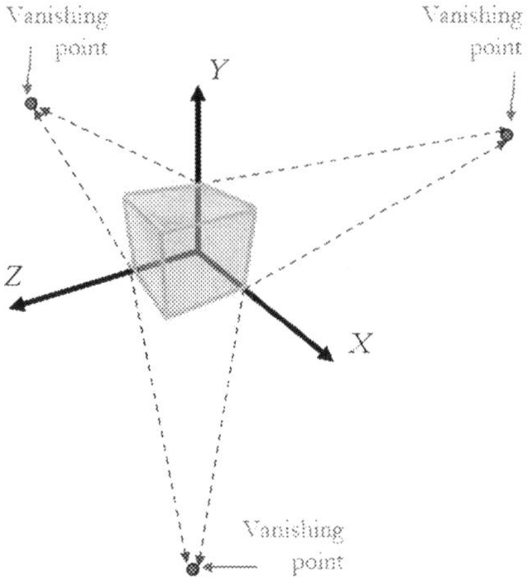


**Fig. 8.30** Three-point perspective projection: The view plane is not parallel to any of the principal axes

The two-point perspective projection for the unit cube drawn on a $0.4 \times 0.4$ grid is shown in Fig. 8.29b. □

### 8.4.3 Three-Point Perspective Projection

The three-point perspective projection exists when the view plane is *not* parallel to any of the principal axes (as shown in Fig. 8.30). Unlike the previous perspective types, the view plane intersects all three axes. Consequently, lines parallel to these three axes converge to three different vanishing points. In case of three-point perspective projection, no component of the normal vector to the view plane is set to zero.

Assuming that the center of projection is at the origin and the normal to the view plane makes an angle $\theta$ with the $yz$-plane and an angle $\varphi$ with the $zx$-plane, the overall three-point perspective projection process can be achieved in three steps.

1. Rotate through an angle $\varphi$ about the $x$-axis so that the normal to the view plane coincides with the $zx$-plane. Let us apply the matrix $\mathtt{M}_1$ where

$$\mathtt{M}_1 = \mathtt{R}_x(\varphi) = \begin{bmatrix} 1 & 0 & 0 & 0 \\ 0 & \cos(\varphi) & -\sin(\varphi) & 0 \\ 0 & \sin(\varphi) & \cos(\varphi) & 0 \\ 0 & 0 & 0 & 1 \end{bmatrix}.$$

2. Perform a two-point perspective projection using Eq. (8.69). Let us apply the matrix $\mathtt{M}_2$ where

$$\mathtt{M}_2 = \mathtt{P}_{per2} = \begin{bmatrix} 1 & 0 & 0 & 0 \\ 0 & 1 & 0 & 0 \\ 0 & 0 & 1 & 0 \\ \frac{\sin(\theta)}{d} & 0 & \frac{\cos(\theta)}{d} & 0 \end{bmatrix}.$$

3. Rotate back through an angle $-\varphi$ about the $x$-axis. Let us apply the matrix $\mathtt{M}_3$ where

$$\mathtt{M}_3 = \mathtt{R}_x(-\varphi) = \begin{bmatrix} 1 & 0 & 0 & 0 \\ 0 & \cos(-\varphi) & -\sin(-\varphi) & 0 \\ 0 & \sin(-\varphi) & \cos(-\varphi) & 0 \\ 0 & 0 & 0 & 1 \end{bmatrix} = \begin{bmatrix} 1 & 0 & 0 & 0 \\ 0 & \cos(\varphi) & \sin(\varphi) & 0 \\ 0 & -\sin(\varphi) & \cos(\varphi) & 0 \\ 0 & 0 & 0 & 1 \end{bmatrix}.$$

Thus, the overall three-point perspective projection is estimated as

$$\begin{aligned} \mathtt{P}_{per3} &= \mathtt{M}_3\mathtt{M}_2\mathtt{M}_1 \\ &= \begin{bmatrix} 1 & 0 & 0 & 0 \\ 0 & \cos(\varphi) & \sin(\varphi) & 0 \\ 0 & -\sin(\varphi) & \cos(\varphi) & 0 \\ 0 & 0 & 0 & 1 \end{bmatrix} \begin{bmatrix} 1 & 0 & 0 & 0 \\ 0 & 1 & 0 & 0 \\ 0 & 0 & 1 & 0 \\ \frac{\sin(\theta)}{d} & 0 & \frac{\cos(\theta)}{d} & 0 \end{bmatrix} \begin{bmatrix} 1 & 0 & 0 & 0 \\ 0 & \cos(\varphi) & -\sin(\varphi) & 0 \\ 0 & \sin(\varphi) & \cos(\varphi) & 0 \\ 0 & 0 & 0 & 1 \end{bmatrix} \\ &= \begin{bmatrix} 1 & 0 & 0 & 0 \\ 0 & 1 & 0 & 0 \\ 0 & 0 & 1 & 0 \\ \frac{\sin(\theta)}{d} & \frac{\cos(\theta)\sin(\varphi)}{d} & \frac{\cos(\theta)\cos(\varphi)}{d} & 0 \end{bmatrix}, \end{aligned} \tag{8.73}$$

where $\mathtt{P}_{per3}$ is the three-point perspective projection matrix when the center of projection is at the origin; and $d$ is the perpendicular distance from the origin to the view plane, which makes an angle $\theta$ with the $yz$-plane and an angle $\varphi$ with the $zx$-plane.

**Example 8.21:** [*Three-point perspective projection—points after projection given view plane orientation when COP is at the origin*]

Figure 8.31 shows a multi-view projections for a 3D model drawn on a $1 \times 1$ grid. If a camera is placed at the origin and the view plane is set such that $\theta = 30°$, $\varphi = 10°$ and $d = 0.8$, determine the three-point perspective projection for each of the corners in this case and show the results on the $xy$-plane.

**Solution 8.21:** The projection matrix is estimated using Eq. (8.73) as

$$\mathtt{P}_{per3} = \begin{bmatrix} 1 & 0 & 0 & 0 \\ 0 & 1 & 0 & 0 \\ 0 & 0 & 1 & 0 \\ \frac{\sin(\theta)}{d} & \frac{\cos(\theta)\sin(\varphi)}{d} & \frac{\cos(\theta)\cos(\varphi)}{d} & 0 \end{bmatrix}$$

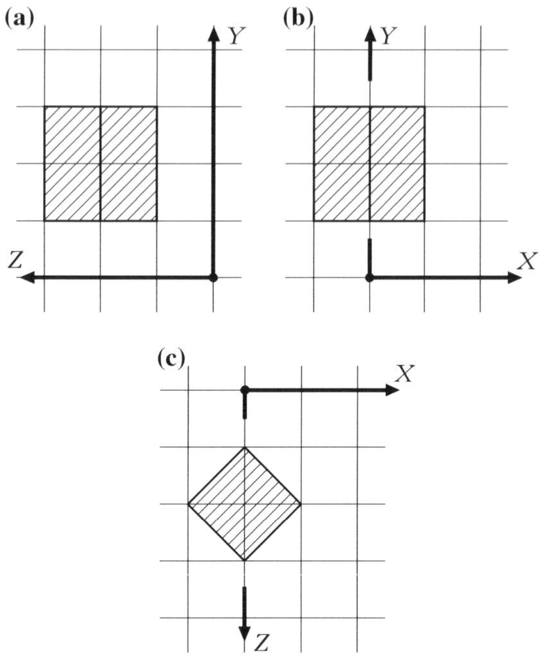


**Fig. 8.31** Multi-view projections for a model drawn on a $1 \times 1$ grid. **a** Side view. **b** Front view. **c** Top view

$$= \begin{bmatrix} 1 & 0 & 0 & 0 \\ 0 & 1 & 0 & 0 \\ 0 & 0 & 1 & 0 \\ \frac{\sin(30)}{0.8} & \frac{\cos(30)\sin(10)}{0.8} & \frac{\cos(30)\cos(10)}{0.8} & 0 \end{bmatrix}$$

$$= \begin{bmatrix} 1 & 0 & 0 & 0 \\ 0 & 1 & 0 & 0 \\ 0 & 0 & 1 & 0 \\ 0.6250 & 0.1880 & 1.0661 & 0 \end{bmatrix}.$$

Let us take the point $\dot{\mathbf{P}} = [1, 1, 2]^T$ as an example:

$$\mathbf{P}' = \underbrace{\begin{bmatrix} 1 & 0 & 0 & 0 \\ 0 & 1 & 0 & 0 \\ 0 & 0 & 1 & 0 \\ 0.6250 & 0.1880 & 1.0661 & 0 \end{bmatrix}}_{\mathrm{P}_{per3}} \underbrace{\begin{bmatrix} x \\ y \\ z \\ 1 \end{bmatrix}}_{\mathbf{P}}$$

$$= \begin{bmatrix} 1 & 0 & 0 & 0 \\ 0 & 1 & 0 & 0 \\ 0 & 0 & 1 & 0 \\ 0.6250 & 0.1880 & 1.0661 & 0 \end{bmatrix} \begin{bmatrix} 1 \\ 1 \\ 2 \\ 1 \end{bmatrix} = \begin{bmatrix} 1 \\ 1 \\ 2 \\ 2.9452 \end{bmatrix}.$$

Similarly, the locations of the corners after projection are obtained using the previous matrix. They are listed in the following table:

| $\dot{\mathbf{P}} = [x, y, z]^T$ | $\mathbf{P}' = \mathrm{P}_{per3}\mathbf{P}$ | $\dot{\mathbf{P}}' = [x', y', z']^T$ |
|---|---|---|
| $[0, 1, 1]^T$ | $[0, 1, 1, 1.2541]^T$ | $[0.0000, 0.7974, 0.7974]^T$ |
| $[0, 3, 1]^T$ | $[0, 3, 1, 1.6300]^T$ | $[0.0000, 1.8405, 0.6135]^T$ |
| $[1, 1, 2]^T$ | $[1, 1, 2, 2.9452]^T$ | $[0.3395, 0.3395, 0.6791]^T$ |
| $[1, 3, 2]^T$ | $[1, 3, 2, 3.3211]^T$ | $[0.3011, 0.9033, 0.6022]^T$ |
| $[0, 1, 3]^T$ | $[0, 1, 3, 3.3862]^T$ | $[0.0000, 0.2953, 0.8859]^T$ |
| $[0, 3, 3]^T$ | $[0, 3, 3., 3.7622]^T$ | $[0.0000, 0.7974, 0.7974]^T$ |
| $[-1, 1, 2]^T$ | $[-1, 1, 2, 1.6952]^T$ | $[-0.5899, 0.5899, 1.1798]^T$ |
| $[-1, 3, 2]^T$ | $[-1, 3, 2, 2.0711]^T$ | $[-0.4828, 1.4485, 0.9657]^T$ |

The three-point perspective projection drawn on a $0.2 \times 0.2$ grid is shown in Fig. 8.32a. □

**Example 8.22:** [*Three-point perspective projection—points after projection given view plane orientation when COP is at the origin*]

Re-solve Problem 8.21 if $\varphi = 0°$ and show the results on the $xy$-plane. Is there a difference? If yes, what is this difference?

**Solution 8.22:** The projection matrix is estimated using Eq. (8.73) as

$$
\begin{aligned}
\mathrm{P}_{per3} &= \begin{bmatrix} 1 & 0 & 0 & 0 \\ 0 & 1 & 0 & 0 \\ 0 & 0 & 1 & 0 \\ \frac{\sin(\theta)}{d} & \frac{\cos(\theta)\sin(\varphi)}{d} & \frac{\cos(\theta)\cos(\varphi)}{d} & 0 \end{bmatrix} \\
&= \begin{bmatrix} 1 & 0 & 0 & 0 \\ 0 & 1 & 0 & 0 \\ 0 & 0 & 1 & 0 \\ \frac{\sin(30)}{0.8} & \frac{\cos(30)\sin(0)}{0.8} & \frac{\cos(30)\cos(0)}{0.8} & 0 \end{bmatrix} \\
&= \begin{bmatrix} 1 & 0 & 0 & 0 \\ 0 & 1 & 0 & 0 \\ 0 & 0 & 1 & 0 \\ 0.6250 & 0 & 1.0825 & 0 \end{bmatrix}.
\end{aligned}
$$

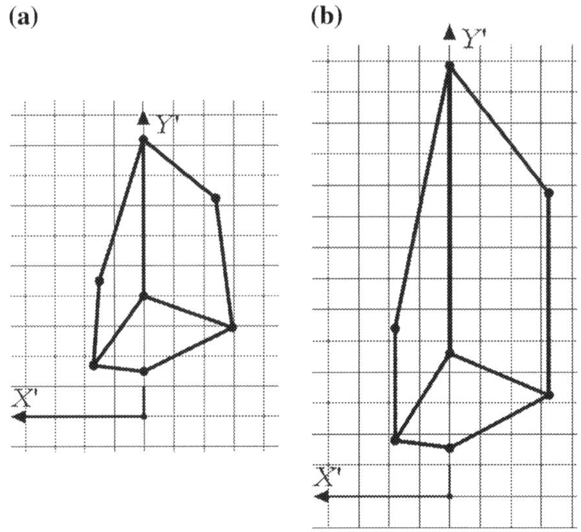


**Fig. 8.32** Perspective projections drawn on a $0.2 \times 0.2$ grid for the model shown in Fig. 8.31 where the center of projection is at the origin. **a** A three-point perspective projection where $\theta = 30°$, $\varphi = 10°$ and $d = 0.8$. **b** A two-point perspective projection where $\theta = 30°$, $\varphi = 0°$ and $d = 0.8$.

The locations of the corners after projection are obtained using the previous matrix. They are listed in the following table:

| $\dot{\mathbf{P}} = [x, y, z]^T$ | $\mathbf{P}' = \mathrm{P}_{per3}\mathbf{P}$ | $\dot{\mathbf{P}}' = [x', y', z']^T$ |
|---|---|---|
| $[0, 1, 1]^T$ | $[0, 1, 1, 1.0825]^T$ | $[0.0000, 0.9238, 0.9238]^T$ |
| $[0, 3, 1]^T$ | $[0, 3, 1, 1.0825]^T$ | $[0.0000, 2.7713, 0.9238]^T$ |
| $[1, 1, 2]^T$ | $[1, 1, 2, 2.7901]^T$ | $[0.3584, 0.3584, 0.7168]^T$ |
| $[1, 3, 2]^T$ | $[1, 3, 2, 2.7901]^T$ | $[0.3584, 1.0752, 0.7168]^T$ |
| $[0, 1, 3]^T$ | $[0, 1, 3, 3.2476]^T$ | $[0.0000, 0.3079, 0.9238]^T$ |
| $[0, 3, 3]^T$ | $[0, 3, 3, 3.2476]^T$ | $[0.0000, 0.9238, 0.9238]^T$ |
| $[-1, 1, 2]^T$ | $[-1, 1, 2, 1.5401]^T$ | $[-0.6493, 0.6493, 1.2986]^T$ |
| $[-1, 3, 2]^T$ | $[-1, 3, 2, 1.5401]^T$ | $[-0.6493, 1.9480, 1.2986]^T$ |

Yes, there is a difference as a two-point perspective projection is generated with $\varphi = 0°$. This two-point perspective projection drawn on a $0.2 \times 0.2$ grid is shown in Fig. 8.32b. □

**Example 8.23:** [*Three-point perspective projection—vanishing points along the x-, y- and z-axes given a general view plane when COP is at the origin*]

Determine the locations of the vanishing points along the $x$-, $y$- and $z$-axes given a general view plane when the center of projection is at the origin.

**Solution 8.23:** A vanishing point along an axis is obtained by applying the perspective transformation to a point at infinity along that axis. A point at infinity along the

$x$-axis can be expressed as $[x, 0, 0, 0]^T$. Hence, the vanishing point along the $x$-axis is estimated as

$$\mathbf{P}' = \begin{bmatrix} 1 & 0 & 0 & 0 \\ 0 & 1 & 0 & 0 \\ 0 & 0 & 1 & 0 \\ \frac{\sin(\theta)}{d} & \frac{\cos(\theta)\sin(\varphi)}{d} & \frac{\cos(\theta)\cos(\varphi)}{d} & 0 \end{bmatrix} \begin{bmatrix} x \\ 0 \\ 0 \\ 0 \end{bmatrix} = \begin{bmatrix} x \\ 0 \\ 0 \\ \frac{x\sin(\theta)}{d} \end{bmatrix}.$$

Dividing by the last term of the homogeneous point $\mathbf{P}'$, the vanishing point $\dot{\mathbf{P}}'$ is expressed as $\left[\frac{d}{\sin(\theta)}, 0, 0\right]^T$. Similarly, points at infinity along the $y$- and $z$-axes can be expressed as $[0, y, 0, 0]^T$ and $[0, 0, z, 0]^T$. Hence, the vanishing points along these axes are estimated as

$$\mathbf{P}' = \begin{bmatrix} 1 & 0 & 0 & 0 \\ 0 & 1 & 0 & 0 \\ 0 & 0 & 1 & 0 \\ \frac{\sin(\theta)}{d} & \frac{\cos(\theta)\sin(\varphi)}{d} & \frac{\cos(\theta)\cos(\varphi)}{d} & 0 \end{bmatrix} \begin{bmatrix} 0 \\ y \\ 0 \\ 0 \end{bmatrix} = \begin{bmatrix} 0 \\ y \\ 0 \\ \frac{y\cos(\theta)\sin(\varphi)}{d} \end{bmatrix}$$

and

$$\mathbf{P}' = \begin{bmatrix} 1 & 0 & 0 & 0 \\ 0 & 1 & 0 & 0 \\ 0 & 0 & 1 & 0 \\ \frac{\sin(\theta)}{d} & \frac{\cos(\theta)\sin(\varphi)}{d} & \frac{\cos(\theta)\cos(\varphi)}{d} & 0 \end{bmatrix} \begin{bmatrix} 0 \\ 0 \\ z \\ 0 \end{bmatrix} = \begin{bmatrix} 0 \\ 0 \\ z \\ \frac{z\cos(\theta)\cos(\varphi)}{d} \end{bmatrix}.$$

Dividing by the last terms of the homogeneous points, the vanishing points along the $y$- and $z$-axes are expressed as $\left[0, \frac{d}{\cos(\theta)\sin(\varphi)}, 0\right]^T$ and $\left[0, 0, \frac{d}{\cos(\theta)\cos(\varphi)}\right]^T$ respectively. □

**The view plane equation:** Since multiplying a homogeneous point by a factor does not change its coordinates (see Sect. B.7), the homogeneous three-point perspective projection matrix of Eq. (8.73) can be re-written as

$$\mathtt{P}_{per3} = \begin{bmatrix} d & 0 & 0 & 0 \\ 0 & d & 0 & 0 \\ 0 & 0 & d & 0 \\ \sin(\theta) & \cos(\theta)\sin(\varphi) & \cos(\theta)\cos(\varphi) & 0 \end{bmatrix}. \tag{8.74}$$

Notice that the first three components of the last row represent a unit vector with projections onto the $x$-, $y$- and $z$-axes as $\sin(\theta)$, $\cos(\theta)\sin(\varphi)$ and $\cos(\theta)\cos(\varphi)$ respectively. Figure 8.33 shows this vector inclining at angles $\theta$ and $\varphi$ with respect to the $yz$- and $zx$-planes respectively. The shaded triangle of Fig. 8.33a shows the $x$-component of the unit vector while Fig. 8.33b shows the $y$- and $z$-components of that vector.

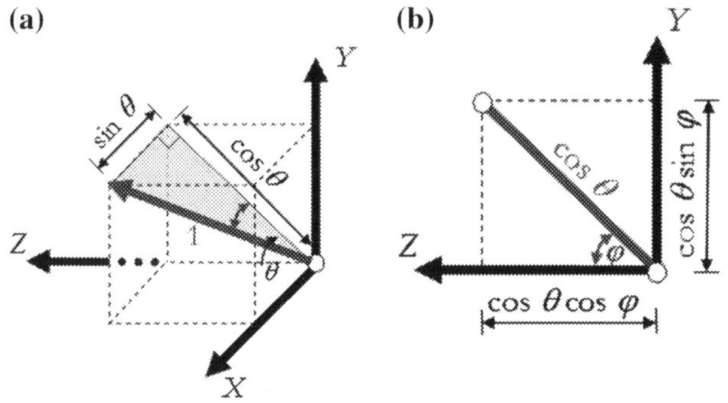


**Fig. 8.33** A unit vector inclined at angles $\theta$ and $\varphi$ with respect to the $yz$- and $zx$-planes respectively. **a** The shaded triangle shows the $x$-component or the projection of the unit vector onto the $x$-axis; i.e., $\sin(\theta)$. **b** The $y$- and $z$-components or the projections of the unit vector onto the $y$- and $z$-axes; i.e., $\cos(\theta)\sin(\varphi)$ and $\cos(\theta)\cos(\varphi)$ respectively.

In fact, Eq. (8.74) represents the general perspective projection matrix given the view plane equation that is expressed as

$$\underbrace{\sin(\theta)}_{n_x} x + \underbrace{\cos(\theta)\sin(\varphi)}_{n_y} y + \underbrace{\cos(\theta)\cos(\varphi)}_{n_z} z = d, \tag{8.75}$$

where $\mathbf{n} = [n_x, n_y, n_z]^T = [\sin(\theta), \cos(\theta)\sin(\varphi), \cos(\theta)\cos(\varphi)]^T$ is the normalized normal vector to the view plane while $d$ is the perpendicular distance from the origin to the view plane.

When $\theta = 0°$ and $\varphi = 0°$, the view plane equation turns to $z = d$ and the perspective projection matrix of Eq. (8.74) is expressed as

$$\mathrm{P}_{per} = \begin{bmatrix} d & 0 & 0 & 0 \\ 0 & d & 0 & 0 \\ 0 & 0 & d & 0 \\ 0 & 0 & 1 & 0 \end{bmatrix}, \tag{8.76}$$

which is the same matrix of Eq. (8.57) representing the one-point perspective projection along the $z$-axis.

When $\theta = 90°$ and $\varphi = 0°$, the view plane equation turns to $x = d$ and the perspective projection matrix of Eq. (8.74) is expressed as

$$\mathrm{P}_{per} = \begin{bmatrix} d & 0 & 0 & 0 \\ 0 & d & 0 & 0 \\ 0 & 0 & d & 0 \\ 1 & 0 & 0 & 0 \end{bmatrix}, \tag{8.77}$$

which is the same matrix of Eq. (8.61) representing the one-point perspective projection along the $x$-axis.

When $\theta = 0°$ and $\varphi = 90°$, the view plane equation turns to $y = d$ and the perspective projection matrix of Eq. (8.74) is expressed as

$$\mathrm{P}_{per} = \begin{bmatrix} d & 0 & 0 & 0 \\ 0 & d & 0 & 0 \\ 0 & 0 & d & 0 \\ 0 & 1 & 0 & 0 \end{bmatrix}, \tag{8.78}$$

which is the same matrix of Eq. (8.63) representing the one-point perspective projection along the $y$-axis.

When $\varphi = 0°$, the view plane equation turns to $\sin(\theta)x + \cos(\theta)z = d$ and the perspective projection matrix of Eq. (8.74) is expressed as

$$\mathrm{P}_{per2} = \begin{bmatrix} d & 0 & 0 & 0 \\ 0 & d & 0 & 0 \\ 0 & 0 & d & 0 \\ \sin(\theta) & 0 & \cos(\theta) & 0 \end{bmatrix}, \tag{8.79}$$

which is the same matrix of Eq. (8.69) representing the two-point perspective projection where the view plane is parallel to the $y$-axis.

Similarly, when $\varphi = 90°$, the view plane equation turns to $\sin(\theta)x + \cos(\theta)y = d$ and the perspective projection matrix of Eq. (8.74) is expressed as

$$\mathrm{P}_{per2} = \begin{bmatrix} d & 0 & 0 & 0 \\ 0 & d & 0 & 0 \\ 0 & 0 & d & 0 \\ \sin(\theta) & \cos(\theta) & 0 & 0 \end{bmatrix}, \tag{8.80}$$

which represents the two-point perspective projection where the view plane is parallel to the $z$-axis.

When $\theta = 0°$, the view plane equation turns to $\sin(\varphi)y + \cos(\varphi)z = d$ and the perspective projection matrix of Eq. (8.74) is expressed as

$$\mathrm{P}_{per2} = \begin{bmatrix} d & 0 & 0 & 0 \\ 0 & d & 0 & 0 \\ 0 & 0 & d & 0 \\ 0 & \sin(\varphi) & \cos(\varphi) & 0 \end{bmatrix}, \tag{8.81}$$

which represents the two-point perspective projection where the view plane is parallel to the $x$-axis.

**Example 8.24:** [*Three-point perspective projection—deriving the projection matrix when COP is at an arbitrary point and the view plane has a general equation* $n_x x + n_y y + n_z z = d$]

If the center of projection is placed at an arbitrary point $[x_0, y_0, z_0]^T$ and the view plane equation is $n_x x + n_y y + n_z z = d$, derive the three-point projection matrix in this case.

**Solution 8.24:** The matrix is obtained in three steps.

1. Translate the center of projection using the translation vector $[-x_0, -y_0, -z_0]^T$ so it coincides with the origin. Let us apply the matrix $\mathtt{M}_1$ where

$$\mathtt{M}_1 = \mathtt{T}([-x, -y, -z]^T) = \begin{bmatrix} 1 & 0 & 0 & -x_0 \\ 0 & 1 & 0 & -y_0 \\ 0 & 0 & 1 & -z_0 \\ 0 & 0 & 0 & 1 \end{bmatrix}.$$

   As mentioned in Example 8.18, make sure that $d$ remains unchanged.
2. Perform a three-point perspective projection using Eq. (8.74). Let us apply the matrix $\mathtt{M}_2$ where

$$\mathtt{M}_2 = \mathtt{P}_{per3} = \begin{bmatrix} d & 0 & 0 & 0 \\ 0 & d & 0 & 0 \\ 0 & 0 & d & 0 \\ n_x & n_y & n_z & 0 \end{bmatrix}.$$

3. Translate back using the translation vector $[x_0, y_0, z_0]^T$. Let us apply the matrix $\mathtt{M}_3$ where

$$\mathtt{M}_3 = \mathtt{T}([x, y, z]^T) = \begin{bmatrix} 1 & 0 & 0 & x_0 \\ 0 & 1 & 0 & y_0 \\ 0 & 0 & 1 & z_0 \\ 0 & 0 & 0 & 1 \end{bmatrix}.$$

Thus, the overall projection is estimated as

$$\begin{aligned} \mathtt{P}_{per3} &= \mathtt{M}_3\mathtt{M}_2\mathtt{M}_1 \\ &= \begin{bmatrix} 1 & 0 & 0 & x_0 \\ 0 & 1 & 0 & y_0 \\ 0 & 0 & 1 & z_0 \\ 0 & 0 & 0 & 1 \end{bmatrix} \begin{bmatrix} d & 0 & 0 & 0 \\ 0 & d & 0 & 0 \\ 0 & 0 & d & 0 \\ n_x & n_y & n_z & 0 \end{bmatrix} \begin{bmatrix} 1 & 0 & 0 & -x_0 \\ 0 & 1 & 0 & -y_0 \\ 0 & 0 & 1 & -z_0 \\ 0 & 0 & 0 & 1 \end{bmatrix} \\ &= \begin{bmatrix} x_0 n_x + d & x_0 n_y & x_0 n_z & -x_0(x_0 n_x + y_0 n_y + z_0 n_z + d) \\ y_0 n_x & y_0 n_y + d & y_0 n_z & -y_0(x_0 n_x + y_0 n_y + z_0 n_z + d) \\ z_0 n_x & z_0 n_y & z_0 n_z + d & -z_0(x_0 n_x + y_0 n_y + z_0 n_z + d) \\ n_x & n_y & n_z & -(x_0 n_x + y_0 n_y + z_0 n_z) \end{bmatrix}. \end{aligned} \tag{8.82}$$

In case the problem is formulated such that the normal to the view plane makes angles $\theta$ and $\varphi$ with the $yz$-plane and the $zx$-plane respectively, substitute the values for the normal vector to the view plane as

$$\begin{bmatrix} n_x \\ n_y \\ n_z \end{bmatrix} = \begin{bmatrix} \sin(\theta) \\ \cos(\theta)\sin(\varphi) \\ \cos(\theta)\cos(\varphi) \end{bmatrix}. \qquad \square$$

**Example 8.25:** [*Three-point perspective projection—vanishing point along an arbitrary direction when COP is at an arbitrary point and the view plane has a general equation* $n_x x + n_y y + n_z z = d$]

All parallel lines diminish to a single vanishing point. Assume that those parallel lines are along the direction vector $\mathbf{d} = [d_x, d_y, d_z]^T$. If the center of projection is an arbitrary point $\dot{\mathbf{P}}_0 = [x_0, y_0, z_0]^T$ and the view plane equation is $n_x x + n_y y + n_z z = d$, determine the location of the vanishing point of the parallel lines.

**Solution 8.25:** A point at infinity along the direction vector $\mathbf{d}$ is expressed as $\mathbf{P}_\infty = [d_x, d_y, d_z, 0]^T$. Plug this point into Eq. (8.82) to get the vanishing point of all lines parallel to the vector $\mathbf{d}$. Thus,

$$\begin{aligned}
\mathbf{P}' &= \mathtt{P}_{per3}\mathbf{P}_\infty \\
&= \begin{bmatrix} x_0 n_x + d & x_0 n_y & x_0 n_z & -x_0(x_0 n_x + y_0 n_y + z_0 n_z + d) \\ y_0 n_x & y_0 n_y + d & y_0 n_z & -y_0(x_0 n_x + y_0 n_y + z_0 n_z + d) \\ z_0 n_x & z_0 n_y & z_0 n_z + d & -z_0(x_0 n_x + y_0 n_y + z_0 n_z + d) \\ n_x & n_y & n_z & -(x_0 n_x + y_0 n_y + z_0 n_z) \end{bmatrix} \begin{bmatrix} d_x \\ d_y \\ d_z \\ 0 \end{bmatrix} \\
&= \begin{bmatrix} x_0(n_x d_x + n_y d_y + n_z d_z) + d_x d \\ y_0(n_x d_x + n_y d_y + n_z d_z) + d_y d \\ z_0(n_x d_x + n_y d_y + n_z d_z) + d_z d \\ n_x d_x + n_y d_y + n_z d_z \end{bmatrix} = \begin{bmatrix} x_0 + \frac{d_x d}{n_x d_x + n_y d_y + n_z d_z} \\ y_0 + \frac{d_y d}{n_x d_x + n_y d_y + n_z d_z} \\ z_0 + \frac{d_z d}{n_x d_x + n_y d_y + n_z d_z} \\ 1 \end{bmatrix}.
\end{aligned}$$

If the center of projection is at $\dot{\mathbf{P}}_0 = [x_0, y_0, z_0]^T$, the normal to the view plane is $\mathbf{n} = [n_x, n_y, n_z]^T$, the equation of the view plane is $n_x x + n_y y + n_z z = d$ and the direction vector is $\mathbf{d} = [d_x, d_y, d_z]^T$, the vanishing point $\dot{\mathbf{P}}'$ is expressed as

$$\dot{\mathbf{P}}' = \begin{bmatrix} x_0 + \frac{d_x d}{\mathbf{n}\cdot\mathbf{d}} \\ y_0 + \frac{d_y d}{\mathbf{n}\cdot\mathbf{d}} \\ z_0 + \frac{d_z d}{\mathbf{n}\cdot\mathbf{d}} \end{bmatrix} = \dot{\mathbf{P}}_0 + \frac{d\mathbf{d}}{\mathbf{n}\cdot\mathbf{d}}, \tag{8.83}$$

where $\cdot$ denotes the dot product. $\square$

**Example 8.26:** [*One-point perspective projection—vanishing point when COP is at the origin and the view plane is at* $z = d$]

Use Eq. (8.83) to get the vanishing point of lines parallel to the $z$-axis when the center of projection is at the origin and view plane is at $z = d$.

**Solution 8.26:** In this case and according to Eq. (8.83), the center of projection is expressed as

$$\dot{\mathbf{P}}_0 = \begin{bmatrix} 0 \\ 0 \\ 0 \end{bmatrix}.$$

Since the $z$-coefficient of the plane equation is 1, the normal to the view plane is expressed as

$$\mathbf{n} = \begin{bmatrix} 0 \\ 0 \\ 1 \end{bmatrix}.$$

We need to get the vanishing point for lines parallel to the $z$-axis; thus, their direction is expressed as

$$\mathbf{d} = \begin{bmatrix} 0 \\ 0 \\ 1 \end{bmatrix}.$$

By applying Eq. (8.83), the vanishing point is expressed as

$$\begin{aligned} \dot{\mathbf{P}}' &= \dot{\mathbf{P}}_0 + \frac{d\mathbf{d}}{\mathbf{n}\cdot\mathbf{d}} \\ &= \begin{bmatrix} 0 \\ 0 \\ 0 \end{bmatrix} + \frac{d\begin{bmatrix} 0 \\ 0 \\ 1 \end{bmatrix}}{\begin{bmatrix} 0 \\ 0 \\ 1 \end{bmatrix}\cdot\begin{bmatrix} 0 \\ 0 \\ 1 \end{bmatrix}} = \begin{bmatrix} 0 \\ 0 \\ d \end{bmatrix}, \end{aligned}$$

which is the same result that should be obtained when applying the general matrix of Example 8.23 when $\theta = \varphi = 0°$ to a point at infinity along the $z$-direction (e.g., $[0, 0, z, 0]^T$). It is also the same result that should be obtained when applying the matrix $\mathtt{P}_{per}$ of Eq. (8.57) to the same point at infinity along the $z$-direction. □

**Example 8.27:** [*Three-point perspective projection—vanishing point when COP is at the origin and the view plane has a general equation* $n_x x + n_y y + n_z z = d$]

Use Eq. (8.83) to get the vanishing point of lines parallel to the $z$-axis when the center of projection is at the origin and view plane has the general equation $n_x x + n_y y + n_z z = d$.

**Solution 8.27:** The center of projection is expressed as

$$\dot{\mathbf{P}}_0 = \begin{bmatrix} 0 \\ 0 \\ 0 \end{bmatrix}.$$

Since the $x$-coefficient is $n_x$, the $y$-coefficient is $n_y$ and the $z$-coefficient is $n_z$, the normal to the view plane is expressed as

$$\mathbf{n} = \begin{bmatrix} n_x \\ n_y \\ n_z \end{bmatrix}.$$

We need to get the vanishing point for lines parallel to the $z$-axis; thus, their direction can be expressed as

$$\mathbf{d} = \begin{bmatrix} 0 \\ 0 \\ 1 \end{bmatrix}.$$

By applying Eq. (8.83), the vanishing point is expressed as

$$\begin{aligned} \dot{\mathbf{P}}' &= \dot{\mathbf{P}}_0 + \tfrac{d\mathbf{d}}{\mathbf{n}\cdot\mathbf{d}} \\ &= \begin{bmatrix} 0 \\ 0 \\ 0 \end{bmatrix} + \frac{d \begin{bmatrix} 0 \\ 0 \\ 1 \end{bmatrix}}{\begin{bmatrix} n_x \\ n_y \\ n_z \end{bmatrix} \cdot \begin{bmatrix} 0 \\ 0 \\ 1 \end{bmatrix}} = \begin{bmatrix} 0 \\ 0 \\ d/n_z \end{bmatrix}, \end{aligned}$$

which is the same result that should be obtained when applying the general matrix of Example 8.23 when $\cos(\theta) + \cos(\varphi) = n_z$. □

**Comparison:** Table 8.2 summarizes the various values for different cases of perspective projections while Table 8.3 lists the main differences among the types of perspective projections.

## 8.5 Parallel/Perspective Comparison

As we have seen in the previous sections, main differences exist between parallel and perspective projections. Table 8.4 list the main differences between these projection types.

**Example 8.28:** [*Projection conditions*] If the normal to the view plane is $[0, 0, 1]^T$, determine whether or not the following projections can be produced:

1. Multi-view projection as a front view.
2. Cabinet projection.
3. Cavalier projection.
4. Isometric projection.

**Table 8.2** Different cases of perspective projections

| Type | $\theta$ | $\varphi$ | **n** | Equation | $\mathtt{P}_{per}$ |
|---|---|---|---|---|---|
| 1-point | 90° | 0° | $\begin{bmatrix}1\\0\\0\end{bmatrix}$ | $x = d$ (i.e., parallel to $yz$-plane) | $\begin{bmatrix}d&0&0&0\\0&d&0&0\\0&0&d&0\\1&0&0&0\end{bmatrix}$ |
| 1-point | 0° | 90° | $\begin{bmatrix}0\\1\\0\end{bmatrix}$ | $y = d$ (i.e., parallel to $zx$-plane) | $\begin{bmatrix}d&0&0&0\\0&d&0&0\\0&0&d&0\\0&1&0&0\end{bmatrix}$ |
| 1-point | 0° | 0° | $\begin{bmatrix}0\\0\\1\end{bmatrix}$ | $z = d$ (i.e., parallel to $xy$-plane) | $\begin{bmatrix}d&0&0&0\\0&d&0&0\\0&0&d&0\\0&0&1&0\end{bmatrix}$ |
| 2-point | | 0° | $\begin{bmatrix}\sin(\theta)\\0\\\cos(\theta)\end{bmatrix}$ | $\sin(\theta)x + \cos(\theta)z = d$ (i.e., parallel to $y$-axis) | $\begin{bmatrix}d&0&0&0\\0&d&0&0\\0&0&d&0\\\sin(\theta)&0&\cos(\theta)&0\end{bmatrix}$ |
| 2-point | | 90° | $\begin{bmatrix}\sin(\theta)\\\cos(\theta)\\0\end{bmatrix}$ | $\sin(\theta)x + \cos(\theta)y = d$ (i.e., parallel to $z$-axis) | $\begin{bmatrix}d&0&0&0\\0&d&0&0\\0&0&d&0\\\sin(\theta)&\cos(\theta)&0&0\end{bmatrix}$ |
| 2-point | 0° | | $\begin{bmatrix}0\\\sin(\varphi)\\\cos(\varphi)\end{bmatrix}$ | $\sin(\varphi)y + \cos(\varphi)z = d$ (i.e., parallel to $x$-axis) | $\begin{bmatrix}d&0&0&0\\0&d&0&0\\0&0&d&0\\0&\sin(\varphi)&\cos(\varphi)&0\end{bmatrix}$ |
| 3-point | | | $\begin{bmatrix}\sin(\theta)\\\cos(\theta)\sin(\varphi)\\\cos(\theta)\cos(\varphi)\end{bmatrix}$ | $\sin(\theta)x + \cos(\theta)\sin(\varphi)y + \cos(\theta)\cos(\varphi)z = d$ | $\begin{bmatrix}d&0&0&0\\0&d&0&0\\0&0&d&0\\\sin(\theta)&\cos(\theta)\sin(\varphi)&\cos(\theta)\cos(\varphi)&0\end{bmatrix}$ |

**Table 8.3** Main differences between perspective projections

| | One-point | Two-point | Three-point |
|---|---|---|---|
| w.r.t. principal axes, there is (are) | One vanishing point | Two vanishing points | Three vanishing points |
| View plane intersects | One principal axis | Two principal axes | Three principal axes |
| View plane is parallel to | Two principal axes/ one principal plane | One principal axis | None of the principal axes |
| Lines parallel to principal axes remain parallel w.r.t. | Two axes | One axis | Not applicable |
| Lines parallel to principal axes converge w.r.t. | One axis | Two axes | Three axes |
| Normal vector to the view plane has | Two components set to zero | One component set to zero | No components set to zero |
| Normal to the view plane is | Parallel to one principal axis | Perpendicular to one principal axis | General |

**Table 8.4** Main differences between parallel and perspective projections

| | **Parallel projections** | **Perspective projections** |
|---|---|---|
| Center of projection is | At infinity | At a finite distance from the view plane |
| Projectors are | Parallel | Not parallel |
| View volume is | Parallelepiped | Pyramidal |
| Lines not parallel to the view plane | Remain parallel | Converge to vanishing points |
| Measurements: | Proportions (not necessarily the actual measurements) are maintained | Away from the center of projection, objects appear smaller |

5. One-point perspective projection.

If more than one projection type can be produced using that same normal vector to the view plane, which is $[0, 0, 1]^T$, what are the other settings that would make such differences among these projections?

**Solution 8.28:** The following are the different options:

1. **Front view** can be produced using $[0, 0, 1]^T$ if the projectors are parallel and perpendicular to view plane.
2. **Cabinet projection** can be produced using $[0, 0, 1]^T$ if the projectors are parallel, not perpendicular to the view plane and $\alpha = 63.4°$.
3. **Cavalier projection** can be produced using $[0, 0, 1]^T$ if the projectors are parallel, not perpendicular to the view plane and $\alpha = 45°$.
4. **Isometric projection** cannot be produced using $[0, 0, 1]^T$.

5. **One-point perspective projection** can be produced using $[0, 0, 1]^T$ if the viewpoint or the center of projection is placed at a finite distance from the view plane (i.e., if the projectors are not parallel to each other as in case of parallel projections).

**Example 8.29:** [*Projection conditions*]

Given a viewing plane represented by the vector $[0, 0, 1, -5]^T$, determine whether or not the following projections can be produced:

1. Multi-view projection as a front view.
2. Dimetric projection.
3. Cabinet projection.
4. One-point perspective projection.
5. Two-point perspective projection.

If more than one projection type can be produced, what are the other settings that would make such differences among these projections? If the plane is rotated about the $x$-axis through an angle of 45°, estimate the plane equation and determine if any of the above projections can be produced.

**Solution 8.29:** The normal to the plane $[0, 0, 1, -5]^T$ is composed of the first three components of the vector (i.e., $\mathbf{n} = [0, 0, 1]^T$). The following are the different options:

1. **Front view** can be produced if the projectors are parallel and perpendicular to view plane.
2. **Dimetric projection** cannot be produced since two of the components of the normal vector are zeros (unless a multi-view projection is considered a special case of dimetric projection).
3. **Cabinet projection** can be produced if the projectors are parallel, not perpendicular to the view plane and $\alpha = 63.4°$.
4. **One-point perspective projection** can be produced if the viewpoint or the center of projection is placed at a finite distance from the view plane (i.e., if the projectors are not parallel to each other as in case of parallel projections).
5. **Two-point perspective projection** cannot be produced since two of the components of the normal vector are zeros.

The plane $[0, 0, 1, -5]^T$ is rotated about the $x$-axis through an angle of 45° using Eq. (5.6) to get the following plane equation:

$$\begin{bmatrix} 1 & 0 & 0 & 0 \\ 0 & \cos(45) & -\sin(45) & 0 \\ 0 & \sin(45) & \cos(45) & 0 \\ 0 & 0 & 0 & 1 \end{bmatrix} \begin{bmatrix} 0 \\ 0 \\ 1 \\ -5 \end{bmatrix} = \begin{bmatrix} 0 \\ -\frac{1}{\sqrt{2}} \\ \frac{1}{\sqrt{2}} \\ -5 \end{bmatrix}.$$

Hence, the normal to the new plane is $\left[0, -\frac{1}{\sqrt{2}}, \frac{1}{\sqrt{2}}\right]^T$; thus,

1. **Front view** cannot be produced since only one component of the normal vector is zero.
2. **Dimetric projection** can be produced if the viewpoint or the center of projection is placed at an infinite distance from the view plane (i.e., if the projectors are parallel).
3. **Cabinet projection** cannot be produced since only one component of the normal vector is zero.
4. **One-point perspective projection** cannot be produced since only one component of the normal vector is zero.
5. **Two-point perspective projection** can be produced if the viewpoint or the center of projection is placed at a finite distance from the view plane (i.e., if the projectors are not parallel to each other as in case of parallel projections). □

## 8.6 Problems

**Problem 8.1:** [*Projections—possibility of projections given a view plane equation*]
Given a view plane represented by the vector $[0, 1, 0, -5]^T$, determine whether or not the following projections can be produced:

1. Multi-view projection as a front view.
2. Dimetric projection.
3. Cabinet projection.
4. One-point perspective projection.
5. Two-point perspective projection.

If more than one projection type can be produced, what are the other settings that would make such differences among these projections?

**Problem 8.2:** [*Projections—possibility of projections given a rotated view plane*]
In Problem 8.1, if the plane is rotated about the $x$-axis through 45°, estimate the plane equation and determine if any of the above projections can be produced.

**Problem 8.3:** [*Multi-view projections—front view projection matrix*]
An image whose origin is its lower left corner can be created for the front view shown in Fig. 8.3a. Assume that each unit in the world coordinate system can be represented by one pixel in the image produced. Also, assume that all points in 3D space have positive $x$- and $y$-coordinates. Write down a front view projection matrix that is used to find the projection of any 3D point (e.g., $\dot{\mathbf{P}} = [x, y, z]^T$) as a 2D image point (e.g., $\dot{\mathbf{p}} = [x, y]^T$).

**Problem 8.4:** [*Multi-view projections—back view projection matrix*]
If the front view is an orthographic projection onto the $xy$-plane with a normal vector $\mathbf{n} = [0, 0, 1]^T$, the back view is an orthographic projection onto the $xy$-plane with a normal vector $\mathbf{n} = [0, 0, -1]^T$. Suppose that a $200 \times 200$ image whose origin is its lower left corner can be created for this back view. Assume that each

unit in the world coordinate system can be represented by one pixel in the image produced. Also, assume that all points in 3D space are within the range $[0, 0, 0]^T$ to $[199, 199, 199]^T$. Write down a single back view projection matrix that is used to find the projection of any 3D point (e.g., $\dot{\mathbf{P}} = [1, 2, 3]^T$) as a 2D image point (e.g., $\dot{\mathbf{p}} = [198, 2]^T$).

**Problem 8.5:** [*Multi-view projections—back view projection matrix*]
In Problem 8.4, if the 3D point (e.g., $\dot{\mathbf{P}} = [1, 2, 3]^T$) is to be projected onto the $xy$-plane as another 3D point whose $z$-coordinate is 0 (i.e., $\dot{\mathbf{P}}' = [198, 2, 0]^T$), write down a single matrix that can be used to perform this transformation.

**Problem 8.6:** [*Isometric projection—points given a view plane equation*]
A view plane has the equation $x + y + z = 12$. If isometric projectors are used to project a point $\dot{\mathbf{P}} = [1, 1, 0]^T$ onto that plane to get another point $\dot{\mathbf{p}}$, where will the projection appear on that plane? In other words, get the location $\dot{\mathbf{p}}$.

**Problem 8.7:** [*Isometric projection—points given a view plane normal vector*]
Consider a unit cube with two of its corners placed at $[0, 0, 0]^T$ and $[1, 1, 1]^T$. Given a view plane with a normal vector $[-1, 1, -1]^T$, determine the isometric projection of its corners.

**Problem 8.8:** [*Isometric projection—projection matrix given a view plane normal vector*]
Estimate the isometric projection matrix when the normal vector to the view plane is having the following values: $[1, 1, -1]^T$, $[1, -1, 1]^T$, $[-1, -1, 1]^T$, $[-1, -1, -1]^T$ and $[1, -1, -1]^T$.

**Problem 8.9:** [*Dimetric projection—projection matrix given a view plane normal vector*]
Estimate the dimetric projection matrix when the normal vector to the view plane is having the following values: $[1, 3, -1]^T$, $[3, -3, 5]^T$ and $[-3, -5, 5]^T$.

**Problem 8.10:** [*Trimetric projection—projection matrix given a view plane normal vector*]
Estimate the trimetric projection matrix when the normal vector to the view plane is having the following values: $[2, 3, -1]^T$, $[1, -6, 3]^T$ and $[-3, -4, 5]^T$.

**Problem 8.11:** [*Cavalier projection—$yz$-plane*]
Equation (8.43) assumes that the view plane is the $xy$-plane. Re-write the equation when the view plane is the $yz$-plane.

**Problem 8.12:** [*Cavalier projection—$zx$-plane*]
Equation (8.44) assumes that the view plane is the $xy$-plane. Re-write the equation when the view plane is the $zx$-plane.

**Problem 8.13:** [*Cabinet projection—$yz$-plane*]
Equation (8.48) assumes that the view plane is the $xy$-plane. Re-write the equation when the view plane is the $yz$-plane.

**Problem 8.14:** [*Cabinet projection—$zx$-plane*]
Equation (8.49) assumes that the view plane is the $xy$-plane. Re-write the equation when the view plane is the $zx$-plane.

**Problem 8.15:** [*General oblique projection—$yz$-plane*]
Equations (8.52) and (8.53) can be used for front view projection when $\alpha = 90°$. Modify them to produce side view projection.

**Problem 8.16:** [*General oblique projection—$zx$-plane*]
Re-write the general oblique projection equation; i.e., Eq. (8.52), such that the view plane is the $zx$-plane.

**Problem 8.17:** [*One-point perspective projection—projection matrix when COP is at $[-d, 0, 0]^T$ and view plane is at $x = 0$*]
The projection matrix of Eq. (8.61) is used when the center of projection is at the origin and the view plane has the equation $x = d$. Modify this matrix so that the center of projection moves to $[-d, 0, 0]^T$ and the view plane moves to $x = 0$.

**Problem 8.18:** [*One-point perspective projection—projection matrix when COP is at $[0, -d, 0]^T$ and view plane is at $y = 0$*]
The projection matrix of Eq. (8.63) is used when the center of projection is at the origin and the view plane has the equation $y = d$. Modify this matrix so that the center of projection moves to $[0, -d, 0]^T$ and the view plane moves to $y = 0$.

**Problem 8.19:** [*Two-point perspective projection—view plane is parallel to the $x$-axis and COP is at the origin*]
The matrix of Eq. (8.69) produces a two-point perspective projection when the view plane is parallel to the $y$-axis. Get the matrix when the view plane is parallel to the $x$-axis and the center of projection is at the origin.

**Problem 8.20:** [*Two-point perspective projection—view plane is parallel to the $z$-axis and COP is at the origin*]
Re-solve Problem 8.19 when the view plane is parallel to the $z$-axis.

**Problem 8.21:** [*Two-point perspective projection—view plane is parallel to the $y$-axis and COP is at the origin*]
If the view plane is parallel to the $y$-axis and passing through points $\dot{\mathbf{P}}_0 = [1, 0, 2]^T$ and $\dot{\mathbf{P}}_1 = [4, 0, 1]^T$ and the COP is located at the origin, derive the projection matrix in this case.

**Problem 8.22:** [*Two-point perspective projection—view plane is parallel to the $y$-axis and COP is at an arbitrary point*]
Re-solve Problem 8.21 if the COP is moved to $[4, 0, 4]^T$.

**Problem 8.23:** [*One-point perspective projection—vanishing point when COP is at the origin and the view plane is at $x = d$*]
Use Eq. (8.83) to get the vanishing point of lines parallel to the $x$-axis when the center of projection is at the origin and view plane is at $x = d$.

**Problem 8.24:** [*One-point perspective projection—vanishing point when COP is at the origin and the view plane is at* $y = d$]

Use Eq. (8.83) to get the vanishing point of lines parallel to the $y$-axis when the center of projection is at the origin and view plane is at $y = d$.

**Problem 8.25:** [*Three-point perspective projection—vanishing point when COP is at the origin and the view plane has the equation* $n_x x + n_y y + n_z z = d$]

Use Eq. (8.83) to get the vanishing point of lines parallel to the $x$-axis when the center of projection is at the origin and view plane has the equation $n_x x + n_y y + n_z z = d$.

**Problem 8.26:** [*Three-point perspective projection—vanishing point when COP is at the origin and the view plane has the equation* $n_x x + n_y y + n_z z = d$]

Use Eq. (8.83) to get the vanishing point of lines parallel to the $y$-axis when the center of projection is at the origin and view plane has the equation $n_x x + n_y y + n_z z = d$.

## Reference

Foley, J.D., van Dam, A., Feiner, S.K., Hughes, J. 1995. The systems programming series. *Computer graphics: principles and practice in C*, 2nd edn. Reading: Addison-Wesley.

# Chapter 9
# View Transformations

**Abstract** Viewing in 3D space deals with more steps than projection transformations and projection types that have already been discussed in Chap. 8. The first step is to determine the view volume that contains the objects to be seen. This includes utilizing the world coordinate system (WCS) to specify a new coordinate system that is called the *view reference coordinate system* (VRC) (also known as *eye coordinate system* or *camera coordinate system*) and doing a normalization step to convert the view volume to what's called the *canonical view volume*. This step is followed by clipping against the view volume so that only objects or parts of objects within the view volume are kept. The projection concepts of Chap. 8 are then applied and mapping into a viewport is performed so that the result is ready to be displayed on the screen at the requested coordinates.

In this chapter, we talk about the viewing process and the use of clipping and projection transformation to obtain a 2D view on the screen as an outcome. In particular, Sect. 9.1 discusses coordinate system transformation according to the camera location and orientation to obtain the view reference coordinate system. Section 9.2 talks about view volume in general and the differences among view volumes in cases of orthographic, oblique and perspective projections. Normalizing the view volume results in a canonical view volume (Sects. 9.3 and 9.4). Clipping against the canonical view volume is discussed in Sect. 9.5. The 3D objects kept following the clipping process are projected (Sect. 9.6) and the positions of the projected objects are determined on the screen in Sect. 9.9 while Sect. 9.10 wraps up all the steps of the viewing pipeline.

## 9.1 View Transformation

In 3D space, objects are defined in world coordinate system. These objects are to be projected onto a viewing surface that is defined by the camera in 3D space as shown in Fig. 9.2. This viewing surface has its own coordinate system, which is called the view reference coordinate system.

R. Elias, *Digital Media*, DOI: 10.1007/978-3-319-05137-6_9, 

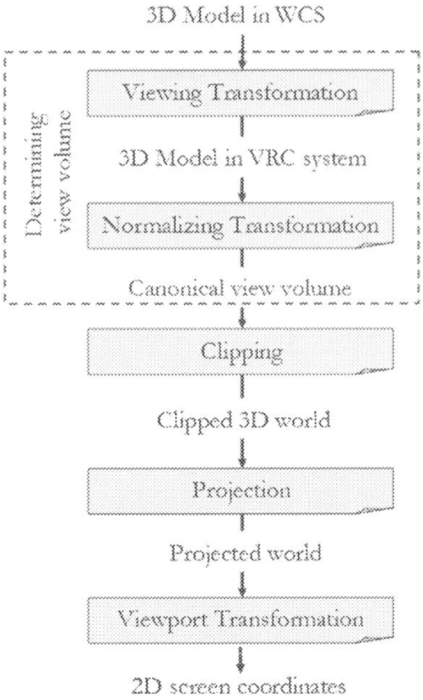


**Fig. 9.1** Viewing pipeline

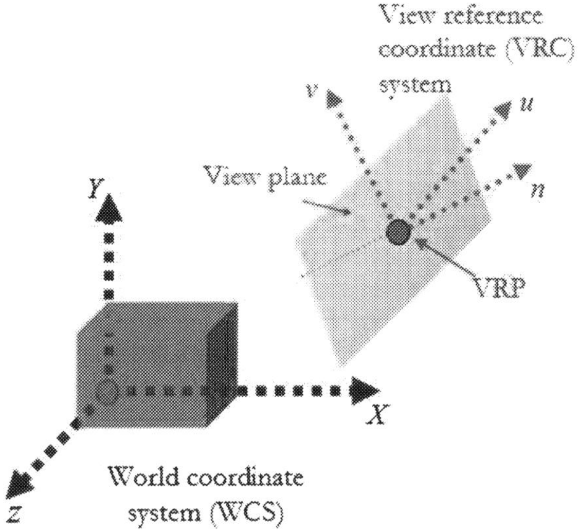


**Fig. 9.2** Objects in 3D space are defined in world coordinates. The viewing surface has its own coordinate system that is called the view reference coordinate system

In general, to transform/convert from the world coordinates to the view reference coordinates, the following steps are required:

1. Define the view reference coordinate system including its origin and its axes. This is discussed in Sect. 9.1.1.
2. For each vertex seen in 3D space, transform the coordinates to the view reference coordinate system. This is discussed in Sect. 9.1.2.

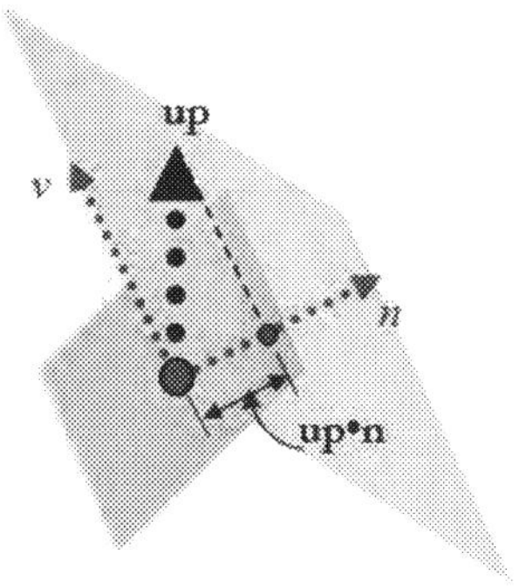


**Fig. 9.3** The **up** vector is *vertical* and *parallel* to the world $y$-axis. Since the **n** vector is normalized, the projection of **up** unto **n** is the dot product $\mathbf{up} \cdot \mathbf{n}$

## *9.1.1 View Reference Coordinate System*

The computer graphics camera is specified through its position, its up direction and where the camera is looking at (Sung et al. 2008). In particular, the view reference coordinate system can be specified by

1. determining the origin of the view reference coordinate system, which is called the view reference point (VRP);
2. determining the view plane normal vector **n** that points in the direction of the $n$-axis as discussed in Sect. 9.1.1.1;
3. determining the view plane vertical axis (i.e., $v$-axis) by specifying a unit vector **v** along that axis as discussed in Sect. 9.1.1.2; and
4. determining the view plane third axis (i.e., $u$-axis) by specifying a unit vector **u** along that axis as discussed in Sect. 9.1.1.3.

In the view reference coordinate system, both of the $u$-axis and the $v$-axis are on the view plane while the $n$-axis is normal (or perpendicular) to the view plane.

### 9.1.1.1 The $n$-Axis

The $n$-axis indicates the direction that is perpendicular to the view plane. The normal vector to the view plane is expressed in world coordinate system as $[x, y, z]^T$. This vector should be normalized (Sect. A.4.1) to get

$$\mathbf{n} = \begin{bmatrix} x_n \\ y_n \\ z_n \end{bmatrix} = \begin{bmatrix} \frac{x}{\sqrt{x^2+y^2+z^2}} \\ \frac{y}{\sqrt{x^2+y^2+z^2}} \\ \frac{z}{\sqrt{x^2+y^2+z^2}} \end{bmatrix}, \tag{9.1}$$

where **n** is a unit vector pointing along the $n$-direction.

#### 9.1.1.2 The $v$-Axis

The $v$-axis represents the vertical axis of the view reference coordinate system and it is indicated by the vector $\mathbf{v}$. But how can we estimate it? Let us proceed by specifying a vertical direction vector $\mathbf{up}$ as shown in Fig. 9.3 (i.e., $\mathbf{up}$ is parallel to the world vertical $y$-axis). Any 3D vector pointing upwards will do; e.g., $[0, 1, 0]^T$ or $[0, 8, 0]^T$ is very good. In other words, keep the first and the last components zeros. At this point, the vector $\mathbf{up}$ does not represent the vector $\mathbf{v}$ that we want. However, the vectors $\mathbf{up}$ and $\mathbf{n}$ span a plane that is perpendicular to the view plane and passing through the VRP as shown in Fig. 9.3. This plane intersects the view plane at the location of the $v$-axis. On this plane, we will get the projection of $\mathbf{up}$ unto $\mathbf{n}$. This can be done using Eq. (A.23):

$$|\text{proj}_{\mathbf{n}}\mathbf{up}| = \frac{\mathbf{up} \cdot \mathbf{n}}{\|\mathbf{n}\|},$$

where $\cdot$ denotes the dot product (Sect. A.4.3.2). Since $\|\mathbf{n}\| = 1$, the projection can be written as

$$|\text{proj}_{\mathbf{n}}\mathbf{up}| = \mathbf{up} \cdot \mathbf{n}.$$

A vector whose length is $\mathbf{up} \cdot \mathbf{n}$ along the $n$-direction can be obtained by multiplying the projection magnitude by the unit vector $\mathbf{n}$ as

$$(\mathbf{up} \cdot \mathbf{n})\mathbf{n}.$$

Notice that both the $\mathbf{up}$ vector as well as the $(\mathbf{up} \cdot \mathbf{n})\mathbf{n}$ vector span the plane that is perpendicular to the view plane. In order to get a vector $\mathbf{up}'$ along the intersection of this plane and the view plane, use vector subtraction as

$$\mathbf{up}' = \mathbf{up} - (\mathbf{up} \cdot \mathbf{n})\mathbf{n}. \tag{9.2}$$

The vector $\mathbf{up}'$ has to be normalized to get the vector $\mathbf{v}$ as

$$\mathbf{v} = \begin{bmatrix} x_v \\ y_v \\ z_v \end{bmatrix} = \frac{\mathbf{up}'}{\|\mathbf{up}'\|}, \tag{9.3}$$

where $\mathbf{v}$ is a unit vector pointing along the $v$-direction.

#### 9.1.1.3 The $u$-Axis

The $u$-axis is represented by the vector $\mathbf{u}$. This vector is perpendicular to both $\mathbf{n}$ and $\mathbf{v}$ vectors defining the other two axes. To establish a right-handed coordinate system as shown in Fig. 9.2, the **u** vector can be estimated by the cross product (Sect. A.4.3.3) as

$$\mathbf{u} = \begin{bmatrix} x_u \\ y_u \\ z_u \end{bmatrix} = \mathbf{v} \times \mathbf{n}. \tag{9.4}$$

In order to establish a left-handed coordinate system, the vector **u** is estimated as

$$\mathbf{u} = \mathbf{n} \times \mathbf{v}. \tag{9.5}$$

The overall rotation matrix used to rotate between the $x$-, $y$- and $z$-axes and the corresponding $u$-, $v$- and $n$-axes is expressed as

$$\dot{\mathrm{R}}_{VRC} = \begin{bmatrix} \mathbf{u}^T \\ \mathbf{v}^T \\ \mathbf{n}^T \end{bmatrix} = \begin{bmatrix} x_u \; y_u \; z_u \\ x_v \; y_v \; z_v \\ x_n \; y_n \; z_n \end{bmatrix}. \tag{9.6}$$

The matrix $\dot{\mathrm{R}}_{VRC}$ has all the properties of rotation matrices mentioned in Sect. 5.2.4. These properties are:

1. The inverse of $\dot{\mathrm{R}}_{VRC}$ is its transpose.
2. The determinant of $\dot{\mathrm{R}}_{VRC}$ has a unit value.
3. $\dot{\mathrm{R}}_{VRC}$ is normalized.
4. $\dot{\mathrm{R}}_{VRC}$ is orthogonal.

### *9.1.2 Coordinates Transformation*

Once the unit vectors representing the $u$-, $v$- and $n$-axes are determined, a 3D point $\dot{\mathbf{P}} = [x, y, z]^T$ previously expressed in the world coordinate system can now be expressed in the view reference coordinate system as $[u, v, n]^T$. The scalar value $u$ can be estimated as the projection of the vector starting from the VRP $\dot{\mathbf{R}} = [x_r, y_r, z_r]^T$ to the 3D point $\dot{\mathbf{P}}$ (i.e., $[\dot{\mathbf{P}} - \dot{\mathbf{R}}]$) onto the unit vector **u**. This can be done as

$$u = [\dot{\mathbf{P}} - \dot{\mathbf{R}}] \cdot \mathbf{u}. \tag{9.7}$$

$v$ and $n$ can be obtained the same way as

$$v = [\dot{\mathbf{P}} - \dot{\mathbf{R}}] \cdot \mathbf{v} \tag{9.8}$$

and

$$n = [\dot{\mathbf{P}} - \dot{\mathbf{R}}] \cdot \mathbf{n}. \tag{9.9}$$

Equations (9.7–9.9) can also be expressed as

$$\begin{bmatrix} u \\ v \\ n \end{bmatrix} = \begin{bmatrix} \mathbf{u}^T \\ \mathbf{v}^T \\ \mathbf{n}^T \end{bmatrix} [\dot{\mathbf{P}} - \dot{\mathbf{R}}] = \underbrace{\begin{bmatrix} x_u \; y_u \; z_u \\ x_v \; y_v \; z_v \\ x_n \; y_n \; z_n \end{bmatrix}}_{\dot{\mathtt{R}}_{VRC}} [\dot{\mathbf{P}} - \dot{\mathbf{R}}], \tag{9.10}$$

where $\dot{\mathbf{P}}$ is the 3D point to be converted; $\dot{\mathbf{R}}$ is the VRP; $\cdot$ represents the dot product; and $[u, v, n]^T$ is the point defined in the view reference coordinate system. In homogeneous coordinates (Sect. B.7), Eq. (9.10) can be expressed in two subsequent steps.

1. Translate point $\dot{\mathbf{P}}$ so that the origin coincides with $\dot{\mathbf{R}}$. This is done using the translation matrix $\mathtt{M}_1$ where

$$\mathtt{M}_1 = \mathtt{T}(-\dot{\mathbf{R}}) = \begin{bmatrix} 1\,0\,0 & -x_r \\ 0\,1\,0 & -y_r \\ 0\,0\,1 & -z_r \\ 0\,0\,0 & 1 \end{bmatrix}.$$

2. Transform to the new coordinate system using the matrix

$$\mathtt{M}_2 = \mathtt{R}_{VRC} = \begin{bmatrix} & & & 0 \\ & \dot{\mathtt{R}}_{VRC} & & 0 \\ & & & 0 \\ 0 & 0 & 0 & 1 \end{bmatrix} = \begin{bmatrix} x_u \; y_u \; z_u \; 0 \\ x_v \; y_v \; z_v \; 0 \\ x_n \; y_n \; z_n \; 0 \\ 0 \;\; 0 \;\; 0 \;\; 1 \end{bmatrix}. \tag{9.11}$$

The overall transformation can then be applied as

$$\begin{aligned} \mathtt{M} &= \mathtt{M}_2\mathtt{M}_1 \\ &= \begin{bmatrix} x_u \; y_u \; z_u \; 0 \\ x_v \; y_v \; z_v \; 0 \\ x_n \; y_n \; z_n \; 0 \\ 0 \;\; 0 \;\; 0 \;\; 1 \end{bmatrix} \begin{bmatrix} 1\,0\,0 & -x_r \\ 0\,1\,0 & -y_r \\ 0\,0\,1 & -z_r \\ 0\,0\,0 & 1 \end{bmatrix} \\ &= \begin{bmatrix} x_u \; y_u \; z_u & -x_u x_r - y_u y_r - z_u z_r \\ x_v \; y_v \; z_v & -x_v x_r - y_v y_r - z_v z_r \\ x_n \; y_n \; z_n & -x_n x_r - y_n y_r - z_n z_r \\ 0 \;\; 0 \;\; 0 & 1 \end{bmatrix} \\ &= \begin{bmatrix} \mathbf{u}^T & -\mathbf{u} \cdot \dot{\mathbf{R}} \\ \mathbf{v}^T & -\mathbf{v} \cdot \dot{\mathbf{R}} \\ \mathbf{n}^T & -\mathbf{n} \cdot \dot{\mathbf{R}} \\ 0 \;\; 0 \;\; 0 & 1 \end{bmatrix}, \end{aligned} \tag{9.12}$$

which performs that same operation as Eq. (9.10).

**Example 9.1:** [*View reference coordinate system—expressing points in view reference coordinate system given their world coordinates*]

A right-handed 3D world coordinate system is defined by an origin at $[0, 0, 0]^T$; an $x$-axis, which is indicated by the unit vector $[1, 0, 0]^T$; a $y$-axis, which is indicated by the unit vector $[0, 1, 0]^T$; and a $z$-axis, which is indicated by the unit vector $[0, 0, 1]^T$.

A new right-handed coordinate system, having the $u$-, $v$- and $n$-axes, is to be defined in terms of the old one. The information available is the new origin that is located at $[4, 5, 6]^T$ and the $n$-axis that is indicated by the vector $[5, 7, -5]^T$.

If there is a 3D point located at $[5, 6, 7]^T$ in terms of the old system, specify its location in terms of the new coordinate system.

**Solution 9.1:** As discussed above, there are two steps:

1. Specify the view reference coordinate system.
   (a) The origin is located at $[4, 5, 6]^T$ as given.
   (b) The $n$-axis is given by the $\mathbf{n}$ vector; however, it is not normalized. To normalize it, divide by its norm as in Eq. (9.1); thus,

$$\mathbf{n} = \begin{bmatrix} \frac{5}{\sqrt{5^2+7^2+(-5)^2}} \\ \frac{7}{\sqrt{5^2+7^2+(-5)^2}} \\ \frac{-5}{\sqrt{5^2+7^2+(-5)^2}} \end{bmatrix} = \begin{bmatrix} 0.5025 \\ 0.7035 \\ -0.5025 \end{bmatrix}.$$

   (c) Determine the $\mathbf{up}'$ vector using Eq. (9.2) where

$$\begin{aligned}\mathbf{up}' &= \mathbf{up} - (\mathbf{up} \cdot \mathbf{n})\mathbf{n} \\ &= \begin{bmatrix} 0 \\ 1 \\ 0 \end{bmatrix} - \left( \begin{bmatrix} 0 \\ 1 \\ 0 \end{bmatrix} \cdot \begin{bmatrix} \frac{5}{3\sqrt{11}} \\ \frac{7}{3\sqrt{11}} \\ -\frac{5}{3\sqrt{11}} \end{bmatrix} \right) \begin{bmatrix} \frac{5}{3\sqrt{11}} \\ \frac{7}{3\sqrt{11}} \\ -\frac{5}{3\sqrt{11}} \end{bmatrix} = \begin{bmatrix} -0.3535 \\ 0.5051 \\ 0.3535 \end{bmatrix}\end{aligned}$$

   and the $\mathbf{v}$ vector using Eq. (9.3) where

$$\mathbf{v} = \frac{\mathbf{up}'}{\|\mathbf{up}'\|} = \begin{bmatrix} \frac{-35}{\sqrt{35^2+50^2+(-35)^2}} \\ \frac{50}{\sqrt{35^2+50^2+(-35)^2}} \\ \frac{35}{\sqrt{35^2+50^2+(-35)^2}} \end{bmatrix} = \begin{bmatrix} -0.4975 \\ 0.7107 \\ 0.4975 \end{bmatrix}.$$

   (d) Determine the $\mathbf{u}$ vector using Eq. (9.4) where

$$\mathbf{u} = \mathbf{v} \times \mathbf{n} = \begin{bmatrix} -0.4975 \\ 0.7107 \\ 0.4975 \end{bmatrix} \times \begin{bmatrix} 0.5025 \\ 0.70353 \\ -0.5025 \end{bmatrix} = \begin{bmatrix} -0.7071 \\ 0 \\ -0.7071 \end{bmatrix}.$$

2. Express the 3D point $[5, 6, 7]^T$ in the view reference coordinate system using Eq. (9.7) through Eq. (9.9). Thus,

$$\begin{aligned} u &= (\dot{\mathbf{P}} - \dot{\mathbf{R}}) \cdot \mathbf{u} \\ &= \left( \begin{bmatrix} 5 \\ 6 \\ 7 \end{bmatrix} - \begin{bmatrix} 4 \\ 5 \\ 6 \end{bmatrix} \right) \cdot \begin{bmatrix} -0.7071 \\ 0 \\ -0.7071 \end{bmatrix} = -1.4142, \end{aligned}$$

$$\begin{aligned} v &= (\dot{\mathbf{P}} - \dot{\mathbf{R}}) \cdot \mathbf{v} \\ &= \left( \begin{bmatrix} 5 \\ 6 \\ 7 \end{bmatrix} - \begin{bmatrix} 4 \\ 5 \\ 6 \end{bmatrix} \right) \cdot \begin{bmatrix} -0.4975 \\ 0.7107 \\ 0.4975 \end{bmatrix} = 0.7107, \end{aligned}$$

$$\begin{aligned} n &= (\dot{\mathbf{P}} - \dot{\mathbf{R}}) \cdot \mathbf{n} \\ &= \left( \begin{bmatrix} 5 \\ 6 \\ 7 \end{bmatrix} - \begin{bmatrix} 4 \\ 5 \\ 6 \end{bmatrix} \right) \cdot \begin{bmatrix} 0.5025 \\ 0.7035 \\ -0.5025 \end{bmatrix} = 0.7035. \end{aligned}$$

Thus, the 3D point located at $[5, 6, 7]^T$ can be expressed in the view reference coordinate system as $[-1.4142, 0.7107, 0.7035]^T$. □

**Example 9.2:** [*Isometric projection—points given a view plane normal vector*]
Consider a unit cube with two of its corners placed at $[0, 0, 0]^T$ and $[1, 1, 1]^T$. Given a view plane with a normal vector $[1, 1, 1]^T$ and view reference point at $[4, 4, 4]^T$, determine the isometric projection of its corners onto the view plane.

**Solution 9.2:** The transformation to the view reference coordinate system can be used to get the isometric projection of the points onto the $uv$-plane. [Note that the same points should be obtained onto the $xy$-plane using the projection matrix of Eq. (8.34).] The steps are as follows:

1. Specify the view reference coordinate system.
   (a) The origin is located at $[4, 4, 4]^T$ as given.
   (b) The $n$-axis is given by the normal vector $[1, 1, 1]^T$; however, it is not normalized. To normalize it, divide by its norm as in Eq. (9.1). Thus,

$$\mathbf{n} = \begin{bmatrix} \frac{1}{\sqrt{1^2+1^2+1^2}} \\ \frac{1}{\sqrt{1^2+1^2+1^2}} \\ \frac{1}{\sqrt{1^2+1^2+1^2}} \end{bmatrix} = \begin{bmatrix} \frac{1}{\sqrt{3}} \\ \frac{1}{\sqrt{3}} \\ \frac{1}{\sqrt{3}} \end{bmatrix} = \begin{bmatrix} 0.5774 \\ 0.5774 \\ 0.5774 \end{bmatrix}.$$

   (c) Determine the $\mathbf{up}'$ vector using Eq. (9.2) where

$$\begin{aligned}\mathbf{up}' &= \mathbf{up} - (\mathbf{up} \cdot \mathbf{n})\mathbf{n} \\ &= \begin{bmatrix} 0 \\ 1 \\ 0 \end{bmatrix} - \left( \begin{bmatrix} 0 \\ 1 \\ 0 \end{bmatrix} \cdot \begin{bmatrix} \frac{1}{\sqrt{3}} \\ \frac{1}{\sqrt{3}} \\ \frac{1}{\sqrt{3}} \end{bmatrix} \right) \begin{bmatrix} \frac{1}{\sqrt{3}} \\ \frac{1}{\sqrt{3}} \\ \frac{1}{\sqrt{3}} \end{bmatrix} = \begin{bmatrix} -\frac{1}{3} \\ \frac{2}{3} \\ -\frac{1}{3} \end{bmatrix} = \begin{bmatrix} -0.3333 \\ 0.6667 \\ -0.3333 \end{bmatrix}\end{aligned}$$

and the $\mathbf{v}$ vector using Eq. (9.3) where

$$\mathbf{v} = \frac{\mathbf{up}'}{\|\mathbf{up}'\|} = \begin{bmatrix} \frac{-\frac{1}{3}}{\sqrt{\left(-\frac{1}{3}\right)^2 + \left(\frac{2}{3}\right)^2 + \left(-\frac{1}{3}\right)^2}} \\ \frac{\frac{2}{3}}{\sqrt{\left(-\frac{1}{3}\right)^2 + \left(\frac{2}{3}\right)^2 + \left(-\frac{1}{3}\right)^2}} \\ \frac{-\frac{1}{3}}{\sqrt{\left(-\frac{1}{3}\right)^2 + \left(\frac{2}{3}\right)^2 + \left(-\frac{1}{3}\right)^2}} \end{bmatrix} = \begin{bmatrix} -\frac{1}{\sqrt{6}} \\ \frac{2}{\sqrt{6}} \\ -\frac{1}{\sqrt{6}} \end{bmatrix} = \begin{bmatrix} -0.4082 \\ 0.8165 \\ -0.4082 \end{bmatrix}.$$

(d) Determine the $\mathbf{u}$ vector using Eq. (9.4) where

$$\mathbf{u} = \mathbf{v} \times \mathbf{n} = \begin{bmatrix} -\frac{1}{\sqrt{6}} \\ \frac{2}{\sqrt{6}} \\ -\frac{1}{\sqrt{6}} \end{bmatrix} \times \begin{bmatrix} \frac{1}{\sqrt{3}} \\ \frac{1}{\sqrt{3}} \\ \frac{1}{\sqrt{3}} \end{bmatrix} = \begin{bmatrix} \frac{1}{\sqrt{2}} \\ 0 \\ -\frac{1}{\sqrt{2}} \end{bmatrix} = \begin{bmatrix} 0.7071 \\ 0 \\ -0.7071 \end{bmatrix}.$$

2. Express the corners of the unit cube in view reference coordinates using Eq. (9.7) through Eq. (9.9). Let us take the point $[1, 0, 0]^T$ as an example. The rest of the points can be obtained the same way. The $u$ and $v$ values are

$$\begin{aligned}u &= (\dot{\mathbf{P}} - \dot{\mathbf{R}}) \cdot \mathbf{u} \\ &= \left( \begin{bmatrix} 1 \\ 0 \\ 0 \end{bmatrix} - \begin{bmatrix} 4 \\ 4 \\ 4 \end{bmatrix} \right) \cdot \begin{bmatrix} \frac{1}{\sqrt{2}} \\ 0 \\ -\frac{1}{\sqrt{2}} \end{bmatrix} = \frac{1}{\sqrt{2}} = 0.7071\end{aligned}$$

and

$$\begin{aligned}v &= (\dot{\mathbf{P}} - \dot{\mathbf{R}}) \cdot \mathbf{v} \\ &= \left( \begin{bmatrix} 1 \\ 0 \\ 0 \end{bmatrix} - \begin{bmatrix} 4 \\ 4 \\ 4 \end{bmatrix} \right) \cdot \begin{bmatrix} -\frac{1}{\sqrt{6}} \\ \frac{2}{\sqrt{6}} \\ -\frac{1}{\sqrt{6}} \end{bmatrix} = -\frac{1}{\sqrt{6}} = -0.4082.\end{aligned}$$

Thus, the corner located at $[1, 0, 0]^T$ is projected onto the $uv$-plane as $[0.7071, -0.4082]^T$. Notice that in this solution, we did only coordinate transformation. Of course, the point after this transformation is a 3D point $[u, v, n]^T$. The third coordinate (i.e., the $n$-coordinate) is neglected as we need a front projection onto the $uv$-plane. The locations of the rest of projected points are given in the following table:

| $\dot{\mathbf{P}} = [x, y, z]^T$ | $\dot{\mathbf{p}} = [u, v]^T$ |
|---|---|
| $[0, 0, 0]^T$ | $[0, 0]^T$ |
| $[1, 0, 0]^T$ | $[0.7071, -0.4082]^T$ |
| $[0, 1, 0]^T$ | $[0, 0.8165]^T$ |
| $[1, 1, 0]^T$ | $[0.7071, 0.4082]^T$ |
| $[0, 0, 1]^T$ | $[-0.7071, -0.4082]^T$ |
| $[1, 0, 1]^T$ | $[0, -0.8165]^T$ |
| $[0, 1, 1]^T$ | $[-0.7071, 0.4082]^T$ |
| $[1, 1, 1]^T$ | $[0, 0]^T$ |

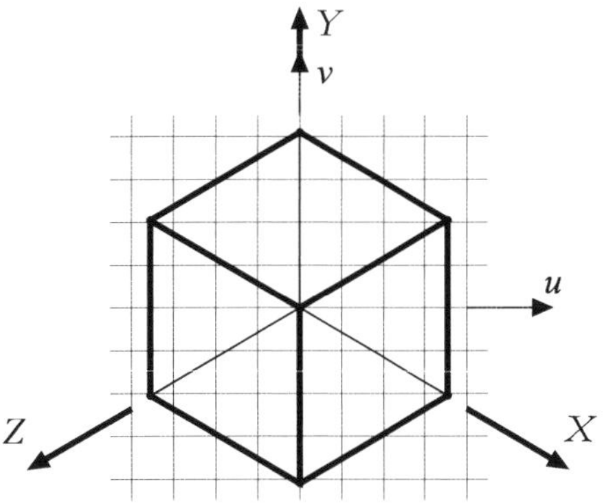


**Fig. 9.4** An isometric projection for a unit cube drawn on a $0.2 \times 0.2$ grid. The normal vector to the view plane is $[1, 1, 1]^T$ and the view reference point is $[4, 4, 4]^T$. Notice that there are two coordinate systems shown; the 3D coordinate system including $x$-, $y$- and $z$-axes as well as the 2D view reference coordinate system including $u$- and $v$-axes

These are the same points obtained using the projection matrix in Example 8.3.

The isometric projection for the unit cube drawn on a $0.2 \times 0.2$ grid is shown in Fig. 9.4. □

**Example 9.3:** [*View reference coordinate system—expressing points in world coordinates given their view reference coordinates*]

If the location $\dot{\mathbf{Q}}$ of a point is defined in view reference coordinate system, write an equation to estimate the same location $\dot{\mathbf{P}}$ in world coordinate system if the following consider world coordinates:

1. A unit vector $\mathbf{u}$ along the $u$-direction.
2. A unit vector $\mathbf{v}$ along the $v$-direction.
3. A unit vector $\mathbf{n}$ along the $n$-direction.
4. A vector $\dot{\mathbf{R}}$ representing the VRP.

**Solution 9.3:** Equation (9.10) is used to get the location of $\dot{\mathbf{Q}}$ as

$$\dot{\mathbf{Q}} = \begin{bmatrix} \mathbf{u}^T \\ \mathbf{v}^T \\ \mathbf{n}^T \end{bmatrix} \left[\dot{\mathbf{P}} - \dot{\mathbf{R}}\right].$$

Hence, $\dot{\mathbf{P}}$ can be obtained as

$$\dot{\mathbf{P}} = \left[ \begin{bmatrix} \mathbf{u}^T \\ \mathbf{v}^T \\ \mathbf{n}^T \end{bmatrix}^{-1} \dot{\mathbf{Q}} \right] + \dot{\mathbf{R}}, \tag{9.13}$$

where $\dot{\mathbf{P}}$ is the location of the point in the world coordinate system; $\dot{\mathbf{Q}}$ is the location of the same point in the view reference coordinate system; and $\mathbf{u}$, $\mathbf{v}$ and $\mathbf{n}$ are the unit vectors along the $u$-, $v$- and $n$-axes respectively. □

**Example 9.4:** [*View reference coordinate system—expressing points in world coordinates given their view reference coordinates*]

Assume that $\dot{\mathbf{Q}} = [-1.4142, 0.7107, 0.7035]^T$ is the location of a point defined in view reference coordinate system. In world coordinate system, if the VRP is located at $[4, 5, 6]^T$, the $n$-axis is indicated by the vector $[5, 7, -5]^T$ and the $v$-axis is indicated by the vector $[-0.4975, 0.7107, 0.4975]^T$, express the location $\dot{\mathbf{P}}$ of the point in world coordinates.

**Solution 9.4:** The vector $[5, 7, -5]^T$ is normalized as

$$\mathbf{n} = \begin{bmatrix} \frac{5}{\sqrt{5^2+7^2+(-5)^2}} \\ \frac{7}{\sqrt{5^2+7^2+(-5)^2}} \\ \frac{-5}{\sqrt{5^2+7^2+(-5)^2}} \end{bmatrix} = \begin{bmatrix} 0.5025 \\ 0.7035 \\ -0.5025 \end{bmatrix}.$$

The norm of the vector $\mathbf{v} = [-0.4975, 0.7107, 0.4975]^T$ is 1; thus, it does not have to be normalized. The vector $\mathbf{u}$ is obtained as

$$\mathbf{u} = \mathbf{v} \times \mathbf{n} = \begin{bmatrix} -0.4975 \\ 0.7107 \\ 0.4975 \end{bmatrix} \times \begin{bmatrix} 0.5025 \\ 0.70353 \\ -0.5025 \end{bmatrix} = \begin{bmatrix} -0.7071 \\ 0 \\ -0.7071 \end{bmatrix}.$$

Consequently, $\dot{\mathbf{P}}$ is estimated using Eq. (9.13) as

$$\begin{aligned} \dot{\mathbf{P}} &= \left[ \begin{bmatrix} \mathbf{u}^T \\ \mathbf{v}^T \\ \mathbf{n}^T \end{bmatrix}^{-1} \dot{\mathbf{Q}} \right] + \dot{\mathbf{R}} \\ &= \left[ \begin{bmatrix} -0.7071 & 0 & -0.7071 \\ -0.4975 & 0.7107 & 0.4975 \\ 0.5025 & 0.70353 & -0.5025 \end{bmatrix}^{-1} \begin{bmatrix} -1.4142 \\ 0.7107 \\ 0.7035 \end{bmatrix} \right] + \begin{bmatrix} 4 \\ 5 \\ 6 \end{bmatrix} = \begin{bmatrix} 5 \\ 6 \\ 7 \end{bmatrix}. \end{aligned}$$ □

**Example 9.5:** [*View reference coordinate system—expressing points in world coordinates given their view reference coordinates*]

Re-solve Example 9.3 using homogeneous coordinates.

**Solution 9.5:** We use the inverse of the transformation matrix of Eq. (9.12). Thus,

$$\mathbf{P} = \begin{bmatrix} \mathbf{u}^T & -\mathbf{u} \cdot \dot{\mathbf{R}} \\ \mathbf{v}^T & -\mathbf{v} \cdot \dot{\mathbf{R}} \\ \mathbf{n}^T & -\mathbf{n} \cdot \dot{\mathbf{R}} \\ 0\ 0\ 0 & 1 \end{bmatrix}^{-1} \mathbf{Q},$$

where $\mathbf{P}$ is a homogeneous point expressed in world coordinates; $\mathbf{u}$, $\mathbf{v}$ and $\mathbf{n}$ are unit vectors along the $u$-, $v$- and $n$-axes of the view reference coordinate system; $\dot{\mathbf{R}}$ is the inhomogeneous representation of the origin of the view reference coordinate system expressed in world coordinates; $\mathbf{Q}$ is the homogeneous representation of the point expressed in view reference coordinates; and $\cdot$ denotes the dot product. □

**Example 9.6:** [*View reference coordinate system—rotation matrix*]
$\dot{\text{R}}_{VRC}$ of Eq. (9.6) represents the rotation operation from the world coordinate system to the view reference coordinate system. The rows of this matrix are the vectors $\mathbf{u}$, $\mathbf{v}$ and $\mathbf{n}$. The sequence of obtaining these vectors is $\mathbf{n}$ followed by $\mathbf{v}$ (using the **up** vector) and finally $\mathbf{u}$. Explain another route for obtaining the same matrix $\dot{\text{R}}_{VRC}$ by getting the vectors $\mathbf{n}$ followed by $\mathbf{u}$ (using the **up** vector) and finally $\mathbf{v}$.

**Solution 9.6:** The steps are as follows:

1. Get the vector $\mathbf{n}$ as done before.
2. Get the vector $\mathbf{u}$: We know that the vectors $\mathbf{up} = [0, 1, 0]^T$, $\mathbf{v}$ and $\mathbf{n}$ originate from the VRP and reside on the same plane that is perpendicular to the vector $\mathbf{u}$. Thus, normalized $\mathbf{u}$ vector is determined as

$$\mathbf{u} = \frac{\mathbf{up} \times \mathbf{n}}{\|\mathbf{up} \times \mathbf{n}\|},$$

   where $\times$ and $\|.\|$ denote the cross product and the norm respectively.
3. Get the vector $\mathbf{v}$ as the cross product of the previous two vectors. Thus,

$$\mathbf{v} = \mathbf{n} \times \mathbf{u}.$$

Hence, the overall rotation is expressed as

$$\dot{\text{R}}_{VRC} = \begin{bmatrix} \mathbf{u}^T \\ \mathbf{v}^T \\ \mathbf{n}^T \end{bmatrix} = \begin{bmatrix} x_u\ y_u\ z_u \\ x_v\ y_v\ z_v \\ x_n\ y_n\ z_n \end{bmatrix}.$$ □

**Example 9.7:** [*View reference coordinate system—expressing points in view reference coordinates given their world coordinates*]
Obtain the vectors $\mathbf{u}$ and $\mathbf{v}$ of Example 9.1 using the method mentioned in Example 9.6.

**Solution 9.7:** From Example 9.1, we know that

$$\mathbf{n} = \begin{bmatrix} \frac{5}{\sqrt{5^2+7^2+(-5)^2}} \\ \frac{7}{\sqrt{5^2+7^2+(-5)^2}} \\ \frac{-5}{\sqrt{5^2+7^2+(-5)^2}} \end{bmatrix} = \begin{bmatrix} 0.5025 \\ 0.7035 \\ -0.5025 \end{bmatrix}.$$

Also, from Example 9.6, we know that

$$\mathbf{u} = \frac{\mathbf{up} \times \mathbf{n}}{\|\mathbf{up} \times \mathbf{n}\|}.$$

So,

$$\mathbf{u} = \frac{\begin{bmatrix} 0 \\ 1 \\ 0 \end{bmatrix} \times \begin{bmatrix} 0.5025 \\ 0.7035 \\ -0.5025 \end{bmatrix}}{\left\| \begin{bmatrix} 0 \\ 1 \\ 0 \end{bmatrix} \times \begin{bmatrix} 0.5025 \\ 0.7035 \\ -0.5025 \end{bmatrix} \right\|} = \begin{bmatrix} -0.7071 \\ 0 \\ -0.7071 \end{bmatrix}$$

Also, from Example 9.6, we know that

$$\mathbf{v} = \mathbf{n} \times \mathbf{u}.$$

So, the vector $\mathbf{v}$ is obtained as

$$\mathbf{v} = \begin{bmatrix} 0.5025 \\ 0.7035 \\ -0.5025 \end{bmatrix} \times \begin{bmatrix} -0.7071 \\ 0 \\ -0.7071 \end{bmatrix} = \begin{bmatrix} -0.4975 \\ 0.7107 \\ 0.4975 \end{bmatrix},$$

which are the same vectors obtained in Example 9.1. □

## 9.2 View Volume

The view volume represents a part of the 3D space under consideration. Objects in the view volume are projected onto the view plane while the rest of the world is neglected (unless reflected off or refracted through surfaces appearing in the view volume); a process that is done by means of clipping.

In order to determine the view volume, a window is determined on the $uv$ view plane, as shown in Fig. 9.5, by specifying the extreme points $[u_{min}, v_{min}]^T$ and $[u_{max}, v_{max}]^T$ in the VRC system. Notice that the center of the window does not have to coincide with the origin of the VRC system (i.e., the VRP). A view volume may be infinite or finite.

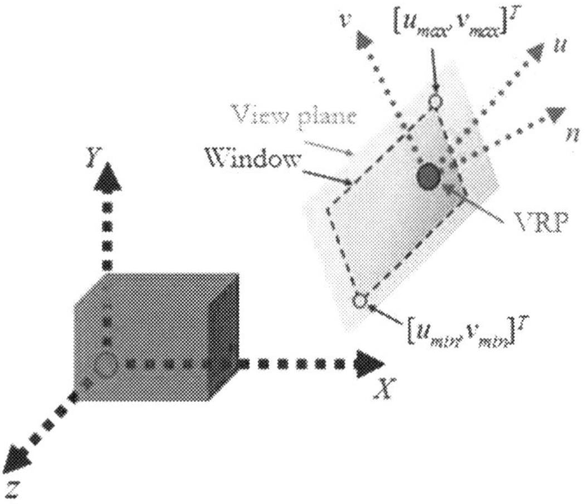


**Fig. 9.5** A window is determined on the view plane by specifying the extreme points $[u_{min}, v_{min}]^T$ and $[u_{max}, v_{max}]^T$ in the VRC system. In this example, the center of the window does not coincide with the VRP

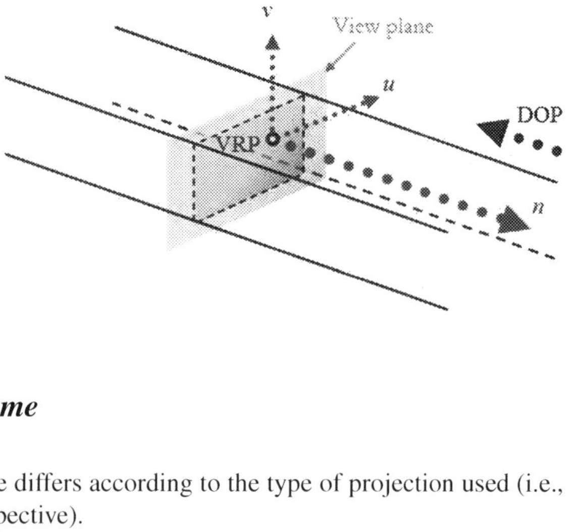


**Fig. 9.6** Infinite parallelepiped view volume of the orthographic projection

## 9.2.1 *Infinite View Volume*

The shape of the view volume differs according to the type of projection used (i.e., orthographic, oblique or perspective).

### 9.2.1.1 Orthographic Projection

In case of orthographic projection, an infinite parallelepiped view volume is considered as shown in Fig. 9.6. In this case, the *direction of projection* (DOP) is parallel to the $n$-axis of the VRC system but points in the opposite direction. Practically, the DOP may be determined by specifying a point, called the *projection reference point* (PRP), and the center of the window on the view plane (i.e., $\left[\frac{u_{min}+u_{max}}{2}, \frac{v_{min}+v_{max}}{2}\right]^T$). The boundaries of the view volume are four planes determined by the four sides of the window and the DOP. Each of those planes is normal to the view plane.

**Example 9.8:** [*Direction of projection—orthographic projection*]

Assume that the view reference coordinate system coincides with the right-handed world coordinate system. If the window of the view plane is determined by the points $[u_{min}, v_{min}]^T = [2, 6]^T$ and $[u_{max}, v_{max}]^T = [6, 8]^T$ and the projection reference point is located at $\dot{\mathbf{P}} = [4, 7, 9]^T$, determine the direction of projection in this case.

**Solution 9.8:** As long as the view reference coordinate system coincides with the right-handed world coordinate system, it can be said that the view plane window is determined by the points $[2, 6, 0]^T$ and $[6, 8, 0]^T$ expressed in world coordinates. Hence, the center of the view plane window is located at

$$\dot{\mathbf{C}} = \frac{1}{2}\left(\begin{bmatrix} 2 \\ 6 \\ 0 \end{bmatrix} + \begin{bmatrix} 6 \\ 8 \\ 0 \end{bmatrix}\right) = \begin{bmatrix} 4 \\ 7 \\ 0 \end{bmatrix}.$$

Notice that the center of the view plane window does not coincide with the VRP; i.e., $[0, 0, 0]^T$, which is not even within the window boundaries. The direction of projection is then determined as

$$\dot{\mathbf{C}} - \dot{\mathbf{P}} = \begin{bmatrix} 4 \\ 7 \\ 0 \end{bmatrix} - \begin{bmatrix} 4 \\ 7 \\ 9 \end{bmatrix} = \begin{bmatrix} 0 \\ 0 \\ -9 \end{bmatrix}.$$

Notice that the direction of projection is pointing opposite to the normal of the view plane. □

**Example 9.9:** [*Clipping planes in world coordinates—infinite orthographic view volume*]

Consider a view reference coordinate system such that the $n$-axis is indicated by the unit vector $\mathbf{n} = \left[\frac{1}{\sqrt{3}}, \frac{1}{\sqrt{3}}, \frac{1}{\sqrt{3}}\right]^T$ and the VRP is positioned at $[4, 4, 4]^T$. If a window that extends from $[u_{min}, u_{max}]^T = [-2, -2]^T$ to $[v_{min}, v_{max}]^T = [2, 2]^T$ on the $uv$-plane is used to specify an infinite orthographic view volume, determine the planes bounding that volume in world coordinates.

**Solution 9.9:** A plane equation can be estimated if the normal to the plane as well as a point on that plane are known. Since the bounding planes are normal (i.e., perpendicular) to the view plane, their normal vectors can be determined using the $\mathbf{u}$ and $\mathbf{v}$ vectors. The extreme $uv$-points (i.e., $[-2, -2]^T$ and $[2, 2]^T$) of the window can be obtained in world coordinates to represent the points on the bounding planes.

As done in previous examples, we determine $\mathbf{up}'$ using Eq. (9.2) as

$$\begin{aligned}
\mathbf{up}' &= \mathbf{up} - (\mathbf{up} \cdot \mathbf{n})\mathbf{n} \\
&= \begin{bmatrix} 0 \\ 1 \\ 0 \end{bmatrix} - \left(\begin{bmatrix} 0 \\ 1 \\ 0 \end{bmatrix} \cdot \begin{bmatrix} \frac{1}{\sqrt{3}} \\ \frac{1}{\sqrt{3}} \\ \frac{1}{\sqrt{3}} \end{bmatrix}\right) \begin{bmatrix} \frac{1}{\sqrt{3}} \\ \frac{1}{\sqrt{3}} \\ \frac{1}{\sqrt{3}} \end{bmatrix} = \begin{bmatrix} -\frac{1}{3} \\ \frac{2}{3} \\ -\frac{1}{3} \end{bmatrix} = \begin{bmatrix} -0.3333 \\ 0.6667 \\ -0.3333 \end{bmatrix}
\end{aligned}$$

and the vector **v** using Eq. (9.3) as

$$\mathbf{v} = \frac{\mathbf{up}'}{\|\mathbf{up}'\|} = \begin{bmatrix} \frac{-\frac{1}{3}}{\sqrt{\left(-\frac{1}{3}\right)^2+\left(\frac{2}{3}\right)^2+\left(-\frac{1}{3}\right)^2}} \\ \frac{\frac{2}{3}}{\sqrt{\left(-\frac{1}{3}\right)^2+\left(\frac{2}{3}\right)^2+\left(-\frac{1}{3}\right)^2}} \\ \frac{-\frac{1}{3}}{\sqrt{\left(-\frac{1}{3}\right)^2+\left(\frac{2}{3}\right)^2+\left(-\frac{1}{3}\right)^2}} \end{bmatrix} = \begin{bmatrix} -\frac{1}{\sqrt{6}} \\ \frac{2}{\sqrt{6}} \\ -\frac{1}{\sqrt{6}} \end{bmatrix} = \begin{bmatrix} -0.4082 \\ 0.8165 \\ -0.4082 \end{bmatrix}.$$

We also determine the vector **u** as the cross product $\mathbf{v} \times \mathbf{n}$. Thus,

$$\mathbf{u} = \mathbf{v} \times \mathbf{n} = \begin{bmatrix} -\frac{1}{\sqrt{6}} \\ \frac{2}{\sqrt{6}} \\ -\frac{1}{\sqrt{6}} \end{bmatrix} \times \begin{bmatrix} \frac{1}{\sqrt{3}} \\ \frac{1}{\sqrt{3}} \\ \frac{1}{\sqrt{3}} \end{bmatrix} = \begin{bmatrix} \frac{1}{\sqrt{2}} \\ 0 \\ -\frac{1}{\sqrt{2}} \end{bmatrix} = \begin{bmatrix} 0.7071 \\ 0 \\ -0.7071 \end{bmatrix}.$$

**Corners of the view plane window in WCS**: Now we get the corners of the *uv*-window in world coordinates. In the VRC system, the corner $[-2, -2]^T$ has the coordinates $\dot{\mathbf{Q}} = [-2, -2, 0]^T$. Its world coordinates are estimated using Eq. (9.13) as

$$\begin{aligned} \dot{\mathbf{P}}_{[-2,-2]^T} &= \left[ \begin{bmatrix} \mathbf{u}^T \\ \mathbf{v}^T \\ \mathbf{n}^T \end{bmatrix}^{-1} \dot{\mathbf{Q}} \right] + \dot{\mathbf{R}} \\ &= \left[ \begin{bmatrix} \frac{1}{\sqrt{2}} & 0 & -\frac{1}{\sqrt{2}} \\ -\frac{1}{\sqrt{6}} & \frac{2}{\sqrt{6}} & -\frac{1}{\sqrt{6}} \\ \frac{1}{\sqrt{3}} & \frac{1}{\sqrt{3}} & \frac{1}{\sqrt{3}} \end{bmatrix}^{-1} \begin{bmatrix} -2 \\ -2 \\ 0 \end{bmatrix} \right] + \begin{bmatrix} 4 \\ 4 \\ 4 \end{bmatrix} = \begin{bmatrix} 3.4023 \\ 2.3670 \\ 6.2307 \end{bmatrix}. \end{aligned}$$

Similarly, the *uv*-point $[2, 2]^T$ is obtained in world coordinates as

$$\dot{\mathbf{P}}_{[2,2]^T} = \left[ \begin{bmatrix} \frac{1}{\sqrt{2}} & 0 & -\frac{1}{\sqrt{2}} \\ -\frac{1}{\sqrt{6}} & \frac{2}{\sqrt{6}} & -\frac{1}{\sqrt{6}} \\ \frac{1}{\sqrt{3}} & \frac{1}{\sqrt{3}} & \frac{1}{\sqrt{3}} \end{bmatrix}^{-1} \begin{bmatrix} 2 \\ 2 \\ 0 \end{bmatrix} \right] + \begin{bmatrix} 4 \\ 4 \\ 4 \end{bmatrix} = \begin{bmatrix} 4.5977 \\ 5.6330 \\ 1.7693 \end{bmatrix}.$$

**Plane equations**: The general equation of a plane is

$$x_n x + y_n y + z_n z = d,$$

where $[x_n, y_n, z_n]^T$ is the normal **n** to the plane; $[x, y, z]^T$ is a point $\dot{\mathbf{P}}$ on the plane; and $d$ is the perpendicular distance from the origin to the plane when **n** is normalized. Hence,

$$d = \mathbf{n} \cdot \dot{\mathbf{P}},$$

where $\cdot$ denotes the dot product.

The left bounding plane is obtained using $\mathbf{u}$ as the normal vector and $\dot{\mathbf{P}}_{[-2,-2]^T}$ as a point on the plane. Thus,

$$\begin{aligned} d_{left} &= \mathbf{u} \cdot \dot{\mathbf{P}}_{[-2,-2]^T} \\ &= \begin{bmatrix} 0.7071 \\ 0 \\ -0.7071 \end{bmatrix} \cdot \begin{bmatrix} 3.4023 \\ 2.3670 \\ 6.2307 \end{bmatrix} = -2. \end{aligned}$$

This means that the equation of the left plane is

$$\frac{x}{\sqrt{2}} - \frac{z}{\sqrt{2}} = -2 \qquad \text{or} \qquad x - z = -2\sqrt{2}.$$

The right bounding plane is obtained using $\mathbf{u}$ and $\dot{\mathbf{P}}_{[2,2]^T}$. Thus,

$$\begin{aligned} d_{right} &= \mathbf{u} \cdot \dot{\mathbf{P}}_{[2,2]^T} \\ &= \begin{bmatrix} 0.7071 \\ 0 \\ -0.7071 \end{bmatrix} \cdot \begin{bmatrix} 4.5977 \\ 5.6330 \\ 1.7693 \end{bmatrix} = 2. \end{aligned}$$

This means that the equation of the right plane is

$$\frac{x}{\sqrt{2}} - \frac{z}{\sqrt{2}} = 2 \qquad \text{or} \qquad x - z = 2\sqrt{2}.$$

The top bounding plane is obtained using $\mathbf{v}$ and $\dot{\mathbf{P}}_{[2,2]^T}$. Thus,

$$\begin{aligned} d_{top} &= \mathbf{v} \cdot \dot{\mathbf{P}}_{[2,2]^T} \\ &= \begin{bmatrix} -0.4082 \\ 0.8165 \\ -0.4082 \end{bmatrix} \cdot \begin{bmatrix} 4.5977 \\ 5.6330 \\ 1.7693 \end{bmatrix} = 2. \end{aligned}$$

This means that the equation of the top plane is

$$-\frac{x}{\sqrt{6}} + \frac{2y}{\sqrt{6}} - \frac{z}{\sqrt{6}} = 2 \qquad \text{or} \qquad -x + 2y - z = 2\sqrt{6}.$$

The bottom bounding plane is obtained using $\mathbf{v}$ and $\dot{\mathbf{P}}_{[-2,-2]^T}$. Thus,

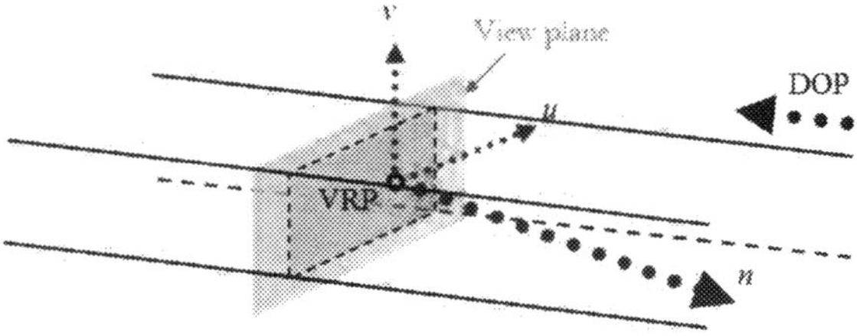


**Fig. 9.7** Infinite parallelepiped view volume of the oblique projection

$$d_{bottom} = \mathbf{v} \cdot \dot{\mathbf{P}}_{[-2,-2]^T} = \begin{bmatrix} -0.4082 \\ 0.8165 \\ -0.4082 \end{bmatrix} \cdot \begin{bmatrix} 3.4023 \\ 2.3670 \\ 6.2307 \end{bmatrix} = -2.$$

This means that the equation of the bottom plane is

$$-\frac{x}{\sqrt{6}} + \frac{2y}{\sqrt{6}} - \frac{z}{\sqrt{6}} = -2 \quad \text{or} \quad -x + 2y - z = -2\sqrt{6}. \qquad \square$$

#### 9.2.1.2 Oblique Projection

In case of oblique projection, an infinite parallelepiped view volume is also considered as shown in Fig. 9.7. Unlike the previous case, the DOP is *not* parallel to the $n$-axis of the VRC system. Like the previous case, the DOP may be determined by specifying the PRP and the center of the window on the view plane (i.e., $\left[\frac{u_{min}+u_{max}}{2}, \frac{v_{min}+v_{max}}{2}\right]^T$). The boundaries of the view volume are four planes determined by the four sides of the window and the DOP. None of those planes is normal to the view plane.

**Example 9.10:** [*Direction of projection—oblique projection*]

Assume that the view reference coordinate system coincides with the right-handed world coordinate system. If the window of the view plane is determined by the points $[u_{min}, v_{min}]^T = [2, 6]^T$ and $[u_{max}, v_{max}]^T = [6, 8]^T$ and the projection reference point is located at $\dot{\mathbf{P}} = [1, 2, 9]^T$, determine the direction of projection in this case.

**Solution 9.10:** Similar to Example 9.8, the center of the view plane window is located at

$$\dot{\mathbf{C}} = \frac{1}{2}\left(\begin{bmatrix} 2 \\ 6 \\ 0 \end{bmatrix} + \begin{bmatrix} 6 \\ 8 \\ 0 \end{bmatrix}\right) = \begin{bmatrix} 4 \\ 7 \\ 0 \end{bmatrix}.$$

The direction of projection is then determined as

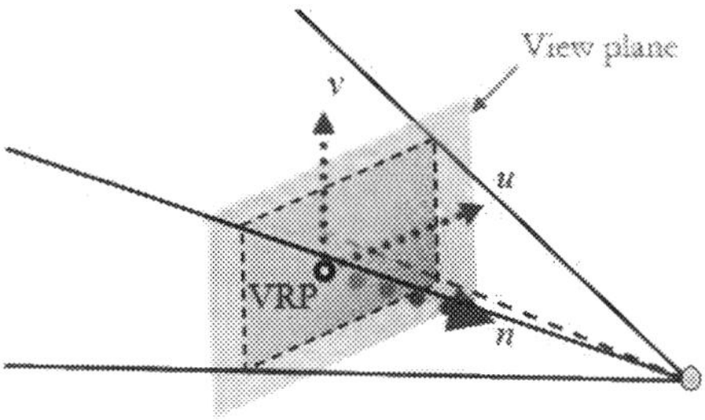


**Fig. 9.8** Semi-infinite pyramidal view volume of the perspective projection

$$\dot{\mathbf{C}} - \dot{\mathbf{P}} = \begin{bmatrix} 4 \\ 7 \\ 0 \end{bmatrix} - \begin{bmatrix} 1 \\ 2 \\ 9 \end{bmatrix} = \begin{bmatrix} 3 \\ 5 \\ -9 \end{bmatrix}. \qquad \square$$

#### 9.2.1.3 Perspective Projection

In case of perspective projection, a semi-infinite pyramidal view volume is considered as shown in Fig. 9.8. In this case, the center of projection (COP) represents the apex of the pyramid. The boundaries of the view volume are four planes determined by the four sides of the window and the COP. In this perspective case, the PRP is the COP and usually is expressed in the VRC system.

**Example 9.11:** [*Expressing projection reference point in world coordinates*]
Consider a view reference coordinate system such that the $n$-axis is indicated by the unit vector $\mathbf{n} = \left[\frac{1}{\sqrt{3}}, \frac{1}{\sqrt{3}}, \frac{1}{\sqrt{3}}\right]^T$ and the VRP is positioned at $[4, 4, 4]^T$. If the PRP is expressed as $[0, 0, 3\sqrt{3}]^T$ in the VRC system, determine its location in the WCS.

**Solution 9.11:** The PRP $[0, 0, 3\sqrt{3}]^T$ in the VRC system is located at $[7, 7, 7]^T$ in the WCS. The steps are left as an exercise. □

**Example 9.12:** [*Clipping planes in world coordinates—semi-infinite perspective view volume*]
Consider a view reference coordinate system such that the $n$-axis is indicated by the unit vector $\mathbf{n} = \left[\frac{1}{\sqrt{3}}, \frac{1}{\sqrt{3}}, \frac{1}{\sqrt{3}}\right]^T$ and the VRP is positioned at $[4, 4, 4]^T$. If a window that extends from $[-1, -1]^T$ to $[3, 3]^T$ on the $uv$-plane is used to specify a semi-infinite perspective view volume whose COP is at $[1, 1, 3\sqrt{3}]^T$ (expressed in the VRC system), determine the planes bounding that volume in world coordinates.

**Solution 9.12:** As calculated in Example 9.9, $\mathbf{v}$ is estimated as $\left[-\frac{1}{\sqrt{6}}, \frac{2}{\sqrt{6}}, -\frac{1}{\sqrt{6}}\right]^T$ and $\mathbf{u}$ is obtained as the cross product $\mathbf{v} \times \mathbf{n}$:

$$\mathbf{u} = \mathbf{v} \times \mathbf{n} = \begin{bmatrix} \frac{1}{\sqrt{2}} \\ 0 \\ -\frac{1}{\sqrt{2}} \end{bmatrix} = \begin{bmatrix} 0.7071 \\ 0 \\ -0.7071 \end{bmatrix}.$$

The corners of the *uv*-window can be obtained in world coordinates. Every two corners along a window edge and the COP determine one of the planes that bound the semi-infinite perspective view volume.

**Corners of the view plane window in WCS**: Let us first obtain the corners in world coordinates. In the VRC system, the corner $[-1, -1]^T$ has the coordinates $\dot{\mathbf{Q}} = [-1, -1, 0]^T$. As done in Example 9.9, its world coordinates are estimated using Eq. (9.13) as

$$\begin{aligned}
\dot{\mathbf{P}}_{[-1,-1]^T} &= \left[ \begin{bmatrix} \mathbf{u}^T \\ \mathbf{v}^T \\ \mathbf{n}^T \end{bmatrix}^{-1} \dot{\mathbf{Q}} \right] + \dot{\mathbf{R}} \\
&= \left[ \begin{bmatrix} \frac{1}{\sqrt{2}} & 0 & -\frac{1}{\sqrt{2}} \\ -\frac{1}{\sqrt{6}} & \frac{2}{\sqrt{6}} & -\frac{1}{\sqrt{6}} \\ \frac{1}{\sqrt{3}} & \frac{1}{\sqrt{3}} & \frac{1}{\sqrt{3}} \end{bmatrix}^{-1} \begin{bmatrix} -1 \\ -1 \\ 0 \end{bmatrix} \right] + \begin{bmatrix} 4 \\ 4 \\ 4 \end{bmatrix} = \begin{bmatrix} 3.7011 \\ 3.1835 \\ 5.1154 \end{bmatrix}.
\end{aligned}$$

The rest of the corners are obtained the same way. The coordinates are listed in the following table:

| Corner | $[u, v]^T$ | $\dot{\mathbf{P}}_{[u,v]^T}$ |
|---|---|---|
| Lower left | $[-1, -1]^T$ | $[3.7011, 3.1835, 5.1154]^T$ |
| Upper left | $[-1, 3]^T$ | $[2.0681, 6.4495, 3.4824]^T$ |
| Lower right | $[3, -1]^T$ | $[6.5296, 3.1835, 2.2869]^T$ |
| Upper right | $[3, 3]^T$ | $[4.8966, 6.4495, 0.6539]^T$ |

**COP expressed in WCS**: As the center of projection is located at $[1, 1, 3\sqrt{3}]^T$ (expressed in the VRC system), the same point $\dot{\mathbf{C}}$ is expressed in world coordinates using Eq. (9.13) as

$$\begin{aligned}
\dot{\mathbf{C}} &= \left[ \begin{bmatrix} \mathbf{u}^T \\ \mathbf{v}^T \\ \mathbf{n}^T \end{bmatrix}^{-1} \dot{\mathbf{Q}} \right] + \dot{\mathbf{R}} \\
&= \left[ \begin{bmatrix} \frac{1}{\sqrt{2}} & 0 & -\frac{1}{\sqrt{2}} \\ -\frac{1}{\sqrt{6}} & \frac{2}{\sqrt{6}} & -\frac{1}{\sqrt{6}} \\ \frac{1}{\sqrt{3}} & \frac{1}{\sqrt{3}} & \frac{1}{\sqrt{3}} \end{bmatrix}^{-1} \begin{bmatrix} 1 \\ 1 \\ 3\sqrt{3} \end{bmatrix} \right] + \begin{bmatrix} 4 \\ 4 \\ 4 \end{bmatrix} = \begin{bmatrix} 7.2989 \\ 7.8165 \\ 5.8846 \end{bmatrix}.
\end{aligned}$$

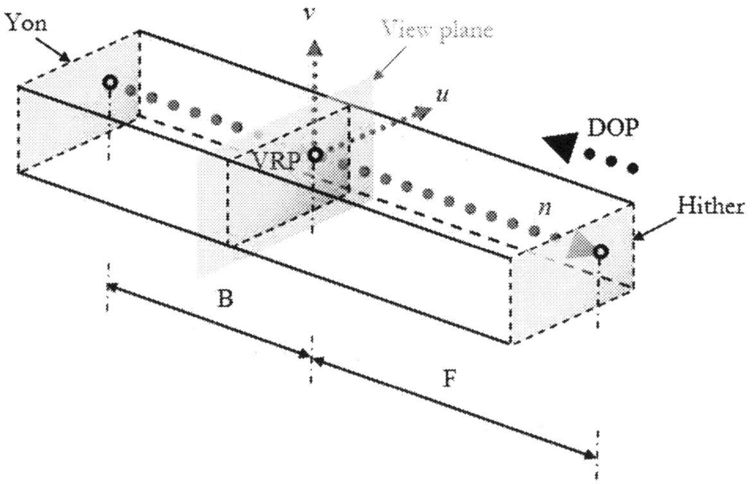


**Fig. 9.9** Finite parallelepiped view volume of the orthographic projection

**Plane equations**: The left plane is obtained using the lower and upper left points of the $uv$-window and the COP (i.e., $\dot{\mathbf{P}}_{[-1,-1]^T} = [3.7011, 3.1835, 5.1154]^T$, $\dot{\mathbf{P}}_{[-1,3]^T} = [2.0681, 6.4495, 3.4824]^T$ and $\dot{\mathbf{C}} = [7.2989, 7.8165, 5.8846]^T$). We get the direction vector from $\dot{\mathbf{C}}$ to $\dot{\mathbf{P}}_{[-1,-1]^T}$ and from $\dot{\mathbf{C}}$ to $\dot{\mathbf{P}}_{[-1,3]^T}$. These are

$$\dot{\mathbf{P}}_{[-1,-1]^T} - \dot{\mathbf{C}} = \begin{bmatrix} 3.7011 \\ 3.1835 \\ 5.1154 \end{bmatrix} - \begin{bmatrix} 7.2989 \\ 7.8165 \\ 5.8846 \end{bmatrix} = \begin{bmatrix} -3.5977 \\ -4.6330 \\ -0.7693 \end{bmatrix}$$

and

$$\dot{\mathbf{P}}_{[-1,3]^T} - \dot{\mathbf{C}} = \begin{bmatrix} 2.0681 \\ 6.4495 \\ 3.4824 \end{bmatrix} - \begin{bmatrix} 7.2989 \\ 7.8165 \\ 5.8846 \end{bmatrix} = \begin{bmatrix} -5.2307 \\ -1.3670 \\ -2.4023 \end{bmatrix}.$$

The normal to the plane is obtained as

$$[\dot{\mathbf{P}}_{[-1,-1]^T} - \dot{\mathbf{C}}] \times [\dot{\mathbf{P}}_{[-1,3]^T} - \dot{\mathbf{C}}] = \begin{bmatrix} -3.5977 \\ -4.6330 \\ -0.7693 \end{bmatrix} \times \begin{bmatrix} -5.2307 \\ -1.3670 \\ -2.4023 \end{bmatrix} = \begin{bmatrix} 10.0781 \\ -4.6188 \\ -19.3157 \end{bmatrix}.$$

This normal vector after normalization becomes

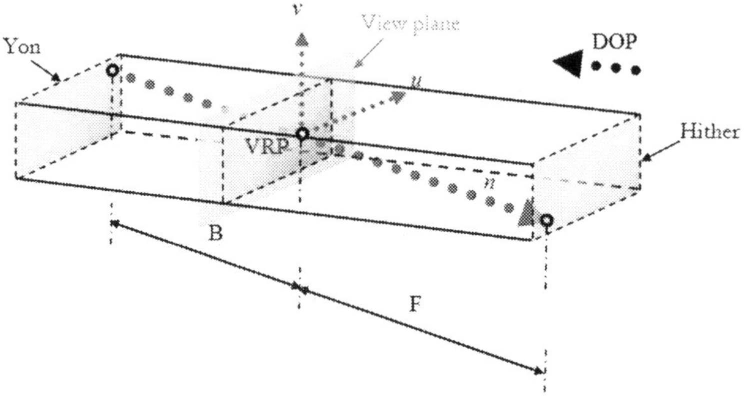


**Fig. 9.10** Finite parallelepiped view volume of the oblique projection

$$\mathbf{n} = \frac{[\dot{\mathbf{P}}_{[-1,-1]^T} - \dot{\mathbf{C}}] \times [\dot{\mathbf{P}}_{[-1,3]^T} - \dot{\mathbf{C}}]}{\|[\dot{\mathbf{P}}_{[-1,-1]^T} - \dot{\mathbf{C}}] \times [\dot{\mathbf{P}}_{[-1,3]^T} - \dot{\mathbf{C}}]\|} = \frac{\begin{bmatrix} 10.0781 \\ -4.6188 \\ -19.3157 \end{bmatrix}}{\left\| \begin{bmatrix} 10.0781 \\ -4.6188 \\ -19.3157 \end{bmatrix} \right\|} = \begin{bmatrix} 0.4525 \\ -0.2074 \\ -0.8673 \end{bmatrix}.$$

Now, we have the normal $\mathbf{n}$ and a point $\dot{\mathbf{C}}$ on the left plane. We can get $d_{left}$ as

$$\begin{aligned} d_{left} &= \mathbf{n} \cdot \dot{\mathbf{C}} \\ &= \begin{bmatrix} 0.4525 \\ -0.2074 \\ -0.8673 \end{bmatrix} \cdot \begin{bmatrix} 7.2989 \\ 7.8165 \\ 5.8846 \end{bmatrix} = -3.4219. \end{aligned}$$

Thus, the left plane can be expressed as

$$0.4525x - 0.2074y - 0.8673z = -3.4219.$$

The right plane is obtained using the lower and upper right points of the $uv$-window and the COP (i.e., $\dot{\mathbf{P}}_{[3,-1]^T} = [6.5296, 3.1835, 2.2869]^T$, $\dot{\mathbf{P}}_{[3,3]^T} = [4.8966, 6.4495, 0.6539]^T$ and $\dot{\mathbf{C}} = [7.2989, 7.8165, 5.8846]^T$). The top plane is obtained using the upper left and right points of the $uv$-window and the COP (i.e., $\dot{\mathbf{P}}_{[-1,3]^T} = [2.0681, 6.4495, 3.4824]^T$, $\dot{\mathbf{P}}_{[3,3]^T} = [4.8966, 6.4495, 0.6539]^T$ and $\dot{\mathbf{C}} = [7.2989, 7.8165, 5.8846]^T$). The bottom plane is obtained using the lower left and right points of the $uv$-window and the COP (i.e., $\dot{\mathbf{P}}_{[-1,-1]^T} = [3.7011, 3.1835, 5.1154]^T$, $\dot{\mathbf{P}}_{[3,-1]^T} = [6.5296, 3.1835, 2.2869]^T$ and $\dot{\mathbf{C}} = [7.2989, 7.8165, 5.8846]^T$). The final plane equations are listed in the following table:

| Plane | Equation |
|---|---|
| Left | $0.4525x - 0.2074y - 0.8673z = -3.4219$ |
| Right | $0.8673x + 0.2074y - 0.4525z = 5.2885$ |
| Top | $0.1736x - 0.9694y + 0.1736z = -5.2885$ |
| Bottom | $0.5884x - 0.5546y + 0.5884z = 3.4219$ |

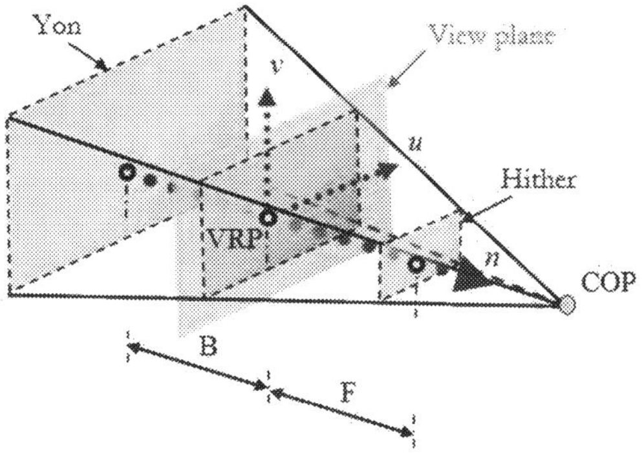


**Fig. 9.11** Finite pyramidal view volume of the perspective projection

## 9.2.2 Finite View Volume

The previous infinite view volumes can be clipped (i.e., turn to finite) by a *front* or *near clipping plane* (also known as the *hither*) and a *back* or *far clipping plane* (also known as the *yon*). The three planes; i.e., the hither, the yon and the view plane are parallel to each other and share the same normal vector along the $n$-axis. The clipped finite view volume for the three types mentioned above are shown in Figs. 9.9, 9.10 and 9.11. The clipped finite view volume for perspective projection is known as the *viewing frustum* (Sect. 10.1). (The viewing frustum can be determined through the field of view (FOV) angle. More on viewing frustum is discussed in Sect. 10.6.1.)

The question now is: How do we determine the locations of the clipping planes (i.e., the hither and the yon) with respect to the view plane? As a matter of fact, this is done by specifying signed quantities along the $n$-axis with respect to the VRP. In Figs. 9.9, 9.10 and 9.11, these quantities are denoted as $F$ and $B$ where the positive distance $F$ is along the positive $n$-axis and the negative distance $B$ is opposite to the direction of the $n$-axis. In general, $F$ and $B$ can be either positive or negative.

**Example 9.13:** [*Clipping planes in world coordinates—finite orthographic view volume*]

If the infinite orthographic view volume of Example 9.9 is truncated using a front and a back clipping planes. The front plane is at $3\sqrt{3}$ world coordinate units along the positive $n$-axis and the back plane is at $2\sqrt{3}$ world coordinate units along the negative $n$-axis. Determine the equations of the front and back clipping planes.

**Solution 9.13:** From Example 9.9, we know that $n$-axis is indicated by the unit vector $\mathbf{n} = \left[\frac{1}{\sqrt{3}}, \frac{1}{\sqrt{3}}, \frac{1}{\sqrt{3}}\right]^T$. This vector represents the normal to the view plane as well as the normal to the front and back clipping planes (as they are parallel to each other).

In order to determine the equations of the front and back planes, we only need a point residing on each of those planes. Since the VRP is positioned at $\dot{\mathbf{R}} = [4, 4, 4]^T$, a point $\dot{\mathbf{P}}_f$ on the front plane can be estimated along the $n$-axis as

$$\begin{aligned}\dot{\mathbf{P}}_f &= \dot{\mathbf{R}} + F\mathbf{n}\\ &= \begin{bmatrix}4\\4\\4\end{bmatrix} + 3\sqrt{3}\begin{bmatrix}\frac{1}{\sqrt{3}}\\\frac{1}{\sqrt{3}}\\\frac{1}{\sqrt{3}}\end{bmatrix} = \begin{bmatrix}7\\7\\7\end{bmatrix}.\end{aligned}$$

Similarly, a point $\dot{\mathbf{P}}_b$ on the back plane can be estimated along the negative $n$-axis as

$$\begin{aligned}\dot{\mathbf{P}}_b &= \dot{\mathbf{R}} - B\mathbf{n}\\ &= \begin{bmatrix}4\\4\\4\end{bmatrix} - 2\sqrt{3}\begin{bmatrix}\frac{1}{\sqrt{3}}\\\frac{1}{\sqrt{3}}\\\frac{1}{\sqrt{3}}\end{bmatrix} = \begin{bmatrix}2\\2\\2\end{bmatrix}.\end{aligned}$$

The front bounding plane is obtained using the normal vector $\mathbf{n}$ and $\dot{\mathbf{P}}_f$. Thus,

$$\begin{aligned}d_{front} &= \mathbf{n} \cdot \dot{\mathbf{P}}_f\\ &= \begin{bmatrix}\frac{1}{\sqrt{3}}\\\frac{1}{\sqrt{3}}\\\frac{1}{\sqrt{3}}\end{bmatrix} \cdot \begin{bmatrix}7\\7\\7\end{bmatrix} = 7\sqrt{3}.\end{aligned}$$

This means that the equation of the front plane is

$$\frac{x}{\sqrt{3}} + \frac{y}{\sqrt{3}} + \frac{z}{\sqrt{3}} = 7\sqrt{3}$$

or

$$x + y + z = 21.$$

Similarly, the back bounding plane is obtained using the normal vector $\mathbf{n}$ and $\dot{\mathbf{P}}_b$. Thus,

$$\begin{aligned}d_{back} &= \mathbf{n} \cdot \dot{\mathbf{P}}_b\\ &= \begin{bmatrix}\frac{1}{\sqrt{3}}\\\frac{1}{\sqrt{3}}\\\frac{1}{\sqrt{3}}\end{bmatrix} \cdot \begin{bmatrix}2\\2\\2\end{bmatrix} = 2\sqrt{3}.\end{aligned}$$

This means that the equation of the back plane is

$$\frac{x}{\sqrt{3}} + \frac{y}{\sqrt{3}} + \frac{z}{\sqrt{3}} = 2\sqrt{3}$$

or

$$x + y + z = 6.$$

Notice that the same results can be obtained without estimating the points $\dot{\mathbf{P}}_f$ and $\dot{\mathbf{P}}_b$. This is done by adding the $F$ value to the $d$ component of the view plane equation to get the front plane equation (or subtracting the $B$ value from the $d$ component of the view plane equation to get the back plane equation). The $d_{view}$ is obtained as

$$\begin{aligned} d_{view} &= \mathbf{n} \cdot \dot{\mathbf{P}}_{view} \\ &= \begin{bmatrix} \frac{1}{\sqrt{3}} \\ \frac{1}{\sqrt{3}} \\ \frac{1}{\sqrt{3}} \end{bmatrix} \cdot \begin{bmatrix} 4 \\ 4 \\ 4 \end{bmatrix} = 4\sqrt{3}. \end{aligned}$$

This means that the equations of the front and back planes are

$$\underbrace{\frac{x}{\sqrt{3}} + \frac{y}{\sqrt{3}} + \frac{z}{\sqrt{3}}}_{\mathbf{n} \cdot [x,y,z]^T} = \underbrace{4\sqrt{3}}_{d_{view}} + \underbrace{3\sqrt{3}}_{F}$$

and

$$\underbrace{\frac{x}{\sqrt{3}} + \frac{y}{\sqrt{3}} + \frac{z}{\sqrt{3}}}_{\mathbf{n} \cdot [x,y,z]^T} = \underbrace{4\sqrt{3}}_{d_{view}} - \underbrace{2\sqrt{3}}_{B},$$

which can be expressed as

$$x + y + z = 21$$

and

$$x + y + z = 6. \qquad \square$$

**Example 9.14:** [*Clipping planes in world coordinates—finite perspective view volume*]

Assume that the camera is located at the origin of the world coordinate system as shown in Fig. 9.12a and the view plane is at a distance $d$ (i.e., the focal length) along the $-z$-axis. If the right and left planes of the frustum intersect the view plane at $x = 1$ and $x = -1$ respectively and the horizontal FOV angle of the frustum is $\alpha$, determine the distance $d$ in terms of $\alpha$.

**Solution 9.14:** Given the horizontal FOV angle $\alpha$, the focal length $d$ is obtained as

$$d = \frac{1}{\tan\left(\frac{\alpha}{2}\right)} = \cot\left(\frac{\alpha}{2}\right). \tag{9.14}$$

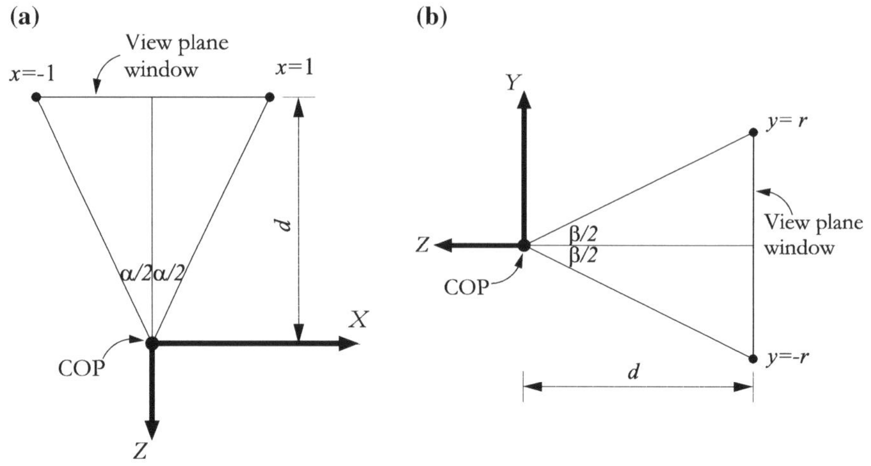


**Fig. 9.12** Finite perspective view volume. **a** Top view. **b** Side view

Notice that changing the FOV angle results in changing the focal length; the greater the angle $\alpha$ the shorter the focal length $d$. □

**Example 9.15:** [*Clipping planes in world coordinates—finite perspective view volume*]

In Example 9.14, if the ratio of image height to image width is denoted by $r$, determine where the top and bottom clipping planes intersect the view plane.

**Solution 9.15:** Since the ratio is $r$ and the image width is 2 as depicted in Fig. 9.12a; thus, the image height is $2r$. It is obvious that the top and bottom clipping planes intersect the view plane at $y = r$ and $y = -r$ respectively. This is shown in Fig. 9.12b. □

**Example 9.16:** [*Clipping planes in world coordinates—finite perspective view volume*]

In Example 9.15, determine the vertical FOV angle $\beta$ in terms of the focal length $d$ and the ratio $r$.

**Solution 9.16:** Since

$$\tan\left(\frac{\beta}{2}\right) = \frac{r}{d},$$

the vertical FOV angle $\beta$ is obtained as

$$\beta = 2\tan^{-1}\left(\frac{r}{d}\right). \qquad (9.15)$$

□

**Example 9.17:** [*Clipping planes in world coordinates—finite perspective view volume*]

In Example 9.16, determine the equations of the left, right, top and bottom clipping planes of the frustum.

**Solution 9.17:** The left plane is expressed as

$$\frac{d}{\sqrt{d^2+1}}x = \frac{1}{\sqrt{d^2+1}}z \quad \text{or} \quad dx = z.$$

The right plane is expressed as

$$\frac{d}{\sqrt{d^2+1}}x = -\frac{1}{\sqrt{d^2+1}}z \quad \text{or} \quad dx = -z.$$

The top plane is expressed as

$$\frac{d}{\sqrt{d^2+r^2}}y = -\frac{r}{\sqrt{d^2+r^2}}z \quad \text{or} \quad dy = -rz.$$

The bottom plane is expressed as

$$\frac{d}{\sqrt{d^2+r^2}}y = \frac{r}{\sqrt{d^2+r^2}}z \quad \text{or} \quad dy = rz.$$

The derivation of these plane equations are left as an exercise. □

## 9.3 Canonical View Volume

In general, the view plane is not perpendicular to the $z$-axis, the direction of projection is not parallel to the $z$-axis and the view volume is not symmetric about the $z$-axis. The planes of the view volume may be used to clip the part of the world we are interested in. This clipped view volume is then projected onto the view plane and consequently transformed into the 2D device coordinates. However, this process may be computationally expensive.

In order to simplify the subsequent steps; especially the clipping step, we should transform the view volume estimated in the previous section to what's called *canonical view volume*; a volume that is easy to clip and project. This process is referred to as *normalizing transformation* (refer to Fig. 9.1).

In the literature, we find conventions exist referring to the canonical view volume for parallel projection. Figure 9.13a shows an example of a canonical view volume for parallel projection. In right-handed coordinate system, the canonical view volume planes are expressed as

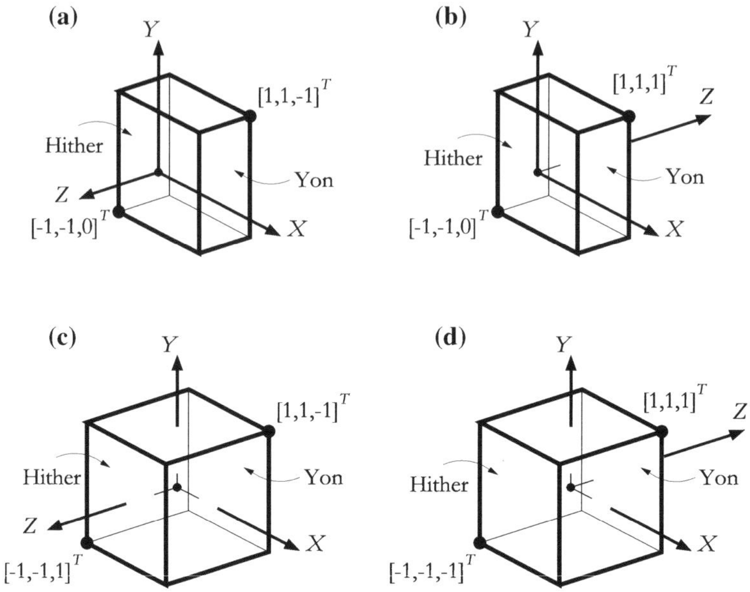


**Fig. 9.13** Canonical view volume for parallel projection. **a** Expressed in Eq. (9.16), viewing is along the negative $z$-axis. **b** Expressed in Eq. (9.17), viewing is along the positive $z$-axis. **c** Expressed in Eq. (9.18), viewing is along the negative $z$-axis. **d** Expressed in Eq. (9.19), viewing is along the positive $z$-axis

$$\begin{aligned} x &= -1, \\ x &= 1, \\ y &= -1, \\ y &= 1, \\ z &= 0, \\ z &= -1. \end{aligned} \tag{9.16}$$

The same canonical view volume planes can be expressed in left-handed coordinate system as

$$\begin{aligned} x &= -1, \\ x &= 1, \\ y &= -1, \\ y &= 1, \\ z &= 0, \\ z &= 1. \end{aligned} \tag{9.17}$$

This is shown in Fig. 9.13b.

Another convention that is regularly used is shown in Fig. 9.13c. In right-handed coordinate system, the canonical view volume planes are expressed as

$$\begin{aligned} x &= -1, \\ x &= 1, \\ y &= -1, \\ y &= 1, \\ z &= 1, \\ z &= -1. \end{aligned} \tag{9.18}$$

The same canonical view volume planes can be expressed in left-handed coordinate system as

$$\begin{aligned} x &= -1, \\ x &= 1, \\ y &= -1, \\ y &= 1, \\ z &= -1, \\ z &= 1. \end{aligned} \tag{9.19}$$

This is shown in Fig. 9.13d. Also, a unit cube extending from $[0, 0, 0]^T$ to $[1, 1, 1]^T$ is sometimes used as a canonical view volume for parallel projection.

For perspective projection, the planes of a canonical view volume are expressed in right-handed system as

$$\begin{aligned} x &= z, \\ x &= -z, \\ y &= z, \\ y &= -z, \\ z &= -z_f, \\ z &= -1. \end{aligned} \tag{9.20}$$

The planes $x = \pm z$ and $y = \pm z$ imply that the FOV in this case is 90°. The same canonical view volume is expressed in left-handed system as

$$\begin{aligned} x &= z, \\ x &= -z, \\ y &= z, \\ y &= -z, \\ z &= z_f, \\ z &= 1. \end{aligned} \tag{9.21}$$

The view volume expressed in right- and left-handed coordinate systems is shown in Fig. 9.14a, b respectively. Other systems use the following canonical perspective view volume:

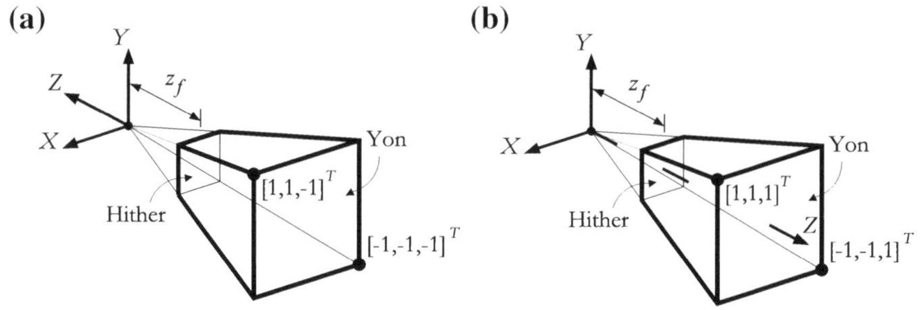


**Fig. 9.14** Canonical view volume for perspective projection. **a** Expressed in Eq. (9.20). **b** Expressed in Eq. (9.21)

$$\begin{aligned} x &= z, \\ x &= -z, \\ y &= z, \\ y &= -z, \\ z &= 1, \\ z &= -1. \end{aligned} \tag{9.22}$$

As illustrated in Fig. 9.1, the remaining steps of the 3D viewing process are as follows:

1. The view volume is transformed into a canonical view volume. Section 9.4 discusses the steps followed to transform an arbitrary view volume (similar to those that handled in Sect. 9.2) into canonical view volumes.
2. Clipping is performed against the canonical view volume as discussed in Sect. 9.5.
3. Projection is applied to project the contents of the view volume. This is discussed in Sect. 9.6.
4. Projected points are then transformed to their final locations on the screen. This is discussed in Sect. 9.9.

Note that the perspective view volume may be transformed into a canonical parallel-projection view volume as discussed in Sect. 9.7. Also, clipping may be performed in homogeneous coordinates as discussed in Sect. 9.8.

## 9.4 Transformation to Canonical View Volume

No matter what the shape of the view volume is, it can be turned to a canonical view volume. Working with canonical view volumes makes the subsequent step of clipping easier.

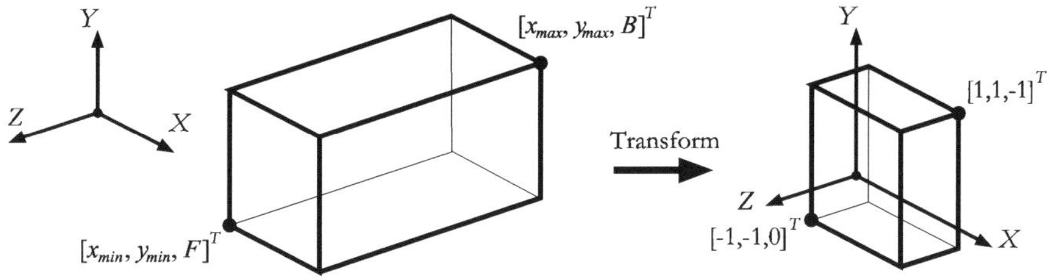


**Fig. 9.15** A view volume with planes parallel to the principal planes and passing through the points $[x_{min}, y_{min}, F]^T$ and $[x_{max}, y_{max}, B]^T$ is transformed into the canonical parallel-projection view volume expressed by Eq. (9.16)

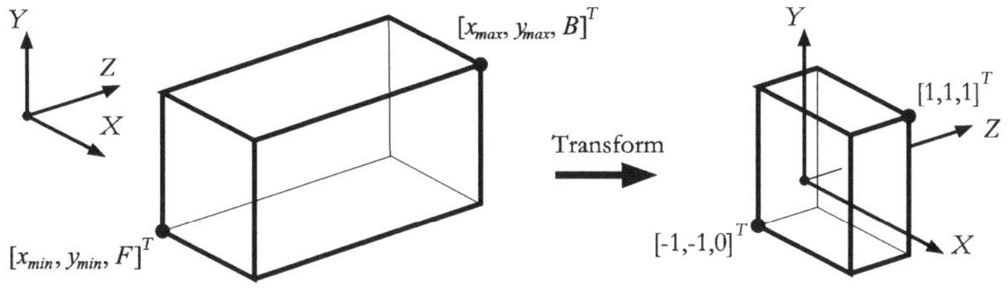


**Fig. 9.16** A view volume with planes parallel to the principal planes and passing through the points $[x_{min}, y_{min}, F]^T$ and $[x_{max}, y_{max}, B]^T$ is transformed into the canonical parallel-projection view volume expressed by Eq. (9.17)

## *9.4.1 Parallel Projection*

Parallel projection view volume; either orthogonal or oblique, is turned to a canonical view volume defined by Eqs. (9.16–9.19). This is done through a series of transformations. The following examples discuss these transformations.

**Example 9.18:** [*Transformation into canonical parallel-projection view volume—from general orthogonal volume*]

Assuming that the view reference coordinate system coincides with the right-handed world coordinate system, consider a view volume with planes parallel to the principal planes and passing through the points $[x_{min}, y_{min}, F]^T$ and $[x_{max}, y_{max}, B]^T$. Derive a matrix to transform this view volume into the canonical parallel-projection view volume expressed by Eq. (9.16) as in Fig. 9.15.

**Solution 9.18:** The canonical parallel-projection view volume expressed by Eq. (9.16) has the origin at the middle of the front plane. Moreover, the size of this canonical view volume is $2 \times 2 \times 1$ along the $x$-, $y$- and $z$-directions respectively. Hence, the transformation is done in two steps.

1. Translate the volume so that the middle point of the front plane is at the origin. The coordinates of the middle point is $\left[\frac{x_{max}+x_{min}}{2}, \frac{y_{max}+y_{min}}{2}, F\right]^T$. Thus, the translation

is done using the translation vector $\left[-\frac{x_{max}+x_{min}}{2}, -\frac{y_{max}+y_{min}}{2}, -F\right]^T$. Let us use the translation matrix $\mathtt{M}_1$ where

$$\mathtt{M}_1 = \mathtt{T}\left(\left[-\frac{x_{max}+x_{min}}{2}, -\frac{y_{max}+y_{min}}{2}, -F\right]^T\right) = \begin{bmatrix} 1 & 0 & 0 & -\frac{x_{max}+x_{min}}{2} \\ 0 & 1 & 0 & -\frac{y_{max}+y_{min}}{2} \\ 0 & 0 & 1 & -F \\ 0 & 0 & 0 & 1 \end{bmatrix}.$$

2. Scale the volume using the scaling factors $\frac{2}{x_{max}-x_{min}}$, $\frac{2}{y_{max}-y_{min}}$ and $\frac{1}{F-B}$. Let us use the scaling matrix $\mathtt{M}_2$ where

$$\mathtt{M}_2 = \mathtt{S}\left(\frac{2}{x_{max}-x_{min}}, \frac{2}{y_{max}-y_{min}}, \frac{1}{F-B}\right) = \begin{bmatrix} \frac{2}{x_{max}-x_{min}} & 0 & 0 & 0 \\ 0 & \frac{2}{y_{max}-y_{min}} & 0 & 0 \\ 0 & 0 & \frac{1}{F-B} & 0 \\ 0 & 0 & 0 & 1 \end{bmatrix}.$$

Therefore, the overall transformation is calculated as

$$\begin{aligned} \mathtt{M} &= \mathtt{M}_2\mathtt{M}_1 \\ &= \mathtt{S}\left(\frac{2}{x_{max}-x_{min}}, \frac{2}{y_{max}-y_{min}}, \frac{1}{F-B}\right)\mathtt{T}\left(\left[-\frac{x_{max}+x_{min}}{2}, -\frac{y_{max}+y_{min}}{2}, -F\right]^T\right) \\ &= \begin{bmatrix} \frac{2}{x_{max}-x_{min}} & 0 & 0 & 0 \\ 0 & \frac{2}{y_{max}-y_{min}} & 0 & 0 \\ 0 & 0 & \frac{1}{F-B} & 0 \\ 0 & 0 & 0 & 1 \end{bmatrix} \begin{bmatrix} 1 & 0 & 0 & -\frac{x_{max}+x_{min}}{2} \\ 0 & 1 & 0 & -\frac{y_{max}+y_{min}}{2} \\ 0 & 0 & 1 & -F \\ 0 & 0 & 0 & 1 \end{bmatrix} \\ &= \begin{bmatrix} \frac{2}{x_{max}-x_{min}} & 0 & 0 & -\frac{x_{max}+x_{min}}{x_{max}-x_{min}} \\ 0 & \frac{2}{y_{max}-y_{min}} & 0 & -\frac{y_{max}+y_{min}}{y_{max}-y_{min}} \\ 0 & 0 & \frac{1}{F-B} & -\frac{F}{F-B} \\ 0 & 0 & 0 & 1 \end{bmatrix}. \quad \square \end{aligned} \tag{9.23}$$

**Example 9.19:** [*Transformation into canonical parallel-projection view volume—from general orthogonal volume*]

In Example 9.18, if the world coordinate system is left-handed, derive a matrix to transform this view volume into the canonical parallel-projection view volume expressed by Eq. (9.17) as in Fig. 9.16.

**Solution 9.19:** Similar to Example 9.18, the transformation is done in two steps.

1. Translate the volume using the translation vector $\left[-\frac{x_{max}+x_{min}}{2}, -\frac{y_{max}+y_{min}}{2}, -F\right]^T$. Let us use the translation matrix $\mathtt{M}_1$ where

$$\mathtt{M}_1 = \mathtt{T}\left(\left[-\frac{x_{max}+x_{min}}{2}, -\frac{y_{max}+y_{min}}{2}, -F\right]^T\right) = \begin{bmatrix} 1 & 0 & 0 & -\frac{x_{max}+x_{min}}{2} \\ 0 & 1 & 0 & -\frac{y_{max}+y_{min}}{2} \\ 0 & 0 & 1 & -F \\ 0 & 0 & 0 & 1 \end{bmatrix}.$$

2. Scale the volume using the scaling factors $\frac{2}{x_{max}-x_{min}}, \frac{2}{y_{max}-y_{min}}$ and $\frac{1}{B-F}$. Let us use the scaling matrix $\mathtt{M}_2$ where

$$\mathtt{M}_2 = \mathtt{S}\left(\frac{2}{x_{max}-x_{min}}, \frac{2}{y_{max}-y_{min}}, \frac{1}{B-F}\right) = \begin{bmatrix} \frac{2}{x_{max}-x_{min}} & 0 & 0 & 0 \\ 0 & \frac{2}{y_{max}-y_{min}} & 0 & 0 \\ 0 & 0 & \frac{1}{B-F} & 0 \\ 0 & 0 & 0 & 1 \end{bmatrix}.$$

Therefore, the overall transformation is calculated as

$$\begin{aligned}
\mathtt{M} &= \mathtt{M}_2\mathtt{M}_1 \\
&= \mathtt{S}\left(\frac{2}{x_{max}-x_{min}}, \frac{2}{y_{max}-y_{min}}, \frac{1}{B-F}\right)\mathtt{T}\left(\left[-\frac{x_{max}+x_{min}}{2}, -\frac{y_{max}+y_{min}}{2}, -F\right]^T\right) \\
&= \begin{bmatrix} \frac{2}{x_{max}-x_{min}} & 0 & 0 & 0 \\ 0 & \frac{2}{y_{max}-y_{min}} & 0 & 0 \\ 0 & 0 & \frac{1}{B-F} & 0 \\ 0 & 0 & 0 & 1 \end{bmatrix} \begin{bmatrix} 1 & 0 & 0 & -\frac{x_{max}+x_{min}}{2} \\ 0 & 1 & 0 & -\frac{y_{max}+y_{min}}{2} \\ 0 & 0 & 1 & -F \\ 0 & 0 & 0 & 1 \end{bmatrix}
\end{aligned}$$

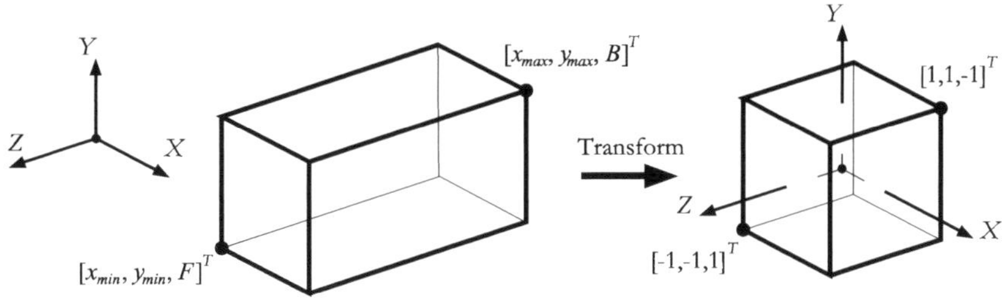


**Fig. 9.17** A view volume with planes parallel to the principal planes and passing through the points $[x_{min}, y_{min}, F]^T$ and $[x_{max}, y_{max}, B]^T$ is transformed into the canonical parallel-projection view volume expressed by Eq. (9.18)

$$= \begin{bmatrix} \frac{2}{x_{max}-x_{min}} & 0 & 0 & -\frac{x_{max}+x_{min}}{x_{max}-x_{min}} \\ 0 & \frac{2}{y_{max}-y_{min}} & 0 & -\frac{y_{max}+y_{min}}{y_{max}-y_{min}} \\ 0 & 0 & \frac{1}{B-F} & -\frac{F}{B-F} \\ 0 & 0 & 0 & 1 \end{bmatrix}. \tag{9.24}$$

□

**Example 9.20:** [*Transformation into canonical parallel-projection view volume—from general orthogonal volume*]

Assuming that the view reference coordinate system coincides with the right-handed world coordinate system, consider a view volume with planes parallel to the principal planes and passing through the points $[x_{min}, y_{min}, F]^T$ and $[x_{max}, y_{max}, B]^T$. Derive a matrix to transform this view volume into the canonical parallel-projection view volume expressed by Eq. (9.18) as in Fig. 9.17.

**Solution 9.20:** The canonical parallel-projection view volume expressed by Eq. (9.18) has the origin at the center of the volume. Moreover, the size of this canonical view volume is $2 \times 2 \times 2$ along the $x$-, $y$- and $z$-directions respectively. Hence, the transformation is done in two steps.

1. Translate the volume so that its center is at the origin. The coordinates of the center point is $\left[\frac{x_{max}+x_{min}}{2}, \frac{y_{max}+y_{min}}{2}, \frac{F+B}{2}\right]^T$. Thus, the translation is done using the translation vector $\left[-\frac{x_{max}+x_{min}}{2}, -\frac{y_{max}+y_{min}}{2}, -\frac{F+B}{2}\right]^T$ and the translation matrix $M_1$ where

$$\begin{aligned}
\mathtt{M}_1 &= \mathtt{T}\left(\left[-\frac{x_{max}+x_{min}}{2}, -\frac{y_{max}+y_{min}}{2}, -\frac{F+B}{2}\right]^T\right) \\
&= \begin{bmatrix} 1 & 0 & 0 & -\frac{x_{max}+x_{min}}{2} \\ 0 & 1 & 0 & -\frac{y_{max}+y_{min}}{2} \\ 0 & 0 & 1 & -\frac{F+B}{2} \\ 0 & 0 & 0 & 1 \end{bmatrix}.
\end{aligned}$$

2. Scale the volume using the scaling factors $\frac{2}{x_{max}-x_{min}}$, $\frac{2}{y_{max}-y_{min}}$ and $\frac{2}{F-B}$. Let us use the scaling matrix $\mathtt{M}_2$ where

$$\begin{aligned}
\mathtt{M}_2 &= \mathtt{S}\left(\frac{2}{x_{max}-x_{min}}, \frac{2}{y_{max}-y_{min}}, \frac{2}{F-B}\right) \\
&= \begin{bmatrix} \frac{2}{x_{max}-x_{min}} & 0 & 0 & 0 \\ 0 & \frac{2}{y_{max}-y_{min}} & 0 & 0 \\ 0 & 0 & \frac{2}{F-B} & 0 \\ 0 & 0 & 0 & 1 \end{bmatrix}.
\end{aligned}$$

Therefore, the overall transformation is calculated as

$$\begin{aligned}
\mathtt{M} &= \mathtt{M}_2\mathtt{M}_1 \\
&= \mathtt{S}\left(\frac{2}{x_{max}-x_{min}}, \frac{2}{y_{max}-y_{min}}, \frac{2}{F-B}\right) \\
&\quad \mathtt{T}\left(\left[-\frac{x_{max}+x_{min}}{2}, -\frac{y_{max}+y_{min}}{2}, -\frac{F+B}{2}\right]^T\right) \\
&= \begin{bmatrix} \frac{2}{x_{max}-x_{min}} & 0 & 0 & 0 \\ 0 & \frac{2}{y_{max}-y_{min}} & 0 & 0 \\ 0 & 0 & \frac{2}{F-B} & 0 \\ 0 & 0 & 0 & 1 \end{bmatrix} \begin{bmatrix} 1 & 0 & 0 & -\frac{x_{max}+x_{min}}{2} \\ 0 & 1 & 0 & -\frac{y_{max}+y_{min}}{2} \\ 0 & 0 & 1 & -\frac{F+B}{2} \\ 0 & 0 & 0 & 1 \end{bmatrix}
\end{aligned}$$

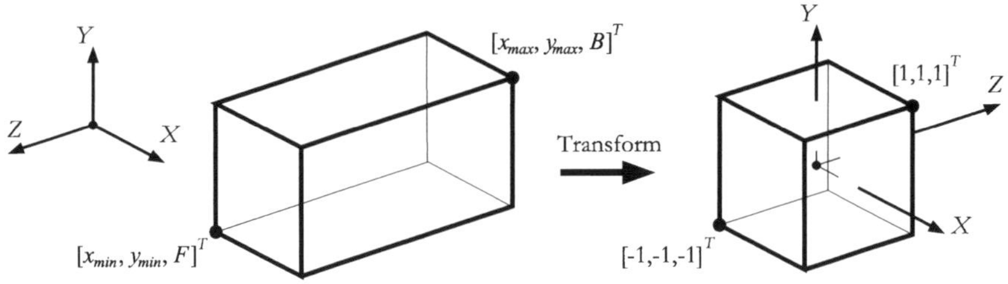


**Fig. 9.18** A view volume with planes parallel to the principal planes and passing through the points $[x_{min}, y_{min}, F]^T$ and $[x_{max}, y_{max}, B]^T$ is transformed into the canonical parallel-projection view volume expressed by Eq. (9.19)

$$= \begin{bmatrix} \frac{2}{x_{max} - x_{min}} & 0 & 0 & -\frac{x_{max} + x_{min}}{x_{max} - x_{min}} \\ 0 & \frac{2}{y_{max} - y_{min}} & 0 & -\frac{y_{max} + y_{min}}{y_{max} - y_{min}} \\ 0 & 0 & \frac{2}{F - B} & -\frac{F + B}{F - B} \\ 0 & 0 & 0 & 1 \end{bmatrix} . \square \tag{9.25}$$

□

**Example 9.21:** [*Transformation into canonical parallel-projection view volume—from general orthogonal volume*]

Assuming that the view reference coordinate system coincides with the right-handed world coordinate system, consider a view volume with planes parallel to the principal planes and passing through the points $[x_{min}, y_{min}, F]^T$ and $[x_{max}, y_{max}, B]^T$. Derive a matrix to transform this view volume into the canonical parallel-projection view volume expressed by Eq. (9.19) as in Fig. 9.18.

**Solution 9.21:** This is similar to Example 9.20; however, Eq. (9.19) assumes a left-handed coordinate system. In order to switch between right- and left-handed coordinate systems, a homogeneous version of Eq. (B.6) may be used. Hence, the transformation is done in three steps.

1. Switch to left-handed coordinate system. In homogeneous coordinates, Eq. (B.6) can be expressed as

$$\begin{aligned} \mathtt{M}_1 &= \mathtt{T}_{rl} \\ &= \begin{bmatrix} 1 & 0 & 0 & 0 \\ 0 & 1 & 0 & 0 \\ 0 & 0 & -1 & 0 \\ 0 & 0 & 0 & 1 \end{bmatrix}. \end{aligned}$$

2. Translate the volume so that its center is at the origin. The coordinates of the center point is $\left[\frac{x_{max}+x_{min}}{2}, \frac{y_{max}+y_{min}}{2}, \frac{F+B}{2}\right]^T$. Thus, the translation is done using the translation vector $\left[-\frac{x_{max}+x_{min}}{2}, -\frac{y_{max}+y_{min}}{2}, -\frac{F+B}{2}\right]^T$ and the translation matrix $\mathtt{M}_2$ where

$$\mathtt{M}_2 = \mathtt{T}\left(\left[-\frac{x_{max}+x_{min}}{2}, -\frac{y_{max}+y_{min}}{2}, -\frac{F+B}{2}\right]^T\right)$$
$$= \begin{bmatrix} 1 & 0 & 0 & -\frac{x_{max}+x_{min}}{2} \\ 0 & 1 & 0 & -\frac{y_{max}+y_{min}}{2} \\ 0 & 0 & 1 & -\frac{F+B}{2} \\ 0 & 0 & 0 & 1 \end{bmatrix}.$$

3. Scale the volume using the scaling factors $\frac{2}{x_{max}-x_{min}}$, $\frac{2}{y_{max}-y_{min}}$ and $\frac{2}{F-B}$. Let us use the scaling matrix $\mathtt{M}_3$ where

$$\mathtt{M}_3 = \mathtt{S}\left(\frac{2}{x_{max}-x_{min}}, \frac{2}{y_{max}-y_{min}}, \frac{2}{F-B}\right)$$
$$= \begin{bmatrix} \frac{2}{x_{max}-x_{min}} & 0 & 0 & 0 \\ 0 & \frac{2}{y_{max}-y_{min}} & 0 & 0 \\ 0 & 0 & \frac{2}{F-B} & 0 \\ 0 & 0 & 0 & 1 \end{bmatrix}.$$

Therefore, the overall transformation is calculated as

$$\begin{aligned} \mathtt{M} &= \mathtt{M}_3\mathtt{M}_2\mathtt{M}_1 \\ &= \mathtt{S}\left(\frac{2}{x_{max}-x_{min}}, \frac{2}{y_{max}-y_{min}}, \frac{2}{F-B}\right) \\ &\quad \mathtt{T}\left(\left[-\frac{x_{max}+x_{min}}{2}, -\frac{y_{max}+y_{min}}{2}, -\frac{F+B}{2}\right]^T\right)\mathtt{T}_{rl} \end{aligned}$$

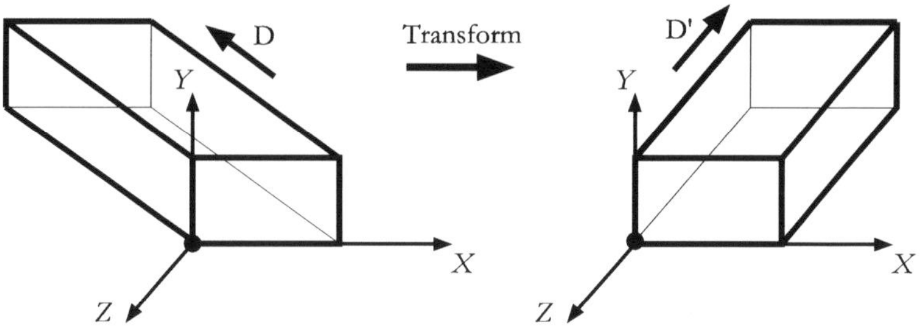


**Fig. 9.19** An oblique view volume is sheared to an orthographic one

$$
= \begin{bmatrix} \frac{2}{x_{max}-x_{min}} & 0 & 0 & 0 \\ 0 & \frac{2}{y_{max}-y_{min}} & 0 & 0 \\ 0 & 0 & \frac{2}{F-B} & 0 \\ 0 & 0 & 0 & 1 \end{bmatrix} \begin{bmatrix} 1 & 0 & 0 & -\frac{x_{max}+x_{min}}{2} \\ 0 & 1 & 0 & -\frac{y_{max}+y_{min}}{2} \\ 0 & 0 & 1 & -\frac{F+B}{2} \\ 0 & 0 & 0 & 1 \end{bmatrix} \cdots
$$
$$
\cdots \begin{bmatrix} 1 & 0 & 0 & 0 \\ 0 & 1 & 0 & 0 \\ 0 & 0 & -1 & 0 \\ 0 & 0 & 0 & 1 \end{bmatrix} \tag{9.26}
$$
$$
= \begin{bmatrix} \frac{2}{x_{max}-x_{min}} & 0 & 0 & -\frac{x_{max}+x_{min}}{x_{max}-x_{min}} \\ 0 & \frac{2}{y_{max}-y_{min}} & 0 & -\frac{y_{max}+y_{min}}{y_{max}-y_{min}} \\ 0 & 0 & -\frac{2}{F-B} & -\frac{F+B}{F-B} \\ 0 & 0 & 0 & 1 \end{bmatrix} . \square
$$

□

**Example 9.22:** [*Shearing the view volume*]
The oblique (left) view volume shown in Fig. 9.19 with the direction of projection **D** is to be sheared so that it takes the orthographic shape (right), which has the direction of projection **D**′. Derive the transformation matrix required.

**Solution 9.22:** Figure 9.20 shows the oblique view volume as multi-view projections where the direction of projection is given by the vector $\mathbf{D} = [x_d, y_d, z_d, 0]^T$. The orthographic view volume (shown as multi-view projections in Fig. 9.21) and the new direction of projection $\mathbf{D}' = [0, 0, z'_d, 0]^T$ can be obtained using the shearing matrix relative to the $z$-axis as in Eq. (5.38). Thus, we have

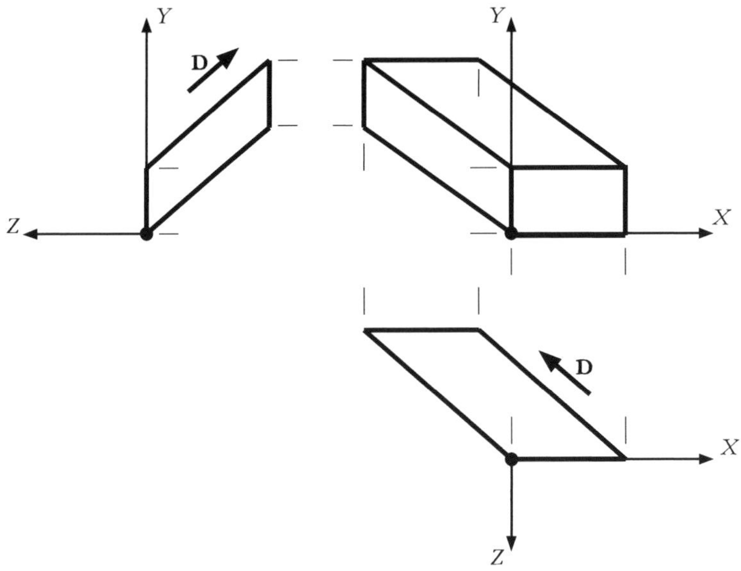


**Fig. 9.20** Multi-view projections for the oblique view volume shown in Fig. 9.19

**Fig. 9.21** Multi-view projections for the view volume shownin Fig. 9.19 after shearing

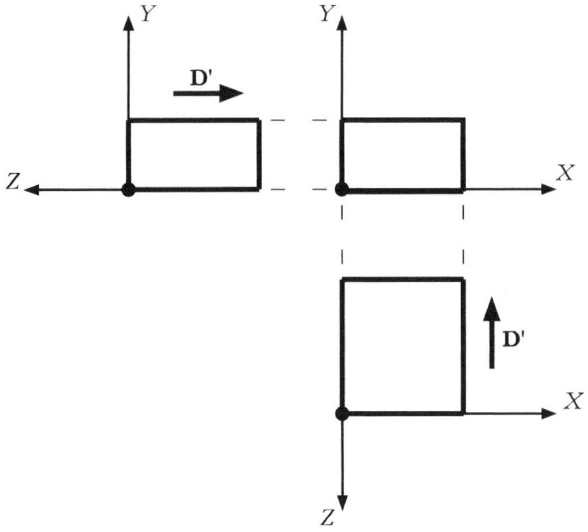


$$\underbrace{\begin{bmatrix} 0 \\ 0 \\ z'_d \\ 0 \end{bmatrix}}_{\mathbf{D}'} = \underbrace{\begin{bmatrix} 1 & 0 & sh_{zx} & 0 \\ 0 & 1 & sh_{zy} & 0 \\ 0 & 0 & 1 & 0 \\ 0 & 0 & 0 & 1 \end{bmatrix}}_{\mathtt{Sh}_z(sh_{zx},sh_{zy})} \underbrace{\begin{bmatrix} x_d \\ y_d \\ z_d \\ 0 \end{bmatrix}}_{\mathbf{D}}.$$

In this case, the $z$-coordinate is not affected. So,

$$z'_d = z_d.$$

The parameters $sh_{zx}$ and $sh_{zy}$ are obtained by solving the equations:

$$\begin{aligned} x_d + sh_{zx} z_d &= 0, \\ y_d + sh_{zy} z_d &= 0. \end{aligned}$$

Therefore,

$$\begin{aligned} sh_{zx} &= -\tfrac{x_d}{z_d}, \\ sh_{zy} &= -\tfrac{y_d}{z_d}. \end{aligned}$$

Hence, the shearing matrix required to do the transformation is

$$\mathtt{Sh}_z\left(-\frac{x_d}{z_d}, -\frac{y_d}{z_d}\right) = \begin{bmatrix} 1 & 0 & -\frac{x_d}{z_d} & 0 \\ 0 & 1 & -\frac{y_d}{z_d} & 0 \\ 0 & 0 & 1 & 0 \\ 0 & 0 & 0 & 1 \end{bmatrix}. \qquad (9.27)$$

□

**Example 9.23:** [*Shearing the view volume*]
In Example 9.22, if the original direction of projection is $\mathbf{D} = [0, 0, z_d, 0]^T$, determine the change in the shearing matrix $\mathtt{Sh}_z$.

**Solution 9.23:** In this case, the original situation is an orthographic view volume and the parameters of the shearing matrix are

$$\frac{x_d}{z_d} = \frac{y_d}{z_d} = 0.$$

Thus, the shearing matrix turns to an identity matrix:

$$\mathtt{Sh}_z(0, 0) = \begin{bmatrix} 1 & 0 & 0 & 0 \\ 0 & 1 & 0 & 0 \\ 0 & 0 & 1 & 0 \\ 0 & 0 & 0 & 1 \end{bmatrix} = \mathtt{I}.$$

This means that the shearing operation has no effect on the view volume in orthographic case. □

**Example 9.24:** [*Shearing the view volume—getting shearing angles*]
Re-express the shearing matrix of Eq. (9.27) in terms of the angles the direction of projection makes with the $x$- and $y$-axes.

**Solution 9.24:** Consider Fig. 9.22. The direction of projection makes the angles $\alpha_x$ and $\alpha_y$ with the $x$- and $y$-axes respectively. Utilizing trigonometry, we can write

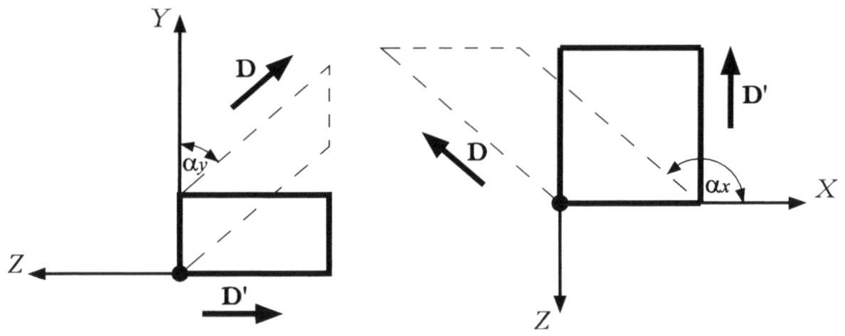


**Fig. 9.22** Using the angles $\alpha_x$ and $\alpha_y$ the direction of projection makes with the $x$- and $y$-axes respectively to shear the view volume

$$-\frac{x_d}{z_d} = -\cot(\alpha_x),$$
$$-\frac{y_d}{z_d} = -\cot(\alpha_y).$$

Therefore, the shearing matrix of Eq. (9.27) can be re-expressed as

$$\mathtt{Sh}_z(-\cot(\alpha_x), -\cot(\alpha_y)) = \begin{bmatrix} 1 & 0 & -\cot(\alpha_x) & 0 \\ 0 & 1 & -\cot(\alpha_y) & 0 \\ 0 & 0 & 1 & 0 \\ 0 & 0 & 0 & 1 \end{bmatrix}. \qquad \square \tag{9.28}$$

**Example 9.25:** [*Transformation into canonical parallel-projection view volume—from general oblique volume*]

The overall transformation from a general oblique view volume into the canonical parallel-projection view volume expressed by Eq. (9.18) involves many steps. What are the steps in sequence?

**Solution 9.25:** The steps are as follows:

1. Translate so that the origin of the view reference coordinate system $\dot{\mathbf{R}} = [x_r, y_r, z_r]^T$ coincides with the origin of the world coordinate system. This is using the vector $-\dot{\mathbf{R}}$ and the translation matrix $\mathtt{M}_1$ where

$$\mathtt{M}_1 = \mathtt{T}(-\dot{\mathbf{R}}) = \begin{bmatrix} 1 & 0 & 0 & -x_r \\ 0 & 1 & 0 & -y_r \\ 0 & 0 & 1 & -z_r \\ 0 & 0 & 0 & 1 \end{bmatrix}.$$

2. Rotate so that the $u$-axis becomes the $x$-axis, the $v$-axis becomes the $y$-axis and the $n$-axis becomes the $z$-axis. This is using the matrix $\mathtt{R}_{VRC}$ of Eq. (9.11) where

$$\mathtt{M}_2 = \mathtt{R}_{VRC} = \begin{bmatrix} x_u & y_u & z_u & 0 \\ x_v & y_v & z_v & 0 \\ x_n & y_n & z_n & 0 \\ 0 & 0 & 0 & 1 \end{bmatrix}.$$

3. Shear so that the bounding planes of the view volume are parallel to the principal planes. This is done by using the matrix $\mathtt{Sh}_z$ of Eq. (9.27) such that

$$\mathtt{M}_3 = \mathtt{Sh}_z\left(-\frac{x_d}{z_d}, -\frac{y_d}{z_d}\right) = \begin{bmatrix} 1 & 0 & -\frac{x_d}{z_d} & 0 \\ 0 & 1 & -\frac{y_d}{z_d} & 0 \\ 0 & 0 & 1 & 0 \\ 0 & 0 & 0 & 1 \end{bmatrix},$$

where $[x_d, y_d, z_d, 0]^T$ is the direction of projection. This shearing step is not required with orthographic projection in which case the matrix $\mathtt{Sh}_z$ turns to the identity matrix (as $x_d = y_d = 0$).
4. Translate so that the center point of the view volume coincides with the origin. From Example 9.20, the translation is done using the translation vector $\left[-\frac{x_{max}+x_{min}}{2}, -\frac{y_{max}+y_{min}}{2}, -\frac{F+B}{2}\right]^T$. The translation matrix is expressed as

$$\mathtt{M}_4 = \mathtt{T}\left(\left[-\frac{x_{max}+x_{min}}{2}, -\frac{y_{max}+y_{min}}{2}, -\frac{F+B}{2}\right]^T\right)$$
$$= \begin{bmatrix} 1 & 0 & 0 & -\frac{x_{max}+x_{min}}{2} \\ 0 & 1 & 0 & -\frac{y_{max}+y_{min}}{2} \\ 0 & 0 & 1 & -\frac{F+B}{2} \\ 0 & 0 & 0 & 1 \end{bmatrix}.$$

Notice that this step differs according to the canonical view volume sought.
5. Scale to comply with the dimensions of the canonical view volume. In case of the canonical view volume expressed by Eq. (9.18), the scaling factors will be $\frac{2}{x_{max}-x_{min}}$, $\frac{2}{y_{max}-y_{min}}$ and $\frac{2}{F-B}$ along the $x$-, $y$- and $z$-axes respectively. The scaling matrix is expressed as

$$\mathtt{M}_5 = \mathtt{S}\left(\frac{2}{x_{max}-x_{min}}, \frac{2}{y_{max}-y_{min}}, \frac{2}{F-B}\right)$$

$$= \begin{bmatrix} \frac{2}{x_{max}-x_{min}} & 0 & 0 & 0 \\ 0 & \frac{2}{y_{max}-y_{min}} & 0 & 0 \\ 0 & 0 & \frac{2}{F-B} & 0 \\ 0 & 0 & 0 & 1 \end{bmatrix}.$$

Notice that this step differs according to the canonical view volume sought.

Therefore, the overall transformation $\mathtt{N}_{par}$ is obtained by concatenating the following matrices:

$$\begin{aligned}
\mathtt{N}_{par} &= \mathtt{M}_5\mathtt{M}_4\mathtt{M}_3\mathtt{M}_2\mathtt{M}_1 \\
&= \mathtt{S}\left(\frac{2}{x_{max}-x_{min}}, \frac{2}{y_{max}-y_{min}}, \frac{2}{F-B}\right) \\
&\quad \mathtt{T}\left(\left[-\frac{x_{max}+x_{min}}{2}, -\frac{y_{max}+y_{min}}{2}, -\frac{F+B}{2}\right]^T\right)\ldots \\
&\quad \ldots \mathtt{Sh}_z\left(-\frac{x_d}{z_d}, -\frac{y_d}{z_d}\right) \mathtt{R}_{VRC}\mathtt{T}(-\dot{\mathbf{R}}) \\
&= \begin{bmatrix} \frac{2}{x_{max}-x_{min}} & 0 & 0 & 0 \\ 0 & \frac{2}{y_{max}-y_{min}} & 0 & 0 \\ 0 & 0 & \frac{2}{F-B} & 0 \\ 0 & 0 & 0 & 1 \end{bmatrix} \begin{bmatrix} 1 & 0 & 0 & -\frac{x_{max}+x_{min}}{2} \\ 0 & 1 & 0 & -\frac{y_{max}+y_{min}}{2} \\ 0 & 0 & 1 & -\frac{F+B}{2} \\ 0 & 0 & 0 & 1 \end{bmatrix} \ldots \\
&\quad \ldots \begin{bmatrix} 1 & 0 & -\frac{x_d}{z_d} & 0 \\ 0 & 1 & -\frac{y_d}{z_d} & 0 \\ 0 & 0 & 1 & 0 \\ 0 & 0 & 0 & 1 \end{bmatrix} \begin{bmatrix} x_u & y_u & z_u & 0 \\ x_v & y_v & z_v & 0 \\ x_n & y_n & z_n & 0 \\ 0 & 0 & 0 & 1 \end{bmatrix} \begin{bmatrix} 1 & 0 & 0 & -x_r \\ 0 & 1 & 0 & -y_r \\ 0 & 0 & 1 & -z_r \\ 0 & 0 & 0 & 1 \end{bmatrix}. \qquad \square
\end{aligned} \tag{9.29}$$

Applying $\mathtt{N}_{par}$ leads to points expressed in *normalized viewing coordinates*. This coordinate system is also known as *normalized device coordinate system* or NDC.

**Example 9.26:** [*Transformation into canonical parallel-projection view volume—from general oblique volume*]

In Example 9.25, if the VRC system coincides with the WCS, derive the matrix $\mathtt{N}_{par}$ in this case.

**Solution 9.26:** The steps are reduced as follows:

1. Shear so that the bounding planes of the view volume are parallel to the principal planes. This is using the matrix $\mathtt{Sh}_z$ of Eq. (9.27):

$$\mathtt{M}_1 = \mathtt{Sh}_z\left(-\frac{x_d}{z_d}, -\frac{y_d}{z_d}\right),$$

where $[x_d, y_d, z_d, 0]^T$ is the direction of projection.

2. Translate so that the center point of the view volume coincides with the origin. The translation matrix is expressed as

$$\mathtt{M}_2 = \mathtt{T}\left(\left[-\frac{x_{max}+x_{min}}{2}, -\frac{y_{max}+y_{min}}{2}, -\frac{F+B}{2}\right]^T\right).$$

3. Scale to comply with the dimensions of the canonical view volume. The scaling matrix is expressed as

$$\mathtt{M}_3 = \mathtt{S}\left(\frac{2}{x_{max}-x_{min}}, \frac{2}{y_{max}-y_{min}}, \frac{2}{F-B}\right).$$

Therefore, the overall transformation $\mathtt{N}_{par}$ is obtained as

$$\begin{aligned}
\mathtt{N}_{par} &= \mathtt{M}_3\mathtt{M}_2\mathtt{M}_1 \\
&= \mathtt{S}\left(\frac{2}{x_{max}-x_{min}}, \frac{2}{y_{max}-y_{min}}, \frac{2}{F-B}\right)\mathtt{T}\left(\left[-\frac{x_{max}+x_{min}}{2}, -\frac{y_{max}+y_{min}}{2}, -\frac{F+B}{2}\right]^T\right)\ldots \\
&\quad\ldots\mathtt{Sh}_z\left(-\frac{x_d}{z_d}, -\frac{y_d}{z_d}\right) \\
&= \begin{bmatrix} \frac{2}{x_{max}-x_{min}} & 0 & 0 & 0 \\ 0 & \frac{2}{y_{max}-y_{min}} & 0 & 0 \\ 0 & 0 & \frac{2}{F-B} & 0 \\ 0 & 0 & 0 & 1 \end{bmatrix}
\begin{bmatrix} 1 & 0 & 0 & -\frac{x_{max}+x_{min}}{2} \\ 0 & 1 & 0 & -\frac{y_{max}+y_{min}}{2} \\ 0 & 0 & 1 & -\frac{F+B}{2} \\ 0 & 0 & 0 & 1 \end{bmatrix}
\begin{bmatrix} 1 & 0 & -\frac{x_d}{z_d} & 0 \\ 0 & 1 & -\frac{y_d}{z_d} & 0 \\ 0 & 0 & 1 & 0 \\ 0 & 0 & 0 & 1 \end{bmatrix}.
\end{aligned} \tag{9.30}$$

**Example 9.27:** [*Transformation into canonical view volume—from general oblique volume*]

Modify the matrix $\mathtt{N}_{par}$ of Eq. (9.29) so that the canonical parallel-projection view volume is expressed using Eq. (9.19) rather than Eq. (9.18).

**Solution 9.27:** The last steps are modified as done in Example 9.21. So, $\mathtt{N}_{par}$ is expressed as

$$
\begin{aligned}
\mathtt{N}_{par} &= \mathtt{M}_6\mathtt{M}_5\mathtt{M}_4\mathtt{M}_3\mathtt{M}_2\mathtt{M}_1\\
&= \mathtt{S}\left(\frac{2}{x_{max}-x_{min}}, \frac{2}{y_{max}-y_{min}}, \frac{2}{F-B}\right)\mathtt{T}\left(\left[-\frac{x_{max}+x_{min}}{2}, -\frac{y_{max}+y_{min}}{2}, -\frac{F+B}{2}\right]^T\right)\dots\\
&\quad \dots\mathtt{Sh}_z\left(-\frac{x_d}{z_d}, -\frac{y_d}{z_d}\right)\mathtt{T}_{rl}\mathtt{R}_{VRC}\mathtt{T}(-\dot{\mathbf{R}})\\
&= \begin{bmatrix} \frac{2}{x_{max}-x_{min}} & 0 & 0 & 0\\ 0 & \frac{2}{y_{max}-y_{min}} & 0 & 0\\ 0 & 0 & \frac{2}{F-B} & 0\\ 0 & 0 & 0 & 1 \end{bmatrix}
\begin{bmatrix} 1 & 0 & 0 & -\frac{x_{max}+x_{min}}{2}\\ 0 & 1 & 0 & -\frac{y_{max}+y_{min}}{2}\\ 0 & 0 & 1 & -\frac{F+B}{2}\\ 0 & 0 & 0 & 1 \end{bmatrix}\dots\\
&\quad \dots\begin{bmatrix} 1 & 0 & -\frac{x_d}{z_d} & 0\\ 0 & 1 & -\frac{y_d}{z_d} & 0\\ 0 & 0 & 1 & 0\\ 0 & 0 & 0 & 1 \end{bmatrix}
\begin{bmatrix} 1 & 0 & 0 & 0\\ 0 & 1 & 0 & 0\\ 0 & 0 & -1 & 0\\ 0 & 0 & 0 & 1 \end{bmatrix}
\begin{bmatrix} x_u & y_u & z_u & 0\\ x_v & y_v & z_v & 0\\ x_n & y_n & z_n & 0\\ 0 & 0 & 0 & 1 \end{bmatrix}
\begin{bmatrix} 1 & 0 & 0 & -x_r\\ 0 & 1 & 0 & -y_r\\ 0 & 0 & 1 & -z_r\\ 0 & 0 & 0 & 1 \end{bmatrix}.
\end{aligned}
\tag{9.31}
$$

Notice that $\mathtt{T}_{rl}$ is used to transform to the left-handed coordinate system expressed by Eq. (9.19). □

### 9.4.2 Perspective Projection

In some cases, a perspective projection view volume is transformed into a canonical perspective-projection view volume defined by Eq. (9.20) or Eq. (9.21). In other cases, a perspective projection view volume is transformed into a canonical parallel-projection view volume defined by Eqs. (9.16), (9.17), (9.18) or (9.19). The next examples discuss some of the transformations.

**Example 9.28:** [*Shearing perspective view volume*]

Assume that the centerline of the perspective view volume goes from the origin of the world coordinate system to a point $\dot{\mathbf{P}} = [5, 6, 7]^T$, which represents the center of the view window in the WCS. Derive a shearing matrix relative to the $z$-axis that forces the centerline of the perspective view volume to coincide with the $z$-axis.

**Solution 9.28:** A shearing matrix relative to the $z$-axis does not change the $z$-coordinates of points. Thus, point $\dot{\mathbf{P}} = [5, 6, 7]^T$ is sheared to $\dot{\mathbf{P}}' = [0, 0, 7]^T$ to reside on the $z$-axis.

Notice that the centerline of the view volume joining the origin to the center of the window (i.e., $\dot{\mathbf{P}}$) is like the direction of projection for parallel projection. Hence, by applying Eq. (9.27), we get

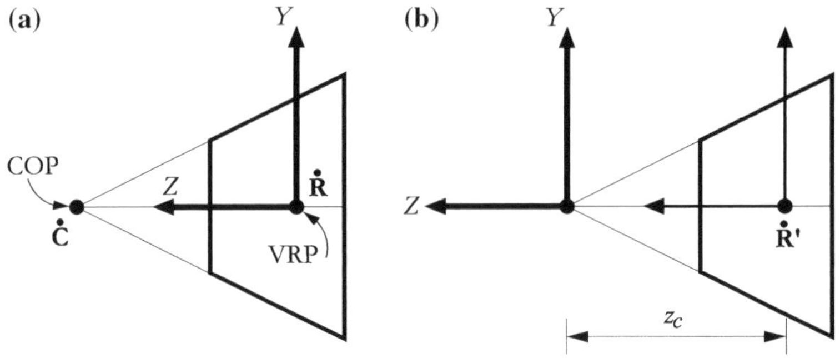


**Fig. 9.23** Cross section of a perspective view volume. **a** The VRP is at the origin of the world coordinate system and the $u$-, $v$- and $n$-axes coincide with the $x$-, $y$- and $z$-axes respectively. **b** The COP is moved to the origin

$$\underbrace{\begin{bmatrix}0\\0\\7\\1\end{bmatrix}}_{\mathbf{P}'} = \underbrace{\begin{bmatrix}1 & 0 & -\frac{x_d}{z_d} & 0\\0 & 1 & -\frac{y_d}{z_d} & 0\\0 & 0 & 1 & 0\\0 & 0 & 0 & 1\end{bmatrix}}_{\mathtt{Sh}_z\left(-\frac{x_d}{z_d},-\frac{y_d}{z_d}\right)} \underbrace{\begin{bmatrix}5\\6\\7\\1\end{bmatrix}}_{\mathbf{P}}.$$

Therefore, the shearing matrix $\mathtt{Sh}_z$ is expressed as

$$\mathtt{Sh}_z = \begin{bmatrix}1 & 0 & -\frac{5}{7} & 0\\0 & 1 & -\frac{6}{7} & 0\\0 & 0 & 1 & 0\\0 & 0 & 0 & 10\end{bmatrix}.$$

□

**Example 9.29:** [*Perspective view volume—translation*]
Assume that the VRP is at the origin of the world coordinate system and the $u$-, $v$- and $n$-axes coincide with the $x$-, $y$- and $z$-axes respectively as shown in Fig. 9.23a. If translation is performed such that the COP is moved to the origin, determine the new location of the VRP.

**Solution 9.29:** The original position of the VRP is $\mathbf{R} = [0, 0, 0, 1]^T$. Figure 9.23b depicts the situation when translation is done such that the COP specified by $\dot{\mathbf{C}} = [x_c, y_c, z_c]^T$ is at the origin. The new location $\dot{\mathbf{R}}'$ of the VRP is then estimated as

$$\underbrace{\begin{bmatrix}x'_r\\y'_r\\z'_r\\1\end{bmatrix}}_{\mathbf{R}'} = \underbrace{\begin{bmatrix}1 & 0 & 0 & -x_c\\0 & 1 & 0 & -y_c\\0 & 0 & 1 & -z_c\\0 & 0 & 0 & 1\end{bmatrix}}_{\mathtt{T}([-x_c,-y_c,-z_c]^T)} \underbrace{\begin{bmatrix}0\\0\\0\\1\end{bmatrix}}_{\mathbf{R}} = \begin{bmatrix}-x_c\\-y_c\\-z_c\\1\end{bmatrix}, \quad (9.32)$$

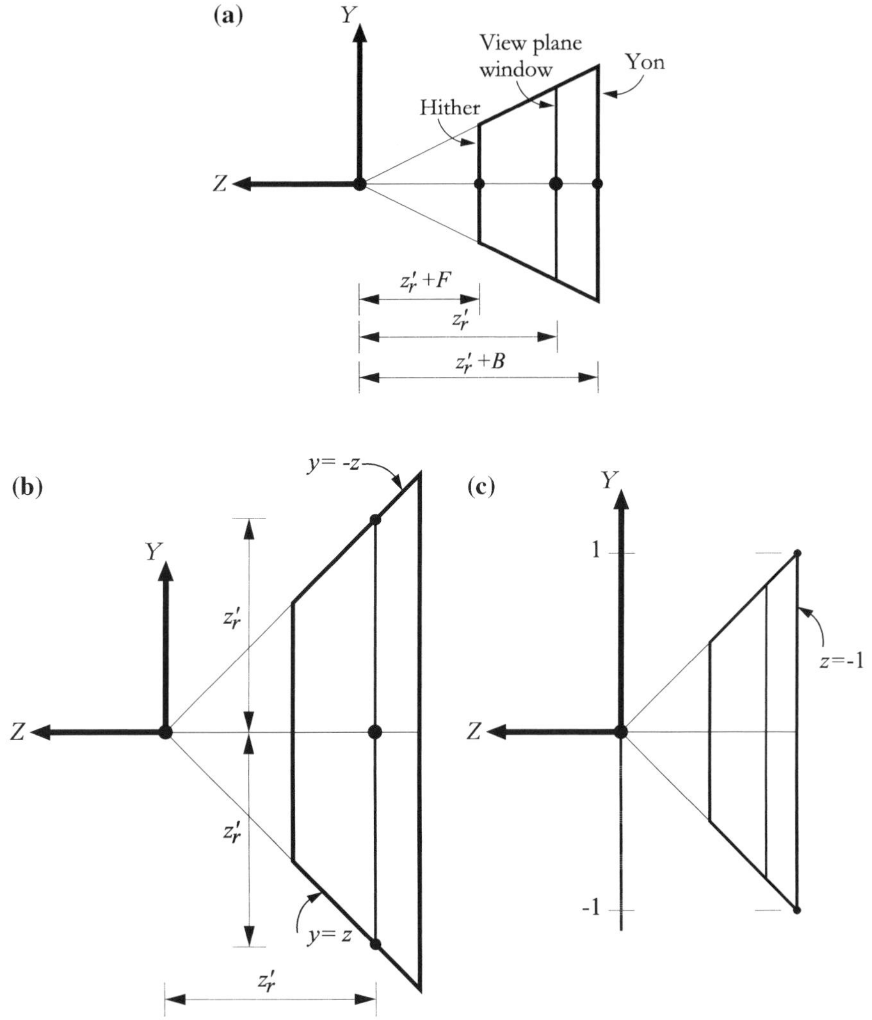


**Fig. 9.24** Cross section of the perspective view volume. **a** Before scaling. **b** After non-uniform scaling along the $x$- and $y$-directions using scaling factors of $\frac{-2z_r'}{u_{max}-u_{min}}$ and $\frac{-2z_r'}{v_{max}-v_{min}}$. **c** After uniform scaling along all directions using a scaling factor of $\frac{-1}{z_r'+B}$. Note that $F$ and $B$ have different signs

which means the new position $\dot{\mathbf{R}}'$ of the VRP is $[-x_c, -y_c, -z_c]^T$. □

**Example 9.30:** [*Perspective view volume—scaling*]

It is required that you scale the perspective view volume we obtained as a result in Example 9.29 (shown in Fig. 9.24a) to comply with that canonical perspective-projection view volume expressed by Eq. (9.20). Get the overall scaling matrix.

**Solution 9.30:** We will perform the scaling in two subsequent steps.

1. Scale along the $x$- and $y$-directions so that the sloped planes have the equations

$$\begin{aligned} x &= z, \\ x &= -z, \\ y &= z, \\ y &= -z. \end{aligned}$$

These equations representing the unit slope of the view volume are the first part of Eq. (9.20). Since the view plane window is centered on the $z$-axis and has the bounds

$$\begin{aligned} -\frac{u_{max}-u_{min}}{2} \leq x \leq \frac{u_{max}-u_{min}}{2}, \\ -\frac{v_{max}-v_{min}}{2} \leq y \leq \frac{v_{max}-v_{min}}{2}, \end{aligned} \tag{9.33}$$

it is scaled to have the size of $-2z'_r \times -2z'_r$. (In other words, we scale the view plane window so that its half-height and half-width are both $z'_r$.) This operation is expressed as

$$\mathtt{M}_1 = \underbrace{\begin{bmatrix} -\frac{2z'_r}{u_{max}-u_{min}} & 0 & 0 & 0 \\ 0 & -\frac{2z'_r}{v_{max}-v_{min}} & 0 & 0 \\ 0 & 0 & 1 & 0 \\ 0 & 0 & 0 & 1 \end{bmatrix}}_{\mathtt{S}\left(-\frac{2z'_r}{u_{max}-u_{min}},-\frac{2z'_r}{v_{max}-v_{min}},1\right)}.$$

2. Scale uniformly along the three axes so that the yon, the back plane, is at $z = -1$ (previously at $z = z'_r + B$). Hence, the uniform scaling factor along the three axes is $-\frac{1}{z'_r+B}$. Note that implementing uniform scaling along all axes ensures that the unit slope of the previous step is intact. Thus, the scaling matrix is expressed as

$$\mathtt{M}_2 = \underbrace{\begin{bmatrix} -\frac{1}{z'_r+B} & 0 & 0 & 0 \\ 0 & -\frac{1}{z'_r+B} & 0 & 0 \\ 0 & 0 & -\frac{1}{z'_r+B} & 0 \\ 0 & 0 & 0 & 1 \end{bmatrix}}_{\mathtt{S}\left(-\frac{1}{z'_r+B},-\frac{1}{z'_r+B},-\frac{1}{z'_r+B}\right)}.$$

The overall scaling operation is then specified as

$$
\begin{aligned}
\mathtt{S} &= \mathtt{M_2 M_1} \\
&= \mathtt{S}\left(-\frac{1}{z'_r+B}, -\frac{1}{z'_r+B}, -\frac{1}{z'_r+B}\right) \mathtt{S}\left(-\frac{2z'_r}{u_{max}-u_{min}}, -\frac{2z'_r}{v_{max}-v_{min}}, 1\right) \\
&= \begin{bmatrix} -\frac{1}{z'_r+B} & 0 & 0 & 0 \\ 0 & -\frac{1}{z'_r+B} & 0 & 0 \\ 0 & 0 & -\frac{1}{z'_r+B} & 0 \\ 0 & 0 & 0 & 1 \end{bmatrix} \begin{bmatrix} -\frac{2z'_r}{u_{max}-u_{min}} & 0 & 0 & 0 \\ 0 & -\frac{2z'_r}{v_{max}-v_{min}} & 0 & 0 \\ 0 & 0 & 1 & 0 \\ 0 & 0 & 0 & 1 \end{bmatrix} \\
&= \begin{bmatrix} \frac{2z'_r}{(u_{max}-u_{min})(z'_r+B)} & 0 & 0 & 0 \\ 0 & \frac{2z'_r}{(v_{max}-v_{min})(z'_r+B)} & 0 & 0 \\ 0 & 0 & \frac{-1}{z'_r+B} & 0 \\ 0 & 0 & 0 & 1 \end{bmatrix}.
\end{aligned}
$$

Notice that the order of applying the subsequent scaling operations will not affect the final matrix. Also, notice that the scaling factors $\frac{2z'_r}{(u_{max}-u_{min})(z'_r+B)}$, $\frac{2z'_r}{(v_{max}-v_{min})(z'_r+B)}$ and $\frac{-1}{z'_r+B}$ are positive since $z'_r$ and $z'_r + B$ are negative. □

**Example 9.31:** [*Perspective view volume—plane equations after scaling*]
Determine the equations of the view, hither and yon planes after the scaling operation performed in Example 9.30.

**Solution 9.31:** Let us get the location of the center of the view plane window (i.e., $[0, 0, z'_r]^T$) after the scaling operation of Example 9.30.

$$
\begin{bmatrix} \frac{2z'_r}{(u_{max}-u_{min})(z'_r+B)} & 0 & 0 & 0 \\ 0 & \frac{2z'_r}{(v_{max}-v_{min})(z'_r+B)} & 0 & 0 \\ 0 & 0 & \frac{-1}{z'_r+B} & 0 \\ 0 & 0 & 0 & 1 \end{bmatrix} \begin{bmatrix} 0 \\ 0 \\ z'_r \\ 1 \end{bmatrix} = \begin{bmatrix} 0 \\ 0 \\ \frac{-z_r}{z'_r+B} \\ 1 \end{bmatrix}. \tag{9.34}
$$

In other words, the view plane equation after scaling becomes

$$
z_{view} = -\frac{z'_r}{z'_r + B}. \tag{9.35}
$$

Similarly, the center of the hither and yon windows before scaling are $[0, 0, z'_r + F]^T$ and $[0, 0, z'_r + B]^T$ respectively. Applying the scaling operation, we will have

$$
\begin{bmatrix} \frac{2z'_r}{(u_{max}-u_{min})(z'_r+B)} & 0 & 0 & 0 \\ 0 & \frac{2z'_r}{(v_{max}-v_{min})(z'_r+B)} & 0 & 0 \\ 0 & 0 & \frac{-1}{z'_r+B} & 0 \\ 0 & 0 & 0 & 1 \end{bmatrix} \begin{bmatrix} 0 \\ 0 \\ z'_r + F \\ 1 \end{bmatrix} = \begin{bmatrix} 0 \\ 0 \\ -\frac{z'_r+F}{z'_r+B} \\ 1 \end{bmatrix} \tag{9.36}
$$

and

$$\begin{bmatrix} \frac{2z'_r}{(u_{max}-u_{min})(z'_r+B)} & 0 & 0 & 0 \\ 0 & \frac{2z'_r}{(v_{max}-v_{min})(z'_r+B)} & 0 & 0 \\ 0 & 0 & \frac{-1}{z'_r+B} & 0 \\ 0 & 0 & 0 & 1 \end{bmatrix} \begin{bmatrix} 0 \\ 0 \\ z'_r + B \\ 1 \end{bmatrix} = \begin{bmatrix} 0 \\ 0 \\ -\frac{z'_r+B}{z'_r+B} \\ 1 \end{bmatrix}. \tag{9.37}$$

In other words, the hither and yon plane equations after scaling become

$$\begin{aligned} z_f &= -\frac{z'_r+F}{z'_r+B}, \\ z_b &= -\frac{z'_r+B}{z'_r+B} = -1. \end{aligned} \tag{9.38}$$

□

**Example 9.32:** [*Transformation into canonical perspective-projection view volume—from general perspective view volume*]

Determine the steps needed to transform a general perspective view volume shown in Fig. 9.25a into the canonical perspective-projection view volume expressed by Eq. (9.20).

**Solution 9.32:** Building on previous examples, the steps are as follows:

1. As in Example 9.25, translate so that the origin of the view reference coordinate system $\dot{\mathbf{R}} = [x_r, y_r, z_r]^T$ coincides with the origin of the world coordinate system. This is using the vector $-\dot{\mathbf{R}}$ and the translation matrix $\mathtt{M}_1$ where

$$\mathtt{M}_1 = \mathtt{T}(-\dot{\mathbf{R}}) = \begin{bmatrix} 1 & 0 & 0 & -x_r \\ 0 & 1 & 0 & -y_r \\ 0 & 0 & 1 & -z_r \\ 0 & 0 & 0 & 1 \end{bmatrix}.$$

   The result of this step is shown in Fig. 9.25b.
2. As in Example 9.25, rotate so that the $u$-axis becomes the $x$-axis, the $v$-axis becomes the $y$-axis and the $n$-axis becomes the $z$-axis. This is using the matrix $\mathtt{R}_{VRC}$ of Eq. (9.11):

$$\mathtt{M}_2 = \mathtt{R}_{VRC} = \begin{bmatrix} x_u & y_u & z_u & 0 \\ x_v & y_v & z_v & 0 \\ x_n & y_n & z_n & 0 \\ 0 & 0 & 0 & 1 \end{bmatrix}.$$

   The result of this step is shown in Fig. 9.25c.
3. As in Example 9.29, translate such that the COP specified by $\dot{\mathbf{C}} = [x_c, y_c, z_c]^T$ is at the origin. The translation matrix is expressed as

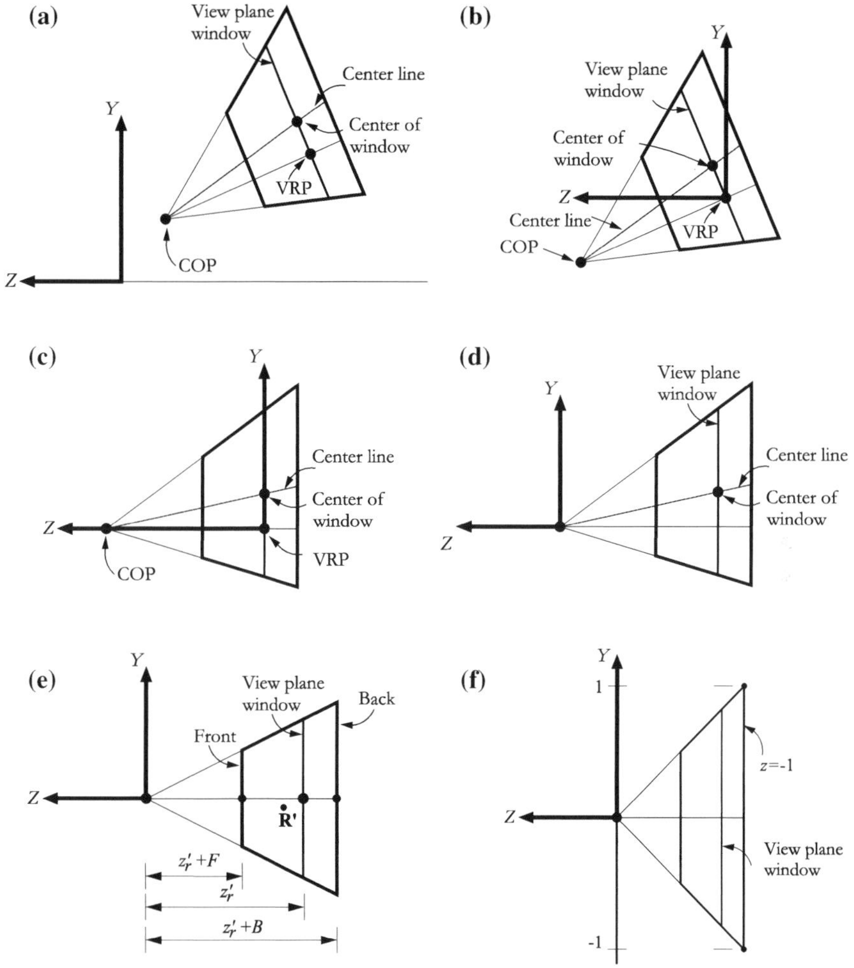


**Fig. 9.25** Turning a general perspective view volume into a canonical perspective-projection view volume. **a** General perspective view volume. **b** After translating the VRP to the origin. **c** After rotating the VRC coordinate system to coincide with the world coordinate system. **d** After translating such that the COP is at the origin of the world coordinate system. **e** After shearing such that the centerline of the view volume coincides with the $z$-axis. **f** After scaling and obtaining the canonical perspective-projection view volume

$$\mathtt{M}_3 = \mathtt{T}([-x_c, -y_c, -z_c]^T) = \begin{bmatrix} 1 & 0 & 0 & -x_c \\ 0 & 1 & 0 & -y_c \\ 0 & 0 & 1 & -z_c \\ 0 & 0 & 0 & 1 \end{bmatrix}.$$

The result of this step is shown in Fig. 9.25d.

4. As in Example 9.28, shear so that the centerline of the perspective view volume (i.e., the line joining the origin of the world coordinate system and the center point of the view plane window) coincides with the $z$-axis. This is using the matrix $\mathtt{Sh}_z$ of Eq. (9.27):

$$\mathtt{M}_4 = \mathtt{Sh}_z\left(-\frac{x_d}{z_d}, -\frac{y_d}{z_d}\right) = \begin{bmatrix} 1 & 0 & -\frac{x_d}{z_d} & 0 \\ 0 & 1 & -\frac{y_d}{z_d} & 0 \\ 0 & 0 & 1 & 0 \\ 0 & 0 & 0 & 1 \end{bmatrix},$$

where $[x_d, y_d, z_d]^T$ is the center of the view plane window before shearing. The result of this step is shown in Fig. 9.25e.

5. As in Example 9.30, scale to transform the view volume into a canonical perspective-projection view volume. The scaling matrix is expressed as

$$\mathtt{M}_5 = \mathtt{S}\left(\frac{2z'_r}{(u_{max}-u_{min})(z'_r+B)}, \frac{2z'_r}{(v_{max}-v_{min})(z'_r+B)}, \frac{-1}{z'_r+B}\right)$$
$$= \begin{bmatrix} \frac{2z'_r}{(u_{max}-u_{min})(z'_r+B)} & 0 & 0 & 0 \\ 0 & \frac{2z'_r}{(v_{max}-v_{min})(z'_r+B)} & 0 & 0 \\ 0 & 0 & \frac{-1}{z'_r+B} & 0 \\ 0 & 0 & 0 & 1 \end{bmatrix}.$$

The result of this step is shown in Fig. 9.25f, which represents the required canonical perspective-projection view volume.

The overall transformation $\mathtt{N}_{per}$ is then estimated as

$$\begin{aligned}\mathtt{N}_{per} &= \mathtt{M}_5\mathtt{M}_4\mathtt{M}_3\mathtt{M}_2\mathtt{M}_1 \\ &= \mathtt{S}\left(\frac{2z'_r}{(u_{max}-u_{min})(z'_r+B)}, \frac{2z'_r}{(v_{max}-v_{min})(z'_r+B)}, \frac{-1}{z'_r+B}\right)\mathtt{Sh}_z\left(-\frac{x_d}{z_d}, -\frac{y_d}{z_d}\right)\ldots \\ &\quad \ldots\mathtt{T}([-x_c, -y_c, -z_c]^T)\mathtt{R}_{VRC}\mathtt{T}(-\dot{\mathbf{R}}) \\ &= \begin{bmatrix} \frac{2z'_r}{(u_{max}-u_{min})(z'_r+B)} & 0 & 0 & 0 \\ 0 & \frac{2z'_r}{(v_{max}-v_{min})(z'_r+B)} & 0 & 0 \\ 0 & 0 & \frac{-1}{z'_r+B} & 0 \\ 0 & 0 & 0 & 1 \end{bmatrix}\begin{bmatrix} 1 & 0 & -\frac{x_d}{z_d} & 0 \\ 0 & 1 & -\frac{y_d}{z_d} & 0 \\ 0 & 0 & 1 & 0 \\ 0 & 0 & 0 & 1 \end{bmatrix}\ldots \\ &\quad \ldots\begin{bmatrix} 1 & 0 & 0 & -x_c \\ 0 & 1 & 0 & -y_c \\ 0 & 0 & 1 & -z_c \\ 0 & 0 & 0 & 1 \end{bmatrix}\begin{bmatrix} x_u & y_u & z_u & 0 \\ x_v & y_v & z_v & 0 \\ x_n & y_n & z_n & 0 \\ 0 & 0 & 0 & 1 \end{bmatrix}\begin{bmatrix} 1 & 0 & 0 & -x_r \\ 0 & 1 & 0 & -y_r \\ 0 & 0 & 1 & -z_r \\ 0 & 0 & 0 & 1 \end{bmatrix}.\end{aligned} \quad (9.39)$$

□

Applying $\mathtt{N}_{per}$ leads to points expressed in *normalized viewing coordinates*.

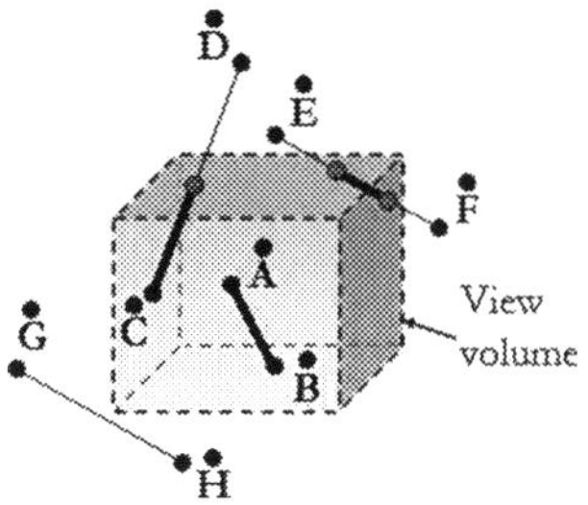


**Fig. 9.26** An example of 3D line clipping. Lines remained after clipping appear thicker

## 9.5 3D Line Clipping

Our discussion here is an extension to that of 2D line clipping (Sect. 2.4). Given a volume specified by two 3D points $[x_{min}, y_{min}, z_{min}]^T$ and $[x_{max}, y_{max}, z_{max}]^T$, a 3D point $[x_1, y_1, z_1]^T$ is within that volume if all the following tests lead to true results:

$$\begin{aligned} x_{min} &\leq x_1 \leq x_{max}, \\ y_{min} &\leq y_1 \leq y_{max}, \\ z_{min} &\leq z_1 \leq z_{max}. \end{aligned} \tag{9.40}$$

Another way for determining whether or not a point is within a volume is explained in Example 9.33.

Now, given a 3D line or a group of 3D lines, a volume can be used to clip those lines so that only lines or portions of lines inside that volume are preserved while the rest of lines or portions of lines are removed. Such an approach is referred to as a *3D line clipping* algorithm. An example of clipping is shown in Fig. 9.26 where lines remained after clipping appear thicker. There are three distinctive cases that may be observed:

1. Both endpoints of the line are *inside* the clip volume as line $\overline{\dot{\mathbf{A}}\dot{\mathbf{B}}}$ shown in Fig. 9.26.
2. One endpoint of the line is *inside* the clip volume while the other endpoint is *outside* the volume as line $\overline{\dot{\mathbf{C}}\dot{\mathbf{D}}}$ shown in Fig. 9.26.
3. Both endpoints of the line are *outside* the clip volume as lines $\overline{\dot{\mathbf{E}}\dot{\mathbf{F}}}$ and $\overline{\dot{\mathbf{G}}\dot{\mathbf{H}}}$ shown in Fig. 9.26.

Dealing with each of the previous cases is different. In the following cases, we assume that the clip volume spans from $[x_{min}, y_{min}, z_{min}]^T$ to $[x_{max}, y_{max}, z_{max}]^T$ and the 3D line goes from $[x_1, y_1, z_1]^T$ to $[x_2, y_2, z_2]^T$.

**Both endpoints are inside the clip volume**: Tests (9.40) can be applied to confirm that both endpoints $[x_1, y_1, z_1]^T$ and $[x_2, y_2, z_2]^T$ are within the volume. In this case, the whole line is preserved and *trivially accepted*.

**Only one endpoint is inside the clip volume**: If tests (9.40) are true for only one of the endpoints, intersection points between the line and the planes of the clip volume

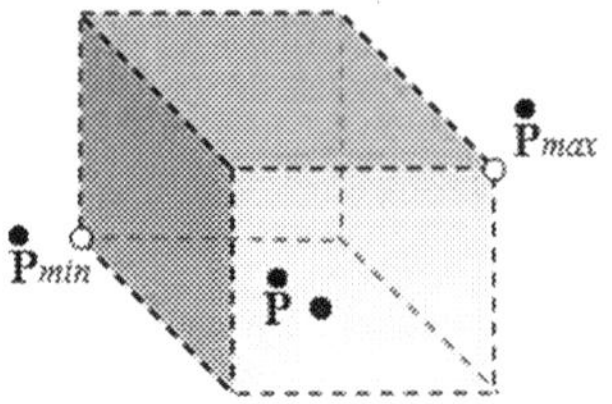


**Fig. 9.27** A point $\dot{\mathbf{P}} = [x, y, z]^T$ falls within a volume bounded by $\dot{\mathbf{P}}_{min} = [x_{min}, y_{min}, z_{min}]^T$ and $\dot{\mathbf{P}}_{max} = [x_{max}, y_{max}, z_{max}]^T$

are detected. (A method for detecting the intersection point between a 3D line and a plane is discussed in Example 9.34. More on detecting intersections is discussed in Sect. 10.6.2.1.)

Note that intersection points may be detected outside the boundaries of the clip volume. Thus, tests (9.40) may be applied to the intersection point to verify that it is within the clip volume. Hence, the portion of the line from the intersection point to the inside endpoint is kept while the rest of the line is removed.

**Both endpoints are outside the clip volume**: If both endpoints are outside the clip volume, the line may be completely outside the clip volume as line $\overline{\dot{\mathbf{G}}\dot{\mathbf{H}}}$ in Fig. 9.26 or part of the line is inside the clip volume as line $\overline{\dot{\mathbf{E}}\dot{\mathbf{F}}}$ in the same figure. In this case, the intersection points between the line and the clip volume must be detected as in the previous case. Caution must be practiced to ensure that an intersection point is within the clip volume by using tests (9.40).

**Example 9.33:** [*3D clipping—point in volume*]

Consider a clip volume that spans from $[x_{min}, y_{min}, z_{min}]^T$ to $[x_{max}, y_{max}, z_{max}]^T$. Determine whether or not a 3D point $\dot{\mathbf{P}} = [x, y, z]^T$ falls within the boundaries of that volume.

**Solution 9.33:** The general equation of a plane is

$$x_n x + y_n y + z_n z - d = 0,$$

where $[x_n, y_n, z_n]^T$ is the normal vector to the plane; and $d$ represents the perpendicular distance to the plane from the origin if $[x_n, y_n, z_n]^T$ is normalized. A point $[x_0, y_0, z_0]^T$ is on the plane if

$$x_n x_0 + y_n y_0 + z_n z_0 - d = 0;$$

otherwise, a signed result is obtained. As the plane splits the space into two halves, all points on one side of the plane will have the same sign when applied to the plane equation while points on the other side will result in the opposite sign when applied to the plane equation. Now, consider Fig. 9.27 where $\dot{\mathbf{P}}_{min}$ is the intersection of the planes $x = x_{min}$, $y = y_{min}$ and $z = z_{min}$ and $\dot{\mathbf{P}}_{max}$ is the intersection of the planes $x = x_{max}$, $y = y_{max}$ and $z = z_{max}$.

A point $\dot{\mathbf{P}} = [x, y, z]^T$ falls within the boundaries of the volume bounded by $\dot{\mathbf{P}}_{min} = [x_{min}, y_{min}, z_{min}]^T$ and $\dot{\mathbf{P}}_{max} = [x_{max}, y_{max}, z_{max}]^T$ if all the following are true:

1. The same sign is obtained when $\dot{\mathbf{P}}$ and $\dot{\mathbf{P}}_{min}$ are applied to the plane $x = x_{max}$.
2. The same sign is obtained when $\dot{\mathbf{P}}$ and $\dot{\mathbf{P}}_{min}$ are applied to the plane $y = y_{max}$.
3. The same sign is obtained when $\dot{\mathbf{P}}$ and $\dot{\mathbf{P}}_{min}$ are applied to the plane $z = z_{max}$.
4. The same sign is obtained when $\dot{\mathbf{P}}$ and $\dot{\mathbf{P}}_{max}$ are applied to the plane $x = x_{min}$.
5. The same sign is obtained when $\dot{\mathbf{P}}$ and $\dot{\mathbf{P}}_{max}$ are applied to the plane $y = y_{min}$.
6. The same sign is obtained when $\dot{\mathbf{P}}$ and $\dot{\mathbf{P}}_{max}$ are applied to the plane $z = z_{min}$. □

**Example 9.34:** [*3D clipping—line-plane intersection in orthographic view volume*]
Consider a clip volume that spans from $[x_{min}, y_{min}, z_{min}]^T$ to $[x_{max}, y_{max}, z_{max}]^T$ and a 3D line that goes from $\dot{\mathbf{P}}_1 = [x_1, y_1, z_1]^T$ to $\dot{\mathbf{P}}_2 = [x_2, y_2, z_2]^T$. Determine the intersection point between the line and the right boundary plane; i.e., $x = x_{max}$.

**Solution 9.34:** Since the clip volume spans from $[x_{min}, y_{min}, z_{min}]^T$ to $[x_{max}, y_{max}, z_{max}]^T$, its bounding planes can be estimated as

$$\begin{aligned} x &= x_{max} \quad \text{(right plane)},\\ x &= x_{min} \quad \text{(left plane)},\\ y &= y_{max} \quad \text{(top plane)},\\ y &= y_{min} \quad \text{(bottom plane)},\\ z &= z_{max} \quad \text{(front plane)},\\ z &= z_{min} \quad \text{(back plane)}. \end{aligned} \tag{9.41}$$

A point $\dot{\mathbf{P}} = [x, y, z]^T$ on the 3D line that goes from $\dot{\mathbf{P}}_1 = [x_1, y_1, z_1]^T$ to $\dot{\mathbf{P}}_2 = [x_2, y_2, z_2]^T$ is expressed as

$$\underbrace{\begin{bmatrix} x \\ y \\ z \end{bmatrix}}_{\dot{\mathbf{P}}} = \underbrace{\begin{bmatrix} x_1 \\ y_1 \\ z_1 \end{bmatrix}}_{\dot{\mathbf{P}}_1} + t \underbrace{\begin{bmatrix} x_2 - x_1 \\ y_2 - y_1 \\ z_2 - z_1 \end{bmatrix}}_{\mathbf{v}} \quad \text{where } t \in [0, 1], \tag{9.42}$$

where $\mathbf{v}$ represents the direction vector $\dot{\mathbf{P}}_2 - \dot{\mathbf{P}}_1$. In order to estimate the intersection point $\dot{\mathbf{P}}$ with the right plane $x = x_{max}$, we substitute the variable $x$ in Eq. (9.42) to get

$$x_{max} = x_1 + t(x_2 - x_1).$$

Thus,

$$t = \frac{x_{max} - x_1}{x_2 - x_1}.$$

Then we substitute the value of $t$ to get the locations of $y$ and $z$. Therefore, the intersection point $\dot{\mathbf{P}}$ is expressed as

**Table 9.1** Assigning outcodes in 3D space

| Bit | Value | Meaning |
|---|---|---|
| 5 | = 1 if endpoint is above the top plane | if $y > y_{max}$ |
| | = 0 otherwise | if $y \leq y_{max}$ |
| 4 | = 1 if endpoint is below the bottom plane | if $y < y_{min}$ |
| | = 0 otherwise | if $y \geq y_{min}$ |
| 3 | = 1 if endpoint is right to the right plane | if $x > x_{max}$ |
| | = 0 otherwise | if $x \leq x_{max}$ |
| 2 | = 1 if endpoint is left to the left plane | if $x < x_{min}$ |
| | = 0 otherwise | if $x \geq x_{min}$ |
| 1 | = 1 if endpoint is behind the back (yon) plane | if $z < z_{min}$ |
| | = 0 otherwise | if $z \geq z_{min}$ |
| 0 | = 1 if endpoint is in front of the front (hither) plane | if $z > z_{max}$ |
| | = 0 otherwise | if $z \leq z_{max}$ |

Bit 5 represents the most-significant bit while bit 0 represents the least-significant bit

$$\begin{bmatrix} x \\ y \\ z \end{bmatrix} = \begin{bmatrix} x_1 + \frac{(x_{max}-x_1)(x_2-x_1)}{x_2-x_1} \\ y_1 + \frac{(x_{max}-x_1)(y_2-y_1)}{x_2-x_1} \\ z_1 + \frac{(x_{max}-x_1)(z_2-z_1)}{x_2-x_1} \end{bmatrix} = \begin{bmatrix} x_{max} \\ y_1 + \frac{(x_{max}-x_1)(y_2-y_1)}{x_2-x_1} \\ z_1 + \frac{(x_{max}-x_1)(z_2-z_1)}{x_2-x_1} \end{bmatrix}. \qquad \square \tag{9.43}$$

### *9.5.1 Clipping Against Canonical View Volume*

The Cohen-Sutherland algorithm discussed in Sect. 2.4.1 can be extended to clip lines in 3D space. In this case, the space is split using the six boundary planes of the view volume resulting in outcodes of 6 bits. Similar to the 2D case, each binary digit indicates where the region is with respect to the view volume that is assigned the outcode 000000. The bits are arranged from left to right as top, bottom, right, left, back and front. Assuming that the view volume spans from $[x_{min}, y_{min}, z_{min}]^T$ to $[x_{max}, y_{max}, z_{max}]^T$, a point $[x, y, z]^T$ is assigned the bit values listed in Table 9.1 starting from the most-significant bit to the least-significant bit.

An outcode for a point $[x, y, z]^T$ is obtained by retrieving the *sign bit* of the following values:

$$\begin{aligned} \text{Bit 5} &\Longrightarrow y_{max} - y, \\ \text{Bit 4} &\Longrightarrow y - y_{min}, \\ \text{Bit 3} &\Longrightarrow x_{max} - x, \\ \text{Bit 2} &\Longrightarrow x - x_{min}, \\ \text{Bit 1} &\Longrightarrow z - z_{min}, \\ \text{Bit 0} &\Longrightarrow z_{max} - z, \end{aligned} \tag{9.44}$$

where bit 5 represents the most-significant bit while bit 0 represents the least-significant bit. A sign bit is 1 for negative values and 0 otherwise. An alternative way to calculate the outcode is by ORing values. If *outcode* is initialized to 000000, it will take the following values:

$$
\begin{aligned}
& outcode = \begin{cases} outcode \text{ OR } 100000, & \text{if } y > y_{max}; \\ outcode \text{ OR } 010000, & \text{if } y < y_{min}; \end{cases} \\
& \text{then} \\
& outcode = \begin{cases} outcode \text{ OR } 001000, & \text{if } x > x_{max}; \\ outcode \text{ OR } 000100, & \text{if } x < x_{min}; \end{cases} \\
& \text{then} \\
& outcode = \begin{cases} outcode \text{ OR } 000010, & \text{if } z < z_{min}; \\ outcode \text{ OR } 000001, & \text{if } z > z_{max}. \end{cases}
\end{aligned}
\tag{9.45}
$$

Now, given two outcodes, we may have the following possibilities:

1. Bitwise-OR the bits. This results in a value of 000000 if both endpoints are in the view volume (i.e., having the same outcode of 000000). In this case, *trivially accept* the line. The OR truth table is listed in Table 2.2
2. Otherwise, bitwise-AND the bits. This results in a value other than 000000 if both endpoints are outside the view volume (i.e., having the same outcode that is not equal to 000000). In this case, *trivially reject* the line. The AND truth table is listed in Table 2.2.
3. Otherwise, segment the line using the bounding planes of the view volume.

**Example 9.35:** [*3D clipping—line-plane intersection in canonical perspective-projection view volume*]

Consider the canonical perspective-projection view volume expressed by Eq. (9.20) and a 3D line that goes from $\dot{\mathbf{P}}_1 = [x_1, y_1, z_1]^T$ to $\dot{\mathbf{P}}_2 = [x_2, y_2, z_2]^T$. Determine the intersection point between the line and the right boundary plane $x = -z$.

**Solution 9.35:** From Eq. (9.42), we know that

$$x = x_1 + t(x_2 - x_1)$$

and

$$z = z_1 + t(z_2 - z_1).$$

At an intersection point on the $x = -z$ plane, we can write

$$
\begin{aligned}
x &= -z \\
x_1 + t(x_2 - x_1) &= -(z_1 + t(z_2 - z_1)).
\end{aligned}
$$

Hence,

$$t = -\frac{x_1 + z_1}{(x_2 - x_1) + (z_2 - z_1)}.$$

Using the value of $t$, the intersection point $\dot{\mathbf{P}}$ on the right bounding plane is expressed as

$$\begin{bmatrix} x \\ y \\ z \end{bmatrix} = \begin{bmatrix} x_1 - \frac{(x_1+z_1)(x_2-x_1)}{(x_2-x_1)+(z_2-z_1)} \\ y_1 - \frac{(x_1+z_1)(y_2-y_1)}{(x_2-x_1)+(z_2-z_1)} \\ z_1 - \frac{(x_1+z_1)(z_2-z_1)}{(x_2-x_1)+(z_2-z_1)} \end{bmatrix}. \qquad \square \tag{9.46}$$

**Example 9.36:** [*3D clipping—canonical perspective-projection view volume*]
Extend the Cohen-Sutherland algorithm to clip 3D lines against the canonical perspective-projection view volume expressed by Eq. (9.20).

**Solution 9.36:** Like the parallel projection case, a 6-bit outcode is to be generated for a given point. The values of the bits are given in the following table which starts from the most-significant bit to the least-significant bit:

| Bit | Value | Meaning |
|---|---|---|
| 5 | = 1 if endpoint is above the top plane | if $y > -z$ |
| | = 0 otherwise | if $y \leq -z$ |
| 4 | = 1 if endpoint is below the bottom plane | if $y < z$ |
| | = 0 otherwise | if $y \geq z$ |
| 3 | = 1 if endpoint is right to the right plane | if $x > -z$ |
| | = 0 otherwise | if $x \leq -z$ |
| 2 | = 1 if endpoint is left to the left plane | if $x < z$ |
| | = 0 otherwise | if $x \geq z$ |
| 1 | = 1 if endpoint is behind the back (yon) plane | if $z < -1$ |
| | = 0 otherwise | if $z \geq -1$ |
| 0 | = 1 if endpoint is in front of the front (hither) plane | if $z > z_f$ |
| | = 0 otherwise | if $z \leq z_f$ |

An outcode for a point $[x, y, z]^T$ is obtained by retrieving the *sign bit* of the following values:

$$\begin{aligned} \text{Bit 5} &\Longrightarrow -z - y, \\ \text{Bit 4} &\Longrightarrow y - z, \\ \text{Bit 3} &\Longrightarrow -z - x, \\ \text{Bit 2} &\Longrightarrow x - z, \\ \text{Bit 1} &\Longrightarrow z + 1, \\ \text{Bit 0} &\Longrightarrow z_f - z, \end{aligned} \tag{9.47}$$

where bit 5 represents the most-significant bit while bit 0 represents the least-significant bit. A sign bit is 1 for negative values and 0 otherwise. An alternative way to calculate the outcode is by using by ORing values. If *outcode* is initialized to 000000, it will take the following values:

$$
\begin{aligned}
outcode &= \begin{cases} outcode \text{ OR } 100000, & \text{if } y > -z; \\ outcode \text{ OR } 010000, & \text{if } y < z; \end{cases} \\
\text{then} & \\
outcode &= \begin{cases} outcode \text{ OR } 001000, & \text{if } x > -z; \\ outcode \text{ OR } 000100, & \text{if } x < z; \end{cases} \\
\text{then} & \\
outcode &= \begin{cases} outcode \text{ OR } 000010, & \text{if } z < -1; \\ outcode \text{ OR } 000001, & \text{if } z > z_f. \end{cases}
\end{aligned}
\tag{9.48}
$$

Identical to the parallel projection case and given two outcodes, we may have the following possibilities:

1. Bitwise-OR the bits. This results in a value of 000000 if both endpoints are in the view volume (i.e., having the same outcode of 000000). In this case, *trivially accept* the line. The OR truth table is listed in Table 2.2.
2. Otherwise, bitwise-AND the bits. This results in a value other than 000000 if both endpoints are outside the view volume (i.e., having the same outcode that is not equal to 000000). In this case, *trivially reject* the line. The AND truth table is listed in Table 2.2.
3. Otherwise, segment the line using the bounding planes of the view volume. Example 9.35 explains how to find intersection points on sloping planes. □

## 9.6 Projection of View Volume Contents

At this stage, projection is performed on the contents of the canonical view volume. Those of the canonical parallel-projection view volume can be projected using the projection matrix of Eq. (8.3). That is

$$
\mathrm{P}_{par} = \begin{bmatrix} 1 & 0 & 0 & 0 \\ 0 & 1 & 0 & 0 \\ 0 & 0 & 0 & 0 \\ 0 & 0 & 0 & 1 \end{bmatrix} \tag{9.49}
$$

and those of the canonical perspective-projection view volume can be projected using the projection matrix of Eq. (8.57). That is

$$
\mathrm{P}_{per} = \begin{bmatrix} 1 & 0 & 0 & 0 \\ 0 & 1 & 0 & 0 \\ 0 & 0 & 1 & 0 \\ 0 & 0 & \frac{1}{d} & 0 \end{bmatrix}, \tag{9.50}
$$

where $d = -1$ for the canonical view volume that is along the $-z$-axis. Thus,

$$\mathtt{P}_{per} = \begin{bmatrix} 1 & 0 & 0 & 0 \\ 0 & 1 & 0 & 0 \\ 0 & 0 & 1 & 0 \\ 0 & 0 & -1 & 0 \end{bmatrix}. \tag{9.51}$$

## 9.7 Perspective Normalization

According to the type of projection, we can use either canonical parallel-projection view volume (Sect. 9.4.1) or canonical perspective-projection view volume (Sect. 9.4.2). The procedure of clipping (Sect. 9.5) that is suitable for the type of the view volume is then applied.

There is a another option that is used by many computer graphics systems and application programming interfaces (API). This is by transforming the perspective view volume into a canonical parallel-projection view volume; a process that is referred to as *perspective normalization*. The rest of the viewing pipeline is performed as done in the parallel projection case. The question now is: How can we apply this perspective normalization step? The answer is detailed in Example 9.37.

**Example 9.37:** [*Transformation into canonical parallel-projection view volume—from perspective view volume*]

Consider the following singular perspective matrix $\mathtt{P}'_{per}$ that projects 3D points onto the $xy$-plane (i.e., $z = 0$):

$$\mathtt{P}'_{per} = \begin{bmatrix} 1 & 0 & 0 & 0 \\ 0 & 1 & 0 & 0 \\ 0 & 0 & 0 & 0 \\ 0 & 0 & -1 & 0 \end{bmatrix}.$$

So a homogeneous point $\mathbf{P} = [x, y, z, 1]^T$ is projected as the homogeneous point $[x, y, 0, -z]^T$ (or equivalently as the inhomogeneous point $\left[-\frac{x}{z}, -\frac{y}{z}, 0, 1\right]^T$). Now consider the following equation:

$$\underbrace{\begin{bmatrix} 1 & 0 & 0 & 0 \\ 0 & 1 & 0 & 0 \\ 0 & 0 & 0 & 0 \\ 0 & 0 & 0 & 1 \end{bmatrix}}_{\mathtt{P}_{par}} \underbrace{\begin{bmatrix} 1 & 0 & 0 & 0 \\ 0 & 1 & 0 & 0 \\ 0 & 0 & \alpha & \beta \\ 0 & 0 & -1 & 0 \end{bmatrix}}_{\mathtt{M}} = \underbrace{\begin{bmatrix} 1 & 0 & 0 & 0 \\ 0 & 1 & 0 & 0 \\ 0 & 0 & 0 & 0 \\ 0 & 0 & -1 & 0 \end{bmatrix}}_{\mathtt{P}'_{per}}.$$

This means that applying the matrix $\mathtt{M}$ followed by applying the front projection matrix [i.e., $\mathtt{P}_{par}$ in Eq. (9.49)] is equivalent to applying the projection matrix $\mathtt{P}'_{per}$. Thus, for a 3D point $\mathbf{P}$, we may write

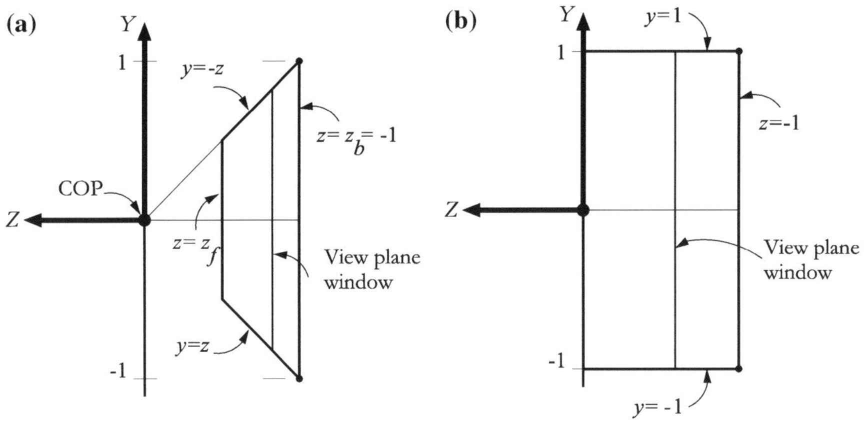


**Fig. 9.28** Turning **a** the canonical perspective-projection view volume expressed by Eq. (9.20) into **b** the canonical parallel-projection view volume expressed by Eq. (9.16)

$$\mathtt{P}_{par}\mathtt{M}\mathbf{P} = \mathtt{P}'_{per}\mathbf{P}.$$

In fact, the matrix M is used as a perspective normalization matrix that transforms the canonical perspective-projection view volume expressed by Eq. (9.20) and shown in Fig. 9.28a into the canonical parallel-projection view volume expressed by Eq. (9.16) and shown in Fig. 9.28b. Estimate the values of $\alpha$ and $\beta$.

**Solution 9.37:** Apply the matrix M to point $\mathbf{P} = [x, y, z, 1]^T$ to get

$$\underbrace{\begin{bmatrix} 1 & 0 & 0 & 0 \\ 0 & 1 & 0 & 0 \\ 0 & 0 & \alpha & \beta \\ 0 & 0 & -1 & 0 \end{bmatrix}}_{\mathtt{M}} \underbrace{\begin{bmatrix} x \\ y \\ z \\ 1 \end{bmatrix}}_{\mathbf{P}} = \underbrace{\begin{bmatrix} x \\ y \\ \alpha z + \beta \\ -z \end{bmatrix}}_{\mathbf{P}'} \Longrightarrow \begin{bmatrix} -\frac{x}{z} \\ -\frac{y}{z} \\ -\frac{\alpha z + \beta}{z} \\ 1 \end{bmatrix}. \tag{9.52}$$

We want to estimate $\alpha$ and $\beta$ such that the $z$-coordinate of the front plane of Eq. (9.20); i.e., $z = z_f$ (where $z_f < 0$) becomes the front plane of Eq. (9.16); i.e., $z = 0$ and the back plane of Eq. (9.20); i.e., $z = z_b = -1$ becomes the back plane of Eq. (9.16); i.e., $z = -1$. Thus, for the front plane, we have

$$-\frac{\alpha z_f + \beta}{z_f} = 0$$

or

$$\beta = -\alpha z_f$$

and for the back plane, we have

$$-\frac{\alpha z_b + \beta}{z_b} = -1.$$

Since $z_b = -1$, we can write

$$\alpha - \beta = 1.$$

Substituting the value of $\beta$, we get

$$\alpha + \alpha z_f = 1.$$

Hence,

$$\alpha = \frac{1}{1 + z_f}.$$

Thus,

$$\beta = -\frac{z_f}{1 + z_f}.$$

So, the perspective normalization matrix can be expressed as

$$\mathtt{M} = \begin{bmatrix} 1 & 0 & 0 & 0 \\ 0 & 1 & 0 & 0 \\ 0 & 0 & \frac{1}{1+z_f} & -\frac{z_f}{1+z_f} \\ 0 & 0 & -1 & 0 \end{bmatrix}, \tag{9.53}$$

where $z_f \neq -1$. The matrix M maps the hither (i.e., the front plane) to $z = 0$, the yon (i.e., the back plane) to $z = -1$ and the side planes to $x = \pm 1$ and $y = \pm 1$.

So, a general *perspective* view volume can be transformed directly to a canonical *parallel*-projection view volume by utilizing the transformation $\mathtt{N}_{per}$ of Eq. (9.39) and the matrix M of Eq. (9.53) to get

$$\begin{aligned} \mathtt{N}'_{per} &= \mathtt{M}\,\mathtt{N}_{per} \\ &= \mathtt{M}\,\mathtt{S}\left(\frac{2z'_r}{(u_{max}-u_{min})(z'_r+B)}, \frac{2z'_r}{(v_{max}-v_{min})(z'_r+B)}, \frac{-1}{z'_r+B}\right)\mathtt{Sh}_z\left(-\frac{x_d}{z_d}, -\frac{y_d}{z_d}\right)\ldots \\ &\quad \ldots\mathtt{T}([-x_c, -y_c, -z_c]^T)\mathtt{R}_{VRC}\mathtt{T}(-\dot{\mathbf{R}}). \end{aligned} \tag{9.54}$$

An example of using the matrix M turning a canonical perspective-projection view volume into a canonical parallel-projection view volume is shown in Fig. 9.29. Notice that the rectangular object is distorted after transformation, which results in correct orthogonal projection.

Applying this perspective normalization step transforms the perspective view volume into a canonical parallel-projection view volume while maintaining the depth order. This step allows a single clipping procedure for both parallel and perspective view volumes, which simplifies clipping in the perspective case. In addition, we work

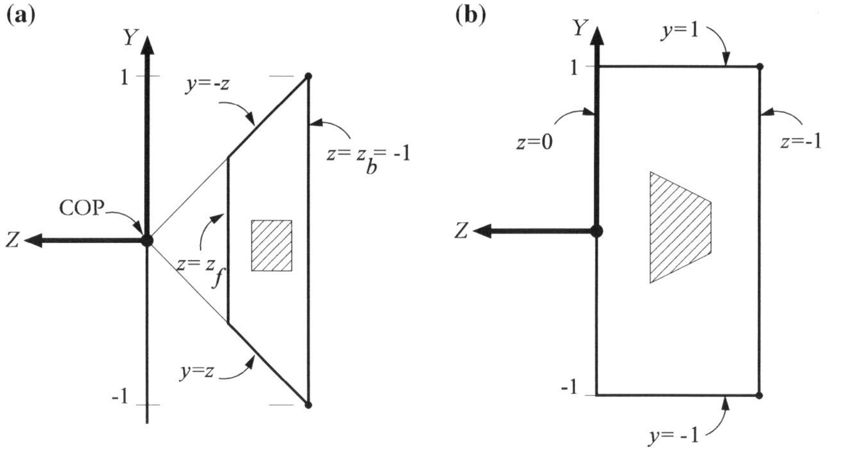


**Fig. 9.29** An example of turning a canonical perspective-projection view volume into a canonical parallel-projection view volume

on the 4D homogeneous coordinates to keep 3D information needed for hidden surface removal (Chap. 10). Also, homogeneous points having negative $W$ (i.e., the fourth term in a homogeneous point 4D vector)[1] can be clipped correctly in homogeneous coordinates in contrary to 3D space. □

**Example 9.38:** [*Transformation into canonical parallel-projection view volume—from perspective view volume*]

Assume that the near or front plane of a perspective view volume defined by the equation $z = -n$ is mapped to the plane $z = -1$ and the far or back plane defined by the equation $z = -f$ is mapped to the plane $z = 1$. Estimate the values of $\alpha$ and $\beta$ in Eq. (9.52) to obtain the canonical view volume expressed by Eq. (9.19).

**Solution 9.38:** Utilizing Eq. (9.52) for the near plane, we have

$$-\frac{\alpha z + \beta}{z} = -1$$

or

$$-\alpha + \frac{\beta}{n} = -1.$$

Thus,

$$\alpha = \frac{\beta}{n} + 1 \tag{9.55}$$

and for the back plane, we have

[1] This may happen due to unusual homogeneous transformations and the use of rational parametric splines (Foley et al. 1995).

$$-\frac{\alpha z + \beta}{z} = 1$$

or

$$-\alpha + \frac{\beta}{f} = 1.$$

So, substituting the value of $\alpha$ from Eq. (9.55), we get

$$-\frac{\beta}{n} - 1 + \frac{\beta}{f} = 1.$$

Hence,

$$\beta = -\frac{2fn}{f - n}.$$

Substituting the value of $\beta$ in Eq. (9.55), we get

$$\alpha = -\frac{f + n}{f - n}.$$

After this normalization step, notice that the positive $z$-coordinates increase with increasing the depth (i.e., a left-handed coordinate system). This can be utilized for determining hidden surfaces (Chap. 10) by applying z-buffering (Sect. 10.4). □

**Example 9.39:** [*Transformation into canonical parallel-projection view volume—from perspective view volume*]

Assume that the near or front plane of a perspective view volume defined by the equation $z = -n$ is mapped to the plane $z = 1$ and the far or back plane defined by the equation $z = -f$ is mapped to the plane $z = -1$. Estimate the values of $\alpha$ and $\beta$ in Eq. (9.52) to obtain the canonical view volume expressed by Eq. (9.18).

**Solution 9.39:** Utilizing Eq. (9.52) for the near plane, we have

$$-\frac{\alpha z + \beta}{z} = 1$$

or

$$-\alpha + \frac{\beta}{n} = 1.$$

Thus,

$$\alpha = \frac{\beta}{n} - 1 \tag{9.56}$$

and for the back plane, we have

$$-\frac{\alpha z + \beta}{z} = -1$$

or

$$-\alpha + \frac{\beta}{f} = -1.$$

So, substituting the value of $\alpha$ from Eq. (9.56), we get

$$-\frac{\beta}{n} + 1 + \frac{\beta}{f} = -1.$$

Hence,

$$\beta = \frac{2fn}{f - n}.$$

Substituting the value of $\beta$ in Eq. (9.56), we get

$$\alpha = \frac{f + n}{f - n}.$$

□

**Example 9.40:** [*Transformation into canonical parallel-projection view volume—from perspective view volume*]

Consider a perspective view volume that is defined in a left-handed coordinate system. Assume that the near or front plane defined by the equation $z = n$ is mapped to the plane $z = 0$ and the far or back plane defined by the equation $z = f$ is mapped to the plane $z = 1$. Estimate the values of $\alpha$ and $\beta$ in Eq. (9.52) to obtain the canonical view volume expressed by Eq. (9.17).

**Solution 9.40:** In this case, $d = 1$ since the view volume is along the $+z$-axis. Hence, the matrix M is modified as

$$\underbrace{\begin{bmatrix} 1 & 0 & 0 & 0 \\ 0 & 1 & 0 & 0 \\ 0 & 0 & \alpha & \beta \\ 0 & 0 & 1 & 0 \end{bmatrix}}_{\mathtt{M}} \underbrace{\begin{bmatrix} x \\ y \\ z \\ 1 \end{bmatrix}}_{\mathbf{P}} = \underbrace{\begin{bmatrix} x \\ y \\ \alpha z + \beta \\ z \end{bmatrix}}_{\mathbf{P}'} \Longrightarrow \begin{bmatrix} \frac{x}{z} \\ \frac{y}{z} \\ \frac{\alpha z+\beta}{z} \\ 1 \end{bmatrix}. \tag{9.57}$$

Continuing as Examples 9.37, 9.38 and 9.39, the final values of $\alpha$ and $\beta$ are obtained as

$$\alpha = -\frac{f}{n - f}$$

and

$$\beta = \frac{nf}{n - f}.$$

The derivation is left as an exercise. □

## 9.8 Clipping in Homogeneous Coordinates

An inhomogeneous 3D point $\dot{\mathbf{P}} = [x, y, z]^T$ can be expressed in homogeneous coordinates as $\mathbf{P} = [X, Y, Z, W]^T$ where $x = \frac{X}{W}$, $y = \frac{Y}{W}$ and $z = \frac{Z}{W}$. Thus, a canonical volume expressed by Eq. (9.16) can be re-expressed as

$$\begin{aligned} X &= -W, \\ X &= W, \\ Y &= -W, \\ Y &= W, \\ Z &= 0, \\ Z &= -W. \end{aligned} \tag{9.58}$$

This volume can be expressed using the following inequalities:

$$\begin{aligned} -1 \le \frac{X}{W} \le 1, \\ -1 \le \frac{Y}{W} \le 1, \\ -1 \le \frac{Z}{W} \le 0 \end{aligned} \tag{9.59}$$

or by multiplying these inequalities by $W$, we get

$$\begin{aligned} -W \le X \le W, \\ -W \le Y \le W, \\ -W \le Z \le 0. \end{aligned} \tag{9.60}$$

This would work well when $W > 0$; however, when $W < 0$, the inequalities change to

$$\begin{aligned} -W \ge X \ge W, \\ -W \ge Y \ge W, \\ -W \ge Z \ge 0. \end{aligned} \tag{9.61}$$

## 9.9 Transforming into Device Coordinates

The final step in the viewing pipeline is to map the clipped environment into a viewport on the screen. It is simply transforming the canonical view volume into another volume that complies with the dimensions of the requested viewport. The following example explains the case for the view volume expressed by Eq. (9.16).

**Example 9.41:** [*Device coordinates—from a view volume to a viewport*]

Determine the steps needed to transform a canonical parallel-projection view volume expressed by Eq. (9.16) into a 3D viewport bounded by the locations $[x_{min}, y_{min}, z_{min}]^T$ and $[x_{max}, y_{max}, z_{max}]^T$.

**Solution 9.41:** The following transformations are applied:

1. Translate such that the corner $[-1, -1, -1]^T$ of the canonical view volume is moved to the origin. This is simply by using the translation vector $[1, 1, 1]^T$. The translation matrix is expressed as

$$\mathtt{M}_1 = \mathtt{T}([1, 1, 1]^T) = \begin{bmatrix} 1 & 0 & 0 & 1 \\ 0 & 1 & 0 & 1 \\ 0 & 0 & 1 & 1 \\ 0 & 0 & 0 & 1 \end{bmatrix}.$$

2. Scale the $2 \times 2 \times 1$ view volume to have the size of $(x_{max} - x_{min}) \times (y_{max} - y_{min}) \times (z_{max} - z_{min})$. This is by using the scaling factors $\frac{x_{max}-x_{min}}{2}$, $\frac{y_{max}-y_{min}}{2}$ and $\frac{z_{max}-z_{min}}{1}$. The scaling matrix is expressed as

$$\begin{aligned} \mathtt{M}_2 &= \mathtt{S}\left(\frac{x_{max}-x_{min}}{2}, \frac{y_{max}-y_{min}}{2}, \frac{z_{max}-z_{min}}{1}\right) \\ &= \begin{bmatrix} \frac{x_{max}-x_{min}}{2} & 0 & 0 & 0 \\ 0 & \frac{y_{max}-y_{min}}{2} & 0 & 0 \\ 0 & 0 & \frac{z_{max}-z_{min}}{1} & 0 \\ 0 & 0 & 0 & 1 \end{bmatrix}. \end{aligned}$$

3. Translate the view volume to the lower left corner of the viewport (i.e., to $[x_{min}, y_{min}, z_{min}]^T$). The translation matrix is expressed as

$$\mathtt{M}_3 = \mathtt{T}([x_{min}, y_{min}, z_{min}]^T) = \begin{bmatrix} 1 & 0 & 0 & x_{min} \\ 0 & 1 & 0 & y_{min} \\ 0 & 0 & 1 & z_{min} \\ 0 & 0 & 0 & 1 \end{bmatrix}.$$

Thus, the overall transformation into the 3D viewport is obtained as

$$\begin{aligned} \mathtt{M} &= \mathtt{M}_3\mathtt{M}_2\mathtt{M}_1 \\ &= \mathtt{T}([x_{min}, y_{min}, z_{min}]^T)\mathtt{S}\left(\frac{x_{max}-x_{min}}{2}, \frac{y_{max}-y_{min}}{2}, \frac{z_{max}-z_{min}}{1}\right)\mathtt{T}([1, 1, 1]^T) \\ &= \begin{bmatrix} 1 & 0 & 0 & x_{min} \\ 0 & 1 & 0 & y_{min} \\ 0 & 0 & 1 & z_{min} \\ 0 & 0 & 0 & 1 \end{bmatrix} \begin{bmatrix} \frac{x_{max}-x_{min}}{2} & 0 & 0 & 0 \\ 0 & \frac{y_{max}-y_{min}}{2} & 0 & 0 \\ 0 & 0 & \frac{z_{max}-z_{min}}{1} & 0 \\ 0 & 0 & 0 & 1 \end{bmatrix} \begin{bmatrix} 1 & 0 & 0 & 1 \\ 0 & 1 & 0 & 1 \\ 0 & 0 & 1 & 1 \\ 0 & 0 & 0 & 1 \end{bmatrix}. \end{aligned} \tag{9.62}$$

It is easy to get the inhomogeneous points (Sect. B.7) after this series of transformations where the 2D position is obtained. As said, the $z$-coordinates may be utilized to remove hidden surfaces (Chap. 10) by applying $z$-buffering (Sect. 10.4).

In case of having a canonical perspective-projection view volume, perspective normalization can be applied to the view volume to get a canonical parallel-projection view volume prior to applying the above translation-scaling-translation operation. □

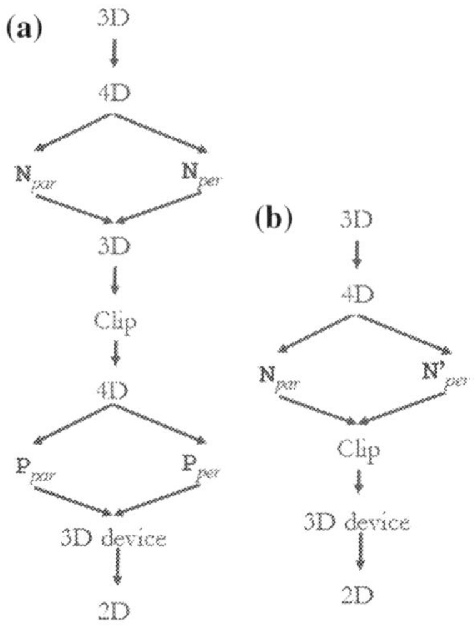


**Fig. 9.30** Viewing pipeline steps **a** when $W > 0$. **b** When $W < 0$ or when a single clipping procedure is desired

## 9.10 Wrapping it up

After defining all the pieces of viewing pipeline, we wrap up our discussion in this section in a few points. Essentially, there are two different routes implementing the viewing process.

1. When $W > 0$: This implementation was shown in Fig. 9.1; however, different coordinate systems are involved and should be emphasized. Thus, given an input as a 3D model in the world coordinate system, the steps are as follows (Fig. 9.30a):
   (a) *Switching coordinates*: Switch from 3D inhomogeneous space into 4D homogeneous space.
   (b) *Viewing transformation*: Apply viewing transformation as in Sect. 9.1. This step may be applied in inhomogeneous coordinates; thus, it may be performed before the previous step.
   (c) *Normalizing transformation*: Perform normalizing transformation. Steps 1b and 1c are applied using $\mathtt{N}_{par}$ for canonical parallel-projection view volume and $\mathtt{N}_{per}$ for canonical perspective-projection view volume. Refer to Sect. 9.4.
   (d) *Switching coordinates*: Switch from 4D homogeneous space into 3D inhomogeneous space.
   (e) *Clipping*: According to the type of the view volume (i.e., parallel or perspective), clipping is performed. Refer to Sect. 9.5.
   (f) *Switching coordinates*: Switch from 3D inhomogeneous space into 4D homogeneous space.
   (g) *Projection*: According to the type of the view volume (i.e., parallel or perspective), projection is performed. Refer to Sect. 9.6.

(h) *Viewport transformation*: Transformation into device coordinates is done as in Sect. 9.9.
(i) *Switching coordinates*: Switching to 2D screen coordinates is done by dividing by $W$.

2. When $W < 0$ or when a single clipping procedure is desired: The steps are as follows (Fig. 9.30b):
   (a) *Switching coordinates*: Switch from 3D inhomogeneous space into 4D homogeneous space.
   (b) *Viewing transformation*: Apply viewing transformation as in Sect. 9.1. This step may be applied in inhomogeneous coordinates; thus, it may be performed before the previous step.
   (c) *Normalizing transformation*: Perform normalizing transformation. Steps 2b and 2c are applied using $\mathrm{N}_{par}$ or $\mathrm{N}'_{per}$ according to the type of view volume considered. Refer to Sects. 9.4 and 9.7.
   (d) *Clipping*: According to whether $W > 0$ or $W < 0$, clipping is performed utilizing Eqs. (9.61) or (9.61).
   (e) *Viewport transformation*: Transformation into device coordinates is done as in Sect. 9.9.
   (f) *Switching coordinates*: Switching to 2D screen coordinates is done by dividing by $W$.

## 9.11 Problems

**Problem 9.1:** [*View reference coordinate system—axes*]
Define the axes of the view reference coordinate system if the VRP is located at $[3, 4, 5]^T$ and the point $[7, 8, 10]^T$ is located along the $n$-axis of the view reference coordinate system. (Both points are expressed in world coordinates.)

**Problem 9.2:** [*View reference coordinate system—expressing points in view reference coordinates given world coordinates*]
Express the position of the world point $[-7, -8, -10]^T$ in terms of the view reference coordinate system established in Problem 9.1.

**Problem 9.3:** [*View reference coordinate system—expressing points in view reference coordinates given world coordinates*]
A unit cube is placed in the world coordinate system such that two corners reside at $[0, 0, 0]^T$ and $[1, 1, 1]^T$. Consider a view reference coordinate system such that the $n$-axis is indicated by the vector $[1, 1, 1]^T$ and the VRP is positioned at $[4, 4, 4]^T$. Determine the locations of the corners $[1, 1, 0]^T$ and $[1, 1, 1]^T$ in view reference coordinates.

**Problem 9.4:** [*Direction of parallel projection*]

If the window of the view plane is determined by the world points $[2, 6, 6]^T$ and $[6, 8, 2]^T$ and the projection reference point is located at $\dot{\mathbf{P}} = [9, 9, 9]^T$ (expressed in world coordinates), determine the direction of projection in this case.

**Problem 9.5:** [*Direction of parallel projection*]

If view reference coordinate system coincides with the world coordinate system, determine whether the projection type in Problem 9.4 is orthographic or oblique. Why?

**Problem 9.6:** [*Clipping planes in world coordinates—infinite orthographic view volume*]

Consider a view reference coordinate system such that the $n$-axis is indicated by the vector $\mathbf{n} = [1, 0, 1]^T$ and the VRP is positioned at $[4, 4, 4]^T$. If a window that extends from $[u_{min}, v_{min}]^T = [-1, -1]^T$ to $[u_{max}, v_{max}]^T = [2, 3]^T$ on the $uv$-plane is used to specify an infinite orthographic view volume, determine the planes bounding that volume in world coordinates.

**Problem 9.7:** [*Clipping planes in world coordinates—infinite oblique view volume*]

Consider a view reference coordinate system such that the $n$-axis is indicated by the unit vector $\mathbf{n} = \left[\frac{1}{\sqrt{3}}, \frac{1}{\sqrt{3}}, \frac{1}{\sqrt{3}}\right]^T$ and the VRP is positioned at $[4, 4, 4]^T$. If a window that extends from $[u_{min}, v_{min}]^T = [-2, -2]^T$ to $[u_{max}, v_{max}]^T = [2, 2]^T$ on the $uv$-plane is used to specify an infinite oblique view volume where the direction of projection is assumed to be $[-1, -1, -2]^T$ in the WCS, determine the planes bounding that volume in world coordinates.

**Problem 9.8:** [*Clipping planes in world coordinates—semi-infinite perspective view volume*]

Consider a view reference coordinate system such that the $n$- axis is indicated by the vector $\mathbf{n} = [1, 0, 1]^T$ and the VRP is positioned at $[4, 4, 4]^T$. If a window that extends from $[u_{min}, v_{min}]^T = [-1, -1]^T$ to $[u_{max}, v_{max}]^T = [2, 3]^T$ on the $uv$-plane is used to specify a semi-infinite perspective view volume whose COP is at $[7, 7, 7]^T$ (expressed in the world coordinate system), determine the planes bounding that volume in world coordinates.

**Problem 9.9:** [*Clipping planes in world coordinates—finite perspective view volume*]

In Example 9.16, determine the normal vectors to the left, right, top and bottom clipping planes of the frustum.

**Problem 9.10:** [*Clipping planes in world coordinates—finite perspective view volume*]

In Example 9.16, determine the equations of the left, right, top and bottom clipping planes of the frustum.

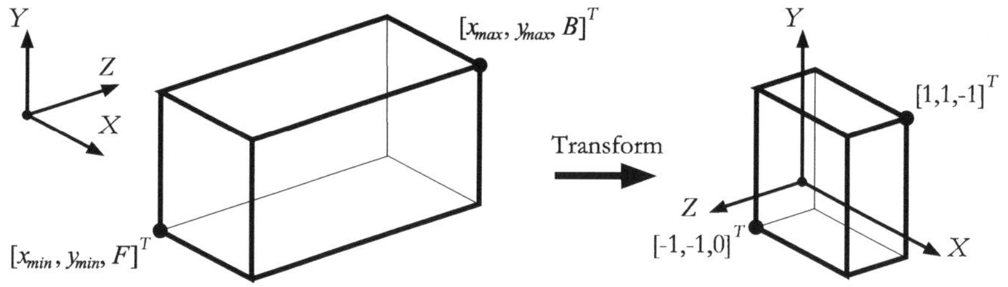


**Fig. 9.31** A view volume with planes parallel to the principal planes and passing through the points $[x_{min}, y_{min}, F]^T$ and $[x_{max}, y_{max}, B]^T$ is transformed into the canonical parallel-projection view volume expressed by Eq. (9.16)

**Problem 9.11:** [*Transformation into canonical parallel-projection view volume—from general orthogonal volume*]

Consider a view volume with planes parallel to the principal planes and passing through the points $[x_{min}, y_{min}, F]^T$ and $[x_{max}, y_{max}, B]^T$. Derive a matrix to transform this view volume into the canonical view volume expressed by Eq. (9.17).

**Problem 9.12:** [*Transformation into canonical parallel-projection view volume—from general orthogonal volume*]

Consider a view volume with planes parallel to the principal planes and passing through the points $[x_{min}, y_{min}, F]^T$ and $[x_{max}, y_{max}, B]^T$. Derive a matrix to transform this view volume into the canonical view volume expressed by Eq. (9.18).

**Problem 9.13:** [*Transformation into canonical parallel-projection view volume—from general orthogonal volume*]

In Example 9.18, if the world coordinate system is left-handed, derive a matrix to transform this view volume into the canonical view volume expressed by Eq. (9.16) as shown in Fig. 9.31.

**Problem 9.14:** [*Transformation into canonical parallel-projection view volume—from general oblique volume*]

Modify the matrix $\mathtt{N}_{par}$ of Eq. (9.29) so that the canonical view volume is expressed using Eq. (9.16) rather than Eq. (9.18).

**Problem 9.15:** [*Transformation into canonical parallel-projection view volume—from general oblique volume*]

Modify the matrix $\mathtt{N}_{par}$ of Eq. (9.29) so that the canonical view volume is expressed using Eq. (9.17) rather than Eq. (9.18).

**Problem 9.16:** [*3D clipping—line-plane intersection*]

Consider a clip volume that spans from $[x_{min}, y_{min}, z_{min}]^T$ to $[x_{max}, y_{max}, z_{max}]^T$ and a 3D line that goes from $\dot{\mathbf{P}}_1 = [x_1, y_1, z_1]^T$ to $\dot{\mathbf{P}}_2 = [x_2, y_2, z_2]^T$. Determine the intersection point between the line and the left boundary plane.

**Problem 9.17:** [*3D clipping—line-plane intersection*]
Consider a clip volume that spans from $[x_{min}, y_{min}, z_{min}]^T$ to $[x_{max}, y_{max}, z_{max}]^T$ and a 3D line that goes from $\dot{\mathbf{P}}_1 = [x_1, y_1, z_1]^T$ to $\dot{\mathbf{P}}_2 = [x_2, y_2, z_2]^T$. Determine the intersection point between the line and the top boundary plane.

**Problem 9.18:** [*3D clipping—line-plane intersection in perspective view volume*]
Consider the canonical perspective-projection view volume expressed by Eq. (9.20) and a 3D line that goes from $\dot{\mathbf{P}}_1 = [x_1, y_1, z_1]^T$ to $\dot{\mathbf{P}}_2 = [x_2, y_2, z_2]^T$. Determine the intersection point between the line and the boundary plane $x = z$.

**Problem 9.19:** [*3D clipping—line-plane intersection in perspective view volume*]
Consider the canonical perspective-projection view volume expressed by Eq. (9.20) and a 3D line that goes from $\dot{\mathbf{P}}_1 = [x_1, y_1, z_1]^T$ to $\dot{\mathbf{P}}_2 = [x_2, y_2, z_2]^T$. Determine the intersection point between the line and the boundary plane $y = -z$.

**Problem 9.20:** [*3D clipping—canonical perspective-projection view volume*]
Extend the Cohen-Sutherland algorithm to clip 3D lines against the canonical perspective-projection view volume expressed by Eq. (9.21).

**Problem 9.21:** [*Transformation into canonical parallel-projection view volume—from perspective view volume*]
Consider a perspective view volume that is defined in a left-handed coordinate system. Assume that the near or front plane defined by the plane $z = n$ is mapped to the plane $z = 0$ and the far or back plane defined by the plane $z = f$ is mapped to the plane $z = 1$. Estimate the values of $\alpha$ and $\beta$ in Eq. (9.52) to obtain the canonical view volume expressed by Eq. (9.17).

**Problem 9.22:** [*Clipping in homogeneous coordinates*]
Express the canonical volume defined by Eq. (9.17) in homogeneous coordinates.

**Problem 9.23:** [*Clipping in homogeneous coordinates*]
Express the canonical volume defined by Eq. (9.18) in homogeneous coordinates.

**Problem 9.24:** [*Clipping in homogeneous coordinates*]
Express the canonical volume defined by Eq. (9.19) in homogeneous coordinates.

**Problem 9.25:** [*Device coordinates—from a view volume to a viewport*]
Determine the steps needed to transform a canonical parallel-projection view volume expressed by Eq. (9.18) into a 3D viewport bounded by the locations $[x_{min}, y_{min}, z_{min}]^T$ and $[x_{max}, y_{max}, z_{max}]^T$.

## References

Foley, J.D., A. van Dam, S.K. Feiner, and J. Hughes. 1995. *Computer graphics: principles and practice in C*, 2nd ed. The systems programming series. Reading: Addison-Wesley.

Sung, K., P. Shirley, and S. Baer. 2008. *Essentials of interactive computer graphics: concepts and implementation*. Wellesley: AK Peters.

# Chapter 10
# Visibility

**Abstract** Rendering is generating a 2D image for a 3D scene and assigning colors to each of the generated pixels. The colors assigned to pixels depend on factors like illumination (Chap. 11), textures (Chap. 12) and radiance flowing out of the surfaces in the scene. When rendering an image, some surfaces will be projected onto that image while others will be hidden behind them. It would be wise to determine which surfaces are visible and which are not in order to eliminate those that are hidden from further processing. This process is known as *visible-surface determination*, *hidden-surface elimination* or *hidden-surface removal*. There are many techniques suggested in the literature to achieve this goal. In this chapter, we will discuss some of these visible-surfaces determination techniques. Also, in this chapter, we will discuss two of the methods that are regarded as the foundation of many rendering algorithms. These are ray casting and ray tracing (Appel 1968; Goldstein and Nagel 1971; Whitted 1980). Both methods use rays emitting from the camera location and penetrating the image plane to objects in 3D space in order to determine which point in the scene contributes to which pixel in the generated image. However, differences exist between them.

## 10.1 Viewing Frustum

The clipped finite view volume for perspective projection or the part of space that can be seen by the camera is referred to as the *viewing frustum* (Chap. 9). Any objects outside this frustum will not appear on the generated image unless they are reflected off or refracted through other objects in the frustum.

The depth of this frustum is determined by two planes; the *hither* and the *yon* planes (also known as the *front* and *back* planes or the *near* and *far* planes with respect to the camera or the eye) as shown in Fig. 10.1. Note that the viewing direction is perpendicular to both planes.

R. Elias, *Digital Media*, DOI: 10.1007/978-3-319-05137-6_10,

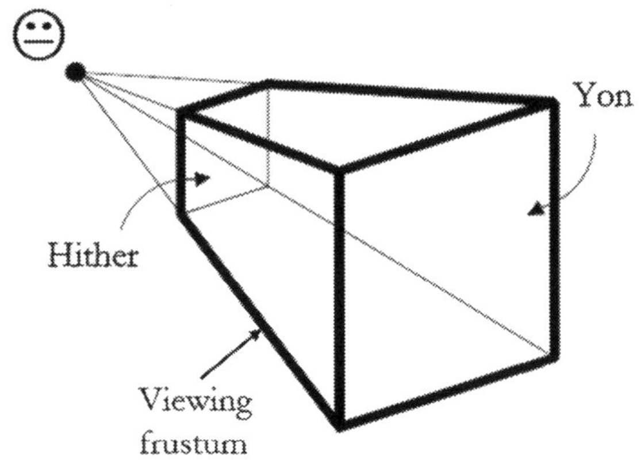


**Fig. 10.1** The viewing frustum is bounded by the hither and the yon (i.e., the near and the far) planes

We should mention that not all objects inside the frustum will appear in the generated image. Some objects may hide others inside the frustum. Also, surfaces of a single object facing away from the camera will not appear in the generated image. Determining surfaces that are hidden is important not only for getting the correct rendering results but for speeding up the rendering process as well by removing hidden surfaces from the calculations. Determining which surface is visible and which is invisible is referred to as the *visibility problem*.

There are many algorithms that are devised to deal with the visibility problem. We will talk about the painter's algorithm, back-face culling, $z$-buffering and space partitioning. Later, we will discuss ray casting and ray tracing.

## 10.2 Painter's Algorithm

The painter's algorithm performs what a simple painter would do to paint different objects having different depths. The first step is to sort all faces or polygons according to their distances (i.e., depths) from the camera location. In case each vertex of a polygon has its own depth, the depth of the whole polygon is determined as the farthest among all its vertices. The sorting order is then used to paint the farthest polygon or face followed by the closer ones. Of course, closer polygons or faces may be painted over farther ones, which results in hiding parts or all of what have been painted before. An example is shown in Fig. 10.2a.

Note that in order to use this algorithm, all faces must be available for sorting before even starting to paint. In some cases where faces and polygons are overlapping, this algorithm will fail. An example of this situation is shown in Fig. 10.2b.

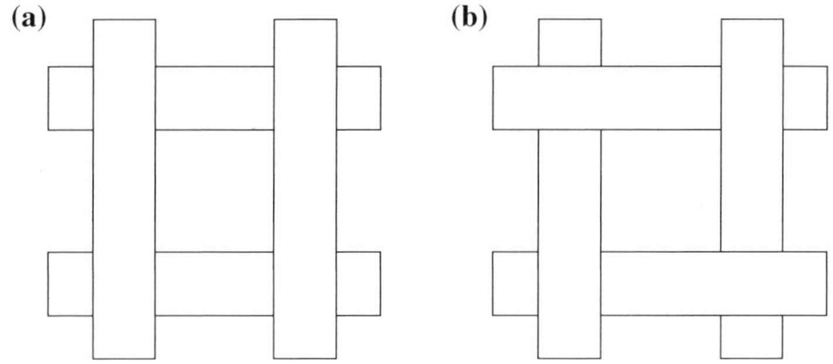


**Fig. 10.2** **a** An example where painter's algorithm succeeds. **b** An example where painter's algorithm fails

**Fig. 10.3** Back-face culling

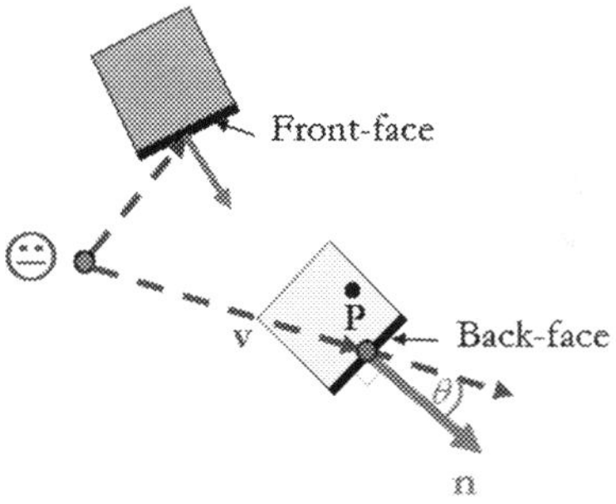


## 10.3 Back-Face Culling

Some surfaces facing away from the camera or the viewer's eye (i.e., back side of some faces) are not visible and should be removed from the calculations. *Back-face culling* or removing is a method used to determine what surfaces are visible and what surfaces are hidden in order to remove the hidden surfaces.

Consider the back-face shown in Fig. 10.3. In order to ensure that this is a back-face, we get the vector $\mathbf{v} = [v_x, v_y, v_z]^T$ extending from the camera location to a point $\dot{\mathbf{P}}$ on the face. Then the normal vector $\mathbf{n} = [n_x, n_y, n_z]^T$ to the face at this point is estimated. The angle $\theta$ enclosed between the vectors $\mathbf{v}$ and $\mathbf{n}$ is calculated. If $\theta$ is between $-90°$ and $90°$, then this is a back-face and should be culled or removed.

The exact value of the angle $\theta$ does not have to be determined. It is only the range $-90° \leq \theta \leq 90°$ that matters. Hence, it is easier to use the dot product (see Sect. A.4.3.2) as follows to detect if $\theta$ falls within this range:

$$\mathbf{n} \cdot \mathbf{v} = \begin{bmatrix} n_x \\ n_y \\ n_z \end{bmatrix} \cdot \begin{bmatrix} v_x \\ v_y \\ v_z \end{bmatrix} = n_x v_x + n_y v_y + n_z v_z, \tag{10.1}$$

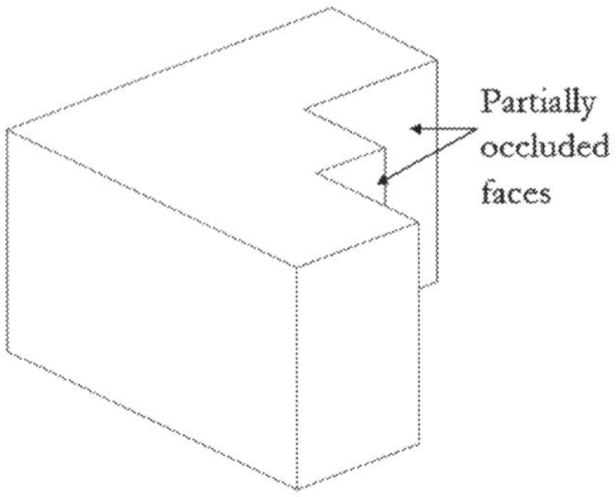


**Fig. 10.4** An example of a concave 3D object. Some front-faces are partially obscured or occluded. Back-face culling test is not enough in such a situation

where $\cdot$ denotes the dot product. Note that

$$\mathbf{n} \cdot \mathbf{v} = \|\mathbf{n}\| \|\mathbf{v}\| \cos(\theta), \tag{10.2}$$

where $\|.\|$ denotes the norm. If the result of $\mathbf{n} \cdot \mathbf{v}$ obtained from Eq. (10.1) is nonnegative, then $\cos(\theta)$ of Eq. (10.2) must be nonnegative; hence, $\theta$ must be between $-90°$ and $90°$ or $\theta \in [-90, 90]$. Consequently, the polygon is back-facing and should be culled. (Notice that the special cases of $\theta = \pm 90°$ means that the vector $\mathbf{v}$ is orthogonal or perpendicular to the vector $\mathbf{n}$.) Almost half the faces can be removed this easy way, which speeds up the rendering process. However, not all hidden surfaces can be removed this way. There are some situations we have to pay attention to when using this back-face culling test. Figure 10.4 shows that when a 3D object is not convex, parts of its front-faces may not be visible. Clearly, back-face culling test is not enough in such a situation.

**Example 10.1:** [*Back-facing culling*]

Assume that a virtual camera is located at $[2, 4, 6]^T$ and pointed towards the point $[7, 8, 9]^T$. Determine whether or not the planar surface with a surface normal $\mathbf{n} = [-2, 5, -5]^T$ is back-facing with respect to this virtual camera.

**Solution 10.1:** The direction vector $\mathbf{v}$ from the camera located at $[2, 4, 6]^T$ to the point $[7, 8, 9]^T$ is calculated as

$$\mathbf{v} = \begin{bmatrix} 7 \\ 8 \\ 9 \end{bmatrix} - \begin{bmatrix} 2 \\ 4 \\ 6 \end{bmatrix} = \begin{bmatrix} 5 \\ 4 \\ 3 \end{bmatrix}.$$

Then the dot product is calculated as

$$\mathbf{n} \cdot \mathbf{v} = \begin{bmatrix} -2 \\ 5 \\ -5 \end{bmatrix} \cdot \begin{bmatrix} 5 \\ 4 \\ 3 \end{bmatrix} = (-2) \times 5 + 5 \times 4 + (-5) \times 3 = -5.$$

The surface is front-facing as the dot product results in a negative result. □

## 10.4 Z-Buffering

The *z-buffer* or *depth buffer* algorithm (Catmull 1975) is an easy algorithm used to solve the visibility problem by maintaining the nearest depth coordinates. Assume that the 3D points are projected onto the $xy$-plane that corresponds to the image plane (see Fig. 10.5). The $z$-buffer algorithm stores the $z$-coordinate of each generated point in a 2D array (i.e., the $z$-buffer or the depth buffer) where each element of the array corresponds to one image pixel. In case a new object projects onto a visited pixel, the new and stored $z$-coordinates are compared and the old value is replaced by the new value if the new one is closer to the viewer (or at the same depth) with respect to the stored one. Consequently, farther objects are hidden behind closer ones. The $z$-buffer algorithm is listed in Algorithm 10.1.

**Algorithm 10.1** *Z-buffer*

**Input:** $x_{min}, x_{max}, y_{min}, y_{max}, polygon\_list$
**Output:** $zBuffer$
**for** ($x = x_{min}$ to $x_{max}$) **do**
  **for** ($y = y_{min}$ to $y_{max}$) **do**
    $zBuffer(x, y) = 0$
  **end for**
**end for**
**for** (each polygon in $polygon\_list$) **do**
  **for** (each pixel $[x, y]^T$ in the polygon) **do**
    $z = z$-value at $[x, y]^T$
    **if** ($z \geq zBuffer(x, y)$) **then**
      $zBuffer(x, y) = z$
    **end if**
  **end for**
**end for**

**end**

**Example 10.2:** [*Z-buffering*]
Consider a $z$-buffer of size $8 \times 8$ pixels where each of the 64 slots is initialized to 0 as shown in Fig. 10.6a. If the planar quadrilateral of Fig. 10.6b (where the numbers indicate the $z$-values) is to be added to the $z$-buffer, determine the final state of the $z$-buffer.

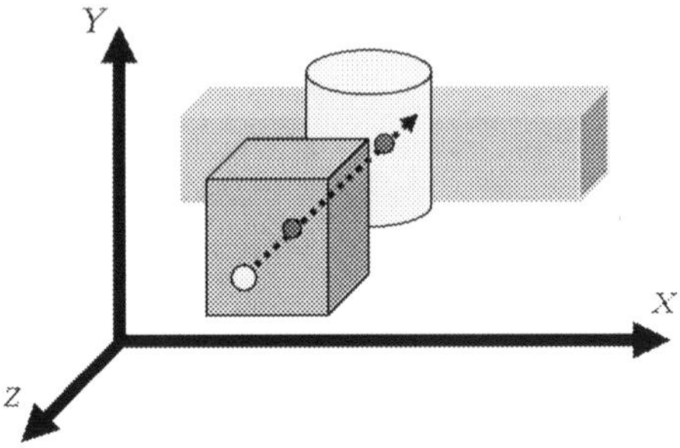

**Fig. 10.5** The $z$-buffer algorithm. A pixel may be shared by multiple 3D points. If this is the case, the $z$-buffer algorithm uses the point that is the closest to the viewer. This example uses a right-handed coordinate system where closer objects have larger $z$-values

**(a)**

| 0 | 0 | 0 | 0 | 0 | 0 | 0 | 0 |
|---|---|---|---|---|---|---|---|
| 0 | 0 | 0 | 0 | 0 | 0 | 0 | 0 |
| 0 | 0 | 0 | 0 | 0 | 0 | 0 | 0 |
| 0 | 0 | 0 | 0 | 0 | 0 | 0 | 0 |
| 0 | 0 | 0 | 0 | 0 | 0 | 0 | 0 |
| 0 | 0 | 0 | 0 | 0 | 0 | 0 | 0 |
| 0 | 0 | 0 | 0 | 0 | 0 | 0 | 0 |
| 0 | 0 | 0 | 0 | 0 | 0 | 0 | 0 |

**(b)**

|   |   |   |   |   |   |   |   |
|---|---|---|---|---|---|---|---|
|   |   |   |   |   |   | 2 |   |
|   |   |   |   |   | 2 | 2 | 2 |
|   |   |   | 2 | 2 | 2 | 2 | 2 |
|   |   |   |   |   | 2 | 2 | 2 |
|   |   |   |   |   |   | 2 |   |
|   |   |   |   |   |   |   |   |
|   |   |   |   |   |   |   |   |

**(c)**

| 0 | 0 | 0 | 0 | 0 | 0 | 0 | 0 |
|---|---|---|---|---|---|---|---|
| 0 | 0 | 0 | 0 | 0 | 2 | 0 | 0 |
| 0 | 0 | 0 | 0 | 2 | 2 | 2 | 0 |
| 0 | 0 | 0 | 2 | 2 | 2 | 2 | 2 |
| 0 | 0 | 0 | 0 | 2 | 2 | 2 | 0 |
| 0 | 0 | 0 | 0 | 0 | 2 | 0 | 0 |
| 0 | 0 | 0 | 0 | 0 | 0 | 0 | 0 |
| 0 | 0 | 0 | 0 | 0 | 0 | 0 | 0 |

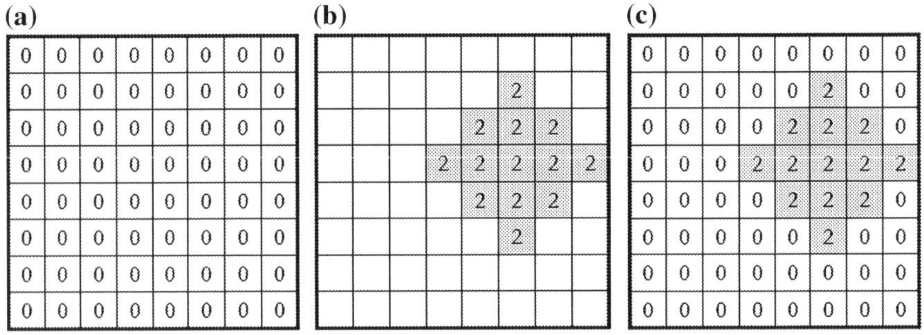

**Fig. 10.6** A $z$-buffer example. **a** A state of the $z$-buffer where slots are initialized to zeros. **b** A square to be added. **c** The final state of the $z$-buffer

**Solution 10.2:** Applying Algorithm 10.1 to this $z$-buffer results in the final state shown in Fig. 10.6c.                                                                                    □

**Example 10.3:** [*Z-buffering and Painter's Algorithm*]
   In Example 10.2, if the painter's algorithm is used instead, will the results change?

**Solution 10.3:** In Example 10.2, the farthest depth (i.e., the background depth of 0) will be considered before the quadrilateral depth (i.e., 2). In other words, there is no depth overlapping. Hence, the results should not change.                                                    □

**Example 10.4:** [*Z-buffering*]
   Consider the $z$-buffer shown in Fig. 10.7a where the numbers indicate the $z$-values. If the square shown in Fig. 10.7b is to be added to the $z$-buffer, determine the final state of the $z$-buffer.

**Solution 10.4:** The final state of the $z$-buffer is shown in Fig. 10.7c.
   Adding various depths to the $z$-buffer will only change its state if the depth values are greater than or equal to the stored $z$-values. Notice that the $z$-values of the pixels

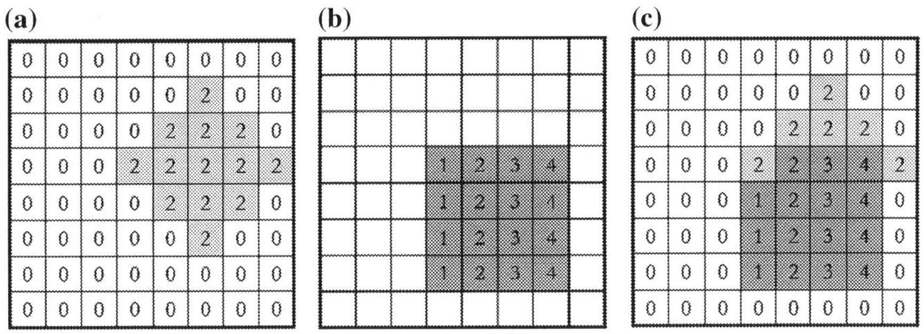


**Fig. 10.7** A $z$-buffer example. **a** A state of the $z$-buffer, which contains one square. **b** Another square to be added. **c** The final state of the $z$-buffer

$[4, 3]^T$ and $[4, 4]^T$ were replaced by those of the new polygon although they have the same values (i.e., 2) due to the existence of the equality on Line 9 of Algorithm 10.1. □

**Example 10.5:** [*Z-buffering*]
Algorithm 10.1 assumes that the coordinate system used is right-handed (see Sect. B.1.1). What change should be made to the algorithm to accommodate left-handed coordinate systems?

**Solution 10.5:** In a right-handed coordinate system, the depth values (i.e., the $z$-values) increases outwards the screen that is represented by the $xy$-plane as shown in Fig. 10.5. In case of using a left-handed system, the depth values (i.e., the $z$-values) should increase inwards the screen. Consequently, the condition appearing on Line 9 of Algorithm 10.1 should change to

$$z \leq zBuffer(x, y).$$

Notice that in case of a left-handed system, the $z$-buffer should be initialized to the largest possible value rather than 0 on Line 3 of Algorithm 10.1. □

**Example 10.6:** [*Z-buffering*]
In Algorithm 10.1 and in case two points having the same depth, which point should be maintained? How may we choose the other point?

**Solution 10.6:** According to Algorithm 10.1 and since that the condition on Line 9 is $z \geq zBuffer(x, y)$, the contribution of the second object will overwrite that of the first one. In case we want to always keep the first contribution in case of equal depth, we change the condition appearing on Line 9 to

$$z > zBuffer(x, y).$$ □

**Table 10.1** Different hyperplanes dividing different spaces

| Space dimension | Space | Hyperplane | Hyperplane divides the space into |
|---|---|---|---|
| 1D | Line | Point | Two rays |
| 2D | Plane | Line | Two half-planes |
| 3D | 3D space | Plane | Two half-spaces |

**Table 10.2** Different space partitioning trees along with the number of dividing hyperplanes, number of sub-spaces formed and space dimension

| Tree | # dividing planes | # sub-spaces formed | Space dimension |
|---|---|---|---|
| BSP tree | 1 | 2 | *n*D |
| Quadtree | 2 | 4 | Usually 2D |
| Octree | 3 | 8 | Usually 3D |

## 10.5 Space Partitioning

*Space partitioning* is a process that partitions the space into two or more disjoint non-overlapping adjacent parts or sub-spaces. Each part or sub-space can be split recursively again into other parts. These parts can be organized into a tree that is referred to as a *space partitioning tree*. Such a tree can be traversed easily to obtain the correct order of the parts in space.

A *hyperplane* is used to partition the space. Points on one side of the hyperplane belong to one of the sub-spaces resulted out of the partitioning process while points on the other side belong to the other sub-space. Practically, points residing on the hyperplane are assigned arbitrarily to any of the sides. A hyperplane may be a point dividing a line into two rays, a line dividing a plane into two half-planes or a plane dividing a 3D space into two half-spaces. A hyperplane is defined as listed in Table 10.1.

Different space partitioning trees (e.g., BSP trees, quadtrees and octrees) are the outcome of different space partitioning techniques where the number of dividing hyperplanes and the number of sub-spaces formed differ as listed in Table 10.2.

In the following section, we will discuss BSP trees as an example of list-priority algorithms that can be used to determine which surfaces are displayed in the beginning and which may overdraw them. In Sect. 10.6.3.4, we will discuss octrees as a method of partitioning the space to accelerate the ray casting process.

### *10.5.1 Binary Space Partitioning Trees*

As listed in Table 10.2, any space can be split or partitioned using a single plane into two sub-spaces. This splitting process can be expressed as a binary tree where a root node representing the whole space has two children representing the two sub-spaces after splitting. This binary tree is referred to as a *binary space partitioning tree* or a *BSP tree*. The BSP tree algorithm (Fuchs et al. 1979a, b, 1980a, b) is an efficient approach to solve the visibility problem for static scenes where objects do not move (while viewpoint moves). We will look at how to construct the BSP tree for a given scene and how to use this tree to render the scene.

#### 10.5.1.1 Constructing BSP Trees

The algorithm of constructing the BSP tree starts with picking up a surface or a polygon to represent the root of the tree. (Note that the BSP tree generated may differ according to the polygon selected to represent the root; however, rendering the scene should be the same regardless of the choice of the root polygon.) The plane of the root polygon is used to split or partition the scene into two sub-spaces. One sub-space is in front of the root polygon according to its surface normal while the other one is behind it. In some cases, polygons may lie on both sides of the partitioning plane. In such cases, those polygons get split into parts by the root partitioning plane. Each part is assigned to the corresponding sub-space.

The same procedure is applied again to the front and back sub-spaces. Thus, for each sub-space, a polygon is picked to be a child of the previous tree root and this child's plane is used to partition this sub-space again into two partitions. The procedure is repeated recursively until each sub-space contains only one polygon. This algorithm for creating the BSP tree is listed in Algorithm 10.2.

**Algorithm 10.2** *BSP_tree*

```
Input: polygon_list
Output: tree
if (polygon_list ≠ NULL) then
    root = select polygon and remove from list (polygon_list)
    back_list = NULL
    front_list = NULL
    for (each polygon in polygon_list) do
        if (polygon in front of root) then
            Add polygon to front_list
        else if (polygon in back of root) then
            Add polygon to back_list
        else
            Split polygon
            Add front part to front_list
            Add back part to back_list
        end if
    end for
    tree = construct_tree(root, BSP_tree(front_list), BSP_tree(back_list))
else
    tree = NULL
end if
end
```

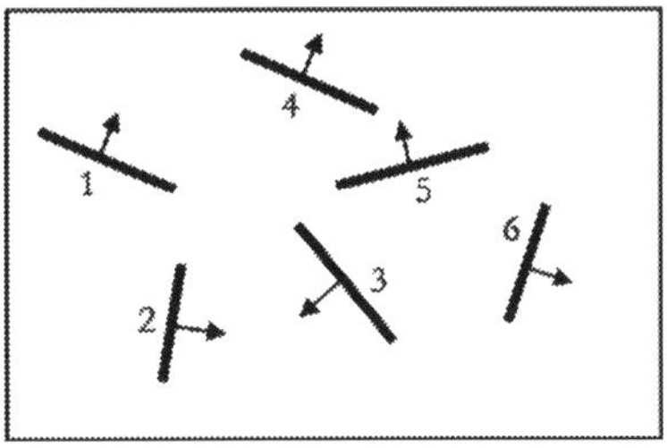


**Fig. 10.8** Top view of a 3D scene. The normal vectors to the surfaces are shown as arrows

**Example 10.7:** [*Partitioning using BSP trees*]
Figure 10.8 shows a top view of a 3D scene that contains six polygons/surfaces where the normal vectors to those surfaces are shown as arrows. It is required to partition this scene using a BSP tree. Use polygon "3" as a root for the tree.

**Solution 10.7:** The partitioning process starts with splitting the space along polygon "3" as shown in Fig. 10.9a. This step corresponds to creating the root of the BSP tree as shown in Fig. 10.9b.

Now, the whole space is split into two sub-spaces; front and back with respect to the normal to polygon "3" that represents the root. We can split the front sub-space along polygon "1" as shown in Fig. 10.9c. This step creates node "1" as a front child node under the root as depicted in Fig. 10.9d. Notice that polygon "2" is in the back of polygon "1"; hence, a back child is created for node "1." Also, notice that no surfaces exist in front of node "1"; hence, no front child is created for this node.

Working with the back sub-space of the root "3," we split along polygon "5" as shown in Fig. 10.9e where there are polygon "4" in the front and polygon "6" in the back. This step creates node "5" as a back child of the root and nodes "4" and "6" as its front and back nodes respectively. □

**Example 10.8:** [*Partitioning using BSP trees—choosing different root*]
Re-solve Problem 10.7 using polygon "5" as a root for the BSP tree.

**Solution 10.8:** The steps of partitioning the space and creating the BSP tree are shown in Fig. 10.10. Notice that the final tree created is different from that created in Fig. 10.9f. □

**Example 10.9:** [*Partitioning using BSP trees*]
A 3D game is designed as consisting of a number of rooms specified by their walls. One of those rooms is shown as a top view in Fig. 10.11a and as a 3D model in Fig. 10.11b. The normal vectors to the planes of these walls are pointed to the inside of the room as shown in Fig. 10.11a. It is required to partition this space using a BSP tree. You may use wall "3" as a root for the tree.

**Solution 10.9:** The partitioning process starts with splitting the space along wall "3" as shown in Fig. 10.12a. This step corresponds to creating the root of the BSP tree as shown in Fig. 10.12b. This also creates two sub-spaces; one in front of wall "3" and the other

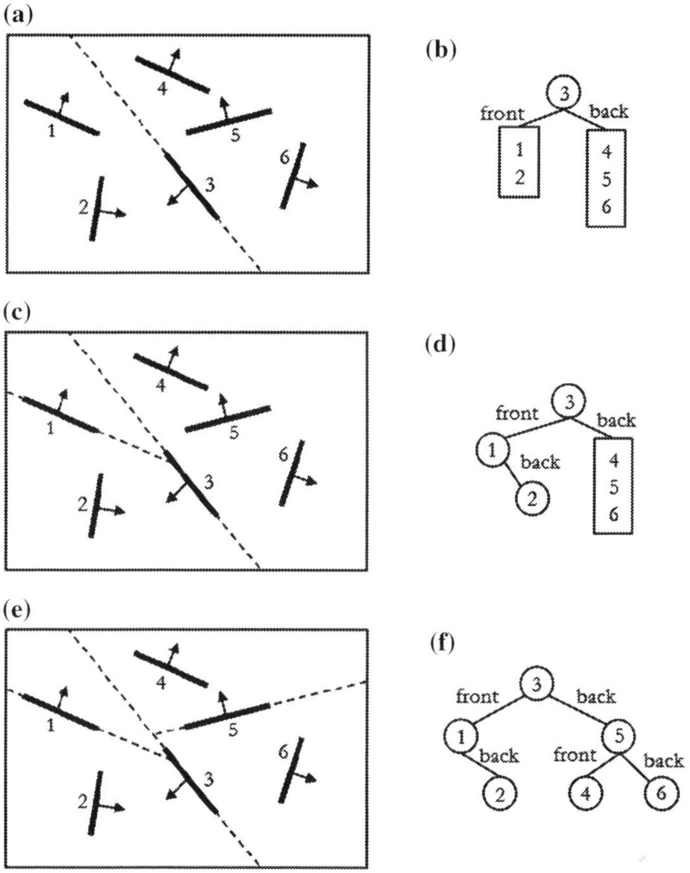


**Fig. 10.9** Partitioning the scene shown in Fig. 10.8 using a BSP tree. **a** Polygon "3" is selected as a root for the tree. **b** The root node is created. **c** The front sub-space of the root node is split along polygon "1." **d** Node "1" is created as a front child of the root while node "2" is created as its back child. **e** The back sub-space of the root node is split along polygon "5." **f** Node "5" is created as a back child of the root while nodes "4" and "6" are created as its front and back children respectively

behind it. Complying with this partitioning, wall "6" is split into two parts; "6a" and "6b" that go with the back and front sub-spaces respectively.

Now, partitioning the front sub-space along wall "6b" (Fig. 10.12c) creates the front child "6b" for the root as shown in Fig. 10.12d. There are no walls in back of wall "6b"; hence, no back child is generated for node "6b." On the contrary, a front child is generated for node "6b" to refer to wall "7."

The same procedure is applied to the back sub-space of the root represented by node "3." This is by partitioning along wall "4," "5" and "1" as shown in Fig. 10.12e, g and i. These steps generate nodes "4," "5," "6a," "1" and "2" as shown in Fig. 10.12f, h and j respectively. The later represents the final BSP tree. □

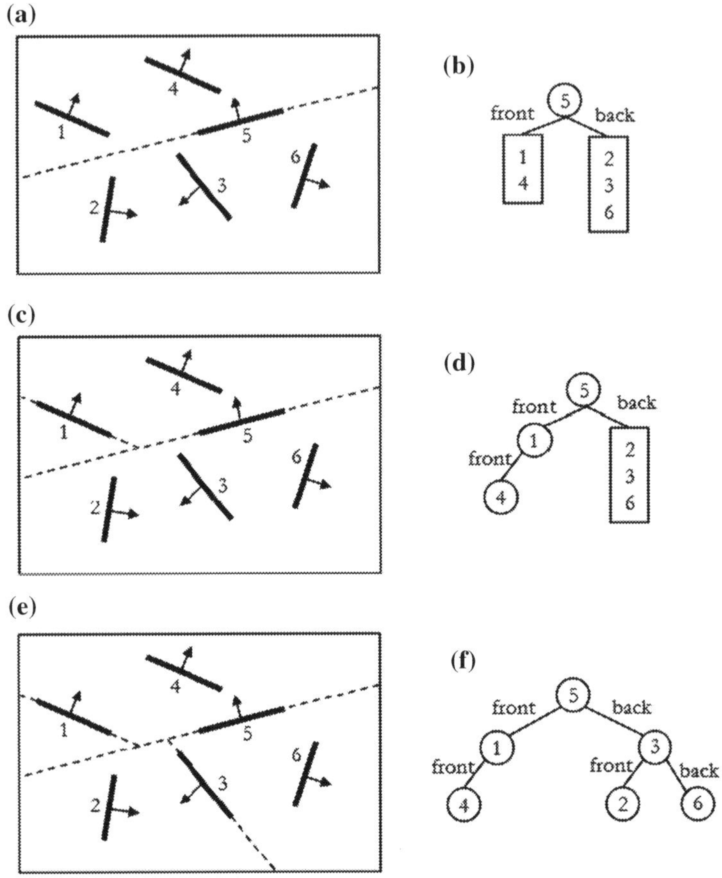


Fig. 10.10 Partitioning the scene shown in Fig. 10.8 using a BSP tree. **a** Polygon "5" is selected as a root for the tree. **b** The root node is created. **c** The front sub-space of the root node is split along polygon "1." **d** Node "1" is created as a front child of the root while node "4" is created as its front child. **e** The back sub-space of the root node is split along polygon "3." **f** Node "3" is created as a back child of the root while nodes "2" and "6" are created as its front and back children respectively

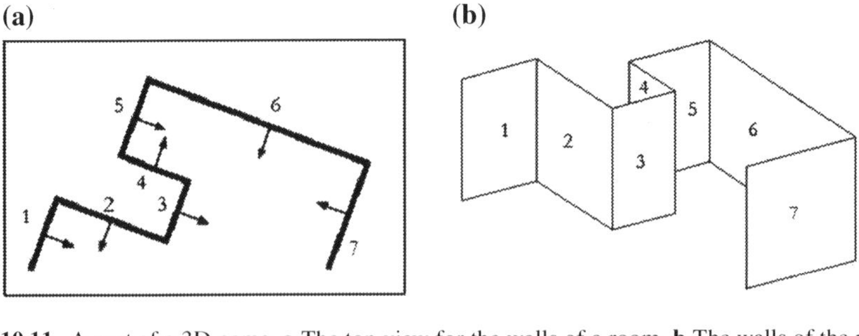


Fig. 10.11 A part of a 3D game. **a** The top view for the walls of a room. **b** The walls of the room shown in 3D space

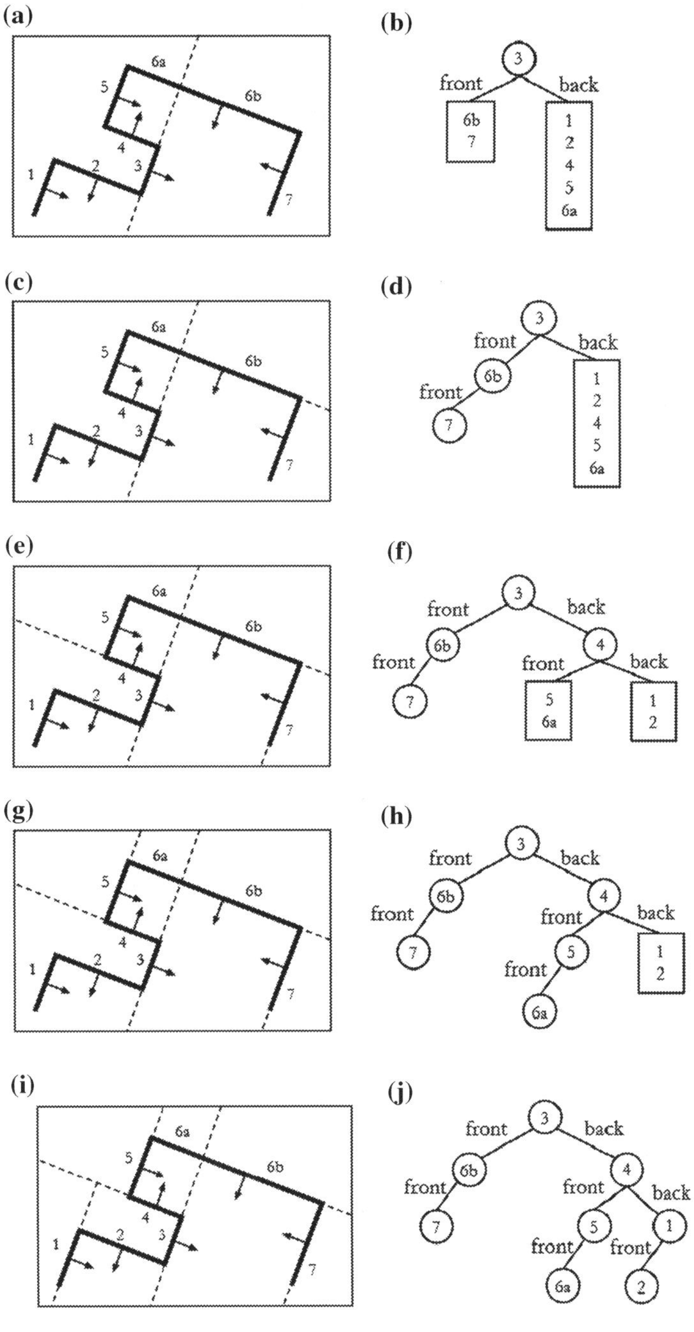


**Fig. 10.12** Partitioning the scene shown in Fig. 10.11 using a BSP tree

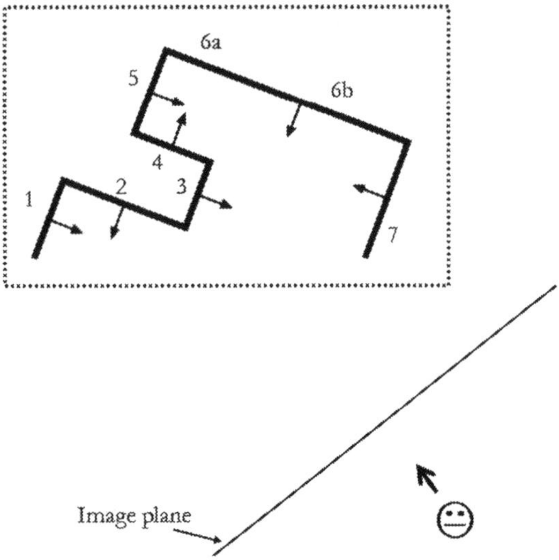


**Fig. 10.13** The top view of a scene with a viewpoint and viewing direction indicated

#### 10.5.1.2 Rendering Using BSP Trees

Once a BSP tree has been built for a given static scene, it can be used to render the scene for an arbitrary viewpoint. The BSP tree can be traversed to lead to a priority-ordered polygon list according to the viewpoint.

Considering the root of the tree, if the viewpoint is in the front side of the root's plane, then polygons in the back side should be displayed first. This is followed by displaying the root that may hide polygons in the back side and then displaying the polygons in the front side, which may hide the root. The order of displaying polygons is reversed if the viewpoint is in the back side of the root. In other words, polygons in the front side are displayed before the root, which is displayed before the polygons in the back side of the root. The algorithm is applied recursively to the root's children. Steps of displaying the scene using the BSP tree is listed in Algorithm 10.3.

**Algorithm 10.3** *BSP_render*

**Input:** *tree*, *viewpoint*
**if** (*tree* $\neq$ NULL) **then**
    **if** (*viewpoint* in front of *tree_root*) **then**
        *BSP_render*(*back_sub_tree*, *viewpoint*)
        display *tree_root*
        *BSP_render*(*front_sub_tree*, *viewpoint*)
    **else**
        *BSP_render*(*front_sub_tree*, *viewpoint*)
        display *tree_root*
        *BSP_render*(*back_sub_tree*, *viewpoint*)
    **end if**
**end if**

**end**

**Example 10.10:** [*Order of displaying polygons given a BSP tree*]

Figure 10.13 shows a top view for a scene while Fig. 10.12j shows the BSP tree used to partition this space. Using the BSP tree, determine the order of displaying the polygons of the scene according to the location of the viewpoint as well as the viewing direction as indicated in Fig. 10.13.

**Solution 10.10:** The first step in the solution is to determine the relative position of the viewpoint with respect to the root node. In our case, the viewpoint is in the front sub-space of the root node. Hence, the back sub-space should be displayed followed by the root followed by the front sub-space.

1. The back sub-tree rooted at node "4": The viewpoint is in back of node "4." Hence, the front sub-space rooted at node "5" should be displayed followed by node "4" followed by the back sub-space.
   a. The front sub-tree rooted at node "5": The viewpoint is in front of node "5." Hence, the back sub-space should be displayed followed by the root followed by the front sub-space.
      i. The back sub-space contains nothing.
      ii. Display node "5."
      iii. The front sub-tree rooted at node "6a": The sub-tree is the leaf node "6a." Thus, display node "6a."
   b. Display node "4."
   c. The back sub-tree rooted at node "1": The viewpoint is in front of node "1." Hence, the back sub-space should be displayed followed by the root followed by the front sub-space.
      i. The back sub-space contains nothing.
      ii. Display node "1."
      iii. The front sub-tree rooted at node "2": The sub-tree is the leaf node "2." Thus, display node "2."
2. Display the main root; node "3."
3. The front sub-tree rooted at node "6b": The viewpoint is in front of node "6b." Hence, the back sub-space should be displayed followed by the root followed by the front sub-space.
   a. The back sub-space contains nothing.
   b. Display node "6b."
   c. The front sub-tree rooted at node "7": The sub-tree is the leaf node "7." Thus, display node "7."

Hence, the sequence of displaying the nodes is "5," "6a," "4," "1," "2," "3," "6b" and "7." The projections of these nodes onto the image plane are shown in Fig. 10.14. Notice that these are the same projections displayed in Fig. 10.11b. □

## 10.6 Ray Casting

*Ray casting* is a technique used to determine the objects seen in an image through a camera by detecting objects intersected by rays. You may think of the image as a window that you use to see what is in the scene. Emt a ray from the camera location (i.e., the

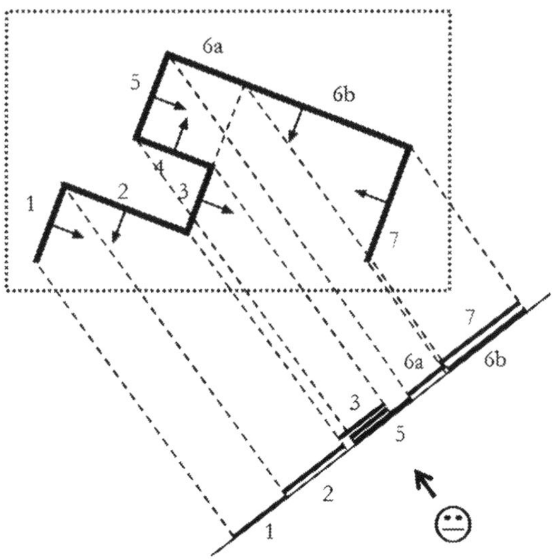


**Fig. 10.14** Projection of different polygons onto the image plane. The sequence of displaying the nodes is: "5," "6a," "4," "1," "2," "3," "6b" and "7"

center of projection) to intersect each and every pixel in the image and extend it until it hits an object in the scene. The point of intersection is the location of what should be seen through that pixel. The color assigned to the pixel under consideration depends on the radiance emanating from the surface of the object at the point of intersection.

### *10.6.1 Rays Through Pixels*

As mentioned above, a ray is constructed for each pixel. In order to determine the equation for the ray, you need to specify the location of the camera in space, which is known (i.e., $\dot{\mathbf{P}}_0$) and the location of the pixel in space (i.e., $\dot{\mathbf{P}}$), which can be estimated. Figure 10.15a shows the location of the camera at $\dot{\mathbf{P}}_0$ along with three vectors; **up**, which points upwards; **towards** which, points towards the image plane; and **right**, which is perpendicular to both **up** and **towards**; i.e., **right** = **towards** × **up**. (Do not get confused between these axes and the view reference coordinate system discussed in Sect. 9.1.1.)

Figure 10.15c shows the dotted triangle $\triangle\dot{\mathbf{P}}_0\dot{\mathbf{P}}_1\dot{\mathbf{P}}_2$ that appears in Fig. 10.15a. From the relationships depicted, we can write

$$\begin{aligned} \dot{\mathbf{P}}_1 &= \dot{\mathbf{P}}_0 + d\,\mathbf{towards} - d\tan(\theta)\,\mathbf{right}, \\ \dot{\mathbf{P}}_2 &= \dot{\mathbf{P}}_0 + d\,\mathbf{towards} + d\tan(\theta)\,\mathbf{right}, \end{aligned} \tag{10.3}$$

where $\dot{\mathbf{P}}_0$ is the 3D location of the camera; $\dot{\mathbf{P}}_1$ and $\dot{\mathbf{P}}_2$ are the 3D locations of the first and last pixels in the current image pixel row; **up** is a 3D unit vector that points upwards; **towards** is a 3D unit vector that points perpendicularly to the image plane; **right** is a 3D unit vector that is perpendicular to both **up** and **towards**; $d$, representing the focal

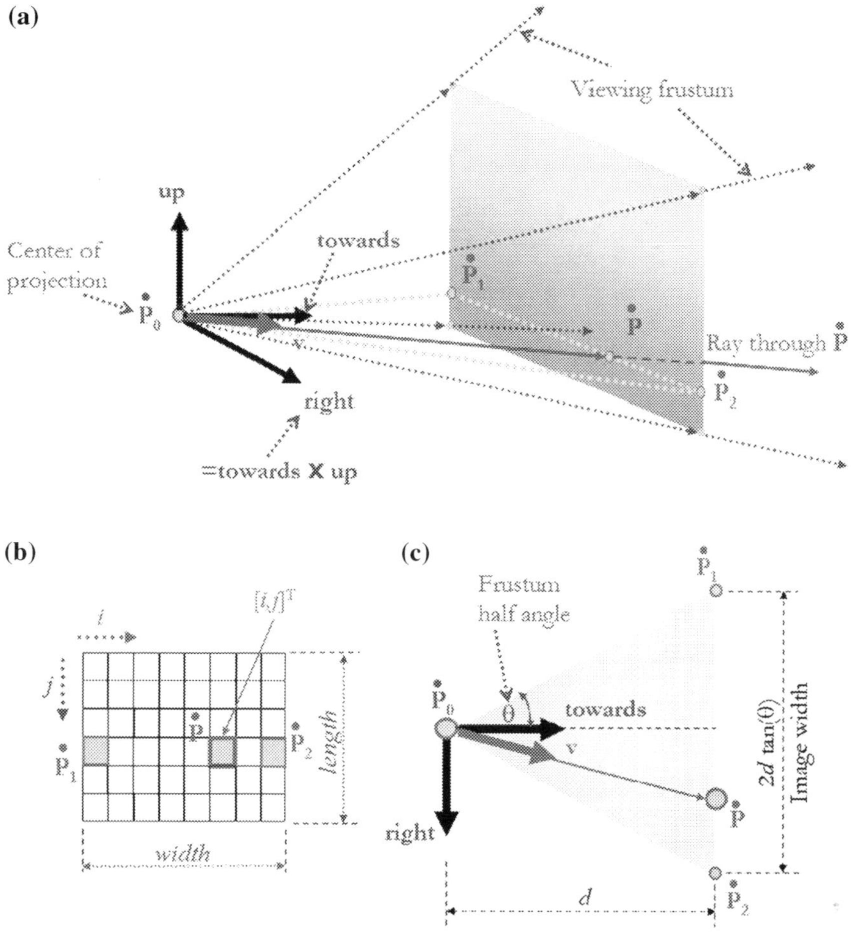


**Fig. 10.15** Ray casting: A ray is emitted from the camera location (i.e., the center of projection) through the pixel location in 3D space. **a** 3D representation. **b** The observed image. **c** Horizontal cross section of **a** showing relationships for a single image row of pixels

length, is the distance along the direction **towards** in world coordinate system units (e.g., millimeters); and $\theta$ is the viewing frustum or field of view (FOV) horizontal half angle. Hence, the 3D location $\dot{\mathbf{P}}$ of the image pixel $[i,\ j]^T$ can be determined as

$$\dot{\mathbf{P}} = \dot{\mathbf{P}}_1 + \left(\frac{i + 0.5}{width}\right)\left(\dot{\mathbf{P}}_2 - \dot{\mathbf{P}}_1\right), \tag{10.4}$$

where $\dot{\mathbf{P}}$ is the 3D location of the pixel under consideration; $\dot{\mathbf{P}}_1$ and $\dot{\mathbf{P}}_2$ are the 3D locations of the first and last pixels in the current image pixel row [obtained using Eq. (10.3)]; $i$

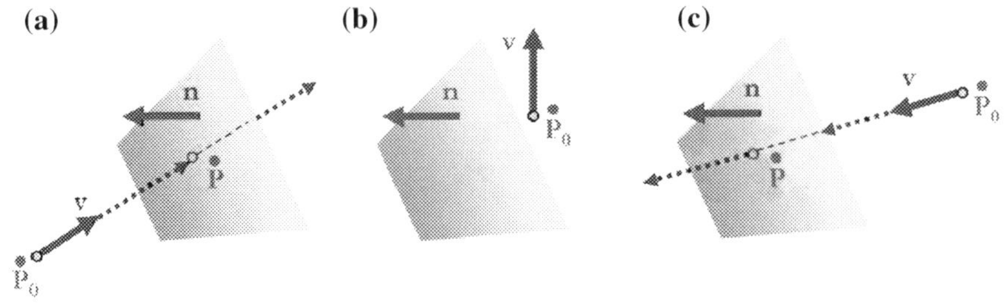


**Fig. 10.16** **a** The ray is pointing towards the plane where $\theta$ is obtuse. **b** The ray is parallel to the plane where $\theta = 90°$. **c** The ray is pointing away from the plane where $\theta$ is acute

is the pixel count in the current row; and *width* is the image width in pixels (i.e., the number of pixels in each image row). Note that $\dot{\mathbf{P}}_2 - \dot{\mathbf{P}}_1 = 2d\tan(\theta)$ **right**. This value represents the image width in world coordinate system units (e.g., millimeters). Also, note that the center of the pixel $[i, j]^T$ is $[i + 0.5, j + 0.5]^T$. This is why the fraction 0.5 appears in the equation.

Thus, given two points $\dot{\mathbf{P}}_0$ and $\dot{\mathbf{P}}$, the ray going through both of them can be expressed as

$$\begin{aligned}\dot{\mathbf{P}} &= \dot{\mathbf{P}}_0 + t\left(\frac{\dot{\mathbf{P}}-\dot{\mathbf{P}}_0}{\|\dot{\mathbf{P}}-\dot{\mathbf{P}}_0\|}\right)\\ &= \dot{\mathbf{P}}_0 + t\mathbf{v},\end{aligned} \tag{10.5}$$

where $\mathbf{v}$ is a unit vector and $t$ is a parameter.

**Example 10.11:** [*Rays and points*]

A ray is emitted from $\dot{\mathbf{P}}_0 = [0, 0, -4]^T$ to $\dot{\mathbf{P}}_1 = [4, 8, 8]^T$. Determine if points $\dot{\mathbf{P}}_2 = [2, 4, 2]^T$ and $\dot{\mathbf{P}}_3 = [6, 12, 14]^T$ obscure or get obscured by $\dot{\mathbf{P}}_1$.

**Solution 10.11:** The equation of the ray extending from $\dot{\mathbf{P}}_0$ to $\dot{\mathbf{P}}_1$ can be expressed as

$$\begin{aligned}\dot{\mathbf{P}} &= \dot{\mathbf{P}}_0 + t\left(\dot{\mathbf{P}}_1 - \dot{\mathbf{P}}_0\right)\\ &= \begin{bmatrix}0\\0\\-4\end{bmatrix} + t\left(\begin{bmatrix}4\\8\\8\end{bmatrix} - \begin{bmatrix}0\\0\\-4\end{bmatrix}\right)\\ &= \begin{bmatrix}0\\0\\-4\end{bmatrix} + t\begin{bmatrix}4\\8\\12\end{bmatrix}\end{aligned}$$

or

$$x_{\dot{\mathbf{P}}} = 4t, \tag{10.6}$$

$$y_{\dot{\mathbf{P}}} = 8t, \tag{10.7}$$

$$z_{\dot{\mathbf{P}}} = -4 + 12t, \tag{10.8}$$

where $t \in [0, 1]$ such that $\dot{\mathbf{P}} = \dot{\mathbf{P}}_0$ at $t = 0$ and $\dot{\mathbf{P}} = \dot{\mathbf{P}}_1$ at $t = 1$. In order to determine whether a point obscures or gets obscured by $\dot{\mathbf{P}}_1$, we need to do the following:

1. We determine whether or not the point is on the ray.
2. If the point is not on the ray, it neither obscures nor gets obscured by $\dot{\mathbf{P}}_1$.
3. If the point is on the ray, determine its relative location from $\dot{\mathbf{P}}_0$ with respect to $\dot{\mathbf{P}}_1$.

Utilizing Eq. (10.6) with the $x$-component of $\dot{\mathbf{P}}_2$, we get $t = 0.5$. At $t = 0.5$, $y_{\dot{\mathbf{P}}} = 4$ and $z_{\dot{\mathbf{P}}} = 2$. In other words, $\dot{\mathbf{P}}_2$ is on the ray. Because $\dot{\mathbf{P}}_2$ is at $t = 0.5$ and $\dot{\mathbf{P}}_1$ is at $t = 1$, then $\dot{\mathbf{P}}_2$ obscures $\dot{\mathbf{P}}_1$. By applying the same procedure, we find that $\dot{\mathbf{P}}_1$ obscures $\dot{\mathbf{P}}_3$. □

**Example 10.12:** [*Rays and points*]
In Example 10.11, determine whether a point $\dot{\mathbf{P}}_4 = [1, 4, 5]^T$ obscures or gets obscured by $\dot{\mathbf{P}}_1$.

**Solution 10.12:** Utilizing Eq. (10.6) with the $x$-component of $\dot{\mathbf{P}}_4$, we get $t = 0.25$. At $t = 0.25$, $y_{\dot{\mathbf{P}}} = 2$ and $z_{\dot{\mathbf{P}}} = -1$. In other words, $\dot{\mathbf{P}}_4$ is *not* on the ray; hence, it cannot obscure or get obscured by point $\dot{\mathbf{P}}_1$. □

## *10.6.2 Ray Intersections*

After establishing the ray equation, rays must be tested for intersections with objects in the scene (e.g., planar triangles, boxes, spheres, cylinders, etc.). In the following, we will discuss how to determine the intersection point between a ray and a general plane. In many cases, surfaces may be approximated by triangles. We will test whether an intersection point falls within the boundaries of a triangle. As an example of ray intersections with curved surfaces, we will talk about how to estimate the intersection point between a ray and a sphere. Intersections with other objects; e.g., a cylinder, a cone, etc. can also be estimated (Vince 2007).

### 10.6.2.1 Ray-Plane Intersection

A plane equation is expressed as

$$ax + by + cz = d, \tag{10.9}$$

where $\mathbf{n} = [a, b, c]^T$ is the normal vector to the plane. In case that $\mathbf{n}$ is normalized to a unit magnitude, $d$ becomes the perpendicular distance from the origin to the plane. If the point of intersection is $\dot{\mathbf{P}}$, Eq. (10.9) can be re-written as

$$\dot{\mathbf{P}} \cdot \mathbf{n} = d, \tag{10.10}$$

where $\cdot$ indicates the dot product. At the ray-plane intersection, we can apply Eq. (10.5) in Eq. (10.10) to have

$$\left[\dot{\mathbf{P}}_0 + t\mathbf{v}\right] \cdot \mathbf{n} = d. \tag{10.11}$$

Consequently, the parameter $t$ along the ray can be estimated as

$$t = \frac{-\left(\dot{\mathbf{P}}_0 \cdot \mathbf{n}\right) + d}{\mathbf{v} \cdot \mathbf{n}}. \tag{10.12}$$

Note that the value $\mathbf{v} \cdot \mathbf{n}$ determines whether or not the ray is pointing towards the plane.

$$\mathbf{v} \cdot \mathbf{n} = \begin{cases} < 0, & \text{ray pointing towards the plane; } \theta \text{ is obtuse as in Fig. 10.16a;} \\ = 0, & \text{ray parallel to the plane; } \theta = 90^\circ \text{ as in Fig. 10.16b;} \\ > 0, & \text{ray pointing away from the plane; } \theta \text{ is acute as in Fig. 10.16c,} \end{cases}$$

where $\theta$ is the angle between the vectors $\mathbf{v}$ and $\mathbf{n}$ (Fig. 10.16).

**Example 10.13:** [*Ray-plane intersection—point of intersection given a ray as two points and the plane equation*]

Determine the point of intersection between a ray and a plane. The ray is going through two points; $\dot{\mathbf{P}}_0 = [3.0, 4.0, 5.0]^T$ and $\dot{\mathbf{P}}_1 = [5.0, -1.5, 4.0]^T$ and the plane equation is given by $6.0x - 2.0y + 1.5z - 4.0 = 0.0$. (Also, the plane equation can be expressed by the vector $[6.0, -2.0, 1.5, -4.0]^T$.)

**Solution 10.13:** The direction vector $\mathbf{v}$ is given by

$$\begin{aligned} \mathbf{v} &= \dot{\mathbf{P}}_1 - \dot{\mathbf{P}}_0 \\ &= \begin{bmatrix} 5.0 \\ -1.5 \\ 4.0 \end{bmatrix} - \begin{bmatrix} 3.0 \\ 4.0 \\ 5.0 \end{bmatrix} = \begin{bmatrix} 2.0 \\ -5.5 \\ -1.0 \end{bmatrix}. \end{aligned}$$

The parameter $t$ is obtained by substituting in Eq. (10.12). Thus,

$$\begin{aligned} t &= \frac{-\left(\dot{\mathbf{P}}_0 \cdot \mathbf{n}\right) + d}{\mathbf{v} \cdot \mathbf{n}} \\ &= \frac{-\left(\begin{bmatrix} 3.0 \\ 4.0 \\ 5.0 \end{bmatrix} \cdot \begin{bmatrix} 6.0 \\ -2.0 \\ 1.5 \end{bmatrix}\right) + 4.0}{\begin{bmatrix} 2.0 \\ -5.5 \\ -1.0 \end{bmatrix} \cdot \begin{bmatrix} 6.0 \\ -2.0 \\ 1.5 \end{bmatrix}} = -0.6279. \end{aligned}$$

The negative value of $t$ means that the intersection happens behind $\dot{\mathbf{P}}_0$. (Note that $t$ equals 0 at $\dot{\mathbf{P}}_0$ and $t$ equals 1 at $\dot{\mathbf{P}}_1$.) Now, substitute the value of $t$ in Eq. (10.5) to get the location of the point of intersection $\dot{\mathbf{P}}$ where

$$\begin{aligned} \dot{\mathbf{P}} &= \dot{\mathbf{P}}_0 + t\mathbf{v} \\ &= \begin{bmatrix} 3.0 \\ 4.0 \\ 5.0 \end{bmatrix} - 0.6279 \begin{bmatrix} 2.0 \\ -5.5 \\ -1.0 \end{bmatrix} = \begin{bmatrix} 1.7442 \\ 7.4535 \\ 5.6279 \end{bmatrix}. \end{aligned}$$

□

#### 10.6.2.2 Ray-Triangle Intersection

In order to detect if a ray intersects a triangle, check for the intersection point with the plane of the triangle as done in Sect. 10.6.2.1. If a point exists, check if its location falls inside the boundaries of the triangle. Note that if the triangle is given as a triplet of 3D points, use cross product (Sect. A.4.3.3) to get the plane equation of the triangle.

**Example 10.14:** [*Plane equation given a number of points*]
Consider a triangle $\triangle\dot{\mathbf{P}}_1\dot{\mathbf{P}}_2\dot{\mathbf{P}}_3$ where $\dot{\mathbf{P}}_1 = [2, 2, 1]^T$, $\dot{\mathbf{P}}_2 = [5, 4, 1]^T$ and $\dot{\mathbf{P}}_3 = [3, 3, 5]^T$. Estimate the plane equation of this triangle.

**Solution 10.14:** Get the direction vectors emitting from $\dot{\mathbf{P}}_1$:

$$\begin{aligned}\mathbf{u} &= \dot{\mathbf{P}}_2 - \dot{\mathbf{P}}_1\\ &= \begin{bmatrix}5\\4\\1\end{bmatrix} - \begin{bmatrix}2\\2\\1\end{bmatrix} = \begin{bmatrix}3\\2\\0\end{bmatrix},\end{aligned}$$

$$\begin{aligned}\mathbf{v} &= \dot{\mathbf{P}}_3 - \dot{\mathbf{P}}_1\\ &= \begin{bmatrix}3\\3\\5\end{bmatrix} - \begin{bmatrix}2\\2\\1\end{bmatrix} = \begin{bmatrix}1\\1\\4\end{bmatrix}.\end{aligned}$$

The vectors $\mathbf{u}$ and $\mathbf{v}$ lie on the plane. So, their cross product (Sect. A.4.3.3) will be perpendicular to both of them. Hence, the normal to the plane of the triangle is obtained as

$$\mathbf{u} \times \mathbf{v} = \begin{bmatrix}3\\2\\0\end{bmatrix} \times \begin{bmatrix}1\\1\\4\end{bmatrix} = \begin{bmatrix}8\\-12\\1\end{bmatrix}.$$

The equation of the plane is given by $ax + by + cz = d$ where $[a, b, c]^T$ represents the normal to that plane. Thus, the equation can be written as

$$8x - 12y + z = d.$$

Apply the coordinates of $\dot{\mathbf{P}}_2$ to get the value of $d$ where

$$d = 8 \times 5 - 12 \times 4 + 1 = -7.$$

Hence, the equation is obtained as

$$8x - 12y + z + 7 = 0.$$

You may check the correctness of the equation by applying the coordinates of the vertices to this equation. □

Now, we will discuss some of the methods that can be used to test whether a point falls inside the boundaries of a triangle.

**Using sum of angles and dot product**: To check if a point $\dot{\mathbf{P}}$ falls inside the triangle $\triangle\dot{\mathbf{P}}_1\dot{\mathbf{P}}_2\dot{\mathbf{P}}_3$:

1. Construct a direction vector from point $\dot{\mathbf{P}}$ to each of the vertices $\dot{\mathbf{P}}_1$, $\dot{\mathbf{P}}_2$ and $\dot{\mathbf{P}}_3$. These vectors are $\dot{\mathbf{P}}_1 - \dot{\mathbf{P}}$, $\dot{\mathbf{P}}_2 - \dot{\mathbf{P}}$ and $\dot{\mathbf{P}}_3 - \dot{\mathbf{P}}$.
2. Using the dot product, get the angles between the vectors (Sect. A.4.3.2). The angles are given by

$$\begin{aligned}\theta_3 &= \cos^{-1}\left(\frac{[\dot{\mathbf{P}}_1 - \dot{\mathbf{P}}] \cdot [\dot{\mathbf{P}}_2 - \dot{\mathbf{P}}]}{\|\dot{\mathbf{P}}_1 - \dot{\mathbf{P}}\|\|\dot{\mathbf{P}}_2 - \dot{\mathbf{P}}\|}\right),\\ \theta_1 &= \cos^{-1}\left(\frac{[\dot{\mathbf{P}}_2 - \dot{\mathbf{P}}] \cdot [\dot{\mathbf{P}}_3 - \dot{\mathbf{P}}]}{\|\dot{\mathbf{P}}_2 - \dot{\mathbf{P}}\|\|\dot{\mathbf{P}}_3 - \dot{\mathbf{P}}\|}\right),\\ \theta_2 &= \cos^{-1}\left(\frac{[\dot{\mathbf{P}}_3 - \dot{\mathbf{P}}] \cdot [\dot{\mathbf{P}}_1 - \dot{\mathbf{P}}]}{\|\dot{\mathbf{P}}_3 - \dot{\mathbf{P}}\|\|\dot{\mathbf{P}}_1 - \dot{\mathbf{P}}\|}\right),\end{aligned} \tag{10.13}$$

   where $\cdot$ denotes the dot product and $\|.\|$ denotes the norm.
3. If point $\dot{\mathbf{P}}$ is inside the boundaries of the triangle, the sum of the angles must be

$$\theta_1 + \theta_2 + \theta_3 = 360^\circ. \tag{10.14}$$

   (Note that it is important to pay attention to round-off errors when testing for equality.) If the point is outside the triangle, then

$$\theta_1 + \theta_2 + \theta_3 \neq 360^\circ. \tag{10.15}$$

**Example 10.15:** [*Ray-triangle intersection—checking if intersection falls inside the triangle*]

Consider a triangle $\triangle\dot{\mathbf{P}}_1\dot{\mathbf{P}}_2\dot{\mathbf{P}}_3$ where $\dot{\mathbf{P}}_1 = [3, 0, 0]^T$, $\dot{\mathbf{P}}_2 = [0, 1, 2]^T$ and $\dot{\mathbf{P}}_3 = [1.5, 0, 1.5]^T$. If a ray is emitting from $[3, 2, 1]^T$ to $[6, 5, 4]^T$, check if its intersection with the triangle plane falls inside the triangle.

**Solution 10.15:** As done previously, the three vertices can be used to get their plane equation as

$$x + y + z = 3.$$

(The steps are omitted as an exercise.) Now, let us get the point of intersection between the ray and the plane. The direction vector $\mathbf{v}$ is given by

$$\mathbf{v} = \begin{bmatrix} 6 \\ 5 \\ 4 \end{bmatrix} - \begin{bmatrix} 3 \\ 2 \\ 1 \end{bmatrix} = \begin{bmatrix} 3 \\ 3 \\ 3 \end{bmatrix}.$$

The parameter $t$ is obtained by substituting in Eq. (10.12). So,

$$
\begin{aligned}
t &= \frac{-(\dot{\mathbf{P}}_0 \cdot \mathbf{n}) + d}{\mathbf{v} \cdot \mathbf{n}} \\
&= \frac{-\left(\begin{bmatrix} 3 \\ 2 \\ 1 \end{bmatrix} \cdot \begin{bmatrix} 1 \\ 1 \\ 1 \end{bmatrix}\right) + 3}{\begin{bmatrix} 3 \\ 3 \\ 3 \end{bmatrix} \cdot \begin{bmatrix} 1 \\ 1 \\ 1 \end{bmatrix}} = -\frac{1}{3} = -0.3333.
\end{aligned}
$$

The location of the point of intersection $\dot{\mathbf{P}}$ is estimated to be

$$
\begin{aligned}
\dot{\mathbf{P}} &= \dot{\mathbf{P}}_0 + t\mathbf{v} \\
&= \begin{bmatrix} 3 \\ 2 \\ 1 \end{bmatrix} - \frac{1}{3} \begin{bmatrix} 3 \\ 3 \\ 3 \end{bmatrix} = \begin{bmatrix} 2 \\ 1 \\ 0 \end{bmatrix}.
\end{aligned}
$$

Notice that we can use $\mathbf{v}$ after normalization. In this case, $t$ should be calculated as

$$
t = \frac{-\left(\dot{\mathbf{P}}_0 \cdot \frac{\mathbf{n}}{\|\mathbf{n}\|}\right) + \frac{d}{\|\mathbf{n}\|}}{\frac{\mathbf{v}}{\|\mathbf{v}\|} \cdot \frac{\mathbf{n}}{\|\mathbf{n}\|}}.
$$

Now, let us check if the intersection point $\dot{\mathbf{P}} = [2, 1, 0]^T$ falls inside the triangle $\triangle \dot{\mathbf{P}}_1 \dot{\mathbf{P}}_2 \dot{\mathbf{P}}_3$. Get the vectors from the intersection point to each of the vertices. These vectors are

$$
\dot{\mathbf{P}}_1 - \dot{\mathbf{P}} = \begin{bmatrix} 3 \\ 0 \\ 0 \end{bmatrix} - \begin{bmatrix} 2 \\ 1 \\ 0 \end{bmatrix} = \begin{bmatrix} 1 \\ -1 \\ 0 \end{bmatrix},
$$

$$
\dot{\mathbf{P}}_2 - \dot{\mathbf{P}} = \begin{bmatrix} 0 \\ 1 \\ 2 \end{bmatrix} - \begin{bmatrix} 2 \\ 1 \\ 0 \end{bmatrix} = \begin{bmatrix} -2 \\ 0 \\ 2 \end{bmatrix},
$$

and

$$
\dot{\mathbf{P}}_3 - \dot{\mathbf{P}} = \begin{bmatrix} 1.5 \\ 0 \\ 1.5 \end{bmatrix} - \begin{bmatrix} 2 \\ 1 \\ 0 \end{bmatrix} = \begin{bmatrix} -0.5 \\ -1 \\ 1.5 \end{bmatrix}.
$$

Using Eq. (10.13), the angles are

$$\theta_3 = \cos^{-1}\left(\frac{[\dot{\mathbf{P}}_1 - \dot{\mathbf{P}}]\cdot[\dot{\mathbf{P}}_2 - \dot{\mathbf{P}}]}{\|\dot{\mathbf{P}}_1 - \dot{\mathbf{P}}\|\|\dot{\mathbf{P}}_2 - \dot{\mathbf{P}}\|}\right)$$

$$= \cos^{-1}\left(\frac{\begin{bmatrix}1\\-1\\0\end{bmatrix}\cdot\begin{bmatrix}-2\\0\\2\end{bmatrix}}{\left\|\begin{bmatrix}1\\-1\\0\end{bmatrix}\right\|\left\|\begin{bmatrix}-2\\0\\2\end{bmatrix}\right\|}\right) = \cos^{-1}\left(-\tfrac{1}{2}\right) = 120^\circ,$$

$$\theta_1 = \cos^{-1}\left(\frac{[\dot{\mathbf{P}}_2 - \dot{\mathbf{P}}]\cdot[\dot{\mathbf{P}}_3 - \dot{\mathbf{P}}]}{\|\dot{\mathbf{P}}_2 - \dot{\mathbf{P}}\|\|\dot{\mathbf{P}}_3 - \dot{\mathbf{P}}\|}\right)$$

$$= \cos^{-1}\left(\frac{\begin{bmatrix}-2\\0\\2\end{bmatrix}\cdot\begin{bmatrix}-0.5\\-1\\1.5\end{bmatrix}}{\left\|\begin{bmatrix}-2\\0\\2\end{bmatrix}\right\|\left\|\begin{bmatrix}-0.5\\-1\\1.5\end{bmatrix}\right\|}\right) = \cos^{-1}\left(\frac{2}{\sqrt{7}}\right) = 40.8934^\circ$$

and

$$\theta_2 = \cos^{-1}\left(\frac{[\dot{\mathbf{P}}_3 - \dot{\mathbf{P}}]\cdot[\dot{\mathbf{P}}_1 - \dot{\mathbf{P}}]}{\|\dot{\mathbf{P}}_3 - \dot{\mathbf{P}}\|\|\dot{\mathbf{P}}_1 - \dot{\mathbf{P}}\|}\right)$$

$$= \cos^{-1}\left(\frac{\begin{bmatrix}-0.5\\-1\\1.5\end{bmatrix}\cdot\begin{bmatrix}1\\-1\\0\end{bmatrix}}{\left\|\begin{bmatrix}-0.5\\-1\\1.5\end{bmatrix}\right\|\left\|\begin{bmatrix}1\\-1\\0\end{bmatrix}\right\|}\right) = \cos^{-1}\left(\frac{1}{2\sqrt{7}}\right) = 79.1066^\circ.$$

Since $\theta_1 + \theta_2 + \theta_3 \neq 360^\circ$; hence, the intersection point is out of the given triangle. □

**Using cross and dot products**: Each edge of a triangle splits its plane into two sides. Points on one side behave differently than points on the other side. Consider the side $\overline{\dot{\mathbf{P}}_1\dot{\mathbf{P}}_3}$ in Fig. 10.17. All the points inside the triangle behave similar to point $\dot{\mathbf{P}}$ (that is inside the triangle) and different than point $\dot{\mathbf{P}}'$ (that is outside the triangle). To express this mathematically, the cross product (Sect. A.4.3.3) can be used as

$$\begin{aligned}\mathbf{n}_{p'} &= \left[\dot{\mathbf{P}}_3 - \dot{\mathbf{P}}_1\right] \times \left[\dot{\mathbf{P}}' - \dot{\mathbf{P}}_1\right],\\ \mathbf{n}_p &= \left[\dot{\mathbf{P}}_3 - \dot{\mathbf{P}}_1\right] \times \left[\dot{\mathbf{P}} - \dot{\mathbf{P}}_1\right].\end{aligned} \tag{10.16}$$

Note that $\dot{\mathbf{P}}$ and $\dot{\mathbf{P}}'$ are on two different sides relative to $\dot{\mathbf{P}}_1\dot{\mathbf{P}}_3$ and $\mathbf{n}_{p'}$ is pointing outwards while $\mathbf{n}_p$ is pointing inwards. Also, notice that all points to the left of $\dot{\mathbf{P}}_1\dot{\mathbf{P}}_3$ will behave similar to $\dot{\mathbf{P}}'$ and all points to the right of $\overline{\dot{\mathbf{P}}_1\dot{\mathbf{P}}_3}$ will behave similar to $\dot{\mathbf{P}}$.

Given an edge $\overline{\dot{\mathbf{P}}_1\dot{\mathbf{P}}_3}$, use the third vertex $\dot{\mathbf{P}}_2$ to determine the direction that corresponds to points inside the triangle. Thus,

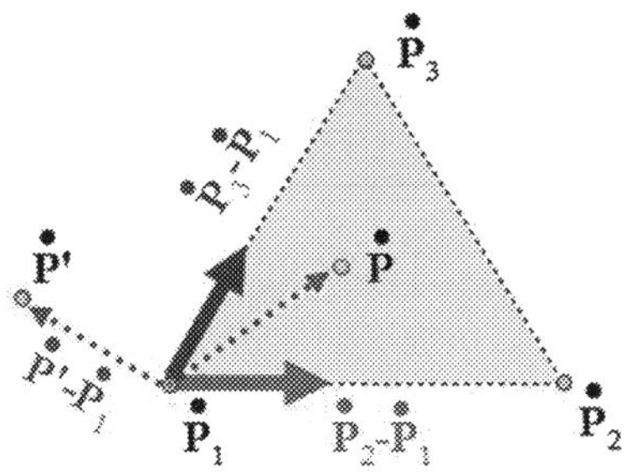


**Fig. 10.17** A point is checked whether it lies inside the triangle using the cross and dot products

$$\mathbf{n}_{p2} = \left[\dot{\mathbf{P}}_3 - \dot{\mathbf{P}}_1\right] \times \left[\dot{\mathbf{P}}_2 - \dot{\mathbf{P}}_1\right]. \tag{10.17}$$

Now, test the direction of $\mathbf{n}_p$ (or $\mathbf{n}_{p'}$) with respect to $\mathbf{n}_{p2}$. This can be done using the dot product (Sect. A.4.3.2) as

$$\begin{aligned} \mathbf{n}_p \cdot \mathbf{n}_{p2} &\geq 0 \Rightarrow in, \\ \mathbf{n}_p \cdot \mathbf{n}_{p2} &< 0 \Rightarrow out. \end{aligned} \tag{10.18}$$

Note that the test must be applied to *all* sides of the triangle.

**Example 10.16:** [*Ray-triangle intersection—checking if a point falls inside a triangle*]
Consider a triangle $\triangle\dot{\mathbf{P}}_1\dot{\mathbf{P}}_2\dot{\mathbf{P}}_3$ where $\dot{\mathbf{P}}_1 = [3, 0, 2]^T$, $\dot{\mathbf{P}}_2 = [9, 0, 7]^T$ and $\dot{\mathbf{P}}_3 = [4, 0, 9]^T$. Check if a point $\dot{\mathbf{P}} = [5, 0, 8]^T$ falls inside this triangle.

**Solution 10.16:** Consider the edge $\overline{\dot{\mathbf{P}}_1\dot{\mathbf{P}}_3}$. Compute $\mathbf{n}_p$ and $\mathbf{n}_{p2}$ and test if $\dot{\mathbf{P}}$ is inside the triangle:

$$\dot{\mathbf{P}}_3 - \dot{\mathbf{P}}_1 = \begin{bmatrix} 4 \\ 0 \\ 9 \end{bmatrix} - \begin{bmatrix} 3 \\ 0 \\ 2 \end{bmatrix} = \begin{bmatrix} 1 \\ 0 \\ 7 \end{bmatrix},$$

$$\dot{\mathbf{P}} - \dot{\mathbf{P}}_1 = \begin{bmatrix} 5 \\ 0 \\ 8 \end{bmatrix} - \begin{bmatrix} 3 \\ 0 \\ 2 \end{bmatrix} = \begin{bmatrix} 2 \\ 0 \\ 6 \end{bmatrix},$$

$$\mathbf{n}_p = \left[\dot{\mathbf{P}}_3 - \dot{\mathbf{P}}_1\right] \times \left[\dot{\mathbf{P}} - \dot{\mathbf{P}}_1\right] = \begin{bmatrix} 1 \\ 0 \\ 7 \end{bmatrix} \times \begin{bmatrix} 2 \\ 0 \\ 6 \end{bmatrix} = \begin{bmatrix} 0 \\ 8 \\ 0 \end{bmatrix},$$

$$\dot{\mathbf{P}}_2 - \dot{\mathbf{P}}_1 = \begin{bmatrix} 9 \\ 0 \\ 7 \end{bmatrix} - \begin{bmatrix} 3 \\ 0 \\ 2 \end{bmatrix} = \begin{bmatrix} 6 \\ 0 \\ 5 \end{bmatrix},$$

$$\mathbf{n}_{p2} = \left[\dot{\mathbf{P}}_3 - \dot{\mathbf{P}}_1\right] \times \left[\dot{\mathbf{P}}_2 - \dot{\mathbf{P}}_1\right] = \begin{bmatrix} 1 \\ 0 \\ 7 \end{bmatrix} \times \begin{bmatrix} 6 \\ 0 \\ 5 \end{bmatrix} = \begin{bmatrix} 0 \\ 37 \\ 0 \end{bmatrix},$$

$$\mathbf{n}_p \cdot \mathbf{n}_{p2} = \begin{bmatrix} 0 \\ 8 \\ 0 \end{bmatrix} \cdot \begin{bmatrix} 0 \\ 37 \\ 0 \end{bmatrix} = 296 \Rightarrow in.$$

Consider the edge $\overline{\dot{\mathbf{P}}_1\dot{\mathbf{P}}_2}$. Compute $\mathbf{n}_p$ and $\mathbf{n}_{p3}$ and test if $\dot{\mathbf{P}}$ is inside the triangle:

$$\dot{\mathbf{P}}_2 - \dot{\mathbf{P}}_1 = \begin{bmatrix} 9 \\ 0 \\ 7 \end{bmatrix} - \begin{bmatrix} 3 \\ 0 \\ 2 \end{bmatrix} = \begin{bmatrix} 6 \\ 0 \\ 5 \end{bmatrix},$$

$$\dot{\mathbf{P}} - \dot{\mathbf{P}}_1 = \begin{bmatrix} 5 \\ 0 \\ 8 \end{bmatrix} - \begin{bmatrix} 3 \\ 0 \\ 2 \end{bmatrix} = \begin{bmatrix} 2 \\ 0 \\ 6 \end{bmatrix},$$

$$\mathbf{n}_p = [\dot{\mathbf{P}}_2 - \dot{\mathbf{P}}_1] \times [\dot{\mathbf{P}} - \dot{\mathbf{P}}_1] = \begin{bmatrix} 6 \\ 0 \\ 5 \end{bmatrix} \times \begin{bmatrix} 2 \\ 0 \\ 6 \end{bmatrix} = \begin{bmatrix} 0 \\ -26 \\ 0 \end{bmatrix},$$

$$\dot{\mathbf{P}}_3 - \dot{\mathbf{P}}_1 = \begin{bmatrix} 4 \\ 0 \\ 9 \end{bmatrix} - \begin{bmatrix} 3 \\ 0 \\ 2 \end{bmatrix} = \begin{bmatrix} 1 \\ 0 \\ 7 \end{bmatrix},$$

$$\mathbf{n}_{p3} = [\dot{\mathbf{P}}_2 - \dot{\mathbf{P}}_1] \times [\dot{\mathbf{P}}_3 - \dot{\mathbf{P}}_1] = \begin{bmatrix} 6 \\ 0 \\ 5 \end{bmatrix} \times \begin{bmatrix} 1 \\ 0 \\ 7 \end{bmatrix} = \begin{bmatrix} 0 \\ -37 \\ 0 \end{bmatrix},$$

$$\mathbf{n}_p \cdot \mathbf{n}_{p3} = \begin{bmatrix} 0 \\ -26 \\ 0 \end{bmatrix} \cdot \begin{bmatrix} 0 \\ -37 \\ 0 \end{bmatrix} = 962 \Rightarrow in.$$

Consider the edge $\overline{\dot{\mathbf{P}}_2\dot{\mathbf{P}}_3}$. Compute $\mathbf{n}_p$ and $\mathbf{n}_{p1}$ and test if $\dot{\mathbf{P}}$ is inside the triangle:

$$\dot{\mathbf{P}}_3 - \dot{\mathbf{P}}_2 = \begin{bmatrix} 4 \\ 0 \\ 9 \end{bmatrix} - \begin{bmatrix} 9 \\ 0 \\ 7 \end{bmatrix} = \begin{bmatrix} -5 \\ 0 \\ 2 \end{bmatrix},$$

$$\dot{\mathbf{P}} - \dot{\mathbf{P}}_2 = \begin{bmatrix} 5 \\ 0 \\ 8 \end{bmatrix} - \begin{bmatrix} 9 \\ 0 \\ 7 \end{bmatrix} = \begin{bmatrix} -4 \\ 0 \\ 1 \end{bmatrix},$$

$$\mathbf{n}_p = [\dot{\mathbf{P}}_3 - \dot{\mathbf{P}}_2] \times [\dot{\mathbf{P}} - \dot{\mathbf{P}}_2] = \begin{bmatrix} -5 \\ 0 \\ 2 \end{bmatrix} \times \begin{bmatrix} -4 \\ 0 \\ 1 \end{bmatrix} = \begin{bmatrix} 0 \\ -3 \\ 0 \end{bmatrix},$$

$$\dot{\mathbf{P}}_1 - \dot{\mathbf{P}}_2 = \begin{bmatrix} 3 \\ 0 \\ 2 \end{bmatrix} - \begin{bmatrix} 9 \\ 0 \\ 7 \end{bmatrix} = \begin{bmatrix} -6 \\ 0 \\ -5 \end{bmatrix},$$

$$\mathbf{n}_{p1} = \left[\dot{\mathbf{P}}_3 - \dot{\mathbf{P}}_2\right] \times \left[\dot{\mathbf{P}}_1 - \dot{\mathbf{P}}_2\right] = \begin{bmatrix} -5 \\ 0 \\ 2 \end{bmatrix} \times \begin{bmatrix} -6 \\ 0 \\ -5 \end{bmatrix} = \begin{bmatrix} 0 \\ -37 \\ 0 \end{bmatrix},$$

$$\mathbf{n}_p \cdot \mathbf{n}_{p1} = \begin{bmatrix} 0 \\ -3 \\ 0 \end{bmatrix} \cdot \begin{bmatrix} 0 \\ -37 \\ 0 \end{bmatrix} = 111 \Rightarrow in.$$

All tests result in positive dot products; thus, point $\dot{\mathbf{P}} = [5, 0, 8]^T$ is inside the triangle. □

**Example 10.17:** [*Ray-triangle intersection—checking if points are on the same side of a line*]

Consider a line segment $\overline{\dot{\mathbf{p}}_1\dot{\mathbf{p}}_2}$ where $\dot{\mathbf{p}}_1 = [3, 2]^T$ and $\dot{\mathbf{p}}_2 = [9, 7]^T$. Determine if points $\dot{\mathbf{q}}_1 = [5, 1]^T$ and $\dot{\mathbf{q}}_2 = [5, 5]^T$ are on the same side of the line $\overline{\dot{\mathbf{p}}_1\dot{\mathbf{p}}_2}$.

**Solution 10.17:** Since all points are on the $xy$-plane, cross product of 2D vectors (Sect. A.4.3.4) may be used. If the 2D cross products $\overline{\dot{\mathbf{p}}_1\dot{\mathbf{q}}_1} \times \overline{\dot{\mathbf{p}}_1\dot{\mathbf{p}}_2}$ and $\overline{\dot{\mathbf{p}}_1\dot{\mathbf{q}}_2} \times \overline{\dot{\mathbf{p}}_1\dot{\mathbf{p}}_2}$ result in the same sign, both $\dot{\mathbf{q}}_1$ and $\dot{\mathbf{q}}_2$ are one the same side of $\overline{\dot{\mathbf{p}}_1\dot{\mathbf{p}}_2}$; otherwise, they are on different sides. Consider the direction vectors $\dot{\mathbf{p}}_2 - \dot{\mathbf{p}}_1$, $\dot{\mathbf{q}}_1 - \dot{\mathbf{p}}_1$ and $\dot{\mathbf{q}}_2 - \dot{\mathbf{p}}_1$:

$$\dot{\mathbf{p}}_2 - \dot{\mathbf{p}}_1 = \begin{bmatrix} 9 \\ 7 \end{bmatrix} - \begin{bmatrix} 3 \\ 2 \end{bmatrix} = \begin{bmatrix} 6 \\ 5 \end{bmatrix},$$

$$\dot{\mathbf{q}}_1 - \dot{\mathbf{p}}_1 = \begin{bmatrix} 5 \\ 1 \end{bmatrix} - \begin{bmatrix} 3 \\ 2 \end{bmatrix} = \begin{bmatrix} 2 \\ -1 \end{bmatrix},$$

$$\dot{\mathbf{q}}_2 - \dot{\mathbf{p}}_1 = \begin{bmatrix} 5 \\ 5 \end{bmatrix} - \begin{bmatrix} 3 \\ 2 \end{bmatrix} = \begin{bmatrix} 2 \\ 3 \end{bmatrix}.$$

Now, determine the 2D cross products:

$$[\dot{\mathbf{q}}_1 - \dot{\mathbf{p}}_1] \times [\dot{\mathbf{p}}_2 - \dot{\mathbf{p}}_1] = \begin{bmatrix} 2 \\ -1 \end{bmatrix} \times \begin{bmatrix} 6 \\ 5 \end{bmatrix} = 2(5) - 6(-1) = 16 \Longrightarrow +ve,$$

$$[\dot{\mathbf{q}}_2 - \dot{\mathbf{p}}_1] \times [\dot{\mathbf{p}}_2 - \dot{\mathbf{p}}_1] = \begin{bmatrix} 2 \\ 3 \end{bmatrix} \times \begin{bmatrix} 6 \\ 5 \end{bmatrix} = 2(5) - 6(3) = -8 \Longrightarrow -ve.$$

Since the 2D cross products result in two different signs, $\dot{\mathbf{q}}_1$ and $\dot{\mathbf{q}}_2$ are on different sides of the line segment $\overline{\dot{\mathbf{p}}_1\dot{\mathbf{p}}_2}$.

This idea can be extended to test whether or not a 2D point falls inside a triangle where the 2D point as well as the vertices of the triangle reside on the same plane. This is left as an exercise (see Problem 10.11). □

**Using barycentric coordinates**: A point $\dot{\mathbf{P}}$ inside a triangle $\triangle\dot{\mathbf{P}}_1\dot{\mathbf{P}}_2\dot{\mathbf{P}}_3$ splits it into three sub-triangles; i.e., $\triangle\dot{\mathbf{P}}\dot{\mathbf{P}}_1\dot{\mathbf{P}}_2$, $\triangle\dot{\mathbf{P}}\dot{\mathbf{P}}_2\dot{\mathbf{P}}_3$ and $\triangle\dot{\mathbf{P}}\dot{\mathbf{P}}_3\dot{\mathbf{P}}_1$ whose areas are $A_3$, $A_1$ and $A_2$ respectively. The total area of the three sub-triangles (i.e., $A_1 + A_2 + A_3$) is equal to the area of the original triangle (i.e., $A$). Barycentric coordinates (Sect. B.3) of the internal point $\dot{\mathbf{P}}$ is given by $\left[\frac{A_1}{A}, \frac{A_2}{A}, \frac{A_3}{A}\right]^T$ where

$$\frac{A_1}{A} + \frac{A_2}{A} + \frac{A_3}{A} = 1. \tag{10.19}$$

(Note that it is important to pay attention to round-off errors when testing for equality.) On the other hand, if the point is outside the triangle, Eq. (10.19) turns to

$$\frac{A_1}{A} + \frac{A_2}{A} + \frac{A_3}{A} \neq 1. \tag{10.20}$$

**Example 10.18:** [*Ray-triangle intersection—checking if a point falls inside a triangle using barycentric coordinates*]

Consider a triangle $\triangle\dot{\mathbf{P}}_1\dot{\mathbf{P}}_2\dot{\mathbf{P}}_3$ where $\dot{\mathbf{P}}_1 = [3, 0, 2]^T$, $\dot{\mathbf{P}}_2 = [9, 0, 7]^T$ and $\dot{\mathbf{P}}_3 = [4, 0, 9]^T$. Use barycentric coordinates to confirm that a point $\dot{\mathbf{P}} = [5, 0, 8]^T$ falls inside this triangle. Heron's formula can be used to calculate the area of a triangle as

$$A = \sqrt{s(s-a)(s-b)(s-c)},$$

where $a$, $b$ and $c$ are the side lengths of the triangle and

$$s = \frac{a+b+c}{2}.$$

**Solution 10.18:** Let us start by calculating the side lengths of the triangle and its sub-triangles.

$$\begin{aligned}
l_{\dot{\mathbf{P}}_1\dot{\mathbf{P}}_2} &= l_{\dot{\mathbf{P}}_2\dot{\mathbf{P}}_1} = \|\dot{\mathbf{P}}_1 - \dot{\mathbf{P}}_2\| = \sqrt{(3-9)^2 + (0-0)^2 + (2-7)^2} = \sqrt{61} = 7.8102,\\
l_{\dot{\mathbf{P}}_2\dot{\mathbf{P}}_3} &= l_{\dot{\mathbf{P}}_3\dot{\mathbf{P}}_2} = \|\dot{\mathbf{P}}_2 - \dot{\mathbf{P}}_3\| = \sqrt{(9-4)^2 + (0-0)^2 + (7-9)^2} = \sqrt{29} = 5.3852,\\
l_{\dot{\mathbf{P}}_3\dot{\mathbf{P}}_1} &= l_{\dot{\mathbf{P}}_1\dot{\mathbf{P}}_3} = \|\dot{\mathbf{P}}_3 - \dot{\mathbf{P}}_1\| = \sqrt{(4-3)^2 + (0-0)^2 + (9-2)^2} = \sqrt{50} = 7.0711,\\
l_{\dot{\mathbf{P}}\dot{\mathbf{P}}_1} &= l_{\dot{\mathbf{P}}_1\dot{\mathbf{P}}} = \|\dot{\mathbf{P}} - \dot{\mathbf{P}}_1\| = \sqrt{(5-3)^2 + (0-0)^2 + (8-2)^2} = \sqrt{40} = 6.3246,\\
l_{\dot{\mathbf{P}}\dot{\mathbf{P}}_2} &= l_{\dot{\mathbf{P}}_2\dot{\mathbf{P}}} = \|\dot{\mathbf{P}} - \dot{\mathbf{P}}_2\| = \sqrt{(5-9)^2 + (0-0)^2 + (8-7)^2} = \sqrt{17} = 4.1231,\\
l_{\dot{\mathbf{P}}\dot{\mathbf{P}}_3} &= l_{\dot{\mathbf{P}}_3\dot{\mathbf{P}}} = \|\dot{\mathbf{P}} - \dot{\mathbf{P}}_3\| = \sqrt{(5-4)^2 + (0-0)^2 + (8-9)^2} = \sqrt{2} = 1.4142.
\end{aligned}$$

For the triangle $\triangle\dot{\mathbf{P}}_1\dot{\mathbf{P}}_2\dot{\mathbf{P}}_3$:

$$s = \frac{l_{\dot{\mathbf{P}}_1\dot{\mathbf{P}}_2} + l_{\dot{\mathbf{P}}_2\dot{\mathbf{P}}_3} + l_{\dot{\mathbf{P}}_3\dot{\mathbf{P}}_1}}{2} = \frac{\sqrt{61} + \sqrt{29} + \sqrt{50}}{2} = 10.1332,$$

$$A = \sqrt{s(s - l_{\dot{\mathbf{P}}_1\dot{\mathbf{P}}_2})(s - l_{\dot{\mathbf{P}}_2\dot{\mathbf{P}}_3})(s - l_{\dot{\mathbf{P}}_3\dot{\mathbf{P}}_1})} = 18.5.$$

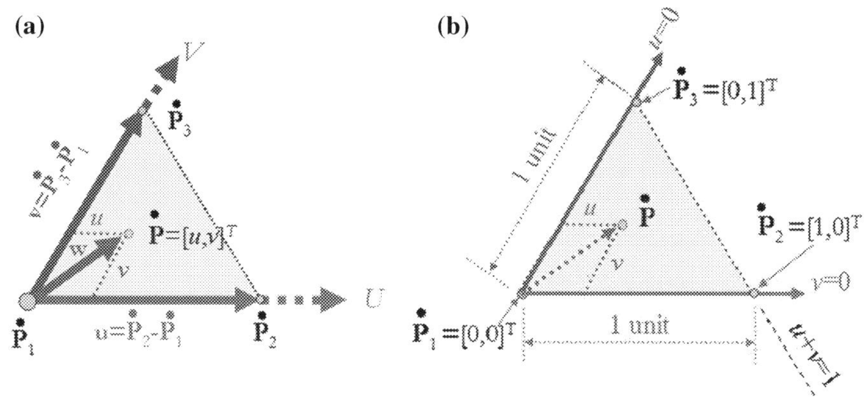


**Fig. 10.18** Parametric coordinates can be used to specify whether a point falls inside a triangle

For the triangle $\triangle\dot{\mathbf{P}}\dot{\mathbf{P}}_1\dot{\mathbf{P}}_2$:

$$s_3 = \frac{l_{\dot{\mathbf{P}}\dot{\mathbf{P}}_1} + l_{\dot{\mathbf{P}}_1\dot{\mathbf{P}}_2} + l_{\dot{\mathbf{P}}_2\dot{\mathbf{P}}}}{2} = \frac{\sqrt{40}+\sqrt{61}+\sqrt{17}}{2} = 9.1290,$$

$$A_3 = \sqrt{s_3(s_3 - l_{\dot{\mathbf{P}}-\dot{\mathbf{P}}_1})(s_3 - l_{\dot{\mathbf{P}}_1-\dot{\mathbf{P}}_2})(s_3 - l_{\dot{\mathbf{P}}_2-\dot{\mathbf{P}}})} = 13.0.$$

For the triangle $\triangle\dot{\mathbf{P}}\dot{\mathbf{P}}_2\dot{\mathbf{P}}_3$:

$$s_1 = \frac{l_{\dot{\mathbf{P}}\dot{\mathbf{P}}_2} + l_{\dot{\mathbf{P}}_2\dot{\mathbf{P}}_3} + l_{\dot{\mathbf{P}}_3\dot{\mathbf{P}}}}{2} = \frac{\sqrt{17}+\sqrt{29}+\sqrt{2}}{2} = 5.4612,$$

$$A_1 = \sqrt{s_1(s_1 - l_{\dot{\mathbf{P}}\dot{\mathbf{P}}_2})(s_1 - l_{\dot{\mathbf{P}}_2\dot{\mathbf{P}}_3})(s_1 - l_{\dot{\mathbf{P}}_3\dot{\mathbf{P}}})} = 1.5.$$

For the triangle $\triangle\dot{\mathbf{P}}\dot{\mathbf{P}}_3\dot{\mathbf{P}}_1$:

$$s_2 = \frac{l_{\dot{\mathbf{P}}\dot{\mathbf{P}}_3} + l_{\dot{\mathbf{P}}_3\dot{\mathbf{P}}_1} + l_{\dot{\mathbf{P}}_1\dot{\mathbf{P}}}}{2} = \frac{\sqrt{2}+\sqrt{50}+\sqrt{40}}{2} = 7.4049,$$

$$A_2 = \sqrt{s_2(s_2 - l_{\dot{\mathbf{P}}\dot{\mathbf{P}}_3})(s_2 - l_{\dot{\mathbf{P}}_3\dot{\mathbf{P}}_1})(s_2 - l_{\dot{\mathbf{P}}_1\dot{\mathbf{P}}})} = 4.0.$$

Since $A_1 + A_2 + A_3 = A$, point $\dot{\mathbf{P}} = [5, 0, 8]^T$ falls inside the triangle. (It is important to pay attention to round-off errors when testing for equality.) □

**Using parametric coordinates**: The same problem can be solved using parametric coordinates as discussed in Sect. B.2. Consider the triangle $\triangle\dot{\mathbf{P}}_1\dot{\mathbf{P}}_2\dot{\mathbf{P}}_3$ shown in Fig. 10.18a.

1. Pick one of the vertices to be the origin of the plane; e.g., $\dot{\mathbf{P}}_1$ is expressed as $[0, 0]^T$ as shown in Fig. 10.18b.
2. Basis vectors are defined to specify points on the plane (and in the triangle). In the example shown, the basis vectors are

$$\mathbf{u} = \dot{\mathbf{P}}_2 - \dot{\mathbf{P}}_1$$

and

$$\mathbf{v} = \dot{\mathbf{P}}_3 - \dot{\mathbf{P}}_1.$$

Thus, the coordinates of $\dot{\mathbf{P}}_2$ and $\dot{\mathbf{P}}_3$ are expressed as $[1, 0]^T$ and $[0, 1]^T$ respectively.
3. A point $\dot{\mathbf{P}}$ can be defined in terms of these basis vectors by starting at the origin $\dot{\mathbf{P}}_1$ and walking some $u$ distance along $\mathbf{u} = \dot{\mathbf{P}}_2 - \dot{\mathbf{P}}_1$ then walking some $v$ distance in the direction $\mathbf{v} = \dot{\mathbf{P}}_3 - \dot{\mathbf{P}}_1$. This can be written as

$$\dot{\mathbf{P}} = \dot{\mathbf{P}}_1 + u[\dot{\mathbf{P}}_2 - \dot{\mathbf{P}}_1] + v[\dot{\mathbf{P}}_3 - \dot{\mathbf{P}}_1]. \tag{10.21}$$

Equivalently, the vector $\mathbf{w}$ is expressed as

$$\begin{aligned}[\dot{\mathbf{P}} - \dot{\mathbf{P}}_1] &= u[\dot{\mathbf{P}}_2 - \dot{\mathbf{P}}_1] + v[\dot{\mathbf{P}}_3 - \dot{\mathbf{P}}_1] \\ \mathbf{w} &= u\mathbf{u} + v\mathbf{v}.\end{aligned} \tag{10.22}$$

The values of $u$ and $v$ are expressed as

$$\begin{aligned}u &= \frac{(\mathbf{u}\cdot\mathbf{v})(\mathbf{w}\cdot\mathbf{v}) - (\mathbf{v}\cdot\mathbf{v})(\mathbf{w}\cdot\mathbf{u})}{(\mathbf{u}\cdot\mathbf{v})^2 - (\mathbf{u}\cdot\mathbf{u})(\mathbf{v}\cdot\mathbf{v})}, \\ v &= \frac{(\mathbf{u}\cdot\mathbf{v})(\mathbf{w}\cdot\mathbf{u}) - (\mathbf{u}\cdot\mathbf{u})(\mathbf{w}\cdot\mathbf{v})}{(\mathbf{u}\cdot\mathbf{v})^2 - (\mathbf{u}\cdot\mathbf{u})(\mathbf{v}\cdot\mathbf{v})}.\end{aligned} \tag{10.23}$$

4. Point $\dot{\mathbf{P}}$ is inside the triangle if *all* the following constraints are true:

$$\begin{aligned}0 \le u \le 1, \\ 0 \le v \le 1, \\ u + v \le 1.\end{aligned} \tag{10.24}$$

This is clarified in Fig. 10.18b.

**Example 10.19:** [*Ray-triangle intersection—checking if a point falls inside a triangle using parametric coordinates*]

Consider a triangle $\Delta\dot{\mathbf{P}}_1\dot{\mathbf{P}}_2\dot{\mathbf{P}}_3$ where $\dot{\mathbf{P}}_1 = [3, 0, 2]^T$, $\dot{\mathbf{P}}_2 = [9, 0, 7]^T$ and $\dot{\mathbf{P}}_3 = [4, 0, 9]^T$. Use parametric coordinates to confirm that a point $\dot{\mathbf{P}} = [5, 0, 8]^T$ falls inside this triangle.

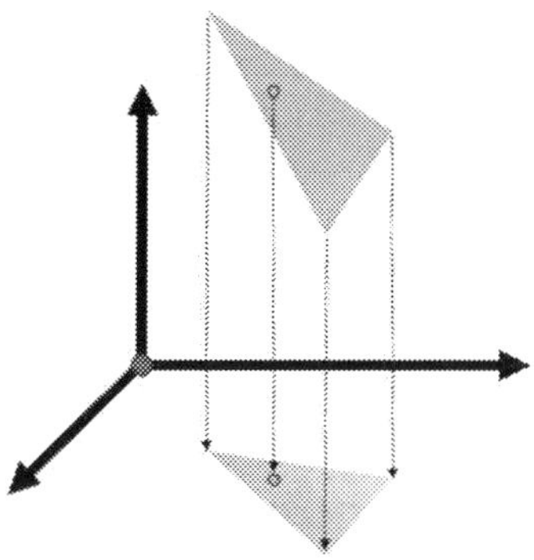

**Fig. 10.19** A triangle in 3D space may be projected onto one of the principal planes

**Solution 10.19:** Get the vectors **u**, **v** and **w**:

$$\begin{aligned}\mathbf{u} &= \dot{\mathbf{P}}_2 - \dot{\mathbf{P}}_1 \\ &= \begin{bmatrix} 9 \\ 0 \\ 7 \end{bmatrix} - \begin{bmatrix} 3 \\ 0 \\ 2 \end{bmatrix} = \begin{bmatrix} 6 \\ 0 \\ 5 \end{bmatrix},\end{aligned}$$

$$\begin{aligned}\mathbf{v} &= \dot{\mathbf{P}}_3 - \dot{\mathbf{P}}_1 \\ &= \begin{bmatrix} 4 \\ 0 \\ 9 \end{bmatrix} - \begin{bmatrix} 3 \\ 0 \\ 2 \end{bmatrix} = \begin{bmatrix} 1 \\ 0 \\ 7 \end{bmatrix},\end{aligned}$$

$$\begin{aligned}\mathbf{w} &= \dot{\mathbf{P}} - \dot{\mathbf{P}}_1 \\ &= \begin{bmatrix} 5 \\ 0 \\ 8 \end{bmatrix} - \begin{bmatrix} 3 \\ 0 \\ 2 \end{bmatrix} = \begin{bmatrix} 2 \\ 0 \\ 6 \end{bmatrix}.\end{aligned}$$

Then,

$$\begin{aligned}u &= \frac{(\mathbf{u}\cdot\mathbf{v})(\mathbf{w}\cdot\mathbf{v}) - (\mathbf{v}\cdot\mathbf{v})(\mathbf{w}\cdot\mathbf{u})}{(\mathbf{u}\cdot\mathbf{v})^2 - (\mathbf{u}\cdot\mathbf{u})(\mathbf{v}\cdot\mathbf{v})} \\ &= \frac{41 \times 44 - 50 \times 42}{41^2 - 61 \times 50} = 0.2162,\end{aligned}$$

$$\begin{aligned}v &= \frac{(\mathbf{u}\cdot\mathbf{v})(\mathbf{w}\cdot\mathbf{u}) - (\mathbf{u}\cdot\mathbf{u})(\mathbf{w}\cdot\mathbf{v})}{(\mathbf{u}\cdot\mathbf{v})^2 - (\mathbf{u}\cdot\mathbf{u})(\mathbf{v}\cdot\mathbf{v})} \\ &= \frac{41 \times 42 - 61 \times 44}{41^2 - 61 \times 50} = 0.7027.\end{aligned}$$

The values of $u$ and $v$ satisfy the constraints (10.24). Thus, point $\dot{\mathbf{P}} = [5, 0, 8]^T$ falls inside the triangle. □

**Using 2D linear equations**: A triangle in 3D space may be projected onto one of the principal planes (i.e., $xy$-, $yz$- or $zx$-plane) along with the tested point in order to eliminate

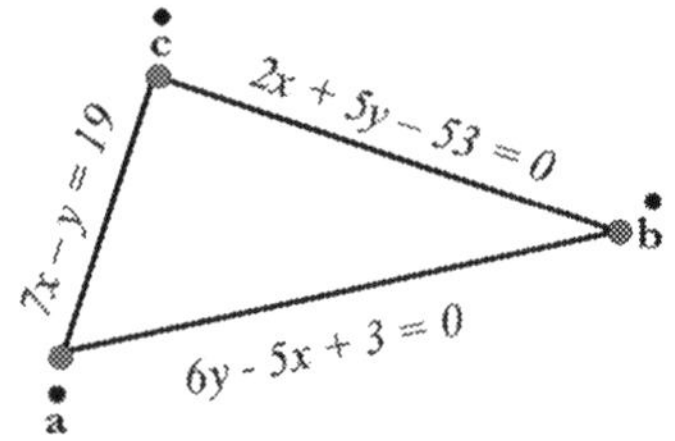


**Fig. 10.20** A triangle is represented by the equations of its sides

one of the dimensions (Fig. 10.19). To achieve this, the coordinate which has the largest component in the plane normal vector may be excluded.

The problem now is converted to the 2D space. We can use 2D linear equations to test whether a point falls inside the triangle. The steps are as follows:

1. Determine the linear equation for each side of the triangle using its vertices.
2. For each side, apply the third vertex to its linear equation obtained above and associate the sign of the value calculated to the current side.
3. Apply the point to be tested to the linear equations of the triangle sides.

A general point $\dot{\mathbf{P}}$ is inside the triangle if it gives the same signs obtained previously when the three vertices are applied to the three linear equations of the sides.

**Example 10.20:** [*Ray-triangle intersection—checking if a point falls inside a triangle expressed as a set of three linear equations*]

A triangle residing on the $xy$-plane and given as a set of three linear equations is shown in Fig. 10.20. Check if a point $[5, 8]^T$ falls inside this triangle.

**Solution 10.20:** There are many ways to solve this problem. One of them is as follows:

1. Get the vertices of the triangle as the intersections of its sides. One of the ways to get the intersection between two lines is by using the cross product (Sect. A.4.3.3) of their two linear equations. Thus,

$$\mathbf{a} = \begin{bmatrix} 7 \\ -1 \\ -19 \end{bmatrix} \times \begin{bmatrix} -5 \\ 6 \\ 3 \end{bmatrix} = \begin{bmatrix} 111 \\ 74 \\ 37 \end{bmatrix} \Rightarrow \dot{\mathbf{a}} = \begin{bmatrix} 3 \\ 2 \end{bmatrix},$$

$$\mathbf{b} = \begin{bmatrix} -5 \\ 6 \\ 3 \end{bmatrix} \times \begin{bmatrix} 2 \\ 5 \\ -53 \end{bmatrix} = \begin{bmatrix} -333 \\ -259 \\ -37 \end{bmatrix} \Rightarrow \dot{\mathbf{b}} = \begin{bmatrix} 9 \\ 7 \end{bmatrix},$$

$$\mathbf{c} = \begin{bmatrix} 2 \\ 5 \\ -53 \end{bmatrix} \times \begin{bmatrix} 7 \\ -1 \\ -19 \end{bmatrix} = \begin{bmatrix} -148 \\ -333 \\ -37 \end{bmatrix} \Rightarrow \dot{\mathbf{c}} = \begin{bmatrix} 4 \\ 9 \end{bmatrix}.$$

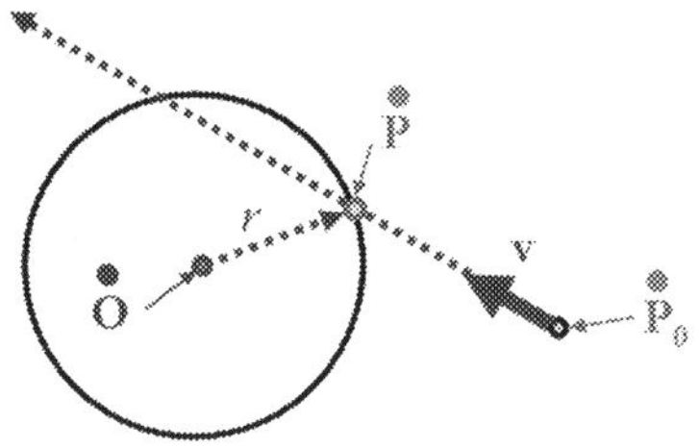


**Fig. 10.21** Solving ray-sphere intersection algebraically

2. Apply vertices to the linear equations.
   a. Get the "inside" signs with respect to the edges:
      Apply $\dot{\mathbf{c}} = [4, 9]^T$ to $\overline{\dot{\mathbf{a}}\dot{\mathbf{b}}}$: $6y - 5x + 3 \Rightarrow 6 \times 9 - 5 \times 4 + 3 \Rightarrow +$.
      Apply $\dot{\mathbf{a}} = [3, 2]^T$ to $\overline{\dot{\mathbf{b}}\dot{\mathbf{c}}}$: $2x + 5y - 53 \Rightarrow 2 \times 3 + 5 \times 2 - 53 \Rightarrow -$.
      Apply $\dot{\mathbf{b}} = [9, 7]^T$ to $\overline{\dot{\mathbf{c}}\dot{\mathbf{a}}}$: $7x - y - 19 \Rightarrow 7 \times 9 - 7 - 19 \Rightarrow +$.
   b. Check if the point $[5, 8]^T$ falls inside this triangle:
      Apply $[5, 8]^T$ to $\overline{\dot{\mathbf{a}}\dot{\mathbf{b}}}$: $6y - 5x + 3 \Rightarrow 6 \times 8 - 5 \times 5 + 3 \Rightarrow +$.
      Apply $[5, 8]^T$ to $\overline{\dot{\mathbf{b}}\dot{\mathbf{c}}}$: $2x + 5y - 53 \Rightarrow 2 \times 5 + 5 \times 8 - 53 \Rightarrow -$.
      Apply $[5, 8]^T$ to $\overline{\dot{\mathbf{c}}\dot{\mathbf{a}}}$: $7x - y - 19 \Rightarrow 7 \times 5 - 8 - 19 \Rightarrow +$.

As long as the same signs are obtained, the point $[5, 8]^T$ falls inside this triangle. □

#### 10.6.2.3 Ray-Sphere Intersection

The problem of finding the intersection between a ray and a sphere may be solved either algebraically or geometrically.

**Algebraic method**: As depicted in Fig. 10.21, a ray emitting from point $\dot{\mathbf{P}}_0$ through direction $\mathbf{v}$ is intersecting a sphere whose radius is $r$ and centered at $\dot{\mathbf{O}}$. It is required to find the point of intersection $\dot{\mathbf{P}}$.

The ray equation

$$\dot{\mathbf{P}} = \dot{\mathbf{P}}_0 + t\mathbf{v}$$

is applied to the sphere equation

$$\left\|\dot{\mathbf{P}} - \dot{\mathbf{O}}\right\|^2 = r^2$$

to get

$$\left\|\left[\dot{\mathbf{P}}_0 + t\mathbf{v}\right] - \dot{\mathbf{O}}\right\|^2 = r^2$$

or

$$\underbrace{\|\mathbf{v}\|^2}_{a} t^2 + \underbrace{\left(2\mathbf{v} \cdot \left[\dot{\mathbf{P}}_0 - \dot{\mathbf{O}}\right]\right)}_{b} t + \underbrace{\left\|\dot{\mathbf{P}}_0 - \dot{\mathbf{O}}\right\|^2 - r^2}_{c} = 0. \tag{10.25}$$

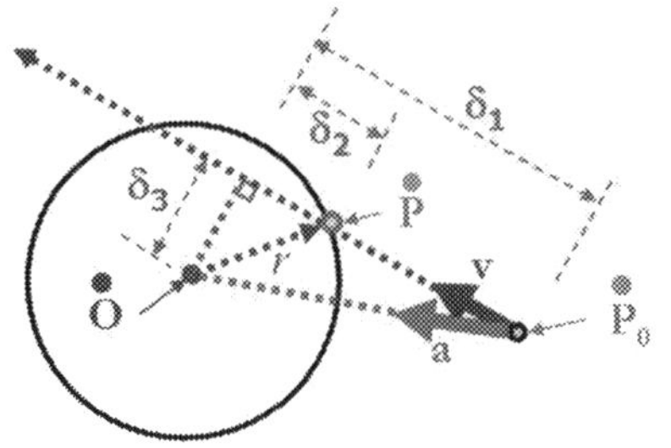


**Fig. 10.22** Solving ray-sphere intersection geometrically

Equation (10.25) is a quadratic equation $at^2 + bt + c = 0$ that may lead to zero to two possible solutions. These three possibilities are when there is no intersection, when ray is touching the sphere and when there are two intersections. The last possibility is shown in Fig. 10.21.

**Geometric method**: The same problem can be solved geometrically. As depicted in Fig. 10.22, the direction vector from $\dot{\mathbf{P}}_0$ to the center of the sphere $\dot{\mathbf{O}}$ is expressed as

$$\mathbf{a} = \dot{\mathbf{O}} - \dot{\mathbf{P}}_0.$$

When the vector $\mathbf{v}$ is normalized to a unit vector, the projection of $\mathbf{a}$ unto $\mathbf{v}$ can be expressed using the dot product (Sect. A.4.3.2) as

$$\delta_1 = \mathbf{a} \cdot \mathbf{v}.$$

Using the Pythagorean theorem, we can write

$$\delta_3 = \sqrt{\mathbf{a} \cdot \mathbf{a} - \delta_1^2}.$$

Using the same theorem, we write

$$\delta_2 = \sqrt{r^2 - \delta_3^2}.$$

Hence, the parameter $t$ along the vector $\mathbf{v}$, can be estimated as

$$t = \delta_1 - \delta_2$$

or

$$t = \mathbf{a} \cdot \mathbf{v} - \sqrt{r^2 - \left(\mathbf{a} \cdot \mathbf{a} - (\mathbf{a} \cdot \mathbf{v})^2\right)}. \tag{10.26}$$

In case $\mathbf{v}$ is not normalized, $t$ is expressed as

$$t = \frac{\mathbf{a} \cdot \mathbf{v}}{\|\mathbf{v}\|} - \sqrt{r^2 - \left(\mathbf{a} \cdot \mathbf{a} - \left(\frac{\mathbf{a} \cdot \mathbf{v}}{\|\mathbf{v}\|}\right)^2\right)}. \tag{10.27}$$

Consequently, in case $\mathbf{v}$ is normalized, the point of intersection

$$\dot{\mathbf{P}} = \dot{\mathbf{P}}_0 + t\mathbf{v}$$

can estimated as

$$\dot{\mathbf{P}} = \dot{\mathbf{P}}_0 + \left(\mathbf{a} \cdot \mathbf{v} - \sqrt{r^2 - \left(\mathbf{a} \cdot \mathbf{a} - (\mathbf{a} \cdot \mathbf{v})^2\right)}\right)\mathbf{v} \tag{10.28}$$

and in case $\mathbf{v}$ is not normalized, the point of intersection is calculated as

$$\dot{\mathbf{P}} = \dot{\mathbf{P}}_0 + \left(\frac{\mathbf{a} \cdot \mathbf{v}}{\|\mathbf{v}\|} - \sqrt{r^2 - \left(\mathbf{a} \cdot \mathbf{a} - \left(\frac{\mathbf{a} \cdot \mathbf{v}}{\|\mathbf{v}\|}\right)^2\right)}\right)\frac{\mathbf{v}}{\|\mathbf{v}\|}. \tag{10.29}$$

**Example 10.21:** [*Ray-sphere intersection—geometric method*]
Equations (10.28) and (10.29) detect the intersection point where the ray first hits the sphere. However, there is another intersection point where the ray leaves the sphere. Adjust these equations to detect this point.

**Solution 10.21:** Referring to Fig. 10.22, the new $t$ value is estimated as

$$t = \delta_1 + \delta_2.$$

Substituting the values of $\delta_1$ and $\delta_2$ obtained previously, $t$ is expressed as

$$t = \mathbf{a} \cdot \mathbf{v} + \sqrt{r^2 - \left(\mathbf{a} \cdot \mathbf{a} - (\mathbf{a} \cdot \mathbf{v})^2\right)}, \tag{10.30}$$

which estimates $t$ in case $\mathbf{v}$ is normalized. Otherwise, $t$ is expressed as

$$t = \frac{\mathbf{a} \cdot \mathbf{v}}{\|\mathbf{v}\|} + \sqrt{r^2 - \left(\mathbf{a} \cdot \mathbf{a} - \left(\frac{\mathbf{a} \cdot \mathbf{v}}{\|\mathbf{v}\|}\right)^2\right)}, \tag{10.31}$$

which estimates $t$ in case $\mathbf{v}$ is not normalized. Notice that Eqs. (10.30) and (10.31) are similar to Eqs. (10.26) and (10.27) respectively except for the sign preceding the square root. Consequently, in case $\mathbf{v}$ is normalized, the other point of intersection can estimated as

$$\dot{\mathbf{P}} = \dot{\mathbf{P}}_0 + \left(\mathbf{a} \cdot \mathbf{v} + \sqrt{r^2 - \left(\mathbf{a} \cdot \mathbf{a} - (\mathbf{a} \cdot \mathbf{v})^2\right)}\right)\mathbf{v} \tag{10.32}$$

and in case $\mathbf{v}$ is not normalized, this point is calculated as

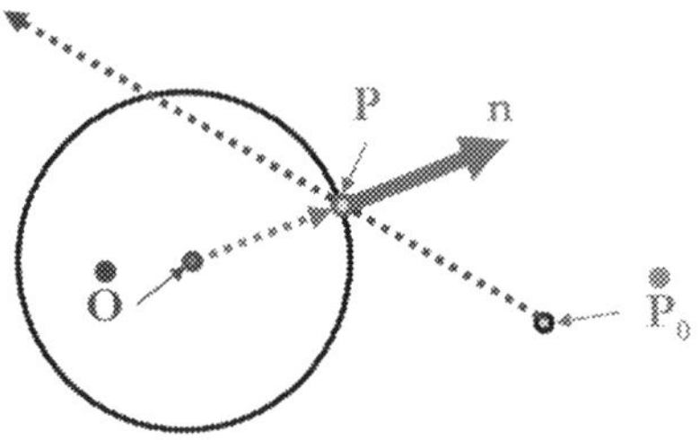


**Fig. 10.23** Normal to the sphere at the point of intersection between the ray and the sphere

$$\dot{\mathbf{P}} = \dot{\mathbf{P}}_0 + \left( \frac{\mathbf{a} \cdot \mathbf{v}}{\|\mathbf{v}\|} + \sqrt{r^2 - \left( \mathbf{a} \cdot \mathbf{a} - \left( \frac{\mathbf{a} \cdot \mathbf{v}}{\|\mathbf{v}\|} \right)^2 \right)} \right) \frac{\mathbf{v}}{\|\mathbf{v}\|}. \tag{10.33}$$

□

The normal vector at the point of intersection between a ray and a sphere (Fig. 10.23) can be calculated as

$$\mathbf{n} = \dot{\mathbf{P}} - \dot{\mathbf{O}}. \tag{10.34}$$

Using Eq. (A.15), the normalized vector is expressed as

$$\hat{\mathbf{n}} = \frac{\dot{\mathbf{P}} - \dot{\mathbf{O}}}{\|\dot{\mathbf{P}} - \dot{\mathbf{O}}\|}. \tag{10.35}$$

**Example 10.22:** [*Ray-sphere intersection—point of intersection given a ray as two points and a sphere as a center point and a radius*]

Determine where the ray starting at $[2, 0, -3]^T$ and passing through $[2, 0, 7]^T$ intersects a sphere centered at $[-1, 0, 0]^T$ and having a radius of 3.

**Solution 10.22:** Calculate the direction vector:

$$\mathbf{v} = \begin{bmatrix} 2 \\ 0 \\ 7 \end{bmatrix} - \begin{bmatrix} 2 \\ 0 \\ -3 \end{bmatrix} = \begin{bmatrix} 0 \\ 0 \\ 10 \end{bmatrix}.$$

The vector normalized is expressed as

$$\hat{\mathbf{v}} = \frac{\mathbf{v}}{\|\mathbf{v}\|} = \begin{bmatrix} 0 \\ 0 \\ 1 \end{bmatrix}.$$

**Algebraic Method**: Note that we can work with the original vector $\mathbf{v}$ or the normalized $\hat{\mathbf{v}}$. The value of the parameter $t$ will be different in both cases but the value $t\mathbf{v}$ and $t\hat{\mathbf{v}}$ must be the same. Hence, we should end up getting the same intersection point.

1. Algebraic method using $\mathbf{v} = [0, 0, 10]^T$:

$$\begin{aligned}
a &= \|\mathbf{v}\|^2 \\
&= 0^2 + 0^2 + 10^2 = 100, \\
b &= 2\mathbf{v} \cdot \left[\dot{\mathbf{P}}_0 - \dot{\mathbf{O}}\right] \\
&= 2 \begin{bmatrix} 0 \\ 0 \\ 10 \end{bmatrix} \cdot \begin{bmatrix} 2+1 \\ 0-0 \\ -3-0 \end{bmatrix} = -60, \\
c &= \left\|\dot{\mathbf{P}}_0 - \dot{\mathbf{O}}\right\|^2 - r^2 \\
&= 3^2 + 0^2 + (-3)^2 - 3^2 = 9.
\end{aligned}$$

Then, the parameter $t$ can be calculated as

$$\begin{aligned}
t &= \frac{-b \pm \sqrt{b^2 - 4ac}}{2a} \\
&= \frac{60 \pm \sqrt{(-60)^2 - 4 \times 100 \times 9}}{2 \times 100} = 0.3.
\end{aligned}$$

(Notice that there is only one value for $t$ as $b^2 = 4ac$; i.e., $\sqrt{b^2 - 4ac} = 0$. This means that the ray is touching the sphere.) Consequently, the point of intersection is calculated as

$$\begin{aligned}
\dot{\mathbf{P}} &= \dot{\mathbf{P}}_0 + t\mathbf{v} \\
&= \begin{bmatrix} 2 \\ 0 \\ -3 \end{bmatrix} + 0.3 \begin{bmatrix} 0 \\ 0 \\ 10 \end{bmatrix} = \begin{bmatrix} 2 \\ 0 \\ 0 \end{bmatrix}.
\end{aligned}$$

Note that $t\mathbf{v} = 0.3[0, 0, 10]^T = [0, 0, 3]^T$.

2. Algebraic method using $\hat{\mathbf{v}} = [0, 0, 1]^T$:

$$\begin{aligned}
a &= \|\hat{\mathbf{v}}\|^2 \\
&= 0^2 + 0^2 + 1^2 = 1, \\
b &= 2\hat{\mathbf{v}} \cdot \left[\dot{\mathbf{P}}_0 - \dot{\mathbf{O}}\right] \\
&= 2 \begin{bmatrix} 0 \\ 0 \\ 1 \end{bmatrix} \cdot \begin{bmatrix} 2+1 \\ 0-0 \\ -3-0 \end{bmatrix} = -6, \\
c &= \left\|\dot{\mathbf{P}}_0 - \dot{\mathbf{O}}\right\|^2 - r^2 \\
&= 3^2 + 0^2 + (-3)^2 - 3^2 = 9.
\end{aligned}$$

Then, the parameter $t$ can be calculated as

$$\begin{aligned} t &= \frac{-b \pm \sqrt{b^2 - 4ac}}{2a} \\ &= \frac{6 \pm \sqrt{(-6)^2 - 4 \times 1 \times 9}}{2 \times 1} = 3. \end{aligned}$$

(Again, notice that there is only one value for $t$. This means that the ray is touching the sphere.) Consequently, the point of intersection is calculated as

$$\begin{aligned} \dot{\mathbf{P}} &= \dot{\mathbf{P}}_0 + t\hat{\mathbf{v}} \\ &= \begin{bmatrix} 2 \\ 0 \\ -3 \end{bmatrix} + 3 \begin{bmatrix} 0 \\ 0 \\ 1 \end{bmatrix} = \begin{bmatrix} 2 \\ 0 \\ 0 \end{bmatrix}. \end{aligned}$$

Note that $t\mathbf{v} = 3[0, 0, 1]^T = [0, 0, 3]^T$, which is the same vector obtained before.

**Geometric Method**: Note that the same value for the parameter $t$ can be obtained using the original vector $\mathbf{v}$ with Eq. (10.29) or the normalized vector $\hat{\mathbf{v}}$ with Eq. (10.28).

1. Geometric method using $\mathbf{v} = [0, 0, 10]^T$ and Eq. (10.29):

$$\begin{aligned} \mathbf{a} &= \dot{\mathbf{O}} - \dot{\mathbf{P}}_0 \\ &= \begin{bmatrix} -1 \\ 0 \\ 0 \end{bmatrix} - \begin{bmatrix} 2 \\ 0 \\ -3 \end{bmatrix} = \begin{bmatrix} -3 \\ 0 \\ 3 \end{bmatrix}, \\ \dot{\mathbf{P}} &= \dot{\mathbf{P}}_0 + \left( \frac{\mathbf{a} \cdot \mathbf{v}}{\|\mathbf{v}\|} - \sqrt{r^2 - \left( \mathbf{a} \cdot \mathbf{a} - \left( \frac{\mathbf{a} \cdot \mathbf{v}}{\|\mathbf{v}\|} \right)^2 \right)} \right) \frac{\mathbf{v}}{\|\mathbf{v}\|} \\ &= \begin{bmatrix} 2 \\ 0 \\ -3 \end{bmatrix} + \left( \frac{30}{10} - \sqrt{3^2 - \left( 18 - \left( \frac{30}{10} \right)^2 \right)} \right) \frac{1}{10} \begin{bmatrix} 0 \\ 0 \\ 10 \end{bmatrix} = \begin{bmatrix} 2 \\ 0 \\ 0 \end{bmatrix}. \end{aligned}$$

Notice that the square root results in a zero; an indication that the ray is touching the sphere.

2. Geometric method using $\hat{\mathbf{v}} = [0, 0, 1]^T$ and Eq. (10.28):

$$\begin{aligned} \mathbf{a} &= \dot{\mathbf{O}} - \dot{\mathbf{P}}_0 \\ &= \begin{bmatrix} -1 \\ 0 \\ 0 \end{bmatrix} - \begin{bmatrix} 2 \\ 0 \\ -3 \end{bmatrix} = \begin{bmatrix} -3 \\ 0 \\ 3 \end{bmatrix}, \\ \dot{\mathbf{P}} &= \dot{\mathbf{P}}_0 + \left( \mathbf{a} \cdot \hat{\mathbf{v}} - \sqrt{r^2 - \left( \mathbf{a} \cdot \mathbf{a} - (\mathbf{a} \cdot \hat{\mathbf{v}})^2 \right)} \right) \hat{\mathbf{v}} \\ &= \begin{bmatrix} 2 \\ 0 \\ -3 \end{bmatrix} + \left( 3 - \sqrt{3^2 - (18 - 3^2)} \right) \begin{bmatrix} 0 \\ 0 \\ 1 \end{bmatrix} = \begin{bmatrix} 2 \\ 0 \\ 0 \end{bmatrix}. \end{aligned}$$

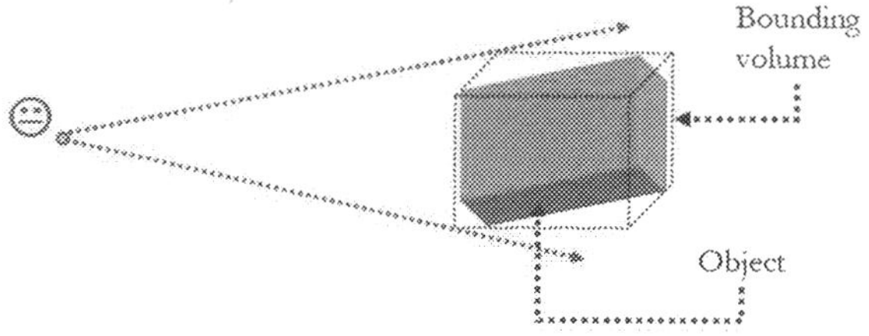


**Fig. 10.24** An object is bounded by a bounding volume

Thus, all the methods result in the same intersection point $\dot{\mathbf{P}} = [2, 0, 0]^T$. □

**Example 10.23:** [*Ray-sphere intersection—point of intersection given a ray as two points and a sphere as a center point and a radius*]

Determine where the ray starting at $[2, 0, -3]^T$ and passing through $[0, 0, 0]^T$ intersects a sphere centered at $[-1, 0, 0]^T$ and having a radius of 3.

**Solution 10.23:** In this case, there are two intersections. These are $[-1.9065, 0, 2.8598]^T$ and $[1.2911, 0, -1.9367]^T$. The details are left as an exercise. □

## *10.6.3 Accelerating the Process*

All intersection situations that were discussed in the previous sections should not be performed for all objects in a 3D scene. Many objects may not exist in the path of a ray and should not be tested for intersections. Such trivial rejections make the process faster. Many techniques may be used in this regard. Among them, bounding volume technique and spatial partitioning techniques including binary space partitioning (BSP) trees, quadtrees and octrees. Other techniques include tracing with cones, beam tracing, pencil tracing (Amanatides 1984; Heckbert and Hanrahan 1984; Shinya and Takahashi 1987), etc.

### 10.6.3.1 Bounding Volume

In this technique, the ray is tested for intersections with the bounding volumes of objects (Fig. 10.24). If the ray does not hit the bounding volume, the contained object should be excluded from further processing (as the ray will not hit its contents). On the other hand, if the ray hits the bounding volume, further testing for the contents must be performed.

In many cases, bounding volumes may overlap. A set of overlapping bounding volumes may be grouped into a larger bounding volume. Thus, a hierarchy can be established where a larger bounding volume acts as a parent and the contained smaller bounding volumes along with their objects become its children. This hierarchy can effectively speed up the process because if the ray does not hit the parent, all the

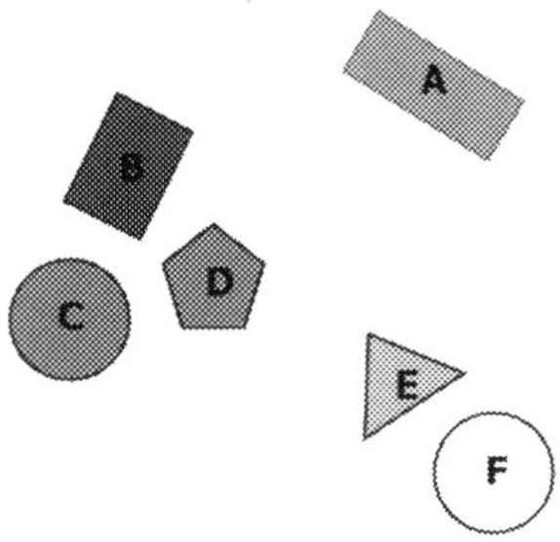


**Fig. 10.25** A 2D scene

children will be excluded from further processing (Rubin and Whitted 1980a, b; Weghorst et al. 1984). An algorithm to traverse such a hierarchy is listed in Algorithm 10.4 (Foley et al. 1995).

**Algorithm 10.4** *traverse_hierarchy*(*ray*, *node*)

**Input:** *ray*, *node*
**if** (*ray* intersects *node*'s bounding volume) **then**
  **if** (*node* is a leaf) **then**
    Calculate intersection between *ray* and *node*'s object
  **else**
    **for** (each *child* of *node*) **do**
      *traverse_hierarchy*(*ray*, *child*)
    **end for**
  **end if**
**end if**

**end**

**Example 10.24:** [*Bounding volume—establishing hierarchy*]
Consider the 2D scene shown in Fig. 10.25. Determine the bounding volumes and establish the bounding volume hierarchy.

**Solution 10.24:** Figure 10.26a shows the bounding volumes of the objects where overlapping occurs. Overlapping volumes are grouped into larger volumes. The hierarchy is shown in Fig. 10.26b. □

**Example 10.25:** [*Bounding volume—intersections given hierarchy*]
Figure 10.27 shows the same previous 2D scene where a ray is shot through the space to intersect an object; i.e., "C." Using the hierarchy constructed previously, show the intersections found (if any) through the space until the ray hits its final destination.

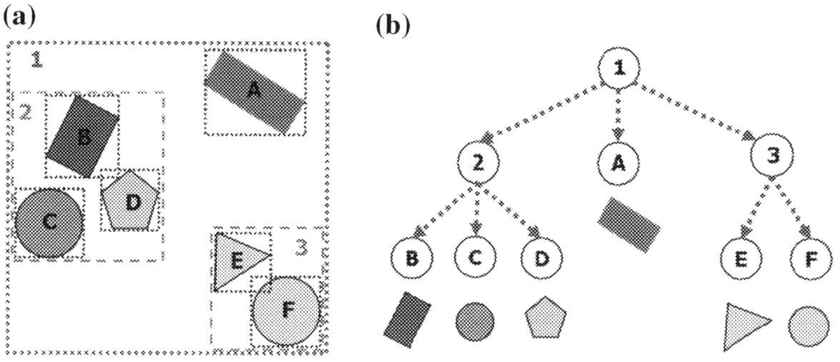


**Fig. 10.26** **a** Bounding volumes surround the objects. **b** Bounding volume hierarchy

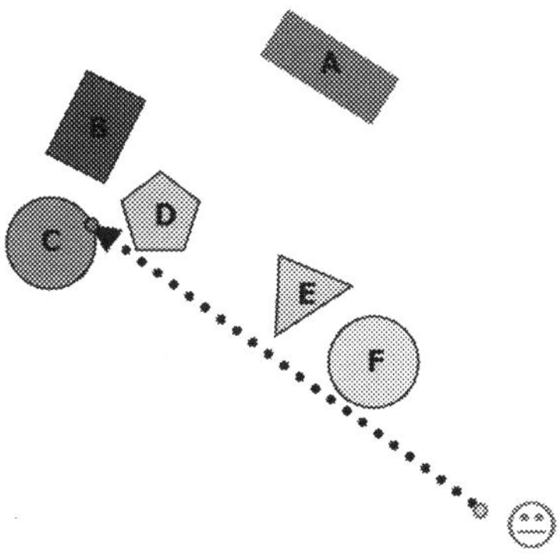


**Fig. 10.27** A 2D scene where a ray is shot towards one of the objects

**Solution 10.25:** Figure 10.28a, which depicts the bounding volumes of the objects, shows that the ray intersects many of the bounding volumes before it hits object "C." The sequence of the steps will be as follows:

1. The ray starts at the camera location.
2. The ray intersects bounding volume "1."
3. The ray intersects bounding volume "3."
4. The ray intersects bounding volume "F."
5. The intersection between the ray and object "F" is tested where no intersection point is found.
6. The ray leaves bounding volume "F."
7. The ray leaves bounding volume "3."
8. The ray walks through bounding volume "1."
9. The ray intersects bounding volume "2."
10. The ray intersects bounding volume "D."
11. The intersection between the ray and object "D" is tested where no intersection point is found.
12. The ray leaves bounding volume "D."

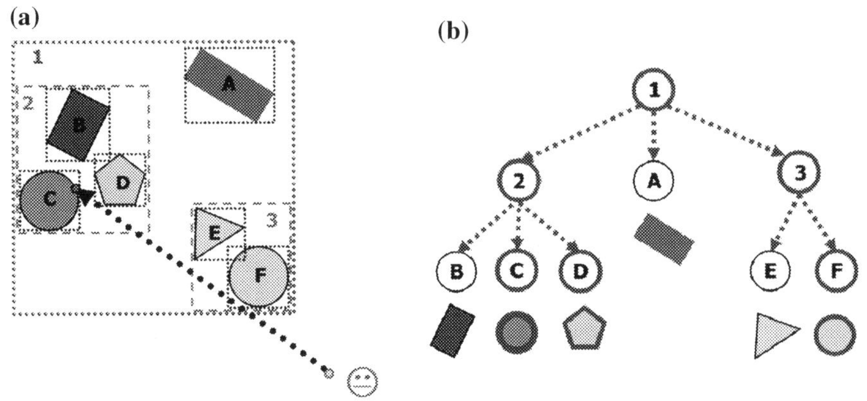


**Fig. 10.28** **a** Bounding volumes surround the objects. **b** Bounding volume hierarchy where the nodes visited are highlighted

13. The ray walks through bounding volume "2."
14. The ray intersects bounding volume "C."
15. The intersection between the ray and object "C" is tested where an intersection point is found.

The visited nodes of the hierarchy are highlighted in Fig. 10.28b.

**Example 10.26:** [*Bounding volume—bounding planes*]
Consider a triangle $\triangle\dot{\mathbf{P}}_1\dot{\mathbf{P}}_2\dot{\mathbf{P}}_3$ where $\dot{\mathbf{P}}_1 = [3, 0, 0]^T$, $\dot{\mathbf{P}}_2 = [0, 1, 2]^T$ and $\dot{\mathbf{P}}_3 = [1.5, 0, 1.5]^T$. Assuming that the planes of its bounding volume are parallel to the principal planes, determine these plane equations.

**Solution 10.26:** We need to determine the minimum and maximum values along the $x$-, $y$- and $z$-directions. Thus,

$$\begin{aligned}
x_{min} &= x_{\dot{\mathbf{P}}_2} = 0,\\
x_{max} &= x_{\dot{\mathbf{P}}_1} = 3,\\
y_{min} &= y_{\dot{\mathbf{P}}_1} = y_{\dot{\mathbf{P}}_3} = 0,\\
y_{max} &= y_{\dot{\mathbf{P}}_2} = 1,\\
z_{min} &= z_{\dot{\mathbf{P}}_1} = 0,\\
z_{max} &= z_{\dot{\mathbf{P}}_2} = 2.
\end{aligned}$$

Therefore, the plane equations are

$$\begin{aligned}
x &= 0,\\
x &= 3,\\
y &= 0,\\
y &= 1,\\
z &= 0,\\
z &= 2.
\end{aligned}$$

□

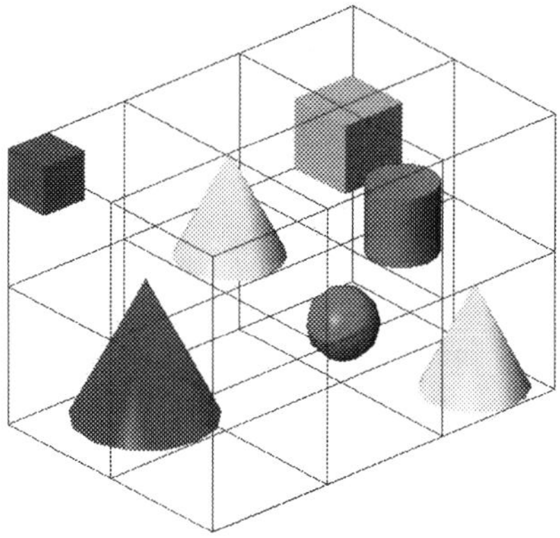

**Fig. 10.29** Partitioning the bounding volume of the whole space using a regular grid of equal-sized units

#### 10.6.3.2 Space Partitioning

In Sect. 10.5, we talked about space partitioning by hyperplanes and arranging subspaces into hierarchies or trees (e.g., BSP trees). The type of hierarchy depends on the number of hyperplanes used for partitioning. In that section, we aimed to prioritize surfaces in order to solve the visibility problem. (Check also Sect. 4.4 where similar hierarchies were used to represent 3D models.)

In this section, we talk about space partitioning from a different point of view. Our aim here is to accelerate the ray casting process where a ray needs to be tested for intersections with objects along its path only. Avoiding intersection testing with other objects saves time.

The idea is to partition the bounding volume of the whole space using a regular grid of equal-sized units in a top-down process. An example is shown in Fig. 10.29. (Notice that in Sect. 10.6.3.1, we start by grouping smaller bounding volumes to form the overall bounding volume for the whole space; a bottom-up process.) A list of objects is then prepared for each partition. A partition list may contain zero, one or more objects while an object may be extended along one or more partitions.

When a ray is shot through the space, it needs to be tested for intersections with objects residing in the partitions it passes through. Examining partitions should be done in the order in which the ray travels. Once an intersection is found, no more partitions along the ray are tested. Notice, however, that in some situations, a partition may contain more than one object and more than one intersection may be found. Hence, all intersections must be detected while the closest one is selected.

**Example 10.27:** [*Regular grid partitioning—testing partitions for intersections*]

Figure 10.30 shows a static 2D space containing some 2D shapes. The space is partitioned using a regular grid. If a ray is shot as indicated, determine the sequence of partitions tested for intersections.

**Solution 10.27:** Assuming that the origin of the regular grid is at the upper left corner, the objects and associated partitions will be as follows:

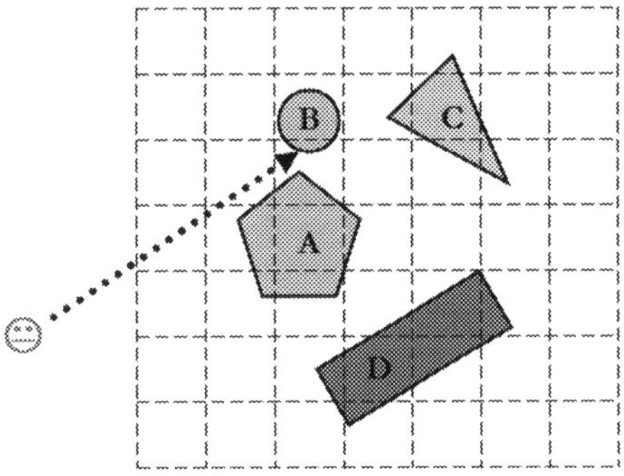


**Fig. 10.30** A 2D space partitioned using a regular grid

1. Object “A” is associated with partitions [1,2], [1,3], [1,4], [2,2], [2,3], [2,4] and [3,3].
2. Object “B” is associated with partitions [2,1] and [2,2].
3. Object “C” is associated with partitions [3,1], [4,0], [4,1], [4,2], [5,1] and [5,2].
4. Object “D” is associated with partitions [2,5], [2,6], [3,4], [3,5], [3,6], [4,4], [4,5], [5,4] and [5,5].
5. All other partitions are empty.

Notice that association of partitions with objects is done only once for the whole static scene and used for all rays afterwards.

When the ray is shot, it passes through the partitions [0,3], [1,3], [1,2] and then [2,2]. The first partition's list is empty; thus, no intersection is tested. The lists associated with partitions [1,3], [1,2] contain object “A” however, no intersections are detected in these partitions. When passing through partition [2,2], we find two objects; “A” and “B.” Examining object “A” for intersections will result in nothing. The intersection is obtained with object “B.” Working with this ray stops at this point. (Practically, the ray is tested only once with an object to avoid recalculations.)

In this example, we worked with four partitions and two objects only. Also, notice that the ray encounters partitions associated with an object (i.e., object “A”) before ending with an intersection with another object (i.e., object “B”). □

#### 10.6.3.3 Quadtrees

Instead of using equal-sized regular grid to partition the space, other adaptive subdivision techniques can be utilized as quadtrees and octrees. As explained in Sect. 4.4.3, a quadtree is used to partition a 2D space into four quadrants, which represent four children for a root node that represents the whole space. If a child is not empty or full, it may be split again into four quadrants representing four children of that node. The splitting continues until we reach a stopping condition (e.g., the leaf node becomes either empty or full, a number of subdivisions is reached or a number

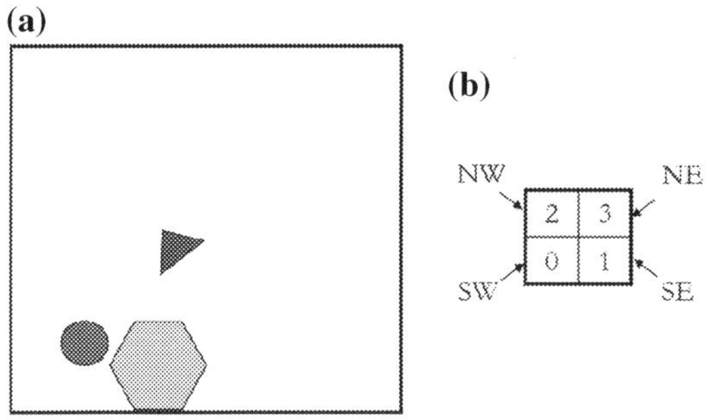


**Fig. 10.31** **a** An example of 2D space. **b** Order of quadrant subdivision

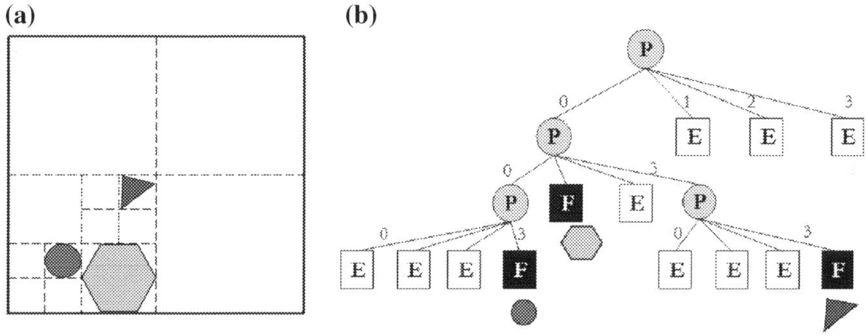


**Fig. 10.32** **a** The 2D space of Fig. 10.31a partitioned using a quadtree. **b** The quadtree used for partitioning

of objects in a node is obtained, etc.). Hence, the whole space is represented as a quadtree.

**Example 10.28:** [*Quadtree partitioning*]
Figure 10.31a shows a 2D space containing some 2D shapes. It is required to partition this space using a quadtree such that a shape cannot be split between partitions and a partition cannot contain more than one shape. The order of quadrants is as shown in Fig. 10.31b where the south west quadrant is followed by the south east, which is followed by the north west and finally followed by the north east.

**Solution 10.28:** The whole 2D space of Fig. 10.31a is represented as a partially full root node in Fig. 10.32b. The space is split into four quadrants corresponding to four children; one is partially full while the other three children are empty. The splitting continues to get the partitions shown in Fig. 10.32a. The partitions as well as the nodes of the quadtree are ordered according to Fig. 10.31b. The corresponding quadtree is shown in Fig. 10.32b. □

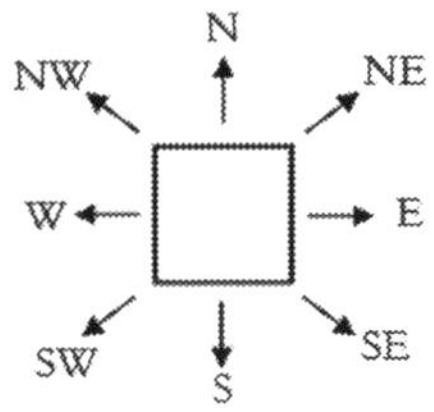


**Fig. 10.33** A ray may pass through one of eight directions

The question now is the following: Given a ray shot from a given center of projection through a direction into a space represented by a quadtree, how can we use such a tree structure to specify the partitions the ray passes through?

To answer this question, we have to know that there are only eight different directions a ray may follow from a certain partition. It may pass to partitions sharing the same edge to the north (N), south (S), east (E) or west (W) of the current partition. Also, it may pass to partitions sharing the same vertex to the north west (NW), north east (NE), south west (SW) or south east (SE) of the current partition as shown in Fig. 10.33.

Let us assume that the ray is going from a partition represented by node "A" through a direction; i.e., N, S, E, W, NW, NE, SW or SE, to another partition represented by node "B." It is a neighbor finding problem (Samet 1989b). The solution may proceed as follows:

1. Start at node "A" of the quadtree and go up until a common ancestor with node "B" is found. The common ancestor is the first node encountered that is not reached from a child on the given direction side of the node. For example, if the direction is N, then the common ancestor is the first node reached from either SW or SE.
2. From the common ancestor, go down the quadtree until the required partition (i.e., node "B") is found. This descending process follows a mirror path from node "A" to the ancestor that is reflected about the common border indicated by the given direction. For example, the common border is N–S for directions N and S and it is SW–NE for directions SW and NE.

**Example 10.29:** [*Quadtree partitioning—ray path on quadtree*]

A ray is shot through the quadtree-partitioned space of Example 10.28 as shown in Fig. 10.34. The figure shows that the ray passes from partition "A" to partition "B" through their shared vertex. Determine the path from partition "A" to partition "B" on the quadtree using the neighbor finding method discussed above.

**Solution 10.29:** The direction to go from partition "A" to partition "B" is SE. As shown in Fig. 10.35, partition "A" is represented as an NW child.

Using the quadtree, we go up from partition "A" to its parent; hence, we reach this ancestor from an NW child while the direction is SE, then we stop at this parent. We go down the quadtree by reflecting about the NW–SE border; thus, we get from NW to SE, which is a leaf node representing partition "B." □

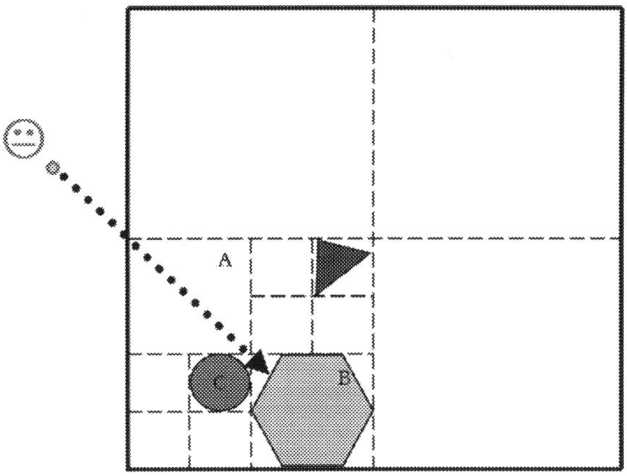


**Fig. 10.34** A ray is shot through the quadtree-partitioned space of Example 10.28

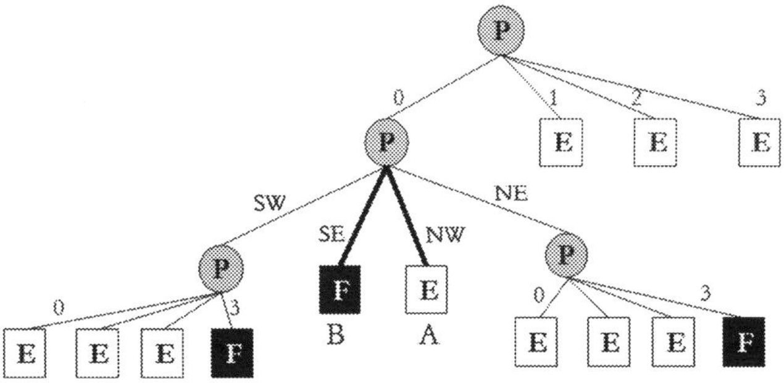


**Fig. 10.35** Quadtree path from partition "A" to partition "B"

**Example 10.30:** [*Quadtree partitioning—ray path on quadtree*]
Re-solve Problem 10.29 if the ray passes from partition "C" to partition "B" through their shared edge as shown in Fig. 10.36. Determine the path from partition "C" to partition "B" on the quadtree using the neighbor finding method discussed above.

**Solution 10.30:** The direction to go from partition "C" to partition "B" is E. As shown in Fig. 10.37, partition "C" is represented as an NE child.

Using the quadtree, we go up from partition "C" to its parent. Thus, we reach this ancestor from an NE child (i.e., an E node) while the direction is E. Hence, we go one step upwards to its grandparent. We reach this ancestor from an SW child (i.e., a W node) while the direction is E. Thus, we stop at this parent. We go down the quadtree by reflecting about the W-E border; thus, we reflect from SW to SE to reach a leaf node representing partition "B." □

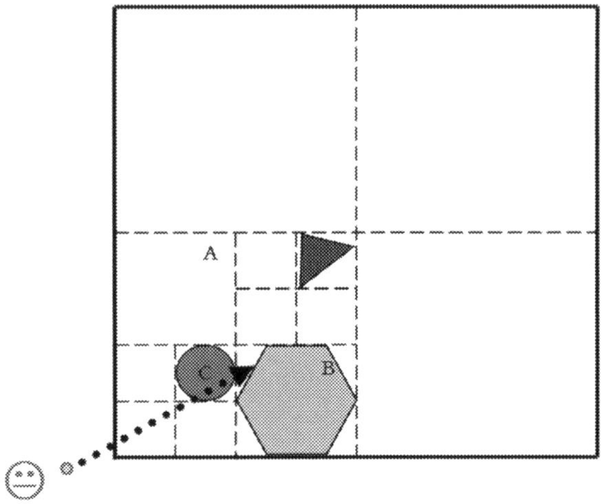


**Fig. 10.36** A ray is shot through the quadtree-partitioned space of Examples 10.28 and 10.29

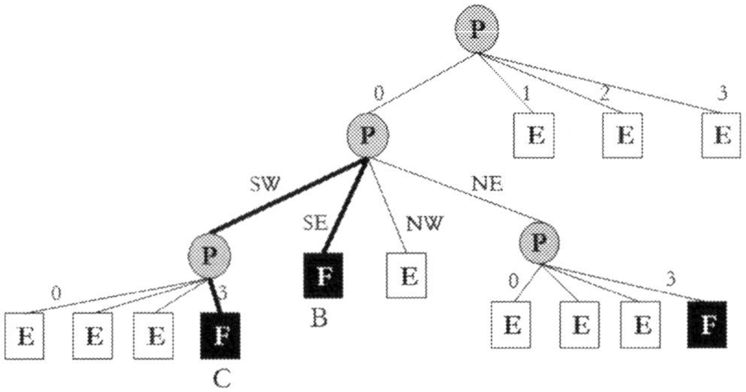


**Fig. 10.37** The quadtree path from partition "C" to partition "B"

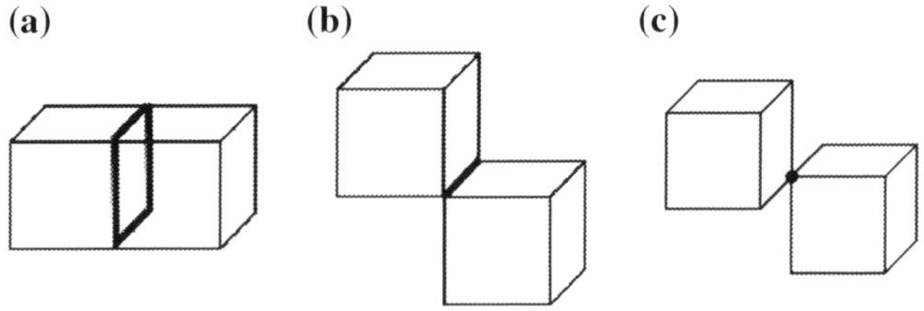


**Fig. 10.38** **a** Neighbors sharing a face. **b** Neighbors sharing an edge. **c** Neighbors sharing a vertex

#### 10.6.3.4 Octrees

An octree is a tree data structure where any node (except for the leaves) has eight children. The partially full 3D space is split into eight octants using three planes such that each of the eight octants is assigned to one of the children. The splitting

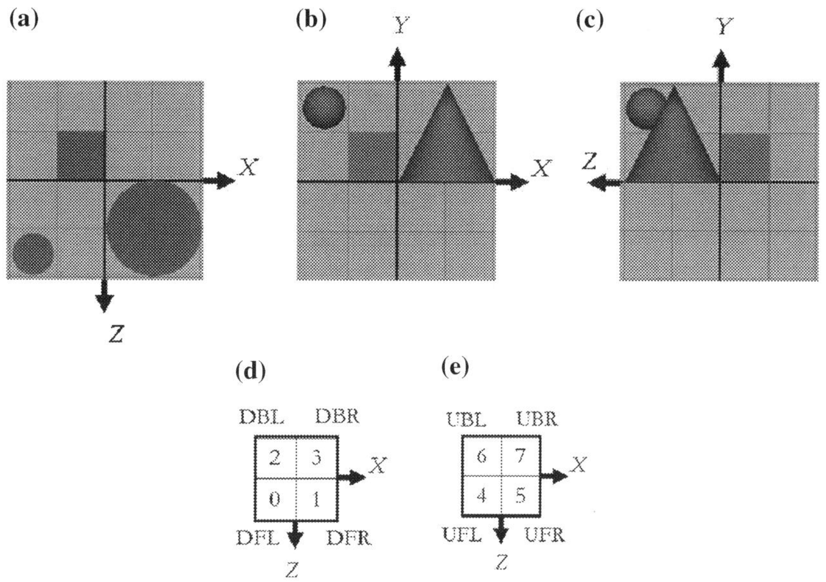


**Fig. 10.39** 3D objects shown as multi-view projections. **a** Top view. **b** Front view. **c** Side view. **d** Order for the $-y$ octants. **e** Order for the $+y$ octants. U, D, F, B, L and R refer to up, down, front, back, left and right respectively

continues recursively as long as a node is partially full. This recursive process halts when a stopping condition is met (e.g., all leaf nodes are either full or empty or the maximum number of levels has been reached, etc.). An adaptive subdivision algorithm is proposed using octrees in Glassner (1984).

As done with quadtrees, when a ray is shot from a given center of projection through a direction into a space represented by an octree, we can specify the partitions the ray passes through using such a tree (Samet 1989a). In contrary to eight possible directions in case of quadtrees, there are 26 possible directions a ray may follow from a certain partition in case of octrees. Out of those 26 possibilities, six neighbors share a face (Fig. 10.38a), 12 neighbors share an edge (Fig. 10.38b) and eight neighbors share a vertex (Fig. 10.38c). Finding an octree path from one partition to another is similar to the approach discussed previously.

**Example 10.31:** [*Octree partitioning*]

A 3D scene is shown as multi-view projections (refer to Chap. 8) in Fig. 10.39a, b and c. If this space is partitioned through three perpendicular planes using an octree such that each leaf node is a cube that is either empty or containing a whole object. The order of constructing nodes is as shown in Fig. 10.39d for the $-y$ octants and in Fig. 10.39e for the $+y$ octants. Construct the octree used for this partitioning.

**Solution 10.31:** For some readers, it may be easier to sketch the objects in 3D space as shown in Fig. 10.40a. Using the order of Fig. 10.39d and e, the octree of the scene is

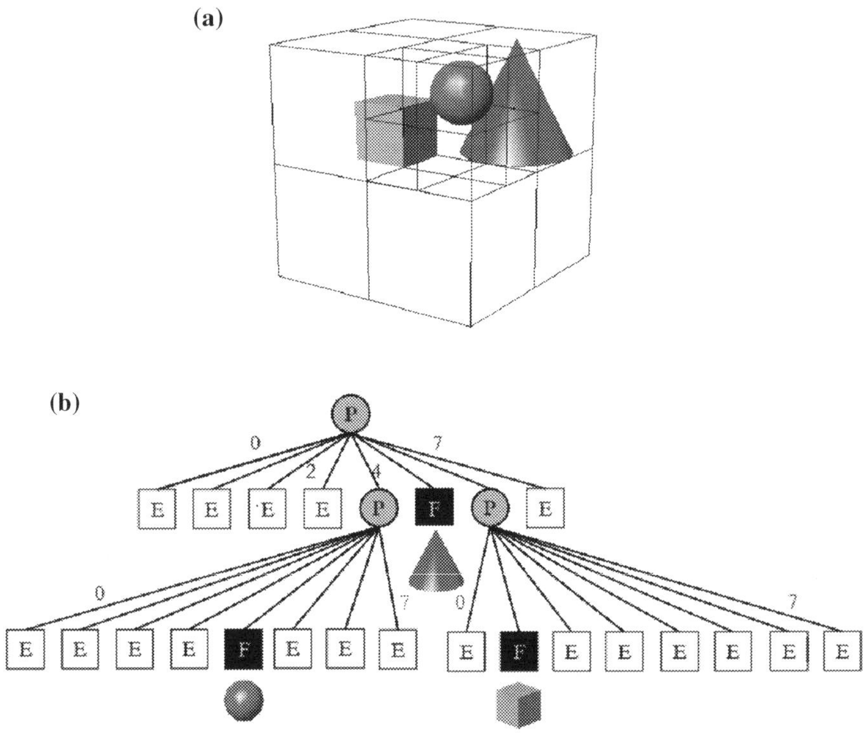


**Fig. 10.40** **a** 3D Objects of Fig. 10.39. **b** The octree used to partition the space shown in **a**

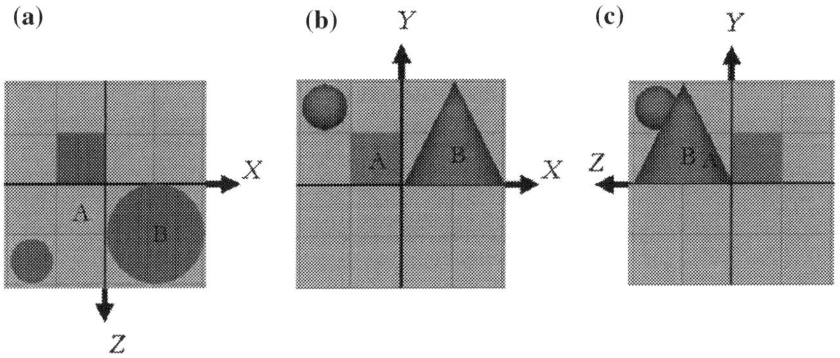


**Fig. 10.41** Partitions "A" and "B" identified

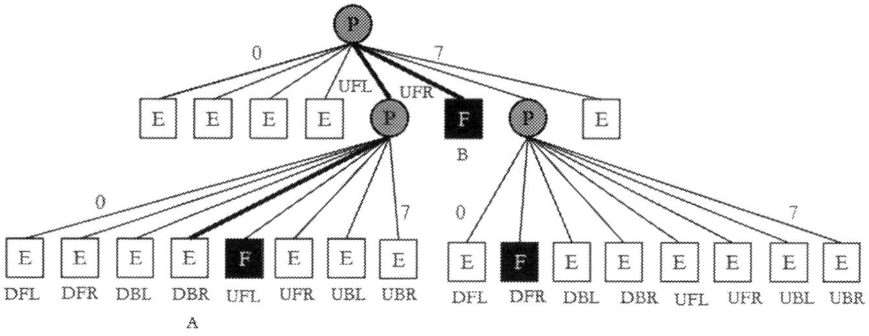


**Fig. 10.42** The path followed from partition "A" to partition "B"

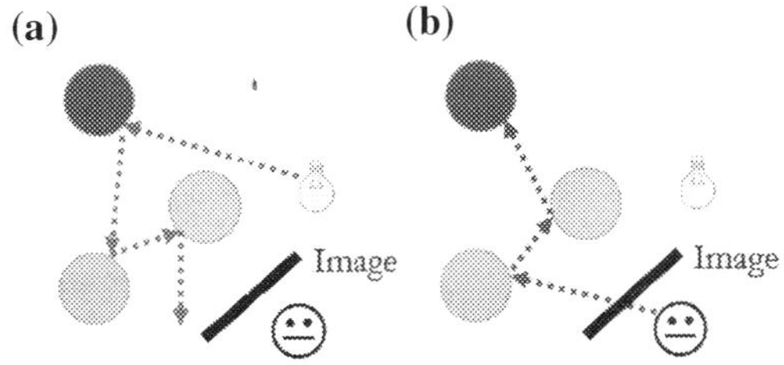


**Fig. 10.43** **a** Light ray tracing where a ray is generated from the light source to objects in 3D space. **b** Eye ray tracing where a ray is generated from the location of the eye to objects in 3D space

shown in Fig. 10.40b. In this example, full leaf nodes are the smallest cubic volumes containing whole objects. □

**Example 10.32:** [*Octree partitioning—ray path on octree*]

A ray is shot through the octree-partitioned space of Problem 10.31. The ray passes from partition "A" to partition "B" containing the cone (shown in Fig. 10.41). Determine the path from partition "A" to partition "B" on the octree using the neighbor finding method discussed above.

**Solution 10.32:** The direction to go from partition "A" to partition "B" is R. As shown in Fig. 10.42, partition "A" is represented as a DBR child.

Using the octree, we go up from partition "A" to its parent. Thus, we reach this parent from a DBR child (i.e., an R node) while the direction is R. Hence, we go one step upwards to the grandparent; the root. In this case, the root is reached from a UFL child; i.e., an L node, while the direction is R. We go down the octree by reflecting about the L-R border; thus, we reflect from UFL to UFR to reach a leaf node representing partition "B." The path is shown in Fig. 10.42. □

## 10.7 Ray Tracing

Light rays are stream of photons that travel through space in straight lines. If these rays intersect, they do not interfere. However, if a ray hits an object, it may get reflected or refracted where the laws of physics for reflection and refraction are obeyed. If this is the case, it continues to travel again. This process in known as *ray tracing* (Appel 1968).

### *10.7.1 Light Versus Eye*

In reality, a ray of light is generated from a light source in space to the object being lit; hence, the laws of physics can be applied. However, if the direction get reversed, the same laws still hold. This is valid for ray tracing too, which has two types.

1. **Light ray tracing**: This is also called *forward ray tracing* where a ray is shot from a light source to the objects in 3D space. This type is shown in Fig. 10.43a. We follow this type in Chap. 11.
2. **Eye ray tracing**: This is also called *backward ray tracing* where a ray is generated from a camera (or an eye) to penetrate pixels on the image plane and hit objects in 3D space. This is the type that was used in Sect. 10.6.1 and it is the type that we follow in this chapter. This is shown in Fig. 10.43b.

### *10.7.2 Tracing Rays*

The ray tracing process includes the ray casting process where a ray is emitted from the location of the eye through pixels and extended until hitting the first object in the scene. The ray tracing process continues by generating three types of rays as shown in Fig. 10.44. These rays are shadow rays, reflected rays and refracted (or transmitted) rays.

#### 10.7.2.1 Shadow Rays

Once a ray hits an object at a point, it should be specified whether the point of intersection lies in the shadow of another object in the scene. In order to determine this, a shadow ray is shot from the point of intersection to each light source in the scene. If such a ray hits another object before reaching the light source, then the point of intersection is in the shadow if that object.

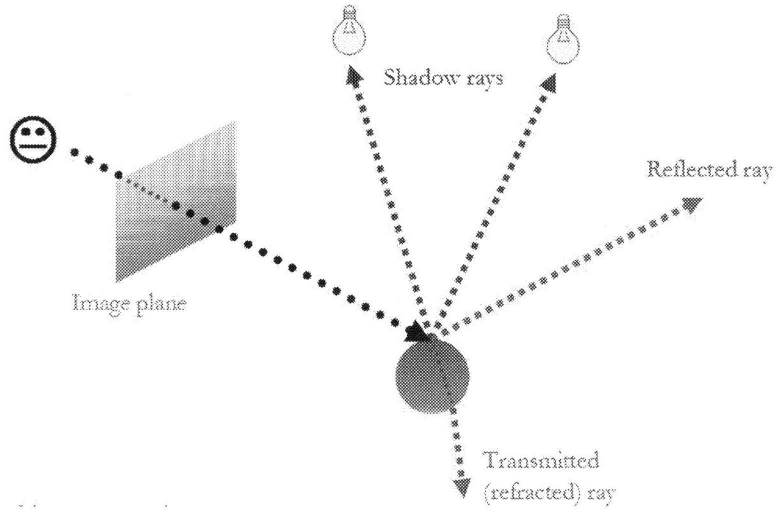


**Fig. 10.44** Shadow, reflection and refraction rays

**Fig. 10.45** When a ray hits an object, a reflection ray (presented by the vector **r**) may be generated at the point of intersection

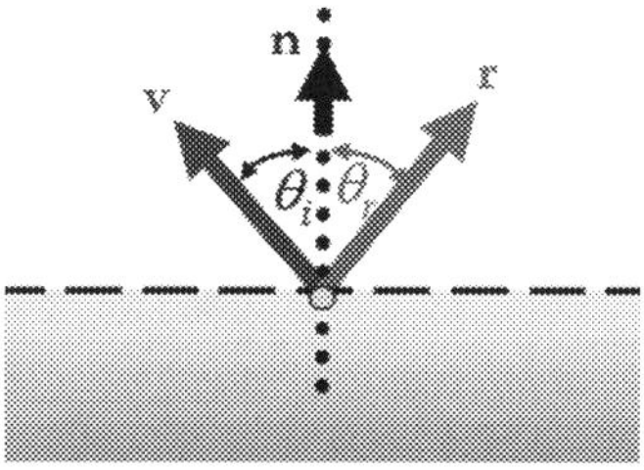


#### 10.7.2.2 Reflection Rays

At the point of intersection between a ray and an object and in addition to shadow rays, a reflection ray may be generated if the surface is reflective. Note that if the normal to the plane **n** and the ray vector **v** are known, the angle of incidence can be calculated using Eq. (A.22) as

$$\theta_i = \cos^{-1}\left(\frac{\mathbf{v} \cdot \mathbf{n}}{\|\mathbf{v}\| \|\mathbf{n}\|}\right). \tag{10.36}$$

Note that Eq. (10.36) assumes that both **v** and **n** are pointing out of the surface. In other words, the vector **v** goes from the intersection point to the camera (or the eye) location.

As shown in Fig. 10.45, the incidence angle $\theta_i$ and the reflection angle $\theta_r$ are related as

$$\theta_i = \theta_r, \tag{10.37}$$

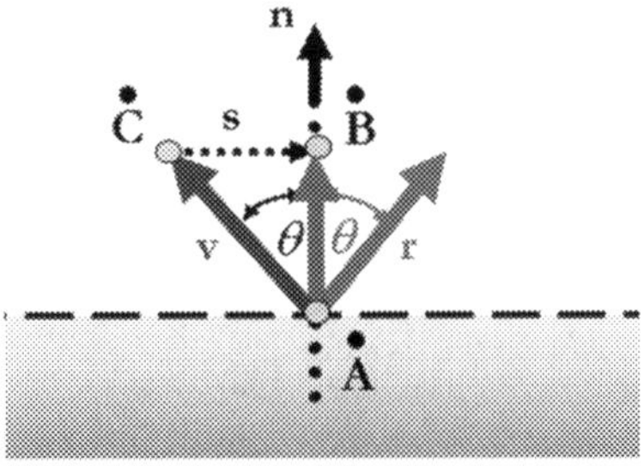


**Fig. 10.46** Reflection ray relationships

where the incidence angle $\theta_i$ is the angle enclosed between the eye ray and the normal to the surface at the point of intersection; and the reflection angle $\theta_r$ is the angle enclosed between the reflected ray and the normal to the surface at the point of intersection.

If $\mathbf{v}$ and $\mathbf{n}$ are normalized, consider the triangle $\triangle\dot{\mathbf{A}}\dot{\mathbf{B}}\dot{\mathbf{C}}$ in Fig. 10.46 where the length of $\overline{\dot{\mathbf{A}}\dot{\mathbf{C}}} = \|\mathbf{v}\| = 1$. In this case, the length of $\overline{\dot{\mathbf{A}}\dot{\mathbf{B}}}$ will be $\cos(\theta) = \cos(\theta_i) = \cos(\theta_r)$; hence, the vector $\dot{\mathbf{B}} - \dot{\mathbf{A}}$ is expressed as $\mathbf{n}\cos(\theta)$. It is obvious that the reflection vector $\mathbf{r}$ can be expressed as

$$\mathbf{r} = \mathbf{n}\cos(\theta) + \mathbf{s}, \tag{10.38}$$

where $\|\mathbf{s}\| = \sin(\theta)$. Note that $\mathbf{s}$ can be expressed as

$$\mathbf{s} = \mathbf{n}\cos(\theta) - \mathbf{v}. \tag{10.39}$$

Substitute the value of $\mathbf{s}$ from Eq. (10.39) in Eq. (10.38); thus, we get

$$\mathbf{r} = 2\mathbf{n}\cos(\theta) - \mathbf{v}. \tag{10.40}$$

Since $\|\mathbf{n}\| = \|\mathbf{v}\| = 1$ and from the definition of the dot product in Eq. (A.21), we can write

$$\mathbf{r} = 2\mathbf{n}\,(\mathbf{n}\cdot\mathbf{v}) - \mathbf{v}. \tag{10.41}$$

**Example 10.33:** [*Incidence and reflection angles*]

Assume that there is a ray emitted from $\dot{\mathbf{P}}_0 = [8, 8, 10]^T$ and pointed towards the origin. Also, assume that a sphere, having a radius of 2 units, is centered at $\dot{\mathbf{O}} = [2, 2, 4]^T$. Get the location where the ray hits the sphere. Also, calculate the incidence angle $\theta_i$ (or reflection angle $\theta_r$) at that point.

**Solution 10.33:** We will solve the ray-sphere intersection problem geometrically. Let $\mathbf{v}'$ be the direction vector from $\dot{\mathbf{P}}_0$ to the origin where

$$\mathbf{v}' = \begin{bmatrix} 0 \\ 0 \\ 0 \end{bmatrix} - \begin{bmatrix} 8 \\ 8 \\ 10 \end{bmatrix} = \begin{bmatrix} -8 \\ -8 \\ -10 \end{bmatrix}.$$

The direction from $\dot{\mathbf{P}}_0$ to the center of the sphere $\dot{\mathbf{O}}$ is given by

$$\begin{aligned} \mathbf{a} &= \dot{\mathbf{O}} - \dot{\mathbf{P}}_0 \\ &= \begin{bmatrix} 2 \\ 2 \\ 4 \end{bmatrix} - \begin{bmatrix} 8 \\ 8 \\ 10 \end{bmatrix} = \begin{bmatrix} -6 \\ -6 \\ -6 \end{bmatrix}. \end{aligned}$$

Then, the point of intersection is given by

$$\begin{aligned} \dot{\mathbf{P}} &= \dot{\mathbf{P}}_0 + \left( \frac{\mathbf{a} \cdot \mathbf{v}'}{\|\mathbf{v}'\|} - \sqrt{r^2 - \left( \mathbf{a} \cdot \mathbf{a} - \left( \frac{\mathbf{a} \cdot \mathbf{v}'}{\|\mathbf{v}'\|} \right)^2 \right)} \right) \frac{\mathbf{v}'}{\|\mathbf{v}'\|} \\ &= \begin{bmatrix} 8 \\ 8 \\ 10 \end{bmatrix} + \left( \frac{156}{2\sqrt{57}} - \sqrt{2^2 - \left( 108 - \left( \frac{156}{2\sqrt{57}} \right)^2 \right)} \right) \frac{1}{2\sqrt{57}} \begin{bmatrix} -8 \\ -8 \\ -10 \end{bmatrix} = \begin{bmatrix} 3.4028 \\ 3.4028 \\ 4.2535 \end{bmatrix}. \end{aligned}$$

(Equivalently, the ray-sphere intersection problem can be solved algebraically.) Now, the unit normal vector at the point of intersection is calculated as

$$\frac{\dot{\mathbf{P}} - \dot{\mathbf{O}}}{\|\dot{\mathbf{P}} - \dot{\mathbf{O}}\|} = \frac{1}{\sqrt{1.4028^2 + 1.4028^2 + 0.2535^2}} \left[ \begin{bmatrix} 3.4028 \\ 3.4028 \\ 4.2535 \end{bmatrix} - \begin{bmatrix} 2 \\ 2 \\ 4 \end{bmatrix} \right] = \begin{bmatrix} 0.7014 \\ 0.7014 \\ 0.1268 \end{bmatrix}.$$

The unit vector from the intersection point to the camera is $\mathbf{v} = -\frac{\mathbf{v}'}{\|\mathbf{v}'\|} = [0.5298, 0.5298, 0.6623]^T$. Thus, the incidence angle $\theta_i$ (or equivalently the reflection angle $\theta_r$) is calculated as

$$\theta_i = \theta_r = \cos^{-1}\left( \frac{\dot{\mathbf{P}} - \dot{\mathbf{O}}}{\|\dot{\mathbf{P}} - \dot{\mathbf{O}}\|} \cdot \mathbf{v} \right) = \cos^{-1}(0.8272) = 34.1909^\circ.\square$$

#### 10.7.2.3 Refraction Rays

In addition to shadow and reflection rays, a refraction ray may be generated at the point of intersection between an eye ray and a surface. This is shown in Fig. 10.47. The relationship between an incidence angle $\theta_i$ and a refraction angle $\theta_t$ is given by Snell's law, which states

$$\eta_i \sin \theta_i = \eta_t \sin \theta_t, \tag{10.42}$$

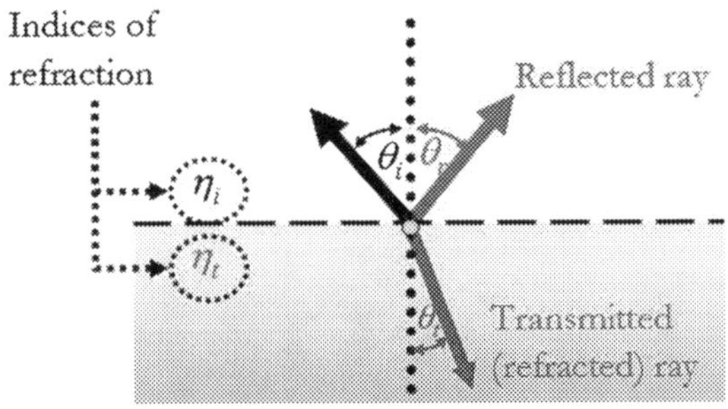


**Fig. 10.47** When a ray hits an object, reflection and refraction rays may be generated at the point of intersection

where $\eta_i$ and $\eta_t$ are the indices of refraction of the two media. From Snell's law, it can be written that

$$\theta_t = \sin^{-1}\left(\frac{\eta_i \sin\theta_i}{\eta_t}\right), \tag{10.43}$$

where $\theta_t$ is the refraction angle. If $\mathbf{v}$ is the direction vector from the point of intersection to the camera (or the eye) and $\mathbf{n}$ is the normal to the surface, the refraction vector $\mathbf{t}$ is given by

$$\mathbf{t} = \left(\frac{\eta_i}{\eta_t}\cos(\theta_i) - \cos(\theta_t)\right)\mathbf{n} - \frac{\eta_i}{\eta_t}\mathbf{v}, \tag{10.44}$$

where $\theta_i$ and $\theta_t$ are the incidence and refraction angles respectively; and $\eta_i$ and $\eta_t$ are the indices of refraction. The proof is left as an exercise.

**Example 10.34:** [*Reflection and refraction angles*]

Consider an eye ray that goes from $[10, 10, 10]^T$ to $[0, 0, 0]^T$. Assume that the medium under the plane $z = 1$ is glass (i.e., the glass occupies everything from $z = +1$ to $z = -\infty$). Get the location where the ray hits the glass. Also, calculate the reflection and refraction angles at that point. Assume that $\eta_{air} = 1.0003$ and $\eta_{glass} = 1.52$.

**Solution 10.34:** Let $\mathbf{v}'$ be the direction vector from $[10, 10, 10]^T$ to $[0, 0, 0]^T$ where

$$\mathbf{v}' = \begin{bmatrix} 0 \\ 0 \\ 0 \end{bmatrix} - \begin{bmatrix} 10 \\ 10 \\ 10 \end{bmatrix} = \begin{bmatrix} -10 \\ -10 \\ -10 \end{bmatrix}.$$

The normal vector $\mathbf{n}$ to the plane $z = 1$ is $[0, 0, 1]^T$ while $d = 1$. The parameter $t$ is obtained by substituting in Eq. (10.12) where

$$t = \frac{-\left(\dot{\mathbf{P}}_0 \cdot \mathbf{n}\right) + d}{\mathbf{v}' \cdot \mathbf{n}}$$

$$= \frac{-\left(\begin{bmatrix} 10 \\ 10 \\ 10 \end{bmatrix} \cdot \begin{bmatrix} 0 \\ 0 \\ 1 \end{bmatrix}\right) + 1}{\begin{bmatrix} -10 \\ -10 \\ -10 \end{bmatrix} \cdot \begin{bmatrix} 0 \\ 0 \\ 1 \end{bmatrix}} = 0.9.$$

Now, substitute the value of $t$ in Eq. (10.5) to get the location of the point of intersection $\dot{\mathbf{P}}$ as

$$\dot{\mathbf{P}} = \dot{\mathbf{P}}_0 + t\mathbf{v}'$$

$$= \begin{bmatrix} 10 \\ 10 \\ 10 \end{bmatrix} + 0.9 \begin{bmatrix} -10 \\ -10 \\ -10 \end{bmatrix} = \begin{bmatrix} 1 \\ 1 \\ 1 \end{bmatrix}.$$

Note that in order to get the incidence angle $\theta_i$, we use $\mathbf{v} = -\mathbf{v}'$ as pointing towards the camera at the intersection point. Hence, using Eq. (10.36), the incidence angle is given by

$$\theta_i = \theta_r = \cos^{-1}\left(\frac{\mathbf{v} \cdot \mathbf{n}}{\|\mathbf{v}\| \|\mathbf{n}\|}\right) 54.7356°.$$

Using Eq. (10.43), the refraction angle is calculated as

$$\theta_t = \sin^{-1}\left(\frac{\eta_{air} \sin\theta_i}{\eta_{glass}}\right) = \sin^{-1}\left(\frac{1.0003 \sin(54.7356)}{1.52}\right) = 32.5021°. \qquad \square$$

## 10.7.3 Recursive Ray Tracing

When a ray gets reflected off a surface, it may hit another object where another reflection ray may be generated. (Think about the case when two mirrors are adjacent to each other.) The same situation may happen with refraction rays. Thus, the whole ray tracing process should start each time a ray (either eye ray, reflection ray or refraction ray) hits an object. However, note that the contribution to a pixel color of an additional ray is attenuated each time the process starts over. This whole process is a recursive one, which should stop if

- the ray escapes the scene;
- no more reflection or refraction happens;
- the maximum recursion number is reached; or
- the contribution of the process gets too small to be considered.

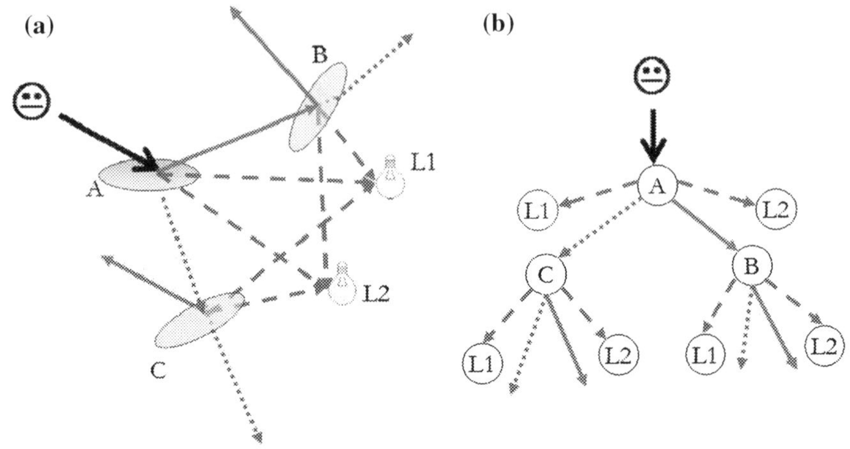


**Fig. 10.48** Recursive ray tracing: **a** An eye ray hits an object "A" where shadow, reflection and refraction rays are generated to hit light sources and other objects in the scene where the process starts over. The shadow rays are represented by the dashed arrows. The reflected rays are represented by the solid arrows. The refracted rays are represented by the dotted arrows. **b** The representation of **a** as a ray tree

Figure 10.48a depicts the recursive ray tracing process where an eye ray hits an object "A" where shadow, reflection and refraction rays are generated to hit the light sources "L1" and "L2" and other objects "B" and "C" in the scene where the process starts over.

The process of recursive ray tracing can be regarded as a tree that is called the *ray tree*. The depth of such a tree must be controlled. A too deep tree means long processing time while a too shallow tree could harm the realistic appearance of the generated image. The ray tree for the scene of Fig. 10.48a is shown in Fig. 10.48b.

## 10.8 Problems

**Problem 10.1:** [*Back-face culling*]

Assume that a virtual camera is located at $[2, 4, 6]^T$ and pointed towards the point $[7, 8, 9]^T$. Determine whether or not the planar surface with a surface normal $\mathbf{n} = [-2, 5, 5]^T$ is back-facing with respect to this virtual camera.

**Problem 10.2:** [*BSP tree partitioning*]

Figure 10.49 shows a top view of a 3D scene that contains five polygons/surfaces where the normal vectors to those surfaces are shown as arrows. It is required to partition this scene using a BSP tree. Use polygon "3" as a root for the tree.

**Problem 10.3:** [*BSP tree partitioning*]

Re-solve Problem 10.2 using polygon "4" as the root of the BSP tree.

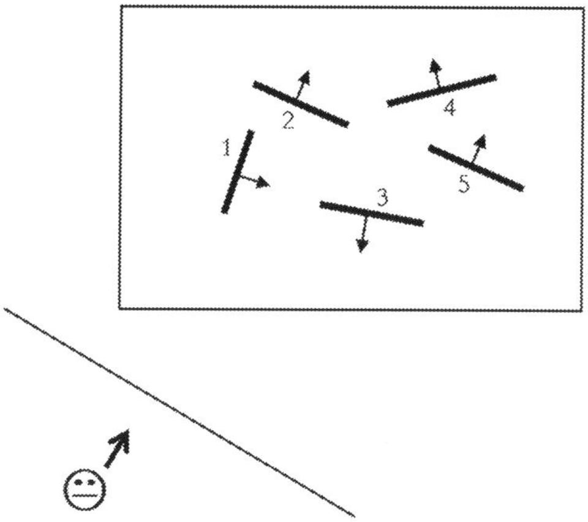


**Fig. 10.49** Top view of a 3D scene

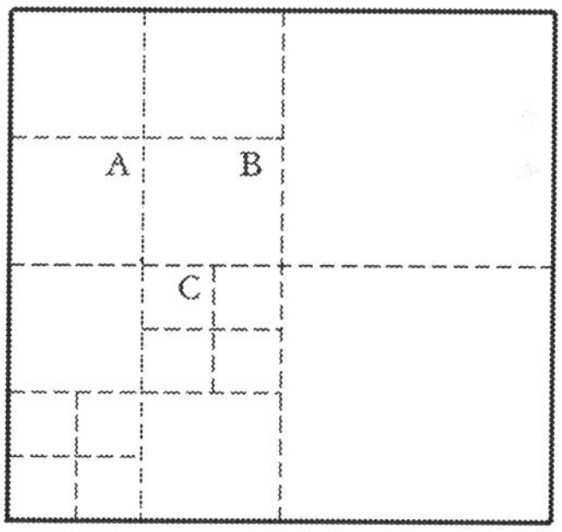


**Fig. 10.50** A 2D space partitioned

**Problem 10.4:** [*BSP trees—displaying polygons*]

Using the BSP trees generated in the above two problems, determine the order of displaying polygons if the image plane and the viewing direction are as shown in Fig. 10.49.

**Problem 10.5:** [*Quadtree partitioning*]

Figure 10.50 shows a 2D space after partitioning. Construct the corresponding quadtree.

**Problem 10.6:** [*Quadtree—neighbor finding*]

In Problem 10.5, determine the path from partition "A" to partition "B" on the quadtree constructed using the neighbor finding method discussed in this chapter. Repeat the solution for the path from partition "C" to partition "B" and from partition "B" to partition "C."

**Problem 10.7:** [*Octree partitioning*]

A 3D scene is shown as multi-view projections in Fig. 10.51a, b and c. If this space is partitioned through three perpendicular planes using an octree such that

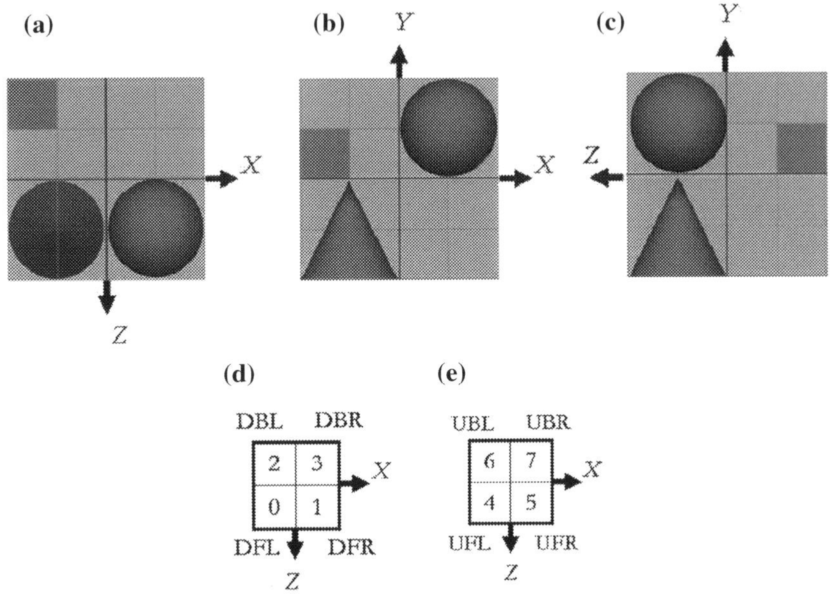


**Fig. 10.51** 3D objects shown as multi-view projections. **a** Top view. **b** Front view. **c** Side view. **d** Order for the $-y$ octants. **e** Order for the $+y$ octants

each leaf node is a cube that is either empty or containing a whole object. The order of constructing nodes is as shown in Fig. 10.51d for the $-y$ octants and in Fig. 10.51e for the $+y$ octants. Construct the octree used for this partitioning.

**Problem 10.8:** [*BSP tree partitioning*]
In Problem 10.7, if the partitioning is to be performed using a BSP tree, determine the maximum depth of that BSP tree. (The depth of a node is the length of the path from the root to the node.)

**Problem 10.9:** [*Octree partitioning*]
A 3D scene is shown as multi-view projections in Fig. 10.52a, b and c. If this space is partitioned through three perpendicular planes using an octree such that each leaf node is a cube that is either empty or containing a whole object. The order of constructing nodes is as shown in Fig. 10.51d for the $-y$ octants and in Fig. 10.51e for the $+y$ octants. Construct the octree used for this partitioning.

**Problem 10.10:** [*BSP tree partitioning*]
In Problem 10.7, if the partitioning is to be performed using a BSP tree, determine the maximum depth of that BSP tree. (The depth of a node is the length of the path from the root to the node.)

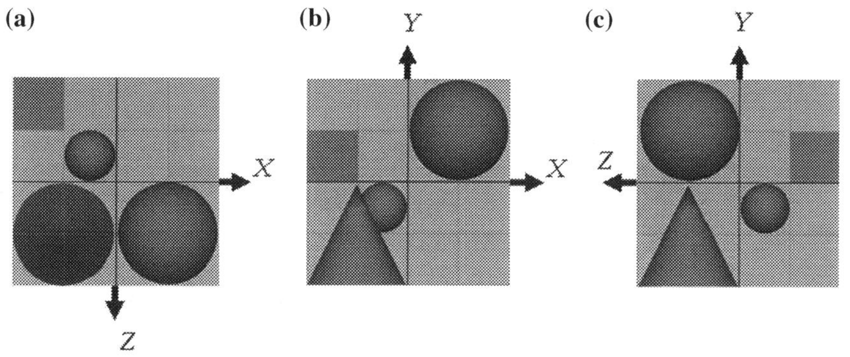


**Fig. 10.52** 3D objects shown as multi-view projections. **a** Top view. **b** Front view. **c** Side view

**Problem 10.11:** [*Checking if a point falls inside a triangle*]
Extend the idea of Example 10.17 to check whether or not a point $\dot{\mathbf{P}} = [5, 5]^T$ falls inside the triangle $\triangle\dot{\mathbf{p}}_1\dot{\mathbf{P}}_2\dot{\mathbf{p}}_3$ where $\dot{\mathbf{p}}_1 = [3, 2]^T$, $\dot{\mathbf{p}}_2 = [9, 7]^T$ and $\dot{\mathbf{p}}_3 = [4, 9]^T$.

**Problem 10.12:** [*Plane equation given a number of points*]
Consider a triangle $\triangle\dot{\mathbf{P}}_1\dot{\mathbf{P}}_2\dot{\mathbf{P}}_3$ where $\dot{\mathbf{P}}_1 = [3, 0, 0]^T$, $\dot{\mathbf{P}}_2 = [0, 1, 2]^T$ and $\dot{\mathbf{P}}_3 = [1.5, 0, 1.5]^T$. Estimate the plane equation of this triangle.

**Problem 10.13:** [*Ray-sphere intersection*]
Determine where the ray starting at $[2, 0, -3]^T$ and passing through $[0, 0, 0]^T$ intersects a sphere centered at $[-1, 0, 0]^T$ and having a radius of 3.

**Problem 10.14:** [*Ray-sphere intersection*]
Assume that there is a ray emitted from $[8, 8, 10]^T$ and pointed at the origin. Also, assume that a sphere, having a radius 2, is centered at $[2, 2, 4]^T$. Algebraically, get the location where the ray hits the sphere.

**Problem 10.15:** [*Normal vector at intersection*]
In Problem 10.14, determine the normal vector at the point where the ray hits the sphere.

**Problem 10.16:** [*Incidence and reflection angles*]
In Problem 10.14, calculate the incidence angle (or the reflection angle) at that point where the ray hits the sphere.

**Problem 10.17:** [*Ray-sphere intersection*]
Re-solve Problem 10.14 geometrically.

**Problem 10.18:** [*Incidence and reflection angles*]
Suppose that a ray starting at $[9, 9, 8]^T$ and passing through $[5, 5, 4]^T$ intersects a sphere centered at $[-1, 0, 0]^T$ and having a radius of 5. Calculate the reflection angle at the point of intersection.

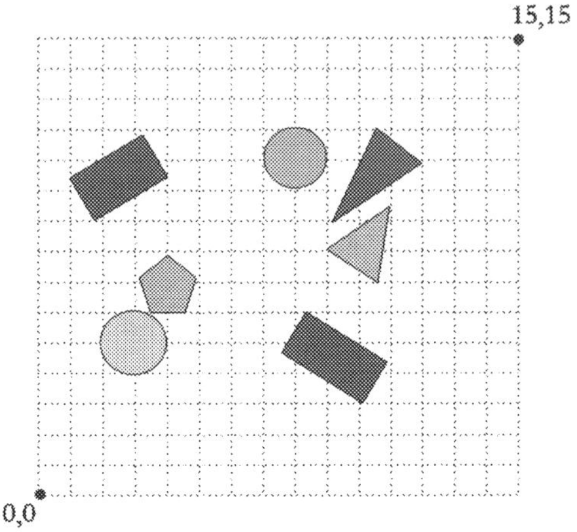


**Fig. 10.53** A 2D scene on a 2D grid

**Problem 10.19:** [*Incidence and reflection angles*]
Assume that there is a ray starting at $[10, 2, 0]^T$ and pointed towards $[0, 5, 5]^T$. If the medium at all negative $x$-coordinates is glass, what would be the reflection angle at the $yz$-plane?

**Problem 10.20:** [*Bounding volume hierarchy*]
Consider the 2D scene that is drawn on a 2D grid and shown in Fig. 10.53. Determine the bounding volumes and establish the bounding volume hierarchy.

**Problem 10.21:** [*Bounding volume hierarchy—intersections*]
In Problem 10.20, if a ray is shot from the point $[15, 1]^T$ to the point $[4, 5]^T$, use the hierarchy constructed to show the intersections found (if any) through the space until the ray hits its final destination.

**Problem 10.22:** [*Refraction vector*]
If $\mathbf{v}$ and $\mathbf{t}$ are the eye and refraction vectors respectively and $\mathbf{n}$ is the normal to the surface, show that

$$\mathbf{t} = \left(\frac{\eta_i}{\eta_t}\cos(\theta_i) - \cos(\theta_t)\right)\mathbf{n} - \frac{\eta_i}{\eta_t}\mathbf{v},$$

where $\theta_i$ and $\theta_t$ are the incidence and refraction angles respectively; and $\eta_i$ and $\eta_t$ are the indices of refraction.

## References

Amanatides, J. 1984. Ray tracing with cones. *Computer Graphics* 18(3): 129–135.
Appel, A. 1968. Some techniques for shading machine renderings of solids. In Proceedings of the spring joint computer conference, AFIPS '68 (Spring), 37–45, New York, USA: ACM.

Catmull, E.E. 1975. Computer display of curved surfaces. In Proceedings of the IEEE conference on computer graphics, pattern recognition, and data structure, 11–17.

Foley, J.D., A. van Dam, S.K. Feiner, and J. Hughes. 1995. *Computer graphics: Principles and practice in C. The systems programming series*, 2nd ed. Boston: Addison-Wesley.

Fuchs, H., Z.M. Kedem, and B. Naylor. 1979a. Predetermining visibility priority in 3-d scenes (preliminary report). In Proceedings of the 6th annual conference on computer graphics and interactive techniques, SIGGRAPH '79, 175–181, New York, USA: ACM.

Fuchs, H., Z.M. Kedem, and B. Naylor. 1979b. Predetermining visibility priority in 3-d scenes (preliminary report). *SIGGRAPH Computer Graphics* 13(2): 175–181.

Fuchs, H., Z.M. Kedem, and B.F. Naylor. 1980a. On visible surface generation by a priori tree structures. *SIGGRAPH Computer Graphics* 14(3): 124–133.

Fuchs, H., Z.M. Kedem, and B.F. Naylor. 1980b. On visible surface generation by a priori tree structures. In Proceedings of the 7th annual conference on Computer graphics and interactive techniques, SIGGRAPH '80, 124–133, New York, USA: ACM.

Glassner, A.S. 1984. Space subdivision for fast raytracing. *IEEE Computer Graphics and Applications* 4(10): 15–22.

Goldstein, R.A., and R. Nagel. 1971. 3d visual simulation. *Simulation* 16(1): 25–31.

Heckbert, P., and P. Hanrahan. 1984. Beam tracing polygonal object. *Computer Graphics* 18(3): 119–127.

Rubin, S.M. and T. Whitted. 1980a. A 3-dimensional representation for fast rendering of complex scenes. In Proceedings of the 7th annual conference on Computer graphics and interactive techniques, SIGGRAPH '80, 110–116, New York, USA: ACM.

Rubin, S.M., and T. Whitted. 1980b. A 3-dimensional representation for fast rendering of complex scenes. *SIGGRAPH Computer Graphics* 14(3): 110–116.

Samet, H. 1989a. Implementing ray tracing with octrees and neighbor finding. *Computers and Graphics* 13(4): 445–460.

Samet, H. 1989b. Neighbour finding in images represented by octrees. *Computer Vision, Graphics and Image Processing* 46(3): 367–386.

Shinya, M., and T. Takahashi. 1987. Principles and applications of pencil tracing. *Computer Graphics* 21(4): 45–54.

Vince, J. 2007. Vector analysis for computer graphics. Berlin: Springer.

Weghorst, H., G. Hooper, and D.P. Greenberg. 1984. Improved computational methods for ray tracing. *ACM Transactions on Graphics* 3(1): 52–69.

Whitted, T. 1980. An improved illumination model for shaded display. *Communication ACM* 23(6): 343–349.

# Chapter 11
# Illumination, Lighting and Shading

**Abstract** In order to achieve good rendering results, the scene under consideration should be illuminated. In this chapter, we will discuss illumination and lighting. *Illumination* is the process of transferring energy from light sources to surfaces. On the other hand, the process of computing the luminous intensity at a surface point is referred to as *lighting*. Light rays may arrive directly from light sources to scene surfaces or they may get reflected off or refracted through other surfaces before arriving at the point being lit. In addition, some objects may cast shadows on others; a situation that affects the final intensity of the points being lit. Thus, illumination of a scene can be direct and/or indirect. Direct and indirect illumination are discussed in Sects. 11.1 and 11.4 respectively. Calculating final intensities at surface points is studied in Sects. 11.2 and 11.3. Also, in this chapter and as parts of the graphics pipeline (Sect. 1.3.1), we will discuss *shading* and *shadowing* as consequences following the presence of light sources in the scene under consideration. Shading and shadowing are different processes. We will study these operations in more details in Sects. 11.5 and 11.6.

## 11.1 Direct Illumination

It is obvious from the term *direction illumination* that light rays arrive *directly* from light sources to scene surfaces. In fact, direct illumination comprises two subsequent steps:

1. Light rays are emitted at a light source. There are many light source models that differ in their impact on the scene being illuminated. These models are discussed in Sect. 11.1.1.
2. Once a ray reaches a scene surface, it may get scattered. This process is affected by surface properties and reflectance models, which are discussed in Sect. 11.1.2.

R. Elias, *Digital Media*, DOI: 10.1007/978-3-319-05137-6_11,

When a light source model in addition to reflectance model are known, a reflection model can be used to calculate the intensity or color of a given pixel. Phong and Blinn-Phong reflection models are discussed in Sects. 11.2 and 11.3.

## *11.1.1 Light Sources*

A light source is the first component of illumination. There are specific parameters affecting the contribution of a light source into the final rendering results. The parameters include

1. the light color (or light intensity),
2. the geometric properties of the light source (e.g., location, direction, etc.), and
3. if the light gets attenuated with large distances or angles.

There are different light sources or light models that can be used. Among those models are

1. ambient light sources,
2. directional light sources,
3. point light sources and
4. spotlight sources.

### 11.1.1.1 Ambient Light

*Ambient light* is used to equally illuminate all points on all surfaces in the scene as shown in Fig. 11.1a. This type of light cannot be used alone to illuminate the scene as all points are treated equally. Practically, it is used with other light sources. You can think of this type as an approximation of indirect illumination (Sect. 11.4). Unlike other light sources, an ambient light does not have any spatial or directional properties (i.e., no location, direction, attenuation, etc.).

An ambient light contributes to ambient reflections; however, it does not contribute to diffuse or specular reflections. Ambient reflection does not depend on the orientation or the position of the surface being illuminated. (More on ambient, diffuse and specular reflections are discussed in Sect. 11.1.2.)

### 11.1.1.2 Directional Light

A *directional light* source emits light in parallel rays as if the light source is placed at an infinite distance from the scene as depicted in Fig. 11.1b. In this type of light sources, no attenuation exists with distance.

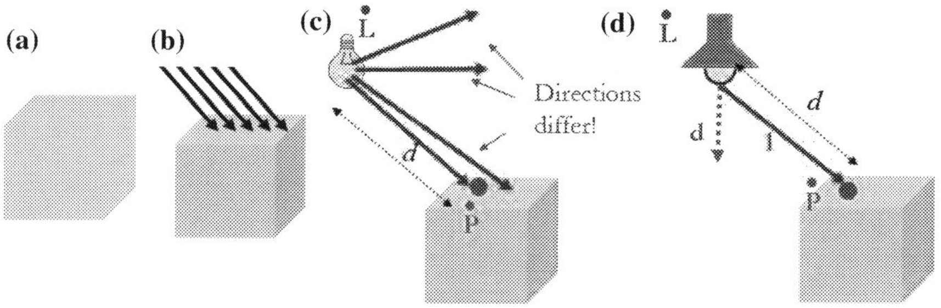


**Fig. 11.1** Light sources. **a** An ambient light where all points on all surfaces in the scene are illuminated equally. **b** A directional light where light rays are parallel. **c** A point light where light rays are shot equally in all directions. The distance from the light source to the 3D point is $d$. **d** A spotlight where light rays are directed. The distance from the light source to the 3D point is $d$

The intensity $I_{light}$ of energy leaving a light source and arriving at an object point $\dot{\mathbf{P}}$ is given by

$$I_{light} = I_p, \tag{11.1}$$

where $I_p$ is the intensity of the directional light source. The direction of light rays is constant for all points in the scene.

A directional light does not contribute to ambient reflections; however, it contributes to diffuse and specular reflections. These contributions depend on the orientation of the surface being illuminated but they do not depend on the location of the surface. (More on ambient, diffuse and specular reflections are discussed in Sect. 11.1.2.)

#### 11.1.1.3 Point Light

A *point light* source shoots light rays equally in *all* directions from the location of the light source as shown in Fig. 11.1c. Consequently and unlike directional lights, the directions of light rays change from one scene point to another according to the direction vectors connecting the light source to each scene point. This means that the light ray directions differ for points that belong to the same surface.

The direction vector connecting the light source at $\dot{\mathbf{L}}$ to a scene point $\dot{\mathbf{P}}$ is calculated as $\dot{\mathbf{P}} - \dot{\mathbf{L}}$. This vector should be normalized to have

$$\mathbf{d} = \frac{\dot{\mathbf{P}} - \dot{\mathbf{L}}}{\|\dot{\mathbf{P}} - \dot{\mathbf{L}}\|}, \tag{11.2}$$

where $\mathbf{d}$ is a unit vector that represents the direction from the light source to the surface point.

The intensity $I_{light}$ of energy leaving the light source and arriving at point $\dot{\mathbf{P}}$ is obtained as

$$I_{light} = \frac{I_p}{k_c + k_l d + k_q d^2}, \tag{11.3}$$

where $d$ is the distance from the light source $\dot{\mathbf{L}}$ to the scene point $\dot{\mathbf{P}}$ (i.e., $d = \|\dot{\mathbf{P}} - \dot{\mathbf{L}}\|$); $I_p$ is the original light intensity; $k_c$ is the constant attenuation factor; $k_l$ is the linear attenuation factor; and $k_q$ is the quadratic attenuation factor. Notice that the intensity $I_{light}$ gets smaller (i.e., attenuated) as the distance $d$ gets larger. Notice also that the attenuation [i.e., $1/(k_c + k_l d + k_q d^2)$] equals 1 in case of directional light or when $k_c = 1$ and $k_l = k_q = 0$ in which case there is no attenuation. Practically, the value $1/(k_c + k_l d + k_q d^2)$ should be less than 1 for attenuation to take effect.

A point light does not contribute to ambient reflections; however, it contributes to diffuse and specular reflections. These contributions depend on the orientation of the surface as well as the position of the point being lit. (More on ambient, diffuse and specular reflections are discussed in Sect. 11.1.2.)

**Example 11.1:** [*Point light—attenuation*]

Assume that the attenuation values of a point light source are modeled by the reciprocal of the quadratic function $0.5 + 0.3d + 0.2d^2$ where $d$ is the distance from light source to the point being lit. Determine the attenuation values such that $d \in \{1, 2, 3, \ldots, 19, 20\}$.

**Solution 11.1:** When $d = 1$, the attenuation is calculated as

$$\begin{aligned} attenuation &= \frac{1}{0.5 + 0.3d + 0.2d^2} \\ &= \frac{1}{0.5 + 0.3 \times 1 + 0.2 \times 1^2} = 1. \end{aligned}$$

When $d = 2$, the attenuation is calculated as

$$attenuation = \frac{1}{0.5 + 0.3 \times 2 + 0.2 \times 2^2} = 0.5263.$$

The attenuation values are summarized in the following table:

| $d$ | Attenuation | $d$ | Attenuation | $d$ | Attenuation | $d$ | Attenuation |
|---|---|---|---|---|---|---|---|
| 1 | 1 | 6 | 0.1053 | 11 | 0.0357 | 16 | 0.0177 |
| 2 | 0.5263 | 7 | 0.0806 | 12 | 0.0304 | 17 | 0.0158 |
| 3 | 0.3125 | 8 | 0.0637 | 13 | 0.0262 | 18 | 0.0141 |
| 4 | 0.2041 | 9 | 0.0515 | 14 | 0.0228 | 19 | 0.0128 |
| 5 | 0.1429 | 10 | 0.0426 | 15 | 0.0200 | 20 | 0.0116 |

These values are drawn in Fig. 11.2. □

**Example 11.2:** [*Point light—light intensity at a point*]

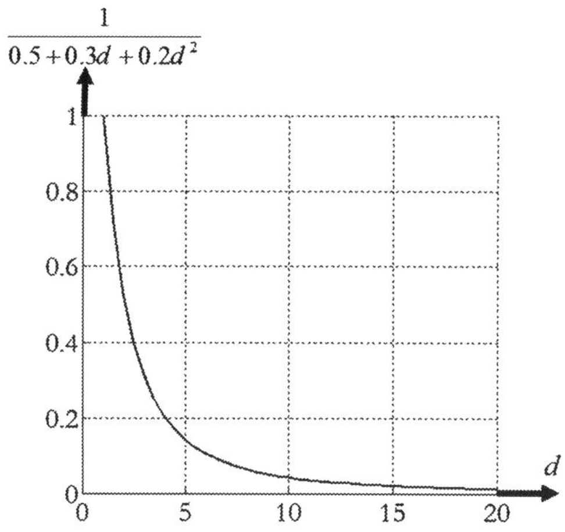


**Fig. 11.2** Representation of the function $\frac{1}{0.5+0.3d+0.2d^2}$

In Example 11.1, assume that the point light source is placed at $\dot{\mathbf{L}} = [4, 5, 6]^T$. At this point, the original intensity $I_p$ of the light is found to be 0.8 (where $I_p \in [0, 1]$). Calculate the intensity $I_{light}$ of energy leaving the light source and arriving at point $\dot{\mathbf{P}} = [8, 7, 10]^T$.

**Solution 11.2:** We should determine the distance $d$ between the light source $\dot{\mathbf{L}}$ and the point $\dot{\mathbf{P}}$ being lit where

$$\begin{aligned} d &= \|\dot{\mathbf{P}} - \dot{\mathbf{L}}\| \\ &= \left\| \begin{bmatrix} 8 \\ 7 \\ 10 \end{bmatrix} - \begin{bmatrix} 4 \\ 5 \\ 6 \end{bmatrix} \right\| = 6. \end{aligned}$$

From Example 11.1, when $d = 6$, the attenuation is 0.1053. Consequently, $I_{light}$ is calculated by applying Eq. (11.3) as

$$\begin{aligned} I_{light} &= \frac{I_p}{k_c + k_l d + k_q d^2} \\ &= 0.8 \times 0.1053 = 0.0842. \end{aligned}$$

In systems where intensities have the range [0, 255], $I_{light}$ has the value $0.0842 \times 255 = 21.4812$. (More on colors can be found in Chap. 13.) □

**Example 11.3:** [*Point light—light color at a point*]

In Example 11.2, assume the original light color is specified as a 3D vector $[255, 0, 200]^T$ representing the red, green and blue channels such that the range of each channel is from 0 to 255. Calculate $I_{light}$ at point $\dot{\mathbf{P}} = [8, 7, 10]^T$.

**Solution 11.3:** Equation (11.3) may be re-written as

$$\mathbf{I}_{light} = \frac{1}{k_c + k_l d + k_q d^2} \mathbf{I}_p, \tag{11.4}$$

where $\mathbf{I}_{light}$ is a 3D vector representing the light color arriving at the point being lit; $d$ is the distance from the light source to the scene point; $\mathbf{I}_p$ is a 3D vector representing the original light color; $k_c$ is the constant attenuation factor; $k_l$ is the linear attenuation factor; and $k_q$ is the quadratic attenuation factor. Hence, $\mathbf{I}_{light}$ is estimated as

$$\begin{aligned}\mathbf{I}_{light} &= \frac{1}{k_c + k_l d + k_q d^2} \mathbf{I}_p \\ &= 0.1053 \begin{bmatrix} 255 \\ 0 \\ 200 \end{bmatrix} = \begin{bmatrix} 26.8421 \\ 0 \\ 21.0526 \end{bmatrix}. \end{aligned}$$ □

#### 11.1.1.4 Spotlight

Figure 11.1d shows an example of a spotlight where light is directed along a main direction (denoted by the vector **d**). This type creates a cone of light specifying boundaries of its effect as illustrated in Fig. 11.3a. Only points within this cone receive light. No effect is extended beyond this cone.

**Cut-off angle:** Assume that the unit vectors **d** and **l** represent the main light direction and the direction from the spotlight to point $\dot{\mathbf{P}}$ respectively as shown in Fig. 11.3b. Point $\dot{\mathbf{P}}$ will be

$$\begin{array}{l}\text{within cone, if } \cos^{-1}(\mathbf{d} \cdot \mathbf{l}) \leq \theta_{in}; \\ \text{outside cone, otherwise,}\end{array} \tag{11.5}$$

where $\cdot$ denotes the dot product; and the angle $\theta_{in}$ represents half the angle of the cone, which is referred to as the *cut-off angle*. Practically, the value $\mathbf{d} \cdot \mathbf{l}$ cannot be negative.

**Spotlight effect and falling-off:** For better spotlight effect, the intensity of a spotlight should decrease from the axis of the light cone to its borders. The falling-off rate can be modeled by the function

$$\text{Falling-off} = \cos(\theta)^f = (\mathbf{d} \cdot \mathbf{l})^f, \tag{11.6}$$

where **d** is a unit vector representing the main direction of the spotlight; **l** is a unit vector representing the direction of the light ray to point $\dot{\mathbf{P}}$; $\theta$ is the angle enclosed between the vectors **d** and **l**; and $f$ is the fall-off factor. Consequently, the intensity $I_{light}$ of energy leaving the light source and arriving at point $\dot{\mathbf{P}}$ is obtained as

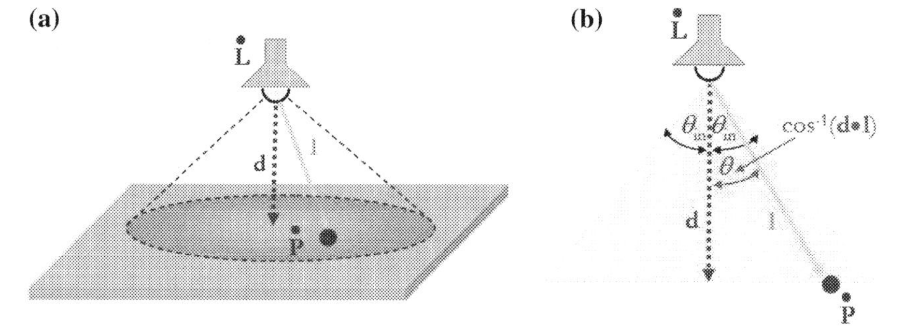


**Fig. 11.3** Spotlight cut-off angle. **a** Spotlight illuminates points within the cone. **b** In order to illuminate a point $\dot{\mathbf{P}}$, the angle $\theta$ should be less than or equal to the cut-off angle $\theta_{in}$

$$I_{light} = \begin{cases} 0, & \text{if } \mathbf{d} \cdot \mathbf{l} < \cos(\theta_{in}); \\ \frac{I_p (\mathbf{d} \cdot \mathbf{l})^f}{k_c + k_l d + k_q d^2}, & \text{otherwise}, \end{cases} \tag{11.7}$$

where $\theta_{in}$ is the cut-off angle; $d$ is the distance from the light source $\dot{\mathbf{L}}$ to the scene point $\dot{\mathbf{P}}$ (i.e., $d = \|\dot{\mathbf{P}} - \dot{\mathbf{L}}\|$); $I_p$ is the original light intensity; and $k_c$, $k_l$ and $k_q$ are the constant, linear and quadratic factors controlling attenuation. Notice that the intensity $I_{light}$ gets smaller (i.e., attenuated) as the distance $d$ gets larger. Also, it gets smaller as the angle, $\theta$, between the vectors $\mathbf{d}$ and $\mathbf{l}$ gets larger (or as the dot product $\mathbf{d} \cdot \mathbf{l} = \cos(\theta)$ gets smaller).

**Example 11.4:** [*Spotlight—light intensity at a point*]

If the light source at $\dot{\mathbf{L}} = [4, 5, 6]^T$ in Example 11.2 is a spotlight whose cut-off angle $\theta_{in}$ is 30° rather than a point light. Calculate the intensity $I_{light}$ of energy leaving the light source and arriving at point $\dot{\mathbf{P}} = [8, 7, 10]^T$ when the spotlight is directed at point $\dot{\mathbf{P}}$; i.e., the main direction of the spotlight is the vector $\dot{\mathbf{P}} - \dot{\mathbf{L}}$.

**Solution 11.4:** The main direction of the spotlight as well as the direction of the light ray to point $\dot{\mathbf{P}}$ are estimated as $\dot{\mathbf{P}} - \dot{\mathbf{L}}$ where

$$\dot{\mathbf{P}} - \dot{\mathbf{L}} = \begin{bmatrix} 8 \\ 7 \\ 10 \end{bmatrix} - \begin{bmatrix} 4 \\ 5 \\ 6 \end{bmatrix} = \begin{bmatrix} 4 \\ 2 \\ 4 \end{bmatrix}.$$

Since $\|\dot{\mathbf{P}} - \dot{\mathbf{L}}\| = 6$, the vector $\dot{\mathbf{P}} - \dot{\mathbf{L}}$ is normalized to get

$$\mathbf{d} = \mathbf{l} = \frac{\dot{\mathbf{P}} - \dot{\mathbf{L}}}{\|\dot{\mathbf{P}} - \dot{\mathbf{L}}\|} = \begin{bmatrix} \frac{4}{6} \\ \frac{2}{6} \\ \frac{4}{6} \end{bmatrix} = \begin{bmatrix} \frac{2}{3} \\ \frac{1}{3} \\ \frac{2}{3} \end{bmatrix}.$$

Thus, $\mathbf{d}\cdot\mathbf{l} = 1$ as expected since point $\dot{\mathbf{P}}$ is along the main direction of the spotlight. In other words, $\theta = 0°$ (i.e., $\theta < \theta_{in}$) and $\cos(\theta) = 1$. Consequently, the result is the same as in Example 11.2. Notice that the result remains unchanged regardless of the fall-off value. □

**Example 11.5:** [*Spotlight—light intensity at a point*]

If the spotlight source of Example 11.4, which is placed at $\dot{\mathbf{L}} = [4, 5, 6]^T$, is directed towards point $\dot{\mathbf{P}}_1 = [8, 7, 8]^T$; i.e., the main direction of the spotlight is the vector $\dot{\mathbf{P}}_1 - \dot{\mathbf{L}}$, calculate the intensity $I_{light}$ of energy leaving the light source and arriving at point $\dot{\mathbf{P}} = [8, 7, 10]^T$ if the fall-off factor is 1. Assume that the cut-off angle $\theta_{in}$ is 45°. Also, assume that the attenuation values are modeled by the reciprocal of the quadratic function $0.5 + 0.3d + 0.2d^2$ where $d$ is the distance from light source to the point being lit and the original intensity $I_p$ of the light $\dot{\mathbf{L}}$ is found to be 0.8 (where $I_p \in [0, 1]$).

**Solution 11.5:** The main direction of the spotlight is estimated as $\dot{\mathbf{P}}_1 - \dot{\mathbf{L}}$ where

$$\dot{\mathbf{P}}_1 - \dot{\mathbf{L}} = \begin{bmatrix} 8 \\ 7 \\ 8 \end{bmatrix} - \begin{bmatrix} 4 \\ 5 \\ 6 \end{bmatrix} = \begin{bmatrix} 4 \\ 2 \\ 2 \end{bmatrix}.$$

The vector $\dot{\mathbf{P}}_1 - \dot{\mathbf{L}}$ is normalized to get

$$\mathbf{d} = \frac{\dot{\mathbf{P}}_1 - \dot{\mathbf{L}}}{\|\dot{\mathbf{P}}_1 - \dot{\mathbf{L}}\|} = \begin{bmatrix} \frac{4}{\sqrt{24}} \\ \frac{2}{\sqrt{24}} \\ \frac{2}{\sqrt{24}} \end{bmatrix} = \begin{bmatrix} \frac{2}{\sqrt{6}} \\ \frac{1}{\sqrt{6}} \\ \frac{1}{\sqrt{6}} \end{bmatrix}.$$

From Example 11.4, we know that $\mathbf{l} = \left[\frac{2}{3}, \frac{1}{3}, \frac{2}{3}\right]^T$; thus,

$$\mathbf{d}\cdot\mathbf{l} = \begin{bmatrix} \frac{2}{\sqrt{6}} \\ \frac{1}{\sqrt{6}} \\ \frac{1}{\sqrt{6}} \end{bmatrix} \cdot \begin{bmatrix} \frac{2}{3} \\ \frac{1}{3} \\ \frac{2}{3} \end{bmatrix} = 0.9526.$$

Since $\mathbf{d}\cdot\mathbf{l} > \cos(45)$, point $\dot{\mathbf{P}}$ falls within the spotlight cone. Hence, $I_{light}$ is obtained using Eq. (11.7) as

$$I_{light} = \frac{I_p(\mathbf{d}\cdot\mathbf{l})^f}{k_c + k_l d + k_q d^2}.$$

Since

$$\begin{aligned} d &= \|\dot{\mathbf{P}} - \dot{\mathbf{L}}\| \\ &= \left\| \begin{bmatrix} 8 \\ 7 \\ 10 \end{bmatrix} - \begin{bmatrix} 4 \\ 5 \\ 6 \end{bmatrix} \right\| = 6 \end{aligned}$$

and

$$\frac{I_p}{k_c + k_l d + k_q d^2} = \frac{0.8}{0.5 + 0.3 \times 6 + 0.2 \times 6^2} = 0.0842$$

as in Example 11.2, $I_{light}$ is calculated as

$$I_{light} = 0.0842 \times 0.9526^1 = 0.0802.$$

In systems where intensities have the range [0, 255], $I_{light}$ has the value $0.0802 \times 255 = 20.4554$. □

**Example 11.6:** [*Spotlight—light color at a point*]
Re-write Eq. (11.7) so that the light color is represented by three channels.

**Solution 11.6:** Equation (11.7) is re-written as

$$\mathbf{I}_{light} = \begin{cases} [0, 0, 0]^T, & \text{if } \mathbf{d} \cdot \mathbf{l} < \cos(\theta_{in}); \\ \dfrac{(\mathbf{d} \cdot \mathbf{l})^f}{k_c + k_l d + k_q d^2} \mathbf{I}_p, & \text{otherwise,} \end{cases} \tag{11.8}$$

where $\mathbf{I}_{light}$ is a 3D vector representing the light color arriving at the point being lit; $\mathbf{d}$ is a unit vector representing the main direction of the spotlight; $\mathbf{l}$ is a unit vector representing the direction of the light ray to a point $\dot{\mathbf{P}}$; $f$ is the fall-off factor; $\mathbf{I}_p$ is a 3D vector representing the original light color; $k_c$, $k_l$ and $k_q$ are the constant, linear and quadratic factors controlling attenuation; and $d$ is the distance from the light source to the scene point. □

**Example 11.7:** [*Spotlight—maximum intensity*]
Suppose that a spotlight source is placed at $[5, 5, 5]^T$ and pointed towards (perpendicular to) the plane represented by the equation $x + y + z = 3$. Calculate the position of maximum intensity produced by that light on the above mentioned plane.

**Solution 11.7:** It is a ray-plane intersection problem (Sect. 10.6.2.1). The intersection point is expressed as

$$\dot{\mathbf{P}} = \dot{\mathbf{P}}_0 + t\mathbf{v}.$$

The light ray goes from $\dot{\mathbf{P}}_0 = [5, 5, 5]^T$. From Eq. (10.9) the normal to the plane $x + y + z = 3$ is $[1, 1, 1]^T$. The direction vector $\mathbf{v}$ is the same as the normal to the plane but along the opposite direction. Thus, $\mathbf{v} = [-1, -1, -1]^T$. Applying Eq. (10.12), $t$ is obtained as

$$\begin{aligned} t &= \frac{-\left(\dot{\mathbf{P}}_0 \cdot \mathbf{n}\right) + d}{\mathbf{v} \cdot \mathbf{n}} \\ &= \frac{-\left(\begin{bmatrix} 5 \\ 5 \\ 5 \end{bmatrix} \cdot \begin{bmatrix} 1 \\ 1 \\ 1 \end{bmatrix}\right) + 3}{\begin{bmatrix} -1 \\ -1 \\ -1 \end{bmatrix} \cdot \begin{bmatrix} 1 \\ 1 \\ 1 \end{bmatrix}} = 4. \end{aligned}$$

Thus, the intersection point $\dot{\mathbf{P}}$ is estimated as

$$\begin{aligned} \dot{\mathbf{P}} &= \dot{\mathbf{P}}_0 + t\mathbf{v} \\ &= \begin{bmatrix} 5 \\ 5 \\ 5 \end{bmatrix} + 4 \begin{bmatrix} -1 \\ -1 \\ -1 \end{bmatrix} = \begin{bmatrix} 1 \\ 1 \\ 1 \end{bmatrix}. \end{aligned}$$

Since the light ray at the intersection point $\dot{\mathbf{P}}$ is perpendicular to the given plane, the angle $\theta = 0°$; i.e., $\cos(\theta) = 1$ and the distance $d$ is the least among all points on the plane. Consequently, the intersection point $\dot{\mathbf{P}}$ is the point of maximum intensity. □

**Umbra and penumbra:** In Fig. 11.4a, the cone emitted from the spotlight is split into two cones; an inner cone that is referred to as the *umbra* and an outer cone that is referred to as the *penumbra*. All points within the inner cone receive full light intensity as in case of point light source. All points outside the outer cone receive no light. Light intensity decreases from the boundaries of the inner cone to the boundaries of the outer cone. Given the unit vectors $\mathbf{d}$ and $\mathbf{l}$ representing the main light direction and the direction from the spotlight to point $\dot{\mathbf{P}}$ respectively as shown in Fig. 11.3b, point $\dot{\mathbf{P}}$ will be

$$\begin{array}{ll} \text{within inner cone,} & \text{if } \cos^{-1}(\mathbf{d} \cdot \mathbf{l}) \leq \theta_{in}; \\ \text{outside outer cone,} & \text{if } \cos^{-1}(\mathbf{d} \cdot \mathbf{l}) > \theta_{out}; \\ \text{between cones,} & \text{otherwise,} \end{array} \tag{11.9}$$

where $\cdot$ denotes the dot product; and $\theta_{in}$ and $\theta_{out}$ represent halves the angles of the inner and outer cones respectively such that $\theta_{in} < \theta_{out}$. Different functions may be used to simulate the falling-off of light between inner and outer cones as the following function:

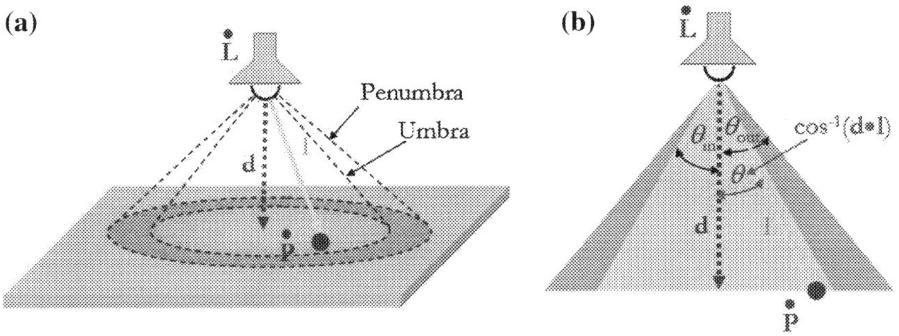


**Fig. 11.4** Spotlight effect. **a** Penumbra (i.e., the outer cone) and umbra (i.e., the inner cone) of the spotlight. **b** Light intensity decreases between the umbra and the penumbra

$$\text{Falling-off} = \left(\frac{\cos(\theta) - \cos(\theta_{out})}{\cos(\theta_{in}) - \cos(\theta_{out})}\right)^f, \tag{11.10}$$

where $\theta$ is the angle enclosed between the vectors **d** and **l**; and $f$ is the fall-off factor. Equation (11.10) produces a value within the interval [0, 1].

Thus, as with Eq. (11.3), assuming that the intensity of the spotlight source is $I_p$, the attenuation factors are $k_c$, $k_l$ and $k_q$, the distance from the light position $\dot{\mathbf{L}}$ to the point $\dot{\mathbf{P}}$ being lit is $d$ (obtained as $\|\dot{\mathbf{P}} - \dot{\mathbf{L}}\|$), the intensity $I_{light}$ of energy leaving the light source and arriving at point $\dot{\mathbf{P}}$ is estimated as

$$I_{light} = \begin{cases} \frac{I_p}{k_c + k_l d + k_q d^2}, & \text{if } \mathbf{d} \cdot \mathbf{l} \geq \cos(\theta_{in}); \\ 0, & \text{if } \mathbf{d} \cdot \mathbf{l} < \cos(\theta_{out}); \\ \frac{I_p \left(\frac{\cos(\theta) - \cos(\theta_{out})}{\cos(\theta_{in}) - \cos(\theta_{out})}\right)^f}{k_c + k_l d + k_q d^2}, & \text{otherwise,} \end{cases} \tag{11.11}$$

A spotlight does not contribute to ambient reflections; however, it contributes to diffuse and specular reflections. These contributions depend on the orientation of the surface as well as the position of the point being lit. (More on ambient, diffuse and specular reflections are discussed in Sect. 11.1.2.)

**Example 11.8:** [*Spotlight—falling-off curve*]

Equation (11.10) determines the amount of falling-off from the umbra to the penumbra. Assuming that $\theta_{in} = 30°$ and $\theta_{out} = 60°$, show the function shape if the fall-off factor $f$ is 1. Also, show the curve when $f = 0.5$ and when $f = 5$.

**Solution 11.8:** The curves are shown in Fig. 11.5. The differences among curves should not much influence the final intensity outcome. Most of the time, $f$ is set to 1 which makes the computation less expensive. □

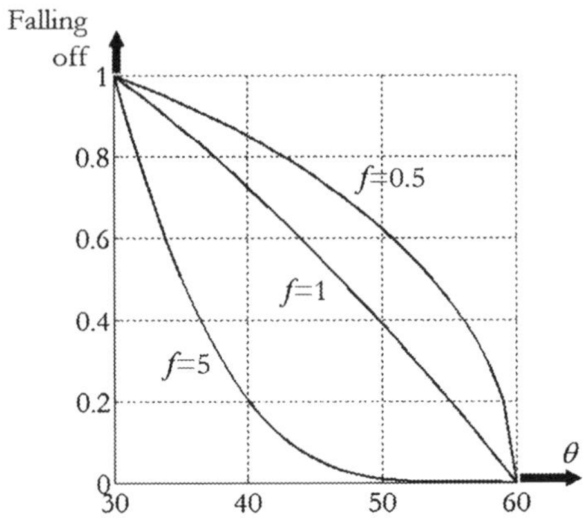


**Fig. 11.5** The shape of the falling-off function changes with the change of the fall-off factor $f$. The angle $\theta$ is measured in degrees

**Table 11.1** Light source types

| Light type | Position | Direction | Attenuation | Contribution | Contrib. affected by surface |
|---|---|---|---|---|---|
| Ambient | No | No | No | Ambient | None |
| Directional | $\infty$ | Parallel rays | No | Diffuse and specular | Orientation |
| Point | Yes | All | Yes | Diffuse and specular | Orientation and position |
| Spot | Yes | Directed | Yes | Diffuse and specular | Orientation and position |

#### 11.1.1.5 Summary of Properties

Table 11.1 summarizes the main properties of different light sources concerning the location of light source, direction of rays and whether or not attenuation exists.

### *11.1.2 Reflectance Models*

The second component affecting direct illumination is related to surface properties, which include its reflectance and its geometric properties as well (e.g., surface location, surface orientation with respect to light, etc.). These properties can be expressed analytically in a reflectance model (e.g., ambient reflection, diffuse reflection and specular reflection).

#### 11.1.2.1 Ambient Reflection

Reflections of light rays off surfaces illuminate other surfaces. This process is approximated by ambient reflection, which produces constant illumination (i.e., same

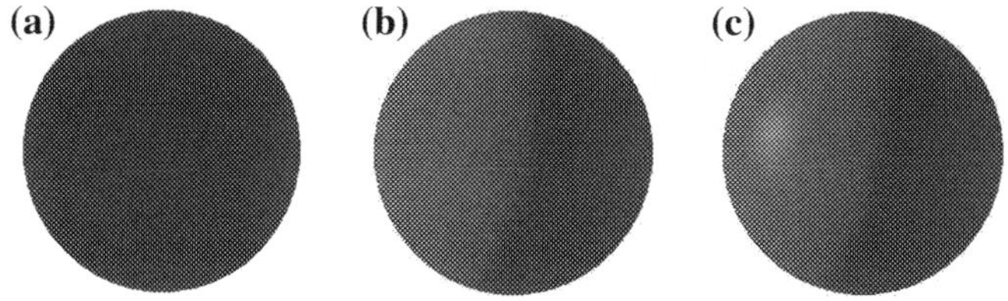


**Fig. 11.6** **a** Ambient reflection. **b** Diffuse and ambient reflections. **c** Specular, diffuse and ambient reflections

**Fig. 11.7** Diffuse reflection. **a** Once a light ray hits a surface, it gets reflected/scattered. **b** The amount of reflected light depends on the angle of incidence $\theta_i$

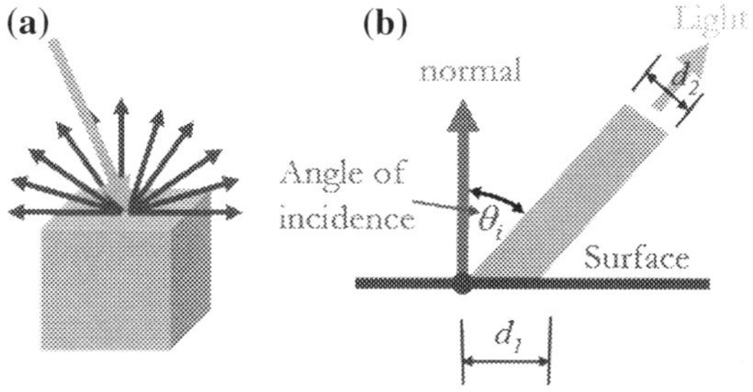


amount of light) on every surface regardless of its geometry, position and/or orientation. Ambient reflection depends on two factors. The first factor is the material's ambient reflectance or ambient reflection coefficient, which is denoted by the factor $k_a$. The second is the intensity $I_a$ of ambient light that is constant for all points in the scene as shown in Fig. 11.6a. This can be expressed as

$$I_{ambient} = k_a I_a, \tag{11.12}$$

where $I_{ambient}$ is the ambient reflection; $k_a$ is the material's ambient reflectance; and $I_a$ is the intensity of ambient light. An example of ambient reflection on a sphere is shown in Fig. 11.6a. Using ambient reflection alone is not good for most scenes as it adds little realism to generated images.

#### 11.1.2.2 Diffuse Reflection

Once a light ray hits a surface, it gets reflected and scattered (even at the microscopic level) as shown in Fig. 11.7a. The amount of reflected light depends on the angle of incidence $\theta_i$ as shown in Fig. 11.7b such that

$$\cos(\theta_i) = \frac{d_2}{d_1}. \tag{11.13}$$

Notice that the area illuminated (that is indicated by $d_1$) gets larger with larger $\theta_i$.

According to Lambert's law, the amount of reflected light is proportional to the cosine of the angle of incidence $\theta_i$, which is enclosed between the light vector $\mathbf{l}$ and the normal $\mathbf{n}$ to the plane. In case $\mathbf{l}$ and $\mathbf{n}$ are normalized, $\cos(\theta_i)$ is calculated by the dot product as

$$\cos(\theta_i) = \mathbf{n} \cdot \mathbf{l}, \tag{11.14}$$

where $\|\mathbf{n}\| = \|\mathbf{l}\| = 1$. It is important to mention that a surface is illuminated by a light ray only if the angle of incidence, $\theta_i$ is between 0° and 90°. The reflected intensity or the *diffuse reflection* (also known as Lambertian reflection) is independent of the direction to the viewer; however, it does depend on the surface orientation with respect to the light source (i.e., the incidence angle $\theta_i$). In addition, the diffuse reflection depends on the intensity $I_{light}$ of light as well as the material's diffuse intensity, which denoted by the factor $k_d$. Hence, the diffuse reflection is calculated as

$$I_{diffuse} = k_d I_{light} \cos(\theta_i), \tag{11.15}$$

where $I_{diffuse}$ is the diffuse reflection; $k_d$ is the material's diffuse intensity or the diffuse reflection coefficient; $I_{light}$ is the intensity of light at the point being lit (after attenuation if applicable); and $\theta_i$ is the incidence angle. Notice that the intensity $I_{diffuse}$ gets lower with larger $\theta_i$. This is in contrast to larger illuminated area with larger $\theta_i$ as stated above. Equation (11.15) can be re-written as

$$I_{diffuse} = k_d I_{light}(\mathbf{n} \cdot \mathbf{l}), \tag{11.16}$$

where $\mathbf{n}$ is a unit vector representing the normal to the surface; $\mathbf{l}$ is a unit vector representing the direction to light; and $\cdot$ denotes the dot product. Practically, $I_{diffuse}$ is only considered if $\mathbf{n} \cdot \mathbf{l} > 0$ as surfaces face away from light (i.e., $\theta_i > 90$) produce negative dot product. An example of diffuse reflection (in addition to ambient reflection) on a sphere is shown in Fig. 11.6b.

**Example 11.9:** [*Diffuse reflection—colors*]
Modify Eq. (11.16) to accommodate color vectors.

**Solution 11.9:** The equation is altered to suit each of the color channels as

$$\mathbf{I}_{diffuse} = \begin{bmatrix} r_{k_d}\, r_{I_{light}} \\ g_{k_d}\, g_{I_{light}} \\ b_{k_d}\, b_{I_{light}} \end{bmatrix} (\mathbf{n} \cdot \mathbf{l}), \tag{11.17}$$

where $\mathbf{I}_{diffuse}$ is a 3D vector representing the final diffuse color; $[r_{k_d}, g_{k_d}, b_{k_d}]^T$ is the material's diffuse color; and $[r_{I_{light}}, g_{I_{light}}, b_{I_{light}}]^T$ is the color of directional, point or spotlight at the point being lit (after attenuation if applicable). □

**Example 11.10:** [*Diffuse reflection—incidence angle*]
Consider a point light ray originating at $\dot{\mathbf{L}} = [12, 10, 14]^T$. Determine the incidence angle at point $\dot{\mathbf{P}} = [3, 1, 5]^T$ residing on the plane $z = 5$.

**Solution 11.10:** The light ray is represented by the normalized vector **l** where

$$\begin{aligned}
\mathbf{l} &= \frac{\dot{\mathbf{L}} - \dot{\mathbf{P}}}{\|\dot{\mathbf{L}} - \dot{\mathbf{P}}\|} \\
&= \frac{\begin{bmatrix} 12 \\ 10 \\ 14 \end{bmatrix} - \begin{bmatrix} 3 \\ 1 \\ 5 \end{bmatrix}}{\left\| \begin{bmatrix} 12 \\ 10 \\ 14 \end{bmatrix} - \begin{bmatrix} 3 \\ 1 \\ 5 \end{bmatrix} \right\|} = \frac{\begin{bmatrix} 9 \\ 9 \\ 9 \end{bmatrix}}{\sqrt{9^2 + 9^2 + 9^2}} = \begin{bmatrix} 0.5774 \\ 0.5774 \\ 0.5774 \end{bmatrix}.
\end{aligned}$$

Since the plane equation is $z = 5$, the normal to this plane is $\mathbf{n} = [0, 0, 1]^T$, which is a normalized vector. Therefore, the incidence angle, $\theta_i$, enclosed between the normalized vectors **n** and **l** is estimated as

$$\begin{aligned}
\theta_i &= \cos^{-1}(\mathbf{n} \cdot \mathbf{l}) \\
&= \cos^{-1}\left( \begin{bmatrix} 0 \\ 0 \\ 1 \end{bmatrix} \cdot \begin{bmatrix} 0.5774 \\ 0.5774 \\ 0.5774 \end{bmatrix} \right) = 54.7356^\circ.
\end{aligned}$$

□

#### 11.1.2.3 Specular Reflection

A hot spot or *specular highlight* is formed when a light ray hits a smooth specular surface. This *specular reflection* depends on the location of the camera. As the camera moves around the scene, the specular highlight location travels with it while keeping everything else unchanged including the surface location, the surface orientation, the surface properties, the light location, the light orientation and the light properties. An example of specular reflection (in addition to ambient and diffuse reflections) on a sphere is shown in Fig. 11.6c.

Consider Fig. 11.8 where **l** represents the light ray, **n** represents the normal to the plane and **r** represents the reflected light ray. According to the law of reflection, the incidence angle $\theta_i$ is equal to the reflection angle $\theta_r$. Also, the three vectors; i.e., **l**, **n** and **r** reside on a single plane. For rough surfaces or non-perfect situations, reflected light rays may get scattered from the optimal **r** direction as shown in Fig. 11.8.

Figure 11.9 shows the direction to the viewer, which is indicated by the vector **v**. Notice that this direction vector **v** varies for different points across the same surface for the same viewer. Also, this direction vector **v** varies when the camera moves while looking at the same point. Hence, unlike diffuse reflection, specular reflection is view-dependent.

Like the previous reflectance models, the specular reflection depends on the material's specular intensity represented by the factor $k_s$ and the intensity $I_{light}$ of light at the point being lit (after attenuation if applicable). In addition, the specular reflection

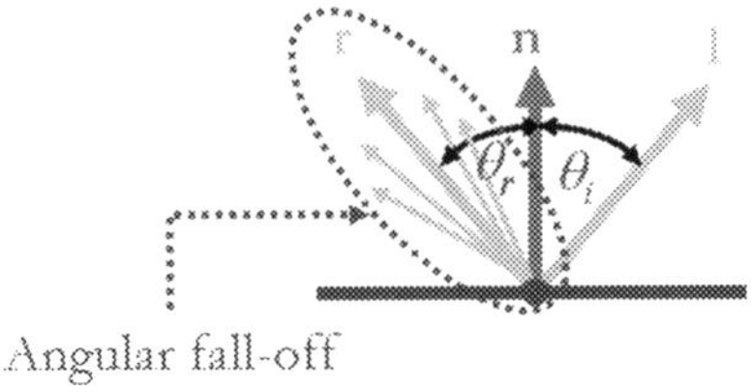


**Fig. 11.8** Angular fall-off: **n** is the normal to the surface; **l** is the light ray; **r** is the reflected ray; $\theta_i$ is the incidence angle; and $\theta_r$ is the reflection angle

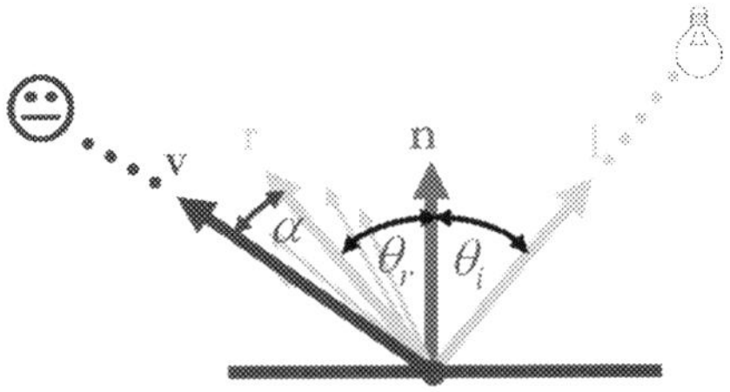


**Fig. 11.9** **n** is the normal to the surface; **l** is the light ray; **r** is the reflected ray; $\theta_i$ is the incidence angle; $\theta_r$ is the reflection angle; **v** is the direction to the camera and $\alpha$ is the angle enclosed between **v** and **r**

depends on the angle $\alpha$ to the camera (i.e., the angle to the viewer) and the rate of angular fall-off $n_s$. This can be expressed as

$$I_{specular} = k_s I_{light} \cos^{n_s}(\alpha), \tag{11.18}$$

where $I_{specular}$ is the specular reflection; $k_s$ is the material's specular intensity or the specular reflection coefficient; $I_{light}$ is the intensity of light at the point being lit (after attenuation if applicable); $\alpha$ is the angle to the viewer; and $n_s$ is a constant varying the rate of falling-off (sometimes called *Phong exponent*). Figure 11.10 shows the behaviour of $\cos^{n_s}(\alpha)$ for different values of $n_s$. Large values of $n_s$ result in shiny surfaces. Like diffuse reflection, specular reflection is only considered when $\mathbf{v}\cdot\mathbf{r} > 0$. Specular reflection is not considered if $\mathbf{n}\cdot\mathbf{l} = 0$. Notice that specular reflection gets lower with larger angle $\alpha$. Equation (11.18) can be re-written as

$$I_{specular} = k_s I_{light} (\mathbf{v}\cdot\mathbf{r})^{n_s}, \tag{11.19}$$

where **r** is a unit vector representing the reflected ray direction; **v** is a unit vector representing the direction to viewer; and · denotes the dot product. According to Eq. (10.41), **r** is calculated as

$$\mathbf{r} = 2\mathbf{n}(\mathbf{n}\cdot\mathbf{l}) - \mathbf{l}, \tag{11.20}$$

where **n** is a unit vector representing the normal vector to the surface; and **l** is a unit vector representing the light vector.

**Example 11.11:** [*Specular reflection—angle between viewing direction and reflected ray*]

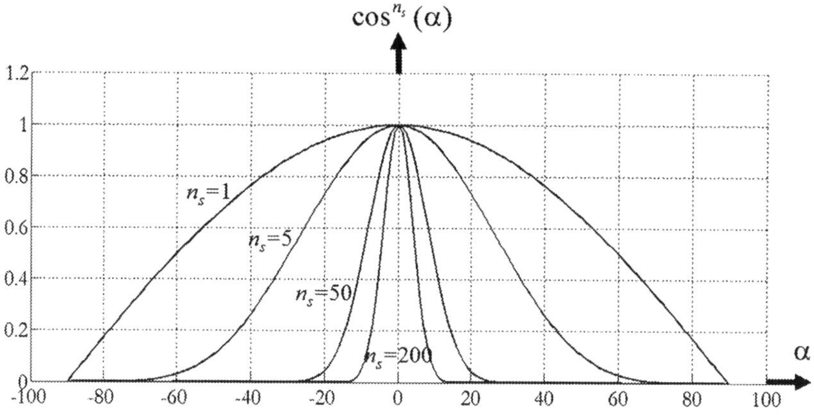


**Fig. 11.10** The behaviour of $\cos^{n_s}(\alpha)$ for different values of $n_s$ where $\alpha$ is measured in degrees

Consider a point light at $\dot{\mathbf{L}} = [7, 10, 12]^T$ that shoots light rays along all directions. If a light ray arrives at a point $\dot{\mathbf{P}} = [3, 4, 5]^T$ on a spherical surface that is centered at the origin and a virtual camera is located in space such that the normalized viewing direction to point $\dot{\mathbf{P}}$ is $\mathbf{v} = [0.2673, 0.5345, 0.8018]^T$, determine the angle between the viewing direction $\mathbf{v}$ and the reflected ray $\mathbf{r}$.

**Solution 11.11:** The normalized light ray is represented by the vector $\mathbf{l}$ where

$$\begin{aligned}
\mathbf{l} &= \frac{\dot{\mathbf{L}} - \dot{\mathbf{P}}}{\|\dot{\mathbf{L}} - \dot{\mathbf{P}}\|} \\
&= \frac{\begin{bmatrix} 7 \\ 10 \\ 12 \end{bmatrix} - \begin{bmatrix} 3 \\ 4 \\ 5 \end{bmatrix}}{\left\| \begin{bmatrix} 7 \\ 10 \\ 12 \end{bmatrix} - \begin{bmatrix} 3 \\ 4 \\ 5 \end{bmatrix} \right\|} = \frac{\begin{bmatrix} 4 \\ 6 \\ 7 \end{bmatrix}}{\sqrt{4^2 + 6^2 + 7^2}} = \begin{bmatrix} 0.3980 \\ 0.5970 \\ 0.6965 \end{bmatrix}.
\end{aligned}$$

The normal to the spherical surface at $\dot{\mathbf{P}}$ is represented by the vector passing from the center of the sphere $\dot{\mathbf{O}} = [0, 0, 0]^T$ to point $\dot{\mathbf{P}}$. Thus, the normalized normal vector $\mathbf{n}$ is obtained as

$$\mathbf{n} = \frac{\dot{\mathbf{P}} - \dot{\mathbf{O}}}{\|\dot{\mathbf{P}} - \dot{\mathbf{O}}\|}$$

$$= \frac{\begin{bmatrix}3\\4\\5\end{bmatrix} - \begin{bmatrix}0\\0\\0\end{bmatrix}}{\left\| \begin{bmatrix}3\\4\\5\end{bmatrix} - \begin{bmatrix}0\\0\\0\end{bmatrix} \right\|} = \frac{\begin{bmatrix}3\\4\\5\end{bmatrix}}{\sqrt{3^2+4^2+5^2}} = \begin{bmatrix}0.4243\\0.5657\\0.7071\end{bmatrix}.$$

According to Eq. (11.20), $\mathbf{r}$ is calculated as

$$\begin{aligned}\mathbf{r} &= 2\mathbf{n}\,(\mathbf{n}\cdot\mathbf{l}) - \mathbf{l}\\ &= 2\begin{bmatrix}0.4243\\0.5657\\0.7071\end{bmatrix}\left(\begin{bmatrix}0.4243\\0.5657\\0.7071\end{bmatrix}\cdot\begin{bmatrix}0.3980\\0.5970\\0.6965\end{bmatrix}\right) - \begin{bmatrix}0.3980\\0.5970\\0.6965\end{bmatrix} = \begin{bmatrix}0.4498\\0.5333\\0.7164\end{bmatrix}.\end{aligned}$$

Therefore, the angle $\alpha$ enclosed between the normalized vectors $\mathbf{v}$ and $\mathbf{r}$ is estimated as

$$\begin{aligned}\alpha &= \cos^{-1}(\mathbf{v}\cdot\mathbf{r})\\ &= \cos^{-1}\left(\begin{bmatrix}0.2673\\0.5345\\0.8018\end{bmatrix}\cdot\begin{bmatrix}0.4498\\0.5333\\0.7164\end{bmatrix}\right) = 11.5583^\circ.\end{aligned}$$ □

**Example 11.12:** [*Specular reflection—colors*]
Modify Eq. (11.19) to accommodate color vectors.

**Solution 11.12:** The equation is altered to suit each of the color channels as

$$\mathbf{I}_{specular} = \begin{bmatrix} r_{k_s}\, r_{I_{light}} \\ g_{k_s}\, g_{I_{light}} \\ b_{k_s}\, b_{I_{light}} \end{bmatrix} (\mathbf{v}\cdot\mathbf{r})^{n_s}, \tag{11.21}$$

where $\mathbf{I}_{specular}$ is a 3D vector representing the final specular color; $[r_{k_s}, g_{k_s}, b_{k_s}]^T$ is the material's specular color; and $[r_{I_{light}}, g_{I_{light}}, b_{I_{light}}]^T$ is the color of directional, point or spotlight at the point being lit (after attenuation if applicable). □

## 11.2 Phong Reflection Model

The *Phong reflection model* (Phong 1975), introduced by Bui-Tuong Phong (Fig. 11.9), is a function that results in the intensity/color of a surface point given information about the light source, the surface and the position of the observer.

This function consists of different components; the ambient component, the diffuse component and the specular component.[1] This can be expressed as

$$I = \underbrace{k_a I_a}_{Ambient} + \underbrace{k_d(\mathbf{n}\cdot\mathbf{l}) I_{light}}_{Diffuse} + \underbrace{k_s(\mathbf{v}\cdot\mathbf{r})^{n_s} I_{light}}_{Specular}. \tag{11.22}$$

Note that the previous equation considers a single light source. In general, a scene may include multiple light sources, which should contribute to the Phong reflection model. However, the ambient component is the same for all surfaces in the scene. Hence, multiple light sources accumulate contributions only to the diffuse and specular components as

$$I = k_a I_a + \sum_i I_i \left(k_d(\mathbf{n}\cdot\mathbf{l}) + k_s(\mathbf{v}\cdot\mathbf{r})^{n_s}\right), \tag{11.23}$$

where $I_i$ represents the intensity $I_{light}$ of light source $i$. Equation (11.23) sums up all diffuse and specular contributions from different light sources. Besides surface properties and light intensities, there are many other factors affecting the result. These factors include the location of each light source, which affects the vector $\mathbf{l}$ (and the vector $\mathbf{r}$) or the incidence angle $\theta_i$ with respect to the light vector (or equivalently, the reflection angle $\theta_r$ with respect to the reflected ray); the location of the point considered, which affects the vectors $\mathbf{v}$ and $\mathbf{l}$; and the location of the camera, which affects the vector $\mathbf{v}$ (or the direction to viewer $\alpha$). In case of color images, Eq. (11.23) can be applied to each color channel independently. This can be re-written as

$$\mathbf{I} = \begin{bmatrix} r_{k_a} r_{I_a} \\ g_{k_a} g_{I_a} \\ b_{k_a} b_{I_a} \end{bmatrix} + \begin{bmatrix} \sum_i r_{I_i}\left(r_{k_d}(\mathbf{n}\cdot\mathbf{l}) + r_{k_s}(\mathbf{v}\cdot\mathbf{r})^{n_s}\right) \\ \sum_i g_{I_i}\left(g_{k_d}(\mathbf{n}\cdot\mathbf{l}) + g_{k_s}(\mathbf{v}\cdot\mathbf{r})^{n_s}\right) \\ \sum_i b_{I_i}\left(b_{k_d}(\mathbf{n}\cdot\mathbf{l}) + b_{k_s}(\mathbf{v}\cdot\mathbf{r})^{n_s}\right) \end{bmatrix}, \tag{11.24}$$

where $\mathbf{I}$ is a 3D vector representing the color calculated for the point being lit; $[r_{I_a}, g_{I_a}, b_{I_a}]^T$ is the ambient light color; $[r_{I_i}, g_{I_i}, b_{I_i}]^T$ is the color of the directional, point or spotlight number $i$; $[r_{k_a}, g_{k_a}, b_{k_a}]^T$ is the ambient reflectance; $[r_{k_d}, g_{k_d}, b_{k_d}]^T$ is the material's diffuse color; and $[r_{k_s}, g_{k_s}, b_{k_s}]^T$ is the material's specular color.[2]

---

[1] Some systems add an emissive component to the standard ambient, diffuse and specular components.

[2] Some systems do not assign different diffuse and specular light colors. Only one color is assigned per light. Other systems assign different ambient, diffuse and specular colors for different lights where the ambient component of the light in this case is different from the global ambient, which is the first part in Eqs. (11.23, 11.24). Also, some systems use RGBA (i.e., red, green, blue and alpha transparency channels) rather than RGB colors.

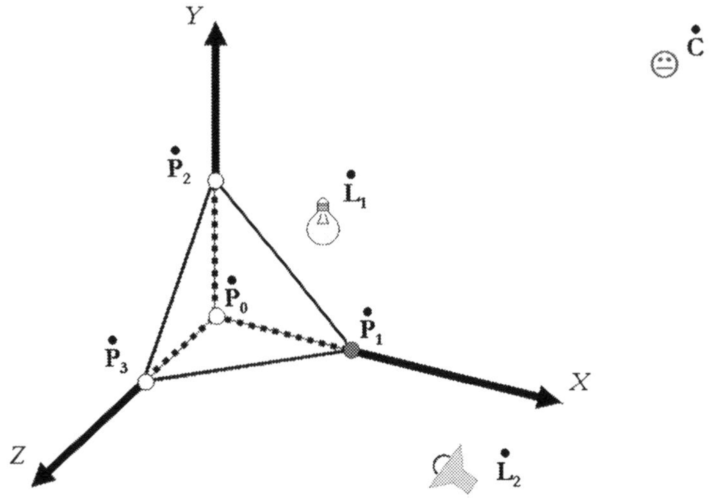


**Fig. 11.11** A pyramid with vertices at $\dot{\mathbf{P}}_0 = [0, 0, 0]^T$, $\dot{\mathbf{P}}_1 = [3, 0, 0]^T$, $\dot{\mathbf{P}}_2 = [0, 3, 0]^T$ and $\dot{\mathbf{P}}_3 = [0, 0, 3]^T$. A point light source $\dot{\mathbf{L}}_1$ is located at $\dot{\mathbf{L}}_1 = [7, 8, 9]^T$ and a spotlight source $\dot{\mathbf{L}}_2$ is placed at $\dot{\mathbf{L}}_2 = [10, 3, 9]^T$ and pointed at the origin $\dot{\mathbf{P}}_0$. A camera is placed at $\dot{\mathbf{C}} = [10, 8, 2]^T$

**Example 11.13:** [*Phong reflection model*]

Figure 11.11 shows a pyramid with vertices at $\dot{\mathbf{P}}_0 = [0, 0, 0]^T$, $\dot{\mathbf{P}}_1 = [3, 0, 0]^T$, $\dot{\mathbf{P}}_2 = [0, 3, 0]^T$ and $\dot{\mathbf{P}}_3 = [0, 0, 3]^T$. A point light source $\dot{\mathbf{L}}_1$, whose diffuse and specular colors are $\mathbf{I}_{\dot{\mathbf{L}}_1} = [1, 0, 0]^T$, is located at $\dot{\mathbf{L}}_1 = [7, 8, 9]^T$. In addition, a spotlight source $\dot{\mathbf{L}}_2$, whose fall-off factor is 1, cut-off angle is 40° and diffuse and specular colors are $\mathbf{I}_{\dot{\mathbf{L}}_2} = [0, 1, 0]^T$, is placed at $\dot{\mathbf{L}}_2 = [10, 3, 9]^T$ and pointed at the origin $\dot{\mathbf{P}}_0$. The constant, linear and quadratic attenuation factors for both lights are 0.1, 0.15 and 0.0 respectively. The attenuation is modeled in point and spot cases using Eqs. (11.4, 11.8) respectively. If the original diffuse and specular colors of the pyramid are $[0.8, 0.1, 0]^T$ each, apply Phong reflection model to get the final color at point $\dot{\mathbf{P}}_1 = [3, 0, 0]^T$ that belongs to the surface $\dot{\mathbf{P}}_1\dot{\mathbf{P}}_2\dot{\mathbf{P}}_3$ if the camera is placed at $\dot{\mathbf{C}} = [10, 8, 2]^T$ and the shininess exponent $n_s$ is 20. Assume that the ambient reflection is $\mathbf{I}_{ambient} = [0, 0.1, 0.1]$ for all points.

**Solution 11.13:** We will determine the contributions of the two light sources to both diffuse and specular components before proceeding to calculate the final color for point $\dot{\mathbf{P}}_1 = [3, 0, 0]^T$.

**Point light:** The distance $d_{\dot{\mathbf{L}}_1\dot{\mathbf{P}}_1}$ between the point light source $\dot{\mathbf{L}}_1$ and $\dot{\mathbf{P}}_1$ is calculated as

$$
\begin{aligned}
d_{\dot{\mathbf{L}}_1\dot{\mathbf{P}}_1} &= \|\dot{\mathbf{P}}_1 - \dot{\mathbf{L}}_1\| \\
&= \left\| \begin{bmatrix} 3 \\ 0 \\ 0 \end{bmatrix} - \begin{bmatrix} 7 \\ 8 \\ 9 \end{bmatrix} \right\| = 12.6886.
\end{aligned}
$$

Since the constant, linear and quadratic attenuation factors (i.e., $k_c$, $k_l$ and $k_q$) are 0.1, 0.15 and 0 respectively, the diffuse or specular color leaving the point light source and arriving at point $\dot{\mathbf{P}}_1$ is calculated by applying Eq. (11.4). Thus,

$$
\begin{aligned}
\mathbf{I}_{\dot{\mathbf{L}}_1\dot{\mathbf{P}}_1} &= \frac{1}{k_c + k_l d_{\dot{\mathbf{L}}_1\dot{\mathbf{P}}_1} + k_q d^2_{\dot{\mathbf{L}}_1\dot{\mathbf{P}}_1}} \mathbf{I}_{\dot{\mathbf{L}}_1} \\
&= \frac{1}{0.1 + 0.15 \times 12.6886 + 0 \times 12.6886^2} \begin{bmatrix} 1 \\ 0 \\ 0 \end{bmatrix} = \begin{bmatrix} 0.4992 \\ 0 \\ 0 \end{bmatrix}.
\end{aligned}
$$

**Spotlight:** The main direction $\mathbf{d}_{\dot{\mathbf{L}}_2\dot{\mathbf{P}}_0}$ of spotlight $\dot{\mathbf{L}}_2$ to the origin $\dot{\mathbf{P}}_0$ is estimated as

$$
\begin{aligned}
\mathbf{d}_{\dot{\mathbf{L}}_2\dot{\mathbf{P}}_0} &= \frac{\dot{\mathbf{P}}_0 - \dot{\mathbf{L}}_2}{\|\dot{\mathbf{P}}_0 - \dot{\mathbf{L}}_2\|} \\
&= \frac{\begin{bmatrix} 0 \\ 0 \\ 0 \end{bmatrix} - \begin{bmatrix} 10 \\ 3 \\ 9 \end{bmatrix}}{\left\| \begin{bmatrix} 0 \\ 0 \\ 0 \end{bmatrix} - \begin{bmatrix} 10 \\ 3 \\ 9 \end{bmatrix} \right\|} = \begin{bmatrix} -0.7255 \\ -0.2176 \\ -0.6529 \end{bmatrix}.
\end{aligned}
$$

The distance $d_{\dot{\mathbf{L}}_2\dot{\mathbf{P}}_1}$ between the point light source $\dot{\mathbf{L}}_2$ and $\dot{\mathbf{P}}_1$ is calculated as

$$
\begin{aligned}
d_{\dot{\mathbf{L}}_2\dot{\mathbf{P}}_1} &= \|\dot{\mathbf{P}}_1 - \dot{\mathbf{L}}_2\| \\
&= \left\| \begin{bmatrix} 3 \\ 0 \\ 0 \end{bmatrix} - \begin{bmatrix} 10 \\ 3 \\ 9 \end{bmatrix} \right\| = 11.7898.
\end{aligned}
$$

The light direction $\mathbf{l}_{\dot{\mathbf{L}}_2\dot{\mathbf{P}}_1}$ from the spotlight $\dot{\mathbf{L}}_2$ to point $\dot{\mathbf{P}}_1$ is estimated as

$$
\mathbf{l}_{\dot{\mathbf{L}}_2\dot{\mathbf{P}}_1} = \frac{\dot{\mathbf{P}}_1 - \dot{\mathbf{L}}_2}{\|\dot{\mathbf{P}}_1 - \dot{\mathbf{L}}_2\|}
$$

$$= \frac{\begin{bmatrix} 3 \\ 0 \\ 0 \end{bmatrix} - \begin{bmatrix} 10 \\ 3 \\ 9 \end{bmatrix}}{\left\| \begin{bmatrix} 3 \\ 0 \\ 0 \end{bmatrix} - \begin{bmatrix} 10 \\ 3 \\ 9 \end{bmatrix} \right\|} = \begin{bmatrix} -0.5937 \\ -0.2545 \\ -0.7634 \end{bmatrix}.$$

Now, make sure that the point under consideration $\dot{\mathbf{P}}$ falls within the cone of the spotlight. This is done by comparing the angle between the vectors $\mathbf{d}_{\dot{\mathbf{L}}_2\dot{\mathbf{P}}_0}$ and $\mathbf{l}_{\dot{\mathbf{L}}_2\dot{\mathbf{P}}_1}$ and the cut-off angle 40°. So,

$$\mathbf{d}_{\dot{\mathbf{L}}_2\dot{\mathbf{P}}_0} \cdot \mathbf{l}_{\dot{\mathbf{L}}_2\dot{\mathbf{P}}_1} = \begin{bmatrix} -0.7255 \\ -0.2176 \\ -0.6529 \end{bmatrix} \cdot \begin{bmatrix} -0.5937 \\ -0.2545 \\ -0.7634 \end{bmatrix} = 0.9845.$$

Since $\cos(40°) < 0.9845$, the spotlight contributes to the illumination of point $\dot{\mathbf{P}}$. As the constant, linear and quadratic attenuation factors (i.e., $k_c$, $k_l$ and $k_q$) are 0.1, 0.15 and 0 respectively, the diffuse or specular color leaving the spotlight source and arriving at point $\dot{\mathbf{P}}_1$ is calculated by applying Eq. (11.8) as

$$\begin{aligned}
\mathbf{I}_{\dot{\mathbf{L}}_2\dot{\mathbf{P}}_1} &= \frac{(\mathbf{d}_{\dot{\mathbf{L}}_2\dot{\mathbf{P}}_0} \cdot \mathbf{l}_{\dot{\mathbf{L}}_2\dot{\mathbf{P}}_1})^f}{k_c + k_l d_{\dot{\mathbf{L}}_2\dot{\mathbf{P}}_1} + k_q d^2_{\dot{\mathbf{L}}_2\dot{\mathbf{P}}_1}} \mathbf{I}_{\dot{\mathbf{L}}_2} \\
&= \frac{\left( \begin{bmatrix} -0.7255 \\ -0.2176 \\ -0.6529 \end{bmatrix} \cdot \begin{bmatrix} -0.5937 \\ -0.2545 \\ -0.7634 \end{bmatrix} \right)^1}{0.1 + 0.15 \times 11.7898 + 0 \times 11.7898^2} \begin{bmatrix} 0 \\ 1 \\ 0 \end{bmatrix} = \begin{bmatrix} 0 \\ 0.5269 \\ 0 \end{bmatrix}.
\end{aligned}$$

In order to compute the diffuse reflection, we need to obtain the normal to plane at the points being lit. At point $\dot{\mathbf{P}}_1$, two vectors are calculated; $\dot{\mathbf{P}}_2 - \dot{\mathbf{P}}_1$ and $\dot{\mathbf{P}}_3 - \dot{\mathbf{P}}_1$ where

$$\dot{\mathbf{P}}_2 - \dot{\mathbf{P}}_1 = \begin{bmatrix} 0 \\ 3 \\ 0 \end{bmatrix} - \begin{bmatrix} 3 \\ 0 \\ 0 \end{bmatrix} = \begin{bmatrix} -3 \\ 3 \\ 0 \end{bmatrix},$$

$$\dot{\mathbf{P}}_3 - \dot{\mathbf{P}}_1 = \begin{bmatrix} 0 \\ 0 \\ 3 \end{bmatrix} - \begin{bmatrix} 3 \\ 0 \\ 0 \end{bmatrix} = \begin{bmatrix} -3 \\ 0 \\ 3 \end{bmatrix}.$$

Now, the normal to the plane of the triangle $\triangle\dot{\mathbf{P}}_1\dot{\mathbf{P}}_2\dot{\mathbf{P}}_3$ is obtained by calculating the cross product $[\dot{\mathbf{P}}_2 - \dot{\mathbf{P}}_1] \times [\dot{\mathbf{P}}_3 - \dot{\mathbf{P}}_1]$ (see Sect. A.4.3.3 ) where

$$[\dot{\mathbf{P}}_2 - \dot{\mathbf{P}}_1] \times [\dot{\mathbf{P}}_3 - \dot{\mathbf{P}}_1] = \begin{bmatrix} -3 \\ 3 \\ 0 \end{bmatrix} \times \begin{bmatrix} -3 \\ 0 \\ 3 \end{bmatrix} = \begin{bmatrix} 9 \\ 9 \\ 9 \end{bmatrix}$$

Normalizing the previous vector, the normal vector $\mathbf{n}$ is estimated as

$$\begin{aligned} \mathbf{n} &= \frac{[\dot{\mathbf{P}}_2 - \dot{\mathbf{P}}_1] \times [\dot{\mathbf{P}}_3 - \dot{\mathbf{P}}_1]}{\|[\dot{\mathbf{P}}_2 - \dot{\mathbf{P}}_1] \times [\dot{\mathbf{P}}_3 - \dot{\mathbf{P}}_1]\|} \\ &= \frac{\begin{bmatrix} 9 \\ 9 \\ 9 \end{bmatrix}}{\left\| \begin{bmatrix} 9 \\ 9 \\ 9 \end{bmatrix} \right\|} = \begin{bmatrix} 0.5774 \\ 0.5774 \\ 0.5774 \end{bmatrix}. \end{aligned}$$

**Diffuse reflection for point light $\dot{\mathbf{L}}_1$:** The normalized light vector $\mathbf{l}_{\dot{\mathbf{P}}_1\dot{\mathbf{L}}_1}$ from point $\dot{\mathbf{P}}_1$ to point light $\dot{\mathbf{L}}_1$ is calculated as

$$\begin{aligned} \mathbf{l}_{\dot{\mathbf{P}}_1\dot{\mathbf{L}}_1} &= \frac{\dot{\mathbf{L}}_1 - \dot{\mathbf{P}}_1}{\|\dot{\mathbf{L}}_1 - \dot{\mathbf{P}}_1\|} \\ &= \frac{\begin{bmatrix} 7 \\ 8 \\ 9 \end{bmatrix} - \begin{bmatrix} 3 \\ 0 \\ 0 \end{bmatrix}}{\left\| \begin{bmatrix} 7 \\ 8 \\ 9 \end{bmatrix} - \begin{bmatrix} 3 \\ 0 \\ 0 \end{bmatrix} \right\|} = \begin{bmatrix} 0.3152 \\ 0.6305 \\ 0.7093 \end{bmatrix}. \end{aligned}$$

The diffuse component resulting from the point light contribution is obtained by applying Eq. (11.17) as

$$\begin{aligned} \mathbf{I}_{diffuse\dot{\mathbf{L}}_1} &= \begin{bmatrix} r_{k_d}\ r_{\mathbf{I}_{\dot{\mathbf{L}}_1\dot{\mathbf{P}}_1}} \\ g_{k_d}\ g_{\mathbf{I}_{\dot{\mathbf{L}}_1\dot{\mathbf{P}}_1}} \\ b_{k_d}\ b_{\mathbf{I}_{\dot{\mathbf{L}}_1\dot{\mathbf{P}}_1}} \end{bmatrix} (\mathbf{n} \cdot \mathbf{l}_{\dot{\mathbf{P}}_1\dot{\mathbf{L}}_1}) \\ &= \begin{bmatrix} 0.8 \times 0.4992 \\ 0.1 \times 0 \\ 0 \times 0 \end{bmatrix} \left( \begin{bmatrix} 0.5774 \\ 0.5774 \\ 0.5774 \end{bmatrix} \cdot \begin{bmatrix} 0.3152 \\ 0.6305 \\ 0.7093 \end{bmatrix} \right) = \begin{bmatrix} 0.3816 \\ 0 \\ 0 \end{bmatrix}. \end{aligned}$$

**Diffuse reflection for spotlight $\dot{\mathbf{L}}_2$:** In order to get the diffuse reflection for the spotlight $\dot{\mathbf{L}}_2$, we need to get the light vector $\mathbf{l}_{\dot{\mathbf{P}}_1\dot{\mathbf{L}}_2}$. We previously calculated $\mathbf{l}_{\dot{\mathbf{L}}_2\dot{\mathbf{P}}_1}$ as $[-0.5937, -0.2545, -0.7634]^T$; thus,

$$\mathbf{l}_{\dot{\mathbf{P}}_1\dot{\mathbf{L}}_2} = -\mathbf{l}_{\dot{\mathbf{L}}_2\dot{\mathbf{P}}_1} = \begin{bmatrix} 0.5937 \\ 0.2545 \\ 0.7634 \end{bmatrix}.$$

The diffuse component resulting from the spotlight contribution is obtained by applying Eq. (11.17) as

$$\begin{aligned}
\mathbf{I}_{diffuse\dot{\mathbf{L}}_2} &= \begin{bmatrix} r_{k_d}\ r_{\mathbf{I}_{\dot{\mathbf{L}}_2\dot{\mathbf{P}}_1}} \\ g_{k_d}\ g_{\mathbf{I}_{\dot{\mathbf{L}}_2\dot{\mathbf{P}}_1}} \\ b_{k_d}\ b_{\mathbf{I}_{\dot{\mathbf{L}}_2\dot{\mathbf{P}}_1}} \end{bmatrix} (\mathbf{n}\cdot\mathbf{l}_{\dot{\mathbf{P}}_1\dot{\mathbf{L}}_2}) \\
&= \begin{bmatrix} 0.8 \times 0 \\ 0.1 \times 0.5269 \\ 0 \times 0 \end{bmatrix} \left( \begin{bmatrix} 0.5774 \\ 0.5774 \\ 0.5774 \end{bmatrix} \cdot \begin{bmatrix} 0.5937 \\ 0.2545 \\ 0.7634 \end{bmatrix} \right) = \begin{bmatrix} 0 \\ 0.049 \\ 0 \end{bmatrix}.
\end{aligned}$$

**Specular reflection for point light $\dot{\mathbf{L}}_1$:** The normalized viewing direction $\mathbf{v}_{\dot{\mathbf{P}}_1\dot{\mathbf{C}}}$ with respect to point $\dot{\mathbf{P}}_1$ is estimated as

$$\begin{aligned}
\mathbf{v}_{\dot{\mathbf{P}}_1\dot{\mathbf{C}}} &= \frac{[\dot{\mathbf{C}} - \dot{\mathbf{P}}_1]}{\|[\dot{\mathbf{C}} - \dot{\mathbf{P}}_1]\|} \\
&= \frac{\begin{bmatrix} 10 \\ 8 \\ 2 \end{bmatrix} - \begin{bmatrix} 3 \\ 0 \\ 0 \end{bmatrix}}{\left\| \begin{bmatrix} 10 \\ 8 \\ 2 \end{bmatrix} - \begin{bmatrix} 3 \\ 0 \\ 0 \end{bmatrix} \right\|} = \begin{bmatrix} 0.6472 \\ 0.7396 \\ 0.1849 \end{bmatrix}.
\end{aligned}$$

The normalized light vector $\mathbf{l}_{\dot{\mathbf{P}}_1\dot{\mathbf{L}}_1}$ from point $\dot{\mathbf{P}}_1$ to point light $\dot{\mathbf{L}}_1$ has been calculated before as $[0.3152, 0.6305, 0.7093]^T$. Thus, the normalized reflected ray $\mathbf{r}_{\dot{\mathbf{P}}_1\dot{\mathbf{L}}_1}$ is estimated using Eq. (11.20) as

$$\begin{aligned}
\mathbf{r}_{\dot{\mathbf{P}}_1\dot{\mathbf{L}}_1} &= 2\mathbf{n}(\mathbf{n}\cdot\mathbf{l}_{\dot{\mathbf{P}}_1\dot{\mathbf{L}}_1}) - \mathbf{l}_{\dot{\mathbf{P}}_1\dot{\mathbf{L}}_1} \\
&= 2 \begin{bmatrix} 0.5774 \\ 0.5774 \\ 0.5774 \end{bmatrix} \left( \begin{bmatrix} 0.5774 \\ 0.5774 \\ 0.5774 \end{bmatrix} \cdot \begin{bmatrix} 0.3152 \\ 0.6305 \\ 0.7093 \end{bmatrix} \right) - \begin{bmatrix} 0.3152 \\ 0.6305 \\ 0.7093 \end{bmatrix} = \begin{bmatrix} 0.7881 \\ 0.4729 \\ 0.3941 \end{bmatrix}.
\end{aligned}$$

According to Eq. (11.21), the specular component related to the point light is estimated as

$$\mathbf{I}_{specular\dot{\mathbf{L}}_1} = \begin{bmatrix} r_{k_s}\ r_{\mathbf{I}_{\dot{\mathbf{L}}_1\dot{\mathbf{P}}_1}} \\ g_{k_s}\ g_{\mathbf{I}_{\dot{\mathbf{L}}_1\dot{\mathbf{P}}_1}} \\ b_{k_s}\ b_{\mathbf{I}_{\dot{\mathbf{L}}_1\dot{\mathbf{P}}_1}} \end{bmatrix} (\mathbf{v}_{\dot{\mathbf{P}}_1\dot{\mathbf{C}}} \cdot \mathbf{r}_{\dot{\mathbf{P}}_1\dot{\mathbf{L}}_1})^{n_s}$$

$$= \begin{bmatrix} 0.8 \times 0.4992 \\ 0.1 \times 0 \\ 0 \times 0 \end{bmatrix} \left( \begin{bmatrix} 0.6472 \\ 0.7396 \\ 0.1849 \end{bmatrix} \cdot \begin{bmatrix} 0.7881 \\ 0.4729 \\ 0.3941 \end{bmatrix} \right)^{20} = \begin{bmatrix} 0.099 \\ 0 \\ 0 \end{bmatrix}.$$

**Specular reflection for spotlight $\dot{\mathbf{L}}_2$:** The normalized viewing direction $\mathbf{v}_{\dot{\mathbf{P}}_1\dot{\mathbf{C}}}$ with respect to point $\dot{\mathbf{P}}_1$ has been obtained as $[0.6585, 0.7526, 0]^T$. Also, the normalized light vector $\mathbf{l}_{\dot{\mathbf{P}}_1\dot{\mathbf{L}}_2}$ from point $\dot{\mathbf{P}}_1$ to point light $\dot{\mathbf{L}}_2$ has been calculated before as $[0.5937, 0.2545, 0.7634]^T$. Therefore, the normalized reflected ray $\mathbf{r}_{\dot{\mathbf{P}}_1\dot{\mathbf{L}}_2}$ is estimated using Eq. (11.20) as

$$\begin{aligned} \mathbf{r}_{\dot{\mathbf{P}}_1\dot{\mathbf{L}}_2} &= 2\mathbf{n}(\mathbf{n} \cdot \mathbf{l}_{\dot{\mathbf{P}}_1\dot{\mathbf{L}}_2}) - \mathbf{l}_{\dot{\mathbf{P}}_1\dot{\mathbf{L}}_2} \\ &= 2 \begin{bmatrix} 0.5774 \\ 0.5774 \\ 0.5774 \end{bmatrix} \left( \begin{bmatrix} 0.5774 \\ 0.5774 \\ 0.5774 \end{bmatrix} \cdot \begin{bmatrix} 0.5937 \\ 0.2545 \\ 0.7634 \end{bmatrix} \right) - \begin{bmatrix} 0.5937 \\ 0.2545 \\ 0.7634 \end{bmatrix} = \begin{bmatrix} 0.4806 \\ 0.8199 \\ 0.311 \end{bmatrix}. \end{aligned}$$

According to Eq. (11.21), the specular component related to the spotlight is estimated as

$$\begin{aligned} \mathbf{I}_{specular\dot{\mathbf{L}}_2} &= \begin{bmatrix} r_{k_s}\, r_{\mathbf{I}_{\dot{\mathbf{L}}_2\dot{\mathbf{P}}_1}} \\ g_{k_s}\, g_{\mathbf{I}_{\dot{\mathbf{L}}_2\dot{\mathbf{P}}_1}} \\ b_{k_s}\, b_{\mathbf{I}_{\dot{\mathbf{L}}_2\dot{\mathbf{P}}_1}} \end{bmatrix} (\mathbf{v}_{\dot{\mathbf{P}}_1\dot{\mathbf{C}}} \cdot \mathbf{r}_{\dot{\mathbf{P}}_1\dot{\mathbf{L}}_2})^{n_s} \\ &= \begin{bmatrix} 0.8 \times 0 \\ 0.1 \times 0.5269 \\ 0 \times 0 \end{bmatrix} \left( \begin{bmatrix} 0.6472 \\ 0.7396 \\ 0.1849 \end{bmatrix} \cdot \begin{bmatrix} 0.4806 \\ 0.8199 \\ 0.311 \end{bmatrix} \right)^{20} = \begin{bmatrix} 0 \\ 0.0317 \\ 0 \end{bmatrix}. \end{aligned}$$

**Final point color:** The final color of $\dot{\mathbf{P}}_1$ is obtained as the sum

$$\begin{aligned} \mathbf{I} &= \mathbf{I}_{ambient} + \mathbf{I}_{diffuse\dot{\mathbf{L}}_1} + \mathbf{I}_{diffuse\dot{\mathbf{L}}_2} + \mathbf{I}_{specular\dot{\mathbf{L}}_1} + \mathbf{I}_{specular\dot{\mathbf{L}}_2} \\ &= \begin{bmatrix} 0 \\ 0.1 \\ 0.1 \end{bmatrix} + \begin{bmatrix} 0.3816 \\ 0 \\ 0 \end{bmatrix} + \begin{bmatrix} 0 \\ 0.049 \\ 0 \end{bmatrix} + \begin{bmatrix} 0.099 \\ 0 \\ 0 \end{bmatrix} + \begin{bmatrix} 0 \\ 0.0317 \\ 0 \end{bmatrix} \\ &= \begin{bmatrix} 0.4806 \\ 0.1807 \\ 0.1 \end{bmatrix}. \end{aligned}$$

□

## 11.3 Blinn-Phong Reflection Model

You might have noticed that the angle $\alpha$ between the vectors $\mathbf{v}$ and $\mathbf{r}$ might be greater than 90°. This situation is illustrated in Fig. 11.12. In such a case, the dot product

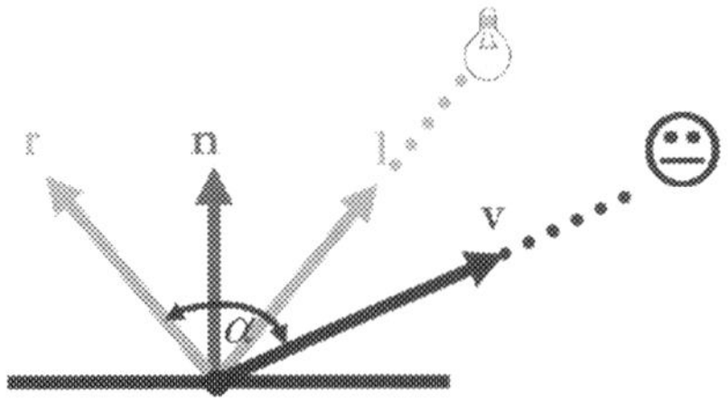


**Fig. 11.12** The angle $\alpha$ between the vectors **v** and **r** might be greater than 90°

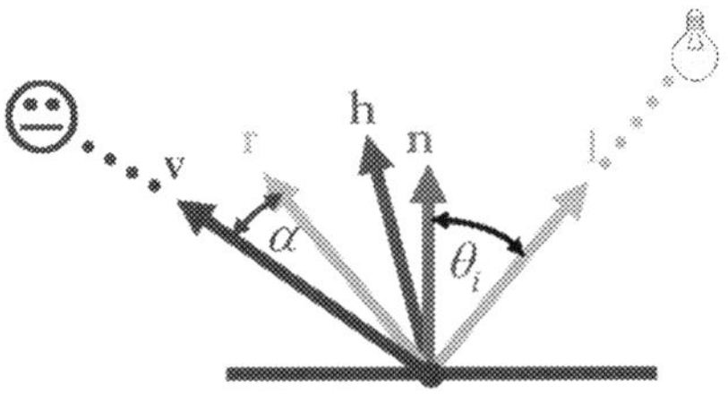


**Fig. 11.13** The half vector **h** that is at the half way between the light vector **l** and the viewing direction **v**

$\mathbf{v} \cdot \mathbf{r}$ will lead to a negative value. If this situation would not be appropriately handled, incorrect outcome should be expected.

Blinn-Phong or Blinn model that was named after James Blinn (Blinn 1977) proposed a modification to the Phong specular component. It introduced a normalized half-angle, half-way or half vector **h** that is at the half way between the light vector **l** and the viewing direction **v** as depicted in Fig. 11.13. It is calculated as

$$\mathbf{h} = \frac{\mathbf{l} + \mathbf{v}}{\|\mathbf{l} + \mathbf{v}\|}, \tag{11.25}$$

where **h** is the half vector; **l** is the light vector; and **v** is the viewing direction. Thus, the specular component can be written as

$$I_{specular} = k_s I_{light} (\mathbf{n} \cdot \mathbf{h})^{n_b}, \tag{11.26}$$

where $I_{specular}$ is the specular reflection; $k_s$ is the material's specular intensity; $I_{light}$ is the intensity of light at the point being lit (after attenuation if applicable); **n** is a unit vector representing the normal to the plane; **h** is a unit vector representing the half vector; $\cdot$ denotes the dot product; and the exponent $n_b$ control the shininess of the surface. In order to produce similar Blinn-Phong and Phong outcomes, the exponent $n_b$ of Blinn specular component should not have the exact same magnitude as that of Phong specular component $n_s$.

Putting the ambient, diffuse and specular components together, the Blinn-Phong reflection model is expressed as

$$I = k_a I_a + \sum_i I_i \left(k_d (\mathbf{n} \cdot \mathbf{l}) + k_s (\mathbf{n} \cdot \mathbf{h})^{n_b}\right). \tag{11.27}$$

In Phong model, the reflected ray **r** has to be re-computed; a value that depends on the normal vector **n**, which changes continually from point to point in case of curved surfaces. In case of Blinn-Phong model, the half vector **h** calculation does not depend on the normal vector **n**. This is computationally less expensive than Phong model especially when light ray vector **l** does not change for directional light sources and when viewing direction **v** remains constant.

Notice that if the viewing direction **v** coincides with the same plane of the light ray **l**, the normal **n** and the reflected ray **r**, the angle enclosed between the vectors **h** and **n** will be half the angle enclosed between the vectors **v** and **r**. This can be written as

$$\cos^{-1}(\mathbf{n} \cdot \mathbf{h}) = \frac{1}{2}\cos^{-1}(\mathbf{v} \cdot \mathbf{r}) = \frac{\alpha}{2}. \tag{11.28}$$

**Example 11.14:** [*Blinn-Phong reflection model—half vector*]

Consider a point light at $\dot{\mathbf{L}} = [7, 10, 12]^T$ that shoots light rays in all directions. Assume that a light ray arrives at a point $\dot{\mathbf{P}} = [3, 4, 5]^T$ on the surface of a sphere centered at the origin. If a virtual camera is located in space such that the normalized viewing direction to point $\dot{\mathbf{P}}$ is $\mathbf{v} = [0.2673, 0.5345, 0.8018]^T$, determine the half vector **h** in this case.

**Solution 11.14:** The normalized light ray is represented by the vector **l** where

$$\begin{aligned}\mathbf{l} &= \frac{\dot{\mathbf{L}} - \dot{\mathbf{P}}}{\|\dot{\mathbf{L}} - \dot{\mathbf{P}}\|}\\ &= \frac{\begin{bmatrix}7\\10\\12\end{bmatrix} - \begin{bmatrix}3\\4\\5\end{bmatrix}}{\left\|\begin{bmatrix}7\\10\\12\end{bmatrix} - \begin{bmatrix}3\\4\\5\end{bmatrix}\right\|} = \frac{\begin{bmatrix}4\\6\\7\end{bmatrix}}{\sqrt{4^2+6^2+7^2}} = \begin{bmatrix}0.3980\\0.5970\\0.6965\end{bmatrix}.\end{aligned}$$

The half vector **h** is calculated using Eq. (11.25) as

$$\begin{aligned}\mathbf{h} &= \frac{\mathbf{l}+\mathbf{v}}{\|\mathbf{l}+\mathbf{v}\|}\\ &= \frac{\begin{bmatrix}0.3980\\0.5970\\0.6965\end{bmatrix} + \begin{bmatrix}0.2673\\0.5345\\0.8018\end{bmatrix}}{\left\|\begin{bmatrix}0.3980\\0.5970\\0.6965\end{bmatrix} + \begin{bmatrix}0.2673\\0.5345\\0.8018\end{bmatrix}\right\|} = \frac{\begin{bmatrix}0.6653\\1.1315\\1.4983\end{bmatrix}}{\sqrt{0.6653^2+1.1315^2+1.4983^2}} = \begin{bmatrix}0.3340\\0.5680\\0.7522\end{bmatrix}. \quad \square\end{aligned}$$

**Example 11.15:** [*Blinn-Phong reflection model—shininess exponent*]

Consider a point light at $\dot{\mathbf{L}} = [7, 10, 12]^T$ that shoots light rays in all directions. Assume that a light ray arrives at a point $\dot{\mathbf{P}} = [3, 4, 5]^T$ on the surface of a sphere centered at the origin. If a virtual camera is located in space such that the normalized viewing direction to point $\dot{\mathbf{P}}$ is $\mathbf{v} = [0.2673, 0.5345, 0.8018]^T$ and if the same amount of specular reflection provided by Phong model is to be obtained using Blinn-Phong model, determine the value of shininess exponent $n_b$ in terms of Phong shininess exponent $n_s$.

**Solution 11.15:** From Example 11.11, the normal vector $\mathbf{n}$ is expressed as $[0.4243, 0.5657, 0.7071]^T$ and the reflected ray $\mathbf{r}$ is expressed as $[0.4498, 0.5333, 0.7164]^T$. From Example 11.14, the half vector $\mathbf{h}$ is expressed as $[0.3340, 0.5680, 0.7522]^T$.

In order to get the same specular reflection from both models and from Eqs. (11.19) and (11.26), we should have

$$\begin{aligned}
(\mathbf{v} \cdot \mathbf{r})^{n_s} &= (\mathbf{n} \cdot \mathbf{h})^{n_b} \\
\left(\begin{bmatrix} 0.2673 \\ 0.5345 \\ 0.8018 \end{bmatrix} \cdot \begin{bmatrix} 0.4498 \\ 0.5333 \\ 0.7164 \end{bmatrix}\right)^{n_s} &= \left(\begin{bmatrix} 0.4243 \\ 0.5657 \\ 0.7071 \end{bmatrix} \cdot \begin{bmatrix} 0.3340 \\ 0.5680 \\ 0.7522 \end{bmatrix}\right)^{n_b} \\
0.9797^{n_s} &= 0.9949^{n_b} \\
\log(0.9797^{n_s}) &= \log(0.9949^{n_b}) \\
n_s \log(0.9797) &= n_b \log(0.9949).
\end{aligned}$$

Hence,

$$n_b = \frac{\log(0.9797)}{\log(0.9949)} n_s = 4.0127\, n_s. \qquad \square$$

## 11.4 Indirect Illumination

In *global* or *indirect illumination*, we have to consider factors of ray tracing discussed in Sect. 10.7. In ray tracing, a ray of sight may get reflected off a surface to form a reflected ray and may penetrate other surfaces to form a refracted ray. Similarly, a light ray may get reflected or refracted. The laws of reflection and refraction also must be obeyed in this case. The *indirect* reflected and refracted light rays contribute to the overall (i.e., *global*) illumination of the scene. In addition, the intensity/color of a surface point that lies in the shadow of another surface may get affected by the presence of that shadow. This should also be considered.

### *11.4.1 Shadow Rays*

The previous Phong reflection model of Eq. (11.23) considers only direct illumination. In other words, it deals with direct light rays coming from light sources to the

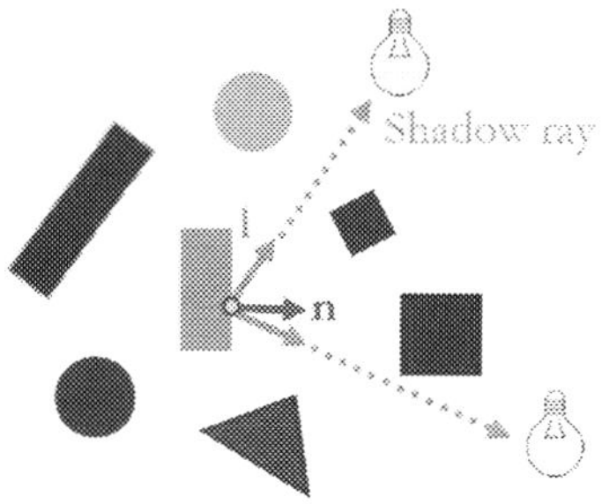


**Fig. 11.14** Shadow rays contribute to illumination. At the point indicated, $S_i = 1$ for both light sources

point being lit as shown in Fig. 11.14. However, if a light ray is blocked, it should be excluded from contributing to the model. This is controlled by a shadow term that modifies Eq. (11.23) to

$$I = k_a I_a + \sum_i S_i I_i \left(k_d(\mathbf{n} \cdot \mathbf{l}) + k_s(\mathbf{v} \cdot \mathbf{r})^{n_s}\right), \tag{11.29}$$

where $S_i$ is the shadow term such that $S_i \in [0, 1]$; and $i$ is the light source number. The shadow term $S_i$ takes one of the following values:

$$S_i = \begin{cases} 0, & \text{light does not contribute if point is in shadow;} \\ 1, & \text{light contributes if point is not in shadow;} \\ (0, 1), & \text{used for soft shadows.} \end{cases} \tag{11.30}$$

Notice that the open interval (0,1) is used with soft shadows to indicate that $S_i$ must be greater than zero and less than one.

## *11.4.2 Reflection Rays*

As said above, a light ray hitting a surface may get reflected as depicted in Fig. 11.15. It obeys the law of reflection

$$\theta_i = \theta_r, \tag{11.31}$$

where $\theta_i$ is the incidence angle measured between the light ray $\mathbf{l}$ and the normal to the surface $\mathbf{n}$; and $\theta_r$ is the reflection angle measured between the reflected ray $\mathbf{r}$ and the normal to the surface $\mathbf{n}$.

The reflected light rays should be traced as they contribute to the illumination of other surfaces when they hit them as shown in Fig. 11.16. Hence, this also should be added to the reflection model of Eq. (11.29) as

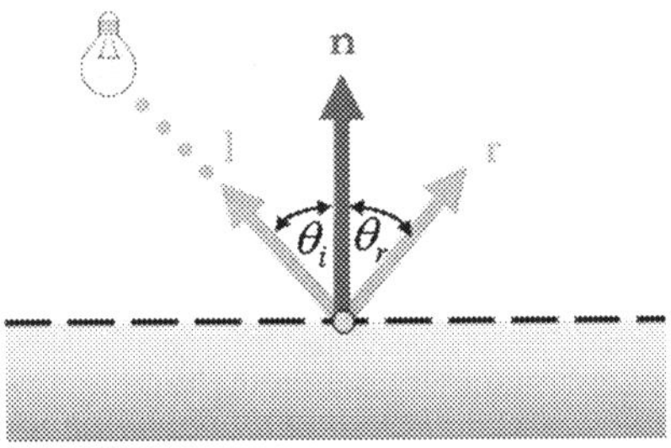


**Fig. 11.15** A light ray may get reflected where the incidence angle $\theta_i$ is equal to the reflection angle $\theta_r$

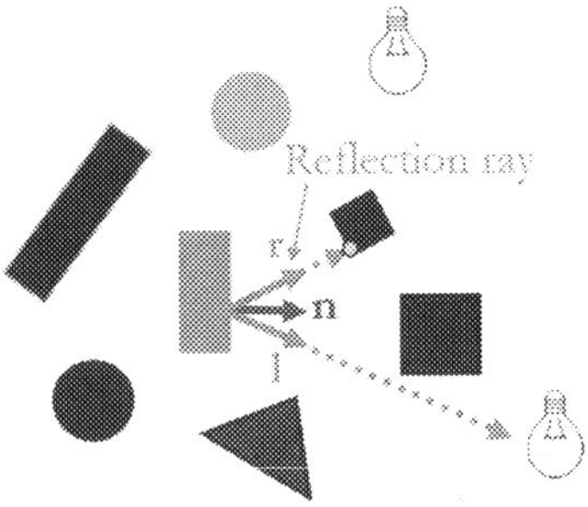


**Fig. 11.16** Reflection rays contribute to illumination. The reflected light ray contributes to the illumination of the point indicated

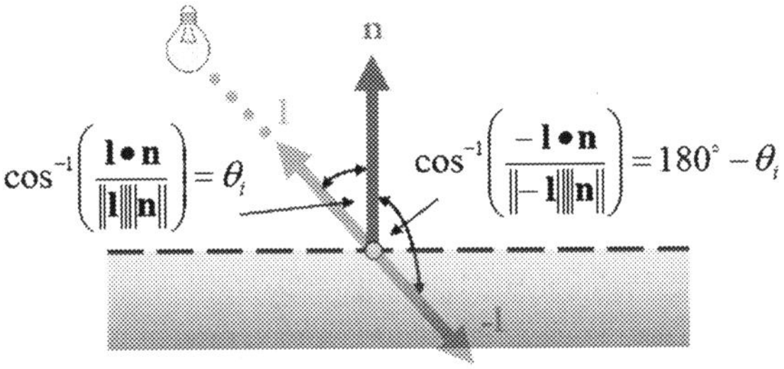


**Fig. 11.17** The incidence angle is calculated when the light vector as well as the normal to the plane are pointing out of the plane

$$I = k_a I_a + \sum_i S_i I_i \left(k_d(\mathbf{n}\cdot\mathbf{l}) + k_s(\mathbf{v}\cdot\mathbf{r})^{n_s}\right) + k_r I_r, \tag{11.32}$$

where $k_r$ is the reflection coefficient; and $I_r$ is the radiance for reflection.

**Example 11.16:** [*Reflection rays—incidence angle*]

A light ray having the direction vector $[-1, -1, -1]$ hits a planar surface having the equation $z = 2$ at a point and reflected off the plane afterwards. Determine the incidence angle.

**Solution 11.16:** Notice that there is no need to obtain the intersection point where the light ray hits the surface. The incidence angle can be estimated as the angle enclosed between the direction vector of the light ray and the normal vector to the plane. This can be calculated using the dot product of the vectors.

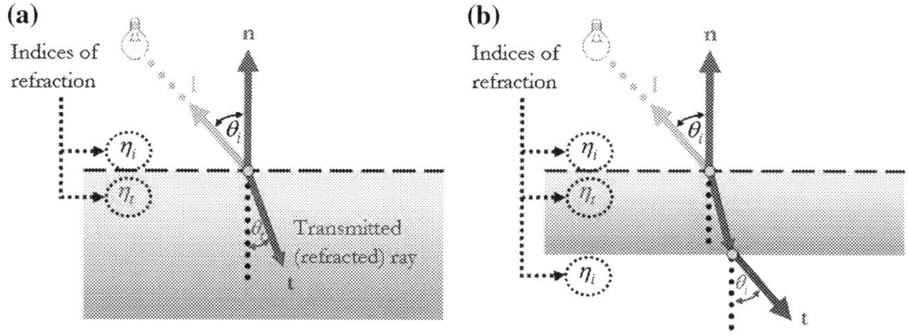


**Fig. 11.18** A light ray gets refracted when passing through different media. **a** The light ray hitting a thick medium where the refraction angle $\theta_t$ is obtained using Snell's law. **b** The light ray hitting a thin medium where the penetrated light ray going out to the original medium makes an angle $\theta_i$ with the normal $-\mathbf{n}$

As depicted in Fig. 11.17, the acute incidence angle is obtained when both light and normal vectors point out of the plane. So, we reverse the direction of the light ray direction vector to get

$$\mathbf{l} = -1 \begin{bmatrix} -1 \\ -1 \\ -1 \end{bmatrix} = \begin{bmatrix} 1 \\ 1 \\ 1 \end{bmatrix}.$$

Since the equation of the planar surface is $z = 2$, the normal to this plane is $[0, 0, 1]^T$. Hence, as in Eqs. (A.22) and (10.36), the incidence angle $\theta_i$ is calculated as

$$\begin{aligned} \theta_i &= \cos^{-1}\left(\frac{\mathbf{l} \cdot \mathbf{n}}{\|\mathbf{l}\| \, \|\mathbf{n}\|}\right) \\ &= \cos^{-1}\left(\frac{\begin{bmatrix} 1 \\ 1 \\ 1 \end{bmatrix} \cdot \begin{bmatrix} 0 \\ 0 \\ 1 \end{bmatrix}}{\sqrt{1^2 + 1^2 + 1^2}\sqrt{0^2 + 0^2 + 1^2}}\right) \\ &= 54.7356^\circ. \end{aligned}$$

Compare this with Example 10.34. □

## *11.4.3 Refraction Rays*

A light ray passing from one medium to another gets refracted at the point of hitting as depicted in Fig. 11.18a. Snell's law of refraction determine the relationship between the incidence angle $\theta_i$ and the refraction angle $\theta_t$ as

Table 11.2 The indices of refraction for some media (neglecting the wavelength of light)

| Medium | $\eta$ |
|---|---|
| Vacuum | 1.0 |
| Air | 1.0003 |
| Water | 1.3333 |
| Glass | 1.52 |
| Diamond | 2.417 |

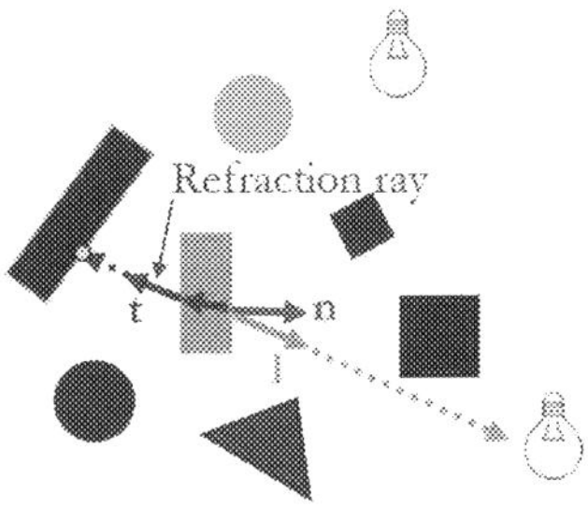


**Fig. 11.19** Refraction rays contribute to illumination. The refracted light ray contributes to the illumination of the point indicated

$$\eta_i \sin \theta_i = \eta_t \sin \theta_t, \tag{11.33}$$

where $\eta_i$ and $\eta_t$ are the indices of refraction of the two media. (Table 11.2 lists the indices of refraction for some materials/media.) Hence, the refraction angle $\theta_t$ is obtained as

$$\theta_t = \sin^{-1}\left(\frac{\eta_i \sin \theta_i}{\eta_t}\right). \tag{11.34}$$

The refraction vector **t** is given by

$$\mathbf{t} = \left(\frac{\eta_i}{\eta_t}\cos(\theta_i) - \cos(\theta_t)\right)\mathbf{n} - \frac{\eta_i}{\eta_t}\mathbf{l}, \tag{11.35}$$

where $\theta_i$ and $\theta_t$ are the incidence and refraction angles respectively; and $\eta_i$ and $\eta_t$ are the indices of refraction.

In case of thin objects as shown in Fig. 11.18b where the light ray penetrate the medium to the original medium, it can be assumed that

$$\mathbf{t} = -\mathbf{l}. \tag{11.36}$$

Consequently, in this case the refracted light ray going out to the original medium makes an angle $\theta_i$ with the normal $-\mathbf{n}$.

As with reflected light rays, refracted or transmitted light rays should be traced as they contribute to the illumination of surfaces when they penetrate other objects as shown in Fig. 11.19. Hence, this also should be added to the reflection model of Eq. (11.32) as

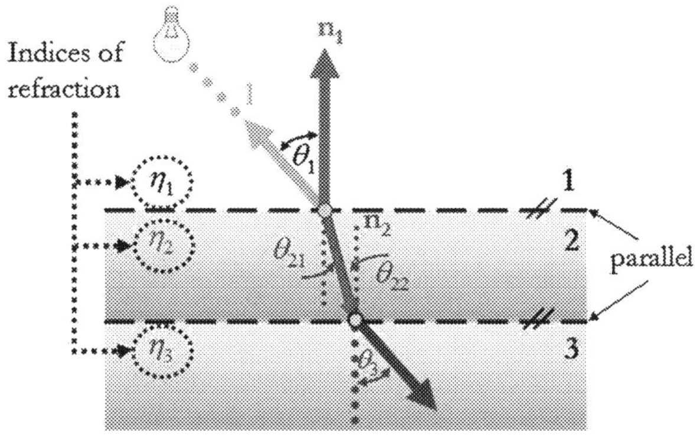


**Fig. 11.20** A ray of light penetrates three different media *1*, *2* and *3*. The plane of intersection between media *1* and *2* is parallel to the plane of intersection between media *2* and *3*

$$I = k_a I_a + \sum_i S_i I_i \left(k_d(\mathbf{n} \cdot \mathbf{l}) + k_s(\mathbf{v} \cdot \mathbf{r})^{n_s}\right) + k_r I_r + k_t I_t, \tag{11.37}$$

where $k_t$ is the transparency (or refractive) coefficient; and $I_t$ is the radiance for refraction. The transparency coefficient may take one of the following values:

$$k_t = \begin{cases} 0, & \text{if the object is opaque;} \\ 1, & \text{if the object is translucent;} \\ (0, 1), & \text{if the object is semi-translucent.} \end{cases} \tag{11.38}$$

Notice that the open interval (0, 1) is used with semi-translucent objects to indicate that $k_t$ is greater than zero and less than one.

**Example 11.17:** [*Refraction rays—refraction angles*]

Figure 11.20 shows a ray of light as penetrating three different media; 1, 2 and 3. It gets refracted while passing from medium 1 to medium 2 and it gets refracted again while passing from medium 2 to medium 3. The plane of intersection between media 1 and 2 is parallel to the plane of intersection between media 2 and 3. Determine the refraction angle $\theta_3$ in terms of the incidence angle $\theta_1$ where $\theta_3$ is the second refraction angle and $\theta_1$ is the first incidence angle.

**Solution 11.17:** Considering the first refraction that happens as the ray passes from medium 1 to medium 2 and according to Eq. (11.33), we have

$$\eta_1 \sin\theta_1 = \eta_2 \sin\theta_{21},$$

where $\eta_1$ and $\eta_2$ are the indices of refraction of media 1 and 2 respectively; $\theta_1$ is the incidence angle in medium 1; and $\theta_{21}$ is the refraction angle in medium 2. Similarly,

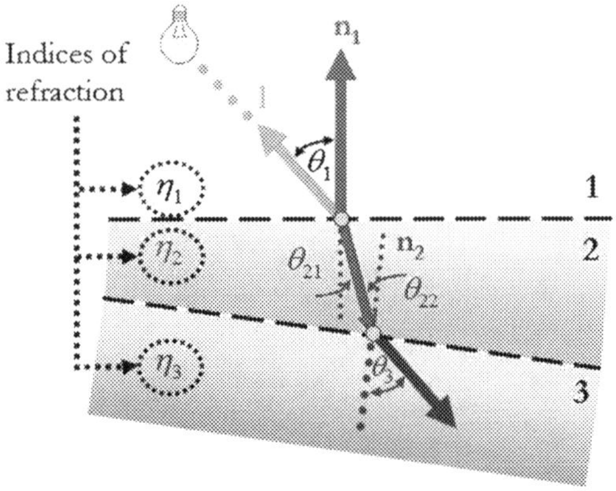


**Fig. 11.21** A ray of light penetrates three different media *1*, *2* and *3*. The plane of intersection between media *1* and *2* is *not* parallel to the plane of intersection between media *2* and *3*

considering the second refraction that happens as the ray passes from medium 2 to medium 3 and according to Eq. (11.33), we have

$$\eta_2 \sin\theta_{22} = \eta_3 \sin\theta_3,$$

where $\eta_2$ and $\eta_3$ are the indices of refraction of media 2 and 3 respectively; $\theta_{22}$ is the incidence angle in medium 2; and $\theta_3$ is the refraction angle in medium 3.

Since the plane of intersection between media 1 and 2 is parallel to the plane of intersection between media 2 and 3, the refraction angle $\theta_{21}$ in medium 2 is equal to the incidence angle $\theta_{22}$ in the same medium. Thus,

$$\eta_1 \sin\theta_1 = \eta_2 \sin\theta_{21} = \eta_2 \sin\theta_{22} = \eta_3 \sin\theta_3.$$

Consequently,

$$\theta_3 = \sin^{-1}\left(\frac{\eta_1 \sin\theta_1}{\eta_3}\right). \qquad \square$$

**Example 11.18:** [*Refraction rays—refraction angles*]

Figure 11.21 shows a ray of light as penetrating three different media; 1, 2 and 3. It gets refracted while passing from medium 1 to medium 2 and it gets refracted again while passing from medium 2 to medium 3. The plane of intersection between media 1 and 2 is *not* parallel to the plane of intersection between media 2 and 3. Determine the refraction angle $\theta_3$ in terms of the incidence angle $\theta_1$ where $\theta_3$ is the second refraction angle and $\theta_1$ is the first incidence angle.

**Solution 11.18:** Considering the first refraction that happens as the ray passes from medium 1 to medium 2 and according to Eq. (11.33), we have

$$\eta_1 \sin\theta_1 = \eta_2 \sin\theta_{21}, \tag{11.39}$$

where $\eta_1$ and $\eta_2$ are the indices of refraction of media 1 and 2 respectively; $\theta_1$ is the incidence angle in medium 1; and $\theta_{21}$ is the refraction angle in medium 2. Similarly, considering the second refraction that happens as the ray passes from medium 2 to medium 3 and according to Eq. (11.33), we have

$$\eta_2 \sin\theta_{22} = \eta_3 \sin\theta_3, \tag{11.40}$$

where $\eta_2$ and $\eta_3$ are the indices of refraction of media 2 and 3 respectively; $\theta_{22}$ is the incidence angle in medium 2; and $\theta_3$ is the refraction angle in medium 3.

Unlike Example 11.17, the refraction angle $\theta_{21}$ in medium 2 is *not* equal to the incidence angle $\theta_{22}$ in the same medium because the plane of intersection between media 1 and 2 is not parallel to the plane of intersection between media 2 and 3.

From Eq. (11.39), the index of refraction $\eta_2$ of the second medium can be expressed as

$$\eta_2 = \eta_1 \frac{\sin\theta_1}{\sin\theta_{21}}.$$

Substituting the value of $\eta_2$ in Eq. (11.40), we get

$$\eta_1 \frac{\sin\theta_1}{\sin\theta_{21}} \sin\theta_{22} = \eta_3 \sin\theta_3.$$

Consequently,

$$\theta_3 = \sin^{-1}\left(\frac{\eta_1 \sin\theta_1 \sin\theta_{22}}{\eta_3 \sin\theta_{21}}\right). \qquad \square$$

## 11.5 Shading Models

In the previous sections, we discussed how lighting effect is estimated using reflection models. Such calculations may be done at surface vertices while the rest of the points comprising the surface are assigned colors through shading. *Shading* is the process of assigning shades of colors to pixels or points based on their angles and distances to light sources (i.e., according to variations in lighting). Different angles and distances with respect to light sources result in different degrees of shading. Figure 11.22a shows a box when no shading effect exists, which results in the same color assigned to all faces of the box. On the other hand, Fig. 11.22b applies shading effect where the same color is assigned to all pixels of a given surface.

In fact, the most common types of shading or shading models used on 3D objects are:

1. Constant shading. An example is shown in Fig. 11.23a.
2. Flat or faceted shading. An example is shown in Fig. 11.23b.

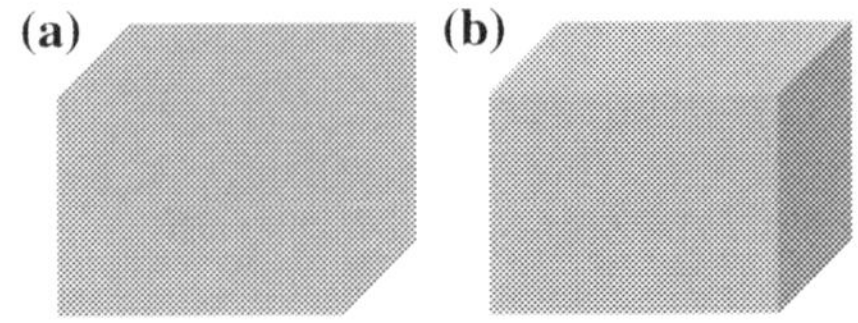


**Fig. 11.22** Shading effect: **a** No shading used or constant shading. **b** Flat shading used where the same color is assigned to all pixels of a given surface

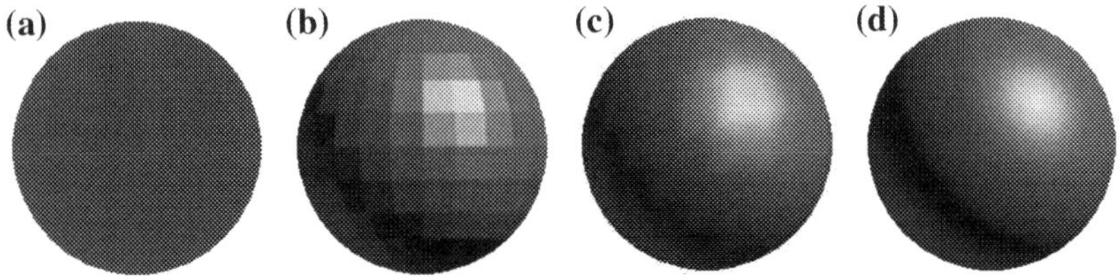


**Fig. 11.23** Shading types: **a** Constant shading. **b** Flat shading. **c** Gouraud shading. **d** Phong shading

3. Gouraud shading. An example is shown in Fig. 11.23c.
4. Phong shading. An example is shown in Fig. 11.23d.

Among these types, the quality of the images produced increases from constant to flat to Gouraud while the best quality is achieved using Phong shading model. Increasing of image shading quality comes with more expensive computation that gradually increases to reach its maximum peak with Phong shading. In the sections to follow, we will discuss each of these shading models.

## 11.5.1 Constant Shading

*Constant* shading applies one color or one shade to all points of the object as shown in Figs. 11.22a and 11.23a. This shading model produces unrealistic images for 3D models.

## 11.5.2 Flat Shading

One of the simplest and easiest shading models is *flat* or *faceted* model. In this model, one color or one shade is assigned to each face or surface as shown in Fig. 11.22b. The important factors affecting the computed color are:

1. The angle between the normal to the surface plane and the vector connecting a point on the plane (e.g., a vertex) and the light source.
2. The intensity/color of the surface.
3. The intensity/color of the light source.

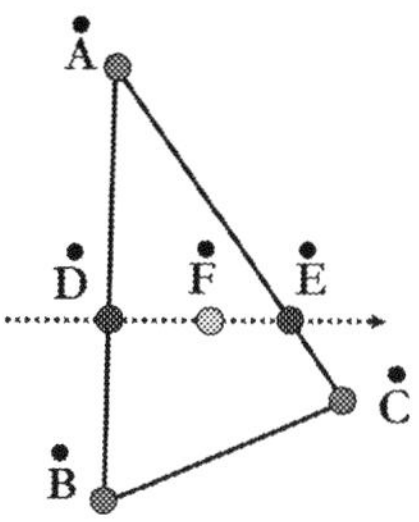


**Fig. 11.24** Scan line interpolation: Shading a point in a triangle

This shading model is computationally inexpensive but produces not-very-realistic images for 3D models especially with curved surfaces and when specular highlights are expected as shown in Fig. 11.23b. Since it is fast, it is suitable for preview purposes.

## *11.5.3 Gouraud Shading*

*Gouraud* shading (Gouraud 1971a, b) (which is named after Henri Gouraud) is used to better simulate gradual shading across polygonal surfaces according to differing effect of light and color. The idea is as follows:

1. For curved surfaces approximated as polygons, obtain the normal vector at each vertex of the polygon being shaded. The normal is calculated as the average normal of all polygons meeting at that vertex.
2. Calculate the intensity, shade or color at this vertex (e.g., using a reflection model).
3. Interpolate colors among vertices to shade internal pixels.

Different methods may be used to assign colors to pixels; however, the same results are expected utilizing any method. The following sections assume that the polygons to be shaded are triangles. We will talk about scan line interpolation and parametric and barycentric coordinates. According to the available input information, one method may be preferred over the other.

### 11.5.3.1 Scan Line Interpolation

Coloring a pixel inside a triangle can be done using a horizontal scan line and bilinear interpolation as discussed in Sect. 12.4. Consider the triangle $\triangle\dot{\mathbf{A}}\dot{\mathbf{B}}\dot{\mathbf{C}}$ shown in Fig. 11.24 with known shades at its vertices. The intensity, shade or color of point $\dot{\mathbf{F}}$ can be estimated by linearly interpolating the shades along $\overline{\dot{\mathbf{A}}\dot{\mathbf{B}}}$ and $\overline{\dot{\mathbf{A}}\dot{\mathbf{C}}}$ to get the shades at $\dot{\mathbf{D}}$ and $\dot{\mathbf{E}}$ as

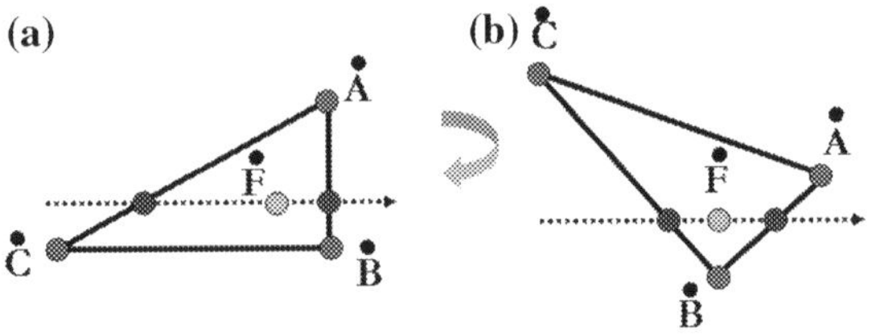


**Fig. 11.25** Scan line interpolation: **a** $\dot{\mathbf{F}}$ gets its shade from $\overline{\dot{\mathbf{A}}\dot{\mathbf{C}}}$ and $\overline{\dot{\mathbf{A}}\dot{\mathbf{B}}}$. **b** $\dot{\mathbf{F}}$ gets its shade from $\overline{\dot{\mathbf{C}}\dot{\mathbf{B}}}$ and $\overline{\dot{\mathbf{A}}\dot{\mathbf{B}}}$

$$I_{\dot{\mathbf{D}}} = I_{\dot{\mathbf{A}}} \frac{\|\dot{\mathbf{B}} - \dot{\mathbf{D}}\|}{\|\dot{\mathbf{B}} - \dot{\mathbf{A}}\|} + I_{\dot{\mathbf{B}}} \frac{\|\dot{\mathbf{A}} - \dot{\mathbf{D}}\|}{\|\dot{\mathbf{B}} - \dot{\mathbf{A}}\|} \tag{11.41}$$

and

$$I_{\dot{\mathbf{E}}} = I_{\dot{\mathbf{A}}} \frac{\|\dot{\mathbf{C}} - \dot{\mathbf{E}}\|}{\|\dot{\mathbf{C}} - \dot{\mathbf{A}}\|} + I_{\dot{\mathbf{C}}} \frac{\|\dot{\mathbf{A}} - \dot{\mathbf{E}}\|}{\|\dot{\mathbf{C}} - \dot{\mathbf{A}}\|}, \tag{11.42}$$

where $I_{\dot{\mathbf{A}}}$, $I_{\dot{\mathbf{B}}}$, $I_{\dot{\mathbf{C}}}$, $I_{\dot{\mathbf{D}}}$ and $I_{\dot{\mathbf{E}}}$ are the intensities, shades or colors at $\dot{\mathbf{A}}$, $\dot{\mathbf{B}}$, $\dot{\mathbf{C}}$, $\dot{\mathbf{D}}$ and $\dot{\mathbf{E}}$ respectively; and $\|.\|$ denotes the norm. Once $I_{\dot{\mathbf{D}}}$ and $I_{\dot{\mathbf{E}}}$ are obtained, $I_{\dot{\mathbf{F}}}$ is estimated by linearly interpolating the shades along $\overline{\dot{\mathbf{D}}\dot{\mathbf{E}}}$ as

$$I_{\dot{\mathbf{F}}} = I_{\dot{\mathbf{D}}} \frac{\|\dot{\mathbf{E}} - \dot{\mathbf{F}}\|}{\|\dot{\mathbf{E}} - \dot{\mathbf{D}}\|} + I_{\dot{\mathbf{E}}} \frac{\|\dot{\mathbf{D}} - \dot{\mathbf{F}}\|}{\|\dot{\mathbf{E}} - \dot{\mathbf{D}}\|}, \tag{11.43}$$

where $I_{\dot{\mathbf{D}}}$, $I_{\dot{\mathbf{E}}}$ and $I_{\dot{\mathbf{F}}}$ are the intensities, shades or colors at $\dot{\mathbf{D}}$, $\dot{\mathbf{E}}$ and $\dot{\mathbf{F}}$ respectively; and $\|.\|$ denotes the norm.

With this technique, a problem may happen when rotating a shape. Consider Fig. 11.25a, which shows a triangle $\triangle\dot{\mathbf{A}}\dot{\mathbf{B}}\dot{\mathbf{C}}$. In this case, point $\dot{\mathbf{F}}$ gets its shade from $\overline{\dot{\mathbf{A}}\dot{\mathbf{C}}}$ and $\overline{\dot{\mathbf{A}}\dot{\mathbf{B}}}$. If this triangle is rotated as shown in Fig. 11.25b, point $\dot{\mathbf{F}}$ gets its shade from $\overline{\dot{\mathbf{C}}\dot{\mathbf{B}}}$ and $\overline{\dot{\mathbf{A}}\dot{\mathbf{B}}}$. Hence, different results might be achieved.

**Example 11.19:** [*Scan line interpolation*]

The vertices of a triangle are placed at the positions $\dot{\mathbf{A}} = [0, 0, 0]^T$, $\dot{\mathbf{B}} = [5, 0, 0]^T$ and $\dot{\mathbf{C}} = [0, 5, 0]^T$. The intensities found at the vertices are 100, 150 and 200 for $\dot{\mathbf{A}}$, $\dot{\mathbf{B}}$ and $\dot{\mathbf{C}}$ respectively. Calculate the intensity at $\dot{\mathbf{P}} = [2, 2, 0]^T$ using the scan line interpolation method.

**Solution 11.19:** The triangle $\triangle\dot{\mathbf{A}}\dot{\mathbf{B}}\dot{\mathbf{C}}$ is depicted in Fig. 11.26. It is easy to show the positions of $\dot{\mathbf{D}} = [0, 2, 0]^T$ and $\dot{\mathbf{E}} = [3, 2, 0]^T$ where $\dot{\mathbf{D}}$ and $\dot{\mathbf{E}}$ are the intersections between the horizontal scan line $y = 2$ and $\overline{\dot{\mathbf{A}}\dot{\mathbf{C}}}$ and $\overline{\dot{\mathbf{B}}\dot{\mathbf{C}}}$ respectively. We perform the following steps:

1. Get the intensity $I_{\dot{\mathbf{D}}}$ at point $\dot{\mathbf{D}}$ using Eq. (11.41) where

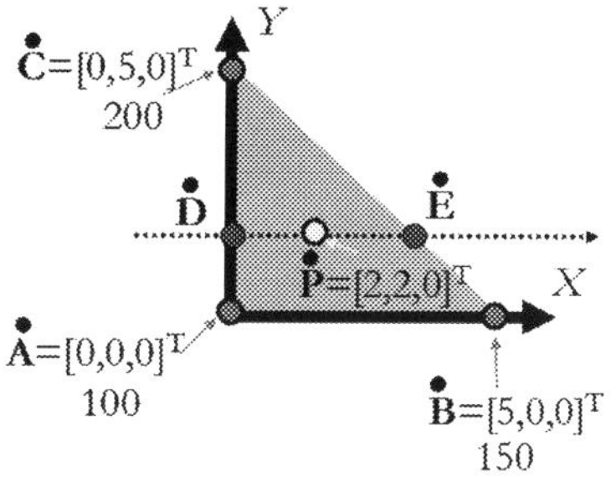


**Fig. 11.26** Given the intensities at the vertices of a triangle, the intensity at an internal point can be calculated using scan line interpolation

$$
\begin{aligned}
I_{\dot{\mathbf{D}}} &= I_{\dot{\mathbf{A}}} \frac{\|\dot{\mathbf{C}} - \dot{\mathbf{D}}\|}{\|\dot{\mathbf{C}} - \dot{\mathbf{A}}\|} + I_{\dot{\mathbf{C}}} \frac{\|\dot{\mathbf{A}} - \dot{\mathbf{D}}\|}{\|\dot{\mathbf{C}} - \dot{\mathbf{A}}\|} \\
&= 100 \frac{\left\| \begin{bmatrix} 0 \\ 5 \\ 0 \end{bmatrix} - \begin{bmatrix} 0 \\ 2 \\ 0 \end{bmatrix} \right\|}{\left\| \begin{bmatrix} 0 \\ 5 \\ 0 \end{bmatrix} - \begin{bmatrix} 0 \\ 0 \\ 0 \end{bmatrix} \right\|} + 200 \frac{\left\| \begin{bmatrix} 0 \\ 0 \\ 0 \end{bmatrix} - \begin{bmatrix} 0 \\ 2 \\ 0 \end{bmatrix} \right\|}{\left\| \begin{bmatrix} 0 \\ 5 \\ 0 \end{bmatrix} - \begin{bmatrix} 0 \\ 0 \\ 0 \end{bmatrix} \right\|} \\
&= 100 \times \frac{3}{5} + 200 \times \frac{2}{5} = 140.
\end{aligned}
$$

2. Get the intensity $I_{\dot{\mathbf{E}}}$ at point $\dot{\mathbf{E}}$ using Eq. (11.42). Thus,

$$
\begin{aligned}
I_{\dot{\mathbf{E}}} &= I_{\dot{\mathbf{B}}} \frac{\|\dot{\mathbf{C}} - \dot{\mathbf{E}}\|}{\|\dot{\mathbf{C}} - \dot{\mathbf{B}}\|} + I_{\dot{\mathbf{C}}} \frac{\|\dot{\mathbf{B}} - \dot{\mathbf{E}}\|}{\|\dot{\mathbf{C}} - \dot{\mathbf{B}}\|} \\
&= 150 \frac{\left\| \begin{bmatrix} 0 \\ 5 \\ 0 \end{bmatrix} - \begin{bmatrix} 3 \\ 2 \\ 0 \end{bmatrix} \right\|}{\left\| \begin{bmatrix} 0 \\ 5 \\ 0 \end{bmatrix} - \begin{bmatrix} 5 \\ 0 \\ 0 \end{bmatrix} \right\|} + 200 \frac{\left\| \begin{bmatrix} 5 \\ 0 \\ 0 \end{bmatrix} - \begin{bmatrix} 3 \\ 2 \\ 0 \end{bmatrix} \right\|}{\left\| \begin{bmatrix} 0 \\ 5 \\ 0 \end{bmatrix} - \begin{bmatrix} 5 \\ 0 \\ 0 \end{bmatrix} \right\|} \\
&= 150 \times \frac{3}{5} + 200 \times \frac{2}{5} = 170.
\end{aligned}
$$

3. Get the intensity $I_{\dot{\mathbf{P}}}$ at point $\dot{\mathbf{P}}$ using Eq. (11.43) where

$$
I_{\dot{\mathbf{P}}} = I_{\dot{\mathbf{D}}} \frac{\|\dot{\mathbf{E}} - \dot{\mathbf{P}}\|}{\|\dot{\mathbf{E}} - \dot{\mathbf{D}}\|} + I_{\dot{\mathbf{E}}} \frac{\|\dot{\mathbf{D}} - \dot{\mathbf{P}}\|}{\|\dot{\mathbf{E}} - \dot{\mathbf{D}}\|}
$$

$$= 140 \frac{\left\| \begin{bmatrix} 3 \\ 2 \\ 0 \end{bmatrix} - \begin{bmatrix} 2 \\ 2 \\ 0 \end{bmatrix} \right\|}{\left\| \begin{bmatrix} 3 \\ 2 \\ 0 \end{bmatrix} - \begin{bmatrix} 0 \\ 2 \\ 0 \end{bmatrix} \right\|} + 170 \frac{\left\| \begin{bmatrix} 0 \\ 2 \\ 0 \end{bmatrix} - \begin{bmatrix} 2 \\ 2 \\ 0 \end{bmatrix} \right\|}{\left\| \begin{bmatrix} 3 \\ 2 \\ 0 \end{bmatrix} - \begin{bmatrix} 0 \\ 2 \\ 0 \end{bmatrix} \right\|}$$

$$= 140 \times \frac{1}{3} + 170 \times \frac{2}{3} = 160.$$

□

#### 11.5.3.2 Parametric Coordinates

As discussed in Sect. B.2.1, considering a triangle $\triangle \dot{\mathbf{A}}\dot{\mathbf{B}}\dot{\mathbf{C}}$ and an internal point $\dot{\mathbf{P}}$, the parametric coordinates $[u, v]^T$ of $\dot{\mathbf{P}}$ are calculated as

$$\begin{aligned} \mathbf{u} &= \dot{\mathbf{B}} - \dot{\mathbf{A}}, \\ \mathbf{v} &= \dot{\mathbf{C}} - \dot{\mathbf{A}}, \\ \mathbf{w} &= \dot{\mathbf{P}} - \dot{\mathbf{A}}, \\ \begin{bmatrix} u \\ v \end{bmatrix} &= \begin{bmatrix} \dfrac{(\mathbf{u}\cdot\mathbf{v})(\mathbf{w}\cdot\mathbf{v}) - (\mathbf{v}\cdot\mathbf{v})(\mathbf{w}\cdot\mathbf{u})}{(\mathbf{u}\cdot\mathbf{v})^2 - (\mathbf{u}\cdot\mathbf{u})(\mathbf{v}\cdot\mathbf{v})} \\ \dfrac{(\mathbf{u}\cdot\mathbf{v})(\mathbf{w}\cdot\mathbf{u}) - (\mathbf{u}\cdot\mathbf{u})(\mathbf{w}\cdot\mathbf{v})}{(\mathbf{u}\cdot\mathbf{v})^2 - (\mathbf{u}\cdot\mathbf{u})(\mathbf{v}\cdot\mathbf{v})} \end{bmatrix}, \end{aligned} \tag{11.44}$$

where $\cdot$ indicates the dot product. Then, the intensity, shade or color at $\dot{\mathbf{P}}$ is defined as

$$I_{\dot{\mathbf{P}}} = I_{\dot{\mathbf{A}}} + u\left(I_{\dot{\mathbf{B}}} - I_{\dot{\mathbf{A}}}\right) + v\left(I_{\dot{\mathbf{C}}} - I_{\dot{\mathbf{A}}}\right), \tag{11.45}$$

where $I_{\dot{\mathbf{A}}}$, $I_{\dot{\mathbf{B}}}$, $I_{\dot{\mathbf{C}}}$ and $I_{\dot{\mathbf{P}}}$ are the intensities, shades or colors at $\dot{\mathbf{A}}$, $\dot{\mathbf{B}}$, $\dot{\mathbf{C}}$ and $\dot{\mathbf{P}}$ respectively; and $[u, v]^T$ represent the parametric coordinates of $\dot{\mathbf{P}}$.

**Example 11.20:** [*Intensity using parametric coordinates*]

The vertices of a triangle are placed at the positions $\dot{\mathbf{A}} = [0, 0, 0]^T$, $\dot{\mathbf{B}} = [5, 0, 0]^T$ and $\dot{\mathbf{C}} = [0, 5, 0]^T$. The intensities found at the vertices are 100, 150 and 200 for $\dot{\mathbf{A}}$, $\dot{\mathbf{B}}$ and $\dot{\mathbf{C}}$ respectively. Calculate the intensity at $\dot{\mathbf{P}} = [2, 2, 0]^T$ using parametric coordinates.

**Solution 11.20:** Consider $\dot{\mathbf{A}}$ to be the origin of the parametric system. Using Eq. (11.44), the parametric coordinates $[u, v]^T$ can be calculated as

$$\mathbf{u} = \dot{\mathbf{B}} - \dot{\mathbf{A}} = \begin{bmatrix} 5 \\ 0 \\ 0 \end{bmatrix} - \begin{bmatrix} 0 \\ 0 \\ 0 \end{bmatrix} = \begin{bmatrix} 5 \\ 0 \\ 0 \end{bmatrix},$$

$$\mathbf{v} = \dot{\mathbf{C}} - \dot{\mathbf{A}} = \begin{bmatrix} 0 \\ 5 \\ 0 \end{bmatrix} - \begin{bmatrix} 0 \\ 0 \\ 0 \end{bmatrix} = \begin{bmatrix} 0 \\ 5 \\ 0 \end{bmatrix},$$

$$\mathbf{w} = \dot{\mathbf{P}} - \dot{\mathbf{A}} = \begin{bmatrix} 2 \\ 2 \\ 0 \end{bmatrix} - \begin{bmatrix} 0 \\ 0 \\ 0 \end{bmatrix} = \begin{bmatrix} 2 \\ 2 \\ 0 \end{bmatrix},$$

$$\begin{aligned} u &= \frac{(\mathbf{u}\cdot\mathbf{v})(\mathbf{w}\cdot\mathbf{v}) - (\mathbf{v}\cdot\mathbf{v})(\mathbf{w}\cdot\mathbf{u})}{(\mathbf{u}\cdot\mathbf{v})^2 - (\mathbf{u}\cdot\mathbf{u})(\mathbf{v}\cdot\mathbf{v})} \\ &= \frac{\left(\begin{bmatrix} 5 \\ 0 \\ 0 \end{bmatrix} \cdot \begin{bmatrix} 0 \\ 5 \\ 0 \end{bmatrix}\right)\left(\begin{bmatrix} 2 \\ 2 \\ 0 \end{bmatrix} \cdot \begin{bmatrix} 0 \\ 5 \\ 0 \end{bmatrix}\right) - \left(\begin{bmatrix} 0 \\ 5 \\ 0 \end{bmatrix} \cdot \begin{bmatrix} 0 \\ 5 \\ 0 \end{bmatrix}\right)\left(\begin{bmatrix} 2 \\ 2 \\ 0 \end{bmatrix} \cdot \begin{bmatrix} 5 \\ 0 \\ 0 \end{bmatrix}\right)}{\left(\begin{bmatrix} 5 \\ 0 \\ 0 \end{bmatrix} \cdot \begin{bmatrix} 0 \\ 5 \\ 0 \end{bmatrix}\right)^2 - \left(\begin{bmatrix} 5 \\ 0 \\ 0 \end{bmatrix} \cdot \begin{bmatrix} 5 \\ 0 \\ 0 \end{bmatrix}\right)\left(\begin{bmatrix} 0 \\ 5 \\ 0 \end{bmatrix} \cdot \begin{bmatrix} 0 \\ 5 \\ 0 \end{bmatrix}\right)} = 0.4, \end{aligned}$$

$$\begin{aligned} v &= \frac{(\mathbf{u}\cdot\mathbf{v})(\mathbf{w}\cdot\mathbf{u}) - (\mathbf{u}\cdot\mathbf{u})(\mathbf{w}\cdot\mathbf{v})}{(\mathbf{u}\cdot\mathbf{v})^2 - (\mathbf{u}\cdot\mathbf{u})(\mathbf{v}\cdot\mathbf{v})} \\ &= \frac{\left(\begin{bmatrix} 5 \\ 0 \\ 0 \end{bmatrix} \cdot \begin{bmatrix} 0 \\ 5 \\ 0 \end{bmatrix}\right)\left(\begin{bmatrix} 2 \\ 2 \\ 0 \end{bmatrix} \cdot \begin{bmatrix} 5 \\ 0 \\ 0 \end{bmatrix}\right) - \left(\begin{bmatrix} 5 \\ 0 \\ 0 \end{bmatrix} \cdot \begin{bmatrix} 5 \\ 0 \\ 0 \end{bmatrix}\right)\left(\begin{bmatrix} 2 \\ 2 \\ 0 \end{bmatrix} \cdot \begin{bmatrix} 0 \\ 5 \\ 0 \end{bmatrix}\right)}{\left(\begin{bmatrix} 5 \\ 0 \\ 0 \end{bmatrix} \cdot \begin{bmatrix} 0 \\ 5 \\ 0 \end{bmatrix}\right)^2 - \left(\begin{bmatrix} 5 \\ 0 \\ 0 \end{bmatrix} \cdot \begin{bmatrix} 5 \\ 0 \\ 0 \end{bmatrix}\right)\left(\begin{bmatrix} 0 \\ 5 \\ 0 \end{bmatrix} \cdot \begin{bmatrix} 0 \\ 5 \\ 0 \end{bmatrix}\right)} = 0.4. \end{aligned}$$

Hence, the intensity, shade or color at point $\dot{\mathbf{P}}$ is estimated using Eq. (11.45) as

$$\begin{aligned} I_{\dot{\mathbf{P}}} &= I_{\dot{\mathbf{A}}} + u\left(I_{\dot{\mathbf{B}}} - I_{\dot{\mathbf{A}}}\right) + v\left(I_{\dot{\mathbf{C}}} - I_{\dot{\mathbf{A}}}\right) \\ &= 100 + 0.4 \times (150 - 100) + 0.4 \times (200 - 100) = 160. \end{aligned}$$ □

#### 11.5.3.3 Barycentric Coordinates

A point in a triangle can be expressed in barycentric coordinates as a triplet of numbers $\left[t_{\dot{\mathbf{A}}}, t_{\dot{\mathbf{B}}}, t_{\dot{\mathbf{C}}}\right]^T$ as discussed in Sect. B.3. These coordinates; i.e., $t_{\dot{\mathbf{A}}}$, $t_{\dot{\mathbf{B}}}$ and $t_{\dot{\mathbf{C}}}$ correspond to the ratios of the sub-triangles formed by the vertices of the triangle and the internal point. Considering a triangle $\triangle\dot{\mathbf{A}}\dot{\mathbf{B}}\dot{\mathbf{C}}$, the barycentric coordinates of an internal point $\dot{\mathbf{P}}$ is estimated as

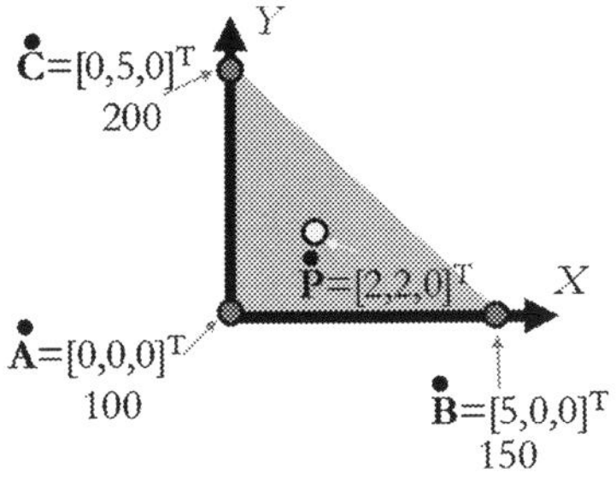


**Fig. 11.27** Given the intensities at the vertices of a triangle, the intensity at an internal point can be calculated using barycentric coordinates

$$\begin{bmatrix} t_{\dot{\mathbf{A}}} \\ t_{\dot{\mathbf{B}}} \\ t_{\dot{\mathbf{C}}} \end{bmatrix} = \frac{1}{A} \begin{bmatrix} A_{\dot{\mathbf{A}}} \\ A_{\dot{\mathbf{B}}} \\ A_{\dot{\mathbf{C}}} \end{bmatrix}, \tag{11.46}$$

where $A_{\dot{\mathbf{A}}}$ is the area of sub-triangle $\triangle\dot{\mathbf{P}}\dot{\mathbf{B}}\dot{\mathbf{C}}$; $A_{\dot{\mathbf{B}}}$ is the area of sub-triangle $\triangle\dot{\mathbf{P}}\dot{\mathbf{C}}\dot{\mathbf{A}}$; $A_{\dot{\mathbf{C}}}$ is the area of sub-triangle $\triangle\dot{\mathbf{P}}\dot{\mathbf{A}}\dot{\mathbf{B}}$; and $A$ is the area of the triangle $\triangle\dot{\mathbf{A}}\dot{\mathbf{B}}\dot{\mathbf{C}}$, which is equal to $A_{\dot{\mathbf{A}}} + A_{\dot{\mathbf{B}}} + A_{\dot{\mathbf{C}}}$. Hence, the intensity, shade or color at $\dot{\mathbf{P}}$ is calculated as

$$I_{\dot{\mathbf{P}}} = I_{\dot{\mathbf{A}}} t_{\dot{\mathbf{A}}} + I_{\dot{\mathbf{B}}} t_{\dot{\mathbf{B}}} + I_{\dot{\mathbf{C}}} t_{\dot{\mathbf{C}}}, \tag{11.47}$$

where $I_{\dot{\mathbf{A}}}$, $I_{\dot{\mathbf{B}}}$, $I_{\dot{\mathbf{C}}}$ and $I_{\dot{\mathbf{P}}}$ are the intensities, shades or colors at $\dot{\mathbf{A}}$, $\dot{\mathbf{B}}$, $\dot{\mathbf{C}}$ and $\dot{\mathbf{P}}$ respectively; and $\left[t_{\dot{\mathbf{A}}}, t_{\dot{\mathbf{B}}}, t_{\dot{\mathbf{C}}}\right]^T$ represent the barycentric coordinates of $\dot{\mathbf{P}}$.

**Example 11.21:** [*Intensity using barycentric coordinates*]

The vertices of a triangle are placed at the positions $\dot{\mathbf{A}} = [0, 0, 0]^T$, $\dot{\mathbf{B}} = [5, 0, 0]^T$ and $\dot{\mathbf{C}} = [0, 5, 0]^T$. The intensities found at the vertices are 100, 150 and 200 for $\dot{\mathbf{A}}$, $\dot{\mathbf{B}}$ and $\dot{\mathbf{C}}$ respectively. Calculate the intensity at $\dot{\mathbf{P}} = [2, 2, 0]^T$ using barycentric coordinates.

**Solution 11.21:** The triangle $\triangle\dot{\mathbf{A}}\dot{\mathbf{B}}\dot{\mathbf{C}}$ is depicted in Fig. 11.27. The area of the triangle $\triangle\dot{\mathbf{A}}\dot{\mathbf{B}}\dot{\mathbf{C}}$ is calculated as

$$A = \frac{5 \times 5}{2} = 12.5.$$

The areas of the sub-triangles $\triangle\dot{\mathbf{P}}\dot{\mathbf{A}}\dot{\mathbf{B}}$, $\triangle\dot{\mathbf{P}}\dot{\mathbf{C}}\dot{\mathbf{A}}$ and $\triangle\dot{\mathbf{P}}\dot{\mathbf{B}}\dot{\mathbf{C}}$ are the following:

$$A_{\dot{\mathbf{C}}} = \frac{2 \times 5}{2} = 5,$$

$$A_{\dot{\mathbf{B}}} = \frac{2 \times 5}{2} = 5,$$

$$A_{\dot{\mathbf{A}}} = 12.5 - 10 = 2.5.$$

Thus, the ratios are calculated using Eq. (11.46) as

$$\begin{bmatrix} t_{\dot{\mathbf{A}}} \\ t_{\dot{\mathbf{B}}} \\ t_{\dot{\mathbf{C}}} \end{bmatrix} = \frac{1}{A} \begin{bmatrix} A_{\dot{\mathbf{A}}} \\ A_{\dot{\mathbf{B}}} \\ A_{\dot{\mathbf{C}}} \end{bmatrix} = \frac{1}{12.5} \begin{bmatrix} 2.5 \\ 5 \\ 5 \end{bmatrix} = \begin{bmatrix} 0.2 \\ 0.4 \\ 0.4 \end{bmatrix}.$$

Hence, the intensity at $\dot{\mathbf{P}} = [2, 2, 0]^T$ is estimated using Eq. (11.47) as

$$\begin{aligned} I_{\dot{\mathbf{P}}} &= I_{\dot{\mathbf{A}}} t_{\dot{\mathbf{A}}} + I_{\dot{\mathbf{B}}} t_{\dot{\mathbf{B}}} + I_{\dot{\mathbf{C}}} t_{\dot{\mathbf{C}}} \\ &= 100 \times 0.2 + 150 \times 0.4 + 200 \times 0.4 = 160. \end{aligned}$$

□

## *11.5.4 Phong Shading*

Gouraud shading model uses the colors calculated at the vertices of a polygon to interpolate shades across the polygon. Consequently, if there is a specular highlight (i.e., a bright spot appearing on shiny objects when illuminated) near the center of the polygon, it will be missed. *Phong* shading model avoids this problem by proceeding as follows:

1. Obtain the normal vectors at each vertex of the polygon being shaded.
2. Interpolate normal vectors for each pixel among vertices to get one normal vector per pixel.
3. Use the normal vector obtained at a pixel after normalization to calculate the intensity, shade or color at this pixel using a reflection model.

Phong shading results in more realistic look than Gouraud shading especially at specular highlight areas. This comes with a cost of more computation.

**Important**: *Phong reflection model is not Phong shading!* A reflection model uses an equation to assign intensity, color or shade to points based on surface normal, material, illumination and viewer direction. On the other hand, Phong shading is an interpolation process that is used to interpolate normals. This shading process may be used with Phong reflection model or any other model in this regard.

### 11.5.4.1 Scan Line Interpolation

Similar to what was done in Sect. 11.5.3.1, the normal vector at point $\dot{\mathbf{F}}$ of Fig. 11.24 can be estimated by linearly interpolating the normal vectors along $\overline{\dot{\mathbf{A}}\dot{\mathbf{B}}}$ and $\overline{\dot{\mathbf{A}}\dot{\mathbf{C}}}$ to get the normal vectors at $\dot{\mathbf{D}}$ and $\dot{\mathbf{E}}$. These are

$$\mathbf{n}_{\dot{\mathbf{D}}} = \mathbf{n}_{\dot{\mathbf{A}}} \frac{\|\dot{\mathbf{B}} - \dot{\mathbf{D}}\|}{\|\dot{\mathbf{B}} - \dot{\mathbf{A}}\|} + \mathbf{n}_{\dot{\mathbf{B}}} \frac{\|\dot{\mathbf{A}} - \dot{\mathbf{D}}\|}{\|\dot{\mathbf{B}} - \dot{\mathbf{A}}\|} \tag{11.48}$$

and

$$\mathbf{n}_{\dot{\mathbf{E}}} = \mathbf{n}_{\dot{\mathbf{A}}} \frac{\|\dot{\mathbf{C}} - \dot{\mathbf{E}}\|}{\|\dot{\mathbf{C}} - \dot{\mathbf{A}}\|} + \mathbf{n}_{\dot{\mathbf{C}}} \frac{\|\dot{\mathbf{A}} - \dot{\mathbf{E}}\|}{\|\dot{\mathbf{C}} - \dot{\mathbf{A}}\|}, \tag{11.49}$$

where $\mathbf{n}_{\dot{\mathbf{A}}}$, $\mathbf{n}_{\dot{\mathbf{B}}}$, $\mathbf{n}_{\dot{\mathbf{C}}}$, $\mathbf{n}_{\dot{\mathbf{D}}}$ and $\mathbf{n}_{\dot{\mathbf{E}}}$ are the normal vectors at $\dot{\mathbf{A}}$, $\dot{\mathbf{B}}$, $\dot{\mathbf{C}}$, $\dot{\mathbf{D}}$ and $\dot{\mathbf{E}}$ respectively; and $\|.\|$ denotes the norm. Once $\mathbf{n}_{\dot{\mathbf{D}}}$ and $\mathbf{n}_{\dot{\mathbf{E}}}$ are obtained, $\mathbf{n}_{\dot{\mathbf{F}}}$ is estimated by linearly interpolating the normal vectors along $\overline{\dot{\mathbf{D}}\dot{\mathbf{E}}}$ as

$$\mathbf{n}_{\dot{\mathbf{F}}} = \mathbf{n}_{\dot{\mathbf{D}}} \frac{\|\dot{\mathbf{E}} - \dot{\mathbf{F}}\|}{\|\dot{\mathbf{E}} - \dot{\mathbf{D}}\|} + \mathbf{n}_{\dot{\mathbf{E}}} \frac{\|\dot{\mathbf{D}} - \dot{\mathbf{F}}\|}{\|\dot{\mathbf{E}} - \dot{\mathbf{D}}\|}, \tag{11.50}$$

where $\mathbf{n}_{\dot{\mathbf{D}}}$, $\mathbf{n}_{\dot{\mathbf{E}}}$ and $\mathbf{n}_{\dot{\mathbf{F}}}$ are the normal vectors at $\dot{\mathbf{D}}$, $\dot{\mathbf{E}}$ and $\dot{\mathbf{F}}$ respectively; and $\|.\|$ denotes the norm.

**Example 11.22:** [*Phong shading—calculating normal vector using scan line interpolation*]

The vertices of a triangle are placed at the positions $\dot{\mathbf{A}} = [0, 0, 0]^T$, $\dot{\mathbf{B}} = [5, 0, 0]^T$ and $\dot{\mathbf{C}} = [0, 5, 0]^T$. The normal vectors at the vertices $\dot{\mathbf{A}}$, $\dot{\mathbf{B}}$ and $\dot{\mathbf{C}}$ are $\mathbf{n}_{\dot{\mathbf{A}}} = [3, 4, 5]^T$, $\mathbf{n}_{\dot{\mathbf{B}}} = [7, 8, 6]^T$ and $\mathbf{n}_{\dot{\mathbf{C}}} = [10, 10, 7]^T$ respectively. If Phong shading is to be applied to this triangle, calculate the normal vector at the position $\dot{\mathbf{P}} = [2, 2, 0]^T$ using scan line interpolation.

**Solution 11.22:** The triangle $\triangle\dot{\mathbf{A}}\dot{\mathbf{B}}\dot{\mathbf{C}}$ is depicted in Fig. 11.26. We proceed as follows:

1. Get the normal vector $\mathbf{n}_{\dot{\mathbf{D}}}$ at point $\dot{\mathbf{D}}$ using Eq. (11.48) where

$$\begin{aligned}
\mathbf{n}_{\dot{\mathbf{D}}} &= \mathbf{n}_{\dot{\mathbf{A}}} \frac{\|\dot{\mathbf{C}} - \dot{\mathbf{D}}\|}{\|\dot{\mathbf{C}} - \dot{\mathbf{A}}\|} + \mathbf{n}_{\dot{\mathbf{C}}} \frac{\|\dot{\mathbf{A}} - \dot{\mathbf{D}}\|}{\|\dot{\mathbf{C}} - \dot{\mathbf{A}}\|} \\
&= \mathbf{n}_{\dot{\mathbf{A}}} \frac{\left\| \begin{bmatrix} 0 \\ 5 \\ 0 \end{bmatrix} - \begin{bmatrix} 0 \\ 2 \\ 0 \end{bmatrix} \right\|}{\left\| \begin{bmatrix} 0 \\ 5 \\ 0 \end{bmatrix} - \begin{bmatrix} 0 \\ 0 \\ 0 \end{bmatrix} \right\|} + \mathbf{n}_{\dot{\mathbf{C}}} \frac{\left\| \begin{bmatrix} 0 \\ 0 \\ 0 \end{bmatrix} - \begin{bmatrix} 0 \\ 2 \\ 0 \end{bmatrix} \right\|}{\left\| \begin{bmatrix} 0 \\ 5 \\ 0 \end{bmatrix} - \begin{bmatrix} 0 \\ 0 \\ 0 \end{bmatrix} \right\|} \\
&= \begin{bmatrix} 3 \\ 4 \\ 5 \end{bmatrix} \frac{3}{5} + \begin{bmatrix} 10 \\ 10 \\ 7 \end{bmatrix} \frac{2}{5} = \begin{bmatrix} 5.8 \\ 6.4 \\ 5.8 \end{bmatrix}.
\end{aligned}$$

2. Get the normal vector $\mathbf{n}_{\dot{\mathbf{E}}}$ at point $\dot{\mathbf{E}}$ using Eq. (11.49). Note that it is easy to show that $\dot{\mathbf{E}} = [3, 2, 0]^T$. Thus,

$$\begin{aligned}
\mathbf{n}_{\dot{\mathbf{E}}} &= \mathbf{n}_{\dot{\mathbf{B}}} \frac{\|\dot{\mathbf{C}} - \dot{\mathbf{E}}\|}{\|\dot{\mathbf{C}} - \dot{\mathbf{B}}\|} + \mathbf{n}_{\dot{\mathbf{C}}} \frac{\|\dot{\mathbf{B}} - \dot{\mathbf{E}}\|}{\|\dot{\mathbf{C}} - \dot{\mathbf{B}}\|} \\
&= \mathbf{n}_{\dot{\mathbf{B}}} \frac{\left\| \begin{bmatrix} 0 \\ 5 \\ 0 \end{bmatrix} - \begin{bmatrix} 3 \\ 2 \\ 0 \end{bmatrix} \right\|}{\left\| \begin{bmatrix} 0 \\ 5 \\ 0 \end{bmatrix} - \begin{bmatrix} 5 \\ 0 \\ 0 \end{bmatrix} \right\|} + \mathbf{n}_{\dot{\mathbf{C}}} \frac{\left\| \begin{bmatrix} 5 \\ 0 \\ 0 \end{bmatrix} - \begin{bmatrix} 3 \\ 2 \\ 0 \end{bmatrix} \right\|}{\left\| \begin{bmatrix} 0 \\ 5 \\ 0 \end{bmatrix} - \begin{bmatrix} 5 \\ 0 \\ 0 \end{bmatrix} \right\|} \\
&= \begin{bmatrix} 7 \\ 8 \\ 6 \end{bmatrix} \frac{3}{5} + \begin{bmatrix} 10 \\ 10 \\ 7 \end{bmatrix} \frac{2}{5} = \begin{bmatrix} 8.2 \\ 8.8 \\ 6.4 \end{bmatrix}.
\end{aligned}$$

3. Get the normal vector $\mathbf{n}_{\dot{\mathbf{P}}}$ at point $\dot{\mathbf{P}} = [2, 2, 0]^T$ using Eq. (11.50) where

$$\begin{aligned}
\mathbf{n}_{\dot{\mathbf{P}}} &= \mathbf{n}_{\dot{\mathbf{D}}} \frac{\|\dot{\mathbf{E}} - \dot{\mathbf{P}}\|}{\|\dot{\mathbf{E}} - \dot{\mathbf{D}}\|} + \mathbf{n}_{\dot{\mathbf{E}}} \frac{\|\dot{\mathbf{D}} - \dot{\mathbf{P}}\|}{\|\dot{\mathbf{E}} - \dot{\mathbf{D}}\|} \\
&= \mathbf{n}_{\dot{\mathbf{D}}} \frac{\left\| \begin{bmatrix} 3 \\ 2 \\ 0 \end{bmatrix} - \begin{bmatrix} 2 \\ 2 \\ 0 \end{bmatrix} \right\|}{\left\| \begin{bmatrix} 3 \\ 2 \\ 0 \end{bmatrix} - \begin{bmatrix} 0 \\ 2 \\ 0 \end{bmatrix} \right\|} + \mathbf{n}_{\dot{\mathbf{E}}} \frac{\left\| \begin{bmatrix} 0 \\ 2 \\ 0 \end{bmatrix} - \begin{bmatrix} 2 \\ 2 \\ 0 \end{bmatrix} \right\|}{\left\| \begin{bmatrix} 3 \\ 2 \\ 0 \end{bmatrix} - \begin{bmatrix} 0 \\ 2 \\ 0 \end{bmatrix} \right\|} \\
&= \begin{bmatrix} 5.8 \\ 6.4 \\ 5.8 \end{bmatrix} \frac{1}{3} + \begin{bmatrix} 8.2 \\ 8.8 \\ 6.4 \end{bmatrix} \frac{2}{3} = \begin{bmatrix} 7.4 \\ 8 \\ 6.2 \end{bmatrix}.
\end{aligned}$$

□

#### 11.5.4.2 Parametric Coordinates

As done in Sect. 11.5.3.2, a point $\dot{\mathbf{P}}$ in a triangle $\triangle\dot{\mathbf{A}}\dot{\mathbf{B}}\dot{\mathbf{C}}$ can be expressed in parametric coordinates $[u, v]^T$ using Eq. (11.44). The coordinates can also be used to get the normal vector at $\dot{\mathbf{P}}$ if the normal vectors at the vertices $\dot{\mathbf{A}}$, $\dot{\mathbf{B}}$ and $\dot{\mathbf{C}}$ are known. This is estimated as

$$\mathbf{n}_{\dot{\mathbf{P}}} = \mathbf{n}_{\dot{\mathbf{A}}} + u\left[\mathbf{n}_{\dot{\mathbf{B}}} - \mathbf{n}_{\dot{\mathbf{A}}}\right] + v\left[\mathbf{n}_{\dot{\mathbf{C}}} - \mathbf{n}_{\dot{\mathbf{A}}}\right], \tag{11.51}$$

where $\mathbf{n}_{\dot{\mathbf{A}}}$, $\mathbf{n}_{\dot{\mathbf{B}}}$, $\mathbf{n}_{\dot{\mathbf{C}}}$ and $\mathbf{n}_{\dot{\mathbf{P}}}$ are the normal vectors at $\dot{\mathbf{A}}$, $\dot{\mathbf{B}}$, $\dot{\mathbf{C}}$ and $\dot{\mathbf{P}}$ respectively; and $[u, v]^T$ represent the parametric coordinates of $\dot{\mathbf{P}}$.

**Example 11.23:** [*Phong shading—calculating normal vector using parametric coordinates*]

The vertices of a triangle are placed at the positions $\dot{\mathbf{A}} = [0, 0, 0]^T$, $\dot{\mathbf{B}} = [5, 0, 0]^T$ and $\dot{\mathbf{C}} = [0, 5, 0]^T$. The normal vectors at the vertices $\dot{\mathbf{A}}$, $\dot{\mathbf{B}}$ and $\dot{\mathbf{C}}$ are $\mathbf{n}_{\dot{\mathbf{A}}} = [3, 4, 5]^T$, $\mathbf{n}_{\dot{\mathbf{B}}} = [7, 8, 6]^T$ and $\mathbf{n}_{\dot{\mathbf{C}}} = [10, 10, 7]^T$ respectively. If Phong shading is to be applied to this triangle, calculate the normal vector at the position $\dot{\mathbf{P}} = [2, 2, 0]^T$ using parametric coordinates.

**Solution 11.23:** Consider $\dot{\mathbf{A}}$ to be the origin of the parametric system. Using Eq. (11.44), the parametric coordinates $[u, v]^T$ can be calculated as

$$\mathbf{u} = \dot{\mathbf{B}} - \dot{\mathbf{A}} = \begin{bmatrix} 5 \\ 0 \\ 0 \end{bmatrix} - \begin{bmatrix} 0 \\ 0 \\ 0 \end{bmatrix} = \begin{bmatrix} 5 \\ 0 \\ 0 \end{bmatrix},$$

$$\mathbf{v} = \dot{\mathbf{C}} - \dot{\mathbf{A}} = \begin{bmatrix} 0 \\ 5 \\ 0 \end{bmatrix} - \begin{bmatrix} 0 \\ 0 \\ 0 \end{bmatrix} = \begin{bmatrix} 0 \\ 5 \\ 0 \end{bmatrix},$$

$$\mathbf{w} = \dot{\mathbf{P}} - \dot{\mathbf{A}} = \begin{bmatrix} 2 \\ 2 \\ 0 \end{bmatrix} - \begin{bmatrix} 0 \\ 0 \\ 0 \end{bmatrix} = \begin{bmatrix} 2 \\ 2 \\ 0 \end{bmatrix},$$

$$\begin{aligned} u &= \frac{(\mathbf{u} \cdot \mathbf{v})(\mathbf{w} \cdot \mathbf{v}) - (\mathbf{v} \cdot \mathbf{v})(\mathbf{w} \cdot \mathbf{u})}{(\mathbf{u} \cdot \mathbf{v})^2 - (\mathbf{u} \cdot \mathbf{u})(\mathbf{v} \cdot \mathbf{v})} \\ &= \frac{\left(\begin{bmatrix} 5 \\ 0 \\ 0 \end{bmatrix} \cdot \begin{bmatrix} 0 \\ 5 \\ 0 \end{bmatrix}\right)\left(\begin{bmatrix} 2 \\ 2 \\ 0 \end{bmatrix} \cdot \begin{bmatrix} 0 \\ 5 \\ 0 \end{bmatrix}\right) - \left(\begin{bmatrix} 0 \\ 5 \\ 0 \end{bmatrix} \cdot \begin{bmatrix} 0 \\ 5 \\ 0 \end{bmatrix}\right)\left(\begin{bmatrix} 2 \\ 2 \\ 0 \end{bmatrix} \cdot \begin{bmatrix} 5 \\ 0 \\ 0 \end{bmatrix}\right)}{\left(\begin{bmatrix} 5 \\ 0 \\ 0 \end{bmatrix} \cdot \begin{bmatrix} 0 \\ 5 \\ 0 \end{bmatrix}\right)^2 - \left(\begin{bmatrix} 5 \\ 0 \\ 0 \end{bmatrix} \cdot \begin{bmatrix} 5 \\ 0 \\ 0 \end{bmatrix}\right)\left(\begin{bmatrix} 0 \\ 5 \\ 0 \end{bmatrix} \cdot \begin{bmatrix} 0 \\ 5 \\ 0 \end{bmatrix}\right)} = 0.4, \end{aligned}$$

$$\begin{aligned} v &= \frac{(\mathbf{u} \cdot \mathbf{v})(\mathbf{w} \cdot \mathbf{u}) - (\mathbf{u} \cdot \mathbf{u})(\mathbf{w} \cdot \mathbf{v})}{(\mathbf{u} \cdot \mathbf{v})^2 - (\mathbf{u} \cdot \mathbf{u})(\mathbf{v} \cdot \mathbf{v})} \\ &= \frac{\left(\begin{bmatrix} 5 \\ 0 \\ 0 \end{bmatrix} \cdot \begin{bmatrix} 0 \\ 5 \\ 0 \end{bmatrix}\right)\left(\begin{bmatrix} 2 \\ 2 \\ 0 \end{bmatrix} \cdot \begin{bmatrix} 5 \\ 0 \\ 0 \end{bmatrix}\right) - \left(\begin{bmatrix} 5 \\ 0 \\ 0 \end{bmatrix} \cdot \begin{bmatrix} 5 \\ 0 \\ 0 \end{bmatrix}\right)\left(\begin{bmatrix} 2 \\ 2 \\ 0 \end{bmatrix} \cdot \begin{bmatrix} 0 \\ 5 \\ 0 \end{bmatrix}\right)}{\left(\begin{bmatrix} 5 \\ 0 \\ 0 \end{bmatrix} \cdot \begin{bmatrix} 0 \\ 5 \\ 0 \end{bmatrix}\right)^2 - \left(\begin{bmatrix} 5 \\ 0 \\ 0 \end{bmatrix} \cdot \begin{bmatrix} 5 \\ 0 \\ 0 \end{bmatrix}\right)\left(\begin{bmatrix} 0 \\ 5 \\ 0 \end{bmatrix} \cdot \begin{bmatrix} 0 \\ 5 \\ 0 \end{bmatrix}\right)} = 0.4. \end{aligned}$$

Hence, the normal vector at $\dot{\mathbf{P}} = [2, 2, 0]^T$ is estimated using Eq. (11.51) as

$$\begin{aligned}\mathbf{n}_{\dot{\mathbf{P}}} &= \mathbf{n}_{\dot{\mathbf{A}}} + u\left[\mathbf{n}_{\dot{\mathbf{B}}} - \mathbf{n}_{\dot{\mathbf{A}}}\right] + v\left[\mathbf{n}_{\dot{\mathbf{C}}} - \mathbf{n}_{\dot{\mathbf{A}}}\right] \\ &= \begin{bmatrix} 3 \\ 4 \\ 5 \end{bmatrix} + 0.4\left[\begin{bmatrix} 7 \\ 8 \\ 6 \end{bmatrix} - \begin{bmatrix} 3 \\ 4 \\ 5 \end{bmatrix}\right] + 0.4\left[\begin{bmatrix} 10 \\ 10 \\ 7 \end{bmatrix} - \begin{bmatrix} 3 \\ 4 \\ 5 \end{bmatrix}\right] = \begin{bmatrix} 7.4 \\ 8 \\ 6.2 \end{bmatrix}. \quad \square\end{aligned}$$

#### 11.5.4.3 Barycentric Coordinates

As done in Sect. 11.5.3.3, a point $\dot{\mathbf{P}}$ in a triangle $\triangle\dot{\mathbf{A}}\dot{\mathbf{B}}\dot{\mathbf{C}}$ can be expressed in barycentric coordinates as a triplet of numbers $\left[t_{\dot{\mathbf{A}}}, t_{\dot{\mathbf{B}}}, t_{\dot{\mathbf{C}}}\right]^T$ using Eq. (11.46). The coordinates can also be used to get the normal vector at $\dot{\mathbf{P}}$ if the normal vectors at the vertices $\dot{\mathbf{A}}$, $\dot{\mathbf{B}}$ and $\dot{\mathbf{C}}$ are known. This is estimated as

$$\mathbf{n}_{\dot{\mathbf{P}}} = \left[\mathbf{n}_{\dot{\mathbf{A}}}\ \mathbf{n}_{\dot{\mathbf{B}}}\ \mathbf{n}_{\dot{\mathbf{C}}}\right] \begin{bmatrix} t_{\dot{\mathbf{A}}} \\ t_{\dot{\mathbf{B}}} \\ t_{\dot{\mathbf{C}}} \end{bmatrix}, \tag{11.52}$$

where $\mathbf{n}_{\dot{\mathbf{A}}}$, $\mathbf{n}_{\dot{\mathbf{B}}}$, $\mathbf{n}_{\dot{\mathbf{C}}}$ and $\mathbf{n}_{\dot{\mathbf{P}}}$ are the normal vectors at $\dot{\mathbf{A}}$, $\dot{\mathbf{B}}$, $\dot{\mathbf{C}}$ and $\dot{\mathbf{P}}$ respectively; and $\left[t_{\dot{\mathbf{A}}}, t_{\dot{\mathbf{B}}}, t_{\dot{\mathbf{C}}}\right]^T$ represent the barycentric coordinates of $\dot{\mathbf{P}}$.

**Example 11.24:** [*Phong shading—calculating normal vector using barycentric coordinates*]

The vertices of a triangle are placed at the positions $\dot{\mathbf{A}} = [0, 0, 0]^T$, $\dot{\mathbf{B}} = [5, 0, 0]^T$ and $\dot{\mathbf{C}} = [0, 5, 0]^T$. The normal vectors at the vertices $\dot{\mathbf{A}}$, $\dot{\mathbf{B}}$ and $\dot{\mathbf{C}}$ are $\mathbf{n}_{\dot{\mathbf{A}}} = [3, 4, 5]^T$, $\mathbf{n}_{\dot{\mathbf{B}}} = [7, 8, 6]^T$ and $\mathbf{n}_{\dot{\mathbf{C}}} = [10, 10, 7]^T$ respectively. If Phong shading is to be applied to this triangle, calculate the normal vector at the position $\dot{\mathbf{P}} = [2, 2, 0]^T$ using barycentric coordinates.

**Solution 11.24:** The area of the triangle $\triangle\dot{\mathbf{A}}\dot{\mathbf{B}}\dot{\mathbf{C}}$ is calculated as

$$A = \frac{5 \times 5}{2} = 12.5.$$

The areas of the sub-triangles $\triangle\dot{\mathbf{P}}\dot{\mathbf{A}}\dot{\mathbf{B}}$, $\triangle\dot{\mathbf{P}}\dot{\mathbf{C}}\dot{\mathbf{A}}$ and $\triangle\dot{\mathbf{P}}\dot{\mathbf{B}}\dot{\mathbf{C}}$ are the following:

$$A_{\dot{\mathbf{C}}} = \frac{2 \times 5}{2} = 5,$$

$$A_{\dot{\mathbf{B}}} = \frac{2 \times 5}{2} = 5,$$

$$A_{\dot{\mathbf{A}}} = 12.5 - 10 = 2.5.$$

Thus, the ratios are calculated using Eq. (11.46) as

$$\begin{bmatrix} t_{\dot{A}} \\ t_{\dot{B}} \\ t_{\dot{C}} \end{bmatrix} = \frac{1}{A}\begin{bmatrix} A_{\dot{A}} \\ A_{\dot{B}} \\ A_{\dot{C}} \end{bmatrix} = \frac{1}{12.5}\begin{bmatrix} 2.5 \\ 5 \\ 5 \end{bmatrix} = \begin{bmatrix} 0.2 \\ 0.4 \\ 0.4 \end{bmatrix}.$$

Hence, the normal vector at $\dot{\mathbf{P}} = [2, 2, 0]^T$ is estimated using Eq. (11.52) as

$$\begin{aligned} \mathbf{n}_{\dot{\mathbf{P}}} &= \begin{bmatrix} \mathbf{n}_{\dot{\mathbf{A}}} & \mathbf{n}_{\dot{\mathbf{B}}} & \mathbf{n}_{\dot{\mathbf{C}}} \end{bmatrix} \begin{bmatrix} t_{\dot{\mathbf{A}}} \\ t_{\dot{\mathbf{B}}} \\ t_{\dot{\mathbf{C}}} \end{bmatrix} \\ &= \begin{bmatrix} 3 & 7 & 10 \\ 4 & 8 & 10 \\ 5 & 6 & 7 \end{bmatrix} \begin{bmatrix} 0.2 \\ 0.4 \\ 0.4 \end{bmatrix} = \begin{bmatrix} 7.4 \\ 8 \\ 6.2 \end{bmatrix}. \end{aligned}$$

□

## 11.6 Shadowing

The *shadow* of an object is an area of darkness the object causes by obstructing the path of a light ray. Casting shadows is the process of generating (or simulating) shadows. Figure 11.28 shows a light source $\dot{\mathbf{L}}$, a triangle $\triangle\dot{\mathbf{P}}_1\dot{\mathbf{P}}_2\dot{\mathbf{P}}_3$ and a horizontal infinite plane. Sharp shadow for the triangle is cast on the horizontal plane to form the triangle $\triangle\dot{\mathbf{P}}'_1\dot{\mathbf{P}}'_2\dot{\mathbf{P}}'_3$. The following algorithm is used to get the locations of the vertices $\dot{\mathbf{P}}'_1$, $\dot{\mathbf{P}}'_2$ and $\dot{\mathbf{P}}'_3$ assuming that the $y$-axis of the world coordinate system is pointing upwards:

1. Get a vector connecting the light source to each vertex; i.e., $\dot{\mathbf{P}}_1$, $\dot{\mathbf{P}}_2$ and $\dot{\mathbf{P}}_3$.
2. Extend these vectors until hitting the horizontal plane. The vertices of the shadow are located at the points of intersection with the horizontal plane.

Thus, the location of $\dot{\mathbf{P}}'_1$ is estimated as

$$\dot{\mathbf{P}}'_1 = \dot{\mathbf{L}} + \left(\frac{y_1 + y_2}{y_1}\right)\left[\dot{\mathbf{P}}_1 - \dot{\mathbf{L}}\right], \tag{11.53}$$

where $\dot{\mathbf{L}}$ and $\dot{\mathbf{P}}_1$ are the locations of the light source and the point for which the shadow is cast as $\dot{\mathbf{P}}'_1$; and $y_1 + y_2$ and $y_2$ are the $y$-components of the vectors $\dot{\mathbf{L}}$ and $\dot{\mathbf{P}}_1$ respectively.

Note that the previous case is not a generic one as it has some restrictions. The first restriction is that the object is a polygon having defined vertices. Also, the shadow generated is sharp. Finally, the case assumes that the shadow is cast on a horizontal infinite plane.

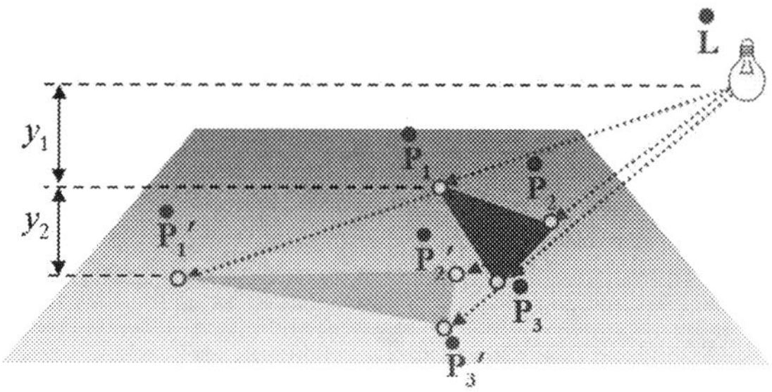


**Fig. 11.28** Sharp shadow is cast on a horizontal infinite plane

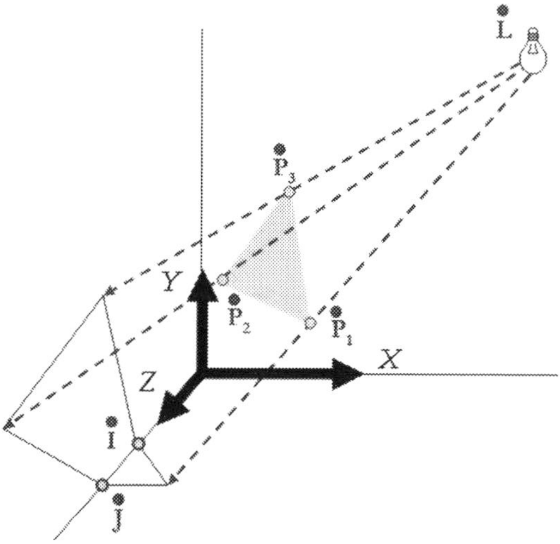


**Fig. 11.29** Sharp shadow is cast on the ground and a wall

**Example 11.25:** [*Shadowing—determining points of sharp shadow*]

Figure 11.29 shows a triangle with vertices $\dot{\mathbf{P}}_1 = [3.7, 3, 5.1]^T$, $\dot{\mathbf{P}}_2 = [4, 6, 7.6]^T$ and $\dot{\mathbf{P}}_3 = [6.8, 8, 8.2]^T$. The triangle is placed in a room as shown near the floor and a wall. The floor coincides with the $zx$-plane and the wall coincides with the $yz$-plane. Also, a light source $\dot{\mathbf{L}}$ located at $[10, 10, 10]^T$ casts a sharp shadow on the floor as well as the wall. Determine the positions of points $\dot{\mathbf{I}}$ and $\dot{\mathbf{J}}$.

**Solution 11.25:** There are more than one way to solve this problem. We will discuss one of them below.

1. Determine the locations where the vertices cast shadow on the floor (i.e., the $zx$-plane) using Eq. (11.53). These are points $\dot{\mathbf{P}}'_1$, $\dot{\mathbf{P}}'_2$ and $\dot{\mathbf{P}}'_3$ where

$$\dot{\mathbf{P}}'_1 = \dot{\mathbf{L}} + \left(\frac{y_{\dot{\mathbf{L}}}}{y_{\dot{\mathbf{L}}} - y_{\dot{\mathbf{P}}_1}}\right)[\dot{\mathbf{P}}_1 - \dot{\mathbf{L}}]$$

$$= \begin{bmatrix} 10 \\ 10 \\ 10 \end{bmatrix} + \left(\frac{10}{7}\right)\left[\begin{bmatrix} 3.7 \\ 3 \\ 5.1 \end{bmatrix} - \begin{bmatrix} 10 \\ 10 \\ 10 \end{bmatrix}\right] = \begin{bmatrix} 1 \\ 0 \\ 3 \end{bmatrix},$$

$$\dot{\mathbf{P}}'_2 = \dot{\mathbf{L}} + \left(\frac{y_{\dot{\mathbf{L}}}}{y_{\dot{\mathbf{L}}} - y_{\dot{\mathbf{P}}_2}}\right)[\dot{\mathbf{P}}_2 - \dot{\mathbf{L}}]$$

$$= \begin{bmatrix} 10 \\ 10 \\ 10 \end{bmatrix} + \left(\frac{10}{4}\right)\left[\begin{bmatrix} 4 \\ 6 \\ 7.6 \end{bmatrix} - \begin{bmatrix} 10 \\ 10 \\ 10 \end{bmatrix}\right] = \begin{bmatrix} -5 \\ 0 \\ 4 \end{bmatrix},$$

$$\dot{\mathbf{P}}'_3 = \dot{\mathbf{L}} + \left(\frac{y_{\dot{\mathbf{L}}}}{y_{\dot{\mathbf{L}}} - y_{\dot{\mathbf{P}}_3}}\right)[\dot{\mathbf{P}}_3 - \dot{\mathbf{L}}]$$

$$= \begin{bmatrix} 10 \\ 10 \\ 10 \end{bmatrix} + \left(\frac{10}{2}\right)\left[\begin{bmatrix} 6.8 \\ 8 \\ 8.2 \end{bmatrix} - \begin{bmatrix} 10 \\ 10 \\ 10 \end{bmatrix}\right] = \begin{bmatrix} -6 \\ 0 \\ 1 \end{bmatrix}.$$

2. The following deals with a line as a path between two 2D points on the $zx$-plane. Thus, points $\dot{\mathbf{P}}'_1$, $\dot{\mathbf{P}}'_2$ and $\dot{\mathbf{P}}'_3$ can be regarded as $\dot{\mathbf{p}}'_1 = [1, 3]^T$, $\dot{\mathbf{p}}'_2 = [-5, 4]^T$ and $\dot{\mathbf{p}}'_3 = [-6, 1]^T$ respectively. Now get the equations of the lines $\overline{\dot{\mathbf{p}}'_3\dot{\mathbf{p}}'_1}$ and $\overline{\dot{\mathbf{p}}'_2\dot{\mathbf{p}}'_1}$. The following uses cross product (Sect. A.4.3.3) of homogeneous points (Sect. B.7):

$$\overline{\dot{\mathbf{p}}'_3\dot{\mathbf{p}}'_1} = \mathbf{p}'_3 \times \mathbf{p}'_1 = \begin{bmatrix} -6 \\ 1 \\ 1 \end{bmatrix} \times \begin{bmatrix} 1 \\ 3 \\ 1 \end{bmatrix} = \begin{bmatrix} -2 \\ 7 \\ -19 \end{bmatrix},$$

$$\overline{\dot{\mathbf{p}}'_2\dot{\mathbf{p}}'_1} = \mathbf{p}'_2 \times \mathbf{p}'_1 = \begin{bmatrix} -5 \\ 4 \\ 1 \end{bmatrix} \times \begin{bmatrix} 1 \\ 3 \\ 1 \end{bmatrix} = \begin{bmatrix} 1 \\ 6 \\ -19 \end{bmatrix}.$$

3. The point $\dot{\mathbf{i}}$ is the intersection between $\overline{\dot{\mathbf{p}}'_3\dot{\mathbf{p}}'_1}$ and the $z$-axis while the point $\dot{\mathbf{j}}$ is the intersection between $\overline{\dot{\mathbf{p}}'_2\dot{\mathbf{p}}'_1}$ and the $z$-axis. Note that the $z$-axis on the $zx$-plane is expressed as $x = 0$ or $[1, 0, 0]^T$. The cross product of two linear equations results in the intersection point between the lines. Therefore, $\mathbf{i}$ and $\mathbf{j}$ are estimated as

$$\mathbf{i} = \begin{bmatrix} -2 \\ 7 \\ -19 \end{bmatrix} \times \begin{bmatrix} 1 \\ 0 \\ 0 \end{bmatrix} = \begin{bmatrix} 0 \\ -19 \\ -7 \end{bmatrix},$$

$$\mathbf{j} = \begin{bmatrix} 1 \\ 6 \\ -19 \end{bmatrix} \times \begin{bmatrix} 1 \\ 0 \\ 0 \end{bmatrix} = \begin{bmatrix} 0 \\ -19 \\ -6 \end{bmatrix}.$$

In inhomogeneous coordinates, $\dot{\mathbf{i}}$ and $\dot{\mathbf{j}}$ can be expressed as (Sect. B.7)

$$\dot{\mathbf{i}} = \begin{bmatrix} 0 \\ \frac{-19}{-7} \end{bmatrix} = \begin{bmatrix} 0 \\ 2.7143 \end{bmatrix},$$

$$\dot{\mathbf{j}} = \begin{bmatrix} 0 \\ \frac{-19}{-6} \end{bmatrix} = \begin{bmatrix} 0 \\ 3.1667 \end{bmatrix}.$$

Hence, the final points are $\dot{\mathbf{I}} = [0, 0, 2.7143]^T$ and $\dot{\mathbf{J}} = [0, 0, 3.1667]^T$.

Can you think of another way to solve this problem? □

## 11.7 Problems

**Problem 11.1:** [*Point light—attenuation*]

Assume that the attenuation value of a point light source is modeled by

$$\frac{1}{0.4 + 0.4d + 0.2d^2},$$

where $d$ is the distance from the light source to the point being lit. Determine the attenuation values such that $d = 2$ and $d = 4$.

**Problem 11.2:** [*Point light—light intensity at a point*]

A point light source is placed at $[8, 5, 6]^T$ where the original intensity $I_p$ of the light is found to be 0.9 (where $I_p \in [0, 1]$). Calculate the intensity $I_{light}$ of energy leaving the light source and arriving at the point $[10, 10, 10]^T$ if the attenuation value of the point light source is obtained by

$$\frac{1}{0.4 + 0.4d + 0.2d^2},$$

where $d$ is the distance from the light source to the point being lit.

**Problem 11.3:** [*Spotlight—light intensity at a point*]

A spotlight source is placed at $[8, 5, 6]^T$ where the original intensity $I_p$ of the light is found to be 0.9 (where $I_p \in [0, 1]$). The spotlight is directed at the point $[10, 10, 10]^T$ and the attenuation value of the light source is modeled by

$$\frac{1}{0.4 + 0.4d + 0.2d^2},$$

where $d$ is the distance from the light source to the point being lit. Calculate the intensity $I_{light}$ of energy leaving the light source and arriving at the point $[10, 10, 10]^T$.

**Problem 11.4:** [*Spotlight—light intensity at a point*]

If the spotlight source of Problem 11.3 is directed at another point $\dot{\mathbf{P}}_1 = [9, 9, 9]^T$, calculate the intensity $I_{light}$ of energy leaving the light source and arriving at the point $\dot{\mathbf{P}} = [10, 10, 10]^T$ if the fall-off factor is 1. Assume that the cut-off angle $\theta_{in}$ is 45°.

**Problem 11.5:** [*Spotlight—falling-off curve*]

Equation (11.6) determines the amount of falling-off from the axis of the cone to its boundaries. Assuming that $\theta_{in} = 60°$, show the function shape if the fall-off factor $f$ is 1. Also, show the curve when $f = 0.5$ and when $f = 5$.

**Problem 11.6:** [*Refraction rays—refraction vector*]

Figure 11.20 shows a ray of light as penetrating three different media 1, 2 and 3. It gets refracted while passing from medium 1 to medium 2 and it gets refracted again while passing from medium 2 to medium 3. The plane of intersection between media 1 and 2 is parallel to the plane of intersection between media 2 and 3. Write down a single equation to express the refraction vector in medium 3.

**Problem 11.7:** [*Refraction rays—refraction vector*]

Figure 11.21 shows a ray of light as penetrating three different media 1, 2 and 3. It gets refracted while passing from medium 1 to medium 2 and it gets refracted again while passing from medium 2 to medium 3. The plane of intersection between media 1 and 2 is *not* parallel to the plane of intersection between media 2 and 3. Write down a single equation to express the refraction vector in medium 3.

**Problem 11.8:** [*Incidence angle*]

Suppose that a spotlight source is placed at $[5, 5, 5]^T$ and pointed towards (perpendicular to) the plane represented by the equation $x + y + z = 3$. Calculate the incidence angle at $[3, 0, 0]^T$.

**Problem 11.9:** [*Multiple-choice questions*]

Two triangles $A$ and $B$ exist in 3D space. The triangle $A$ is bounded by the vertices $\dot{\mathbf{A}}_1 = [3, 6, 6]^T$, $\dot{\mathbf{A}}_2 = [2, 2, 7]^T$ and $\dot{\mathbf{A}}_3 = [1, 2, 1]^T$ while the vertices of triangle $B$ are $\dot{\mathbf{B}}_1 = [6, 8, 5]^T$, $\dot{\mathbf{B}}_2 = [4, 4, 6]^T$ and $\dot{\mathbf{B}}_3 = [5, 5, 3]^T$. Also, there is a light source at $[9, 9, 9]^T$. Choose the correct answer. The floating point numbers are given precision up to two digits to the right of the decimal point.

1. The normal to triangle $A$ is:
   (a) $[-1, -4, 1]^T$.
   (b) $[-2, -4, 5]^T$.
   (c) $[24, -7, -4]^T$.
   (d) None of the above.
2. The perpendicular distance from the origin to triangle $A$ is:
   (a) 6.
   (b) 4.

(c) 5.
(d) None of the above.

3. The equation of triangle $A$ plane is:

   (a) $[9, 9, 9, 5]^T$.
   (b) $[24, -7, -4, -6]^T$.
   (c) $6x + 8y + 5z + 6 = 0$.
   (d) None of the above.

4. If the ray going from the light source to vertex $\dot{\mathbf{B}}_1$ is given by the equation $\dot{\mathbf{P}} = \dot{\mathbf{P}}_0 + \mathbf{v}t$, then:

   (a) $\dot{\mathbf{P}}_0 = [9, 9, 9]^T$.
   (b) $\dot{\mathbf{P}}_0 = [6, 8, 5]^T$.
   (c) $\dot{\mathbf{P}}_0 = [3, 1, 4]^T$.
   (d) None of the above.

5. If the ray going from the light source to vertex $\dot{\mathbf{B}}_1$ is given by the equation $\dot{\mathbf{P}} = \dot{\mathbf{P}}_0 + \mathbf{v}t$, then:

   (a) $\mathbf{v} = [9, 9, 9]^T$.
   (b) $\mathbf{v} = [6, 8, 5]^T$.
   (c) $\mathbf{v} = [-3, -1, -4]^T$.
   (d) None of the above.

6. Determine if the above ray is pointing towards triangle $A$.

   (a) It points away from triangle $A$.
   (b) It points towards triangle $A$.
   (c) The ray is parallel to triangle $A$.
   (d) None of the above.

7. If there is an intersection, the intersection point is:

   (a) $[6.32, 1.04, -5.87]^T$.
   (b) $[1.47, 6.49, -1.04]^T$.
   (c) There is no intersection.
   (d) None of the above.

**Problem 11.10:** [*Phong reflection model—colors*]
Apply Phong reflection model to get the final colors at points $\dot{\mathbf{P}}_2 = [0, 3, 0]^T$ and $\dot{\mathbf{P}}_3 = [0, 0, 3]^T$ of Example 11.13.

**Problem 11.11:** [*Blinn-Phong reflection model—half vector*]
Derive a single equation to estimate the angle enclosed between the half and normal vectors (i.e., **h** and **n**) in terms of the viewing and light directions (i.e., **v** and **l**). You may assume that the viewing direction **v** coincides with the same plane of the light ray **l**, the normal **n** and the reflected ray **r**.

**Problem 11.12:** [*Blinn-Phong reflection model—shininess exponent*]
If the same amount of specular reflection provided by Phong model is to be obtained using Blinn-Phong model, derive an equation to obtain the value of the shininess exponent $n_b$ in terms of Phong shininess exponent $n_s$.

**Problem 11.13:** [*Shading—scan line interpolation*]
Consider a triangle in 2D space with vertices at $[10, 8]^T$, $[12, 4]^T$ and $[8, 2]^T$. The colors assigned at these vertices are 100, 200, 50 respectively. Use scan line interpolation to get the shade value at the point $[10, 4]^T$.

**Problem 11.14:** [*Shading—parametric coordinates*]
Solve Problem 11.13 using parametric coordinates.

**Problem 11.15:** [*Shading—barycentric coordinates*]
Solve Problem 11.13 using barycentric coordinates.

**Problem 11.16:** [*Normal vector—parametric coordinates*]
Consider a triangle $\triangle\dot{\mathbf{A}}\dot{\mathbf{B}}\dot{\mathbf{C}}$ where $\dot{\mathbf{A}} = [1, 3, 1]^T$, $\dot{\mathbf{B}} = [4, 2, 0]^T$ and $\dot{\mathbf{C}} = [2, 2, 3]^T$. The normal vectors at these vertices are $\mathbf{n}_{\dot{\mathbf{A}}} = [0, 1, 0]^T$, $\mathbf{n}_{\dot{\mathbf{B}}} = [1, 0, 0]^T$ and $\mathbf{n}_{\dot{\mathbf{C}}} = [0, 0, 1]^T$. Assuming that $\dot{\mathbf{A}}$ is the origin of a parametric coordinate system, estimate the normal vector for the point whose coordinates are 0.2 and 0.3.

**Problem 11.17:** [*Normal vector—parametric coordinates*]
In Problem 11.16, if the origin was at point $\dot{\mathbf{B}}$ instead of $\dot{\mathbf{A}}$, determine the parametric coordinates of the previous point in this case. Check to see if the normal vector would change in this case (i.e., after changing the origin).

**Problem 11.18:** [*Normal vector—barycentric coordinates*]
Consider a triangle $\triangle\dot{\mathbf{A}}\dot{\mathbf{B}}\dot{\mathbf{C}}$ where $\dot{\mathbf{A}} = [1, 3, 1]^T$, $\dot{\mathbf{B}} = [4, 2, 0]^T$ and $\dot{\mathbf{C}} = [2, 2, 3]^T$. The normal vectors at these vertices are $\mathbf{n}_{\dot{\mathbf{A}}} = [0, 1, 0]^T$, $\mathbf{n}_{\dot{\mathbf{B}}} = [1, 0, 0]^T$ and $\mathbf{n}_{\dot{\mathbf{C}}} = [0, 0, 1]^T$. Estimate the normal vector for a point $\dot{\mathbf{P}}$ whose barycentric coordinates are $t_{\dot{\mathbf{A}}} = 0.3$, $t_{\dot{\mathbf{B}}} = 0.3$ and $t_{\dot{\mathbf{C}}} = 0.4$.

**Problem 11.19:** [*Normal vector—barycentric coordinates*]
Consider a triangle $\triangle\dot{\mathbf{A}}\dot{\mathbf{B}}\dot{\mathbf{C}}$ where the normal vectors at the vertices $\dot{\mathbf{A}}$ and $\dot{\mathbf{B}}$ are known. Also, the normal vector at an internal point $\dot{\mathbf{P}}$ whose barycentric coordinates are $[t_{\dot{\mathbf{A}}}, t_{\dot{\mathbf{B}}}, t_{\dot{\mathbf{C}}}]^T$ is known. Write a single equation to estimate the normal vector at the vertex $\dot{\mathbf{C}}$.

**Problem 11.20:** [*Shadowing*]
Two triangles $A$ and $B$ exist in 3D space. The triangle $A$ is bounded by the vertices $[3, 6, 6]^T$, $[2, 2, 7]^T$ and $[1, 2, 1]^T$ while the vertices of triangle $B$ are $[6, 8, 5]^T$, $[4, 4, 6]^T$ and $[5, 5, 3]^T$. If there is a light source at $[9, 9, 9]^T$, determine if the vertex $[6, 8, 5]^T$ will cast shadow on triangle $A$. Repeat the calculations for vertices $[4, 4, 6]^T$ and $[5, 5, 3]^T$.

# References

Blinn, J.F. 1977. Models of light reflection for computer synthesized pictures. In Proceedings of the 4th annual conference on computer graphics and interactive techniques, SIGGRAPH '77, 192–198, New York, NY, USA. ACM.

Gouraud, H. 1971a. Computer display of curved surfaces. PhD thesis, The University of Utah. AAI7127878.

Gouraud, H. 1971b. Continuous shading of curved surfaces. *IEEE Transactions on Computers* C-20(6):623–629.

Phong, B.T. 1975. Illumination for computer generated pictures. *Communications of the ACM* 18(6): 311–317.

# Chapter 12
# Mapping Techniques

**Abstract** The concept of mapping centers around applying images (sometimes real-world images) to graphical objects to achieve more interesting computer-generated images or to add realism to rendered images without computing additional geometry. The images used in this regard are referred to as *maps*. Maps add new characteristics to the materials and hence to the objects under consideration. For example, diffuse or texture mapping is used to paint an image onto a surface. Bump maps use their intensities to add wrinkles and grooves to the final images. Other maps add the illusion of reflection of objects that do not exist as 3D models in the scene. Similarly, refraction maps are used to give the effect that objects that do not exist in 3D space are seen through other objects. Other types of mapping exist as well. Different spaces are considered when working with maps; map space, 3D space and final image space. Transformations among these spaces should be handled appropriately. Also, mapping treatment of planar surfaces is different from that of curved surfaces. One may think of the mapping process in different ways. For example, a 3D vertex may be projected onto the output image and the map. Then transformation is utilized to apply the information of the map to the output image. The process of mapping can be viewed another way where the surface meshes of the 3D model are flattened and map information is applied to the flattened meshes. In this chapter, we will discuss different issues regarding mapping. This includes mapping spaces (Sect. 12.1), mapping steps (Sect. 12.2), transformations for mapping onto planar surfaces (Sect. 12.3), mapping onto curved surfaces (Sect. 12.5) and different mapping types (Sect. 12.6).

## 12.1 Mapping Spaces

Three spaces or coordinate systems (Fig. 12.1) are observed for mapping.

1. The first is the modeling space or the space in which the models/objects are created. As shown in Fig. 12.1a, this space may be a 3D space with three principal axes (i.e., a 4D space in homogeneous coordinates).

R. Elias, *Digital Media*, DOI: 10.1007/978-3-319-05137-6_12,

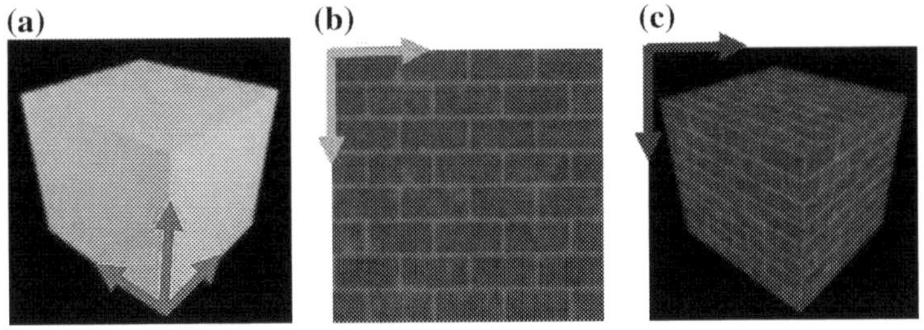


**Fig. 12.1** Spaces in mapping. **a** A 3D object in 3D space. **b** A map or an array of texels in 2D space. **c** An image for the model after mapping in 2D space

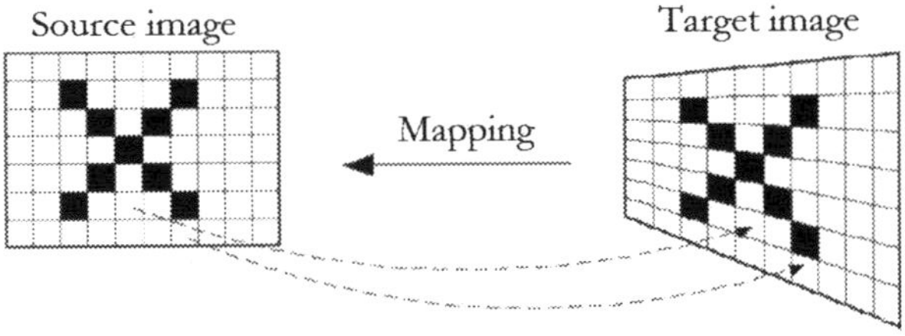


**Fig. 12.2** Mapping is performed from the destination image to the source image

2. The second is a space containing information that will be mapped to objects. It is often an image that is referred to as a *map*, a *uv-map* or a texture array. Its information is in discrete pieces that correspond to pixels. Each of these pieces is called a *texel* or a texture element. As shown in Fig. 12.1b, this is a 2D space with two axes (i.e., a 3D space in homogeneous coordinates).
3. The third is the output image after mapping. Similar to the previous, this is a 2D space with two axes as depicted in Fig. 12.1c (i.e., a 3D space in homogeneous coordinates).

## 12.2 Mapping Steps

A 3D vertex is projected to a 2D point on the output image using a projection technique (Chap. 8). This projection represents the transformation from the first coordinate system mentioned above to the third one. Also, the same 3D vertex can be projected onto the map (i.e., the second coordinate system above) to determine its location on the that map. Patches surrounded by three to four projected points can be transformed from the map; i.e., the source image, to the output, i.e., the destination or target image. On the contrary to logical thinking, mapping is performed from the destination image to the source image as depicted in Fig. 12.2. Specifically, mapping process is implemented in a number of steps.

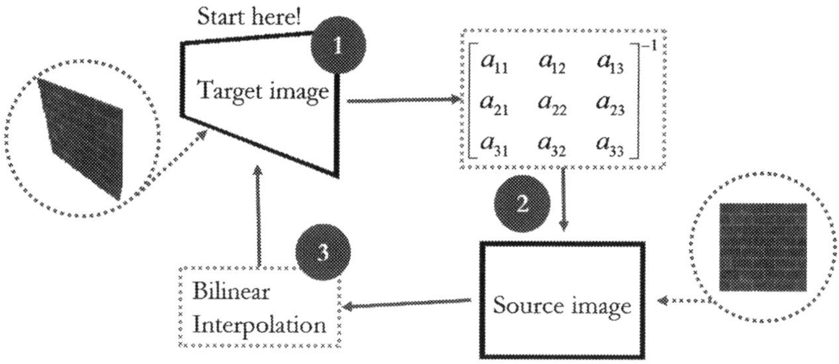


**Fig. 12.3** Mapping is performed from the destination image to the source image

1. Start with a pixel in the target image.
2. Jump to its corresponding location in the source image and retrieve its color. This is done through a transformation matrix. This is discussed in Sect. 12.3.
3. If the location in the source image falls between pixels (i.e., position contains fractions), bilinear interpolation should be used as discussed in Sect. 12.4.

These steps are depicted in Fig. 12.3.

## 12.3 Transformation for Mapping

As depicted in Fig. 12.3, Step 2 represents a transformation process from the target image to the source image. For planar surfaces, this transformation may be achieved through different methods (e.g., homography matrix or affine matrix).

### *12.3.1 Homography Transformation*

In order to map four points $[x_1, y_1]^T$, $[x_2, y_2]^T$, $[x_3, y_3]^T$ and $[x_4, y_4]^T$ to four other points $[x'_1, y'_1]^T$, $[x'_2, y'_2]^T$, $[x'_3, y'_3]^T$ and $[x'_4, y'_4]^T$, eight equations must be solved simultaneously to produce plane projective transformation matrix, which is represented by a $3 \times 3$ matrix that is called *homography matrix*, $\mathtt{H}$. This matrix is used to accurately map a source point $\dot{\mathbf{p}} = [x, y]^T$ to another destination one $\dot{\mathbf{p}}' = [x', y']^T$. That is

$$\mathbf{p}' = \mathtt{H}\mathbf{p}, \tag{12.1}$$

where $\mathbf{p}$ and $\mathbf{p}'$ are the homogeneous source and destination points. Equation (12.1) can be re-written as

$$\underbrace{\begin{bmatrix} x' \\ y' \\ 1 \end{bmatrix}}_{\mathbf{p}'} = \underbrace{\begin{bmatrix} h_{11} & h_{12} & h_{13} \\ h_{21} & h_{22} & h_{23} \\ h_{31} & h_{32} & h_{33} \end{bmatrix}}_{\mathtt{H}} \underbrace{\begin{bmatrix} x \\ y \\ 1 \end{bmatrix}}_{\mathbf{p}}. \tag{12.2}$$

*How to estimate the homography matrix*? A pair of corresponding points contributes to two linear equations for the elements of $\mathtt{H}$. Removing the scale factor by dividing by the third component, we get

$$x' = \frac{h_{11}x + h_{12}y + h_{13}}{h_{31}x + h_{32}y + h_{33}} \tag{12.3}$$

and

$$y' = \frac{h_{21}x + h_{22}y + h_{23}}{h_{31}x + h_{32}y + h_{33}}. \tag{12.4}$$

Consequently,

$$x'(h_{31}x + h_{32}y + h_{33}) = h_{11}x + h_{12}y + h_{13} \tag{12.5}$$

and

$$y'(h_{31}x + h_{32}y + h_{33}) = h_{21}x + h_{22}y + h_{23}. \tag{12.6}$$

The homography matrix, $\mathtt{H}$, has 8° of freedom and can be defined through four corresponding pairs. Having four correspondences results in eight linear equations, which are sufficient to solve for $\mathtt{H}$ up to a scale factor. We choose one matrix term to have a certain value; e.g., $h_{33} = 1$. Thus, the eight equations can be written as

$$\overbrace{\begin{bmatrix} x_1 & y_1 & 1 & 0 & 0 & 0 & -x'_1x_1 & -x'_1y_1 \\ 0 & 0 & 0 & x_1 & y_1 & 1 & -y'_1x_1 & -y'_1y_1 \\ x_2 & y_2 & 1 & 0 & 0 & 0 & -x'_2x_2 & -x'_2y_2 \\ 0 & 0 & 0 & x_2 & y_2 & 1 & -y'_2x_2 & -y'_2y_2 \\ x_3 & y_3 & 1 & 0 & 0 & 0 & -x'_3x_3 & -x'_3y_3 \\ 0 & 0 & 0 & x_3 & y_3 & 1 & -y'_3x_3 & -y'_3y_3 \\ x_4 & y_4 & 1 & 0 & 0 & 0 & -x'_4x_4 & -x'_4y_4 \\ 0 & 0 & 0 & x_4 & y_4 & 1 & -y'_4x_4 & -y'_4y_4 \end{bmatrix}}^{\mathtt{M}} \overbrace{\begin{bmatrix} h_{11} \\ h_{12} \\ h_{13} \\ h_{21} \\ h_{22} \\ h_{23} \\ h_{31} \\ h_{32} \end{bmatrix}}^{\mathbf{h}} \overset{=}{=} \overbrace{\begin{bmatrix} x'_1 \\ y'_1 \\ x'_2 \\ y'_2 \\ x'_3 \\ y'_3 \\ x'_4 \\ y'_4 \end{bmatrix}}^{\mathbf{x}}. \tag{12.7}$$

Consequently, a solution can be obtained as

$$\mathbf{h} = \mathtt{M}^{-1}\mathbf{x}. \tag{12.8}$$

where $\mathbf{h}$ is an 8D vector that consists of the components of the homography matrix $\mathtt{H}$; i.e., $h_{11}, h_{12}, \ldots, h_{31}, h_{32}$. If the location in the synthesized target image is $\dot{\mathbf{p}}'$, then the location in the source image, $\dot{\mathbf{p}}$, is given by

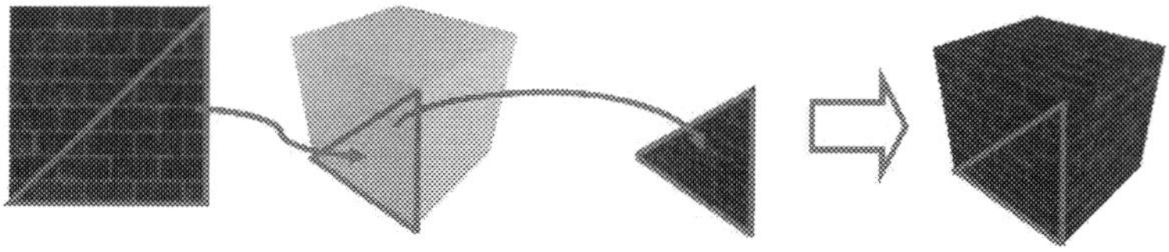

**Fig. 12.4** Any surface can be split into triangles where affine transformation may be applied to each of those triangles

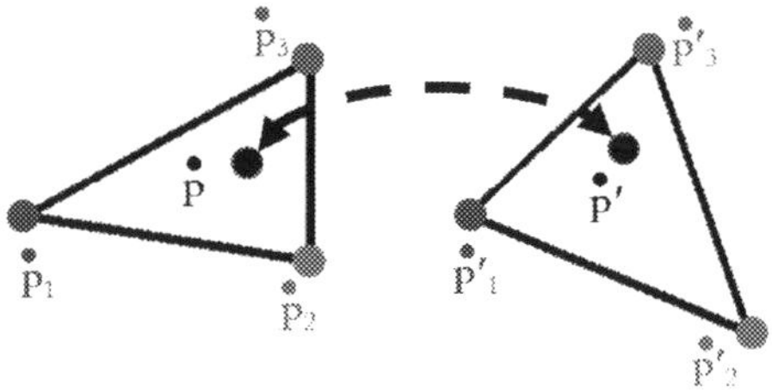


**Fig. 12.5** A source triangle $\triangle\dot{\mathbf{p}}_1\dot{\mathbf{p}}_2\dot{\mathbf{p}}_3$ is mapped to a destination triangle $\triangle\dot{\mathbf{p}}'_1\dot{\mathbf{p}}'_2\dot{\mathbf{p}}'_3$

$$\mathbf{p} = \mathrm{H}^{-1}\mathbf{p}'. \tag{12.9}$$

Bilinear interpolation may be used at this point to get the intensity of the synthesized image at the location $\dot{\mathbf{p}}'$.

## 12.3.2 *Affine Transformation*

Instead of working with quadrilaterals and homography matrices, it may be easier to split each surface into triangles and work with triangles as shown in Fig. 12.4. In this case, a $3 \times 3$ affine matrix can be created to approximate the actual results of the homography matrix. The affine transformation matrix is a simpler type of transformation and has 6° of freedom; hence, it can be fully estimated using three pairs of points; i.e., mapping one triangle to another.

As depicted in Fig. 12.5, suppose that a triangle $\triangle\dot{\mathbf{p}}_1\dot{\mathbf{p}}_2\dot{\mathbf{p}}_3$ where $\dot{\mathbf{p}}_1 = [x_1, y_1]^T$, $\dot{\mathbf{p}}_2 = [x_2, y_2]^T$ and $\dot{\mathbf{p}}_3 = [x_3, y_3]^T$ is to be mapped to another triangle $\triangle\dot{\mathbf{p}}'_1\dot{\mathbf{p}}'_2\dot{\mathbf{p}}'_3$ where $\dot{\mathbf{p}}'_1 = [x'_1, y'_1]^T$, $\dot{\mathbf{p}}'_2 = [x'_2, y'_2]^T$ and $\dot{\mathbf{p}}'_3 = [x'_3, y'_3]^T$. In other words, we need to find a $3 \times 3$ transformation matrix $\mathrm{A}$ that maps a point $\dot{\mathbf{p}}$ in the source triangle to another point $\dot{\mathbf{p}}'$ in the destination triangle. Thus,

$$\mathbf{p}' = \mathrm{A}\mathbf{p}, \tag{12.10}$$

where $\mathbf{p}$ and $\mathbf{p}'$ are the homogeneous source and destination points. We can re-write Eq. (12.10) as

$$\underbrace{\begin{bmatrix} x' \\ y' \\ 1 \end{bmatrix}}_{\mathbf{p}'} = \underbrace{\begin{bmatrix} \mathbf{a}_1^T \\ \mathbf{a}_2^T \\ \mathbf{a}_3^T \end{bmatrix}}_{\mathtt{A}} \underbrace{\begin{bmatrix} x \\ y \\ 1 \end{bmatrix}}_{\mathbf{p}}. \tag{12.11}$$

where $\mathbf{a}_1^T$, $\mathbf{a}_2^T$ and $\mathbf{a}_3^T$ are the rows of the affine matrix. Since we have three pairs of points, we can write

$$\begin{bmatrix} x_1' \\ x_2' \\ x_3' \end{bmatrix} = \begin{bmatrix} \mathbf{p}_1^T \\ \mathbf{p}_2^T \\ \mathbf{p}_3^T \end{bmatrix} \mathbf{a}_1, \tag{12.12}$$

where $\dot{\mathbf{p}}_1$, $\dot{\mathbf{p}}_2$ and $\dot{\mathbf{p}}_3$ are the three source vertices; and $\dot{\mathbf{p}}_1' = [x_1', y_1']^T$, $\dot{\mathbf{p}}_2' = [x_2', y_2']^T$ and $\dot{\mathbf{p}}_3' = [x_3', y_3']^T$ are the three destination vertices. Then, the first row in matrix $\mathtt{A}$ can be written as

$$\mathbf{a}_1 = \begin{bmatrix} \mathbf{p}_1^T \\ \mathbf{p}_2^T \\ \mathbf{p}_3^T \end{bmatrix}^{-1} \begin{bmatrix} x_1' \\ x_2' \\ x_3' \end{bmatrix}. \tag{12.13}$$

Similarly, the second and the third rows can be expressed as

$$\mathbf{a}_2 = \begin{bmatrix} \mathbf{p}_1^T \\ \mathbf{p}_2^T \\ \mathbf{p}_3^T \end{bmatrix}^{-1} \begin{bmatrix} y_1' \\ y_2' \\ y_3' \end{bmatrix} \tag{12.14}$$

and

$$\mathbf{a}_3 = \begin{bmatrix} \mathbf{p}_1^T \\ \mathbf{p}_2^T \\ \mathbf{p}_3^T \end{bmatrix}^{-1} \begin{bmatrix} 1 \\ 1 \\ 1 \end{bmatrix}. \tag{12.15}$$

As done with the homography matrix, the transformation from a destination point $\dot{\mathbf{p}}'$ to its corresponding source point $\dot{\mathbf{p}}$ can be expressed as

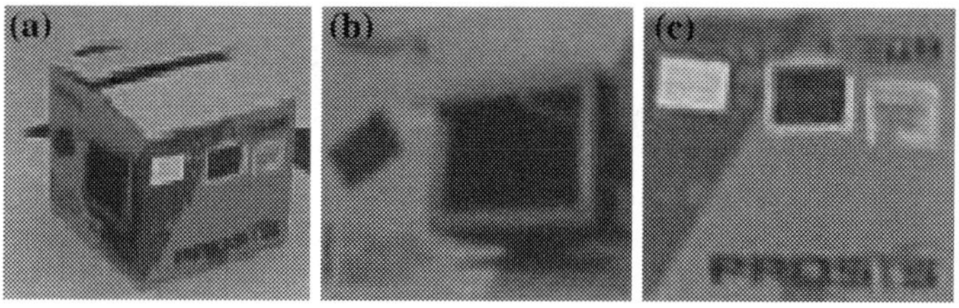


**Fig. 12.6** **a** A box. **b** and **c** Box sides transformed through affine matrix

$$
\begin{aligned}
\mathbf{p} &= \begin{bmatrix} \mathbf{a}_1^T \\ \mathbf{a}_2^T \\ \mathbf{a}_3^T \end{bmatrix}^{-1} \mathbf{p}' \\
\begin{bmatrix} x \\ y \\ 1 \end{bmatrix} &= \underbrace{\begin{bmatrix}
\left[\begin{bmatrix} x_1 & y_1 & 1 \\ x_2 & y_2 & 1 \\ x_3 & y_3 & 1 \end{bmatrix}^{-1} \begin{bmatrix} x'_1 \\ x'_2 \\ x'_3 \end{bmatrix}\right]^T \\
\left[\begin{bmatrix} x_1 & y_1 & 1 \\ x_2 & y_2 & 1 \\ x_3 & y_3 & 1 \end{bmatrix}^{-1} \begin{bmatrix} y'_1 \\ y'_2 \\ y'_3 \end{bmatrix}\right]^T \\
\left[\begin{bmatrix} x_1 & y_1 & 1 \\ x_2 & y_2 & 1 \\ x_3 & y_3 & 1 \end{bmatrix}^{-1} \begin{bmatrix} 1 \\ 1 \\ 1 \end{bmatrix}\right]^T
\end{bmatrix}^{-1}}_{\mathtt{A}^{-1}} \begin{bmatrix} x' \\ y' \\ 1 \end{bmatrix}.
\end{aligned}
\tag{12.16}
$$

Equation (12.16) has been used to generate the box sides shown in Fig. 12.6 by splitting each four-sided area into two triangles and then mapping through affine transformation thereafter.

**Example 12.1:** [*Affine transformation matrix for mapping*]

Derive the affine transformation matrix used for mapping from triangle $\triangle\dot{\mathbf{p}}_1\dot{\mathbf{p}}_2\dot{\mathbf{p}}_3$ where $\dot{\mathbf{p}}_1 = [5, 3]^T$, $\dot{\mathbf{p}}_2 = [3, 2]^T$ and $\dot{\mathbf{p}}_3 = [5, 5]^T$ to triangle $\triangle\dot{\mathbf{p}}'_1\dot{\mathbf{p}}'_2\dot{\mathbf{p}}'_3$ where $\dot{\mathbf{p}}'_1 = [3, 8]^T$, $\dot{\mathbf{p}}'_2 = [9, 6]^T$ and $\dot{\mathbf{p}}'_3 = [7, 4]^T$.

**Solution 12.1:** Equation (12.16) can be used. Thus,

$$
\begin{bmatrix} x_1 & y_1 & 1 \\ x_2 & y_2 & 1 \\ x_3 & y_3 & 1 \end{bmatrix}^{-1} = \begin{bmatrix} 5 & 3 & 1 \\ 3 & 2 & 1 \\ 5 & 5 & 1 \end{bmatrix}^{-1} = \begin{bmatrix} 0.75 & -0.5 & -0.25 \\ -0.5 & 0 & 0.5 \\ -1.25 & 2.5 & -0.25 \end{bmatrix}.
$$

(If you do not remember how to calculate the inverse of a matrix, refer to Sect. A.2.2.) Hence, in order to map from the source triangle to the destination one, we will use the affine matrix $\mathtt{A}$ where

$$
\mathtt{A} = \begin{bmatrix}
\left[\begin{bmatrix} x_1 & y_1 & 1 \\ x_2 & y_2 & 1 \\ x_3 & y_3 & 1 \end{bmatrix}^{-1} \begin{bmatrix} x'_1 \\ x'_2 \\ x'_3 \end{bmatrix}\right]^T \\
\left[\begin{bmatrix} x_1 & y_1 & 1 \\ x_2 & y_2 & 1 \\ x_3 & y_3 & 1 \end{bmatrix}^{-1} \begin{bmatrix} y'_1 \\ y'_2 \\ y'_3 \end{bmatrix}\right]^T \\
\left[\begin{bmatrix} x_1 & y_1 & 1 \\ x_2 & y_2 & 1 \\ x_3 & y_3 & 1 \end{bmatrix}^{-1} \begin{bmatrix} 1 \\ 1 \\ 1 \end{bmatrix}\right]^T
\end{bmatrix}
$$

$$
= \begin{bmatrix}
\left[\begin{bmatrix} 0.75 & -0.5 & -0.25 \\ -0.5 & 0 & 0.5 \\ -1.25 & 2.5 & -0.25 \end{bmatrix} \begin{bmatrix} 3 \\ 9 \\ 7 \end{bmatrix}\right]^T \\
\left[\begin{bmatrix} 0.75 & -0.5 & -0.25 \\ -0.5 & 0 & 0.5 \\ -1.25 & 2.5 & -0.25 \end{bmatrix} \begin{bmatrix} 8 \\ 6 \\ 4 \end{bmatrix}\right]^T \\
\left[\begin{bmatrix} 0.75 & -0.5 & -0.25 \\ -0.5 & 0 & 0.5 \\ -1.25 & 2.5 & -0.25 \end{bmatrix} \begin{bmatrix} 1 \\ 1 \\ 1 \end{bmatrix}\right]^T
\end{bmatrix}
= \begin{bmatrix} -4 & 2 & 17 \\ 2 & -2 & 4 \\ 0 & 0 & 1 \end{bmatrix}. \qquad \square
$$

## 12.4 Bilinear Interpolation

Applying the inverse of a $3 \times 3$ transformation matrix will locate the position $\dot{\mathbf{p}}$ of the source intensity/color. In homogeneous coordinates, the result is a 3D vector $\mathbf{p} = [x, y, s]^T$ and in order to get the real 2D location, each element must be divided by the third element $s$. Thus, the source intensity/color position is expressed as $\left[\frac{x}{s}, \frac{y}{s}\right]^T$. These operations may result in fractions (i.e., position falls between pixels as shown in Fig. 12.7). In order to get the intensity/color at the in-between point, bilinear interpolation must be used.

Bilinear interpolation consists of successively interpolating intensity/color values along the two principal directions; i.e., the rows and columns.

1. Interpolate along rows:

$$
\begin{aligned}
I\left(\tfrac{x}{s}, \left\lfloor \tfrac{y}{s} \right\rfloor\right) &= I\left(\left\lfloor \tfrac{x}{s} \right\rfloor, \left\lfloor \tfrac{y}{s} \right\rfloor\right)\left(\left\lceil \tfrac{x}{s} \right\rceil - \tfrac{x}{s}\right) + I\left(\left\lceil \tfrac{x}{s} \right\rceil, \left\lfloor \tfrac{y}{s} \right\rfloor\right)\left(\tfrac{x}{s} - \left\lfloor \tfrac{x}{s} \right\rfloor\right), \\
I\left(\tfrac{x}{s}, \left\lceil \tfrac{y}{s} \right\rceil\right) &= I\left(\left\lfloor \tfrac{x}{s} \right\rfloor, \left\lceil \tfrac{y}{s} \right\rceil\right)\left(\left\lceil \tfrac{x}{s} \right\rceil - \tfrac{x}{s}\right) + I\left(\left\lceil \tfrac{x}{s} \right\rceil, \left\lceil \tfrac{y}{s} \right\rceil\right)\left(\tfrac{x}{s} - \left\lfloor \tfrac{x}{s} \right\rfloor\right).
\end{aligned} \tag{12.17}
$$

2. Interpolate along columns:

$$
I\left(\tfrac{x}{s}, \tfrac{y}{s}\right) = I\left(\tfrac{x}{s}, \left\lfloor \tfrac{y}{s} \right\rfloor\right)\left(\left\lceil \tfrac{y}{s} \right\rceil - \tfrac{y}{s}\right) + I\left(\tfrac{x}{s}, \left\lceil \tfrac{y}{s} \right\rceil\right)\left(\tfrac{y}{s} - \left\lfloor \tfrac{y}{s} \right\rfloor\right), \tag{12.18}
$$

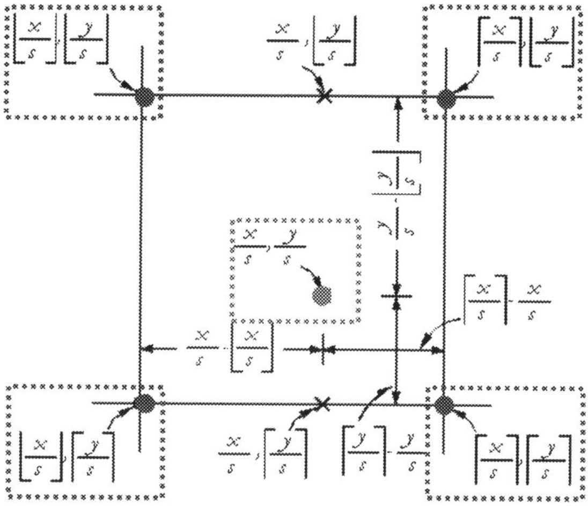

Fig. 12.7 Bilinear interpolation is used to determine the intensity/color of a point between pixels

(a)

| Y \ X | 0 | 1 | 2 | 3 | 4 |
|---|---|---|---|---|---|
| 0 | 100 | 102 | 104 | 102 | 106 |
| 1 | 102 | 105 | 107 | 106 | 106 |
| 2 | 104 | 108 | 108 | 109 | 110 |
| 3 | 105 | 110 | 104 | 106 | 109 |
| 4 | 107 | 105 | 103 | 107 | 105 |

(b)

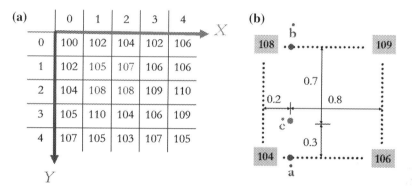

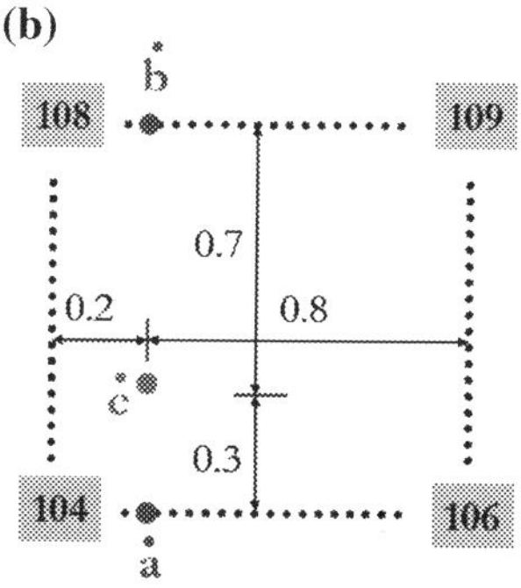


**Fig. 12.8** **a** The upper left corner of an image. **b** $\dot{\mathbf{c}}$ is the point at $[2.2, 2.7]^T$

where $I\left(\frac{x}{s}, \frac{y}{s}\right)$ is the intensity at $\left[\frac{x}{s}, \frac{y}{s}\right]^T$. Note that switching these two steps (i.e., interpolation along columns then interpolation along rows) results in the same outcome.

**Example 12.2:** [*Intensity using bilinear interpolation*]

Figure 12.8a shows the upper left corner of an image; e.g., the intensity at $[0, 0]^T$ is 100 and the intensity at $[3, 2]^T$ is 109. Use bilinear interpolation to get the intensity at $[2.2, 2.7]^T$.

**Solution 12.2:** Consider Fig. 12.8b which shows point $\dot{\mathbf{c}}$ at $[2.2, 2.7]^T$ and use Eq. (12.17) to interpolate along the rows. Thus,

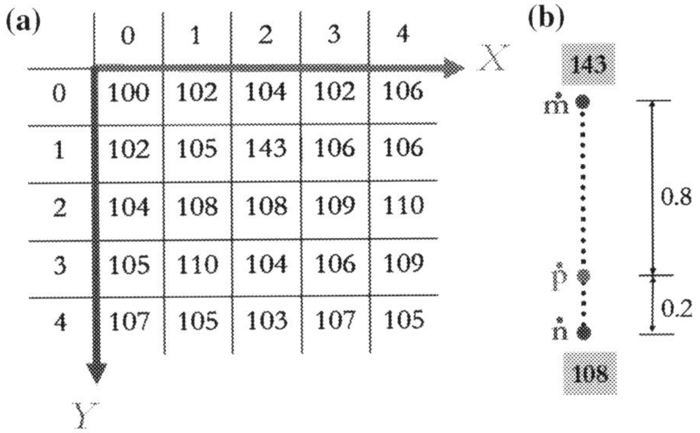


**Fig. 12.9** **a** The upper left corner of an image. **b** Point $\dot{\mathbf{p}}$ has barycentric coordinates of $[0.4, 0.3, 0.3]^T$

$$I(x_{\dot{\mathbf{c}}}, \lfloor y_{\dot{\mathbf{c}}} \rfloor) = I(\lfloor x_{\dot{\mathbf{c}}} \rfloor, \lfloor y_{\dot{\mathbf{c}}} \rfloor)\,(\lceil x_{\dot{\mathbf{c}}} \rceil - x_{\dot{\mathbf{c}}}) + I(\lceil x_{\dot{\mathbf{c}}} \rceil, \lfloor y_{\dot{\mathbf{c}}} \rfloor)\,(x_{\dot{\mathbf{c}}} - \lfloor x_{\dot{\mathbf{c}}} \rfloor)$$

$$\begin{aligned} I_{\dot{\mathbf{b}}}(2.2, 2) &= I(2, 2) \quad (3 - 2.2) \quad + I(3, 2) \quad (2.2 - 2) \\ &= 108 \quad (0.8) \quad + 109 \quad (0.2) \quad = 108.2, \end{aligned}$$

$$I(x_{\dot{\mathbf{c}}}, \lceil y_{\dot{\mathbf{c}}} \rceil) = I(\lfloor x_{\dot{\mathbf{c}}} \rfloor, \lceil y_{\dot{\mathbf{c}}} \rceil)\,(\lceil x_{\dot{\mathbf{c}}} \rceil - x_{\dot{\mathbf{c}}}) + I(\lceil x_{\dot{\mathbf{c}}} \rceil, \lceil y_{\dot{\mathbf{c}}} \rceil)\,(x_{\dot{\mathbf{c}}} - \lfloor x_{\dot{\mathbf{c}}} \rfloor)$$

$$\begin{aligned} I_{\dot{\mathbf{a}}}(2.2, 3) &= I(2, 3) \quad (3 - 2.2) \quad + I(3, 3) \quad (2.2 - 2) \\ &= 104 \quad (0.8) \quad + 106 \quad (0.2) \quad = 104.4. \end{aligned}$$

Then, use Eq. (12.18) to interpolate along the columns. So,

$$I(x_{\dot{\mathbf{c}}}, y_{\dot{\mathbf{c}}}) = I(x_{\dot{\mathbf{c}}}, \lfloor y_{\dot{\mathbf{c}}} \rfloor)\,(\lceil y_{\dot{\mathbf{c}}} \rceil - y_{\dot{\mathbf{c}}}) + I(x_{\dot{\mathbf{c}}}, \lceil y_{\dot{\mathbf{c}}} \rceil)\,(y_{\dot{\mathbf{c}}} - \lfloor y_{\dot{\mathbf{c}}} \rfloor)$$

$$\begin{aligned} I_{\dot{\mathbf{c}}}(2.2, 2.7) &= I_{\dot{\mathbf{b}}}(2.2, 2) \quad (3 - 2.7) \quad + I_{\dot{\mathbf{a}}}(2.2, 3) \quad (2.7 - 2) \\ &= 108.2 \quad (0.3) \quad + 104.4 \quad (0.7) \quad = 105.54. \end{aligned}$$

The intensity at $[2.2, 2.7]^T$ should be approximated to the nearest integer; i.e., $I_{\dot{\mathbf{c}}}(2.2, 2.7)$ is approximated to 106. □

**Example 12.3:** [*Intensity using bilinear interpolation—barycentric coordinates*]
Figure 12.9a shows the upper left corner of an image. Consider the triangle with vertices $\dot{\mathbf{a}} = [2, 0]^T$, $\dot{\mathbf{b}} = [4, 2]^T$ and $\dot{\mathbf{c}} = [0, 4]^T$. Determine the intensity of a point $\dot{\mathbf{p}}$ whose barycentric coordinates are $[0.4, 0.3, 0.3]^T$. (A discussion about barycentric coordinates can be found in Sect. B.3.)

**Solution 12.3:** The answer to this problem has two steps:

1. Get the Cartesian coordinates of point $\dot{\mathbf{p}}$ whose barycentric coordinates are $[0.4, 0.3, 0.3]^T$. This can be done using Eq. (B.16) as

$$\begin{aligned}\dot{\mathbf{p}} &= t_{\dot{\mathbf{a}}}\,\dot{\mathbf{a}} + t_{\dot{\mathbf{b}}}\,\dot{\mathbf{b}} + t_{\dot{\mathbf{c}}}\,\dot{\mathbf{c}}\\ &= 0.4 \times \begin{bmatrix}2\\0\end{bmatrix} + 0.3 \times \begin{bmatrix}4\\2\end{bmatrix} + 0.3 \times \begin{bmatrix}0\\4\end{bmatrix} = \begin{bmatrix}2\\1.8\end{bmatrix}.\end{aligned}$$

2. Get the intensity of point $\dot{\mathbf{p}}$, which lies along column number 2 as shown in Fig. 12.9b. We use Eq. (12.18) to interpolate along this column. Thus,

$$I_{\dot{\mathbf{p}}}\left(x_{\dot{\mathbf{p}}}, y_{\dot{\mathbf{p}}}\right) = I\left(x_{\dot{\mathbf{p}}}, \lfloor y_{\dot{\mathbf{p}}}\rfloor\right)\left(\lceil y_{\dot{\mathbf{p}}}\rceil - y_{\dot{\mathbf{p}}}\right) + I\left(x_{\dot{\mathbf{p}}}, \lceil y_{\dot{\mathbf{p}}}\rceil\right)\left(y_{\dot{\mathbf{p}}} - \lfloor y_{\dot{\mathbf{p}}}\rfloor\right)$$

$$\begin{aligned}I_{\dot{\mathbf{p}}}(2, 1.8) &= I_{\dot{\mathbf{m}}}(2, 1) \quad (2 - 1.8) \quad + I_{\dot{\mathbf{n}}}(2, 2) \quad (1.8 - 1)\\ &= 143 \quad (0.2) \quad + 108 \quad (0.8) \quad = 115.\square\end{aligned}$$

**Example 12.4:** [*Mapping using barycentric coordinates*]

We discussed how to map one triangle $\triangle\dot{\mathbf{p}}_1\dot{\mathbf{p}}_2\dot{\mathbf{p}}_3$ to another triangle $\triangle\dot{\mathbf{p}}'_1\dot{\mathbf{p}}'_2\dot{\mathbf{p}}'_3$ using Cartesian coordinates. The mapping process can be performed using barycentric coordinates (Sect. B.3) of both triangles. Suggest the steps that may be followed to achieve the mapping.

**Solution 12.4:** For every point $\dot{\mathbf{p}}' = [x', y']^T$ in the destination triangle, do the following:

1. Get its barycentric coordinates $[t_{\dot{\mathbf{p}}'_1}, t_{\dot{\mathbf{p}}'_2}, t_{\dot{\mathbf{p}}'_3}]^T$. Equation (B.14) may be used to get these coordinates as

$$\begin{bmatrix}t_{\dot{\mathbf{p}}'_1}\\ t_{\dot{\mathbf{p}}'_2}\\ t_{\dot{\mathbf{p}}'_3}\end{bmatrix} = \frac{1}{\left|[\dot{\mathbf{p}}'_2 - \dot{\mathbf{p}}'_1][\dot{\mathbf{p}}'_3 - \dot{\mathbf{p}}'_1]\right|}\begin{bmatrix}\left|[\dot{\mathbf{p}}'_2 - \dot{\mathbf{p}}'][\dot{\mathbf{p}}'_3 - \dot{\mathbf{p}}']\right|\\ \left|[\dot{\mathbf{p}}'_3 - \dot{\mathbf{p}}'][\dot{\mathbf{p}}'_1 - \dot{\mathbf{p}}']\right|\\ \left|[\dot{\mathbf{p}}'_1 - \dot{\mathbf{p}}'][\dot{\mathbf{p}}'_2 - \dot{\mathbf{p}}']\right|\end{bmatrix}.$$

2. Use the above-obtained barycentric coordinates $[t_{\dot{\mathbf{p}}'_1}, t_{\dot{\mathbf{p}}'_2}, t_{\dot{\mathbf{p}}'_3}]^T$ along with the vertices of the source triangle to get the Cartesian coordinates $[x, y]^T$ of the corresponding point $\dot{\mathbf{p}}$ in the source triangle. Equation (B.16) may be used to get the Cartesian coordinates as

$$\dot{\mathbf{p}} = \begin{bmatrix}x\\y\end{bmatrix} = t_{\dot{\mathbf{p}}'_1}\,\dot{\mathbf{p}}_1 + t_{\dot{\mathbf{p}}'_2}\,\dot{\mathbf{p}}_2 + t_{\dot{\mathbf{p}}'_3}\,\dot{\mathbf{p}}_3.$$

3. If the location of point $\dot{\mathbf{p}}$ falls between pixels, use bilinear interpolation to get its intensity. Start by interpolating along the rows. Thus,

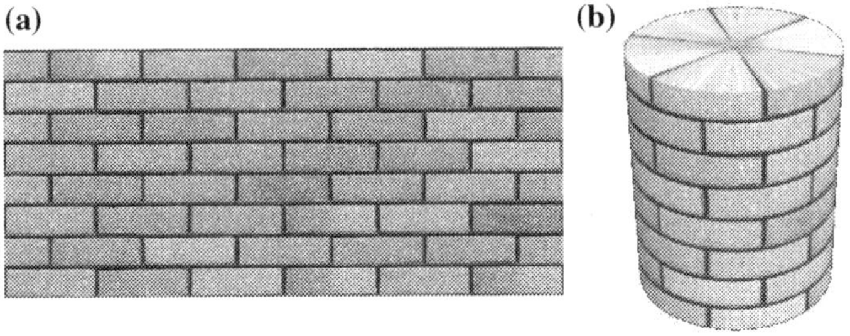


Fig. 12.10 Cylindrical map projection. **a** A map. **b** The map after wrapping on a cylinder

$$I\left(x_{\dot{\mathbf{p}}}, \lfloor y_{\dot{\mathbf{p}}} \rfloor\right) = I\left(\lfloor x_{\dot{\mathbf{p}}} \rfloor, \lfloor y_{\dot{\mathbf{p}}} \rfloor\right)\left(\lceil x_{\dot{\mathbf{p}}} \rceil - x_{\dot{\mathbf{p}}}\right) + I\left(\lceil x_{\dot{\mathbf{p}}} \rceil, \lfloor y_{\dot{\mathbf{p}}} \rfloor\right)\left(x_{\dot{\mathbf{p}}} - \lfloor x_{\dot{\mathbf{p}}} \rfloor\right),$$

$$I\left(x_{\dot{\mathbf{p}}}, \lceil y_{\dot{\mathbf{p}}} \rceil\right) = I\left(\lfloor x_{\dot{\mathbf{p}}} \rfloor, \lceil y_{\dot{\mathbf{p}}} \rceil\right)\left(\lceil x_{\dot{\mathbf{p}}} \rceil - x_{\dot{\mathbf{p}}}\right) + I\left(\lceil x_{\dot{\mathbf{p}}} \rceil, \lceil y_{\dot{\mathbf{p}}} \rceil\right)\left(x_{\dot{\mathbf{p}}} - \lfloor x_{\dot{\mathbf{p}}} \rfloor\right).$$

Then, continue to interpolate along the columns as

$$I_{\dot{\mathbf{p}}}\left(x_{\dot{\mathbf{p}}}, y_{\dot{\mathbf{p}}}\right) = I\left(x_{\dot{\mathbf{p}}}, \lfloor y_{\dot{\mathbf{p}}} \rfloor\right)\left(\lceil y_{\dot{\mathbf{p}}} \rceil - y_{\dot{\mathbf{p}}}\right) + I\left(x_{\dot{\mathbf{p}}}, \lceil y_{\dot{\mathbf{p}}} \rceil\right)\left(y_{\dot{\mathbf{p}}} - \lfloor y_{\dot{\mathbf{p}}} \rfloor\right).$$

The intensity of point $\dot{\mathbf{p}}'$ is $I_{\dot{\mathbf{p}}}\left(x_{\dot{\mathbf{p}}}, y_{\dot{\mathbf{p}}}\right)$. □

## 12.5 Map Projection

From the previous discussion, we can say that texture mapping is like projecting an image onto a 3D surface. This 3D surface may be planar (i.e., what has been discussed in this chapter so far) or curved (e.g., a sphere or a cylinder) so that the map is wrapped around it. Thus, different mapping coordinates appear. The common types are planar map projection, box map projection, cylindrical map projection and spherical map projection.

In planar map projection, the map is projected onto a flat surface. Similarly, in box map projection, the map is projected onto all surfaces of a box where each side can be regarded as a single planar map projection. Determining which pixel in the map is projected to which point on the surface may be harder in case of curved surfaces. We will talk about the cases of cylindrical and spherical surfaces.

### *12.5.1 Cylindrical Map Projection*

Cylindrical map projection wraps a map around a cylindrical surface as shown in Fig. 12.10. Planar map projection may be used for capping. Cylindrical coordinates are used to locate a point on a cylindrical surface as discussed in Sect. B.5 where the base of the cylinder, whose height is $h$, is centered at the origin on the $xy$-plane. A point is defined by a radial coordinate $r$ and an angular coordinate $\theta$ [where $\theta \in [0, 2\pi)$] measured about the $z$-axis from the positive $x$-axis. This is in addition to a height coordinate $z$. Refer to Fig. B.9a for illustration. The Cartesian coordinates $[x, y, z]^T$ of a point $[r, \theta, z]^T$ in cylindrical system can be expressed as

$$\begin{bmatrix} x \\ y \\ z \end{bmatrix} = \begin{bmatrix} r\cos(\theta) \\ r\sin(\theta) \\ z \end{bmatrix}. \tag{12.19}$$

A point on the $uv$-map (that it to be wrapped around the cylinder) is expressed as $[u, v]^T$ where $u \in [0, 1]$ and $v \in [0, 1]$. If the map is to be wrapped completely around the cylinder and according to the interval of $\theta$ and the height $h$ of the cylinder, the width of the map can be expressed as $2\pi$ and the height as $h$. Thus, it can be said that

$$\begin{aligned} u &= \frac{\theta}{2\pi}, \\ v &= \frac{z}{h}, \end{aligned} \tag{12.20}$$

which represent the location of a point on the $uv$-map given the cylindrical coordinates of the 3D point. Hence, Eq. (12.19) can be re-written as

$$\begin{bmatrix} x \\ y \\ z \end{bmatrix} = \begin{bmatrix} r\cos(2\pi u) \\ r\sin(2\pi u) \\ hv \end{bmatrix}. \tag{12.21}$$

Accordingly, from the $x$-component, $u$ is estimated as

$$u = \frac{\cos^{-1}\left(\frac{x}{r}\right)}{2\pi} = \frac{\cos^{-1}\left(\frac{x}{\sqrt{x^2+y^2}}\right)}{2\pi} \tag{12.22}$$

and from the $z$-component, $v$ is estimated as

$$v = \frac{z}{h}. \tag{12.23}$$

This means that the location of a point on the $uv$-map can be obtained if the $x$-, $y$- and $z$-coordinates of the point as well as the height of the cylinder are known. Equations (12.22) and (12.23) are used when the base of the right cylinder, whose height is $h$, is centered at the origin on the $xy$-plane.

**Example 12.5:** [*Cylindrical mapping—points in Cartesian coordinates*]
Consider a right cylinder with a lower base residing on the $zx$-plane. The base is having a radius $r$ and centered at the origin. The angle $\theta$ is measured about the $y$-axis from the positive $z$-axis and the height $h$ of the cylinder is considered along the $y$-axis. Determine the Cartesian coordinates of the point $[r, y, \theta]^T$.

**Solution 12.5:** According to Sect. B.5.2, a point $[r, y, \theta]^T$ on the cylindrical surface has its Cartesian coordinates $[x, y, z]^T$ expressed as

$$\begin{bmatrix} x \\ y \\ z \end{bmatrix} = \begin{bmatrix} r\sin(\theta) \\ y \\ r\cos(\theta) \end{bmatrix}. \qquad \square \quad (12.24)$$

**Example 12.6:** [*Cylindrical mapping—points on a uv-map*]
In Example 12.5, determine the location $[u, v]^T$ of the point $[r, y, \theta]^T$ on a map when wrapped completely on the cylindrical surface.

**Solution 12.6:** A point on the $uv$-map is expressed as $[u, v]^T$ where $u \in [0, 1]$ and $v \in [0, 1]$. When the map is wrapped completely around the cylindrical surface, the width of the map can be expressed as $2\pi$ and the height as $h$ (i.e., the height of the cylinder). Hence,

$$\begin{aligned} u &= \frac{\theta}{2\pi}, \\ v &= \frac{y}{h}, \end{aligned} \qquad (12.25)$$

which represent the location of a point on the $uv$-map given the cylindrical coordinates of the 3D point. $\square$

**Example 12.7:** [*Cylindrical mapping—Cartesian points in terms of uv-coordinates*]
Re-write Eq. (12.24) in terms of $uv$-coordinates.

**Solution 12.7:** Substituting the values of $\theta$ and $y$ from Eq. (12.25), we may re-write Eq. (12.24) as

$$\begin{bmatrix} x \\ y \\ z \end{bmatrix} = \begin{bmatrix} r\sin(2\pi u) \\ hv \\ r\cos(2\pi u) \end{bmatrix} = \begin{bmatrix} \sqrt{x^2+z^2}\sin(2\pi u) \\ hv \\ \sqrt{x^2+z^2}\cos(2\pi u) \end{bmatrix}. \qquad \square \quad (12.26)$$

**Example 12.8:** [*Cylindrical mapping—uv points in terms of Cartesian coordinates*]
Re-write Eq. (12.25) in terms of Cartesian coordinates.

**Solution 12.8:** From the $x$-component of Eq. (12.26), $u$ is estimated as

$$u = \frac{\sin^{-1}\left(\frac{x}{r}\right)}{2\pi} = \frac{\sin^{-1}\left(\frac{x}{\sqrt{x^2+z^2}}\right)}{2\pi}. \qquad (12.27)$$

Also, from the $z$-component, $u$ is estimated as

$$u = \frac{\cos^{-1}\left(\frac{z}{r}\right)}{2\pi} = \frac{\cos^{-1}\left(\frac{z}{\sqrt{x^2+z^2}}\right)}{2\pi} \tag{12.28}$$

and from the $y$-component, $v$ is estimated as

$$v = \frac{y}{h}. \tag{12.29}$$

This means that the location of a point on the $uv$-map can be obtained if the $x$-, $y$- and $z$-coordinates of the point as well as the height of the cylinder are known. Equations (12.27), (12.28) and (12.29) are used when the base of the right cylinder, whose height is $h$, is centered at the origin on the $zx$-plane. □

**Example 12.9:** [*Cylindrical mapping—intensity of pixels*]
In texture mapping, you are dealing with different spaces and coordinates systems:

1. A 3D modeling space using right-handed system.
2. A 2D map that contains the texels where the $y$-axis is pointing downwards.
3. A 2D output image where the $y$-axis is pointing downwards.

Consider the following assumptions:

1. You have a cylinder (e.g., a can of Coke) with lower base residing on the $zx$-plane. This lower base, whose radius $r$ is 100 units, is centered at $[100, 0, -100]^T$. The height $h$ of the cylinder is 350 units.
2. You have a map of size 480 × 350 texels. For simplicity, the intensities can be obtained as

$$I(x_u, y_v) = \left\lceil \frac{3}{2} x_u \% y_v \right\rceil,$$

   where $I(x_u, y_v)$ is the intensity at $[x_u, y_v]^T$; $\lceil . \rceil$ represents the ceiling operation; and % represents the modulus.
3. The whole map is wrapped onto the curved surface of the cylinder so that this curved surface is fully covered by the map and the whole map appears on the cylinder. The wrapping starts and ends where the cylinder touches the $yz$-plane.
4. A front view whose normal is $[0, 0, 1]^T$ is obtained for the cylinder and an output image of 200 × 350 is created.

Get the intensity of the output pixel $[150, 25]^T$.

**Solution 12.9:** Notice that the height of the cylinder is equal to the height of the map (as well as the output image) and the diameter of the cylinder is equal to the width of the output image. Figure 12.11 shows the three coordinate systems considered and also shows how the angle $\theta$ is estimated. We can work with the cylindrical coordinates to get the map coordinates $u$ and $v$ and use those coordinates to get the intensity of the corresponding pixel. The steps of the solution are the following:

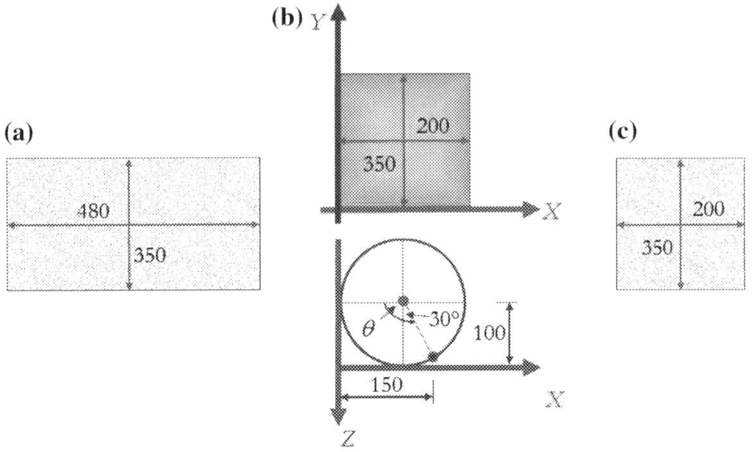


**Fig. 12.11** Cylindrical map projection: An example. **a** The map. **b** The 3D coordinate system shown as multi-view projections. **c** The output image

1. Get the location of the point in 3D space (in cylindrical coordinates). Thus,

$$
\begin{aligned}
r &= 100, \\
\theta &= 90 + \sin^{-1}\left(\frac{50}{100}\right) = 120^\circ, \\
y &= h - 25 = 350 - 25 = 325.
\end{aligned}
$$

   Pay attention that the height of the cylinder in this example is along the $y$-axis. Also, notice that the angle $\theta$ is measured starting from the negative $x$-direction to simplify the current case of front projection.
2. Get the location on the map as $[u, v]^T$ as

$$
\begin{aligned}
u &= \frac{\theta}{2\pi} = \frac{120}{360} = \frac{1}{3}, \\
v &= \frac{h-y}{h} = \frac{350-325}{350} = \frac{1}{14}.
\end{aligned}
$$

   Note that we used $h - y$ as the $y$-axis of the map is pointing downwards while the $y$-axis of the 3D coordinate system is pointing upwards (as it is a right-handed coordinate system).
3. Get the location of $[u, v]^T$ in pixels $[x_u, y_v]^T$ as

$$
\begin{aligned}
x_u &= 480u = \frac{480}{3} = 160, \\
y_v &= 350v = \frac{350}{14} = 25.
\end{aligned}
$$

**Fig. 12.12** Spherical map projection. **a** A map. **b** The map after wrapping on a sphere

4. Get the intensity of the source point as

$$I(x_u, y_v) = \left\lceil \frac{3}{2} x_u \, \% y_v \right\rceil = \left\lceil \frac{3}{2} 160 \, \% 25 \right\rceil = 15.$$

Thus, the intensity of the output pixel $[150, 25]^T$ is 15. □

## 12.5.2 Spherical Map Projection

Spherical map projection wraps a map around a spherical surface as shown in Fig. 12.12. Spherical coordinates are used to locate a point on a spherical surface as discussed in Sect. B.6. Considering a sphere whose radius is $r$ and centered at the origin, two angles are used to determine the point spherical coordinates. These angles are $\theta$ and $\phi$ where $\theta \in [0, 2\pi)$ and $\phi \in [0, \pi]$. The first angle $\theta$ is the azimuth angle in the $xy$-plane from the positive $x$-axis while the second angle $\phi$ is the zenith angle from the positive $z$-axis. You may refer to Fig. B.10a for illustration. The Cartesian coordinates $[x, y, z]^T$ of a point $[r, \theta, \phi]^T$ in spherical system can be expressed as

$$\begin{bmatrix} x \\ y \\ z \end{bmatrix} = \begin{bmatrix} r\cos(\theta)\sin(\phi) \\ r\sin(\theta)\sin(\phi) \\ r\cos(\phi) \end{bmatrix}. \tag{12.30}$$

A point on the $uv$-map (that it to be wrapped around the sphere) is expressed as $[u, v]^T$ where $u \in [0, 1]$ and $v \in [0, 1]$. If the map is to be wrapped completely around the sphere and according to the intervals of $\theta$ and $\phi$, the width of the map can be expressed as $2\pi$ and the height as $\pi$. Thus, it can be said that

$$\begin{aligned} u &= \frac{\theta}{2\pi}, \\ v &= \frac{\phi}{\pi}, \end{aligned} \tag{12.31}$$

which represent the location of a point on the $uv$-map given the spherical coordinates of the 3D point. Hence, Eq. (12.30) can be re-written as

$$\begin{bmatrix} x \\ y \\ z \end{bmatrix} = \begin{bmatrix} r\cos(2\pi u)\sin(\pi v) \\ r\sin(2\pi u)\sin(\pi v) \\ r\cos(\pi v) \end{bmatrix}. \tag{12.32}$$

Accordingly, from the $z$-component, $v$ is estimated as

$$v = \frac{\cos^{-1}\left(\frac{z}{r}\right)}{\pi} = \frac{\cos^{-1}\left(\frac{z}{\sqrt{x^2+y^2}}\right)}{\pi} \tag{12.33}$$

and from the $x$-component, $u$ is estimated as

$$u = \frac{\cos^{-1}\left(\frac{x}{r\sin(\pi v)}\right)}{2\pi} = \frac{\cos^{-1}\left(\frac{x}{\sqrt{x^2+y^2}\sin(\pi v)}\right)}{2\pi}. \tag{12.34}$$

Alternatively, $u$ is estimated from the $y$-component as

$$u = \frac{\sin^{-1}\left(\frac{y}{r\sin(\pi v)}\right)}{2\pi} = \frac{\sin^{-1}\left(\frac{y}{\sqrt{x^2+y^2}\sin(\pi v)}\right)}{2\pi}. \tag{12.35}$$

This means that the location of a point on the $uv$-map can be obtained if the $x$-, $y$- and $z$-coordinates of the point are known. Equations (12.33), (12.34) and (12.35) are used when the azimuth angle is measured in the $xy$-plane from the positive $x$-axis while the zenith angle is measured from the positive $z$-axis.

**Example 12.10:** [*Spherical mapping—points on a map when the azimuth angle is measured about the y-axis and the zenith angle is measured from the positive y-axis*]

In case the azimuth angle $\theta$ is measured about the $y$-axis and the zenith angle $\phi$ is measured from the positive $y$-axis, determine the location of a point $[u, v]^T$ on the map when wrapped completely on a sphere of radius $r$ that is centered at the origin.

**Solution 12.10:** According to Sect. B.6.2, a point $[r, \phi, \theta]^T$ on the spherical surface has its Cartesian coordinates $[x, y, z]^T$ expressed as

$$\begin{bmatrix} x \\ y \\ z \end{bmatrix} = \begin{bmatrix} r\sin(\theta)\sin(\phi) \\ r\cos(\phi) \\ r\cos(\theta)\sin(\phi) \end{bmatrix}. \tag{12.36}$$

A point on the $uv$-map is expressed as $[u, v]^T$ where $u \in [0, 1]$ and $v \in [0, 1]$. When the map is wrapped completely around the spherical surface, the width of the map can be expressed as $2\pi$ and the height as $\pi$. Hence,

$$
\begin{aligned}
u &= \frac{\theta}{2\pi},\\
v &= \frac{\phi}{\pi},
\end{aligned}
\tag{12.37}
$$

which represent the location of a point on the $uv$-map given the spherical coordinates of the 3D point. Equation (12.36) can be re-written as

$$
\begin{bmatrix} x \\ y \\ z \end{bmatrix} = \begin{bmatrix} r \sin(2\pi u)\sin(\pi v) \\ r\cos(\pi v) \\ r\cos(2\pi u)\sin(\pi v) \end{bmatrix}. \tag{12.38}
$$

Accordingly, from the $y$-component, $v$ is estimated as

$$
v = \frac{\cos^{-1}\left(\frac{y}{r}\right)}{\pi} = \frac{\cos^{-1}\left(\frac{y}{\sqrt{x^2+z^2}}\right)}{\pi} \tag{12.39}
$$

and from the $z$-component, $u$ is estimated as

$$
u = \frac{\cos^{-1}\left(\frac{z}{r\sin(\pi v)}\right)}{2\pi} = \frac{\cos^{-1}\left(\frac{z}{\sqrt{x^2+z^2}\sin(\pi v)}\right)}{2\pi}. \tag{12.40}
$$

Alternatively, $u$ is estimated from the $x$-component as

$$
u = \frac{\sin^{-1}\left(\frac{x}{r\sin(\pi v)}\right)}{2\pi} = \frac{\sin^{-1}\left(\frac{x}{\sqrt{x^2+z^2}\sin(\pi v)}\right)}{2\pi}. \tag{12.41}
$$

This means that the location of a point on the $uv$-map can be obtained if the $x$-, $y$- and $z$-coordinates of the point are known. Equations (12.39), (12.40) and (12.41) are used when the azimuth angle is measured in the $zx$-plane from the positive $z$-axis while the zenith angle is measured from the positive $y$-axis. □

**Example 12.11:** [*Spherical mapping—points on a map when the azimuth angle is measured about the z-axis*]

Consider a sphere whose radius $r$ is 5 and centered at $[3, 3, 3]^T$. If the azimuth angle is measured about the $z$-axis, determine the $uv$-coordinates for the point $[8, 3, 3]^T$.

**Solution 12.11:** The center of the sphere must be translated to the origin; thus, the point $[8, 3, 3]^T$ is translated to

$$
\begin{bmatrix} 8 \\ 3 \\ 3 \end{bmatrix} - \begin{bmatrix} 3 \\ 3 \\ 3 \end{bmatrix} = \begin{bmatrix} 5 \\ 0 \\ 0 \end{bmatrix}.
$$

Utilizing Eq. (12.33), $v$ is estimated as

$$v = \frac{\cos^{-1}\left(\frac{z}{r}\right)}{\pi} = \frac{\cos^{-1}\left(\frac{0}{5}\right)}{180} = 0.5$$

and $u$ is estimated using Eq. (12.34) as

$$u = \frac{\cos^{-1}\left(\frac{x}{r\sin(\pi v)}\right)}{2\pi} = \frac{\cos^{-1}\left(\frac{5}{5\sin(0.5\pi)}\right)}{2\times 180} = 0.$$

Alternatively, $u$ is estimated using Eq. (12.35) as

$$u = \frac{\sin^{-1}\left(\frac{y}{r\sin(\pi v)}\right)}{2\pi} = \frac{\sin^{-1}\left(\frac{0}{5\sin(0.5\pi)}\right)}{2\times 180} = 0.$$

□

**Example 12.12:** [*Spherical mapping—points on a map when the azimuth angle is measured about the y-axis*]

Re-solve Problem 12.11 if the azimuth angle is measured about the $y$-axis.

**Solution 12.12:** The center of the sphere must be translated to the origin; thus, the point $[8, 3, 3]^T$ is translated to

$$\begin{bmatrix}8\\3\\3\end{bmatrix} - \begin{bmatrix}3\\3\\3\end{bmatrix} = \begin{bmatrix}5\\0\\0\end{bmatrix}.$$

Utilizing Eq. (12.39), $v$ is estimated as

$$v = \frac{\cos^{-1}\left(\frac{y}{r}\right)}{\pi} = \frac{\cos^{-1}\left(\frac{0}{5}\right)}{180} = 0.5$$

and $u$ is estimated using Eq. (12.40) as

$$u = \frac{\cos^{-1}\left(\frac{z}{r\sin(\pi v)}\right)}{2\pi}$$

$$= \frac{\cos^{-1}\left(\frac{0}{5\sin(0.5\pi)}\right)}{2 \times 180} = 0.25.$$

Alternatively, $u$ is estimated using Eq. (12.41) as

$$u = \frac{\sin^{-1}\left(\frac{x}{r\sin(\pi v)}\right)}{2\pi}$$
$$= \frac{\sin^{-1}\left(\frac{5}{5\sin(0.5\pi)}\right)}{2 \times 180} = 0.25. \quad \square$$

## 12.6 Mapping Types

There are many types of mapping; maps that affect the main color components and maps that add new characteristics to the material. For example, *ambient* and *specular mapping* are used where the map is applied to the ambient and specular areas of the object respectively. Other mapping types may include *shininess mapping* that affects the locations of highlights where lighter areas in a shininess map result in shiny regions; *self-illumination mapping* that lets us use a map to affect the intensity in different areas of a self-illuminated surface according to the intensity levels of the map where lighter areas of the map result in self-illuminated regions on the surface; and *filter color mapping* that applies a transparent color to the object under consideration where the appearance of this color depends on the intensities of the map pixels. Below are some other important types of mapping.

### 12.6.1 Diffuse Mapping

*Diffuse mapping* affects the basic appearance of a material. It may alter the original color assigned previously to a material into an image. Applying a diffuse map is like painting an image on the surface of an object. For example, to render a wall made of brick, we can apply a brick bitmap image as a diffuse map. This is shown in Fig. 12.13. An example of diffuse mapping is shown in Fig. 12.14.

### 12.6.2 Bump Mapping

*Bump mapping* (Blinn 1978) is an important concept that is used to add roughness or wrinkles to a smooth surface. It helps us make features on surfaces look raised or sunk; i.e., it alters the height appearance, without altering the geometry of the object

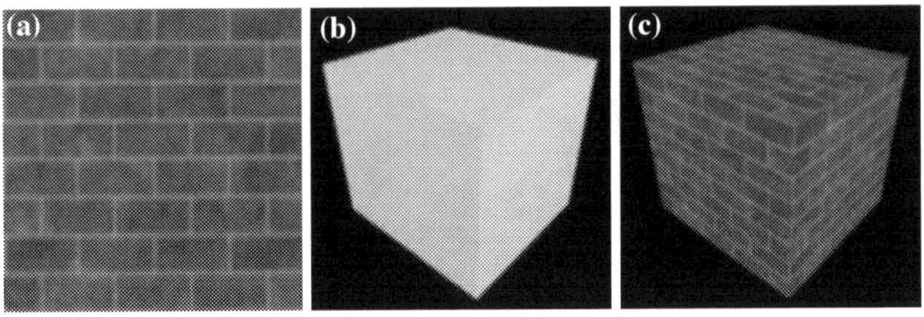


**Fig. 12.13** Using diffuse mapping to paint an image of a brick wall on an object. **a** A bitmap image. **b** A cube. **c** The image in (**a**) is diffuse-mapped on cube (**b**)

**Fig. 12.14** An example of diffuse mapping. Part of the floor is magnified to show the effect of diffuse mapping

under consideration. In order to do that, bump mapping uses the brightness values of an image. Bright regions will look raised while dark regions look sunk. This is done by perturbing the normal to the surface vector by another vector that depends on the values in the bump map space. This mapping type could be used to obtain coarse texture in walls for instance. Refer to Fig. 12.15. Thus, although the appearance of coarse surface, the surface itself remains smooth. This is in contrast to *displacement mapping* (Cook et al. 1987) where the surface is displaced or modified. An example of bump mapping is shown in Fig. 12.16.

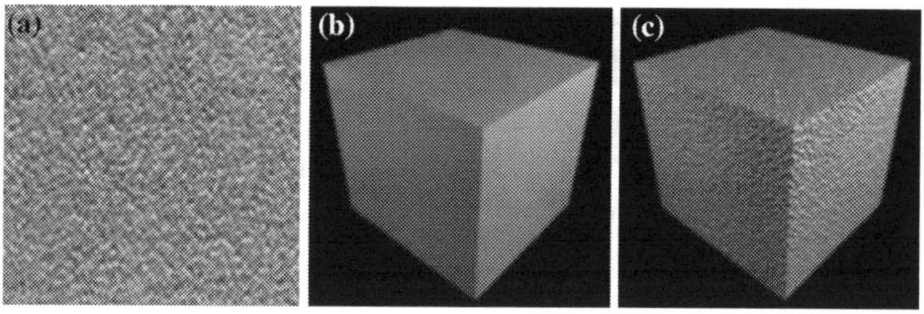


**Fig. 12.15** Using bump mapping to provide coarse texture. **a** A bitmap image. **b** A cube. **c** The image in (**a**) is bump-mapped on cube (**b**). Notice that the image in (**a**) only affected the texture while the color remains unchanged

**Fig. 12.16** An example of bump mapping. Skirting is magnified to show the effect of bump mapping

## *12.6.3 Reflection Mapping*

*Reflection mapping* is also known as *environment mapping* (Blinn and Newell 1976). Reflection mapping calculates the reflection direction of a ray from the viewer to the point being shaded. This type of mapping creates the effect of a scene reflected on the surface of a shiny or reflective object; e.g., mirror, glass or brass. For example, this mapping type can be used to get the effect of reflection of the sky on windows as seen in Fig. 12.17. Note that with this type of mapping, if the reflective surface moves in the environment, the image reflected on it does not move with the surface. However, the map does move with changes in viewpoints. This is different from

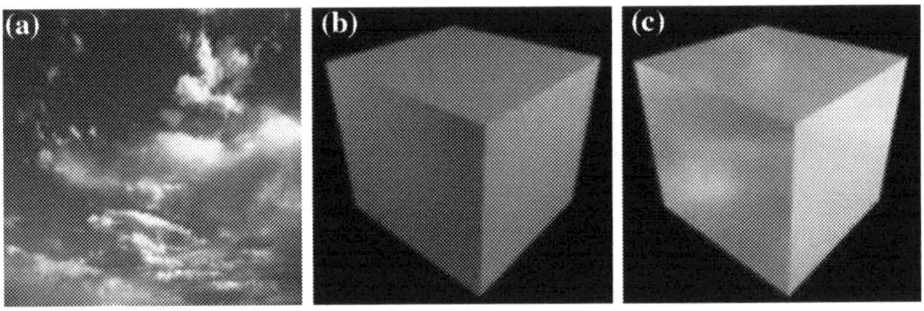


**Fig. 12.17** Using reflection mapping to get the effect of reflection of the sky. **a** A bitmap image. **b** A cube. **c** The image in (**a**) is reflection-mapped on cube (**b**)

**Fig. 12.18** An example of reflection mapping. Part of a window is magnified to show the effect of reflection of the sky

diffuse mapping, for example, where the map is attached to the surface and moves with it. An example of reflection mapping is shown in Fig. 12.18.

### *12.6.4 Refraction Mapping*

Instead of reflecting the map off the surface as in the previous type, *refraction mapping* allows the map to be perceived as if it is seen through the object. This is illustrated in Fig. 12.19. Similar to reflection mapping, refraction mapping depends on the viewpoint rather than the movement of the object.

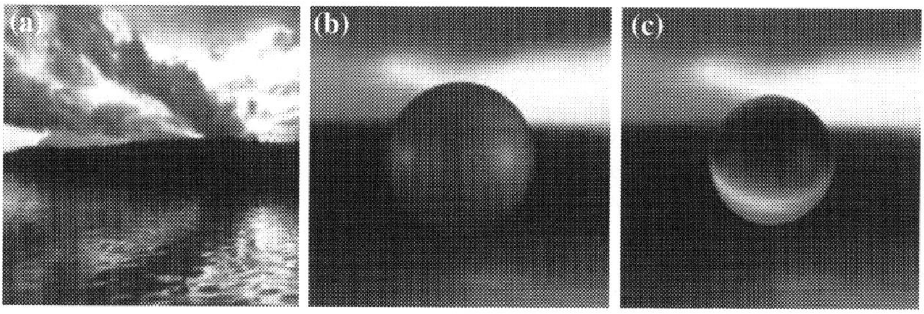


**Fig. 12.19** Using refraction mapping lets us perceive the map as if it is seen through the object. **a** A bitmap image. **b** A sphere. **c** The image in (**a**) is refraction-mapped on sphere (**b**)

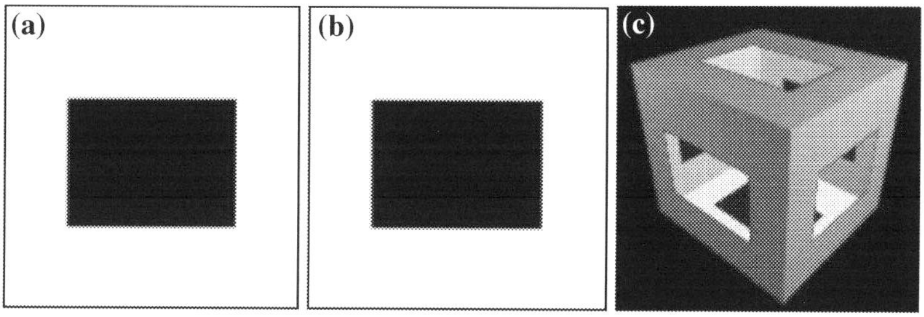


**Fig. 12.20** Using opacity mapping to alter the opacity of a surface. **a** A bitmap image. **b** A cube. **c** The image in (**a**) used as an opacity map results in a transparent region on the faces of the cube

### *12.6.5 Opacity Mapping*

*Opacity mapping* affects the opacity or transparency of objects. It uses the intensity levels of the opacity map image to alter the opacity of a surface. For example, dark areas when mapped onto an object result in more translucent regions while lighter areas result in more opaque regions. This is illustrated in Fig. 12.20.

## 12.7 Problems

**Problem 12.1:** [*Affine transformation matrix*]

Derive the affine transformation matrix used for mapping from triangle $\triangle\dot{\mathbf{p}}_1\dot{\mathbf{p}}_2\dot{\mathbf{p}}_3$ where $\dot{\mathbf{p}}_1 = [1, 1]^T$, $\dot{\mathbf{p}}_2 = [3, 3]^T$ and $\dot{\mathbf{p}}_3 = [4, 1]^T$ to triangle $\triangle\dot{\mathbf{p}}'_1\dot{\mathbf{p}}'_2\dot{\mathbf{p}}'_3$ where $\dot{\mathbf{p}}'_1 = [3, 4]^T$, $\dot{\mathbf{p}}'_2 = [7, 6]^T$ and $\dot{\mathbf{p}}'_3 = [5, 2]^T$.

**Problem 12.2:** [*Affine matrix—destination points*]

Using the derived matrix in Problem 12.1, what location in the destination triangle a source point $[3, 2]^T$ is mapped to?

**Problem 12.3:** [*Affine matrix—source points*]
Using the derived matrix in Problem 12.1, what location in the source triangle a destination point $[5, 4]^T$ is mapped to? And if the intensities (from left to right and top to bottom) of the surrounding source pixels are 100, 110, 103, 107, calculate the intensity of the source point.

**Problem 12.4:** [*Intensity using bilinear interpolation*]
Figure 12.8a shows the upper left corner of an image; e.g., the intensity at $[0, 0]^T$ is 100 and at $[3, 2]^T$ is 109. Use bilinear interpolation to get the intensity at $[1.2, 3.7]^T$.

**Problem 12.5:** [*Intensity using bilinear interpolation—barycentric coordinates*]
Figure 12.9a shows the upper left corner of an image. Consider the triangle with vertices $\dot{\mathbf{a}} = [0, 0]^T$, $\dot{\mathbf{b}} = [4, 1]^T$ and $\dot{\mathbf{c}} = [0, 4]^T$. Determine the intensity of a point $\dot{\mathbf{p}}$ whose barycentric coordinates are $[0.4, 0.3, 0.3]^T$. (Refer to Sect. B.3 for a discussion about barycentric coordinates.)

**Problem 12.6:** [*Intensity using bilinear interpolation—parametric coordinates*]
Figure 12.9a shows the upper left corner of an image. The triangle $\triangle\dot{\mathbf{a}}\dot{\mathbf{b}}\dot{\mathbf{c}}$ defines a parametric coordinate system where $\dot{\mathbf{a}} = [0, 0]^T$, $\dot{\mathbf{b}} = [4, 1]^T$ and $\dot{\mathbf{c}} = [0, 4]^T$. The origin of the parametric coordinate system is at $\dot{\mathbf{b}}$ and the unit vectors along the $u$- and $v$-axes are determined using points $\dot{\mathbf{c}}$ and $\dot{\mathbf{a}}$ respectively. Determine the intensity of a point $\dot{\mathbf{p}}$ whose parametric coordinates are $[0.3, 0.5]^T$. (Refer to Sect. B.2 for a discussion about parametric coordinates.)

**Problem 12.7:** [*Intensity using bilinear interpolation—polar coordinates*]
Figure 12.9a shows the upper left corner of an image. Determine the intensity of a point $\dot{\mathbf{p}}$ whose polar coordinates are $[3, 25°]^T$. (Refer to Sect. B.4 for a discussion about polar coordinates.)

**Problem 12.8:** [*Mapping using parametric coordinates*]
We discussed how to map one triangle $\triangle\dot{\mathbf{p}}_1\dot{\mathbf{p}}_2\dot{\mathbf{p}}_3$ to another triangle $\triangle\dot{\mathbf{p}}'_1\dot{\mathbf{p}}'_2\dot{\mathbf{p}}'_3$ using Cartesian coordinates. The mapping process can be performed using parametric coordinates (Sect. B.2) of both triangles. Suggest the steps that may be followed to achieve the mapping.

## References

Blinn, J.F. 1978. Simulation of wrinkled surfaces. *SIGGRAPH Computer Graphics* 12(3): 286–292.
Blinn, J.F., and M.E. Newell. 1976. Texture and reflection in computer generated images. *Communications of the ACM* 19(10): 542–547.
Cook, R.L., L. Carpenter, and E. Catmull. 1987. The reyes image rendering architecture. *SIGGRAPH Computer Graphics* 21(4): 95–102.

# Chapter 13
# Color Spaces

**Abstract** Since images are better in color, colors represent an essential component in computer graphics . Working with colors is not only important because of the good look colors provide to images but also because of the more information they pass to humans to perceive. A color is represented through what is called *color space*, *color model* or *color system*. This refers to a 3D space in which any color can be represented by a 3D vector where each element in the vector represents one color component. There are many color spaces, color models or color coordinate systems; e.g., RGB, HSV, etc. The same color may be represented by different 3D vectors in different color spaces. Discussing color theory and the science of colors may fill several volumes of books, which is out of our scope. In this chapter, we will discuss some color spaces, models or coordinate systems and how to convert among them. Readers interested to learn more about colors may refer to other resources; e.g., (Velho et al. in Image processing for computer graphics and vision (texts in computer science). Springer 2009).

## 13.1 RGB Color Space

The most famous color model is called the RGB color space where the primary colors are red, green and blue colors. Any other color can be obtained my mixing different quantities from the three primary colors. For example, Fig. 13.1a shows a color image. Each pixel is composed of three components; one for each primary color. All *red components* for all pixels, shown in Fig. 13.1b, represent the *red channel* for the image. The same goes for the green and blue components that are shown in Fig. 13.1c and d respectively.

The RGB coordinate system is formed by three perpendicular axes representing the red, green and blue components. The whole spectrum of colors is enclosed in a cube with Cartesian coordinates as shown in Fig. 13.2.

R. Elias, *Digital Media*, DOI: 10.1007/978-3-319-05137-6_13, 

**Fig. 13.1** **a** A color image. **b** The *red* ($R$) channel. **c** The *green* ($G$) channel. **d** The *blue* ($B$) channel

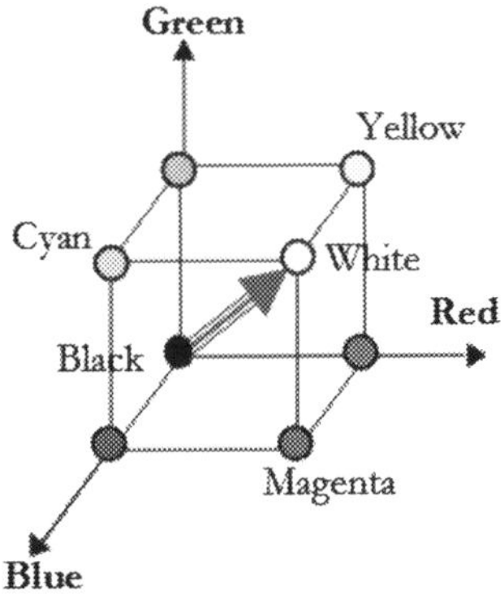


**Fig. 13.2** The RGB coordinate system is formed by three perpendicular axes representing the *red*, *green* and *blue* components. The whole spectrum of colors is enclosed in a cube

Each point on or inside the cube represents a color where the coordinates of this point represent the components of the primary colors that contribute to the color. Each component should have a value from 0 to 255 (or from 0.0 to 1.0). In Fig. 13.2, the gray arrow from $[0, 0, 0]^T$ to $[255, 255, 255]^T$ (or from $[0, 0, 0]^T$ to $[1, 1, 1]^T$) represents the shades of gray from black to white. The main color values are listed in Table 13.1.

From the values of this table, we can write

$$\begin{array}{ccccccc} W & = & R & + & G & + & B \\ \begin{bmatrix} 1 \\ 1 \\ 1 \end{bmatrix} & = & \begin{bmatrix} 1 \\ 0 \\ 0 \end{bmatrix} & + & \begin{bmatrix} 0 \\ 1 \\ 0 \end{bmatrix} & + & \begin{bmatrix} 0 \\ 0 \\ 1 \end{bmatrix} \end{array}. \tag{13.1}$$

**Table 13.1** Main color components in RGB space. **a** Range of values is [0, 255]. **b** Range of values is [0, 1]

**(a)**

| Color | Sym. | $R$ | $G$ | $B$ |
|---|---|---|---|---|
| Black | $B$ | 0 | 0 | 0 |
| Red | $R$ | 255 | 0 | 0 |
| Green | $G$ | 0 | 255 | 0 |
| Blue | $B$ | 0 | 0 | 255 |
| Yellow | $Y$ | 255 | 255 | 0 |
| Magenta | $M$ | 255 | 0 | 255 |
| Cyan | $C$ | 0 | 255 | 255 |
| White | $W$ | 255 | 255 | 255 |

**(b)**

| Color | Sym. | $R$ | $G$ | $B$ |
|---|---|---|---|---|
| Black | $B$ | 0 | 0 | 0 |
| Red | $R$ | 1 | 0 | 0 |
| Green | $G$ | 0 | 1 | 0 |
| Blue | $B$ | 0 | 0 | 1 |
| Yellow | $Y$ | 1 | 1 | 0 |
| Magenta | $M$ | 1 | 0 | 1 |
| Cyan | $C$ | 0 | 1 | 1 |
| White | $W$ | 1 | 1 | 1 |

Considering the RGB cube, Eq. (13.1) means that reaching white (i.e., $[1, 1, 1]^T$) from black (i.e., $[0, 0, 0]^T$) is done in three steps or additions.

1. When going from $[0, 0, 0]^T$ (i.e., black) through a unit vector along the red axis, you reach the point $[1, 0, 0]^T$ (i.e., red).
2. When going from $[1, 0, 0]^T$ (i.e., red) through a unit vector along the green axis, you reach the point $[1, 1, 0]^T$ (i.e., yellow).
3. When going from $[1, 1, 0]^T$ (i.e., yellow) through a unit vector along the blue, axis, you reach the point $[1, 1, 1]^T$ (i.e., white).

Also, Eq. (13.1) says that the *red* component of white equals to the *red* component of red plus the *red* component of green plus the *red* component of blue. The same is true for the other components.

**Example 13.1:** [*RGB color space—component range*]

The components of an RGB color $[100, 200, 50]^T$ are within the range [0, 255]. Express the same color to occupy the range [0, 1].

**Solution 13.1:** The color is expressed as

$$\begin{bmatrix} R \\ G \\ B \end{bmatrix} = \begin{bmatrix} \frac{100}{255} \\ \frac{200}{255} \\ \frac{50}{255} \end{bmatrix} = \begin{bmatrix} 0.3922 \\ 0.7843 \\ 0.1961 \end{bmatrix}. \qquad \square$$

**Example 13.2:** [*RGB color space—component range*]

The components of an RGB color $[0.3922, 0.7843, 0.1961]^T$ are within the range [0, 1]. Express the same color to occupy the range [0, 255].

**Solution 13.2:** The color is expressed as

$$\begin{bmatrix} R \\ G \\ B \end{bmatrix} = \begin{bmatrix} 0.3922 \times 255 \\ 0.7843 \times 255 \\ 0.1961 \times 255 \end{bmatrix} = \begin{bmatrix} 100 \\ 200 \\ 50 \end{bmatrix}. \qquad \square$$

## 13.2 CMY Color Space

Two complementary colors are diagonally opposite in the RGB cube shown in Fig. 13.2. Complementary colors are those colors that when mixed produce white or gray in general. From that perspective, we can say that red and cyan (where cyan is a mixture of green and blue) are complementary colors that produce white.

$$\begin{array}{ccccc} W & = & R & + & C \\ \begin{bmatrix} 1 \\ 1 \\ 1 \end{bmatrix} & = & \begin{bmatrix} 1 \\ 0 \\ 0 \end{bmatrix} & + & \begin{bmatrix} 0 \\ 1 \\ 1 \end{bmatrix} \end{array}. \tag{13.2}$$

The same goes for green with magenta (which is a mixture of red and blue) and blue with yellow (which is a mixture of red and green). Thus, we can write

$$\begin{array}{ccccc} W & = & G & + & M \\ \begin{bmatrix} 1 \\ 1 \\ 1 \end{bmatrix} & = & \begin{bmatrix} 0 \\ 1 \\ 0 \end{bmatrix} & + & \begin{bmatrix} 1 \\ 0 \\ 1 \end{bmatrix} \end{array} \tag{13.3}$$

and

$$\begin{array}{ccccc} W & = & B & + & Y \\ \begin{bmatrix} 1 \\ 1 \\ 1 \end{bmatrix} & = & \begin{bmatrix} 0 \\ 0 \\ 1 \end{bmatrix} & + & \begin{bmatrix} 1 \\ 1 \\ 0 \end{bmatrix} \end{array}. \tag{13.4}$$

Utilizing the same previous concept with Eq. (13.2), it can be said that the *red* component of white is equal to the *red* component of red plus the *red* component of cyan. Consequently, it is natural to say that the *red* component of red is equal to the *red* component of white minus the *red* component of cyan. In other words, red is the complement of cyan or $R = 1 - C$. Similarly, green is the complement of magenta or $G = 1 - M$ and blue is the complement of yellow or $B = 1 - Y$. These relations can be written as (Agoston 2005)

$$\begin{bmatrix} R \\ G \\ B \end{bmatrix} + \begin{bmatrix} C \\ M \\ Y \end{bmatrix} = \begin{bmatrix} 1 \\ 1 \\ 1 \end{bmatrix}. \tag{13.5}$$

The CMY colors are *subtractive* colors. They indicate what should be *subtracted* from white rather than what should be *added* to black. The CMY colors are used for devices as printers and plotters.

The cyan, magenta and yellow channels for the color image of Fig. 13.1a are shown in Fig. 13.3b, c and d respectively.

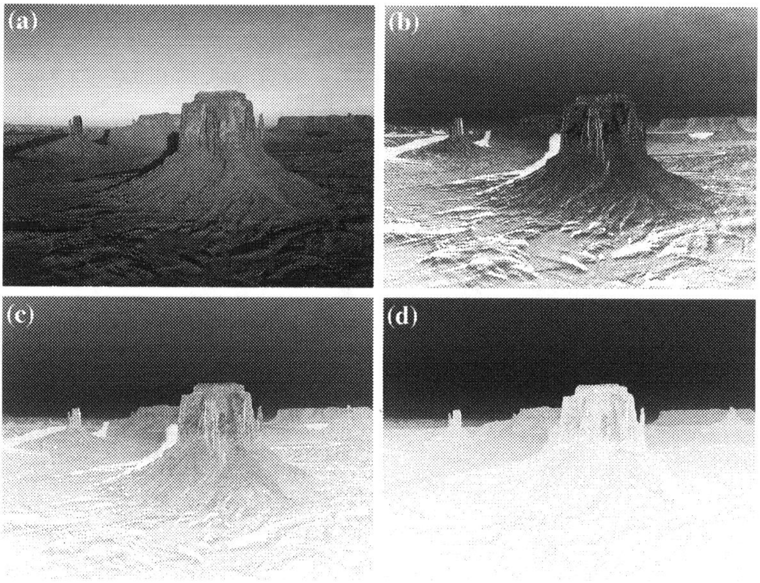

**Fig. 13.3** **a** A color image. **b** The *cyan* ($C$) channel. **c** The *magenta* ($M$) channel. **d** The *yellow* ($Y$) channel

### *13.2.1 RGB to CMY Transformation*

Transformation from the RGB space to the CMY space can be performed as

$$\begin{bmatrix} C \\ M \\ Y \end{bmatrix} = \begin{bmatrix} 1 \\ 1 \\ 1 \end{bmatrix} - \begin{bmatrix} R \\ G \\ B \end{bmatrix}. \tag{13.6}$$

where $R, G, B, C, M, Y \in [0.0, 1.0]$.

### *13.2.2 CMY to RGB Transformation*

Transformation from the CMY space to the RGB space can be performed as

$$\begin{bmatrix} R \\ G \\ B \end{bmatrix} = \begin{bmatrix} 1 \\ 1 \\ 1 \end{bmatrix} - \begin{bmatrix} C \\ M \\ Y \end{bmatrix}, \tag{13.7}$$

where $R, G, B, C, M, Y \in [0.0, 1.0]$.

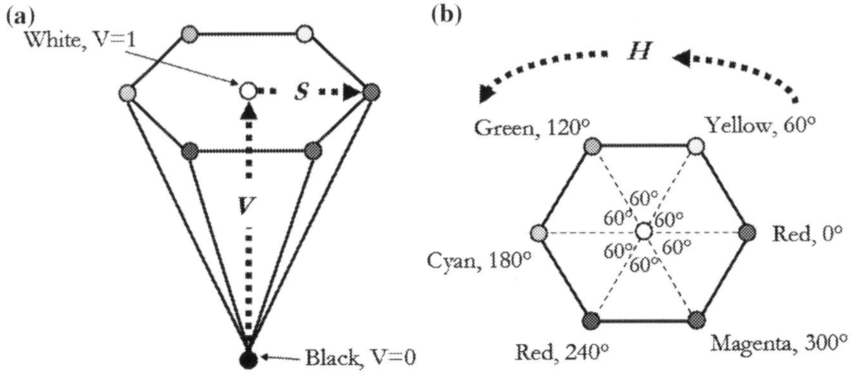


**Fig. 13.4** HSV color space. **a** HSV hexcone: the value component is indicated along the centerline of the hexcone. The saturation is indicated as the radial distance from the centerline of the hexcone. **b** The hue component is given by the angle about the centerline of the hexcone, which takes a value from 0° to 360°

## 13.3 HSV Color Space

The *HSV* color model (Velho et al. 2009), also known as *HSB*, defines a color space in terms of hue, saturation and value (or brightness). The HSV color space is derived from the RGB color space. Consider the RGB cube shown in Fig. 13.2. If you look at this cube along the black–white diagonal, you will notice a hexagon that is surrounded by six vertices representing red, yellow, green, cyan, blue and magenta. These colors along with the black at the tip and white at the center of the base form a hexcone that is called the *HSV hexcone*. This hexcone is shown in Fig. 13.4a.

The three color components are the following:

**Value**: The *value* component, also called the *brightness* component, indicates how dark (i.e., towards black) or bright (i.e., towards white) the color is. The value component is indicated along the centerline of the hexcone. It goes from 0 to 1. The black color (value of 0) is at the lower tip of the hexcone while the white color (value of 1) is at the center point of the upper circle/hexagon. Shades of gray are represented along this line. The value axis is shown in Fig. 13.4a. Notice that this axis corresponds to the diagonal of the RGB cube that goes from black to white. Note that some systems define the value to occupy the range [0, 255] instead of [0.0, 1.0].

**Saturation**: The *saturation* component defines the purity or the vibrancy of color and whether it is mixed with other colors. The saturation is indicated as the radial distance from the centerline of the hexcone. The saturation takes a value from 0 (i.e., a gray color) to 1 (i.e., a pure color). The saturation axis is shown in Fig. 13.4a.

**Hue**: The *hue* component is used to define the color (e.g., red, green, etc.). The hue is given by the angle about the centerline of the hexcone, which takes a value from

**Table 13.2** Angles of different colors in HSV color space

| Hue | Angle |
|---|---|
| Red | 0°/360° |
| Yellow | 60° |
| Green | 120° |
| Cyan | 180° |
| Blue | 240° |
| Magenta | 300° |

0° to 360° as shown in Fig. 13.4b. Table 13.2 lists the angles of different colors. Notice that every two complementary colors are 180° apart from each other. Note that some systems define the hue component to occupy the range [0.0, 1.0) instead of [0.0, 360.0).

The hue, saturation and value channels for the color image of Fig. 13.1a are shown in Fig. 13.5b, c and d respectively.

### 13.3.1 RGB to HSV Transformation

In order to convert or transform from an RGB color to an HSV color, Eq. (13.8) can be used (Agoston 2005). Note that this equation assumes that the values of R, G and B components are within the range [0.0, 1.0].

$$
\begin{aligned}
H &= \begin{cases} \text{undefined (set to } 0^\circ), & \text{if } MAX = MIN; \\ 60^\circ \times \frac{G-B}{MAX-MIN} + 0^\circ, & \text{if } MAX = R \text{ and } G \geq B; \\ 60^\circ \times \frac{G-B}{MAX-MIN} + 360^\circ, & \text{if } MAX = R \text{ and } G < B; \\ 60^\circ \times \frac{B-R}{MAX-MIN} + 120^\circ, & \text{if } MAX = G; \\ 60^\circ \times \frac{R-G}{MAX-MIN} + 240^\circ, & \text{if } MAX = B, \end{cases} \\
S &= \begin{cases} 0, & \text{if } MAX = 0; \\ \frac{MAX-MIN}{MAX}, & \text{otherwise,} \end{cases} \\
V &= MAX,
\end{aligned}
\tag{13.8}
$$

where $MAX$ is the maximum value among the R, G and B components and $MIN$ is the minimum value among the R, G and B components. The resulting HSV color has S and V components within the range [0.0, 1.0] while its H component lies within the range [0.0°, 360.0°); i.e., the value 360.0° is not included in the range.

**Example 13.3:** [*RGB to HSV transformation*]
Transform the red color $[255, 0, 0]^T$ to the HSV space.

**Fig. 13.5** **a** A color image. **b** The hue (*H*) channel. **c** The saturation (*S*) channel. **d** The value (*V*) channel

**Solution 13.3:** In order to use Eq. (13.8), the range of R, G and B components must be within [0.0, 1.0]. Thus, the first step is to change the range from [0, 255] to [0.0, 1.0] by dividing each component by 255.

$$RGB = \left[\frac{255}{255}, \frac{0}{255}, \frac{0}{255}\right]^T = [1.0, 0.0, 0.0]^T$$

Hence,

$$MAX = 1.0 \text{ and } MIN = 1.0.$$

Utilizing Eq. (13.8), we will have the following values for H, S and V:

$$\begin{aligned} H &= 60 \times \frac{G-B}{MAX-MIN} \\ &= 60 \times \frac{0.0-0.0}{1.0-0.0} = 0.0^\circ, \\ S &= \frac{MAX-MIN}{MAX} \\ &= \frac{1.0-0.0}{1.0} = 1.0, \\ V &= MAX \\ &= 1.0. \end{aligned}$$

Thus, the red color $[255, 0, 0]^T$ is $[0.0^\circ, 1.0, 1.0]^T$ in HSV space. □

**Example 13.4:** [*RGB to HSV transformation*]
Transform the RGB color $[100, 200, 50]^T$ to the HSV space.

**Solution 13.4:** In order to use Eq. (13.8), the range of R, G and B components must be within [0.0, 1.0]. Thus, the first step is to change the range from [0, 255] to [0.0, 1.0] by dividing each component by 255.

$$RGB = \left[\frac{100}{255}, \frac{200}{255}, \frac{50}{255}\right]^T = [0.3922, 0.7843, 0.1961]^T.$$

Hence,

$$MAX = 0.7843 \text{ and } MIN = 0.1961.$$

Utilizing Eq. (13.8), we will have the following values for H, S and V:

$$\begin{aligned} H &= 60 \times \frac{B-R}{MAX-MIN} + 120 \\ &= 60 \times \frac{0.1961-0.3922}{0.7843-0.1961} + 120 = 100°, \end{aligned}$$

$$\begin{aligned} S &= \frac{MAX-MIN}{MAX} \\ &= \frac{0.7843-0.1961}{0.7843} = 0.75, \end{aligned}$$

$$\begin{aligned} V &= MAX \\ &= 0.7843. \end{aligned}$$

Thus, the RGB color $[100, 200, 50]^T$ is $[100°, 0.75, 0.7843]^T$ in HSV space. □

## 13.3.2 HSV to RGB Transformation

In order to convert or transform from an HSV color to an RGB color, Eq. (13.9) can be used to get the values of $H_i$, $p$, $q$ and $t$, which are used to get the final RGB values.

$$\begin{aligned} H_i &= \left\lfloor \frac{H}{60} \right\rfloor, \\ f &= \frac{H}{60} - H_i \\ p &= V(1-S), \\ q &= V(1-fS), \\ t &= V(1-(1-f)S), \end{aligned} \tag{13.9}$$

$$[RGB] = \begin{cases} [V, t, p], & H_i = 0; \\ [q, V, p], & H_i = 1; \\ [p, V, t], & H_i = 2; \\ [p, q, V], & H_i = 3; \\ [t, p, V], & H_i = 4; \\ [V, p, q], & H_i = 5, \end{cases}$$

where $H \in [0.0°, 360.0°)$ and $S, V, R, G, B \in [0.0, 1.0]$.

**Example 13.5:** [*HSV to RGB transformation*]
Transform the HSV color $[100.34°, 0.74, 0.78]^T$ to the RGB space.

**Solution 13.5:** Use Eq. (13.9) to get the values of $H_i$, $p$, $q$ and $t$.

$$\begin{aligned} H_i &= \left\lfloor \frac{H}{60} \right\rfloor \\ &= \left\lfloor \frac{100.34}{60} \right\rfloor = 1, \end{aligned}$$

$$\begin{aligned} f &= \frac{H}{60} - H_i \\ &= \frac{100.34}{60} - 1 = 0.6723, \end{aligned}$$

$$\begin{aligned} p &= V(1 - S) \\ &= 0.78 \times (1 - 0.74) = 0.2028, \end{aligned}$$

$$\begin{aligned} q &= V(1 - fS) \\ &= 0.78 \times (1 - 0.6723 \times 0.74) = 0.3919, \end{aligned}$$

$$\begin{aligned} t &= V(1 - (1 - f)S) \\ &= 0.78 \times (1 - (1 - 0.6723) \times 0.74) = 0.5909. \end{aligned}$$

Thus, the representation of the HSV color $[100.34°, 0.74, 0.78]^T$ in RGB space can be written as $[0.3919, 0.78, 0.2028]^T$. □

**Example 13.6:** [*HSV to CMY transformation*]
Transform the HSV color $[110.7°, 0.3, 0.5]^T$ to the CMY color space.

**Solution 13.6:** The steps are the following:

1. Transform to the RGB color space using Eq. (13.9). The values of $H_i$, $p$, $q$ and $t$ are obtained as

$$\begin{aligned} H_i &= \left\lfloor \frac{H}{60} \right\rfloor \\ &= \left\lfloor \frac{110.7}{60} \right\rfloor = 1, \end{aligned}$$

$$
\begin{aligned}
f &= \frac{H}{60} - H_i \\
&= \frac{110.7}{60} - 1 = 0.845, \\
p &= V(1 - S) \\
&= 0.5 \times (1 - 0.3) = 0.35, \\
q &= V(1 - fS) \\
&= 0.5 \times (1 - 0.845 \times 0.3) = 0.37325, \\
t &= V(1 - (1 - f)S) \\
&= 0.5 \times (1 - (1 - 0.845) \times 0.3) = 0.4768.
\end{aligned}
$$

Hence, the color expressed in RGB space is $[0.37325, 0.5, 0.35]^T$.

2. Transform to the CMY color space using Eq. (13.6):

$$
\begin{aligned}
\begin{bmatrix} C \\ M \\ Y \end{bmatrix} &= \begin{bmatrix} 1 \\ 1 \\ 1 \end{bmatrix} - \begin{bmatrix} R \\ G \\ B \end{bmatrix} \\
&= \begin{bmatrix} 1 \\ 1 \\ 1 \end{bmatrix} - \begin{bmatrix} 0.37325 \\ 0.5 \\ 0.35 \end{bmatrix} = \begin{bmatrix} 0.62675 \\ 0.5 \\ 0.65 \end{bmatrix}.
\end{aligned}
$$

Hence, the HSV color $[110.7°, 0.3, 0.5]^T$ is expressed in CMY color space as $[0.62675, 0.5, 0.65]^T$. □

## 13.4 HLS Color Space

The *HSL* color model (Velho et al. 2009), also known as *HLS*, defines a color space in terms of hue, saturation and lightness (or luminance). As opposite to a single hexcone that is used to represent the HSV color space, a double-hexcone is used to represent the HSL color space as shown in Fig. 13.6a. The hexagonal base is shown in Fig. 13.6b.

The three color components are the following:

**Lightness**: The *lightness* component, also called the *luminance* component, indicates how dark (i.e., towards black) or bright (i.e., towards white) the color is. The lightness component is indicated along the centerline of the double-hexcone. It goes from 0 to 1. The black color (value of 0) is at the lower tip of the lower hexcone while the white color (value of 1) is at the upper tip of the upper hexcone. Shades of gray are represented along this line (i.e., represents a black–white axis). The lightness axis is shown in Fig. 13.6a.

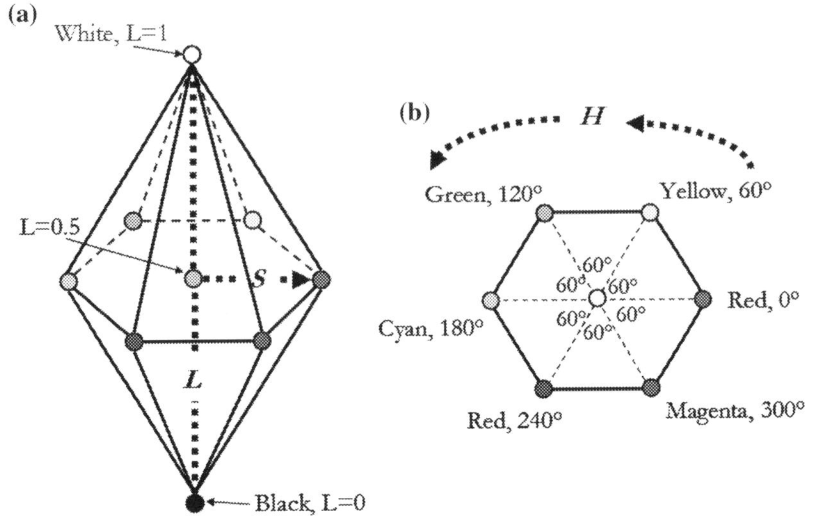


**Fig. 13.6** HSL (or HLS) color space. **a** HLS double-hexcone: The lightness component is indicated along the centerline of the double-hexcone. The saturation is indicated as the radial distance from the centerline of the double-hexcone. **b** The hue component is given by the angle about the centerline of the double-hexcone, which takes a value from 0° to 360°

**Saturation**: Also, similar to the HSV color space, the *saturation* component of the HSL color space is indicated as the radial distance from the centerline of the double-hexcone. The saturation takes a value from 0 to 1. The saturation axis is shown in Fig. 13.6a.

**Hue**: As with the HSV color space, the *hue* component of the HSL color space is used to define the color. It is given by the angle about the centerline of the double-hexcone, which takes a value from 0° to 360° as shown in Fig. 13.6b. The angles of different colors are the same as those listed in Table 13.2. Again, notice that every two complementary colors are 180° apart from each other.

The hue, saturation and lightness channels for the color image of Fig. 13.1a are shown in Fig. 13.7b, c and d respectively. In the examples presented in the rest of this section, the triplets of numbers representing HLS colors will be expressed as $[H, S, L]^T$ rather than $[H, L, S]^T$.

### 13.4.1 RGB to HLS Transformation

In order to convert or transform from an RGB color to an HLS color, Eq. (13.10) can be used. Note that this equation assumes that the values of R, G and B components are within the range [0.0, 1.0].

**Fig. 13.7** **a** A color image. **b** The hue ($H$) channel. **c** The saturation ($S$) channel. **d** The lightness ($L$) channel

$$
\begin{aligned}
H &= \begin{cases} \text{undefined (set to } 0^\circ), & \text{if } MAX = MIN; \\ 60^\circ \times \frac{G-B}{MAX-MIN} + 0^\circ, & \text{if } MAX = R \text{ and } G \geq B; \\ 60^\circ \times \frac{G-B}{MAX-MIN} + 360^\circ, & \text{if } MAX = R \text{ and } G < B; \\ 60^\circ \times \frac{B-R}{MAX-MIN} + 120^\circ, & \text{if } MAX = G; \\ 60^\circ \times \frac{R-G}{MAX-MIN} + 240^\circ, & \text{if } MAX = B, \end{cases} \\
L &= \frac{MAX+MIN}{2}, \\
S &= \begin{cases} 0, & \text{if } MAX = 0; \\ \frac{MAX-MIN}{MAX+MIN}, & \text{if } L \leq 0.5; \\ \frac{MAX-MIN}{2-MAX-MIN}, & \text{otherwise,} \end{cases}
\end{aligned}
\qquad (13.10)
$$

where $MAX$ is the maximum value among the R, G and B components and $MIN$ is the minimum value among the R, G and B components. The resulting HLS (or HSL) color has S and L components within the range [0.0, 1.0] while its H component lies within the range [0.0°, 360.0°); i.e., the value 360.0° is not included in the range.

**Example 13.7:** [*RGB to HLS (or HSL) transformation*]

Transform the red color $[255, 0, 0]^T$ to the HLS (or HSL) space.

**Solution 13.7:** In order to use Eq. (13.10), the range of R, G and B components must be within [0.0, 1.0]. Thus, the first step is to change the range from [0,255] to [0.0, 1.0] by dividing each component by 255.

$$RGB = \left[\frac{255}{255}, \frac{0}{255}, \frac{0}{255}\right]^T = [1.0, 0.0, 0.0]^T.$$

Hence,

$$MAX = 1.0 \text{ and } MIN = 0.0.$$

Utilizing Eq. (13.10), we will have the following values for H, L and S:

$$\begin{aligned} H &= 60 \times \frac{G - B}{MAX - MIN} \\ &= 60 \times \frac{0.0 - 0.0}{1.0 - 0.0} = 0.0°, \end{aligned}$$

$$\begin{aligned} L &= \frac{MAX + MIN}{2} \\ &= \frac{1.0 + 0.0}{2} = 0.5, \end{aligned}$$

$$\begin{aligned} S &= \frac{MAX - MIN}{MAX + MIN} \\ &= \frac{1.0 - 0.0}{1.0 + 0.0} = 1.0. \end{aligned}$$

Thus, the red color $[255, 0, 0]^T$ is expressed as $[0.0°, 1.0, 0.5]^T$ in HLS space. □

**Example 13.8:** [*RGB to HLS (or HSL) transformation*]
Transform the RGB color $[100, 200, 50]^T$ to the HLS (or HSL) space.

**Solution 13.8:** In order to use Eq. (13.10), the range of R, G and B components must be within [0.0, 1.0]. Thus, the first step is to change the range from [0,255] to [0.0, 1.0] by dividing each component by 255.

$$RGB = \left[\frac{100}{255}, \frac{200}{255}, \frac{50}{255}\right]^T = [0.3922, 0.7843, 0.1961]^T.$$

Hence,

$$MAX = 0.7843 \text{ and } MIN = 0.1961.$$

Utilizing Eq. (13.10), we will have the following values for H, L and S:

$$\begin{aligned} H &= 60 \times \frac{B - R}{MAX - MIN} + 120 \\ &= 60 \times \frac{0.1961 - 0.3922}{0.7843 - 0.1961} + 120 = 100°, \end{aligned}$$

$$\begin{aligned} L &= \frac{MAX + MIN}{2} \\ &= \frac{0.7843 + 0.1961}{2} = 0.4902, \end{aligned}$$

$$\begin{aligned} S &= \frac{MAX - MIN}{MAX + MIN} \\ &= \frac{0.7843 - 0.1961}{0.7843 + 0.1961} = 0.6. \end{aligned}$$

Thus, the RGB color $[100, 200, 50]^T$ is $[100°, 0.6, 0.4902]^T$ in HLS space. □

**Example 13.9:** [*CMY to HLS (or HSL) transformation*]
Transform the CMY color $[0.61, 0.22, 0.8]^T$ to the HLS color space.

**Solution 13.9:** The steps are the following:

1. Transform to the RGB color space using Eq. (13.7).

$$\begin{aligned} \begin{bmatrix} R \\ G \\ B \end{bmatrix} &= \begin{bmatrix} 1 \\ 1 \\ 1 \end{bmatrix} - \begin{bmatrix} C \\ M \\ Y \end{bmatrix} \\ &= \begin{bmatrix} 1 \\ 1 \\ 1 \end{bmatrix} - \begin{bmatrix} 0.61 \\ 0.22 \\ 0.8 \end{bmatrix} = \begin{bmatrix} 0.39 \\ 0.78 \\ 0.2 \end{bmatrix}. \end{aligned}$$

2. Transform to the HLS color space using Eq. (13.10):

$$\begin{aligned} H &= 60° \times \frac{B - R}{MAX - MIN} + 120° \\ &= 60° \times \frac{0.2 - 0.39}{0.78 - 0.2} + 120° = 100.3448°, \end{aligned}$$

$$\begin{aligned} L &= \frac{MAX + MIN}{2} \\ &= \frac{0.78 + 0.2}{2} = 0.49, \end{aligned}$$

$$\begin{aligned} S &= \frac{MAX - MIN}{MAX + MIN} \\ &= \frac{0.78 - 0.2}{0.78 + 0.2} = 0.5918. \end{aligned}$$

Thus, the CMY color $[0.61, 0.22, 0.8]^T$ is expressed in HLS space as $[100.3448°, 0.5918, 0.49]^T$. □

### 13.4.2 HLS to RGB Transformation

In order to convert or transform from an HLS color to an RGB color, Eq. (13.11) can be used to get the values of $h$, $p_1$ and $p_2$, which are used to get the final RGB values.

$$
\begin{aligned}
p_2 &= \begin{cases} L(1+S), & L \le 0.5; \\ L+S-LS, & \text{otherwise}, \end{cases} \\
p_1 &= 2L - p_2, \\
h &= \begin{cases} H+120, & \text{red}; \\ H, & \text{green}; \\ H-120, & \text{blue}, \end{cases} \\
&\text{if } h < 0 \Rightarrow h = h + 360, \\
&\text{if } h > 360 \Rightarrow h = h - 360, \\
R/G/B &= \begin{cases} p_1 + \frac{(p_2-p_1)h}{60}, & h < 60; \\ p_2, & h < 180; \\ p_1 + \frac{(p_2-p_1)(240-h)}{60}, & h < 240; \\ p_1, & \text{otherwise}, \end{cases}
\end{aligned}
\tag{13.11}
$$

where $H \in [0.0°, 360.0°)$ and $L, S, R, G, B \in [0.0, 1.0]$.

**Example 13.10:** [*HLS (or HSL) to RGB transformation*]
Convert the HLS color $[200°, 0.6, 0.49]^T$ to the RGB space expressed in the range [0, 255].

**Solution 13.10:** Apply Eq. (13.11):

$$
\begin{aligned}
p_2 &= L(1+S) \\
&= 0.49 \times (1+0.6) = 0.784,
\end{aligned}
$$

$$
\begin{aligned}
p_1 &= 2L - p_2 \\
&= 2 \times 0.49 - 0.784 = 0.196,
\end{aligned}
$$

$$
h = \begin{cases} H + 120 = 200 + 120 = 320, & \text{red}, \\ H = 200, & \text{green}, \\ H - 120 = 200 - 120 = 80, & \text{blue}, \end{cases}
$$

$$
\begin{aligned}
R &= p_1 \\
&= 0.196, \\
G &= p_1 + \frac{(p_2 - p_1)(240 - h)}{60} \\
&= 0.196 + \frac{(0.784 - 0.196)(240 - 200)}{60} = 0.588,
\end{aligned}
$$

$$\begin{aligned} B &= p_2 \\ &= 0.784. \end{aligned}$$

Thus, the HLS color $[200°, 0.6, 0.49]^T$ is expressed in RGB color space as $[0.196, 0.588, 0.784]^T$, which is within the range [0.0,1.0]. In order to switch to the range [0,255], multiply each component by 255. Thus, the final color is $[49.98, 149.94, 199.92]^T$. □

**Example 13.11:** [*HLS (or HSL) to CMY transformation*]
Transform the HLS color $[300°, 0.7, 0.8]^T$ to the CMY color space.

**Solution 13.11:** The steps are the following:

1. Transform to the RGB color space using Eq. (13.11). The values of $H_i$, $p$, $q$ and $t$ are obtained as

$$\begin{aligned} p_2 &= L + S - LS \\ &= 0.8 + 0.7 - 0.8 \times 0.7 = 0.94, \end{aligned}$$

$$\begin{aligned} p_1 &= 2L - p_2 \\ &= 2 \times 0.8 - 0.94 = 0.66, \end{aligned}$$

$$h = \begin{cases} H + 120 = 300 + 120 = 420 & \text{red,} \\ \Rightarrow 420 - 360 = 60, & \\ H = 300, & \text{green,} \\ H - 120 = 300 - 120 = 180, & \text{blue,} \end{cases}$$

$$\begin{aligned} R &= p_2 = 0.94, \\ G &= p_1 = 0.66, \\ B &= p_1 + \tfrac{(p_2 - p_1)(240 - h)}{60} \\ &= 0.66 + \frac{(0.94 - 0.66)(240 - 180)}{60} = 0.94. \end{aligned}$$

Hence, the color expressed in RGB space is $[0.94, 0.66, 0.94]^T$.

2. Transform to the CMY color space using Eq. (13.6):

$$\begin{aligned} \begin{bmatrix} C \\ M \\ Y \end{bmatrix} &= \begin{bmatrix} 1 \\ 1 \\ 1 \end{bmatrix} - \begin{bmatrix} R \\ G \\ B \end{bmatrix} \\ &= \begin{bmatrix} 1 \\ 1 \\ 1 \end{bmatrix} - \begin{bmatrix} 0.94 \\ 0.66 \\ 0.94 \end{bmatrix} = \begin{bmatrix} 0.06 \\ 0.34 \\ 0.06 \end{bmatrix}. \end{aligned}$$

Hence, the HLS color $[300°, 0.7, 0.8]^T$ is expressed in CMY color space as $[0.06, 0.34, 0.06]^T$. □

## 13.5 Problems

**Problem 13.1:** RGB to CMY transformation Eq. (13.6) assumes that $R, G, B, C, M, Y \in [0.0, 1.0]$. Modify this equation so that $R, G, B, C, M, Y \in [0, 255]$.

**Problem 13.2:** CMY to RGB transformation Eq. (13.7) assumes that $R, G, B, C, M, Y \in [0.0, 1.0]$. Modify this equation so that $R, G, B, C, M, Y \in [0, 255]$.

**Problem 13.3:** HLS (or HSL) to RGB transformation Convert the following HLS colors to RGB color space: $[100.34°, 0.74, 0.78]^T$, $[100°, 0.49, 0.60]^T$, $[200°, 0.49, 0.60]^T$ and $[300°, 0.8, 0.7]^T$.

**Problem 13.4:** HLS (or HSL) to CMY transformation Convert the following HLS colors to CYM color space: $[100.34°, 0.74, 0.78]^T$, $[100°, 0.49, 0.60]^T$, $[200°, 0.49, 0.60]^T$ and $[300°, 0.8, 0.7]^T$,

**Problem 13.5:** HLS (or HSL) to HSV transformation Convert the following HLS colors to HSV color space: $[100.34°, 0.74, 0.78]^T$, $[100°, 0.49, 0.60]^T$, $[200°, 0.49, 0.60]^T$ and $[300°, 0.8, 0.7]^T$.

## References

Agoston, M.K. 2005. *Computer graphics and geometric modeling*. Heidelberg: Springer.
Velho, L., A.C. Frery, J. Gomes, and S. Levy. 2009. *Image processing for computer graphics and vision (texts in computer science)*, 2nd ed. Heidelberg: Springer.

# Appendix A
# Linear Algebra

This appendix surveys some of the important basic concepts in linear algebra that often appear in computer graphics literature. It is not meant to be a complete reference for linear algebra; however, it covers the concepts required to read this book. Skilled readers may skip this appendix.

## A.1 Matrices

A matrix is an array of numbers, entries, components, terms or elements. An $n \times m$ matrix $\mathtt{A}$ consists of $n$ rows and $m$ columns and is expressed as

$$\mathtt{A} = \begin{bmatrix} a_{11} & a_{12} & \dots & a_{1m} \\ a_{21} & a_{22} & \dots & a_{2m} \\ \vdots & \vdots & \ddots & \vdots \\ a_{n1} & a_{n2} & \dots & a_{nm} \end{bmatrix}. \tag{A.1}$$

A matrix is called *square* if the number of rows and the number of columns are equal (i.e., if $n = m$); otherwise, it is called *rectangular* (i.e., if $n \neq m$).

A square matrix is *orthogonal* when the dot product (Sect. A.4.3.2) of any pair of rows or any pair of columns is zero and when the columns and the rows are unit vectors (Sect. A.4.1). Also, the inverse (Sect. A.2.2) and the transpose (Sect. A.2.3) of an orthogonal matrix are equal.

### *A.1.1 Identity Matrix*

An *identity* matrix $\mathtt{I}$ is a square matrix where $a_{ij} = 1$ when $i = j$ and $a_{ij} = 0$ otherwise. Hence, an identity matrix is expressed as

R. Elias, *Digital Media*, DOI: 10.1007/978-3-319-05137-6,

$$\mathtt{I} = \begin{bmatrix} 1\,0 \dots 0 \\ 0\,1 \dots 0 \\ \vdots\,\vdots \ddots \vdots \\ 0\,0 \dots 1 \end{bmatrix}. \tag{A.2}$$

As a convention, the identity matrix is always referred to by the letter $\mathtt{I}$.

## A.1.2 Diagonal Matrix

A *diagonal* matrix $\mathtt{D}$ is a square matrix with zero entries except for those of the main diagonal (i.e., where $i = j$). In other words, an $n \times n$ matrix $\mathtt{D}$ is diagonal if $a_{ij} = 0 \mid i \neq j \;\forall\, i, j \in \{1, 2, \dots, n\}$. Hence, a diagonal matrix is expressed as

$$\mathtt{D} = \begin{bmatrix} a_{11} & 0 & \dots & 0 \\ 0 & a_{22} & \dots & 0 \\ \vdots & \vdots & \ddots & \vdots \\ 0 & 0 & \dots & a_{nn} \end{bmatrix}. \tag{A.3}$$

The same diagonal matrix may also be denoted as $\mathtt{D} = \mathrm{diag}(a_{11}, a_{22}, \dots, a_{nn})$ where $a_{11}, a_{22}, \dots, a_{nn}$ are the elements of the main diagonal. *Matrix diagonalization* is converting a square matrix into a diagonal matrix.

## A.1.3 Symmetric Matrix

A *symmetric* matrix is a square matrix where $a_{ij} = a_{ji}$. For an $n \times n$, it can be expressed as

$$\mathtt{A} = \begin{bmatrix} a_{11} & a_{12} & \dots & a_{1n} \\ a_{12} & a_{22} & \dots & a_{2n} \\ \vdots & \vdots & \ddots & \vdots \\ a_{1n} & a_{2n} & \dots & a_{nn} \end{bmatrix}. \tag{A.4}$$

In this case, $\mathtt{A} = \mathtt{A}^T$. This implies that $\mathtt{A}^{-1}\mathtt{A}^T = \mathtt{I}$.

## A.1.4 Anti-Symmetric Matrix

An *anti-symmetric* or *skew symmetric* matrix is a square matrix where $a_{ij} = -a_{ji}$. For an $n \times n$, it can be expressed as

$$\mathtt{A} = \begin{bmatrix} 0 & a_{12} & \dots & a_{1n} \\ -a_{12} & 0 & \dots & a_{2n} \\ \vdots & \vdots & \ddots & \vdots \\ -a_{1n} & -a_{2n} & \dots & 0 \end{bmatrix}. \tag{A.5}$$

An anti-symmetric matrix must have zeros on its diagonal. In this case, $\mathtt{A} = -\mathtt{A}^T$. This implies that $-\mathtt{A}^{-1}\mathtt{A}^T = \mathtt{I}$.

## A.2 Matrix Operations

Some matrix operations are applied to single matrices (e.g., determinant, inverse, transpose and scalar multiplication) while others are applied to pairs of matrices (e.g., addition, subtraction and multiplication). In the following sections, we will talk about some of the most important matrix operations.

### *A.2.1 Matrix Determinant*

A matrix determinant is defined for a square matrix. A $2 \times 2$ matrix determinant $|\mathtt{A}|$ is defined as

$$\begin{aligned} |\mathtt{A}| &\equiv \det \begin{bmatrix} a_{11} & a_{12} \\ a_{21} & a_{22} \end{bmatrix} \equiv \begin{vmatrix} a_{11} & a_{12} \\ a_{21} & a_{22} \end{vmatrix} \\ &= a_{11}a_{22} - a_{12}a_{21}. \end{aligned} \tag{A.6}$$

A $3 \times 3$ matrix determinant $|\mathtt{A}|$ is defined as

$$\begin{aligned} |\mathtt{A}| &\equiv \det \begin{bmatrix} a_{11} & a_{12} & a_{13} \\ a_{21} & a_{22} & a_{23} \\ a_{31} & a_{32} & a_{33} \end{bmatrix} \equiv \begin{vmatrix} a_{11} & a_{12} & a_{13} \\ a_{21} & a_{22} & a_{23} \\ a_{31} & a_{32} & a_{33} \end{vmatrix} \\ &= a_{11} \begin{vmatrix} a_{22} & a_{23} \\ a_{32} & a_{33} \end{vmatrix} - a_{12} \begin{vmatrix} a_{21} & a_{23} \\ a_{31} & a_{33} \end{vmatrix} + a_{13} \begin{vmatrix} a_{21} & a_{22} \\ a_{31} & a_{32} \end{vmatrix} \\ &= a_{11}(a_{22}a_{33} - a_{23}a_{32}) - a_{12}(a_{21}a_{33} - a_{23}a_{31}) + a_{13}(a_{21}a_{32} - a_{22}a_{31}). \end{aligned} \tag{A.7}$$

### *A.2.2 Matrix Inverse*

The inverse of a square matrix $\mathtt{A}$ is another square matrix $\mathtt{A}^{-1}$ such that $\mathtt{A}\mathtt{A}^{-1} = \mathtt{I}$. If $\mathtt{A} = \begin{bmatrix} a_{11} & a_{12} \\ a_{21} & a_{22} \end{bmatrix}$ then the inverse $\mathtt{A}^{-1}$ is calculated as

$$\begin{aligned} \mathtt{A}^{-1} &= \frac{1}{|\mathtt{A}|}\begin{bmatrix} a_{22} & -a_{12} \\ -a_{21} & a_{11} \end{bmatrix} \\ &= \frac{1}{a_{11}a_{22} - a_{12}a_{21}}\begin{bmatrix} a_{22} & -a_{12} \\ -a_{21} & a_{11} \end{bmatrix}. \end{aligned} \tag{A.8}$$

For a $3 \times 3$ matrix $\mathtt{A}$, the inverse $\mathtt{A}^{-1}$ is defined as

$$\mathtt{A}^{-1} = \frac{1}{|\mathtt{A}|}\begin{bmatrix} \begin{vmatrix} a_{22} & a_{23} \\ a_{32} & a_{33} \end{vmatrix} & \begin{vmatrix} a_{13} & a_{12} \\ a_{33} & a_{32} \end{vmatrix} & \begin{vmatrix} a_{12} & a_{13} \\ a_{22} & a_{23} \end{vmatrix} \\ \begin{vmatrix} a_{23} & a_{21} \\ a_{33} & a_{31} \end{vmatrix} & \begin{vmatrix} a_{11} & a_{13} \\ a_{31} & a_{33} \end{vmatrix} & \begin{vmatrix} a_{13} & a_{11} \\ a_{23} & a_{21} \end{vmatrix} \\ \begin{vmatrix} a_{21} & a_{22} \\ a_{31} & a_{32} \end{vmatrix} & \begin{vmatrix} a_{12} & a_{11} \\ a_{32} & a_{31} \end{vmatrix} & \begin{vmatrix} a_{11} & a_{12} \\ a_{21} & a_{22} \end{vmatrix} \end{bmatrix}. \tag{A.9}$$

**Example A.1** [*Matrices–inverse*]

Compute the inverse for the following matrix:

$$\mathtt{A} = \begin{bmatrix} 1 & 1 & 1 \\ 3 & 3 & 1 \\ 4 & 1 & 1 \end{bmatrix}.$$

**Solution A.1** There are two steps:

1. Get the determinant $|\mathtt{A}|$ by applying Eq. (A.7). Thus,

$$|\mathtt{A}| = 1 \times (3 \times 1 - 1 \times 1) - 1 \times (3 \times 1 - 4 \times 1) + 1 \times (3 \times 1 - 3 \times 4) = -6.$$

2. Get the inverse $\mathtt{A}^{-1}$ by applying Eq. (A.9) as

$$\begin{aligned} \mathtt{A}^{-1} &= \frac{1}{-6}\begin{bmatrix} \begin{vmatrix} 3 & 1 \\ 1 & 1 \end{vmatrix} & \begin{vmatrix} 1 & 1 \\ 1 & 1 \end{vmatrix} & \begin{vmatrix} 1 & 1 \\ 3 & 1 \end{vmatrix} \\ \begin{vmatrix} 1 & 3 \\ 1 & 4 \end{vmatrix} & \begin{vmatrix} 1 & 1 \\ 4 & 1 \end{vmatrix} & \begin{vmatrix} 1 & 1 \\ 1 & 3 \end{vmatrix} \\ \begin{vmatrix} 3 & 3 \\ 4 & 1 \end{vmatrix} & \begin{vmatrix} 1 & 1 \\ 1 & 4 \end{vmatrix} & \begin{vmatrix} 1 & 1 \\ 3 & 3 \end{vmatrix} \end{bmatrix} \\ &= \frac{1}{-6}\begin{bmatrix} 2 & 0 & -2 \\ 1 & -3 & 2 \\ -9 & 3 & 0 \end{bmatrix} \end{aligned}$$

$$= \begin{bmatrix} -\frac{1}{3} & 0 & \frac{1}{3} \\ -\frac{1}{6} & \frac{1}{2} & -\frac{1}{3} \\ 1\frac{1}{2} & -\frac{1}{2} & 0 \end{bmatrix}. \qquad \square$$

## A.2.3 Matrix Transpose

The transpose of a matrix A is the matrix obtained by replacing all elements $a_{ij}$ with $a_{ji}$ (i.e., columns become rows and rows become columns). The transpose of A is denoted by $A^T$. Thus, we can write $(A^T)^T = A$.

**Example A.2** [*Matrices–transpose*]

Get the transpose of A where $A = \begin{bmatrix} 1 & 2 & 3 \\ 4 & 5 & 6 \end{bmatrix}$.

**Solution A.2** The inverse can be expressed as

$$A^T = \begin{bmatrix} 1 & 2 & 3 \\ 4 & 5 & 6 \end{bmatrix}^T = \begin{bmatrix} 1 & 4 \\ 2 & 5 \\ 3 & 6 \end{bmatrix}. \qquad \square$$

## A.2.4 Addition and Subtraction

Matrices of the same size can be added together (or subtracted from each other) by adding (or subtracting) the corresponding elements. Thus, for two matrices A and B of size $n \times m$, we may have

$$\begin{aligned} A + B &= \begin{bmatrix} a_{11} & a_{12} & \dots & a_{1m} \\ a_{21} & a_{22} & \dots & a_{2m} \\ \vdots & \vdots & \ddots & \vdots \\ a_{n1} & a_{n2} & \dots & a_{nm} \end{bmatrix} + \begin{bmatrix} b_{11} & b_{12} & \dots & b_{1m} \\ b_{21} & b_{22} & \dots & b_{2m} \\ \vdots & \vdots & \ddots & \vdots \\ b_{n1} & b_{n2} & \dots & b_{nm} \end{bmatrix} \\ &= \begin{bmatrix} a_{11} + b_{11} & a_{12} + b_{12} & \dots & a_{1m} + b_{1m} \\ a_{21} + b_{21} & a_{22} + b_{22} & \dots & a_{2m} + b_{2m} \\ \vdots & \vdots & \ddots & \vdots \\ a_{n1} + b_{n1} & a_{n2} + b_{n2} & \dots & a_{nm} + b_{nm} \end{bmatrix} \end{aligned} \tag{A.10}$$

or

$$\text{A}-\text{B}=\begin{bmatrix} a_{11} & a_{12} & \dots & a_{1m} \\ a_{21} & a_{22} & \dots & a_{2m} \\ \vdots & \vdots & \ddots & \vdots \\ a_{n1} & a_{n2} & \dots & a_{nm} \end{bmatrix} - \begin{bmatrix} b_{11} & b_{12} & \dots & b_{1m} \\ b_{21} & b_{22} & \dots & b_{2m} \\ \vdots & \vdots & \ddots & \vdots \\ b_{n1} & b_{n2} & \dots & b_{nm} \end{bmatrix}$$
$$= \begin{bmatrix} a_{11}-b_{11} & a_{12}-b_{12} & \dots & a_{1m}-b_{1m} \\ a_{21}-b_{21} & a_{22}-b_{22} & \dots & a_{2m}-b_{2m} \\ \vdots & \vdots & \ddots & \vdots \\ a_{n1}-b_{n1} & a_{n2}-b_{n2} & \dots & a_{nm}-b_{nm} \end{bmatrix}. \tag{A.11}$$

**Example A.3** [*Matrices–addition and subtraction*]

Consider two matrices A and B where $\text{A} = \begin{bmatrix} 1 & 2 & 3 & 4 \\ 5 & 6 & 7 & 7 \end{bmatrix}$ and $\text{B} = \begin{bmatrix} 3 & 5 & 5 & 6 \\ 7 & 8 & 9 & 10 \end{bmatrix}$. Calculate the addition $\text{A}+\text{B}$ and the subtractions $\text{A}-\text{B}$ and $\text{B}-\text{A}$.

**Solution A.3** The addition is performed by adding corresponding terms as

$$\text{A}+\text{B} = \begin{bmatrix} 1 & 2 & 3 & 4 \\ 5 & 6 & 7 & 7 \end{bmatrix} + \begin{bmatrix} 3 & 5 & 5 & 6 \\ 7 & 8 & 9 & 10 \end{bmatrix}$$
$$= \begin{bmatrix} 1+3 & 2+5 & 3+5 & 4+6 \\ 5+7 & 6+8 & 7+9 & 7+10 \end{bmatrix}$$
$$= \begin{bmatrix} 4 & 7 & 8 & 10 \\ 12 & 14 & 16 & 17 \end{bmatrix}.$$

The subtraction is performed by subtracting corresponding terms as

$$\text{A}-\text{B} = \begin{bmatrix} 1 & 2 & 3 & 4 \\ 5 & 6 & 7 & 7 \end{bmatrix} - \begin{bmatrix} 3 & 5 & 5 & 6 \\ 7 & 8 & 9 & 10 \end{bmatrix}$$
$$= \begin{bmatrix} 1-3 & 2-5 & 3-5 & 4-6 \\ 5-7 & 6-8 & 7-9 & 7-10 \end{bmatrix}$$
$$= \begin{bmatrix} -2 & -3 & -2 & -2 \\ -2 & -2 & -2 & -3 \end{bmatrix}$$

$$\text{B}-\text{A} = \begin{bmatrix} 3 & 5 & 5 & 6 \\ 7 & 8 & 9 & 10 \end{bmatrix} - \begin{bmatrix} 1 & 2 & 3 & 4 \\ 5 & 6 & 7 & 7 \end{bmatrix}$$
$$= \begin{bmatrix} 3-1 & 5-2 & 5-3 & 6-4 \\ 7-5 & 8-6 & 9-7 & 10-7 \end{bmatrix}$$
$$= \begin{bmatrix} 2 & 3 & 2 & 2 \\ 2 & 2 & 2 & 3 \end{bmatrix}.$$

Notice that $\text{B}-\text{A} = -[\text{A}-\text{B}]$. □

**Example A.4** [*Matrices–addition and subtraction*]

Consider two matrices A and B where $\mathtt{A} = \begin{bmatrix} 1 & 2 & 3 \\ 5 & 6 & 7 \end{bmatrix}$ and $\mathtt{B} = \begin{bmatrix} 3 & 5 \\ 7 & 8 \end{bmatrix}$. Calculate the addition $\mathtt{A}+\mathtt{B}$ and the subtractions $\mathtt{A}-\mathtt{B}$ and $\mathtt{B}-\mathtt{A}$.

**Solution A.4** Since the sizes of the matrices are different, none of the operations can be performed. □

## A.2.5 Scalar Multiplication

Scalar multiplication is an operation performed by multiplying each of the elements of a matrix by a scalar value. Thus, for a $n \times m$ matrix A and a scalar value $s$, we can write

$$s\mathtt{A} = s \begin{bmatrix} a_{11} & a_{12} & \dots & a_{1m} \\ a_{21} & a_{22} & \dots & a_{2m} \\ \vdots & \vdots & \ddots & \vdots \\ a_{n1} & a_{n2} & \dots & a_{nm} \end{bmatrix} = \begin{bmatrix} sa_{11} & sa_{12} & \dots & sa_{1m} \\ sa_{21} & sa_{22} & \dots & sa_{2m} \\ \vdots & \vdots & \ddots & \vdots \\ sa_{n1} & sa_{n2} & \dots & sa_{nm} \end{bmatrix}. \tag{A.12}$$

**Example A.5** [*Matrices–scalar multiplication*]

If a matrix A is defined as $\mathtt{A} = \begin{bmatrix} 1 & 2 & 3 \\ 4 & 5 & 6 \end{bmatrix}$, get the result of $s\mathtt{A}$ where $s = 2.5$.

**Solution A.5** The scalar value is multiplied by each matrix term individually. Thus,

$$s\mathtt{A} = 2.5 \begin{bmatrix} 1 & 2 & 3 \\ 4 & 5 & 6 \end{bmatrix} = \begin{bmatrix} 2.5 & 5 & 7.5 \\ 10 & 12.5 & 15 \end{bmatrix}.$$ □

**Example A.6** [*Matrices–scalar multiplication and addition/subtraction*]

Consider two matrices A and B where $\mathtt{A} = \begin{bmatrix} 1 & 2 & 3 & 4 \\ 5 & 6 & 7 & 7 \end{bmatrix}$ and $\mathtt{B} = \begin{bmatrix} 3 & 5 & 5 & 6 \\ 7 & 8 & 9 & 10 \end{bmatrix}$. Calculate $\mathtt{A}+2\mathtt{B}$ and $2\mathtt{A}-\mathtt{B}$.

**Solution A.6**

$$\begin{aligned} \mathtt{A}+2\mathtt{B} &= \begin{bmatrix} 1 & 2 & 3 & 4 \\ 5 & 6 & 7 & 7 \end{bmatrix} + 2 \begin{bmatrix} 3 & 5 & 5 & 6 \\ 7 & 8 & 9 & 10 \end{bmatrix} \\ &= \begin{bmatrix} 1 & 2 & 3 & 4 \\ 5 & 6 & 7 & 7 \end{bmatrix} + \begin{bmatrix} 6 & 10 & 10 & 12 \\ 14 & 16 & 18 & 20 \end{bmatrix} \\ &= \begin{bmatrix} 1+6 & 2+10 & 3+10 & 4+12 \\ 5+14 & 6+16 & 7+18 & 7+20 \end{bmatrix} \\ &= \begin{bmatrix} 7 & 12 & 13 & 16 \\ 19 & 22 & 25 & 27 \end{bmatrix}. \end{aligned}$$

$$
\begin{aligned}
2\mathtt{A} - \mathtt{B} &= 2\begin{bmatrix} 1 & 2 & 3 & 4 \\ 5 & 6 & 7 & 7 \end{bmatrix} - \begin{bmatrix} 3 & 5 & 5 & 6 \\ 7 & 8 & 9 & 10 \end{bmatrix} \\
&= \begin{bmatrix} 2 & 4 & 6 & 8 \\ 10 & 12 & 14 & 14 \end{bmatrix} - \begin{bmatrix} 3 & 5 & 5 & 6 \\ 7 & 8 & 9 & 10 \end{bmatrix} \\
&= \begin{bmatrix} 2-3 & 4-5 & 6-5 & 8-6 \\ 10-7 & 12-8 & 14-9 & 14-10 \end{bmatrix} \\
&= \begin{bmatrix} -1 & -1 & 1 & 2 \\ 3 & 4 & 5 & 4 \end{bmatrix}.
\end{aligned}
$$

□

## A.2.6 Matrix Multiplication

In order to multiply two matrices A and B, the number of columns of the first matrix A must be equal to the number of rows of the second B. The resulting matrix has the same number of rows as the first and the same number of columns as the second. Thus, if A is of size $n \times m$ and B is of size $m \times k$, the resulting matrix C will be of size $n \times k$. This can be written as

$$
\begin{aligned}
\mathtt{AB} &= \mathtt{C} \\
&= \begin{bmatrix} c_{11} & c_{12} & \dots & c_{1k} \\ c_{21} & c_{22} & \dots & c_{2k} \\ \vdots & \vdots & \ddots & \vdots \\ c_{n1} & c_{n2} & \dots & c_{nk} \end{bmatrix} \\
&= \begin{bmatrix} \sum_{i=1}^{i<=m} a_{1i}b_{i1} & \sum_{i=1}^{i<=m} a_{1i}b_{i2} & \dots & \sum_{i=1}^{i<=m} a_{1i}b_{ik} \\ \sum_{i=1}^{i<=m} a_{2i}b_{i1} & \sum_{i=1}^{i<=m} a_{2i}b_{i2} & \dots & \sum_{i=1}^{i<=m} a_{2i}b_{ik} \\ \vdots & \vdots & \ddots & \vdots \\ \sum_{i=1}^{i<=m} a_{ni}b_{i1} & \sum_{i=1}^{i<=m} a_{ni}b_{i2} & \dots & \sum_{i=1}^{i<=m} a_{ni}b_{ik} \end{bmatrix},
\end{aligned}
\tag{A.13}
$$

where $\mathtt{A} = \begin{bmatrix} a_{11} & a_{12} & \dots & a_{1m} \\ a_{21} & a_{22} & \dots & a_{2m} \\ \vdots & \vdots & \ddots & \vdots \\ a_{n1} & a_{n2} & \dots & a_{nm} \end{bmatrix}$ and $\mathtt{B} = \begin{bmatrix} b_{11} & b_{12} & \dots & b_{1k} \\ b_{21} & b_{22} & \dots & b_{2k} \\ \vdots & \vdots & \ddots & \vdots \\ b_{m1} & b_{m2} & \dots & b_{mk} \end{bmatrix}$.

**Example A.7** [*Matrices–multiplication*]

Consider two matrices A and B where $A = \begin{bmatrix} 1 & 2 & 3 \\ 4 & 5 & 6 \end{bmatrix}$ and $B = \begin{bmatrix} 3 & 4 & 5 \\ 6 & 7 & 8 \\ 1 & 2 & 3 \end{bmatrix}$. Calculate the multiplications (a) AB. (b) BA. (c) $BA^T$.

**Solution A.7** (a) The multiplication AB:

$$
\begin{aligned}
AB &= \begin{bmatrix} 1 & 2 & 3 \\ 4 & 5 & 6 \end{bmatrix} \begin{bmatrix} 3 & 4 & 5 \\ 6 & 7 & 8 \\ 1 & 2 & 3 \end{bmatrix} \\
&= \begin{bmatrix} 1 \times 3 + 2 \times 6 + 3 \times 1 & 1 \times 4 + 2 \times 7 + 3 \times 2 & 1 \times 5 + 2 \times 8 + 3 \times 3 \\ 4 \times 3 + 5 \times 6 + 6 \times 1 & 4 \times 4 + 5 \times 7 + 6 \times 2 & 4 \times 5 + 5 \times 8 + 6 \times 3 \end{bmatrix} \\
&= \begin{bmatrix} 18 & 24 & 30 \\ 48 & 63 & 78 \end{bmatrix}.
\end{aligned}
$$

(b) The multiplication BA: This operation cannot be performed since the number of columns of B (i.e. 3) is not equal to the number of rows of A (i.e., 2).
(c) The multiplication $BA^T$:

$$
\begin{aligned}
BA^T &= \begin{bmatrix} 3 & 4 & 5 \\ 6 & 7 & 8 \\ 1 & 2 & 3 \end{bmatrix} \begin{bmatrix} 1 & 2 & 3 \\ 4 & 5 & 6 \end{bmatrix}^T \\
&= \begin{bmatrix} 3 & 4 & 5 \\ 6 & 7 & 8 \\ 1 & 2 & 3 \end{bmatrix} \begin{bmatrix} 1 & 4 \\ 2 & 5 \\ 3 & 6 \end{bmatrix} \\
&= \begin{bmatrix} 3 \times 1 + 4 \times 2 + 5 \times 3 & 3 \times 4 + 4 \times 5 + 5 \times 6 \\ 6 \times 1 + 7 \times 2 + 8 \times 3 & 6 \times 4 + 7 \times 5 + 8 \times 6 \\ 1 \times 1 + 2 \times 2 + 3 \times 3 & 1 \times 4 + 2 \times 5 + 3 \times 6 \end{bmatrix} \\
&= \begin{bmatrix} 26 & 62 \\ 44 & 107 \\ 14 & 32 \end{bmatrix}.
\end{aligned}
$$

□

**Example A.8** [*Matrices–multiplication*]

Consider two matrices A and B where $A = \begin{bmatrix} \frac{1}{3} & 0 \\ -\frac{2}{3} & \frac{1}{3} \end{bmatrix}$ and $B = \begin{bmatrix} 3 & 0 \\ 6 & 3 \end{bmatrix}$. Calculate the multiplications (a) AB. (b) BA.

**Solution A.8** (a) The multiplication AB:

$$
\begin{aligned}
\text{AB} &= \begin{bmatrix} \frac{1}{3} & 0 \\ -\frac{2}{3} & \frac{1}{3} \end{bmatrix} \begin{bmatrix} 3 & 0 \\ 6 & 3 \end{bmatrix} \\
&= \begin{bmatrix} \frac{1}{3} \times 3 + 0 \times 6 & \frac{1}{3} \times 0 + 0 \times 3 \\ -\frac{2}{3} \times 3 + \frac{1}{3} \times 6 & -\frac{2}{3} \times 0 + \frac{1}{3} \times 3 \end{bmatrix} \\
&= \begin{bmatrix} 1 & 0 \\ 0 & 1 \end{bmatrix}.
\end{aligned}
$$

(b) The multiplication BA:

$$
\begin{aligned}
\text{BA} &= \begin{bmatrix} 3 & 0 \\ 6 & 3 \end{bmatrix} \begin{bmatrix} \frac{1}{3} & 0 \\ -\frac{2}{3} & \frac{1}{3} \end{bmatrix} \\
&= \begin{bmatrix} 3 \times \frac{1}{3} + 0 \times -\frac{2}{3} & 3 \times 0 + 0 \times \frac{1}{3} \\ 6 \times \frac{1}{3} + 3 \times -\frac{2}{3} & 6 \times 0 + 3 \times \frac{1}{3} \end{bmatrix} \\
&= \begin{bmatrix} 1 & 0 \\ 0 & 1 \end{bmatrix}.
\end{aligned}
$$

Notice that AB = BA = I. This implies that $\text{A}^{-1} = \text{B}$ and $\text{B}^{-1} = \text{A}$. □

## A.3 Vectors

The number of components, terms or elements in a vector determines its dimension (e.g., a 2D vector contains two elements and an $n$D vector contains $n$ elements). There are two types of vectors; column vectors and row vectors. A *column vector* $\mathbf{v}_1$ is a matrix of one column that contains multiple values. It can be indicated as

$$
\mathbf{v}_1 = \begin{bmatrix} v_1 \\ v_2 \\ v_3 \end{bmatrix} = [v_1, v_2, v_3]^T.
$$

A *row vector* $\mathbf{v}_2$ is a matrix of one row that contains multiple values. It can be indicated as

$$
\mathbf{v}_2 = [v_1, v_2, v_3].
$$

By convention, if the type is not indicated, it is assumed to be a column vector. Two vectors $\mathbf{u} = [u_1, u_2, u_3]$ and $\mathbf{v} = [v_1, v_2, v_3]$ are equal if their corresponding elements are equal (i.e., $u_1 = v_1$, $u_2 = v_2$ and $u_3 = v_3$).

**Example A.9** [*Vectors–equal vectors*]
If the vectors $\mathbf{u} = [2x, x+z, 3y]$ and $\mathbf{v} = [2.5y, 2y, 12]$ are equal, find the values of $x$, $y$ and $z$.

**Solution A.9** Since the vectors $\mathbf{u}$ and $\mathbf{v}$ are equal, their corresponding elements are equal. Thus, we can write

$$\begin{aligned} 2x &= 2.5y, \\ x + z &= 2y, \\ 3y &= 12. \end{aligned}$$

Solving these three equations yields

$$\begin{aligned} x &= 5, \\ y &= 4, \\ z &= 3. \end{aligned}$$

□

# A.4 Vector Operations

There are many operations that can be performed on vectors. Some of these operations deal with single vectors (e.g., vector normalization and scalar multiplication) while others handle pairs of them (e.g., addition, subtraction, dot product and cross product).

## A.4.1 Normalization and Unit Vectors

The *norm* of a vector $\mathbf{v}$ indicates its length. It is denoted as $\|\mathbf{v}\|$. (Some references denote the norm of a vector $\mathbf{v}$ as $|\mathbf{v}|$.) The norm is defined as the square root of the sum of the squares of all elements. For an $n$D vector, it can be calculated as

$$\|\mathbf{v}\| = \sqrt{v_1^2 + v_2^2 + \cdots + v_n^2}. \tag{A.14}$$

**Example A.10** [*Vectors–norm of a vector*]
Get the norm of the vector $\mathbf{v} = [2, 5, 8, 9]$.

**Solution A.10** The norm is obtained using Eq. (A.14) as

$$\|\mathbf{v}\| = \sqrt{2^2 + 5^2 + 8^2 + 9^2} = \sqrt{174} = 13.1909.$$

□

In case $\|\mathbf{v}\| = 1$, the vector $\mathbf{v}$ is said to be a *unit vector*. A unit vector can be treated as a direction. For example, unit vectors along the $x$-, $y$- and $z$-axes are $\mathbf{i} = [1, 0, 0]^T$, $\mathbf{j} = [0, 1, 0]^T$ and $\mathbf{k} = [0, 0, 1]^T$ respectively. These are called *unit Cartesian vectors*. On the other hand, any vector can be converted to a unit vector through a process that is called *normalization*. In order to normalize a vector $\mathbf{v}$, divide each of its elements by its norm $\|\mathbf{v}\|$ to get

$$\hat{\mathbf{v}} = \frac{\mathbf{v}}{\|\mathbf{v}\|}, \tag{A.15}$$

where $\hat{\mathbf{v}}$ is a unit vector (i.e., $\|\hat{\mathbf{v}}\| = 1$). Throughout this book, the context clarifies whether or not the vector under consideration is a unit vector.

**Example A.11** [*Vectors–normalization of a vector*]
Normalize the vector $\mathbf{v} = [2, 5, 8, 9]$.

**Solution A.11** The norm of $\mathbf{v}$, $\|\mathbf{v}\|$, is $\sqrt{174}$ as computed in Example A.10. Hence, $\hat{\mathbf{v}}$ is computed using Eq. (A.15) as

$$\begin{aligned}
\hat{\mathbf{v}} &= \tfrac{\mathbf{v}}{\|\mathbf{v}\|} \\
&= \tfrac{[2,5,8,9]}{\sqrt{174}} \\
&= \left[\tfrac{2}{\sqrt{174}}, \tfrac{5}{\sqrt{174}}, \tfrac{8}{\sqrt{174}}, \tfrac{9}{\sqrt{174}}\right] \\
&= [0.1516, 0.3790, 0.6065, 0.6823].
\end{aligned}$$

□

## A.4.2 Addition and Subtraction

Vectors of the same size can be added together (or subtracted from each other) by adding (or subtracting) the corresponding elements. Thus, for two vectors $\mathbf{u}$ and $\mathbf{v}$ of size $n$, we have

$$\mathbf{u} \pm \mathbf{v} = \begin{bmatrix} u_1 \\ u_2 \\ \vdots \\ u_n \end{bmatrix} \pm \begin{bmatrix} v_1 \\ v_2 \\ \vdots \\ v_n \end{bmatrix} = \begin{bmatrix} u_1 \pm v_1 \\ u_2 \pm v_2 \\ \vdots \\ u_n \pm v_n \end{bmatrix}. \tag{A.16}$$

Given two 3D points $\dot{\mathbf{P}}_1 = [x_1, y_1, z_1]^T$ and $\dot{\mathbf{P}}_2 = [x_2, y_2, z_2]^T$, vector subtraction can be used to define a direction vector $\mathbf{u}$ from $\dot{\mathbf{P}}_1$ to $\dot{\mathbf{P}}_2$ as

$$\mathbf{u} = \begin{bmatrix} x_2 - x_1 \\ y_2 - y_1 \\ z_2 - z_1 \end{bmatrix}. \tag{A.17}$$

**Example A.12** [*Vectors–addition and subtraction*]
Consider two vectors $\mathbf{u} = [5, 6, 7, 8]^T$ and $\mathbf{v} = [9, 3, 8, 1]^T$. Calculate the addition $\mathbf{u}+\mathbf{v}$ and the subtractions $\mathbf{u}-\mathbf{v}$ and $\mathbf{v}-\mathbf{u}$.

**Solution A.12** The addition is performed by adding corresponding terms as

$$\mathbf{u}+\mathbf{v}=\begin{bmatrix}5\\6\\7\\8\end{bmatrix}+\begin{bmatrix}9\\3\\8\\1\end{bmatrix}=\begin{bmatrix}5+9\\6+3\\7+8\\8+1\end{bmatrix}=\begin{bmatrix}14\\9\\15\\9\end{bmatrix}.$$

The subtraction is performed by subtracting corresponding terms as

$$\mathbf{u}-\mathbf{v}=\begin{bmatrix}5\\6\\7\\8\end{bmatrix}-\begin{bmatrix}9\\3\\8\\1\end{bmatrix}=\begin{bmatrix}5-9\\6-3\\7-8\\8-1\end{bmatrix}=\begin{bmatrix}-4\\3\\-1\\7\end{bmatrix}.$$

$$\mathbf{v}-\mathbf{u}=\begin{bmatrix}9\\3\\8\\1\end{bmatrix}-\begin{bmatrix}5\\6\\7\\8\end{bmatrix}=\begin{bmatrix}9-5\\3-6\\8-7\\1-8\end{bmatrix}=\begin{bmatrix}4\\-3\\1\\-7\end{bmatrix}.$$

Notice that $\mathbf{u}-\mathbf{v}=-[\mathbf{v}-\mathbf{u}]$. □

## A.4.3 *Multiplication*

There are different types of multiplication operations that can be applied to vectors.

### A.4.3.1 Scalar Multiplication

*Scalar multiplication* or *vector scaling* is an operation performed by multiplying each of the elements of a vector by a scalar value. Thus, for an $n$D vector $\mathbf{v}$ and a scalar value $s$, we can write

$$s\mathbf{v}=s\begin{bmatrix}v_1\\v_2\\\vdots\\v_n\end{bmatrix}=\begin{bmatrix}sv_1\\sv_2\\\vdots\\sv_n\end{bmatrix}. \tag{A.18}$$

Note that if the scalar $s$ is positive, the vector $s\mathbf{v}$ is in the *same* direction as the vector $\mathbf{v}$; however, its length is $s$ times the length of $\mathbf{v}$. On the other hand, if the scalar $s$ is negative, the vector $s\mathbf{v}$ is in the *opposite* direction with respect to the vector $\mathbf{v}$ and its length is $s$ times the length of $\mathbf{v}$. (This implies that the vectors $-\mathbf{v}$ and $\mathbf{v}$ point in opposite directions with respect to each other although they have the same length; i.e., $\|\mathbf{v}\|=\|-\mathbf{v}\|$.)

Vector scaling and addition can be used with unit Cartesian vectors to define the position vector of any 3D point $\dot{\mathbf{P}} = [x, y, z]^T$ as

$$\dot{\mathbf{P}} = x\mathbf{i} + y\mathbf{j} + z\mathbf{k}, \tag{A.19}$$

where $\mathbf{i} = [1, 0, 0]^T$, $\mathbf{j} = [0, 1, 0]^T$ and $\mathbf{k} = [0, 0, 1]^T$ are the unit vectors along the $x$-, $y$- and $z$-axes (i.e., unit Cartesian vectors) respectively.

**Example A.13** [*Vectors–scalar multiplication*]
Consider the vector $\mathbf{u} = [5, 6, 7, 8]^T$. Get the result of $s\mathbf{u}$ where $s = 2.5$.

**Solution A.13** The scalar value is multiplied by each vector term individually. Thus,

$$s\mathbf{u} = 2.5 \begin{bmatrix} 5 \\ 6 \\ 7 \\ 8 \end{bmatrix} = \begin{bmatrix} 12.5 \\ 15 \\ 17.5 \\ 20 \end{bmatrix}.$$

□

**Example A.14** [*Vectors–scalar multiplication and addition/subtraction*]
Consider two vectors $\mathbf{u} = [5, 6, 7, 8]^T$ and $\mathbf{v} = [9, 3, 8, 1]^T$. Calculate $2\mathbf{u} + 3\mathbf{v}$ and $3\mathbf{u} - 2\mathbf{v}$.

**Solution A.14** The operations are performed as

$$2\mathbf{u} + 3\mathbf{v} = 2 \begin{bmatrix} 5 \\ 6 \\ 7 \\ 8 \end{bmatrix} + 3 \begin{bmatrix} 9 \\ 3 \\ 8 \\ 1 \end{bmatrix} = \begin{bmatrix} 10 \\ 12 \\ 14 \\ 16 \end{bmatrix} + \begin{bmatrix} 27 \\ 9 \\ 24 \\ 3 \end{bmatrix} = \begin{bmatrix} 10+27 \\ 12+9 \\ 14+24 \\ 16+3 \end{bmatrix} = \begin{bmatrix} 37 \\ 21 \\ 38 \\ 19 \end{bmatrix}$$

and

$$3\mathbf{u} - 2\mathbf{v} = 3 \begin{bmatrix} 5 \\ 6 \\ 7 \\ 8 \end{bmatrix} - 2 \begin{bmatrix} 9 \\ 3 \\ 8 \\ 1 \end{bmatrix} = \begin{bmatrix} 15 \\ 18 \\ 21 \\ 24 \end{bmatrix} - \begin{bmatrix} 18 \\ 6 \\ 16 \\ 2 \end{bmatrix} = \begin{bmatrix} 15-18 \\ 18-6 \\ 21-16 \\ 24-2 \end{bmatrix} = \begin{bmatrix} -3 \\ 12 \\ 5 \\ 22 \end{bmatrix}.$$

□

#### A.4.3.2 Dot Product

The *dot product* or *scalar product* is an operation performed on two vectors of the same dimension. The symbol '·' is used to denote this operation. It results in a single scalar value. The dot product may be calculated as the sum of the component-wise products of the vectors. Thus, if the two vectors are $\mathbf{u} = [u_1, u_2, u_3]$ and $\mathbf{v} = [v_1, v_2, v_3]$, the dot product is computed as

$$\mathbf{u} \cdot \mathbf{v} = u_1 v_1 + u_2 v_2 + u_3 v_3. \tag{A.20}$$

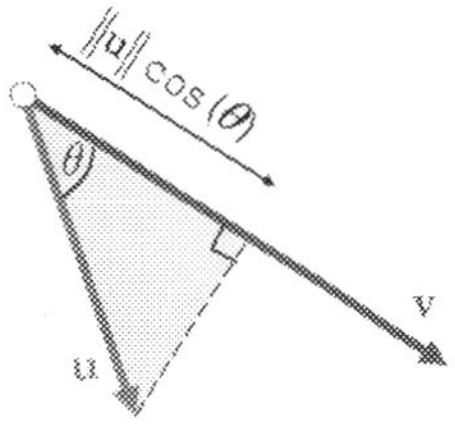


**Fig. A.1** The dot product of two vectors can be used to compute the projection of one vector onto the other

Note that the $\|\mathbf{u}\| = \sqrt{\mathbf{u} \cdot \mathbf{u}}$. Alternatively, the dot product can be computed as the product of lengths of the two vectors times the cosine of the angle between them. In other words,

$$\mathbf{u} \cdot \mathbf{v} = \|\mathbf{u}\| \, \|\mathbf{v}\| \cos(\theta), \tag{A.21}$$

where $\theta$ is the angle between the two vectors. Notice that if the two vectors **u** and **v** are parallel (i.e., $\theta = 0°$ or $\theta = 180°$), the dot product will be the product of their lengths with the sign saying whether they are oriented in the same or opposite directions since $\cos(0) = 1$ and $\cos(180) = -1$. If vectors are orthogonal (i.e., $\theta = 90°$), the dot product will be 0 since $\cos(90) = 0$. If the angle between the vectors is acute, then the dot product will be positive, no matter what orientations of the vectors are, because the cosine of any angle between $-90°$ and $90°$ is positive. On the other hand, if the angle between them is obtuse, then the dot product will be negative.

Also, Eq. (A.21) implies that the angle between two vectors can be computed if the norms and the dot product are known. It can be estimated as

$$\theta = \cos^{-1}\left(\frac{\mathbf{u} \cdot \mathbf{v}}{\|\mathbf{u}\| \, \|\mathbf{v}\|}\right). \tag{A.22}$$

Moreover, Eq. (A.21) lets us compute the projection of one vector onto the other. Consider Fig. A.1, which shows two vectors **u** and **v**. Construct a right triangle in which one side is the vector **u**. It is obvious that the projection of **u** onto **v** equals to $\|\mathbf{u}\| \cos(\theta)$. This can be written as

$$|\text{proj}_{\mathbf{v}}\mathbf{u}| = \|\mathbf{u}\| \cos(\theta) = \frac{\mathbf{u} \cdot \mathbf{v}}{\|\mathbf{v}\|}. \tag{A.23}$$

**Example A.15** [*Dot product and vector norm*]
Given a vector $\mathbf{u} = [u_1, u_2, u_3]^T$, show that $\mathbf{u} \cdot \mathbf{u} = \|\mathbf{u}\|^2$.

**Solution A.15**

$$\mathbf{u} \cdot \mathbf{u} = u_1 u_1 + u_2 u_2 + u_3 u_3 = u_1^2 + u_2^2 + u_3^2 = \|\mathbf{u}\|^2. \qquad \square$$

**Example A.16** [*Dot product–orthogonal vectors*]
If the vectors $\mathbf{u} = [-3, 3s, 10]^T$ and $\mathbf{v} = [2s, 5, 1.8]^T$ are orthogonal, estimate the value of $s$.

**Solution A.16** Since the dot product of two orthogonal vectors is 0, then

$$\begin{aligned} \mathbf{u} \cdot \mathbf{v} &= 0 \\ -3 \times 2s + 3s \times 5 + 10 \times 1.8 &= 0 \\ 9s &= -18. \end{aligned}$$

Hence,

$$s = -2. \qquad \square$$

**Example A.17** [*Dot product–vector projection*]
Suppose that two vectors $\mathbf{u}$ and $\mathbf{v}$ are emitted from the origin $[0, 0, 0]^T$ to the points $[2, -4, 0]^T$ and $[5, -3, 0]^T$ respectively. Using the dot product, determine the length of the projection of $\mathbf{u}$ onto $\mathbf{v}$.

**Solution A.17** We can follow these steps:

1. Calculate the dot product using Eq. (A.20) as

$$\mathbf{u} \cdot \mathbf{v} = 2 \times 5 + (-4) \times (-3) + 0 \times 0 = 22.$$

2. Get the norm of the second vector using Eq. (A.14) as

$$\|\mathbf{v}\| = \sqrt{5^2 + (-3)^2 + 0^2} = \sqrt{34} = 5.8310.$$

3. Get the projection of $\mathbf{u}$ unto $\mathbf{v}$ using Eq. (A.23). Thus, we have

$$|\text{proj}_{\mathbf{v}}\mathbf{u}| = \frac{\mathbf{u} \cdot \mathbf{v}}{\|\mathbf{v}\|} = 3.7730. \qquad \square$$

**Example A.18** [*Dot product–vector projection*]
Consider the column vectors $\mathbf{a} = [2, 2, 1]^T$, $\mathbf{b} = [5, 4, 2]^T$. Calculate the projection of $\mathbf{a}$ unto $\mathbf{b}$.

**Solution A.18** We follow the same steps as in Example A.17:

1. Calculate the dot product using Eq. (A.20) as

$$\mathbf{a} \cdot \mathbf{b} = 2 \times 5 + 2 \times 4 + 1 \times 2 = 20.$$

2. Get the norm of vector **b** using Eq. (A.14) as

$$\|\mathbf{b}\| = \sqrt{5^2 + 4^2 + 2^2} = 3\sqrt{5} = 6.7082.$$

3. Get the projection of **a** unto **b** using Eq. (A.23). Thus, we have

$$|\text{proj}_{\mathbf{b}}\mathbf{a}| = \frac{\mathbf{a} \cdot \mathbf{b}}{\|\mathbf{b}\|} = 2.9814.$$ □

**Example A.19** [*Dot product–angle between vectors*]
In Example A.18, calculate the angle between the vectors **a** and **b**.

**Solution A.19** The norm of vector **a** is calculated as

$$\|\mathbf{a}\| = \sqrt{2^2 + 2^2 + 1^2} = 3.$$

Using the values of $\mathbf{a} \cdot \mathbf{b}$ and $\|\mathbf{b}\|$ from Example A.18, the angle between the vectors can be calculated using Eq. (A.22) as

$$\theta = \cos^{-1}\left(\frac{\mathbf{a} \cdot \mathbf{b}}{\|\mathbf{a}\|\,\|\mathbf{b}\|}\right) = \cos^{-1}\left(\frac{20}{9\sqrt{5}}\right) = 6.3794^{\circ}.$$ □

**Example A.20** [*Vectors–normalization and dot product*]
Consider two vectors $\mathbf{u} = [1, 2, 5]^T$ and $\mathbf{v} = [7, 8, 6]^T$. Normalize them. Calculate the angle between the normalized vectors and the projection of **u** onto **v** after normalization.

**Solution A.20** Using Eq. (A.14), the norms of the vectors are

$$\|\mathbf{u}\| = \sqrt{1^2 + 2^2 + 5^2} = \sqrt{30} = 5.4772$$

and

$$\|\mathbf{v}\| = \sqrt{7^2 + 8^2 + 6^2} = \sqrt{149} = 12.2066.$$

Using Eq. (A.15), the normalized vectors are

$$\hat{\mathbf{u}} = \frac{\mathbf{u}}{\|\mathbf{u}\|} = \begin{bmatrix} \frac{1}{\sqrt{30}} \\ \frac{2}{\sqrt{30}} \\ \frac{5}{\sqrt{30}} \end{bmatrix} = \begin{bmatrix} 0.1826 \\ 0.3651 \\ 0.9129 \end{bmatrix}$$

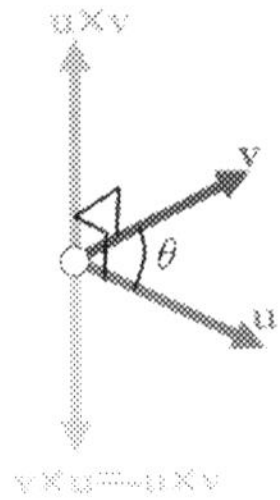


**Fig. A.2** The cross product of two vectors results in a third vector perpendicular to their plane

and

$$\hat{\mathbf{v}} = \frac{\mathbf{v}}{\|\mathbf{v}\|} = \begin{bmatrix} \frac{7}{\sqrt{149}} \\ \frac{8}{\sqrt{149}} \\ \frac{6}{\sqrt{149}} \end{bmatrix} = \begin{bmatrix} 0.5735 \\ 0.6554 \\ 0.4915 \end{bmatrix}.$$

Calculate the dot product of the unit vectors using Eq. (A.20) as

$$\hat{\mathbf{u}} \cdot \hat{\mathbf{v}} = \frac{1}{\sqrt{30}} \times \frac{7}{\sqrt{149}} + \frac{2}{\sqrt{30}} \times \frac{8}{\sqrt{149}} + \frac{5}{\sqrt{30}} \times \frac{6}{\sqrt{149}} = \frac{53}{\sqrt{4470}} = 0.7927.$$

The angle between the vectors can be calculated using Eq. (A.22) as

$$\theta = \cos^{-1}\left(\hat{\mathbf{u}} \cdot \hat{\mathbf{v}}\right) = \cos^{-1}\left(\frac{53}{\sqrt{4470}}\right) = 37.5592^\circ.$$

Finally, the projection of $\hat{\mathbf{u}}$ onto $\hat{\mathbf{v}}$ is calculated using Eq. (A.23) as

$$|\mathrm{proj}_{\hat{\mathbf{v}}}\hat{\mathbf{u}}| = \hat{\mathbf{u}} \cdot \hat{\mathbf{v}} = 0.7927.$$ □

#### A.4.3.3 Cross Product of 3D Vectors

The *cross product* or *vector product* is an operation performed on two 3D vectors. The symbol '×' is used to denote this operation. It results in another 3D vector that is perpendicular to both vectors (i.e., normal/orthogonal to their plane) as shown in Fig. A.2.

Notice that there are two directions for two normals depending on the order of multiplication. To get the correct direction in a right-handed coordinate system (Sect. B.1.1), curl the fingers of your right hand from the first vector to the second, your right thumb will point in the direction of the cross product. Thus, given the vectors $\mathbf{u} = [u_1, u_2, u_3]$ and $\mathbf{v} = [v_1, v_2, v_3]$, the following cross products are equivalent:

$$\mathbf{u} \times \mathbf{v} = -\mathbf{u} \times -\mathbf{v} = -\mathbf{v} \times \mathbf{u} = \mathbf{v} \times -\mathbf{u}.$$

Similarly, the following cross products are equivalent:

$$\mathbf{v} \times \mathbf{u} = -\mathbf{v} \times -\mathbf{u} = -\mathbf{u} \times \mathbf{v} = \mathbf{u} \times -\mathbf{v}.$$

In order to calculate the cross product $\mathbf{u} \times \mathbf{v}$, assume that the unit vectors along the $x$-, $y$- and $z$-axes are $\mathbf{i} = [1, 0, 0]^T$, $\mathbf{j} = [0, 1, 0]^T$ and $\mathbf{k} = [0, 0, 1]^T$, then the cross product can be calculated as

$$\begin{aligned}\mathbf{u} \times \mathbf{v} &= \det \begin{bmatrix} \mathbf{i} & \mathbf{j} & \mathbf{k} \\ u_1 & u_2 & u_3 \\ v_1 & v_2 & v_3 \end{bmatrix} \\ &= \mathbf{i} \begin{vmatrix} u_2 & u_3 \\ v_2 & v_3 \end{vmatrix} - \mathbf{j} \begin{vmatrix} u_1 & u_3 \\ v_1 & v_3 \end{vmatrix} + \mathbf{k} \begin{vmatrix} u_1 & u_2 \\ v_1 & v_2 \end{vmatrix} \\ &= \begin{bmatrix} u_2 v_3 - v_2 u_3 \\ v_1 u_3 - u_1 v_3 \\ u_1 v_2 - v_1 u_2 \end{bmatrix}.\end{aligned} \tag{A.24}$$

The same cross product can be obtained through matrix multiplication by constructing an anti-symmetric matrix $[\mathbf{u}]_\times$ from the first vector $\mathbf{u}$ and multiplying it by the second $\mathbf{v}$ as

$$\begin{aligned}\mathbf{u} \times \mathbf{v} &= \underbrace{\begin{bmatrix} 0 & -u_3 & u_2 \\ u_3 & 0 & -u_1 \\ -u_2 & u_1 & 0 \end{bmatrix}}_{[\mathbf{u}]_\times} \underbrace{\begin{bmatrix} v_1 \\ v_2 \\ v_3 \end{bmatrix}}_{\mathbf{v}} \\ &= \begin{bmatrix} u_2 v_3 - v_2 u_3 \\ v_1 u_3 - u_1 v_3 \\ u_1 v_2 - v_1 u_2 \end{bmatrix}.\end{aligned} \tag{A.25}$$

Considering two 3D vectors $\mathbf{u}$ and $\mathbf{v}$, the length of the resulting vector $\mathbf{u} \times \mathbf{v}$ is the product of the two vector lengths times the sine of the angle between them. This can be written as

$$\|\mathbf{u} \times \mathbf{v}\| = \|\mathbf{u}\| \, \|\mathbf{v}\| \sin(\theta), \tag{A.26}$$

where $\theta$ is the angle between the two vectors. Notice that if the two vectors $\mathbf{u}$ and $\mathbf{v}$ are parallel (i.e., $\theta = 0°$ or $\theta = 180°$), the length of their cross product will be 0 since $\sin(0) = \sin(180) = 0$. This implies that $\mathbf{u} \times \mathbf{v} = \mathbf{0} = [0, 0, 0]^T$ where $\mathbf{0}$ is the *null vector* or *zero vector*. If they are orthogonal (i.e., $\theta = 90°$), their cross product will have a length equal to the product of the two lengths (i.e., $\|\mathbf{u} \times \mathbf{v}\| = \|\mathbf{u}\| \, \|\mathbf{v}\|$) since $\sin(90) = 1$. If $\mathbf{u}$ and $\mathbf{v}$ are both unit vectors, the length of their cross product is the sine of the enclosed angle (i.e., $\|\mathbf{u} \times \mathbf{v}\| = \sin(\theta)$).

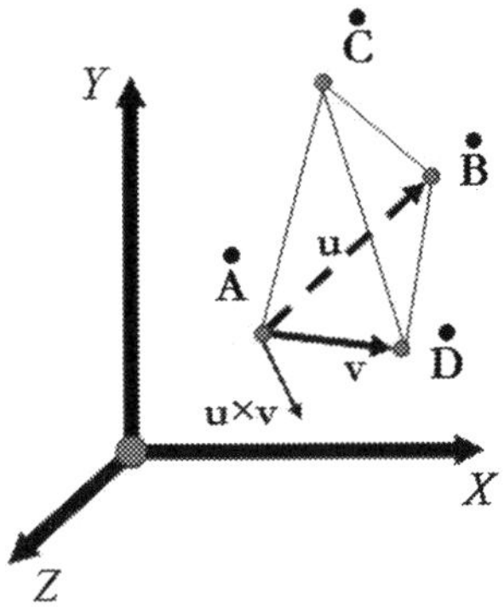


**Fig. A.3** A pyramid with a normal vector $\mathbf{u} \times \mathbf{v}$ perpendicular to the face $\dot{\mathbf{A}}\dot{\mathbf{B}}\dot{\mathbf{D}}$

The cross product may be used to obtain the area of a triangle. Given a triangle $\triangle\dot{\mathbf{A}}\dot{\mathbf{B}}\dot{\mathbf{C}}$, its area $A$ is calculated as

$$A = \frac{1}{2} \left\| [\dot{\mathbf{B}} - \dot{\mathbf{A}}] \times [\dot{\mathbf{C}} - \dot{\mathbf{A}}] \right\| . \tag{A.27}$$

**Example A.21** [*Cross product–normal vector to a plane*]

Consider a pyramid whose vertices are $\dot{\mathbf{A}} = [2, 2, 1]^T$, $\dot{\mathbf{B}} = [5, 4, 1]^T$, $\dot{\mathbf{C}} = [3, 7, 1]^T$ and $\dot{\mathbf{D}} = [3, 3, 5]^T$. What is the normal to the face $\dot{\mathbf{A}}\dot{\mathbf{B}}\dot{\mathbf{D}}$?

**Solution A.21** Figure A.3 illustrates the problem. We start by obtaining the direction vectors emitting from $\dot{\mathbf{A}}$ as

$$\begin{aligned} \mathbf{u} &= \dot{\mathbf{B}} - \dot{\mathbf{A}} \\ &= \begin{bmatrix} 5 \\ 4 \\ 1 \end{bmatrix} - \begin{bmatrix} 2 \\ 2 \\ 1 \end{bmatrix} = \begin{bmatrix} 3 \\ 2 \\ 0 \end{bmatrix} \end{aligned}$$

and

$$\begin{aligned} \mathbf{v} &= \dot{\mathbf{D}} - \dot{\mathbf{A}} \\ &= \begin{bmatrix} 3 \\ 3 \\ 5 \end{bmatrix} - \begin{bmatrix} 2 \\ 2 \\ 1 \end{bmatrix} = \begin{bmatrix} 1 \\ 1 \\ 4 \end{bmatrix}. \end{aligned}$$

The normal to the face $\dot{\mathbf{A}}\dot{\mathbf{B}}\dot{\mathbf{D}}$ is the cross product $\mathbf{u} \times \mathbf{v}$, which can be calculated using Eq. (A.24) as

$$\mathbf{u} \times \mathbf{v} = \det \begin{bmatrix} \mathbf{i} & \mathbf{j} & \mathbf{k} \\ u_1 & u_2 & u_3 \\ v_1 & v_2 & v_3 \end{bmatrix}$$

$$= \mathbf{i} \begin{vmatrix} u_2 & u_3 \\ v_2 & v_3 \end{vmatrix} - \mathbf{j} \begin{vmatrix} u_1 & u_3 \\ v_1 & v_3 \end{vmatrix} + \mathbf{k} \begin{vmatrix} u_1 & u_2 \\ v_1 & v_2 \end{vmatrix}$$

$$= \begin{bmatrix} u_2 v_3 - v_2 u_3 \\ v_1 u_3 - u_1 v_3 \\ u_1 v_2 - v_1 u_2 \end{bmatrix}$$

$$= \begin{bmatrix} 2 \times 4 - 1 \times 0 \\ 1 \times 0 - 3 \times 4 \\ 3 \times 1 - 1 \times 2 \end{bmatrix} = \begin{bmatrix} 8 \\ -12 \\ 1 \end{bmatrix}.$$

The same vector can be calculated using Eq. (A.25) as

$$\mathbf{u} \times \mathbf{v} = \underbrace{\begin{bmatrix} 0 & -u_3 & u_2 \\ u_3 & 0 & -u_1 \\ -u_2 & u_1 & 0 \end{bmatrix}}_{[\mathbf{u}]_\times} \underbrace{\begin{bmatrix} v_1 \\ v_2 \\ v_3 \end{bmatrix}}_{\mathbf{v}}$$

$$= \begin{bmatrix} u_2 v_3 - v_2 u_3 \\ v_1 u_3 - u_1 v_3 \\ u_1 v_2 - v_1 u_2 \end{bmatrix}$$

$$= \begin{bmatrix} 0 & 0 & 2 \\ 0 & 0 & -3 \\ -2 & 3 & 0 \end{bmatrix} \begin{bmatrix} 1 \\ 1 \\ 4 \end{bmatrix} = \begin{bmatrix} 8 \\ -12 \\ 1 \end{bmatrix}.$$

□

**Example A.22** [*Cross product–equation of a plane*]
Building on Example A.21, estimate the plane equation of the face $\dot{\mathbf{A}}\dot{\mathbf{B}}\dot{\mathbf{D}}$.

**Solution A.22** The general equation of a plane is

$$ax + by + cz = d,$$

where $[a, b, c]^T$ is the normal to the plane; and $d$ is the perpendicular distance from the origin to the plane when the normal vector $[a, b, c]^T$ is normalized. According to Example A.21, the normal to the plane is $[8, -12, 1]^T$. Substituting the values of $a$, $b$ and $c$, we get

$$8x - 12y + z = d.$$

Since point $\dot{\mathbf{A}} = [2, 2, 1]^T$ is on the plane, $d$ is estimated as

$$d = 8 \times 2 - 12 \times 2 + 1 \times 1 = -7.$$

Hence, the equation of the plane is expressed as

$$8x - 12y + z + 7 = 0. \qquad \square$$

#### A.4.3.4 Cross Product of 2D Vectors

Although less frequently used, we sometimes need to calculate the cross product of two 2D vectors $\mathbf{u} = [u_1, u_2]$ and $\mathbf{v} = [v_1, v_2]$. In this case, these vectors lie on a single plane (e.g., $xy$-plane); thus, we can write them as $\mathbf{u} = [u_1, u_2, 0]$ and $\mathbf{v} = [v_1, v_2, 0]$. By applying Eq. (A.24), we may have

$$\begin{aligned} \mathbf{u} \times \mathbf{v} &= \det \begin{bmatrix} \mathbf{i} & \mathbf{j} & \mathbf{k} \\ u_1 & u_2 & 0 \\ v_1 & v_2 & 0 \end{bmatrix} \\ &= \mathbf{i} \begin{vmatrix} u_2 & 0 \\ v_2 & 0 \end{vmatrix} - \mathbf{j} \begin{vmatrix} u_1 & 0 \\ v_1 & 0 \end{vmatrix} + \mathbf{k} \begin{vmatrix} u_1 & u_2 \\ v_1 & v_2 \end{vmatrix} \\ &= \begin{bmatrix} 0 \\ 0 \\ u_1 v_2 - v_1 u_2 \end{bmatrix}. \end{aligned} \tag{A.28}$$

Thus, in order to obtain the cross product of two 2D vectors, calculate the determinant of the $2 \times 2$ matrix composed of the two vectors. Note that $\begin{vmatrix} u_1 & u_2 \\ v_1 & v_2 \end{vmatrix} = \begin{vmatrix} u_1 & v_1 \\ u_2 & v_2 \end{vmatrix} = u_1 v_2 - u_2 v_1$.

## A.5 Problems

**Problem A.1** [*Matrices–determinant*]
Compute the determinant for the following matrix:

$$\mathtt{A} = \begin{bmatrix} 3 & 4 & 5 \\ 1 & 6 & 7 \\ 1 & 8 & 9 \end{bmatrix}.$$

**Problem A.2** [*Matrices–inverse*]
Compute the inverse for matrix $\mathtt{A}$ that is defined in Problem A.1.

**Problem A.3** [*Matrices–addition and subtraction*]
Consider the matrices $\mathtt{A}$ and $\mathtt{B}$ where

$$\mathtt{A} = \begin{bmatrix} 3\,4\,5 \\ 1\,6\,7 \\ 1\,8\,9 \end{bmatrix}$$

and

$$\mathtt{B} = \begin{bmatrix} 1\,4\,0 \\ 1\,6\,0 \\ 1\,8\,4 \end{bmatrix}.$$

Calculate $\mathtt{A}+\mathtt{B}$, $\mathtt{A}-\mathtt{B}$ and $\mathtt{B}-\mathtt{A}$.

**Problem A.4** [*Matrices–multiplication*]
Consider matrices A and B of Problem A.3. Determine whether or not $\mathtt{AB}=\mathtt{BA}$.

**Problem A.5** [*Matrices–multiplication*]
Assume that a matrix B is defined to be

$$\mathtt{B} = \begin{bmatrix} 1\,4 \\ 1\,6 \\ 1\,8 \end{bmatrix}.$$

If matrix A keeps all its elements as in Problem A.3, calculate AB and BA. If the multiplications cannot be performed, mention the reason.

**Problem A.6** [*Vectors–vector normalization*]
Normalize the vector $\mathbf{v} = [7, 3, 6]$.

**Problem A.7** [*Vectors–angle between vectors*]
Suppose that two 3D line segments are extended from $[1, 5, 0]^T$ to $[2, 3, 0]^T$ to $[4, 4, 0]^T$. What is the angle between them at $[2, 3, 0]^T$?

**Problem A.8** [*Vectors–angle between vectors*]
Suppose that two 3D line segments are extended from $[1, 5, 0]^T$ to $[2, 3, 0]^T$ to $[4, 4, 0]^T$. Without calculating its value, determine whether the angle between them is acute or obtuse.

**Problem A.9** [*Vectors–orthogonal vectors*]
Suppose that two 3D line segments are extended from $[0, 0, 0]^T$ to $[3, 3, 0]^T$ and from $[2, 2, 0]^T$ to $[2, 2, 4]^T$. Show that their direction vectors are orthogonal.

**Problem A.10** [*Vectors–dot and cross products*]
Consider two parallel vectors each of length 3.5. Determine their dot product. Also, determine the magnitude of their cross product.

**Problem A.11** [*Vectors–dot and cross products*]
Consider two orthogonal vectors each of length 3.5. Determine their dot product. Also, determine the magnitude of their cross product.

**Problem A.12** [*Vectors–vector projection*]

Suppose that two vectors **u** and **v** are emitted from the origin $[0, 0, 0]^T$ to the points $[2, -4, 0]^T$ and $[5, -3, 0]^T$ respectively. Using the dot product, determine the length of the projection of **u** onto **v**.

**Problem A.13** [*Vectors–plane normal vectors*]

Consider the tetrahedron whose vertices are located at $[1, 1, 1]^T$, $[0, 1, 1]^T$, $[0, 0, 1]^T$ and $[0, 0, 0]^T$. What are the normals to the four triangles that bound the tetrahedron where each normal is pointing to the outside?

**Problem A.14** [*Vectors–plane equations*]

Consider the tetrahedron whose vertices are located at $[1, 1, 1]^T$, $[0, 1, 1]^T$, $[0, 0, 1]^T$ and $[0, 0, 0]^T$. Determine the plane equation for each of its faces.

# Appendix B
# Coordinate Systems

There are many coordinate systems that appear in computer graphics literature. These systems include the most usable Cartesian coordinate system both in 2D and 3D spaces with its perpendicular axes. Other coordinate systems include parametric and barycentric that are usually used with triangles. Coordinates do not have to be represented by straight axes. On the contrary, angles may be used to represent separate coordinates as in polar, cylindrical and spherical coordinates. Homogeneous coordinates are very important in computer graphics to facilitate operations like transformations.

This appendix gives a short description for each of those coordinate systems, which are important for the reader of this book to know. In addition to the descriptions of the coordinate systems, we will discuss how to convert from the Cartesian coordinates to each of these systems and vice versa. Skilled readers may skip this appendix.

## B.1 Cartesian Coordinate Systems

A Cartesian coordinate system may be specified in 2D space or in 3D space. In 2D space, the system is split into four quadrants by two axes (i.e., the $x$- and $y$-axes). Points are represented by two real numbers (e.g., $\dot{\mathbf{p}} = [x, y]^T$); each representing the distance from the origin to that point along the $x$- and $y$-axes as shown in Fig. B.1a. This can be written as

$$\underbrace{\begin{bmatrix} x \\ y \end{bmatrix}}_{\dot{\mathbf{p}}} = x \underbrace{\begin{bmatrix} 1 \\ 0 \end{bmatrix}}_{\mathbf{i}} + y \underbrace{\begin{bmatrix} 0 \\ 1 \end{bmatrix}}_{\mathbf{j}}, \tag{B.1}$$

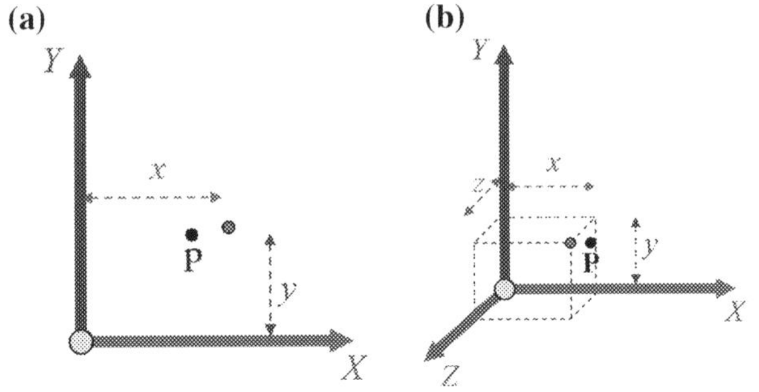


**Fig. B.1** Right-handed coordinate systems. **a** 2D Cartesian coordinate system showing a point $\dot{\mathbf{p}}$ specified as $[x, y]^T$. **b** 3D Cartesian coordinate system showing a point $\dot{\mathbf{P}}$ specified as $[x, y, z]^T$

where $\mathbf{i} = [1, 0]^T$ and $\mathbf{j} = [0, 1]^T$ are the unit vectors along the $x$- and $y$-axes respectively. Each of the four quadrants contains points with the same algebraic signs in each component.

In 3D space, the system is split into eight octants by three axes (i.e., the $x$-, $y$- and $z$-axes). Points are represented by three real numbers (e.g., $\dot{\mathbf{P}} = [x, y, z]^T$); each representing the distance from the origin to that point along the $x$-, $y$- and $z$-axes as shown in Fig. B.1b. As done in Eq. (B.1), this can be written as

$$\underbrace{\begin{bmatrix} x \\ y \\ z \end{bmatrix}}_{\dot{\mathbf{P}}} = x \underbrace{\begin{bmatrix} 1 \\ 0 \\ 0 \end{bmatrix}}_{\mathbf{i}} + y \underbrace{\begin{bmatrix} 0 \\ 1 \\ 0 \end{bmatrix}}_{\mathbf{j}} + z \underbrace{\begin{bmatrix} 0 \\ 0 \\ 1 \end{bmatrix}}_{\mathbf{k}}, \tag{B.2}$$

where $\mathbf{i} = [1, 0, 0]^T$, $\mathbf{j} = [0, 1, 0]^T$ and $\mathbf{k} = [0, 0, 1]^T$ are the unit vectors along the $x$-, $y$- and $z$-axes respectively. Each of the eight octants contains points with the same algebraic signs in each component.

## *B.1.1 Right-Versus Left-Handed Coordinate Systems*

A coordinate system may be either right-handed or left-handed (Vince 2008).

### B.1.1.1 Right-Handed Coordinate Systems

In *2D right-handed* system, the $x$-axis coincides with the $y$-axis if it rotates through an angle of 90° about the origin in a *counter-clockwise* direction as in Fig. B.1a. In *3D right-handed* system, if you hold your *right* hand in space with your fingers along the $x$-axis and curl your fingers towards the $y$-axis, your thumb will point in

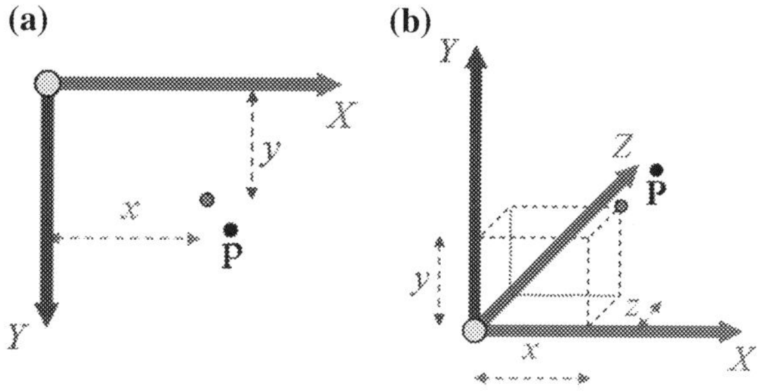


**Fig. B.2** Left-handed coordinate systems. **a** 2D Cartesian coordinate system showing a point $\dot{\mathbf{p}}$ specified as $[x, y]^T$. **b** 3D Cartesian coordinate system showing a point $\dot{\mathbf{P}}$ specified as $[x, y, z]^T$

the $z$-axis direction, which is perpendicular to both the $x$- and $y$-axes. Figure B.1b illustrates the 3D right-handed coordinate systems.

### B.1.1.2 Left-Handed Coordinate Systems

The above concepts hold for the *left-handed* coordinate systems. In *2D left-handed* system, the $x$-axis coincides with the $y$-axis if it rotates through an angle of 90° about the origin in a *clockwise* direction as shown in Fig. B.2a. In *3D left-handed* system, if you hold your *left* hand in space with your fingers along the $x$-axis and curl your fingers towards the $y$-axis, your thumb will point in the $z$-axis direction, which is perpendicular to both the $x$- and $y$-axes as illustrated in Fig. B.2b.

### B.1.1.3 Right-/Left-Handed Coordinate Systems Transformations

Switching between right- and left-handed coordinate systems in 2D space is performed by switching signs along the $y$-coordinates to get

$$\begin{aligned} x_l &= x_r, \\ y_l &= -y_r, \end{aligned} \tag{B.3}$$

where $[x_l, y_l]^T$ is a 2D point expressed in 2D left-handed coordinate system and $[x_r, y_r]^T$ is the same 2D point expressed in 2D right-handed coordinate system. This relationship can be expressed in matrix form as

$$\begin{bmatrix} x_l \\ y_l \end{bmatrix} = \begin{bmatrix} 1 & 0 \\ 0 & -1 \end{bmatrix} \begin{bmatrix} x_r \\ y_r \end{bmatrix}. \tag{B.4}$$

Note that turning between right- and left-handed coordinate systems in 2D space is equivalent to reflecting about the $x$-axis. (More discussion about 2D reflection can be found in Chap. 3.)

The same idea is extended to 3D space. Thus, transformation between right- and left-handed coordinate systems in 3D space is performed by switching signs along the $z$-coordinates to get

$$\begin{aligned} x_l &= x_r, \\ y_l &= y_r, \\ z_l &= -z_r, \end{aligned} \tag{B.5}$$

where $[x_l, y_l, z_l]^T$ is a 3D point expressed in 3D left-handed coordinate system and $[x_r, y_r, z_r]^T$ is the same 3D point expressed in 3D right-handed coordinate system. This relationship can be expressed in matrix form as

$$\begin{bmatrix} x_l \\ y_l \\ z_l \end{bmatrix} = \begin{bmatrix} 1 & 0 & 0 \\ 0 & 1 & 0 \\ 0 & 0 & -1 \end{bmatrix} \begin{bmatrix} x_r \\ y_r \\ z_r \end{bmatrix}. \tag{B.6}$$

Similar to the 2D version of the transformation, switching between right- and left-handed coordinate systems in 3D space is equivalent to reflecting about the $xy$-plane. (More discussion about 3D reflection can be found in Chap. 5.)

#### B.1.1.4 Images and Coordinate Systems

The 2D left-handed coordinate system is usually used with raster images. In this case, the origin is located at the upper left corner of the image and the $y$-axis is pointing downwards. Converting between these systems is done using the following formula:

$$\begin{bmatrix} x_r \\ y_r \end{bmatrix} = \begin{bmatrix} x_l \\ y_{max} - y_l \end{bmatrix}, \tag{B.7}$$

where $[x_l, y_l]^T$ is a pixel expressed in 2D left-handed coordinate system; $[x_r, y_r]^T$ is the same pixel expressed in 2D right-handed coordinate system; and $y_{max}$ is the height of the image in pixels.

### *B.1.2 Distances*

The distance $d(\dot{\mathbf{p}}_1, \dot{\mathbf{p}}_2)$ between two 2D points $\dot{\mathbf{p}}_1 = [x_1, y_1]^T$ and $\dot{\mathbf{p}}_2 = [x_2, y_2]^T$ is given by

$$d(\dot{\mathbf{p}}_1, \dot{\mathbf{p}}_2) = \sqrt{(x_2 - x_1)^2 + (y_2 - y_1)^2}. \tag{B.8}$$

Similarly, the distance $d(\dot{\mathbf{P}}_1, \dot{\mathbf{P}}_2)$ between two 3D points $\dot{\mathbf{P}}_1 = [x_1, y_1, z_1]^T$ and $\dot{\mathbf{P}}_2 = [x_2, y_2, z_2]^T$ is given by

$$d(\dot{\mathbf{P}}_1, \dot{\mathbf{P}}_2) = \sqrt{(x_2 - x_1)^2 + (y_2 - y_1)^2 + (z_2 - z_1)^2}. \tag{B.9}$$

$d(\dot{\mathbf{p}}_1, \dot{\mathbf{p}}_2)$ and $d(\dot{\mathbf{P}}_1, \dot{\mathbf{P}}_2)$ are referred to as *Euclidean distances* in 2D and 3D spaces respectively. Note that the Euclidean distance between two vectors $\mathbf{v}_1$ and $\mathbf{v}_2$ represents the norm of the direction vector $\mathbf{v}_2 - \mathbf{v}_1$ and it is denoted as $\|\mathbf{v}_2 - \mathbf{v}_1\|$. More is discussed in Sect. A.4.1.

**Example B.1** [*Euclidean distance–2D points*]
Determine the Euclidean distance between points $\dot{\mathbf{p}}_1 = [4, 7]^T$ and $\dot{\mathbf{p}}_2 = [7, 8]^T$.

**Solution B.1** Equation (B.8) is used to get the distance from $\dot{\mathbf{p}}_1$ to $\dot{\mathbf{p}}_2$ as

$$\begin{aligned} d(\dot{\mathbf{p}}_1, \dot{\mathbf{p}}_2) &= \sqrt{(x_2 - x_1)^2 + (y_2 - y_1)^2} \\ &= \sqrt{(7-4)^2 + (8-7)^2} \\ &= \sqrt{10}. \end{aligned}$$

□

**Example B.2** [*Euclidean distance–3D points*]
Determine the Euclidean distance between points $\dot{\mathbf{P}}_1 = [4, 7, 6]^T$ and $\dot{\mathbf{P}}_2 = [7, 8, 3]^T$.

**Solution B.2** Equation (B.9) is used to get the distance from $\dot{\mathbf{P}}_1$ to $\dot{\mathbf{P}}_2$ as

$$\begin{aligned} d(\dot{\mathbf{P}}_1, \dot{\mathbf{P}}_2) &= \sqrt{(x_2 - x_1)^2 + (y_2 - y_1)^2 + (z_2 - z_1)^2} \\ &= \sqrt{(7-4)^2 + (8-7)^2 + (3-6)^2} \\ &= \sqrt{19}. \end{aligned}$$

□

## B.2 Parametric Coordinate System

Parametric coordinates can be regarded as a generalization of Cartesian coordinates. In a parametric coordinates system, axes do not have to be orthogonal to each other as shown in Fig. B.3.

In 2D space, points are represented by two real numbers (e.g., $\dot{\mathbf{p}} = [u, v]^T$); each representing the distance from the origin $[0, 0]^T$ to that point along the $u$- and $v$-axes. In other words, you start at the origin and walk $u$ distance along $\mathbf{u}$ then walk $v$ distance in the direction $\mathbf{v}$. This can be written as

$$\underbrace{\begin{bmatrix} u \\ v \end{bmatrix}}_{\dot{\mathbf{p}}} = u \underbrace{\begin{bmatrix} 1 \\ 0 \end{bmatrix}}_{\mathbf{u}} + v \underbrace{\begin{bmatrix} 0 \\ 1 \end{bmatrix}}_{\mathbf{v}}, \tag{B.10}$$

where $\mathbf{u} = [1, 0]^T$ and $\mathbf{v} = [0, 1]^T$ are unit vectors along the $u$- and $v$-axes respectively.

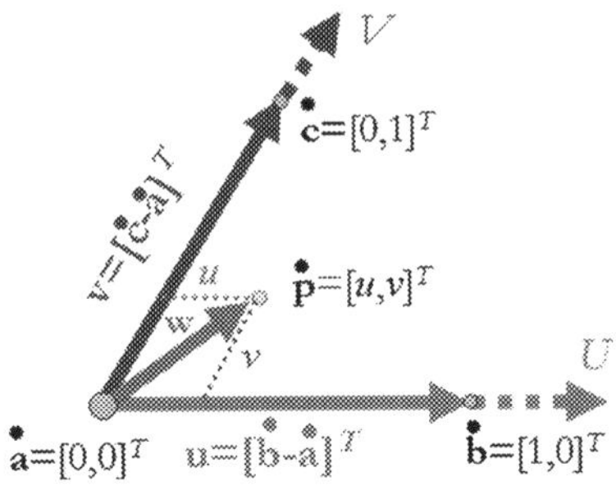


Fig. B.3 Parametric coordinates

## B.2.1 Cartesian-Parametric Transformation

A point $[x, y]^T$ in Cartesian coordinates can be expressed in parametric coordinates $[u, v]^T$ as

$$\begin{aligned}\mathbf{u} &= \dot{\mathbf{b}} - \dot{\mathbf{a}},\\ \mathbf{v} &= \dot{\mathbf{c}} - \dot{\mathbf{a}},\\ \mathbf{w} &= \dot{\mathbf{p}} - \dot{\mathbf{a}},\\ \begin{bmatrix} u \\ v \end{bmatrix} &= \begin{bmatrix} \dfrac{(\mathbf{u}\cdot\mathbf{v})(\mathbf{w}\cdot\mathbf{v}) - (\mathbf{v}\cdot\mathbf{v})(\mathbf{w}\cdot\mathbf{u})}{(\mathbf{u}\cdot\mathbf{v})^2 - (\mathbf{u}\cdot\mathbf{u})(\mathbf{v}\cdot\mathbf{v})} \\ \dfrac{(\mathbf{u}\cdot\mathbf{v})(\mathbf{w}\cdot\mathbf{u}) - (\mathbf{u}\cdot\mathbf{u})(\mathbf{w}\cdot\mathbf{v})}{(\mathbf{u}\cdot\mathbf{v})^2 - (\mathbf{u}\cdot\mathbf{u})(\mathbf{v}\cdot\mathbf{v})} \end{bmatrix},\end{aligned} \tag{B.11}$$

where $\dot{\mathbf{a}}$, $\dot{\mathbf{b}}$, $\dot{\mathbf{c}}$ and $\dot{\mathbf{p}}$ are expressed in Cartesian coordinates; $\cdot$ indicates the dot product; and $u$ and $v$ are the parametric coordinates of the point.

**Example B.3** [*Cartesian-parametric transformation*]

Consider a triangle $\triangle\dot{\mathbf{a}}\dot{\mathbf{b}}\dot{\mathbf{c}}$ where $\dot{\mathbf{a}} = [1, 1]^T$, $\dot{\mathbf{b}} = [10, 2]^T$ and $\dot{\mathbf{c}} = [6, 5]^T$. Also, consider a point $\dot{\mathbf{p}} = [7, 3]^T$ inside the triangle. Express $\dot{\mathbf{p}}$ in parametric coordinates if the $u$- and $v$-axes go along $\overline{\dot{\mathbf{a}}\dot{\mathbf{b}}}$ and $\overline{\dot{\mathbf{a}}\dot{\mathbf{c}}}$ respectively.

**Solution B.3** To do this conversion, Eq. (B.11) is used. Thus,

$$\begin{aligned}\mathbf{u} &= \dot{\mathbf{b}} - \dot{\mathbf{a}}\\ &= \begin{bmatrix} 10 \\ 2 \end{bmatrix} - \begin{bmatrix} 1 \\ 1 \end{bmatrix} = \begin{bmatrix} 9 \\ 1 \end{bmatrix},\end{aligned}$$

$$\begin{aligned}\mathbf{v} &= \dot{\mathbf{c}} - \dot{\mathbf{a}}\\ &= \begin{bmatrix} 6 \\ 5 \end{bmatrix} - \begin{bmatrix} 1 \\ 1 \end{bmatrix} = \begin{bmatrix} 5 \\ 4 \end{bmatrix},\end{aligned}$$

$$\begin{aligned}\mathbf{w} &= \dot{\mathbf{p}} - \dot{\mathbf{a}} \\ &= \begin{bmatrix} 7 \\ 3 \end{bmatrix} - \begin{bmatrix} 1 \\ 1 \end{bmatrix} = \begin{bmatrix} 6 \\ 2 \end{bmatrix}.\end{aligned}$$

Hence,

$$\begin{aligned}\begin{bmatrix} u \\ v \end{bmatrix} &= \begin{bmatrix} \dfrac{(\mathbf{u}\cdot\mathbf{v})(\mathbf{w}\cdot\mathbf{v}) - (\mathbf{v}\cdot\mathbf{v})(\mathbf{w}\cdot\mathbf{u})}{(\mathbf{u}\cdot\mathbf{v})^2 - (\mathbf{u}\cdot\mathbf{u})(\mathbf{v}\cdot\mathbf{v})} \\ \dfrac{(\mathbf{u}\cdot\mathbf{v})(\mathbf{w}\cdot\mathbf{u}) - (\mathbf{u}\cdot\mathbf{u})(\mathbf{w}\cdot\mathbf{v})}{(\mathbf{u}\cdot\mathbf{v})^2 - (\mathbf{u}\cdot\mathbf{u})(\mathbf{v}\cdot\mathbf{v})} \end{bmatrix} \\
&= \begin{bmatrix} \dfrac{\left(\begin{bmatrix} 9 \\ 1 \end{bmatrix}\cdot\begin{bmatrix} 5 \\ 4 \end{bmatrix}\right)\left(\begin{bmatrix} 6 \\ 2 \end{bmatrix}\cdot\begin{bmatrix} 5 \\ 4 \end{bmatrix}\right) - \left(\begin{bmatrix} 5 \\ 4 \end{bmatrix}\cdot\begin{bmatrix} 5 \\ 4 \end{bmatrix}\right)\left(\begin{bmatrix} 6 \\ 2 \end{bmatrix}\cdot\begin{bmatrix} 9 \\ 1 \end{bmatrix}\right)}{\left(\begin{bmatrix} 9 \\ 1 \end{bmatrix}\cdot\begin{bmatrix} 5 \\ 4 \end{bmatrix}\right)^2 - \left(\begin{bmatrix} 9 \\ 1 \end{bmatrix}\cdot\begin{bmatrix} 9 \\ 1 \end{bmatrix}\right)\left(\begin{bmatrix} 5 \\ 4 \end{bmatrix}\cdot\begin{bmatrix} 5 \\ 4 \end{bmatrix}\right)} \\ \dfrac{\left(\begin{bmatrix} 9 \\ 1 \end{bmatrix}\cdot\begin{bmatrix} 5 \\ 4 \end{bmatrix}\right)\left(\begin{bmatrix} 6 \\ 2 \end{bmatrix}\cdot\begin{bmatrix} 9 \\ 1 \end{bmatrix}\right) - \left(\begin{bmatrix} 9 \\ 1 \end{bmatrix}\cdot\begin{bmatrix} 9 \\ 1 \end{bmatrix}\right)\left(\begin{bmatrix} 6 \\ 2 \end{bmatrix}\cdot\begin{bmatrix} 5 \\ 4 \end{bmatrix}\right)}{\left(\begin{bmatrix} 9 \\ 1 \end{bmatrix}\cdot\begin{bmatrix} 5 \\ 4 \end{bmatrix}\right)^2 - \left(\begin{bmatrix} 9 \\ 1 \end{bmatrix}\cdot\begin{bmatrix} 9 \\ 1 \end{bmatrix}\right)\left(\begin{bmatrix} 5 \\ 4 \end{bmatrix}\cdot\begin{bmatrix} 5 \\ 4 \end{bmatrix}\right)} \end{bmatrix} \\
&= \begin{bmatrix} 0.4516 \\ 0.3871 \end{bmatrix}.\end{aligned}$$

□

## B.2.2 Parametric-Cartesian Transformation

A point $[u, v]^T$ in parametric coordinates can be expressed in Cartesian coordinates $[x, y]^T$ as

$$\begin{bmatrix} x \\ y \end{bmatrix} = \dot{\mathbf{a}} + u[\dot{\mathbf{b}} - \dot{\mathbf{a}}] + v[\dot{\mathbf{c}} - \dot{\mathbf{a}}], \tag{B.12}$$

where $\dot{\mathbf{a}}$, $\dot{\mathbf{b}}$ and $\dot{\mathbf{c}}$ are expressed in Cartesian coordinates; $u$ and $v$ are the parametric coordinates; and $x$ and $y$ are the Cartesian coordinates of the point.

**Example B.4** [*Parametric-Cartesian transformation*]
Consider a triangle $\triangle\dot{\mathbf{a}}\dot{\mathbf{b}}\dot{\mathbf{c}}$ where $\dot{\mathbf{a}} = [1, 1]^T$, $\dot{\mathbf{b}} = [10, 2]^T$ and $\dot{\mathbf{c}} = [6, 5]^T$. If a parametric coordinate system is defined such that the $u$- and $v$-axes go along $\overline{\dot{\mathbf{a}}\dot{\mathbf{b}}}$ and $\overline{\dot{\mathbf{a}}\dot{\mathbf{c}}}$ respectively, express the parametric point $[0.4516, 0.3871]^T$ in Cartesian coordinates.

**Solution B.4** This transformation is performed using Eq. (B.12). Thus,

$$
\begin{aligned}
\begin{bmatrix} x \\ y \end{bmatrix} &= \dot{\mathbf{a}} + u[\dot{\mathbf{b}} - \dot{\mathbf{a}}] + v[\dot{\mathbf{c}} - \dot{\mathbf{a}}] \\
&= \begin{bmatrix} 1 \\ 1 \end{bmatrix} + 0.4516 \left[ \begin{bmatrix} 10 \\ 2 \end{bmatrix} - \begin{bmatrix} 1 \\ 1 \end{bmatrix} \right] + 0.3871 \left[ \begin{bmatrix} 6 \\ 5 \end{bmatrix} - \begin{bmatrix} 1 \\ 1 \end{bmatrix} \right] \\
&= \begin{bmatrix} 7 \\ 3 \end{bmatrix},
\end{aligned}
$$

which is the same point of Example B.3. □

## B.3 Barycentric Coordinate System

Barycentric coordinates are triplets of numbers $[t_{\dot{\mathbf{a}}}, t_{\dot{\mathbf{b}}}, t_{\dot{\mathbf{c}}}]^T$ corresponding to masses placed at the vertices $\dot{\mathbf{a}}$, $\dot{\mathbf{b}}$ and $\dot{\mathbf{c}}$ of a triangle $\triangle\dot{\mathbf{a}}\dot{\mathbf{b}}\dot{\mathbf{c}}$. A point inside the triangle can be treated as the geometric centroid of the three masses (Vince 2010). This point is identified with coordinates $[t_{\dot{\mathbf{a}}}, t_{\dot{\mathbf{b}}}, t_{\dot{\mathbf{c}}}]^T$.

Figure B.4 shows a point $\dot{\mathbf{p}}$ that lies inside the triangle $\triangle\dot{\mathbf{a}}\dot{\mathbf{b}}\dot{\mathbf{c}}$. The barycentric coordinates of $\dot{\mathbf{p}}$ are represented as a triplet $[t_{\dot{\mathbf{a}}}, t_{\dot{\mathbf{b}}}, t_{\dot{\mathbf{c}}}]^T$ where $t_{\dot{\mathbf{a}}}$, $t_{\dot{\mathbf{b}}}$ and $t_{\dot{\mathbf{c}}}$ are proportional to the three areas of the sub-triangles created by point $\dot{\mathbf{p}}$ and the vertices $\dot{\mathbf{a}}$, $\dot{\mathbf{b}}$ and $\dot{\mathbf{c}}$ respectively.

### *B.3.1 Cartesian-Barycentric Transformation*

The barycentric coordinates $[t_{\dot{\mathbf{a}}}, t_{\dot{\mathbf{b}}}, t_{\dot{\mathbf{c}}}]^T$ of point $\dot{\mathbf{p}}$ that lies inside the triangle $\triangle\dot{\mathbf{a}}\dot{\mathbf{b}}\dot{\mathbf{c}}$ (Fig. B.4) can be expressed as

$$
\begin{bmatrix} t_{\dot{\mathbf{a}}} \\ t_{\dot{\mathbf{b}}} \\ t_{\dot{\mathbf{c}}} \end{bmatrix} = \frac{1}{A} \begin{bmatrix} A_{\dot{\mathbf{a}}} \\ A_{\dot{\mathbf{b}}} \\ A_{\dot{\mathbf{c}}} \end{bmatrix}, \tag{B.13}
$$

where $A_{\dot{\mathbf{a}}}$ is the area of the sub-triangle $\triangle\dot{\mathbf{p}}\dot{\mathbf{b}}\dot{\mathbf{c}}$; $A_{\dot{\mathbf{b}}}$ is the area of the sub-triangle $\triangle\dot{\mathbf{p}}\dot{\mathbf{c}}\dot{\mathbf{a}}$; $A_{\dot{\mathbf{c}}}$ is the area of the sub-triangle $\triangle\dot{\mathbf{p}}\dot{\mathbf{a}}\dot{\mathbf{b}}$; and $A$ is the area of the triangle $\triangle\dot{\mathbf{a}}\dot{\mathbf{b}}\dot{\mathbf{c}}$, which is equal to $A_{\dot{\mathbf{a}}} + A_{\dot{\mathbf{b}}} + A_{\dot{\mathbf{c}}}$. Note that $t_{\dot{\mathbf{a}}} + t_{\dot{\mathbf{b}}} + t_{\dot{\mathbf{c}}} = 1$.

**Example B.5** [*Cartesian-barycentric transformation*]
Consider a triangle $\triangle\dot{\mathbf{a}}\dot{\mathbf{b}}\dot{\mathbf{c}}$ where $\dot{\mathbf{a}} = [1, 1]^T$, $\dot{\mathbf{b}} = [10, 2]^T$ and $\dot{\mathbf{c}} = [6, 5]^T$. Also, consider a point $\dot{\mathbf{p}} = [7, 3]^T$ inside the triangle. Express $\dot{\mathbf{p}}$ in barycentric coordinates.

**Solution B.5** Let us assume that $A_{\dot{\mathbf{a}}}$ represents the area of the triangle $\triangle\dot{\mathbf{p}}\dot{\mathbf{b}}\dot{\mathbf{c}}$, $A_{\dot{\mathbf{b}}}$ represents the area of the triangle $\triangle\dot{\mathbf{p}}\dot{\mathbf{c}}\dot{\mathbf{a}}$, $A_{\dot{\mathbf{c}}}$ represents the area of the triangle $\triangle\dot{\mathbf{p}}\dot{\mathbf{a}}\dot{\mathbf{b}}$ and $A$ represents the whole area of the triangle $\triangle\dot{\mathbf{a}}\dot{\mathbf{b}}\dot{\mathbf{c}}$. Many equations may be used to obtain the area of a triangle. Equation (A.27) can be utilized.

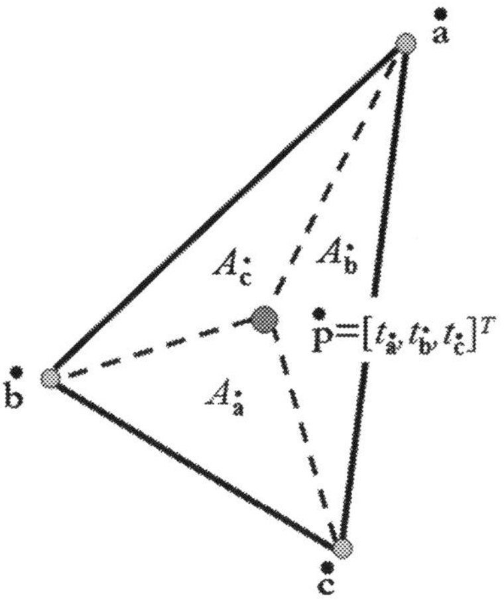


**Fig. B.4** Barycentric coordinates. The barycentric values $t_{\dot{\mathbf{a}}}$, $t_{\dot{\mathbf{b}}}$ and $t_{\dot{\mathbf{c}}}$ are proportional to the three areas $A_{\dot{\mathbf{a}}}$, $A_{\dot{\mathbf{b}}}$ and $A_{\dot{\mathbf{c}}}$ of the sub-triangles created by point $\dot{\mathbf{p}}$ and the vertices $\dot{\mathbf{a}}$, $\dot{\mathbf{b}}$ and $\dot{\mathbf{c}}$

Thus,

$$\begin{aligned} A &= \tfrac{1}{2}\left\|[\dot{\mathbf{b}}-\dot{\mathbf{a}}]\times[\dot{\mathbf{c}}-\dot{\mathbf{a}}]\right\| \\ &= \tfrac{1}{2}\left\|\left[\begin{bmatrix}10\\2\end{bmatrix}-\begin{bmatrix}1\\1\end{bmatrix}\right]\times\left[\begin{bmatrix}6\\5\end{bmatrix}-\begin{bmatrix}1\\1\end{bmatrix}\right]\right\|. \end{aligned}$$

Notice that the cross product of 2D vectors is the determinant as discussed in Sect. A.4.3.4 and the norm of a scalar value is its absolute value. Thus,

$$A = \frac{1}{2}\begin{vmatrix}9 & 5\\1 & 4\end{vmatrix} = 15.5.$$

Similarly, we have

$$\begin{aligned} A_{\dot{\mathbf{a}}} &= \frac{1}{2}\left\|[\dot{\mathbf{b}}-\dot{\mathbf{p}}]\times[\dot{\mathbf{c}}-\dot{\mathbf{p}}]\right\| \\ &= \frac{1}{2}\left\|\left[\begin{bmatrix}10\\2\end{bmatrix}-\begin{bmatrix}7\\3\end{bmatrix}\right]\times\left[\begin{bmatrix}6\\5\end{bmatrix}-\begin{bmatrix}7\\3\end{bmatrix}\right]\right\| \\ &= \frac{1}{2}\begin{vmatrix}3 & -1\\-1 & 2\end{vmatrix} = 2.5, \end{aligned}$$

$$\begin{aligned} A_{\dot{\mathbf{b}}} &= \frac{1}{2}\left\|[\dot{\mathbf{c}}-\dot{\mathbf{p}}]\times[\dot{\mathbf{a}}-\dot{\mathbf{p}}]\right\| \\ &= \frac{1}{2}\left\|\left[\begin{bmatrix}6\\5\end{bmatrix}-\begin{bmatrix}7\\3\end{bmatrix}\right]\times\left[\begin{bmatrix}1\\1\end{bmatrix}-\begin{bmatrix}7\\3\end{bmatrix}\right]\right\| \\ &= \frac{1}{2}\begin{vmatrix}-1 & -6\\2 & -2\end{vmatrix} = 7 \end{aligned}$$

and

$$
\begin{aligned}
A_{\dot{\mathbf{c}}} &= \tfrac{1}{2}\left\|[\dot{\mathbf{a}} - \dot{\mathbf{p}}] \times [\dot{\mathbf{b}} - \dot{\mathbf{p}}]\right\| \\
&= \frac{1}{2}\left\|\left[\begin{bmatrix}1\\1\end{bmatrix} - \begin{bmatrix}7\\3\end{bmatrix}\right] \times \left[\begin{bmatrix}10\\2\end{bmatrix} - \begin{bmatrix}7\\3\end{bmatrix}\right]\right\| \\
&= \frac{1}{2}\begin{vmatrix}-6 & 3\\ -2 & -1\end{vmatrix} = 6.
\end{aligned}
$$

Notice that $A_{\dot{\mathbf{a}}} + A_{\dot{\mathbf{b}}} + A_{\dot{\mathbf{c}}} = A$. The barycentric coordinates can be expressed using Eq. (B.13) as

$$
\begin{aligned}
\begin{bmatrix} t_{\dot{\mathbf{a}}} \\ t_{\dot{\mathbf{b}}} \\ t_{\dot{\mathbf{c}}} \end{bmatrix} &= \frac{1}{A}\begin{bmatrix} A_{\dot{\mathbf{a}}} \\ A_{\dot{\mathbf{b}}} \\ A_{\dot{\mathbf{c}}} \end{bmatrix} \\
&= \frac{1}{15.5}\begin{bmatrix} 2.5 \\ 7 \\ 6 \end{bmatrix} = \begin{bmatrix} 0.1613 \\ 0.4516 \\ 0.3871 \end{bmatrix}.
\end{aligned}
$$

□

**Example B.6** [*Cartesian-barycentric transformation*]
If the area of the triangle $\triangle\dot{\mathbf{a}}\dot{\mathbf{b}}\dot{\mathbf{c}}$ is obtained as

$$
A = \frac{1}{2}\left\|\left[\dot{\mathbf{b}} - \dot{\mathbf{a}}\right] \times \left[\dot{\mathbf{c}} - \dot{\mathbf{a}}\right]\right\|
$$

and a point $\dot{\mathbf{p}}$ inside this triangle is expressed in Cartesian coordinates, write down a single equation to express $\dot{\mathbf{p}}$ in barycentric coordinates given the Cartesian points $\dot{\mathbf{a}}$, $\dot{\mathbf{b}}$, $\dot{\mathbf{c}}$ and $\dot{\mathbf{p}}$.

**Solution B.6** The total area of the triangle can be written as

$$
A = \frac{1}{2}\left\|\left[\dot{\mathbf{b}} - \dot{\mathbf{a}}\right] \times \left[\dot{\mathbf{c}} - \dot{\mathbf{a}}\right]\right\| = \tfrac{1}{2}\left|\left[\dot{\mathbf{b}} - \dot{\mathbf{a}}\right]\left[\dot{\mathbf{c}} - \dot{\mathbf{a}}\right]\right|,
$$

where $|.|$ denotes the determinant of the $2 \times 2$ matrix $\left[\dot{\mathbf{b}} - \dot{\mathbf{a}}\right] | \left[\dot{\mathbf{c}} - \dot{\mathbf{a}}\right]$. Similarly, we can write

$$
\begin{aligned}
A_{\dot{\mathbf{a}}} &= \tfrac{1}{2}\left|\left[\dot{\mathbf{b}} - \dot{\mathbf{p}}\right]\left[\dot{\mathbf{c}} - \dot{\mathbf{p}}\right]\right|, \\
A_{\dot{\mathbf{b}}} &= \tfrac{1}{2}\left|\left[\dot{\mathbf{c}} - \dot{\mathbf{p}}\right]\left[\dot{\mathbf{a}} - \dot{\mathbf{p}}\right]\right|, \\
A_{\dot{\mathbf{c}}} &= \tfrac{1}{2}\left|\left[\dot{\mathbf{a}} - \dot{\mathbf{p}}\right]\left[\dot{\mathbf{b}} - \dot{\mathbf{p}}\right]\right|.
\end{aligned}
$$

**Fig. B.5** Barycentric coordinates

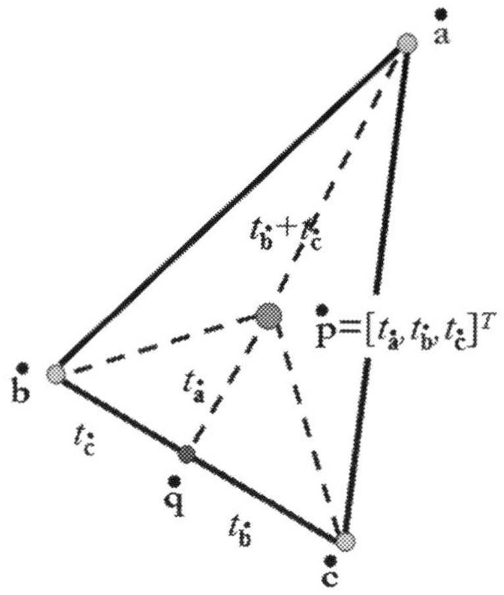


By substituting in Eq. (B.13), we get

$$
\begin{bmatrix} t_{\dot{\mathbf{a}}} \\ t_{\dot{\mathbf{b}}} \\ t_{\dot{\mathbf{c}}} \end{bmatrix} = \frac{1}{A} \begin{bmatrix} A_{\dot{\mathbf{a}}} \\ A_{\dot{\mathbf{b}}} \\ A_{\dot{\mathbf{c}}} \end{bmatrix}
= \frac{1}{\left|\left[\dot{\mathbf{b}} - \dot{\mathbf{a}}\right] \left[\dot{\mathbf{c}} - \dot{\mathbf{a}}\right]\right|} \begin{bmatrix} \left|\left[\dot{\mathbf{b}} - \dot{\mathbf{p}}\right] \left[\dot{\mathbf{c}} - \dot{\mathbf{p}}\right]\right| \\ \left|\left[\dot{\mathbf{c}} - \dot{\mathbf{p}}\right] \left[\dot{\mathbf{a}} - \dot{\mathbf{p}}\right]\right| \\ \left|\left[\dot{\mathbf{a}} - \dot{\mathbf{p}}\right] \left[\dot{\mathbf{b}} - \dot{\mathbf{p}}\right]\right| \end{bmatrix}. \tag{B.14}
$$

□

## B.3.2 Barycentric-Cartesian Transformation

Consider Fig. B.5 where a point $\dot{\mathbf{p}}$ lies inside a triangle $\triangle\dot{\mathbf{a}}\dot{\mathbf{b}}\dot{\mathbf{c}}$. If you draw a line from $\dot{\mathbf{a}}$ to $\dot{\mathbf{p}}$ and extend it to $\dot{\mathbf{q}}$ that lies on $\overline{\dot{\mathbf{b}}\dot{\mathbf{c}}}$, $t_{\dot{\mathbf{a}}}$ will represent the distance $\|\dot{\mathbf{p}} - \dot{\mathbf{q}}\|$ while $t_{\dot{\mathbf{b}}} + t_{\dot{\mathbf{c}}}$ will represent the distance $\|\dot{\mathbf{p}} - \dot{\mathbf{a}}\|$ (i.e., $\|\dot{\mathbf{p}} - \dot{\mathbf{q}}\|+\|\dot{\mathbf{p}} - \dot{\mathbf{a}}\| = 1$ in terms of barycentric coordinates). At the same time, $t_{\dot{\mathbf{b}}}$ will represent the distance $\|\dot{\mathbf{c}} - \dot{\mathbf{q}}\|$ while $t_{\dot{\mathbf{c}}}$ will represent the distance $\|\dot{\mathbf{b}} - \dot{\mathbf{q}}\|$.

Utilizing the above relations, the Cartesian coordinates of point $\dot{\mathbf{q}}$ can be obtained using linear interpolation if $\dot{\mathbf{b}}$, $\dot{\mathbf{c}}$, $t_{\dot{\mathbf{b}}}$ and $t_{\dot{\mathbf{c}}}$ are known. So,

$$
\dot{\mathbf{q}} = \frac{t_{\dot{\mathbf{b}}}}{t_{\dot{\mathbf{b}}} + t_{\dot{\mathbf{c}}}} \dot{\mathbf{b}} + \frac{t_{\dot{\mathbf{c}}}}{t_{\dot{\mathbf{b}}} + t_{\dot{\mathbf{c}}}} \dot{\mathbf{c}}, \tag{B.15}
$$

where $\dot{\mathbf{q}}$, $\dot{\mathbf{b}}$ and $\dot{\mathbf{c}}$ are represented in Cartesian coordinates; and $t_{\dot{\mathbf{a}}}$, $t_{\dot{\mathbf{b}}}$ and $t_{\dot{\mathbf{c}}}$ are scalars representing the barycentric coordinates. Consequently, the Cartesian coordinates $[x, y]^T$ of point $\dot{\mathbf{p}}$ can be obtained as $\dot{\mathbf{a}}$, $\dot{\mathbf{q}}$, $t_{\dot{\mathbf{a}}}$, $t_{\dot{\mathbf{b}}}$ and $t_{\dot{\mathbf{c}}}$ are known. This can be written as

$$\dot{\mathbf{p}} = t_{\dot{a}}\,\dot{\mathbf{a}} + (t_{\dot{b}} + t_{\dot{c}})\,\dot{\mathbf{q}}.$$

Substituting the location of $\dot{\mathbf{q}}$ from Eq. (B.15), we get

$$\begin{bmatrix} x \\ y \end{bmatrix} = t_{\dot{a}}\,\dot{\mathbf{a}} + t_{\dot{b}}\,\dot{\mathbf{b}} + t_{\dot{c}}\,\dot{\mathbf{c}}, \tag{B.16}$$

where $\dot{\mathbf{a}}$, $\dot{\mathbf{b}}$ and $\dot{\mathbf{c}}$ are the Cartesian coordinates of the triangle vertices; $[t_{\dot{a}}, t_{\dot{b}}, t_{\dot{c}}]^T$ are the barycentric coordinates of point $\dot{\mathbf{p}}$ and $[x, y]^T$ are the Cartesian coordinates of the same point $\dot{\mathbf{p}}$. Note that the same coordinates must be obtained if you extend $\overline{\dot{\mathbf{b}}\dot{\mathbf{p}}}$ to intersect $\overline{\dot{\mathbf{c}}\dot{\mathbf{a}}}$ or if you extend $\overline{\dot{\mathbf{c}}\dot{\mathbf{p}}}$ to intersect $\overline{\dot{\mathbf{a}}\dot{\mathbf{b}}}$.

**Example B.7** [*Barycentric-Cartesian transformation*]
Consider a triangle $\triangle\dot{\mathbf{a}}\dot{\mathbf{b}}\dot{\mathbf{c}}$ where $\dot{\mathbf{a}} = [1, 1]^T$, $\dot{\mathbf{b}} = [10, 2]^T$ and $\dot{\mathbf{c}} = [6, 5]^T$. If a point $\dot{\mathbf{p}}$ inside the triangle is expressed in barycentric coordinates $[t_{\dot{a}}, t_{\dot{b}}, t_{\dot{c}}]^T$ as $[0.1613, 0.4516, 0.3871]^T$, express the same point in Cartesian coordinates.

**Solution B.7** Since $\dot{\mathbf{a}}$, $\dot{\mathbf{b}}$, $\dot{\mathbf{c}}$, $t_{\dot{a}}$, $t_{\dot{b}}$ and $t_{\dot{c}}$ are known, point $\dot{\mathbf{p}}$ can be expressed in Cartesian coordinates by applying Eq. (B.16) as

$$\begin{aligned}\begin{bmatrix} x \\ y \end{bmatrix} &= t_{\dot{a}}\,\dot{\mathbf{a}} + t_{\dot{b}}\,\dot{\mathbf{b}} + t_{\dot{c}}\,\dot{\mathbf{c}} \\ &= 0.1613\begin{bmatrix} 1 \\ 1 \end{bmatrix} + 0.4516\begin{bmatrix} 10 \\ 2 \end{bmatrix} + 0.3871\begin{bmatrix} 6 \\ 5 \end{bmatrix} = \begin{bmatrix} 7 \\ 3 \end{bmatrix}.\end{aligned}$$ □

**Example B.8** [*Barycentric-parametric transformation*]
Consider a triangle $\triangle\dot{\mathbf{a}}\dot{\mathbf{b}}\dot{\mathbf{c}}$. If a point $\dot{\mathbf{p}}$ inside the triangle is expressed in barycentric coordinates as $[t_{\dot{a}}, t_{\dot{b}}, t_{\dot{c}}]^T$, express the same point in parametric coordinates if the parametric $u$- and $v$-axes are along $\overline{\dot{\mathbf{a}}\dot{\mathbf{b}}}$ and $\overline{\dot{\mathbf{a}}\dot{\mathbf{c}}}$ respectively.

**Solution B.8** As depicted in Fig. B.6, this problem can be solved in two steps:

1. Transform from barycentric coordinates to Cartesian coordinates. By applying Eq. (B.16), point $\dot{\mathbf{p}} = [t_{\dot{a}}, t_{\dot{b}}, t_{\dot{c}}]^T$ is expressed in Cartesian coordinates as

$$\dot{\mathbf{p}} = \begin{bmatrix} x \\ y \end{bmatrix} = t_{\dot{a}}\,\dot{\mathbf{a}} + t_{\dot{b}}\,\dot{\mathbf{b}} + t_{\dot{c}}\,\dot{\mathbf{c}}.$$

2. Transform from Cartesian coordinates to parametric coordinates. The vector $\mathbf{w}$ is obtained as

$$\mathbf{w} = \dot{\mathbf{p}} - \dot{\mathbf{a}}.$$

From Step 1, $\mathbf{w}$ is expressed as

$$\begin{aligned}\mathbf{w} &= t_{\dot{a}}\,\dot{\mathbf{a}} + t_{\dot{b}}\,\dot{\mathbf{b}} + t_{\dot{c}}\,\dot{\mathbf{c}} - \dot{\mathbf{a}} \\ &= (t_{\dot{a}} - 1)\dot{\mathbf{a}} + t_{\dot{b}}\,\dot{\mathbf{b}} + t_{\dot{c}}\,\dot{\mathbf{c}}.\end{aligned}$$

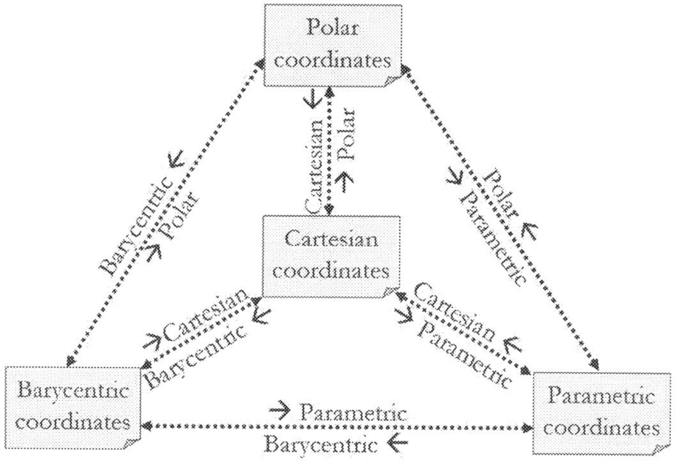


**Fig. B.6** Barycentric to parametric coordinate transformation may be done in two steps by transforming to Cartesian coordinates as a middle step. The same may be applied to the opposite transformation. Other transformations may be applied the same way

Hence, to transform from barycentric to parametric coordinates, we substitute the value of $\mathbf{w}$ Eq. (B.11). Thus, we have

$$\begin{aligned}
\mathbf{u} &= \dot{\mathbf{b}} - \dot{\mathbf{a}} \\
\mathbf{v} &= \dot{\mathbf{c}} - \dot{\mathbf{a}} \\
\mathbf{w} &= (t_{\dot{\mathbf{a}}} - 1)\dot{\mathbf{a}} + t_{\dot{\mathbf{b}}}\,\dot{\mathbf{b}} + t_{\dot{\mathbf{c}}}\,\dot{\mathbf{c}} \\
\begin{bmatrix} u \\ v \end{bmatrix} &= \begin{bmatrix} \dfrac{(\mathbf{u}\cdot\mathbf{v})(\mathbf{w}\cdot\mathbf{v}) - (\mathbf{v}\cdot\mathbf{v})(\mathbf{w}\cdot\mathbf{u})}{(\mathbf{u}\cdot\mathbf{v})^2 - (\mathbf{u}\cdot\mathbf{u})(\mathbf{v}\cdot\mathbf{v})} \\ \dfrac{(\mathbf{u}\cdot\mathbf{v})(\mathbf{w}\cdot\mathbf{u}) - (\mathbf{u}\cdot\mathbf{u})(\mathbf{w}\cdot\mathbf{v})}{(\mathbf{u}\cdot\mathbf{v})^2 - (\mathbf{u}\cdot\mathbf{u})(\mathbf{v}\cdot\mathbf{v})} \end{bmatrix}.
\end{aligned} \tag{B.17}$$

□

**Example B.9** [*Barycentric-parametric transformation*]

Consider a triangle $\triangle\dot{\mathbf{a}}\dot{\mathbf{b}}\dot{\mathbf{c}}$ where $\dot{\mathbf{a}} = [1, 1]^T$, $\dot{\mathbf{b}} = [10, 2]^T$ and $\dot{\mathbf{c}} = [6, 5]^T$. Also, consider a barycentric point $\dot{\mathbf{p}} = [0.1613, 0.4516, 0.3871]^T$ inside the triangle. Express $\dot{\mathbf{p}}$ in parametric coordinates if the $u$- and $v$-axes go along $\overline{\dot{\mathbf{a}}\dot{\mathbf{b}}}$ and $\overline{\dot{\mathbf{a}}\dot{\mathbf{c}}}$ respectively.

**Solution B.9** To do this conversion, Eq. (B.17) is used. Thus,

$$\begin{aligned}
\mathbf{u} &= \dot{\mathbf{b}} - \dot{\mathbf{a}} \\
&= \begin{bmatrix} 10 \\ 2 \end{bmatrix} - \begin{bmatrix} 1 \\ 1 \end{bmatrix} = \begin{bmatrix} 9 \\ 1 \end{bmatrix},
\end{aligned}$$

$$\begin{aligned}
\mathbf{v} &= \dot{\mathbf{c}} - \dot{\mathbf{a}} \\
&= \begin{bmatrix} 6 \\ 5 \end{bmatrix} - \begin{bmatrix} 1 \\ 1 \end{bmatrix} = \begin{bmatrix} 5 \\ 4 \end{bmatrix},
\end{aligned}$$

$$\begin{aligned}
\mathbf{w} &= (t_{\dot{\mathbf{a}}} - 1)\dot{\mathbf{a}} + t_{\dot{\mathbf{b}}}\dot{\mathbf{b}} + t_{\dot{\mathbf{c}}}\dot{\mathbf{c}} \\
&= (0.1613 - 1)\begin{bmatrix} 1 \\ 1 \end{bmatrix} + 0.4516\begin{bmatrix} 10 \\ 2 \end{bmatrix} + 0.3871\begin{bmatrix} 6 \\ 5 \end{bmatrix} \\
&= \begin{bmatrix} 6 \\ 2 \end{bmatrix}.
\end{aligned}$$

Hence,

$$\begin{aligned}
\begin{bmatrix} u \\ v \end{bmatrix} &= \begin{bmatrix} \dfrac{(\mathbf{u}\cdot\mathbf{v})(\mathbf{w}\cdot\mathbf{v}) - (\mathbf{v}\cdot\mathbf{v})(\mathbf{w}\cdot\mathbf{u})}{(\mathbf{u}\cdot\mathbf{v})^2 - (\mathbf{u}\cdot\mathbf{u})(\mathbf{v}\cdot\mathbf{v})} \\ \dfrac{(\mathbf{u}\cdot\mathbf{v})(\mathbf{w}\cdot\mathbf{u}) - (\mathbf{u}\cdot\mathbf{u})(\mathbf{w}\cdot\mathbf{v})}{(\mathbf{u}\cdot\mathbf{v})^2 - (\mathbf{u}\cdot\mathbf{u})(\mathbf{v}\cdot\mathbf{v})} \end{bmatrix} \\
&= \begin{bmatrix} \dfrac{\left(\begin{bmatrix} 9 \\ 1 \end{bmatrix}\cdot\begin{bmatrix} 5 \\ 4 \end{bmatrix}\right)\left(\begin{bmatrix} 6 \\ 2 \end{bmatrix}\cdot\begin{bmatrix} 5 \\ 4 \end{bmatrix}\right) - \left(\begin{bmatrix} 5 \\ 4 \end{bmatrix}\cdot\begin{bmatrix} 5 \\ 4 \end{bmatrix}\right)\left(\begin{bmatrix} 6 \\ 2 \end{bmatrix}\cdot\begin{bmatrix} 9 \\ 1 \end{bmatrix}\right)}{\left(\begin{bmatrix} 9 \\ 1 \end{bmatrix}\cdot\begin{bmatrix} 5 \\ 4 \end{bmatrix}\right)^2 - \left(\begin{bmatrix} 9 \\ 1 \end{bmatrix}\cdot\begin{bmatrix} 9 \\ 1 \end{bmatrix}\right)\left(\begin{bmatrix} 5 \\ 4 \end{bmatrix}\cdot\begin{bmatrix} 5 \\ 4 \end{bmatrix}\right)} \\ \dfrac{\left(\begin{bmatrix} 9 \\ 1 \end{bmatrix}\cdot\begin{bmatrix} 5 \\ 4 \end{bmatrix}\right)\left(\begin{bmatrix} 6 \\ 2 \end{bmatrix}\cdot\begin{bmatrix} 9 \\ 1 \end{bmatrix}\right) - \left(\begin{bmatrix} 9 \\ 1 \end{bmatrix}\cdot\begin{bmatrix} 9 \\ 1 \end{bmatrix}\right)\left(\begin{bmatrix} 6 \\ 2 \end{bmatrix}\cdot\begin{bmatrix} 5 \\ 4 \end{bmatrix}\right)}{\left(\begin{bmatrix} 9 \\ 1 \end{bmatrix}\cdot\begin{bmatrix} 5 \\ 4 \end{bmatrix}\right)^2 - \left(\begin{bmatrix} 9 \\ 1 \end{bmatrix}\cdot\begin{bmatrix} 9 \\ 1 \end{bmatrix}\right)\left(\begin{bmatrix} 5 \\ 4 \end{bmatrix}\cdot\begin{bmatrix} 5 \\ 4 \end{bmatrix}\right)} \end{bmatrix} \\
&= \begin{bmatrix} 0.4516 \\ 0.3871 \end{bmatrix}.
\end{aligned}$$

□

**Example B.10** [*Parametric-barycentric transformation*]

Consider a triangle $\triangle\dot{\mathbf{a}}\dot{\mathbf{b}}\dot{\mathbf{c}}$. If a point $\dot{\mathbf{p}}$ inside the triangle is expressed in parametric coordinates as $[u, v]^T$ where the parametric $u$- and $v$-axes are along $\overline{\dot{\mathbf{a}}\dot{\mathbf{b}}}$ and $\overline{\dot{\mathbf{a}}\dot{\mathbf{c}}}$ respectively, get its barycentric coordinates $[t_{\dot{\mathbf{a}}}, t_{\dot{\mathbf{b}}}, t_{\dot{\mathbf{c}}}]^T$.

**Solution B.10** This problem can be solved in two steps as illustrated in Fig. B.6:

1. Transform from parametric coordinates to Cartesian coordinates.
2. Transform from Cartesian coordinates to barycentric coordinates.

The details of the solution are left as an exercise. □

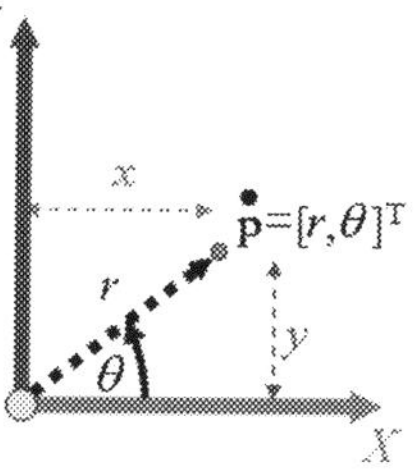


**Fig. B.7** Polar coordinates

## B.4 Polar Coordinate System

In polar coordinate system, a point is defined by a polar coordinate (or radial coordinate) $r$ and a polar angle (or angular coordinate) $\theta$. This is shown in Fig. B.7. Thus, a point $\dot{\mathbf{p}}$ in polar system is defined as $[r, \theta]^T$.

### *B.4.1 Cartesian-Polar Transformation*

A point $\dot{\mathbf{p}} = [x, y]^T$ in Cartesian system can be expressed in polar coordinates $[r, \theta]^T$ as

$$\begin{bmatrix} r \\ \theta \end{bmatrix} = \begin{bmatrix} \sqrt{x^2 + y^2} \\ \tan^{-1}\left(\frac{y}{x}\right) \end{bmatrix}, \tag{B.18}$$

where $r$ is the radial coordinate and $\theta$ is the angular coordinate.

**Example B.11** [*Cartesian-polar transformation*]
Express the Cartesian point $[3, 4]^T$ in polar coordinates such that the origin of the polar system coincides with the origin of the Cartesian system and the $x$-axis corresponds to $\theta = 0°$.

**Solution B.11** Applying Eq. (B.18), $[3, 4]^T$ is expressed in polar coordinates as

$$\begin{aligned} \begin{bmatrix} r \\ \theta \end{bmatrix} &= \begin{bmatrix} \sqrt{x^2 + y^2} \\ \tan^{-1}\left(\frac{y}{x}\right) \end{bmatrix} \\ &= \begin{bmatrix} \sqrt{3^2 + 4^2} \\ \tan^{-1}\left(\frac{4}{3}\right) \end{bmatrix} = \begin{bmatrix} 5 \\ 53.1301° \end{bmatrix}. \end{aligned}$$ □

### *B.4.2 Polar-Cartesian Transformation*

A point $\dot{\mathbf{p}} = [r, \theta]^T$ in polar system can be expressed in Cartesian coordinates $[x, y]^T$ as

$$\begin{bmatrix} x \\ y \end{bmatrix} = \begin{bmatrix} r\cos(\theta) \\ r\sin(\theta) \end{bmatrix}. \tag{B.19}$$

**Example B.12** [*Polar-Cartesian transformation*]
The point $[5, 53.1301°]^T$ is expressed in polar coordinates. Transform this point to Cartesian coordinates such that the origin of the Cartesian system coincides with the origin of the polar system and the $x$-axis corresponds to $\theta = 0°$.

**Solution B.12** Applying Eq. (B.19), we get

$$\begin{aligned} \begin{bmatrix} x \\ y \end{bmatrix} &= \begin{bmatrix} r\cos(\theta) \\ r\sin(\theta) \end{bmatrix} \\ &= \begin{bmatrix} 5\cos(53.1301) \\ 5\sin(53.1301) \end{bmatrix} = \begin{bmatrix} 3 \\ 4 \end{bmatrix}. \end{aligned}$$

□

**Example B.13** [*Barycentric-polar transformation*]
Consider a triangle $\triangle\dot{\mathbf{a}}\dot{\mathbf{b}}\dot{\mathbf{c}}$. If a point $\dot{\mathbf{p}}$ inside the triangle is expressed in barycentric coordinates as $[t_{\dot{\mathbf{a}}}, t_{\dot{\mathbf{b}}}, t_{\dot{\mathbf{c}}}]^T$, express the same point in polar coordinates if

1. the origin of the Cartesian system expressing the vertices $\dot{\mathbf{a}}$, $\dot{\mathbf{b}}$ and $\dot{\mathbf{c}}$ is the same as the origin of the polar system; and
2. the $x$-axis of the Cartesian system has an angular coordinate of 0°.

**Solution B.13** Similar to Example B.8, this problem can be solved in two steps:

1. Transform from barycentric coordinates to Cartesian coordinates. By applying Eq. (B.16), point $\dot{\mathbf{p}} = [t_{\dot{\mathbf{a}}}, t_{\dot{\mathbf{b}}}, t_{\dot{\mathbf{c}}}]^T$ is expressed in Cartesian coordinates as

$$\begin{aligned} \dot{\mathbf{p}} = \begin{bmatrix} x \\ y \end{bmatrix} &= t_{\dot{\mathbf{a}}}\,\dot{\mathbf{a}} + t_{\dot{\mathbf{b}}}\,\dot{\mathbf{b}} + t_{\dot{\mathbf{c}}}\,\dot{\mathbf{c}} \\ &= t_{\dot{\mathbf{a}}}\begin{bmatrix} x_{\dot{\mathbf{a}}} \\ y_{\dot{\mathbf{a}}} \end{bmatrix} + t_{\dot{\mathbf{b}}}\begin{bmatrix} x_{\dot{\mathbf{b}}} \\ y_{\dot{\mathbf{b}}} \end{bmatrix} + t_{\dot{\mathbf{c}}}\begin{bmatrix} x_{\dot{\mathbf{c}}} \\ y_{\dot{\mathbf{c}}} \end{bmatrix}. \end{aligned}$$

2. Transform from Cartesian coordinates to polar coordinates by substituting the value of $[x, y]^T$ obtained from Step 1 in Eq. (B.18). So,

$$\begin{bmatrix} r \\ \theta \end{bmatrix} = \begin{bmatrix} \|t_{\dot{\mathbf{a}}}\,\dot{\mathbf{a}} + t_{\dot{\mathbf{b}}}\,\dot{\mathbf{b}} + t_{\dot{\mathbf{c}}}\,\dot{\mathbf{c}}\| \\ \tan^{-1}\left(\dfrac{t_{\dot{\mathbf{a}}}y_{\dot{\mathbf{a}}} + t_{\dot{\mathbf{b}}}y_{\dot{\mathbf{b}}} + t_{\dot{\mathbf{c}}}y_{\dot{\mathbf{c}}}}{t_{\dot{\mathbf{a}}}x_{\dot{\mathbf{a}}} + t_{\dot{\mathbf{b}}}x_{\dot{\mathbf{b}}} + t_{\dot{\mathbf{c}}}x_{\dot{\mathbf{c}}}}\right) \end{bmatrix}. \tag{B.20}$$

□

**Example B.14** [*Polar-barycentric transformation*]
Consider a triangle $\triangle\dot{\mathbf{a}}\dot{\mathbf{b}}\dot{\mathbf{c}}$. If a point $\dot{\mathbf{p}}$ inside the triangle is expressed in polar coordinates as $[r, \theta]^T$ where

1. the origin of the Cartesian system expressing the vertices $\dot{\mathbf{a}}$, $\dot{\mathbf{b}}$ and $\dot{\mathbf{c}}$ is the same as the origin of the polar system; and

2. the $x$-axis of the Cartesian system has an angular coordinate of 0°,

express the same point in barycentric coordinates $\left[t_{\dot{\mathbf{a}}}, t_{\dot{\mathbf{b}}}, t_{\dot{\mathbf{c}}}\right]^T$.

**Solution B.14** Also, this problem can be solved in two steps:

1. Transform from polar coordinates to Cartesian coordinates.
2. Transform from Cartesian coordinates to barycentric coordinates.

The details of the solution are left as an exercise. □

**Example B.15** [*Parametric-polar transformation*]
Consider a triangle $\triangle\dot{\mathbf{a}}\dot{\mathbf{b}}\dot{\mathbf{c}}$. If a point $\dot{\mathbf{p}}$ inside the triangle is expressed in parametric coordinates as $[u, v]^T$ such that the $u$- and $v$-axes are along $\overline{\dot{\mathbf{a}}\dot{\mathbf{b}}}$ and $\overline{\dot{\mathbf{a}}\dot{\mathbf{c}}}$ respectively, express the same point in polar coordinates if

1. the origin of the Cartesian system expressing the vertices $\dot{\mathbf{a}}$, $\dot{\mathbf{b}}$ and $\dot{\mathbf{c}}$ is the same as the origin of the polar system; and
2. the $x$-axis of the Cartesian system has an angular coordinate of 0°.

**Solution B.15** The problem can be solved in two steps:

1. Transform from parametric coordinates to Cartesian coordinates. By applying Eq. (B.12), point $\dot{\mathbf{p}} = [u, v]^T$ is expressed in Cartesian coordinates as

$$\begin{bmatrix} x \\ y \end{bmatrix} = \dot{\mathbf{a}} + u[\dot{\mathbf{b}} - \dot{\mathbf{a}}] + v[\dot{\mathbf{c}} - \dot{\mathbf{a}}]$$
$$= \begin{bmatrix} x_{\dot{\mathbf{a}}} \\ y_{\dot{\mathbf{a}}} \end{bmatrix} + u \begin{bmatrix} x_{\dot{\mathbf{b}}} - x_{\dot{\mathbf{a}}} \\ y_{\dot{\mathbf{b}}} - y_{\dot{\mathbf{a}}} \end{bmatrix} + v \begin{bmatrix} x_{\dot{\mathbf{c}}} - x_{\dot{\mathbf{a}}} \\ y_{\dot{\mathbf{c}}} - y_{\dot{\mathbf{a}}} \end{bmatrix}.$$

2. Transform from Cartesian coordinates to polar coordinates by substituting the value of $[x, y]^T$ obtained from Step 1 in Eq. (B.18). Therefore,

$$\begin{bmatrix} r \\ \theta \end{bmatrix} = \begin{bmatrix} \|\dot{\mathbf{a}} + u[\dot{\mathbf{b}} - \dot{\mathbf{a}}] + v[\dot{\mathbf{c}} - \dot{\mathbf{a}}]\| \\ \tan^{-1}\left(\dfrac{(1-u-v)y_{\dot{\mathbf{a}}} + uy_{\dot{\mathbf{b}}} + vy_{\dot{\mathbf{c}}}}{(1-u-v)x_{\dot{\mathbf{a}}} + ux_{\dot{\mathbf{b}}} + vx_{\dot{\mathbf{c}}}}\right) \end{bmatrix}. \tag{B.21}$$

□

**Example B.16** [*Polar-parametric transformation*]
Consider a triangle $\triangle\dot{\mathbf{a}}\dot{\mathbf{b}}\dot{\mathbf{c}}$. If a point $\dot{\mathbf{p}}$ inside the triangle is expressed in polar coordinates as $[r, \theta]^T$ where

1. the origin of the Cartesian system expressing the vertices $\dot{\mathbf{a}}$, $\dot{\mathbf{b}}$ and $\dot{\mathbf{c}}$ is the same as the origin of the polar system; and
2. the $x$-axis of the Cartesian system has an angular coordinate of 0°,

express the same point in parametric coordinates $[u, v]^T$ such that the $u$- and $v$-axes are along $\overline{\dot{\mathbf{a}}\dot{\mathbf{b}}}$ and $\overline{\dot{\mathbf{a}}\dot{\mathbf{c}}}$ respectively.

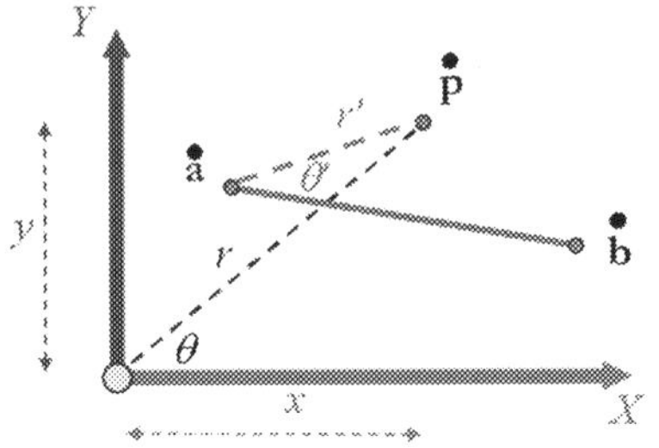


**Fig. B.8** Two polar coordinate systems

**Solution B.16** Like similar problems, this problem can be solved in two steps:

1. Transform from polar coordinates to Cartesian coordinates.
2. Transform from Cartesian coordinates to parametric coordinates.

The details of the solution are left as an exercise. □

**Example B.17** [*Polar-polar transformation*]

Consider Fig. B.8 where a point $\dot{\mathbf{p}}$ is expressed in Cartesian coordinates as $[x, y]^T$ and in polar coordinates as $[r, \theta]^T$ such that $r = \sqrt{x^2 + y^2}$ and $\theta = \tan^{-1}\left(\frac{y}{x}\right)$. If a new polar system is defined using a line segment extending from a point $\dot{\mathbf{a}}$ to another point $\dot{\mathbf{b}}$ where point $\dot{\mathbf{a}}$ is the origin and point $\dot{\mathbf{b}}$ has angular coordinate of 0° in the new polar coordinate system. Express point $\dot{\mathbf{p}}$ in the new polar coordinate system as $[r', \theta']^T$ where 1 $r$ unit = 1 $r'$ unit.

**Solution B.17** The new radial coordinate $r'$ represents the distance from the new origin $\dot{\mathbf{a}}$ to point $\dot{\mathbf{p}}$ (as depicted in Fig. B.8) and it can be determined as a Euclidean distance (Sect. B.1.2). Using Eq. (B.8), $r'$ is expressed as

$$r' = d(\dot{\mathbf{a}}, \dot{\mathbf{p}}) = \sqrt{(x_{\dot{\mathbf{p}}} - x_{\dot{\mathbf{a}}})^2 + (y_{\dot{\mathbf{p}}} - y_{\dot{\mathbf{a}}})^2}$$

or equivalently by the norm (Sect. A.4.1) as in Eq. (A.14):

$$r' = \|\dot{\mathbf{p}} - \dot{\mathbf{a}}\| = \sqrt{(x_{\dot{\mathbf{p}}} - x_{\dot{\mathbf{a}}})^2 + (y_{\dot{\mathbf{p}}} - y_{\dot{\mathbf{a}}})^2}.$$

The angular coordinate $\theta'$ is obtained as the angle enclosed between $\dot{\mathbf{a}}\dot{\mathbf{b}}$ and $\dot{\mathbf{a}}\dot{\mathbf{p}}$ (refer to Fig. B.8). Using the dot product (Sect. A.4.3.2) as in Eq. (A.22), this angle can be obtained as

$$\theta' = \cos^{-1}\left(\frac{[\dot{\mathbf{b}} - \dot{\mathbf{a}}] \cdot [\dot{\mathbf{p}} - \dot{\mathbf{a}}]}{\|\dot{\mathbf{b}} - \dot{\mathbf{a}}\| \, \|\dot{\mathbf{p}} - \dot{\mathbf{a}}\|}\right).$$

Thus, the new polar coordinates of point $\dot{\mathbf{p}}$ is expressed as

$$\begin{bmatrix} r' \\ \theta' \end{bmatrix} = \begin{bmatrix} \|\dot{\mathbf{p}} - \dot{\mathbf{a}}\| \\ \cos^{-1}\left(\frac{[\dot{\mathbf{b}} - \dot{\mathbf{a}}] \cdot [\dot{\mathbf{p}} - \dot{\mathbf{a}}]}{\|\dot{\mathbf{b}} - \dot{\mathbf{a}}\| \, \|\dot{\mathbf{p}} - \dot{\mathbf{a}}\|}\right) \end{bmatrix}.$$ □

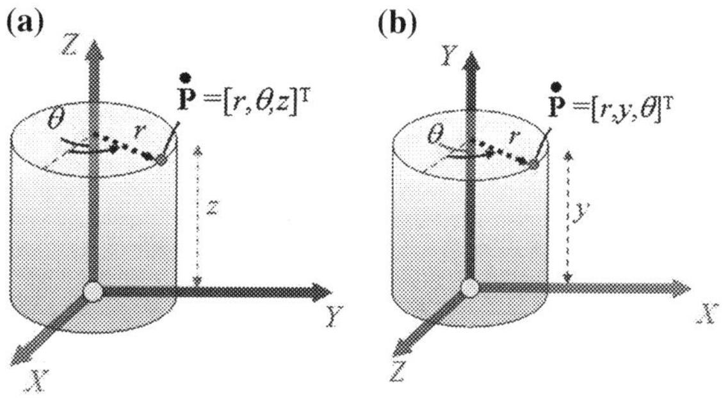


**Fig. B.9** Cylindrical coordinates. **a** The cylinder height is considered along the $z$-axis. **b** The cylinder height is considered along the $y$-axis

## B.5 Cylindrical Coordinate System

Cylindrical coordinates are used to describe a point on a cylindrical surface. The cylindrical coordinate system is an extension to the polar coordinate system in 3D space by adding another dimension representing the height as the $z$-axis. In cylindrical coordinate system, a point is defined by a polar coordinate (or radial coordinate) $r$ and a polar angle (or angular coordinate) $\theta$ (also known as the azimuth angle) in addition to a height coordinate $z$. This is shown in Fig. B.9a. Thus, a point $\dot{\mathbf{P}}$ in polar system is defined as $[r, \theta, z]^T$.

Some systems consider the height as being along the $y$-axis and the base as residing on the $zx$-plane. This is shown in Fig. B.9b.

### *B.5.1 Cartesian-Cylindrical Transformation*

A point $\dot{\mathbf{P}} = [x, y, z]^T$ in Cartesian system can be expressed in cylindrical coordinates $[r, \theta, z]^T$ as

$$\begin{bmatrix} r \\ \theta \\ z \end{bmatrix} = \begin{bmatrix} \sqrt{x^2 + y^2} \\ \tan^{-1}\left(\frac{y}{x}\right) \\ z \end{bmatrix}. \tag{B.22}$$

If the height of the cylinder is along the $y$-axis, point $\dot{\mathbf{P}} = [x, y, z]^T$ in Cartesian system can be expressed in cylindrical coordinates $[r, y, \theta]^T$ as

$$\begin{bmatrix} r \\ y \\ \theta \end{bmatrix} = \begin{bmatrix} \sqrt{z^2 + x^2} \\ y \\ \tan^{-1}\left(\frac{z}{x}\right) \end{bmatrix}. \tag{B.23}$$

**Example B.18** [*Cartesian-cylindrical transformation*]
Express the Cartesian point $[3, 4, 5]^T$ in cylindrical coordinates such that the origin of the cylindrical system coincides with the origin of the Cartesian system, the $x$-axis corresponds to $\theta = 0°$ and the height is along the $z$-axis.

**Solution B.18** Applying Eq. (B.22), $[3, 4, 5]^T$ is expressed in cylindrical coordinates as

$$\begin{bmatrix} r \\ \theta \\ z \end{bmatrix} = \begin{bmatrix} \sqrt{x^2 + y^2} \\ \tan^{-1}\left(\frac{y}{x}\right) \\ z \end{bmatrix}$$
$$= \begin{bmatrix} \sqrt{3^2 + 4^2} \\ \tan^{-1}\left(\frac{4}{3}\right) \\ 5 \end{bmatrix} = \begin{bmatrix} 5 \\ 53.1301° \\ 5 \end{bmatrix}. \qquad \square$$

## *B.5.2 Cylindrical-Cartesian Transformation*

A point $\dot{\mathbf{P}} = [r, \theta, z]^T$ in cylindrical system can be expressed in Cartesian coordinates $[x, y, z]^T$ as

$$\begin{bmatrix} x \\ y \\ z \end{bmatrix} = \begin{bmatrix} r\ \cos(\theta) \\ r\ \sin(\theta) \\ z \end{bmatrix}. \tag{B.24}$$

If the height of the cylinder is along the $y$-axis, point $\dot{\mathbf{P}} = [r, y, \theta]^T$ in cylindrical system can be expressed in Cartesian coordinates $[x, y, z]^T$ as

$$\begin{bmatrix} x \\ y \\ z \end{bmatrix} = \begin{bmatrix} r\ \sin(\theta) \\ y \\ r\ \cos(\theta) \end{bmatrix}. \tag{B.25}$$

**Example B.19** [*Cylindrical-Cartesian transformation*]
The point $[5, 53.1301, 5]^T$ is defined in cylindrical coordinates. Express it in Cartesian coordinates such that the origin of the cylindrical system coincides with the origin of the Cartesian system, the $x$-axis corresponds to $\theta = 0°$ and the height is along the $z$-axis.

**Solution B.19** Applying Eq. (B.24), $[5, 53.1301, 5]^T$ is expressed in Cartesian coordinates as

$$\begin{bmatrix} x \\ y \\ z \end{bmatrix} = \begin{bmatrix} r\ \cos(\theta) \\ r\ \sin(\theta) \\ z \end{bmatrix}$$
$$= \begin{bmatrix} 5\ \cos(53.1301) \\ 5\ \sin(53.1301) \\ 5 \end{bmatrix} = \begin{bmatrix} 3 \\ 4 \\ 5 \end{bmatrix}. \qquad \square$$

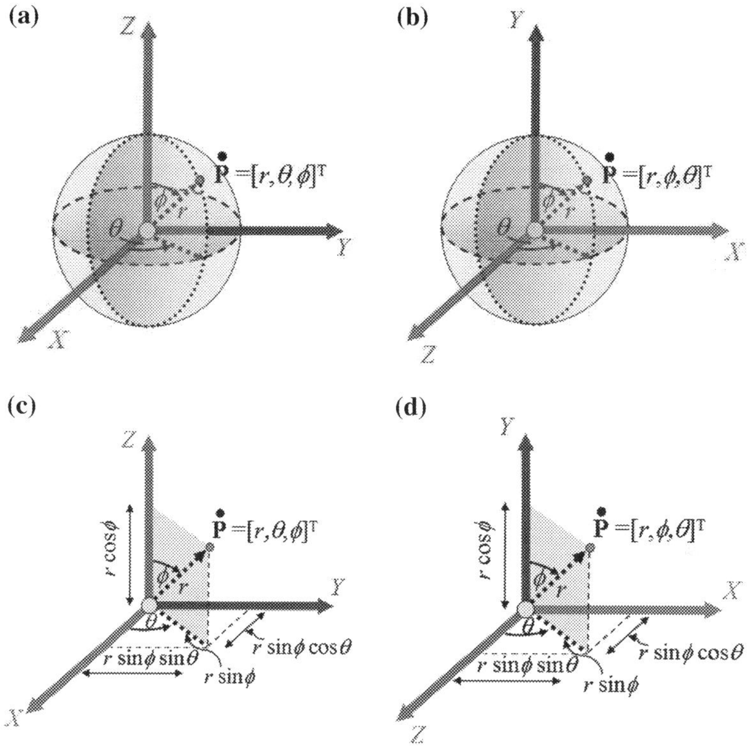


**Fig. B.10** Spherical coordinates. **a** $\theta$ is the angle in the $xy$-plane from the positive $x$-axis, $\phi$ is the angle from the positive $z$-axis. **b** $\theta$ is the angle in the $zx$-plane from the positive $z$-axis, $\phi$ is the angle from the positive $y$-axis. **c** Cartesian components for **a**. **d** Cartesian components for **b**

## B.6 Spherical Coordinate System

Spherical coordinates are used to describe a point on a spherical surface as depicted in Fig. B.10a. In this system, a point $\dot{\mathbf{P}} = [r, \theta, \phi]^T$ is described using two angles $\theta$ and $\phi$ in addition to a radial distance $r$. Considering a sphere centered at the origin, $\theta$ is the azimuth angle in the $xy$-plane from the positive $x$-axis, $\phi$ is the zenith angle from the positive $z$-axis while $r$ is the radial distance from the origin to the point.

Some systems consider the azimuth angle $\theta$ as being the angle in the $zx$-plane from the positive $z$-axis and the zenith angle $\phi$ as being the angle from the positive $y$-axis. This is shown in Fig. B.10b.

### *B.6.1 Cartesian-Spherical Transformation*

A point $\dot{\mathbf{P}} = [x, y, z]^T$ in Cartesian system can be expressed in spherical coordinates $[r, \theta, \phi]^T$ as

$$\begin{bmatrix} r \\ \theta \\ \phi \end{bmatrix} = \begin{bmatrix} \sqrt{x^2 + y^2 + z^2} \\ \tan^{-1}\left(\frac{y}{x}\right) \\ \cos^{-1}\left(\frac{z}{r}\right) \end{bmatrix}. \tag{B.26}$$

If the angle $\theta$ is measured about the $y$-axis and $\phi$ is measured from the positive $y$-axis as in Fig. B.10b, point $\dot{\mathbf{P}} = [x, y, z]^T$ in Cartesian system can be expressed in spherical coordinates $[r, \phi, \theta]^T$ as

$$\begin{bmatrix} r \\ \phi \\ \theta \end{bmatrix} = \begin{bmatrix} \sqrt{x^2 + y^2 + z^2} \\ \cos^{-1}\left(\frac{y}{r}\right) \\ \tan^{-1}\left(\frac{x}{z}\right) \end{bmatrix}. \tag{B.27}$$

**Example B.20** [*Cartesian-spherical transformation*]

Express the Cartesian point $[3, 4, 5]^T$ in spherical coordinates such that the origin of the spherical system coincides with the origin of the Cartesian system, $\theta$ is measured in the $xy$-plane from the positive $x$-axis and $\phi$ is measured from the positive $z$-axis.

**Solution B.20** Applying Eq. (B.26), $[3, 4, 5]^T$ is expressed in spherical coordinates as

$$\begin{bmatrix} r \\ \theta \\ \phi \end{bmatrix} = \begin{bmatrix} \sqrt{x^2 + y^2 + z^2} \\ \tan^{-1}\left(\frac{y}{x}\right) \\ \cos^{-1}\left(\frac{z}{r}\right) \end{bmatrix}$$

$$= \begin{bmatrix} \sqrt{3^2 + 4^2 + 5^2} \\ \tan^{-1}\left(\frac{4}{3}\right) \\ \cos^{-1}\left(\frac{5}{5\sqrt{2}}\right) \end{bmatrix} = \begin{bmatrix} 7.0711 \\ 53.1301^\circ \\ 45^\circ \end{bmatrix}.$$

□

### *B.6.2 Spherical-Cartesian Transformation*

A point $\dot{\mathbf{P}} = [r, \theta, \phi]^T$ in spherical system can be expressed in Cartesian coordinates $[x, y, z]^T$ as

$$\begin{bmatrix} x \\ y \\ z \end{bmatrix} = \begin{bmatrix} r\cos(\theta)\sin(\phi) \\ r\sin(\theta)\sin(\phi) \\ r\cos(\phi) \end{bmatrix}. \tag{B.28}$$

These Cartesian coordinates are shown in Fig. B.10c. If the azimuth angle $\theta$ is measured about the $y$-axis and the zenith angle $\phi$ is measured from the positive $y$-axis as in Fig. B.10b, point $\dot{\mathbf{P}} = [r, \phi, \theta]^T$ in spherical system can be expressed in Cartesian coordinates $[x, y, z]^T$ as

$$\begin{bmatrix} x \\ y \\ z \end{bmatrix} = \begin{bmatrix} r\ \sin(\theta)\ \sin(\phi) \\ r\ \cos(\phi) \\ r\ \cos(\theta)\ \sin(\phi) \end{bmatrix}. \tag{B.29}$$

These Cartesian coordinates are shown in Fig. B.10d.

**Example B.21** [*Spherical-Cartesian transformation*]

The point $[5\sqrt{2}, 53.1301, 45]^T$ is defined in spherical coordinates. Express it in Cartesian coordinates such that the origin of the spherical system coincides with the origin of the Cartesian system, $\theta$ is measured in the $xy$-plane from the positive $x$-axis and $\phi$ is measured from the positive $z$-axis.

**Solution B.21** Applying Eq. (B.28), $[5\sqrt{2}, 53.1301, 45]^T$ is expressed in Cartesian coordinates as

$$\begin{aligned} \begin{bmatrix} x \\ y \\ z \end{bmatrix} &= \begin{bmatrix} r\ \cos(\theta)\ \sin(\phi) \\ r\ \sin(\theta)\ \sin(\phi) \\ r\ \cos(\phi) \end{bmatrix} \\ &= \begin{bmatrix} 5\sqrt{2}\ \cos(53.1301)\ \sin(45) \\ 5\sqrt{2}\ \sin(53.1301)\ \sin(45) \\ 5\sqrt{2}\ \cos(45) \end{bmatrix} = \begin{bmatrix} 3 \\ 4 \\ 5 \end{bmatrix}. \end{aligned}$$

□

## B.7 Homogeneous Coordinates

In order to express a 2D point in homogeneous coordinates, simply add a third term whose value is 1 to the point vector (i.e., a 2D point is represented as a 3D vector in homogeneous coordinates). For example, the point $[3, 4]^T$ is represented homogeneously as $[3, 4, 1]^T$. In general, a 2D point $[x, y]^T$ is expressed as $[a_1, a_2, a_3]^T$ such that $a_3 \neq 0$, $x = \frac{a_1}{a_3}$ and $y = \frac{a_2}{a_3}$. Hence, the overall scaling $a_3$ of the homogeneous coordinates is not important. Thus, the homogeneous 2D points $[3, 4, 1]^T$, $[6, 8, 2]^T$ and $[1.5, 2, 0.5]^T$ are the same. Two homogeneous points $[a_1, a_2, a_3]^T$ and $[b_1, b_2, b_3]^T$ are identical if and only if

$$\begin{vmatrix} a_2 & a_3 \\ b_2 & b_3 \end{vmatrix} = \begin{vmatrix} a_3 & a_1 \\ b_3 & b_1 \end{vmatrix} = \begin{vmatrix} a_1 & a_2 \\ b_1 & b_2 \end{vmatrix} = 0, \tag{B.30}$$

where $|.|$ indicates the determinant (Sect. A.2.1). Thus,

$$a_2b_3 - a_3b_2 = a_3b_1 - a_1b_3 = a_1b_2 - a_2b_1 = 0. \tag{B.31}$$

If the third term of a homogeneous point is zero, this point is a point at infinity or a direction (Elias 2008, 2012). We can use such points to get the vanishing point of a group of parallel lines as explained in Chap. 8.

Similarly, to express a 3D point in homogeneous coordinates, simply add a fourth term whose value is 1 to the point vector (i.e., a 3D point is represented as a 4D vector in homogeneous coordinates). For example, the point $[3, 4, 2]^T$ is represented homogeneously as $[3, 4, 2, 1]^T$. In general, a 3D point $[x, y, z]^T$ is expressed as $[a_1, a_2, a_3, a_4]^T$ such that $a_4 \neq 0$, $x = \frac{a_1}{a_4}$, $y = \frac{a_2}{a_4}$ and $z = \frac{a_3}{a_4}$. (If $a_4 = 0$, the point becomes a point at infinity or a direction.) Hence, the overall scaling $a_4$ of the homogeneous coordinates is not important. Thus, the homogeneous 3D points $[3, 4, 2, 1]^T$, $[6, 8, 4, 2]^T$ and $[1.5, 2, 1, 0.5]^T$ are the same.

**Example B.22** [*Homogeneous coordinates–points*]
Determine if the following homogeneous points are the same: $[2, 3, 1]^T$ and $[4, 6, 3]^T$.

**Solution B.22** The homogeneous coordinates refer to the same point when the proportions are maintained; i.e., when there is a single number to be multiplied by all the components of one point to get the other. Since no single number exists in this problem, the points $[2, 3, 1]^T$ and $[4, 6, 3]^T$ are different.

The same conclusion can be obtained using Eq. (B.30) or (B.31). The determinants are

$$\begin{vmatrix} a_2 & a_3 \\ b_2 & b_3 \end{vmatrix} = a_2b_3 - a_3b_2 = 3 \times 3 - 1 \times 6 = 3,$$

$$\begin{vmatrix} a_3 & a_1 \\ b_3 & b_1 \end{vmatrix} = a_3b_1 - a_1b_3 = 1 \times 4 - 2 \times 3 = -2$$

and

$$\begin{vmatrix} a_1 & a_2 \\ b_1 & b_2 \end{vmatrix} = a_1b_2 - a_2b_1 = 2 \times 6 - 3 \times 4 = 0.$$

Since

$$a_2b_3 - a_3b_2 \neq a_3b_1 - a_1b_3 \neq 0,$$

the points not identical. (You may stop calculating once a determinant results in a value other than 0.) □

## B.8 Problems

**Problem B.1** [*Cartesian-barycentric transformation*]
A triangle is given by the vertices $[1, 0]^T$, $[3, 1]^T$ and $[0, 3]^T$. Determine the barycentric coordinates of the points $[1, 2]^T$ and $[2, 1]^T$.

**Problem B.2** [*Barycentric-Cartesian transformation*]
Consider the triangle with vertices $[2, 0]^T$, $[4, 2]^T$ and $[0, 4]^T$. Determine the Cartesian coordinates of the barycentric point $[0.4, 0.3, 0.3]^T$.

**Problem B.3** [*Barycentric-Cartesian transformation*]
The vertices of a triangle are placed at the positions $[0, 0, 0]^T$, $[2, 3, 0]^T$ and $[3, 1, 0]^T$. Determine the points represented by the following set of barycentric coordinates: $[0, 1, 0]^T$, $\left[\frac{2}{3}, \frac{1}{3}, 0\right]^T$, $\left[\frac{1}{3}, \frac{1}{3}, \frac{1}{3}\right]^T$, $[0.8, 0.1, 0.1]^T$ and $\left[\frac{4}{3}, \frac{2}{3}, -1\right]^T$.

**Problem B.4** [*Cartesian-parametric transformation*]
A triangle is given by the vertices $[1, 0]^T$, $[3, 1]^T$ and $[0, 3]^T$. Determine the parametric coordinates of the points $[1, 2]^T$ and $[2, 1]^T$ if $[1, 0]^T$ is considered as the origin of the system and the $u$- and $v$-axes are passing through $[3, 1]^T$ and $[0, 3]^T$ respectively.

**Problem B.5** [*Parametric-Cartesian transformation*]
Consider a triangle $\triangle\dot{\mathbf{a}}\dot{\mathbf{b}}\dot{\mathbf{c}}$ where $\dot{\mathbf{a}} = [1, 0]^T$, $\dot{\mathbf{b}} = [3, 1]^T$ and $\dot{\mathbf{c}} = [0, 3]^T$. If a parametric coordinate system is defined such that the $u$- and $v$-axes go along $\overline{\dot{\mathbf{a}}\dot{\mathbf{b}}}$ and $\overline{\dot{\mathbf{a}}\dot{\mathbf{c}}}$ respectively, express the parametric points $[0.2857, 0.5714]^T$, $[0.5714, 0.1429]^T$ and $[0, 0]^T$ in Cartesian coordinates.

**Problem B.6** [*Parametric-barycentric transformation*]
Consider a triangle $\triangle\dot{\mathbf{a}}\dot{\mathbf{b}}\dot{\mathbf{c}}$. If a point $\dot{\mathbf{p}}$ inside the triangle is expressed in parametric coordinates as $[u, v]^T$ where the parametric $u$- and $v$-axes are along $\overline{\dot{\mathbf{a}}\dot{\mathbf{b}}}$ and $\overline{\dot{\mathbf{a}}\dot{\mathbf{c}}}$ respectively, get its barycentric coordinates $[t_{\dot{\mathbf{a}}}, t_{\dot{\mathbf{b}}}, t_{\dot{\mathbf{c}}}]^T$. *Hint:* You may refer to Example B.10 for steps.

**Problem B.7** [*Barycentric-polar transformation*]
Consider a triangle $\triangle\dot{\mathbf{a}}\dot{\mathbf{b}}\dot{\mathbf{c}}$. If a point $\dot{\mathbf{p}}$ inside the triangle is expressed in barycentric coordinates as $[t_{\dot{\mathbf{a}}}, t_{\dot{\mathbf{b}}}, t_{\dot{\mathbf{c}}}]^T$, express the same point in polar coordinates if the origin of the polar system is at $\dot{\mathbf{a}}$ and point $\dot{\mathbf{b}}$ has an angular coordinate of 0°.

**Problem B.8** [*Polar-barycentric transformation*]
Consider a triangle $\triangle\dot{\mathbf{a}}\dot{\mathbf{b}}\dot{\mathbf{c}}$. If a point $\dot{\mathbf{p}}$ inside the triangle is expressed in polar coordinates as $[r, \theta]^T$ where

1. the origin of the Cartesian system expressing the vertices $\dot{\mathbf{a}}$, $\dot{\mathbf{b}}$ and $\dot{\mathbf{c}}$ is the same as the origin of the polar system; and
2. the $x$-axis of the Cartesian system has an angular coordinate of 0°,

express the same point in barycentric coordinates $[t_{\dot{\mathbf{a}}}, t_{\dot{\mathbf{b}}}, t_{\dot{\mathbf{c}}}]^T$. *Hint:* You may refer to Example B.14 for steps.

**Problem B.9** [*Polar-barycentric transformation*]
Consider a triangle $\triangle\dot{\mathbf{a}}\dot{\mathbf{b}}\dot{\mathbf{c}}$ such that the vertices $\dot{\mathbf{a}}$, $\dot{\mathbf{b}}$ and $\dot{\mathbf{c}}$ are expressed in Cartesian coordinates. If a point $\dot{\mathbf{p}}$ inside the triangle is expressed in polar coordinates as $[r, \theta]^T$ where

1. the origin of the polar system is at vertex $\dot{\mathbf{a}}$; and
2. the edge $\overline{\dot{\mathbf{a}}\dot{\mathbf{b}}}$ has an angular coordinate of 0°,

express the same point in barycentric coordinates $[t_{\dot{\mathbf{a}}}, t_{\dot{\mathbf{b}}}, t_{\dot{\mathbf{c}}}]^T$.

**Problem B.10** [*Polar-parametric transformation*]
Consider a triangle $\triangle\dot{\mathbf{a}}\dot{\mathbf{b}}\dot{\mathbf{c}}$. If a point $\dot{\mathbf{p}}$ inside the triangle is expressed in polar coordinates as $[r, \theta]^T$ where

1. the origin of the Cartesian system expressing the vertices $\dot{\mathbf{a}}$, $\dot{\mathbf{b}}$ and $\dot{\mathbf{c}}$ is the same as the origin of the polar system; and
2. the $x$-axis of the Cartesian system has an angular coordinate of 0°,

express the same point in parametric coordinates $[u, v]^T$ such that the $u$- and $v$-axes are along $\overline{\dot{\mathbf{a}}\dot{\mathbf{b}}}$ and $\overline{\dot{\mathbf{a}}\dot{\mathbf{c}}}$ respectively. *Hint:* You may refer to Example B.16 for steps.

**Problem B.11** [*Polar-parametric transformation*]
Consider a triangle $\triangle\dot{\mathbf{a}}\dot{\mathbf{b}}\dot{\mathbf{c}}$ such that the vertices $\dot{\mathbf{a}}$, $\dot{\mathbf{b}}$ and $\dot{\mathbf{c}}$ are expressed in Cartesian coordinates. If a point $\dot{\mathbf{p}}$ inside the triangle is expressed in polar coordinates as $[r, \theta]^T$ where

1. the origin of the polar system is at vertex $\dot{\mathbf{a}}$; and
2. the edge $\overline{\dot{\mathbf{a}}\dot{\mathbf{b}}}$ has an angular coordinate of 0°,

express the same point in parametric coordinates $[u, v]^T$ if the parametric $u$- and $v$-axes are along $\overline{\dot{\mathbf{a}}\dot{\mathbf{b}}}$ and $\overline{\dot{\mathbf{a}}\dot{\mathbf{c}}}$.

**Problem B.12** [*Barycentric coordinates–3D space*]
The following equation determines the barycentric coordinates of a point $\dot{\mathbf{p}}$ inside a 2D triangle bounded by the vertices $\dot{\mathbf{a}}$, $\dot{\mathbf{b}}$ and $\dot{\mathbf{c}}$:

$$\begin{bmatrix} t_{\dot{\mathbf{a}}} \\ t_{\dot{\mathbf{b}}} \\ t_{\dot{\mathbf{c}}} \end{bmatrix} = \frac{1}{\left\|[\dot{\mathbf{b}}-\dot{\mathbf{a}}]\,[\dot{\mathbf{c}}-\dot{\mathbf{a}}]\right\|} \begin{bmatrix} \left\|[\dot{\mathbf{b}}-\dot{\mathbf{p}}]\,[\dot{\mathbf{c}}-\dot{\mathbf{p}}]\right\| \\ \left\|[\dot{\mathbf{c}}-\dot{\mathbf{p}}]\,[\dot{\mathbf{a}}-\dot{\mathbf{p}}]\right\| \\ \left\|[\dot{\mathbf{a}}-\dot{\mathbf{p}}]\,[\dot{\mathbf{b}}-\dot{\mathbf{p}}]\right\| \end{bmatrix}.$$

Can we use the same equation to obtain the barycentric coordinates of a 3D point $\dot{\mathbf{P}}$ inside a 3D triangle bounded by the vertices $\dot{\mathbf{A}}$, $\dot{\mathbf{B}}$ and $\dot{\mathbf{C}}$? If no, write down the correct equation.

**Problem B.13** [*Cartesian-cylindrical transformation*]
Express the Cartesian point $[3, 4, 5]^T$ in cylindrical coordinates such that the origin of the cylindrical system coincides with the origin of the Cartesian system, $\theta = 0°$ corresponds to the $z$-axis and the height is along the $y$-axis.

**Problem B.14** [*Cylindrical-Cartesian transformation*]
The point $[5, 53.13, 5]^T$ is defined in cylindrical coordinates. Express it in Cartesian coordinates such that the origin of the cylindrical system coincides with the origin of the Cartesian system, $\theta = 0°$ corresponds to the $z$-axis and the height is along the $y$-axis.

**Problem B.15** [*Cartesian-spherical transformation*]

Express the Cartesian point $[3, 4, 5]^T$ in spherical coordinates such that the origin of the spherical system coincides with the origin of the Cartesian system, $\theta$ is measured in the $zx$-plane from the positive $z$-axis and $\phi$ is measured from the positive $y$-axis.

**Problem B.16** [*Spherical-Cartesian transformation*]

The point $[5\sqrt{2}, 53.13, 45]^T$ is defined in spherical coordinates. Express it in Cartesian coordinates such that the origin of the spherical system coincides with the origin of the Cartesian system, $\theta$ is measured in the $zx$-plane from the positive $z$-axis and $\phi$ is measured from the positive $y$-axis.

**Problem B.17** [*Homogeneous coordinates–points*]

Determine if the following homogeneous points are the same: $[2, 3, 1]^T$ and $[4, 6, 2]^T$.

## References

Elias, R. 2008. Geometric modeling in computer vision: An introduction to projective geometry. In *Wiley encyclopedia of computer science and engineering*, ed. B.W. Wah, 1400–1416. New Jersey: Wiley.

Elias, R. 2012. *3D surface geometry and reconstruction: Developing concepts and applications, chapter projective geometry for 3D modeling of objects*. Hershey, PA, USA: IGI Global.

Vince, J. 2008. *Geometric algebra for computer graphics*. Berlin: Springer.

Vince, J. 2010. Mathematics for computer graphics, 3rd edn. Undergraduate Topics in Computer Science. Springer

# Index



R. Elias, *Digital Media*, DOI: 10.1007/978-3-319-05137-6,